✧ **W9-ANQ-164**

K-4

NOTICE

If this book, when loaned to you, is in any way defective, notify the teacher before accepting it. If this is not done you will be held responsible for its condition when it is returned.

WORLD HISTORY
THE HUMAN EXPERIENCE

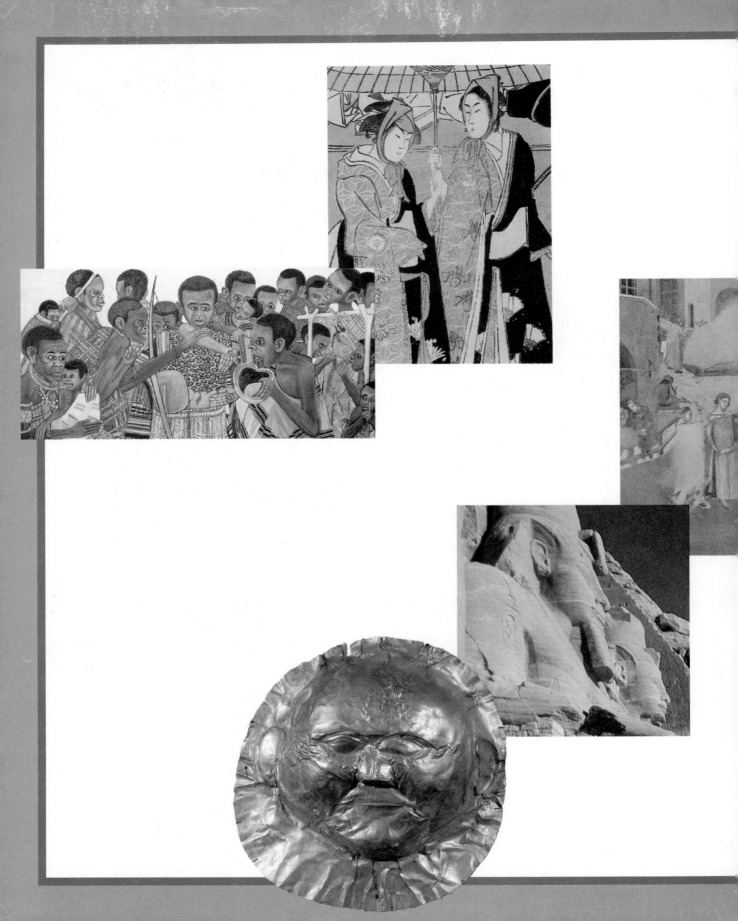

WORLD HISTORY

THE HUMAN EXPERIENCE

Third Edition

Mounir Farah
Andrea Berens Karls

GLENCOE
Macmillan/McGraw-Hill

Lake Forest, Illinois
Columbus, Ohio
Mission Hills, California
Peoria, Illinois

AUTHORS

Mounir Farah is Department Chair of Social Studies in the Monroe, Connecticut, public schools and an adjunct lecturer of Social Science at Western Connecticut State University. He has taught history at New York University and has lectured at many nationwide teachers' conferences and workshops. Past president of the Connecticut Council for Social Studies and a member of the Middle East Institute, the Middle East Studies Association, and the International Activities Committee of the National Council for the Social Studies, Dr. Farah has been a contributing writer to several works and has authored numerous articles and reviews. He is coauthor of Glencoe's *Global Insights*.

Andrea Berens Karls is an educator and coauthor of Glencoe's *Global Insights*. Educated at Wellesley College and Harvard University, she has taught at both the elementary and secondary levels. Ms. Karls was formerly Program Associate at Global Perspectives in Education, Inc., where she edited and wrote curriculum materials and worked with teachers. She is a member of the National Council for the Social Studies and the American Historical Association.

CONSULTANTS

Geography Consultant

W. Randy Smith, PhD
Professor of Geography
The Ohio State University
Columbus, Ohio

Multicultural Consultant

Donna M. Gollnick
Deputy Executive Director
National Council for the
  Accreditation of Teacher Education
Washington, D.C.

Religion Consultants

Austin B. Creel, PhD
Professor of Religion
University of Florida
Gainesville, Florida

Nicolas Piediscalzi, PhD
Past President of the National
  Council on Religion and Public
  Education and Visiting Scholar
University of California
Santa Barbara, California

Copyright © 1992 by the Glencoe Division of Macmillan/McGraw-Hill School Publishing Company. Copyright © 1990, 1985 by Merrill Publishing Company. All rights reserved. Except as permitted under the United States Copyright Act, no part of this publication may be reproduced or distributed in any form or by any means, or stored in a database or retrieval system, without prior written permission of the publisher.

Send all inquiries to:
Glencoe Division, Macmillan/McGraw-Hill, 936 Eastwind Drive, Westerville, Ohio 43081

ISBN 0-02-800200-8 (student text)   ISBN 0-02-800201-6 (Teacher's Wraparound Edition)

Printed in the United States of America.
2 3 4 5 6 7 8 9 10 VH 00 99 98 97 96 95 94 93 92

Cover: Detail of the throne of King Tutankhamen showing him with Queen Ankhesenamen.
  Photo by Lee Boltin

CONTENT HISTORIANS

Ancient History

D. Brendan Nagle, Ph.D
Associate Professor
University of Southern California
Los Angeles, California

Medieval History

Penny Schine Gold, Ph.D.
Associate Professor of History
Knox College
Galesburg, Illinois

Early Modern History

Charles Carlton, Ph.D.
Professor of History
North Carolina State University
Raleigh, North Carolina

Nineteenth-Century History

Gerald H. Davis, Ph.D.
Professor of History
Georgia State University
Atlanta, Georgia

Twentieth-Century History

Donald L. Niewyk, Ph.D.
Professor of History
Southern Methodist University
Dallas, Texas

Latin American Studies

Dr. Jesus Mendez, Ph.D.
Associate Professor of History
Barry University
Miami Shores, Florida

Asian Studies

Geraldine Forbes, Ph.D.
Professor of History
State University of New York
Oswego, New York

History of Eastern Europe and the Soviet Union

Barbara Engel, Ph.D.
Associate Professor of History
University of Colorado
Boulder, Colorado

African Studies

Boniface Obichere, Ph.D.
Professor of History
University of California
Los Angeles, California

Middle Eastern Studies

Joseph Rosenbloom, Ph.D.
Professor of Classics
Washington University
St. Louis, Missouri

TEACHER REVIEWERS

C. June Bryant
Creekside High School
Fairburn, Georgia

Richard Dean Barlow
West Forsyth High School
Clemmons, North Carolina

Daniel M. Jarvis
Hinkley High School
Aurora, Colorado

Gerald Mason
Northside High School
San Antonio, Texas

Mary Gentry
Manzano High School
Albuquerque, New Mexico

Patrick S. McGee
Madera High School
Madera, California

Sue H. Dickson
Murrah High School
Jackson, Mississippi

Deidre R. Foreman
Calcasieu Parish School Board
Lake Charles, Louisiana

Tim Moore
Simon Kenton High School
Florence, Kentucky

Jerry W. Gray
Oxford High School
Oxford, Alabama

Cheryl A. Menke
Broadneck Senior High School
Annapolis, Maryland

Ruby Wanland
Miami Beach Senior High School
Miami Beach, Florida

CONTENTS

xii

FEATURES

CONNECTIONS

History and the Environment

Science and Technology

Geography in History

SKILLS

MAPS

PERSONAL PROFILES

CHARTS AND DIAGRAMS

FOOTNOTES TO HISTORY

THE STRUCTURE OF THIS BOOK

This book contains eight units, each with its own border pattern. Each unit is divided into chapters; each chapter is divided into sections. This structure, together with special features, helps you focus on people and events that are part of the larger story of the human experience.

A unit timeline records important political, scientific, and cultural or social events from all over the world.

The unit opener lists the time span and chapters found in the unit. A quote, a brief introduction, and an artifact from the period set the mood for the chapters that follow.

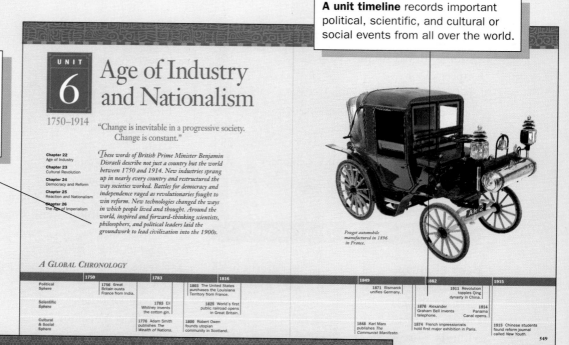

UNIT 6

Age of Industry and Nationalism

1750–1914

"Change is inevitable in a progressive society. Change is constant."

Chapter 22
Age of Industry

Chapter 23
Cultural Revolution

Chapter 24
Democracy and Reform

Chapter 25
Reaction and Nationalism

Chapter 26
The Age of Imperialism

These words of British Prime Minister Benjamin Disraeli describe not just a country but the world between 1750 and 1914. New industries sprang up in nearly every country and restructured the way societies worked. Battles for democracy and independence raged as revolutionaries fought to win reform. New technologies changed the ways in which people lived and thought. Around the world, inspired and forward-thinking scientists, philosophers, and political leaders laid the groundwork to lead civilization into the 1900s.

Peugot automobile manufactured in 1896 in France.

A GLOBAL CHRONOLOGY

	1750	1783	1816	1849	1882	1915
Political Sphere	1756 Great Britain ousts France from India.		1803 The United States purchases the Louisiana Territory from France.	1871 Bismarck unifies Germany.	1911 Revolution topples Qing dynasty in China.	
Scientific Sphere		1793 Eli Whitney invents the cotton gin.	1825 World's first public railroad opens in Great Britain.	1876 Alexander Graham Bell invents telephone.	1914 Panama Canal opens.	
Cultural & Social Sphere		1776 Adam Smith publishes *The Wealth of Nations.*	1800 Robert Owen founds utopian community in Scotland.	1848 Karl Marx publishes *The Communist Manifesto.*	1874 French impressionists hold first major exhibition in Paris.	1915 Chinese students found reform journal called *New Youth.*

549

CHAPTER 9

Byzantines and Slavs

A.D. 400-1500

1 The New Rome

2 Byzantine Civilization

3 The Eastern Slavs

The awestruck visitor arriving in A.D. 600 in the city of Constantinople in southeastern Europe scarcely knew where to turn. Splendid public buildings as well as simple private homes lined the streets; the scent of rare spices perfumed the air; people dressed in fine silk thronged the church of Hagia Sophia. "One might imagine that one has chanced upon a meadow in full bloom," the Greek historian Procopius wrote about the newly built church. "For one would surely marvel at the purple hue of some [columns], the green of others, at those on which the crimson blooms, at those that flash with white, at those, too, which nature, like a painter, has varied with the most contrasting colors." The church's grandeur reflected that of Constantinople, "city of the world's desire," capital of a prosperous empire that controlled east–west trade and laid the basis for the Greek and Slavic civilizations of modern Europe.

The subject and style of this painting are typical of religious art throughout the Byzantine Empire.

CHAPTER PREVIEW

Key Terms to Define: clergy, laity, icons, iconoclast, schism, mosaic, illuminated manuscript, steppe, boyar, tsar

People to Meet: Constantine, Justinian, Theodora, Leo III, Cyril, Seljuk Turks, Ottoman Turks, Rurik, Vladimir, Alexander Nevsky, Ivan III

Places to Discover: Constantinople, Balkan Peninsula, Asia Minor, Adriatic Sea, Black Sea, Manzikert, Dnieper River, Kiev, Moscow, Volga River

Objectives to Learn:
1. What made Constantinople such a rich and powerful city?
2. What role did the Church play in Byzantine and Slavic societies?
3. What caused the split between the Roman and Byzantine churches?
4. Why did Constantinople suffer almost constant attack?
5. What factors contributed to the development of Eastern Slavic culture?
6. How did the Eastern Slavic lands become isolated from western Europe?

The chapter opener displays a map to help you locate the parts of the world you will study. The **chapter preview** lists key terms, people, and places you will get to know. The questions and concepts here guide your reading.

212

Each chapter is divided into two to six sections. Primary-source quotes, photographs, fine art, and maps work with the text to make history come to life.

SECTION 5

The Catholic Reformation

Most of the people in Spain, France, Italy, Portugal, Hungary, Poland, and southern Germany remained Catholic during the Protestant Reformation. Nevertheless, Catholicism's power was threatened by Protestantism's increasing popularity in northern Europe. To counter the Protestant challenge, Catholics decided to reform Church practices. The Catholic Church had had a history of periodic reform since the Middle Ages. Thus, in the movement that came to be known as the Counter-Reformation, or Catholic Reformation, the Catholic Church eliminated many abuses, clarified its theology, and reestablished the pope's authority over Church members.

Redefining Catholicism

In 1536 Pope Paul III established a distinguished commission of cardinals and bishops to prepare a report on the need for reform and how such reform might be undertaken. The completed report blamed church leaders, including popes, for many abuses. It also called for reforms that would convince Protestants to rejoin the Church.

The reforms undertaken as a result of this report were only partially carried out. The Church's financial problems had increased, and the Church was unable to respond quickly and effectively to the Protestant threat.

By the 1540s Catholic Church leaders, sensing the importance of checking the spread of Protestantism, finally decided to embark on an ambitious reform program. The goals were to introduce a rebirth of faith among its followers, reassess the Church's principles, and halt the spread of Protestantism.

The Inquisition In 1542 the Church gave full powers to an Inquisition, a church court based in Italy, to find, try, and judge heretics—especially Protestants. The purpose of this Inquisition, however, was not merely to rid Italy of non-Catholics. The purge was also intended to restore the pope's authority over church members. With the imposition of rigid repression, the pope succeeded in restoring his authority over the entire Italian peninsula. The Church also introduced censorship to curtail the humanist thinking that had fueled Italy's Renaissance. In 1543 the Inquisition published the first Index of Prohibited Books.

The Council of Trent One of the needs of the Church was to clearly state and defend Catholic teaching. In 1545 Pope Paul III called a council of bishops at Trent, Italy, to define official doctrine. The Council of Trent met in several sessions from 1545 to 1563.

The Council strictly and clearly defined Catholic doctrine, especially teachings that the Protestants had challenged. Salvation, the Council declared, could not be achieved by faith alone, but only by faith and works together. The Latin Vulgate translation of the Bible was made the only acceptable version of scripture. In addition, the Church hierarchy alone was to decide the interpretation of the Bible.

The Council of Trent also put an end to many Church abuses that had been practiced for

Learning from Art *The decisions of the Council of Trent brought needed reforms to the Catholic Church. The Council's influence was so strong that more than 300 years passed before the Church deemed it necessary to hold another Church council.* **How did the Council of Trent result in an enthusiasm for baroque art and music?**

RELIGIONS OF EUROPE 1560

Learning from Maps *By 1560 many northern Europeans had become Protestants. Most southern Europeans, however—including those in two of the most powerful countries, Spain and France—remained Catholic.* **What were the results of this religious division?**

---

began negotiating a free-trade agreement with the United States. This agreement would remove all quotas, tariffs, and other barriers to trade between the two countries. Salinas hoped this plan would lure United States investors and their industries into Mexico, thereby increasing job opportunities.

To further enhance the economy, Salinas began to sell off government-owned industries to private investors. He was setting out to reverse the policy that had been followed between the 1930s and the 1980s, when the government of Mexico had purchased control of the oil industry, the system of railroads and other transportation systems, and most communications industries. Salinas hoped that private ownership would run these industries with greater efficiency than had the government. One of the first industries sold to investors was the telephone company.

Cuba

Unlike Mexico, which has been politically stable since World War II, the Caribbean island nation of Cuba was the scene of a dramatic revolution. In 1953 Fidel Castro began a guerrilla movement against dictator Fulgencio Batista, who had ruled Cuba for most of the previous 20 years. Batista had allowed the Cuban economy, by the early 1950s, United States companies, taking full advantage of the island's lenient policy, owned almost 90 percent of the island's mines, ranches, and oil and about 50 percent of its sugar. Little wealth trickled down to the poverty-stricken masses. For six years, Castro and his soldiers carried out daring and successful raids on Batista's forces, slowly winning popular support. On January 1, 1959, Batista fled the country, and Castro assumed control.

Castro's Domestic Policies Castro pushed through reforms quickly. For example, he passed laws to improve wages, health, and education. More important, he began a program of land reform to redistribute ownership of land. In the process, the government seized control of sugar plantations and major industries.

These reforms opened a period of progress. Over the next 20 years, per capita income increased from $210 to $1,975. Food production quadrupled, and industrial output tripled. However, the reforms also angered many people when they were first instituted. Thousands of upper-class Cubans—landowners, professionals, and business people—fled to the United States. In retaliation for some of Castro's policies, the United States cut off all sugar imports from the tiny island in 1960. Castro turned to the Soviet Union for help. Soviet Premier Nikita Khrushchev agreed to buy Cuban sugar and sell arms to Castro. Two years after the revolution, Castro's dictatorship was openly Communist, and Castro's willingness to stand up to the United States made him a Latin American folk hero.

Cuba and the United States Castro's friendship with the Soviets made Cuba the key cold-war battleground in the Western Hemisphere. Castro supported guerrilla movements and governments in Latin America and Africa, most of which opposed U.S.-backed heroes. He called on people around the world to combat U.S. policies:

The revolution will triumph in America and throughout the world, but it is not for revolutionaries to sit in the doorways of their houses waiting for the corpse of imperialism to pass by.

—From a 1962 speech by Fidel Castro

IMAGES OF THE TIME

Mexico Today

With one of the world's biggest cities and a large rural population, Mexico is a land of great variety.

Traditional crafts are still highly valued today. These clay figures are by a contemporary Mexican artist.

Mexico City, one of North America's oldest cities, is Mexico's cultural, governmental, and economic center.

Vibrant market days take place in many Mexican towns where people come to sell the foods they grow and the products they make.

Hand woven textiles of wool and of cotton are an important industry in many rural areas.

Reflecting on the Times
What sort of problems would the rising population in Mexico City pose?

Artifacts and photographs bring you to another place in time and help capture the richness of the human experience

Images of the Time features in each chapter serve as journeys through the past, giving you a sense of what life was like at different periods of history.

SPECIAL FEATURES

Throughout the book, you will find special feature pages. Each unit contains a literature selection from or about the era dealt with in the unit. Each chapter contains several other features to give you in-depth views of the many different issues and personalities of history.

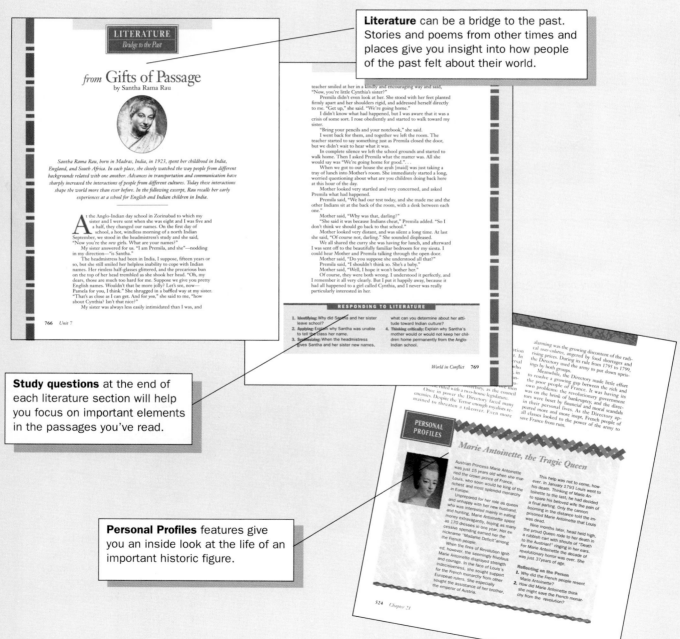

Literature can be a bridge to the past. Stories and poems from other times and places give you insight into how people of the past felt about their world.

Study questions at the end of each literature section will help you focus on important elements in the passages you've read.

Personal Profiles features give you an inside look at the life of an important historic figure.

Connections show how geography, the environment, and science and technology have influenced history. You will see how people have shaped and been shaped by their surroundings.

CONNECTIONS: SCIENCE AND TECHNOLOGY

At the Doctor's

Here, an Islamic man is shown preparing medicine.

Making the Connection
1. Why was Islamic medicine far ahead of the Western medicine during the Middle Ages?
2. What new methods of treatment have doctors developed in the past 50 years?

Islam 251

HISTORY AND THE ARTS

The Mask of Tutankhamen

Slowly . . . the remains of passage debris . . . were removed, until at last we had the whole door clear before us. The decisive moment had arrived. With trembling hands I inserted a tiny breach in the upper left-hand corner. . . . widening the hole a little, I inserted the candle and peered in. . . . At first I could see nothing, . . . but presently, as my eyes grew accustomed to the light, details of the room within emerged slowly from the mist, strange animals, statues, and gold . . . everywhere the glint of gold.

—Howard Carter and A.C. Mace, *The Tomb of Tut-ankh-Amen*, 1923

This is British archaeologist Howard Carter's account of his suspense as he opened Tutankhamen's tomb. For years Carter had sought the ruler's burial place in the Valley of the Kings, where Egyptian pharaohs were traditionally buried. On November 26, 1922, Carter opened a chamber that had been shrouded in silence and darkness for over 3,000 years.

The mask of Tutankhamen, who ruled from about 1334 to 1325 B.C., is among the most spectacular works of art to have survived from Egypt's New Kingdom. The mask, made of pure gold and decorated with lapis lazuli, quartz, and colored glass, covered the head and shoulders of the linen-wrapped mummy. The beard on Tutankhamen's funeral mask associates him with Osiris, the god of the afterworld. The vulture and cobra at his brow symbolize Upper and Lower Egypt, the two regions over which he ruled.

Unlike Egyptian tomb sculpture of earlier times, Tutankhamen's mask seems to be a true portrait. Earlier images of pharaohs were often idealized, using symbols and inscriptions to indicate who was portrayed. Even though the artist who made Tutankhamen's mask used such symbols, he or she personalized the mask, making it look like the young king.

As impressive as Tutankhamen's tomb is, this pharaoh was not an important king in ancient Egypt. He came to the throne when only a boy, and died before reaching age 20. His tomb is unique because it was not robbed of its treasures as many Egyptian tombs were.

Responding to the Arts
1. What symbols of kingship did Egyptian artists include on Tutankhamen's mask?
2. Why were so many elaborate objects buried with the pharaoh?

History and the Arts features provide a close-up views of artists and artworks from all over the world. These features will show you how art is a reflection of an artist's culture and times.

Skills pages will help you learn and apply map and graphic, critical thinking, and study and writing skills.

CRITICAL THINKING SKILLS

CLASSIFYING

Can you imagine the frustration of shopping in a store where merchandise is not arranged in departments? A similar frustration may occur when you try to read and understand large quantities of information about a subject. You can learn more by sorting data into categories. Classifying involves sorting items based on shared characteristics. Classifying makes it easier to detect patterns or to see relationships among items in order to draw conclusions or make comparisons.

The royal children . . . were privately tutored . . . frequently joined by the one of the great noble families. . . . The most sought-after profession in Egypt was that of scribe. . . . The most important subjects were reading and writing . . . history, literature, geography, [and] ethics. Arithmetic was almost certainly part of the curriculum. . . . Boys who were to specialize in medicine, law or religious liturgy would perhaps have devoted some of their time to elementary studies in these fields.

Formal education for [a son from] the lower classes . . . was not selected for him because he wished to become an artist or goldsmith or a farmer . . . be entered a trade because it was his father's work. The sons of artists and craftsmen were apprenticed and went to train at one of the temples or state workshops . . . the sons of peasants would have joined their fathers in the field at an early age.

A. Rosalie David,
The Egyptian Kingdoms, 1975

Explanation

When faced with lengthy or difficult material, use these steps to classify data:
1. Read the information, noticing items with shared features or characteristics.
2. Sort items with shared characteristics into categories (technology, economy, housing, culture, education).
3. Label each group of items.
4. Check the original selection for other items that could be added to each category. Continue sorting until all possible items are placed in a category.
5. Review the items within each category. If necessary subdivide, combine, or rename categories.
6. After classifying, formulate new conclusions or generalizations from the data.

Example

If you read the above passage about life in ancient Egypt, you could classify the information by listing items with shared characteristics. The selection describes the education of nobles and of commoners. The words *scribe*, *medicine*, and *law* share the characteristic of being occupations of the nobility. The chart below shows one way in which other information could be classified.

Application

Read about life in Harappan civilization in the Indus River Valley on pages 51–53 in Section 3. Use the steps above to classify that information.

Practice

Turn to Practicing Skills in the Chapter Review on page 67 for further practice in the skill of classifying information.

CLASSIFICATION CHART

	Nobles' Education	Commoners' Education
Areas of Study	reading, writing, history, ethics, literature, geography, arithmetic	apprenticeships, field work
Occupations	scribes, priests, doctors, lawyers	artisans, farmers, craftspeople

Early Civilizations 57

Each skill has four sections: Explanation, Examples, Application, and Practice.

REVIEWING WHAT YOU KNOW

Review sections appear throughout the book. Each section and chapter has its own review. The Unit Synopsis and Unit Review will help you tie together what you've learned before you move on to the next unit.

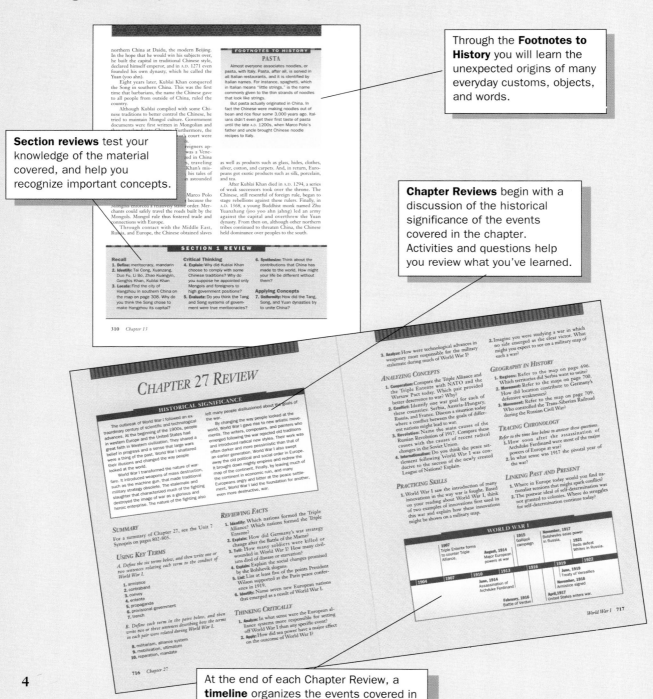

Through the **Footnotes to History** you will learn the unexpected origins of many everyday customs, objects, and words.

Section reviews test your knowledge of the material covered, and help you recognize important concepts.

Chapter Reviews begin with a discussion of the historical significance of the events covered in the chapter. Activities and questions help you review what you've learned.

At the end of each Chapter Review, a **timeline** organizes the events covered in the chapter in an easy-to-read format.

***Human/Environment
Interaction*** *focuses on how
people respond to and alter their
environment. To live comfortably
or even to survive in many parts
of the world, people must make
changes in the environment or
adapt to conditions they cannot
change, or both.*

*How people choose to change
their environment depends on
their attitude toward the natural
setting and on the technology they
have available to change it.*

*Over time, humans increasingly
have been able to manipulate the
environment. Mountains are no
longer barriers—you can fly over
them or tunnel through them.
People have rerouted rivers when
they get in the way of highways or
other construction. Human actions
that change the environment may
also influence regional or global
systems.*

▲
**In Holland, people have created a
series of dikes and canals to
control the water, which otherwise would flood the low land.**

►

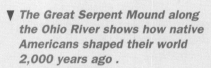

**Wildlife conservation includes
protection of animals, including
the elephant, shown here in
Kenya, East Africa.**

▼ **The Great Serpent Mound along
the Ohio River shows how native
Americans shaped their world
2,000 years ago .**

The **Movement** of people and things between places means that events in other places can have an impact on you personally. Transportation routes, communication systems, and trade connections link people and places throughout the world. Products, ideas, and information are sent around

▼ This Sherpa family in Nepal uses yaks to carry wood through steep mountain passes in the Himalayas.

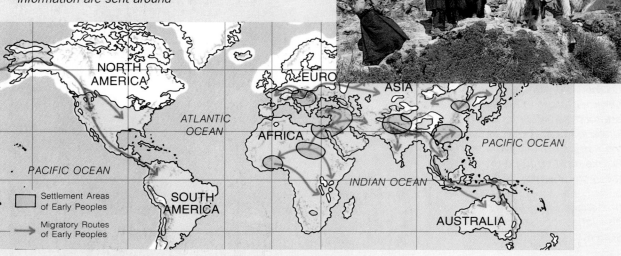

NORTH AMERICA

ATLANTIC OCEAN

EUROPE

ASIA

AFRICA

PACIFIC OCEAN

PACIFIC OCEAN

INDIAN OCEAN

SOUTH AMERICA

AUSTRALIA

▢ Settlement Areas of Early Peoples

→ Migratory Routes of Early Peoples

▲ This map traces the migration routes of early humans during the Ice Age.

the globe, either slowly by ship or almost instantaneously by electronics.

The movement of people is particularly important because it can spread ideas and cultural characteristics from one place to another. Sometimes those ideas or characteristics are accepted in the new location, and the culture is changed by that linkage.

Movement enables you to see that each place is part of the broader system of places, each one dependent upon, and in some way influenced by, the other.

▲ At left, medieval crusaders prepare for a long, hard voyage. Today, satellites transmit information almost instantly (right).

10

A **Region** is an area that is unified by some feature or a mixture of features. These features can be language, landscape, religion, location, occupation of people, or a legal definition such as "county." Because you cannot learn in detail the geography of every place, a region is used to generalize about parts of the earth's surface in either physical or human terms. A neighborhood is an example of a small region, while a cultural region that shares a common language, such as Quebec, would be a larger region. Other regions could be economic, such as a "corn belt," or a political region where the same type of political system is followed (the unification of Germany in the 1800s and again in 1990).

While studying the history of the world, you will be learning about the people and the events that have shaped the past and provide the framework for the future. As you read a World History: The Human Experience, *pay special attention to the ways in which geography has influenced history and fashioned the world in which you live.*

▲
The Berlin Wall divided the city of Berlin into two political zones. When the people tore down the wall, it was a symbol of their desire to reunite Germany, their country.

◄
A traditional men's dance in Papua New Guinea helps to define the region's culture.

The ruins of the ancient city of Machu Picchu atop a mountain in the Peruvian Andes of South America are evidence of the ability of the Inca to adapt to their environment.
▼

11

U N I T

1

Prehistory–500 B.C.

Rise of Civilizations

"At such moments the emotions evade verbal expression, complex and stirring as they are."

Thus British archaeologist Howard Carter reflected on the moment when he had first gazed with awe on the mummy of an ancient Egyptian pharaoh, whose tomb he had spent six years carefully excavating. These words describing his moment of discovery might also have been voiced by any number of others—those who unearthed the skull of the earliest human being found so far, who first made out the marvelous beasts painted on subterranean cave walls, or who cracked the code of ancient pictographs.

A GLOBAL CHRONOLOGY

	2,000,000 B.C.	1,500,000 B.C.	500,000 B.C.	50,000 B.C.	35,000 B.C.
Political Sphere					c. 35,000 Cro-Magnons invent bow and arrow.
Scientific Sphere	c. 2,000,000 Early humans make stone tools.	c. 1,400,000 Early humans discover fire.			
Cultural & Social Sphere			c. 500,000 Early humans acquire language.	c. 50,000 Neanderthal burials prepare dead for afterlife.	

Bust of bearded man from Indus River civilization

4,000 B.C.	3000 B.C.	2000 B.C.	1000 B.C.
c. 3500 Sumerians build first cities.	**c. 3000** Narmer unites Upper and Lower Egypt.		**c. 1150** Olmec civilization begins in Mexico.
	c. 3400 Corn and beans cultivated in the Americas.	**c. 1800** Stonehenge monument built.	
	c. 2000 Chinese writing on oracle bones		**c. 1200** Gilgamesh epic recorded.

Human Beginnings

The toolmaker, sitting near the tall grass in prehistoric Europe, hefted his treasured hammerstone and took careful aim at the nodule of flint he had found. His granddaughter—his apprentice—almost held her breath as she watched silently. Striking the gray flint precisely, again and again, the old man chipped away flake after flake. Then, with eyes skilled from years of experience, he selected a perfectly oval flake, its cutting edge sharp. With some finishing touches, he would have a knife that could cut through an animal's thick hide or bones. The young woman cradled the new tool in her hand. She was proud that her grandfather had chosen her to learn the time-honored craft passed down to him by his ancestors. She did not know that 70,000 years later another woman— sifting through the dirt at the same spot—would pick up the stone knife, excited at her archaeological find.

CHAPTER PREVIEW

Key Terms to Define: prehistory, anthropologist, archaeologist, artifact, radiocarbon dating, culture, technology, nomad, civilization, economy, artisan, cultural diffusion, myth

People to Meet: Donald C. Johanson, Neanderthals, Cro-Magnons

Places to Discover: Hadar, Olduvai Gorge, Neander Valley, Lascaux, Çatal Hüyük

Objectives to Learn:
1. What were the probable origins of the first human beings? What methods do scientists use to prove this?
2. What were the achievements of prehistoric people?

14

In 1940, these prehistoric cave paintings were discovered in Lascaux, France.

3. What economic, political, and social changes resulted from the rise of cities?

Concepts to Understand:

• Movement—Migrations of prehistoric peoples resulted in their spread throughout the world. Sections 1,2

• Innovation—Paleolithic people produced clothing, fire, stone tools, and language. Section 1

• Change—The earliest civilizations began with the evolution of farming settlements into the first cities. Section 2

SECTION 1

The First Humans

History tells the story of humankind. Because historians mostly use written records to gather information about the past, history is said to begin with the invention of writing about 5,500 years ago. But the story of humankind really begins in the time *before* people developed writing—the period called **prehistory.**

Using the best available evidence, scientists have traced the existence on Earth of the first humanlike creatures back to about 4 million years ago. Human beings and the humanlike creatures that preceded them together belong to a group of beings named hominids (HAHM uh nuhds). The scientific study of hominids—their physical features, development, and behavior—is called anthropology. Physical **anthropologists** (an thruh PAHL uh juhsts) compare hominid bones and other fossil remains, looking for changes in such features as brain size and posture. Anthropologists work closely with other researchers, such as **archaeologists** (ahr kee AHL uh justs), who investigate prehistoric life by unearthing and interpreting the **artifacts** left behind by prehistoric people. These artifacts include any objects that were shaped by human hands—tools, pots, and beads, for example—as well as other remains of human life, such as bits of charcoal.

Reaching Back into Prehistory

It was almost noon on November 30, 1974, when a physical anthropologist named Dr. Donald C. Johanson made an extraordinary discovery. For several weeks he had been searching for fossils at Hadar, Ethiopia, a place he described as "a wasteland of bare rock, gravel, and sand." That day, he and his companion, Tom Gray, decided to survey a little gully that other workers had examined earlier. Part of the way up the gully's slope, Johanson spotted a piece of bone that looked like a bit of an arm. Nearby lay the back of a small skull, and a few feet away was a thighbone.

When Johanson recovered all the pieces of bone, including several vertebrae and part of a pelvis, they turned out to be about 40 percent of the skeleton of one individual. Johanson nicknamed her Lucy, after a popular song of the period, "Lucy in the Sky with Diamonds." Hers was the most nearly complete skeleton of any erect-walking prehuman found up to that time.

Johanson later commented about how much his findings depended on luck.

> *If I had not followed a hunch that morning with Tom Gray, Lucy might never have been found. . . . If I had waited another few years, the next rains might have washed many of her bones down the gully. They would have been lost, or at least badly scattered; it would not have been possible to establish that they belonged together.*
>
> —Johanson's account of his discovery in *Lucy: The Beginnings of Humankind,* 1981

Of course, luck played only one part in Johanson's discovery. Skill also helped. Johanson admitted, "Some people are good at finding fossils. Others are hopelessly bad at it. It's a matter of practice, of training your eyes to see what you need to see." Other scientific specialists helped, too, both in making the discovery and in interpreting it. Tom Gray, for example, is a paleoclimatologist (PAY lee oh kly muh TAHL uh juhst), a scientist who studies prehistoric climate. He examined fossil animals and plants around Hadar to understand the environment in which Lucy lived.

Dating Ancient Artifacts   As they unearth the remains of prehuman and human settlements, archaeologists and physical anthropologists face the additional problem of dating what they find. It is easy to determine the relative sequence in which events happened: more recent remains are usually found above older ones. The problem lies in assigning a definite age to fossil bones, tools, and other remains.

Among the techniques for determining the age of organic remains is **radiocarbon dating**. Organic matter includes once-living things like wood artifacts, campfire ashes, hair, and cotton cloth. A very small percentage of the carbon atoms absorbed by every living thing is radioactive. When any living thing dies, it stops absorbing carbon. Then, because radioactive carbon decays at a known rate, archaeologists can measure how much the radioactive carbon in organic remains has decayed and figure out when the animal or plant died.

Radiocarbon dating, however, can be used only for organic matter that is less than 70,000 years old. Researchers have devised other techniques for studying earlier periods. By measuring the rate of decay for chemical elements other than carbon, researchers can date older fossils as far back as 2.6 billion years. These extremely sophisticated methods are not infallible, of course, but they do enable scientists to peer far into the past.

Uncovering Human Origins   Scientists disagree about many aspects of the story of human beginnings. Some interpret the evidence in one way and some in another. As scientists unearth more clues to solve the puzzle, newer evidence may require them to reinterpret older evidence.

According to one of the generally accepted theories, the first prehuman hominids, of whom Lucy is an example, date back about 4 million years. Known as *Australopithecus* (aw stray loh PITH uh kuhs), or "southern ape," they stood about 3.5 to 4.0 feet (1.1 to 1.2 meters) tall and walked on two legs. The brain was small, the nose flat, and the teeth large. *Australopithecus* lived in the humid forests of eastern and southern Africa, where they fed on fruits, leaves, and nuts.

About 3 million years ago, a worldwide climatic change occurred. Africa became cooler and drier, and grassy plains replaced much of the tropical rain forest. Some hominids adapted to the change over many generations by evolving

Learning from Photographs   *Together, archaeologists Mary and Louis Leakey uncovered thousands of fossils and stone artifacts in their search for early hominids at Olduvai, Tanzania, where erosion had carved a nine-mile-long gorge.* **Why would a deep gorge be a likely location for finding very old fossils?**

powerful teeth that enabled them to chew the roots and tubers they found. Others developed larger brains.

Scientists use the Latin word *Homo*, which means "man," to name these large-brained hominids who lived 2 million years ago—and to name all later human beings as well. Anthropologists today are still not certain whether a direct relationship connected *Australopithecus* and human beings or exactly when hominids became truly human. Scientists divided *Homo*—the human genus—into three species that differ somewhat in body structures. These three human or humanlike species arose at different times in prehistory. The earliest of the three was *Homo habilis*, or "person with ability," who lived until about 1.5 million years ago. After *Homo habilis* lived the second type of early human—*Homo erectus*, or "person who walks upright"—who was, in turn, followed about 200,000 years ago by *Homo sapiens*, or "person who thinks." All people living today belong to the species *Homo sapiens*.

Facing the Ice Ages

Even after early human beings appeared, climatic changes continued to play a part in the development of humankind. Between 2 million and 10 thousand years ago, Earth experienced four long periods of cold climate, known as the Ice Ages. During each such period, average temperatures in many parts of the world fell to below freezing, and massive glaciers spread out from the poles, scarring the landforms over which they crept. The northern glaciers covered large portions of Europe, Asia, and North America, and the ice fields of Antarctica stretched over wide regions in the Southern Hemisphere. Only the middle latitudes remained warm enough to support human and animal life. Between glacial periods, Earth's climate warmed overall, and abundant rains brought lush plant growth—until the next glacial period began.

As the sheets of ice formed, the level of the oceans dropped more than 300 feet (90 meters). As a result, some areas that are now separated by water were connected by bridges of land. One

such land bridge joined Japan and mainland Korea, another connected Great Britain and Ireland to western Europe, a third led from the Malay Peninsula through the Indonesian islands almost all the way to Australia, and a fourth connected Asia and North America at the Bering Strait.

Early human beings responded to the environmental changes of the Ice Ages in several ways. Some migrated to warmer places. Others found techniques for keeping warm, such as clothing and fire. Those who could not adapt died from starvation or exposure.

Human Culture

Clothing and fire had become part of the **culture,** or way of life, of prehistoric people. Culture also includes the knowledge of a people, the language they speak, the ways in which they eat and dress, their religious beliefs, and their achievements in art and music.

One of the earliest aspects of culture that people formed was the use of tools. At first they dug roots and tubers out of the ground with wooden digging sticks. Later, they made crude tools of stone, which enabled them to skin small animals and cut off pieces of meat. As their **technology** improved—that is, the skills and useful knowledge available to them for collecting material and making the objects necessary for survival—early people began to create specialized tools, such as food choppers, skin scrapers, and spear points.

The Stone Age   The use of stone tools by early people led historians to apply the name Stone Age to the period before writing became established. Scholars divided the Stone Age into three shorter periods, depending on differences in toolmaking techniques. The first period, the Paleolithic (pay lee uh LITH ik) or "old stone" period, began about 2 million years ago with the first toolmaking by *Homo habilis* and lasted until about 12,000 B.C. The Mesolithic (mez uh LITH ik) or "middle stone" period is usually dated from 12,000 to about 8000 B.C. The Neolithic (nee uh LITH ik) or "new stone" period lasted from about 8000 to 5000 B.C.

Paleolithic Hunter-Gatherers   As yet, archaeologists do not know a great deal about the culture of the early humans called *Homo habilis*, who lived during the first quarter of the Paleolithic period. It seems probable, however, that these prehistoric people made their homes in the trees. They had limited powers of speech, but they were beginning to cooperate with one another in gathering food. Much of the evidence for *Homo habilis* has come from research by Mary and Louis Leakey, and later their son Richard, at Olduvai (OHL duh vy) Gorge and other sites in eastern Africa.

Homo erectus, who succeeded *Homo habilis*, lived on the ground in bands of about 40 to 60 related members. Much more information has been gathered about *Homo erectus* than about *Homo habilis*. These early humans who walked upright lived as **nomads,** using up the food supply in one place and then moving on to another. They were nomadic within their home territory, which averaged 2 square miles (5.2 square kilometers) for each member of the band. High death rates left them with an average life expectancy of 20 years.

During the first part of the Paleolithic period, the early human beings were mostly food gatherers. Scientists think the females gathered fruits, nuts, and seeds, and the males scavenged for meat—either searching for an animal that

CONNECTIONS: HISTORY AND THE ENVIRONMENT

First Migration to America

The United States island Little Diomedes, shown with its modern Inuit village, is separated by about 2 miles (3.2 kilometers) of water from the Soviet Union's Big Diomedes. Both islands in the Bering Strait were part of the Beringia land bridge.

One of the land bridges that formed during the Ice Ages joined Siberia, the easternmost part of Asia, with Alaska, the westernmost part of the Americas. Today, historians have named this land bridge Beringia, after the shallow Bering Strait that covers it today.

Approximately 30,000 years ago, groups of Cro-Magnons began crossing Beringia from Asia to the Americas. According to most anthropologists, these groups were nomadic hunting bands who came in search of migrating herds of animals. We do not know whether the migrants crossed all at once or in successive waves.

From the north the migrants gradually moved south into new territory. Anthropologists estimate that their journey all the way to the southernmost tip of South America took about 600 generations. This is equivalent to a rate of migration of about 18 miles (29 kilometers) per generation, over 18,000 years.

About 10,000 years ago, while the migrants were moving south through the Americas, the last Ice Age ended and the glaciers retreated toward the poles. As the ice sheets melted, large quantities of water poured into the oceans and the sea level rose, covering Beringia and similar land bridges throughout the world. As a result, the Inuit, or Eskimos, who migrated to North America from Asia about 2,000 years ago, arrived by boat rather than on foot.

Making the Connection
1. Why were the Inuit unable to migrate from Asia to North America by land?
2. Predict the effects on human life today of major changes in global climate, either warmer or colder.

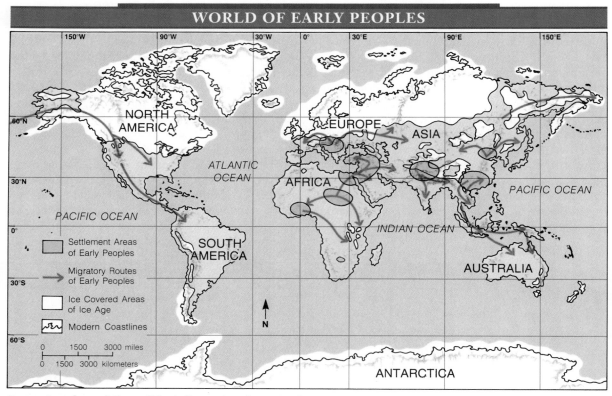

WORLD OF EARLY PEOPLES

Legend:
- Settlement Areas of Early Peoples
- Migratory Routes of Early Peoples
- Ice Covered Areas of Ice Age
- Modern Coastlines

0 1500 3000 miles
0 1500 3000 kilometers

NORTH AMERICA · ATLANTIC OCEAN · PACIFIC OCEAN · SOUTH AMERICA · EUROPE · ASIA · AFRICA · INDIAN OCEAN · PACIFIC OCEAN · AUSTRALIA · ANTARCTICA

Learning from Maps *The information shown in this map spans more than a million years. The glaciers advanced and retreated at least four times during the Ice Ages. Likewise, the early human migrations seem to have occurred gradually in successive waves.* **What was the homeland of Homo erectus *and where did these early people migrate to?***

had died of natural causes or yelling and waving their arms to frighten carnivores away from a kill. By about 500,000 years ago, however, the males had become hunters, using spears and clubs to kill such small prey as deer, pigs, and rabbits. The females, whose movements were restricted by the constant demands of child care, continued to forage close to home for vegetable food.

At about the same time, these early humans also had learned how to make fire. This discovery allowed them to keep warm, cook food, and scare away threatening animals. It also enabled them to live in caves. Before, they had protected themselves from the weather by digging shallow pits and covering these with branches. Now, they were able to drive bears and tigers out of caves and use the caves themselves.

Paleolithic people by this time not only had fire, but were also making clothing. Initially they simply wrapped themselves in animal skins, having first scraped hair and tissue off the inner side of the skins. Later, they laced the skins together with strips of leather.

With clothing, *Homo erectus* could migrate from warm, dry areas to places that were cooler or wetter. Unlike *Homo habilis*, who never moved out of eastern Africa, *Homo erectus* migrated from their native Africa to Europe and Asia. Skeletal remains found in Java have led anthropologists to conclude that *Homo erectus* reached the Indonesian islands 800,000 years ago. *Homo erectus* was clearly well established in China by 460,000 years ago, and the earliest skeletal traces in Europe may also date back around 400,000 years.

Early human beings also were talking to each other about 500,000 years ago instead of just making sounds to indicate emotions and directions. Language was one of humanity's greatest achievements. It enabled individuals to work with one another—to organize a hunting group, for example, or to give specific instructions about where to find a spring of fresh water. It enabled individuals to exchange ideas, such as how the world began or what caused animals to migrate across the plains. Individuals could sit around a hearth fire, eat together, and talk about the day's events. Perhaps most helpful, speech made it possible for the older generation to pass its culture on to the younger generation, enabling new generations to build upon the knowledge of the past.

Learning from Art *Cro-Magnon artists portrayed bison, aurochs (oxlike animals), horses, and deer. These animals, drawn with great accuracy, were always shown in profile.* **What does the accuracy of the representations suggest?**

Early Peoples

Homo erectus discovered, used, and elaborated numerous aspects of culture that are basic to present-day life. These accomplishments occurred extremely slowly, however, taking place over many thousands of years. When *Homo sapiens*, the modern human species, appeared, cultural changes began occurring with much greater frequency.

The Neanderthals Evidence of early *Homo sapiens* dates back about 200,000 years. The first *Homo sapiens* probably were the Neanderthals (nee AN duhr thawlz). Anthropologists named them after the Neander Valley in Germany where their remains were first discovered in the A.D. 1850s. Fossil evidence indicates that Neanderthal people originated in Africa and began spreading into Europe and Asia about 100,000 years ago.

Neanderthals stood about 5.5 feet (1.7 meters) tall. Their brains were slightly larger than those of modern humans, and their bodies were stocky, with thick bones and very muscular necks and shoulders.

Like their predecessors, Neanderthals were nomadic hunter-gatherers who used fire for warmth and for cooking their food, but their toolmaking ability was more sophisticated than that of *Homo erectus*. Neanderthals made their major technological advances in housing. Although they still lived mostly in caves, they improved the cave by digging drainage ditches in the dirt floor to carry away water. They also piled rocks around the cave mouth to cut down on drafts. If they could not find caves, the Neanderthals built shelters. They covered wood

---

FOOTNOTES TO HISTORY

THE FIRST RAZORS

Archaeologists have unearthed evidence that prehistoric men were shaving as early as 18,000 B.C. Some Cro-Magnon cave paintings portray beardless men, and early Cro-Magnon gravesites contain sharpened shells that were the first razors. Later, people hammered razors out of bronze, and eventually, out of iron.

Men's beards have gone in and out of fashion throughout history. The ancient Egyptians, for example, considered a clean-shaven face a symbol of high status. The ancient Persians, however, wore their beards long and curled. Alexander the Great, the conqueror who spread the culture of ancient Greece from Egypt to India, forbade his men to wear beards in battle because in hand-to-hand combat they gave opponents something to grab hold of.

frames with animal skins and held the skins on with mammoth bones.

The Neanderthals also apparently had a belief in life after death. They covered the bodies of their dead with flowers and buried them in shallow graves with food, tools, and weapons.

The Cro-Magnons   About 40,000 years ago a new group of *Homo sapiens* arose. They are known as Cro-Magnons, after the rock shelter in France where their remains were first found in the A.D. 1860s. Taller but less robust than the Neanderthals, the Cro-Magnons looked much like present-day people. Most anthropologists think that the Cro-Magnons first appeared in southwestern Asia and then spread into other parts of the world.

The fossil evidence found so far has been ambiguous about whether or not Cro-Magnons and Neanderthals lived in the same place at the same time, and researchers are uncertain why the Neanderthals disappeared. By about 35,000 B.C., however, the Cro-Magnons had completely replaced the Neanderthals, perhaps by conquest or because they were culturally more advanced. All people on Earth today probably are descended from the Cro-Magnons.

The many advances the Cro-Magnons made in their toolmaking technology transformed human life. They invented the knife and the chisel, and as a result they could work with new materials, such as bone. Soon they were fishing with bone fishhooks and using bone needles to sew fitted leather clothes.

With their invention of the stone axe, Cro-Magnons could chop down trees and shape them into canoes. Soon they were traveling down rivers and along seacoasts. They even crossed 50 miles (80 kilometers) of open sea to reach Australia.

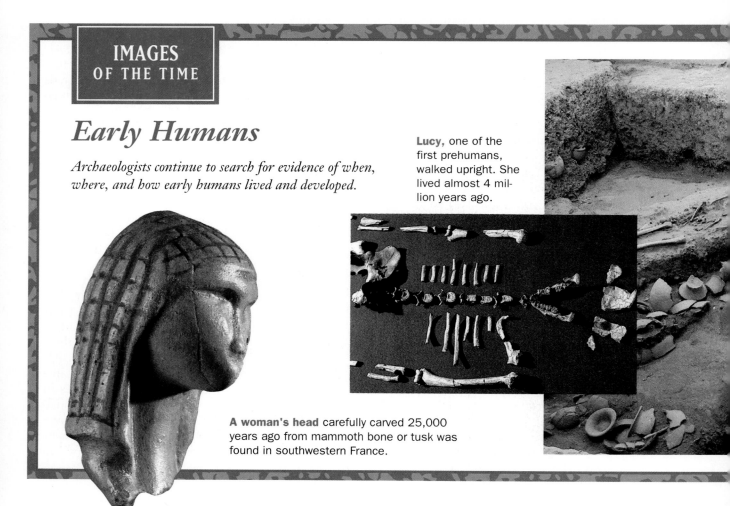

IMAGES OF THE TIME

Early Humans

Archaeologists continue to search for evidence of when, where, and how early humans lived and developed.

Lucy, one of the first prehumans, walked upright. She lived almost 4 million years ago.

A woman's head carefully carved 25,000 years ago from mammoth bone or tusk was found in southwestern France.

Cro-Magnon hunters also invented long-distance weapons—the spear-thrower and the bow and arrow. Now they could hunt several animals at once and larger animals, too, such as wooly mammoths and bison. The food supply increased and with it the number of people on Earth. Anthropologists estimate that by 20,000 B.C., the world population of human beings stood at 3 million.

The increased food supply had political and social consequences as well. Because it was not possible for a lone band of Cro-Magnons to carry out a big game hunt, it became necessary for four or five unrelated bands to cooperate, often for weeks at a time. The cooperating bands probably needed formal rules in order to get along, giving rise in turn to leaders who devised and enforced the rules. The evidence for Cro-Magnon leaders consists of high-status burials. Archaeologists have discovered certain Cro-Magnons buried with ivory daggers, amber beads, and other signs of high rank.

To their technological advances, the Cro-Magnons added accomplished artistry. They created cave paintings like those found at Lascaux (La SKOH), France. Researchers so far can only speculate on the purpose behind the mysterious wall images. Perhaps the hunting scenes were educational, designed to teach young hunters how to recognize prey. On the other hand, the Cro-Magnon painters may have been reaching out to the spiritual world, creating images meant to have mystical powers that would help the hunters.

Archaeologists have discovered some Cro-Magnon figures sculpted from clay or carved from reindeer antlers. They have also found figures of ivory and bone decorated with animal-drawings and abstract designs. Some of these artifacts may well have been used in magic rituals

Archaeologists must record their observations carefully as they excavate ancient sites (left). The hand axe (below) was made 200,000 years ago of carefully chipped stone.

Reflecting on the Times
What sort of observations do archaeologists need to make about the sites they excavate?

EARLY HUMANS				
	Homo habilis	**Homo erectus**	**Homo sapiens**	
Years ago	2.5-1.5 million	1.5 million-200,000	200,000-35,000	40,000-8,000
			Neanderthal	**Cro-Magnon**
Technological Innovations	•Crude stone tools	•Hand-axes and other flaked stone tools •Caves used and pits dug •Clothing of animal skins •Fire controlled for warmth, protection, and cooking	•Spear points and hide scrapers •Shelters built or caves improved •Skins laced for clothing	•Knives, chisel, spearthrower, bow and arrow •Bone tools: needle, fish hook, harpoon •Fish nets, canoes •Sewed leather clothing •Sun-hardened pottery
Social Behaviors	•Limited speech •Food gathering and scavenging	•Language •Nomadic bands •Hunting-gathering	•Planned burials of dead •Care for handi-capped members of community	•Cooperative big game hunts •Status burials for leaders •Possible magic rituals with cave painting and carved, sculpted artifacts

Learning from Charts *The category "Technological Innovations" describes items found in archaeological digs and dated to a specific period. Interpretation of likely prehistoric social behaviors, however, depends mostly on inferences made by archaeologists and anthropologists.* **What evidence do researchers have to support their theory that the social behaviors listed above really existed?**

and probably reflect Cro-Magnon beliefs about spirits that live in animals, plants, the earth, and the sky.

The Neolithic Revolution

During the Neolithic and immediately after, humanity made one of its greatest cultural advances. Over some 5,000 years, people gradually shifted from gathering and hunting food to producing food. Because new agricultural methods led to tremendous changes in life styles, this period is usually called the Neolithic Revolution.

The Mesolithic Period   In a sense, the Mesolithic period was a forerunner of the Neolithic Revolution. Most of the cultural changes of the Mesolithic came in methods of obtaining food. People domesticated the dog and used it to help them hunt small game. They also domesticated the goat to use for meat. Early farmers invented the sickle for cutting wild grains so that they could eat the seeds. Pottery, made from sun-hardened clay, was far more effective for carrying and storing food and water than the pouches of animal skin they had used previously.

The expanded food supply increased the average life expectancy to 30 years. It also increased world population to about 10 million.

The Neolithic Period   The Neolithic Revolution not only took place slowly, but also it began at different times in different parts of the world. Archaeologists have found evidence of agriculture in the Middle East dating as far back as 8000 B.C. In contrast, China did not have agriculture until about 5000 B.C.

The crops that Neolithic people domesticated varied from place to place, depending on the varieties of wild plants and on the crops best adapted to the region's climate—wheat and barley in the Middle East, rice in Southeast Asia, and corn in the Americas. Farmers in Africa cultivated bananas and yams, and farmers in South America grew potatoes.

Neolithic people supplemented crops by domesticating animals. They used cattle, pigs, and sheep for meat and sometimes milk. Chickens provided eggs as well as meat.

Now that they could produce food, many more people survived. Anthropologists estimate that by 4000 B.C. the world population had risen to 90 million. Once they had agriculture, people could also settle in communities instead of wandering as nomads. Soon, agricultural villages of about 200 or so inhabitants could be found where soil was fertile and water abundant. Archaeologists date one of the earliest such villages—Jericho, in the Israeli-occupied West Bank—back to 8000 B.C. Another ancient village, Çatal Hüyük (chah TUHL hoo YOOK), in today's Turkey, was inhabited between 7000 and 6300 B.C.

Çatal Hüyük is the largest Neolithic village that archaeologists have so far discovered. Its people built rectangular, flat-roofed houses of mud bricks placed in wooden frames. Houses of several related families made up a compound with shared walls. People had to walk across roofs. The villagers also painted the interior walls of their windowless houses with vivid scenes of hunting and other activities.

Neolithic farmers eventually made their work easier and more productive by inventing the plow and by training oxen to pull it. They also learned how to fertilize their fields with ashes, fish, and manure.

The relatively steady food supply quickened the pace of technological advance. Neolithic villagers invented the loom and began weaving textiles of linen and wool. They invented the wheel and used it for transportation; found a way to bake clay bricks for construction; and learned how to hammer the metals copper, lead, and gold to make jewelry and weapons.

The agricultural way of life led to many other changes. People created calendars to measure the seasons and determine when to plant crops. Because their food supply depended on land ownership, people now cared about such matters as boundary lines and rules of inheritance. Warfare probably came into being as villages competed for land and water.

Neolithic people also believed in many deities. The spirits that supposedly surrounded them throughout nature were transformed into humanlike gods and goddesses with the power to help or hurt people. The people of Çatal Hüyük, for example, set up shrines at which they prayed, danced, and offered gifts in honor of their deities. Their most worshiped goddess, the Earth Mother or the goddess of fertility, brought good harvests and many children.

SECTION 1 REVIEW

Recall

1. **Define:** prehistory, anthropologist, archaeologist, artifact, radiocarbon dating, culture, technology, nomad
2. **Identify:** Donald Johanson, Paleolithic period, Neanderthals, Cro-Magnons, Neolithic Revolution
3. **Locate:** Tell where each of these locations is and why each is valuable in archaeological research: Hadar, Olduvai Gorge, Neander Valley, Lascaux, Çatal Hüyük.
4. **List:** What innovations were made during the Neolithic period?

Critical Thinking

5. **Analyze:** Compare and contrast the culture of *Homo erectus* with that of early *Homo sapiens*. Think about housing, technology, mobility, and religious beliefs.
6. **Evaluate:** Does the use of agriculture deserve to be called a revolution? Give reasons.

Applying Concepts

7. **Movement:** Explain how changes in climate affected the migration of early peoples from one part of the world to another.

Emergence of Civilization

Gradually, over thousands of years, some of the early agricultural villages evolved into highly complex societies, known as **civilizations.** The people of a civilization lived in a highly organized society with an advanced knowledge of farming, trade, government, art, and science. The word *civilization* comes from the Latin word *civitas*, meaning "city," and most historians equate the rise of civilizations with that of cities. Because inhabitants of most cities learned the art of writing, the rise of cities also marks the beginning of history.

As with agriculture, cities formed at different times in different parts of the world. But many of the earliest civilizations had one thing in common: they rose from agricultural settlements in river valleys like that of the Nile in Egypt. The earliest cities that archaeologists have uncovered so far lie in the valley of the Tigris and Euphrates (yoo FRAYT eez) rivers in southwest Asia and date back to about 3500 B.C. Cities arose in the Indus River Valley in south Asia some 1,000 years later. The first urban communities in east Asia appeared about 1500 B.C. in the Huang He (hwong huh) Valley. By about 1000 B.C. cities were flourishing in Europe and in the Americas, and by 750 B.C. in sub-Saharan Africa.

Besides the newly created writing and cities, the early river valley civilizations shared several other basic features. People's labor was specialized, with different men and women doing different jobs. The civilization depended on advanced technology, such as metalworking skills. Each civilization invariably had some form of government to coordinate large-scale cooperative efforts such as building irrigation systems. And the people in each civilization shared a complex system of values and beliefs.

You will read more about specific river valley civilizations in Chapter 2; in this section we focus on the features that all civilizations have shared. Not all societies formed civilizations, however. Some people continued to live in small agricultural villages and others by hunting and gathering. Some nomadic people built a specialized culture that relied on moving herds of domesticated animals in search of good pasture.

The Economy of a Civilization

The ways in which people use their environment to meet their material needs is known as an **economy.** Any civilization's economy depends on its farmers' growing surplus food. With extra food, fewer men and women needed to farm and more could earn their living in other occupations.

First Irrigation Systems A major reason that farmers could produce surpluses of grain crops was that early civilizations built massive irrigation systems. Neolithic farmers had relied at first on rainfall to water their crops. Later, farmers transported water to grow the crops by digging ditches from a nearby river to their fields. Then they began building small canals and simple reservoirs.

Farmers also built earthen dikes and dams to control flooding in their valley by the river itself. They could now count on a reasonably steady flow of water and prevent destructive flooding.

Specialization of Labor As men and women continued to specialize in ways of earning a living, **artisans,** or workers skilled in a craft, became increasingly productive and creative. The longer they worked at one task, such as producing storage vessels, the more they learned about how to handle available materials,

Learning from Photographs *Archaeologists in the 1920s excavated the ancient city of Mohenjo-Daro near the Indus River in Pakistan.* **What do the remains of a large-scale construction project, such as a walled city with a rectangular grid of streets, suggest about the civilization that built it?**

such as different types of clay. Gradually they turned out larger quantities of goods and improved the quality of their products. Potters shaped delicate jars for ceremonial purposes as well as the thick containers they made for everyday use. Textiles became richer and more elaborate. Artisans decorated the handles of weapons with elaborate designs.

Metalworking Technology

In a major advance over the Neolithic period techniques, metalworkers in the early civilizations learned to make alloys, or mixtures of metals. The most important alloy was bronze, a reddish-brown metal made by mixing melted copper and tin. Historians refer to the period that followed the Stone Age as the Bronze Age, when bronze replaced flint and stone as the chief material for weapons and tools.

Bronze, harder than either copper or tin alone, took a sharper cutting edge. Artisans also found it much easier to cast bronze—that is, shape the liquid metal by pouring it into a mold to harden. Because the copper- and tin-containing ores needed to make bronze were scarce, however, the metal was expensive and therefore used only by kings, priests, and soldiers. Bronze was so useful that cities often sent out trading expeditions to search for new sources of copper and tin.

Long-Distance Trade

The search for new sources of copper and tin is an example of the long-distance trade that accompanied the rise of early civilizations. At first farmers and artisans traded within their own communities. They would exchange their goods and services, perhaps trading a length of linen cloth for a basket of grain or a freshly slaughtered goat for medical advice.

Eventually ancient people began traveling to nearby communities to exchange goods. After a while merchants, a specialized class of traders, began to handle the exchange of goods, and trading expeditions soon were covering longer routes.

Some long-distance trade moved overland by means of animal caravans. Some goods were transported by water. People floated down rivers on rafts. They made boats, propelling them in shallow water with poles and, in deeper water, with paddles and oars. After a time, people learned how to harness the force of the wind, and rivers and seacoasts became filled with sailing ships. By about 2200 B.C., traders were crossing the open waters of the Arabian Sea.

Along with goods, ideas were actively shared. This exchange of goods and ideas when cultures come in contact is known as **cultural diffusion.** Although early civilizations came up with many similar ideas independently, other

The Bronze Age

The baby elephant, on the back of the larger elephant, is the handle for the lid of this Shang bronze vessel.

The Bronze Age began as early as 5,000 years ago in the Tigris-Euphrates and Nile river valleys. In Bronze Age China, in the valley of the Huang He River, skilled artisans working for the rulers of the Shang dynasty (1600s to 1000s B.C.) produced hundreds of elaborate bronze vessels of the highest technical and artistic quality. Chinese bronze casting may have begun long before the beginning of the Shang dynasty. Tin and copper, the two metal ores used to produce bronze, were readily available in the Huang He region.

Most Shang bronzes seem to have been ritual vessels made for use in ceremonies honoring ancestors. They were made in various shapes, each apparently meant for a specific use. Some vessels held sacrificial meat; others were used for wine. Many, like the ritual wine vessel shown, were animal-shaped.

The technique of bronze casting used by Shang metalworkers took a great deal of work. First, the artist formed a clay model of the vessel to be made. This model was then elaborated with the basic decoration that would appear on the piece. Once this clay model was complete, sections of fresh clay were used to take impres-sions of the model. These impressions were then carefully baked to retain their shape and detail. After baking, they were pieced together to form a mold. This mold was then filled with molten bronze. Once cooled, the clay mold was removed, and the bronze vessel remained. The metalworker would then work further on the piece, adding the finishing touches to the decoration and polishing the surface.

Shang bronzes are remarkable for the vitality of their detailed designs. Often shaped as animals (either real or imaginary), they are further decorated with animals, figures, and abstract designs. These objects, because of their dynamic shapes and designs, seem to have a life of their own.

Shang metalworkers were probably esteemed in their day for their fine work. In exploring the remains of Shang cities, archaeologists have discovered that bronze casters lived near the royal residence or in very specific sections of the city. This suggests that they probably led a privileged life, and that their works and skills were highly valued.

Responding to the Arts
1. What technique of bronze casting did Shang metalworkers use?
2. What were Shang bronze vessels used for?

ideas arose in a few areas and then spread throughout the world by cultural diffusion. When ancient peoples learned about the technology and other ideas of different civilizations, the new knowledge stimulated them to improve their own skills and way of life.

Living Together in Cities

Gradually, civilizations grew both more prosperous and more complex. Early cities had from 5,000 to 30,000 inhabitants. A population of this size could not function in the same way that a Neolithic farming village of 200 inhabitants had.

Planning and Leadership Ancient cities confronted several problems unknown in the Neolithic period. Because city residents depended on farmers for their food, they had to make certain that farmers regularly brought their surplus food to city markets. At the same time, farmers could not build dams, dig irrigation ditches, and maintain reservoirs on their own. As civilizations prospered, they drew the attention and envy of nomadic groups, who would repeatedly raid and pillage outlying farms and attack traveling merchants. In short, the first cities needed a way of supervising and protecting agriculture and trade.

The early city dwellers found two solutions to these problems. First, ancient cities organized a group of government officials whose job it was to oversee the collection, storage, and distribution of agricultural surpluses. These officials also organized and directed the labor force needed for large-scale construction projects, such as irrigation systems, public buildings, and city walls. Second, ancient cities hired a class of professional soldiers to guard their territory and trade routes.

At the head of the army and government officials was a ruling class often led by a king, although women also held positions of authority. The ruling class justified its position and power by means of religion. According to ancient beliefs, the land produced food only if the gods and goddesses looked on the people with favor. One of the king's main functions, therefore, was to carry out religious ceremonies to ensure an abundant harvest. The first kings were probably elected, but in time they began to inherit their positions.

Levels of Social Standing Archaeological evidence for the position of the ruling class can be found both in the treasures with which they were buried and in the physical layout of the ancient cities. At the city's center was an area that held the most imposing religious and government buildings. Nearby stood the residences of the ruling class. Next to these came the houses of the merchants. Farther out, the shops and dwellings of specific groups of artisans—such as weavers or smiths—were established in special streets or quarters. Farmers, as well as sailors and fishermen, lived on the city's outskirts. Archaeological evidence suggests too that slaves, who were probably captured in battle, lived in many parts of the city.

At the center of the early cities lived a specialized group—the priesthood. Priests and priestesses were responsible for daily sacrifices and other special ceremonies to keep the deities favorably disposed toward the people. But the influence of the priesthood extended into other areas as well.

Invention of Writing Many archaeologists think that writing originated with the records that priests kept of the wheat, cloth, livestock, and other items they received as religious offerings. At first the priests used marks and pictures, called pictograms, to represent products. After a time they used the marks and pictures to represent abstract ideas and, later still, to represent sounds. Priestly records listed the individual men and women who were heads of households, landowners, and merchants. Soon the priests were also recording such information as the king's battle victories, along with legal codes, medical texts, and observations of the stars.

Systems of Values

Among the materials recorded by the priesthoods in early civilizations were **myths,** traditional stories explaining how the world was formed, how people came into being, and what they owed their creator. Ancient Sumerian priests in the Tigris-Euphrates River Valley wrote their myth of creation, for example, on seven clay tablets.

According to the story, before creation there were two gods, Apsu the First Father and Tiamat the First Mother. They married and had many children. "But each generation of gods grew taller than its parents . . . [and] the younger gods could do things their parents had never tried to do." Eventually Apsu's great-grandson Ea made a magic spell and killed Apsu. Ea's son Marduk killed Tiamat. Then:

> M*arduk turned again to the body of Tiamat.*
> *He slit her body like a shellfish into two parts.*
> *Half he raised on high and set it up as sky. . . .*
> *He marked the places for the stars. . . .*
> *He planned the days and nights, the months and years.*
> *From the lower half of Tiamat's body, Marduk made the earth.*
> *Her bones became its rocks.*
> *Her blood its rivers and oceans. . . .*
> *"We need creatures to serve us," he said.*
> *"I will create man and woman who must learn to plow land to plant, and make the earth bring forth food and drink for us.*
> *I will make them of clay." . . .*

> —Sumerian account of creation from *The Seven Tablets of Creation*, date unknown

After relating how the people drained marshes for farmland, built walled cities, learned to make bricks, and built a great temple at the center of their biggest city, the myth continues:

> D*aily they sang praises to Marduk, supreme among the gods*
> *He who created the vast spaces and fashioned earth and men;*
> *He who both creates and destroys; who is god of storms and of light;*
> *He who directs justice; a refuge for those in trouble;*
> *From whom no evil doer can escape;*
> *His wisdom is broad. His heart is wide. His sympathy is warm.*

Creation myths have been found in every civilization. Because these myths vary from place to place, historians often examine them for evidence of a people's customs and values. For example, the archaeologists who unearthed and translated the seven Sumerian clay tablets could easily infer information about Sumer's values and beliefs. To begin with, the clay tablets reveal that Marduk, though not the first god, had become—at the time the tablets were recorded—the leading one in the hierarchy of deities by supplanting the goddess Tiamat. The Sumerians seemed to believe too that evil should—and would—be punished. Apparently they also thought it was effective to praise and worship Marduk. Of course, the inferences an archaeologist can reasonably make from a myth are often limited and leave many unanswered questions.

SECTION 2 REVIEW

Recall
1. **Define:** civilization, economy, artisan, cultural diffusion, myth
2. **Describe:** List briefly the basic features of a civilization.
3. **Locate:** In which four river valleys did the earliest civilizations in the world evolve? Where are these river valleys located?

Critical Thinking
4. **Analyze:** Explain the relationship between the rise of cities and large-scale irrigation systems, labor specialization, long-distance trade, and well-organized government.
5. **Synthesize:** Imagine that you rule a city in an early civilization. What instructions would

you give to your government officials to improve the living conditions of your people?

Applying Concepts
6. **Innovation:** Explain how the technological innovations of the first civilizations improved toolmaking and the transportation of trade goods.

UNDERSTANDING MAP PROJECTIONS

Have you ever wondered why Greenland appears to be a larger land mass than Australia on some world maps? Yet, an almanac states that Australia has a larger land area than Greenland.

Explanation

The reason for this contradiction is because when map makers attempt to transfer the three-dimensional surface of the earth to a flat surface, some inaccuracies occur. Mapmakers use *projections*, drawings on a flat surface, showing a globe's grid lines. These projections may stretch or shrink the Earth's features, depending on the map's intended use.

Maps can show one of three things. There are two major kinds of projections. A *conformal map* shows land areas in their true shapes, while distorting their actual size. An *equal area map* shows land areas in correct proportion to one another, but distorts shapes.

Notice the map on this page. It is called a *Cylindrical (Mercator) Projection*. Imagine wrapping a cylinder of paper around a globe. A light from within projects the globe's surface on the paper. The resulting projection is conformal—Alaska apppears larger than Mexico, but in reality the opposite is true. Distortion is greatest nearest the poles. This kind of map is used for plotting navigation routes, as it allows for a true measurement of compass direction.

A *conic projection* is formed by placing a cone of paper over a lighted globe. The projection is a compromise between the conformal and the equal area maps. Neither the size nor the shape is perfect, but neither are greatly distorted. This projection is best to show areas in middle latitudes.

Use the following steps to help you understand map projections:
- Determine what type of map projection—conformal or equal area—was used.
- Identify the purpose for the projection—true shape or correct proportions.

Application

Turn to the map on pages 984–985. Compare the sizes and shapes of the features on this map to those on a globe. Based on this comparison, answer the following questions:

1. What is the map's projection?
2. How does the map distort Earth's features?
3. In what way does this map accurately present Earth's features?
4. Can you think of reasons why the mapmaker chose this projection?

Practice

Turn to Practicing Skills on page 33 of the Chapter Review for further practice in understanding map projections.

Cylindrical Projection *(Mercator): This projection is accurate along the line where the cylinder touches the globe, with great distortion near the poles. The projection is useful for plotting navigation routes, because a line connecting any two points gives the compass direction between them.*

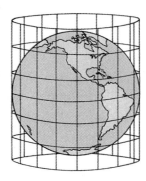

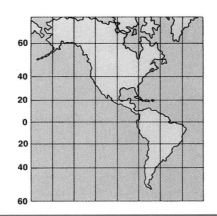

CHAPTER 1 REVIEW

HISTORICAL SIGNIFICANCE

During the 2 million years of the Stone Age, prehistoric people created many fundamentals of human life—for example, toolmaking technology, cooperation among individuals and groups, communication of culture through language, and religious belief. The basic structures of civilizations, however, were formed at the end of the Neolithic period, when surplus foods were produced, labor became specialized, and, later, cities arose. City life was essential to development of ancient civilizations because it enabled large numbers of people to live together and, by pooling their efforts, promoted creative activity and further improvements in the way they lived. Throughout the centuries, as civilizations rose and fell, many of their cities fell into ruin, sometimes to be rebuilt several times. Today the populations of most cities are more than 100 times that of these first cities. Modern cities serve as centers for a complex economic, cultural, and political network in a world that has become, in many ways, one global civilization.

SUMMARY

For a summary of Chapter 1, see the Unit 1 Synopsis on pages 82–85.

USING KEY TERMS

Write a sentence about each group of words below. The sentences should show how the words are related.

1. technology, artisan
2. myth, civilization
3. nomad, economy
4. anthropologist, prehistory
5. radiocarbon dating, archaeologist, artifact
6. culture, cultural diffusion

REVIEWING FACTS

1. **Describe:** Which four land bridges that people used for migrating during the Ice Ages are underwater today?
2. **Locate:** Where did the Cro-Magnons seem to have originated before spreading into other parts of the world?
3. **Tell:** Why is the acquisition of language one of humanity's greatest achievements?
4. **Explain:** How did invention of the spear-thrower and the bow and arrow change the Cro-Magnons' food supply?

5. **List:** What two major problems faced by inhabitants of ancient cities did not exist in the Neolithic period?
6. **Explain:** What do many archaeologists consider to be the relationship between religion and the origin of writing?

THINKING CRITICALLY

1. **Apply:** How did climatic changes affect the development of humankind?
2. **Analyze:** What were the major cultural features of each period in the Stone Age?
3. **Synthesize:** How do you think invention of the stone axe might have changed the culture of people who lived along the banks of a navigable river?
4. **Evaluate:** What do you think was the most valuable skill that prehistoric people learned during the Paleolithic period? during the Neolithic period?

ANALYZING CONCEPTS

1. **Movement:** Describe the migrations of human beings from their place of origin to other parts of the world.
2. **Change:** In what ways did city life in the early civilizations differ from village life in the first agricultural settlements?

3. Innovation: How did the discovery of fire affect the tools prehistoric people used and the way they lived?

PRACTICING SKILLS

1. Imagine you were using a map of South America that was created with the Mercator projection as it is shown on page 31 in Understanding Map Projections. What two assumptions could you make about the map based on your knowledge of these projections?
2. Turn to the map of South Asia on page 995. Can you think of a reason why the Mercator projection is used to show this portion of the globe? If the equator is the point at which distortion is least, which country on this map will be most distorted?
3. Look at the maps on pages 986 and 987. In the azimuthal equal area projection used for these maps, distances are most accurate at the center of the map but more distorted closer to the edges. Why does this projection work well for the continents of North and South America?

GEOGRAPHY IN HISTORY

1. **Location:** In what part of the world have archaeologists found the earliest evidence of agriculture and cities?

2. **Place:** What were the physical characteristics of humanity's place of origin?
3. **Human-environment relationships:** Why did the first civilizations form in river valleys?

TRACING CHRONOLOGY

Refer to the time line below to answer these questions.
1. For about how many years has our modern species of human beings lived?
2. How soon after the last Ice Age did prehistoric people begin to use agriculture?
3. Which event on the time line marks the beginning of the Paleolithic period?

LINKING PAST AND PRESENT

1. Many aspects of human culture are passed down from generation to generation. What cultural achievements of *Homo erectus*—from more than 200,000 years ago—do we still use today?
2. Government officials 5,000 years ago organized and directed the large labor forces needed for large-scale construction projects such as irrigation systems, public buildings, and city walls. They oversaw the collection, storage, and distribution of agricultural surpluses. How do government officials' activities in the early river valley civilizations compare with those of government officials in your community?

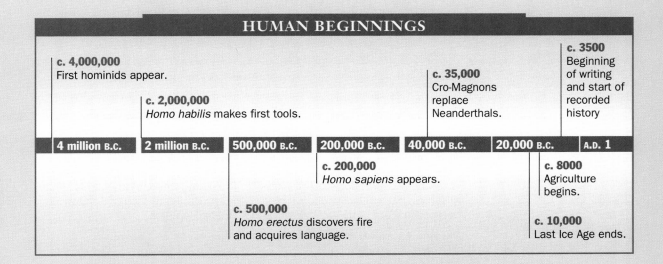

HUMAN BEGINNINGS

c. 4,000,000 First hominids appear.

c. 2,000,000 *Homo habilis* makes first tools.

c. 35,000 Cro-Magnons replace Neanderthals.

c. 3500 Beginning of writing and start of recorded history

| 4 million B.C. | 2 million B.C. | 500,000 B.C. | 200,000 B.C. | 40,000 B.C. | 20,000 B.C. | A.D. 1 |

c. 200,000 *Homo sapiens* appears.

c. 8000 Agriculture begins.

c. 500,000 *Homo erectus* discovers fire and acquires language.

c. 10,000 Last Ice Age ends.

Early Civilizations

*U*nder the blazing Egyptian sun, a gigantic stone structure began to emerge from the desert sand. A hundred thousand men toiled together, building a burial pyramid for Khufu, a king of Egypt about 2500 B.C. Gangs of laborers dragged blocks of limestone, each weighing 2.5 short tons (2.3 metric tons), along log roadways from the quarries. Others ferried stone blocks across the Nile River and hauled the immense stone blocks up winding ramps of dirt and brick to pile layer upon layer of stone. Farmers during the rest of the year, these laborers were compelled to work for the three or four months during which the annual flooding of the Nile made farming impossible. It would take 20 years of their forced labor and more than 2 million blocks of stone before the Egyptians completed the massive pyramid. Today, the Great Pyramid so many slaved over still stands at Giza, near the city of Cairo.

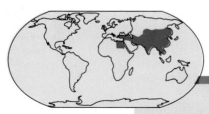

CHAPTER PREVIEW

Key Terms to Define: monarchy, dynasty, theocracy, bureaucracy, pharaoh, empire, polytheism, hieroglyphics, city-state, cuneiform, monsoon, mandate

People to Meet: Narmer, Ahmose, Hatshepsut, Thutmose III, Akhenaton, Sargon I, Hammurabi, Yu the Great

Places to Discover: Nile River, Tigris and Euphrates rivers, Fertile Crescent, Mesopotamia, Ebla, Indus River, Harappa, Mohenjo-Daro, Huang He River

Objectives to Learn:
1. How did geography and climate affect early civilizations?
2. What features were common to all the river valley civilizations?

Colossal statues of Egyptian pharaoh Ramses II guard the entrance to a temple to the god Amon-Ra.

3. In what ways were each of the river valley civilizations unique?

Concepts to Understand:

• Relation to environment—The river valley civilizations learned to control the floodwaters of the rivers upon which their agriculture relied. Sections 1,2,3,4

• Cooperation—The peoples of the early civilizations worked together to build irrigation systems and cities. Sections 1,2,3,4

• Innovation—The river valley civilizations created writing systems and devised many new technologies. Sections 1,2,3,4

• Cultural diffusion—The rise of the first empires led to the spread of ideas, technologies, and ways of living. Sections 1,2

Ancient Egypt

Many years after the early period of Egyptian history, the Greek historian Herodotus (hih RAHD uh tuhs) observed about Egypt that "there is no land that possesses so many wonders, nor any that has such a number of works that defy description." Of the four early river valley civilizations, people today probably know the most about the ancient civilization in the valley along the Nile River. People still marvel at its remains in modern Egypt—especially the enormous Sphinx, the wondrous pyramids, and the mummies buried in lavish tombs.

Learning from Photographs *Because the prevailing winds in the Nile Valley blow south, or upstream, Egyptian boats can sail up the Nile River with the wind or can drift downstream against the wind, carried by the current.* **What has the Nile River contributed to Egypt besides a means of transportation?**

A River Valley and Its People

Running like a ribbon through great expanses of desert in northeastern Africa, the Nile River for thousands of years has shaped the lives of those who have dwelled on its banks. Egypt and the surrounding region receive little rainfall, but people have relied instead on the Nile's predictable yearly floods to bring them water.

At 4,160 miles (6,660 kilometers) in length, the Nile River is the longest river in the world. Several sources in the highlands of east Africa, including Lake Victoria, feed the Nile. The river then takes a northward route to the Mediterranean Sea. On its course through Egypt it crosses six cataracts, or waterfalls. Because of the cataracts the Nile is not completely navigable until it reaches its last 650 miles (1,040 kilometers). Before emptying into the Mediterranean, the Nile splits into many branches, forming a marshy, fan-shaped delta.

The Gifts of the River   The lush, green Nile Valley contrasts sharply with the vast areas of desert that stretch for hundreds of miles on either side. Rich black soil covers the river's banks and extends about 10 miles (16 kilometers) beyond—farther into the Nile Delta. In late spring and in summer, heavy tropical rains in central Africa and melting mountain snow in east Africa add to the Nile's volume. As a result the river overflows its banks and floods the land nearby. The floodwaters recede in late fall, leaving behind thick deposits of silt carried down from the highlands.

As early as 5000 B.C., nomadic hunter-gatherers who had roamed throughout northeastern Africa began to settle by the Nile. They took up a farming life regulated by the river's seasonal rise and fall, cultivating cereal crops such as wheat and barley. The Nile offered these

Neolithic farmers other resources as well—ducks and geese in its marshlands and fish in its waters. The early Egyptians also harvested papyrus growing wild along the banks of the Nile, using the long, thin reeds to make rope, matting, sandals, baskets, and later on, sheets of paperlike writing material.

Uniting Egypt Protected from foreign invasion by the deserts and the cataracts, the early agricultural villages by the river grew and prospered. In time a few strong leaders joined villages together into small kingdoms, or **monarchies,** each under the absolute or unrestricted rule of its king. Eventually the weaker kingdoms gave way to the stronger. By 4000 B.C. ancient Egypt consisted of two large kingdoms: Lower Egypt in the north, in the Nile Delta, and Upper Egypt in the south, in the Nile Valley.

Around 3000 B.C., Narmer, also known as Menes (MEE neez), a king of Upper Egypt, gathered the forces of the south and led them north to invade and conquer Lower Egypt. Narmer established the first government that ruled all of the country. He united Upper and Lower Egypt and governed both lands from a capital city he had built at Memphis, near the border of the two kingdoms.

Narmer's reign marked the beginning of the first Egyptian **dynasty,** or line of rulers from one family. From 3000 until 332 B.C., a series of 30 dynasties ruled Egypt. Historians have

CONNECTIONS:
HISTORY
AND THE
ENVIRONMENT

Stemming the Flood

A farmer uses a shadoof to lift water for irrigation.

Akhet, the time of the flood; *peret,* the time when the land emerged again from the floodwaters; *shomu,* the time when water was in short supply—these were the three seasons in the Egyptian year. The year, and life itself, revolved around the Nile River.

To flourish, even to survive, the people of Egypt had to take control of their environment. At first, farmers used water from the river more or less passively, merely scattering seeds in the wet mud after the flood had subsided. Over the years they devised actual irrigation systems—ditches and canals to carry the floodwaters to basins. There the silt settled and served as fertilizer for planting crops. In some places, machines, such as the *shadoof,* lifted water to cultivated land. Eventually farmers built dams and reservoirs, making year-round irrigation possible.

Today, the Aswan High Dam in southeastern Egypt traps the waters of the Nile for later irrigation in a huge reservoir. Built in the 1960s, the Aswan High Dam generates electrical power and protects crops and people against seasonal flooding. Although the dam has benefited agricultural production, it also has affected the environment. Because the dam prevents the Nile from flowing over the valley land, the floodwaters no longer deposit fertile silt annually. Today, farmers must add expensive chemical fertilizers to their fields. The absence of silt has also increased land erosion along the Nile Delta.

Making the Connection
1. How did the Egyptians gradually manage to control the waters of the Nile?
2. Why might people today object to the building of a dam?

organized the dynasties into three great periods: the Old Kingdom, the Middle Kingdom, and the New Kingdom.

The Old Kingdom

The Old Kingdom lasted from about 2700 to 2200 B.C. During the first centuries of the unified kingdom, Upper and Lower Egypt kept their separate identities. In time, however, Egypt built a strong national government under its kings. It also developed the basic features of its civilization.

The Egyptian Monarchy   The Egyptians eventually saw themselves as subjects of one unified kingdom as they began to look upon their king as a god who ruled all Egyptians. Such a government, in which the same person is both the religious leader and the political leader, is called a **theocracy**.

As a god, the king performed many ritual acts believed to benefit the entire kingdom, such as cutting the first ripe grain to ensure a good harvest. As political leader, the king wielded absolute power, issuing commands regarded as the law of the land.

Unable to carry out all official duties himself, the king delegated many administrative responsibilities to a **bureaucracy**, a group of government officials headed by the king's vizier, or prime minister. Through the vizier and other bureaucrats the king controlled trade and collected taxes. He also indirectly supervised the building of dams, canals, and storehouses for grain—all crucial to survival for an agriculture-based civilization.

Pyramids: A Lasting Legacy   To honor their god-kings and to provide them with an eternal place of rest, the Egyptians of the Old Kingdom built lasting monuments—the pyramids. The Step Pyramid, built in the mid-2600s B.C. overlooking Memphis for King Zoser, was the first large, all-stone building in the world. The masons who constructed it first cut the stone into small bricks, which they then pieced together to build the pyramid. About 75 years later, however, the Egyptians had learned how

to move masses of stone and so began to build with huge stones. The three pyramids at Giza stand today as testimony to the Egyptians' new technology and engineering skills. The Great Pyramid, built around 2500 B.C. for King Khufu, stands 481 feet (144 meters) high and is the largest of the three. Long, narrow passageways lead to the king's burial chamber deep within the pyramid.

The Egyptians believed that a king's soul continued to guide the affairs of the kingdom after death. Before entombing a dead king in his pyramid, they first preserved the king's body from decay by a procedure called embalming. Next they wrapped the dried, shrunken body—called a mummy—with long strips of linen and placed it in an elaborate coffin. Only then could the coffin lie in the burial chamber of the pyramid along with the king's clothing, weapons, furniture, and jewelry—personal possessions the king could enjoy in the afterlife.

The Middle Kingdom

Around 2200 B.C., the kings in Memphis began to lose their grip on power as ambitious nobles fought each other for control of Egypt. The stable, ordered world of the Old Kingdom crumbled into a period of upheaval and violence. Then around 2050 B.C., a new dynasty reunited Egypt and moved the capital south to Thebes, a city in Upper Egypt. This new kingdom, known as the Middle Kingdom, would last until after 1800 B.C.

In time Theban kings became as powerful as the rulers of the Old Kingdom and brought unruly local governments under their control. They supported irrigation projects that added thousands of acres to the land already under cultivation. The Theban dynasty seized new territory for Egypt, setting up fortresses along the Nile to capture Nubia (part of modern Sudan) and launching military campaigns against Syria. Theban kings also ordered construction of a canal between the Nile and the Red Sea, and as a result, Egyptian ships traded along the coasts of the Arabian Peninsula and east Africa.

In the 1700s B.C., local leaders began to challenge the kings' power again, shattering the peace and general prosperity of the Middle Kingdom. At the same time, Egypt also faced its first serious threat—invasion by the Hyksos (HIHK sahs), a people from western Asia. The Hyksos swept across the desert into Egypt with new tools for war—bronze weapons and horse-drawn chariots. So armed, they quickly conquered the Egyptians, who fought on foot with copper and stone weapons. The Hyksos established a new dynasty which ruled for more than 150 years.

The New Kingdom

The Egyptians despised their Hyksos masters. To overthrow Hyksos rule, the Egyptians learned to use Hyksos weapons and adopted the fighting style of their conquerors. In about 1600 B.C. Ahmose (ah MOH suh), an Egyptian prince, raised an army and drove the Hyksos out.

Pharaohs Rule an Empire After defeating the Hyksos, Ahmose founded a new Egyptian dynasty—the first of the New Kingdom. Ahmose and the monarchs who succeeded him assumed the title **pharaoh**, an Egyptian word meaning "great house of the king."

Ahmose devoted his energies to rebuilding Egypt, restoring abandoned temples and reopening avenues of trade. The pharaohs who directly followed him, however, used large armies to realize their dreams of conquest and expansion. They pressed farther to the east and into the rest of Africa than had the kings of the Middle Kingdom.

Around 1480 B.C., Queen Hatshepsut (hat shehp' soot) came to power in Egypt. She first ruled with her husband and then took the throne as regent, ruling on behalf of her stepson Thutmose (thoot MOH suh) III, who was too young to govern. Finally she had herself crowned pharaoh. Hatshepsut assumed all the royal trappings of power, including the false beard traditionally worn by Egyptian kings. Hatshepsut carried out an extensive building program, which included a great funeral temple and a tomb built into the hills of what is now called the Valley of the Kings. The decorated walls of her temple tell of the trading expedition

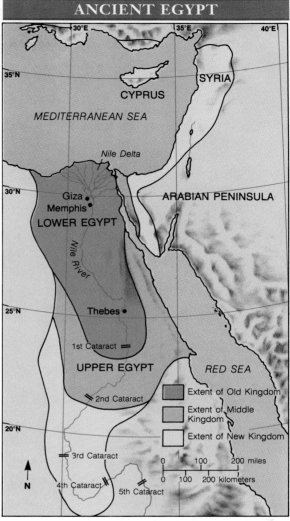

ANCIENT EGYPT

Learning from Maps *Throughout most of Egyptian history a land bridge, where the Suez Canal is now located, connected Africa and Asia.* **How did this land connection contribute to cultural diffusion between ancient Egypt and the rest of the Middle East?**

she sent south to Punt (probably in modern Somalia or Ethiopia) which returned with gold, myrrh, baboons, and animal skins.

Thutmose III did reclaim the throne at Hatshepsut's death and soon after marched with a large army out of Egypt toward the northeast. He conquered Syria and pushed the Egyptian frontier to its easternmost point at the northern

The Mask of Tutankhamen

Slowly . . . the remains of passage debris . . . were removed, until at last we had the whole door clear before us. The decisive moment had arrived. With trembling hands I made a tiny breach in the upper left-hand corner. . . . widening the hole a little, I inserted the candle and peered in. . . . At first I could see nothing, . . . but presently, as my eyes grew accustomed to the light, details of the room within emerged slowly from the mist, strange animals, statues, and gold . . . everywhere the glint of gold.

—Howard Carter and A.C. Mace, *The Tomb of Tut-ankh-Amen*, 1923

This is British archaeologist Howard Carter's account of his suspense as he opened Tutankhamen's tomb. For years Carter had sought the ruler's burial place in the Valley of the Kings, where Egyptian pharaohs were traditionally buried. On November 26, 1922, Carter opened a chamber that had been shrouded in silence and darkness for over 3,000 years.

The mask of Tutankhamen, who ruled from about 1334 to 1325 B.C., is among the most spectacular works of art to have survived from Egypt's New Kingdom. The mask, made of pure gold and decorated with lapis lazuli, quartz, and colored glass, covered the head and shoulders of the linen-wrapped mummy. The beard on Tutankhamen's funeral mask associates him with Osiris, the god of the afterworld. The vulture and cobra at his brow symbolize Upper and Lower Egypt, the two regions over which he ruled.

Unlike Egyptian tomb sculpture of earlier times, Tutankhamen's mask seems to be a true portrait. Earlier images of pharaohs were often idealized, using symbols and inscriptions to indicate who was portrayed. Even though the artist who made Tutankhamen's mask used such symbols, he or she personalized the mask, making it look like the young king.

As impressive as Tutankhamen's tomb is, this pharaoh was not an important king in ancient Egypt. He came to the throne when only a boy, and died before reaching age 20. His tomb is unique because it was not robbed of its treasures as many Egyptian tombs were.

Responding to the Arts

1. What symbols of kingship did Egyptian artists include on Tutankhamen's mask?
2. Why were so many elaborate objects buried with the pharaoh?

Euphrates River. In a short time, Thutmose III had established an **empire** for Egypt, bringing many different territories under the rule of one government.

The Egyptian empire grew rich from both commerce and tribute from the conquered territories. The capital of Thebes, with its palaces, temples, and carved stone obelisks reflected the wealth won by conquest. No longer isolated from other cultures, Egyptians benefited from cultural diffusion within their empire. They began to appreciate the artistry of the objects received in trade or tribute, and they may even have incorporated new gods and goddesses into Egyptian religion.

Akhenaton Founds a Religion   Other religious changes happened when Pharaoh Amenhotep IV (ahm uhn HOH tehp) assumed power about 1370 B.C. Supported by his wife, Nefertiti, Amenhotep broke with the Egyptian tradition of worshiping many deities. He declared that Egyptians should worship only Aton, the sun-disk god, as the one supreme deity. Claiming to be Aton's equal, Amenhotep changed his royal name to Akhenaton (ahk uh NAHT uhn), which means "spirit of Aton." To stress the break with the past, Akhenaton moved the capital from Thebes to a new city in central Egypt dedicated to Aton.

These controversial changes had an unsettling effect on Egypt. Many of the common people rejected the worship of Aton, a god without human form, and continued to believe in many deities. The priests of the old religion resented their loss of power. At the same time, the army was unhappy about Egypt's loss of territories under Akhenaton's weak rule.

After Akhenaton's death, the priests restored the old religion. They also made Akhenaton's successor, Tutankhamen, return the capital to Thebes. Shortly thereafter, the head of the Egyptian army overthrew the dynasty and created a new one.

Recovery and Decline   During the 1200s B.C. the pharaohs were mostly military leaders who regained some of the territory and prestige that Egypt had lost during the previous century. One of these pharaohs, Ramses II, reigned for 67 years. He built many temples and erected large statues of himself.

In the 1100s B.C., another pharaoh also named Ramses led Egypt into a long and costly war for the control of Syria. Ramses III barely escaped assassination, and after his war, Egypt entered a long period of decline. Eventually it split into two kingdoms. Beginning in 945 B.C., Egypt came under control by foreigners—among them the Libyans from the west and the Kushites from the south.

Life in Ancient Egypt

At the height of its glory, ancient Egypt was home to some 8 million persons, most of whom lived in the Nile Valley and its delta. Even though Egyptian society was divided into classes, ambitious people in the lower classes could improve their social status somewhat.

Levels of Egyptian Society   Royalty, nobles, and priests formed the top of the social pyramid. They controlled religious and political affairs. Members of the wealthy upper class lived in the cities or on estates along the Nile River. There they built large, elaborately decorated homes surrounded by magnificent gardens, pools, and orchards.

Below the upper class on the pyramid was the middle class. Its members—artisans, scribes, merchants, and tax collectors—carried out the business activities of Egypt. Middle-class

---

FOOTNOTES TO HISTORY

EYE MAKEUP

c. 4000 B.C.—When applying cosmetics, the ancient Egyptians—both men and women—focused on adorning their eyes. They favored an eye shadow made from powdered malachite (a green copper ore) but also used eye glitter, made by crushing the iridescent shells of beetles. With a black paste called kohl they outlined their eyes and darkened their lashes and eyebrows. Many women shaved their eyebrows and applied false ones, striving for the ideal look of eyebrows that met above the nose.

Learning from Art *In early Egypt, women of the lower class worked along with their husbands in the fields, harvesting wheat and barley.* **What clues does this painting offer you about Egyptian life?**

homes—mostly in the cities—were comfortable but not elegant. During the New Kingdom, the middle class profited from the empire's prosperity. Some of its members became very wealthy and moved into the upper class.

The majority of Egyptians belonged to the poor lower class. Many were farmers. For the land they farmed, they paid rent to the king—usually a large percentage of their crop. Farmers also worked on building projects for the king, and some members of the lower class served the priests and the nobles. They lived in small villages of simple huts on or near the large estates along the Nile.

Egyptian Families   In the cities and in the upper class the husband, wife, and children made up the family group. Outside the cities, especially among farmers and laborers, a family also included grandparents and other relatives, who took an active part in the life of the household. An Egyptian child was taught great respect for his or her parents, with a son particularly expected to maintain his father's tomb.

The status of Egyptian women changed somewhat as the centuries passed. Literature of the Old Kingdom portrayed women as the property of their husbands and as valued producers of children. Wise men reminded children to cherish their mothers for bearing them, nourishing them, and loving and caring for them. By the time of the empire, documents indicate that women's legal rights had improved. Women could buy, own, and sell property in their own names, testify in court, and start divorce and other legal proceedings. The lives of Hatshepsut and some of the queens of the later pharaohs,

like Nefertiti, suggest that privileged women of the royalty could attain prominence.

Worshiping Many Gods and Goddesses
Religion guided every aspect of Egyptian life. Egyptian religion was based on **polytheism**, or the worship of many deities, except during the controversial rule of Akhenaton. Often gods and goddesses were represented as part human and part animal—Horus, the sky god, had the head of a hawk. The Egyptians in each region worshiped local deities, but rulers and priests promoted the worship of specific gods and goddesses over all of Egypt. These deities included Ra, the sun god, whom the Theban pharaohs joined with their favorite god Amon to make one god, Amon-Ra.

The popular god Osiris, initially the powerful god of the Nile, became the god responsible for the life, death, and rebirth of all living things. The Egyptians worshiped Osiris and his wife, the goddess Isis, as rulers of the realm of the dead. They believed that Osiris determined a person's fate after death.

Because their religion stressed an afterlife, Egyptians devoted much time and wealth to preparing for survival in the next world. At first they believed that only kings and wealthy people could enjoy an afterlife. By the time of the New Kingdom, however, poor people could also hope for eternal life with Osiris's help.

Writing with Pictures   In their earliest writing system, called **hieroglyphics**, the Egyptians carved onto pieces of slate picture symbols, or hieroglyphs, to stand for objects, ideas, and sounds. For everyday business, however, the

Egyptians used a cursive, or flowing, script known as hieratic, which simplified and connected the picture symbols.

Few people in ancient Egypt could read or write. But some Egyptians did prepare at special schools for a career as a scribe in government or commerce. Scribes learned to write hieratic script on paper made from the papyrus reed.

After the decline of ancient Egypt, hieroglyphs fell from use, and their meaning remained a mystery to the world's scholars for nearly 2,000 years. Then in A.D. 1799 French soldiers in Egypt found near the town of Rosetta a slab of stone dating to the 200s B.C., carved with Greek letters and two forms of Egyptian writing. In A.D. 1822, a French archaeologist named Jean-Francois Champollion (shan pawl YOHN) figured out how the Greek text on the Rosetta stone matched the Egyptian texts. Using the Greek version, he was able to decipher the Egyptian hieroglyphics.

Some of the oldest writings from the Old Kingdom were carved on the inner walls of the pyramids. Scribes also copied many prayers and hymns to the gods and goddesses. The Book of the Dead collected texts telling how to reach a happy afterlife, recording more than 200 prayers and magic formulas.

The ancient Egyptians also wrote secular, or nonreligious, works such as collections of proverbs. One vizier gave this advice: "Do not repeat slander; you should not hear it, for it is the result of hot temper. Repeat a matter seen, not what is heard." And the Egyptians enjoyed adventure stories, fairy tales, and love stories:

*N*ow I'll lie down inside
and act as if I'm sick.
My neighbors will come in to visit,
and with them my girl.
She'll put the doctors out,
for she's the one to know my hurt.

— A love poem by a young Egyptian, date unknown

Achievements in Science   Pyramids, temples, and other monuments—their walls covered with paintings of deities, people, animals, and plants—bear witness to the architectural and artistic achievement of Egyptian artisans. But these works would not have been possible without advances in disciplines such as mathematics. The Egyptians developed a number system that enabled them to calculate area and volume, and they used principles of geometry to survey flooded land.

The Egyptians worked out an accurate 365-day calendar by basing their year not only on the movements of the moon but also on Sirius, the bright Dog Star. Sirius rises annually in the sky just before the Nile's flood begins.

Egyptians also developed medical expertise recognized throughout the ancient world, having first learned about human anatomy in their practice of embalming. Egyptian doctors wrote directions on papyrus scrolls for using splints, bandages, and compresses when treating fractures, wounds, and diseases. Other ancient civilizations would acquire much of their medical knowledge from the Egyptians.

SECTION 1 REVIEW

Recall

1. **Define:** monarchy, dynasty, theocracy, bureaucracy, pharaoh, empire, polytheism, hieroglyphics
2. **Identify:** Narmer, the Hyksos, Ahmose, Hatshepsut, Thutmose III, Akhenaton, Ramses II, Ramses III
3. **Explain:** How did a bureaucracy become part of government in ancient Egypt?

Critical Thinking

4. **Apply:** Select the class of Egyptian society to which you would have preferred to belong. Provide a brief explanation for your choice.
5. **Evaluate:** Compare the reigns of Ahmose, Hatshepsut, and Thutmose III. Which reign do you think contributed most to the development of Egypt? Support your opinion.

Applying Concepts

6. **Cultural diffusion:** Describe the period of greatest cultural diffusion in early Egypt.

SECTION 2

The Fertile Crescent

About 5000 B.C.—at the same time as Egyptian nomads moved into the valley of the Nile River—groups of herders started to journey north from the Arabian Peninsula. Rainfall had declined over the years in the peninsula, and the lakes and grasslands there had begun to dry up. Other peoples—from the highlands near present-day Turkey—moved south at this time. Driven by poor weather, they also fled war and overpopulation.

Both groups of migrants were headed into the crescent-shaped strip of relatively fertile land that stretched from the Mediterranean Sea to the Persian Gulf, curving around northern Syria. Called the Fertile Crescent, this region included portions of the modern nations of Israel, Jordan, Lebanon, Turkey, Syria, and Iraq.

Many of the peoples migrating from the north and south chose to settle in Mesopotamia (mehs uh puh TAY mee uh), the eastern part of the Fertile Crescent. Located on a low plain lying between the Tigris and Euphrates rivers, the name *Mesopotamia* means "land between the rivers" in the Greek language. The two rivers begin in the hills of present-day eastern Turkey and later run parallel to each other through what is now Iraq on their way to the Persian Gulf. In this region, the newcomers built villages and farmed the land.

The Twin Rivers

Beginning with Neolithic farmers, people used the Tigris and Euphrates rivers to water their crops. Unlike the Nile River, however, the twin rivers did not provide a regular supply of water. In the summer no rain fell, and the Mesopotamian plain was dry. As a result, water shortages often coincided with the fall planting season. By the spring harvest season, however, the rivers swelled with rain and melting snow. Clogged with deposits of silt, the Tigris and Euphrates rivers often overflowed onto the plain. Sometimes strong floods swept away whole villages and fields. The time of year of such flooding, however, was never predictable, and the water level of the rivers often varied from year to year.

The early Mesopotamian villages cooperated in order to meet the rivers' challenges. Together they first built dams and escape channels to control the seasonal floodwaters and later constructed canals and ditches to bring river water to irrigate their fields. As a result of their determined efforts, Mesopotamian farmers were producing food, especially grain crops, in abundance by 4000 B.C.

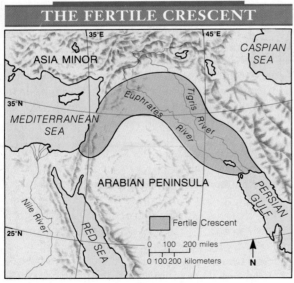

THE FERTILE CRESCENT

Learning from Maps The Fertile Crescent of the ancient world curved through parts of today's Middle East region. **What is the distance from the Mediterranean Sea to the Persian Gulf?**

The Sumerian Civilization

Around 3500 B.C. a people from either Central Asia or Asia Minor—the Sumerians—arrived in Mesopotamia. They settled in the lower part of the Tigris-Euphrates river valley, known as Sumer. Sumer became the birthplace of what historians have considered the world's first cities.

The Sumerian City-States By 3000 B.C. the Sumerians had established 12 **city-states** in the Tigris-Euphrates valley, including Ur, Uruk, and Eridu. A typical Sumerian city-state consisted of the city itself and the land and villages surrounding it. The population of each city-state ranged from 20,000 to 250,000.

The people of Sumer shared a common culture, speaking the same language and worshiping the same gods and goddesses. Sumerian city-states also shared some physical features. A ziggurat (ZIHG uh rat), or temple, made of sun-dried brick and decorated with colored tile, was built in each city-state. Sumerians built a ziggurat as a series of terraces, with each terrace smaller than the one below. A monumental staircase climbed to a shrine atop the ziggurat. Only priests and priestesses were allowed to enter the shrine, which was dedicated to the city-state's chief deity. In form a ziggurat resembled a pyramid—both being massive stepped or peaked structures—but the feeling and emphasis of the two differed. A pyramid hid a sunless tomb reachable only through winding passageways. A ziggurat raised a shrine to the sky, accessible by mounting stairs in the broad sun.

Each Sumerian city-state usually governed itself independently of the others. In the city-state of Uruk, for example, a council of nobles and a general assembly of citizens controlled political affairs at first. But later, as city-states faced threats of foreign invaders and began to vie with each other for land and water rights, the citizens of each city-state typically chose a military leader from among themselves. By 2700 B.C. the leaders of several city-states ruled as kings. Soon after, the kingships became hereditary.

A Sumerian king served not only as military leader but as the high priest, who represented the god or goddess of the city-state. Thus the

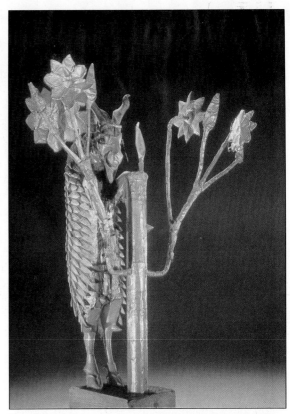

Learning from Art *Some archaeologists have inferred that this Sumerian statue of a goat behind the branches of a flowering tree symbolized agricultural fertility.* **Why would religious rituals for agriculture have been powerful in ancient times?**

governments of the city-states were not only monarchies but theocracies. Because the Sumerians believed that much of the land belonged to a city-state's god or goddess, a king and his priests closely supervised farming. A king also enforced the law and set penalties for lawbreakers. Most punishments consisted of fines and did not involve bodily injury or loss of life. The following Sumerian law is only one example of this system: "If a man has broken another man's bones with a weapon, he shall pay one mina [unit of weight or value] of silver."

The Roles of Men and Women Sumerian law extensively regulated family life and outlined the roles of men and women. As the heads of households, men exercised great authority over their wives and children. According to Sumerian

Learning from Artifacts *Sumerian students memorized hundreds of cuneiform symbols by writing on clay tablets about the size of a postcard.* ***Why were scribes so highly respected in ancient Sumer?***

law codes, a man could sell his wife or children into slavery if he needed the money to pay a debt. He could also divorce his wife for the slightest cause. For a Sumerian woman, on the other hand, the law codes made divorce much more difficult. Women did enjoy some legal rights, however. Like Egyptian women, they could buy and sell property. They could also operate their own businesses and own and sell their own slaves.

Writing on Clay Tablets   Commerce and trade were important economic activities in the Sumerian city-states. The Sumerians quickly developed a system of writing so they could keep accounts, record transactions, and prepare documents. Archaeologists believe that the writing system the Sumerians invented is the oldest in the world, dating to about 3100 B.C. The **cuneiform** (kyoo NEE uh fawrm) system of writing began with pictograms—as did Egyptian hieroglyphics—and consisted of hundreds of wedge-shaped markings made by pressing the end of a sharpened reed on wet clay tablets. Then the Sumerians dried or baked the tablets until they were hard. Eventually cuneiform evolved into a script that became—2,000 years later—a model for alphabetic systems of writing.

Sumerians wishing to learn cuneiform and become scribes studied for many years at special schools called eddubas. As educated professionals, scribes rose to high positions in Sumerian society. They produced business records, lists of historical dates, and literary works.

One of these literary works, the epic poem about Gilgamesh, was written down before 1800 B.C. Scholars believe that the Gilgamesh epic may be the oldest story in the world. The scribes probably based the stories of Gilgamesh, a godlike man who performs heroic deeds, on an actual king of the city-state of Uruk.

The Many Deities of Sumer   The Sumerians, like the Egyptians, developed a polytheistic religion. The numerous Sumerian deities presided over a specific natural force—rain, moon, air—or over a human activity—plowing or brickmaking, for example. An, the highest Sumerian deity, was responsible for the seasons. Another important god—Enlil, god of winds and agriculture—created the hoe. Although Sumerians honored all the deities, each city-state claimed as its own one god or goddess, to whom its citizens prayed and offered sacrifices.

The Sumerians pictured their gods and goddesses as unpredictable, selfish beings who had little regard for human beings. The Sumerians believed that if deities became angry, they would cause misfortunes such as floods or famine. To appease their temperamental gods and goddesses, Sumerian priests and priestesses performed religious ceremonies and rituals.

FOOTNOTES TO HISTORY

THE UMBRELLA

1400 B.C.—Umbrellas actually originated under the sunny skies of Mesopotamia. As close relatives of the fan, the first palm frond or feather umbrellas shielded the head from the harsh rays and scorching heat of the Middle Eastern sun. The word umbrella is itself derived from the Latin umbra, meaning "shade." In Mesopotamia and Egypt, umbrella-toting servants trotted alongside kings and queens and other members of the upper class. An umbrella also signified high rank for women in ancient Greece. Roman women were the first to raise umbrellas to rainy skies, oiling their sunshades to waterproof them.

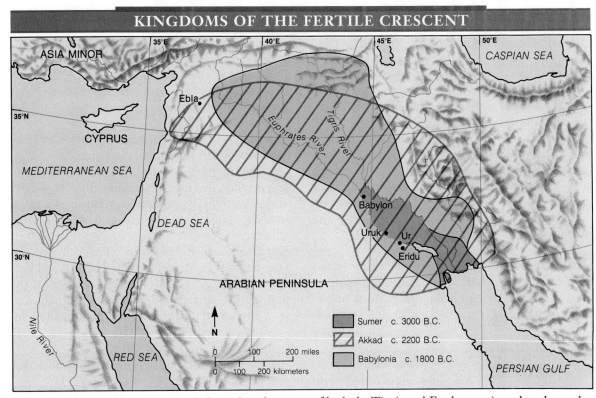

Learning from Maps *Scholars believe that the course of both the Tigris and Euphrates rivers has changed a great deal since the first Sumerian city-states were built.* **What present-day countries fall within the boundaries of the Akkadian and Babylonian empires?**

Unlike the Egyptians, the Sumerians felt that humans had little control over their lives and could not expect a happy life after death. Only a grim underworld, empty of light and air, awaited them—an afterlife where the dead were only pale shadows.

Sumerian Inventions Historians credit the Sumerians with numerous technological innovations. The Sumerians developed the wagon wheel, for example, to better transport people and goods, the arch to build sturdier buildings, the potter's wheel to shape containers, and the sundial to keep time. They developed a number system based on 60 and devised a 12-month calendar based on the cycles of the moon. The Sumerian civilization also was the first to make bronze out of copper and tin and to develop a metal plow. These and other Sumerian achievements have prompted one scholar to observe that "history begins at Sumer."

First Mesopotamian Empires

After a long period of conquest and reconquest, the Sumerian city-states eventually fell to foreign invaders in the 2000s B.C. The invaders of Sumer, like the Egyptians of the New Kingdom, were inspired by dreams of empire.

Sargon Leads the Akkadians The first empire builder in Mesopotamia—Sargon I—may have been born a herder or a farmer's son. According to legend his mother abandoned him as a baby, setting him out on the Euphrates River in a reed basket. Downstream a farmer irrigating his fields pulled Sargon ashore and raised him as his own.

Sargon's people, the Akkadians, were Semites, one of the nomadic groups that had migrated from the Arabian Peninsula to the Fertile Crescent around 5000 B.C. The Akkadians established a kingdom called Akkad (AHK ahd)

in northern Mesopotamia. When Sargon assumed power in Akkad around 2300 B.C. he immediately launched a military campaign of expansion. First he marched south and took Sumer. Then he moved north. Sargon united all of the city-states of Mesopotamia in one empire, which predated the empire of the Egyptian New Kingdom by more than 800 years.

Under Sargon's rule the people of Mesopotamia began to use the Akkadian language instead of Sumerian. But the Akkadians adopted various Sumerian religious and agricultural practices. After Sargon's death, however, his dynasty ruled with less success, and the Akkadian Empire disintegrated.

The Kingdom of Ebla   No one really knows how far Sargon's empire extended. Historians do know, however, that Ebla, a kingdom in the eastern part of the Fertile Crescent in what is

now northern Syria, fought unsuccessfully against Sargon for control of the Euphrates River trade. When Sargon's grandson captured Ebla, he burned the royal archives. Yet fire did not destroy the thousands of clay tablets of cuneiform writing stored there. These tablets and other finds from recent excavations at Ebla have convinced historians that highly developed Semitic civilizations prospered in that area of Syria earlier than previously believed.

The overland trade that passed between Egypt and Mesopotamia made Ebla a wealthy and powerful city-state. Ebla controlled a number of neighboring towns, from which it exacted tribute.

The kings of Ebla were elected for seven-year terms. In addition to their political and military role, they looked after the welfare of the poor. If the kings failed, they could be removed by a council of elders. After 2000 B.C., Ebla de-

IMAGES OF THE TIME

Mesopotamia

In the valley of the Tigris and Euphrates rivers, the people of Mesopotamia depended on their environment.

Even today the Euphrates River dominates the surrounding countryside.

Votive figures were placed at shrines so that worshipers could offer eternal prayers.

clined and eventually was destroyed by the Amorites, a Semitic people from western Syria.

Hammurabi's Babylonian Empire

Around the same time that they destroyed Ebla, the Amorites saw an opening for themselves beyond Syria. After the Akkadian empire disintegrated, the Sumerian civilization had briefly recovered under the leadership of the kings of Ur, but soon it was again in decline. The Amorites poured into Mesopotamia and overran many Sumerian centers, including Babylon (about 50 miles, or 80 kilometers, south of modern Iraq's capital, Baghdad). The dynasty that they founded at Babylon later produced a ruler who would dominate Mesopotamia: Hammurabi.

Hammurabi, the sixth king of the dynasty at Babylon, used his might to put down other kings in Mesopotamia, including fellow Amorites. He eventually brought the entire region under his control, reorganizing the tax system and ordering local officials to build and repair irrigation canals. Under his rule, Babylon became a major trade center. Merchants from as far away as India and China paid gold and silver for the grain and cloth the Babylonians produced.

Historians consider Hammurabi's greatest achievement his effort "to make justice appear in the land." Hammurabi collected laws of the various Mesopotamian city-states and created a law code covering the entire region. When completed, Hammurabi's code consisted of 282 sections dealing with most aspects of daily life. It clearly stated which actions were considered violations and assigned a specific punishment for each. Hammurabi's code penalized wrongdoers more severely than did the old Sumerian laws. Instead of fining violators, it exacted what the Bible later expressed as "an eye for an eye, and a tooth for a tooth." According to his harsh approach:

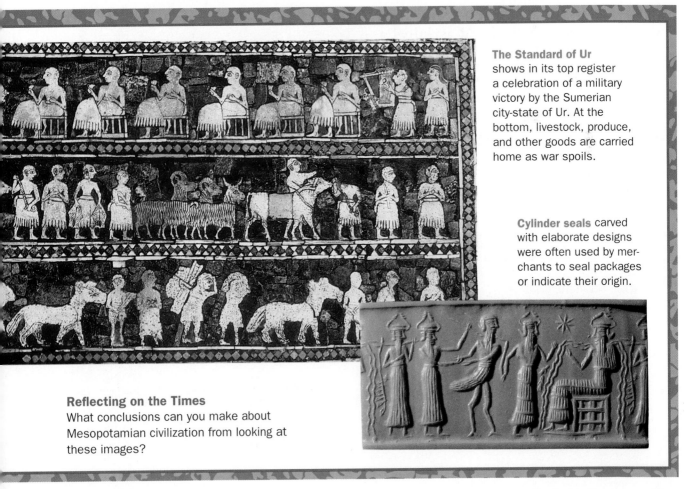

The Standard of Ur shows in its top register a celebration of a military victory by the Sumerian city-state of Ur. At the bottom, livestock, produce, and other goods are carried home as war spoils.

Cylinder seals carved with elaborate designs were often used by merchants to seal packages or indicate their origin.

Reflecting on the Times
What conclusions can you make about Mesopotamian civilization from looking at these images?

If a builder has built a house for a man and has not made his work sound, so that the house he has made falls down and causes the death of the owner of the house, that builder shall be put to death. If it causes the death of the son of the owner of the house, they shall kill the son of that builder.

Other sections of Hammurabi's code covered the property of married women, adoption and inheritance, interest rates on loans, and damage to fields by cattle. Some laws were attempts to protect the less powerful—for example, protecting wives against beatings or neglect by their husbands.

Historians have been able to infer from Hammurabi's code a threefold division of Babylonian social classes—the kings, priests, and nobles at the top; the artisans, small merchants, scribes, and farmers next; and slaves as the lowest group. His laws varied according to the class of the person offended against, with more severe penalties if the criminal had assaulted a landowner than if he had hurt a slave. Most slaves had been captured in war or had failed to pay their debts.

Hammurabi's dynasty ended and his empire fell apart when the Hittites, a people from Asia Minor, raided Babylon—about 1600 B.C. However, as you will learn in Chapter 3, Babylon would again play a role in Mesopotamian civilization in the 600s B.C. as the capital of a new empire under the Chaldeans.

Learning from Artifacts *At the top of the stone slab inscribed in cuneiform with Hammurabi's code of laws, King Hammurabi is pictured standing in front of the sun god Shamesh—the supreme judge—who delivers the laws to him.* **Why were Hammurabi's laws carved in stone for public display?**

SECTION 2 REVIEW

Recall

1. **Define:** city-state, cuneiform
2. **Identify:** the Sumerians, Gilgamesh, Sargon I, the Akkadians, the Amorites, Hammurabi
3. **Locate:** Find the Fertile Crescent on the maps on pages 44 and 47. Describe the region of the Fertile Crescent in which the ancient Sumerian civilization developed.

4. **Explain:** What was the purpose of the religious ceremonies and rituals performed by Sumerian priests and priestesses?

Critical Thinking

5. **Analyze:** Contrast Hammurabi's code with Sumerian law. Which do you think served justice better? Explain your answers.

6. **Synthesize:** Imagine that you are a citizen in the general assembly of the Sumerian city-state of Uruk. Do you favor the establishment of a monarchy at Uruk? Explain your answer.

Applying Concepts

7. **Innovation:** Explain why the Sumerians developed their writing system.

Early India

A third civilization, surpassing both Egypt and Sumer in land area, developed in the Indus River Valley far to the east, in South Asia. It reached its height at about the time of the Akkadian and Babylonian empires between about 2500 and 1500 B.C.

Subcontinent of South Asia

Three modern nations—India, Pakistan, and Bangladesh—trace their cultural roots to the Indus River Valley civilization. These countries are located on the subcontinent of South Asia, a large, triangular-shaped landmass that juts into the Indian Ocean.

Bounded by Mountains Natural barriers separate the subcontinent of South Asia from the rest of Asia. Water surrounds the landmass on the east and west. To the north rise two lofty mountain ranges—the Himalayas and the Hindu Kush (see the map on page 52). Throughout history, invaders who wished to penetrate the subcontinent by land have had to traverse the few high mountain passes of the Hindu Kush.

Plains dominate the landscape to the south of the mountains. Beyond the plains lies the Deccan Plateau, separated from the plains by a range of hills called the Vindhya (VIHN dyuh). The Ghats, low mountains that descend to coastal plains, border the plateau east and west.

Three rivers flow from the Himalayas across the plains of the subcontinent, fed by rain and melting mountain snow. The Indus River drains into the Arabian Sea, and the Ganges (GAN jeez) and Brahmaputra (brahm uh PYOO truh) rivers join and empty into the Bay of Bengal, forming a wide delta. The Ganges-Brahmaputra delta and the plain that lies between the Indus and Ganges rivers are alluvial, built from soils deposited by the rivers. Like the valley and delta of the Nile and the plains of the Tigris and Euphrates, fertile alluvial areas of South Asia have supported vast numbers of people over the ages.

Seasonal Winds The northern mountains ensure generally warm or hot weather in South Asia. Like a wall, they block blasts of cold air from central Asia. Two seasonal winds called **monsoons** rule the climate, however, and shape the pattern of life on the subcontinent.

The northeast, or winter, monsoon blows from November to March—the southwest, or summer, monsoon from May or June to September. The northeast wind brings dry air from the cool mountains, and the average winter temperatures of the Indus-Ganges plain remain mild—above 60°F (16°C). By June, temperatures have soared, sometimes exceeding 100°F (38°C), and the people of the subcontinent welcome the rain-bearing southwest wind blowing off the ocean.

Because of the torrential downpours of the southwest monsoon, however, the rivers swell rapidly, then widen across the flat plains and rush to the sea. The flooding enriches the soil, but in some years abnormally heavy rains drown people and animals and destroy whole villages. In other years the monsoon arrives late or rainfall is light; then crops are poor and people go hungry. The people of the plains are dependent on the monsoons.

The Indus Valley Civilization

Less than a century ago, archaeologists working in the valley of the Indus River first identified an ancient civilization on the subcontinent of South Asia. They dated this early civilization to about 2500 B.C.

Centrally Planned Cities Archaeologists named the Indus Valley settlements "Harappan civilization" after one of its major cities, Harappa (huh RAP uh), located in what is now northern Pakistan. Mohenjo-Daro (moh HEHN joh DAHR oh), another important Harappan city, lay nearer the Arabian Sea.

The ruins of Harappa and Mohenjo-Daro are outstanding examples of urban planning. A citadel, or fortress, built on a brick platform overlooked each city—possibly serving as government and religious center. The citadel enclosed a granary, a grand hall, and a public bath, perhaps used for religious ceremonies.

Below the citadel Harappan engineers skillfully laid out each city in a grid pattern of straight streets crossing each other at right angles. The Harappans used oven-baked brick to build houses with flat wooden roofs, and some houses rose to several stories and enclosed courtyards. Almost every house had at least one bathroom, with drains and chutes connected to a brick sewer system beneath the streets.

Harappan Life Most of the Harappan people worked the land. In the fields of the Indus Valley floodplain they grew a surplus of wheat, barley, and rice. They also cultivated cotton. Farmers often dug ditches and canals to irrigate their crops. Sometimes they also planted at the beginning or end of the flood season and relied on the drenched land to provide the necessary water for their crops.

Supported by the agricultural surplus from these farms, Harappan city dwellers could engage in industry and commerce. Some artisans worked bronze and copper into axes, spears, knives, and chisels. Others made silver vessels

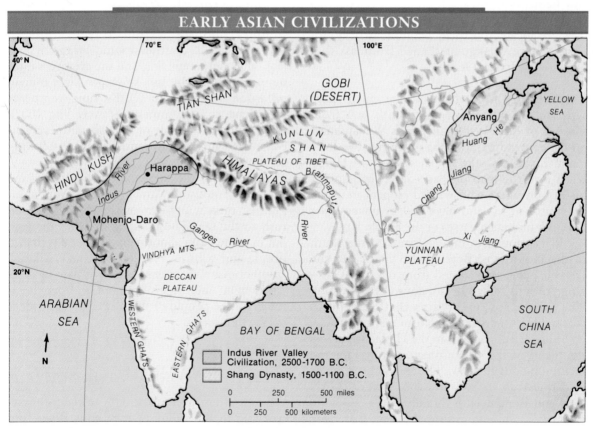

EARLY ASIAN CIVILIZATIONS

Indus River Valley Civilization, 2500–1700 B.C.

Shang Dynasty, 1500–1100 B.C.

Learning from Maps *Two unique Asian civilizations developed independently— one in the Indus Valley and one on the plain of the Huang He.* **Where on this map would the boundaries of present-day countries be?**

and gold, shell, and ivory jewelry. They also mass-produced clay pots, and they spun and wove cotton cloth. Merchants who handled these goods used soapstone seals to identify bundles of merchandise. The discovery by archaeologists of Harappan seals in Mesopotamia indicates that Indus Valley people traded with the Mesopotamians as early as 2300 B.C.

Clues About Language and Religion

The Harappans inscribed pictograms on the seals they placed on packages of goods. Linguists, or scholars who study languages, have yet to decipher these inscriptions—almost the only known examples of the written language of the Harappan civilization. Some believe that the Harappans devised their pictograms after adopting the idea of writing from the Mesopotamians.

The lack of written records has made it difficult to learn as much about the Harappan civilization as is known about Egypt and Mesopotamia. Artifacts found in the ruins, however, have provided archaeologists with some clues. For example, the many children's toys found suggest that the Harappans delighted in play, and the absence of weapons leads archaeologists to question whether these people had enemies. Animal and humanlike figurines suggest that the Harappans worshiped gods associated with natural forces, possibly believing that these gods lived in water, trees, and animals. A mother goddess seems to have been honored as the source of growing things.

Collapse of a Civilization

About 2000 B.C. the once-thriving Harappan civilization began to fade. By 1500 B.C. it had disappeared.

Learning from Artifacts *The pictograms inscribed above the bull carved on this Harappan seal have yet to be deciphered.* **What is a likely explanation for archaeologists' finding seals like this in Mesopotamia?**

Historians have many theories for what caused the collapse of this civilization. Evidence of disastrous floods, for example, possibly suggests climate changes.

In the ruins at Mohenjo-Daro are signs that some of its residents may have met a violent end. At Harappa, the discovery of a different pottery style suggests the arrival of outsiders. Archaeological evidence shows that various peoples did cross into the subcontinent after about 1750 B.C., among them the nomadic Aryans of Central Asia. Whether the Aryans contributed to the fall of Harappa and Mohenjo-Daro, however, is not known.

SECTION 3 REVIEW

Recall
1. **Define:** monsoon
2. **Identify:** Which three modern nations trace their roots to the Indus Valley civilization?

Critical Thinking
3. **Analyze:** What do clues at Mohenjo-Daro and Harappa suggest about the collapse of Harappan Civilization?
4. **Evaluate:** Considering facts that written records have revealed about Egyptian and Sumerian civilizations, predict what archaeologists might learn if they could interpret extensive Harappan written records.

Applying Concepts
5. **Relation to environment:** Examine how the land and climate of South Asia affected Harappan agriculture.

Early China

Even as the Harappans were meeting their mysterious fate, China's first dynasty had begun to assert its power over another river valley. This fourth river valley civilization has endured into the twentieth century.

For many centuries the Chinese lived in relative isolation from the rest of the world. They called their homeland *Zhong Guo* (joohng gwah), or the Middle Kingdom. To them it was the center of the whole world and the one truly supreme civilization. The lack of outside contacts allowed the Chinese to develop one culture across many regions and a strong sense of national identity as well. As a result, China has the oldest continuous civilization in the world.

China's Varied Geography

The landforms of China account for the early isolation of the Chinese (see the map on page 52). Everywhere stand barriers to communication and movement. Mountains make up about a third of China's area. The Himalayas close off China to the southwest. Just north of this range is the formidable Plateau of Tibet, sometimes called the "roof of the world." The Kunlun Shan and Tian Shan ranges rise on the western border north of the Plateau of Tibet. To the east of the Tian Shan stretches the vast Gobi, an inhospitable desert extending over China's northern frontier. These physical features hindered contacts with lands to the north, south, and west, curtailing cultural diffusion both into and out of China for many centuries.

On the east, the coastline of China lies open along the Pacific Ocean. Although some Chinese became enthusiastic seafarers, they mostly concentrated on developing the agriculture of eastern China's fertile river valleys, plains, and hills. Unlike the land to the west and

northwest with its forbidding terrain—high, cold mountains and plateaus and arid tracts of desert—the east welcomed life. For centuries large numbers of Chinese have farmed in the region's North China Plain.

Three major rivers drain eastern China: the Huang He, or Yellow River; the Chang Jiang (chahng jyahng), known also as the Yangtze (YANG see); and the Xi Jiang (shee jyahng), also called the West River. The Huang He flows more than 2,900 miles (4,640 kilometers) from the northern highlands eastward to empty into the Yellow Sea. On its way it cuts through thick layers of loess (lehs), a rich yellow soil. The river carries away large quantities of loess, which it deposits farther down its course. The abundance of yellow soil suspended in the water of the Huang He gives it the name Yellow River. The Chinese sometimes call the Huang He "the Great Sorrow" because of the tragedy it brings with its floods. However, the deposits of silt that the flooding Huang He also brings have transformed the North China Plain into rich farmland.

A favorable climate also contributes to successful farming on the North China Plain. Melting snow from the mountains and the monsoon rains between July and October feed the Huang He. Farmers of the region have long depended on the well-defined seasonal rhythm of temperature and precipitation.

The Shang Dynasty

Very little is known about the origins of Chinese civilization. In the 1920s, archaeologists in the Huang He Valley excavated traces of Neolithic culture in China. The magnificent painted pots of the Yang-shao (yahng show) culture unearthed by the archaeologists date back to 3000–1500 B.C. Archaeologists have found that the Lungshan culture, 3000–2500 B.C., used a potter's wheel to make delicate pots and goblets with legs, spouts, and handles. These and other Neolithic finds dated to earlier than 5000 B.C. make it clear that the Huang He Valley, like the river valleys of Egypt, the Fertile Crescent, and South Asia, invited settlement from very early times.

Over the centuries the Chinese have developed many myths to explain their remote past. One myth tells how the universe was created from the body of a giant named Pan Gu (pahn goo), who hatched from an egg. Other legends celebrate the deeds of hero-kings. These larger-than-life rulers included Yao (yow), a person in the form of a mountain and Shun, the master of elephants. Another, Yu the Great, was a miraculous engineer. According to a myth about Yu:

> *When widespread waters swelled to Heaven and serpents and dragons did harm, Yao sent Yu to control the waters and to drive out the serpents and dragons. The waters were controlled and flowed to the east. The serpents and dragons plunged to their places.*

The myth about Yu—written much later than the event itself—may reflect stories about the attempts of one or many early rulers to channel the floodwaters of the Huang He.

Yu the Great supposedly founded China's first dynasty, named Xia (syah), around 2000 B.C. But archaeologists have yet to find evidence of the legendary Xia. The first historical dynasty to be dated from written records in China is the Shang (shahng). One noble of the Shang family named Tang (tahng) roused others of his class in a successful rebellion against a cruel Xia king. The dynasty Tang founded, the Shang, ruled China from about 1700 to 1000 B.C.

Early Religion   Though the Shang kings were political leaders, they also performed very important religious duties. As high priests, they could communicate with the deities of nature on behalf of the people. They prayed, made offerings, and performed sacrifices and other religious rituals to gain a good harvest, a change in

Learning from Artifacts   *The Shang probably used this bronze wine vessel, in the form of two owls back to back, for offering sacrifices to the wise spirits of their ancestors.* **What did the Shang metalworkers combine to make the alloy bronze?**

the weather, or victory in battle. Kings also had special powers for calling upon their ancestors. To do so, they had a priest scratch a question on an animal bone or sometimes on a tortoise shell. The priest then applied intense heat to the bone. The bone would crack, and the priest would interpret the splintered pattern of cracks as the answer to the king's question. The bones helped the kings to predict the future—for example, the outcome of a battle or the likelihood of a good harvest. The scratchings on the oracle bones, as they are called, are the first known examples of writing in China.

Important Achievements   The priests writing on the oracle bones used a script with many characters. The characters represented objects, ideas, or sounds and are written in vertical columns. The Chinese of the Shang period probably developed the script over several centuries from a much older system of pictograms. To use the script with ease, a writer had to memorize each character. Because only a small percentage of the population could master all the characters, few people in ancient China could read and write. Later, the Chinese script spread to other parts of East Asia.

Not only did the Chinese of this period develop a written script, but they also perfected their metal-casting skills and produced some of the finest bronze objects ever made. These included figurines, ritual urns, and massive ceremonial caldrons that stood on legs. Bronze fittings adorned hunting chariots, and warriors carried bronze daggers. Artisans of the Shang dynasty also carved beautiful ivory and jade statues. They wove silk into elegantly colored cloth for the upper class and fashioned pottery from kaolin, a fine white clay.

The Chinese built their first cities under the Shang. Seven capital cities, including the important city of Anyang (ahn yahng), have been identified by archaeologists. Excavations reveal the general layout of Anyang. A palace and temple stood at the center of the city, as in the cities of other early river valley civilizations, and public buildings and homes of government officials circled the royal sanctuary. Beyond the city's center stood various workshops and other homes. Archaeologists have discovered burial grounds in the outlying area. Here they have unearthed thousands of hidden oracle bones. Other Shang sites share features with Anyang, including large earthen walls enclosing them.

Shang Expansion   The early Shang kings ruled over a small area that included Anyang and nearby territories in northern China. Later Shang kings, their armies equipped with bronze weapons and chariots, conquered more distant territories and finally took over most of the valley of the Huang He (see the map on page 52).

The Shang dynasty lacked strong leaders, however, and in time grew weak. As a result, local nobles gained control of the more remote areas under Shang domination. Around 1000 B.C., Wu, a ruler of a former Shang territory in the northwest, marshaled his forces and marched on the capital. Wu killed the Shang king and established a new dynasty. Wu's dynasty, known as the Zhou (joe), ruled China for 800 years.

Many Centuries of Dynasties

From the beginning of its recorded history until the present century, dynasties have ruled China. When writing about China's past, Western historians have followed the Chinese practice of dividing their history into periods based on the reigns of these ruling families.

The Chinese believed that their rulers governed according to a principle known as the Mandate of Heaven. If rulers were just and effective, they received a **mandate**, or authority to rule, from heaven. If rulers did not govern properly—as indicated by poor crops or losses in battle—they lost the mandate to someone else who then started a new dynasty. The principle first surfaced during the Zhou dynasty. Indeed the Zhou, as did later rebels, probably found the Mandate of Heaven a convenient way to explain away their overthrow of an unpopular dynasty.

SECTION 4 REVIEW

Recall

1. **Define:** mandate
2. **Identify:** Yu the Great, Xia dynasty, Tang, Shang dynasty, Mandate of Heaven
3. **Locate:** Use the map on page 52 to list the major physical features of China. Explain how these physical features affected the development of Chinese civilization.

Critical Thinking

4. **Apply:** Why were oracle bones an especially significant archaeological find?
5. **Analyze:** Compare the Chinese Mandate of Heaven principle with the way Egyptian kings justified their rule.

Applying Concepts

6. **Cooperation:** Identify an achievement of the Shang dynasty that must have required great planning and organization of many people.

CLASSIFYING

Can you imagine the frustration of shopping in a store where merchandise is not arranged in departments? A similar frustration may occur when you try to read and understand large quantities of information about a subject. You can learn more by sorting data into categories. Classifying involves sorting items based on shared characteristics. Classifying makes it easier to detect patterns or to see relationships among items in order to draw conclusions or make comparisons.

> *The royal children . . . were privately tutored . . . frequently joined by the sons of the great noble families. . . . The most sought-after profession in Egypt was that of scribe. . . . The most important subjects were reading and writing . . . history, literature, geography, [and] ethics. Arithmetic was almost certainly part of the curriculum. . . . Boys who were to specialize in medicine, law or religious liturgy would perhaps have devoted some of their time to elementary studies in these fields.*
>
> *Formal education for [a son from] the lower classes . . . was not selected for him because he wished to become an artist or goldsmith or a farmer . . . he entered a trade because it was his father's work. The sons of artists and craftsmen were apprenticed and went to train at one of the temples or state workshops, . . . the sons of peasants would have joined their fathers in the field at an early age.*
>
> A. Rosalie David,
> *The Egyptian Kingdoms*, 1975

Explanation

When faced with lengthy or difficult material, use these steps to classify data:

1. Read the information, noticing items with shared features or characteristics.
2. Sort items with shared characteristics into categories (technology, economy, housing, culture, education).
3. Label each group of items.
4. Check the original selection for other items that could be added to each category. Continue sorting until all possible items are placed in a category.
5. Review the items within each category. If necessary subdivide, combine, or rename categories.
6. After classifying, formulate new conclusions or generalizations from the data.

Example

If you read the above passage about life in ancient Egypt, you could classify the information by listing items with shared characteristics. The selection describes the education of nobles and of commoners. The words *scribe, medicine,* and *law* share the characteristic of being occupations of the nobility. The chart below shows one way in which other information could be classified.

Application

Read about life in Harappan civilization in the Indus River Valley on pages 51–53 in Section 3. Use the steps above to classify that information.

Practice

Turn to Practicing Skills in the Chapter Review on page 67 for further practice in the skill of classifying information.

CLASSIFICATION CHART

	Nobles' Education	Commoners' Education
Areas of Study	reading, writing, history, ethics, literature, geography, arithmetic	apprenticeships, field work
Occupations	scribes, priests, doctors, lawyers	artisans, farmers, craftspeople

from Gilgamesh

retold by Herbert Mason

*Like people today, ancient Sumerians loved adventure tales
featuring extraordinary heroes battling the forces of evil. Many Sumerian myths
featured a king, Gilgamesh, who lived around 2700 B.C. The earliest known written
accounts of Gilgamesh's adventures date from about 1850 B.C., making them the oldest
surviving examples of epic poetry. An epic is a long poem recalling the exploits of a
legendary hero. Gilgamesh, after the death of his friend Enkidu, searched for the secret of
eternal life, which he hoped to share with his departed friend. In the following excerpt,
Gilgamesh, hoping to learn how to escape death, listens to a mysterious elderly man,
Utnapishtim, recount how he survived a great flood.*

There was a city called Shurrupak
On the bank of the Euphrates.
It was very old, and so many were the gods
Within it. They converged in their complex hearts
On the idea of creating a great flood.
There was Anu, their aging and weak-minded father,
The military Enlil, his adviser,
Ishtar, the sensation-craving one,
And all the rest. Ea, who was present
At their council, came to my house
And, frightened by the violent winds that filled the air,
Echoed all that they were planning and had said.
Man of Shurrupak, he said, tear down your house
And build a ship. Abandon your possessions

And the works that you find beautiful and crave,
And save your life instead. Into the ship
Bring the seed of all the living creatures.

I was overawed, perplexed,
And finally downcast. I agreed to do
As Ea said, but I protested: What shall I say
To the city, the people, the leaders?

Tell them, Ea said, you have learned that Enlil
The war god despises you and will not
Give you access to the city anymore.
Tell them for this Ea will bring the rains.

That is the way gods think, he laughed. His tone
Of savage irony frightened Gilgamesh
Yet gave him pleasure, being his friend.
They only know how to compete or echo.

But who am I to talk? He sighed as if
Disgusted with himself; I did as he
Commanded me to do. I spoke to them,
And some came out to help me build the ship
Of seven stories, each with nine chambers.
The boat was cube in shape, and sound; it held
The food and wine and precious minerals
And seed of living animals we put
In it. My family then moved inside,
And all who wanted to be with us there:
The game of the field, the goats of the steppe,
The craftsmen of the city came, a navigator
Came. And then Ea ordered me to close
The door. The time of the great rains had come.
O there was ample warning, yes, my friend,
But it was terrifying still. Buildings
Blown by the winds for miles like desert brush.
People clung to branches of trees until
Roots gave way. New possessions, now debris,
Floated on the water with their special
Sterile vacancy. The riverbanks failed
To hold the water back. Even the gods
Cowered like dogs at what they had done.
Ishtar cried out like a woman at the height
Of labor: O how could I have wanted
To do this to my people! They were *hers*,
Notice. Even her sorrow was possessive.
Her spawn that she had killed too soon.
Old gods are terrible to look at when
They weep, all bloated like spoiled fish.
One wonders if they ever understand

Art and Literature *On a wall relief from one of Sargon's palaces,*
Akkadian riverboats transport timber for palace construction. The artist
depicted a river teeming with animal life.

That they have caused their grief. When the seventh day
Came, the flood subsided from its slaughter
Like hair drawn slowly back
From a tormented face.
I looked at the earth and all was silence.
Bodies lay like alewives [a type of fish], dead
And in the clay. I fell down
On the ship's deck and wept. Why? Why did they
Have to die? I couldn't understand. I asked
Unanswerable questions a child asks
When a parent dies—for nothing. Only slowly
Did I make myself believe—or hope—they
Might all be swept up in their fragments
Together
And made whole again
By some compassionate hand.
But my hand was too small
To do the gathering.
I have only known this feeling since
When I look out across the sea of death,
This pull inside against a littleness—myself—
Waiting for an upward gesture.

O the dove, the swallow and the raven
Found their land. The people left the ship.
But I for a long time could only stay inside.
I could not face the deaths I knew were there.

Then I received Enlil, for Ea had *chosen* me;
The war god touched my forehead; he blessed
My family and said:
Before this you were just a man, but now
You and your wife shall be like gods. You
Shall live in the distance at the rivers' mouth,
At the source. I allowed myself to be
Taken far away from all that I had seen.
Sometimes even in love we yearn to leave mankind.
Only the loneliness of the Only One
Who never acts like gods
Is bearable.
I am downcast because of what I've seen,
Not what I still have hope to yearn for.
Lost youths restored to life,
Lost children to their crying mothers,
Lost wives, lost friends, lost hopes, lost homes,
I want to bring these back to them.
But now there is you.
We must find something for you.
How will you find eternal life
To bring back to your friend?
He pondered busily, as if
It were just a matter of getting down to work
Or making plans for an excursion.
Then he relaxed, as if there were no use
In this reflection. I would grieve
At all that may befall you still,
If I did not know you must return
And bury your own loss and build
Your world anew with your own hands.
I envy you your freedom.

As he listened, Gilgamesh felt tiredness again
Come over him, the words now so discouraging,
The promise so remote, so unlike what he sought.
He looked into the old man's face, and it seemed changed,
As if this one had fought within himself a battle
He would never know, that still went on.

RESPONDING TO LITERATURE

1. **Comprehending:** How did Utnapishtim survive the great flood?
2. **Analyzing:** How were the reactions to the flood of the gods and of Utnapishtim similar?
3. **Synthesizing:** What questions would you ask Utnapishtim if you could meet him?
4. **Thinking Critically:** What aspects of this tale might apply to other cultures in other places and at other times?

CHAPTER 2 REVIEW

HISTORICAL SIGNIFICANCE

The four early river valley civilizations—the Nile, Tigris and Euphrates, Indus, and the Huang He—each followed a unique pattern of development, partly because the physical geography of each place differed. Yet these civilizations also shared many features because, although far apart, they confronted similar problems—for example, how to survive destructive floods, defend against greedy neighbors, organize the construction of public buildings, keep records of commerce, and explain the mysteries of natural forces. All four river valley civilizations attempted solutions to these problems through cooperation, government, technology, and religion. Thus these ancient peoples built cities and monuments, created dynasties, developed writing systems, and devised law codes. These earliest civilizations left behind far more than their ruins and artifacts. They passed on political ideas, social institutions, and cultural achievements to later civilizations and laid the foundations for the civilization we know today.

SUMMARY

For a summary of Chapter 2, see the Unit 1 synopsis on pages 82–85.

USING KEY TERMS

Write the key term that best completes each sentence below.

a. bureaucracy
b. city-state
c. cuneiform
d. dynasty
e. empire
f. hieroglyphics
g. mandate
h. monarchy
i. monsoon
j. pharaoh
k. polytheism
l. theocracy

1. Each ancient ___ was directed by a king.
2. The first historical ___ in China was the Shang.
3. The Egyptian writing system, ___, used picture symbols.
4. ___ consisted of hundreds of wedge-shaped markings.
5. The southwest ___ brings rain to the South Asia subcontinent.
6. The title ___ was used by Egyptian kings.
7. Egyptian government was considered a ___ because a pharaoh was both god and king.
8. A typical Sumerian ___ included the city itself and surrounding land and villages.
9. ___ was the basis of Egyptian religion except during the rule of Akhenaton.
10. Sargon I united all of the Mesopotamian city-states in a single ___.
11. The Chinese believed that their rulers received a ___ to rule from heaven.
12. Governmental officials in the ___ handled administrative responsibilities.

REVIEWING FACTS

1. **Explain:** How did the early Mesopotamians control the Tigris and Euphrates rivers?
2. **Describe:** How does the southwest monsoon affect life on the South Asia subcontinent?
3. **Identify:** What archaeological discovery indicates that there was contact between the Mesopotamian and Harappan cultures?
4. **List:** What achievements of the ancient Chinese exemplify their artistic innovation?
5. **Describe:** How did the Himalayas affect two early river valley civilizations?

THINKING CRITICALLY

1. **Apply:** What clues do artifacts found in the ruins at Harappa and Mohenjo-Daro provide about the Harappan religion?
2. **Analyze:** Compare and contrast the powers of the Egyptian kings and the Shang kings.

3. **Synthesize:** What reaction would you have had to Akhenaton's reforms if you had been a priest of Amon-Ra?
4. **Evaluate:** Predict what might have happened if Sumerians never invented cuneiform.

ANALYZING CONCEPTS

1. **Relation to Environment:** What flood-control methods of the ancient river valley peoples are still in use?
2. **Cooperation:** Identify areas in city life today in which cooperation is as important as it was when ancient peoples built the earliest cities.
3. **Innovation:** Explain how each of these was an innovation: the Step Pyramid, the Great Pyramid, cuneiform.
4. **Cultural Diffusion:** What advances in the twentieth century have made cultural diffusion easier and faster than in ancient times?

PRACTICING SKILLS

1. Considering what you have learned about life in Babylonia, suggest a system to classify all 282 laws in the Code of Hammurabi. Label at least four categories with at least two items in each. You may use examples from the text as well as laws you think Hammurabi might have decreed.
2. Classify the factors that led to the rise of ancient Chinese culture. Include as much information from the chapter as possible.

GEOGRAPHY IN HISTORY

1. **Human-environment Interaction:** What special advantages did river valleys have for human settlement?
2. **Place:** What topographical features isolated the early Chinese?

TRACING CHRONOLOGY

Refer to the time line below to answer these questions.
1. When did peoples begin to move toward the Nile Valley and the Fertile Crescent?
2. Which two dates in the time line show the time span from the beginning of the Old Kingdom to the end of the New Kingdom in Egypt?
3. Which four events given in the timeline were key events in the history of the region of Mesopotamia?

LINKING PAST AND PRESENT

1. Hatshepsut was only one of the women who held prominent positions in ancient Egypt. What women have held high government positions in modern times?
2. Physical features isolated the Chinese from the rest of the world for centuries. What moves have the Chinese made recently to make greater contact with other cultures? To what extent have they maintained their traditional isolation?

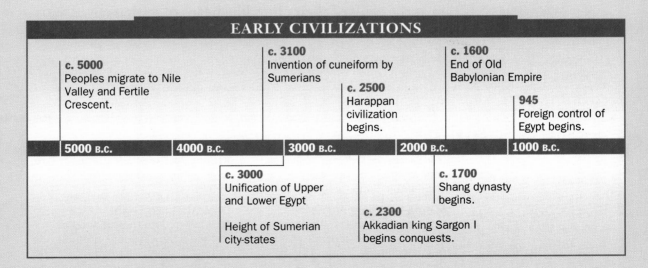

EARLY CIVILIZATIONS

c. 5000 Peoples migrate to Nile Valley and Fertile Crescent.

c. 3100 Invention of cuneiform by Sumerians

c. 2500 Harappan civilization begins.

c. 1600 End of Old Babylonian Empire

945 Foreign control of Egypt begins.

5000 B.C.	4000 B.C.	3000 B.C.	2000 B.C.	1000 B.C.

c. 3000 Unification of Upper and Lower Egypt

Height of Sumerian city-states

c. 2300 Akkadian king Sargon I begins conquests.

c. 1700 Shang dynasty begins.

Kingdoms and Empires in the Middle East

*A*shurbanipal, the last great Assyrian king, reigned in the mid-600s B.C. The dim rooms were almost still in Ashurbanipal's great palace at Nineveh, the splendid capital of his empire. Men with shoulder-length hair and squared-off beards glided in their tunics and sandals through the vast hallways. But the stone reliefs that decorated the palace walls told a less peaceful story. In intricately carved scenes, the impassive hunter in his chariot lets fly with a volley of arrows into a staggering lion, and the valiant general on the battlefield proudly waves his sword above the defeated enemy legions.

Ashurbanipal proudly followed a long line of ruthless Assyrian conquerors, such as Tiglath-pileser, who boasted, "I made their blood to flow over all the ravines and high places of mountains. I cut off their heads and piled them up at the walls of their cities like heaps of grain."

CHAPTER PREVIEW

Key Terms to Define: alphabet, colony, barter, monotheism, covenant, exodus, prophet

People to Meet: Aramaeans, Phoenicians, Lydians, Abraham, Moses, David, Solomon, Hittites, Nebuchadnezzar, Cyrus, Darius, Zoroaster

Places to Discover: Canaan, Tyre, Asia Minor, Jerusalem, Nineveh, Babylon

Objectives to Learn:
1. What did the trading peoples in the Fertile Crescent contribute to neighboring civilizations?
2. What part do slavery, exile, and return play in the history of the Hebrews?

In this detail of an Assyrian relief, Judaean exiles carry provisions after their defeat by Assyria.

3. What was the succession of empires in the Middle East between 2000 and 400 B.C.?

Concepts to Understand:
- Diversity—The Middle Eastern empires were composed of many different peoples. Sections 1,2,3
- Cultural Diffusion—Merchants and armies spread ideas throughout the Middle East. Sections 1,2,3
- Conflict—A series of empires— Hittite, then Assyrian, then Chaldean, then Persian—each swallowed up the previous one. Section 3
- Innovation—The Phoenicians developed a working alphabet, and the Hebrews contributed to the world the concept of monotheism. Sections 1,2

Trading Peoples

The magnificent civilizations of Mesopotamia and Egypt greatly influenced neighboring peoples in the Fertile Crescent—among them the Aramaeans (ar uh MEE uhnz) and the Phoenicians (fih NEESH uhnz). In turn, these trading peoples helped to spread their own cultures throughout the region and into much of the ancient world. Traveling on sailing ships and by caravan, traders from the Fertile Crescent brought language, customs, and ideas along with their trade goods.

The Aramaeans

One of the most active peoples in early Middle Eastern trade, the Aramaeans settled in central Syria around 1200 B.C. Although Aramaean kings established a capital at Damascus, provincial leaders frequently challenged their authority. Split by internal feuding, the Aramaeans were easily overrun by invaders from Mesopotamia. Despite military and political weaknesses, the Aramaeans—famed for their

IMAGES OF THE TIME

The Phoenicians

For more than 1,000 years, the Phoenicians were the most successful traders and experienced seafarers in the Mediterranean.

Phoenician glass was highly valued throughout the Mediterranean. The Phoenician artisans originally learned glassmaking from the Egyptians.

Phoenician ships carried a wealth of trade items to and from foreign lands. Wood from the cedars of the Lebanese mountains was one of the most valuable resources that the Phoenician merchants traded.

trading skills—gained control of the rich overland trade between Egypt and Mesopotamia.

Because Aramaean caravans crossed and recrossed the Fertile Crescent on business, people throughout the region learned Aramaic, the language of the Aramaeans. Until the A.D. 800s, the majority of the people living in the Fertile Crescent spoke Aramaic, a language closely related to Hebrew and Arabic. In addition, some parts of the Bible were written in Aramaic.

The Phoenicians

Between ancient Egypt and Syria lay the land of Canaan, today made up of Lebanon, Israel, and Jordan. The Phoenicians, one of the Semitic groups that migrated from the Arabian Peninsula about 3000 B.C., settled in the northern part of Canaan. Their neighbors in Canaan, the Philistines, came from the eastern Mediterranean. The Greeks would later call Canaan "Palestine," the Greek name for the Philistines.

In contrast to the Aramaeans, who trekked overland to reach their markets, the Phoenicians sailed the seas. On a narrow strip of land between the mountains of western Syria and the Mediterranean Sea, Phoenicia lacked enough arable land for farming, and many Phoenicians turned to the sea to earn a living. They harvested timber from the cedar forests on nearby slopes to build strong, fast ships.

By 1200 B.C. the Phoenicians had built a string of cities and towns along their coast. Many of these scattered ports grew to become city-states, the largest of which were Tyre, Byblos, Sidon, and Berytus (later Beirut). The city-state of Tyre often provided the leadership for what remained a loose union of independent Phoenician city-states. According to the Bible:

In Byblos, Lebanon, modern buildings overlook the ruins of Phoenician fortifications on the eastern coast of the Mediterranean.

A Phoenician coin bears an image of a ship, recalling the importance of seafaring to the Phoenicians.

Reflecting on the Times
Why did the Phoenicians make a success of trading and seafaring?

Who was like Tyre . . .
In the midst of the sea?
When your wares were unloaded from the seas,
You satisfied many peoples;
With your great wealth and merchandise
You enriched the kings of the earth.

—Ezekiel 27:32-33

The Phoenicians sailed from their coastal city-states throughout the Mediterranean. Expert navigators, they learned to plot their voyages with great accuracy by means of the sun and the stars. After 1100 B.C. Phoenicians reached the southern coast of Spain and the western coast of Africa. Some historians believe they even ventured as far as the British Isles.

Astute traders and businesspeople, the Phoenicians soon took charge of Mediterranean shipping and trade. At ports of call, they exchanged cedar logs, textiles dyed a beautiful purple, glass objects, and elegant jewelry for precious metals. They also brought new business practices, such as bills of sale and contracts.

An advantage that Phoenician merchants held over their competitors when keeping track of complex business deals was an improved **alphabet**—a series of written symbols that represent sounds. Phoenicians developed their efficient alphabet about 1000 B.C. from earlier, more complicated systems from southern Canaan and northwest Syria. The concise Phoenician alphabet used just 22 characters, each character representing a consonant sound. Readers mentally supplied vowels in the proper places.

The Phoenician system later became the foundation of several alphabets, including Greek, which in turn became the basis of all Western alphabets. Because the Phoenician alphabet did not require years of study to master, merchants no longer needed the services of specially trained scribes to keep records.

To protect and resupply their ships, Phoenician sailors and traders set up along the coasts of the Mediterranean a network of temporary trading posts and **colonies**, or settlements of Phoenician emigrants. For example, people from Tyre, in about 750 B.C., founded a colony named Carthage on the coast of what is today Tunisia. Carthage eventually became the most powerful city in the western Mediterranean.

The Lydians

The Lydians (LIHD ee uhnz) lived in Asia Minor—the peninsula jutting westward between the Mediterranean, Aegean, and Black seas. Lydian merchants and artisans were well situated to prosper in the growing regional trade. By the late 600s B.C., the Lydians had developed a wealthy and independent kingdom famous for its rich gold deposits.

Most traders from neighboring cultures still relied on a system of **barter** for their transactions—that is, exchanging their wares for other goods. The Lydians, however, began to set prices and developed a money system using coins as a medium of exchange. Each Lydian coin—a bean-shaped lump made from a mixture of silver and gold—bore a stamp to show that the king of Lydia guaranteed it to be the same size as any other coin. Soon Greek and Persian rulers began to stamp their own coins, and the concept of money spread beyond Lydia.

SECTION 1 REVIEW

Recall

1. **Define:** alphabet, colony, barter
2. **Identify:** the Aramaeans, the Phoenicians, the Lydians
3. **Describe:** Next to which bodies of water are Canaan and Asia Minor located?

Critical Thinking

4. **Apply:** How was Aramaic a "universal language"?
5. **Analyze:** Compare and contrast the Aramaeans, Phoenicians, and Lydians.
6. **Evaluate:** Why did the Phoenician city-states remain independent of each other?

Applying Concepts

7. **Innovation:** Explain why the Phoenician alphabet was significant.

The Hebrews

As you learned in Chapter 2, people in the ancient world usually worshiped many gods and goddesses, a practice called polytheism. The Phoenicians, for example, worshiped three principal deities: a head god known as El, Baal, or Melqart; an earth-mother goddess called Ashtart; and a young god named Adonis, whose annual death and resurrection reflected the cycle of the seasons.

The Hebrews—another people living in Canaan—were an exception among the ancient polytheistic cultures. They brought a new idea to the world, **monotheism**, or the belief in one all-powerful God. The Hebrews believed that God, whom they called "Yahweh," determined right and wrong and expected people to deal justly with each other and to accept moral responsibility for their actions. The teachings of the Hebrews exist today as the religion of Judaism, which in turn has influenced two other monotheistic religions—Christianity and Islam.

The Land of Canaan

The Bible remains one of the main sources of ancient history in the Fertile Crescent. Rooted in the geography of the Middle East, the Bible describes many notable sites. The story of the tower of Babel, for instance, refers to the great ziggurat built for the god Marduk in the city of Babylon in Mesopotamia.

As a record of the early Hebrews, the Bible helps trace their origins to Abraham, a herder and trader who lived in the Mesopotamian city of Ur. Around 1900 B.C. Abraham and his household left Ur and settled in Canaan at the command of Yahweh, or God. The Hebrews believed that God made a **covenant**, or agreement, with Abraham at this time. "I will make of you a great nation" was God's promise to bless

Abraham and his descendants if they would remain faithful to God.

Once in the land of Canaan, the Hebrews shared the varied land with several other peoples, such as the Phoenicians and Philistines. Canaan contained rocky hills and desert, fertile plains and grassy slopes, with the best farming in the valley of the Jordan River. Most Hebrews lived as nomads herding sheep and goats.

The Exodus from Egypt

Abraham's grandson Jacob, also named Israel, raised twelve sons in Canaan, and each son led a separate family group, or tribe. These groups became the twelve tribes of Israel, and the Hebrews became known as the Israelites.

After a severe drought struck Canaan and brought a terrible famine to the land, the Israelites migrated to Egypt, perhaps during the time that the Hyksos ruled. The Israelites lived peacefully in the Egyptian province of Goshen for several generations, until the pharaohs decided to enslave them.

Moses as Leader   "The Egyptians," according to the Bible, "ruthlessly . . . made life bitter for [the Israelites] with hard labor at mortar and bricks and with all sorts of tasks in the field." In the 1200s B.C., the Israelite leader Moses rallied his people and led them out of Egypt in an **exodus**, or departure, into the Sinai Desert. Every year during the festival of Passover, Jews today retell the story of the Exodus from Egypt.

The Ten Commandments   During the long trek across the desert of the Sinai Peninsula, God, according to the Bible, renewed the covenant made with Abraham. Moses and the

Israelites pledged to reject all gods other than the one true God and to obey God's laws, the most important of which would be called the Ten Commandments.

I the Lord am your God who brought you out of the land of Egypt, the house of bondage: You shall have no other gods beside Me.

You shall not make for yourself a sculptured image. . . .

You shall not swear falsely by the name of the Lord your God. . . .

Remember the sabbath day and keep it holy. . ..

Honor your father and your mother, that you may long endure on the land that the Lord your God is giving you.

You shall not murder.

You shall not commit adultery.

You shall not steal.

You shall not bear false witness against your neighbor.

You shall not covet . . . anything that is your neighbor's.

—Exodus 20:2–14

In return for their loyalty, God promised the Israelites a safe return to the land of Canaan.

Settling the Land

Moses died before reaching Canaan, but his successor, Joshua, led the Israelites across the Jordan River into Canaan. For about 200 years, the Israelites struggled to gain the region. They fought the Philistines and the Canaanites who now occupied the land.

The Fighting Judges   Lack of unity among the twelve tribes of Israel prolonged the military campaign to acquire Canaan. Leaders known as "judges" ruled each tribe. Serving as both judicial and military leaders, some of the judges attempted to rally the Israelites. The Bible relates how Deborah, a judge widely admired for her wisdom, planned an attack on a Canaanite army camped near Mount Tabor. Through God's intervention, the Israelites won the battle.

The Davidic Monarchy   Around 1020 B.C. the continual warfare with their neighbors in Canaan led most of the Israelite tribes to unite under one king, Saul. Although he was popular at first, Saul's power waned when he proved unable to defeat the Philistines. David, who had once fought the Philistine Goliath on Saul's behalf, took the throne in 1012 B.C. and ruled for the next 40 years. King David set up a capital at

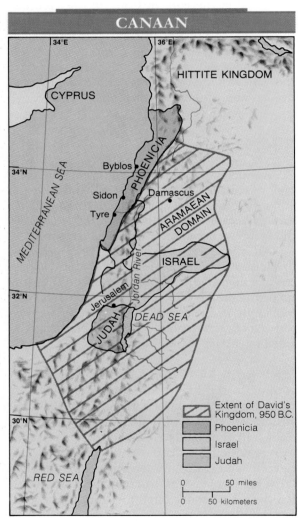

CANAAN

Learning from Maps *Located in the western portion of the Fertile Crescent, the land of Canaan was important throughout ancient history as a trade route, marketplace, and battlefield.* **Where was Canaan in relation to Egypt and to Babylon?**

Jerusalem, organized a central government, and enlarged the borders of his kingdom. During his reign, the Israelites enjoyed a period of economic prosperity.

David's son Solomon succeeded his father in 973 B.C. Solomon founded new cities and rebuilt old ones. He also lavished money on building projects, constructing a magnificent temple to God in Jerusalem.

The Israelites resented Solomon's high taxes and his requirement of all men to work on his projects without pay. After Solomon's death in 922 B.C., the ten northern tribes broke away from the two tribes remaining in the south. The northern tribes continued to call their kingdom Israel. The two southern tribes called their kingdom Judah, and kept Jerusalem as their capital. The word *Jew* comes from the name *Judah*.

Exile and Return

Although split politically, the people of Israel and Judah continued to share one religion. However, the two kingdoms were too weak to resist invasions by powerful neighbors from the east. In 722 B.C. the Assyrians of Mesopotamia swept in and conquered the kingdom of Israel, scattering the people of the ten northern tribes throughout the Assyrian Empire. Then, in 586

PERSONAL PROFILES

Solomon

A Christian artist of the A.D. 1400s painted Solomon on a wall mural in a church on the Mediterranean island of Cyprus.

According to biblical accounts, shortly after Solomon succeeded his father, David, as king of Israel, he had a dream in which God offered him whatever he wanted. Solomon asked for wisdom so that he might govern well. Pleased at the young king's answer, God granted him not only wisdom but also long life and riches.

Solomon gained particular fame for his wisdom. Once two women brought to him their quarrel over which was the mother of a child. The king ordered that the child be cut in two so that each woman could have half. One woman accepted the decision; the other instantly gave up her claim in order to spare the child. Solomon recognized the second woman as the mother.

Solomon's kingdom grew rich from trading and from taxing trade. Solomon's friendship with the Phoenicians gave his merchants the chance to travel by Phoenician ships as far as Arabia and Africa. The king made allies of neighbors and trading partners by marrying into each ruling family, eventually taking 700 wives. He maintained his household lavishly.

Solomon's greatest project was the building of the Temple in Jerusalem. He imported expensive materials, required forced labor, and raised taxes to pay for it.

Despite their pride in the Temple and their ruler, the Israelites grew resentful of the cost of Solomon's works and life-style. Upon his death, the nation that he had ruled so brilliantly broke apart.

Reflecting on the Person
1. By which characteristic and for which activity is Solomon primarily remembered?
2. Was Solomon wise in the modern sense of the word? Explain.

B.C., another Mesopotamian people, the Chaldeans (kal DEE uhnz), gained control of Judah. After suppressing a Hebrew revolt, the Chaldeans destroyed the Temple in Jerusalem. They enslaved some of the city's residents and carried them off to exile in the Chaldean capital city of Babylon.

During this difficult period, **prophets**— preachers who interpreted God's will—arose among the Israelites, who were called Jews after the Babylonian exile. Some prophets, such as Jeremiah, condemned abuses in society and blamed the Babylonian exile on the Jews' forgetting their duties to God and to one another. The prophets also helped the people of Judah retain their culture during the Babylonian captivity and exile.

While in Babylon, the Jews no longer had an elegant temple in which to worship God. Instead, small groups of Jews began to meet on the Sabbath, the holy day of rest, for prayer and discussion. The institution of local synagogues developed from these gatherings.

Many Jews continued to hope for a return to Jerusalem. Finally, in 539 B.C., the Persians conquered the Chaldeans. The Persian king, Cyrus II, allowed the Jewish exiles to return to Judah and to rebuild the Temple in Jerusalem. In the 400s B.C., under the leadership of a scribe named Ezra, Jewish holy writings were collected and organized into the Torah, made up of the five books of Genesis, Exodus, Leviticus, Numbers, and Deuteronomy.

Although a new Jewish community flourished in Jerusalem, many Jews chose to remain in Babylon, and some migrated to other areas in the Middle East. Ever since this time, communities of Jews have existed outside their homeland in what has become known as the *Diaspora*, a Greek word meaning "scattered."

A Lasting Legacy

Their troubled history—with its cycles of slavery, exile, and return—made the Jews keenly aware of their past. Seeing events as having a God-directed purpose, the Jews recorded their history and examined it for meaning. The Jewish Bible, called the Old Testament by Christians, begins with the Torah and includes the writings of the prophets. As the Jews scattered beyond Canaan, they took the Torah with them, and its teachings spread around the world.

From the Torah has come the concept that every human being, made in the image of God, has infinite worth. Further, humans work in partnership with God, striving to achieve a perfect world, and this link between God and humans makes people accountable for what happens in the world. The Jewish prophet Micah expressed his vision for the world as follows:

*A*nd they shall beat their swords
    into plowshares,
And their spears into pruning hooks.
Nation shall not take up
Sword against nation;
They shall never again know war;
But every man shall sit
Under his grapevine or fig tree
With no one to disturb him.

              —Micah 4:3–4

SECTION 2 REVIEW

Recall

1. **Define:** monotheism, covenant, exodus, prophet
2. **Identify:** Abraham, Jacob, Moses, Deborah, Saul, David, Solomon, *Diaspora*
3. **Locate:** Find Jerusalem on the map on page 70. What was the significance of Jerusalem to Jews in exile in Babylon?

Critical Thinking

4. **Analyze:** Create a chronology of the migrations of the Hebrews.
5. **Evaluate:** Why have the Jews survived as a people, while other ancient peoples have altogether disappeared?

Applying Concepts

6. **Cultural diffusion:** Examine the role that the Jews' *Diaspora* has played in spreading their religious ideas.

Empire Builders

The Phoenicians, Aramaeans, Lydians, and Hebrews contributed to the world their alphabet, language, commercial practices, and religious beliefs. But these peoples lacked the military power of their neighbors, and the conquering armies of a series of warlike empires came to dominate the Fertile Crescent.

The Hittites Rule Asia Minor

Around 2000 B.C., the Hittites—perhaps coming from areas beyond the Black Sea—conquered the local people of Asia Minor. The Hittites set up several city-states on a large, central plateau called Anatolia, and by about 1650 B.C., they had established a well-organized kingdom. Archaeologists have deciphered the writing on some of the clay tablets found in the ruins of Hattusas, the Hittite capital. Other information about the Hittites comes from records of people they confronted as they expanded their empire. An Egyptian source, for example, described the Hittite custom of wearing their hair in a long, thick pigtail that hung down in back.

The kings who ruled the Hittites assembled a fearsome army—the first in the Middle East to wield iron weapons extensively. The army employed light, spoked-wheel chariots that could carry two soldiers and a driver. This gave the Hittites a decided advantage in battle, because they were able to field twice as many troops as their foes in two-person chariots. Overwhelming any army that stood in their way, the Hittites pushed eastward and conquered the city of Babylon about 1595 B.C. The Hittite Empire—spanning Asia Minor, Syria, and part of Mesopotamia—lasted until about 1200 B.C.

Although their culture was largely borrowed from Mesopotamia and Egypt, the Hittites contributed to Middle Eastern civilization a legal system considered less harsh than Hammurabi's code of law. Hittite law emphasized payments for damages rather than harsh punishments.

Assyrian Conquests

The Assyrians, a people living in the hilly country of northern Mesopotamia, had faced constant invasions from adjoining Asia Minor—including those by the Hittites. About 900 B.C. the Assyrians finally became strong enough to repel attacks from the west. They also began to launch their own military campaigns to subdue their Mesopotamian neighbors.

A Powerful Army   The Assyrian army earned a reputation after 900 B.C. as the most lethal fighting force in the Middle East. The Assyrians organized their professional soldiers into units of foot soldiers, charioteers, and fast-moving cavalry fighting on horseback. They were described as warriors "whose arrows were sharp and all their bows bent, the horses' hooves were like flint, and their [chariot] wheels like a whirlwind." Like the Hittites, the Assyrians fought with iron weapons. They also used battering rams against the walls of the cities they attacked.

The Assyrians treated conquered peoples cruelly. They burned cities and tortured and killed thousands of captives. The Assyrians routinely deported entire populations from their homelands. Resettling the land with people from other parts of the empire, the Assyrians forced these settlers to pay heavy taxes.

Assyrian Empire   By about 650 B.C., the Assyrian kings controlled an empire stretching from the Persian Gulf to Egypt and into Asia Minor. They divided their empire into provinces, each headed by a governor directly

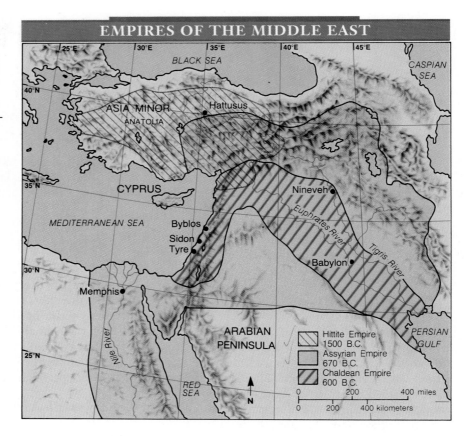

Learning from Maps
Ancient peoples used the wealth gained from their empires to support building projects in their capital cities—the Hittites in Hattusus, the Assyrians in Nineveh, and the Chaldeans in Babylon. **When did the Egyptian city labeled on this map become a capital city?**

EMPIRES OF THE MIDDLE EAST

BLACK SEA

CASPIAN SEA

ASIA MINOR
ANATOLIA

Hattusus

CYPRUS

Nineveh

MEDITERRANEAN SEA

Byblos
Sidon
Tyre

Euphrates River

Babylon

Tigris River

Memphis

Nile River

ARABIAN PENINSULA

PERSIAN GULF

RED SEA

N

Hittite Empire 1500 B.C.
Assyrian Empire 670 B.C.
Chaldean Empire 600 B.C.

0   200   400 miles
0   200   400 kilometers

responsible to the king. Officials sent from the imperial government collected taxes to be used to bolster the army and to fund building projects in Nineveh, the Assyrian capital. To improve communication, the Assyrians built a network of roads connecting the provinces. Imperial messengers and Aramaean merchants traveled these roads, protected by soldiers from bandits.

In spite of these links, the Assyrian Empire eventually began to fracture as conquered peoples continually rebelled. In 612 B.C., the Chaldeans, who lived in the ancient city of Babylon, formed an alliance with the Medes from the east. The alliance captured Nineveh and brought down the Assyrian Empire.

The Chaldeans of Babylon

Soon after the Assyrians fell, the Chaldean Empire succeeded in dominating the entire Fertile Crescent. Most of the Chaldeans—some-

times called the New Babylonians—were descended from people of Hammurabi's Babylonian Empire of the 1700s B.C.

The Chaldeans reached the apex of their power during the reign of one of their greatest rulers, King Nebuchadnezzar (nehb uh kuhd NEZ uhr), from 604 to 561 B.C. He extended the boundaries of the Chaldean Empire as far west as Syria and Canaan, conquering the city of Jerusalem and the Phoenician city-state of Tyre and forcing the people of the kingdom of Judah into a Babylonian exile in 586 B.C. Nebuchadnezzar also amassed great wealth and rebuilt Babylon into one of the largest, most stunning cities of the ancient world.

Historians of the time counted two features of Babylon among the so-called Seven Wonders of the World—its wall and its Hanging Gardens. An immense, snaking wall surrounded the city, standing 50 feet (15 meters) high and bristling with watchtowers every 100 yards (90 meters). Nebuchadnezzar created the Hanging Gardens

The Ishtar Gate to Babylon

In March of A.D. 1899, German archaeologist Robert Koldewey began to uncover the ruins of the ancient city of Babylon. Ruled by King Nebuchadnezzar in the 500s B.C., Babylon was one of the most magnificent cities of the time. But by A.D. 1899, only crumbled ruins remained. The one structure Koldewey would find standing was Babylon's main entrance, dedicated to the goddess Ishtar.

Sheathed in colored, glazed bricks, the Ishtar Gate is adorned with reliefs, or raised sculptures, of fantastic animals. Rows of bulls and dragons (575 in all) seem to parade around and through the gate. In Babylonian mythology, the bulls stood for the weather god Adad; the dragons, or *mushhushshu* (threatening beasts part viper, part lion, part bird of prey, and part scorpion), were associated with Babylon's city-god, Marduk.

Originally, a road led up to the gate, paved with colorful stone and flanked by glazed brick walls. The walls showed rows of lions in profile, as though they were walking in a procession. This passageway, with yellow lions set against a deep blue background, was often used for religious processions honoring Marduk. Beyond the gate was Babylon's main avenue. Along the avenue were a soaring ziggurat, Nebuchadnezzar's shining palace, and the famous Hanging Gardens the king had ordered built for his wife.

The elaborate road leading to the Ishtar Gate was not intended simply as decoration. It was also part of the city's defense system. The long walls on either side of the road would trap an attacking army trying to enter the city through the Ishtar Gate. Then the city's guards could rain arrows down upon the attackers from the battlements atop the gate and the surrounding walls.

Visible for miles on the plains around the city, Babylon must have seemed like a mirage to many approaching travelers. Glimmering sunlight reflecting off the Ishtar Gate's glazed brick and the brilliant colors of the deep blue walls with yellow and white animals would announce to any visitor that the city inside was a wondrous place.

Responding to the Arts

1. What functions did the Ishtar Gate serve in ancient Babylon?
2. What were the meanings behind the animals depicted on the gate?

for his wife. Constructed on several levels and designed to be visible from any point in Babylon, the elaborate park was fed by water pumped from a nearby river.

The Chaldeans were also noted for their interest in astrology. They recorded their observations of the stars and made maps that showed the position of the planets and the phases of the moon. Their studies laid the foundations for the science of astronomy.

After Nebuchadnezzar's death, a series of weak kings held the throne. Poor harvests and slow trade further sapped the strength of an empire whose people had been severely taxed and plundered. Then, in 539 B.C., the Persians under Cyrus II came from the mountains to the northeast, seized Babylon, and then conquered the short-lived Chaldean Empire.

The Persians' Large Empire

The Persians had originated from a larger group of people now called Indo-Europeans. As warriors and cattle herders on the lookout for new grasslands, the Persians and the Medes, another Indo-European group, migrated out of central Asia in about 2000 B.C. They settled on a plateau between the Persian Gulf and the Caspian Sea, today part of the country of Iran.

CONNECTIONS: SCIENCE AND TECHNOLOGY

Counting the Days

This modern sundial follows the practice devised by Babylonian astronomers of dividing daylight into 12 hours, nighttime into 12 hours, and each hour into 60 minutes.

How many days are there in a week? Different ancient peoples had more than one answer to this simple question. The Assyrians used a five-day week while the Egyptians favored groupings of ten.

The modern week may trace its origins to the Jewish custom of observing a Sabbath day every seven days. Alternatively, our week may have originated in the Babylonian belief in the sacredness of the number seven—a belief probably linked either to the four seven-day phases of the moon or to the seven planets then visible in the heavens.

Ancient peoples often developed lunar calendars, based on the length of time it takes the moon to circle Earth, approximately 29 days. Of course, the lunar year of about 354 days did not line up properly with the solar, or agricultural, year of 365 days. To solve this problem, Babylonian rulers added an extra month to certain years by royal decree.

Astronomers continued to try to adjust calendars to match the annual cycle of seasons. In 46 B.C. the Roman ruler Julius Caesar decreed that months should be longer than a lunar month. He also introduced January 1 as the first day of a new year. But not until A.D. 1582 were errors in the Julian calendar corrected by Pope Gregory XIII, who formalized a self-correcting system of leap years. The Gregorian calendar used today by most people in the Western world closely matches the solar year.

Making the Connection

1. How did the Babylonians resolve differences between the lunar year and the solar year?
2. How does our modern calendar differ from the ancient Babylonian calendar?

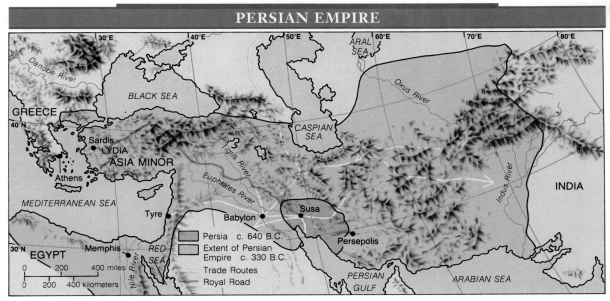

Learning from Maps *The Persians created four capital cities for their empire: Persepolis, Susa, Babylon, and Sardis.* **What was the distance between Susa and Sardis along the Royal Road?**

The Conquests of Cyrus   During the 540s B.C., Cyrus had developed a strong army, conquered the Medes, and advanced into neighboring lands. He quickly added northern Mesopotamia, Syria, Canaan, and the Phoenician cities to his empire and brought an end to the Jews' Babylonian exile. Cyrus also took over the kingdom of Lydia and the Greek city-states in Asia Minor. In 525 B.C., Cyrus's son Cambyses (kam BY seez) conquered Egypt, bringing all the Middle East under Persian control.

The Persian Empire, then second to none, stretched from the Nile River to the Indus River, a distance of 3,000 miles (4,800 kilometers). Within this immense empire, the Persians ruled more than 50 million people.

Darius's Empire   The best organizer among the Persian kings was Darius I, who reigned from 522 to 486 B.C. To administer his empire effectively, Darius divided the realm into provinces and assigned provincial governors to rule. Military officials and tax inspectors, chosen by the king from among the conquered people themselves, assisted governors in carrying out the king's decrees in the provinces. In addition,

inspectors called "Eyes and Ears of the King" made unannounced tours of the provinces.

In contrast to the Assyrians, the Persians were tolerant rulers who allowed conquered peoples to retain their own languages, religions, and laws. The Persians won the loyalty of conquered peoples by respecting local customs.

Darius brought artisans from many of his conquered lands to build Persepolis, the most magnificent city in the empire. To encourage trade among the peoples of the empire and aid

FOOTNOTES TO HISTORY

POSTAL SERVICE

In the 500s B.C., a relay system of runners and mounted couriers carried the imperial mail across the Persian Empire. As described by the Greek historian Herodotus, "Neither snow, nor rain, nor heat, nor gloom of night stays these couriers from the swift completion of their appointed rounds." Many centuries later, the United States Postal Service adopted these words as its motto.

Kingdoms and Empires of the Middle East   **77**

Learning from Art *On this enameled brick panel found in Susa, Iran, the artist placed above the two winged sphinxes a winged disk, symbolic of Ahura Mazda.* **What did Zoroaster teach about Ahura Mazda?**

(ZUHRK seez) led the forces of Persia in a disastrous campaign to conquer Greece in 480 B.C., crippling the Persian Empire in the process.

Persian Religion and Culture　Before the Persian Empire, the Persian people worshiped many gods associated with the sky, sun, and fire. Then, about 570 B.C., a prophet named Zoroaster (ZOHR uh was tuhr) began to call for reform of the Persian religion. Zoroaster preached that the world was divided by a struggle between good and evil. The god Ahura Mazda led the forces of good, and another god, Ahriman, commanded the forces of evil. At the end of time, Ahura Mazda would triumph over Ahriman.

According to Zoroaster, all humans who fought on the side of Ahura Mazda against evil would be rewarded with eternal life. Those who chose Ahriman would be condemned after death to eternal darkness and misery. Darius I had the following statement carved on a cliff:

*O*n this account Ahura Mazda brought me health . . .
Because I was not wicked, nor was I a liar, nor was I a tyrant, neither I nor any of my line. We had ruled according to righteousness.

Some scholars believe that Zoroaster's teachings about paradise, hell, and the Last Judgment—or the separation of good and evil at the end of time—may have influenced Judaism, Christianity, and Islam. Other aspects of Persian culture lived on, too, and mixed with Greek culture when Alexander the Great absorbed the Persians into his own empire in the 300s B.C.

the movement of soldiers, he had Persian engineers improve and expand the network of roads first laid down by the Assyrians.

The Royal Road, the most important thoroughfare in the Persian Empire, stretched more than 1,500 miles (2,400 kilometers) from Susa in Persia to Sardis in Asia Minor. Every 14 miles (22.4 kilometers), stations along the Royal Road provided travelers with food, water, and fresh horses. Royal messengers could travel the length of the road in just seven days, a journey that had taken three months before the road was built.

During his reign, Darius waged war against the Greeks over the control of city-states in Asia Minor. After Darius died, his son Xerxes

---

SECTION 3 REVIEW

Recall
1. **Identify:** Hittites, Nebuchadnezzar, Cyrus, Darius, Zoroaster
2. **Locate:** Find the Hittite, Assyrian, Chaldean, and Persian empires on the maps on pages 74 and 77. Rank them in order of approximate size.

Critical Thinking
3. **Analyze:** Compare how the Persians and Assyrians treated their conquered peoples.
4. **Evaluate:** Why might other religions have adopted certain aspects of the Zoroastrian religion?

Appplying Concepts
5. **Conflict:** Describe how the Hittites and the Assyrians both changed the way peoples of the time fought military battles and the way they dealt with the conquered peoples in their empires.

NOTETAKING

Your history teacher assigned 20 pages of text for you to read for homework tonight. You will be tested on the material tomorrow. You wonder how you will remember all those facts.

Explanation

Notetaking, or writing information in a brief and logical manner, will help you to remember. Notetaking clarifies and orders information. This order can be chronological, based on the importance of events, or based on relationships between events or topics. To master the skill of notetaking, follow these steps:

- Read the material carefully to identify the main ideas.
- Look for patterns or connections between ideas.
- Decide on a method of notetaking. One way to take notes is to use graphic organizers such as the following: **time line**—lists events and dates in chronological order; **cause-and-effect chart**—clarifies the causes of events and describes the effects, using arrows to show sequence; **problem-and-solution chart**—connects problem to corresponding solution; **semantic web**—defines a term or topic by highlighting its characteristics; **category frame**—organizes data about people and places into categories.

- Paraphrase the information, or put it into your own words.

Example

To practice taking notes, refer to Section 2, pages 69-72. Skim the heads and the text itself. Try to identify main ideas, such as the Hebrews' influence on other religions. You will see that the principal focus of the section is Hebrew religion. An appropriate method of notetaking would be to create a semantic web. The center of the web contains the topic "Hebrew Religion." Radiating from the center are the subtopics—"Beliefs," "Writings," and "Influences on Other Religions." Each subtopic could be expanded. "Hebrew Writings" might include "Torah" and "prophetic writings." To the topic "Hebrew Beliefs" you could add "monotheism" and "humans are made in God's image."

Application

Use a semantic web as you take notes on Section 1, Trading Peoples.

Practice

Turn to Practicing Skills on page 85 of the Chapter Review for further practice in notetaking.

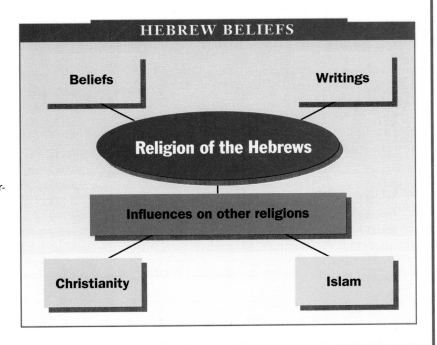

HEBREW BELIEFS

Beliefs

Writings

Religion of the Hebrews

Influences on other religions

Christianity

Islam

CHAPTER 3 REVIEW

HISTORICAL SIGNIFICANCE

Trading peoples and empire builders both enriched the culture of the ancient Middle East and strongly influenced later civilizations, including those beyond the region itself. Historians can trace the origins of many of the foundations of modern life to this place and to the period of time covered in this chapter.

One of the most significant innovations of the period, for example, was the concise and easy-to-learn Phoenician alphabet, which spread communication, enhanced trade, and eventually evolved into the alphabet used to spell the words on this page.

Spiritual life also evolved dramatically, through the adherence of the Hebrews to a belief in one God, who required people to follow moral commandments. The concept of monotheism and the ethical laws recorded in Hebrew teachings have endured in the modern religions of Judaism, Christianity, and Islam.

SUMMARY

For a summary of Chapter 3, see the Unit Synopsis on pages 82–85.

USING KEY TERMS

Write the definition of each key term below. Then explain how each term is related to one of the Concepts to Understand listed in the Chapter Preview on page 65—diversity, cultural diffusion, conflict, or innovation.

1. alphabet
2. barter
3. colony
4. covenant
5. exodus
6. monotheism
7. prophet

REVIEWING FACTS

1. **Explain:** How did Aramaic come to be spoken throughout the Fertile Crescent?
2. **Identify:** What practices did the Phoenicians introduce to Mediterranean business and trade, and what advantage did the Phoenicians have over their competitors?
3. **Describe:** How did the Hebrews interpret and apply the new idea of monotheism?
4. **List:** Name the peoples with which the Israelites came into conflict after the Exodus from Egypt and return to Canaan.

5. **Identify:** What contribution did the Hittites make to the civilization of the Middle East?
6. **Locate:** What were the boundaries of the Hittite, Assyrian, Chaldean, and Persian empires at their peak?

THINKING CRITICALLY

1. **Apply:** What natural resource supported the Lydians' development of a money system to replace the barter system?
2. **Analyze:** Differentiate among the gods and beliefs of the Phoenicians, the Hebrews, and the Persians.
3. **Synthesize:** Create a model hypothetical civilization, drawing on the best features of the civilizations described here. What political, social, religious, economic, and legal features would you give it, and why?
4. **Evaluate:** Which development of this period do you believe was most important for the future of world history, and why?
5. **Analyze:** What actions taken by Darius I made his administration of the Persian Empire so effective?
6. **Synthesize:** If you were to go back in time to live under one of the governments in the ancient Middle East, which government would you choose? What position in society would you select? Would you want to be a man or a woman? Explain your answer.

ANALYZING CONCEPTS

1. **Diversity:** Do you think the Persian Empire resembles or differs from the United States in its absorption and tolerance of diverse peoples? Explain your answer.
2. **Cultural diffusion:** What kinds of ideas, do you think, are people most likely to adopt from other cultures?
3. **Conflict:** Make a list of what aims might have motivated conquerors such as the Hittites, Assyrians, Chaldeans, and Persians to incorporate their neighbors into empires.
4. **Innovation:** From a modern perspective, do you see any drawbacks in the replacement of the barter system with a money system? Explain your answer.

PRACTICING SKILLS

1. Refer to the Chapter Preview on pages 64–65. Describe a graphic organizer that would be useful in taking notes for discussing each of the following:
   a. Key Terms to Define
   b. People to Meet
   c. Places to Discover
   d. Objectives to Learn, number 3
2. Create a cause-and-effect chart to organize the events in the history of the Hebrews from 1020 to 538 B.C., discussed in Section 2 of this chapter.

GEOGRAPHY IN HISTORY

1. **Place:** Why did the Phoenicians turn to the sea to make a living, and how did they use the land to pursue a seafaring life?
2. **Movement:** Why did the Israelites migrate to Egypt, and why did they flee from Egypt sometime later?

TRACING CHRONOLOGY

Refer to the time line below to answer these questions.

1. What event important to modern Jews is represented on the time line?
2. Identify the four important Middle Eastern empires represented in the time line, and list them chronologically.
3. The Hittites and the Lydians both lived in Asia Minor, but about how many years separated them?

LINKING PAST AND PRESENT

1. Does the legal system of our country parallel Hittite law or Hammurabi's code? Provide a brief explanation of your view.
2. The Hebrews, ancestors of the Jews, moved to Canaan around 1900 B.C. and shared that land with several other peoples. What peoples live today in what was the land of Canaan, and what is the status of the struggles of these peoples for homelands?

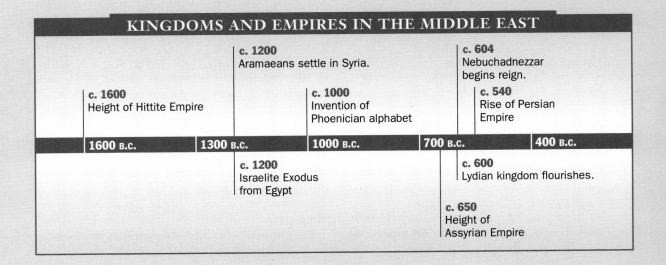

KINGDOMS AND EMPIRES IN THE MIDDLE EAST

c. 1200
Aramaeans settle in Syria.

c. 604
Nebuchadnezzar begins reign.

c. 1600
Height of Hittite Empire

c. 1000
Invention of Phoenician alphabet

c. 540
Rise of Persian Empire

1600 B.C.   1300 B.C.   1000 B.C.   700 B.C.   400 B.C.

c. 1200
Israelite Exodus from Egypt

c. 600
Lydian kingdom flourishes.

c. 650
Height of Assyrian Empire

UNIT 1 SYNOPSIS

The bones of early human beings as well as other fossil remains, archaeological artifacts, and written records hold many clues for researchers studying the past. Although historians consider history to have begun about 5,500 years ago, when early civilizations created writing systems, the human story extends much further into the past—into more than 2 million years of prehistory.

In prehistoric times, early human beings set many cultural patterns that continued into historic times. They adapted to their changing environment. They migrated in search of more hospitable living conditions. They cooperated with one another to obtain food and came into conflict over land and water. They invented new ways of doing things and adopted from one another new methods and ideas.

Some early peoples quit their wandering life and settled down as farmers. They began to live together in villages and later built cities. Many historians set the beginning of history at the formation of cities, for it was there that writing and other activities of early civilization evolved. The ancient cities founded in the river valleys of Egypt, the Fertile Crescent, South Asia, and China spawned several great civilizations. Some of these civilizations shared their ideas and way of life with other peoples through trade, conquest, and empire. Some disappeared; some were overcome but rose again; some have continued in one form or another into the twentieth century.

CHAPTER 1
Human Beginnings

Using research techniques such as radiocarbon dating to date plant and animal matter, anthropologists and archaeologists have been able to establish a time frame for prehistoric human life. Scientists do not agree about all aspects of how or when the first human beings became truly human, but fossil evidence suggests that the first prehuman hominids lived about 4 million years ago. Over the next few million years, the hominids gradually adapted to changes in their environment, such as a colder climate, in various ways. Some hominids evolved larger brains.

Early Humans   Two large-brained hominids, *Homo habilis* and *Homo erectus*, as well as all modern human beings, are scientifically classified in the genus *Homo*—man. During the Ice Ages—periods of cold climate and glaciation—some early people migrated to warmer areas, and others perished from the cold or lack of food. Others learned techniques for staying warm. Clothing and fire became part of the culture of prehistoric people, as did the use of stone tools. The early human beings of the Stone Age invented many new technological and social skills, including spoken language. Changes were relatively slow, however, until the modern human species, *Homo sapiens*, appeared around 200,000 years ago. Two groups of *Homo sapiens*, the Neanderthals and the Cro-Magnons, made significant advances in housing and in tool and weapon making, but the greatest achievement came in the final few thousand years of the Stone Age—the Neolithic period—with the shift from hunting and food gathering to agriculture. This change in the way of life was so radical that it is often referred to as the Neolithic Revolution.

Civilizations   The development of agriculture was an essential stepping stone to civilization. Initially farming allowed people to give up their nomadic life and settle in communities. Eventually, with a relatively steady food supply, many men and women could devote their time to economic activities other than farming. As time passed, some of the early agricultural villages grew into the first cities, which were home to highly organized societies, or civilizations. All early civilizations shared some basic features. They had specialized labor; cooperative methods for producing surplus food, such as irrigation; and metalworking technology. Under an organized government they formed social classes and maintained an army. They undertook long-distance trade. With a system of values and religious beliefs, they were sophisticated enough to have written records.

Learning from Art *Cro-Magnon artists often painted their vivid animal images on the ceilings of caves that they reached only through twisted networks of underground tunnels.* ***Why do you think they chose such inaccessible locations?***

CHAPTER 2
Early Civilizations

Cities and civilizations arose at different times in different parts of the world. Many of the earliest civilizations had one thing in common, however: they grew out of agricultural settlements in river valleys. Civilization is said to have been born around 3500 B.C. in the Tigris-Euphrates River Valley in the Fertile Crescent, but it also arose soon thereafter in the Nile Valley of Egypt, and again later in the Indus River Valley of the South Asia subcontinent and in the Huang He Valley in China.

Ancient Egypt and Mesopotamia In the Nile Valley, nomads who had left the desert to settle along the fertile banks of the Nile founded villages. These villages then banded together in small kingdoms, which were later united under a king, who was a religious and political leader and head of a governmental bureaucracy.

The ancient Egyptians built a magnificent civilization. With innovative irrigation and flood-control techniques, they used the seasonally fluctuating Nile waters to their advantage. They undertook ambitious building projects, such as the pyramids, which required new engineering skills. The writing system early Egyptians invented and the script that formed from it were put to use both for everyday purposes and for decorating their massive monuments. The prosperity achieved by Egyptian civilization encouraged later pharaohs to expand the frontiers of their country and to build an empire. The cultural diffusion made possible by the empire further enriched Egyptian civilization.

In Mesopotamia, the land between the Tigris and Euphrates rivers, the pattern of development was much the same. Peoples fleeing war and overpopulation, as well as poor climate, settled in villages on the fertile river plain. Although the early Mesopotamians, unlike the Egyptians, could not depend on a regular supply of water, they managed to meet the challenges of the twin rivers by cooperating with one another and devising methods of irrigation and flood control. The Sumerians, a group who migrated to the region from central Asia, built the world's first cities and a civilization that reached its height sometime before that of the Egyptians. The complex organization of their civilization was evident in the governments of the Sumerian city-states and their laws and religion. The innovative Sumerians created cuneiform, perhaps the world's oldest writing system, and they also invented the wheel. The prosperous Sumerian city-states eventually fell to empire builders, first the Akkadians and later the Babylonians.

First Asian Civilizations At about the same time as the rise of empires in Mesopotamia, a third river valley civilization to the east, the Harappans, reached its peak. Adapting to the unique seasonal winds and flood patterns of their environment, the people of the South Asia subcontinent prospered in the Indus River Valley. They produced a surplus of food and varied goods, which they traded with the Mesopotamians, among others. The pictograms on the seals used to identify merchandise from the Indus Valley suggest that the Harappan people also exchanged ideas with their trading partners. Although the remains of Harappan cities such as Mohenjo-Daro indicate that the people of the Indus Valley were expert urban planners, why the cities were destroyed and what caused their civilization to collapse remains a mystery.

The fourth river valley civilization, which began in ancient China, has continued into the twentieth century. Isolated from other cultures for many centuries by formidable landforms, the Chinese formed one culture and a strong sense of national identity. From Neolithic times, people settled and flourished in the Huang He Valley. Written records and other finds indicate that under the Shang dynasty, which controlled the river valley from about 1700 to 1000 B.C., the Chinese built their first cities, created a complex writing system, and perfected their skill in casting bronze. The replacement of the Shang dynasty by the Zhou dynasty was just one of many transitions between the dynasties that successively ruled China.

CHAPTER 3
Kingdoms and Empires in the Middle East

The Fertile Crescent, where civilization began, continued to be home for diverse peoples after the earliest river valley civilizations fell. Many people in the region were active in trade and thus promoted cultural diffusion and also made lasting cultural and economic contributions to later civilizations.

Traders and Herders Prominent among the trading peoples of the Middle East were the Phoenicians. They not only navigated the Mediterranean Sea and beyond with ease, controlling shipping and trade and founding

Learning from Art *Sumerian artists, working about 2500 B.C., inlaid two wooden panels—called the Standard of Ur—with a mosaic of shell and semiprecious stones to illustrate scenes of peace and war. The peace panel is shown here.* **Why is the Standard of Ur valuable to historians?**

colonies, but created an alphabet that was a major breakthrough in writing and the model for later alphabets. Among the other trading peoples in the region, the Aramaeans introduced the Aramaic language into the everyday life of many other peoples, and the Lydians left a lasting mark on the economies of other civilizations by using coins as a medium of exchange.

The Hebrews, a nomadic people in this region, made lasting cultural contributions. Foremost among these was monotheism—the belief in one all-powerful God—an idea that formed the basis of Judaism, Christianity, and Islam. During their troubled history, the Hebrews several times came into conflict with neighboring peoples and were enslaved and exiled.

Empire Builders Many peoples in the Fertile Crescent suffered as warlike empires successively dominated the region and neighboring regions as well. The Hittites were the first of these aggressors, coming to Asia Minor from Europe or central Asia. With many advantages in battle-fighting tactics, the Hittites overwhelmed the region and established an empire that spanned Asia Minor, Syria, and part of Mesopotamia. The Assyrians, a Mesopotamian people, were the next conquerors in the Middle East. They too had great expertise on the battlefield, and cruelly treated the peoples they conquered. The well-organized and extensive Assyrian Empire fell to the Chaldeans (descendants of the Babylonians), but in less than 100 years the Chaldean Empire was in turn overthrown by the Persians. The Persians, who originated in central Asia and settled in the land that today is Iran, built an empire that was second to none, stretching from

Learning from Art *The Ishtar Gate, with its brightly glazed brickwork, stands today in a museum in Berlin.* **Why do you think this artifact of ancient Babylon is found in a European museum?**

the Nile River to the Indus River. The Persians surpassed their predecessors in administering a vast area and in tolerating the languages, religions, and customs of subject peoples. Communication and cooperation characterized the Persian approach to ruling an empire.

SURVEYING THE UNIT

1. **Making Connections:** How did the Neolithic Revolution become a stepping stone to the rise of the first civilizations?

2. **Defending a Point of View:** Do you think that cultural diffusion benefits or hinders the growth of a civilization? Explain your reasoning, supporting your point of view by citing examples from your reading.

3. **Making Comparisons:** Compare and contrast the empires that came to dominate the Fertile Crescent and neighboring regions, from the Akkadians to the Persians.

UNIT 1 REVIEW

REVIEWING THE MAIN IDEAS

1. **Describe:** What was the Neolithic Revolution? What technological and social developments are associated with it?
2. **Locate:** Where were the four early civilizations described in Chapter 2 located? What physical feature was common to them all?
3. **Identify:** Name the peoples who inhabited the Middle East between 2000 and 500 B.C. and tell about one accomplishment of each.

THINKING CRITICALLY

1. **Apply:** Use the information in the text to make a chart illustrating the religious beliefs of the Neanderthals, the Cro-Magnons, the Neolithic peoples, the Egyptians, the Sumerians, the Harappans, the early Chinese, the Phoenicians, the Hebrews, and the Persians.
2. **Analyze:** What caused each of these events in the history of the Hebrews: migration to Egypt, exodus from Egypt, union of Israelite tribes under Saul, split by Israelite tribes into two kingdoms after Solomon, and Babylonian exile?
3. **Synthesize:** Why did some societies never develop civilizations?
4. **Evaluate:** Rank the writing systems of the Egyptians, Sumerians, early Chinese, and Phoenicians in order of complexity and of usefulness.

A GLOBAL PERSPECTIVE

Refer to the time line on pages 12–13 to answer these questions.

1. What was happening in the Americas at the same time as the Sumerians were building their first cities?
2. About how many years after civilization arose in the Fertile Crescent did it appear in the Americas?

3. Compare (a) the time between the first manufacture of stone tools and the discovery of fire with (b) the time between the Chinese writing on oracle bones and Sumerians' recording *Gilgamesh*.
4. Why is acquisition of language by early people the first event shown in the time line for the cultural and social sphere?
5. Which three events in the cultural, social, and scientific spheres predate the appearance of *Homo sapiens*?
6. The Great Pyramid was built about 500 years after Narmer united Upper and Lower Egypt. How much later were the monuments at Stonehenge erected?

LINKING PAST AND PRESENT

1. The increased food supply that followed the Cro-Magnons' invention of long-distance weapons encouraged unrelated bands to cooperate in big game hunts. How effectively do nations today cooperate to provide food for all people? What problems today influence feeding for all people, and do you think these problems can be solved? Cite specific examples and explain your reasoning.
2. Archaeological artifacts have told us a great deal about early civilizations. Name five objects or technological advances in our era that would carry significant information about our own civilization if it were to disappear. What would each of the five reveal?
3. Many groups made their home in the Middle East between 2000 and 500 B.C., sometimes coexisting in peace but more often fighting with each other. The Middle East is still troubled by much conflict and political turmoil. Describe two recent events that demonstrate the continuing struggles among the peoples of the Middle East. What do you think will come of these events?

ANALYZING VISUALS

The earliest works of art known to historians seem to have been made about 30,000 years ago. Prehistoric art can be classified into two categories: mural art, or wall paintings, and portable art, such as the small carved head shown here. Although this piece and others like it predate written history, they can tell us a number of things about the society that produced them. This woman's head was found in Brassempouy, in southwestern France. Only 1.4 inches (3.5 cm) high, the carving has fascinated historians who study early humans. Probably made about 22,000 years ago, it is an example of fairly advanced craftsmanship. The woman's delicate features and the detailed carving of the hair show a sophistication not seen in many other early carvings. The extensive detail of the piece is remarkable, considering that the only carving tools available were probably pieces of chipped flint.

1. What can you deduce about the society that made this object from the fact that it is not a tool or weapon?
2. What do you think the function of this piece might have been? Can you provide any evidence or logic to back up your ideas?

3. Even though this carving was done 22,000 years ago, it is easy for us to understand and relate to, and enables us to think about the artist who created it in a personal way. Why do you think this is?

USING LITERATURE

Refer to the excerpt from Gilgamesh *on pages 58–61 to answer these questions.*

1. What part of the excerpt seems especially to reflect the Sumerians' own experience and special relation to their environment?
2. Which details in the selection support what you have learned about Sumerian civilization?
3. What evidence in the poem shows that the Sumerians, like some other early peoples, saw a connection between natural forces and their gods and goddesses?

WRITING ABOUT HISTORY

1. Do research on the Cro-Magnon cave paintings in France and Spain. Find out how the paintings were discovered, what they depict, and how they have been interpreted. Then imagine that you were the first person in modern times to see the cave paintings. Compose a brief journal entry describing the experience and its meaning for you and for humankind. Use the information you have gathered to make your account appear authentic.
2. Reread the chapters in Unit 1 to determine which early people or civilization was the most innovative. Write an essay explaining the rationale behind your choice. Support your argument with facts from the text and from outside sources if you wish to do research on the question.
3. Refer to the Book of Exodus (20:2) in the Bible for the complete text of the Ten Commandments. Write a paraphrase of each law in your own words. Conclude with a brief discussion on how each of the Ten Commandments relates to the lives of modern people.

UNIT 2

Flowering of Civilizations

2000 B.C.–A.D. 500

"No one is so savage that he cannot become civilized, if he will lend a patient ear to culture."

With these words the poet Horace described a dominant value of the Roman civilization in which he lived almost 2,000 years ago. Rome not only preserved Greek culture but spread the Latin language, cities, a legal system, roads, and aqueducts throughout Europe as well. During the same time in which Greco-Roman culture reached its height, two other major civilizations were flourishing in Asia. There—in India and China—Hinduism, Buddhism, Confucianism, and Daoism arose.

A GLOBAL CHRONOLOGY

	2000 B.C.	1500 B.C.	1000 B.C.
Political Sphere		**c. 1500** Aryans cross the Hindu Kush into South Asia.	
Scientific Sphere	**c. 1700** Babylonian Empire adapts Sumerian calendar.		
Cultural & Social Sphere		**c. 1200** Vedic Age begins in India.	**c. 800** Ionians introduce Phoenician alphabet to Greece.

Etruscan pottery from about 600 B.C.

500 B.C.		A.D. 1		A.D. 500	
	31 Augustus establishes the *Pax Romana.*		**476** Western Roman Empire falls.		
	c. 330 Aristotle advances scientific method.		**c. 150** Ptolemy collects astronomical information.		**c. 600** The Chinese invent block printing.
551 Confucius is born.	**c. 33** Crucifixion of Jesus Christ	**c. 100** Kushite merchants cross the Sahara by camel caravan.			

The Rise of Ancient Greece

*A*n eager crowd gathered in the sun-drenched sports arena just outside King Minos's palace at Knossos on the Aegean island of Crete. According to legend, Minos ruled over the Minoan civilization in the 2000s B.C. The Minoans' favorite event—bull leaping—was about to begin. The crowd gasped as a raging bull, representing the earthquakes that shook Crete, charged a young male gymnast who stood motionless. Just before the collision, the gymnast grabbed the bull's horns and somersaulted onto the bull's back. Then his body arched into the air, and he completed a back flip, landing in the arms of his female partner waiting nearby. The exultant crowd cheered at the conclusion of this spectacle, part sport and part religious ritual. By leaping over the bull, the gymnast had shown that no matter how much the earth trembled, the Minoans would stay on Crete.

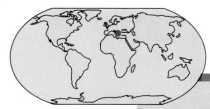

CHAPTER PREVIEW

Key Terms to Define: polis, citizens, aristocrats, tyrant, oligarchy, democracy, rhetoric

People to Meet: Sir Arthur Evans, Minoans, Mycenaeans, Heinrich Schliemann, Homer, Draco, Solon, Peisistratus, Cleisthenes, Pheidippides, Themistocles, Pericles

Places to Discover: Balkan Peninsula, Aegean Sea, Crete, Knossos, Mycenae, Ionia, Troy, Sparta, Peloponnesus, Athens, Attica, Marathon, Thermopylae, Salamis

Objectives to Learn:
1. Where and how did the early civilizations of Greece develop?
2. What aspects of life did Greek deities explain?

In this Minoan fresco from Knossos, a family brings ceremonial offerings to their goddess.

3. What different Greek values did Sparta and Athens represent?

4. What was the impact of the Persian Wars and the Peloponnesian War?

Concepts to Understand:

• Relation to environment—Closeness to the sea helped make the early Greeks seafarers. Section 1

• Movement—The Greeks founded colonies throughout the area of the Mediterranean and Black seas. Section 2

• Conflict—Greek city-states together fought the Persians; then the city-states, led by rivals Athens and Sparta, fought each other. Sections 3,4

91

Beginnings

Any observer of the Mediterranean region in the year 500 B.C. probably would have predicted that the Persians would strongly influence future civilizations. Instead, it was the ancient Greeks who set their stamp on the Mediterranean region and who also contributed greatly to the way we live today. Every time people of today go to the theater or watch the Olympic games on television, they enjoy an activity that has its roots in ancient Greece. Modern public buildings often reflect Greek architectural styles. And above all, the ancient Greeks developed the Western concept of democratic government.

The Aegean Area

Ancient Greece consisted of two parts: a mainland—the southern part of Europe's Balkan Peninsula—and a group of small, rocky islands. A few of the islands lay west of the peninsula, but most dotted the Aegean (ih JEE uhn) Sea between the mainland and Asia Minor.

Low-lying but rugged mountains make up about three-fourths of the Greek mainland. Between the mountain ranges and along the coast lie fertile plains suitable for farming. Short, swift rivers flow from the interior to the sea, and the long, indented coastline provides many fine harbors. The climate is mild, with rainy winters. Afternoon breezes carrying cooler air from the sea offset the hot, dry summers.

The mountains both protected and isolated Greeks on the mainland. Besides making attacks by foreigners difficult, the mountains limited travel and communication between communities. The Greek people, therefore, never united under one government, although they spoke one language and practiced the same religion.

Because of the numerous harbors and because no place in Greece is more than 50 miles (80 kilometers) from the coast, many Greeks turned to the sea to earn their living. They became fishermen, traders, and even pirates.

In addition, the mild climate allowed the ancient Greeks to spend much of their time outdoors. People assembled for meetings in the

Learning from Photographs *This modern view shows a harbor on one of the Greek islands in the Aegean Sea.* **In what ways did the sea become part of the economic and social life of ancient Greek civilization?**

public square, teachers met their students in public gardens, and actors performed plays in unroofed theaters.

Aegean Civilizations

Greek myths referred to an early civilization on the island of Crete, southeast of the Greek mainland, but for a long time historians disputed this. Then, about A.D. 1900, British archaeologist Sir Arthur Evans unearthed remains of the Minoan civilization, which flourished from about 2500 to 1450 B.C.

The Minoans At Knossos (NAHS uhs) on Crete, Evans excavated the palace of legendary King Minos. Passageways twisted and turned in all directions to form a labyrinth, or maze. The palace contained indoor bathrooms with running water and portable fireboxes to keep off the night chill. Evans found workshops where artisans had produced beautifully decorated pottery as thin as eggshells, and an archives where scribes kept records of goods that moved in and out of the palace.

The brightly colored murals that decorate palace walls provide considerable information about the Minoans. The murals show that both men and women curled their hair, bedecked themselves with gold jewelry, and set off their narrow waists with wide metal belts. The Minoans were fond of dancing and sporting events, such as boxing matches.

Minoan women apparently enjoyed a higher status than women in other civilizations. For example, they were permitted to attend sporting events. Furthermore, Minoan religion had more goddesses than gods. The chief deity of Crete was the Great Goddess, or Earth Mother, whom the Minoans believed caused the growth of all living things.

The Minoans earned their living from sea trade. Crete's forests of oak and cedar provided wood for ships. In addition, the island's location enabled Minoan traders to act as middlemen for the empires of Egypt and Mesopotamia. By 2000 B.C., Minoan fleets dominated the eastern Mediterranean, carrying goods and keeping the seas free from pirates. The ships also guarded

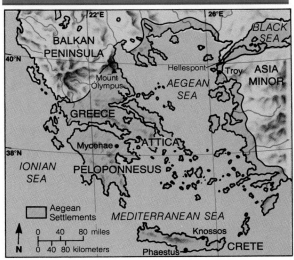

AEGEAN CIVILIZATIONS 1400 B.C.

Learning from Maps *Greek civilization grew out of earlier civilizations that flourished in the Aegean area from about 3000 to about 1000 B.C.* **Which two civilizations dominated the Aegean area during that period?**

Crete against outside attack, which is why the Minoans did not surround their cities with walls.

Minoan civilization reached its peak around 1600 B.C. Some 250 years later, it collapsed. Some historians think that its cities were destroyed by huge tidal waves resulting from an undersea earthquake. Others think that a people from the Greek mainland, the Mycenaeans (my suh NEE uhnz), succeeded in invading Crete.

The Mycenaeans In A.D. 1876 Heinrich Schliemann, a businessman turned amateur archaeologist, found evidence of the Mycenaean civilization. As he reported in a telegram to the Greek king:

I am overwhelmed with joy to inform Your Majesty that I have uncovered the tombs which tradition . . . knew as the sepulchres of Agamemnon, Cassandra . . . and their fellows. . . . Inside the tombs I found a vast mass of treasure consisting of archaic objects made of solid gold. These alone are enough to fill a great museum, which will be the wonder of the world.

Learning from Art
Young Minoan men and women participated in the ritual of leaping over bulls, shown in this fresco—a mural painted on plaster—from Knossos. The bull is also important in the myth of the Minotaur of Crete, a monster half man and half bull. **What purpose might myths about monsters have served?**

The Mycenaean civilization, which flourished from about 2000 to 1100 B.C., would eventually combine with the Minoan civilization to form ancient Greece. The Mycenaeans originated among the Indo-European peoples of central Asia. About 2000 B.C., as a result of the rapid growth of their population, they began moving out from their homeland. After pushing west into Europe, they turned south into the Balkan Peninsula, where they gradually intermarried with the local population—known as Hellenes—and set up a group of kingdoms.

Each Mycenaean kingdom centered around a hilltop on which was built a royal fortress that dominated the surrounding plain. Stone walls circled the fortress, providing a shelter for the kingdom's inhabitants in times of danger. Warrior-nobles lived on their estates outside the walls. They would turn out in armor when the king needed them to supply horse-drawn chariots. The slaves and tenants who farmed the land lived in villages on these estates.

The palaces in the city of Mycenae served as centers of both government administration and production. Inside, artisans tanned leather, sewed clothes, fashioned jars for storing wine and olive oil, and made bronze swords and ox-hide shields. To help in collecting taxes, government officials kept records of the wealth of every person in the kingdom. They collected taxes in the form of wheat, livestock, and honey, to be stored in the palace to pay government employ-

ees and to reimburse the king for providing military protection.

Minoan traders visited the Greek mainland soon after the Mycenaeans set up their kingdoms. Gradually, the Mycenaeans adopted many elements of Minoan culture—metalworking and shipbuilding techniques and navigation by the sun and the stars. And the Mycenaeans worshiped the Minoan Earth Mother as well.

By the mid-1400s B.C., the Mycenaeans had conquered the Minoans and controlled the Aegean area. But by 1100 B.C., fighting among the Mycenaeans had destroyed the great hilltop fortresses. Soon after, a new wave of invaders, the Greek-speaking Dorians, entered Greece from the north. Armed with iron weapons, the Dorians easily overran the mainland.

Historians call the next 300 years of Greek history a "dark age." Written language disappeared and the illiterate Dorians kept no records. During this dark age, overseas trade stopped, poverty increased, and people lost the skills once practiced by Mycenaean artisans. Thousands of refugees fled the mainland and settled in Ionia—the west coast of Asia Minor and its adjoining islands.

By 750 B.C. the Ionians had reintroduced crafts and skills to their homeland, including an alphabet used by Phoenician traders. The dark age had ended. The Greeks began to write again, and a new Greek civilization with Mycenaean elements emerged. The new civilization—

Mycenaean Warrior Kings

Discovered in a deep shaft grave, the mask below probably shows the face of a Mycenaean warrior-king who lived during the 1500s B.C. Several masks like this one have been discovered in the Mycenaean tombs of central and southern Greece. Made from a sheet of gold, the mask is a true "death mask." That is, the mask seems to have been shaped directly from the face of the dead person. Once the general form of the face was made, an artist added more stylized details to the mask to show the outline of the closed eyes, the ears, and the mouth.

The discovery of Mycenaean shaft graves, with their abundant treasures of gold, silver, and jeweled objects, has told historians a great deal about the ancient Mycenaean culture. Gold was not a metal native to Mycenaean lands, but Mycenaean tombs of the 1500s B.C. contain many ornate gold objects. Historians believe that Mycenaean rulers either traded or fought to acquire gold and other riches. During this period, Egypt was the leading source of gold in the Mediterranean. It seems likely that mercenaries, or paid warriors, from Mycenae may have fought for the Egyptians. From 1700 to 1580 B.C., the Egyptians were trying to secure the Nile Delta

from the Hyksos, a people from Asia. Mycenaean soldiers who fought with the Egyptians in these wars may have received gold as payment for their help.

The tradition of including a death mask in a ruler's grave also may have come from the Egyptians. Those who traveled to Egypt may have seen and learned about Egyptian burial customs. Impressed by the beauty and splendor of Egyptian royal burials, the Mycenaeans may have chosen to adopt some of these traditions for their own burials. In effect, the Mycenaean mask shown here may be a part of the same tradition that was behind the pharaoh Tutankhamen's funerary mask.

The Mycenaean economic system brought its rulers great wealth when times were good, but was extremely vulnerable because it relied so heavily on foreign trade. By 1300 B.C. the system had collapsed. Trade with Egypt declined, and before the end of the century, Mycenaean culture was destroyed by a Dorian invasion from the north. The art objects buried in Mycenaean royal graves are among the few links historians have to this early period of Greek history.

Responding to the Arts

1. How were Mycenaean death masks made?
2. What sort of contact between the Mycenaeans and the Egyptians does this mask suggest?

called Hellenic, after the original inhabitants of Greece—flourished from about the 700s B.C. until 336 B.C.

Poets and Heroes

Bards, or singing storytellers, had kept alive Mycenaean traditions during the dark age. With their new ability to write, the Greeks began to record the epic poems that the bards had passed from generation to generation.

The *Iliad* and the *Odyssey*   According to tradition, a blind poet named Homer who lived during the 700s B.C. composed the two most famous Greek epics—the *Iliad* and the *Odyssey*. Homer set the *Iliad* and the *Odyssey* during and after the legendary Trojan War. The Mycenaeans had supposedly fought the people of Troy in the mid-1200s B.C. In A.D.1870 Heinrich Schliemann proved that Troy actually existed and was a major trading city in Asia Minor.

The *Iliad* begins when a Trojan prince named Paris falls in love with Helen, the wife of a Mycenaean king, and takes her with him to Troy. To avenge Helen's kidnapping, the Mycenaeans lay siege to Troy for 10 years, but they cannot capture the city. Finally, they trick the Trojans by building a huge, hollow wooden horse. The best Mycenaean soldiers hide inside the horse, while the rest board their ships and pretend to sail away. The joyful Trojans, thinking themselves victorious, bring the gift horse into the city. That night, the Greeks creep out of the horse, slaughter the Trojan men, enslave the women and children, and burn the city to the ground. Ever since, the expression *Trojan horse* has meant something or someone who destroys from within.

The *Odyssey* describes the homeward wanderings of the Mycenaean king Odysseus after the fall of Troy. Because it took him 10 years to return to Greece, people refer to any long, adventure-filled journey as an *odyssey*.

Teaching Greek Values   Eventually, schools in ancient Greece used the *Iliad* and the *Odyssey* to present to students many of the values of Hellenic civilization. For example, in an exciting description of men marching to war, the *Iliad* taught students to be proud of their Greek heritage and their heroic ancestors.

As a ravening fire blazes over a vast forest on the mountains, and its light is seen afar, so while they marched the sheen from their forest of bronze [spears] went up dazzling into high heaven.

As flocks of wildfowl on the wing, geese or cranes or long-necked swans fly this way and that way over the Asian meadows, proud of the power of their wings, and they settle on and on honking as they go until they fill the meadow with sound: so flocks of men poured out of their camp onwards over the Scamandrian plain, and the ground thundered terribly under the tramp of horses and of men.

—Homer, from the *Iliad*, mid-700s B.C.

The *Iliad* and the *Odyssey* also represented other values of Hellenic civilization, such as a love for nature, the importance of husband-wife relationships and tender feelings, and loyalty between friends. Hellenic schools also used the two epics to teach students to always strive for excellence and to meet with dignity whatever fate had in store.

A Family of Deities

In Greek religion, the activities of gods and goddesses explained why people behaved the way they did and why their lives took one direction rather than another. The Greeks also believed that their powerful deities caused the events of the physical world to occur—such as the coming of spring or violent storms with thunder and lightning.

The gods and goddesses of ancient Greece combined features of both Minoan and Mycenaean deities. For example, different Greek goddesses took over different aspects of the Earth Mother. Athena became the goddess of wisdom and art, Demeter became the goddess of agriculture, and Aphrodite became the goddess of love and beauty. Each community chose a particular god or goddess as its patron and protector, but all Greeks worshiped as their chief deity the Mycenaean god Zeus.

Much more than other civilizations did, the Greeks humanized their deities. Unlike the half-animal gods and goddesses of Egypt, Greek deities had totally human forms. They behaved like humans, too—marrying, having children, lying, and murdering. Frequently jealous of one another, the Greek deities quarreled and sometimes played tricks on one another. They also possessed superhuman powers. Since the Greeks saw their deities as sources of power, both physical and mental, they tried to be like them by doing everything to the best of their ability.

Greeks believed that the 12 most important Greek deities lived on high Mount Olympus, an actual mountain in Greece. Each of these deities controlled a specific part of the natural world. For example, Zeus was thought to rule the sky, weather, and thunderstorms; his brother Poseidon was thought to rule the sea; and another brother, Hades, was thought to rule the underworld, where the dead spent eternity.

Zeus's son Apollo, the god of light, drove the sun across the sky every day in his chariot. Because the Greeks also considered Apollo to be the god of prophecy, they would bring gifts to the oracle at Delphi—a sanctuary to honor Apollo—and ask to have hidden knowledge revealed. Like the Shang in ancient China, the Greeks believed that oracles could predict the future. At the Delphic oracle, they would ask questions and the priests and priestesses would interpret Apollo's replies.

As Hellenic civilization developed, certain religious festivals became an important part of

GREEK DEITIES

Zeus	king of the gods
Hera	wife of Zeus; goddess of marriage
Poseidon	god of the sea
Apollo	god of the sun and of prophecy
Ares	god of war
Athena	goddess of wisdom and art
Aphrodite	goddess of love and beauty
Dionysus	god of wine and fertility
Artemis	goddess of the hunt
Hermes	messenger of the gods
Hephaestus	god of fire
Hades	god of the underworld
Demeter	goddess of agriculture
Hestia	goddess of home and family

Learning from Charts *The gods and goddesses living on Mount Olympus had distinct personalities and responsibilities.* **In what ways did the ancient Greeks humanize their superpowerful deities?**

Greek life. Every four years the Greeks held a series of athletic contests "for the greater glory of Zeus." Because these contests were held at the city of Olympia, they were called the Olympic Games. The Greeks also originated the play—a celebration in honor of Dionysus, the god of wine and fertility.

SECTION 1 REVIEW

Recall
1. **Identify:** Sir Arthur Evans, Minoans, Mycenaeans, Heinrich Schliemann, Homer
2. **Desribe:** What routes would the Mycenaeans have taken to reach Troy and Knossos from their home city of Mycenae?

Critical Thinking
3. **Apply:** Use Zeus and Apollo as examples to illustrate some ways that the Greeks viewed their deities.
4. **Analyze:** What have historians learned from the Homeric epics?

Applying Concepts
5. **Relation to environment:** Illustrate how the geography and climate of the mainland of Greece and of the Aegean islands affected the development of the ancient Minoan and Mycenaean civilizations.

The Polis

The English language offers evidence of how ancient Greeks have influenced modern life. Words such as *police* and *politics*, for example, derive from the Greek word *polis*. The **polis**, or city-state, was the basic political unit of Hellenic civilization. Each polis developed its own pattern of life independently but shared certain features with other city-states.

The Typical Polis

A typical polis included a city and the surrounding villages, fields, and orchards. At the center of the city on the top of a fortified hill, or acropolis (uh KRAHP uh luhs)—stood the temple of the local deity. At the foot of the acropolis, the agora, or public square, served as the political center of the polis. **Citizens**—those who took part in government —gathered in the agora to discuss public affairs, choose their officials, and pass their laws. Artisans and merchants also conducted business in the agora.

A polis had to be small enough so that all of its citizens could participate in public business. Accordingly, the typical polis measured about three days' walking distance across and included between 5,000 and 10,000 male citizens. Only a few large city-states, like Athens, had as many as 40,000 male citizens. Citizens, however, made up only a minority of the inhabitants of a polis. In Athens, slaves and those who were foreign-born were excluded from citizenship, and before 500 B.C. so were men who did not own land. Greek women had no political or legal rights.

Male citizens had both rights and responsibilities. They could vote, hold public office, own property, and speak for themselves in court. In return, the polis expected them to participate in government and to defend the polis in time of war. As the Athenian leader Pericles said, "We

do not say that a man who takes no interest in politics minds his own business. We say he has no business here at all."

Greek Colonies and Trade

As prosperity gradually returned after the dark age, the population of Greece increased. By 700 B.C. Greek farmers no longer grew enough grain to feed everyone. As a result, each polis sent out groups of people to coastal areas around the Mediterranean and Black seas. There, they established some 250 colonies, from Spain in the west to Crimea in the north.

Each colony kept close economic ties with its metropolis, or "mother city." A colony supplied its metropolis with grain—wheat and barley. Farmers on the Greek mainland could thus use their land to produce profitable cash crops for export, such as wine and olive oil. Because vineyards and olive groves needed fewer workers than did grain fields, many farmers moved to the cities, where they learned crafts such as metalworking and pottery making. With more goods to sell, Greek merchants began trading throughout the Mediterranean region.

The Greeks learned about coined money from the Lydians in the 600s B.C. Finding trade easier with coins, Greeks replaced their barter system with a money economy, and their overseas trade expanded further. Merchants issued their own coins, but eventually individual city-states took over this responsibility.

Political and Social Change

Increased trade changed Greek political life. During the dark age and for 100 years after, one king governed each Greek community. By the

700s B.C., however, the kings had lost power to landholding **aristocrats**, or nobles, who as members of the upper class provided cavalry for the king's military ventures. As overseas trade developed, the aristocracy—once only hereditary—expanded to include wealthy merchants and manufacturers.

By 650 B.C. disputes arose between the aristocrats and the common people, especially in the polis of Athens. Farmers often needed credit until harvest time. To obtain loans from the wealthy aristocrats, they had to pledge their fields as security. But the farmers often could not grow enough in their small fields to feed themselves and also repay the loans. As a result, many farmers lost their land to the aristocrats and became either sharecroppers or day laborers in the cities. Some former farmers even had to sell themselves into slavery. In protest, farmers demanded political reforms.

The farmers, who were foot soldiers, were becoming more valuable to Greek armies than the aristocrats, who were cavalry. As Greek armies came to rely on the phalanx—rows of foot soldiers closely arrayed with their shields forming a solid wall—aristocrats began to lose influence. Middle-class, non-landowning merchants and artisans, thus far excluded from citizenship, wanted a voice in the government and joined the farmers in their demands. Merchants

CONNECTIONS: GEOGRAPHY IN HISTORY

Sailing the Aegean

This Minoan fresco from the 1400s B.C. depicts the importance of trade to ancient Greek civilization.

The ancient Greeks took advantage of the many natural harbors along their coasts by transporting most goods by sea. Sea travel made good sense, given the rugged mountains of the Greek mainland. Besides, pack animals could carry only small loads short distances. Merchants found sea transport of bulky cargo—grain, timber, and even jugs of olive oil—to be practical and inexpensive.

Greek sailors could sail easily only when the wind was behind them. The prevailing northerly winds made the voyage from Athens to the Black Sea slow and difficult, but the return trip was quick and easy. Likewise, Greek ships could coast to Egypt, but they had to struggle to get home. Most ships managed only one round-trip per year.

The typical Greek freighter was broad—about 25 feet wide compared to a length of 80 feet (7.5 meters by 24 meters). Rigged with a large square sail, this sturdy ship averaged only about 5 knots with the wind. Merchant ships usually sailed in fleets escorted by warships—galleys propelled by banks of oarsmen.

Compare the ancient ships with today's diesel-driven behemoths. A container ship makes the round-trip between the United States and Europe in 21 days. It holds cargo in 1,000 containers—two of which are the size of one Greek freighter.

Some things have not changed, however. The Greek merchant fleet of today ranks among the largest in the world.

Making the Connection
1. Why were the prevailing winds a problem for Greek sailors?
2. Besides larger, faster ships, how has cargo transport changed since ancient times?

The Rise of Ancient Greece **99**

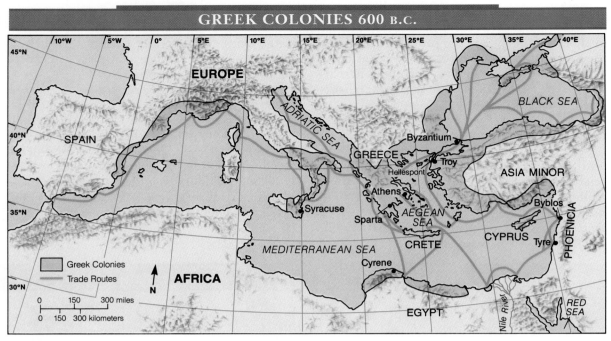

GREEK COLONIES 600 B.C.

Learning from Maps *The overcrowded city-states on the Greek mainland established colonies in the coastal areas their trading ships reached.* **How did these colonists support the economy of their homeland?**

and artisans also wanted the polis to advance their interests by encouraging industry and by protecting overseas trade routes.

As a result of the unrest, tyrannies arose. A tyranny was created when one man, called a **tyrant**, seized power and ruled the polis single-handedly. Although most often an aristocrat himself, the new tyrant made promises to the middle and lower classes and generally treated the people fairly. Tyrants promoted trade, carried out many public works projects, and abolished debt slavery. The harshness of a few tyrants, however, gave *tyranny* its present meaning—rule by a cruel and unjust person.

Tyrants ruled various Greek city-states until about 500 B.C. From then until 336 B.C., the citizens of most city-states restructured their government into an oligarchy or a democracy. In an **oligarchy**, a few wealthy people hold power over the larger group of citizens. In a **democracy**, or government by the people, power lies in the hands of all the citizens. Two democracies of ancient Greece—Sparta and Athens—became the most famous of the city-states.

SECTION 2 REVIEW

Recall

1. **Define:** polis, citizen, aristocrat, tyrant, oligarchy, democracy
2. **Describe:** What were the social and political functions served by an acropolis and an agora in a Greek polis?

Critical Thinking

3. **Analyze:** Compare the rights and responsibilities of a U.S. citizen with those of a citizen of a Greek polis.
4. **Synthesize:** What arguments might a citizen of a polis pre-

sent for or against changing citizenship?

Applying Concepts

5. **Movement:** Describe the relationship between a Greek colony and its metropolis.

Rivals

The two leading city-states in ancient Greece—Sparta and Athens—stood in sharp contrast to each other. Though citizens of both Sparta and Athens participated in polis government, the two city-states differed greatly from each other in their values, cultures, and accomplishments.

Sparta

The descendants of the Dorian invaders of the dark age founded Sparta. It was located in the Peloponnesus (pehl uh puh NEE suhs), a peninsula of southern Greece. Like other city-states, Sparta based its economy on agriculture.

Most other city-states responded to the population increase and the shortage of arable land in the 700s B.C. by setting up new colonies and expanding overseas trade, but the Spartans adopted a different approach. They invaded neighboring city-states, taking over the farmlands and enslaving the local people. The polis of Sparta owned many slaves, known as helots (HEHL uhts), and assigned them to farm the estates of individual Spartans. In addition, a group of free individuals called *perioeci* (peh REE ee sy)—artisans and merchants from the conquered territories—worked for the Spartans. Helots and *perioeci* together outnumbered Spartans by about 200,000 to 10,000.

Around 650 B.C., the helots revolted against their Spartan masters. It took 30 years, but the Spartans managed to suppress the revolt. They then decided that the only way they could maintain power was to establish a military society.

A Military Society   All life in Sparta revolved around the army. Spartan men strove to become first-rate soldiers, and Spartan women aspired to become mothers of soldiers. Spartans despised the other Greeks who lived behind city walls, believing that a city defended by Spartan soldiers did not need walls.

In Sparta, government officials examined newborn infants to see if they were healthy. If not, an official left the sickly infant on a hillside to die. At the age of seven, Spartan boys were taken away from their homes and placed in military barracks. Their training included learning to read, write, and use weapons. To toughen their bodies, the boys went barefoot and had only one garment to wear, even in winter. The boys received little to eat, so that they could learn to fight on an empty stomach if necessary. They learned how to forage by stealing grain and chickens from neighboring farms. If a boy got caught, the public whipping he received taught all of the boys to bear pain in silence.

At age 20, Spartan men became soldiers and were sent to frontier areas. At age 30, they were expected to marry. But Spartan men did not

---

FOOTNOTES TO HISTORY
WORDS FROM SPARTA

Many words that have become part of the English language came from the Spartans. Today the word *spartan* means "avoiding luxury and comfort" and "being as simple and frugal as possible." Another English word that came from the Spartans is *laconic*. Laconia was the plain in the southeastern part of the Peloponnesus where Sparta was situated. The Spartans were not impressed by oratory. On the contrary, they trained their young men to walk in silence and to say only what was absolutely necessary. The English word *laconic* refers to a person whose speaking style is short, sharp, and to the point.

maintain households of their own. Instead they continued to live in military barracks until age 60, when they could retire from the army.

The Role of Women　The Spartans brought up women to be, like the Spartan men, as healthy and strong as possible. Female infants received as much food as their brothers, which was not the case elsewhere in Greece. Young Spartan girls trained in gymnastics, wrestling, and boxing. The women in Sparta married at age 19 rather than at 14—the average marrying age in most of Greece—which increased the likelihood that their children would be healthy.

Sparta gave its women more personal rights and freedoms than the women of other Greek city-states received. Spartan women could go shopping in the marketplace, attend dinners at which nonfamily members were present, own property in their own names, and express opin-

ions on public issues. They could not, however, take part in the government of the polis.

Spartan Government　Two kings, who ruled jointly, officially governed Sparta. Except for leading the army and conducting religious services, however, Spartan kings had little power. The Assembly, made up of all male citizens over the age of 20, passed laws and made decisions concerning war and peace. Each year the Assembly elected five overseers, known as ephors (EHF uhrs), to administer public affairs. The ephors could also veto legislation. A Council of Elders, consisting of 28 men over the age of 60, proposed laws to the Assembly and also served as a supreme court.

Results of Militarism　The Spartans succeeded in maintaining their power over the helots and *perioeci* for almost 250 years. But they

IMAGES OF THE TIME

Athenian Life

In the 400s B.C., having defeated the Persians, Athens became wealthy and powerful. Athenian culture flourished, and great monuments were built.

This silver coin, called a tetradrachm, shows an owl, a symbol of Athena. It was used as payment for public works in Athens.

The Acropolis (right) sits on a hilltop above Athens. Here people gathered to celebrate civic festivals and to honor the gods and goddesses of the city. The temples in the Acropolis complex were decorated with elaborate sculptural reliefs (above).

paid a price. Suspicious of any new ideas that might change their society, the Spartans lagged far behind other city-states in developing trade and manufacturing. As a result, they were much poorer than the other Greeks. The Spartans also lagged in intellectual accomplishments. The Athenians created a vast body of literature and made important discoveries in science. The Spartans did not. The Spartans were, however, exceptional athletes who almost always won the Olympic Games, and Spartan soldiers played key roles in defending Greece against invaders.

Athens

Northeast of the Peloponnesus—on a peninsula of central Greece named Attica—people descended from the Mycenaeans established the city-state of Athens. They named their polis after the goddess Athena. Like the early rulers of the other city-states, Athenian kings and aristocrats in the 600s B.C. faced demands by their small farmers, merchants, and artisans for economic and political reforms.

Around this time, the governing methods of Athens and Sparta diverged. Athens gradually expanded its definition of citizenship to encompass more people. Initially, only a man whose father and maternal grandfather had been citizens could be a citizen; however, non-landowning citizens could not participate in Athens's Assembly. Athenians called the many free (nonslave) foreigners who lived in Athens *metics*. These people could not own land or participate in government. By 507 B.C., however, the constitution of Athens stipulated that all free men were citizens regardless of what class they belonged to, and that they could participate in the Assembly regardless of whether they owned land.

A memorial to a loved one, this stele, or grave marker, (right) portrays a woman with her servant. Many grave markers like this one have been found in Athens.

Reflecting on the Times
Why do you think upper-class Athenians devoted so much of their wealth to public buildings?

Reforms by Tyrants   A successsion of four tyrants engineered most of the changes in Athenian government. Draco, the first of these tyrants, issued an improved code of laws in 621 B.C. By distinguishing between intentional and unintentional killing, for example, Draco's code helped end family feuds. The penalties given to offenders, however, were extremely harsh. Even minor offenses, like stealing a cabbage, were punishable by death, and creditors could make slaves of their debtors.

As a later Greek lawgiver said, "Draco's laws were not written with ink, but blood." And over time, the word *draconian* has come to describe something that is very cruel and severe. On the other hand, because Draco's laws were written down, everyone knew exactly what the laws were. Aristocrats could no longer dictate what was legal and what was not.

The next series of reforms took place under the tyrant Solon, who became the leader of Athens in 594 B.C. Solon first turned his attention to improving economic conditions. He canceled all land debts and freed debtors from slavery. Solon also placed limits on the amount of land any one individual could own. By urging farmers to grow cash crops rather than grain, he promoted trade. He also promoted industry by ordering fathers to teach their sons a trade and by extending citizenship to artisans and merchants who were not born Athenians.

Next, Solon turned his attention to the political conflict between aristocrats and commoners. He did this by setting up a two-house legislature. Aristocrats belonged to the Council of 400, while landowning commoners made up the Assembly. The Council drafted measures that then went to the Assembly for approval.

After Solon left office, however, grumbling and discontent disrupted Athens. Aristocrats thought Solon had gone too far in his reforms, while farmers thought he had not gone far enough. Only middle-class merchants and artisans believed Solon had wisely followed a moderate course.

In 546 B.C., the tyrant Peisistratus (py SIHS truht uhs) took over the government of Athens. Peisistratus pushed reforms in an even more radical direction than had Solon. He divided large estates among landless farmers and extended citizenship to men who did not own land. Peisistratus provided the poor with loans and put many of them to work building temples and other public works projects.

Cleisthenes (KLYS thuh neez), the fourth tyrant to help reform Athens, came to power in 508 B.C. The following year he introduced a series of laws that established democracy for Athens.

Athenian Democracy   The Assembly remained the major political institution in Cleisthenes' democracy. All citizens could belong to the Assembly, in which they were considered equal before the law and guaranteed freedom of speech. The Assembly passed laws and also served as a supreme court. In addition, each year the Assembly chose 10 generals to run the army and navy. A Council of 500 administered everyday government business such as taxes, treaties, and public works.

Each year in a lottery, Athenians chose members of the Council. They favored a lottery over the ballot, believing that, except for running a military campaign, all citizens were competent to hold public office. In addition, they considered elections unfair because rich men, men who boasted a well-known family name, or men who spoke effectively in public would have an advantage. Besides, all citizens were supposed to take part in government.

Athenian democracy included a jury system to decide court cases. Juries contained from 201 to 1,001 members, with a majority vote needed to reach a verdict. The Athenians reasoned that the large size of their juries would keep jurors from being influenced by threats, bribes, or prejudice.

Athenian democracy also included a system called ostracism. Each year, citizens could write the name of an undesirable politician on a piece of baked clay called an ostracon. If a person's name appeared on 6,000 ostraca, the polis exiled him for 10 years.

Cleisthenes' reforms lasted for almost 200 years, until the Macedonians living to the north conquered the Greeks. Even though the Athenians excluded several groups from citizenship, ancient Athens indeed laid the foundation for the Western concept of democratic government.

Athenian Education   Because Athens expected every citizen to hold public office at some time in his life, they required Athenian citizens to educate their sons. With few exceptions, Athenian girls—who would not participate in governing the democracy of Athens—did not receive a formal education. Instead, a girl learned household duties, such as weaving and baking, from her mother.

Private tutors educated the boys from wealthy upper-class families, while other students paid a small fee to attend a private school. Much of their education was picked up in the agora, through daily conversations and discussions in the Assembly.

Athenian boys entered school at age 7 and graduated at age 18. Their main textbooks were the *Iliad* and the *Odyssey*, and students learned each epic by heart. They studied arithmetic, geometry, drawing, and music in the morning and gymnastics in the afternoon. When boys reached their teens, they added **rhetoric,** or the art of public speaking, to their studies. Because lawyers did not represent participants in a court case, an Athenian needed to be accomplished in rhetoric to argue his own position.

When young Athenian men reached age 18, they left school for two years of military service. Before entering the army, however, they went with their fathers to the temple of Zeus, where they swore the following oath:

Learning from Art *This painting on a Greek pottery jar from the 500s B.C. shows a woman on a swing. Even though slaves relieved an upper-class Athenian woman of many household duties, she had to spend most of her time within the privacy of her own house.* **What clues about daily life in ancient Greece can you find in this painting?**

I will not bring dishonor upon my weapons nor desert the comrade by my side. I will strive to hand on my fatherland greater and better than I found it. I will not consent to anyone's disobeying or destroying the constitution, but will prevent him, whether I am with others or alone. I will honor the temples and the religion my forefathers established.

—Oath of enrollment in Epheboi corps, early 400s B.C.

SECTION 3 REVIEW

Recall
1. **Define:** rhetoric
2. **Identify:** Draco, Solon, Peisistratus, Cleisthenes,
3. **Locate:** Find Athens and Sparta on the map on page 100. In which peninsula of Greece was each polis located?

Critical Thinking
4. **Analyze:** Contrast Athens and Sparta in their idea of citizenship; type of education; and position of women.
5. **Evaluate:** Do you think the reasons the Athenians gave for choosing government officials by lottery were good reasons? Explain your answer.

Applying Concepts
6. **Conflict:** Evaluate the choice by the Spartans to become a military society in order to control the helots and *perioeci.*

 War, Glory, and Decline

As the 400s B.C. opened, the Persian Empire—then the strongest military power in the ancient world—stood poised to extend its influence into Europe. Surprisingly, the Greek city-states not only cooperated with each other in resisting the Persian attack, they succeeded in throwing Persia's armed forces back into Asia.

After their victory against Persia, the Greeks—especially the Athenians—enjoyed a "golden age" of remarkable achievements in the arts and sciences. Then, as the Mycenaean kingdoms had, the Greek city-states began to fight among themselves. This bitter and devastating war lasted for more than 27 years.

The Persian Wars

In 546 B.C. the Persian armies, led by Cyrus, conquered the Greek city-states of Ionia, in Asia Minor. Despite the mildness of Persian rule, the Ionians disliked their conquerors. The Ionians considered the non-Greek–speaking Persians to be barbarians. In addition, an all-powerful king ruled the Persian Empire, whereas the Greek population of Ionia believed that citizens should choose their own government.

Finally, in 499 B.C., the Ionians revolted against the Persians. Even though Athens and another mainland polis sent some warships to help the Ionians, Darius I of Persia soon defeated the Ionians. Darius then decided to punish the mainland Greeks for helping the rebels.

Marathon Darius first tried to send an army around the northern coast of the Aegean Sea. However, a storm destroyed his supply ships, forcing him to turn back. Two years later, in 490 B.C., Darius tried again. This time he sent his fleet directly across the Aegean to the coastal plain of Marathon, about 25 miles (40 kilometers) north of Athens. For several days, the Persians awaited the Athenians. But the Athenians, outnumbered 20,000 to 10,000, did nothing. Finally, the Persians decided to stop waiting and attack Athens directly. They loaded their ships with the cavalry—the strongest part of their army—and then began loading the infantry.

Not waiting for the Persians to take the offensive, the Athenians struck. The Athenian general ordered his well-disciplined foot soldiers to charge down the hills above Marathon at the Persian infantry, which stood in shallow water waiting to board the ships. This tactic astounded the Persians, who believed that infantrymen would fight only with the support of horsemen and archers. Marathon was a terrible defeat for the Persians, who reportedly lost 6,400 men

FOOTNOTES TO HISTORY
MARATHON

Two thousand years after the victory of the Athenians over the Persians, writers continued to call upon the name of Marathon to symbolize humanity's struggle for freedom. The nineteenth-century English poet Lord Byron, who fought for Greek independence from the Ottoman Empire, penned the following verse:

The mountains look on Marathon—
And Marathon looks on the sea;
And musing there an hour alone,
I dream'd that Greece might still be free;
For standing on the Persians' grave,
I could not deem myself a slave.

—George Gordon, Lord Byron, from the poem *Don Juan*, 1821

PERSIAN WARS

Learning from Maps
The battles of Marathon and Salamis proved important to later history because the Greek victories prevented the spread of the powerful Persian Empire into Europe. **Whose revolt in 499 B.C. triggered the Persian Wars?**

Map legend:
- Greek States
- Persian Empire
- Revolt by Greek States
- Persian Invasions
  - 490 B.C.
  - 480 B.C.
- ★ Major Battles

0 50 100 miles
0 50 100 kilometers
N

Map labels: GREECE, SEA OF MARMARA, Hellespont, AEGEAN SEA, PERSIAN EMPIRE, Thermopylae, Marathon, Athens, Sardis, IONIA, Salamis, ATTICA, Miletus, PELOPONNESUS, Sparta, CRETE, MEDITERRANEAN SEA, 22°E, 26°E, 30°E, 40°N, 38°N, 36°N

compared to only 192 Greek casualties. According to legend, the Athenians sent a messenger named Pheidippides (fy DIHP uh deez) to carry news of the victory back to Athens. Although Pheidippides had previously run 280 miles (448 kilometers) in four days, he barely managed to reach the agora of the city and cry out *"Nike!"*— the Greek word for victory—before he fell to the ground, dead from exhaustion. Ever since, people have used the word *marathon* to describe a long-distance race.

Salamis   After Marathon, the Persians withdrew to Asia Minor, but they returned 10 years later. In 480 B.C., Darius's son and successor, Xerxes, invaded Greece from the north, this time with 200,000 soldiers. Because so huge an army could not live off the land, offshore supply ships accompanied them.

Once again the Greeks, this time under the leadership of Sparta, faced the Persians. A few years before, the oracle at Delphi had said that Greece would be safe behind a "wooden wall." The Athenian general Themistocles (thuh MIHS tuh kleez) tried to convince his Greek allies that a "wooden wall" meant a fleet of ships and that the way to defeat the Persians was to challenge them at sea.

To do this, the Greek army had to set up a delaying action on land. They chose Thermopylae (thuhr MAHP uh lee) as the place—a mountain pass north of Athens. There, 7,000 Greeks led by King Leonidas of Sparta stood firm against the Persians for three days. Then a Greek traitor showed the enemy a trail over which they could attack the Greeks from the rear. Realizing that he would soon be surrounded, Leonidas sent off most of his troops. But he and 300 fellow Spartans remained obedient to the law of their polis—never surrender on the battlefield but fight until victory or death.

They [the Spartans] *defended themselves to the last, such as still had swords using them, and the others resisting with their hands and teeth; till the barbarians* [Persians] *. . . overwhelmed and buried the remnant left beneath showers of missile weapons.*

—Herodotus, from *History*, 400s B.C.

The Rise of Ancient Greece   **107**

Learning from Art *This woodcut illustrates the battle between the small Spartan-led Greek force and the invading Persian army at the narrow pass of Thermopylae.* **Why did the Spartans resist so heroically against great odds?**

The heroic stand of Leonidas and the Spartans gave Themistocles enough time to carry out his plan. He drew the Persian fleet into the strait of Salamis, a narrow body of water between Athens and the island of Salamis. Themistocles reasoned that the heavy Persian ships would bunch up in the strait and make easy targets for the lighter but faster and more maneuverable Greek ships. The plan worked, and the outnumbered ships of the Greek navy destroyed almost the entire Persian fleet.

After the battle at Salamis, the Greeks gained the upper hand. By 479 B.C. the Persians had once again retreated to Asia Minor, this time for good. With the end of the Persian Wars, the Greek city-states resumed their traditional quarrels.

The Golden Age of Athens

Greek culture reached its peak after the Persian Wars. Most historians refer to the period from 461 to 429 B.C. as the Golden Age of Athens because most Greek achievements in the arts and sciences took place in Athens during this time.

Pericles in Charge The Athenian general Pericles, beginning in the 450s B.C., led Athens through its golden age. The polis continued to reelect Pericles to the position of general for more than 30 years. Pericles was responsible for many of the magnificent marble buildings we associate with ancient Greece. The Persians had

burned Athens during the Persian Wars, but beginning in 447 B.C., Pericles was determined to rebuild Athens. When the rebuilt temples and palaces crowned its acropolis, Athens became the most beautiful city in Greece. The most famous structure built under Pericles, the Parthenon (the temple of Athena), still stands.

Pericles wanted the polis of Athens to stand for all that was best in Greek civilization. A persuasive speaker, he expressed his ideas in a famous funeral oration quoted by the Greek historian Thucydides (thyoo SIHD uh deez):

We are called a democracy [because power] *is in the hands of the many and not the few. . . . When it is a question of putting one person before another in positions of public responsibility, what counts is not membership of a particular class, but the actual ability which the man possesses. . . . We are prevented from doing wrong by respect . . . for the laws. . . . We are lovers of the beautiful, yet simple in our tastes, and we cultivate the mind without the loss of manliness. . . . To avow poverty with us is no disgrace; the true disgrace is in doing nothing to avoid it. . . . Athens is the school of Hellas* [Greece].

Athenian Daily Life Athenians lavished money on public buildings, but they kept their private structures simple. The typical Athenian house contained two main rooms and several smaller ones built around a central courtyard. In one main room, the dining room, the men entertained guests and ate while reclining on couches. An Athenian woman joined her husband for dinner only if company was not invited. In the other main room, the wool room, the women spun and wove cloth. In the courtyard stood an altar, a wash basin, and sometimes a well. The courtyard also contained the family's chickens and goats.

Athenian men usually worked in the morning as farmers, artisans, and merchants. Then they spent the afternoon attending the Assembly or exercising in the gymnasium. Slaves—who were mostly foreigners and prisoners of war and who made up about one-third of the population—did most of the heavy work in craft production and mining. Many slaves also worked as teachers and household servants. Most Athenian women spent their time at home, cooking and making wool cloth, but poor women worked in the open-air markets as food sellers and cloth weavers.

Upper-class Athenian men—as well as citizens from other city-states—enjoyed the symposium as a form of recreation. Wives were excluded from a symposium, which was a drinking session following a banquet. The men at a symposium were entertained by female dancers and singers as well as by acrobats and magicians. The guests also spent much of the evening entertaining each other, telling riddles and discussing literature, philosophy, and public issues.

The Peloponnesian War

Even after the Persian Wars ended, the Persian threat remained. Athens persuaded most of the city-states—but not Sparta—to ally against the enemy. This alliance became known as the Delian League because the treasury was kept on the sacred island of Delos. Athens provided the principal naval and land forces, while the other city-states furnished money and ships. Over the next several decades, the Delian League succeeded in freeing Ionia from Persian rule and sweeping the Aegean free of pirates. Overseas trade expanded, and Greece grew richer.

Gradually, however, Athens began to dominate the other city-states, especially after Peri-

cles was elected general. Pericles, for example, used part of the Delian League's treasury to build the Parthenon. He insisted that criminal cases be tried only in Athens and that other city-states adopt the Athenian coinage system. He also interfered in the internal affairs of other city-states by sending Athenian troops to support revolts by commoners against aristocrats. In short, the policies of Pericles more or less transformed the Delian League from what had been an anti-Persian defense alliance into an Athenian empire.

As Athens's trade and political influence grew, several city-states reacted by forming an alliance opposed to Athens. Sparta, a long-standing Athenian rival, became the leader of the anti-Athens alliance. Since Sparta was located in the Peloponnesus, historians have called the war against Athens and its allies the Peloponnesian War.

The Peloponnesian War lasted from 431 to 404 B.C., excluding one brief period of peace. At first it seemed as if Athens could hold out indefinitely, since Sparta had no navy. But its fear and jealousy of Athens were so strong that Sparta made a deal with the Persians to return Ionia to Persian control. In exchange, Sparta received gold, which it used to build its own fleet. Then, in 430 B.C., a disastrous plague—probably typhus—weakened Athens. More than a third of its population died, including Pericles.

After Pericles died in 429 B.C., some Athenians wanted to make peace with Sparta and its allies, while other Athenians wanted to keep on fighting. No decision was made, and the war continued deadlocked for many more years. Eventually, several allies of Athens defected to join the Spartan-led alliance. Then, with their Persian-financed navy, the Spartans destroyed the Athenian fleet. After the Spartans laid siege to Athens itself, the Athenians finally surrendered in 404 B.C.

The Peloponnesian War brought disaster to Athens and to other Greek city-states, both victors and vanquished. Many city-states declined in population. Fighting had devastated many fields and orchards. Unemployment became so widespread that thousands of young men emigrated and became mercenaries, or hired soldiers, in the Persian army.

Learning from Maps
The alliance of city-states led by Sparta, known as the Peloponnesian League, attacked the Athenian Empire because it feared the growing power of Athens. **Why had Athens and its allied city-states originally formed the Delian League?**

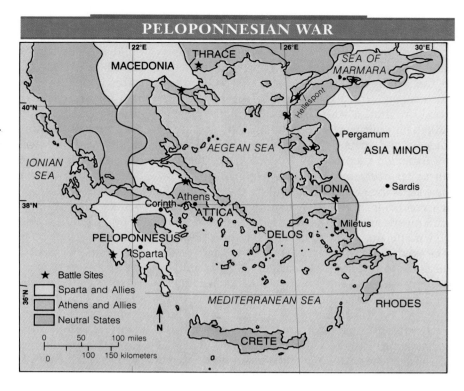

PELOPONNESIAN WAR

Worst of all, the Greeks lost their ability to govern themselves. The length and cost of the war made people forget about the common good of their polis and think only about making money. According to the Greek historian Thucydides, "war is a stern teacher; in depriving them of the power of easily satisfying their daily wants, it brings most people's minds down to the level of their actual circumstances." Feelings between aristocrats and commoners grew increasingly bitter. Many Greeks, losing faith in democracy, even came to look down on free po-litical discussion and began to believe that might makes right.

For a time, Sparta tried to rule the other city-states. Then, in 371 B.C., a new alliance of city-states led by Thebes overthrew the harsh, incompetent Spartan rulers. The Thebans, however, also made poor rulers and were also overthrown. As a result of almost continual fighting, the city-states became weaker than ever. When a new invader, the Macedonians, threatened Greece in the 350s B.C., the city-states were unable to resist.

SECTION 4 REVIEW

Recall

1. **Identify:** Darius, Pheidippides, Xerxes, Themistocles, Leonidas, Pericles
2. **Locate:** Find Ionia, Marathon, Thermopylae, and Salamis on the map on page 107. Explain the significance of each.

3. **Describe:** What were the daily activities of an Athenian husband? an Athenian wife?

Critical Thinking

4. **Apply:** How did the Peloponnesian War affect the system of city-states?

5. **Evaluate:** Judge whether Pericles' rule was beneficial for Athens. Explain your answer.

Applying Concepts

6. **Conflict:** Why didn't loyalty to the polis prevent Greeks from uniting against Persia?

MAKING COMPARISONS

Which book did you like best? What were the strengths and weaknesses of Sparta and Athens? These questions involve *making comparisons*. Making comparisons means determining similarities and differences between objects. This is useful to know when you want to draw conclusions.

Explanation

To make a comparison:
- Determine the purpose for making the comparison.
- Examine the information and take notes.
- Classify the information.
- Identify similarities and differences.
- Draw conclusions based on the comparisons you made.

Example

Read the excerpts at the top right of this page.

Refer to the chart that compares the military strength of Athens and Sparta. The information has been classified and grouped into categories. The chart tells you that the Spartans had a large force.

You see that both sides seem to be evenly matched. You might conclude, however, that a superior navy would give Athens an advantage during the war.

We [Spartans] have many reasons to expect success,—first, superiority in numbers and in military experience, and second our general and unvarying obedience in the execution of orders. The naval strength which they possess shall be raised by us from . . . the monies at Olympia and Delphi. A loan from these enables us to seduce their foreign sailors by the offer of higher pay . . . A single defeat at sea is in all likelihood their ruin.

—Thucydides, account of a Corinthian envoy to the Congress at Sparta, 432 B.C.

Personally engaged in the cultivation of their land, without funds either private or public, the Peloponnesians [Spartans] are also without experience in long wars across the sea. . . . Our naval skill is of more use to us for service on land, than their military skill for service at sea. Even if they were to . . . try to seduce our foreign sailors by the temptation of higher pay . . . none of our foreign sailors would consent to become an outlaw from his own country, and to take service with them.

—Pericles, account to Athenian Ecclesia, 432 B.C.

Application

Using the steps outlined above, compare these aspects of the Athenian and Spartan society: social structure and economy.

Practice

Turn to Practicing Skills on page 113 in the Chapter Review for further practice in making comparisons.

MILITARY FORCES

	Sparta	Athens
Army	• large numbers of disciplined and experienced soldiers	• small numbers of soldiers
Navy	• small force • capable of hiring foreigners	• large numbers of skilled sailors • adaptable force able to fight on land

CHAPTER 4 REVIEW

A Greek polis developed a sense of community by encouraging its citizens to consider the common good as well as their individual welfare. Those city-states with democratic assemblies also encouraged male citizens to develop their abilities to the fullest because what each citizen said or did mattered to the community. Ancient Greece provided the world with its first democracy, an example that more and more nations are following today. Because the limited number of citizens in a city-state permitted direct participation by all citizens, political scientists describe the democracy that Cleisthenes developed in Athens as a *direct* democracy. In the United States today, where we elect senators and representatives who are responsible to us, the form of government qualifies both as a republic and as a *representative* democracy. In contrast to citizenship in ancient Greece, U.S. citizenship has broadened to include women and people of all races and, additionally, naturalized foreign-born citizens.

SUMMARY

For a summary of Chapter 4, see the Unit 2 Synopsis on pages 204–207.

USING KEY TERMS

Write the key term that best completes each sentence .

a. aristocrat e. polis
b. citizen f. rhetoric
c. democracy g. tyrant
d. oligarchy

1. The basic political unit of ancient Greece was the ___.
2. A woman in ancient Greece was not considered to be a full ___ with political rights.
3. A ___ usually promised to help farmers, merchants, and artisans.
4. Athenian boys studied ___ in school.
5. ___ gradually became more important than kings in early Greek city-states.
6. Both Athens and Sparta were ___ .
7. Democracy alternated with ___ as the form of government of most Greek city-states.

REVIEWING FACTS

1. **List:** What elements of Minoan culture did the Mycenaeans adopt?

2. **Tell:** What values of Hellenic civilization did the *Iliad* and the *Odyssey* teach?
3. **Explain:** How did the attitude of the Greeks toward their deities differ from the attitude of the Egyptians?
4. **Explain:** How did Sparta's response in the 700s B.C. to the problems of increased population and a shortage of arable land differ from the response of most other Greek city-states?
5. **Tell:** What were the advantages and disadvantages of Draco's laws?
6. **Describe:** For the Ionians, what was the major difference between the Greeks and the Persians?

THINKING CRITICALLY

1. **Apply:** How did Sparta's values affect its educational system?
2. **Analyze:** How did increased trade affect Greek political life?
3. **Synthesize:** What might have been the outcome of the Persian Wars if Themistocles had not convinced the Greeks to build a fleet of ships?
4. **Evaluate:** Do you think that having juries contain from 201 to 1,001 members—as opposed to 12-member juries in the United States—is a good idea?

ANALYZING CONCEPTS

1. **Relation to environment:** How did Greece's relation to the sea affect the ways in which the city-states tried to solve the problems of overpopulation and a shortage of arable land?
2. **Movement:** What role did trade play in the development of Greek civilization?
3. **Conflict:** Explain why several Greek city-states, led by Sparta, formed an alliance in the mid-400s B.C. to fight against Athens and the Delian League.

PRACTICING SKILLS

1. Compare the political system of ancient Athens with that of the cities and towns, states, and national government of the United States today.
2. Read the following passage:

   The Greeks found in Homer the source of their history and their mythology; he was the center of Greek education, and it was not uncommon for Greek boys to know both the Iliad *and the* Odyssey *by heart.*

   Compare the education of ancient Greeks with a typical American education today. Use information from the chapter as well as the passage above. Which aspects are similar and which are different?

GEOGRAPHY IN HISTORY

1. **Location:** How did the location of Crete influence the way in which Minoans earned a living?
2. **Place:** In what ways did the city-states resemble Mycenaean kingdoms?
3. **Regions:** What determined the size of the average city-state?

TRACING CHRONOLOGY

Refer to the time line below to answer these questions.

1. About how many years after Mycenaean civilization had reached its peak did Homer compose the *Iliad* and the *Odyssey*?
2. Would Cleisthenes have studied about the Persian Wars in school?
3. About how many years after the defeat of Athens by the Spartan-led alliance did Macedonia invade Greece?

LINKING PAST AND PRESENT

1. During times of unrest in ancient Athens, tyrants seized power to institute political and economic reforms. Do you think a tyrant could establish a dictatorship in the United States at a time of crisis? Explain your answer.
2. Why might students at the U.S. Naval Academy study the Persian Wars?

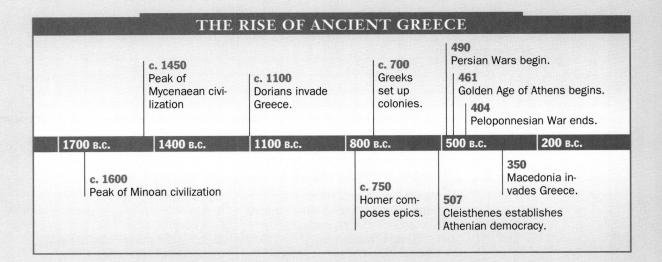

THE RISE OF ANCIENT GREECE

c. 1450 Peak of Mycenaean civilization
c. 1100 Dorians invade Greece.
c. 700 Greeks set up colonies.
490 Persian Wars begin.
461 Golden Age of Athens begins.
404 Peloponnesian War ends.

1700 B.C. — 1400 B.C. — 1100 B.C. — 800 B.C. — 500 B.C. — 200 B.C.

c. 1600 Peak of Minoan civilization
c. 750 Homer composes epics.
507 Cleisthenes establishes Athenian democracy.
350 Macedonia invades Greece.

The Triumph of Greek Civilization

*A*n outwardly unimpressive man—he was stout and short, with a snub nose, a wide mouth, and prominent eyes—Socrates was nonetheless an intellectual giant in the Athens of the late 400s B.C. One of his devoted followers described Socrates' routine. "At early morning he was to be seen betaking himself to one of the promenades or wrestling grounds; at noon he would appear with the gathering crowds in the marketplace; and as day declined, wherever the largest throng might be encountered, there was he to be found, talking for the most part, while anyone who chose might stop and listen." Socrates was a supreme questioner who succeeded in getting people to analyze their own behavior. Although he never held a position in a school and never received pay for teaching, 2,000 years after his death Socrates' reputation lives on as one of the greatest teachers of all time.

In this Roman mosaic, the Greek philosopher Plato teaches geometry at his Academy.

3. What were Alexander the Great's goals for his empire, and how successful was he in achieving them?

4. How did Hellenistic culture differ from Hellenic culture?

Concepts to Understand:

• Innovation—Ancient Greeks believed in reason and in the individual. Sections 1,2

• Diversity—Alexander the Great's empire included diverse ethnic groups and cultures. Section 3

• Cultural diffusion—A mix of Greek and Middle Eastern cultures spread throughout the Hellenistic world. Section 3

SECTION 1

Quest for Beauty and Meaning

During the mid-400s B.C., with the Persian Wars over, Greek civilization reached its cultural peak, particularly in the wealthy and powerful city-state of Athens. This period of brilliant cultural achievement has been called ancient Greece's Golden Age. Artists of the golden age excelled in architecture, sculpture, and painting. They created works characterized by beautiful simplicity and graceful balance, an artistic style now called **classical**.

Classical Greek art, copied soon after in Roman artistic styles, set lasting standards of beauty still admired today. The writers and thinkers of ancient Greece also made enduring intellectual achievements in literature and drama, creating works read through the centuries and still considered classics today. Many cultural traditions of Western civilization—that is, the civilization of Europe and those parts of the world influenced by Europeans—began with Greece's Golden Age.

Buildings for the Gods

The Greeks, wrote the Athenian leader Pericles, were "lovers of the beautiful." Each Greek city-state tried to turn its acropolis into an architectural treasure.

The Parthenon—the temple to Athena built on the summit of the Acropolis in Athens—best exemplified classical Greek architecture. It was begun in 447 B.C. and finished in 432 B.C., under the rule of Pericles. Because the Greeks worshiped either in their homes or at outdoor altars, they did not need large sanctuaries. Instead, they built temples as places where their deities would live.

The Parthenon has an ingeniously simple design. It is a rectangle surrounded by 46 fluted columns. At the same time, the Parthenon is extremely beautiful. In the right light, because of iron in its white marble, the Parthenon gleams a soft gold against the blue sky.

Part of the beauty of the Parthenon, and of Greek architecture in general, has to do with carefully chosen building sites. Architects considered how a building would fit in with its surroundings and how it would look when viewed from a distance. They often built on mountains, like the Acropolis in Athens, or on cliffs overlooking the sea.

The Parthenon's graceful proportions perfectly balance width, length, and height. To the Greeks the Parthenon represented the ideal of "nothing to excess," an ideal sometimes called

Learning from Photographs *The Porch of the Maidens—part of the Erechtheum temple—faces the Parthenon on the Acropolis. A draped female figure used as a column is called a* caryatid. ***Why do you think the classical style of architecture has been imitated over the centuries?***

the Golden Mean, or the midpoint between two extremes.

The architects of the Parthenon also understood perspective and optical illusions. Thus, they made the temple's columns thicker in the middle and thinner at the top so that the columns appeared straight when viewed from a distance. The steps leading up to the Parthenon, actually lower in the center than at either end, likewise appear straight. The Athenians wanted to create the impression of perfection—and they succeeded.

Greek Arts

The Greek love of beauty was expressed in the fine arts as well as in architecture. In both painting and sculpture, the Greeks—because they emphasized the individual—excelled at portraying the human form.

Painting on Vases   Although the Greeks painted murals, as had the Minoans, no originals have survived. We know of Greek murals only from written descriptions or Roman copies. But today we can still see examples of their work in the paintings on Greek vases.

Greek pottery was a major item of trade in the Mediterranean world. The word ceramic comes from the Kerameikos, the district in Athens where the city's potters worked.

The Greeks designed their pottery with different shapes that were suited for different functions. For example, Greek potters gave the *krater*—a small two-handled vase—a wide mouth in which it was easy to mix wine with water. On the other hand, they gave the *lekythos* a narrow neck so that oil could be poured out slowly and in small quantities.

Most Greek pottery remaining from the classical period is either red on a black background or black on a red background. The varied subjects of the paintings depended on the size and use of the vase. Potters usually decorated an *amphora*—a large vase for storing bulk supplies such as oil—with scenes from mythology and legend. On the other hand, a *kylix*—a wide, shallow two-handled drinking cup—showed scenes of everyday life: children attend-

Learning from Art   *In the painting on this vase from about 525 B.C., women carry water from a public well or fountain house. Athenian homes did not have indoor plumbing.* **Why might the women actually enjoy collecting water?**

ing school, shoemakers and carpenters plying their trades, a farmer guiding the plow behind a team of oxen, a merchant ship braving the winds. Greek potters skillfully adapted their designs and decorations to the curves and shape of the vase.

Sculpting the Human Body   Greek sculpture, like Greek architecture, reached its height in Athens during the time of Pericles. Myron, one of the greatest sculptors of Greece's Golden Age, portrayed in his statues idealized views of what people *should* look like rather than actual persons. When Myron sculpted his *Discus Thrower* poised to hurl the discus, he carved the lines of the body to indicate an athlete's excellent physical condition as well as his mental control over what he was doing.

The great sculptor Phidias (FIHD ee uhs) was in charge of the Parthenon's sculptures. Phidias himself carved the towering statue of Athena that was placed inside the Parthenon. The statue, made of gold and ivory plates attached to a wooden framework, showed the goddess in her warlike aspect, carrying a shield, spear, and helmet. A small statue of Nike, the winged goddess of victory, stood in Athena's right hand.

A hundred years after the Golden Age of Athens, the work of another famous Greek sculptor—Praxiteles (prak SIHT uhl eez)—reflected the changes that had occurred in Greek life and outlook. The sculptures of Myron and Phidias had been full of power and striving for perfection, as befitted a people who had defeated the mighty Persian Empire. By the time of Praxiteles, the Greeks had suffered through the Peloponnesian War and had lost their self-confidence. Accordingly, Praxiteles and his colleagues favored life-sized statues rather than massive works. They emphasized grace rather than power. The sculptors of the Golden Age had carved only deities and heroes, but the sculptors of the 300s B.C. carved ordinary people too.

Drama and Theater

The Greeks also explored the human condition through theatrical dramas. They were the first people to write and perform plays, which they presented twice a year at festivals to honor Dionysus, the god of wine and fertility.

Aeschylus The earliest Greek plays were tragedies. In a **tragedy**, the lead character struggled against fate only to be doomed—after much suffering—to an unhappy, or tragic, ending. Aeschylus (EHS kuh luhs), the first of the great writers of tragedies in the 400s B.C., wrote 90 plays. Seven have survived. His *Oresteia* is a trilogy—a set of three plays with a related theme—and is famous for the grandeur of its language.

The *Oresteia* shows how the consequences of one's deeds are carried down from generation to generation. The first play in the trilogy tells about the return of King Agamemnon from the Trojan War and his murder by his wife Clytemnestra in revenge for Agamemnon's sacrifice of their daughter Iphigenia before the Greeks sailed for Troy. The second play describes how Agamemnon's son Orestes in turn avenges his father's death by killing his mother. The third play has Orestes standing trial in Athens for his bloody deed. When the jury splits six to six, the goddess Athena intervenes and casts the deciding vote in favor of mercy. The overall moral of the trilogy is that the law of the community, not personal revenge, should decide the punishment for wrongdoers.

Sophocles The next great tragedian, Sophocles (SAHF uh kleez), had served as a general in the Athenian army and had lived through most of the Peloponnesian War. Sophocles accepted human suffering as an unavoidable part of life. At the same time, he stressed human courage and compassion.

In one of his most famous plays, *Oedipus Rex*, Sophocles deals with the plight of Oedipus, a king who is doomed by the deities to kill his father and marry his mother. Despite Oedipus' efforts to avoid his fate, all that the deities have decreed comes true. When Oedipus discovers what he has done, he blinds himself in despair and goes into exile.

Euripides Unlike Aeschylus and Sophocles, the last of the three great Greek tragedians—Euripides (yu RIHP uh deez)—rarely dealt with the influence of the gods and goddesses on human lives. Instead, he focused on the qualities human beings possess that bring disaster on themselves.

Euripides also hated war, and many of his 19 surviving plays show the misery war brings. In *The Trojan Women*, the Trojan princess Cassandra explains why the Greeks, despite their victory, are no better off than the Trojans.

A nd when [the Greeks] *came to the banks*
of the Scamander those thousands died.
And why?
No man had moved their landmarks
or laid siege to their high-walled towns.
But those whom war took never saw their
children.
No wife with gentle hands shrouded them
for their grave.
They lie in a strange land. And in their homes
are sorrows, too, the very same.
Lonely women who died, old men who waited
for sons that never came—no son left to them
to make the offering at their graves.
That was the glorious victory they won.

—Euripides, from his tragedy
The Trojan Women, c. 415 B.C.

Greek Drama

The earliest Greek plays took place around 600 B.C. at festivals honoring Dionysus, the Greek god of wine and fertility. The audience sat on a hillside around an open space, where a chorus chanted a story about Dionysus and danced to the sound of a flute. Eventually, cities began building permanent amphitheaters, carving a hillside into a semicircle, adding rows of stone seats, and paving the stage area, or orchestra. A low building erected behind the orchestra served as a dressing room and backstage area for the players.

As the years passed, theater performances changed. Around 550 B.C. the dramatist Thespis began including an actor to recite poems explaining the songs and dances of the chorus. Gradually, more actors were added, and the words they recited became dialogue. The word *thespian*, meaning actor or actress, derives from Thespis's name.

All the actors in Greek theater were men; women were allowed only as spectators. Each actor would play several parts, wearing a large mask to show the age, sex, and mood of each of his characters. A funnel-shaped mouth in the mask helped carry his voice to the audience. To make themselves more visible to the audience on the hillside, the actors wore padding under their robes and boots with thick soles to make themselves larger and taller.

In building their theaters, the Greeks took advantage of the beauty in natural settings. The theater at Epidaurus is set in a hillside with a vista of distant mountains. The acoustics, or the way sound travels, are so good that from the top rows—about 200 feet (60 meters) away—a person on the stage can be heard to whisper and even breathe.

The ancient Greeks believed that the dramatic arts were a vital part of their culture. Public officials were responsible for deciding which plays to present, and leading citizens funded and organized them. Those citizens who could not afford the price of admission to a drama were admitted free. In this way, Greek society ensured that all citizens had the chance to enjoy and learn from the arts.

Responding to the Arts
1. How did Greek drama originate?
2. How is modern theater similar to or different from ancient Greek theater?

A Comedy Tonight Eventually the Greeks also wrote **comedies**, plays with humorous themes and happy endings. Aristophanes (ar uh STAHF uh neez), the most famous writer of comedies, created imaginative social satire. In his works he made witty comments about leading figures—such as Euripides—and about issues of his day. In his play *The Clouds*, Aristophanes had a character named Strepsiades ask where Athens was on a map. When the polis's location was pointed out to him, Strepsiades replied: "Don't be ridiculous, that can't be Athens, for I can't see even a single law court in session."

The Olympic Games

Believing that healthy bodies made the best use of nature's gifts, the ancient Greeks stressed athletics in their school curriculum. Greek men who could afford the leisure time usually spent all or part of their afternoons practicing sports in their polis's gymnasiums.

The ancient Greeks held the Olympic Games—their best-known sporting event—in Olympia every four years. Because the Olympic Games were a religious festival in honor of Zeus, trading and fighting stopped while they were going on. The Greek calendar began with the supposed date of the first Olympic Games: 776 B.C.

Athletes came from all over the Greek-speaking world to compete in the Olympics. Only male athletes, however, were allowed to take part, and women were not permitted even

Learning from Art *Wrestling was one of the more popular Greek sports. This sculpture idealizes the wrestlers' excellent physical condition.* **Why did the Greeks value sports?**

as spectators. Games that honored the goddess Hera were held at a different location than Olympia and gave Greek women an opportunity to participate in running races.

In line with the Greek emphasis on the individual, Olympic competition took the form of individual rather than team events. These consisted at first of only a footrace. Later other events—the broad jump, the discus throw, boxing, and wrestling—were added.

The Greeks regarded Olympic winners as heroes. They crowned the victors with wreaths of olive leaves and held parades in their honor. Some city-states even excused outstanding athletes from paying taxes.

SECTION 1 REVIEW

Recall
1. **Define:** classical, tragedy, comedy
2. **Identify:** Western civilization, Myron, Phidias, Praxiteles, Aeschylus, Sophocles, Euripides, Aristophanes
3. **Describe:** Tell how worship of Greek deities influenced architecture, art, and athletics.

Critical Thinking
4. **Apply:** Show how the Greek emphasis on the individual was demonstrated both in the Olympic Games and in the fine arts.
5. **Analyze:** Compare an Aeschylus tragedy with an Aristophanes comedy. Why do you think both were popular?

6. **Synthesize:** What event do you imagine influenced Euripides' attitude toward war?

Applying Concepts
7. **Innovation:** Illustrate the ancient Greeks' intellectual innovations with examples from architecture, sculpture, and drama.

The Greek Mind

The Greeks believed the human mind capable of understanding everything. As a result, the **philosophers**, or thinkers, of ancient Greece produced some of the most remarkable ideas the world has ever known. Through philosophy—which means "the seeking of wisdom"—they laid the foundations for such disciplines as history, political science, biology, and **logic**, or the science of reasoning.

The Sophists

In the 400s B.C., higher education was provided by professional teachers called Sophists. Although Sophists traveled from polis to polis, many congregated in Athens, possibly for the freedom of speech allowed there. Sophists, meaning "knowers," claimed that they could find the answers to all questions. As the Peloponnesian War brought about changes in the political cohesiveness of the polis, in the late 400s B.C. Sophists participated in the intellectual discussions that accompanied political change.

Many Sophists rejected the belief that the gods and goddesses influenced human behavior. They also did not believe in absolute moral and legal standards. Instead, they asserted that "man is the measure of all things" and that truth is different for each individual. Rather than wonder how the world came into being, they focused on issues that grew out of everyday life, such as "What is a state?" and "What is justice?"

Not only did Sophists challenge certain traditional Greek beliefs, they took money for their teaching. Many of them also seemed most intent on teaching young men how to win a political argument and get ahead in the world. Many Greeks, including two of Greece's greatest philosophers—Socrates (SAHK ruh teez) and his pupil Plato—criticized the Sophists severely.

Socrates

Socrates, an Athenian born to a poor family in 470 B.C., had served as a soldier in the Peloponnesian War. Although a sculptor by trade, he spent most of his time teaching.

Unlike the Sophists, Socrates believed in absolute rather than relative truth. His main interest did not lie in teaching rhetoric or in imparting information. Rather, Socrates was attracted to the process by which people learned how to think for themselves.

To encourage his students to clear away mistaken ideas and discover the truth, Socrates originated a teaching technique—known as the Socratic method. He would ask students pointed questions without giving them answers and then oppose the students' answers with clear logical arguments. Through this method, he forced his students to defend their statements and to clarify their thinking. For example, in discussing the topic of justice, Socrates proceeded as follows:

Socrates: Does falsehood then exist among mankind?

Euthydemus: It does assuredly.

Socrates: Under which head [justice or injustice] shall we place it?

Euthydemus: Under injustice, certainly.

Socrates: Well then . . . if a father, when his son requires medicine, and refuses to take it, should deceive him, and give him the medicine as ordinary food, and, by adopting such deception, should restore him to health, under which head must we place such an act of deceit?

Euthydemus: It appears to me that we must place it under [justice]. . . . I retract what I said before.

—Xenophon, from *Memorabilia*, early 300s B.C.

Learning from Art *The philosopher Socrates discusses answers given by his young students.* **Why did Socrates think that asking questions made students good thinkers?**

Socrates gained many followers because of his sincerity and sharp intellect. Some prominent Athenians, however, viewed his teachings as a threat to the polis. In 399 B.C. they accused Socrates of "corrupting the young" and of "not worshiping the gods worshiped by the state" and had him brought to trial.

Socrates argued in his own defense that a person who *knew* what was right would always *do* what was right and that the intellectual search for truth was the most important thing in the world. "A man who is good for anything ought not to calculate the chance of living or dying; he ought only to consider whether . . . he is doing right or wrong."

Despite Socrates' eloquence, a jury of 501 citizens found him guilty and sentenced him to death. Although Socrates had the right to ask for a lesser penalty, such as exile, he refused to do so. He had lived all his life under the laws of his polis, and he would not avoid obeying them now.

Socrates carried out the sentence of his fellow citizens himself. He drank poisonous hemlock juice and died quietly among his grieving followers.

Plato

Socrates did not leave any writings when he died. We know about his ideas and his teaching technique from the works of his pupil Plato.

Born an Athenian aristocrat, Plato thought at first of entering politics. However, after Socrates' death, Plato—at age 30—became a teacher and opened his Academy, a school that remained in existence until A.D. 529.

From memory Plato recorded dialogues, or conversations, between Socrates and fellow Athenians, and he also wrote the earliest book on political science, *The Republic.* In this book, he presented a plan for what he considered would be the ideal society and government.

Plato disliked Athenian democracy and preferred the government of Sparta. He gave more importance to the state than to the individual. Like the Spartans, he believed that each person should place service to the community above strictly personal goals. Plato also believed that the result of people having too much freedom is social disorder. People should do what they are best suited to do. Plato distrusted the lower classes and wanted only the most intelligent and best-educated citizens to participate in government. As he explained in *The Republic*:

Until philosophers are kings, or the kings and princes of this world have the spirit and power of philosophy, and political greatness and wisdom meet in one, and those commoner natures who pursue either to the exclusion of the other are compelled to stand aside, cities will never have rest from their evils, no, nor the human race.

Plato's political views were part of an all-embracing philosophy by which he tried to search for "truth." Plato rejected the senses—seeing, hearing, touch, smell, and taste—as a source of truth, believing that the many things that could be perceived by these senses were only "appearance." Reality, the "real" world, was constructed from ideas, or ideal "forms," which could be understood through logical thought and reasoning.

Aristotle

The third great philosopher of ancient Greece was Aristotle (AR uh staht uhl), who had studied with Plato at the Academy for 20 years. Aristotle then tutored the young Alexander of Macedonia, who later would be known as Alexander the Great. In 335 B.C. Aristotle opened a school in Athens called the Lyceum. Besides teaching, he wrote or edited more than 200 books on topics ranging from astronomy to poetry and from political science to the weather. Because of Aristotle's wide range of knowledge, the Italian poet Dante later called him "the master of those who know."

Aristotle influenced later philosophers with his work on logic. He developed the syllogism, a means for presenting an argument in such a way that one can determine whether or not the conclusion follows logically from the premises, or basic statements.

Aristotle also influenced scientific work. He was the first person to observe facts, then classify them according to their similarities and their differences, and finally develop generalizations from his data. Some of his specific beliefs—notably, that Earth is the center of our solar system—were incorrect, but Aristotle's views would come to dominate European scientific thinking for centuries. Nevertheless, his technique for analyzing information was so useful that scientists still follow his methods today.

Many of Aristotle's writings were focused on political science. Unlike Plato, he did not theorize about idealized principles of government. Instead, he examined the political structure of 158 city-states, analyzing their advantages and disadvantages. Only then did he spell out his conclusions in a book called *Politics*. Aristotle believed that democracies, oligarchies, and tyrannies are all workable, depending on circumstances. He preferred, however, to have power rest with the middle class, because they knew how to both command *and* obey.

Writers of History

The Greeks also used their intellectual skills in writing history. Until the 400s B.C., the Greeks had considered literary legends as history. Herodotus, the first Greek historian, decided to separate fact from legend. Historians still consider him "the father of history."

Herodotus chose as his subject the Persian Wars and called his work the *Historia*, or "investigation." Herodotus traveled throughout the Persian Empire and also visited many Greek colonies. Everywhere he went, he asked questions, recorded answers, and indicated which of his sources he thought were reliable and which were not. However, he accepted some statements that were not true, especially exaggerated numbers—such as how many Persians died at Marathon. He also sometimes offered supernatural explanations of events.

Herodotus did not limit himself to describing military and political events. He also wrote about outstanding individuals, social customs, and religious beliefs and practices. Later historians have learned a great deal from the *Historia* about the culture of the period and about the civilizations that Herodotus visited.

The second noted historian of ancient Greece, Thucydides, wrote about the Peloponnesian War. Thucydides is regarded as the first scientific historian because he completely rejected the idea that the deities played a part in human history. Only human beings make history, Thucydides said. He was also as accurate and impartial as possible. He visited battle sites, carefully examined documents, and accepted only the evidence of actual eyewitnesses to events.

Thucydides did not simply recite facts, however. He also offered explanations as to why events took place and what motivated political leaders. He believed that future generations could learn from the past.

The First Scientists

The ancient Greeks believed that the world is ruled by natural laws and that human beings can discover these laws by using reason. Lacking

THE ATOM

During the 300s B.C., Greek philosophers pondered this question: Is all matter composed of a basic ingredient? One of these thinkers, Democritus, came up with the idea of a solid particle of matter so small that it was both invisible and uncuttable. He named this particle *atom*, meaning "indivisible." Democritus argued that objects in the world look different because the atoms from which they are built —all consisting of the same substance—have different shapes.

Today, scientists know that atoms are in fact "divisible" and incorporate more than 30 separate and smaller types of matter. But the basic idea of atomic physics can be traced back to Democritus.

scientific equipment, the Greek scientists made most of their discoveries by observation and thought.

The first prominent Greek scientist was Thales (THAY leez) of Miletus, a Greek city-state in Ionia. Born in the mid-600s B.C., Thales studied astronomy at Babylon and mathematics in Egypt and could foretell a solar eclipse. He also formulated a theory that water was the basic substance of which everything in the world is made.

During the 500s B.C., Pythagoras (puh THAG uh ruhs) tried to explain everything in mathematical terms. He contributed to music by showing that the pitch of a string depended on its length; the shorter the string, the higher the pitch. Students of geometry still learn the Pythagorean theorem about the hypotenuse of a right triangle. Pythagoras also taught that the world was round and revolved around a fixed point.

Greek scientists also contributed to the field of medicine. Called the "father of medicine," Hippocrates (hihp AHK ruh teez) believed that diseases had natural, not supernatural, causes. Basing his work in the late 400s B.C. on observation, he traveled all over Greece diagnosing illnesses and treating sick people. He urged fellow doctors to keep records of their cases and to exchange information with one another. He strongly advocated proper hygiene, a sound diet, and plenty of rest. According to tradition, Hippocrates drafted this ethical code:

The regimen I adopt shall be for the benefit of my patients according to my ability and judgment, and not for their hurt or for any wrong. I will give no deadly drug to any, though it be asked of me. . . . Whatever house I enter, there I will go for the benefit of the sick, refraining from all wrongdoing or corruption. . . . Whatsoever things I see or hear . . . in my attendance on the sick . . . I will keep silence thereon, counting such things to be as sacred secrets.

Hippocrates' code for ethical medical conduct has guided the practice of medicine for more than 2,000 years. Many doctors today recite the Hippocratic Oath when they receive their medical degree.

SECTION 2 REVIEW

Recall
1. **Define:** philosopher, logic
2. **Identify:** Sophists, Socrates, Plato, Aristotle, Herodotus, Thucydides, Thales, Pythagoras, Hippocrates
3. **Explain:** How were Plato, Socrates, and Aristotle related?

Critical Thinking
4. **Analyze:** Compare the political views of Plato and Aristotle and their attitudes regarding observations made through the senses.
5. **Evaluate:** Do you think Herodotus deserves to be called the "father of history"? Explain your answer.

Applying Concepts
6. **Innovation:** Illustrate Greek intellectual innovations with examples from Socrates and Hippocrates.

Alexander's Empire

In the early 400s B.C., the Persians under Darius I, and then under his son Xerxes, had tried to conquer the Greek city-states but failed. Some 150 years later the Macedonians, a people who lived just north of Greece in the Balkan Peninsula, made a similar attempt—and succeeded.

Rise of Macedonia

The Macedonians, like the Spartans, were descended from the Dorians, and the Macedonian language incorporated many Greek words. The Greeks, however, looked down on the Macedonians as "backward mountaineers."

In 359 B.C. Philip II became king of Macedonia. During his youth he had been a hostage for three years in the Greek city-state of Thebes. There he had learned to admire both Greek culture and military organization. As king, Philip determined to do three things: create a strong standing army, unify the quarreling Greek city-states under Macedonian rule, and destroy the Persian Empire.

Philip increased his army's fighting power by organizing his infantry into Greek-style phalanxes. Arrayed in close formation 16 rows deep, Philip's lance-bearing foot soldiers fought as a single unit.

For the next 23 years, Philip pursued his ambition. Sometimes he conquered a polis or bribed a polis's leaders to surrender. Sometimes he allied a polis through marriage; Philip had a total of six or seven wives.

The Greek city-states, weakened and dispirited by the Peloponnesian War, would not cooperate in resisting Philip. The great Athenian orator Demosthenes (dih MAHS thuh neez) appealed to his fellow citizens to fight for their liberty.

[Philip] cannot rest content with what he has conquered; he is always taking in more, everywhere casting his net round us, while we sit idle and do nothing. When, Athenians, will you take the necessary action? What are you waiting for?

—Demosthenes, *First Philippic*, 351 B.C.

But Demosthenes' words were to no avail. By 338 B.C., Philip had conquered all of Greece except Sparta. Philip then announced that he would lead the Greeks and Macedonians in a war against Persia. But in 336 B.C., just as he was ready to carry out his plans, Philip was murdered—either by a Persian agent or by an assassin hired by his first wife, Olympias. Olympias' son Alexander became king.

Alexander the Great

Alexander was only 20 when he became the ruler of Macedonia and Greece. A commander in the Macedonian army since he was 16, Alexander was highly respected by his soldiers for his courage and military skill. He was also extremely well educated, for his father had him tutored by Aristotle for four years. Alexander loved reading the *Iliad* and other literary works. He became so interested in science that he added a staff of scientists to his army to map the land and collect specimens of unusual plants and animals. Alexander also traveled with a historian to write about his campaigns.

Early Conquests   In 334 B.C. Alexander led 35,000 soldiers and 7,000 cavalry into Asia to open his campaign of "West against East." The first major encounter with the Persians took place at the Granicus River in western Asia

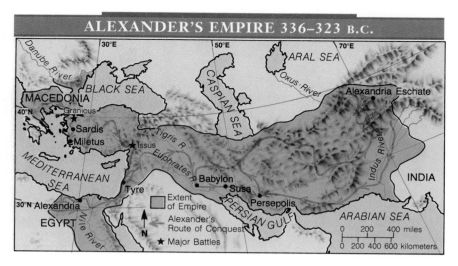

ALEXANDER'S EMPIRE 336–323 B.C.

Minor. Alexander's forces won, and he sent 300 suits of Persian armor to Athens as an offering to the goddess Athena. He then marched along the coast of Asia Minor, freeing the Ionian city-states from Persian rule.

The second major battle between the Greeks and Persians took place in 333 B.C. at Issus, Syria. Once again, Alexander's superb tactics resulted in victory, forcing the Persian king Darius III to flee.

Instead of pursuing Darius, Alexander and his troops moved south along the Mediterranean coast. First they captured the seaports of Phoenicia and cut off the Persian fleet from its main supply bases. The fleet soon surrendered. Next, turning west, they invaded Egypt where the people, discontented under Persian rule, welcomed them and declared Alexander a pharaoh. In Egypt, Alexander established a new city and named it Alexandria after himself.

Final Campaigns In 331 B.C. Alexander again turned his attention eastward. He invaded Mesopotamia and smashed Darius's main army in the battle of Gaugamela near the Tigris River. He went on to capture the key cities of the Persian Empire: Babylon, Persepolis, and Susa. When Darius was killed by one of his own generals, Alexander declared himself King of Kings, ruler of the Persian Empire.

Even this elevation was not enough for the young conqueror. In 327 B.C. he led his soldiers into India, and after three years they reached the Indus River Valley. Alexander hoped to go farther yet, but his Macedonian veterans refused. Alexander therefore reluctantly turned around and went to Babylon, which he had made the capital of his empire. But the hardships of the journey had undermined his health, and he fell ill with a fever, probably malaria. In 323 B.C. Alexander the Great died at the age of 33.

Imperial Goals

When Alexander first set out with his army, his goal was to avenge himself on Persia for its invasion of Greece 150 years earlier. But as more and more territory came under his control, his views changed. Instead of "West *against* East," he now wanted "West *and* East"—in other words, an empire that would permanently unite Europe and Asia and combine the best of Greek and Persian cultures into one civilization.

Alexander tried to promote this goal by example. He wore Persian dress and imitated the court life of Persian kings, wearing a crown as a sign of royal authority and having his courtiers kiss his hand as a mark of respect. He married a daughter of Darius III—and encouraged 10,000 of his soldiers to marry Persian women. He enrolled 30,000 Persians in his army. And he founded approximately 70 cities that served both as military outposts and as centers for spreading the Greek language and culture throughout his empire.

Divided Domain

Following Alexander's death, three of his generals—Ptolemy (TAHL uh mee), Seleucus (suh LOO kuhs), and Antigonus—eventually divided his vast empire into separate domains. Ptolemy and his descendants ruled Egypt, Libya, and part of Syria. The most famous Ptolemaic ruler was Cleopatra VII, who lost her kingdom to the Romans in 31 B.C.

Seleucus and his descendants at first controlled the rest of Syria, as well as Mesopotamia, Iran, and Afghanistan. After a while, however, they were forced to give up their eastern territory and withdraw to Syria. In 167 B.C. Jewish guerrillas led by Judah Maccabee challenged the Seleucid control of Palestine. The Seleucid Antiochus IV had ordered the Jews to worship the Greek deities, but many Jews refused to abandon their religion. In 165 B.C. Judah Maccabee succeeded in reoccupying Jerusalem and rededicating the Temple, an event commemorated by the Jewish festival of Hanukkah. The kingdom of Judah would remain independent until its defeat by Rome in 63 B.C. The Seleucids likewise ruled in Syria until the coming of the Romans.

The domain of Antigonus and his heirs consisted at first of Macedonia and Greece. But the Greek city-states soon declared their independence and once again began fighting with each

---

CONNECTIONS: GEOGRAPHY IN HISTORY

An Economic Region

These drachmas (ancient Greek coins) are stamped with the portrait of Alexander the Great.

When geographers or historians divide the world into regions, they may define a region by physical topography, by political boundaries, or by economic features, such as trade routes and uniform currency. The empire of Alexander the Great came to be one economic region.

A tremendous expansion of international sea trade characterized both Alexander's empire and its successor domains. The Ptolemies, in particular, began using the monsoons to sail directly across the Indian Ocean between Africa and Asia instead of hugging the coast. As a result, luxury items from India and Arabia became common in Mediterranean cities.

An increase in public works projects also spread through the region. Alexander and his successors used the vast sums of gold and silver captured in Persia to finance road construction and harbor development.

A uniform currency held Alexander's empire together economically. Prior to Alexander, the Greek city-states, Egypt, and Persia all had coined their own money. Alexander circulated a coin bearing his profile, which merchants could use everywhere. Even if a kingdom coined its own money, it used Macedonian currency as a standard.

After Alexander's death, his empire fractured politically into rival kingdoms. The people in the overall geographic area, however, still shared a culture. And because of the trade routes linking commercial centers, the cities Alexander built continued to interact.

Making the Connection

1. List three regional economic characteristics of Alexander's empire.
2. What are the boundaries of the region in which you live?

---

other. In the 100s B.C., the growing Roman Empire would conquer and absorb Macedonia and Greece.

Hellenistic Culture

The political unity of Alexander's empire disappeared with his death, but the Greek language, systems of thought, and way of life continued to spread and flourish in the lands he had conquered. There, Hellenic culture mixed with elements of Middle Eastern culture to form a new culture, called Hellenistic.

City Life Hellenistic culture was concentrated in cities. The largest and wealthiest of these was Alexandria in Egypt. Alexandria's straight streets intersected each other at right angles, in contrast to the crooked streets of older cities. Its

palaces and temples, finished with white stucco over a stone base, gleamed brilliantly in the sun.

The city's economic position benefited from a double harbor that could hold 1,200 ships at a time. Another asset to trade was the city's lighthouse, which was visible from 35 miles (56 kilometers) out at sea.

Alexandria was also a major intellectual center. Its museum was the first ever and included a library of nearly a million volumes, an institute for scientific research, a zoo, and a botanical garden. Scientists came from all over the Hellenistic world. Around 250 B.C. Jewish scholars in Alexandria translated the Hebrew Bible into Greek. This translation, known as the Septuagint, was later used by the apostle Paul and is still used in the Eastern Orthodox Church.

During Hellenic times, the Greeks had been intensely involved with their particular polis. In Hellenistic society, however, the Greeks formed

IMAGES
OF THE TIME

The Hellenistic Age

The diverse traditions of the Mediterranean and the Middle East contributed to Hellenistic culture.

Alexander the Great brought together many different cultures in a single empire.

The Winged Victory of Samothrace, commemorating a military victory, is one of the most famous sculptures of the Hellenistic age.

the upper class of Alexandria and other cities in the Middle East and Asia Minor that were ruled by kings. Rather than being loyal to their king or kingdom, professional Greek soldiers and bureaucrats moved from place to place, wherever job opportunities were best.

In Alexandria and other Hellenistic cities, the social status of upper-class Greek women improved over their traditional status in Athens. No longer secluded, women could move about freely. They learned how to read and write and entered such occupations as real estate, banking, and government. Such opportunities were not, however, available to commoners.

Hellenistic Philosophers Hellenistic philosophers shunned political and social questions. Instead, they focused on personal behavior, especially the question of how to achieve peace of mind. Three systems of thought attracted most Hellenistic intellectuals: Cynicism, Epicureanism, and Stoicism.

The best known Cynic was Diogenes (dy AHJ uh neez). He criticized materialism and asserted that people would be happy if they gave up luxuries and lived simply, in accord with nature. The story is told that Alexander the Great urged Diogenes, "Ask me whatever gift you like." Diogenes responded, "Get out of my sunlight." In other words, not even a king could give Diogenes anything that nature had not already provided. Alexander was reportedly so impressed that he said, "If I were not Alexander, I would choose to be Diogenes."

Epicureans based their philosophy on the ideas of the scholar Epicurus. He argued that people should avoid both joy and pain by accepting the world as it was, ignoring politics, and living simply and quietly with a few close friends.

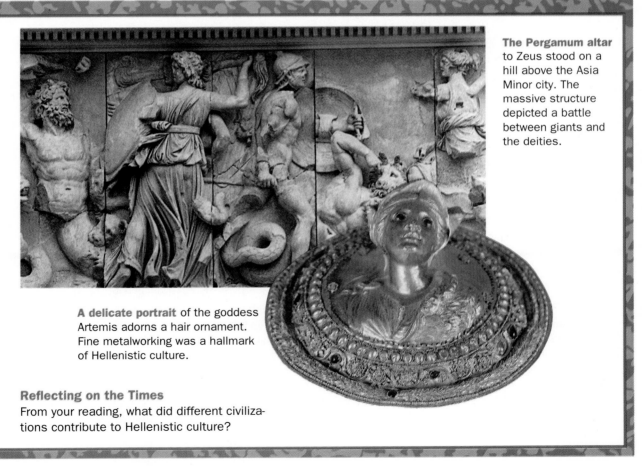

The Pergamum altar to Zeus stood on a hill above the Asia Minor city. The massive structure depicted a battle between giants and the deities.

A delicate portrait of the goddess Artemis adorns a hair ornament. Fine metalworking was a hallmark of Hellenistic culture.

Reflecting on the Times
From your reading, what did different civilizations contribute to Hellenistic culture?

The Triumph of Greek Civilization **129**

A thinker named Zeno founded Stoicism. The name *Stoicism* comes from the *Stoa Poikile*, or "painted porch," in which Zeno lectured. The Stoics believed that what happened to people was governed by natural laws. Accordingly, people could gain happiness by ignoring their emotions, and instead following their reason. In this way, they were able to accept even the most difficult circumstances of life and do their duty. Stoicism later affected both Roman intellectuals and early Christian thinkers.

Hellenistic Art and Literature

During the Hellenistic era, artists departed from both the subjects and the style of Hellenic times. Instead of carving idealized individuals, Hellenistic sculptors showed people in the grip of powerful emotions. They also carved numerous portrait heads, because art—no longer devoted to adorning the polis—had become a business.

Hellenistic playwrights usually wrote comedies rather than tragedies. Like Hellenistic philosophers, they ignored the problems of the outside world as much as possible. Menander, the most renowned Hellenistic playwright, specialized in comedies about everyday life. Well-known lines from his works include "Whom the gods love die young" and "We live not as we will, but as we can."

Science, Medicine, and Mathematics

Although limited by their simple instruments, scientists of the Hellenistic period performed many experiments and formed new theories, particularly in astronomy. Aristarchus (ar uh STAHR kuhs) of Samos concluded that the sun is larger than the earth, that the earth revolves around the sun, and that the stars lie at immense distances from both. In Alexandria, Eratosthenes (ehr uh TAHS thuh neez) estimated the earth's circumference to within one percent of the correct figure. He also asserted that the earth's land area was surrounded by water and that a ship could sail from Spain to India by going westward across the Atlantic. Most historians believe that Christopher Columbus based his voyage in large part on Eratosthenes' ideas.

Hellenistic doctors dissected corpses in order to learn more about human anatomy. They discovered the nervous system, studied the brain and the liver, and learned how to use drugs to relieve pain.

The Hellenistic period also saw great developments in mathematics and physics. About 300 B.C. Euclid of Alexandria wrote *The Elements of Geometry*, a book that collected and organized all information about geometry. Students until 1900 used the book as their introductory text.

Archimedes (ahr kuh MEED eez) of Syracuse was an excellent engineer and inventor. He invented the compound pulley, which moves heavy objects easily, and the cylinder-screw, which farmers still use to lift water for irrigation. Archimedes discovered the principle of buoyancy, which explains why some objects float and others sink. He also demonstrated the principle of the lever and said that if he had a lever and a place to stand, he could move the world. In the 100s B.C., when the Roman Empire began to absorb the Hellenistic world, the Romans would borrow heavily from the knowledge of Hellenistic scholars and scientists.

SECTION 3 REVIEW

Recall

1. **Identify:** Philip II of Macedon, Alexander the Great, Diogenes, Menander, Eratosthenes, Euclid, Archimedes
2. **Locate:** Find Macedonia and Alexandria on the map on page 126. What does Alexandria owe to the Macedonians?

Critical Thinking

3. **Analyze:** Compare and contrast Alexander the Great's original goal and the goal he finally chose for his empire. Why did his goals change?
4. **Evaluate:** Does Alexander deserve to be called "the Great"? Explain your answer.

5. **Synthesize:** Why was the position of upper-class women in Hellenistic cities higher than it had been in Hellenic cities?

Applying Concepts

6. **Cultural diffusion:** Explain how and why Hellenistic arts differed from Hellenic arts.

FINDING EXACT LOCATION ON A MAP

Your geography teacher has just asked you to state the exact location of your home town. To find the answer, you first need to understand the meaning of the term "exact location."

Explanation

To *find the exact location* of any place on Earth, cartographers use a grid system formed by imaginary lines called *lines of latitude and longitude.*

Lines of latitude run east and west around the earth and always remain the same distance from each other. For this reason, they are sometimes called *parallels.* Latitude is used to calculate distance north and south and is measured in degrees.

The starting point for measuring latitude is the Equator, which is a line of latitude and is designated as 0°. Each line of latitude is one degree from the next. One degree of latitude equals 69 miles (110 kilometers). There are 90 lines of latitude from the Equator to each pole. Those lines north of the Equator are usually marked with an "N," while those lines south of the Equator are labelled with an "S."

Lines of longitude run north and south from pole to pole. Unlike lines of latitude, lines of longitude are not always the same distance from one another. They are farthest apart at the Equator and closest together at the poles. Longitude is used to calculate distance east and west and is measured in degrees from the Prime Meridian, a line of longitude that runs through Greenwich, England, and is designated as 0°. Thus, sometimes lines of longitude are referred to as *meridians.* Those lines east of the Prime Meridian are usually marked with an "E" to 180° E and those lines west of it are labelled with a "W" to 180° W. You can locate a particular place by its "grid address" or the degrees at which the latitude and longitude lines meet.

Use the following steps to find the grid address, or exact location of a place:

- Find on the map the line of latitude nearest the designated place.
- Follow along the line of latitude until it crosses the nearest line of longitude. The point where the lines intersect is the grid address.

Example

For example, to determine the grid address of New York City, you would consult a map of the United States and find the line of latitude closest to New York City. This line turns out to be 41° N. Then, you would follow along the line of latitude until it cuts across the nearest line of longitude, which is 74° W. These latitude and longitude coordinates tell you the exact location or grid address of New York City—41° N, 74° W.

On the other hand, suppose you haven't been given a designated place and you want to locate a spot found at 40° N latitude and 20° E longitude. First, refer to the world map on pages 984–985 in the Atlas of your textbook and look for the line of latitude marked 40° N. Then, find the line of longitude marked 20° E. Follow these lines to the point where they intersect, and you will find the exact location of the grid address—the west coast of Greece.

Application

Refer to the map on page 126 of your textbook and answer the following questions:

1. What is the approximate grid address of Babylon?
2. What city is located at approximately 31° N and 30° E?
3. What is the approximate grid address of Tyre?
4. What body of water extends between 40° and 50° N and has a longitude of 50° E?
5. What is the approximate grid address of Persepolis?

Practice

Turn to Practicing Skills on page 137 of the Chapter Review for further practice finding exact location.

from Antigone

by Sophocles

The Greek playwright Sophocles (about 496–406 B.C.) wrote about the conflict between conscience and authority in his play Antigone. *After Antigone's two brothers died battling each other for the throne of Thebes, her uncle, Creon, became king. Creon allowed one brother, Eteocles, an honorable burial. He declared, however, that the other brother, Polyneices, was a traitor whose body should be left for the "birds and scavenging dogs." Anyone attempting to bury Polyneices, he warned, would be stoned to death. Antigone's sister, Ismene, obeys Creon. Antigone, however, out of respect for her brother, buries him.*

CREON [*slowly, dangerously*]. And you, Antigone,
   You with your head hanging—do you confess this thing?

ANTIGONE. I do. I deny nothing.

CREON [*to* SENTRY].   You may go. [*Exit* SENTRY]
   [*To* ANTIGONE] Tell me, tell me briefly:
   Had you heard my proclamation touching this matter?

ANTIGONE. It was public. Could I help hearing it?

CREON. And yet you dared defy the law.

ANTIGONE.   I dared.
   It was not God's proclamation. That final justice
   That rules the world below makes no such laws.

Your edict, King, was strong,
But all your strength is weakness itself against
The immortal unrecorded laws of God.
They are not merely now: they were, and shall be,
Operative forever, beyond man utterly.

I knew I must die, even without your decree:
I am only mortal. And if I must die
Now, before it is my time to die,
Surely this is no hardship: can anyone
Living, as I live, with evil all about me,
Think death less than a friend? This death of mine
Is of no importance; but if I had left my brother
Lying in death unburied, I should have suffered.
Now I do not.
         You smile at me. Ah Creon,
Think me a fool, if you like; but it may well be
That a fool convicts me of folly. . . .
Creon, what more do you want than my death?

CREON.   Nothing.
  That gives me everything.

ANTIGONE.   Then I beg you: kill me.
This talking is a great weariness: your words
Are distasteful to me, and I am sure that mine
Seem so to you. And yet they should not seem so:
I should have praise and honor for what I have done.
All these men here would praise me
Were their lips not frozen shut with fear of you.
[*Bitterly*] Ah the good fortune of kings,
Licensed to say and do whatever they please!

CREON. You are alone here in that opinion.

ANTIGONE. No, they are with me. But they keep their tongues in
  leash.

CREON. Maybe. But you are guilty, and they are not.

ANTIGONE. There is no guilt in reverence for the dead.

CREON. But Eteocles—was he not your brother too?

ANTIGONE. My brother too.

CREON.   And you insult his memory?

ANTIGONE [*softly*]. The dead man would not say that I insult it.

Art and Literature *Each actor in Greek drama wore masks, such as those depicted in a Roman mosaic, to indicate the several characters played. Men played all the women's roles.*

CREON. He would: for you honor a traitor as much as him.

ANTIGONE. His own brother, traitor or not, and equal in blood.

CREON. He made war on his country. Eteocles defended it.

ANTIGONE. Nevertheless, there are honors due all the dead.

CREON. But not the same for the wicked as for the just.

ANTIGONE. Ah Creon, Creon.
 Which of us can say what the gods hold wicked?

CREON. An enemy is an enemy, even dead.

ANTIGONE. It is my nature to join in love, not hate.

CREON [*finally losing patience*]. Go join them, then; if you must
   have your love,
 Find it in hell!

CHORAGOS [*leader of a group of 15 citizens*]. But see, Ismene comes:
 [*Enter* ISMENE, *guarded.*] Those tears are sisterly, the cloud
 That shadows her eyes rains down gentle sorrow.

CREON. You too, Ismene,
 Snake in my ordered house, sucking my blood

Stealthily—and all the time I never knew
That these two sisters were aiming at my throne!

                                         Ismene,
Do you confess your share in this crime, or deny it?
Answer me.

ISMENE. Yes, if she will let me say so. I am guilty.

ANTIGONE [*coldly*]. No, Ismene. You have no right to say so.
   You would not help me, and I will not have you help me.

ISMENE. But now I know what you meant; and I am here
   To join you, to take my share of punishment.

ANTIGONE. The dead man and the gods who rule the dead
   Know whose act this was. Words are not friends.

ISMENE. Do you refuse me, Antigone? I want to die with you:
   I too have a duty that I must discharge to the dead.

ANTIGONE. You shall not lessen my death by sharing it.

ISMENE. What do I care for life when you are dead?

ANTIGONE. Ask Creon. You're always hanging on his opinions.

ISMENE. You are laughing at me. Why, Antigone?

ANTIGONE. It's a joyless laughter, Ismene.

ISMENE.   But can I do nothing?

ANTIGONE. Yes. Save yourself. I shall not envy you.
   There are those who will praise you; I shall have honor, too.

ISMENE. But we are equally guilty!

ANTIGONE.   No more, Ismene.
   You are alive, but I belong to death.

RESPONDING TO LITERATURE

1. **Comprehending:** Explain what Antigone means when she says to Creon, "But all your strength is weakness itself against the immortal unrecorded laws of God."

2. **Applying:** Quote a passage that demonstrates Antigone's bravery.

3. **Synthesizing:** Explain whether you would like to live in a society in which individuals followed only their consciences.

4. **Thinking Critically:** Predict whether Creon actually had Antigone stoned to death.

CHAPTER 5 REVIEW

HISTORICAL SIGNIFICANCE

Greek culture has influenced Western civilization in many ways. Contemporary sculptors of the human form have studied the Greek sculptures. Architects throughout Europe and the United States, inspired by the ruins of classical buildings, have designed public buildings in the "neoclassical" style. The ancient Greeks invented the play, and some of the tragedies and comedies they wrote are still acted in modern theaters. The Socratic method of teaching is widely used in colleges and universities, and the way classical thinkers used reasoning has influenced science and other intellectual achievements. For example, scientists follow Aristotle's technique of investigating and analyzing data before reaching a conclusion.

Greek philosophers also laid the foundation for the disciplines of history, political science, and logic. The founders of the United States took inspiration from the ideals recorded in classical literature, such as belief in the worth and importance of the individual. The founders' belief in a democratic form of government—as the one best suited to enabling people to enhance their abilities—also derived from ancient Greece.

SUMMARY

For a summary of Chapter 5, see the Unit 2 Synopsis on pages 204–207.

USING KEY TERMS

Write the definition of each key term below. Then write one or two sentences that show how the terms are related to the concept of innovation.

1. classical
2. comedy
3. logic
4. philosopher
5. tragedy

REVIEWING FACTS

1. **Locate:** Where was the Parthenon built and for what purpose?
2. **Describe:** What were the main philosophical differences between the Sophists and Socrates?
3. **Outline:** What are the main steps in the scientific method as constructed by Aristotle?
4. **Explain:** Why is Thucydides considered the first scientific historian?

5. **List:** What are the major contributions that Hippocrates made to medicine?
6. **Identify:** Which two major cultures contributed to Hellenistic civilization?
7. **Tell:** How did Eratosthenes influence Christopher Columbus?

THINKING CRITICALLY

1. **Apply:** How did the Peloponnesian War affect Greek drama and philosophy?
2. **Analyze:** In what ways did Alexander the Great demonstrate his love of learning?
3. **Synthesize:** What reasons might Alexander's Macedonian veterans have given for refusing to go beyond the Indus River Valley?
4. **Evaluate:** Whose political ideas does the government of the United States more closely follow, those of Plato or those of Aristotle?

ANALYZING CONCEPTS

1. **Innovation:** What might contemporary theater be like if such playwrights as Aristophanes and Menander had not lived?
2. **Diversity:** What might be the benefits in having different ethnic groups living under a common government?

3. **Cultural diffusion:** How did Alexander the Great's founding of approximately 70 cities help spread Greek culture?

PRACTICING SKILLS

1. Imagine that you had a grid address that read simply 20° latitude and 120° longitude. What other information would you need? What are the four possible locations of this place?
2. Suppose you were plotting Alexander the Great's military campaigns on a map. In which hemispheres would you expect your grid address to be?
3. Very few places are located at the exact junction of a latitude line and a longitude line on a map. How would you figure the grid address of a place like Athens? (See the map on page 988.)

GEOGRAPHY IN HISTORY

1. **Location:** What factors enabled Alexandria to become a major center of commerce?
2. **Place:** Why do you think many scientists and scholars traveled to Alexandria to study?
3. **Movement:** What changes in international trade came about as a result of the conquests of Alexander the Great?
4. **Human–environment interaction:** How did Greek architects choose building sites?

TRACING CHRONOLOGY

Refer to the time line below to answer these questions.
1. Which event in the time line is related to the period of Pericles and the rise of Athens as a cultural center?
2. Why was Aeschylus, the writer of Greek tragedies, listed in the time line and not Sophocles or Euripedes?
3. Which date on the time line could be thought of as signaling the beginning of Hellenistic civilization?

LINKING PAST AND PRESENT

1. The Olympic Games were revived in 1896. In what ways do the modern Olympic Games resemble those of ancient Greece? In what ways do they differ?
2. The inclusion of diverse territories in Alexander the Great's empire led to widespread cultural diffusion. What aspects of Greek culture spread during the Hellenistic period? What aspects of American culture have spread beyond the borders of the United States?
3. Some American and European theaters have recently staged revivals of Greek plays. What do you think might be the appeal of these ancient plays to modern directors? How might modern audiences react to plays written more than 2,000 years ago?

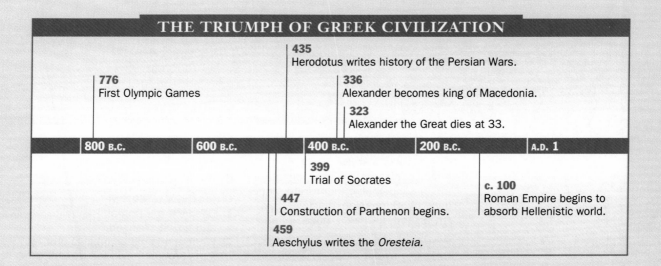

THE TRIUMPH OF GREEK CIVILIZATION

435
Herodotus writes history of the Persian Wars.

776
First Olympic Games

336
Alexander becomes king of Macedonia.

323
Alexander the Great dies at 33.

800 B.C. **600 B.C.** **400 B.C.** **200 B.C.** **A.D. 1**

399
Trial of Socrates

447
Construction of Parthenon begins.

c. 100
Roman Empire begins to absorb Hellenistic world.

459
Aeschylus writes the *Oresteia.*

The Legacy of Rome

*W*ar trumpets rang over the shouts and cheers of the people of Rome who crowded the narrow way to view the triumphal grand parade. Then sweating horses jerking at their harnesses rattled the victor's chariot over the broad paving stones, and the people's cries became deafening. On this day in 146 B.C., the Roman people were celebrating General Lucius Mummius's conquest of the last of the free Greek city-states.

Ironically, however, over the next several centuries Greek culture would actually come to form the basis of Roman culture and society. Greek slaves would teach the children of Roman aristocrats. Texts written by Greeks would form the base of Roman knowledge in many areas of study. By the A.D. 600s and 700s, the Greek language would even replace Latin as the official language of the eastern Roman Empire.

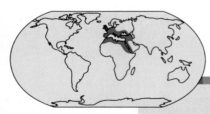

CHAPTER PREVIEW

Key Terms to Define: patrician, republic, plebeian, consul, dictator, tribune, indemnity, triumvirate, aqueduct, sect, messiah, disciple, martyr, bishop, patriarch, pope, inflation

People to Meet: Hannibal, Julius Caesar, Augustus Caesar, Nero, Jesus, Paul, Constantine, Attila

Places to Discover: Etruria, Rome, Sicily, Gaul, Nazareth

Objectives to Learn:
1. Describe the Roman Republic and how it changed.
2. What economic and social problems brought down the republic?
3. What was life like in the Roman Empire during the *Pax Romana*?

In A.D. 312–315 Emperor Constantine had his triumphal arch erected near the Colosseum in Rome.

4. What did Jesus of Nazareth teach?

5. What caused the decline of the western Roman Empire?

Concepts to Understand:

- Conflict—Roman armies conquer most of the Mediterranean world. Sections 1,2
- Change—The Roman political system evolves as Rome grows from a city-state to the capital of a vast empire. Sections 1,2
- Cultural diffusion—The Romans build an empire and spread Latin culture. Section 3
- Innovation—Christianity becomes dominant in the West. Section 4
- Change—Germanic invasions and cultural weaknesses destroy the Roman Empire. Section 5

139

The Roman Republic

The peoples of Italy first came into contact with the Greeks around 900 B.C., when Greek traders sailed up both the east and west coasts of the Italian peninsula. The Greeks gradually built an active trade relationship with the Italians. Then, from about 750 to 500 B.C., the Greeks began establishing farming communities in southern Italy and in Sicily, an island southwest of the Italian peninsula. These Greek colonists planted olive trees for the oil yielded and grapevines from which they could produce wine, thus introducing these two major products to Italy. The Greeks also introduced the Greek alphabet, which the Italians accepted and used in writing down their laws, their literature, and their history.

The Italian Peninsula

The Greeks were interested in colonizing Italy for several reasons, one of which was Italy's central location in the Mediterranean. A narrow, boot-shaped peninsula, Italy extends from Europe toward the shores of Africa, dividing the Mediterranean almost in half. Thus, Italy was ideally situated to be the center of trade among three continents: Asia, Europe, and Africa. Italy's rich soil and mild, moist climate also attracted the Greek colonists. Beyond the mountains and foothills that covered three-quarters of the peninsula lay plains with soil enriched by the silt deposits of mountain streams. On these plains vegetables, grains, and fruits thrived.

However, the silt washing down Italy's short and shallow rivers blocked the mouths of many rivers, creating mosquito-infested swamps. The people of Italy suffered recurrent epidemics of malaria and other diseases carried by mosquitoes.

Because of Italy's mountainous topography, the early inhabitants of the peninsula generally traveled solely within Italy and traded among themselves. Italy's only land connection—with Europe in the north—was cut off by the Alps. Furthermore, Italy's coastline, long though rocky and marshy, lacked good harbors. To increase trade, the Italians eventually overcame geographic obstacles and mastered the ways of the sea, but until that time came, they remained attached to the land.

Latins and Etruscans

Archaeologists have found evidence suggesting that people lived in Italy long before the Greeks arrived or Roman civilization began. In fact, the remains of human settlements suggest that Neolithic cultures began to form in Italy as early as about 5000 B.C. The Italians of Neolithic times built villages and farms, moving on whenever they had exhausted the land around their settlements. Between 2000 and 1000 B.C., waves of Indo-European immigrants overwhelmed these Neolithic peoples. By the time the Greek colonists arrived, many peoples inhabited Italy—including Umbrians in the north, Latins in the central plain called Latium (LAY shee uhm), and Oscans in the south. Like the Greeks, most of these peoples spoke the Indo-European languages.

The most mysterious of these peoples were the Etruscans. From about 900 to 500 B.C.—just when Greeks were colonizing southern Italy—the Etruscans were ruling most of northern Italy from city-states on the plains of Etruria. No one knows definitely where the Etruscans came from—whether their ancestors were Neolithic people from Italy or whether they migrated from Asia Minor. The Etruscans did not, at any rate, speak an Indo-European language as did most migrant peoples from Asia Minor.

Etruscan Culture

Historians have not deciphered much Etruscan writing and cannot read first-hand accounts of Etruscan history. The mud, bricks, and wood from which Etruscans constructed their buildings have disintegrated. And, although archaeologists have unearthed foundations of some Etruscan cities, these tell little about Etruscan culture. Only the many burial chambers provide clues about Etruscan culture. Thus, most knowledge about ancient Etruria comes from evidence in the tombs.

The murals and sculptures in the tombs depict life in ancient Etruria. Many tomb paintings show sports, religious ceremonies, and people enjoying music and feasts. Some tombs have murals that show funeral banquets. In these, the scene on one wall shows banqueters, and on the other walls dancers or musicians.

The many objects in Etruscan tombs—from furniture and clothing, pottery, tools, and food to jewelry and elaborate funerary art—also reveal much about Etruscan culture. Because many of the objects seem Greek or Near Eastern, the Etruscans probably traded with these peoples. The luxury items also suggest that Etruscan society had a wealthy upper class. These speculations are confirmed by the writings of other cultures, describing Etruscans as important and wealthy Mediterranean traders.

Etruscan tombs reveal less about Etruscan culture than historians might wish. By studying tomb artifacts, however, historians have begun to understand much about Etruscan culture. They have learned of the Etruscans' economic standing, and they have also begun to learn what these people valued.

Responding to the Arts
1. Why are Etruscan tombs so vital in studying ancient Etruria?
2. What conclusions have historians drawn from objects in Etruscan tombs?

ITALY 500 B.C.

Greeks
Etruscans
Latins

0   50   100 miles
0   50   100 kilometers

Learning from Maps *Find Etruria and Latium on the map. Notice that Latium divides Etruscan territory.* **What advantage might this location have provided the Latins when they set out to conquer the Etruscans?**

Such sculptures ornamented the homes of the wealthy overlords or aristocratic priests. Historians have determined that Etruscan society probably consisted of wealthy overlords, aristocratic priests, and a slave-labor force made up of conquered peoples. Wealthy overlords enslaved these peoples to provide themselves with comforts, and aristocratic priests sacrificed prisoners of war or forced them to duel to the death to appease angry gods.

After repeated revolts, the Etruscan lower classes and the other Italian peoples subject to Etruscan rule eventually freed themselves from domination by these wealthy overlords and priests. Chief among those who overthrew the Etruscans were the Latins of Rome.

The Rise of Rome

According to a legend of the Latins, in 753 B.C. a stocky man named Romulus was building the wall of a city on a hill overlooking the Tiber River. His twin brother, Remus, came over from the hillside opposite, where he too had been laying foundations for a city. The Roman historian Livy tells what happened next:

Remus, by way of jeering at his brother, jumped over the half-built walls of the new settlement, whereupon Romulus killed him in a fit of rage, adding the threat, "So perish whoever else shall overleap my battlements."

—Livy, *Ab Urbe Condita*, 29 B.C.

Setting more stone on the stains of his brother's blood, Romulus is said to have continued his building. In time, his namesake city—Rome—grew to include his brother's hill and all six of the nearby hills. Romulus was so effective a military ruler, the myth tells us, that Rome became the greatest city in that part of the peninsula.

In actuality, the origins of Rome were probably much less violent. At some time between 800 and 700 B.C., the Latin people huddled in the straw-roofed huts of the villages on the seven hills apparently agreed to join and form one community. It was this community that came to be called Rome.

Furthermore, although the people wrote in an alphabet borrowed from the Greeks, scholars have been able to decipher only a few Etruscan words, such as the names of gods and goddesses.

Although Etruscan writings still baffle our understanding, Etruscan art is expressive, needing no translation. In wall paintings, Etruscan figures dance and play music, enjoying a rich and pleasant life. In Etruscan sculpture, men and women feast and converse, triumphant soldiers brandish their spears, and hauntingly beautiful gods smile and gesture.

Etruscan Rule   Sometime during the late 600s B.C., the Etruscans gained control of Rome. An aristocratic Etruscan family, the Tarquins, set themselves up as kings over the Romans. The Tarquins taught the Latins to build with brick and to roof their houses with tile. They drained the marshy lowlands around the Roman hills and laid out streets where disease-carrying mosquitoes had once swarmed. At the center of the growing city they created a square called the Forum, which became the seat of Roman government and law. The Tarquins also built temples, taught the Romans many of the Etruscans' religious rituals, and placed Rome among the wealthiest cities in Italy.

But in 534 B.C., the tyrannical Tarquin the Proud came to power. This king's cruelties so angered the Romans that in 509 B.C. they drove the Tarquins out. Skilled Etruscan workers and artists stayed on in Rome, however, helping the city continue to grow and prosper.

Social Groups   Under Etruscan rule, a new wealthy aristocratic class had come into being in Rome—Latin nobles called **patricians.** Once the Etruscan rulers were driven out, the patricians declared Rome a **republic,** a community in which the people elect their leaders.

The majority of Rome's inhabitants, however, were **plebeians** (plih BEE yuhns). The plebeian class included wealthy, nonaristocratic townspeople and landowners as well as merchants, artisans, shopkeepers, small farmers, and laborers. As citizens, both the plebeians and the patricians had rights, such as the right to vote, and responsibilities, such as the duty to pay taxes and serve in the military. However, plebeians could not hold public office as patricians could.

The Roman Republic   The patricians organized the government of the republic into an executive branch and a legislative branch. Two patrician officials elected for one-year terms headed the executive branch, running the city's day-to-day affairs. These officials were called **consuls** because they had to consult each other before acting. They understood that either consul could veto the other's decisions. The word *veto* is Latin for "I forbid." The consuls oversaw other executive officials, such as praetors, or

judges, and censors, or keepers of tax and population records. Only a **dictator,** a leader whose word was law, could overrule the consuls. But dictators were temporarily appointed to lead the Romans only in times of crisis.

The Roman legislative branch initially consisted of the Assembly of Centuries and the Senate, both under patrician control. Members of the Assembly of Centuries (named for a military formation of 100—or *centum*—men) elected officials of the executive branch. But the power of the Senate—a group of 300 patrician men who served for life—outweighed the Assembly of Centuries. The senators advised the consuls, debated foreign policy, proposed laws, and approved contracts for constructing roads, temples, and defenses.

Plebeians Against Patricians

The plebeians bitterly resented their lack of power in the new republic—especially because they knew that the patricians could not maintain the republic without them. In 471 B.C., to obtain a greater voice in government, the plebeians went on strike—at first refusing to serve in the army and then leaving the city altogether to set up a republic of their own.

FOOTNOTES TO HISTORY
A ROMAN DINNER PARTY

Around 300 B.C., the dinner guests of wealthy Romans would recline on couches while slaves served them delicacies. Their appetizers might include snails fed on milk; smoked pig's stomach stuffed with brains, pine nuts, and peppercorns; or minced sea-crayfish tails. These delectables would be followed by main course dishes, which might include boiled stingray garnished with hot raisins; boiled crane with turnips; roast hare in white sauce; leg of boar; wood pigeon baked in a pie; or roast flamingo cooked with Jericho dates, dried onion, honey, and wine. The leisurely banquet would not be complete, however, without several similarly exotic offerings for dessert.

Tribunes   The patricians, frightened at being abandoned by those who composed their military and work forces, soon agreed to meet some of the plebeians' demands. The patricians agreed to recognize the plebeians' chosen representatives, the **tribunes.** They also granted tribunes the power to veto any government decision and ensured that they would be protected by law. Tribunes could not be arrested, and any person who dared to injure a tribune could be put to death. The patricians also formally recognized the Assembly of Tribes, the plebeians who elected the tribunes.

Old and New Laws   The plebeians did not stop fighting for their rights after winning these concessions. Up to that time no one had ever put Roman laws into writing—and only the patricians knew what the laws said. As a result, plebeians usually found out about a law only upon being charged with breaking that law. To make sure that judges applied the laws fairly, the plebeians insisted that the government write down the laws.

After decades of struggle, the plebeians finally got the patricians to engrave the laws on 12 bronze tablets in 451 B.C. and to set them in the Forum for all to see. The Twelve Tables, as these tablets were called, became the basis for all future Roman law.

Soon after, plebeians also won the right to serve in some public offices, although few of them could bear the cost of an unsalaried public position. Then, in 287 B.C., plebeians won their greatest success, establishing their right to make laws for the republic in the Assembly of Tribes. Rome was now very nearly a true democracy.

Religion and the Family

For almost five centuries, Rome thrived under a republican government. During this time, the Romans were powerfully influenced by Greek culture—brought to Italy by Greek colonists and, later, by Romans who conquered Greece. The Romans borrowed Greek gods and goddesses, giving them Roman names. Aphrodite, the Greek goddess of love, became the Roman goddess Venus. Ares, the Greek god of war, became Mars. They also made their old gods look Greek, giving the Etruscan god Jupiter the characteristics of the Greek Zeus.

Roman life remained distinctly Roman, however. Families privately worshiped their ancestral spirits and their storeroom guardians, as well as Vesta, goddess of the hearth.

In Roman families the father was absolute head of the household. He conducted the religious ceremonies; he was in charge of his wife, children, married sons and their families, any relatives who lived with him, and his slaves. Poor households were held together by equally strong bonds.

Roman wives had few legal rights. Occasionally they did find loopholes and acquired their own property and businesses. Wealthy women, with slaves to do their work, could study Greek literature, arts, and fashions. Lower-class women spent their time at household tasks and in family-run shops.

Yet, rich or poor, most Romans held the same values: thrift, discipline, self-sacrifice, and devotion to the family and the republic. Long after the Roman Republic ended, nostalgic reformers saw these as traditional Roman values.

SECTION 1 REVIEW

Recall
1. **Define:** patrician, republic, plebeian, consul, dictator, tribune
2. **Identify:** Tarquins
3. **Locate:** Find Latium, Etruria, and Rome on the map on page 142. How were the people of these three places connected?

Critical Thinking
4. **Analyze:** The French emperor Napoleon said that it is better to have one bad general than two good ones. Would the Romans have agreed with Napoleon's remark? Why or why not?

5. **Evaluate:** How might the struggle between patricians and plebeians have weakened Rome?

Applying Concepts
6. **Change:** Why did political change occur in the Roman Republic from 471 to 287 B.C.?

Expansion and Crisis

From about 500 to 300 B.C., Rome faced threats from its many neighbors in Italy. To protect their republic, the Romans either conquered these opponents or forced them to ally with Rome. In this way the Romans subdued one rival after another, until by 264 B.C., Rome ruled the entire peninsula.

Roman Legions

The Roman armies initially used the tactics of Greek phalanx warfare. But Roman generals learned that phalanxes were too large and slow to be effective. Innovative generals reorganized their troops into legions of 6,000 men. They divided these further into small, mobile units of 60 to 120 soldiers that could shatter the slow-moving phalanxes of their enemies.

Roman soldiers—called legionaries—were well trained and disciplined. Deserters were punished by death. With such iron discipline, the legionaries would conquer an empire.

In a time when victors routinely slaughtered or enslaved whole cities, Rome treated conquered foes remarkably well. Some conquered peoples were allowed to keep their own governments if they contributed soldiers or ships to help fight Rome's wars. Rome gave other peoples partial rights, and to some peoples even granted citizenship.

The Romans established permanent military settlements—called *coloniae*—throughout Italy to defend strategic heights and river crossings. To link these *coloniae*, the legions forged a chain of roads up and down the Italian peninsula. As war yielded gradually to peace, some of these roads became major trade routes.

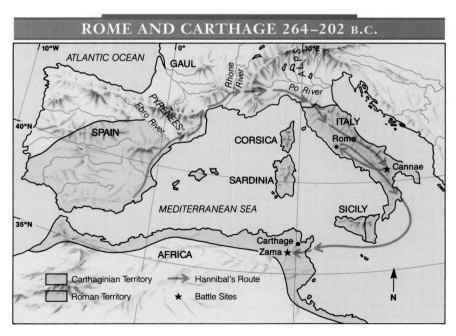

ROME AND CARTHAGE 264–202 B.C.

Learning from Maps
Locate Carthage, Italy, and Sicily on the map. **Why do you suppose the Romans and Carthaginians fought so fiercely for control of Sicily?**

Learning from Art *For the elephants in Hannibal's army, crossing rivers posed as great a problem as crossing the Alps. Here the elephants had to be floated on barges to make the crossing. But the treacherous journey across the Alps, combined with the bitter cold of a north Italian winter, cost Hannibal even more elephants than did the rivers.* **How successful was Hannibal's campaign after crossing into Italy?**

Rome Against Carthage

In Chapter 3 you read how Carthage became the wealthiest city in the Mediterranean region. To expand their commerce and protect their trade routes, the Carthaginians had then gone on to conquer the Spanish coast and most of Sicily by about 300 B.C. The Romans decided to check the expansion of the Carthaginians—the Punici, as the Romans called them.

The First Punic War In 264 B.C. the Carthaginians threatened to gain control over the Strait of Messina, a narrow passage between Sicily and Italy. When the Romans sent a force to prevent the Carthaginians from securing the strategic waterway, a full-scale war erupted.

The Romans' strong army conquered most of the Carthaginian colonies in Sicily. However, the Carthaginians—lords of the sea—lashed out at the Romans with their huge and powerful fleet. For a time this naval superiority gave Carthage the advantage.

Undaunted, the Romans built a larger fleet than the Carthaginians. In a battle off the coast of Africa, they stunned the Carthaginians with a new tactic: they snared the enemy's ships with grappling hooks, boarded them, and defeated the enemy in hand-to-hand combat. This enabled the Romans to make battles between ships like the land battles they excelled at. Thus, they were able to force the Carthaginians to retreat.

Although the war raged on until 241 B.C., the Carthaginians never regained control of Sicily or the sea. Threatened with invasion of their homeland, they agreed to give up their Sicilian cities and to hand the Romans a huge **indemnity,** or payment for damages.

The Second Punic War In 221 B.C. a 25-year-old soldier named Hannibal became general of the Carthaginian army in Spain. To get revenge against the Romans, Hannibal provoked a new war with Rome. In 218 B.C. he grabbed one of Rome's allied cities in Spain. His next move was even more audacious—to take the war into

Italy itself. Leading 40,000 soldiers and 50 elephants, he marched out of Spain, crossed southern Gaul, and started up the Alps. But his soldiers were terrified by the sight of those chilly heights, and their fears were well founded. Before they reached Italy, cold, snow, hunger, sickness, and attacks by mountain peoples killed half of Hannibal's army and most of the elephants.

Although outnumbered, Hannibal's troops defeated the Roman armies sent against them. By 216 B.C., in a battle at Cannae in southeastern Italy, Hannibal's soldiers had all but annihilated the Roman army. But the Romans rallied, refusing to admit defeat, and raised dozens of new volunteer legions. Their general, Publius Scipio, attacked Carthage itself to force Hannibal's recall to Africa. Scipio's attack had the desired result: Hannibal was called home.

In 202 B.C. Scipio's forces defeated Hannibal's army at Zama, near Carthage. At Scipio's demand, the Carthaginians gave up their lands in Spain, handed over all but 10 of their warships, and agreed to another large indemnity.

The Third Punic War   After 50 years of peace, Carthage regained its prosperity. Although Carthage was still no threat to Rome, Rome decided to end Carthaginian independence for good. In 149 B.C., when Carthaginians fought—and lost—a defensive skirmish against a Roman ally in Africa, the Romans used the battle as a pretext for war. They burned Carthage, sold its surviving population into slavery, and sowed salt in its soil so that no crops would grow. This victory gave the Romans complete control of the western Mediterranean.

The Republic in Crisis

While Roman armies were fighting the Punic Wars in the west, their forces were also engaged in conflicts in the east. Between 230 and 210 B.C., Rome brought the entire eastern Adriatic coast under its rule. The Romans also defeated King Philip V of Macedonia in his attempt to block Rome's expansion in the Adriatic region. Later, in 188 B.C., they forced the Seleucid king Antiochus III, who was supported by Hannibal, to give the Romans all his territories

in Asia Minor. In 133 B.C., Roman legions seized Pergamum, a kingdom in Asia Minor. Although the Romans left Syria and Egypt independent, they forced the rulers into obedient alliances.

By 130 B.C. the Romans were undisputed masters of the Mediterranean from Spain to Asia Minor. In fact, they had begun to call the Mediterranean *mare nostrum*—"our sea."

Maintaining and protecting such a vast territory created considerable difficulties. Political leaders could not readily adapt Rome's form of government—which had been created to meet the needs of a small city-state—to govern these numerous peoples. Political problems led to social and economic upheaval as well.

Exploiting the Provinces   Rome organized its non-Italian territories into provinces that had to pay tribute to Rome and recognize its authority. At first the provinces seemed a source of endless wealth. The Senate-appointed governors, called proconsuls, often accepted bribes and robbed the provincial treasuries. The publicans—officials who collected the taxes—also extorted money from the provinces. Soon, extorting money from the provinces became an accepted way for the rich to become richer.

In response to this treatment, the provinces rebelled. It became necessary to permanently station Roman legions in most provinces. Because putting down revolts cost Rome troops and money, the provinces began to strain its resources. However, the people in the provinces did adjust to Roman rule.

Changing the Countryside   By expanding, the Roman government acquired properties in the provinces. These holdings were rented to wealthy Romans, who joined individual units into large estates called latifundia (lat uh FUHN dee uh). Latifundia owners used slaves to work the land. Because slave labor was less expensive than paid labor, latifundia owners could produce crops that cost less than those grown by small farmers in Italy. By offering low prices for grain, latifundia owners in the provinces captured the grain market and thus brought great wealth to the provinces.

The latifundia owners also forced small farmers out of business. Then, just as they had done in the provinces, proconsuls and publicans began buying up small farms in Rome to create latifundia. Wisely, rather than try to compete in the grain market against provincial latifundia, these owners devoted their estates to sheep ranching and to raising olives and fruits. Thus, latifundia owners captured these markets too, putting even more farmers out of work.

Crowding the Cities Poor farmers streamed into Rome, where bread cost pennies and public shows and games were free. In the cities the poor discovered that many jobs were already being done by slaves. Angry and hopeless, the free poor eked out a living and voted for any leader who promised cheaper food and more amusements. Although often jobless, these people clung proudly to their status as free citizens.

While the urban poor proliferated, so too did a new social class between the plebeians and the old patrician families who filled the Senate and held most public offices. Made up of people who had obtained wealth in the provinces, in working their latifundia, or in businesses, this new social class took the old title of *equites* (EHK wuh teez). The title *equites*, or knights, had once applied to those wealthy enough to ride horses in battle but not noble enough to be patricians. The new *equites* saw more value in wealth than in nobility or character, influencing most Romans to adopt similar values.

Reformers and Generals

Many Romans viewed with dismay the changes brought on by Roman expansion. They claimed that the latifundia were ruining Italy and had to be reduced. They also thought that someone had to help the urban poor before these plebeians toppled the state.

The Gracchi As grandson of General Scipio, a patrician career lay open to Tiberius Gracchus. Instead, he threw in his lot with the plebeians, winning the office of tribune in 133 B.C. As tribune, Tiberius at once proposed a law to take back some of the land from the latifundia and give it to landless citizens. Despite stiff op-

position from the patrician Senate, Tiberius passed the law through the plebeian Assembly of Tribes. Opponents organized a riot in which Tiberius and 300 of his followers were killed. His murder, the first political violence in Rome in 400 years, would begin a trend.

Elected tribune a decade later, Tiberius's brother Gaius pushed through more reforms. A fiery orator, he persuaded the plebeian Assembly to give more land to farmers. To help the urban poor, he set up a government program to sell grain at low prices. Because the Senate refused to convict corrupt provincial governors—members of their social class—Gaius started a new court with members drawn from the *equites*.

Gaius too met with a violent end. In 122 B.C., he was killed in a riot planned by his enemies. And, by 111 B.C., the Senate had put a stop to the land reforms.

Marius and Sulla In 108 B.C. General Gaius Marius was elected consul. A reformer, he gave poor people jobs by enlisting them in the army. He paid them money for their service and promised them land when they were discharged. For the first time, Rome had a professional army in which soldiers owed allegiance to their commander, not to the republic.

In 88 B.C. this new army was used against Gaius Marius. General Lucius Cornelius Sulla sought to end his dispute with Marius over who should command the army in the east. Sulla persuaded his legions to capture Rome and drive Marius into exile. After seven years of civil war, Sulla appointed himself dictator. He tried to strengthen the Senate and take power away from the Assembly of Tribes. But by then the army had become the most powerful element in Roman politics, and violence overtook law.

The First Triumvirate In 70 B.C. General Gnaeus Pompey and the politician Marcus Licinius Crassus were elected consuls. They gained the support of Julius Caesar, a rising young aristocrat. Then, in 60 B.C., the three formed a **triumvirate**, a group of three persons with equal power, to control the government. But the triumvirate proved to be unstable.

Politically ambitious, Caesar took a military command in Gaul, which was inhabited by

Indo-Europeans known as Celts. Caesar conquered the Celts, forcing them to accept Roman rule. He then pushed northward, greatly increasing Rome's landholdings in northwestern Europe and elevating his own status as well.

Meanwhile Crassus, attempting to prove that he too was a great military leader, was killed in battle in 53 B.C. Fearing that Caesar might use his own legions to seize power, Pompey and the Senate then ordered Caesar to leave his legions north of the Rubicon River, the legal border of Roman Italy, and return to Rome. According to legend, however, upon arriving at the Rubicon, Caesar saw an apparition that encouraged him to cross, and exclaimed to his troops, "Let us accept this as a sign from the gods, and follow where they beckon, in vengeance on our double-dealing enemies. The die is cast."

By crossing the Rubicon, Caesar officially committed treason and started civil war. Within two months he had captured all Italy and driven Pompey and his allies out of the country. The civil war then escalated, spreading to the entire Mediterranean region, with Caesar and his legions hunting down their enemies and overwhelming Pompey's armies.

Julius Caesar In 45 B.C. Caesar took over the government as dictator for life, to rule very much like a monarch. Under his leadership, the government gave jobs to the unemployed, public land to the poor, and citizenship to many people in the provinces. Caesar also added representatives from the provinces to the Senate.

Many Romans believed that Caesar was a wise ruler who had brought order and peace back to Rome. Others, however, considered him to be a tyrant who meant to end the republic and make himself king. To prevent this, on March 15, 44 B.C., a group of senators led by Marcus Brutus and Gaius Cassius assassinated Caesar as he entered the Senate.

End of the Republic

After the death of Julius Caesar, his 18-year-old grandnephew Octavian joined forces with Marc Antony and Marcus Lepidus, two of Caesar's top government officers. Together this second triumvirate defeated Caesar's assassins in 42 B.C. and condemned to death hundreds of senators and thousands of *equites*. Then, while keeping up the appearance of republican government, these three generals divided the Roman world among themselves. Octavian took command in Italy and the west, Antony ruled in Greece and the east, and Lepidus took charge of North Africa.

The second triumvirate did not last long, however. Octavian forced Lepidus to retire from political life. When Antony married Cleopatra, the queen of Egypt, Octavian persuaded the Romans that Antony intended to conquer and rule them with his foreign queen by his side, and so Octavian declared war on Antony in Rome's name. In 31 B.C. Octavian scattered the forces of his enemies in a critical naval battle at Actium in Greece. A year later, to evade capture by Octavian, Antony and Cleopatra committed suicide in Egypt. With Antony dead, Octavian became the undisputed ruler of Rome.

SECTION 2 REVIEW

Recall
1. **Define:** indemnity, triumvirate
2. **Identify:** Hannibal, Scipio, Tiberius Gracchus, Gaius Gracchus, Marius, Sulla, Julius Caesar, Octavian, Marc Antony
3. **Locate:** Find Sicily and Gaul on the map on page 145. What was the importance of each place in the military history of the Roman Republic?

Critical Thinking
4. **Analyze:** Compare the events that started the First and Third Punic Wars. Why might one war be called justified and the other unjustified?

5. **Synthesize:** Do you agree with the way in which the Romans treated the people in their provinces? Why or why not?

Applying Concepts
6. **Conflict:** Explain how Roman conquests overseas affected Rome's development.

The Roman Empire

Under the Roman Republic, laws had proven too weak to control social changes, while generals had become too strong, taking power away from elected officials. Thus, Octavian and his supporters believed that Rome needed a new form of government—with one strong leader. The Senate—filled with Octavian's supporters—agreed and appointed Octavian consul, tribune, and commander in chief for life in 27 B.C. Octavian gave himself the title *Augustus*, or Majestic One.

The First Emperors

Augustus claimed to support the republic, but he actually laid the foundation for a new state called the Roman Empire. In practice, he became Rome's first emperor, or absolute ruler.

Augustus Caesar   In the 40 years of his reign—from 27 B.C. to A.D. 14—Augustus rebuilt the city of Rome and became a great patron of the arts. He also introduced many reforms to Rome and the empire. Proconsuls could no longer exploit the provinces. Publican tax collectors were replaced with permanent government employees. Grain was imported from North Africa so that all in Rome would be fed. New roads were built and old ones repaired. Magnificent public buildings were constructed throughout the empire. Augustus boasted that he had "found Rome a city of brick and left it a city of marble."

In 31 B.C. there began the *Pax Romana*, or Roman Peace, which lasted about 200 years. The only major disturbances during those years occurred when new emperors came to power. For, although Augustus chose his own successor carefully, he failed to devise any law for the selection of later emperors.

The Julian Emperors   Historians call the four emperors who ruled from A.D. 14 to 68 the Julians because each was related in some way to Julius Caesar. Each showed promise when he became emperor, but later revealed great faults. Augustus's adopted son Tiberius, who succeeded Augustus Caesar as emperor, spoiled his able leadership by accusing many innocent people of treason against him. Caligula, Tiberius's grand-nephew and successor in A.D. 37, became mentally disturbed after a serious illness and was assassinated by a palace guard in A.D. 41. Caligula's uncle, Claudius, was a renowned scholar full of fresh ideas, but as he grew older he had difficulty concentrating on affairs of state. Nero, Claudius's stepson, who became emperor in A.D. 54, was cruel, vain, and probably insane. Nero was willing to bankrupt Rome to pay for his own twin pleasures—horse racing and music. Furthermore, suspecting others of plotting to kill him, he murdered his wife and his mother and had many senators executed. In A.D. 68 the Senate, with the backing of the palace guard, sentenced Nero to death for crimes against the state. Before he committed suicide, reportedly he cried, "What a loss I shall be to the arts!"

In the 28 years following Nero's end, eight new emperors rose to power. But, although each had his flaws and committed various crimes, on the whole the Roman people prospered during the rule of the emperors.

The Good Emperors   Then, in A.D. 96, the Senate chose its own candidate for emperor: Nerva. Historians consider Nerva the first of the so-called Good Emperors; the others were Trajan, Hadrian, Antoninus Pius, and Marcus Aurelius. The Emperor Trajan, who succeeded Nerva, increased the empire to its greatest size. Hadrian then strengthened Rome's fortifications along the frontiers. Antoninus Pius succeeded

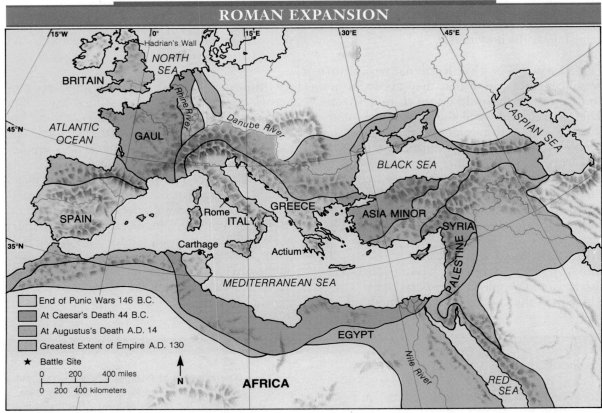

ROMAN EXPANSION

Map legend:
- End of Punic Wars 146 B.C.
- At Caesar's Death 44 B.C.
- At Augustus's Death A.D. 14
- Greatest Extent of Empire A.D. 130
- ★ Battle Site

0   200   400 miles
0 200 400 kilometers

Learning from Maps *Examine the pattern Roman expansion took. Notice that most Roman land bordered the Mediterranean Sea. Thus, each conquest further strengthened Rome's control of the Mediterranean region.* **During whose reign did the Roman Empire reach its greatest size?**

him, maintaining the empire's prosperity. And the Stoic philosopher Marcus Aurelius brought the empire to the height of its economic prosperity. All these Good Emperors ruled according to the system created by Augustus and lived by the principle of Stoic philosophy best expressed by Marcus Aurelius in *Meditations:* "Every moment think steadily as a Roman and a human being how to do what you have in hand with perfect and simple dignity."

Roman Rule

By the time Augustus had come to power in 27 B.C., between 70 and 100 million people were living in the Roman Empire. To rule so many

people effectively, Augustus had to institute many changes in government.

Imperial Government   Augustus improved the working of the empire by carefully choosing professional governors rather than letting the Senate appoint inexperienced proconsuls every year. In some provinces, such as Judea, he left local kings in charge under his command. Under the republic, the Senate had often remained ignorant of what was happening in the outlying provinces. Augustus ordered new roads built so that he could keep in touch with all parts of the empire, and he personally inspected the provinces frequently.

Augustus also dignified his own position by serving as *pontifex maximus,* or chief priest of

The Legacy of Rome   **151**

Rome. Thus he and each later emperor became the head of a national religion that further helped unify the provinces.

The Law   As the Romans won more provinces, they found that they needed a new kind of law that would apply to noncitizens. They therefore created the *jus gentium*, or the law that dealt with foreigners or noncitizens, as opposed to the *jus civile*, or citizen law. Over the centuries, however, emperors granted citizenship rights to the peoples of so many nearby cities and provinces that by the early A.D. 200s, all free males in the empire had been made full citizens of Rome, and the two kinds of laws became one.

In their laws Romans generally stressed the authority of the state over the individual. They also accorded people definite legal rights, one of which was that an accused person should be considered innocent until proven guilty. The Roman system of law has formed the basis for the legal systems of many Western nations and of the Christian Church.

An Imperial Army   Augustus and later emperors maintained the professional army that Marius had created in 107 B.C. As conditions became more peaceful, Augustus reduced the number of legions from 60 to 28 and supplemented this fighting force with auxiliaries—troops that were recruited from the provincial peoples. Even with the legions and the auxiliaries combined, the emperor could count on having only about 300,000 troops, which was not enough to defend a border with a length of about 4,000 miles (6,440 kilometers). Therefore, by the time Marcus Aurelius was in power, invasions by peoples outside the empire had become a chronic problem.

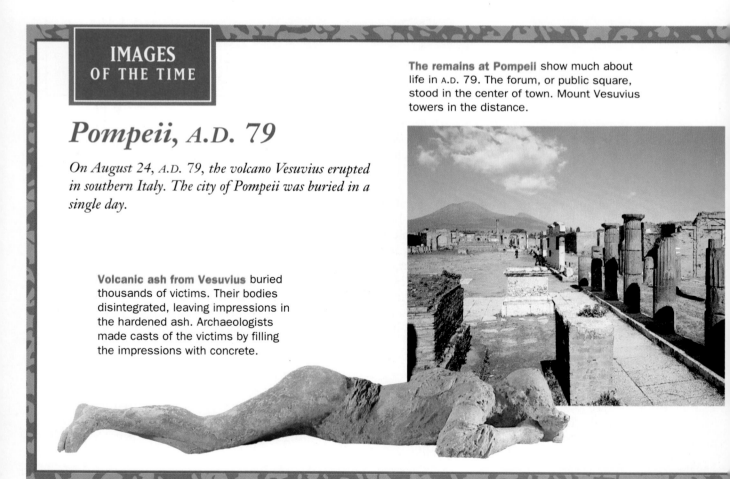

IMAGES OF THE TIME

Pompeii, A.D. 79

On August 24, A.D. 79, the volcano Vesuvius erupted in southern Italy. The city of Pompeii was buried in a single day.

The remains at Pompeii show much about life in A.D. 79. The forum, or public square, stood in the center of town. Mount Vesuvius towers in the distance.

Volcanic ash from Vesuvius buried thousands of victims. Their bodies disintegrated, leaving impressions in the hardened ash. Archaeologists made casts of the victims by filling the impressions with concrete.

Roman Civilization

The order and stability of the *Pax Romana* fostered trade and enabled people to enhance the quality of their daily lives and to fashion lasting accomplishments in Roman architecture and Latin literature. The Latin author Tertullian described this time:

Everywhere roads are built, every district is known, every country is open to commerce . . . the [fields] are planted; the marshes drained. There are now as many cities as there were once solitary cottages. . . . Wherever there is a trace of life, there are houses and human habitations, well-ordered governments, and civilized life.

—Tertullian,
Concerning the Soul, c. A.D. 180

The Economy of the Empire   Tertullian's description of economic growth under the empire was not exaggerated. In the first century A.D., production centers in Italy made pottery, woven cloth, blown glass, and jewelry for sale in the peninsula and the provinces. The provinces in turn sent goods to Italy—often luxury items for Italy's wealthy, such as silk cloth and spices gathered in trade with China, India, and southeast Asian countries. Dockworkers at Rome's harbor, Ostia, unloaded raw materials such as tin from Britain, iron from Gaul, and lead from Spain. In the A.D. 100s shrewd business owners in Gaul and in the Rhine River district began making pottery and glassware that outsold even the competing products in Italy. Soon skillful Greek traders within the empire were doing business in Zanzibar off the coast of southern Africa, in southeast Asia, and, in A.D. 166, at the court of the Chinese emperor Huan-ti.

Mosaics and frescoes decorated the houses of wealthy Romans. At left is a floor mosaic showing marine life; below, a portrait of a young girl holding a book.

Reflecting on the Times
Why do the remains at Pompeii tell historians more than the fragmentary artifacts of other ancient cities?

Learning from Photographs *To better protect the empire's borders, Hadrian oversaw the construction of a wall in northern Britain that is approximately 73 miles (117 kilometers) long.* **Why might this fortification have been necessary?**

Life During the *Pax Romana* With these economic changes came alterations in life-style as well. The family gradually became less significant than it had been during the republic. Romans had fewer children and were likely to divorce and remarry several times. Fathers lost some of the absolute power they had during the republic, and wives gained some legal rights. Society became less stable. Patricians might go bankrupt, *equites* might take a place in the Senate, and a poor man might even make a fortune in manufacturing and rise to the middle class.

Within each class, a consistent pattern of life formed. The wealthy often held public office, owned large farms in the countryside, ran factories, or oversaw trading firms. They lived comfortably in luxurious homes with marble walls, mosaic floors, running water, and baths.

The prosperity of the *Pax Romana* sometimes trickled down to the people of average means—the shopkeepers and artisans. Although fewer people became extremely rich, more became moderately well off. The majority in Rome, however, were still poor. There were no private baths for them; instead they bathed at crowded public facilities built under Augustus

and later emperors. Most Romans lived in flimsy wooden tenements of six or seven stories that readily collapsed or caught fire.

Public Amusements And yet, despite the conditions under which they lived, the poor did not rebel against the government, because it offered them both free bread and free entertainment. By the time of Marcus Aurelius, Romans celebrated 130 holidays a year. On some days, teams of jockeys or charioteers competed in violent races in the Circus Maximus, an arena that could seat more than 150,000. On other holidays, crowds could watch armed slaves called gladiators fight each other to the death or battle wild animals in stadiums like the Colosseum.

Architecture, Engineering, and Science
The Romans constructed many impressive buildings during the *Pax Romana* besides the Circus Maximus and the Colosseum. Between A.D. 118 and 128, Hadrian rebuilt the Pantheon, a temple for all the gods and goddesses, with a soaring dome and a huge skylight. To build the Pantheon, the Romans mixed concrete—a new building material—with various kinds of stone.

As they constructed public buildings and a vast network of roads, the Romans engineered **aqueducts,** or artificial channels for carrying water. These lofty arches built out of stone enabled water to flow into Rome from as far away as 30 miles (about 48 kilometers). One Roman-built aqueduct in Segovia, Spain, was so well constructed that it is still used today—nearly 1,900 years after it was completed.

The Romans excelled at taking discoveries made by others, combining them, refining them, and using them in new—and often more practical—ways. They adapted the Etruscan arch and dome to construct aqueducts and the Pantheon, and borrowed the design for columns from the Greek temple to support porches they built around Roman city squares.

Roman scientists also relied upon foreign resources—information that had been collected and organized from other cultures. The medical ideas of the ancient world compiled by the Greek physician Galen formed the basis of Roman medical science. Likewise, the notes and observations on astronomy that were compiled and written into a text by the Egyptian astronomer Ptolemy formed the foundation of Roman astronomy. Galen's works influenced medical science for 14 centuries, and Ptolemy's work made it possible for later astronomers to predict with accuracy the motion of the planets.

Learning and Literature   The Romans studied their borrowed knowledge avidly. Wealthy boys and girls received private lessons at home. Young men from these wealthy families went on to academies—where former Greek slaves often taught—to learn geometry, astronomy, philosophy, and oratory. The daughters of the wealthy did not attend academies. Many upper-class women continued to be given private lessons at home, however, and often became as well educated as Roman men. People in the lower classes usually had at least the rudimentary knowledge of reading, writing, and arithmetic they needed to conduct business.

Latin, Rome's official language, had a vocabulary far smaller than that of Greek or modern English; thus, many words had to do multiple duty, expressing several meanings. Nevertheless, Latin remained the *lingua franca*, or common language, of Europe as late as the A.D. 1500s; it is still used in some church services. Latin also forms the basis of the so-called Romance languages—Italian, French, Spanish,

---

CONNECTIONS: HISTORY AND THE ENVIRONMENT

Roman Origins of Cultural Centers

Romans built aqueducts throughout Europe.

Although most people do not think of Bonn, Vienna, London, or Paris as Roman, these cities were founded by the Romans.

In the Roman Empire, when soldiers at a military camp retired, they moved into houses nearby. Gradually, these houses formed a *colonia*—an officially recognized military town. Castra Bonnensia was one such town. Today Castra (camp) Bonnensia is the German city of Bonn. Vienna was also originally a military camp.

Other Roman cities grew out of marketplaces that were centers of trade serving the entire empire. For instance, London, once called Londinium, began as a trading post on the Thames River in Britain from which merchants would set sail for Europe. Paris, once Roman Lutetia, blossomed on the left bank of the Seine River during the upsurge in Roman trade in the first century A.D.

Today, a visitor to any of these cities can see traces of Rome's influence. For the Roman governors of these cities encouraged city residents to use the technology invented by the Romans. Thus, residents built aqueduct systems and public baths modeled after those in the city of Rome. They also constructed public arenas and theaters like those in Rome so that they too could have the races, gladiatorial games, and other amusements commonly enjoyed by Romans.

Making the Connection
1. What modern cities were originally Roman military camps?
2. How did trading centers lead to the growth of Roman cities?

during the reign of Augustus, Latin literature achieved an elegance and enduring power that began its so-called Golden Age. Cicero, a Roman senator, published his own beautifully written speeches. Horace, a poet, wrote odes, satires, and letters on many themes such as the shortness of life and the rewards of companionship. And Horace's friend Virgil wrote the *Aeneid*, an epic poem comparable to those of Homer. In one passage of this poem, Virgil expresses both the humility and pride of Romans:

> *O*thers, no doubt, will better mould the
> bronze
> To the semblance of soft breathing, draw, from
> marble,
> The living countenance; and others plead
> With greater eloquence, or learn to measure,
> Better than we, the pathways of the heaven,
> The risings of the stars: remember, Roman,
> To rule the people under law, to establish
> The way of peace, to battle down the haughty,
> To spare the meek. Our fine arts, these,
> forever.

—Virgil, the *Aeneid*, c. 20 B.C.

Learning from Photographs *Roman engineers were ordered to build a road that would last forever. Called the Queen of Roads, the Appian Way was used for 1,000 years.* **Why were roads so vital to the Roman emperors?**

Portuguese, and Romanian—and supplies the roots for more than half of English words.

Although they initially modeled their writing on Greek literature, Roman writers also originated their own works of genius. In fact,

Later writers expressed other points of view. Livy wrote a monumental history of Rome that glorified the patriotism and heroism of early Romans. The historian Tacitus, on the other hand, condemned the tyranny of the Julian emperors with subtle but scathing irony.

SECTION 3 REVIEW

Recall

1. **Define:** aqueduct
2. **Identify:** Augustus, *Pax Romana*, Tiberius, Caligula, Claudius, Nero, Marcus Aurelius, Galen, Ptolemy, Virgil, Livy

Critical Thinking

3. **Analyze:** Contrast the quotation by Nero on page 150 with the one by Marcus Aurelius on page 151. How do the two quotations show these two emperors' different attitudes toward their responsibilities as leaders?
4. **Synthesize:** The expression "bread and circuses" has often been used to describe cheap, short-term measures taken by a government to prevent the poor from causing political upheaval. Explain whether you believe the description "bread and circuses" is applicable to any aspects of contemporary life in the modern United States. If so, to what aspects of modern life does it apply?

Applying Concepts

5. **Cultural diffusion:** List some of the advantages and disadvantages to a province of adopting Latin culture.

The Rise of Christianity

The early Romans worshiped nature spirits. Under Etruscan influence they came to think of these spirits as gods and goddesses. Later, the Romans adopted much of Greek religion and mythology, identifying Greek gods and goddesses with their own deities and honoring them as the Roman government required. Beginning with Augustus, the government also began expecting people throughout the empire to honor the emperor as Rome's chief priest. Nevertheless, the empire's people were still allowed to worship freely—and they did. A variety of religions flourished in the Roman Empire.

Then, at about the time of Augustus, a new monotheistic religion called Christianity began to be practiced by the Jews in the eastern Mediterranean. At first, both the Roman authorities and the followers of Christianity thought of the new religion as a **sect,** or group, within Judaism. As Christians won over non-Jewish followers, however, their faith diverged further and further from its Jewish roots, and Christianity eventually became a separate religion in its own right.

Judaism and the Empire

In A.D. 6, about 100 years after the people of Judah had won their freedom from the Seleucids, the Emperor Augustus turned the kingdom of Judah into the Roman province of Judea. The Roman government in Judea still allowed the Jews to practice their religion, but it was particularly corrupt and cruel in its treatment of the Jews. Many Jews therefore began to hope that a **messiah,** or savior, would come to save them and restore the dynasty of David. The coming of a messiah had long been foretold by Jewish prophets.

Others took matters into their own hands. In A.D. 66 the Jews rebelled against the Roman governor and easily overpowered the small Roman army in Jerusalem. But only four years later, in A.D. 70, the Romans retook Jerusalem, destroying the Temple—which had been rebuilt only a few years before—and killing thousands of Jews.

Then, after another unsuccessful rebellion in A.D. 132, the Romans banned the Jews from living in Jerusalem. The Jews were forced to resettle in other parts of the Mediterranean and the Middle East. In their diaspora, or scattered communities, the Jews continued to cherish their study of the Torah, the entire body of Jewish religious law and learning. They established special academies called yeshivas to promote its study. Furthermore, between A.D. 200 and 500, rabbis—scholars trained in the yeshivas—assembled their various teachings and interpretations of the Torah into a book known as the Talmud. To this day the Talmud remains an important book of Jewish law.

Jesus of Nazareth

A few decades before the revolts of the Jews—at about the time Augustus had established the Roman province of Judea—a Jew named Jesus was born near the town of Nazareth. After a traditional Jewish education, Jesus traveled through Judea from about A.D. 26 to 30, preaching a new message to his fellow Jews and winning **disciples,** or followers.

Proclaiming that the kingdom of God was close at hand, Jesus urged people to repent their mistakes and change their behavior. He said that God was loving and forgiving toward all those who repented, no matter what evil they had done or how lowly they were. Addressing people of every class, he often used parables, or symbolic stories, to get his message across. With the parable below, Jesus urged his followers to give up everything so that they would be ready for God's kingdom:

> *The kingdom of heaven is like treasure lying buried in a field. The man who found it, buried it again; and for sheer joy went and sold everything he had, and bought that field.*
>
> —Matthew 13:44–46

Jesus' disciples began to believe that he was the long-awaited messiah. Other Jews, believing that the messiah had not yet come, did not think Jesus deserved to be called messiah and so viewed him as an impostor. This disagreement soon became a fiercely debated controversy.

The controversy troubled Roman officials in Palestine. They believed that anyone who aroused such strong feelings in the public could jeopardize Roman authority. In about A.D. 33, the Roman governor arrested Jesus as a political troublemaker and ordered that he be crucified—hung from a cross until dead. This was the customary Roman way of punishing criminals.

Learning from Art *Jesus said that he would make his disciples fishers of men, meaning that he would teach them to convert others to Christianity.* **What Christian teaching might have fostered such a missionary spirit?**

The Spread of Christianity

After the death of Jesus, his disciples claimed that he had been resurrected, or had risen from the dead, and had appeared to them. They pointed to this as further evidence that he was the messiah. His followers began preaching that Jesus was the Son of God and the way of salvation. Jews and non-Jews who accepted this message and followed Jesus' teachings became known as Christians—*Christos* was Greek for "messiah." They formed churches—communities for worship, fellowship, and instruction.

A convert named Paul contributed to the spread of Christianity, especially among non-Jews. He traveled widely and wrote on behalf of the new religion. Paul's epistles to various churches were later combined with the Gospels, or stories about Jesus, and the writings of other early Christian leaders. Together, these works form the New Testament of the Bible.

Meanwhile, other apostles, or Christian missionaries, were spreading Christianity throughout the Roman world. It is believed that Peter, the leader of the group, came to Rome and helped found a church in that city. Other churches were established in Egypt, Asia Minor, Greece, and later in Gaul and Spain.

Persecution and Competition

Christians taught that their religion was the only true faith. They refused to honor the emperor as a god, rejected military service, and criticized Roman festivals and games. As a result, many Romans came to dislike the Christians and accused them of treason.

The Romans feared that by scorning all gods but their own, the Christians would incur the wrath of the Roman gods, bringing calamity. Therefore, although they did not hunt out the Christians, if Roman authorities thought a Christian community was causing trouble, they might have the members of the community killed. Roman magistrates frequently threw these Christian **martyrs**—people who chose to die rather than give up their religious beliefs—into the stadiums to be killed by wild beasts in front of cheering crowds of thousands.

Such persecution, which lasted until the early A.D. 300s, deterred many people from becoming Christians. To win converts to their religion, Christians had to overcome this deterrent. Christianity also had to compete for converts with polytheistic religions and mystery religions—so named for their mythical heroes and secret rituals—and with Judaism.

Beginning in the A.D. 200s and 300s, people in the Roman world began to feel dissatisfied with their polytheistic and mystery religions. The empire was beginning to collapse, causing people to believe that these religions and values had failed them. Well-educated people began to heed the teachings of Greek and Roman philosophers who had long cast doubt on the foundations of older polytheistic religions. And mystery religions, which could never generate more than limited appeal because they usually excluded people from some social groups, began to attract even fewer people to their ranks. Rejecting these religions, many people turned instead to the monotheism and moral ethics of Judaism—and to Christianity, finding it to be a source of strength and hope. The Christian emphasis on salvation for all and doing good for others appealed especially to the poor, whose lot in life was difficult. As conditions in the empire worsened, the wealthy too turned to Christianity for comfort.

Romans Adopt Christianity

According to legend, in A.D. 312, as the Roman general Constantine led his army into battle, a flaming cross appeared in the sky and beneath it in fiery letters appeared the Latin words *In hoc signo vinces:* "With this as your standard you will have victory." Apparently because of this vision, Constantine ordered his soldiers to paint the Christian symbol of the cross on their shields. When his army won the battle, Constantine credited the victory to the God of the Christians.

Named emperor of Rome in A.D. 312, Constantine thus became a defender of Christianity. Through his influence all religious groups throughout the empire, including Christians, gained complete freedom to worship as they pleased. Calling conferences of Christian leaders, Constantine resolved differences that had arisen among them. He also ordered churches to be constructed at the sites of Christian shrines in Rome and Jerusalem.

At least half the population in the eastern part of the empire had become Christian by this time, but there were far fewer Christians in Italy and the western part of the empire. Constantine's policies began to change that situation. During the A.D. 300s, Christians increased throughout the entire Roman world. Then, in A.D. 392, the emperor Theodosius (thee uh DOH shuhs) made Christianity the official religion of the Roman Empire, outlawing the old Hellenistic and Roman religions.

The Early Christian Church

From early times Christians recognized that their organization, the Church, would prosper only if it was unified. They also felt they must state Christian teachings clearly to avoid differences of opinion that might divide the Church. Consequently, the Christians greatly valued the teachings of Augustine, a scholar who attempted to explain many Christian beliefs.

Teachings of St. Augustine Augustine was born in Hippo, in North Africa, in the year A.D. 354. In his autobiography, *Confessions,* he says that he spent his youth pursuing pleasure and studying pagan philosophers. He then describes how, at the age of 32, he was moved to read a chapter from the Bible, which converted him to Christianity:

> *I* heard from a neighboring house a voice, as of a boy or girl, I know not, chanting, and oft repeating, "Take up and read; Take up and read." . . . So . . . I arose, interpreting it to be no other than a command from God, to open the book, and read the first chapter I should find.
>
> —Augustine, *Confessions,* c. A.D. 398

So powerful was Augustine's intellect and his leadership ability that within 10 years of his

Learning from Art *The image of Jesus as a shepherd was intended to convey the message that Jesus shepherded people to God.* **What did Jesus urge people to do?**

conversion he had become the leading church official in Hippo, where he vigorously defended Christian beliefs. In this post he wrote books, letters, and sermons that influenced Western Christian thought during his own time and continue to do so up to the present time. For instance, he wrote *The City of God*—the first history of humanity from the Christian point of view. Centuries after his death, the Church declared Augustine a saint.

Church Structure   By Augustine's time, Christian leaders had organized the Church as a hierarchy—that is, into levels of authority, each level more powerful than the level below it. At the lowest level were the local gatherings of Christians, which were called parishes, each led by a full-time priest. Several parishes together formed a diocese, each overseen by a **bishop**. Bishops interpreted Christian beliefs, managed Church property, and provided aid for the poor and the needy. The most powerful bishops—who were known as archbishops—governed Christians in the larger cities of the empire. The archbishops of the five leading Christian cities—Rome, Constantinople, Alexandria, Antioch, and Jerusalem—were called **patriarchs.**

During the A.D. 400s, the bishop of Rome began to claim authority over the other patriarchs. Originally addressed by the Greek or Latin word *papa*, his title today is rendered *pope* in the English language. Latin-speaking Christians in the West regarded the **pope** as the head of all of the churches. Greek-speaking Christians in the East, however, would not accept the authority of the pope over their churches. Eventually these churches and those of the Latin West separated from each other. In time, the Latin churches as a group became known as the Roman Catholic Church. The Greek churches as a group became known as the Eastern Orthodox Church.

SECTION 4 REVIEW

Recall

1. **Define:** sect, messiah, disciple, martyr, bishop, patriarch, pope
2. **Identify:** the Talmud, Jesus of Nazareth, Paul, the Gospels, Peter, Constantine, Judea, Jerusalem, Theodosius, Augustine

Critical Thinking

3. **Evaluate:** Why might the Romans in Judea especially have responded harshly toward anyone arousing strong feelings among the Jewish people?
4. **Analyze:** What was one major difference between the political structure of the Roman Re-

public and the early structure of the Christian Church?

Applying Concepts

5. **Innovation:** List some of the ways in which Christianity diverged from Judaism to become a distinct religion rather than a sect.

Roman Decline

During the A.D. 200s, at the same time as the Christian Church was gaining a following in the Roman Empire, Germanic tribes began to overrun the western half of the empire. In this poem, Rutilius Namatianus describes the devastation he saw on a journey from Rome to his native land, Gaul.

The fields of Gaul . . . have been disfigured by immeasurably long wars. . . . It would be wrong to overlook these endless disasters any longer; they are made worse by a failure to remedy them promptly. Now is the time to rebuild, after these fierce fires have ruined our farms, even if the best we can do is to put up a few huts for our shepherds.

—Rutilius Namatianus,
On His Return, c. A.D. 420

But Germanic tribes had always been a threat to the empire. Why were they so much more successful now than they were during the times of Marcus Aurelius?

The Empire's Problems

The Romans had a brief rest from cruel rulers and violent power struggles during the reign of the five Good Emperors. When Marcus Aurelius died in A.D. 180, however, a new period of violence and corruption brought the *Pax Romana* to an end.

Political Instability   The time of confusion began with the installation of Emperor Commodus, Marcus Aurelius's son. Like Nero, he spent so much state money on his own pleasures that he bankrupted the treasury. In A.D. 192 Commodus's own troops conspired to kill him.

From A.D. 192 to 284, army legions installed 28 emperors, only to kill most of them off in rapid succession. At one time the troops actually sold the position of emperor to the highest bidder. During this era of political disorder, Rome's armies were busier fighting each other than they were defending the empire's borders. Germanic tribes such as the Goths, the Alemanni, the Franks, and the Saxons repeatedly and successfully attacked the empire.

Economic Decline   Political instability led to economic decline. Warfare disrupted travel, production, and trade. For artisans and merchants, profits declined sharply, forcing many out of business. Invaders ruined many production centers in Gaul and the Rhine region. Warfare also destroyed farmland, causing food shortages, which sent food prices soaring.

To cope with the combination of falling incomes and soaring food prices, the government minted more coins. It hoped the increase would make it easier to pay its soldiers. However, because the government had already drained its stores of gold and silver, the new coins contained less of the precious metals—cutting their value. To continue getting the same return for their goods, merchants raised prices. Thus, the government's policy sparked severe **inflation**—a rise in prices responding to a decrease in the value of money—throughout the empire.

The spiraling decline in wealth affected almost all parts of the empire. To sustain a fighting force, the Roman government had to keep up with this inflation by continually raising soldiers' wages. Taxing landowners heavily seemed the only way to meet this expense, but as increased taxes made farming less profitable, more and more farmers abandoned their lands. As a result, the output of crops shrank even more, worsening the food shortage.

Unsuccessful Reforms

During the late A.D. 200s and early 300s, two emperors—Diocletian (dy uh KLEE shuhn) and later, Constantine—struggled to halt the decline of the empire. Their reforms did preserve the government in the eastern part of the empire for more than 1,000 years. In the west, they succeeded only in briefly delaying the Germanic tribes' invasion of Rome.

Diocletian   General Diocletian came to power in A.D. 284 by slaying the murderer of the preceding emperor. To hold back invasions, he raised the number of legions in the Roman army to 60 and spent his time traveling from one part of the empire to another to oversee defenses. Recognizing, however, that the empire had simply grown too large to be governed adequately by one person, Diocletian divided the empire into two administrative units. Diocletian set himself up as coemperor of the eastern provinces and set up General Maximian as coemperor of the western provinces.

Diocletian also tried to stop the empire's economic disintegration. To slow inflation, he issued an order called the Edict of Prices. In this edict he froze wages and set maximum prices for goods. Yet, even though the penalty for breaking the law was death, the edict failed completely. Citizens merely sold their goods on the black market—that is, through unofficial and illegal trade. To stop farmers from abandoning their lands and heavily taxed people from changing their professions to avoid being taxed, Diocletian required farmers who rented land from latifundia never to leave their land and all workers to remain at the same job throughout their lives.

Constantine   After Diocletian retired in A.D. 305, civil wars broke out again. Then, in A.D. 312, Constantine came to power.

Constantine worked to stabilize the empire once more. He made it legal for landowners to chain their workers to keep them on the farm. He declared most jobs hereditary; the sons of landowners, city officials, soldiers, farmers, and laborers *all* had to follow their fathers' occupations. In A.D. 330 he moved the capital of the eastern empire to the Greek town of Byzan-

tium—an ideal site for trade and well protected by natural barriers—and renamed it Constantinople.

Theodosius   After Constantine's death in A.D. 337, civil war flared anew until Theodosius I succeeded Constantine. During Theodosius's rule, the empire still suffered internal problems, and again the western half suffered more. To lessen the problems, Theodosius willed upon his death that the eastern and western sections should be declared separate empires. In A.D. 395 this division came to pass. To distinguish the two, historians refer to the eastern empire as the Byzantine Empire—after Byzantium, the town that became the capital—and the western empire as the Roman Empire.

Germanic Invasions

Germanic tribes entered the Roman Empire for many reasons. Beginning in the late A.D. 300s, large numbers of Germanic people migrated into the empire's territory because they sought a warmer climate and better grazing land. Others crossed the empire's borders hoping to gain a share of Rome's wealth. Most, however, came because they were fleeing the Huns, fierce nomadic invaders from central Asia.

Warrior Groups   Germanic warriors lived mostly by raising cattle and farming small plots. Despite their interest in the empire's trade goods, they themselves had little surplus to trade and were poor compared with the citizens of the empire. Each warrior group consisted of warriors, their families, and a chief. This chief governed the group and also led the warriors into battle. As the bands of warriors were numerous, so too were the chiefs. Often the only unifying factor among these Germanic groups was their language, which to the Romans sounded like unintelligible babbling. The Romans labeled the Germanic peoples barbarians, a reference to the sounds they made.

The Visigoths   In A.D. 378 a Germanic group called the Visigoths defeated a Roman army at Adrianople in the Balkan Peninsula, killing the eastern Roman emperor. His successor managed to buy peace by giving the Visigoths land in the Balkans. Then in A.D. 410 the Visigoth chief, Alaric, led his people into Italy, capturing and sacking Rome. After Alaric's death the Visigoths retreated into Gaul.

The Huns The next threat to the empire was invasion by the Huns. Led by their chief, Attila, the Huns raided the eastern empire; then they moved north into Gaul. In A.D. 451 the Romans and the Visigoths combined to fight and stop the Huns in central Gaul. Foiled in the provinces, Attila turned upon Italy. There his horde plundered the larger cities and terrified the people. Eventually plague and famine took their toll on the Huns. After Attila died in A.D. 453, they retreated to eastern Europe.

End of the Western Empire

With the Huns gone and Italy devastated, nothing remained to prevent Germanic tribes from taking over. The Vandals raided and thoroughly sacked Rome in A.D. 455. Franks and Goths divided Gaul among themselves. Finally, in A.D. 476, a German soldier named Odoacer seized control of Rome by killing the emperor and keeping the emperor's son Romulus Augus-

---

PERSONAL PROFILES

Zenobia, Rebel Against Rome

Many artists have portrayed Zenobia's beauty, learning, and wealth.

Zenobia, queen of Palmyra from A.D. 267 to 272, was one of the most celebrated women in the Roman Empire. As queen, she helped her husband lead the army and rule the lands entrusted to him. She became known for her leadership and bravery.

But Zenobia was not content with sharing the throne. In A.D. 267 she killed her husband and stepson and made herself sole ruler. Despite her treachery, the people of Palmyra supported her, for she was a just ruler who selected competent advisers and was tolerant of others' beliefs.

Zenobia wanted to expand Palmyra. In A.D. 269 she seized Egypt, conquered most of Asia Minor, and declared her country independent from Rome. From A.D. 270 until 272, Zenobia was the ruler of the eastern Roman Empire.

Then Aurelian became emperor of Rome. He marched two armies east to fight Palmyra. Zenobia's forces battled fiercely, even Zenobia herself sometimes joining them in battle. But in A.D. 272 they were at last defeated by the Romans. Palmyra's capital was then destroyed and Zenobia was captured and taken to Rome in gold chains.

After being promenaded down the streets of Rome she would have been slain, but the emperor was so impressed by Zenobia's courage that he spared her life. Because of her beauty, learning, and wealth, Zenobia became a popular figure in Roman high society. She married a senator and spent the rest of her life in a villa outside the city of Rome.

Reflecting on the Person
1. What traits and achievements made Zenobia memorable?
2. Would Zenobia have been more or less respected today? Why?

Learning from Maps
In A.D. 472 Germanic tribes controlled only about 20 percent of the territory that had belonged to the western Roman Empire. The Huns so thoroughly devastated the western Roman Empire, however, that by A.D. 476 these Germanic tribes were able to take over the remaining 80 percent of the weakened empire. **Why do you suppose most of these Germanic tribes focused their attacks on the western Roman Empire and not on the Byzantine Empire?**

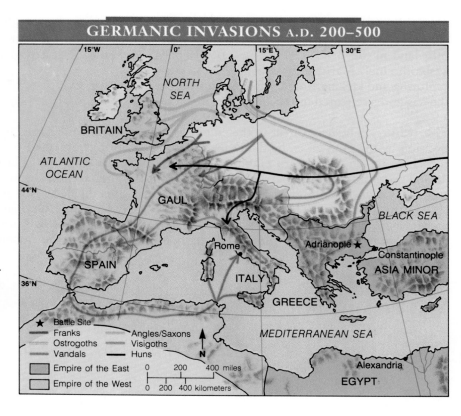

GERMANIC INVASIONS A.D. 200–500

tulus from power. Odoacer then named himself king of Italy.

Because Odoacer called himself king and never named a substitute emperor, people today refer to A.D. 476 as the year in which the Roman Empire "fell." However, this event no more signifies the collapse of the empire than any other event. Its end was caused by a complex interaction of events between A.D. 200 and 500.

More accurately, the Roman Empire ended in the late A.D. 400s. However, it did not mean the end of Roman culture, for the new Germanic rulers accepted the Latin language, Roman laws, and the Christian Church. In the Byzantine Empire, however, aspects of Roman culture were gradually supplanted by Hellenistic culture. By the A.D. 700s, Greek had even replaced Latin as the language of the Byzantine Empire.

SECTION 5 REVIEW

Recall

1. **Define:** inflation
2. **Identify:** Commodus, Diocletian, Constantine, Maximian, Alaric, Theodosius, Zenobia, Attila, Odoacer
3. **Locate:** Find Adrianople on the map on this page. What significant event occurred there during the time of the "fall" of the Roman Empire?

Critical Thinking

4. **Evaluate:** Which half of the Roman Empire would have benefited most by becoming officially separated from the other? Why?

5. **Synthesize:** Which do you think had a greater impact on the fall of Rome, internal difficulties or outside invaders? Why?

Applying Concepts

6. **Change:** Explain how conflict both created and destroyed the Roman Empire.

RELEVANT AND IRRELEVANT INFORMATION

Suppose you go to a department store sale and see tennis shoes that you want to buy.

"How much are they?" you ask.

"Prices have been slashed," the sales clerk replies.

"But how much?" you repeat.

"These shoes are a great deal!"

The clerk's replies do not help you. You try again.

"You've told me they're discounted and that I can get a great deal. But how much are they?"

"They're $39.95—plus tax."

Finally, you have the information you need.

Explanation

As you see in the example above, there are two kinds of information—relevant information and irrelevant information. Relevant information is information related to a particular topic, issue, or main idea. It defines, explains, illustrates, or describes a cause or consequence of a main idea. Irrelevant information is information not related to the topic. In the example above, the fact that the shoes are a great deal is irrelevant. What is relevant is the price —$39.95. When you are studying history, you also need to be able to distinguish relevant from irrelevant information.

Use the following steps to help you *distinguish relevant information from irrelevant information:*

- Read or listen carefully and determine the topic or main idea.
- Examine each sentence if you are working with written material or review your notes item by item if the material was oral.
- Decide if each sentence or item deals with the main idea by looking for information that defines, explains, illustrates, or describes a cause or consequence of the main idea.

Example

These steps are used to distinguish relevant from irrelevant information in the following paragraph, the topic of which is the importance of the Italian peninsula in ancient times.

The Greeks were interested in colonizing Italy for several reasons, the most important of which was Italy's central location in the Mediterranean. (cause) A narrow boot-shaped peninsula, Italy extends from Europe toward Africa, dividing the Mediterranean almost in half. (cause) Thus Italy was ideally situated to be the center of trade among three continents: Asia, Europe, and Africa. (consequence) Italy's rich soil and moist climate also attracted Greek colonists. (cause) The silt washing down Italy's rivers, however, created mosquito-infested swamps at the mouths of rivers. (irrelevant)

By the time Greek colonists arrived, many peoples inhabited Italy, including Umbrians, Latins, and Oscans. (irrelevant)

Application

Use the outlined steps to determine which of the following statements are relevant or irrelevant to the main idea—"The Decline of the Roman Empire." Explain.

1. During the A.D. 200s, at the same time as the Christian Church was gaining a following in the Roman Empire, Germanic tribes began to overrun the western half of the empire.
2. From A.D. 192 to 284, army legions installed 28 emperors, only to kill most of them off in rapid succession.
3. The Romans built aqueducts throughout Europe.
4. Political instability led to economic decline.
5. The Roman baths served as popular meeting places for social and business purposes.
6. Long after the Roman Empire had collapsed, Latin continued in use as the written language of the Roman Catholic Church.

Practice

Turn to Practicing Skills on page 167 of the Chapter Review for further practice in distinguishing relevant from irrelevant information.

CHAPTER 6 REVIEW

HISTORICAL SIGNIFICANCE

The Romans established a common Greco-Roman culture among the diverse peoples of the Roman Empire. As people throughout the provinces built upon Greco-Roman ideas, accomplishments, and traditions, they became more closely unified. Rome's legal system, social and political hierarchies, engineering feats, and styles of art and architecture formed the foundations and structures of many provincial cities. Christianity, another legacy of Greco-Roman culture, also helped to unify the diverse peoples in the empire.

Only when Rome's generals began battling for power among themselves, pitting one Roman legion against another, did the empire begin to decline. These frequent civil wars triggered a chain of events that led to changes in the very structure of Roman society and, eventually, to economic and political collapse.

Lasting legacies of the Roman Empire to Western civilization are its Latin language, which provided the roots of the Romance languages; and its engineering skills, its transmission of Greek culture, and Christianity.

SUMMARY

For a summary of Chapter 6, see the Unit 2 Synopsis on pages 204–207.

USING KEY TERMS

A. Write one or two sentences explaining the difference between the terms in each of these pairs in the context of the history of Rome or the Church or both. Use the words in parentheses in your explanations.

1. patrician, plebeian (noble)
2. consul, tribune (class)
3. dictator, triumvirate (rule)
4. messiah, martyr (Christian)
5. patriarch, pope (bishop)

B. Write one or two sentences to define the meaning of each of these terms and to describe a context in which you might use it.

6. sect
7. inflation
8. republic
9. bishop

REVIEWING FACTS

1. **Explain:** What was the main source of conflict between Rome and Carthage?

2. **Describe:** In what way did Rome's political system change when Augustus Caesar came to power?
3. **Explain:** What was the difference between the *jus gentium* and the *jus civile*?
4. **Discuss:** How did Roman governors make provincial cities more like Rome?
5. **Tell:** How did Augustus strengthen the bonds between the city of Rome and provincial cities?

THINKING CRITICALLY

1. **Apply:** How did the reforms introduced during Marius's reign hasten the end of the Roman Republic?
2. **Analyze:** What evidence suggests that Roman society was more stable during the republic than during the time of the empire?
3. **Evaluate:** In what ways did the Romans' treatment of the peoples they conquered differ from the ways in which other victors usually treated the peoples they conquered? How might the Romans' attitudes toward conquered peoples have strengthened the empire?
4. **Analyze:** What conditions in Rome might have caused people to convert to Christianity? Why?

ANALYZING CONCEPTS

1. **Conflict:** Describe a conflict between nations that has occurred in the recent past and explain the ways in which it is similar to conflicts between Romans and other peoples of the Mediterranean region.
2. **Change:** What factors necessitated a change in the Roman government by the time of Augustus?
3. **Cultural diffusion:** How might Roman roads have helped to foster cultural diffusion?
4. **Innovation:** What was the basis of the religious controversy among the Jews of Palestine? How might this division have furthered Christianity's evolution as a separate religion?

PRACTICING SKILLS

A student preparing a talk about the fall of the Roman Empire wants to illustrate her speech with photographs of Roman ruins. Which of the following photographs would be relevant to her topic? Identify each image that would be appropriate and explain how it applies.

- a. the Forum
- b. the Pantheon
- c. Circus Maximus
- d. an aqueduct still in use in Spain
- e. the Colosseum

GEOGRAPHY IN HISTORY

1. **Location:** How did Italy's location help the Romans to dominate Mediterranean trade?
2. **Place:** What geographic features of the Italian peninsula discouraged Italians from seafaring?
3. **Relationships within places:** How did the Tarquins change the environment? How did this alteration promote the growth of Rome?

TRACING CHRONOLOGY

Refer to the time line below to answer these questions.
1. What happened when the Romans drove out the Tarquin kings?
2. In what year did the *Pax Romana* come to an end? What event marks its beginning?
3. Which of the individuals named on the time line do you think most deeply and extensively affected Western civilization? Why?

LINKING PAST AND PRESENT

Recently, the executive branch of the United States government has tried to win the power to veto parts of budget laws passed by the legislative branch. Do you think the executive branch should be granted this power? Why or why not? Use examples from Roman history to support your answer.

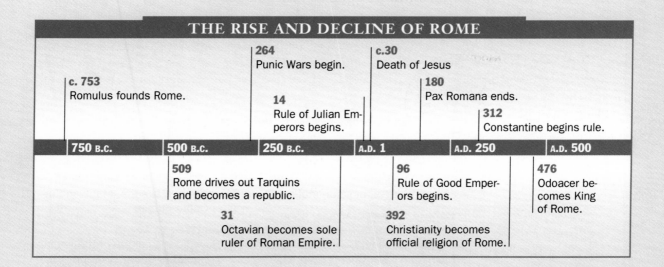

THE RISE AND DECLINE OF ROME

- **c. 753** Romulus founds Rome.
- **264** Punic Wars begin.
- **14** Rule of Julian Emperors begins.
- **c.30** Death of Jesus
- **180** Pax Romana ends.
- **312** Constantine begins rule.

| 750 B.C. | 500 B.C. | 250 B.C. | A.D. 1 | A.D. 250 | A.D. 500 |

- **509** Rome drives out Tarquins and becomes a republic.
- **31** Octavian becomes sole ruler of Roman Empire.
- **96** Rule of Good Emperors begins.
- **392** Christianity becomes official religion of Rome.
- **476** Odoacer becomes King of Rome.

India's Great Civilization

1 Origins of Hindu India

2 Rise of Buddhism

3 Indian Empires

The Mahabharata, an epic poem written in ancient India, relates an intriguing event. A battle raged, but the warrior prince Arjuna did not want to fight. After all, among his foes were members of his own family. Arjuna took his case to the god Krishna: "O Krishna, when I see my own people ready to fight and eager for battle, my limbs shudder, my mouth is dry, my body shivers, and my hair stands on end. . . . I can see no good in killing my own kinsmen."

Krishna answered, "As a Kshatriya [a member of the warrior caste], your duty is to fight a righteous battle. . . . Arise, O Arjuna, and be determined to fight. Get ready for battle without thought of pleasure and pain, gain and loss, victory and defeat."

As a warrior, Arjuna understood Krishna's words. A warrior must fight. It was his duty.

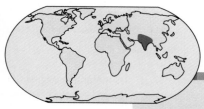

CHAPTER PREVIEW

Key Terms to Define: rajah, epic, *varna, jati*, dharma, reincarnation, karma, ahimsa, nirvana, stupa

People to Meet: Aryans, Kshatriyas, Brahmans, Vaisyas, Sudras, pariahs, Buddha, Chandragupta Maurya, Asoka, Chandragupta I, Chandragupta II

Places to Discover: Indus River Valley, Ganges Plain, Hindu Kush Mountains, Magadha, Mauryan Empire, Gupta Empire

Objectives to Learn:
1. How did the culture of the Aryan conquerors and that of the people they conquered develop into the culture of Hindu India?

Temples such as the Visvanatha in Khajuraho, India, are dedicated to divinities.

2. In what ways is Hinduism both a religion and a way of life in India?

3. Why did Buddhism appeal to many people in India, Southeast Asia, and East Asia?

4. What achievements of the Gupta dynasty resulted in the era known as India's Golden Age?

Concepts to Understand:

•Movement—Aryans invade the Indian subcontinent and bring new ideas and practices. Section 1

•Innovation—Hinduism and Buddhism emerge and become the dominant religions in much of Asia. Sections 1,2

•Cultural diffusion—Mauryan and Gupta rulers bring unity to northern India and encourage cultural achievements. Section 3

Origins of Hindu India

Into the Indus River Valley raced horse-drawn chariots carrying tall, light-skinned warriors—Aryans from eastern Europe north of the Black and Caspian seas. The invasion began around 1200 B.C. Over several generations, waves of Aryans swept through passes in the Hindu Kush Mountains into the Indus River Valley and from there into northern India.

Learning from Artifacts *This Vedic sculpture from about 100 A.D. depicts a* Yakshi, *or female nature spirit.* **How did Vedic culture influence religious life in early India?**

Aryans

After conquering the people of the Indus River Valley, the Aryans moved southeast into the Ganges Plain. There they subdued the local inhabitants and developed a new civilization that eventually spread over much of South Asia. Aspects of this civilization—especially its religious contributions—endure today.

Ways of Life The Aryans were loosely organized into tribes of nomadic herders. Each tribe was led by a **rajah,** or chief. Ancient Aryan legends and hymns describe people who delighted in waging war, gambling on chariot races, and singing and dancing at festivals. Cattle were the basis of their diet and economy, even serving as money. Wealth was measured in cattle, and so the Aryans raided each other's herds. They were often at war.

The fertile Indus Valley was ideal for farming, and the Aryans soon settled down into an agricultural way of life. Dozens of Aryan words describe cattle, indicating their continued prominence in Aryan life. Cattle provided meat, fresh milk, and ghee, or liquid butter. The Aryans also hunted game and butchered sheep and goats from their herds. Later, their herds would be considered so sacred that a ban was placed on eating meat. The Aryans also ate cucumbers, bananas, and barley cakes.

Men dominated the Aryan world. Although a woman had some say in choosing a husband, the man she married expected no challenge to his authority. Even so, women took part in religious ceremonies and social affairs, and they were allowed to remarry if they were widowed—freedoms they would lose in the centuries to come. Both girls and boys from families of high rank attended school, where they learned Aryan traditions.

Language and Traditions   As a nomadic people, the Aryans had no written language. Sanskrit, their spoken language, evolved slowly and became one of the major languages of India. As part of the great Indo-European language family, Sanskrit has many of the same root words as English, Spanish, French, and German.

The Aryan warrior-herders sang rousing hymns and recited **epics**, long poems celebrating their heroes. For centuries these hymns and poems were passed by word of mouth from generation to generation. Families of warriors and priests were responsible for preserving this oral heritage. Over and over they repeated the legends, striving for complete accuracy.

Eventually, the Aryans developed a written form of Sanskrit. Priests collected the hymns, poems, legends, and religious rituals into holy books known as Vedas (VAY duhz), or "Books of Knowledge," which formed the basis of Aryan religious practices.

Indeed, the Vedas are extremely valuable sources of knowledge, for without them historians would know little about the Aryans. Unlike the Indus River Valley people, the Aryans left no artifacts or structures. Whatever we know of their life and culture we know from the Vedas. In fact, Indian history from 1200 to 500 B.C. is known as the Vedic Age. The oldest of the four Vedas, the *Rig-Veda*, dates from around 1000 B.C. It records legends that tell us about Aryan life. The *Rig-Veda* is the world's oldest religious text still in use.

Social Structure   The Vedas reveal the complex social system of ancient India. The invading Aryans brought a system of four main social classes, or *varnas*. At first the warriors, called Kshatriyas (kuh SHA tree yuhz), were the most honored *varna*. They were followed by the priests, or Brahmans; merchants, artisans, and farmers, called Vaisyas (VISH yuhz); and unskilled laborers and servants, known as Sudras (SHOO druhz).

Only priests and warrior families were allowed to hear and recite the Vedas. Over the years, rituals grew more secret and complex, and priests replaced warriors as the most honored members of society. The priests alone knew how to make sacrifices properly and to repeat the

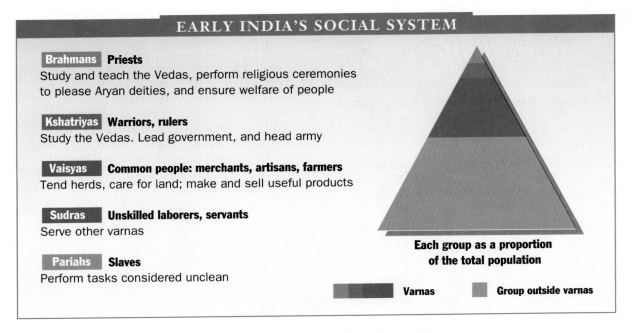

EARLY INDIA'S SOCIAL SYSTEM

Brahmans **Priests**
Study and teach the Vedas, perform religious ceremonies to please Aryan deities, and ensure welfare of people

Kshatriyas **Warriors, rulers**
Study the Vedas. Lead government, and head army

Vaisyas **Common people: merchants, artisans, farmers**
Tend herds, care for land; make and sell useful products

Sudras **Unskilled laborers, servants**
Serve other varnas

Pariahs **Slaves**
Perform tasks considered unclean

Each group as a proportion of the total population

■ Varnas   ■ Group outside varnas

Learning from Charts *India's early social system classified people according to their caste.* **How did belonging to a certain caste affect what people did to earn a living?**

appropriate hymns. The social system changed to reflect the importance of priests.

Each *varna* had its own duties and took pride in doing them well. The Brahmans performed the elaborate rituals and studied the Vedas; only they could teach the Vedas. As warriors, Kshatriyas took charge of the army and the government. They led the councils of elders who ran small villages. Kshatriyas could study the Vedas but were not allowed to teach them. Vaisyas had the important tasks of tending the cattle, lending money, trading goods, and caring for the land. The Sudras' job was to serve the other *varnas*. They worked in the fields and acted as servants.

By 500 B.C. the division among the four *varnas* had become more rigid. *Varnas* were divided into smaller groups knows as **jati**. *Jati* were formed according to occupations: shoemakers,

potters, farmers, and so on. Priests were higher than cultivators, and cultivators were higher than carpenters, for example. *Jati* had their own rules for diet, marriage, and social customs. Groups lived in separate neighborhoods and did not mix socially with others.

Centuries later, Europeans named the Indian system of *varnas* and *jati* the caste system. The word *caste* has no one definition, but how it worked is clear. Within the system people were always ranked. They were born into a group, and that group could not be changed. People married within their own group. In fact, that group determined a great deal about people's everyday lives. Members of the group lived in the same neighborhoods and did not mix socially with those outside.

Outside the system of *varnas* and *jati* were a group later called the pariahs. They did work

Hindu Beliefs

Hinduism encompasses several religious systems. Many Hindu symbols and traditions have ancient origins.

The Mahabharata, a Hindu epic, took shape in the Gupta period. This illustration from the epic shows a battle between Arjuna and Karna.

Hindu temples, towering into the sky, were intended to symbolize a cosmic pillar, allowing for communication with the gods.

that was considered unclean, such as skinning animals and tanning their hides for leather. Sometimes called "outcastes" or "untouchables," the pariahs lived outside the villages and were shunned by most other people.

Concept of Duty   The Vedas outlined the **dharma**, or duties, of the males who belonged to each *varna*. Members of each *varna* were urged to do their duty. The epic poem called the *Mahabharata* (muh HAH BAH rah tuh) makes the concept clear. One eloquent section, called the *Bhagavad Gita* (BUHG uh vuhd GEE tah), or "Song of the Lord," includes the story you read at the beginning of this chapter. Arjuna's decision—to fight no matter what the personal cost—illustrates the importance of dharma in Indian life. As a warrior, Arjuna had to do his duty, even if it meant fighting against family.

The concept of dharma included doing what was proper for one's age. For instance, a male student would follow an occupation that was appropriate for his class. He then took a wife, and assumed responsibility for a family. In old age, he retired. As he neared death, he withdrew from his friends and family to pray. A woman was educated in household tasks. She married and served her husband and family until he died or retired, at which time she was expected to retire from active life and be taken care of by her sons and daughters-in-law. This concept of duty affected every member of society.

India's Two Epics   The tale of Arjuna is a small part of the *Mahabharata*, which is 100,000 verses in length—as long as the first five books of the Bible. The epic—like the Bible—is a collection of writings by several authors. Some

Siva, an important Hindu god in earliest times, dances in a circle of fire, symbolizing the cycle of creation, death, and rebirth.

Hindus bathe in the Ganges, India's most sacred river. They believe the water of the Ganges will purify them.

Reflecting on the Times
How do these images show the timeless, universal concerns addressed by Hinduism?

characters are historical, while other characters represent human ideals and various deities. Woven into the story of two families' struggle for power are discussions of religion and philosophy.

One passage tells of how the need for a king arose when dharma no longer guided people in everyday life.

Bhishma said: . . . Neither kingship nor king was there in the beginning, neither scepter nor the bearer of the scepter. All people protected one another by means of righteous conduct (dharma). Thus, while protecting another by means of righteous conduct, O Bharata, men eventually fell into a state of spiritual lassitude [weariness]. Then delusion overcame them . . . their sense of righteous conduct was lost. When understanding was lost, all men . . . became victims of greed.

Learning from Art *Half elephant and half human, Ganesa is the Hindu god of wisdom and good fortune.* **What is the primary religious goal of each Hindu?**

Later, the God Vishnu chooses " . . . that one person among mortals who alone is worthy of high eminence." A man named Virajas is brought forth, and he becomes the first king.

A second epic, the well-loved *Ramayana*, grew to 24,000 verses before it was written down. It presents the moving tale of Rama and Sita (SEE tuh). Rama was the ideal king; Sita, his faithful wife. Vividly describing the struggle between good and evil, the *Ramayana* tells how the demon Ravana captures Sita. When Rama finds that she is missing, he cries:

Sita! Gentle Sita! If you have wanted to prove my love, if you are hiding from us, let the agony of my fear suffice. Come to me, my love, come to me!"

He stood there, both his arms held wide, as though half hoping she might run forward to his embrace. The country lay very still around him. Only the old tree shivered in every leafy spray and seemed to wring its hands for pity.

Slowly that gleam of hope quite faded, and his arms fell to his sides.

Rama at first doubted Sita; but later she is saved, and they are reunited. Like other Indian epics, the *Ramayana* ends happily, with good winning over evil.

Indian Beliefs

The Aryan conquerors believed in many deities and thought their gods and goddesses had power over the forces of nature. They worshiped Agni, the god of fire; Indra, the god of thunder and war; and Usha, the goddess of dawn. Aryan priests created elaborate rituals and offered sacrifices to appease the gods and win their favor.

Over the centuries, as political and social organizations evolved, the Aryan religion slowly changed into Hinduism and became the national religion of India.

Universal Spirit   Hinduism was not founded on the teachings of one person, nor did it have one holy book. Instead it was based on different beliefs and practices, many of which had their roots in the Vedas and the Indian epics.

Other ideas that became part of Hinduism came from religious thinkers who had grown discontented with complex Vedic rituals. Between 800 and 400 B.C., their search for wisdom and truth was reflected in the religious writings known as the *Upanishads* (oo PAN uh SHADZ).

The *Upanishads* tell of a universal spirit present within all life, "a light that shines beyond all things on earth." All living things, according to these writings, have souls. Thus, Hindus came to regard animals as sacred and forbade killing them. All souls, say the *Upanishads*, are part of the one eternal spirit, sometimes called Brahman Nerguna. Their bodies tie them to the material world, but only for a short time. To know true freedom, a soul must be separated from the material world and united with Brahman Nerguna: "As a lump of salt thrown in water dissolves, and cannot be taken out again as salt, though wherever we taste the water it is salt."

The authors of the *Upanishads* taught that forms of self-denial such as fasting helped people achieve union with the universal spirit. They encouraged the practice of yoga, a discipline that combines physical and mental exercises designed to help one achieve a state of tranquillity.

Cycle of Rebirth   Another idea that came from the *Upanishads* was that of **reincarnation,** or the rebirth of the soul. Hindus believe the soul passes through many lifetimes before it finally achieves union with the universal spirit. The *Upanishads* offer this picture of rebirth:

As a caterpillar, having reached the end of a blade of grass, takes hold of another blade, then draws its body from the first, so the Self, having reached the end of his body, takes hold of another body, then draws itself from the first.

The cycle of rebirth is determined by a principle called **karma.** According to this principle, how a person lives his or her life determines what form the person will take in the next life. To move toward the universal spirit, one must live a good life and fulfill one's dharma. For example, a conscientious diplomat, a Kshatriya, might be reborn as a Brahman. The souls of those who fail to fulfill their dharma, however, might be reborn in a lower *varna*, or perhaps even as snakes or insects.

The concept of karma creates the desire to live a good life, for "By good deeds a man becomes what is good, by evil deeds what is bad." Out of that desire arose the practice of nonviolence toward all living things—still important to Hindus today. Called **ahimsa** (uh HIHM sah), this practice requires the believer to protect humans, animals, and even insects and plants.

The ultimate aim of life was *moksha*, or release from the pain and suffering of rebirth after rebirth. In *moksha* a person finds freedom from reincarnation in a state of complete oneness with Brahman Nerguna. Hindus taught that prayer, religious rituals, strict self-denial, and rejection of all worldly possessions helped a person to achieve *moksha*.

SECTION 1 REVIEW

Recall
1. **Define:** rajah, epic, *varna, jati,* dharma, reincarnation, karma, ahimsa
2. **Identify:** Aryans, Sanskrit, Vedas, *Mahabharata, Bhagavad Gita, Ramayana,* Hinduism, *Upanishads*
3. **Locate:** How did geography affect Aryan life?

4. **Explain:** How did the Aryans influence the development of early Indian society?

Critical Thinking
5. **Apply:** Illustrate the Hindu concept of dharma by telling the story of Arjuna.
6. **Analyze:** Compare the Hindu concept of *moksha* and the beliefs of Western religions concerning the afterlife, including the meaning of each concept and how it encourages correct behavior.

Applying Concepts
7. **Movement:** Describe how the Aryan invasion affected Indian culture.

Rise of Buddhism

During the 500s B.C., changes occurred in Indian religious life. Many devout Hindus became dissatisfied with external rituals and wanted a more spiritual faith. They left the towns and villages and looked for solitude in the hills and forests. Through meditation, many of these religious seekers developed new insights and became religious teachers. Their ideas and practices often led to the rise of new religions. The most influential of the new religions was Buddhism.

The Buddha

Siddharta Gautama (sid DAHR tuh GOWT uh muh), the founder of Buddhism, began his life as a Kshatriya prince. Born the son of a prince in northern India around 566 B.C., Gautama was raised in luxury. As a young man he continued to live a sheltered life, shielded from sickness and poverty. Tradition states that one day Gautama's charioteer drove him around his estates, and for the first time Gautama saw sickness, old age, and death. Shocked at these scenes of misery, Gautama decided to find out why people suffered and how suffering could be ended. At the age of 29, he left his wife and newborn son and wandered throughout India in what is known as the Great Renunciation.

For seven years Gautama lived as a hermit, seeking the truth through fasting and self-denial. This did not lead him to the truth, however. One day, while meditating under a tree, Gautama gained a flash of insight that he felt gave him an answer to the problem of suffering. He began to share with others the meaning of his "enlightenment." Dressed in a yellow robe, he preached his message to people and began to gather followers. His closest friends began calling him the Buddha, or "Enlightened One."

Four Noble Truths The Buddha developed a new religious philosophy. He outlined his main ideas in the Four Noble Truths. First, as he had discovered, all people suffer and know sorrow, an idea that he explained in the following words:

O monks, I will tell you the truth about suffering. Suffering is birth, suffering is old age, suffering is sickness, suffering is death. You are bound to that which you hate: [which causes] suffering; you are separated from that which you love: suffering; you do not obtain that which you desire: suffering. To cling to bodies, to sensations, to forms, to impressions, to perceptions: suffering, suffering, suffering.

Next, said the Buddha, people suffer because their desires bind them to the cycle of rebirth. He told his followers:

The thirst for existence leads from rebirth to rebirth; lust and pleasure follow. Power alone can satisfy lust. The thirst for power, the thirst for pleasure, the thirst for existence; there, O monks, is the origin of suffering.

The third truth, said the Buddha, was that people could end their suffering by eliminating their desires. And according to the fourth truth, one could eliminate desire by following the Eightfold Path.

The Eightfold Path The Buddha urged his disciples to do eight things: know the truth, resist evil, say nothing to hurt others, respect life, work for the good of others, free their minds of evil, control their thoughts, and practice meditation. By avoiding extremes and following the Eightfold Path, a person could attain **nirvana,** a state of freedom from the cycle of rebirth.

The Ajanta Caves

In 1819 several British soldiers were on a tiger hunt along the rushing Wagurna River in the Deccan region of India. One day they made an astonishing discovery. On the inner side of a 70-foot (22-meter) granite cliff, they found 29 caves carved into the rock. What they found inside the caves was even more amazing: elaborate rooms decorated with many fine sculptures and splendid wall paintings.

The caves became known as the Ajanta caves. Buddhist monks who lived between A.D. 300 and 600 had carved out these rooms to serve as monasteries, temples, and shelters for their monastic community.

Study of the caves has shown that the monks began their construction by carving out the ceilings of the chambers. Then they worked their way downward, cutting out the walls and floors. Finally, sculptors and painters decorated the entrances and interiors of the caves with murals, statues, and carved pillars.

To prepare the cave walls for painting, artists plastered them with a coating made from clay, cow ma-nure, animal hair, and crushed rice husks. Next, they applied a smooth coat of lime, or plaster, over the coating. On the plaster, they outlined their figures with cinnabar, a red mineral. They modeled the faces and bodies skillfully, making each one an individual with a distinct personality.

Once they had completed the sketches, the artists painted the graceful figures with rich colors made from plants and minerals. After coloring an entire wall, they drew flowing brown or black lines around the figures to emphasize their shapes and provide a sense of movement. When the artists had finished the paintings, they polished the surfaces of the wall.

Most of the Ajanta cave paintings illustrate *jataka* (JAH duh kuh) tales, stories from the Buddha's previous lives. Some paintings show everyday life in early India. Others show Gupta kings and queens and their royal courts. Still others are images of ships, elaborate buildings, and animals such as elephants, bulls, and tigers. Art historians believe that the subjects and styles of the Ajanta cave paintings spread to other parts of India and eventually influenced Buddhist art throughout Asia.

Responding to the Arts

1. Who built the Ajanta caves? How and why did they build them?
2. What subjects do the sculptures and paintings show?

Nirvana is not a place, like heaven, but a state of extinction. In fact, the root meaning of the word *nirvana* is "a blowing out," as of a candle. In nirvana, a person would be in a state of oneness with the universe.

Although the Buddha taught that desire causes suffering, he did not teach that people must always be poor. He encouraged hard work and diligence. It was all right to be wealthy as long as wealth was gained lawfully and used well, which meant sharing it with others.

The Buddha rejected the *varna* system. He taught that a person's place in life depended on the person, not on the person's birth. He taught that anyone, regardless of caste, could attain enlightenment. He did not believe in the Hindu gods. He believed in reincarnation but taught that one could escape the cycle of suffering and reach nirvana by following the Eightfold Path.

Spread of Buddhism

The Buddha spent 45 years teaching the Four Noble Truths and the Eightfold Path. He gathered thousands of disciples around him. After their master's death, traveling monks carried the new religion beyond India and eventually around the world.

First, they took it northward through snowy mountain passes to central Asia. Missionaries and merchants carried it eastward along the trade routes to China, and Chinese Buddhists later carried it to Korea and Japan.

Buddhist missionaries joined traders heading southeast across the Indian Ocean to Siam, Malaysia, and Indonesia. As a result of these efforts, Buddhism became the dominant faith in East Asia.

Buddhism's spread to new areas led to a flowering of architecture and the arts. Buddhist architects built **stupas,** or large stone mounds over the bones of Buddhist holy people. Stupas were known for their elaborately carved stone railings and gateways. Paintings and statues of the Buddha, carved of polished stone or wood covered with gilt, adorned stupas and cave temples. Exquisite smaller statues were made from fine porcelain. Books about the Buddha's life and teaching were often beautifully illustrated.

Divisions As Buddhism spread, disagreements developed among the Buddha's followers. Two distinct branches of Buddhism soon arose. One branch, known as Theravada, was established in South Asia. It remained fairly close in practice to the original teachings of the Buddha, regarding him as simply a teacher.

The other branch of Buddhism was known as Mahayana. It became dominant in China, Korea, and Japan. Mahayana encouraged the worship of Buddha as a divine being and savior.

Today, only a few Indians are Buddhists. Most are Hindus, with a few Jains, Christians, and others. Recently, however, Buddhism has gained new followers in India, especially among the pariahs. And outside India, Buddhism has a vast following in the West as well as the East.

SECTION 2 REVIEW

Recall

1. **Define:** nirvana, stupa
2. **Identify:** Siddharta Gautama, Four Noble Truths
3. **Locate:** Find the Asian countries to which monks and merchants carried the teachings of the Buddha: China, Japan, Korea, Burma, Malaysia, Indonesia. How did the monks and merchants help to assure the survival of Buddhism as a worldwide religion?

Critical Thinking

4. **Synthesize:** Compare Hinduism and Buddhism, explaining which Hindu beliefs and practices the Buddha accepted and which he rejected.
5. **Hypothesize:** Recently, a number of India's pariahs have converted from Hinduism to Buddhism. Explain the special appeal that Buddhism might have for pariahs.

Applying Concepts

6. **Innovation:** Decide how your own life and goals would be different if you tried to live by the Four Noble Truths and the Eightfold Path.

Indian Empires

Despite the formidable mountain barriers in the north, India has never been completely cut off from other lands. The Aryans marched through the mountain passes to invade the Indus River Valley; later, others followed. In the 500s B.C., Persian ruler Darius I conquered lands in the Indus River Valley. Alexander the Great invaded the same area in 327 B.C., and Indian merchants carried on a busy trade with the Roman Empire. In all that time, however, no Indian king or foreign conqueror had ever succeeded in uniting the separate kingdoms into one Indian nation.

At the time of Darius's invasion, one Indian kingdom, Magadha, was expanding in the north. King Bimbisara, who ruled Magadha from 542 to 495 B.C., added to its territory by conquest and marriage. He appointed trained officials and sent ambassadors to other Indian kingdoms. To make travel easier, he had roads and bridges built. Although Magadha declined after Bimbisara's death, it was to become the center of India's first empire.

The Mauryan Empire

At the time of Alexander's invasion, Magadha was only one of many small warring states in northern India. Then, in 321 B.C., a military officer named Chandragupta Maurya (CHUHN druh GUP tuh MAH oor yuh) overthrew the Magadhan king and proclaimed himself ruler.

Chandragupta Maurya was a skilled administrator whose achievements included the development of an efficient postal system. He kept control of his empire by maintaining a strong army and by using an extensive spy network. He founded a Mauryan kingdom that included most of northern and central India and lasted until 184 B.C.

Asoka's Enlightened Rule   Indian civilization blossomed during the reign of Chandragupta's grandson, Asoka (uh SOH kuh). Asoka's rule began in 274 B.C. with fierce wars of conquest. His merciless armies swept across the plains and into the forests and cities, hunting down and killing their enemies. He built an empire that covered two-thirds of the subcontinent. Indian accounts tell of 100,000 people being killed in these wars. An even greater number were captured and enslaved or died of starvation and disease.

After one particularly brutal battle, according to his own account, Asoka rode out to view the battlefield. As he looked on the bloodied bodies of the dead and maimed, the Indian ruler was horrified.

The experience changed his life. Determined never again to rule by force and terror, Asoka renounced war. Henceforth, he announced, he would follow the teachings of the Buddha and become a man of peace. Asoka kept his word. During his reign, missionaries spread the Buddha's message of respect for life and truth throughout India and other parts of Asia. Later, other missionaries carried Buddhism to Syria, Egypt, Sri Lanka, and Southeast Asia.

Asoka issued laws stressing compassion and concern for other human beings. To make sure these laws became widely known, Asoka wrote them in the local languages rather than in Sanskrit. The laws, known today as the Rock Edicts, were carved on rocks and on tall stone pillars throughout the vast empire.

Asoka's public projects reflected the same care for people. He provided free hospitals and veterinary clinics. He built fine roads, with rest houses and shade trees for the travelers' comfort.

Asoka personally encouraged the spread of Buddhism. His daughter made a pilgrimage to

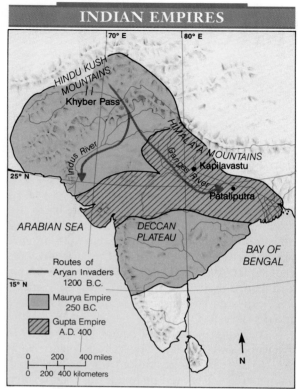

70° E   80° E

HINDU KUSH MOUNTAINS
Khyber Pass

Indus River

HIMALAYA MOUNTAINS

Ganges River
Kapilavastu

25° N

Pataliputra

ARABIAN SEA

DECCAN PLATEAU

BAY OF BENGAL

Routes of
Aryan Invaders
1200 B.C.

15° N

Maurya Empire
250 B.C.

Gupta Empire
A.D. 400

0   200   400 miles
0   200   400 kilometers

N

Learning from Maps *Under Mauryan rule, India's borders were expanded to include new territories. Gupta rule, on the other hand, resulted in a weakening of Indian unity.* **What territories were conquered by the Mauryan Empire? How was the Gupta Empire weakened?**

obtain a branch of the tree that the Buddha was sitting under when he attained enlightenment. A Buddhist mission that Asoka sent to Sri Lanka reportedly resulted in the conversion of 40,000 people.

But even though he promoted Buddhism, Asoka permitted his non-Buddhist subjects to continue to practice Hinduism if they wished. The Hindu caste system continued.

Collapse of Mauryan Empire The Mauryan Empire declined after Asoka's death in 232 B.C. because his successors were not as enlightened as he was. They levied heavy taxes on the goods sold by merchants and seized large portions of the crops grown by peasants. Such harsh policies caused the people to turn against the

Mauryas. When the last Mauryan ruler was murdered in 184 B.C., northern India again split into many small warring kingdoms.

The Gupta Empire

After the Mauryan Empire, 500 years passed before much of India was again united. About A.D. 310, Chandragupta I began to build an empire. He was not related to Chandragupta Maurya, but like that earlier ruler he made Magadha the base of his kingdom.

Chandragupta I introduced the Gupta dynasty, which ruled northern India for more than 200 years. The arts and sciences flourished, and the Gupta period would later be called India's Golden Age.

The Guptas governed a much smaller empire than the Mauryas. They never gained control of the Indus River Valley or of the Deccan, the broad plateau that forms most of India's southern peninsula. The Guptas did manage to build a strong state, however, and worked to maintain unquestioned authority. They trained soldiers; they used spies and political assassins. In short, they did whatever they felt had to be done to maintain power.

FOOTNOTES TO HISTORY

HIGHWAY REST STOPS

The highway rest stops that travelers enjoy today had their counterpart in the Mauryan Empire. Asoka set up wayside resting places to provide lodging and wells along highways throughout his empire. Many included stone pillars engraved with Buddhist teachings—Asoka's Rock Edicts. In one of these, Asoka explained:

I have ordered banyan trees to be planted along the roads to give shade to men and animals. I have ordered mango groves to be planted. I have ordered wells to be dug every [half-mile]*, and I have ordered rest houses built.*

— The Edicts of Asoka

Gupta Religion   The Gupta rulers encouraged learning based on the ideas in the *Upanishads*. They made Hinduism the religion of their empire. Hindu temples were built—elaborate structures with brightly painted sculptures depicting tales in the *Mahabharata* and the *Ramayana*. Although each temple had its presiding god or goddess, the Hindus viewed the many deities as different ways of worshiping Brahman Nerguna, the eternal spirit.

Gupta Life   The Gupta Empire reached its height under Chandragupta II, who ruled from A.D. 375 to 415. Faxian (fah SHEE ehn), a Buddhist monk from China, traveled to India and in one of the first historical accounts of Indian life, he recorded in his diary:

> *In the Gupta Empire, people are numerous and happy; only those who cultivate the royal land have to pay [in] grain. . . . If they want to go, they go; if they want to stay, they stay. The king governs without decapitation [cutting off heads] or corporal [bodily] punishment. . . . The leaders of Vaisya families have houses in the cities for dispensing charity and medicine.*

Faxian may have exaggerated the benefits of Gupta rule, but he provided a useful glimpse

CONNECTIONS: HISTORY AND THE ENVIRONMENT

Buddhism Then and Now

A Buddhist family participates in turning prayer wheels in Nepal.

Established in India and founded by an Indian, Buddhism remains a major religion. Still, fewer than one percent of India's people are Buddhists.

Asoka's support began to transform Buddhism from a local faith into a world religion. Monks carried the Buddha's message to other Asian lands. Some crossed mountains to bring Buddhism to China; others traveled by sea to convert southeast Asia.

Scholars offer various explanations for the eventual end of Buddhism in India. Gupta rulers supported Hinduism, making it almost a state religion. Over time, Indian Buddhism absorbed elements of Hinduism and lost its distinctiveness. The Buddha was even made a minor deity of a Hindu sect.

Hinduism took on certain elements of Buddhism. Hindu practice became more a matter of personal devotion and less one of ritual and sacrifice. As a result, Hinduism regained thousands of followers it had lost to Buddhism.

Much later, in the A.D. 1200s, thousands of Indian Buddhists were killed or driven to Nepal or Tibet by Muslim conquerors. Not until modern times would a significant number of Buddhists inhabit India.

Today, Buddhism has over 250 million followers. A few are in India, but most are in Sri Lanka, Japan, and the nations of the Southeast Asian mainland. Large numbers of Buddhists inhabit most parts of Asia— but not the Buddha's homeland.

Making the Connection

1. What are some explanations for the almost total disappearance of Buddhism from India?
2. What environmental barriers did Buddhists overcome to spread their faith to other Asian lands?

into Indian life in this Golden Age. By easing tax burdens, Chandragupta II gave people more freedom. Of all the Gupta monarchs, he was the most chivalrous and heroic. Though he expanded the empire, he is remembered for far more than conquest. Gupta rulers believed they had reached a high level of civilization. They began to write down rules for everything, from grammar to drama to politics. The Sanskrit of the Gupta court became the major language in the north.

In one respect, though, daily life did not improve. The status of Indian women had declined since Aryan times. Aryan women often had a say about whom they would marry. By Gupta times, parents were choosing mates for their children, and child marriages were common. Women and mothers were highly respected, but they had little power or independence.

Art and Learning Learning flourished under the Guptas. The court welcomed poets, playwrights, philosophers, and scientists. Much of the writing was concentrated on religion, but folk tales were also popular. A collection of tales called the *Panchatantra* presented moral lessons through animals who acted like humans. Many of these stories eventually spread to the Middle East and the West, where they were retold by other authors. Drama was also important during Gupta times. Kalidasa, the most famous playwright, wrote *Shakuntala*, a play about romantic love between a king and a forest maiden.

Gupta mathematicians contributed significantly to mathematics as it is today, making major advances in developing the principles of algebra. They also explained the concept of infinity and invented the concept of zero. The symbols they devised for the numbers one to nine were adopted by traders from the Middle East and so came to be called "Arabic numerals" in the West.

Gupta astronomers used these mathematical discoveries to advance their understanding of the universe. They realized that the earth is round, and they had some knowledge of gravity. In medicine, Gupta doctors set bones, performed operations, and invented hundreds of medical instruments.

Many countries benefited from Gupta achievements, as both ideas and products traveled the land and sea trade routes that connected India to the rest of the world. Indian exporters traded such items as gems, spices, cotton, teak, and ebony for horses from Arabia and central Asia, silk from China, and gold from Rome.

The Golden Age Ends After Chandragupta II's death in A.D. 415, the Gupta Empire began to fail. As the government weakened, the Guptas faced invasions along India's northwestern border. By A.D. 600, the Gupta Empire had dissolved into a collection of small states.

However, much of the culture that was uniquely Indian survived. Many aspects of India's life today grew out of the social structures and religions, the arts and sciences, that were born during the 2,000 years that followed the Aryan invasions.

Recall

1. **Identify:** Chandragupta Maurya, Asoka, Chandragupta I, Chandragupta II, *Panchatantra, Shakuntala*
2. **Locate:** On the map on page 180, find the Mauryan Empire and the Gupta Empire. Compare and contrast their sizes and features.

Critical Thinking

3. **Explain:** Tell what happened that caused dramatic changes in Asoka's life and reign. What were some of the changes?
4. **Describe:** Tell why the Gupta era came to be called India's Golden Age.
5. **Analyze:** How did the rulers of India's empires have an effect on the religious life of the Indian people?
6. **Synthesize:** Compare and contrast Hinduism and the religions of the West.

Applying Concepts

7. **Cultural diffusion:** What aspects of early India have had a lasting impact?

IDENTIFYING CAUSE-EFFECT RELATIONSHIPS

As you read a mystery novel, you may try to figure out which events or actions caused the principal character to act in specific ways. When you read history, it also helps you to make sense of historical events if you can identify *cause-and-effect relationships.*

Explanation

A *cause* is any condition, person, or event that makes something happen. What happens as a result of a cause is known as an *effect.* Any event generally has more than one cause and produces more than one effect. A cause may have both immediate and long-term effects. An *immediate cause* leads directly to an event. For example, if you are exposed to a virus, you may catch a cold. Other indirect, underlying causes, however, may have contributed to the cold, such as lack of sleep or poor diet.

You can identify immediate and underlying cause-effect relationships by determining either the effects or the causes of an event or condition. To identify causes or effects, follow these steps:

- Select an event.
- Compare and contrast the situation at the time of the event with the situation before (causes) and after it (effects). Look for clue words such as *because, as a result of, led to,* and *brought about.*

- Look for logical relationships between events.
- To test your findings, look for a similar event in another time or place, and examine that event for similar causes and effects.

Analyzing historical events to identify cause-effect relationships, however, is not always simple. Facts may not be available. What is worse, ideas cannot be tested as in a science experiment. Consequently, explanations of cause-effect relationships must rely on logic and cannot be proved.

Example

Consider this question: *What causes led to the greatness* (effect) *of Asoka's reign?* In comparing the period of greatness with the years preceding it, you note one major difference—the country was at peace for most of Asoka's reign. You decide then that one cause for the era of achievement was Asoka's renunciation of war after the period of conflict.

You also notice that during the early years of Asoka's reign, before he renounced war, his kingdom grew because of his military conquests. You decide that unifying so many peoples was another cause of greatness.

When you test your idea of peace being a cause of greatness against another situation, you recall that the earlier Indus Valley civilization was destroyed during a

time of peace. You therefore decide that peace alone was not a sufficient cause but that Asoka's military strength—whether or not he chose to use it—was another underlying cause for his reign's greatness.

Application

Read the following excerpt from Section 1:

As a nomadic people, the Aryans had no written language. Sanskrit, their spoken language, evolved slowly and became one of the major languages of India. As part of the Indo-European family of languages, Sanskrit has many of the same root words as English, Spanish, French, and German.

The Aryan warrior-herders sang rousing hymns and recited epics, long poems celebrating their heroes. For centuries these epics were passed by word of mouth from generation to generation.

Use what you know about the Aryans to explain the causes that made Sanskrit (effect) a major Indian language.

Practice

Turn to Practicing Skills on page 185 of the Chapter Review for further practice in identifying cause-effect relationships.

CHAPTER 7 REVIEW

HISTORICAL SIGNIFICANCE

The civilization that developed in India between 1200 B.C. and A.D. 500 produced two of the world's great religions. Hinduism became not only India's dominant faith but also its way of life, defining people's roles in Indian society and restricting their diet and marriage choices, for example. Buddhism rejected many Hindu social practices and affirmed a disciplined life to achieve peace and deliverance from suffering. The belief in nonviolence has influenced modern leaders in their struggle for peace and human rights. Over the centuries, the two religions have inspired magnificent achievements in art and architecture.

SUMMARY

For a summary of Chapter 7, see the Unit 2 Synopsis on pages 204–207.

USING KEY TERMS

Write the key term that best completes each sentence below.

a. ahimsa	f. nirvana
b. dharma	g. rajah
c. epic	h. reincarnation
d. *jati*	i. stupa
e. karma	j. *varna*

1. Buddhists strive to attain freedom from the cycle of rebirth, a state called ___ .
2. An Aryan leader was known as a ___ .
3. In Aryan society, priests became the most honored ___ .
4. To ensure rebirth in a higher state, each Hindu group must properly perform its ___.
5. The *Mahabharata* and the *Ramayana* are ___ that reflect basic Hindu beliefs.
6. Hindus believe in ___ , a process of rebirth in which the soul resides in many bodies before it finally unites with the universal spirit.
7. A person's ___ determines whether he or she will be closer to the universal spirit in the next life.
8. Buddhist architects built elaborate ___ over the remains of holy people.
9. Each *varna* was made up of groups called ___ that were defined by occupation.

REVIEWING FACTS

1. **Identify:** Who was Chandragupta Maurya?
2. **Explain:** In your own words, explain the Four Noble Truths of Buddhism.
3. **Define:** What is *ahimsa*?
4. **Identify:** What is the *Bhagavad Gita*?
5. **Locate:** Where did the Aryan invaders come from, and how did they enter what would later become Pakistan and northern India?
6. **List:** What are some of the achievements of Gupta mathematicians?
7. **Identify:** Who was Siddhartha Gautama?

THINKING CRITICALLY

1. **Apply:** How could a person use the principle of *ahimsa* as a force for social change?
2. **Analyze:** How did ideas in the Hindu religion help to maintain the separation of classes in Indian society?
3. **Synthesize:** What might have happened if Asoka had not been horrified while viewing the carnage after a fierce battle? State your reasoning.
4. **Synthesize:** When do you think India's *varna* system was stronger, under Asoka or under Chandragupta II?
5. **Synthesize:** What linguistic evidence suggests that the Aryans migrated to other places in addition to the Indian subcontinent?
6. **Evaluate:** How did the social status of women differ during the Vedic Age and the Gupta Empire?

ANALYZING CONCEPTS

1. **Movement:** How was India affected by the Aryan invasions?
2. **Innovation:** What might make Buddhism attractive to people from different cultures?
3. **Cultural Diffusion:** Why did Gupta achievements in science and the arts spread quickly to other parts of the world, both eastern and western?

PRACTICING SKILLS

1. What examples do we have of the effects Gupta achievements have had on modern American literature and math?
2. What caused Asoka to change the methods by which he ruled?

GEOGRAPHY IN HISTORY

1. **Place:** Why did the Aryans discard their nomadic life-style after conquering the people of the Indus River Valley?
2. **Location:** Refer to the map on page 180. What provides a natural barrier between India and China?
3. **Location:** Refer to the map on page 180. In what present-day country is the Indus River Valley located?
4. **Region:** Refer to the map on page 180. Define the borders of the Indian subcontinent.

5. **Movement:** Why are the numerals devised by the Guptas referred to as "Arabic"?

TRACING CHRONOLOGY

Refer to the time line below to answer these questions.
1. How long after its founding did Buddhism spread widely beyond India?
2. For how many years did the Mauryan Empire exist?
3. Which is the older religious text, the Vedas or the *Upanishads*?
4. How many years separated the Aryan conquest of the Indus River Valley from Alexander the Great's conquest of the same region?

LINKING PAST AND PRESENT

1. The *varna* system created a huge underclass that Europeans called the untouchables. How do you think this system created problems for modern India?
2. Religion has always had a major part in Indian society. How have religious differences hindered Indian unity in modern times?
3. Early in the 1900s, India applied the Hindu principle of nonviolence to help win its independence from Great Britain. Do you think people can still use nonviolence effectively to win freedom and human rights?

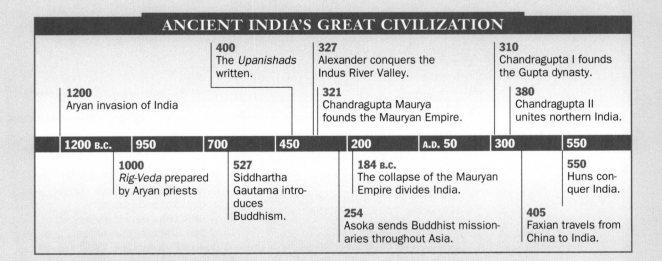

ANCIENT INDIA'S GREAT CIVILIZATION

400 The *Upanishads* written.

1200 Aryan invasion of India

327 Alexander conquers the Indus River Valley.

321 Chandragupta Maurya founds the Mauryan Empire.

310 Chandragupta I founds the Gupta dynasty.

380 Chandragupta II unites northern India.

1200 B.C. | **950** | **700** | **450** | **200** | **A.D. 50** | **300** | **550**

1000 *Rig-Veda* prepared by Aryan priests

527 Siddhartha Gautama introduces Buddhism.

184 B.C. The collapse of the Mauryan Empire divides India.

254 Asoka sends Buddhist missionaries throughout Asia.

550 Huns conquer India.

405 Faxian travels from China to India.

China's Flourishing Civilization

*W*hom do you agree with in the following conversation, dating from the 500s B.C.? What is right, or "straightness," in this case?

The Governor of She said to Confucius: "In our village there is a man nicknamed Straight Body. When his father stole a sheep, he gave evidence against him." Confucius answered, "In our village those who are straight are quite different. Fathers cover up for their sons, and sons cover up for their fathers. Straightness is to be found in such behavior."

This conversation involves a clear conflict between law and family. Confucius's view, however—that family should always take precedence—reflects an attitude toward families that was dominant in Chinese culture long before Confucius lived—and long after.

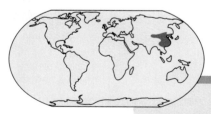

CHAPTER PREVIEW

Key Terms to Define: civil service, mandarin, ethics, acupuncture

People to Meet: Qin Shihuangdi, Liu Bang, Wudi, Zhang Qian, Kongzi, Laozi, Sima Qian

Places to Discover: Great Wall of China, Silk Road, Shandong Province

Objectives to Learn:

1. What major advances did the Chinese make under each dynasty— Zhou, Qin, and Han?
2. What Confucian ideals helped to shape China's government, and how did they shape it?
3. What Confucian ideals helped to shape the structure of China's families and social classes?

The Great Wall warded off invaders in Northern China during the Han dynasty.

Concepts to Understand:
- Uniformity—The Qin and Han dynasties establish and maintain a strong central government. Section 1
- Innovation—The Chinese formulate ethical philosophies and make scientific and technological advances. Sections 2,3
- Cultural diffusion—Buddhism is brought to China from India, and traders carry ideas along the Silk Road. Sections 2,3

187

Three Great Dynasties

Around 1100 B.C., the Chinese people were fashioning ideas that would result in a unique civilization. From then until the 200s A.D., the Chinese lived under three dynasties, or ruling families—the Zhou (joh), the Qin (chin), and the Han (hahn). The first of these, the Zhou, ruled the nation for more than 800 years, longer than any other Chinese dynasty.

The Enduring Zhou

The Zhou conquered the last Shang dynasty king around 1028 B.C., claiming the Mandate of Heaven, or heaven's approval. They called their king the Son of Heaven, saying that the Shang had lost the mandate by ruling poorly.

Eventually, the Zhou held a vast realm. To control their holdings, Zhou kings set up an agricultural system, in which nobles owned the land and serfs, or peasants, worked it. They appointed their relatives to govern, giving each one a city-state—a walled town and the surrounding countryside.

Each local lord had total authority on his own lands and built his own army. At first all the lords pledged allegiance to the Son of Heaven. In time, though, some grew strong enough to challenge the king's authority.

In 771 B.C. a frivolous king named Yu (yoo), the thirteenth ruler of the Zhou dynasty, suffered a severe defeat. King Yu had often amused his court by lighting signal fires that summoned the army. When the soldiers came, the king greeted them with jeers and laughter. Once, however, the attack was real; the army ignored the signal fires, and the king's enemies killed him and destroyed his capital.

After that, the Zhou had little political power, which fell instead to local nobles. In the next centuries, the nobles fought small wars until by the 200s B.C., several city-states were locked in a struggle that ended the Zhou era.

Even though Zhou rulers lost their power, the Zhou are remembered for numerous technological advances. During the Zhou period the Chinese built and improved roads and expanded foreign trade. They obtained horses from western nomads, forming a cavalry of mounted warriors and horse-drawn chariots. The Zhou also added a deadly weapon: the crossbow. They further elaborated the system of picture writing begun by the Shang, a system that is the ancestor of modern Chinese writing. Under the Zhou, iron plows were invented, irrigation systems were developed, and flood-control systems were initiated. These and other advances led to population growth, and Zhou China became the world's most densely populated country.

The Mighty Qin

Meanwhile, several small states were struggling for control in China. Among them was a state on the western border ruled by the Qin. By 221 B.C., the Qin had wiped out the Zhou and conquered the rest of northern China, uniting much of the nation under a strong central authority for the first time. Westerners would later call the nation China after the Qin, whose first ruler added the title Shihuangdi (shur hwang dee), or First Emperor, to his name.

A tireless ruler, Qin Shihuangdi set out to create a government directly under his control. He reorganized the empire into 36 military districts, appointing officials to govern them. This system prevented local lords from becoming strong enough to challenge the power of the central government—the problem that had led to the downfall of the Zhou.

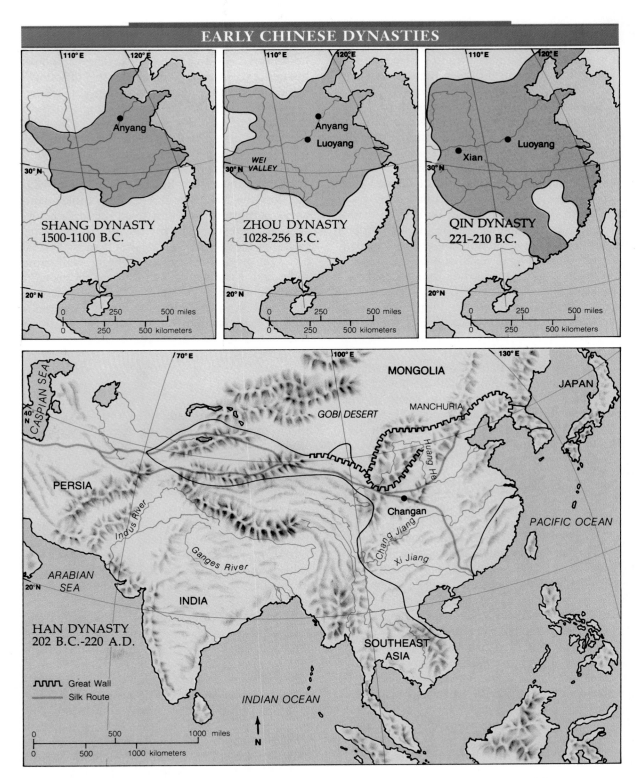

EARLY CHINESE DYNASTIES

SHANG DYNASTY
1500-1100 B.C.

Anyang

ZHOU DYNASTY
1028-256 B.C.

Anyang
Luoyang
WEI VALLEY

QIN DYNASTY
221–210 B.C.

Xian
Luoyang

MONGOLIA

JAPAN

GOBI DESERT

MANCHURIA

CASPIAN SEA

PERSIA

Huang He

Changan

PACIFIC OCEAN

Indus River

Ganges River

Chang Jiang

Xi Jiang

ARABIAN SEA

INDIA

HAN DYNASTY
202 B.C.-220 A.D.

ⅢⅢⅢ Great Wall
⸺ Silk Route

INDIAN OCEAN

SOUTHEAST ASIA

N

Learning from Maps *What natural features isolated China from the rest of the world?*

The First Emperor made other changes to further centralize his control. He devised a system of weights and measures to replace the various systems used in different regions. He standardized coins, instituted a uniform writing system, and set up a law code throughout China.

Qin had grandiose plans for his empire, and he used forced labor to accomplish them. Gangs of Chinese peasants dug canals and built roads radiating from the capital.

To Qin, one building project seemed especially urgent—shoring up China's defenses to the north. Earlier rulers had built walls to prevent attacks by nomadic barbarians. Qin ordered those walls connected and the entire wall completed. Over several years, some 300,000 peasants toiled—and thousands died—before the work was done. Eventually, the wall stretched more than 1,400 miles (2,254 kilometers). Today the Great Wall of China stands as a monument to Qin's ambition and to the peasants who carried out their emperor's will.

Qin Shihuangdi imposed a new order on Chinese society. He eliminated the power of the local lords by taking land from many of them and imposing a tax on landowners. He appointed educated men instead of nobles as officials to run his government.

FOOTNOTES TO HISTORY

COURT MAGIC

During Wudi's reign, a court magician claimed he had made a potion that would give the emperor immortality, which Wudi had sought all his life. Before the magician could give him the vial, the scholar Dong Fangso seized it and drank its contents. Furious, Wudi sentenced Dong Fangso to a painful death.

The scholar, though, persuaded Wudi to let him live. If the potion was genuine, he argued, the emperor would not be able to kill him. If the potion was a fake, Dong Fangso had done no harm.

Wudi had to agree. It turned out that Dong Fangso had indeed exposed a fraud. Although the exact date of Dong Fangso's death is not known, it did occur.

Qin even imposed an early form of censorship, clamping down on scholars who discussed books and ideas. In 213 B.C. he ordered all books burned except those dealing with "practical" subjects like agriculture, medicine, and magic. In this way, he hoped to cut off people's ties to the past. He agreed with his adviser, who said, "anyone referring to the past to criticize the present . . . should be put to death." About 460 scholars resisted and were executed.

Qin's subjects saw him as a cruel tyrant who had lost the Mandate of Heaven. Nobles were angry because he had destroyed the aristocracy; scholars detested him for burning books; and peasants hated his forced-labor gangs. In 210 B.C. Qin died, and soon the dynasty itself came to an end. Even so, the rule of the Qin brought lasting changes. The most influential changes were new ways of organizing the nation, establishing foundations for the imperial Chinese state that would last 2,000 years.

The Glorious Han

In 207 B.C. Liu Bang (lee OO BONG) overthrew the Qin government. A military official from a peasant background, Liu was proud to be the son of a country farmer. In 202 B.C. he defeated his most powerful rival and declared himself the emperor of a new dynasty, the Han.

The Han governed China until A.D. 220, more than 400 years. The Han emperors used the same forms of centralized power that the Qin had set up but without the harshness of Qin rule. Han China rivaled the Roman Empire in its prosperity, power, and achievement.

Advances under Wudi   The Han dynasty reached its peak during the reign of Wudi (woo dee), the sixth Han emperor, who ruled from 141 to 87 B.C. Wudi, one of the most talented and dynamic rulers in Chinese history, personally supervised all aspects of his government.

An ambitious ruler, Wudi extended his empire. He sent huge armies against the nomadic barbarians and other non-Chinese peoples. He conquered lands to the north, including Korea and Manchuria; south into Southeast Asia; and west as far as northern India.

Eternal Guardians

Guardians of the emperor's tomb, the figures shown in the photo are part of an army of life-sized figures buried more than 2,000 years ago with the body of Emperor Qin Shihuangdi. The tomb is one of the most important archaeological finds the world has ever known. Qin came to power when he was only 13 years old. Almost as soon as he ascended the throne, he ordered laborers to begin work on his tomb, a project believed to have taken 36 years to complete.

Shown here is only a small section of the massive clay army of up to 6,000 figures buried with the emperor. Most of the figures, standing in formation, originally held weapons—bronze spears and swords, crossbows, or bows and arrows. The tomb was rigged with booby-trapped crossbows intended to protect the emperor's remains against grave robbers. But robbers found and looted the tomb, and most of the soldiers' weapons were pilfered centuries ago.

The tomb was found by chance in 1974 near the ancient city of Xian (shee YAHN) in the Huang He valley.

These soldiers are only a small contingent of Qin Shihuangdi's clay army of 6,000.

Chinese peasants who were digging a well uncovered one of its gateway chambers. The roof that once stood over Qin's army had collapsed, damaging many of the terra-cotta, or baked clay, statues. Nevertheless, the contents of the tomb are in remarkably good condition and are easy to view.

The workmanship of the statues is exceptional. The buried army includes all types of military figures—archers, officers, charioteers, and horses. Although the figures were molded of ordinary red-brown clay, the details were done carefully. The soldiers' uniforms were brightly painted in a variety of colors: red, green, blue, and lavender. The heads and hands were individually crafted, with attention even to such details as the hair and eyelashes.

Each statue was apparently modeled after a specific soldier—an astounding feat, considering the vast number of statues. Some figures have a stamp on the back of the head bearing a name, probably of the soldier or of the artist who created his likeness. Standing in long, straight ranks, the clay soldiers appear intent on their duty, guarding the tomb of their mighty emperor.

Responding to the Arts

1. What are some remarkable features of the clay figures found in Qin Shihuangdi's tomb?
2. How do the contents of Qin's tomb reflect the emperor himself and the society he ruled?

In 139 B.C. Wudi sent out an expedition led by Zhang Qian (jahng chyee YAHN), a general and explorer. Thirteen years later, Zhang staggered back. His troops had been nearly wiped out by barbarian attacks, and the general had endured more than 10 years of captivity.

Although he had made no conquests, Zhang brought back amazing tales he had heard on his travels. He told of a great empire to the west, with huge cities full of people "who cut their hair short, wear embroidered garments, and ride in very small chariots." Zhang, who was describing Rome, gave Han rulers their first hint of another civilization as advanced as their own.

Wudi's new interest in the West, fed by news of Zhang Qian's explorations, led to the expansion of trade routes later known as the Silk Road. Winding past deserts and through mountain passes, the Silk Road linked East and West. It allowed traders to exchange China's fine silk and porcelain for Middle Eastern and European products, such as gold, glassware, and wool and linen fabrics.

Pax Sinica   Under the Han, China enjoyed a 400-year period of prosperity and stability, later referred to as the *Pax Sinica* (PAHKS SI nuh kuh), the Chinese Peace. The *Pax Sinica* coincided with the *Pax Romana* in the West.

During the *Pax Sinica*, Wudi adopted an economic policy designed to prevent food shortages and high prices. Government agents stored surplus food during years of plenty and sold it when harvests were poor. Under this system, China was able to feed a population that had been growing steadily since Zhou times.

Before Wudi, emperors had chosen as their officials members of their families or of the aristocracy, a practice that led easily to corruption in government. Wudi wanted talented people to govern, and so he initiated changes. First, he asked people to recommend candidates for public posts. These candidates took long, difficult written examinations. After an official "graded" the tests, the emperor evaluated the results and appointed those with the highest scores.

Wudi's examinations evolved into the **civil service,** a system that allowed anyone with ability to attain public office. At least, that was the theory. In practice, the system favored the wealthy, for education was expensive, and usually the wealthy alone could afford to obtain enough education to pass the exams.

The civil service system made scholars the most respected members of Chinese society. A new class of well-educated civil servants, called **mandarins,** controlled the government, and they would continue to do so until the 1900s.

After Wudi's reign, Han power declined, and wealthy landowners regained power. The Han dynasty fell in A.D. 220. Afterward, warring factions again divided China, and barbarians swept across the land. For the next three and a half centuries, the peace that China had enjoyed under the Han would be only a vague memory.

But many accomplishments from the *Pax Sinica* were lasting. Han astronomers and mathematicians made great advances, Han technology produced items such as paper, and Han writers and artists left valuable records. These and other achievements explain why, even today, some Chinese call themselves "sons of Han."

SECTION 1 REVIEW

Recall
1. **Define:** civil service, mandarins
2. **Identify:** Qin Shihuangdi, Liu Bang, Zhang Qian, Wudi
3. **Locate:** Great Wall of China, Silk Road
4. **List:** What were two of the major achievements the Chinese made under each dynasty—the Zhou, the Qin, and the Han?
5. **Analyze:** Compare and contrast China's government and politics under the Zhou, Qin and Han dynasties.

Critical Thinking
6. **Evaluate:** What were the three most important developments during the *Pax Sinica*?
7. **Analyze:** Did Wudi's civil service system offer equal opportunity? Explain.

Applying Concepts
8. **Uniformity:** How did Qin Shihuangdi unify China?

Three Ways of Life

In the latter half of the Zhou era, two major philosophies appeared in China—Confucianism and Daoism. Neither dealt with the supernatural or with eternal life; both were focused instead on life in this world.

Confucianism

Confucianism grew out of the teachings of Kongzi (kong dzuh), a government official from Shandong Province. Known in the West as Confucius, he was born about 551 B.C. to a poor family. Before reaching age 16, he left his home and wandered around northern China for 12 to 14 years, seeking a position as adviser to a ruler. He hoped that in such a position he could help end the personal, political, and social disorder he saw everywhere. He was never able to get the government position he wanted, but he found a group of students who were eager to learn his ideas about people and government. At age 22 he began to teach.

Family and Government   Promoting order was Confucius's principal concern. He believed that everyone had a proper role in society. If each person would accept that role and perform the related duties, social and political disorder would end.

Individuals, Confucius taught, should live according to principles of **ethics**—good conduct and moral judgment. Ethics began with respect for family, especially elders, and reverence for the past and its traditions. Ethics should govern each person's behavior in these five primary relationships: ruler and subject, parent and child, husband and wife, old and young, friend and friend.

Confucius cared especially about "filial piety," or children's respect for their parents. In fact, for Confucius, the family represented society in miniature. He said:

> *The superior man spreads his culture to the entire nation by remaining at home. . . . The teaching of filial piety is a preparation for serving the ruler of the state; the teaching of respect for one's elder brothers is a preparation for serving all the elders of the community; and the teaching of kindness in parents is a training for ruling over people. . . . When individual families have learned kindness, then the whole nation has learned kindness.*

Governments too had a duty: to set an example of right conduct. The ethical ruler had integrity, was righteous, inspired loyalty, understood proper behavior, followed the appropriate rituals, and appreciated culture.

When a student asked Confucius for one single word that could serve as a principle for conduct, he responded: "Perhaps the word *reciprocity* will do. Do not do unto others what you would not want others to do unto you." This rule is similar to a familiar teaching of Judaism and Christianity, sometimes called the Golden Rule: "Do unto others as you would have others do unto you."

Confucianism After Confucius   The Zhou government did not accept Confucius's teachings during his lifetime. Within a century after his death in 479 B.C., however, Confucian ethics were widely followed in China. Later scholars added their ideas, and Confucianism eventually went far beyond the teachings of Confucius.

The Qin rulers rejected books, especially those that looked to the past as Confucius had. But in the Han dynasty, Confucius's teachings provided the basis for Wudi's civil service

The First Seismograph

Zhang Heng's seismoscope from the A.D. 100s is the first known attempt to detect distant earthquakes.

In 1989 millions watched on television as a powerful earthquake rocked San Francisco shortly before baseball's World Series. That quake's tremors brought death and destruction around the Bay area.

Today we know that the shifting in the earth's crust causes earthquakes. This movement sends "seismic waves" across the earth's surface, much as dropping a pebble in a pond sends ripples across water.

People living in Han China believed that angry spirits caused earthquakes to express their displeasure with society. Scholars studied quakes closely, believing they were interpreting a divine message.

In A.D. 132 Zhang Heng invented the world's first seismograph, an instrument for detecting and measuring earthquakes. Zhang's device resembled a domed, cylindrical urn. Each of eight dragons around the top held a ball in its jaws. At the base of the urn sat eight toads with upturned heads and open mouths, each directly under a dragon.

When a tremor occurred, a mechanism caused one of the balls to fall into a toad's mouth. This action showed that somewhere an earthquake was taking place. The side of the seismograph where that toad was sitting indicated the quake's direction. As the ball popped into the toad's mouth, the loudness may have indicated the tremor's strength.

Zhang Heng's seismograph had one quality that today's instruments lack: it was also a work of art.

Making the Connection

1. How was Zhang Heng's seismograph like and unlike today's?
2. Why might Han emperors want to know about earthquakes?

---

system. Though Han scholars reinterpreted Confucianism, they retained its devotion to ethical behavior and just government. Indeed, Confucius's teachings would serve as a basis for Chinese society and government until the 1900s.

Daoism

At about the same time as Confucius, during the late Zhou period, a man called Laozi (low dzuh), or "Old Master," taught ideas that in some ways seem the opposite of Confucianism. He rejected formal social structures and the idea that people must fill specific roles in society.

Also in contrast to Confucius, Laozi shunned public life, leaving anything we know of him heavily mixed with legend. According to tradition, as an old man Laozi climbed onto a purple water buffalo and rode off toward the western wilderness. At the frontier, a guard stopped him and asked him to leave an account of his teaching, the Dao, or "Way." The old man replied:

The Dao that can be told is not the eternal Dao.
The name that can be named is not the eternal name.
The nameless is the beginning of heaven and earth.

Laozi's ideas are recorded in the *Dao De Jing*, one of the best-known of all Chinese classics. Daoists believed people should renounce wealth, power, and ambition. They also rejected social structures and formal codes of behavior. Daoists believed people should attune themselves to nature and the Dao, which is the eternal force that permeates everything in nature. They followed examples from nature, as these lines suggest:

> *The highest good is like water.*
> *Water gives life to the ten thousand things and*
> *   does not strive.*
> *It flows in places men reject and so is like the*
> *   Dao.*
> *In dwelling, be close to the land.*
> *In meditation, go deep in the heart.*
> *In dealing with others, be gentle and kind.*
> *In speech, be true.*
> *In ruling, be just.*

By emphasizing harmony with nature and its underlying spirit, Daoists profoundly influenced Chinese arts, particularly painting and poetry. Their influence lingers in painting, poetry, and other arts to this day.

Daoist simplicity seems to oppose Confucian formalism, but a person could be both a Confucianist and a Daoist. Confucianism provided the pattern for government and one's place in the social order, and Daoism emphasized harmony within the individual attuned to nature. Because the emphasis of each was different, a person could easily be both.

A Chinese theory related to Daoist ideas was the concept of yin and yang, the two opposing forces believed to be present in all nature. Yin was cool, dark, female, and submissive, while yang was warm, light, male, and aggressive. Everything had both elements. For harmony the two elements had to be in balance. Human life and natural events, including the changing seasons, resulted from the interplay between yin and yang.

The concept of yin and yang helped the Chinese reconcile seeming opposites—like Dao simplicity and Confucian formalism. No doubt, it also helped them accept Buddhist ideas brought to China by monks and traders from India.

Buddhism

Buddhism reached China just as the Han Empire was collapsing, and its beliefs were eagerly adopted by many people. Peasants whose lives were torn apart by constant warfare welcomed the opportunity Buddhism offered for an escape from suffering. Confucianists could walk its "eightfold path." Daoists admired its use of meditation.

Buddhism never replaced or greatly threatened the ideas of Confucianism and Daoism. Instead, it added a spiritual influence with its emphasis on personal salvation in Nirvana. By the 400s A.D., Buddhism was widely embraced in China, adding one more color to the rich mosaic of Chinese life and thought.

SECTION 2 REVIEW

Recall
1. **Define:** ethics
2. **Identify:** Kongzi, Laozi
3. **Locate:** Shandong Province
4. **Explain:** Why did Confucius want to become an adviser to a ruler? What was his goal in life, and was he successful?
5. **Analyze:** How did Confucius apply the idea of filial piety to governments as well as to families?

Critical Thinking
6. **Analyze:** Compare and contrast Confucius and Laozi in their ideas and also in their ways of life.
7. **Synthesize:** Explain why the Qin strongly opposed the teachings of Confucius, though Han rulers like Wudi promoted Confucianism.

Applying Concepts
8. **Innovation:** How did the concept of yin and yang help the Chinese deal with ideas in Daoism that seemed opposed to Confucianism?

Society and Culture

Confucian values governed all aspects of personal and social life in Han China. "With harmony at home, there will be order in the nation," Confucius had said. "With order in the nation, there will be peace in the world." And indeed, the family was supreme in Chinese society. It was the focus of life, bound together strongly by mutual love, loyalty, and dependence.

Family Life

The members of a Chinese family of the Han era lived and worked together. In an ideal family every member knew his or her role and the duties that went with it.

Family members did not relate to each other as equals; instead, the family was a strict hierarchy. The oldest male in the home, usually the father, was dominant—a genuine head of his house. Next in rank was the oldest son, followed by all the younger sons and all the females. The mother came before the daughters, and finally—at the bottom—the youngest daughter or childless daughter-in-law. Each family member expected obedience from those who were further down in the hierarchy, and each obeyed and respected those who were above.

Strict rules governed the relationships between husbands and wives, parents and grandparents, uncles and aunts, brothers and sisters, first and second cousins, and a tangle of in-laws. Each family member knew his or her place and understood its duties, and each was careful not to bring "dishonor" on the family by failing in those duties. And the duty to family members did not stop at death; all were expected to pay proper respect to departed ancestors.

Typical homes in Han China did not have the multigenerational, or "extended," families that would later be typical. Rather, they had what we call today the "nuclear" family, consisting of parents and their children. The father was king, and his home was indeed his castle. He assigned his children's careers, determined their education, arranged their marriages, meted out rewards or punishments, and controlled the family finances. All family members turned over their earnings to him, and he determined how to redistribute the income among them. The family also provided support for members who could not themselves contribute—the aged, the young, the sick, and even the lazy.

No doubt the system offered many opportunities for exploiting those further down in the hierarchy. Nevertheless, few fathers were tyrants. Like other family members, they practiced ethical principles of kindness and compassion, either from genuine love or from fear of the disapproval of others and the scorn of their ancestors.

Status of Women   Under the Confucian social system, women were subordinate to men. Confucius himself had little regard for women, saying, "Women and uneducated people are the most difficult to deal with."

Girls began life subservient to their fathers and brothers. Later their husbands and in-laws were their superiors, and eventually even a mother came under the authority of her own sons. Parents valued baby girls far less than baby boys. A poor family had to work hard to raise and support a child, and if that child was a daughter, she left home to become part of her husband's family as soon as she married.

Some women were able to gain respect in Chinese homes. With marriage and motherhood, they became revered. Other opportunities for women, such as education, were limited. One first-century Chinese scholar wrote:

Females should be strictly grave and sober, and yet adapted to the occasion. Whether in waiting on her parents, receiving or reverencing her husband, rising up or sitting down, when pregnant, in times of mourning, or when fleeing in war, she should be perfectly decorous. Rearing the silkworm and working cloth are the most important employments of the female; preparing food for the household and setting in order sacrifices follow next, each of which must be attended to. After that, study and learning can fill up the time.

In spite of Confucianism's predominance, women fared far better under the Han than they would in later centuries. They could inherit property, even own it after they married, and they could remarry after a husband's death.

Society and Economy   Chinese society consisted of three main classes: landowners, peasants, and merchants. Landowning families were wealthy. They lived in tile-roofed mansions with courtyards and gardens. They surrounded their homes with walls to protect them from bandits. They filled their rooms with fine furniture and adorned them with silk scrolls and carpets. The wealthy family feasted on a rich variety of foods.

The landholders' wealth and power were generally limited, however, and families rarely kept their holdings for more than a few generations. When a family's land was divided, it went to *all* the sons, not just the oldest, with the result that in time individual landowners had less and less property.

Probably 90 percent of the Chinese people were peasants. The wealth that supported the life-styles of the rich was gained from the hard labor of the peasants who cultivated the land. Unlike Western farmers, who usually lived on the land they farmed, most Chinese peasants lived in rural villages and worked fields outside their mud walls. Their homes were simple, and they ate a plain diet that featured millet, rice, beans, turnips, and fish.

The peasants raised livestock and toiled long hours in the grain fields. One writer of the time described their lives in this way: "All year round they cannot afford to take even a day's rest." Peasants faced constant threats from floods and from famines. As rent for the land, they turned over part of their produce to the landowner. The government required them to pay taxes and to work one month each year on public works projects such as road building. In times of conflict, peasants were drafted into the army as soldiers.

At the bottom of the social hierarchy were merchants—a group that included shopkeepers, traders, service workers, and even bankers. The merchants lived in towns and provided goods and services for the wealthy. In spite of the great wealth that many merchants accumulated, Chinese society generally held them in contempt. Confucianism taught that the pursuit of profit was an unworthy pastime for the "superior" individual. Thus, merchants were considered the lowest and least honorable class. Of all the people in Han society, only merchants were not allowed to take the civil service examinations and enter government service.

For all others, the civil service system provided opportunities for advancement, though the expense of education blocked most of the poor from competing. Still, poor but talented individuals sometimes rose to positions of power and influence. And just as peasants might climb the social ladder, landowners could also fall into poverty.

Literature

Although the Qin burned thousands of books, many survived in royal libraries and secret private collections. Particularly prized was a collection of books called the Five Classics, some of which were written before Confucius. All candidates for the civil service were required to master them. No better example is recorded of the Chinese reverence for history.

The oldest of the Five Classics, the *Book of Songs*, preserves 305 of the earliest Chinese poems, written between 1000 and 600 B.C. The poems deal with political themes, ritual, and romance, and even the oldest show that they belonged to an advanced literary tradition. Many seem modern, with their everyday topics and simple, concrete imagery—this one, for example:

Near the East Gate
Young women go
Like so many clouds all day.
Like drifting clouds
A thought of them
Soon blows away.

There. White robe
and a blue scarf—
she makes my day.

Near the Great Tower and Wall
Go slender girls
Like reeds by river's edge:
Like bending reeds
A thought of them
Soon passes by.

The *Book of Documents* records political speeches and documents from early in the Zhou dynasty, including the earliest statement of the Mandate of Heaven. The *Book of Changes* presents a complex system for foretelling the future and choosing a course of action. In *Spring and Autumn Annals* Confucius reported major events that occurred in the state of Lu between 722 and 481 B.C. Although accounts were brief, a scholar of the 300s B.C. declared this work to be as important to China as the legendary flood thousands of years before.

Followers of Confucius scoured the *Spring and Autumn Annals* and other ancient writings to find events that might provide meaning for their own time. Scholars diligently read and studied every line to determine all of its possible meanings.

The Classics were thought to carry solutions to most problems. Officials studied them

IMAGES OF THE TIME

Han China

The Han Dynasty was a golden age of Chinese history. Important political, economic, and cultural changes took place.

An elegant bronze from the Han era shows a horse balanced in midair.

A decorated tile portrays the meeting of two officials. Scholars of Confucius held important positions in the centralized government.

closely to find support for their positions, such as the conduct of political leaders. Accounts of solar eclipses, meteor showers, and droughts were used to show what terrifying events and disasters could befall poor political leaders.

Another great collection of books, the Thirteen Classics, included the *Analects*—Confucius's sayings compiled by his students after his death. Many appeared as answers to questions. For example, Confucius was asked about the gentleman, or the "superior man." Among other replies he gave this one: "What the gentleman seeks, he seeks within himself; what the small man seeks, he seeks in others."

The Han Chinese encouraged literary pursuits and made literature available to everyone. An especially valuable work produced during the Han dynasty era was the *Historical Record*. Written by Sima Qian during the reign of Wudi, it is the first true history of ancient China.

Science and Technology

Besides literature and philosophy, China made major contributions in science and technology. By the 300s B.C., Chinese astronomers had calculated the length of the solar year as 365 1/4 days. They gazed through bronze tubes equipped with a device that divided the sky into measured segments, allowing them to make accurate measurements. They kept valuable records of solar and lunar eclipses and comet sightings. In 240 B.C. Chinese astronomers recorded the appearance of the object that would later be called Halley's comet—many centuries before Halley's birth.

Chinese physicians recognized nutrition as vital and realized that some diseases resulted from vitamin deficiencies. Although they did not identify vitamins as such, they discovered and prescribed foods that would correct some prob-

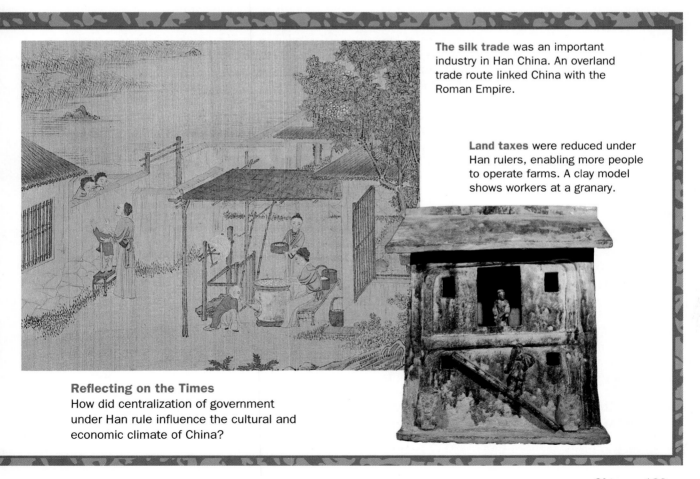

The silk trade was an important industry in Han China. An overland trade route linked China with the Roman Empire.

Land taxes were reduced under Han rulers, enabling more people to operate farms. A clay model shows workers at a granary.

Reflecting on the Times
How did centralization of government under Han rule influence the cultural and economic climate of China?

lems. They also understood that many herbs had medicinal value.

Chinese doctors treated ailments and relieved pain with **acupuncture,** a technique in which the skin is pierced with thin needles at vital points. They believed acupuncture restored the balance between yin and yang in a person's body.

Under the Han, many improvements occurred in agriculture and transportation. Complex irrigation systems drained swamps and diverted rivers to quench parched fields. Advances in fertilizing crops helped farmers produce enough to feed China's growing population. Veterinary medicine helped save many farm animals. New canals and improved roadways reduced the cost of distributing food, made it easier to ship goods to market, and permitted ideas and information to spread more rapidly throughout the country.

Three inventions in ancient China were especially vital to Chinese life and the economy. Made by the Chinese since prehistoric times, silk was in great demand as a trade item; its worth was attested to by the name of one of history's greatest trade routes—the Silk Road. Caravans carried the precious cargo as far as the city of Rome.

The Chinese discovered that the cocoon of the silkworm could be unwound to make a mile of thread. Han weavers created beautiful damasks of several colors. Designs included geometric patterns and cloud forms punctuated with images of exotic creatures. These luxurious textiles were enjoyed by Mongolian warriors and Egyptian rulers alike.

Paper was probably invented by 100 B.C., although it was officially credited to an inventor of about 200 years later. Artisans pounded tree bark, hemp, or rags into a pulp. By treating it with gelatin, they discovered that they could then make paper. Used first for wrapping and clothing, paper was soon recognized as an ideal writing material.

The invention of paper benefited the bureaucratic Han government. Its centralized structure resulted in an explosion in the number of documents. Most were written on strips of wood, which were fragile and cumbersome to work with. The use of paper had many obvious advantages.

The third critical invention of the period was porcelain, which has come to be called "china." Centuries before European artisans could imitate this white, translucent material, potters supplied Chinese people with everyday utensils and rare works of art, which were collected by emperors.

These are only a few examples from a list of Chinese "firsts," which also includes the first printed books, the earliest technologies for casting bronze and iron, the suspension bridge, the compass, the wheelbarrow, and gunpowder. Such achievements as these caused China to remain far ahead of Europe in science and technology until the 1300s.

SECTION 3 REVIEW

Recall

1. **Define:** acupuncture
2. **Identify:** Five Classics, *Spring and Autumn Annals, Analects,* Sima Qian
3. **Analyze:** Explain how families and government during the Han era reflected the Confucian idea of order.

Critical Thinking

4. **Analyze:** Compare a typical Han Chinese family with families you consider typical of America today.
5. **Synthesize:** Think about how merchants were viewed in Han society and why. How might America be different if we felt that way about merchants?
6. **Compare:** Make a chart that describes the three main classes of Chinese society. Then compare these divisions with classes in other societies.
7. **Evaluate:** What negative outcomes might result for a society with the view of women held by Confucius and later by Han society?

Applying Concepts

8. **Cultural diffusion:** What ideas and products from ancient China have become popular in the West in recent years? Why?

DETERMINING THE RELIABILITY OF A SOURCE

Which class in auto mechanics would you take—one taught by a respected professional mechanic or one taught by your friend's older brother who fixes his own car? You probably would choose the course taught by the professional mechanic because he is a reliable source of information.

Explanation

When gathering data for a research report or paper, you may need to *determine the reliability of the sources* you plan to use. A reliable source is one that provides accurate information.

When determining the reliability of a source, use the following steps:

- Examine the author's background. What credentials does the writer have that qualify him or her to write about the topic in question? Was the author able to report events accurately? For example, was this a first- or secondhand account?
- Determine if the author has a particular bias that could cause inaccuracy or subjectivity.
- Identify the author's purpose in writing and the author's targeted audience.
- Verify the methods the author used in writing the source. For example, did the author include footnotes or a bibliography? Are the author's claims supported by facts?

Example

Confucius gathered and updated hundreds of ancient documents and compiled them into texts later known as the *Shujing* or the *Book of Documents*. But in 213 B.C., these and many other books were burned by Shihuangdi. Some scholars, however, memorized the complete works of Confucius and passed them down to succeeding generations.

Read the following excerpt from the *Shujing:*

Our king Tsu Yi came and fixed on Keng for his capital. He did so from a deep concern for our people, because he would not have them all die where they cannot help one another to preserve their lives. I have consulted with the tortoise shell and obtained the reply: "This is no place for us." When the former kings had any important business they gave reverent heed to the commands of Heaven. . . . The great inheritance of the former kings will be continued and renewed.

Consider how the steps can be used to determine the reliability of *Shujing*. Confucius was a clerk, not a historian. He reported events secondhand from ancient writings. Confucius believed China had been governed by heroic leaders who unified the empire. His bias comes through in the refer-

ence to the king's "deep concern" for his people and to the "great inheritance of the former kings." Confucius' purpose was to inspire his pupils with the glorious deeds of their ancestors. Since there are no other sources for this period, and the original texts were burned, the *Shujing* must not be considered a reliable source.

Application

Use the outlined steps to determine the reliability of the following excerpt from *The Female Instructor* written by the first-century Chinese scholar Luhchau. You will need to consult an encyclopedia or other library resources.

In conversation, a female should not be forward and garrulous, but observe strictly what is correct, whether in suggesting advice to her husband, in remonstrating with him, or teaching her children. . . humbly imparting her experience.

1. Was Luhchau a contemporary of Confucius?
2. What people or events influenced Luhchau's work?

Practice

Turn to Practicing Skills on page 203 of the Chapter Review for further practice in determining the reliability of a source.

CHAPTER 8 REVIEW

HISTORICAL SIGNIFICANCE

Today, some hold Confucian ideas at least partly responsible for China's recent troubled past. They point to the denial of women's rights and the blind submission to authority, saying that these legacies of Confucianism have caused China to lag behind the West.

On the other hand, remember that Confucianism was instrumental in launching China into its golden age. Its emphasis on tradition and stability helped Han rulers build and maintain a strong government and a unified empire. Confucius's ideas about family and government resulted in a more ethical and compassionate society. As for modern times, some contend that Confucianism has been an influence for positive change. Confucius considered it society's duty to overthrow an incompetent ruler and to establish a just government. And for some, his call for equalizing wealth has resounded loudly.

SUMMARY

For a summary of Chapter 8, see the Unit 2 Synopsis on pages 204–207.

USING KEY TERMS

Write the key term that best completes each sentence.

a. acupuncture   c. ethics
b. civil service   d. mandarin

1. Wudi created a school that helped students prepare for examinations for positions in the ___ .
2. China based its ideal of family structure and government on Confucian ___ .
3. The administration of China's government came under the control of the ___ , a class of educated officials.
4. To relieve pain and cure some ailments, Chinese physicians employed a technique known as ___ .

REVIEWING FACTS

1. **Identify:** Who was Kongzi?
2. **Explain:** How did Qin Shihuangdi organize his government?
3. **List:** Name the five relationships identified by Confucius.
4. **Define:** What is the *Book of Songs?*
5. **Explain:** Why did Qin Shihuangdi order construction of the Great Wall?
6. **Locate:** Where is the Silk Road?
7. **Identify:** Who was Wudi?
8. **Explain:** How did Qin Shihuangdi try to control the flow of ideas among his subjects?
9. **Name:** Who was Laozi?
10. **Define:** What was the *Pax Sinica?*
11. **List:** Identify three main groups that made up Chinese society during the Han era.
12. **Locate:** Where did Qin Shihuangdi build the Great Wall of China?

THINKING CRITICALLY

1. **Evaluate:** Do you think merchants deserved the low status they held in Chinese society?
2. **Analyze:** Contrast the basic principles of Daoism and Confucianism.
3. **Apply:** How does your society make use of the Han concept of appointing officials on the basis of their abilities?
4. **Synthesize:** How would you respond if your government adopted the social policies of the Qin dynasty?
5. **Analyze:** Differentiate between the Zhou and Qin systems of government.
6. **Synthesize:** If you lived in China during the Han era, which would interest you most—Confucianism, Daoism, or Buddhism?

7. **Evaluate:** Decide whether its strong family structure was a positive or negative influence on Chinese society.

ANALYZING CONCEPTS

1. **Innovation:** Choose a technological development of ancient China and discuss its significance.
2. **Cultural diffusion:** How did Buddhism reach China?
3. **Innovation:** How did the ethical philosophy of Confucius influence Chinese society?
4. **Uniformity:** What methods did Qin Shihuangdi use to unify China?
5. **Cultural diffusion:** Discuss the importance of the Silk Road.

PRACTICING SKILLS

1. Describe a news account in which you doubted the reliability of a source. (A terrorist reporting on how happy his hostages are.) Follow the criteria to determine the reliability of a source.

GEOGRAPHY IN HISTORY

1. **Movement:** How did improved roads help to unify China?
2. **Place:** How did the Chinese use rivers to improve their economy?

3. **Location:** Refer to the map on page 189. Which river lies farthest south—the Chang Jiang, the Huang He, or the Xi Jiang?
4. **Place:** The Zhou and the Qin originally came from the Wei valley on China's western border. How might their location have contributed to their military abilities?

TRACING CHRONOLOGY

Refer to the time line below to answer the questions.
1. How long did the Qin dynasty exist?
2. Zhang Qian began his journey west in 139 B.C. How long did his journey last, and in what year did he return?
3. How many years did the Han dynasty exist?
4. For how long did the Qin dynasty survive its founder?

LINKING PAST AND PRESENT

1. The Qin tried to control people's ideas by limiting the books they could read. Provide an example of a modern government that limits the information its people receives.
2. The Han government forced peasants to work one month of each year on public projects. Was forced labor justified?
3. All candidates for China's civil service were required to master the Five Classics. Can you think of literature from our own culture that everyone should know?

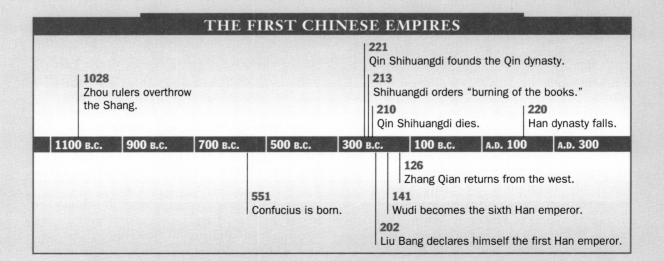

THE FIRST CHINESE EMPIRES

1028 Zhou rulers overthrow the Shang.

221 Qin Shihuangdi founds the Qin dynasty.

213 Shihuangdi orders "burning of the books."

210 Qin Shihuangdi dies.

220 Han dynasty falls.

1100 B.C. | 900 B.C. | 700 B.C. | 500 B.C. | 300 B.C. | 100 B.C. | A.D. 100 | A.D. 300

551 Confucius is born.

126 Zhang Qian returns from the west.

141 Wudi becomes the sixth Han emperor.

202 Liu Bang declares himself the first Han emperor.

UNIT 2 SYNOPSIS

During the years from about 2000 B.C. to about A.D. 500, four major civilizations formed in different parts of the world. Although each civilization had distinctive characteristics, they shared such features as a stable political system, one or more major religions, and interest in the arts and sciences. The people of Greece, Rome, India, and China made numerous achievements whose influence has lasted to the present.

CHAPTER 4
The Rise of Ancient Greece

Although Greece's mountains protected against invaders, they also limited travel and communication among the Greeks and prevented them from uniting under one government. Numerous harbors and proximity to the sea encouraged the Greeks to become traders, and eventually they established colonies around the Mediterranean Sea.

Greek civilization grew out of the Minoan civilization of Crete and the Mycenaean civilization brought in by Indo-Europeans. A significant event early in Greek history was the Trojan War, in which the Mycenaeans fought the people of Troy, a major trading city in Asia Minor. The Trojan War was later immortalized in two epic poems, the *Iliad* and the *Odyssey*. These epics served as textbooks in Greek schools to teach such values as courage, dignity, and love of beauty. The Greeks worshiped a family of gods and goddesses—who were both humanlike and superpowerful—and imitated their deities by themselves striving for excellence.

The polis—the Greek city-state—served as the political as well as the geographic center of Greek life. Each polis, especially Athens, encouraged participation by its citizens in self-government. Women, however, had no political rights, and slaves and foreign-born men were excluded from citizenship.

After being ruled by kings, landholding aristocrats, and tyrants, most city-states became either oligarchies or democracies. The two dominant Greek democracies were Sparta and Athens. Sparta was a militaristic society that used its army to control noncitizens rigidly. Athens built a much freer society that laid the foundation for the Western concept of democratic government.

During the 500s B.C., the Greek city-states, led by Athens, defeated invading armies from the Persian Empire in a series of wars. A Golden Age of cultural achievement in Athens followed the Persian War. Athens transformed the anti-Persian Delian League into a sort of empire, and resentment against Athenian dominance led to the Peloponnesian War between Athens and an alliance of city-states led by Sparta. The war resulted in defeat for Athens and decline for the Greek city-state system.

CHAPTER 5
Triumph of Greek Civilization

During the 400s B.C., Athens became the center of Greek civilization. The classical style of art and architecture from the Golden Age of Athens and the classical works of literature have endured in Western civilization. The Athenians expressed their love of beauty and balance in such architectural masterpieces as the Parthenon. They decorated their pottery with paintings and created masterworks in sculpture. The Greeks were the first to write and perform plays. Aeschylus, Sophocles, and Euripides were the leading writers of tragedy, and Aristophanes was the most famous writer of comedies. The Olympic Games were a religious festival in honor of Zeus, the chief Greek god.

Greek thinkers, questioning all things, believed they could explain the world by applying reason; their philosophy flowered in the 400s and 300s B.C. To help his students clarify their thinking, the philosopher Socrates constructed a technique known as the Socratic method. Plato, another great philosopher, studied human behavior and wrote the first book on political science. The philosopher Aristotle formulated the analytical system now called the scientific method, and also wrote on logic, rhetoric, poetry, and political science, among other topics. The Greeks also gave us the first true historians, Herodotus and Thucydides, and the father of medicine, Hippocrates.

By 338 B.C., King Philip II of Macedonia conquered Greece and, by 330 B.C., his son Alexander defeated the Persian Empire and conquered an area stretching from the Nile to the Indus. Alexander the Great tried to combine the best of Greek and Persian cultures into one civilization. After his death his empire was divided among three of his generals.

Although political unity disappeared, Greek culture spread through the Mediterranean region and mixed with Middle Eastern culture to form a Hellenistic civilization. This new civilization formed around its cities, especially Alexandria, Egypt. During the Hellenistic era, the Greeks excelled in astronomy, geography, mathematics, and physics.

Learning from Art *The artist who decorated this Greek vase showed human figures as black silhouettes.* ***How did painting on pottery restrict the artist's creativity?***

Chapter 6
The Legacy of Rome

In 509 B.C. the Romans overthrew their Etruscan king and established a republic that lasted almost 500 years. The republic was ruled primarily by patrician consuls and the Senate, although after a while representatives of the plebeians—tribunes and the Assembly of Tribes—also played a part in government.

Organized in legions, the Roman army conquered the Italian peninsula by 280 B.C. Rome then fought three Punic Wars against the Carthaginians, finally defeating them in 146 B.C. Rome's military successes and acquisition of territory brought the Roman Republic wealth but also substituted slave labor on large estates for small, independent citizen-farmers. The latter crowded into Rome, where they voted for any leader who promised cheaper food and more public amusements. After several unsuccessful attempts at political and economic reform by both tribunes and generals, Julius Caesar took over the government in 49 B.C. In 27 B.C. his grandnephew Octavian, later known as Augustus, became the first Roman emperor.

From 27 B.C. to A.D. 180, the Roman Empire enjoyed a time of peace, order, and prosperity known as the *Pax Romana*. During this period the Romans greatly expanded and strengthened their system of laws and built numerous roads, aqueducts, and public buildings. Great literary figures include the poets Horace and Virgil and the historians Livy and Tacitus.

Christianity, based on the life and teachings of Jesus, began as a sect of Judaism but quickly spread through the Roman world as a new religion. After great persecution, Christianity became the official religion of the empire in A.D. 392. During the A.D. 400s, the bishop of Rome began to claim authority over the other patriarchs of the Christian Church and eventually became known as pope.

During the A.D. 200s, the Roman Empire began to decline because of political instability, severe inflation, and invasions by Germanic and other barbarian tribes. Valiant efforts at reform by Diocletian and Constantine preserved the

Learning from Art *Jesus taught his followers that they, as individuals, were responsible only to God and to their fellow human beings.* **Why did many Romans oppose Christianity?**

eastern part of the empire but succeeded in delaying the downfall of the western part of the empire only until the late A.D. 400s.

CHAPTER 7
India's Great Civilization

About 1200 B.C. Aryan invaders conquered northern India, bringing with them the Sanskrit language and a social structure that divided people into *varnas*, four social classes. The system of *varnas* and *jati* evolved into the caste system of India. The *Rig-Veda*, dating from the Aryan period, is one of the oldest religious texts still in use. Between 900 and 500 B.C., the two Aryan epic poems, the *Mahabharata* and the *Ramayana*, were recorded. These epics and later religious writings, the *Upanishads*, taught the principles of Hinduism, India's major religion. Hinduism includes belief in a universal spirit, reincarnation, and the obligation to perform the duties of one's caste.

During the 500s B.C., Siddhartha Gautama founded Buddhism, which spread from India to East and Southeast Asia. Known as the Buddha, or Enlightened One, he taught that people can escape the cycle of rebirth by eliminating desire and by following rules of behavior, the Eightfold Path. Buddhist artists created paintings and statues of the Buddha throughout Asia.

The Mauryas, who ruled from 322 to 184 B.C., founded an empire in northern India, and the Mauryan ruler Asoka helped spread Buddhism throughout India and beyond. About 500 years later, the Guptas reunited India, and their empire lasted from A.D. 320 to 600. Under the Guptas, writers and scientists made numerous advances. These include Arabic numerals and the concept of zero.

CHAPTER 8
China's Flourishing Civilizations

The Zhou, who replaced the Shang dynasty about 1000 B.C., ruled China until 256 B.C.—their dynasty lasting longer than any other Chinese dynasty. Under the Zhou, China made many technological advances and began to experience steady population growth.

After an interval in which various states warred continually with one another, the Qin ruler conquered all other states in northern China and created the first true Chinese empire in 221 B.C. He called himself Shihuangdi, or First Emperor, and adopted many techniques for unifying China, including standardized coins, one writing system, and a uniform system of weights and measures. Qin Shihuangdi had the separate walls that protected China's northern borders against nomadic barbarians combined into the Great Wall. He also tried to control people's thinking by burning many books.

The Qin dynasty was overthrown by the Han, who ruled from 202 B.C. to A.D. 220. Under the Han emperor Wudi, the government adopted a civil-service system in which officials were appointed on the basis of examinations. The Han defeated the barbarians and also explored as far west as the Caspian Sea. The 400 years of peace under the Han were later referred to as the *Pax Sinica*. After the Han dynasty came to an end, China split into three states.

Learning from Art *This Chinese painting on silk depicts one stage in the silk-making process—boiling silkworm cocoons.* **During which dynasty did the Silk Road trade begin?**

Two major philosophies appeared during the Zhou period: Confucianism and Daoism. Confucianism was developed by Kongzi, also known as Confucius. He emphasized basic ethical relationships, especially those between ruler and ruled and between parent and child. Confucianism also stressed the ideal of a courteous, knowledgeable individual. Daoism, which is associated with a semilegendary man named Laozi, emphasizes living in harmony with nature. Toward the end of the Han dynasty, Buddhism entered China.

The Chinese family of the Han era played an important role in Chinese society and was dominated by the oldest male. The family functioned as an economic unit to which all members gave their earnings and which supported the old, the young, and the sick. Chinese society was divided into three main groups—landowners, peasants, and merchants—of which merchants were considered the lowest and least honorable.

Producing numerous literary works, the Chinese also made great contributions in science and technology. These include the first printed book and the invention of paper, gunpowder, the compass, porcelain, the wheelbarrow, and acupuncture.

SURVEYING THE UNIT

1. **Making Comparisons:** In what ways did the peoples of India and China differ in their general attitudes toward life?
2. **Analyzing Viewpoints:** What do you think the attitude of the ancient Greeks would have been about Qin Shihuangdi's policy toward books and dissident scholars? Give reasons for your answer.
3. **Predicting Developments:** What do you think might have happened if Diocletian and Constantine had lived about 100 years earlier than they did?

UNIT 2 REVIEW

REVIEWING THE MAIN IDEAS

1. **Describe:** What are the primary values and beliefs in the Chinese philosophies of Confucianism and Daoism?
2. **Explain:** What was the relationship between people and their government in the polis of Athens and in the Roman Republic?
3. **Describe:** What was the position of women in each of the ancient civilizations discussed in Unit 2?
4. **Explain:** How significant was international trade in the economies of Greece and Rome?
5. **Identify:** Give an example of how one of the civilizations discussed in Unit 2 influenced another of the civilizations.
6. **Outline:** Outline the evolution of the caste system in India as it was introduced by the Aryans.

THINKING CRITICALLY

1. **Apply:** How did belief in the power of the mind influence Greek contributions to history? to science?
2. **Analyze:** What were the political and economic changes that brought about the end of the Roman Republic? of the western Roman Empire?
3. **Synthesize:** Why did the South Asia subcontinent attract so many invaders—for example, the Aryans and Alexander the Great—in spite of its difficult climate?
4. **Evaluate:** Do you think belief in reincarnation makes people more or less willing to accept difficult social circumstances?
5. **Evaluate:** Do you think that the reign of Qin Shihuangdi was good or bad for China? Give reasons to support your answer.
6. **Synthesize:** Both the rule of Pericles in Athens and that of the Guptas in India are referred to as golden ages. Using these periods as examples, explain what distinguishes a golden age in history.

A GLOBAL PERSPECTIVE

Refer to the time line on pages 88–89 to answer these questions.

1. About A.D. 100 the Chinese invented paper. How much later did they invent block printing?
2. Gautama Buddha was born in 566 B.C. What other Asian religious or philosophical leader was born in the same century?
3. About how many years after the *Pax Romana* began did the fall of the western Roman Empire occur?
4. Which came first, the work of the Babylonian astronomers or the astronomical work of Ptolemy?
5. How many years after Phoenician traders controlled the eastern Mediterranean did trans-Saharan trade develop?
6. What was happening in the political sphere during the lifetime of Jesus Christ?

LINKING PAST AND PRESENT

1. Athens organized the Delian League, an alliance of Greek city-states initially meant to resist the Persian Empire. Name one international alliance organized by the United States since World War II and describe its purpose.
2. Which of these Greek accomplishments do you think has most profoundly influenced the modern world: drama, architecture, or government? Give examples to defend your choice.
3. Using a dictionary, list the words in the Preamble to the United States Constitution that are derived from Latin words and give the meanings of the Latin roots.
4. How does the Confucian system of care for the aged compare with the system followed in the United States today? What are the advantages and the disadvantages in each system?

ANALYZING VISUALS

Although this statue was made after the period covered in this unit, it sums up the underlying concepts of Hinduism in many ways. The Hindu god Shiva, along with the gods Vishnu and Sakti, had his origins in earlier religions. It was during the Kushan period, when Hinduism became more formalized, that the personality and attributes of Shiva began to be clearly defined. Shiva, the Lord of the Dance, has both creative and destructive powers. In this image, he dances in a circle of fire. The circle frames Shiva and symbolizes the unending cycle of creation, death, and rebirth. This symbolism relates very clearly to the Hindu belief in a universal spirit and reincarnation.

1. Compare Hinduism to the other major religious systems you have studied in this unit: Greek, Roman, Buddhist, and Judeo-Christian. What concerns and issues are common to all of them?

2. How is the Hindu belief in reincarnation represented in this sculpture?

3. Hinduism continues to be one of the world's major religions. In what regions of the world is Hinduism practiced?

USING LITERATURE

Refer to the excerpt from Antigone *on pages 132–135 to answer these questions.*

1. Compare and contrast Antigone's attitude toward the laws of the community with that of the Greek philosopher Socrates.

2. Would the authors of the *Mahabharata* have agreed or disagreed with Antigone's behavior? Why do you think so?

3. Do you think Qin Shihuangdi would have supported Creon's condemnation of Antigone? Give reasons for your opinion.

4. Do you think people have the moral right to disobey a law they believe is unjust? Why or why not? Can you give examples from the twentieth century in which people have followed this reasoning?

5. Suppose the inhabitants of a community were to decide to follow the dictates of individual conscience rather than obey the laws of their community. Under what circumstances might the community be able to function? Why might it fall apart?

WRITING ABOUT HISTORY

1. Write a one-week diary for one of these individuals:
   a. a Carthaginian soldier under Hannibal
   b. an Indian woman during the Gupta Empire
   c. a government official in Han China
   d. a Greek woman living in Hellenistic Alexandria

2. Imagine that you are a newscaster on television. Write an eyewitness account of the assassination of Julius Caesar.

3. Make an illustrated chart showing the scientific accomplishments of each of the four civilizations that you studied in this unit. Be sure to include the disciplines of astronomy, engineering, mathematics, medicine, and technology.

UNIT 3
Regional Civilizations

A.D. 400–1500

> "The first key to wisdom is this constant and frequent questioning . . . by questioning we arrive at the truth."

A popular philosopher of the early 1100s, Peter Abelard was a man in search of the truth. His words above reflect the desire for knowledge following the emergence of western Europe from the Early Middle Ages. Isolated for centuries, Europe was beginning to make contact with other peoples and nations. Meanwhile, African, North American, and South American civilizations were establishing their places in the world. An exciting age of growth and discovery was about to begin.

A GLOBAL CHRONOLOGY

	A.D. 500	A.D. 700	A.D. 900
Political Sphere	**527** Justinian becomes Byzantine emperor.	**637** Jerusalem conquered by Arabs.	
Scientific Sphere		**850** Astrolabe perfected by Arabs.	
Cultural & Social Sphere		**622** Muhammad flees Mecca (Islamic Year 1).	**960** Northern Song dynasty in China

Byzantine incense burner in the form of a church

A.D. 1100		A.D. 1300	A.D. 1500

1095
Crusades
begin.

1215
Magna Carta

1453 Gutenberg prints Bible.

c. 1000 Chinese
invent gunpowder.

1271 Marco Polo
begins travels in China.

1347
Black Death
strikes Europe.

211

Byzantines and Slavs

*T*he awestruck visitor arriving in A.D. 600 in the city of Constantinople in southeastern Europe scarcely knew where to turn. Splendid public buildings as well as simple private homes lined the streets; the scent of rare spices perfumed the air; people dressed in fine silk thronged the church of Hagia Sophia. "One might imagine that one has chanced upon a meadow in full bloom," the Greek historian Procopius wrote about the newly built church. "For one would surely marvel at the purple hue of some [columns], the green of others, at those on which the crimson blooms, at those that flash with white, at those, too, which nature, like a painter, has varied with the most contrasting colors." The church's grandeur reflected that of Constantinople, "city of the world's desire," capital of a prosperous empire that controlled east–west trade and laid the basis for the Greek and Slavic civilizations of modern Europe.

CHAPTER PREVIEW

Key Terms to Define: clergy, laity, icons, iconoclast, schism, mosaic, illuminated manuscript, steppe, boyar, tsar

People to Meet: Constantine, Justinian, Theodora, Leo III, Cyril, Seljuk Turks, Ottoman Turks, Rurik, Vladimir, Alexander Nevsky, Ivan III

Places to Discover: Constantinople, Balkan Peninsula, Asia Minor, Adriatic Sea, Black Sea, Manzikert, Dnieper River, Kiev, Moscow, Volga River

Objectives to Learn:
1. What made Constantinople such a rich and powerful city?
2. What role did the Church play in Byzantine and Slavic societies?

The subject and style of this painting are typical of religious art throughout the Byzantine Empire.

3. What caused the split between the Roman and Byzantine churches?

4. Why did Constantinople suffer almost constant attack?

5. What factors contributed to the development of Eastern Slavic culture?

6. How did the Eastern Slavic lands become isolated from western Europe?

Concepts to Understand:

- Conflict—Byzantines fight off invaders and struggle over use of icons. Section 1
- Innovation—Byzantines develop Eastern Orthodox theology and distinctive art forms. Section 2
- Cultural diffusion—Trade routes and invasions spread beliefs and ideas. Sections 1,2,3

213

The New Rome

As you read in Chapter 6, after the Roman Empire was formally divided in A.D. 395, the eastern half became known as the Byzantine Empire. At its height in the A.D. 500s, the Byzantine Empire included most of the Balkan Peninsula, Asia Minor, Syria, and Egypt. Its major population group, the Greeks, lived mainly in the central part of the empire. Also included in the Byzantine population were Egyptians, Syrians, Arabs, Armenians, Jews, Persians, Slavs, and Turks. The many peoples and their varied cultures gave Byzantine civilization an international character.

Byzantine Foundations

The location of Constantinople, the Byzantine capital, reinforced the civilization's multicultural character. The city was situated near the strongholds of early Christian faith as well as major trade routes.

A Strategic City   In A.D. 324 the Roman emperor Constantine built Constantinople at a strategic place where Europe and Asia meet. Located on a peninsula, Constantinople overlooked the Bosporus, the narrow strait between the Sea of Marmara and the Black Sea. A second strait, the Dardanelles, connects the Sea of Marmara and the Aegean Sea, which leads to the Mediterranean. These straits gave the occupiers of the peninsula control over movement between the Mediterranean and the Black Sea and, as a result, over the routes leading east to Asia and north to northern Europe. The site of Constantinople itself offered superb natural protection from attack at a time when Germanic invaders were assaulting Rome. Water protected the city on three sides, and triple walls fortified the side open to attack by land. Eventually a

huge chain was strung across the narrow mouth of the deep harbor on the city's north side for still greater protection.

The straits also made the peninsula a natural crossroad for trade. By Constantine's time the Byzantine capital had become the wealthiest part of the Roman Empire, handling rich cargoes from Asia, Europe, and Africa.

Cultural Blend   After the fall of Rome, the Byzantine Empire was regarded as heir to Roman power and traditions. Constantinople was known as the New Rome because its emperors were Romans who spoke Latin and many of its aristocratic families came from Rome. Despite these ties, the Byzantine Empire was more than a continuation of the old Roman Empire.

Lands that were once part of the Greek world formed the heart of the Byzantine Empire. The Byzantine people not only spoke Greek but also stressed their Greek heritage. Eventually Byzantine emperors and officials also used Greek rather than Latin. Religious scholars expressed their ideas in Greek and developed a distinct form of Christianity known as Eastern Orthodoxy. In addition to the Byzantine Empire's classical Greek heritage and Christian religion came cultural influences from eastern civilizations such as Persia. This mixture of cultures created a distinct Byzantine civilization. Between A.D. 500 and 1200, this civilization was one of the most advanced in the world and had a higher standard of living than western Europe.

Justinian's Rule   At its height the Byzantine Empire was ruled by Justinian, the son of prosperous peasants from Macedonia in the western part of the empire. Justinian was called the Emperor Who Never Sleeps. While a young man in the court of his uncle, Emperor Justin I, he often worked late into the night at his studies of law, music, religion, and architecture. Justinian retained this work pattern after he became emperor in A.D. 527, at age 44.

Theodora's Support

Justinian's wife, Theodora, was beautiful, intelligent, and ambitious. Justinian had married her in spite of court objections to her occupation as an actress—a profession held in low esteem in the empire. A capable empress, Theodora participated actively in the government, rewarding friends with positions and using dismissals to punish enemies.

Theodora was especially concerned with improving the social standing of women. She persuaded Justinian to issue a decree giving a wife the right to own land equal in value to the wealth she brought with her at marriage. This land gave a widow the income she needed to support her children without the assistance of the government .

In A.D. 532 Theodora's political astuteness helped save Justinian's throne. When a tax revolt in Constantinople threatened the government, Justinian's advisers urged him to leave the city. As flames roared through Constantinople and the rebels battered at the palace gates, Justinian prepared to flee. Theodora, however, persuaded him to remain in control.

Inspired by his wife's determination, Justinian reasserted his power. His army crushed the rebels, killing 30,000 people. From that time until his death in A.D. 565, Justinian ruled without challenge.

Military Campaigns

Justinian envisioned a restored Roman Empire. In A.D. 533 he began the reconquest of Italy, North Africa, and Spain—Roman lands that had fallen to Germanic invaders. By A.D. 554 he had achieved his goal.

The successful reconquest, however, proved costly for the empire. The wars exhausted most of the Byzantine resources. Funds were low for defending the eastern borders, which faced attack by an expanding Persian Empire. Justinian's conquests did not last. Within a generation of his death, the empire lost many of its outlying territories.

Code of Laws

Justinian's reform of the legal system did last, affecting Western law even today. Faced with a tangle of Roman laws, many of them outmoded or overly complicated, Justinian commissioned ten scholars to collect and reorganize them. The result of their six years' labor was a collection of books known as the *Corpus of Civil Law*, or the Justinian Code. This monumental work preserved the legal heritage of Rome and later served as the basis for most European legal systems.

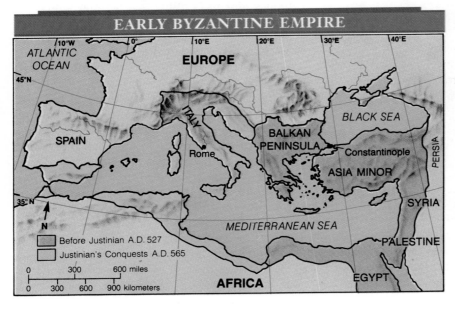

Learning from Maps
Emperor Justinian's conquests extended Byzantine rule in the West. ***What effect did this have on the Byzantine Empire?***

Byzantine Religion

Strong ties existed between the Byzantine emperors and the church. The emperors were regarded as Christ's representatives on earth. Starting in the A.D. 400s, Byzantine emperors were crowned by the patriarch of Constantinople and took an oath to defend the Christian faith.

Byzantine emperors frequently played a major role in church affairs. They appointed church officials, defined the style of worship, and used the wealth of the church for government purposes.

Justinian strengthened this control over the church by intervening in disputes over church beliefs. He also tried to unify the empire under one Christian faith, a practice that sometimes led to persecution of Jews and non-Greek Christians.

Learning from Art *Icons were one source of religious controversy in the Byzantine Empire during the A.D. 700s and 800s.* **What were other sources of conflict?**

Religious Controversy Both Byzantine **clergy**—church officials such as priests and bishops—and **laity**—church members who were not clergy—were intensely interested in religious matters. In their homes, markets, and shops, Byzantines often engaged in heated theological discussions.

In the A.D. 700s, a major religious dispute broke out over the use of **icons** (EYE kahnz), or religious images. Although Christians had disagreed about this practice since the A.D. 200s, the use of icons in churches had become a political issue by the A.D. 700s.

Those who objected to the use of icons in Christian worship argued that the Old Testament prohibited such images in the Ten Commandments. Defenders stressed the symbolic nature and creative value of icon worship. The leading champion of icons was the Byzantine theologian John of Damascus. Although a resident of the Islamic Empire, he wrote many religious articles defending the use of icons.

Believing that icons encouraged superstition and the worship of idols, in A.D. 726 Emperor Leo III ordered all icons removed from the churches. The emperor's supporters—mostly military leaders, government officials, and many of the people in Asia Minor—became known as **iconoclasts**, or image breakers.

Church leaders and other Byzantines resisted the order to get rid of their cherished images, and were supported by the church in Rome, which was as prestigious a center of Christianity as Constantinople. The Roman pope's involvement in the controversy strained relations between the Eastern and Western churches.

Feeling his authority was being challenged, Leo asserted his power and suppressed demonstrations held in favor of icons. Although several later emperors followed Leo's lead, they were not supported by the people. In A.D. 787 a church council at Nicaea approved the use of icons. Soon after, the Empress Irene—the first woman to hold the Byzantine throne in her own right—permitted the use of icons as long as they were not given the worship due to God. The Eastern church further resolved the issue in A.D. 843, allowing the use of pictures, but not statues, in worship.

Hagia Sophia

Emperor Justinian commanded his architects to create the most spectacular religious building of all time. Construction of Constantinople's church of Hagia Sophia, or Holy Wisdom, began in A.D. 532. Workers completed the church in only five years. At its consecration, Justinian is supposed to have said, "Solomon, I have outdone you," referring to the ancient Hebrew king who had built a magnificent temple.

For Justinian, building this church was important for religious and political reasons. First, as the church of the imperial court, Hagia Sophia symbolized the importance of Orthodox Christianity in the Byzantine Empire. Second, by commissioning important buildings and art, Justinian asserted his authority as well as the church's role in Byzantine society. Hagia Sophia proclaimed Justinian's goals for all to see.

The design of Hagia Sophia was radically new. Justinian turned to two noted mathematicians to create his spectacular building. Thus, the building's plan reflected logical geometric forms on a scale never seen before. Its dome, supported by four arches, was larger and more prominent than any the world had ever known.

From the inside of the building, the visual effect of the architecture was one of mystery and splendor. The huge dome, pierced by windows and covered with glimmering mosaics, appeared to hover, weightless, above the vast church. Light streamed into the church from all directions and reflected off decorated surfaces.

To an extent, Justinian succeeded in his goal of creating the greatest religious monument of his time. It was centuries before a building of equal size and splendor was built in the Mediterranean world.

Responding to the Arts
1. What sort of effect did the interior of Hagia Sophia have on its viewers?
2. How did the splendor of the church of Hagia Sophia serve Justinian's goals?

Learning from Art
Justinian is surrounded by court officials, soldiers, and priests in this Byzantine mosaic. Justinian's efforts to protect the eastern border and restore the Roman Empire were not successful. **What lands did he seek to conquer?**

Conflict with Rome   Since the A.D. 300s, the Eastern and Western churches had disagreed on a number of religious and political issues. As centuries passed, the disagreements intensified.

The iconoclastic controversy was but one of many reasons that divided the two churches. The most serious issue concerned the source of religious authority. The pope in Rome and the patriarch of Constantinople did not agree on their roles in the Christian Church. The pope stated that he was supreme leader of the Church; the patriarch refused to recognize this claim. In addition, the two church leaders also disagreed over points of doctrine. They challenged each other for control of the new churches in the Balkan Peninsula.

Relations between Eastern and Western churches worsened in the A.D. 700s when the Germanic Lombards invaded Italy. When the Byzantine emperor refused to give the pope military protection, the pope turned to the Franks, a Germanic Catholic people in western Europe. After the Franks defeated the Lombards, the pope gave the Frankish leader, Pepin the Short, the title of emperor—a title which only the Byzantine ruler could legally grant. This action made the Byzantines even more bitter toward the pope.

By A.D. 1054, doctrinal, political, and geographical differences finally led to a **schism** (SIHZ uhm), or separation, of the church into the Roman Catholic Church in the West and the Eastern Orthodox Church in the East. The split further weakened the Byzantine Empire, which had faced attacks from numerous peoples since its founding.

SECTION 1 REVIEW

Recall
1. **Define:** clergy, laity, icon, iconoclast, schism
2. **Identify:** Constantine, Justinian, Theodora, Leo III,
3. **Locate:** Constantinople, Balkan Peninsula, Asia Minor, the Bosporus, the Dardanelles.

Why was Constantinople's location significant?

Critical Thinking
4. **Analyze:** How did the Byzantines promote Christianity?
5. **Synthesize:** Examine Constantine's reasons for his location

of Constantinople. What other factors are of concern in the location of a city?

Applying Concepts
6. **Conflict:** Explain how religious controversy affected Byzantine politics.

Byzantine Civilization

From A.D. 500 to 800, when western Europe was in decline, the Byzantine Empire was a brilliant center of civilization. Its scholars preserved Greek philosophy and literature; Roman political and legal ideas; and Christian theology, or religious teachings. The Byzantines also created new art forms and spread the religion of the Eastern Orthodox Church into eastern Europe.

Byzantine Life

Byzantine society was divided into a hierarchy of social groups. Yet, there were few barriers to prevent a person from moving from one group to another. This flexibility brought variety and change to Byzantine life.

Family Life The family was the center of social life for most Byzantines. Both the Church and the government supported marriage as a sacred institution. Divorce was difficult to obtain, and the Church generally forbade more than one remarriage.

Byzantine women were expected to live partly in seclusion, and so rooms in homes and churches were set aside for their sole use. Nevertheless, women had gained some rights through Theodora's efforts. Like the empress herself, some women became well educated and influential in the government. Several governed as regents, or temporary rulers, and a few ruled in their own right as empresses.

The Economy Most Byzantines made a living through farming, herding, or working as laborers. Farmers paid heavy taxes that supported the government.

Although the base of the Byzantine economy was agricultural, commerce thrived in cities such as Constantinople, which was the site of a natural crossroad for trade. Byzantine ships loaded with cargo sailed between the Mediterranean and Black seas by way of the Bosporus and Dardanelles. At the eastern shore of the Black Sea, goods could be shipped overland through Asia. Rivers such as the Dnieper, which flowed from the Black Sea north to the Baltic, provided access to northern Europe.

Merchants traded Byzantine agricultural goods and furs and slaves from northern Europe for luxury goods from the East. To Constantinople's busy harbor, called the Golden Horn, ships brought cloves and sandalwood from the East Indies; pepper, copper, and gems from India and Ceylon (now Sri Lanka); and silk from China.

The major Byzantine industry was weaving silk. It developed after A.D. 550, when Justinian sent two monks to China, the center of the silk industry. On a visit to a silk factory the monks stole some silkworm eggs, hid them in hollow bamboo canes, and smuggled their precious cargo out of China. Transplanted to Constantinople, the silkworms fed on mulberry leaves and spun the silk that made the empire wealthy.

Byzantine Art and Learning

Among the products of Byzantine culture were beautiful icons, jewel-encrusted crosses, and carved ivory boxes for sacred items. These art forms were adopted by eastern Europe and also influenced western Europe and the Middle East.

Art Religious subjects were the sources of most Byzantine art. Icons, the most popular art form, portrayed saints and other religious figures. Icons were displayed on the walls of churches, homes, and shrines. Magnificent churches were embellished with gold and silver, polished and carved marble, ivory, and jewels, as well as icons and other religious images.

The Byzantines also excelled in the art of **mosaic**, or pictures made of many tiny pieces of colored glass or flat stone set in plaster. The most masterly mosaics captured the finest gradations of skin tones and textures of clothing—a skill even painters found difficult to master. Byzantine emperor Constantine VII, historian, painter, and author, described one mosaic:

As you move, the figures seem to move, too. You could swear that their eyes are turning and shining and that their garments are rustling . . . the Byzantine mosaicist has succeeded in creating the illusion that his jig-saw puzzle has come to life.

Religious scholars of the Byzantine Empire created another art form, the **illuminated manuscript**. These were books decorated with elaborate designs, beautiful lettering, and miniature paintings. The brilliantly colored paintings portrayed religious themes as well as scenes of Byzantine daily life. Adopted in western Europe, the art of illuminating manuscripts provided a vivid record of daily life between A.D. 300 and 1200.

Education   Schools and learning also played an important role in Byzantine culture. The government-supported University of Constantinople, established in A.D. 850, trained scholars and lawyers for government jobs; the Eastern Orthodox Church provided religious schools to train priests and theological scholars. Beyond the religious subjects that reflected the primary role of the church, areas of study

IMAGES OF THE TIME

Byzantine Society

Byzantine civilization consolidated political, religious, and cultural elements from all over the Mediterranean world.

Constantinople, on a peninsula between Europe and Asia, was the empire's most important city. Its harbor, shown here, was a major port for trade.

Precious objects like this icon of the archangel Michael were the work of skilled artists. Icons were placed and revered, not only in churches but also in homes.

included medicine, law, philosophy, arithmetic, geometry, astronomy, grammar, and music. Wealthy people sometimes hired tutors to instruct their children, particularly their daughters, who were usually not admitted to schools and universities.

Byzantine literature focused on salvation of the soul and obedience to God's will. Writers composed hymns and poems in praise of Christ and his mother, Mary. Instead of popular fiction, Byzantine authors wrote books about the lives of the saints, which provided readers with moral lessons as well as accounts of the saints' miracles and adventures.

The foremost occupation of Byzantine scholars, however, was copying the writings of the ancient Greeks and Romans. By preserving ancient works on science, medicine, and mathematics, the Byzantines helped spread classical knowledge to the Western world.

Spread of Christianity   Church missionaries—people who carry a religious message to others—taught neighboring peoples about Eastern Orthodoxy and converted many of them to their faith. They also spread Byzantine arts and learning.

Among the most successful missionaries were the brothers Cyril and Methodius. They reasoned that Christianity would be more acceptable to the Slavic peoples who lived north of the empire if it were presented in their own language. About A.D. 860 Cyril devised an alphabet for the Slavic languages. Known today as the Cyrillic (sih RIHL ihk) alphabet in honor of its inventor, this script is still used by Russians, Ukrainians, Bulgarians, and Serbs. When Cyril and Methodius presented the Slavs with Cyrillic translations of the Bible and church ceremonies, they won many converts to Orthodox Christianity.

Monasteries and churches throughout the empire were financed by the emperor and by wealthy citizens. The architecture of many of these buildings, like this one in Greece, showed the influence of Constantinople.

A marriage ring bears an inscription asking God to protect the married couple.

Reflecting on the Times
How do these images reveal the prosperity of the Byzantine Empire?

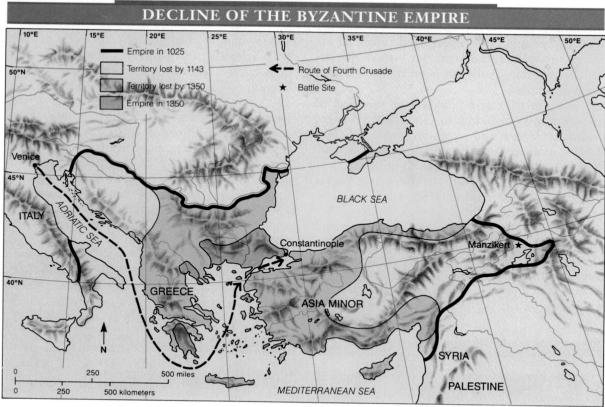

DECLINE OF THE BYZANTINE EMPIRE

Key:
- Empire in 1025
- Territory lost by 1143
- Territory lost by 1350
- Empire in 1350
- ← Route of Fourth Crusade
- ★ Battle Site

Venice • ITALY • ADRIATIC SEA • GREECE • BLACK SEA • Constantinople • Manzikert ★ • ASIA MINOR • SYRIA • PALESTINE • MEDITERRANEAN SEA

Learning from Maps *Compare this map with the map on page 215.* **What territory did the Byzantine Empire lose between A.D. 565 and 1350?**

Decline and Fall

From its founding, the Byzantine Empire suffered frequent attacks by invading armies. Among them were Germanic Lombards, Slavs, Avars, Bulgars, Persians, and Arabs.

Unending Attacks   After Justinian died in A.D. 565, the Germanic Lombards took over most of Italy, the Avars attacked the northern frontier, Slavic peoples moved into the Balkans, and the Persians resumed their attacks in the east. By A.D. 626 the Persians were at the walls of Constantinople. Although a brilliant counterattack stopped their advance, a new enemy—the Arabs from the Middle East—entered the scene. Followers of the new religion of Islam, the Arabs sought to spread their faith and acquire wealth. By the A.D. 630s, they occupied Syria and Palestine and expanded into Persia and across North Africa. The Byzantines stopped the Arabs at Constantinople, but could not regain the lost territories in the Middle East and North Africa.

By A.D. 700 the Byzantine Empire was reduced to the territories that were primarily Greek. The loss of the non-Greek lands actually helped strengthen the empire because it now had one religion, one language, and one culture.

Christian Conquest   In A.D. 1071 northern European people called Normans seized the Byzantine lands in southern Italy. Venice, an Italian trading city on the Adriatic Sea, agreed to help the Byzantines' effort to regain the lands in return for trading privileges in Constantinople. The attempt failed, however, and the Byzantines soon lost control of trade, badly weakening an economy already strained by war.

In the same year, the Seljuk (SEHL johk) Turks, who had come from central Asia and converted to Islam, defeated the Byzantines at the town of Manzikert. As the invaders advanced, the Byzantine emperor asked the pope's help in defending Christianity. Expeditions sent by the pope against the Islamic forces were more interested in taking over Palestine.

In A.D. 1204 Christian soldiers from western Europe agreed to help the Venetians attack Constantinople. For three days the attackers burned and looted the city, stealing and destroying priceless manuscripts and works of art. Their actions were so brutal that Pope Innocent III publicly condemned them:

These defenders of Christ, who should have turned their swords only against the infidels [followers of Islam], have bathed in Christian blood. They have respected neither religion, nor age, nor sex. . . . It was not enough for them to squander the treasures of the Empire and to rob private individuals, whether great or small. . . . They have dared to lay their hands on the wealth of the churches. They have been seen tearing from the altars the silver adornments, breaking them in fragments, over which they quarrelled, violating the sanctuaries, carrying away the icons, crosses, and relics.

The western Christians established "a Latin empire" in Constantinople. The Byzantine people resisted this rule successfully and reestablished their own culture in A.D. 1261.

FOOTNOTES TO HISTORY
GREEK FIRE

How did the Byzantine Empire survive frequent attack? The answer lay in a terrifying weapon known as Greek fire, one of the earliest uses of chemicals in warfare.

Squirted from tubes or thrown in clay pots that shattered on impact, Greek fire burst into flames the moment it hit water and kept burning even under water. The formula remains a secret; it probably included highly flammable oil, pitch, quicklime, sulfur, and resin.

Fall of Constantinople   The years of fighting had severely weakened the Byzantine Empire. Soon Serbs and Bulgars took over Balkan territory. New invaders from central Asia, the Ottoman Turks, attacked the eastern provinces. By the late A.D. 1300s, the Byzantine Empire consisted of only Constantinople and part of Greece.

About 100,000 people still lived in the capital; food was scarce, and wealth was gone. In A.D. 1453 the Ottomans laid siege to Constantinople. For six weeks their huge cannon blasted away at the city's walls. The Byzantines fought fiercely until their last emperor was killed.

For a thousand years, the Byzantine Empire had protected the Christian lands to its north. With the fall of Constantinople, central Europe lay open to attack by Islamic forces. Despite the empire's fall, the Byzantine heritage lived on in the civilization developed by the Eastern Slavs.

SECTION 2 REVIEW

Recall
1. **Define** mosaic, illuminated manuscript.
2. **Identify:** Constantine VII, Cyril, Methodius, Seljuk Turks, Ottoman Turks.
3. **Locate** Adriatic Sea, Black Sea, Venice, Syria, Palestine, Manzikert.

4. Why are the Bosporus and the Dardanelles strategic waterways?

Critical Thinking
5. **Analyze:** How did trade affect the Byzantine Empire?
6. **Analyze:** Examine how the split between the Roman Catholic

Church and the Eastern Orthodox Church contributed to the Byzantine Empire's decline.

Applying Concepts
7. **Innovation:** What do Byzantine mosaics and icons tell you about the focus of Byzantine art?

The Eastern Slavs

One of the Byzantine trade routes ran north across the Black Sea and up the Dnieper River, then overland to the Baltic Sea. From trading posts along the river grew the roots of a civilization that would combine features of several cultures.

The Setting and the People

North of the Black Sea are vast plains, thick forests, and mighty rivers. Much of the land is an immense plain called the **steppe**. Ukrainian author Nikolai Gogol vividly captures its spirit in his *Cossack Tales*:

The farther the steppe went the grander it became. . . . one green uninhabited waste. No plow ever furrowed its immense wavy plains of wild plants; the wild horses, which herded there, alone trampled them down. The whole extent of the steppe was nothing but a green-gold ocean, whose surface seemed besprinkled with millions of different colored flowers.

Although the steppe has rich black soil, the harsh climate makes farming difficult and crop failures common. Too far inland to be reached by moist ocean breezes, the steppe often has scanty rainfall. In addition, most of the land lies in the same latitudes as Canada and has the same short growing season. During the long, hard winter, blasts of Arctic air roar across the land and bury it deep in snow.

North of the steppe stretch seemingly endless forests of evergreens, birch, oak, and other hardwoods. North–south flowing rivers such as the Dnieper, Dniester, and Volga cross the steppe and penetrate the forests, providing the easiest means of transportation. Yet travel is difficult for much of the year. In winter, deep drifts

of snow cover the earth, and in the spring thaw the land turns to knee-deep mud.

The People   The major population group in this area was known as the Slavs. No one knows the origin of the first Slavic peoples, but by about A.D. 500, they formed three distinct groups. The West Slavs—Poles, Czechs, and Slovaks—settled where Poland and Czechoslovakia are today. Their religious ties came to be with the Roman Catholic Church, and their cultural ties were with western Europe. The South Slavs—Serbs, Croats, and Slovenes—settled in the Balkans, where Yugoslavia now lies, and had frequent contacts with the Byzantines.

The third and largest Slavic group, the Eastern Slavs, includes those now known as Ukrainians, Russians, and Belorussians. They lived north of the Black Sea between the Dnieper and Dniester rivers and had contacts mainly with the Byzantine Empire and northern Europe.

Most of the Eastern Slavs were farmers who hunted wild game and birds to supplement the wheat, rye, and oats they grew. In the forests they cleared land by cutting and burning trees and scattering the ash to enrich the soil. On the steppes they ignited a "sea of flame" to burn off the grass for planting.

Most farm homes were sturdy log houses called *izbas*. With knife, chisel, and ax the peasants skillfully shaped the logs, notching them so that they would fit together without nails. They used the same tools to carve their wooden furniture as well as their cooking and eating utensils.

Kievan Rus

Around A.D. 1100 Slavic traditions were written down in the *Primary Chronicle*, a record that combines legends and facts. According to the *Chronicle*, in about A.D. 860 the Slavic people from the northern forest village of Novgorod asked Vikings from Scandinavia for aid: "Our land is great and rich, but there is no order in it. Come to rule and reign over us." The Viking leader Rurik accepted the invitation. The Slavs called the Vikings and the area they controlled *Rus*; the word *Russia* is probably derived from this name.

Rise of Kiev

In about A.D. 880, Rurik's successor, Prince Oleg, conquered the fortress-village of Kiev to the south. Built high on a bluff where the forest meets the steppe, Kiev prospered because it lay on the Dnieper River trade route. Some still call it the mother of Eastern Slavic cities.

Kiev was the major city in Kievan Rus, a collection of principalities, or regions ruled by princes. A council of landowners and wealthy merchants called **boyars** assisted the princes. In return for military protection, these princes paid tribute to the Grand Prince of Kiev. Included in this tribute were valuable forest products—furs of sable and ermine, honey, amber, and beeswax for candles—as well as grain and slaves. The Grand Princes of Kiev exchanged this tribute for Byzantine silk, jewels, and wine. Proof of the Slavic city's commercial prominence are the more than 200,000 Arabic and Byzantine coins archaeologists have unearthed in Sweden. Income from this trade helped build Kiev's magnificent churches, schools, and libraries.

Trade was soon accompanied by religion. In A.D. 911, the *Chronicle* says, Grand Prince Oleg made a treaty with the Byzantines that guaranteed Kievan traders six months' supplies when they reached Constantinople. "After agreeing on the tribute and mutually binding themselves by oath, they [the Byzantines] kissed the cross, and invited Oleg to . . . swear an oath likewise." Oleg, however, swore by his weapons and the pagan gods of thunder and cattle rather than a Christian god. The people of Kiev did not become Christians until Vladimir (VLAD uh mihr) became Grand Prince in A.D. 988.

Arrival of Christianity

Vladimir's grandmother Olga had visited Constantinople in A.D. 957 and had become the first of the Kievan no-

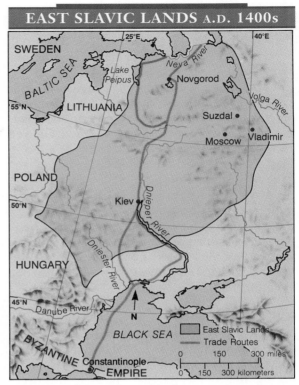

EAST SLAVIC LANDS A.D. 1400s

Learning from Maps *Trade routes through eastern Slavic lands extended the Byzantine culture.* ***How did this trade benefit Kiev in particular?***

bility to convert to Christianity. The Grand Prince, however, was originally a pagan, worshiping such deities as Perun, god of thunder and lightning, and the Great Mother, goddess of the lands and harvest.

Contact with the sophisticated Byzantine culture eventually convinced Vladimir that a new religion would help the Eastern Slavs become a more powerful civilization. According to one legend, he sent observers abroad to examine Judaism, Roman Catholicism, Eastern Orthodoxy, and Islam. Only the beautiful ceremony in the splendid Byzantine church of Hagia Sophia impressed the observers. In A.D. 989, after his own conversion to Eastern Orthodoxy, Vladimir ordered a mass baptism in the Dnieper River for his people.

The conversion to Eastern Orthodoxy brought Byzantine culture to Kievan Rus. Byzantine artisans taught the Eastern Slavs the arts of painting icons, making mosaics, and building churches in the Byzantine style. The Kievans also learned to write their language in the Cyrillic alphabet that Cyril had devised. Schools were established for the sons of boyars, priests, and merchants.

Acceptance of Eastern Orthodoxy also tended to isolate the Eastern Slavs. The Orthodox practice of translating the Bible into local languages meant that the Slavs learned Church Slavonic rather than Greek or Latin. As a result, they did not deepen their knowledge of the heritage of western European civilization. Instead, the Eastern Slavs turned for inspiration to the traditions of their own local cultures.

The schism between the Eastern and Western churches further deepened the gap and prevented the Eastern Slavs from sharing in the Renaissance that took place in western Europe after A.D. 1400.

Kiev at Its Height   When Vladimir's son, Yaroslav the Wise, became Grand Prince in A.D. 1019, Kievan culture reached its height. Yaroslav encouraged the spread of learning by establishing the first library in Kiev. Yaroslav also organized the Kievan legal system, drawing from Justinian's code. Written primarily for the princes and merchants, the code treated crimes of property as more serious than crimes against persons.

A skilled diplomat, Yaroslav arranged for his daughters and sisters to marry kings in Norway, Hungary, France, and Poland. To the Europeans, who were just arising from the isolation and disorder of the early Middle Ages, Kiev was a glittering capital whose culture outshone that of any in western Europe.

Decline of Kiev   After Yaroslav's death, Kiev declined in power and wealth for several reasons. First, Yaroslav began the practice of dividing up his lands among all his sons instead of willing them to one heir. Since no law established a clear line of succession, the heirs battled one another over control of Kiev. Second, the Latin Christian state created in Constantinople disrupted trade with the Byzantines and weakened Kiev's economy. Finally, in A.D. 1240 Mongol invaders from central Asia captured Kiev and completely destroyed it.

Learning from Art *East Slavic churches reflected the skills of their builders. Note the onion-shaped domes, which were based on Byzantine architecture.* **What Christian church became established in Kiev?**

Mongol Rule

The Mongols, or Tatars, as the Slavs called them, defeated the armies of the Russian princes and conquered most of the country except for Novgorod. They sacked towns and villages and killed thousands. Mongols sought to tax the peoples they conquered, rather than impose their culture. The Slavs were allowed to practice their Christian faith, but the Mongols required allegiance to the Mongol ruler and service in the Mongol army.

For two centuries, Mongol rule isolated the Eastern Slavs from European civilization. Although the occupation helped unify the Eastern Slavs, it also further distanced them from ideas and trends of the Western world.

Rise of Muscovy

As city life in the south declined after Kiev fell, the Eastern Slavs moved into the remote northern forests in order to escape Mongol rule. By the late A.D. 1200s, the principalities of Vladimir–Suzdal and Novgorod were the strongest Slavic territories.

Alexander Nevsky   The Mongols had never advanced as far north as Novgorod because the spring thaw turned the land into a swamp they could not cross. Instead, the city faced attacks in the Baltic Sea area from Swedes and Germans who wanted to convert the Eastern Slavs to Roman Catholicis... a ferocious battle on the Neva River in A.D. ... Alexander, prince of Novgorod, defeated ... ding Swedes. This victory earned him t... ame Alexander Nevsky, Alexander "of t... and his victory established Novgorod... ... independent principality.

Muscovy Develops   Da... son of Alexander Nevsky, b... Moscow, a small but prosperou... near vital land and water routes. ...est diplomatic marriages, the princes o... Muscovy, gradually expanded their s... tory. Muscovy's importance grew in ...

CONNECTIONS: GEOGRAPHY IN HISTORY

The Steppes

The steppe that is at the heart of the Eastern Slavic lands is part of a plain that stretches west to the Atlantic Ocean and east into central Asia. Even the Ural Mountains, the division between Europe and Asia, are so low that they present little obstacle to invaders.

Since ancient times this open, rolling plain has served as a highway for mounted nomads—Huns, Magyars, Mongols, and Turks—who were bent on plundering the richer lands to the west. Later from the west have come Polish and Lithuanian conquerors and French and German invaders.

It is little wonder that the Russians, a branch of the Eastern Slavs, tried to build a protective zone around the Kiev–Novgorod–Moscow heartland. In the late 1500s, the Russian rulers solved the problem of invasion from the east by expanding their domain in all directions. One of the areas that they made part of their large empire was Siberia, the huge arctic area east of the Urals.

In the early twentieth century, the Russian Empire became the Soviet Union following a revolution. The Soviet Union has faced periodic challenges from invaders. During World War II, it suffered a devastating invasion by Germans from the west. By keeping control over the countries of Eastern Europe after the war, the Soviets effectively widened the zone that protected their borders.

Making the Connection

1. Why did the Russians pursue a policy of expanding their territory?
2. Did the expansion of the United States from the Atlantic to the Pacific develop from similar motives? Explain.

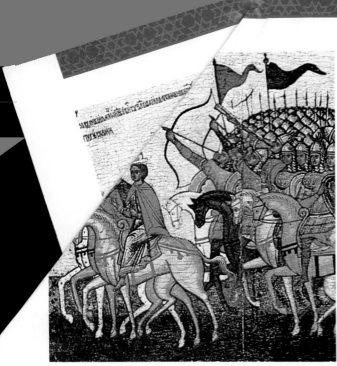

Learning from Art *The defense of Novgorod in A.D. 1169 against the rival city of Vladimir–Suzdal is depicted in this fifteenth-century Russian icon.* **What other forces attacked Novgorod?**

Muscovite forces defeated the Mongols at the Battle of Kulikovo in A.D. 1380. The tide had turned in favor of Muscovy. Over the next hundred years, the Eastern Slavs steadily drove out the Mongols. In A.D. 1480 during the rule of Ivan III, Moscow finally refused to pay taxes to the Mongols. The long submission to the Asian rulers was over. Today, Ivan is known as Ivan the Great because he was able to bring all the Slavic principalities under his rule. His major gain was Novgorod, which controlled territory all the way east to the Ural Mountains, the traditional division between Europe and Asia.

The Third Rome   Other factors helped to strengthen the power of Moscow's rulers. After Constantinople fell to the Ottoman Turks in A.D. 1453, Muscovy stood alone as the center of the Eastern Orthodox Church. In A.D. 1472 when Ivan III married Sophia, niece of the last Byzantine emperor, he took the title **tsar**, or caesar, the title used by the Roman and Byzantine emperors.

In A.D. 1493 Ivan added the title "Sovereign of All Russia." The lands he ruled, now known as Russia, were a hundred times as large as the original Muscovite state. The people spoke one language, and the princes served one tsar. The Russian Orthodox Church, which identified its interests with those of the Muscovite ruler, proclaimed that Russia was the Third Rome. The church regarded Ivan as both the successor of the Byzantine emperor and protector of the Eastern Orthodox Church, a claim all succeeding Russian tsars would also make.

when the metropolitan, or leader of the Orthodox Church in the Eastern Slavic lands, was transferred there from Vladimir–Suzdal. By the late A.D. 1400s, Moscow had become the most powerful city. Cooperation with Mongol policies had kept it free from outside interference. In fact, Daniel's son, Prince Ivan I, became known as Money Bag because the Mongols trusted him to collect taxes for them.

SECTION 3 REVIEW

Recall

1. **Define:** steppe, boyar, tsar
2. **Identify:** Rurik, Vladimir, Alexander Nevsky, Ivan III
3. **Locate:** Dnieper River, Kiev, the steppe, Moscow

Critical Thinking

4. **Describe:** How did Christianity affect Eastern Slavs?

5. **Explain:** What role did the Vikings play in Slavic and Byzantine history?
6. **Analyze:** Contrast the Kievan state with Muscovy. How was each dependent on geography? What role did the church play in each?
7. **Synthesize:** Imagine that you are a Russian boyar under

Ivan III. Would you resist calling him tsar? Explain.

Applying Concepts

8. **Cultural diffusion:** What traditions that had originated with Rome became part of Russian culture? How did Russian culture differ from the civilization of western Europe? Why?

DISTINGUISHING BETWEEN FACT AND OPINION

Imagine that it is the year of a presidential election and that your history teacher has given you the assignment to watch a televised debate between the two principal candidates. After watching the debate, you are asked to decide whom you would vote for and to give a list of reasons for your decision. In order to decide, you would have to be able to *distinguish between the facts and the opinions* the candidates used during the debate.

Explanation

A fact is a statement or piece of information that can be proved or verified by evidence. An opinion, though, presents a personal viewpoint that cannot be proved true or false.

Use these steps to help distinguish between fact and opinion in written material and visual media presentations.

- While reading or listening to informational material, think about the distinctions between fact and opinion.
- Look for words and phrases that indicate opinion, such as *I think, I believe, probably, seems to me, may, might, could, ought, in my judgment,* or *in my view.*
- Examine the material for expressions of approval and disapproval, such as *good, bad, poor,* and *satisfactory.*

- Be aware of such superlatives as *greatest, worst, finest,* and *best.*
- Look for words that have negative meanings such as *squander, contemptible,* and *disgrace.*
- Note the use of generalizations that include words like *none, every,* and *always.*
- Look for specific data that support a statement of fact.
- Determine whether information is fact or opinion.

Example

Examine the following statements to identify examples of fact and opinion.

1. (a) The Byzantine Empire came to a pitiful end at the hands of the savage Turks. (Opinion: uses negative words—*pitiful* and *savage*—to imply disapproval.)
   (b) The Byzantine Empire ended when Constantine XI died while defending Constantinople from invading Turks in A.D. 1453. (Fact: can be verified by reading a scholar's article or text.)
2. (a) The Ten Commandments are found in the Old Testament of the Bible. (Fact: can be verified by looking in the Bible.)
   (b) Icon worship promotes idolatry and is wrong. (Opinion: uses negative wording to judge and evaluate cultural and artistic value.)

3. (a) In the A.D. 900s, Kiev was the most isolated, uncivilized place and possessed little in the way of culture. (Opinion: uses superlative *most* and negative words *uncivilized* and *little*.)
   (b) The alliance with the Byzantine Empire made Kiev a major trading link between Europe and Asia and between Scandinavia and the Middle East. (Fact: Archaeologists in Sweden have unearthed Arabic and Byzantine coins, evidence that extensive trade occurred.)

Application

Read the following statements. Determine which are factual and which express opinion. Give reasons for your choices.

1. The *Primary Chronicle* states that in A.D. 911 Grand Prince Oleg agreed on a peace treaty with the Byzantine Emperors Leo and Alexander.
2. The Volga River is longer than the Danube River.
3. The Russian Orthodox Church is the only religion I would join.
4. Nomads wandered aimlessly throughout the steppes and lived in flimsy shelters.

Practice

Turn to Practicing Skills on page 231 in the Chapter Review for further practice in distinguishing between fact and opinion.

CHAPTER 9 REVIEW

HISTORICAL SIGNIFICANCE

As a crossroads of trade, the Byzantine Empire was a center for cultural diffusion. The code of laws that developed under Justinian preserved Roman law and in time served as the foundation for legal systems in most of Europe. By preserving the writings of ancient Greek and Roman authors, Byzantine scholars made the learning of the past available to western Europe.

The Byzantine Church spread Christianity by sending missionaries to convert the Slavs. In addition, the Byzantines were innovators. Their icons became part of the religious art of the Eastern Slavs, and their architecture inspired building styles in Eastern Europe and the Middle East.

Through ties to the Eastern Orthodox Church and marriage into the Byzantine imperial family, the rulers of Russia claimed to be heirs of Rome and protectors of the Eastern Orthodox Church. Prevented from sharing in the ideas from the West by their use of the Cyrillic alphabet and by the schism between the Eastern and Western churches, Eastern Slavs were suspicious of outsiders. The long isolation during Mongol rule fortified this attitude, which persisted into modern times.

SUMMARY

For a summary of Chapter 9, see the Unit 3 Synopsis on pages 354–357.

USING KEY TERMS

Write the key term that best completes each sentence below.

a. boyar
b. clergy
c. icon
d. iconoclast
e. illuminated manuscript
f. laity
g. mosaic
h. schism
i. steppe
j. tsar

1. Priests are members of the ___ , and ordinary church goers are ___ .
2. Tiny stones set in plaster are called ___ .
3. The year A.D. 1054 marks the ___ between the churches of East and West.
4. Emperor Leo III was considered an ___ .
5. Those who assisted the princes in Kiev were called ___ .
6. Byzantine scholars often preserved ancient writings in ___ .
7. Eastern Slavs lived in an area called the ___.
8. Ivan II took the title of ___.
9. ___ are religious images.

REVIEWING FACTS

1. **Explain:** Why was the Justinian Code significant?
2. **Describe:** How did religious art become the center of a controversy in the Eastern Orthodox Church?
3. **Explain:** What contribution did Cyril make to learning?
4. **Identify:** Who are the three groups of Slavs and in what part of modern Europe is each found?
5. **Explain:** How did the Russians become isolated from the rest of Europe?

THINKING CRITICALLY

1. **Analyze:** Explain how the title of New Rome was both suitable and unsuitable for Constantinople.
2. **Analyze:** Why was the preservation of Greek and Roman learning a significant contribution of Byzantine civilization?
3. **Analyze:** Examine the reasons for the schism in the Christian church. Could the split have been prevented? Explain.
4. **Synthesize:** Compare and contrast the Byzantine and Roman empires.

ANALYZING CONCEPTS

1. **Conflict:** How does conflict such as the iconoclast controversy in the Byzantine Empire weaken a government?
2. **Innovation:** Do you believe that one society's ideas can be adapted to other societies? Explain.
3. **Cultural Diffusion:** How can two cultures be enriched by sharing cultural aspects?

PRACTICING SKILLS

1. Write three factual statements and three value judgments based on the material in this chapter. State why each is a fact or value judgment.
2. Read the following statements from *Byzantium and Europe* by Speros Vryonis. Determine which are value judgments and explain why.
   a. "His [Justinian's] personality and genius inspired and permeated all the great achievements that were accomplished during his long rule."
   b. "But in the hostilities which ensued, Constantinople was forced to concede to Charlemagne the title of Basileus in 812."
   c. "The succession of the incompetent and brutal Phocas marked the low point of the decline which followed Justinian's death."

GEOGRAPHY IN HISTORY

1. **Location:** Refer to the map on page 215. What made Constantinople a natural crossroad for trade?
2. **Movement:** Refer to the map on page 225. Describe the trade route from Constantinople to the Baltic Sea.
3. **Region:** Refer to the maps on pages 215 and 222. Trace the changes in the Byzantine Empire from A.D. 565 to A.D. 1054.

TRACING CHRONOLOGY

Refer to the time line below to answer these questions.
1. How long did the Byzantine Empire last after it was separated from Rome?
2. How long after Leo III banned icons did the split between the Eastern and Western churches occur?
3. How long were the Eastern Slavs under Mongol rule?

LINKING PAST AND PRESENT

1. Investigate the role the Bosporus played in World Wars I and II.
2. Explain the historical reasons for the Soviet decision to make the Eastern European nations its satellites after World War II.
3. Investigate the historical roots of religious controversies in modern societies.

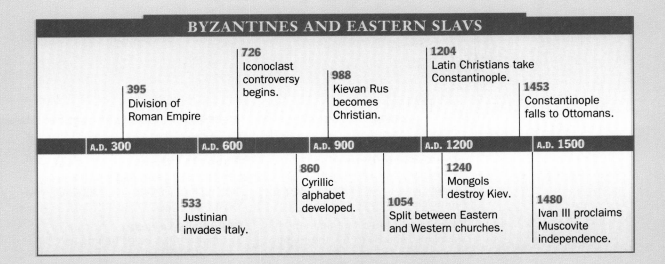

BYZANTINES AND EASTERN SLAVS

395 Division of Roman Empire

726 Iconoclast controversy begins.

988 Kievan Rus becomes Christian.

1204 Latin Christians take Constantinople.

1453 Constantinople falls to Ottomans.

A.D. 300 — A.D. 600 — A.D. 900 — A.D. 1200 — A.D. 1500

533 Justinian invades Italy.

860 Cyrillic alphabet developed.

1054 Split between Eastern and Western churches.

1240 Mongols destroy Kiev.

1480 Ivan III proclaims Muscovite independence.

Islam

I was in Mecca at last," writes a devout Muslim woman about her pilgrimage in 1974 to Mecca, the holiest city of the religion of Islam. She continues, "Before me was the Kaaba, a great black cube partly submerged in a torrent of white-robed pilgrims circling round and round. Around us, like a great dam containing the torrent, stood the massive walls and the seven slim minarets of the Sacred Mosque. High above, the muezzin began the evening call to prayer: 'Allahu Akbar! . . . God is Most Great!'. . .

"Around the Kaaba . . . repeating the customary prayers, swirled men and women of every race and nation, from every corner of the earth. . . . "

All believers of Islam hope to participate in this event at least once in their lives. Since the A.D. 600s, it has been one of the unifying events for all Muslims.

CHAPTER PREVIEW

Key Terms to Define: sheikh, revelation, *shari'ah*, imam, hajj, caliph, jihad, *madrasa,* arabesque, chronicle

People to Meet: Muhammad, Muslims, Abu Bakr, Ali, the Rightly Guided Caliphs, Mu'awiyah, Husayn, Umayyads, Abbasids, al-Razi, Ibn Sina, Moses Maimonides, Ibn Khaldun

Places to Discover: the Arabian Peninsula, Mecca, Medina, the Islamic state, Damascus, Baghdad, Cordoba

Objectives to Learn:
1. What are the basic beliefs and practices of Islam?
2. How did the Islamic state expand and why did it decline?
3. How did Islam affect Muslims?

Mosques serve as places of worship for followers of Islam.

4. What were the achievements of the Islamic state, and how were they spread to other cultures?

Concepts to Understand:

• Innovation—The faith and principles of Islam that Muhammad first preached in the Arabian Peninsula became the basis of a new civilization. Section 1

• Movement—Armies and traders spread Islam through the Middle East and North Africa, and into Spain and Asia. Section 2

• Diversity—Contributions from many cultures and peoples enriched the Islamic state. Section 3

• Cultural diffusion—The ideas and achievements of the Muslim world were spread to others. Section 3

233

Rise of Islam

South of Asia Minor was the Arabian Peninsula, home of the Arabs. This location placed the Arabs at the furthest reaches of the great Middle East civilizations. Like the ancient Hebrews, Phoenicians, and Chaldeans, whom you read about in Chapter 3, the Arabs were descended from Semitic tribes. Archaeologists have traced Arab civilizations in the Arabian Peninsula, or Arabia, to at least 3000 B.C.

Arab Life

The relative geographic remoteness of the Arabian Peninsula kept the empires in the northern part of the region from invading Arab lands. Their isolation allowed the Arabs to create their own civilization.

The Setting   The Arabian Peninsula is a wedge of land of about 1 million square miles (2.6 million square kilometers) between the Red Sea and the Persian Gulf. The peninsula is made up of two distinct regions. The southwestern area, across from the northeast coast of Africa, has well-watered valleys nestled between mountains. The rest of the peninsula, however, consists of arid plains and deserts. Mountains block moist air from reaching the interior, which is hot and dry. Drifting sand dunes cover most of the southeastern part of the peninsula. This area, about the size of Texas, is so barren that it is called the Empty Quarter.

Yet the peninsula is not entirely forbidding. Grass grows quickly during the showers of the rainy season, and oases, the fertile areas around springs and water holes, provide a permanent source of water for farmers, herders, and travelers. For centuries, nomadic herders and caravans have crisscrossed the desert, traveling from oasis to oasis.

Lives of the Bedouin   In ancient times many of the Arabs were bedouin (BEHD uh wihn), nomads who herded sheep, camels, and goats and lived in tents made of felt from camel or goat hair. They ate mainly fresh or dried dates or cakes made of dates pounded together, and they drank milk from their herds; on special occasions they added mutton to their diet.

The bedouin lived in tribes, each made up of related families. Arabs valued family ties because they ensured protection and survival in the harsh desert environment. Leading each tribe was a **sheikh**, or chief, appointed by the heads of the families. A council of elders advised the sheikh, who ruled as long as he had the tribe's consent. Survival in the desert depended on everyone's obeying tribal rules based on such values as honor, generosity, loyalty, and bravery.

Warfare was part of bedouin life. The Arab tribes went on raids to gain camels and horses and battled one another over pastures and water holes, the most precious resources in the desert. To protect their honor and their possessions, the bedouins believed in retaliation—"an eye for an eye, and a tooth for a tooth." Raids often led to blood feuds, quarrels in which a tribe sought revenge against an enemy tribe. Sometimes a blood feud went on for generations.

For entertainment bedouins enjoyed a variety of activities. Camel and horse races and other games sharpened the men's abilities as warriors, and then everyone enjoyed an evening of storytelling around the campfires, an oral tradition through which children learned the history of their tribe.

Poets composed and recited poems about battles, deserts, camels and horses, and love. Yearly, poets from different tribes met to compete. The Arabs regarded each line, or *bayt*, in a poem as very important. In these lines Sheikh Al Abbas Ibn Merdas states his view of war:

*From the cup of peace
drink your fill;
but from the cup of war
a sip will suffice.*

Growth of Towns

By the A.D. 500s, many tribes had settled around oases or in fertile valleys to pursue either agriculture or trade. Groups of merchants soon emerged and founded prosperous market towns—Yathrib, an oasis of fertile farms and villages; Taif, a mountain refuge where wealthy Arabs spent the sweltering summer months; and Mecca, a crossroads of commerce about 50 miles (80 kilometers) inland from the Red Sea. Of these towns, Mecca was by far the most prominent.

Trade and Religion in Mecca

People from all over the Arabian Peninsula traveled to Mecca to trade animal products for weapons, dates, grain, spices, jewels, ivory, silk, and perfumes. Enormous caravans from the fertile southwest passed through Mecca en route to Syria. Caravans heading east from the Red Sea passed through Mecca on the way to Iraq and the overland route that led east to China.

Arabs also visited Mecca to worship at Arabia's holiest shrine, the Kaaba, which contained statues of the many Arab deities. In one corner, set in silver, was the Black Stone, which the Arabs believed the angel Gabriel had given to Abraham. The business the pilgrims brought to Mecca made its merchants wealthy.

Signs of Change

As business ties began to replace tribal ties in the trading towns, the old tribal rules were no longer adequate. At the same time, the Byzantine and Persian empires were threatening to take over Arab lands. The Arabs had a common language, but they lacked a sense of unity and had no central government to solve these new problems. Nevertheless, several regional Arab kingdoms did flourish at the time. One was in Yemen in southwest Arabia. Two others were in southern Syria and Iraq. The Christian Arab kingdom of the Ghassanids (gus AH nids) in southern Arabia was an ally of the Byzantines and fought against the Arab kingdom of the Lakhmids (LAH kmids) in southern Iraq, which was allied with the Persians.

Religious ideas were also changing. Contacts with the Byzantines, the Persians, and the Ethiopians introduced the teachings of the monotheistic religions of Judaism and Christianity. Moreover, a number of Christian and Jewish Arabs lived in the peninsula. Dissatisfied with their old beliefs, many idol-worshiping Arabs searched for a new religion. Holy men known as hanifs (hah NEEFS) denounced the worship of idols and believed in one god. They rejected Judaism and Christianity, however, pre-

Learning from Art *In towns and oases along caravan routes were fortified inns. Built for the safety and care of travelers, these inns contained a hospital, lodgings, and a mosque. Traveling merchants were often provided with water, food, and sleeping quarters before the real business of trading began.* **How did trade affect tribal life?**

ferring to find a uniquely Arab form of monotheism.

This ferment in Arab religious life contributed to the emergence of a new religion, known as Islam, which means "submission to the will of God." This new faith would bring the Arabs into contact with other civilizations and change Arab history.

Revelation of Islam

The founder of Islam, Muhammad, was born in the bustling city of Mecca around A.D. 570. Muslim traditions state that Muhammad was orphaned at an early age and raised by an uncle.

Life of Muhammad   During his teens, Muhammad worked as a caravan leader on a prosperous trade route. His reputation as an exceptionally honest and able person prompted his employer, a wealthy widow of 40 named Khadija (kuh DEE juh), to put him in charge of her business affairs. When Muhammad was about 25 years old, Khadija proposed marriage to him.

It was his marriage to Khadija that relieved Muhammad of financial worries and gave him time to reflect on the meaning of life. He was troubled by the greed of Mecca's wealthy citizens, the worship of idols, the immorality of city life, and the mistreatment of the poor. Seeking guidance, Muhammad began to spend time alone praying and fasting in a cave outside the city.

Revelation   Islamic tradition holds that, in A.D. 610, Muhammad experienced a **revelation**, or vision. He heard a voice calling him to be the apostle of the one true deity—Allah, the Arabic word for God. Three times the voice proclaimed, "Recite!" When Muhammad asked what he should recite, the voice replied:

*R*ecite in the name of your Lord, the Creator,
Who created man from clots of blood.
Recite! Your Lord is the most bountiful One
Who by the pen has taught mankind things
  they did not know.

A second revelation commanded Muhammad to "rise and warn" the people about divine judgment. Although Muhammad had doubts about the revelations, he finally accepted his divine mission.

In A.D. 613, Muhammad began sharing his revelations with his family and friends. He preached to the people of Mecca that there was only one God and that people everywhere must worship and obey him. He also declared that all who believed in God were equal. Therefore the rich should share their wealth with the poor. Muhammad also preached that God measured the worth of people by their devotion and good deeds. He told the people of Mecca to live their lives in preparation for the day of judgment, when God would punish evildoers and reward the just.

Muhammad made slow progress in winning converts to his message. Khadija and members of Muhammad's family became the first Muslims, or followers of Islam. Most of the other converts came from Mecca's poor, who were attracted by Muhammad's call for social justice.

Opposition to Islam   The majority of Meccans rejected Muhammad's message. Wealthy merchants and religious leaders were upset by the prophet's attacks on the images at the Kaaba. They feared that monotheistic worship would end the pilgrimages to Mecca, threaten their livelihood, and undermine the wealth and prestige of the city. Driven by these fears, the Meccan merchants began to persecute Muhammad and the Muslims.

Muhammad persisted in his preaching until threats against his life forced him to seek help outside the city. He found it in Yathrib, a small town north of Mecca. At the time, Yathrib was torn by a quarrel between two rival tribes. Its citizens agreed to protect Muhammad and the Muslims if he would settle their dispute.

In A.D. 622, Muhammad sent about 60 Muslim families from Mecca to Yathrib; soon after, he followed them in secret. His departure to Yathrib is known in Muslim history as the *Hijrah* (HIH jruh), or emigration. The year in which the *Hijrah* took place, A.D. 622, marks the beginning of the Islamic era and is the first year of the Muslim calendar.

Persian Manuscripts

The art of Islam has taken many forms over the centuries. Among the most beautiful objects produced by Islamic artists were miniatures, or manuscript paintings. The Persian tradition of painting was one of Islam's most spectacular. Usually made as book illustrations, Persian miniatures embellished widely varied texts: scientific treatises, heroic epics, romances, and poems.

This Persian manuscript painting from the 1500s depicts pilgrims on their way to Mecca.

Miniatures were produced by skilled artists who often worked together in studios or workshops. In the A.D. 1400s and 1500s, Persian royal studios produced many beautiful books. Work was divided among several specialized artists. One artist might be responsible for laying out the pages, and others would produce the paintings, borders, gold decoration, and calligraphy.

The Persian manuscript pictured here shows a caravan of pilgrims on their way to Mecca. It has several features typical of Islamic painting in the early 1500s. One of these characteristics is the use of colorful, lively patterns. Here, the attention to patterns is most evident in the clothing and saddle blankets and in the scattered plants that carpet the ground. The overall composition, or arrangement, of the picture emphasizes the two-dimensional pattern of the page rather than depth or perspective. Instead of using one figure or group as a focal point, the artist gave each portion of the picture almost equal emphasis.

The schematic landscape setting is also typical of Persian painting of this time. With the high horizon line, the artist essentially tilts the ground up, as though we are looking down upon it. Figures within the landscape are shown as though seen from the side, not from above. The figures at the top of the composition are most distant from the viewer. Using this method, the artist was able to treat all figures in the painting with the same intensity and exactitude.

The art of the book in Persian culture had a long tradition—not only of literary history but also of picture-making. Made for private ownership and enjoyment, the primary function of Persian miniatures was to delight the eye with the beautiful rhythm and color of the painted page.

Responding to the Arts

1. What features of Persian painting around 1500 does this manuscript show?
2. What sort of texts did images like the one shown here illustrate?

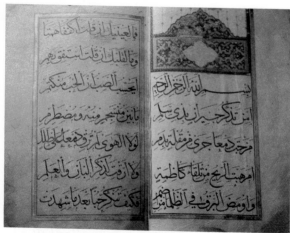

Learning from Art *A distinguishing characteristic of Islamic books is the beauty of writing combined with abstract designs.* **What is the most important book of Islam?**

Islamic Community Grows

The people of Yathrib accepted Muhammad as the messenger of God and the ruler of their city. As the center of Islam, Yathrib became known as Madinat al-Nabi, "the city of the prophet," or Medina (muh DEE nuh).

Origin of the Islamic State   Muhammad proved that he was a skilled political and religious leader. In the Medina Compact of a.d. 624, Muhammad decreed that all Muslims were to place loyalty to the Islamic community above loyalty to their tribe. The Islamic community, he proclaimed, must be based on greater allegiance—loyalty to God—and on obedience to divine law, not tribal law, which encouraged blood feuds. Disputes were to be settled by Muhammad, who was declared the community's lawgiver and commander-in-chief. All areas of life were placed under the divine law given to Muhammad and recorded in the Quran (kuh RAHN), the holy scriptures of Islam. Muhammad also extended protection to Jews and Christians who accepted the political authority of the Islamic community.

The Medina Compact shows that Muhammad was a gifted political organizer and a wise decision maker as well as an inspired prophet.

The Medina Compact created an Islamic state and culture as well as a religion.

Islam's Triumph   Although the Muslims were safe in Medina, opposition from Mecca continued. Muhammad began to lead the Muslims in raids against the caravans moving north from Mecca. His forces defeated the Meccans in two battles, and Muhammad won the support of Arab tribes outside Medina.

When Muhammad and his followers entered Mecca in A.D. 630, they faced little resistance. The Meccans accepted Islam and acknowledged Muhammad as God's prophet. The Muslims destroyed the idols in the Kaaba and turned the shrine into a place of worship for Muslim pilgrims. Mecca became the spiritual capital of Islam, and Medina remained its political capital.

Following their victory in Mecca, the Muslims extended their control into other parts of Arabia. By A.D. 631 the Islamic state included the entire peninsula and was supported by a strong army recruited from all the Arab tribes.

After a brief illness, Muhammad died at Medina in A.D. 632. He left behind two major achievements: a new monotheistic religion that stood on an equal level with Judaism and Christianity and a well-organized political-religious community that increased the Arabs' power and influence.

Beliefs and Practices of Islam

Muhammad established basic beliefs and practices for his followers based on his revelations. In spite of social and political changes, these beliefs and practices have remained remarkably stable.

The Quran   According to Muslim tradition, the angel Gabriel revealed divine messages to Muhammad over a 22-year period. Faithful Muslims wrote down or memorized these messages, but they were not compiled into one written collection until after Muhammad died. Then his successor, Abu Bakr, ordered Muslims to retrieve these messages from wherever they could be found, from the "ribs of palm-leaves and tablets of white stone and from the breasts of men." It took 20 years before the messages were compiled into the holy book of Islam, the Quran, whose name means "recital." For all Muslims, the Quran is the final authority in matters of faith and practice.

Written in Arabic, the Quran is believed to contain God's message as revealed to Muhammad. This message is expressed in stories, legends, and poems. Some of the stories—such as Noah's ark and Jonah in the belly of the whale—are variations of those found in the Bible.

Moral Values   The Quran presents the basic moral values of Islam, which are similar to those of Judaism and Christianity. Muslims are commanded to honor their parents, show kindness to their neighbors, protect orphans and widows, and give generously to the poor. Murder, stealing, lying, and adultery are condemned.

The Quran also lays down specific rules to guide Muslims in their daily activities. It forbids gambling, eating pork, or drinking alcoholic beverages. It also contains rules governing marriage, divorce, property inheritance, and business practices.

Law   Law cannot be separated from religion in Islamic society. Although Islam has no ranked order of clergy, generations of legal scholars and theologians have organized Islamic moral rules into a code of law known as the **shari'ah** (shuh REE uh). Based on the Quran and the *Hadith*, or sayings of Muhammad, the *shari'ah* covers all aspects of Muslim private and public life.

Five Pillars of Islam

The Quran presents the Five Pillars of Islam, or the five essential duties that all Muslims are to fulfill. They are the confession of faith, prayer, almsgiving, fasting, and the pilgrimage to Mecca.

Faith   The first pillar is the confession of faith, or creed, which affirms the oneness of an all-powerful, just, and merciful God. All Muslims are required to submit completely to the will of God as revealed in the Quran.

Learning from Artifacts   *This mihrab made of ceramic tiles is completely covered with geometric and flowery patterns and verses from the Quran in Arabic script.* **Why is Islamic art so abstract and symbolic?**

The creed stresses Muhammad's role as a prophet; he is not considered divine. Muslims view him as the last and most important of several prophets, messengers who have brought God's word to different peoples. To Muslims, Allah is the same god as the God of the Jews and the Christians; and Abraham, Moses, and Jesus are considered prophets.

Prayer   Verses, or suras, in the Quran open with the phrase "In the name of God, the Merciful and Compassionate" as an acknowledgment of God's power, justice, and mercy. Muslims express their devotion in prayers offered five times each day—sunrise, noon, afternoon, sunset, and evening. Worshipers pray while facing Mecca, always using the same set of words and motions—kneeling, bowing, and touching one's forehead to the ground as a sign of submission to God.

Muslims can offer their daily prayers outside or inside, at work or at home. At noon on Fridays, many pray together in a mosque, a building that may serve as a place of worship, a school, a court of law, and a shelter.

Learning from Paintings *The faithful traveled to Mecca bearing palm leaves as a sign that they were on a pilgrimage. The hajj is the fifth pillar of Islam. What are the other four?*

An imam (ih MAM), or prayer leader, guides believers in prayer, and a sermon sometimes follows. Any male Muslim with the proper religious education can serve as an imam, or preacher.

Alms   The third pillar of Islam is the giving of alms, or charity. It reflects the Islamic view that the wealthy should assist the poor and weak. Almsgiving is practiced privately through contributions to the needy and publicly through a state tax that supports schools and aids the poor.

Fasting   The fourth pillar of Islam, fasting, occurs in the month of Ramadan (ram uh DAHN), the ninth month in the Muslim calendar. During Ramadan, Muhammad received the first revelation. From sunrise to sunset Muslims neither eat nor drink, although they work as usual. Children, pregnant women, travelers, and the sick are exempt from fasting. At sunset the call for prayer—and in large cities the sound of a cannon—announces the end of the fast. Muslims then sit down to eat their "evening breakfast." In the cool evening hours, people stream out into the streets to greet their friends. At the end of Ramadan, there is a three-day celebration for the end of the fast.

Pilgrimage   The fifth pillar of the religion of Islam is the annual pilgrimage, or **hajj,** to Mecca. Every able-bodied Muslim who can afford the trip is expected to make the pilgrimage at least once in his or her lifetime. Those who perform the hajj are especially honored in the community.

The hajj takes place about two months after the Ramadan fast and involves three days of ceremony, prayer, and sacrifice. Today, hundreds of thousands of Muslims like the woman at the beginning of the chapter, come together to worship at the Kaaba and other shrines of Islam in Mecca and Medina. A visible expression of Muslim unity, the hajj allows a continuing exchange of ideas among the peoples of Africa, Europe, Asia, North America, and South America who follow Islam.

SECTION 1 REVIEW

Recall

1. **Define:** sheikh, revelation, *shari'ah*, imam, hajj
2. **Identify:** Muhammad, Muslims, *Hijrah,* Quran, Medina Compact
3. **Locate:** Arabian Peninsula, Mecca, Medina
4. **Explain:** What made life possible in the harsh environment of the Arabian Peninsula?

Critical Thinking

5. **Analyze:** In what ways was Islam a new religion? In what ways was it an extension or a continuation of other religions that were also founded in this region—Judaism and Christianity?
6. **Synthesize:** Contrast the unity of the bedouin tribe and the unity of the Islamic community.

7. **Analyze:** Why do you think Abu Bakr wanted to compile Muhammad's revelations into one written collection?

Applying Concepts

8. **Innovation:** Describe the Five Pillars of Islam and the Medina Compact and tell how they changed life in the Arabian Peninsula.

Spread of Islam

When Muhammad died in A.D. 632, he had left no clear instructions about who was to succeed him as the leader of Islam. Muslims knew that no one could take Muhammad's place as the messenger of God. They realized, however, that the Islamic community needed a strong political-religious leader who could preserve its unity and guide its daily affairs. A group of prominent Muslims met and chose a leader, whom they called *khalifah* (ku LEE fuh) or **caliph** (KAY lihf), meaning "successor." This caliph was Muhammad's successor only as a leader of the Muslim community, not as a prophet.

The Rightly Guided Caliphs

The first four caliphs were elected for life. All were close friends or relatives of Muhammad. The first caliph was Muhammad's father-in-law and close friend, Abu Bakr (uh BOO BAHK er). The last, his son-in-law Ali (uh LEE), was married to Muhammad's daughter Fatimah (FAH ti muh). The first four caliphs followed the prophet's example, kept in close touch with the people, and asked the advice of other Muslim leaders. For these reasons, Muslims have called them the Rightly Guided Caliphs.

Early Conquests   The Rightly Guided Caliphs sought to protect and spread Islam. They conducted military expeditions that carried Islam beyond the Arabian Peninsula. The Arabs were eager to spread Islam and acquire the agricultural wealth of the Byzantine and Persian empires to meet the needs of the growing population.

Arab armies swept forth against the weakened Byzantine and Persian empires. By A.D. 650, these armies had acquired Palestine, Syria, Iraq, Persia, and Egypt. The conquests reduced the Asian territories of the Byzantine Empire to Asia Minor and the area around Constantinople and brought the Persian Empire completely under Muslim control.

The Arab armies were successful for several reasons. Their faith united them in seeking a common goal that they considered holy—to carry Islam to other peoples. According to the Quran, Muslims had a religious duty to struggle for the faith, even by armed force. The Islamic state, therefore, viewed the conquests as a **jihad** (jih HAHD), or holy war, against infidels, or unbelievers. Islamic teaching promised that warriors who died in a jihad would immediately enter paradise. Furthermore, the two empires that the Muslims defeated, the Byzantine and the Persian, had been weakened militarily and economically by the wars they had been fighting with each other for many years. The Byzantine Empire was further weakened by the religious controversies you read about in Chapter 9.

Division Within Islam   While Muslim armies were achieving military success, rival groups fought for control of the caliphate, the office of the caliph. The struggle began when Ali was elected the fourth caliph in A.D. 656.

One of Ali's most powerful rivals was Mu'awiyah (moo UH wee uh), governor of Syria and nephew of the third caliph, Uthman, who had been murdered. Mu'awiyah wanted revenge for that murder and accused Ali's supporters of encouraging it. When Ali tried to depose the Syrian governor, Mu'awiyah refused to step down.

In the battle that followed, Mu'awiyah's defeat seemed certain. Then the Syrian soldiers tied copies of pages from the Quran to the tips of their lances and charged, shouting, "Let Allah

{God} decide!" Unwilling to strike an enemy bearing the word of God, Ali was forced to negotiate with Mu'awiyah.

While Ali was trying to reassert his control as caliph, Mu'awiyah took over Egypt and raided Iraq. In A.D. 661, Ali was fatally stabbed by a disillusioned follower, and his older son renounced his claim to the caliphate. Mu'awiyah became the first caliph of the powerful Umayyad (oo MY ahd) dynasty.

Followers of Ali, known as Shiites (SHEE aits), never accepted Mu'awiyah's rule. When he died in A.D. 680, they claimed the caliphate for Ali's son, Husayn, then in Medina. Husayn's followers in Iraq invited him to lead them as caliph. When he arrived in Iraq with his family and a small group of followers, Umayyad troops massacred all but the women and a young son. The leader sent Husayn's head to Mu'awiyah's son, who had assumed the caliphate.

The murder of Muhammad's grandson shocked all Muslims. In some parts of the Islamic world today, the anniversary of Husayn's murder is still observed as a period of mourning.

The murders of Ali and Husayn also led to a permanent schism in the Islamic world. The majority of Muslims, known as Sunnis (SUHN eez), or "followers of the way," follow the teachings of Muhammad, the tradition followed by the Rightly Guided Caliphs. In Sunni Islam, the caliph may be any devout Muslim who is accepted by the people.

The Shiites, the smaller group of Muslims, live mostly in Iraq and Iran. They believe the caliphate should be held only by descendants of Muhammad through his daughter Fatimah and her husband Ali. The Shiites stress the imam's power as a spiritual leader. Over the centuries they also developed the belief that the imam was divinely appointed and saintly.

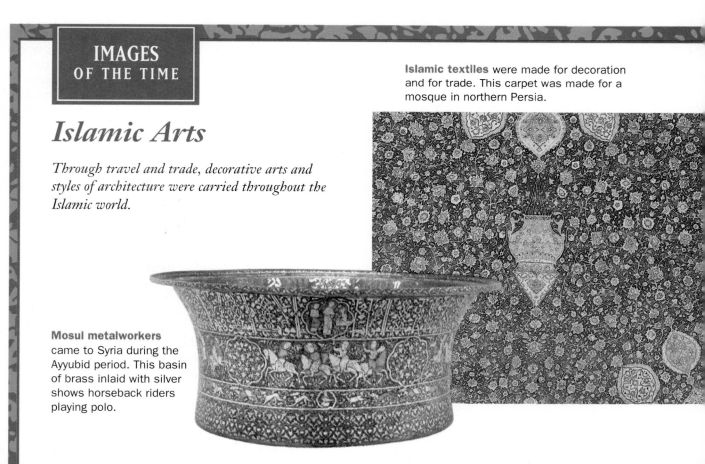

IMAGES
OF THE TIME

Islamic Arts

Through travel and trade, decorative arts and styles of architecture were carried throughout the Islamic world.

Islamic textiles were made for decoration and for trade. This carpet was made for a mosque in northern Persia.

Mosul metalworkers came to Syria during the Ayyubid period. This basin of brass inlaid with silver shows horseback riders playing polo.

The Islamic State

The Umayyad dynasty, which was founded by Mu'awiyah, ruled the Muslims for nearly a century, from A.D. 661 to 750, a period of tremendous change and achievement. The Umayyads moved the capital from Medina to Damascus, Syria, which was more centrally located in the expanding state.

Umayyad Conquests   In the next century, Umayyad warriors carried Islam east, to the borders of India and China. In the west, they swept across North Africa and into Spain, the southernmost area of Christian western Europe.

By A.D. 716 the Muslims ruled almost all of Spain. They advanced halfway into France before the Frankish leader Charles Martel stopped them (see Chapter 11). The Battle of Tours in A.D. 732 occurred just a hundred years after the death of Muhammad and halted the spread of Islam into western Europe.

Life in the Umayyad State   The Umayyads built a powerful Islamic state that stressed the political importance rather than the religious importance of their office. As time went by, they ruled more like kings and less like the earlier caliphs.

The Umayyads did, however, help to unite the lands they ruled. They made Arabic the official language, minted the first Arabic currency, built roads, and established postal routes. Their efficient administration depended on a civil service made up of the well-trained bureaucrats who had served as officials in the Byzantine and Persian empires.

Umayyad rule also improved conditions for many, particularly Jews and non-Greek Christians, who had often suffered discrimination

From minarets, or towers, muezzins called the faithful of the Islamic world to prayer. In Istanbul, minarets rise above the city.

Pottery decorations varied from region to region. This bowl is typical of Persian pottery of the A.D. 800s.

Reflecting on the Times
Why do you think the decorative arts flourished in the Islamic world during this period?

under Byzantine rule. They had to pay a special tax, but they were tolerated because they believed in one God. The great Arab commander Khalid ibn al-Walid, who had led the conquest of Syria and Persia, described Muslim policy:

*I*n the name of Allah, the compassionate, the merciful, this is what Khalid ibn al-Walid would grant to the inhabitants of Damascus. . . . He promises to give them security for their lives, property and churches. Their city wall shall not be demolished, neither shall any Muslim be quartered in their houses. Thereunto we give to them the pact of Allah and the protection of His Prophet, the Caliphs and the believers. So long as they pay the tax, nothing but good shall befall them.

Opposition to Umayyad Rule   Despite this enlightened outlook, Umayyad rule caused dissatisfaction among non-Arab Muslims. They paid higher taxes, received lower wages in the army and government, and were discriminated against socially. Discontent was particularly strong in Iraq and Persia, the center of the Shiite opposition to Umayyad rule.

The Abbasids   In the year A.D. 747, the anti-Umayyad Arabs and the non-Arab Muslims in Iraq and Persia joined forces, built an army, and, in three years of fighting, overwhelmed the Umayyads. The new caliph, Abu'l-'Abbas, was a descendant of one of Muhammad's uncles. He established the Abbasid (uh BAHS ihd) dynasty and had a new city, Baghdad, built on the banks of the Tigris River.

Situated on a fertile plain, Baghdad lay at the crossroads of the great land and water trade routes that stretched from the Mediterranean to the Far East. More than 100,000 skilled workers from every region of the empire worked for four years on the city. Baghdad was shaped like a cir-

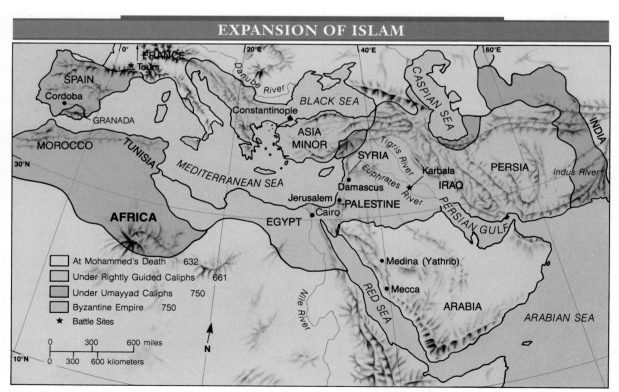

EXPANSION OF ISLAM

At Mohammed's Death   632
Under Rightly Guided Caliphs   661
Under Umayyad Caliphs   750
Byzantine Empire   750
★ Battle Sites

0   300   600 miles
0   300   600 kilometers

Learning from Maps   *By A.D. 750, the Islamic state stretched from western Europe to southern Asia.* **Which caliphs added most of the territory in Europe and North Africa? Which added most of the territory in Asia?**

cle. Three walls pierced by four gates surrounded it; two main roads connected the gates.

The two highways led to different parts of the empire and divided Baghdad into four pie-shaped sections. By the A.D. 900s, about 1.5 million people lived in Baghdad. At its heart stood the great mosque and the caliph's magnificent palace, where he ruled in splendor like the Persian rulers. Between the innermost wall and the middle wall were the luxurious homes of court members and army officials. City architects provided an open area for defense and a large park for recreation between the middle and outer walls. A deep moat surrounded the outer wall. Beyond this wall and the moat were the homes of the common people of Baghdad.

Breakup of the Islamic State The Abbasids ruled the Islamic state from A.D. 750 to 1258; during this time, however, large portions of the lands that had been won by the Umayyads broke free from Baghdad. One of the last Umayyad princes escaped assassination by the Abbasids, fled to Spain, and continued Umayyad rule there. The Egyptian dynasty, the Fatimids, gained control over Palestine, Syria, and most of North Africa and western Arabia, rivaling Baghdad for power. Much of Persia also came under the control of rival rulers. By the A.D. 1000s, the Abbasids ruled little more than the area around Baghdad.

In A.D. 1055, Baghdad was captured by Seljuk Turks from Central Asia, the same invaders who defeated the Byzantines at Manzikert. The Seljuks permitted the Abbasid caliph to remain on the throne, but he had to carry out

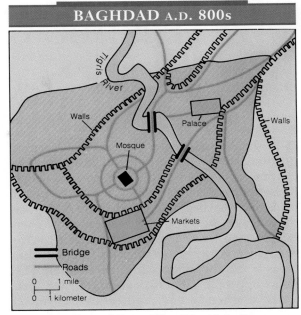

BAGHDAD A.D. 800s

Learning from Maps *The Abbasids built a new capital in Iraq called Baghdad.* **How was the city protected?**

their orders. By A.D. 1100, the Seljuk conquests had been divided up among the captains in the army. At the same time, Christian soldiers from western Europe, united in a holy war against Islam, conquered Palestine. A crushing defeat for what remained of the Islamic state came in A.D. 1258. Asian invaders called Mongols attacked Baghdad. In the ferocious assault, they burned palaces, libraries, and schools and slaughtered 50,000 inhabitants, among them the last Abbasid caliph.

SECTION 2 REVIEW

Recall
1. **Define:** caliph, jihad
2. **Identify:** Abu Bakr, Ali, Mu'awiyah, Shiites, Sunnis, Umayyads, Abbasids
3. **Locate:** Turn to the map on page 244 and locate the cities of Damascus and Baghdad. Why did the caliphs move the capital of the Islamic state to each of these cities?

Critical Thinking
4. **Analyze:** Why did the murders of Ali and Husayn cause a permanent split in Islam?
5. **Evaluate:** What were the strengths and weaknesses of Umayyad rule? State your reasoning.

Applying Concepts
6. **Movement:** How did Islamic expansion affect the racial and ethnic composition of the Islamic empire? How did it affect the empire's stability?

Islamic Civilization

In the Abbasid state, the arts and learning flourished despite political disunity. The time of conquest had ended, and the people had enough leisure to enjoy the fruits of the lands that they had subdued. Because Arabic was the language of the Quran, it became the common language. Its widespread use enabled scientists, rulers, writers, and pilgrims from different lands to communicate with one another. This influx of people and ideas gave the Islamic state a new multiracial and multicultural character and helped create a golden age.

Muslim Society

Islam set the guidelines for the way people lived. It laid down rules for family life and business as well as for religious practices.

Family Life Early Islam stressed the equality of all believers before God; however, as in the case of contemporary Christian and Jewish communities, in Islamic communities men and women had distinct roles and rights. The Quran told male Muslims that "men are responsible for women." A woman's social position was therefore defined by her relationship as wife, mother, daughter, or sister to the male members of her family. She was rarely considered a person in her own right. "Good women are obedient," Muhammad proclaimed.

Islam did, however, improve the position of women. It forbade the tribal custom of killing female infants and also limited polygamy (puh LIGH uh mee), or the practice that allowed a man to have more than one wife. A Muslim could have as many as four wives, but all were to be treated as equals and with kindness. Also, although a woman was subject to the will of her husband, she had complete control over her own property. If she were divorced, she could keep the property she had brought with her when she married. A woman could also inherit property from her father and remarry.

Many Muslim women learned to read and write, and several women in the caliph's court, particularly during the Abbasid period, were renowned for their poetry. They were not always happy with their lives, though, as indicated by this poem written by Maisuna, the bedouin wife of Mu'awiyah. Her comments made Mu'awiyah so furious that he sent her back to the desert.

*The coarse cloth worn in the serenity
of the desert
  Is more precious to me than the luxurious
robes of a queen;
  I love the bedouin's tent, caressed by the
murmuring breeze, and standing amid
boundless horizons,
  More than the gilded halls of marble in
all their royal splendor.
  I feel more at ease with my simple crust,
  Than with the delicacies of the court;
  I prefer to rise early with the caravan,
  Rather than be in the golden glare of
the sumptuous escort.
  The barking of a watchdog keeping away
strangers
  Pleases me more than the sounds of the
tambourine played by the court singers;
  I prefer a desert cavalier, generous and poor,
  To a fat lout in purple living behind closed
doors.*

—Najib Ullah, from *Islamic Literature*

Women were expected to stay at home and do household tasks, and they could not participate in public life except to go shopping and sometimes to go to the mosque on Friday. Even in the mosque, women were assigned a special room for prayer.

At home, a married woman was entitled to her own rooms and cooking and sleeping conveniences. Household servants, some of them slaves, helped with the housekeeping. Girls usually married young; they prepared for marriage by learning from their mothers or servants how to manage a household.

Outside the home, Islamic society was a man's world. Muslim men worked at a variety of businesses or in the fields. For leisure they visited public baths and meeting places where they relaxed, talked, listened to the debates of scholars, and enjoyed the tales told by professional storytellers. Men also played chess, practiced gymnastics, or watched horse racing, a continuation of a bedouin tradition.

Education   When Muslim boys reached age seven, they entered mosque schools, which cost little and were open to all boys. Those families that could afford to, paid tuition, but many poor children were admitted without charge. Being able to speak Arabic fluently and to write with grace and ease were skills that Muslims valued. For all but the sons of the wealthy, however, schooling ended with learning to read and write. Some young men continued their studies at *madrasas*, or theological schools. Those who were to become leaders in Muslim society studied the classical literature of Islam, memorized poetry, and learned to compose original verses.

City and Country

Although most Arabs lived in rural or desert places, the leadership of the Islamic state came from the cities. Muslim cities were divided into distinct business and residential districts. A maze of narrow streets, often covered to protect pedestrians from the scorching sun, separated the closely packed buildings.

Urban Centers   City homes were designed to provide maximum privacy and to keep the occupants cool in the blazing heat. Houses were centered around courtyards; in wealthy homes, these courtyards had fountains and gardens. Thick walls of dried mud or brick and few windows kept the interior dim and cool. Usually a lattice or an ornamental wood grating protected the windows so that women could look out without being seen.

The main religious, government, and business buildings were at the center of the city. Dominating the skyline were the graceful silhouettes of mosques and their slender minarets, or towers from which people were called to prayer. Unlike Byzantine churches, which usually followed a general style, mosques had no common layout, although they usually included a prayer hall where worshipers gathered on Fridays. At one end of this hall a mihrab, or niche, marked the direction of Mecca. Often mosques included schools and shelters for travelers.

Trade and the Bazaar   Muslim merchants dominated trade throughout the Middle East and North Africa until the A.D. 1400s. Caravans traveled overland from Baghdad to China. Muslim traders roved the Indian Ocean gathering cargoes of Indian rubies, dyes, and silver; Chinese silk, paper, and porcelain; and Southeast

---

FOOTNOTES TO HISTORY

MAGIC CARPETS

The magic carpet that glides through the air is a familiar form of transportation in *The Arabian Nights.* The real magic of carpets from the Islamic world is found in their glowing colors and intricate designs of interwoven leaves and flowers, geometric figures, and, in some rugs, animal figures. From the silk rugs that adorned caliphs' palaces to the carpets of sheep's wool that served as walls between different sections of a tent, carpets were far more than floor coverings. Most Muslims owned small rugs that they used in daily prayer. These prayer rugs usually had a design that was oriented in one direction, and thus, like the mihrab in a mosque, could point toward Mecca. Today, carpets from Iran, Afghanistan, and other parts of the Islamic world still give their magic to modern walls and floors.

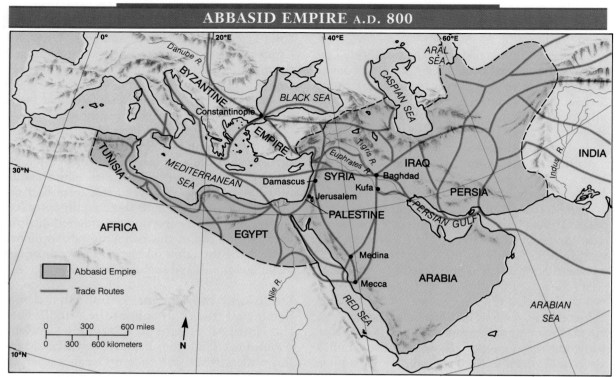

ABBASID EMPIRE A.D. 800

Learning from Maps *Trade united the Islamic state. **What were the different routes that caravans and trading vessels could take from Baghdad to Asia and to Europe?***

Asian spices. Gold, ivory, and slaves came from Africa. From the Islamic world came spices and medicines, textiles of silk and a woven cotton called damask, hand-blown glass, glazed tiles, utensils of copper and brass, and finely woven prayer rugs and carpets that were used to decorate the walls of tents and houses alike.

The destination of these goods were the city bazaars, or marketplaces, that served as the heart of a far-flung commerce. In major cities, such as Baghdad, Damascus, and Cairo, goods were sold in fabulous bazaars, mazes of shops and stalls, often enclosed to shut out the glare of the sun. Buyers at the major bazaars included Venetians who purchased Asian goods, shipped them across the Mediterranean to Venice and then on to other parts of Europe.

Rural Areas   Because of the dry climate and the scarcity of water, growing food was difficult in most of the Islamic state. However, good use

was made of the few areas that were capable of sustaining crops. Farmers produced good yields by irrigating their fields, rotating crops, and fertilizing the land. Most productive land was held by large landowners who received grants from the government. They had large estates and employed farmers from nearby villages to work the land. Muslim farms produced wheat, rice, beans, melons, cucumbers, celery, and mint. From orchards came almonds and olives. Many farmers specialized in such fruits as dates, apricots, and figs, which could be dried and thus survive long journeys to market. Farmers also cultivated flowers for use in perfume.

After Arab irrigation methods were introduced into Spain, Muslims there could cultivate valuable new crops, including cherries, apples, pears, pomegranates, and bananas. Seville, Cordoba, and other Spanish cities in the Islamic state grew rich from the agricultural goods they produced and sold in international trade.

248   *Chapter 10*

Islamic Achievements

The use of Arabic not only promoted trade but also encouraged communication among the different peoples in the Islamic state. From these peoples the state built a rich storehouse of knowledge and scientific discovery.

The House of Wisdom According to Muslim tradition, the Abbasid caliph Ma'mun (mah MOON) founded the House of Wisdom at Baghdad in A.D. 830. This research center and library specialized in the translation into Arabic of Greek, Persian, and Indian scientific texts. Ma'mun staffed the institute with salaried Christian, Jewish, and Muslim scholars who used Arabic to share ideas from different intellectual traditions. They performed scientific experiments, made mathematical calculations, and studied and built upon the ideas of the ancients. The House of Wisdom, therefore, served as a catalyst for many mathematical and scientific achievements in the Islamic world.

Mathematics As you read in Chapter 7, Gupta mathematicians in India devised the numerals we know as Arabic numerals and the concept of zero. Muslim mathematicians adopted these numerals and used them in a place-value system. In this system, today used worldwide, a number's value is determined by the position of its digits. The place-value system made possible great achievements in mathematics.

Muslim mathematicians invented algebra and expressed equations to define curves and lines. Their work in geometry led to the development of trigonometry, which was used to calculate the distance to a star and the speed of a falling object. Mathematicians spent hours trying to stump each other with intricate mathematical puzzles. They were also interested in practical applications, such as devising hydraulic pumps and fountains and applying their skills to building, surveying, and the manufacture of musical instruments.

Astronomy and Geography At Ma'mun's observatory in Baghdad, astronomers checked the findings of the ancient Greeks, made observations of the skies, and produced physical and mathematical models of the universe. They accurately described eclipses of the sun and proved that the moon affects the oceans.

Muslim astronomers improved on a Greek device called the astrolabe, with which they determined the positions of stars, the movements of planets, and the time. The astrolabe made navigation easier and safer. It was also useful in religious practices, enabling Muslims to ascertain the direction of Mecca, the beginning of Ramadan, and the hours of prayer.

Using the astrolabe, Muslim geographers measured the size and circumference of the earth with accuracy unmatched until the 1900s. From such studies, geographers concluded that the earth was round, although most continued to accept the Greek theory that heavenly bodies revolve around the earth.

By the A.D. 1100s, Muslim geographers had determined the basic outlines of Asia, Europe, and North Africa and had produced the first accurate maps of the eastern hemisphere. They also traveled widely to gain first-hand knowledge of the earth's surface, its climates, and its peoples.

Chemistry and Medicine Does your high school chemistry lab stock equipment such as beakers, flasks, vials, balance scales, crucibles, and crystallization dishes? If so, it reflects the contributions of Muslim alchemy, the branch of chemistry that attempted to change lead into gold. Although alchemists never succeeded in their goal, they did develop tools and processes that are still used in modern chemistry.

The renowned chemist and physician al-Razi (ahl RAH zee), who lived from A.D. 865 to 925, classified chemical substances as animal, mineral, or vegetable, a classification system that remains in use today. Al-Razi also made invaluable contributions to medicine. Among his nearly 200 works are a medical encyclopedia that describes the origin of disease and a handbook identifying the differences between smallpox and measles.

In the A.D. 900s, the doctor Ibn Sina (ih bin SEE nuh) produced the *Canon of Medicine*, a monumental volume that was an attempt to summarize all the medical knowledge of that time. It described the circulation of the blood and the functions of the kidneys and the heart. It also offered diagnosis and treatment for many diseases, as well as advice on diet and hygiene.

Muslim physicians founded the science of optics, or the study of sight. Ibn al-Haytham, the founder of optics, discovered that the eye sees because it receives light from the object seen. Earlier physicians believed the opposite: the eye sees because it produces rays that *give* light to the object seen. Muslim medicine, in fact, was centuries ahead of the medicine practiced in the West.

Art and Architecture   While Islamic scientists studied how people see, artists and architects enhanced the beauty of what people saw. Like mathematics and science, Islamic art and architecture profited from the cultural diversity of the Islamic state.

The nomadic Arabs had little visual art or architecture. Muslim theologians, fearful of idol worship, did not allow artists to make images or pictures of living creatures. Instead, artists used the beautiful script of written Arabic in an art form known as calligraphy (kuh LIHG ruh fee), or the art of elegant handwriting, to decorate public walls with passages from the Quran. Often calligraphy was accompanied by geometric designs entwined with plant stems, leaves, flowers, and stars. These **arabesques** (air uh BEHSKS) decorated books, carpets, swords, and entire walls. The artists who designed the walls of the Alhambra, a dazzling palace in Muslim Spain, often combined calligraphy and arabesques on the same wall or panel.

Gardens and water, both precious in the arid Islamic lands, also became artistic objects. Sun-drenched courtyards in mosques, palaces, and wealthy homes had trees to provide cool shade and flowers to delight the eye and nose; splashing fountains and running water refreshed both eye and ear.

Literature   Until the A.D. 600s, Arabic literature consisted mostly of poetry passed orally from one generation to the next. After the rise of Islam, religion had much influence in the creation of Arabic literature. The Quran, the first and greatest work in Arabic prose, was familiar to every Muslim, and its style influenced Islamic writing. Considered a model of classical Arabic, the Quran set the standard by which other Arabic literature was judged. Devout Muslims memorized long passages for their beauty of expression and forcefulness of ideas.

During the A.D. 700s, nonreligious prose appeared that was designed both to instruct and to entertain. The most famous of these writings was *Kalila and Dimna*, a collection of animal fables that presented moral lessons.

During the Abbasid period, Islamic literature blossomed as a result of contact with Greek

Learning from Photographs   *The Alhambra was built by rulers of Islamic Granada. A fortified palace, the Alhambra was constructed around a series of open courtyards.* **What details characterized the interior walls of the palace?**

At the Doctor's

Here, an Islamic man is shown preparing medicine.

Today we take it for granted that the doctor can make us better when we get sick. In A.D. 765, however, the caliph Mansur was not so fortunate. His personal physicians—the best in Baghdad—could find no remedy for chronic indigestion.

The caliph had heard that physicians in a Persian medical school based their practices on rational Greek methods for treating disease. Traditional Arab medicine was based mainly on magic or superstition.

When the caliph asked the medical school for help, the chief physician, a Christian named Jurjis ibn Bakhtishu, cured Mansur. This encouraged other Muslim doctors to practice medicine based on the methods of the Greeks and Persians.

Muslim doctors were the first to discover the functions of internal organs and to diagnose illnesses such as meningitis. They also advanced surgery, carrying out head and stomach operations with the aid of anesthetics such as opium.

Believing that medicine required long training, Muslim doctors studied in hospitals and medical schools. Doctors based their treatments upon careful observation of their patients rather than superstition. They also diagnosed diseases such as measles and smallpox, prescribed treatments, and performed surgery. Such practices were unknown in the West until the A.D. 1000s and 1200s, when Islamic knowledge reached western Europe.

Making the Connection
1. Why was Islamic medicine far ahead of the Western medicine during the Middle Ages?
2. What new methods of treatment have doctors developed in the past 50 years?

thought, Hindu legends, and Persian court epics. The upper classes valued elegant speech and the ability to handle words cleverly. Reading and appreciating literature became the sign of a good upbringing; every wealthy person took pride in having a well-stocked library. Cordoba, the Umayyad capital in Spain, had 70 libraries and more than half a million books. In contrast, the largest library in the Christian monasteries, at that time the center of European learning, held only a few hundred volumes.

In the A.D. 1000s, Persian became a second literary language in the Muslim world. Persian authors wrote epics about warrior-heroes, religious poetry, and verses about love. One of the best known works of this time is the *Rubaiyyat* of Omar Khayyam, a Persian mathematician and poet. You may also have heard some of the stories found in *A Thousand and One Nights*, also known as *The Arabian Nights*—stories such as "Sinbad the Sailor," "Aladdin and His Lamp," and "Ali Baba and the Forty Thieves." Originating in Arabia, India, Persia, Egypt, and other lands, the tales reflect the multinational character of the Islamic state and the exciting nature of life between the A.D. 800s and 1500s.

Philosophy and History   Muslim philosophers tried to construct systems of thought that would reconcile the teachings of the Quran with

Learning from Artifacts *This oil lamp from a mosque shows the creative ability of Islamic artists.* ***What are other examples of Islamic art?***

Greek philosophy. They believed that religious truths could be analyzed and defended using logic. Many of their works were translated into Latin and later brought a new understanding of philosophy to western Europe. Ibn Sina, known for his work in medicine, also wrote 68 books on logic and theology. Ibn-Rushd, a judge in Cordoba, was the most noted Islamic philosopher, and Christian scholars later used his commentaries on Aristotle.

Moses Maimonides, a Spanish Jew born in A.D. 1135, fled to Morocco and then Egypt to escape persecution. Maimonides became a leader in the Jewish community and a doctor to the Egyptian ruler. Like several Muslim scholars, Maimonides attempted to reconcile his faith with the teachings of Aristotle. One of his major contributions was the *Mishne Torah*, a 14-volume work on Jewish law and tradition, written in Hebrew. His philosophical works gained him recognition as one of the great philosophers of the Middle Ages.

Like Judaism and Christianity, Islam traces its origins to historical events. Therefore, Islamic scholars were interested in writing history. At first they wrote **chronicles,** or accounts in which events are arranged in the order in which they occurred. The most famous of the Islamic chroniclers were al Tabari (al tah BAH ree), who in the early A.D. 900s wrote a multivolume history of the world, and Ibn al-Athir (ih bin ahl ah THEER), who wrote an extensive history during the early A.D. 1200s.

Later, historians began to organize their accounts around events in the lives of rulers and others. The first Muslim historian to examine history scientifically was a North African diplomat named Ibn Khaldun (khahl DOON). He looked for laws and cause-and-effect relationships to explain historical events and human behavior. Ibn Khaldun believed that history was a process in which human affairs were shaped by geography, climate, and economics, as well as by moral and spiritual forces. His work later influenced historical writing in western Europe.

SECTION 3 REVIEW

Recall
1. **Define:** *madrasa*, arabesque, chronicle,
2. **Identify:** House of Wisdom, al-Razi, Ibn Sina, *Rubaiyyat*, Moses Maimonides, Ibn Khaldun
3. **Locate:** Using the map on page 248, locate the major trade routes used by Muslim merchants. What features gave the Islamic state its multicultural character?

Critical Thinking
4. **Analyze:** What were some Islamic achievements in science and art?
5. **Evaluate:** Were Islamic theologians justified in their fear that people might worship paintings or sculptures of people or animals? Explain your answer.

Applying Concepts
6. **Cultural diffusion:** Identify examples of the cultural diffusion in the Islamic state of (a) art, (b) mathematics, (c) commerce, and (d) literature.

PREPARING FOR AND TAKING TESTS

How do you react when your teacher announces a test? For many students, taking a test is a dreaded ordeal. Learning some test-taking strategies, however, can make this unavoidable experience less forbidding. For tests that measure knowledge of a specific subject, an organized plan of study will help you do your best.

Explanation

In *planning to take a test*, allow adequate time for a review. Simply plowing through your notes can waste your time. Your plan of study should include these steps:

- Identify what you need to know. Usually your teacher will state which lessons or chapters the test will cover.
- Begin to list topics and concepts for study. First, refer to your class notes and then add to the list any material your teacher emphasized in class. Next, skim the textbook for headings, graphics, preview items, and review questions. Often these appear in boldface. Add key places, people, events, movements, and concepts to your list. Then, review previous quizzes or tests. This survey will not only give you an idea about the type of questions you can expect, but also additional key points.
- Identify what you already know. Turn your list of topics and concepts into questions and test yourself on them. Write the answers to these questions.
- Identify what you need to find out. Evaluate your self test and make another list of topics and concepts that you feel you need to study more.
- At this point, you can study alone, or work with a friend. If you choose the latter, take turns quizzing each other, using the types of questions you anticipate and topics that require more study.
- If your teacher schedules class time for review, discuss your problem areas.
- When you take the test, begin by previewing it. Evaluate how much time you will need to complete each section. Essay questions, for example, need more time than short answer questions. Answer easy questions first. On multiple-choice questions, read all the choices before marking any. If you are not sure, mark your best guess. On essay questions, make sure you understand what is being asked. Allow yourself time for a fast check of your answers.

Example

Suppose your teacher announces a quiz tomorrow about life on the Arabian Peninsula around A.D. 500. Today, you review your notes and see that class time on this subject was devoted to a film about Bedouin life. You write that broad topic at the top of your study list.

In the textbook you find that the first heading in Section 1 is "The Arabian Peninsula"; you decide you can concentrate your review on a few pages from Section 1. You look at the subheadings and add several more key topics to the topic list—the physical characteristics of the Arabian Peninsula, the formation of towns, and life in Mecca.

You add a few more topics from a previous test, and turn your list of topics into a list of possible test questions. Notice any topics about which you are not sure and focus your attention on them. Soon, you are ready for the quiz.

Application

Examine "The Revelation of Islam" on pages 235–236. Outline the strategies to use for studying for a test on this material, making sure you determine what you need to know, what you already know, and what you need to find further information about.

Practice

Turn to Practicing Skills on page 255 of the Chapter Review for further practice in preparing for and taking tests.

CHAPTER 10 REVIEW

HISTORICAL SIGNIFICANCE

Out of the revelations that Muhammad experienced in the A.D. 600s grew the monotheistic religion of Islam, which now includes more than a billion worshipers and ranks with Judaism and Christianity as one of the world's most widely practiced religions. The equality among believers that Islam stresses has contributed to a sense of community among Muslims all over the world. This feeling is reinforced by the pilgrimage that many Muslims make to their sacred city of Mecca. Today, Muslims make up the majority of the population in the Middle East, North Africa, and parts of sub-Saharan Africa and Southeast Asia. Other parts of the world have significant Muslim minorities.

Forming a common bond between people of many lands, Islam has also made major contributions to world knowledge and culture. While western Europe struggled to rise from the long decline following the collapse of Rome, people in the Islamic state were establishing centers of learning and preserving much of the knowledge of the ancient world. Muslim scientists made medical advances and discovered new methods in chemistry, physics, and mathematics. Artists and architects built on the skills and ideas of the multicultural Islamic state. This knowledge and these skills, passed on to western Europe, greatly enriched Western science, mathematics, and literature.

SUMMARY

For a summary of Chapter 10, see the Unit 3 Synopsis on pages 354–357.

USING KEY TERMS

Write the key term that best completes each sentence.

a. arabesque
b. caliph
c. chronicle
d. hajj
e. imam
f. jihad
g. *madrasa*
h. revelation
i. *shari'ah*
j. sheikh

1. A ___ ruled a tribe if he had consent.
2. Muhammad experienced a ___ in A.D. 610.
3. Islam's moral rules have been organized into a code of law known as ___ .
4. A ___ guides Islamic believers in prayer.
5. The fifth pillar of Islam is the pilgrimage to Mecca, or ___ .
6. After Muhammad's death in A.D. 632, a group of prominent Muslims chose a ___ .
7. Muslims believed they had a religious duty to struggle for their faith through conquests known as ___ .
8. Young men continued their religious studies at a ___ .
9. Geometric designs entwined with plant stems, leaves, flowers, and stars that accompany calligraphy are known as ___ .
10. ___ is an account in which events are related in the order they occurred.

REVIEWING FACTS

1. **Identify:** What created an atmosphere of change in the Arabian Peninsula in the A.D. 600s?
2. **Explain:** How did the Medina Compact lay the basis for the Islamic state?
3. **Outline:** What events led to the schism between Muslims?
4. **Explain:** Why did some Muslims revolt against the Umayyads?
5. **Describe:** What was the status of women in the Islamic state?

THINKING CRITICALLY

1. **Analyze:** Contrast bedouin society with the society that formed under Islam.

2. **Apply:** Would there have been a struggle for the caliphate if Muhammad had named a successor before his death?

3. **Synthesize:** Imagine that the hajj was not among the Five Pillars of Islam. How might its omission have affected the Islamic state?

4. **Evaluate:** How did Muslim scholars contribute to the world's knowledge?

ANALYZING CONCEPTS

1. **Innovation:** Why was Islam an innovation in the way people of the Arabian Peninsula worshiped?

2. **Movement:** How was the Umayyad decision to move the nation's capital from Medina to Damascus a result of Islamic expansion?

3. **Diversity:** How did Umayyad failure to embrace non-Arab Muslims destroy Umayyad rule?

4. **Cultural diffusion:** How did cultural diffusion affect the wealth of Spanish cities?

PRACTICING SKILLS

1. You are given a five-part test on Section 2 of this chapter. Part A has eight completion questions; Parts B, C, and D—multiple-choice, true-false, and analogy questions, respectively—have five items each; and Part E has three essay questions. Describe how you would schedule your time (40 minutes).

2. List the steps you would follow to prepare for a test on this chapter.

GEOGRAPHY IN HISTORY

1. **Migration:** Turn to the map on page 244. What geographical features encouraged the Arabs to expand their territory beyond the Arabian Peninsula?

2. **Interaction with the environment:** How did the bedouins survive the harsh desert?

3. **Place:** Turn to the map on page 248. Explain why each of these places is significant in Muslim history and culture: Mecca, Medina, Damascus, Baghdad.

TRACING CHRONOLOGY

Refer to the time line below to answer the questions.

1. How many years did Muhammad preach in Mecca before fleeing to Yathrib?

2. Between which years did the Rightly Guided Caliphs lead the Islamic state?

3. Under which caliphate did the Sunni-Shiite split take place? Why did it occur?

LINKING PAST AND PRESENT

1. What evidence can you find in today's world of the split between Sunnis and Shiites?

2. How have students today benefited from the work done at the House of Wisdom?

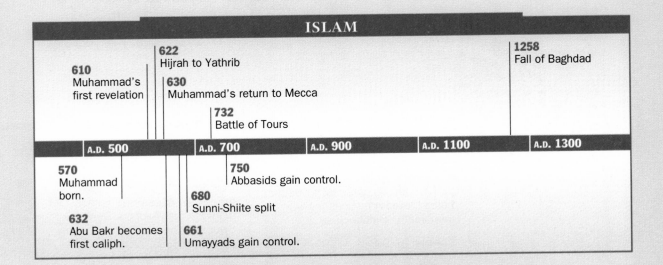

ISLAM

610 Muhammad's first revelation	**622** Hijrah to Yathrib				**1258** Fall of Baghdad
	630 Muhammad's return to Mecca				
		732 Battle of Tours			
A.D. 500	**A.D. 700**	**A.D. 900**	**A.D. 1100**	**A.D. 1300**	
570 Muhammad born.	**750** Abbasids gain control.				
632 Abu Bakr becomes first caliph.	**680** Sunni-Shiite split				
	661 Umayyads gain control.				

The Rise of Medieval Europe

*I*t was tournament day. As trumpets flourished, the marshal shouted, "In the name of God and St. Michael, do your battle!" Knights on horseback thundered toward each other and met with a deafening clash. Lords and ladies cheered as their favorite unhorsed his opponent. The victor was awarded a prize from the lady whose colors he wore.

Such tournaments provided more than just entertainment. A contemporary historian wrote:

"A knight cannot distinguish himself in [war] if he has not trained for it in tourneys. He must have seen his blood flow, heard his teeth crack under fist blows, . . . and, after being twenty times unhorsed, have risen twenty times to fight."

After the fall of Rome, wars were frequent. A professional warrior class—the knights—led the new, vigorous, competitive society that would reshape western Europe.

CHAPTER PREVIEW

Key Terms to Define: feudalism, fief, vassal, chivalry, manorialism, serf, abbot, cardinal, lay investiture, heresy, excommunication, friar, mendicant, middle class

People to Meet: Clovis, Charles Martel, Charlemagne, Benedict, Pope Gregory I, Pope Innocent III, Francis of Assisi, Dominic, Alfred the Great, William the Conqueror, Hugh Capet, Philip the Fair, Otto the Great, Henry IV, Pope Gregory VII

Places to Discover: France, Germany, Rome, Aachen, Denmark, Sweden, Norway, England, Cluny, Paris, Canossa, Worms

Objectives to Learn:
1. In what way was Charlemagne an exceptional ruler for his time?

The Très Riches Heures du Duc de Berry *presents an elaborate depiction of medieval life.*

2. How were loyalties maintained in a fragmented and violent Europe?

3. What role did the Catholic Church play in the rebuilding of Europe?

4. What were the achievements of medieval European monarchs?

Concepts to Understand:

• Movement—Invasions by Vikings, Magyars, and Muslims influence medieval Europe. Section 1

• Cooperation—Nobles, Church officials, and peasants develop ties of loyalty and service to one another. Section 2

• Uniformity—Roman Catholicism affects every aspect of medieval life. Section 3

• Conflict—European kings, feudal lords, and popes struggle for political dominance. Section 4

257

Frankish Rulers

By A.D 500, Germanic invasions had all but destroyed the urban world of the Roman Empire. Trade declined. Cities, bridges, and roads fell into disrepair and disuse. Law and order vanished, and education almost disappeared. Money was no longer used. For most people, life did not extend beyond the tiny villages where they were born, lived, and died.

Compared with other contemporary societies—Islamic, Byzantine, or Chinese—western Europe was so backward that scholars once called the early part of this period the Dark Ages. Later scholars combined the Latin terms *medium* (middle) and *aveum* (age) to form the term *medieval*, recognizing that this period was an era of transition between ancient and modern times. Out of this violent medieval period, or Middle Ages, a dynamic and highly competitive civilization arose. It combined elements of Germanic and Roman culture with Christian beliefs, and would make western Europe a leading force in the rest of the world.

Merovingian Rulers

During the A.D. 400s, the Franks, who settled in what is now France and western Germany, emerged as the strongest Germanic group. Their early rulers, known as Merovingian (mehr oh VIN gih uhn) kings for the ruler Meroveg, held power until the early A.D. 700s.

Clovis   In A.D. 481 a brutal and wily warrior named Clovis became king of the Franks. To please his Christian wife Clothilda, in A.D. 496 Clovis vowed to convert to Catholicism if he was victorious in a battle against his enemies. Following his victory, King Clovis stood in front of a huge crowd to fulfill his promise. The bishop of Reims asked the king to burn his idols and agree to worship the Christian God: "Bow thy neck in meekness . . . adore what thou hast burned and burn what thou hast adored."

Of course, Clovis's conversion had a reason beyond pleasing his wife. Catholicism was the religion of the bishops and people he had conquered. His conversion identified him with Rome and the people; his military strength won him the following of other Frankish leaders.

However, Clovis did not leave a unified realm behind him when he died. Instead, he followed Frankish custom and divided his kingdom among his male heirs. This led to several hundred years of son fighting son for the larger share of the inheritance. By A.D. 700 real power had passed from the bloodline kings to government officials known as **mayors of the palace.**

Charles Martel   In A.D. 719 Charles Martel, or "Charles the Hammer," became mayor of the palace. When Muslim forces threatened Europe in A.D. 732, Charles led the successful defense of Tours, in France. This victory won him great prestige. As you read in Chapter 10, the victory ensured that Christianity would remain the dominant religion of Europe.

Pepin the Short   Charles's son, Pepin the Short, succeeded his father and became mayor of the palace in A.D. 741. Pepin—unlike his father, who never assumed the royal title—wished to be named king of the Franks. Since he had no blood claim to the throne, Pepin used his influence with the Frankish bishops and the pope to bring about a change in dynasties. In a show of support, the pope journeyed to France and anointed King Pepin I with holy oil.

In return for the Church's blessing, Pepin was to defend the pope against his enemies. In A.D. 754 the new king forced the Lombards, a Germanic people, to withdraw from Rome.

Pepin seized a large tract of Lombard territory around Rome and gave it to the pope. Known as the Donation of Pepin, it became part of the territory known as the Papal States. Until the late 1800s, popes still governed it.

Pepin's relations with the pope set new precedents. The Catholic Church effectively turned away from the Byzantine Empire and toward the West. Cultural unity between Catholicism and western Europe would continue.

Charlemagne's Empire

In A.D. 768 Pepin's son, Charlemagne, became the Frankish king. Charlemagne, or Charles the Great, was one of Europe's great monarchs. In Latin his name is written Carolus Magnus, which gave the name Carolingian to his dynasty. The king cut an imposing figure. His biographer, a monk named Einhard, described him this way:

Charles was large and strong, and of lofty stature, though not disproportionally tall . . . nose a little long, hair fair, and face laughing and merry. . . . He used to wear the national, that is to say, the Frankish, dress—next his skin a linen shirt and linen breeches, and above these a tunic fringed with silk; while hose fastened by bands covered his lower limbs and shoes his feet, and he protected his shoulders and chest in winter by a close-fitting coat of otter or marten skins. Over all he flung a blue cloak, and he always had a sword girt about him.

Charlemagne nearly doubled the borders of his Frankish kingdom to include Germany, France, northern Spain, and most of Italy. For the first time since the fall of Rome, most Europeans were ruled by one government.

To govern effectively and to successfully convert conquered peoples to Catholicism, Charlemagne needed to restore literacy to his empire. Since the decline of the Roman Empire, reading and writing had almost died out in western Europe. Therefore, Charlemagne made his court a center for education and research. Scholars from all over Europe gathered to teach in the palace school. These scholars helped preserve classical learning by making accurate Latin copies of ancient religious manuscripts and Roman classics. In addition, Charlemagne's government functioned better with literate administrators and officials.

A Christian Realm   By A.D. 800 the Frankish Empire under Charlemagne included nearly all the area that was to be the center of western European civilization. Indeed, once the Franks controlled what is now Italy, they also came to dominate the papacy and the Catholic Church. In recognition of this new empire and of the developing unity between the Church and the West, Charlemagne traveled to Rome in A.D. 800 to defend the pope against Roman nobles. To show his gratitude, Pope Leo III crowned Charlemagne Emperor of the Romans on Christmas Day of that year.

As ruler of much of western Europe and protector of the Catholic Church, Charlemagne

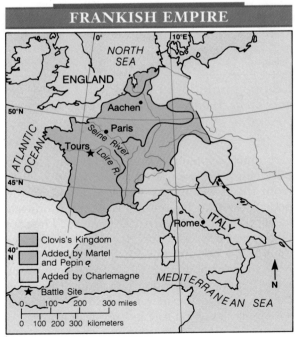

FRANKISH EMPIRE

Clovis's Kingdom
Added by Martel and Pepin
Added by Charlemagne
★ Battle Site

Learning from Maps *During the A.D. 400s, the Franks emerged as the strongest of all Germanic peoples.* **What modern countries did the Franks control?**

Learning from Maps *Foreign invasions were a constant in western Europe at this time.* **What effects did they have on the Carolingian kingdoms?**

very much wanted the title of emperor. He had misgivings, however, about receiving the office from the pope. By crowning a monarch, the pope seemed to be saying that Church officials were superior to political leaders. Despite Charlemagne's reservations, his crowning cemented the relationship that had been growing between the popes and the Frankish kings since King Pepin's coronation. The alliance between the papacy and the new Holy Roman emperor would play a central role in European history.

Charlemagne's Government Charlemagne relied on local officials called counts to help him rule his huge empire. Carefully instructed in the duties of office, the counts solved local problems, settled disputes, and raised armies.

Each year Charlemagne's messengers, the *missi dominici,* went on inspections in which they informed Charlemagne about the performance of the counts and administrators. Charlemagne also made regular tours from his court at Aix-la-Chapelle, which is today Aachen, Germany.

Collapse of Charlemagne's Empire
More than anything else, Charlemagne's forceful personality held his empire together. His death in A.D. 814 left a vacuum that his only surviving son, Louis the Pious, could not fill. After Louis's death, Charlemagne's three grandsons fought one another for control of the empire.

In A.D. 843 the three brothers agreed in the Treaty of Verdun to divide the Carolingian lands. Charles the Bald took the western part, an area that covered most of present-day France. Louis the German acquired the eastern portion, which today is Germany. Lothair, who became the Holy Roman emperor, took a strip of land in the middle of the empire stretching from the North Sea southward to Italy.

Invasions Increase Disunity

By the late A.D. 800s, Charlemagne's empire lay in ruins. Weak Carolingian monarchs had proved unable to control the nobles of their kingdoms. The nobles had gained so much power that they now elected their own kings.

Internal feuding also weakened the Carolingian kingdoms, but a series of terrifying outside invasions nearly destroyed them. Muslims swept out of North Africa to seize Sicily, Sardinia, and Corsica as well as the western Mediterranean coast. The Slavs marched out of the east to invade central Europe. From Asia a new group of fierce nomads called Magyars galloped west, leaving a trail of destruction. The most threatening attacks, however, came from the Vikings, raiders from Scandinavia to the north.

Viking Invaders   In medieval Scandinavian, to *go a-viking* means to fight as a pirate or warrior. The Viking warriors traveled in long, deckless ships that had one sail and were designed to slide swiftly through the water propelled by long oars. These boats were sturdy enough to cross the Atlantic Ocean, shallow enough to navigate Europe's rivers, and light enough to be carried past fortified bridges. The Vikings became known for surprise attacks and speedy retreats. What they could not steal they burned. No place in Europe seemed safe from attack.

Boasting names like Eric Bloodax and Harald Bluetooth, the Vikings sought riches and adventure. In the A.D. 800s, they left their overpopulated homeland, which later became the kingdoms of Norway, Denmark, and Sweden. Viking warriors fought ferociously and showed little mercy to their victims.

The Vikings, however, were more than just raiders. They were also explorers and settlers. Skilled in sailing and trading, they moved along the Atlantic and Mediterranean coasts of Europe. The Norwegians settled the North Atlantic islands of Greenland and Iceland, and even reached North America. The Danes temporarily held England and established the Viking state of Normandy in northwestern France. The Swedes settled in the Ukraine and Russia, where they helped organize the Slavic population.

The people of western Europe suffered at the hands of Vikings and other invaders. These raids isolated European communities and severely weakened the central authority of monarchs. Trade declined, and many areas faced economic collapse. As a result of royal weakness, nobles and local officials took over the local defense. Beginning in the A.D. 900s, a new political and social system took hold in western Europe.

SECTION 1 REVIEW

Recall
1. **Define:** mayor of the palace
2. **Identify:** Clovis, Charles Martel, Pepin, Charlemagne, Treaty of Verdun, Vikings
3. **Locate:** Germany, France, Tours, Aachen
4. **Explain:** What problem resulted when Charlemagne was crowned by the pope?

Critical Thinking
5. **Analyze:** Contrast Charlemagne with his weak successors. Why do you think Charlemagne was successful in enlarging and maintaining his empire?
6. **Evaluate:** Predict what might have happened if scholars had not preserved learning in an age when hardly anyone could read or write. If learning had not been preserved, would life today be different?

Applying Concepts
7. **Movement:** Explain the reasons why the Vikings, the Magyars, and the Slavs left their homelands and invaded the lands of western Europe.

Medieval Life

As the Carolingian Empire disintegrated and as attacks by invaders devastated the lands, a new political system known as **feudalism** developed in Europe. Feudalism was a highly decentralized form of government that stressed alliances of mutual protection between monarchs and nobles of varying degrees of power. The system was based on giving land to nobles in exchange for loyalty and military aid. With the land came peasants to farm it and many of the powers usually reserved for governments. Feudalism took firm hold in northern France around A.D. 900 and spread through England and western Europe by the A.D. mid-1000s.

Feudal Relationships

The tie between military service and land ownership that characterized feudalism began during the rule of Charles Martel. At that time, Charles was fighting the Muslims. Unlike the Europeans, the Muslim soldiers used saddles with stirrups that enabled them to fight on horseback, using a sword or lance. Charles wanted to adopt the stirrup and develop a cavalry. However, the cost of such an enterprise required a new type of military system. To raise such a cavalry, Martel began giving tracts of land to warriors so they would have a source of income to buy the weapons and horses. With each tract of land, called a **fief,** came peasant laborers to work it.

Frankish kings later enlarged this system by giving fiefs to counts and local officials. In time, such nobles assumed many of the powers usually held by government: raising armies, dispensing justice, and in some cases even minting coins. In return, the nobles swore an oath of loyalty and pledged military support to the king.

By the A.D. 900s, such arrangements emerged as feudalism. Lords who had been granted fiefs were allowed to pass their lands on to their heirs. In return, these nobles were to provide knights, or mounted warriors, for the royal army. However, confusing social and legal distinctions often blurred this relationship.

In theory, feudal relationships were like a pyramid. The king was at the top. In the middle were various ranks of lords. Each lord was a **vassal,** that is, a noble who served a lord of the next higher rank. At the bottom of the pyramid were the knights. In practice, however, a noble might be both a lord and a vassal, since a noble could pledge his allegiance to more than one lord. In fact, one German warrior, Siboto of Falkenstein, was vassal to twenty different lords. Of course, conflicts of loyalty arose if one of a vassal's lords went to war with another.

Feudal Obligations   A solemn ceremony called homage established a contract—not usually put in writing—between a new vassal and

---

FOOTNOTES TO HISTORY

IDENTIFYING A KNIGHT

Once knights began to use closed helmets, it was impossible to tell one knight from another. To identify themselves, knights had individual designs painted on the shields they carried to ward off blows. Later, the loose tunics they wore over their armor had the same designs embroidered on them. The designs became known as a knight's coat of arms. In noble families, coats of arms were passed down from father to son. The flags of some modern countries are derived from the system of designs that were developed by the knights.

Roman Town to Medieval Village

The strength and security of the Roman Empire made city life safe and popular. Indeed, small cities made up the bulk of the empire. When the Roman army proved unable to hold back the foreign invasions, Roman cities fell into decline. People began to use the bricks and stones from Roman monuments to patch their houses and build walls to keep out the invaders.

During the early Middle Ages, nine out of ten western Europeans lived in the countryside, where they could grow their own food. Carving farmland out of forest, they centered their villages around a manor house or castle, where they could run for protection in case of attack. Other villages grew up around monasteries.

In those violent times, village settlements differed in two main ways from Roman cities. First, because trade had practically disappeared, medieval villages had to be almost completely self-sustaining. Second, the idea of protection was uppermost in the minds of the people in medieval villages. Castles and monasteries were sheltered behind strong fortifications, moats, and walls.

When European city life reawakened between A.D. 1100 and 1200, many walled villages and monasteries became part of the re-emerging cities. Their remains can be seen today in many of Europe's oldest cities.

Making the Connection
1. Why did cities of the Roman Empire fall into decline?
2. In 1920, for the first time, more than half of the U.S. population lived in cities or towns. Why do you think the majority of the U.S. population lives in urban areas today?

---

his lord. In return for a fief, the vassal pledged to perform certain duties. The most important obligation was military service. The vassal agreed to provide his lord with a certain number of knights for battle during a period of 40 to 60 days each year. In addition, the vassal agreed to serve in the lord's court, to provide food and lodging when the lord came visiting, and to contribute funds when the lord's son became a knight or when his oldest daughter married. Vassals also pledged to pay ransom in the event of the lord's capture in battle.

A Time of Warfare The lack of a strong central government led to frequent battles and small-scale wars between feudal lords hoping to gain land or to add to their wealth. The Church tried to limit these battles by issuing a set of decrees. The Peace of God forbade fighting in places such as churches, while the Truce of God prohibited battles on holidays and weekends. Eventually fighting was legal on only 80 days each year. However, since the Church lacked the power to enforce its decrees, private wars continued throughout western Europe.

Castles for Defense The power and security of a lord depended largely on his ability to withstand attack. As a result, lords built fortified dwellings, or castles, to protect their lands. The

The Rise of Medieval Europe **263**

first castles were wooden buildings with high fences of logs or mounds of hard-packed earth around them. By the A.D. 1100s, castles were built of stone, with thick walls and turrets, or small towers. At the first sign of an attack, the peasants working in the fields around the castle rushed inside to safety.

A castle usually sat on top of a hill or a mound so sentries could easily spot attackers. Sometimes a deep ditch called a moat surrounded the castle as another obstacle for attackers. Often the moat was filled with water and could only be crossed by a drawbridge that would be raised during an attack.

The main building within the walls of the castle was the keep, a square tower with thick walls and slotted windows. It included storage rooms for grain and wine, barracks where the knights and their attendants lived, and rooms for the lord and his family. The castle also had a well so that defenders would have water if the castle came under siege. Other buildings inside the castle walls included a chapel, storage rooms, and stables.

Life of the Nobility

Kings, lords, knights, and ladies made up the nobility of the Middle Ages. Although the nobles lived much easier lives than the peasants who worked for them, their lives can hardly be called glamorous. Castles were built for security, not comfort, and were largely cold, dingy, and damp.

Within his fief, a lord had almost total authority. He collected rents from peasants and administered justice in disputes between his vassals. Any outside attempt to seize the land or control the inhabitants of his fief was met with violent resistance.

In contrast, a noblewoman had few, if any, rights. A noblewoman could be wed as early as her twelfth birthday to a man her father selected. Her primary duties lay in raising children and taking care of the household. Noblewomen took pride in their needlework, turning out cloth and fine embroidery. They also learned to make effective medicines from plants and herbs. Some women shared the supervision of the es-

tate with the lord and took over their husband's duties while the men were away at war.

Entertainment   Nobles looked forward to tournaments—mock battles between knights—as a show of military skills. They also loved to hunt, and both men and women learned the art of falconry and archery. A dinner featuring several dishes of game and fish might follow. In castles' large halls, nobles and their guests ate while being entertained by minstrels such as Robert Le Maine. He described his skills this way:

I can sing a song well and make tales and fables. I can tell a story against any man, I can make love verses to please young ladies, and can play the gallant for them if necessary. Then I can throw knives into the air and catch them without cutting my fingers. . . . I can throw a somersault and walk on my head.

Becoming a Knight   A nobleman's son began training for knighthood at age 7. Beginning as a page, or assistant, in the house of a lord, he learned manners and the use of weapons. A book of medieval manners, *Babees Book*, details rules of conduct for a page:

When you enter your lord's place, say "God Speed" and with humble cheer greet all who are there present. Do not rush in rudely, but enter with head up and at an easy pace and kneel on only one knee only to your lord. . . . Make obeisance [bow] to your lord always when you answer, otherwise stand as still as a stone unless he speak.

At 15, the page became a squire who assisted a knight and practiced using weapons. Once he proved himself in battle, the squire was knighted in an elaborate ceremony.

The behavior of knights was governed by a code of **chivalry.** This code called for knights to be brave in battle, fight fairly, keep promises, defend the Church, and treat women of noble birth in a courteous manner. Chivalry eventually became the basis for the development of good manners in Western society.

The Manorial System

The wealth of the feudal lords came from the labor of the peasants who lived on and worked their land. Since the last years of the Roman Empire, many peasants had worked for large landowners, in part because they could not afford their own land and in part for protection. By the Middle Ages, economic life across Europe centered around a system of agricultural production called **manorialism.** It provided lords and peasants with food, shelter, and protection.

Manors, or estates, varied in size from several hundred to several hundred thousand acres. Each manor included the lord's manor house, pastures for livestock, fields for crops, forest areas, and a village where the peasants lived. While feudalism describes the political relationships between nobles, manorialism concerns economic ties between nobles and peasants.

In return for the lord's protection, the peasants provided various services for the lord. Chief among the obligations were to farm the lord's land and to make various payments of goods. For example, each time a peasant ground grain at the lord's mill, he was obligated to leave a portion for the lord. If he baked in the lord's oven, he left a loaf behind for the lord. In addition, peasants were obligated to set aside a number of days each year to provide various types of labor, such as road or bridge repair.

Warfare and invasions made trade almost impossible, so the manor had to produce nearly everything its residents needed. Most of the peasants farmed or herded sheep. A few worked as skilled artisans, for each manor needed a blacksmith to make tools, a carpenter for building, a shoemaker, a miller to grind grain, a vintner to make wine, and a brewer to make beer. Peasant women made candles, sheared sheep, spun wool, and sewed clothing.

Peasants rarely left the manor. In fact, most were **serfs,** people who were bound to the manor and could not leave it without permission. But the serfs were not slaves—they could not be "sold" apart from the land they lived on.

Increased Production   The manorial system normally produced only enough food to support the peasants and the lord's household. However, a number of improvements gradually boosted productivity and eased the threat of famine.

The first improvement was the development of a new, heavier type of plow. The new plow made deeper cuts in the ground and had a device called a mould-board that pushed the soil sideways. The heavier plow meant less time in the fields for peasant farmers. As a result, farmers developed a better method of planting.

Instead of dividing plots of land into two fields, one of which lay fallow, or unsown, each year, farmers began to use a three-field system. One field might be planted with winter wheat, a second with spring wheat and vegetables, and a third left fallow. The next year, different crops were planted in the fallow field. One of the two remaining fields was planted and the other one

Learning from Art *This illumination from the A.D. 1200s, "The Laborer and His Plow," depicts medieval life.* **What can you tell about medieval dress and technology from it?**

was left fallow until the next year. This system produced more crops than the old system and helped to preserve the soil.

Peasant Life

Poverty and hardship were the staples of peasant life, and few serfs lived beyond the age of 40. Famine and disease were constant dangers. In times of war, the peasants were the first and hardest hit. Invading knights trampled crops and burned villages, causing famine and loss of life. To support the war, their lord might require additional payments of crops or labor. A monk of Canterbury described an English serf's account of his day:

I work very hard. I go out at dawn, driving the oxen to the field, and I yoke them to the plough; however hard the winter I dare not stay home for fear of my master; but, having yoked the oxen and made the ploughshare and coulter fast to the plough, every day I have to plough a whole acre or more.

—from Aelfric, *Colloquy*, A.D. 1005

Serfs like this man lived in tiny, one-room houses with dirt floors, no chimney, and one or two crude pieces of furniture—perhaps a table and stools. People slept huddled together for warmth. Coarse bread, a few vegetables from their gardens, and grain for porridge made up their usual diet. Meat was a rarity.

Yet peasants did have opportunities to relax. On holidays they enjoyed religious dramas, singing, dancing, wrestling, and archery. A few children found their way out of serfdom by becoming part of the clergy. Most, however, lived and died on the manor where they had been born.

Despite the obvious differences between the life and rights of a serf and the life and rights of a lord, the two groups did share a common interest: the land. Without peasants to farm it, the land was useless to the lord. Without the lord's protection from violence, the peasants could not survive. These mutually reciprocal interests often turned into a common bond. No lord wanted to be so oppressive that the peasants fled the land; no peasant wanted to be without protection. These mutual obligations created a complex number of different social stations and relationships between peasants, lords, and the Church.

Medieval Christians believed that every person was equal in the "eyes of the Lord." In practice, however, society was viewed as a hierarchy with ranked leaders from top to bottom. Each person—no matter what his or her place might be in the hierarchy—had certain duties and obligations that were attached to his or her station in life. In general, people did not question their station—or their obligations—in life. Although the manorial system seemed to lack freedom and opportunity for most of the people involved in it, it did create a very stable and secure way of life during a time in history that was generally violent and uncertain.

SECTION 2 REVIEW

Recall

1. **Define:** feudalism, fief, vassal, chivalry, manorialism, serf
2. **Explain:** Use a chart to describe the interlocking system of rights and responsibilities for kings, lords, knights, and peasants.
3. **Explain:** What were the stages necessary to become a knight?

Critical Thinking

4. **Analyze:** Contrast the daily responsibilities and life-style of a noble with those of a serf.
5. **Analyze:** Compare and contrast the feudal class structure with the structure of the *varna* system discussed in Chapter 7.
6. **Synthesize:** Make a list of duties for serfs to carry out in the fall, keeping in mind the need to provide for the medieval manor during the long winter months.

Applying Concepts

7. **Cooperation:** Diagram the ways nobles, clergy, knights, and peasants cooperated during the medieval period.

The Medieval Church

During the Middle Ages, the Catholic Church and its teachings assumed a new influence in western Europe. For most people—whether men or women, young or old, of noble or humble birth—the Church was the center of life.

The Medieval Church

Although the primary mission of the Church was spiritual, the fall of Rome in A.D. 476 and the accompanying collapse of central government led the Church to assume many political and social responsibilities. With the end of the line of Roman emperors, the bishop of Rome, now called the pope, became the strongest political figure in western Europe. As the spiritual leader of the Church in the West, the pope exercised authority over all Christians throughout this region. The pope based his authority on the tradition that Peter the Apostle, the first bishop of Rome, had been chosen by Jesus to be head of the Church. Although there were many pagan groups that did not accept papal authority, they were gradually converted, and the vast majority of Europeans came to be loyal to Rome and the pope.

Religious Role The Catholic Church taught that all people were sinners. Good lives in this world and salvation after death were dependent on the grace, or favor, of God. The only way to receive grace was by taking part in the **sacraments,** or formal Church rituals: baptism, penance, eucharist, confirmation, matrimony, anointing of the sick, and holy orders. The most important sacrament was the eucharist, or holy communion, which commemorated Christ's death on the cross. People shared in the eucharist at a mass, or worship service. At each mass, the priest blessed wheat wafers and a cup of wine that stood on an altar. According to Catholic teaching, Jesus was invisibly present in the eucharist. The priest and the worshipers received his presence in the forms of the bread and wine.

Although people were deeply religious, they had a limited understanding of Church ceremonies. Masses were said in Latin, a language that few people understood. In addition, many village priests were poorly educated and did not preach effectively. Moreover, few worshipers could read or write. What the average person learned about Christianity came from the statues, paintings, and later the stained glass windows that adorned most medieval churches.

Church Organization The Church hierarchy, which was described in Chapter 6, remained largely the same during the Middle Ages. The contact most people had with the Church was through parish priests, who conducted services, administered the sacraments, and generally oversaw the spiritual life of the community. Occasionally bishops visited a parish to supervise the priests and the extensive Church lands.

The pope, bishops, and priests formed what is called the secular clergy because they lived *in saeculo*, a Latin phrase that means "in the world." Other clergy were known as regular clergy, those who lived by a *regula*, or rule. Regular clergy included monks and nuns who lived apart from the mainstream of society. These Christians played an important role in changing and strengthening the medieval Church.

Benedict's Rule In A.D. 520 a former Roman official named Benedict established a monastery at Monte Cassino in Italy. His monastery became a model for monks in other communities. Based on the maxims that "idleness is an enemy of the soul" and that "to labor is to pray," Benedict drew up a list of rules that alternated hard work with meditation and prayer.

According to the Benedictine rule, monks could not own goods, must never marry, and were bound to obey the laws of the monastery. Their life was one of poverty, chastity, and obedience to an **abbot,** or monastery head.

Monastic Life   Monks dressed in simple, long, loose robes made of coarse material and tied at the waist by a cord. They ate one or two plain meals each day. Most monasteries had a rule of silence; monks could not converse with one another except for a short time each day. In some monasteries total silence was the rule. During meals one monk might read passages from the Bible while the others meditated.

Women took part in monastic life by living in a convent under the supervision of an abbess. Known as nuns, they wore simple clothes—a gown and a veil—and wrapped a white cloth called a wimple around their face and neck. They alternated prayer with spinning, weaving, and embroidering items such as tapestries, altarpieces, and banners to adorn churches. They also taught needlework and the medicinal use of herbs to the daughters of nobles.

Influence of Monastics   Although monks and nuns lived apart from society, they were not completely isolated. Indeed, they played a crucial role in medieval intellectual and social life. Since few people could read or write, the regular clergy preserved ancient religious works and the classical writings of Greece and Rome. Scribes laboriously copied books by hand, working in a small drafty room with only a candle or small

IMAGES OF THE TIME

Monastic Life

Although monasteries were closed religious communities, their members often worked in the outside world.

Travelers are offered food and drink in this image of a Spanish monastery. Many monasteries served as inns for weary travelers.

Nuns and monks performed various works of charity. Here, they tend the sick, counsel the wrongdoer, and feed the hungry.

window for light. For pens they used a sharpened goose quill or feather; for paper, costly parchment made from the skins of animals such as sheep. Illuminated manuscripts decorated with rich colors and intricate pictures indicate that, although the task was tedious, it was lovingly done. One scribe added this note to the bottom of his manuscript: "He who does not know how to write imagines that it is no labor, but though only three fingers hold the pen the whole body grows weary."

Monasteries and convents provided schools for young people, hospitals for the sick and injured, food distribution centers for the needy, and guest houses for weary travelers. They taught peasants carpentry and weaving and made improvements in agriculture that they passed on to others. Some monks and nuns became missionaries who spread Christian teachings to non-Christians.

Missionary Efforts   Pope Gregory I was so impressed with the Benedictine Rule that he adopted it to spread Christianity in Europe. In A.D. 597 he sent monks to England, where they converted the Anglo-Saxons—the dominant group there—to Catholicism. From England, missionaries carried Christianity to northern Germany. During the A.D. 600s, monasteries in Ireland sent missionaries throughout the North Atlantic and western Europe. Although the Irish were isolated from the pope in Rome, their missionaries won many converts. By the A.D. mid-1000s, western Europeans shared one faith.

Power of the Church

During the Middle Ages, the Catholic Church helped to govern western Europe. Bishops and abbots played an important part in the

Each monastery had a cloister, a courtyard surrounded by a walkway. Here, monks could pray and meditate on holy writings. Many cloisters had elaborately carved stonework (right).

Reflecting on the Times
How do the monastic activities shown here reflect the ideals of medieval Christianity?

The Rise of Medieval Europe   **269**

Learning from Art *A seated pope confers authority on a king.* **What was the relationship between medieval religion and politics?**

feudal system. Because many of them came from noble families, they received land from kings in return for military service. Since they were religious leaders, however, these vassals could not fight. They fulfilled their military obligation by giving some of their land to knights who would fight for them.

These feudal ties boosted the Church's wealth and political power. The Church also received donations of land and money from rich nobles who wanted to perform acts of piety or pay for their children's education. As a result, local lords began to exert control over many Church offices and lands, contrary to Church tradition. They often appointed close relatives as bishops or abbots, instead of awarding those offices to the most qualified people. In addition, as religious leaders and monasteries grew wealthier, many Church officials became increasingly careless about carrying out their religious duties.

Church Reform

By the A.D. 900s, many sincere Christians were calling for reform. The reform movement began in the monasteries and spread throughout much of western Europe. Most famous was the monastery at Cluny in eastern France, whose monks won respect for leading lives of pious simplicity. The abbots of Cluny sent emissaries to other monasteries all over Europe to help them undertake similar reforms.

Another group of Church leaders tried to free the Church from the control of feudal lords. They wanted the Church, not the state, to be the final authority in Western society. In 1059 a Church council declared that political leaders could no longer choose the pope. Instead, the pope would be elected by a gathering of **cardinals**—high Church officials in Rome ranking directly below the pope. In addition, the reformers insisted that the pope, not secular rulers such as lords and kings, should be the one to appoint bishops and priests and other officials to Church offices.

In A.D. 1073 the cardinals elected a reform-minded monk named Hildebrand as Pope Gregory VII. Gregory believed that the pope should have complete jurisdiction over all Church officials. He especially criticized the practice of **lay investiture,** in which secular rulers gave the symbols of office, such as a ring and a staff, to the bishops they had appointed.

Elimination of Heresy   Innocent III, who was the pope at the height of the papacy's power, also tried to reform the Catholic Church. In A.D. 1215 he convened a council that condemned drunkenness, feasting, hawking, and dancing among the clergy. The council also laid down strict rules for stopping the spread of **heresy,** or the denial of basic Church teachings. Heresy had increased as corruption and scandal had rocked the Church. In the Middle Ages, heresy was regarded as seriously as the crime of treason is viewed today.

At first, the Catholic Church tried to convert heretics, or those who challenged its teachings. When that failed, however, heretics were threatened with **excommunication,** or expulsion from the Church. An excommunicated person was not allowed to take part in Church sacraments and was also outlawed from any contact with Christian society. Since participation in the sacraments was considered to be essential for salvation, banishment was an especially severe penalty.

Early in the A.D. 1200s, for example, the Church became concerned about a group of heretics in France known as Albigensians (al bih JEHN chuhnz). The Albigensian belief that all life was evil and only the spirit was good caused a few of its members to commit suicide, which the Church regarded as a deadly sin. To end the heresy, Pope Innocent III sent French knights to crush the group.

The Inquisition   In order to seek out and punish people who were suspected of heresy, the Church developed a court in A.D. 1232 known as the Inquisition. Those brought before the court were urged to confess their heresy and to ask forgiveness. Often, however, Inquisition officials accused people of heresy without sufficient proof; sometimes they even used torture to obtain confessions. The Church welcomed back those who repented, but those who did not repent were punished. Punishment ranged from imprisonment to loss of property and even execution. According to Church teachings, these punishments were necessary to save the souls of the heretics.

Friars Inspire Reform   Other Church reformers during the early A.D. 1200s were **friars,** or wandering preachers. At a time when Church leaders were widely criticized for their love of wealth and power, the friars lived simply and owned no possessions. Because they depended on gifts of food and shelter to survive, the friars were called **mendicants,** or religious beggars.

The mendicants followed monastic rules but did not isolate themselves from the rest of the Christian community. The best-known friars were the Franciscan Friars and the Dominican Friars. They kept many western Europeans loyal to the Roman Catholic Church because they were well known and liked.

Francis of Assisi, the son of a wealthy Italian cloth merchant, founded the Franciscan friars in A.D. 1200. Francis and his followers sought to follow the simple life of Jesus and his disciples. St. Francis's Rule declared:

The brothers shall appropriate nothing to themselves, neither a house, nor a place, nor anything; but as pilgrims and strangers in this world, in poverty and humility serving God, they shall confidently go seeking for alms.

The Franciscans became known for their cheerful trust in God and their respect for nature as a divine gift.

A Spanish priest named Dominic organized the Dominican friars in A.D. 1220. Like the Franciscans, the Dominicans lived a life of poverty and service. In addition, they stressed the importance of well-educated, persuasive preachers who could reply to the arguments of heretics.

Church councils, the Inquisition, and the efforts of the mendicants were all signs of Church power. By the A.D. 1000s, however, that power was increasingly being challenged by secular rulers.

SECTION 3 REVIEW

Recall

1. **Define:** sacrament, abbot, cardinal, lay investiture, heresy, excommunication, friar, mendicant
2. **Identify:** Benedict, Gregory I, Gregory VII, Innocent III, Francis of Assisi, Dominic
3. **Locate:** Monte Cassino, Cluny
4. **Explain:** How did the Roman Catholic Church provide the link between the past and the medieval world?

Critical Thinking

5. **Synthesize:** Imagine that you are a religious, but superstitious, peasant. Invent an explanation for the famine that has struck your village.
6. **Analyze:** Contrast the atmosphere that led to the Inquisition with our greater tolerance for differences in religious belief and practice.

Applying Concepts

7. **Uniformity:** Examine the effectiveness of the actions the Catholic Church took to ensure uniformity of people's beliefs and practices during the medieval period.

Rise of European Monarchy

After the decline of the Roman Empire, government in western Europe grew increasingly decentralized. Small feudal states ruled by nobles replaced a large state ruled by a strong, central government. Except for Charlemagne's brief reign in the late A.D. 700s, central authority had disappeared. Kings were rulers in name only, their lands and power gradually lost to feudal lords. However, beginning in the A.D. 1100s, many European monarchs succeeded in building strong states. The Holy Roman emperors, once the most powerful rulers in Europe, eventually weakened through disputes with the Church and powerful nobles.

Medieval England

After the Romans abandoned Britain in the A.D. 400s, the island was invaded by Germanic Angles, Saxons, and Jutes. These groups took over much of Britain from the native Celts (keltz) and set up several kingdoms. In the late A.D. 800s, the Danes, Vikings from the Scandinavian kingdom of Denmark, posed another threat. King Alfred of Wessex, known as Alfred the Great, united the Anglo-Saxon kingdoms and defeated the Danes in A.D. 886. His united kingdom eventually became known as "Angleland," or England.

Anglo-Saxon England   Alfred ruled Anglo-Saxon England from A.D. 871 to 899. Like Charlemagne, he was acutely interested in the revival of learning. The English king founded schools, and he hired scholars to translate many books from Latin to Anglo-Saxon, the language of the country. He also commissioned a history of England, known as the *Anglo-Saxon Chronicle*, which continued to be updated for 250 years after his death.

The kings who followed Alfred were weak rulers. When the last Anglo-Saxon king, Edward the Confessor, died in A.D. 1065, three rivals claimed the throne.

The Norman Conquest   One of the claimants to the throne was William, the Duke of Normandy. A cousin of the late English king and vassal of the king of France, William had a strong feudal organization in the area of northwestern France where the Vikings had settled about a century earlier. Gathering a force of several hundred boats and some 6,000 men, he invaded England in 1066. At the Battle of Hastings, William defeated Harold Godwinson, another rival for the throne. The victory won William the English crown and the title William I, as well as the name William the Conqueror.

To crush potential revolts and keep the loyalty of his Norman vassals, William gave them the lands of the Anglo-Saxon church leaders and nobles. He also established a Great Council of royal officials, bishops, and nobles to advise him and used local officials called sheriffs to collect taxes.

To find out how much money he could collect from the populace, William sent officials throughout the land to conduct the first census in western Europe since Roman times. Every person, every farm, every town and manor, every cow and pig, every horse and sheep became an entry in the *Domesday Book*.

Strong Royal Power   William's grandson, Henry I, ruled from A.D. 1100 to 1135 and continued to strengthen the power of the English monarchy. He established the Exchequer, or department of royal finances, and set up a system of royal courts.

The court system continued to develop under Henry's son, Henry II. In place of the old

The Bayeux Tapestry

The Bayeux Tapestry, made between A.D. 1073 and 1083, is a remarkable work of late Anglo-Saxon art. In fact, the Bayeux Tapestry is not a tapestry at all. By definition, a tapestry is a textile woven of different-colored threads to produce a design or picture. The Bayeux Tapestry is really a work of embroidery, a band of linen upon which pictures and patterns are stitched in colored wool. Twenty inches high and 230 feet long, it probably once decorated the walls of an entire room.

The 72 scenes on the tapestry illustrate William the Conqueror's invasion of England in A.D. 1066. The story is shown in a series of individual scenes, much as a story is told in a comic book today. The tapestry even includes words to indicate what is happening in each scene. The images are lively and simple. No complicated settings are shown; only the people or objects necessary to the story appear. For the most part, the people depicted are shown in motion.

The scene shown here depicts the Duke's boats at Pevensey. William and his men landed in England at Pevensey, near Hastings, with no opposition. The water is indicated by two simple, wavy lines. This simplicity of style can also be seen in the way the horses in the boats are shown.

Just the heads of the horses are visible, and although the boat is clearly not big enough to contain the rest of the horse, the heads are enough to indicate that horses were carried in the boats. Despite the simple style of the figures and objects, however, many informative details are included. From the embroidery, we can see what kind of clothing and armor were worn at the time, as well as what kind of boats and carts were common.

The figures themselves are outlined in a cartoonlike fashion, giving a sense of movement and vitality. The men who stand in the prow of two of the boats call ahead to the next boat. The bold outline of the figures, and their gesture of holding their hand to their mouth to help carry their voice, convey a vivid sense that they are shouting.

The Bayeux Tapestry was probably the work of Matilda (the wife of William the Conqueror) and the ladies of her court. Such textiles seem to have been common in the Middle Ages, and were often used to decorate castles and the homes of wealthy clerics. The Bayeux Tapestry is a part of this decorative tradition.

Responding to the Arts

1. What story is told by the Bayeux Tapestry?
2. How did the artists of the Bayeux Tapestry convey a sense of movement in the scenes depicted?

feudal rules, which differed from lord to lord, Henry II established a **common law** that applied throughout the kingdom. In each community, judges began to meet with a **grand jury,** a group of men who submitted the names of people suspected of crimes. Soon a system of trial by jury was developed to establish the guilt or innocence of the accused. The kind of jury used in these cases was called a **petty jury.**

Limits on the Monarch

Henry's sons, Richard I and John, were ineffective rulers. John lost some English land to France and became unpopular when he increased taxes and punished his enemies without trial. Alarmed at the loss of their feudal rights, a group of nobles met at Runnymede in A.D. 1215. They forced John to sign the Magna Carta, or Great Charter, one of the most important documents in the history of representative government.

The Magna Carta placed clear limits on royal power. Now even a king was bound by law. The charter prevented the king from collecting taxes without the consent of the Great Council. It also assured freemen the right of trial by jury. Article 39 stated:

> *No freeman shall be taken, or imprisoned, or disseized [dispossessed], or outlawed, or exiled, or in any way harmed—nor will we go upon or send upon him—save by the lawful judgment of his peers [equals] or by the law of the land.*

The nobles intended the Magna Carta to protect their feudal rights. Over time, however, it became a guarantee of the rights of all English people.

Rise of Parliament

During the reign of John's son, Henry III, towns began to reappear in England as a result of population growth. A new social class—the middle class—was emerging. The **middle class** did not fit in the medieval social order of nobles, clergy, and peasants. Their income came from business and trade, not from the land. This group played an increasingly important role in local politics.

In recognition of their growing power, Henry III added knights and burgesses, or important townspeople, to the Great Council that advised the king. By that time the Great Council was called Parliament, the name by which it is still known.

In A.D. 1295 Henry's son, Edward I, summoned Parliament with the words, "let that which toucheth all be approved by all," a phrase that reformers later used as the basis for widening representation. Known as the Model Parliament, the session included representatives from the clergy, nobility, and burgesses: the government of England was becoming more representative. Edward encouraged members of Parliament to advise him on business matters, submit petitions to him, and meet frequently. During his reign, Parliament reaffirmed provisions of the Magna Carta.

By A.D. 1400 Parliament had divided into two chambers. Nobles and clergy met as the House of Lords, while knights and burgesses met as the House of Commons.

France

Like England, France developed a strong monarchy in the late Middle Ages. But the type of government that emerged in France differed considerably from the increasingly representative government in England.

Beginnings of Central Government

After Charlemagne's death, the Frankish lands disintegrated into many separate territories governed by feudal lords. These lords defended their own land and were virtually independent rulers.

In A.D. 987 a noble named Hugh Capet seized the French throne from the weak Carolingian king. Capet controlled only the city of Paris and a strip of land between the Seine and Loire rivers in northern France. The Capetian (kah PEE shahn) dynasty he established, however, lasted for more than three centuries. The Capetians strengthened the power of the monarchy and brought French feudal lords under royal control.

As in England, the number of towns in France increased during the A.D. 1100s. Louis VI, who became king in A.D. 1108, used the townspeople to strengthen the royal government at the expense of the nobles. Louis awarded both the townspeople and the clergy positions on his court of advisers and also granted self-government to towns, freeing them from obligations to feudal lords. These measures led officials to be loyal to the monarch rather than to feudal lords.

Strengthening the Monarchy   Philip II, known as Philip Augustus, ruled France from 1180 to 1223. Barely 15 when he succeeded to the throne, Philip had said, "I desire that at the end of my reign the monarchy shall be as powerful as in the time of Charlemagne." Indeed, during his 43-year reign Philip doubled the area of his domain, acquiring some territory through marriage and recapturing French land from England. By appointing local officials who were loyal to the king and forming a semipermanent royal army, Philip further weakened the power of feudal lords.

A Saintly Ruler   Philip's grandson became King Louis IX in A.D. 1226. Louis made royal courts dominant over feudal courts and decreed that only the king had the right to mint coins. Bans on private warfare and the bearing of arms further promoted the French monarch.

An intensely religious man, Louis was proclaimed a saint in A.D. 1297. The king was regarded as the ideal for his chivalry and high moral character. His advice to his son reveals these characteristics:

> [Have] *a tender pitiful heart for the poor . . . [and] hold yourself steadfast and loyal toward your subjects and your vassals, without turning either to the right or to the left, but always straight, whatever may happen. And if a poor man have a quarrel with a rich man, sustain the poor rather than the rich, until the truth is made clear, and when you know the truth, do justice to them.*

Signs of a Strong Monarchy   Louis IX's grandson, Philip IV, was so handsome he was nicknamed Philip the Fair. The blond, blue-eyed Philip increased France's territory and trade by defeating both England and Flanders in

war. To pay for the wars, he raised taxes and taxed new groups, such as the clergy. Although Pope Boniface VIII objected to taxing the clergy, he could not force the French king to back down.

Before he died in A.D. 1314, Philip established the Estates-General, an assembly of nobles, clergy, and townspeople. He intended to use the assembly to allow him to raise taxes on a national level rather than locally. However, the assembly never became an important political body. French kings exercised an almost absolute rule over the people.

The Holy Roman Empire

While monarchs in England and France were building strong central governments, rulers in Germany remained weak and often powerless. One of the major reasons was their entanglement in the politics of the papacy and the Italian states.

Learning from Art *Eleanor of Aquitaine, wife of Louis VII of France and later Henry II of England, tried to raise the status of medieval women.* **Pictured here on a crusade to Palestine, how might she have affected attitudes of the day?**

"Emperor of the Romans" During the A.D. 1000s and 1100s, German kings posed the biggest threat to the pope's authority. King Otto I, or Otto the Great as he was called, of Germany tried to restore Charlemagne's empire. After defeating the Magyars at the Battle of Lechfeld in A.D. 955, King Otto set his sights on Italy. In A.D. 961 his army seized the crown of Lombardy. The following year, Pope John XII sought Otto's help against Roman nobles who opposed the pope. In return for the German king's help, the pope crowned Otto Emperor of the Romans.

Problems of the Holy Roman Empire

Otto and his successors claimed the right to approve or disapprove the election of popes, and Otto himself appointed and deposed several popes. The pope, as you have read, claimed the right to anoint and depose kings. These two conflicting claims led to centuries of dispute between the Holy Roman emperors and the Roman Catholic popes.

Powerful German lords also prevented the Holy Roman emperors from building a strong, unified state. Their challenges to imperial power caused several civil wars. Numerous wars with the Slavic states—Poland and Bohemia—and with Hungary also weakened the emperor's power.

Emperor and Pope Collide During the rule of Henry IV, a major quarrel broke out with Pope Gregory VII. In A.D. 1073 the pope condemned lay investiture, hoping to free the Church from secular control. Since the bishops were important allies in Henry's struggle with the feudal lords, the emperor refused to halt the practice.

The pope promptly proclaimed Henry deposed and excommunicated and urged the German nobles to elect another ruler. Henry gave in. In A.D. 1077 he made his way southward in bitter January weather across the snowy mountains to Canossa, Italy, where the pope was staying. Gregory later described how Henry showed his repentance:

There, having laid aside all the belongings of royalty, wretchedly, with bare feet and clad in wool, he continued for three days to stand before the gate of the castle. Nor did he desist from imploring with many tears the aid and consolation of the apostolic mercy.

Gregory pardoned Henry, but the struggle between the Holy Roman emperor and the pope resumed later. Finally, in A.D. 1122, Church officials, nobles, and representatives of the Holy Roman emperor reached a compromise at the German city of Worms (vurmz). The Concordat of Worms allowed the emperor to name bishops and grant them land. It also gave the pope the right to refuse to approve unworthy candidates.

Popes and monarchs would continue to struggle over power and territory in the coming years. The increasing strength of Europe's monarchies not only threatened the absolute authority of the Church, but it also paved the way toward other changes on the European scene.

SECTION 4 REVIEW

Recall

1. **Define:** common law, grand jury, petty jury, middle class
2. **Identify:** Alfred the Great, William the Conqueror, Magna Carta, Parliament, Hugh Capet, Philip Augustus, Otto the Great, Henry IV
3. **Locate:** Hastings, Paris, Canossa, Worms

4. **Explain:** What factors account for the differences in the way French and English monarchs built strong states?

Critical Thinking

5. **Evaluate:** Judge the importance of the English Parliament in the development of representative government.

6. **Synthesize:** Imagine the scene at Canossa, and compose Henry's speech of apology to Pope Gregory.

Applying Concepts

7. **Conflict:** Identify reasons for conflict between popes and monarchs. Could they have been resolved peacefully?

MAKING INFERENCES

Imagine that just as you leave home to catch your school bus, you hear a news report that fire fighters are battling a fire near the bus garage. When your bus arrives 45 minutes late, you know without being told that the fire disrupted the bus schedule.

Explanation

In the situation above, you *made an inference.* That is, you formed a conclusion that was not based on direct information but was suggested by the facts given. When you read, making inferences enables you to "read between the lines," or to draw conclusions that are not stated directly in the text. Good inferences are based on logical thinking and a careful analysis of information.

Use the following steps to help you make inferences:

- Read or listen carefully for stated facts and ideas.
- Summarize the information and list the pertinent facts.
- Use other information you know about the same subject.
- Decide what inferences or conclusions can be made based on what was read or heard but was not stated directly.

Example

By applying these steps to the passage about Pepin the Short on pages 258–259, you can make in-ferences about information not stated directly in the text.

Charles's son, Pepin the Short, succeeded his father and be-came mayor of the palace in A.D. 741. Pepin—unlike his father, who never assumed the royal title—wished to be named king of the Franks. Since he had no blood claim to the throne, Pepin used his influence with the Frank-ish bishops and the pope to bring about a change in dynasties. In a show of support, the pope jour-neyed to France and anointed King Pepin I with holy oil.

In return for the Church's blessing, Pepin was to defend the pope against his enemies. In A.D. 754 the new king forced the Lombards, a Germanic people, to withdraw from Rome. Pepin seized a large tract of Lombard territory around Rome and gave it to the pope.

List the facts from the passage and think about information you have learned about Pepin, the pope, and the Germanic people.

- Pepin wanted to be king, but had no blood claim to the throne.
- Pepin appealed to the pope.
- The pope anointed Pepin king.
- In return for the pope's sup-port, Pepin forced the Lom-bards to withdraw from Rome, seized some of their territory, and gave it to the pope.

- Popes governed this territory until the late 1800s.

Using these facts, you can now make some inferences about Pepin and European political af-fairs. Since Pepin appealed to the pope in his quest to be king, you can infer that the pope exerted a great deal of power in Europe. You can also infer that the Lombards were enemies of the Franks, since Pepin forced the Lombards to give up much of their territory.

Application

Read the following passage, listing the stated facts. Then, based on the facts and your knowledge about knights and life in the Middle Ages, make infer-ences about a knight's appear-ance and the length of his career.

A knight cannot distinguish himself in [war] if he has not trained for it in tourneys. He must have seen his blood flow, heard his teeth crack under fist blows, felt his opponent's weight bear down upon him as he lay on the ground and, after being twen-ty times unhorsed, have risen twenty times to fight.

Practice

Turn to Practicing Skills on page 279 of the Chapter Review for further practice in making infer-ences.

CHAPTER 11 REVIEW

HISTORICAL SIGNIFICANCE

In the early Middle Ages, a new European civilization arose that combined elements of Roman and Germanic culture with Christian beliefs. While feudalism offered limited stability, it led to a struggle between powerful lords and monarchs seeking to build strong, unified states. The outlines of modern England and France arose during this time, and parliamentary government and the English trial system had their beginnings. The medieval Church preserved ancient manuscripts and established schools, thus laying the basis for later advances in learning. Church and secular authorities, however, became locked in a stormy partnership in which each depended on the other, but both sought to be dominant.

SUMMARY

For a summary of Chapter 11, see the Unit 3 Synopsis on pages 354–357.

USING KEY TERMS

Choose the term from the list that matches best with each phrase below.

a. abbot
b. cardinal
c. chivalry
d. excommunication
e. feudalism
f. fief
g. friar
h. heresy
i. manorialism
j. mendicant
k. middle class
l. petty jury
m. sacrament
n. serf
o. vassal

1. head of a monastery
2. formal Church ritual
3. code of conduct
4. disbelieving Church doctrine
5. land a noble provided his vassal
6. a new social group
7. a wandering preacher
8. medieval agricultural system
9. a religious beggar
10. noble who served the lord of the manor
11. peasant bound to the manor
12. banishment from the Church
13. a political system
14. high-ranking Church official
15. people who decided guilt or innocence

REVIEWING FACTS

1. **List:** What invaders attacked the Carolingians?
2. **Describe:** How and when did the tie between military service and land ownership begin?
3. **Explain:** What important part did Church leaders play in the feudal system?
4. **Outline:** Sketch briefly how missionaries carried Christianity across Europe.
5. **List:** Give factors that helped maintain religious uniformity in feudal times.

THINKING CRITICALLY

1. **Apply:** Until the 1970s, "good manners" required a man to help a woman with her coat, and push in her chair. How do these customs relate to chivalry?
2. **Analyze:** What did the bishop of Reims mean by the order he gave Clovis (page 258)?
3. **Evaluate:** Every society has to develop ways to deal with ignorance, ill health, hunger, and homelessness. Compare the way feudal society handled these problems with the way modern society handles them.
4. **Synthesize:** Use a diagram to describe what goods and services were exchanged among nobles, knights, and peasants.

ANALYZING CONCEPTS

1. **Movement:** How can movement both have created and crippled Frankish society?
2. **Cooperation:** How were lords and peasants mutually dependent?
3. **Uniformity:** How is uniformity implied in the term *regular clergy*?
4. **Conflict:** How did the conflict between King John and the nobles eventually have positive results for all English people?

PRACTICING SKILLS

1. Review the description of a castle on pages 263–264. Make an inference about the peasants' living conditions inside the castle during conflict.
2. Many men and women adopted the monastic life-style. What inferences can you make about their motivations?

GEOGRAPHY IN HISTORY

1. **Location:** Refer to the map on page 988 to explain why the Irish Church was isolated from Rome.
2. **Place:** How did Vikings use technology to overcome obstacles along the routes to the places they wished to conquer?
3. **Relationships within places:** How did the three-field system of crop rotation and soil preser-

vation allow farmers to better use their environment?
4. **Movement:** How was movement important to Charlemagne's government?

TRACING CHRONOLOGY

Refer to the time line below to answer these questions.

1. A Church council took the right to elect popes away from political leaders in A.D. 1059. What does the time line suggest as a positive consequence of that action?
2. Contrast the effect of events in England and on the Continent in the early A.D. 1200s on freedom.
3. Examine the events from A.D. 719 to 987. What do they have in common?

LINKING PAST AND PRESENT

1. Great Britain, defended by its isolation, has not been invaded since A.D. 1066. What structure has recently been built that will reduce Great Britain's physical isolation from the rest of Europe?
2. People often cherish a romantic view of medieval life. Do you think such a view is justified by historical evidence?
3. Improvements changed farming in Europe around A.D. 1000. What improvements today will increase farm productivity? What far-reaching effects will they have?

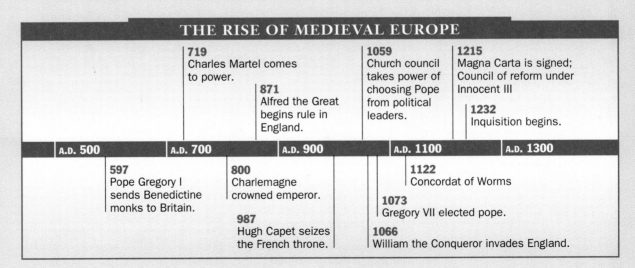

THE RISE OF MEDIEVAL EUROPE

719 Charles Martel comes to power.

871 Alfred the Great begins rule in England.

1059 Church council takes power of choosing Pope from political leaders.

1215 Magna Carta is signed; Council of reform under Innocent III

1232 Inquisition begins.

A.D. 500   A.D. 700   A.D. 900   A.D. 1100   A.D. 1300

597 Pope Gregory I sends Benedictine monks to Britain.

800 Charlemagne crowned emperor.

987 Hugh Capet seizes the French throne.

1122 Concordat of Worms

1073 Gregory VII elected pope.

1066 William the Conqueror invades England.

Medieval Europe at Its Height

*W*ell-beloved father," wrote a medieval student, "I have not a penny, nor can I get any save through you, for all things at the University are so dear: nor can I study in my [law books], for they are all tattered. Moreover, I owe ten crowns in dues to the [university administrator], and can find no man to lend them to me.

"Well-beloved father, to ease my debts . . . at the baker's, with the doctor . . . and to pay . . . the laundress and the barber, I send you word of greetings and of money."

This letter from a medieval student sounds very much like something a modern student might write. At that time, however, the university was something new. It was part of the cultural awakening that took place in the High Middle Ages.

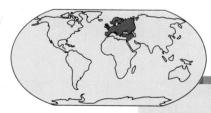

CHAPTER PREVIEW

Key Terms to Define: crusade, money economy, guild, master, apprentice, journeyman, charter, scholasticism, troubadour, vernacular

People to Meet: Seljuk Turks, Pope Urban II, Saladin, Richard I, Peter Abelard, Thomas Aquinas, Dante Alighieri, Geoffrey Chaucer, Edward III, Philip IV, Joan of Arc,

Henry Tudor, John Wycliffe, Jan Hus, Lollards, Hussites

Places to Discover: Jerusalem, Constantinople, Crécy, Orléans, Burgundy, Castile, Aragon, Avignon, Bohemia

Objectives to Learn:
1. What were the results of the crusades?

This painting depicts the crusaders battling Muslims at Antioch, in what is now Turkey.

2. What effect did the growth of towns have on medieval society?
3. How did European monarchs consolidate power?
4. Why was the Church under pressure to reform?

Concepts to Understand:
- Cultural diffusion—The crusades increase European contact with other areas. Section 1
- Innovation—Advances in commerce, learning, and the arts change Europe. Section 2
- Conflict—England and France battle while monarchs gain power. Section 3
- Conflict—The Church faces a split from within and dissent from without. Section 4

281

The Crusades

Life in the Early Middle Ages was characterized by decentralized and destabilized government, warfare and invasions, cultural isolation, famine, and wretched living conditions. Trade was sparse, and agricultural production—the mainstay of the economy—was inefficient.

By A.D. 1100, however, conditions in Europe had begun to improve. Some European monarchs succeeded in building strong, central governments. Better farming methods led to larger crop yields and a growth in population. Towns and trade began to reappear. The Church held a powerful sway over the emotions and energies of the people. Changes in religion, society, politics, and economics made the High Middle Ages—the period between A.D. 1050 and 1270—a springboard for a new and brilliant civilization in western Europe.

The transformation of medieval society began with a holy war over the city of Jerusalem. European Christians undertook a series of military expeditions—nine in all—to recover the Holy Land from the Muslims. These expeditions were called **crusades**, from the Latin word *crux*, meaning "cross." Those who fought were called crusaders because they vowed to "take up the cross."

Call for a Crusade

Jerusalem was a holy city for people of three faiths. Jews treasured it as Zion, God's own city, and as the site of the ancient temple built by Solomon. To Christians, the city was holy because it was the place where Jesus was crucified and resurrected. Muslims regarded Jerusalem as their third holiest city, after Mecca and Medina. According to tradition, Muhammad ascended to heaven from Jerusalem.

Jerusalem and the entire region of Palestine fell to Arab invaders in the A.D. 600s. Mostly Muslims, the Arabs tolerated other religions. Christians and Jews were allowed to live in Jerusalem as long as they paid their taxes and followed certain regulations. European traders and religious pilgrims traveled to Palestine without interference.

In the late 1000s, however, Seljuk Turks—a Muslim people from central Asia—took control of Jerusalem and closed the city to Jewish and Christian pilgrims. The Seljuks also threatened the Byzantine Empire, especially Constantinople. As a result of this threat, the Byzantine emperor wrote to the pope in 1095 requesting military assistance from the West. Reports of persecution against Christians in Palestine gave added urgency to the emperor's request.

First Crusade   On a cold November day in 1095, Pope Urban II mounted a platform outside the church at Clermont, France. His voice shaking with emotion, he addressed the assembled throng, asking for a volunteer army to take Jerusalem and Palestine from the Seljuks:

I exhort you . . . to strive to expel that wicked race from our Christian lands. . . . Christ commands it. Remission of sins will be granted for those going thither. . . . Let those who are accustomed to wage private war wastefully even against believers go forth against the infidels. . . . Let those who have lived by plundering be soldiers of Christ; let those who formerly contended against brothers and relations rightly fight barbarians; let those who were recently hired for a few pieces of silver win their eternal reward.

"Deus vult!" (God wills it!) shouted the crowd. Knights and peasants alike vowed to join

the expedition to the Holy Land. For knights, the crusade was a happy chance to employ their fighting skills. For peasants, the crusade meant freedom from feudal bonds while on the crusade. All were promised immediate salvation in heaven if they were killed freeing the Holy Land from non-Christians. Adventure and the possibility of wealth were other reasons to join the crusade. In preparation for the holy war, red crosses of cloth were stitched on clothing as a symbol of service to God.

Historians estimate that as many as 30,000 crusaders left western Europe between 1096 and 1099 to fight in the First Crusade. Led by French nobles, three armies marched across Europe and met in Constantinople in 1097. From there, the crusaders crossed into Asia Minor, enduring the hardships of hunger and disease, the trials of desert travel, and quarrels among their leaders. At Antioch—in present-day Syria—the crusaders met and defeated a large Muslim garrison. Sweeping southward, the crusaders made their way on to Jerusalem.

In June 1099, the army reached Jerusalem and began to attack the city. After a siege of almost two months, the city fell. Crusaders swarmed into the city and slaughtered most of its Muslim and Jewish inhabitants.

The success of the First Crusade reinforced the authority of the Church and strengthened the self-confidence of western Europeans. The religious zeal of the crusaders soon cooled, however, and many knights returned home. Those who stayed set up feudal states in Syria and Palestine. Contact between the crusaders and the relatively more sophisticated civilizations of the Byzantines and the Muslims would continue for the next 100 years and become a major factor in ending the cultural isolation of western Europe.

Second Crusade   Less than 50 years after the First Crusade, the Seljuks conquered part of the crusader states in Palestine. Pope Eugenius IV called for a Second Crusade to regain the territory. Eloquent sermons by the monk Bernard of Clairvaux (klair VOH) persuaded King Louis VII of France and Holy Roman Emperor Conrad III to lead armies to Palestine. The Second Crusade, which lasted from 1147 to 1149, was unsuccessful. Louis VII and Conrad III quarreled constantly and were ineffective militarily. They were easily defeated by the Seljuks.

Third Crusade   A diplomatic and forceful leader named Saladin (SAL uhd uhn) united the Muslim forces and then captured Jerusalem in 1187. The people of western Europe were stunned and horrified. Holy Roman Emperor Frederick Barbarossa of Germany, King Philip Augustus of France, and King Richard I of England assembled warriors for the Third Crusade. This "Crusade of Kings" lasted from 1189 to 1192 and was no more successful than the Second Crusade. Frederick Barbarossa died on the way to Palestine, and his army returned home. Philip Augustus returned to France before the army reached Jerusalem. Richard continued the struggle alone.

Although his army defeated the Muslims in several battles, Richard could not win a decisive victory over Saladin's well-trained and dedicated forces. After three years of fighting, Richard signed a truce with the Muslims and tried to persuade Saladin to return Jerusalem to the Christians. "Jerusalem," he wrote to the Muslim leader, "we are resolved not to renounce as long as we have a single man left." Saladin's reply to Richard showed his equal determination to keep the city:

Learning from Art *Shown here are crusaders preparing to leave for Jerusalem.* **How do you think the crusades might have benefited Italian port cities?**

To us Jerusalem is as precious, aye and more precious, than it is to you, in that it was the place whence our Prophet made his journey by night to heaven and is destined to be the gathering place of our nation at the last day. Do not dream that we shall give it up to you. . . . It belonged to us originally, and it is you who are the real aggressors. When you seized it, it was only because of the suddenness of your coming and the weakness of those [Muslims] who then held it. So long as the war shall last God will not suffer you to raise one stone upon another.

Although Saladin refused to turn over Jerusalem, he allowed Christian pilgrims access .

Other Crusades   In 1198 Pope Innocent III called for a crusade that proved to be disastrous for the Byzantine Empire. In this Fourth Crusade, lasting between 1202 and 1204, crusaders sacked Constantinople, the capital of the Byzantine Empire, instead of trying to recover Jerusalem. The motivations for the attack were religious, commercial, and military.

In part, the crusaders turned against the city for money: they were heavily in debt to Venetian bankers for supplies. The crusaders also were motivated by a hatred for the Orthodox Church.

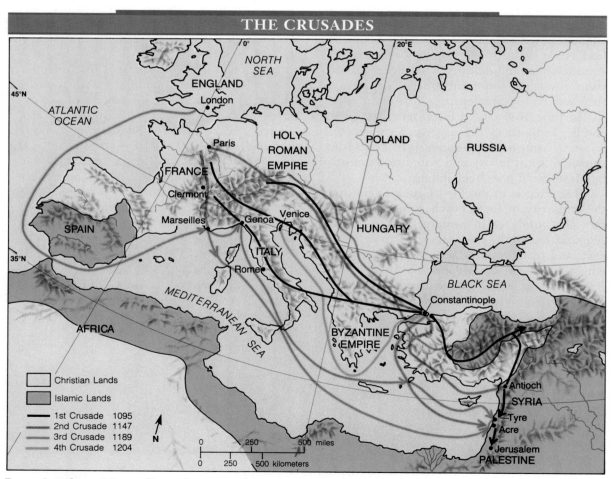

THE CRUSADES

☐	Christian Lands
▦	Islamic Lands
▬▬	1st Crusade 1095
▬▬	2nd Crusade 1147
▬▬	3rd Crusade 1189
▬▬	4th Crusade 1204

Learning from Maps *Trace the routes of the crusaders from western Europe to Palestine.* **About how far did crusaders on the First Crusade travel before reaching Jerusalem?**

284   *Chapter 12*

For three terrible days in 1204, the crusaders burned libraries, desecrated churches, and stole valuable works of art, jewels, and gold. The attack not only opened the Byzantines to attack from foreign invaders; it embittered the Byzantines toward the West for hundreds of years to come. During the Fourth Crusade, the spirit of the crusades—the religious goals—were lost, replaced by a hunger for wealth and power.

Other crusades followed, including the strange and tragic Children's Crusade. In 1212 thousands of peasant children between the ages of 10 and 18 set out from France and Germany for Jerusalem. They believed that God would deliver the Holy City to them because they were poor and faithful; many of the children starved or froze to death on the long march south to the Mediterranean sea. When the sea did not part for them to cross safely to Jerusalem—a miracle they expected—the children began returning home in shame. Many were captured and sold into slavery by Muslims.

None of the later crusades succeeded in winning permanent Christian control of Palestine. In fact, the Muslims eventually reconquered all the territories remaining in Christian hands. Acre—the last Christian stronghold in Palestine—fell in 1291, nearly 200 years after Pope Urban had begun the crusades.

By this time, western Europeans had lost sight of the original religious goal of the crusades. They were now more concerned about political and economic gain than about recovering territory from the Muslims. As a result, European rulers lost interest in Palestine and shifted their attention in new directions.

Effects of the Crusades

The crusades failed to free the Holy Land from the Muslims. Nonetheless, the crusades had a major impact on the development of western Europe. In Europe, the crusades helped break down feudalism and increase the authority of kings. Kings levied taxes and raised large armies of fighting forces. Some nobles died in battle without leaving heirs, and their lands passed to kings. To raise money for weapons and supplies, many lesser nobles sold their estates or allowed their serfs to buy their freedom to become freeholders on the land or artisans in the towns.

European contact during the crusades with the more advanced Byzantine and Muslim civilizations helped to bring classical texts back to the West. This knowledge fueled a renewed interest in literature and art that later swept across Europe.

In addition, European cities—especially Venice and Genoa in Italy—became more prosperous and powerful due to increased trading in the Mediterranean. Contact with the East spurred a new demand for luxury goods: spices, sugar, melons, tapestries, silk, and other items previously hard to come by.

Finally, the crusades improved European technology. From the Muslims, the crusaders learned how to build better ships and make more accurate maps. They began to use the magnetic compass to tell direction. The crusaders also learned new military skills, especially in siege techniques. Weaponry significantly improved as well.

SECTION 1 REVIEW

Recall

1. **Define:** crusade
2. **Identify:** Seljuk Turks, Pope Urban II, Richard I, Saladin
3. **Locate:** Find Jerusalem and Constantinople on the map on page 284.
4. **Explain:** Why did both Christians and Muslims feel that Jerusalem should belong to them?

Critical Thinking

5. **Apply:** The crusades were both a sign of European recovery and a stimulant of further growth. Explain how this could be so.

6. **Analyze:** In what ways were the crusades a success? In what ways were they a failure?

Applying Concepts

7. **Cultural diffusion:** Describe how cultural diffusion in the Middle Ages occurred as a result of the crusades.

Economic and Cultural Revival

The crusades accelerated the transformation of western Europe from a society that was crude, backward, and violent—showing little cultural and technological advancement—to a civilization that exhibited some early features of modern Western civilization. Towns grew, trade expanded, and learning and the arts thrived.

Economic Expansion

The economy of western Europe had begun to show vigor around A.D. 1000. Agricultural production increased. Expanding opportunities in trade encouraged the growth of towns, and the lively atmosphere of the towns in turn stimulated creative thought and innovations in art.

Agriculture Improves   Plows during the Early Middle Ages were light and did not cut much below the surface of the soil. The invention of a new, heavier plow made it possible to cut through the rich, damp soils of northwestern Europe. This plow enabled farmers to produce more and to cultivate new lands, increasing food production. Nobles and freeholders—peasants not bound to the land—migrated to new areas, clearing forests, draining swamps, and building villages. In one of the largest migrations of the time, the Germans moved to eastern Europe, doubling the territory they controlled.

About the same time, the collar harness replaced the ox yoke. Horses were choked by the ox yoke, but the new harness shifted weight off the neck and onto the shoulders, allowing farmers to replace oxen with horses. Horses pulled the plow faster than oxen, allowing farmers to plant and plow more crops.

As you read in Chapter 11, the three-field system of planting also made the land more pro-ductive. As the land began to feed more people, the population naturally increased.

Trade Expands   The revival of towns caused a rapid expansion of trade. Soon the sea-lanes and roads were filled with traders carrying goods to market. Important sea and river routes connected western Europe with the Mediterranean, eastern Europe, and Scandinavia. The repaired and rebuilt Roman road system carried international traders to and from Europe.

Italian towns such as Venice, Pisa, and Genoa controlled the Mediterranean trade after 1200, bringing silks and spices from Asia to Europe. The towns of Flanders, a region that today is the northeastern part of France and Belgium, became the center of trade on Europe's northern coast. The textiles produced by these towns were traded at Middle Eastern markets for porcelain, velvet and silk, and silver. Towns along the Baltic coast controlled trade between eastern Europe and the North Atlantic.

The merchandise for sale in a town was varied and seemingly endless. This was especially true during trade fairs. Each year hundreds of traders met at large trade fairs in places convenient to land and water routes. Feudal lords charged the merchants fees, charged taxes on goods, and offered protection to the merchants. The most famous fair was at Champagne in eastern France, located in almost the exact center of western Europe. For four to six weeks each year, Champagne was a distribution point for goods from around the world.

Banking   Early merchants used the barter system, trading one good for another without using money. Before long, however, merchants found this system impractical. Moreover, some of the merchants who supplied luxury goods such as silk would only accept money in payment. European merchants therefore needed a common medium of exchange.

The rise of a **money economy,** or an economy based on money, had far-reaching consequences for the growth of Europe. Initially, it led to the growth of banking. Since traders came from many countries, they carried different currencies with different values. Moneychangers—often Jews or Italians—determined the value of the various currencies and exchanged one currency for another. They also developed procedures for transferring funds from one place to another, received deposits, and arranged loans, thus becoming the first bankers in Europe. In fact, the word *bank* comes from the *banca,* or bench, that the moneychangers set up at fairs.

As the money economy grew, it put the feudal classes in an economic squeeze. Kings, clergy, and nobles became dependent on money from banks to pay their expenses. To pay off their loans, they had to raise taxes, sell their lands, or demand money in place of traditional feudal services. As serfs became able to buy their freedom, the feudal system declined.

Growth of Towns

The number of towns in western Europe grew tremendously in the 1000s and 1100s. Many grew up beside well-traveled roads or near waterways. Although warfare had declined, settlements still faced bandits. To protect themselves, townspeople built walls around their towns. At first these enclosures were simple wooden fences. As the population grew, stone walls were built, with guard towers at the gates.

Inside the walls narrow, winding streets bustled with people, carts drawn by horses and oxen, and farm animals on the way to market. A din of noise and overpowering smells attacked the senses. Church bells chimed the hours; carts piled high with goods creaked and rumbled through streets that were little more than alleys. Shops lined the streets at ground level, and the shop owners often lived in quarters above. Most buildings were of wood and had thatch roofs, making fire a constant hazard.

Medieval towns had almost no sanitation facilities, and a constant stench assailed the people from the garbage and sewage tossed into the streets. These unsanitary conditions caused the rapid spread of diseases such as diphtheria, typhoid, influenza, and malaria. In crowded towns such diseases often turned into epidemics and took many lives. The worst of these epidemics ravaged Europe between A.D. 1346 and 1352, killing one-third of the population and earning the name the Black Death.

Guilds   During the 1100s, merchants and artisans organized themselves into business associations called **guilds.** The primary function of the merchant guild was to maintain a monopoly of the local market for its members. To accomplish this end, merchant guilds severely restricted trading by foreigners in their city and enforced uniform pricing. The following regulations from Southampton, England, indicate the power of the merchant guilds:

> *A*nd no one shall buy honey, fat, salt herrings, or any kind of oil, or millstones, or fresh hides, or any kind of fresh skins, unless he is a guildsman; nor keep a tavern for wine, nor sell cloth at retail, except in market or fair days. . .

Craft guilds, on the other hand, regulated the work of artisans: carpenters, shoemakers, blacksmiths, masons, tailors, and weavers. Women working as laundresses, seamstresses and embroiderers, and maidservants had their own trade associations.

Craft guilds established strict rules concerning prices, wages, and employment. A member of the shoemakers' guild could not charge more (or less) for a pair of shoes than other shoemakers, nor could he advertise or in any way induce people to buy his wares. Although the guilds prohibited competition, they set standards of quality to protect the public from shoddy goods.

Craft guilds were controlled by **masters,** or artisans who owned their own shops and tools and employed less-skilled artisans as helpers. To become a master at a particular craft, an artisan served an apprenticeship, the length of which varied according to the difficulty of the craft. **Apprentices** worked for a master without pay. An apprentice then became a **journeyman** and received pay. However, a journeyman could only work under a master. To become a master, a journeyman submitted a special sample of his work—a masterpiece—to the guild for approval. If the sample was approved, the journeyman became a master and could set up his own shop.

Aside from business activities, guilds provided benefits for their members such as medical care and unemployment relief. Guilds also organized social and religious life by sponsoring banquets, holy day processions, and outdoor plays.

Rise of the Middle Class The medieval town, or *burg*, created the name for a new class of people. In Germany they were called *burghers;* in France, the *bourgeoisie* (burzh wah ZEE); and in England, *burgesses.* The name originally referred to anyone living in a town. Gradually it came to mean the people who made money through the developing money economy. They were a middle class made up of merchants, bankers, and artisans who no longer had to rely on the land to make a living.

The middle class helped turn towns into organized municipalities. Businessmen created councils to administer town affairs and gained political power for themselves. As the money economy spread, kings began to depend on the middle class for loans and for income from the taxes they paid. The leading merchants and bankers became advisers to lords and kings.

Town Government Conflict developed between the feudal classes and the burghers. City dwellers did not fit into the feudal system; they resented owing taxes and services to lords. They wanted to run their own affairs and have their own laws. At the same time, feudal lords feared the growing wealth and power of the middle class. To try to keep the burghers in line, the lords began to strictly enforce feudal laws.

IMAGES OF THE TIME

Medieval Life

In the later Middle Ages, commerce became more important throughout Europe, and cities grew.

Many medieval cities were fortified to protect the town from possible attack. Towers and sheltered walkways allowed guards to defend the city.

Stories of romance and heroic deeds were popular in the later Middle Ages. This embroidered purse shows a man and woman courting.

The money economy gave the towns the income and power they needed to win the struggle against the lords. In the 1000s Italian towns formed groups called communes. Using the political power they gained from the growing money economy, the communes made the Italian towns into independent city-states. In other areas of Europe, kings and nobles granted townspeople **charters,** documents that gave them the right to control their own affairs.

Education

During the Early Middle Ages, most people were illiterate. Education was controlled by the clergy. In monastery and cathedral schools, students prepared for monastery life or for work as church officials. In addition to religious subjects such as church music and theology—the study of religious thought—students learned the seven liberal arts: grammar, rhetoric, logic, arithmetic, geometry, astronomy, and music.

As towns grew, the need for educated officials stimulated a new interest in learning. The growth of courts and other legal institutions created a need for lawyers. As a result, around 1150, students and teachers began meeting away from monastery and cathedral schools.

At first the university was not so much a place as it was a group of scholars organized like a guild for the purpose of learning. Classes were held in rented rooms or churches or in the open air. Books were scarce. In most classes a teacher read the text and discussed it, while students took notes on slates or committed as much information as possible to memory. Classes did, however, meet on a regular schedule. University rules established the obligations of students and teachers toward each other. To qualify as a

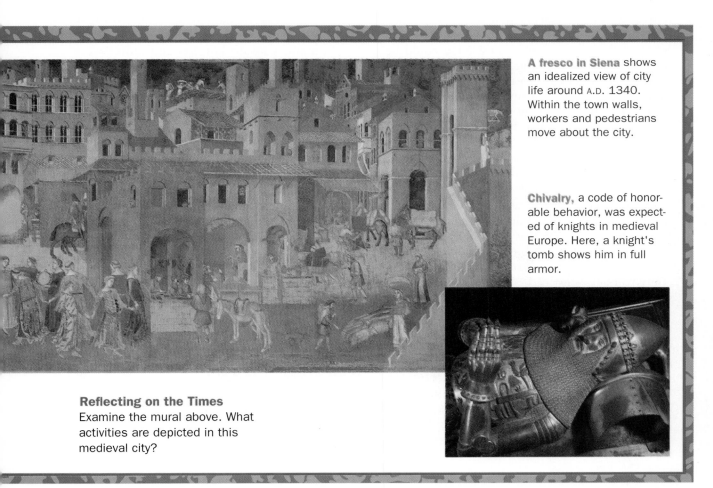

A fresco in Siena shows an idealized view of city life around A.D. 1340. Within the town walls, workers and pedestrians move about the city.

Chivalry, a code of honorable behavior, was expected of knights in medieval Europe. Here, a knight's tomb shows him in full armor.

Reflecting on the Times
Examine the mural above. What activities are depicted in this medieval city?

teacher, students had to pass an examination leading to a degree, or certificate of completion. Access to the subjects of law, theology, and medicine were controlled by the teachers' guild.

By the end of the 1200s, universities had spread throughout Europe. Most southern European universities were modeled after the law school at Bologna (buh LOHN yuh), Italy, and specialized in law and medicine. Universities in northern Europe, on the other hand, specialized in liberal arts and theology. These were generally modeled after the University of Paris.

New Learning   At medieval universities, scholars studied Latin classics and Roman law in depth. They also acquired knowledge from the works of the Greek philosopher Aristotle and from Islamic scholarship in the sciences. This interest in the physical world eventually led to the rise of Western science.

Many church leaders opposed the study of Aristotle's works, fearing that his ideas threatened Christian teachings. In contrast, some scholars thought the new knowledge could be used to support Christian ideas. They applied Aristotle's philosophy to theological questions and developed a system of thought called **scholasticism.** This new type of learning emphasized reason as well as faith in the interpretation of Christian doctrine. Scholastics sought to reconcile classical philosophy with Church teachings. They believed all knowledge could be integrated into a coherent whole.

One early scholastic teacher, Peter Abelard, taught theology in Paris during the early 1100s. In his book *Sic et Non* (yes and no), he collected statements from the Bible and the writings of early Christian leaders that showed both sides of controversial questions. Abelard then had his students reconcile the differences through logic.

In the 1200s the most important scholastic thinker was Thomas Aquinas (uh KWY nuhs), a brilliant theologian and philosopher who taught philosophy in Paris and Naples. In his work *Summa Theologica* (a summary of religious thought), Aquinas claimed that reason was a gift from God that could provide answers to basic philosophical questions. The Catholic Church later accepted and promoted Aquinas's way of teaching and thinking.

Medieval Literature and Art

The spread of universities and the revival of intellectual endeavor stimulated advances in literature and the arts. Songs and epics of the Early Middle Ages were put in writing for the first time. One of the earliest works, *Beowulf*, was an epic poem of almost 3,200 lines. Handed down by oral tradition for two centuries, it was finally written down in an early form of English known as Old English (Anglo-Saxon) by an unknown poet in about A.D. 700. In colorful verses and exciting narrative, the epic describes how the Anglo-Saxon warrior Beowulf defeats a horrible monster named Grendel.

French epics called *chansons de geste*, or songs of high deeds, celebrated and often embellished the courage of feudal warriors. The *Song of Roland*, written around 1100, gives an account of the chivalrous defense of Christianity by Charlemagne's knights. The hero of the epic is a loyal and fearless knight named Roland, who may have been the nephew of Charlemagne.

Romances about knights and ladies were also popular. These love stories usually presented an idealized picture of feudal society. In southern France in the 1100s and 1200s, traveling poet-musicians called **troubadours** composed short lyric poems and songs about love and the feats of knights. They helped define the ideal knight celebrated in the code of chivalry.

Most medieval literature was written in the **vernacular,** or language of everyday speech, of the writer. Instead of using Latin as a common language, people spoke the language of their own country—English, German, French, Italian, or Spanish. These vernacular languages helped give each kingdom of Europe a separate identity. Use of vernacular languages in writing made literature accessible to more people.

Some outstanding works of literature were written in the vernacular in the 1300s. Dante Alighieri (DAHN tay al uhg YEHR ee) wrote the *Divine Comedy*, an epic poem in Italian. Written over a period of several years, the poem discusses medieval ideas of life after death by describing an imaginary journey from hell to heaven. The *Divine Comedy* presents the important theological concepts of the Middle Ages and has influenced numerous writers since that time.

Trail of the Black Death

This French illumination of the 1400s depicts the Black Death.

Some thought it was retribution for wickedness; others feared it was the end of the world. The mysterious disease seemed to burst out of nowhere and kill everyone in its path. Outbreaks of the disease—then known as the Black Death but today called the bubonic plague—erupted throughout Europe in the 1340s. It continued at 10-year intervals throughout the Middle Ages. The worst epidemic, which claimed nearly 25 million lives between 1347 and 1351, originated in China. The first victims were nomadic Mongol horsemen who were infected by flea-carrying rats. The plague spread swiftly across Asia.

When ships from Asia reached the Mediterranean the disease spread to Sicily, North Africa, and western Europe. People in crowded towns with poor sanitation—and rats—were at greater risk than those in the countryside. Whole families were wiped out.

About one-third of Europe's population died in this single epidemic. It was not until 1906 that rats were identified as the carrier of the Black Death.

The plague brought many changes to western Europe. Wars stopped, and trade slowed. People were forbidden to gather in groups, religious services were suspended, and infected homes were sealed off. Businesses shut their doors and many city people fled to the country.

The plague changed the social, economic, and religious face of Europe forever. It would take two centuries for western Europe to regain its pre-1347 level of population.

Making the Connection

1. How was the plague brought to western Europe?
2. How is the spread of disease still related to human movement?

In England a government official named Geoffrey Chaucer began the *Canterbury Tales* in 1386 and continued the series of tales probably right up to his death in 1400. The narrative poems brilliantly describe a group of pilgrims, representing people of various classes and occupations, who tell stories to amuse one another on their way to a shrine at Canterbury, England. Chaucer's worldly approach to the pilgrims and their stories delight readers to this day.

Medieval Art Early medieval churches were built in a style called Romanesque, which combined features of Roman and Byzantine structures. Romanesque churches had thick walls, columns set close together, heavy curved arches, and small windows. Colorful tapestries, wall paintings, and gilded statues that reflected the glow from hundreds of candles lighted the dark interior.

In the mid–1100s, French architects began to build in a new style called Gothic. They overcame the structural limitations of Romanesque architectual—heavy walls and low arches—by two innovations. On the outside, they built flying buttresses, or stone beams that extended out from the wall. These supports took the weight of the building off the walls and allowed walls to be thinner, with more window space. The ceiling inside was supported by pointed arches

Learning from Art
In The Canterbury Tales, *each of the 29 pilgrims was to tell a tale for the others on the way to Canterbury. Chaucer only completed 22 of the tales before his death.* **What are some other examples of literature during the Middle Ages?**

made of narrow stone ribs reaching out from tall pillars. These supports allowed architects to build higher ceilings and more open interiors. The lofty pointed spires of Gothic cathedrals seemed to soar into the heavens. The sun shining through the beautiful stained-glass windows filled the interior with a rich, warm glow.

Medieval painters turned their attention to a smaller art form, the illuminated manuscript.

The demand for this art form increased as the newly moneyed middle class began to collect libraries of bibles, psalters or hymnbooks, and books of hours—devotional calendars—as well as secular works like the *Canterbury Tales.* Adorned with brilliantly colored illustrations and often highlighted with gold leaf, these works were miniature masterpieces whose beauty has endured to the present day.

SECTION 2 REVIEW

Recall

1. **Define:** money economy, guild, master, apprentice, journeyman, charter, scholasticism, troubadour, vernacular
2. **Identify:** Peter Abelard, Thomas Aquinas, *Beowulf,* Dante Alighieri, Geoffrey Chaucer
3. **Describe:** Write a description of trade fairs in the Middle Ages.
4. **Explain:** Why was membership in a guild advantageous for a medieval artisan? Why was it disadvantageous

Critical Thinking

5. **Synthesize:** Create an imaginary medieval town. Briefly explain its physical characteristics. Then describe what a typical day for an artisan working there would be like.

6. **Evaluate:** What would have happened if medieval Europe had remained an agriculture-based society?

Applying Concepts

7. **Innovation:** Choose one of the following and trace its effect on medieval society: three-field system, money economy, guilds.

Strengthening of Monarchy

During the Middle Ages, power rested in the hands of nobles who owned feudal estates. But as trade flourished and towns grew, feudalism weakened in the face of an increasingly complex society. Beginning in the 1100s, power in western Europe began to shift from nobles to kings or queens. Gradually the influence of the clergy and nobles diminished as educated common people and laymen became advisers to monarchs. At the outset, however, a period of violent warfare swept through western Europe.

Hundred Years' War

During the 1300s, feudal disputes often led to wars among Europe's monarchs. The Hundred Years' War between England and France grew out of such a dispute. The war—actually a series of wars—lasted from 1337 to 1453, before the French claimed victory.

Causes Ever since William of Normandy conquered England in 1066, conflicting feudal claims had caused great bitterness between the English and French kings. Because William had been duke of Normandy—an area in northwestern France—before becoming king of England, his successors in England saw themselves as rulers of Normandy and England. English control over French lands increased in 1152, when Henry II married Eleanor of Aquitaine, heir to lands in southwestern France. As a result of the marriage, Henry II controlled more land in France than did the French king.

The French monarch Philip II regained most of the northern lands held by England by defeating Eleanor's son, King John, in the early 1200s. But the French kings wanted all of the lands claimed by the English.

Matters between the English and French worsened in 1328, when the French king died without leaving a direct heir. King Edward III of England, a grandson of the French king, declared himself king of France and announced that he would not recognize French sovereignty over his lands in France. The successor to the French throne, Philip of Valois—himself only a nephew of the dead king—quietly began to prepare for war with England.

Major Battles Despite being poorer and less populated than France, England won the early battles of the Hundred Years' War. English unity contributed to this success. English kings received popular support from the nation and financial support from Parliament. Superior military tactics also gave England an edge.

When French knights arrived at the small village of Crécy (kray SEE) in 1346, they outnumbered the English two to one. They were surprised to see foot soldiers fighting alongside the English knights. These soldiers carried a new weapon, the Welsh longbow. As tall as a man, longbows could shoot steel-tipped arrows capable of piercing heavy armor at 400 yards (360 meters). French swords and crossbows were useless at such a distance. French historian Jean Froissart described the battle:

> *Then the English archers stept forth one pace and let fly their arrows so wholly* [together] *and so thick, that it seemed snow. When the* [soldiers] *felt the arrows piercing through heads, arms and breasts, many of them cast down their cross-bows and did cut their strings and* [retreated]. . . .

At Crécy the English forces also used the first portable firearm in European warfare: a long iron tube mounted on a pole. This cumbersome firearm led to the development of the cannon, which became a major weapon in later fighting.

By the late 1300s, France was in disarray. War and plague were ravaging the country. Although a peasant revolt was quickly put down, it added to the disorder. At the battle of Agincourt (ah zhan KOOR) in 1415, the English army once more triumphed, though again outnumbered, this time by a margin of three to one. Just as French fortunes had sunk to their lowest, a young woman helped bring about a dramatic reversal.

Joan of Arc   Born just three years before the French defeat at Agincourt, Joan of Arc grew up in the small French village of Domremy. Like most peasants, she did not learn to read or write. Joan left home at the age of 17, insisting that she had received messages from God telling her to help drive the English from France.

In 1429 Joan arrived at Chinon (shee NYON) to persuade Charles, heir to the French throne, to give her command of his troops. After several tests of her unique powers, Charles gave her armor, a banner, and command of troops.

Joan then set off to Orléans (ohr lay AYN), a town in northern France that had been besieged by English troops for several months. Inspired by her piety and sincerity, French soldiers broke the siege of Orléans in only 10 days, and the English fled. Under the leadership of the Maid of Orléans, as Joan of Arc came to be known, French soldiers fought their way to Reims, where Charles was officially crowned King Charles VII.

In 1430 Joan was captured by rivals of the French king and sold to the English. After nearly a year in prison and a long trial in which she steadfastly insisted on the truth of her visions, Joan of Arc was condemned to be burned at the stake as a witch and a heretic. On a mild May day in 1431, onlookers wept as Joan calmly went to her fate. Twenty-four years after her death, a new trial proclaimed her innocence.

Joan's courage and devotion rallied the French around the king and drove the English out of France. When the war finally ended in 1453, the port of Calais was the only French territory still in English hands.

Effects of the War   During the Hundred Years' War, France suffered more severely than England, since all of the fighting occurred on French soil. Yet victory gave the French a new sense of unity that enabled them to rebuild their country.

Although England had been spared destruction, English nobles who had owned lands in France were bitter about the defeat. For the rest of the 1400s, England was torn by civil war. In the long run, however, the loss of French lands contributed to national unity and encouraged the English to concentrate on problems at home.

The Hundred Years' War also hastened the decline of feudalism. The use of the longbow and firearms made feudal methods of fighting obsolete. Monarchs replaced feudal soldiers with national armies made up of hired soldiers. Finally, threats to the monarchy, both in France and England, decreased as a result of the large numbers of nobles killed in the war.

France

By the end of the Hundred Years' War, the French monarchy had gained much power and prestige. Warfare emergencies allowed kings to collect national taxes and maintain standing, or permanent, armies. Therefore, after Charles VII defeated the English, he was able to renew the royal tradition of ruling the country assertively.

Louis XI, son of Charles VII, set out to unite France by taking back lands held by French nobles that had once been part of the royal territory. Louis especially wanted Burgundy, one of the most prosperous regions of Europe. However, its ruler, Charles the Bold, wanted Burgundy to be an independent state.

Louis was a shrewd diplomat. Rather than fight Charles openly, he encouraged quarrels between Burgundy and the neighboring Swiss. After Charles was killed in a battle with the Swiss in 1477, Burgundy was divided into two parts: the northern half, Flanders, went to Charles's daughter Mary; the remainder became part of France.

Through a series of reforms, Louis strengthened the bureaucracy of government, kept the

Stained Glass

This is part of the Jesse Tree window in Notre Dame Cathedral in Chartres, France.

During the High Middle Ages, the arts flourished under the patronage of the aristocracy and the Catholic Church. Among the most spectacular achievements of medieval art were the beautiful stained-glass windows produced for Gothic cathedrals. Because architects had developed a new technology for building cathedrals, builders were able to "open up" the walls of cathedrals, making room for large stained-glass windows. Colored light streamed into the cathedral, creating a breathtaking, mystical space.

Although earlier churches had used colored glass, during the High Middle Ages, stained glass was produced and used on an unprecedented scale. Medieval glaziers, or stained-glass makers, produced windows showing stories from the Bible and portraits of prophets and saints. Symbolic figures representing the seasons, the months, and the zodiac were also shown in cathedral windows, along with other subjects.

Windows were often donated by wealthy individuals or by local guilds. In some windows, a coat of arms or portrait was included to indicate who the donor was. In others, windows showed artisans of various guilds at work. Shown here is part of the Jesse Tree window from Notre Dame Cathedral in Chartres, France. The Jesse Tree was essentially Jesus Christ's "family tree"—the figures shown are kings, priests, and prophets from biblical history.

To make stained-glass windows, glaziers added metals or chemicals to molten glass to produce the desired color. The molten glass was poured into sheets to cool. Pieces of glass were then cut to fit the shapes needed for the window design. Once pieces were cut to the correct shapes, lead bars were fitted to frame each piece of glass and hold the window together. Details of shading or facial features were brushed on in a paste of glass mixed with iron filings.

Rising above towns and villages, beautiful stone cathedrals were the grand masterpieces of the Middle Ages. A town's cathedral, with its soaring towers and elaborate decoration, was often its most magnificent sight. The finished cathedral was not only a religious monument, but also a monument to the townspeople's dedication, labor, and donations. The interior of a Gothic cathedral, bathed in glowing colors, was unlike anything else to be found in medieval Europe.

Responding to the Arts

1. How were stained-glass windows made in medieval Europe?
2. What subjects were shown in medieval stained-glass windows?

nobles under royal control, and promoted trade and agriculture. By the end of his reign, France was strong and unified, and its monarch ruled with increased power.

England

After the Hundred Years' War, England became mired in a struggle for the English throne. The 30-year conflict, known as the Wars of the Roses (because of the symbols of the rival royal families), began in 1455. The royal house of Lancaster bore the red rose; its rival, the house of York, a white rose.

FRANCE IN THE 1400s

Burgundian Lands
French Lands
English Possessions
★ Battle Sites

0   50   100   150 miles
0 50 100 150 kilometers

Learning from Maps *The Hundred Years' War was actually a series of conflicts between England and France that lasted from 1337 to 1453.* **What were some of the reasons for the on-going conflict between these countries?**

During the Wars of the Roses, Edward, duke of York, overthrew the weak Lancaster dynasty and became King Edward IV. When Edward died in 1483, his son, also named Edward, was only 12. Edward IV had named his uncle, Richard, as the boy's guardian. Through a series of political maneuvers, Richard took the throne. As king, Richard III imprisoned Prince Edward and his younger brother in the Tower of London. Not long after, they were found murdered. Many suspected Richard—who himself fell to the forces of Henry Tudor, a Lancaster noble, on Bosworth Field in 1485.

Henry became King Henry VII, the first Tudor king. Henry steadily eliminated rival claimants to the throne, avoided expensive foreign wars, and gradually reasserted royal power over the lords and nobles. As a result, the English monarchy emerged from the Wars of the Roses strengthened and with few challengers. The Tudor dynasty ruled England for more than 100 years until 1603.

Spain

During the late 1400s, Spain emerged from a period of turmoil and warfare to become an important European power. Even before Pope Urban called for the crusades, the Christian kingdoms of northern Spain were engaged in the *Reconquista* (rai kohn KEES tuh), or reconquest, of the lands the Muslims had taken in the 700s. By 1250 Spain consisted of three Christian kingdoms: Portugal in the west, Castile in the center, and Aragon on the Mediterranean coast. Only Granada in the south remained in the hands of the Moors, or Spanish Muslims.

In 1469 Ferdinand of Aragon and Isabella of Castile were married. The two kingdoms maintained separate governments, however, and the power of their monarchs was limited by local interests and large minority religious groups. The Christian settlers who had been moved into the reconquered territories and the large Jewish and Muslim communities in Castile and Aragon had their own laws and elected their own officials. Special royal charters allowed many towns to keep their own courts and local customs. Finally, assemblies known as *cortes* (KOR tays), in which nobles were powerful, had the right to review the monarchs' policies.

The two monarchs strengthened the powers of the Crown in Castile. Royal officials governed the towns, and special courts enforced royal laws. In 1492 their armies forced the surrender of the last Moorish stronghold at Granada. Shortly afterward, Ferdinand and Isabella ended the traditional policy of toleration for minority groups. They believed that all Spaniards had to be Catholic if Spain was to become one nation. Spanish Jews and Muslims were given the choice to either become Catholic or leave Spain. Later the two monarchs set up the Spanish Inquisition, a court that enforced Catholic teachings. The fear caused by the Inquisition further strengthened the power and authority of the Spanish monarchs.

The Holy Roman Empire

During the 900s and 1000s, the Holy Roman Empire was the most powerful state in Europe. By the 1300s the Holy Roman Empire was still the largest political unit in Europe, including mostly German and Slav territories in the central part of the continent. But it was far from a unified state. While most European monarchs inherited their thrones, the Holy Roman emperor was elected to office by a diet, or assembly of German princes. These princes governed their lands as independent rulers. They were able to keep the emperor weak because they ruled on his requests for taxes and soldiers. Moreover, the Holy Roman emperors

Learning from Art *In this contemporary painting, Henry VII is depicted as a man of peace by means of a red and white rose, a symbol of the reunion between the houses of York and Lancaster.* ***How long did the Tudor dynasty rule England?***

continued to be involved in a struggle with the pope that went back to the time of Henry IV and Gregory VII. This hostility to the papacy would become important in the early 1500s.

SECTION 3 REVIEW

Recall
1. **Identify:** Joan of Arc, Edward IV, Richard III, Henry VII
2. **Locate:** Find the following places on the map on page 296: London, Flanders, Crécy, Agincourt, Orléans, Calais, Burgundy, Paris, Champagne, Avignon.

3. **Explain:** What were the causes and results of the Hundred Years' War?

Critical Thinking
4. **Apply:** Select one European country and describe how its monarchy changed during the Middle Ages.

5. **Analyze:** Contrast the political and geographic relationship of England and France before and after the Hundred Years' War.

Applying Concepts
6. **Conflict:** Explain the reasons for the struggles between the various European monarchies.

The Troubled Church

During the upheavals of the Late Middle Ages—caused by warfare, the plague, and religious controversy—many people turned to the Church for comfort and reassurance. Religious ceremonies multiplied, and thousands of people went on religious pilgrimages. In spite of this increase in religious devotion, the temporal authority of the Church was weakening due to the influence of strong monarchs and national governments. A growing middle class of educated townspeople and a general questioning of Church teachings also contributed to this decline.

Babylonian Captivity

During the early 1300s, the papacy came under the influence of the French monarchy. In 1305 a French archbishop was elected Pope Clement V. Clement decided to move his court from Rome to Avignon (ah vee NYOHN), a small city in southern France, to escape the civil wars that were disrupting Italy. While in France, the pope appointed only French cardinals. Pope Clement V and his successors—all French—remained in Avignon until 1377.

This long period of the exile of the popes at Avignon came to be known as the Babylonian Captivity, after the period of the exile of the Hebrews in Babylon in the 500s B.C. For centuries, Rome had been the center of the western Church. With the pope in France, people feared that the papacy would be dominated by French monarchs. Others disliked the concern the Avignon popes showed for increasing Church taxes and making Church administration more efficient. They believed the popes had become corrupted by worldly power and were neglecting their spiritual duties. The Italian poet Petrarch complained:

Here reign the successors of the poor fishermen of Galilee; they have strangely forgotten their origin. I am astounded . . . to see these men loaded with gold and clad in purple, boasting of the spoils of princes and nations.

Great Schism

Finally, in 1377, Pope Gregory XI left Avignon and returned to Rome. After his death, Roman mobs forced the College of Cardinals to elect an Italian as pope. They later declared the election invalid, insisting they had voted under pressure. The cardinals elected a second pope, who settled in Avignon. When the Italian pope refused to resign, the Church faced the dilemma of being led by two popes.

This controversy became known as the Great Schism because it caused serious divisions in the Church. The Great Schism lasted from 1378 until 1417 and seriously undermined the pope's authority. People wondered how they

FOOTNOTES TO HISTORY
SILVER SPOONS

Etiquette in the Early Middle Ages often meant knowing which fingers to use in picking up food. Later, hunting knives (which were used to carve up a roast or an enemy with equal ease) and pewter spoons became the standard utensils. In the 1400s silver "apostle spoons," bearing the image of a child's patron saint, were favored gifts for newborns in Italy. Only the wealthy could afford such a luxury. From these apostle spoons comes the saying that a privileged child is "born with a silver spoon in his mouth."

could regard the pope as the infallible leader of Christianity when there was more than one person claiming to be the single, unquestioned head of the Church.

The Babylonian Captivity and the Great Schism aroused great resentment against the powers of the papacy. Many kings, princes, and Church scholars called for a reform of Church government. The most popular remedy was a general church council. However, this solution posed many problems. First, such councils were traditionally called by popes. No pope was willing to call a council that would limit his authority. However, the legality of a council would be questionable if it did not receive papal approval. Second, different rulers in Europe supported particular popes for political reasons. Such political divisions made it almost impossible to reach agreement on even the site of a council, let alone to reach agreement on the deeper and more important issues involved.

By 1400 many western Europeans were committed to the idea of a church council. In 1409 a council met at Pisa, Italy, to unite the Church behind one pope. It resulted in the election of a third pope, since neither the pope at Rome nor the pope at Avignon would resign. Finally, in 1415, another council met at Constance, Germany. It forced the resignation of all three popes and then elected Pope Martin V, ending the Great Schism. The long period of disunity, however, had seriously weakened the political influence of the Church. Moreover, many Europeans had come to feel a greater sense of loyalty to their monarchs than to the pope.

Calls for Reform

Church authority was also weakened by people's distaste for abuses within the Church. The clergy used many unpopular means to raise money. Fees were charged for almost every type of Church service. Common people especially disliked simony—the selling of Church positions—because the price of buying these positions was passed on to them. The princely lifestyles of the clergy further eroded regard for the Church. Many Europeans called for reform.

Two of the clearest voices belonged to an English scholar and a Bohemian preacher.

John Wycliffe   John Wycliffe (WIHK lihf), a scholar at England's Oxford University, criticized the Church's wealth, corruption among the clergy, and the pope's claim to absolute authority. He wanted secular rulers to remove Church officials who were immoral or corrupt.

Wycliffe claimed that the Bible was the sole authority for religious truth. He began to translate the Bible from Latin into English so people could read it themselves. Since Church doctrine held that only the clergy could interpret God's word in the Bible, this act was regarded as revolutionary. Some of Wycliffe's followers, known as Lollards, angrily criticized the Church. They destroyed images of saints, ridiculed the Mass, and ate communion bread with onions to show that it was no different from ordinary bread.

Widespread antipapal feelings made it difficult for the English government to suppress the Lollards. Wycliffe was persuaded to moderate his views and received only a mild punishment. He died peacefully in 1384, but his ideas spread.

Among those who supported the Lollards was Bohemian-born Queen Anne, the wife of King Richard II. Anne sent copies of Wycliffe's writings to her homeland in the Holy Roman Empire, where they influenced another great religious reformer.

Jan Hus   During the late 1300s and early 1400s, the Slavs of Bohemia, known as Czechs, became more aware of their own national identity. They wanted to end German control of their country and backed reforms in the Catholic Church in Bohemia, which had many German clergy. Their religious and political grievances combined to produce an explosive situation.

The Czechs produced religious pamphlets and copies of the Bible in Czech and criticized the corruption of leading Church officials, many of whom were German. The leader of the Czech reform movement was Jan Hus, a popular preacher and professor at the University of Prague. When Hus and his works were condemned by Church and political leaders, a wave of riots swept across Bohemia.

Learning from Art
After the death of Pope Gregory, the Italian archbishop, Bartolomeo Prignano, was elected pope as Urban VI. Prignano —considered a modest and peaceable bishop—alienated his political allies with his harsh and condemning behavior. It was believed—as this painting shows—that he killed five cardinals who had plotted against him. **How did Urban's behavior contribute to the Great Schism?**

Faced with a possible full-scale rebellion against the Church, in 1415 the council at Constance demanded that Hus appear before them to defend his views. The Holy Roman emperor promised Hus safe conduct to Constance, Germany, but this guarantee was ignored. Hus was burned at the stake as a heretic, but many Czechs rallied around their new martyr.

From 1420 to 1436, Hus's peasant supporters, called Hussites, resisted the Church with the Holy Roman emperor, and the Church launched five crusades against the Hussites. All five failed. Using firearms and the tactic of forming movable walls with farm wagons, Hussites defeated the "crusading" knights.

In 1436, representatives of the pope and the Holy Roman emperor reached a compromise with the Hussite leaders. They gave the Hussites certain religious liberties in return for their allegiance to the Church. The ideas of Jan Hus, however, continued to spread throughout Europe to influence later and more radical reformers. While this agreement gave the appearance that the Church had successfully met the challenges to its authority, the basic spiritual questions raised by Hus and others did not go away.

SECTION 4 REVIEW

Recall
1. **Identify:** John Wycliffe, Lollards, Jan Hus, Hussites, Babylonian Captivity, Great Schism
2. **Locate:** Locate Avignon on the map on page 296. Why did Pope Clement V choose this location for his court?
3. **Explain:** What were the effects of the Babylonian Captivity and the Great Schism on the Church?

Critical Thinking
4. **Evaluate:** Predict what might have happened if the Church had not reunited after the Great Schism.
5. **Synthesize:** Imagine you are a follower of Jan Hus just after his execution. How would you feel about carrying on his work? How might you be able to do this?

Applying Concepts
6. **Conflict:** Explain the rise of dissent among many devout Europeans. Why were they against the Church and its leadership?

ANALYZING HISTORICAL MAPS

When you walk through your town, you may see changes in progress. A new restaurant may be opening, or workers may be building a new housing development.

Explanation

Change, on a larger scale, also takes place across nations and continents. These changes become part of the historical record, and one way to show them is on a historical map. Historical maps tell about a region's history.

Use the following steps to help you analyze a *historical map:*

- Identify the thematic information on the map. For example, a historical map of the United States might show U.S. land acquisitions. In this case, the theme of the map would be United States expansion. Often, the map title reflects its theme. In some cases, historical maps also show additional information. The U.S. expansion map, for example, might also indicate the nation from which each area was acquired.
- Identify the chronology of the events on the map. Historical maps often show how an area has changed over time. In the case of the U.S. expansion map, each acquisition may be dated. Or, the areas may be shaded to represent the particular time periods in which they were acquired.

Example

The map on this page is a historical map of Europe. The theme of the map, as indicated by the title, is the spread of the Black Death in Europe. The map uses color to indicate how the Black Death spread from one country to another over time.

Application

Use the map "France in the 1400s" on page 296 to answer the following questions:

1. What is the theme of this map?
2. How does the map indicate possession of French land?
3. What other historical information is included on the map?
4. Can you learn how the land possession in France changed over time from this map? Explain your answer.

Practice

Turn to Practicing Skills on page 303 of the Chapter Review for further practice in analyzing historical maps.

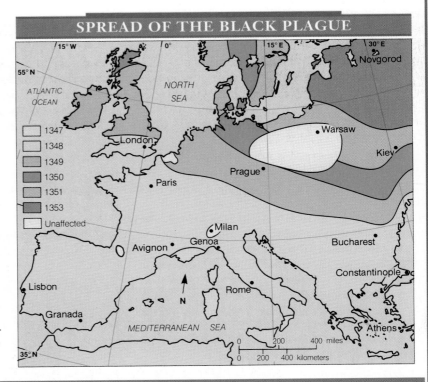

SPREAD OF THE BLACK PLAGUE

Legend:
- 1347
- 1348
- 1349
- 1350
- 1351
- 1353
- Unaffected

CHAPTER 12 REVIEW

HISTORICAL SIGNIFICANCE

The High Middle Ages was a period of change and consolidation that laid the foundations for many features of modern Western civilization. The crusades forged new international contacts, and monarchs prepared the way for the emergence of new nations. Trade networks linked many people and different countries together. Many of modern Europe's great cities were born in the Middle Ages, and their medieval history can still be seen in Romanesque and Gothic cathedrals. Merchant and craft guilds were forerunners of the modern labor union, although the latter eventually took on different characteristics. The university was born during this period. National languages flourished, thanks to medieval authors who popularized the use of the vernacular. Finally, the middle class, which plays a tremendously important political, economic, and social role in the world today, had its beginnings during the High Middle Ages.

SUMMARY

For a summary of Chapter 12, see the Unit 3 Synopsis on pages 354–357.

USING KEY TERMS

Write the key term that best completes each sentence below.

a. apprentice
b. charter
c. crusade
d. guild
e. journeyman
f. master
g. money economy
h. scholasticism
i. troubadour
j. vernacular

1. A military expedition to free the Holy Land from the Muslims was called a (an) ___ .
2. A ___ could only ply his trade under supervision.
3. The ___ gave towns in the Middle Ages power against the feudal lords.
4. Most medieval literature was written in the language of everyday speech, known as the ___ .
5. The system of theological and philosophical teachings set forth by Thomas Aquinas was known as ___ .
6. An artisan had to be a member of a ___ to sell goods in a town.
7. While a (an) ___ learned his trade, he had to work without pay.
8. A poet-musician attached to the courts who composed and sang poems and love songs was a ___ .
9. Only a ___ could open his own shop.
10. A ___ is a formal document granting the right to self-rule.

REVIEWING FACTS

1. **List:** Name the various medieval crusades and their results.
2. **Describe:** What were several agricultural improvements in the Middle Ages?
3. **Outline:** What steps did an apprentice take to become a master?
4. **Describe:** What was a typical medieval town like?
5. **Identify:** Who were the bourgeoisie?
6. **List:** What were the key events in the Hundred Years' War?
7. **Identify:** Name two Church reformers and a major event in the life of each.

THINKING CRITICALLY

1. **Apply:** How did the medieval middle class change society?
2. **Analyze:** Examine the various forces that led to Europe's economic growth.
3. **Evaluate:** How would Europe be different today if there had been no crusades?

ANALYZING CONCEPTS

1. **Cultural diffusion:** How did a mix of cultures affect medieval Europe?
2. **Innovation:** Choose one medieval innovation and describe its implications for medieval society; do the same for a modern innovation and modern society.
3. **Conflict:** How did conflict between England and France strengthen the monarchies of those countries?
4. **Conflict:** Why was there religious dissent in the Catholic Church?

PRACTICING SKILLS

1. Suppose you wanted to create a historical map that shows how towns in Europe expanded greatly in the A.D. 1000–1100s. You know that these towns grew up along trade routes. How would you present this information on a historical map?
2. Imagine you are looking at a map that shows how feudal systems were declining in the A.D. 1100–1400s. The map also shows how strong central monarchies emerged around this time. What conclusions might you draw by viewing this map?
3. How would a historical map help improve someone's understanding of the events of the Hundred Years' War? What do you think such a map should emphasize?

GEOGRAPHY IN HISTORY

1. **Movement:** Refer to the map on page 284. Trace the routes of the crusades. Why do you think routes changed?
2. **Location:** Name some of the major export products in the Middle Ages of the following places: the Baltic coast, Flanders, Asia, the Middle East.
3. **Location:** Refer to the map on page 296. Locate the region King Louis XI wanted to add to the royal territory of France.

TRACING CHRONOLOGY

Refer to the time line below to answer these questions.
1. How many years did the Babylonian Captivity last? Why did this period of Church history end?
2. How long after the Hundred Years' War ended did the English power struggle for the throne begin?
3. How old was Joan of Arc when she was burned at the stake?

LINKING PAST AND PRESENT

1. The crusades were a series of "holy wars." Can you find examples of holy wars in the modern period?
2. Compare the rise of the towns in medieval times with the same phenomenon in Ameri-

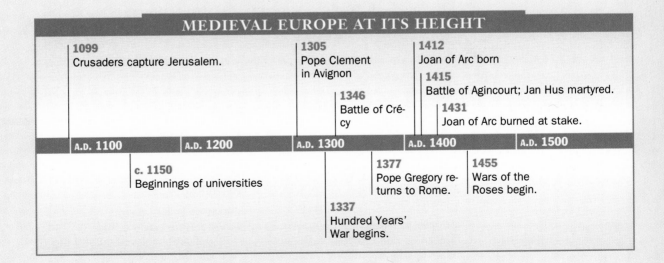

MEDIEVAL EUROPE AT ITS HEIGHT

- **1099** Crusaders capture Jerusalem.
- **1305** Pope Clement in Avignon
- **1412** Joan of Arc born
- **1346** Battle of Crécy
- **1415** Battle of Agincourt; Jan Hus martyred.
- **1431** Joan of Arc burned at stake.

A.D. 1100 A.D. 1200 A.D. 1300 A.D. 1400 A.D. 1500

- **c. 1150** Beginnings of universities
- **1377** Pope Gregory returns to Rome.
- **1455** Wars of the Roses begin.
- **1337** Hundred Years' War begins.

East and South Asia

*I*n China, in the year A.D. 1200, a lone student sat behind a desk in a room furnished only with a lamp, some paper, a writing brush, and an inkstone. He labored over a grueling government exam designed to test his knowledge of Confucian texts. He worried because examiners could fail a person for even a single misquotation. If he passed, he would be one of the Song emperor's officials, and he could move his family into a luxurious household. If he failed, the money his family paid to have him tutored would have earned them nothing. And, ashamed, he would have to hawk cheap goods in the streets.

Civil service examinations helped ancient China to maintain a consistent government no matter which dynasty was in power. Later, the neighboring countries of Korea and Japan adopted these civil service examinations as well as other aspects of Chinese culture.

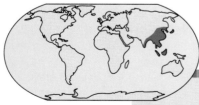

CHAPTER PREVIEW

Key Terms to Define: meritocracy, mandarin, archipelago, animism, shamanism, shogun, shogunate, samurai, daimyo

People to Meet: Tai Cong, Wu, Xuanzang, Zhao Kuangyin, Genghis Khan, Kublai Khan, Marco Polo, Suryavarman II, Trung sisters, Sejong, Yi-Sun-shin, Amaterasu, Shotoku, Yoritomo

Places to Discover: Chang-an, Kaifeng, Hangzhou, Angkor Wat, Heian Kyo

Objectives to Learn:
1. What were some of the significant achievements of the ancient Chinese?
2. What elements of Chinese and Indian culture were adopted by East and Southeast Asians?

To become government officials in the Tang dynasty, men had to pass the difficult civil service exam.

3. How did the Koreans and Japanese accept China's culture?

Concepts to Understand:
- Uniformity—A centralized government, a state religion, and a common language maintained China's cultural continuity. Section 1
- Cultural diffusion—The cultures of Asian civilizations influenced their neighbors. Sections 1,2,3
- Movement—Mongols conquered China and parts of Europe. Section 1
- Regionalism—Feudal Japan was controlled by regional leaders. Section 3
- Innovation—The Chinese developed inventions that changed the world; Japan and Korea created unique arts and traditions. Sections 1,2,3

China

For more than 350 years after the collapse of the Han dynasty in A.D. 220, Chinese kingdoms and invaders from the north rivaled each other for control of China. Then in A.D. 589, a northern official named Yang Jian (yahng jyen) united China by conquering both the north and the south. Yang Jian took the title Emperor Wen and founded the Sui (sway) dynasty. Emperor Wen renewed many of the goals and traditions that had been accepted during the reign of the Han dynasty. He organized public works projects such as the rebuilding of the former Han capital city at Chang-an (chong on), the repair of the Great Wall, and the construction of a Grand Canal to link northern and southern China. However, to accomplish these projects he used crews of forced laborers, which made him quite unpopular with the peasants.

The Tang Dynasty

In A.D. 618, peasant uprisings against the Sui dynasty enabled a rebellious lord named Li Yuan (lee yoo ahn) to take control of the country and proclaim himself emperor. He established the Tang (tong) dynasty, which lasted from A.D. 618 to 907. Under the Tang, the Chinese Empire expanded its borders to include new territories.

Government and Society   The military genius behind the early Tang expansion was a son of Li Yuan who took the name Tai Cong (tie tsoong). Not only was Tai Cong a warrior, but he was also a shrewd administrator. By restoring a strong central government in China, he maintained control of his enormous empire while continuing to expand it.

To obtain a position in the Tang government, candidates had to pass civil service examinations. Under Tang rule, these tests measured the degree to which candidates had mastered Confucian principles. According to Confucianism, an individual was expected to obey the emperor and serve his government just as a son was expected to obey his father.

Because almost any male could take these examinations, the Chinese government claimed that it was a **meritocracy**—a system in which people are chosen and promoted for their talents and performance. But in practice it did not meet that ideal. Few boys from poor families could afford to pay tutors to help them prepare for the exams. Most could not spare the time away from their labor to study on their own.

Nevertheless, some peasants benefited from the Tang dynasty's rule. The Tang government gave land to farmers and enforced the peace that enabled them to till their land. In the Chang Jiang (Yangtze River) region, farmers were able to experiment with new strains of rice and better methods for growing it—both of which led to greater crop yields. With more food available, the Chinese population increased as well.

Foreign Influences   Tang rulers also devoted resources to the construction of roads and waterways. These routes made travel within China and to neighboring countries much easier. These routes helped government officials to perform their duties. They also enabled Chinese merchants to increase trade with people from Japan, India, and the Middle East.

Chinese luxury goods, such as silk and pottery, passed through central Asia along a route called the Silk Road. Beginning in central China, traders' camel caravans traveled north to the Great Wall and then headed west, crossing into central Asia just north of the Tibetan plateau. Some traveled as far west as Syria. These caravans brought Chinese goods and ideas to other cultures and returned with foreign products and new ideas as well. The Buddhist, Christian, and Islamic religions came to China by way of the Silk Road. During the Tang dynasty, Buddhism especially became very popular in China.

As trade increased the wealth of the empire, the Tang capital at Chang-an grew into the largest city in the world. Dazzling tales attracted merchants and scholars from countries throughout Asia to this city of 2 million people. Visitors to Chang-an spoke of wide, tree-shaded avenues and two vast market squares where merchants sold goods from Asia and the Middle East. They said that acrobats, jugglers, and dancers performed in the streets and that wealthy Chinese—including women—played the Persian games of chess and polo.

The Arts   In A.D. 649 Gaozong (gow dzahng) succeeded Tai Cong as emperor of China. But Gaozong's wife, Empress Wu, actually controlled the empire. She was a brilliant political leader under whose control China continued to thrive.

In A.D. 712 Empress Wu's grandson, Xuanzang (see wahn dzong), became emperor of China. Because Xuanzang welcomed artists to his splendid court, during his reign the arts flourished. Tang artisans made a fine translucent pottery that became a prized commodity known in the West as "china." Two of China's greatest poets, Duo Fu and Li Bo, produced their works in Xuanzang's court. Scholars compiled encyclopedias, dictionaries, and official histories of China. Writers popularized stories about ghosts, crime, and love. And while European monks were still slowly and laboriously copying texts by hand, Chinese Buddhist monks invented the more efficient technique of block printing. They carved the text of a page into a block of wood. Then they reproduced the page by inking the wood and pressing a piece of paper onto it.

Decline of the Tang   For a time the cultural splendor of Xuanzang's court masked its military weakness. But the Tang ruler's vulnerability to attack was revealed in A.D. 751, when Turkish armies in central Asia successfully revolted against China. They cut off China's trade routes to the Middle East and they put an end to the

Learning from Art *Tai Cong, founder of the Tang dynasty, instituted many reforms in Chinese government and education.* **What other accomplishments came under his rule?**

thriving exchange of goods and ideas along the Silk Road.

In A.D. 755, some of the emperor's own troops—led by a governor named An Lushan (on lyoo shon)—rebelled against him, causing him to flee the capital. An Lushan's rule weakened the government even more severely. During the 10 years he controlled the central government, provincial leaders disregarded any orders from the central government.

By the time the emperor's son regained the throne in A.D. 766, he found that military governors and generals had much more power than before, but the central government had much less. Furthermore, with goods and ideas no longer traveling the Silk Road, China was gradually turning inward, rejecting foreign ideas and styles. Chinese officials even closed Buddhist temples and monasteries.

Border wars with the Tibetans and rebellions in famine-stricken provinces plagued the Tang from A.D. 766 on. In A.D. 907 this turmoil caused the fall of the Tang dynasty.

The Song Dynasty

From A.D. 907 to 960, China was ruled by military dynasties. Then a military general named Zhao Kuangyin (jow kwong yin) seized the throne and established the Song dynasty.

Song emperors kept peace with a group of Mongols in the north, the Khitan, by paying them large amounts of silver. But in A.D. 1127, the Jurchen, a nomadic people, captured the Song capital of Kaifeng (ky fuhng). The Song set up court in the southern city of Hangzhou (hong joh).

Cultural Contributions   Song scholars, resentful of foreign influences, produced an official state philosophy called neo-Confucianism. This philosophy combined Confucian values with elements of the most popular belief systems in China at the time—Buddhism and Daoism.

Song rulers also more firmly entrenched the civil service system that the Tang had resurrected. They saw to it that determining one's knowledge of Confucian curriculum was the main focus of these tests. The scholars who had passed the tests eventually formed a wealthy elite group, called **mandarins** by Westerners. The mandarins dominated Chinese society. Some of them also used their position to enrich themselves.

Rich and Poor   During the Song dynasty, China experienced unprecedented economic growth, partly because Song rulers used tax revenues to fund several public-works projects that benefited the economy. For example, they used these revenues to fund the digging of irrigation ditches and canals, which in turn helped farmers increase their crop yields.

The introduction of new crops from Southeast Asia, such as tea and a faster-growing rice plant, further boosted China's farming economy. It also led to an increase in China's sea trade and commerce with India and Southeast Asia. With farming, trade, and commerce all thriving, urban centers prospered.

The urban wealthy lived in spacious homes and enjoyed going to teahouses, restaurants, and luxurious bathhouses. The capital of the dynasty, Hangzhou, grew to nearly 1 million residents.

Of course, the country still had many urban poor. Although they could enjoy watching jugglers, animal trainers, dancers, and singers at bazaars called "pleasure grounds," they derived less pleasure from city life than did the wealthy. The urban poor lived in flimsy houses. To survive they hawked cheap goods in the streets, worked as manual laborers, begged, or stole.

Song Arts and Sciences   Song achievements in the arts and sciences were many. The cuisine which people recognize today as distinctively Chinese originated during the Song dynasty. Experts regard Song porcelain as the best ever made. Landscape painting reached its peak during Song rule. Song inventors perfected the compass, a tool that enabled Chinese seamen to navigate on journeys far offshore. They also produced gunpowder, first used in fireworks and later in military weapons. In fact, bamboo-tube rocket launchers charged with gunpowder made the Song army a powerful fighting force.

China's enemies, however, were eventually able to obtain the secrets of Song military technology. Thus, using the Song empire's own technology against it, the Mongols were able to completely capture northern China in A.D. 1234 and bring about the fall of the Song dynasty in southern China in A.D. 1279.

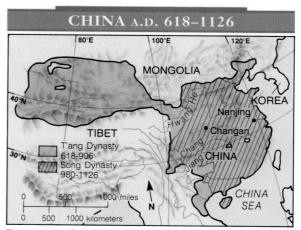

CHINA A.D. 618–1126

Learning from Maps *Notice that the Song dynasty governed a much smaller territory than did the Tang—yet neither dynasty expanded very far to the southwest.* **What physical barriers prevented expansion in that direction?**

PERSONAL
PROFILES

Empress Wu

Chinese tomb figurine of a woman holding a vase

When the Tang emperor Tai Cong died in A.D. 650, the women of his court were sent into exile. But Gaozong, his son, recalled one beauty, Wu. Wu quickly displaced the new emperor's first wife and, after having this first wife and another rival killed, she also came to dominate her husband. She eventually gained control of all the major political offices.

When Gaozong died, Wu had one of their sons put on the throne. She hoped to control him as she had his father and thereby continue to control the government. When the young man proved to be too independent for her to manipulate, she had his younger brother replace him. Then, in A.D. 690, Wu stopped pretending that she was acting only as an aide to her son and took the title of empress.

Empress Wu became the first and only woman in Chinese history to reign in her own. Wu received little aristocracy. To con lack, she built up th ess, tem and appointed th trators she could find. justly, she won the loyal cials. She promoted Budo arts, and literature. She als ed the country's borders effe recovering by force lands that been lost not long before. In fact, Empress Wu was so strong a ruler that not until she had reached her 80s could she be overthrown.

Reflecting on the Person

1. Explain the steps by which Wu managed to gain control of the government.
2. In what ways did China benefit politically and culturally during Empress Wu's rule?

The Mongols

The Mongols were nomadic people who lived on the grassy plains of Mongolia, northwest of China. Because these plains were not suitable for farming, Mongol clans raised herds of sheep, horses, and yaks, traveling from pasture to pasture. Children were practically raised on horseback, and they grew into hardy fighters.

Genghis Khan In A.D. 1206 a fierce young Mongol warrior named Temujin won control of all the Mongol tribes and took the title Genghis Khan, or Universal Ruler. Thus, having united all the Mongols for the first time, he turned them into an organized fighting force. He as-

sembled the various Mongolian laws into a code of law called the *yasa*. He also brought together an assembly of local chiefs to plan military campaigns and appoint leaders.

In A.D. 1211 a force of 100,000 Mongol horsemen led by Genghis Khan devastated northern China. They used gunpowder, storming ladders, and battering rams to overwhelm the Chinese. Then the Mongols swept westward through central Asia into Europe, conquering everyone in their path.

Kublai Khan In A.D. 1260 Genghis Khan's grandson, Kublai, was chosen the Great Khan. In A.D. 1267, so that he could more easily rule over his subjects, Kublai set up his capital in

... e modern Beijing.
... in his subjects over,
northern China at Dai... ...itional Chinese style,
In the hope that her, and in A.D. 1271 even
he built the cap...asty, which he called the
declared him...
founded...hern China. This was the first
Yuan ...rians, the name the Chinese gave
... from outside of China, ruled the

...ough Kublai complied with some Chi-
...aditions to better control the Chinese, he
... to maintain Mongol culture. Government
...cuments were first written in Mongolian and
...en translated into Chinese. Furthermore, the
highest positions in the emperor's court were
given to Mongols or other foreigners.

The most famous of these foreigners appointed to a government position was a Venetian named Marco Polo. Polo arrived in China
in A.D. 1275 and stayed 17 years, traveling
through Mongol territory on the Khan's missions. After Polo returned to Italy, his tales of
the splendor of Chinese civilization astounded
Europeans.

Mongol Peace and Decline Marco Polo
was able to travel throughout China because the
Mongols enforced a relatively stable order. Merchants could safely travel the roads built by the
Mongols. Mongol rule thus fostered trade and
connections with Europe.

Through contact with the Middle East,
Russia, and Europe, the Chinese obtained slaves

FOOTNOTES TO HISTORY

PASTA

Almost everyone associates noodles, or
pasta, with Italy. Pasta, after all, is served in
all Italian restaurants, and it is identified by
Italian names. For instance, spaghetti, which
in Italian means "little strings," is the name
commonly given to the thin strands of noodles
that look like strings.

But pasta actually originated in China. In
fact the Chinese were making noodles out of
bean and rice flour some 3,000 years ago. Italians didn't even get their first taste of pasta
until the late A.D. 1200s, when Marco Polo's
father and uncle brought Chinese noodle
recipes to Italy.

---

as well as products such as glass, hides, clothes,
silver, cotton, and carpets. And, in return, Europeans got exotic products such as silk, porcelain,
and tea.

After Kublai Khan died in A.D. 1294, a series
of weak successors took over the throne. The
Chinese, still resentful of foreign rule, began to
stage rebellions against these rulers. Finally, in
A.D. 1368, a young Buddhist monk named Zhu
Yuanzhang (joo yoo ahn jahng) led an army
against the capital and overthrew the Yuan
dynasty. From then on, although other northern
tribes continued to threaten China, the Chinese
held dominance over peoples to the south.

SECTION 1 REVIEW

Recall

1. **Define:** meritocracy, mandarin
2. **Identify:** Tai Cong, Xuanzang, Duo Fu, Li Bo, Zhao Kuangyin, Genghis Khan, Kublai Khan
3. **Locate:** Find the city of Hangzhou in southern China on the map on page 991. Why do you think the Song chose to make Hangzhou its capital?

Critical Thinking

4. **Explain:** Why did Kublai Khan choose to comply with some Chinese traditions? Why do you suppose he appointed only Mongols and foreigners to high government positions?
5. **Evaluate:** Do you think the Tang and Song systems of govern-ment were true meritocracies?

6. **Synthesize:** Think about the contributions that China has made to the world. How might your life be different without them?

Applying Concepts

7. **Uniformity:** How did the Tang, Song, and Yuan dynasties try to unite China?

Southeast Asia

Although China was the most culturally diverse and influential society in Asia from about A.D. 220 until 1300, other Asian civilizations were simultaneously creating distinct and influential cultures of their own. Southeast Asian cultures were among these new societies.

South of China and east of India is the region known as Southeast Asia. Southeast Asia includes the present-day countries of Burma, Thailand, Vietnam, Laos, Cambodia, Malaysia, Singapore, Brunei, Indonesia, and the Philippines. Located in the tropics, many of these countries have the fertile soils, warm climates and abundant rainfall that make them excellent for agricultural development.

Geographically, Southeast Asia is divided into mainland and maritime Southeast Asia. The latter includes more than 10,000 islands of the Philippine and Indonesian **archipelagos,** or chains of islands.

During the A.D. 100s, an exchange of goods and ideas began between India and Southeast Asia. This exchange led Southeast Asia to adopt many elements of Indian culture. For instance, at that time, traveling Indian traders and scholars introduced to Southeast Asia the Sanskrit language and the religions of Hinduism and Buddhism. Indian epics such as the *Ramayana* were interwoven with Southeast Asian stories and legends. Indian architecture, law codes, and political ideas also deeply influenced the cultures of the region. As contact with India increased, Indian culture gradually spread throughout Southeast Asia.

Southeast Asians nevertheless retained many of their own traditions, arts, and beliefs. They continued to perform the art of shadow puppetry, to make intricately patterned cloth called batik, and to play their own unique instruments and music—all achievements that Southeast

Asians originated without Indian influence. They also continued to believe in **animism,** the idea that spirits inhabit living and nonliving things. Southeast Asians did, however, adopt some elements of the Indian religious beliefs as well.

Learning from Maps *Find Angkor Wat on the Indochina Peninsula to locate Cambodia.* ***What river runs near Angkor Wat?***

The Khmer

In A.D. 802 the Khmer people of the mainland Southeast Asian country of Cambodia established a great Hindu-Buddhist empire with its capital at Angkor. Borrowing from the Indian idea of kingship, Khmer rulers presented themselves as incarnations of the Hindu gods or as future Buddhas, which served to enhance their power.

Cambodia's wealth came primarily from its rice production. Elaborate hydraulic engineering projects enabled the Khmer to irrigate and produce three crops of rice a year.

With the wealth from this bountiful harvest, Khmer rulers subsidized mammoth construction projects. Adapting Indian building techniques to create their own distinctive architecture, the Khmer built hundreds of temples that glorified Hindu and Buddhist religious figures. They also constructed roads, reservoirs, irrigation canals, harbors, and hospitals. Furthermore, the rulers bedecked themselves in elaborate finery and filled their palaces with ornate thrones and beautiful furnishings. A Chinese traveler named Zhou Dakuan (joh dah kwon) described the splendor of a Khmer king in dress and manner:

His crown of gold is high and pointed like those on the heads of the mighty gods. When he does not wear his crown, he wreathes his chignon [hair gathered in a bun] in garlands of sweet-scented jasmine. His neck is hung with ropes of huge pearls (they weigh almost three pounds); his wrists and ankles are loaded with bracelets and on his fingers are rings of gold set with cats' eyes. He goes barefoot—the soles of his feet, like the palms of his hands, are rouged with a red stuff. When he appears in public he carries the Golden Sword.

IMAGES OF THE TIME

Angkor Wat

Angkor Wat (meaning "temple of the capital") was built in the A.D. 1100s by the Khmer ruler Suryavarman II. Suryavarman believed he was an incarnation of the Hindu god Vishnu.

A bronze three-headed serpent, or *naga,* was found at Angkor Wat. Most *nagas* were demons but were believed to guard the life-giving energy of water.

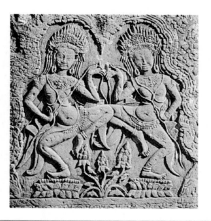

Dancing figures sculpted in this relief portray stories about rulers and gods from the ancient Khmer civilization.

During the A.D. 1100s, under the rule of King Suryavarman II, the Khmer kingdom reached the height of its power. Having expanded Cambodia by conquest to include parts of areas known today as Laos, Vietnam, and Thailand, the king decided to glorify both the Hindu god Vishnu and himself. He ordered the construction of Angkor Wat, a temple complex that covers nearly a square mile. Carvings depicting the Hindu gods cover the walls of Angkor Wat, and, at the center of the complex, the sanctuary stands 130 feet high. The Khmer king poured so much of the empire's wealth into building Angkor Wat, however, that he severely weakened the kingdom. This excess, along with Thai rebellions against Khmer rule and infighting between members of the royal family, further crippled the empire. In A.D. 1431 Thai armies captured the capital city of Angkor, bringing an end to Khmer rule there.

Vietnam

East of Cambodia and south of China lies the area today called Vietnam. Because of Vietnam's proximity to China and because the Chinese dominated Vietnam for more than 1,000 years, Vietnam's culture in some ways came to resemble that of China.

The Vietnamese absorbed elements of Chinese belief systems such as Confucianism, Daoism, and Buddhism. The Vietnamese also adopted Chinese forms of writing and government. Just as in China, Vietnamese officials were selected through civil service exams based on Confucian principles.

The Vietnamese retained many of their own traditions, however. They adopted Chinese religions and beliefs, but they continued to believe in animism. The Vietnamese built a *dinh*, or spirit house, in each village. This tiny house

The temple complex at Angkor Wat is encircled by a three-mile moat. The temples and monuments within the complex honored the god-king Suryavarman II and impressed visitors with their size and detailed ornamentation.

Reflecting on the Times
Looking at these images of Angkor Wat, what values do you think were important to the Khmer?

served as the home for the guardian spirit of a village. The Vietnamese wore their hair long and tattooed their skin. They wrote and spoke their own Vietnamese language, although in writing it they used Chinese characters. Even though the Chinese controlled Vietnam almost continuously from about 200 B.C. to A.D. 939, the Vietnamese fought hard to retain—and then to regain—their independence.

T̲he Viets [Vietnamese] were very difficult to defeat. They did not come out to fight, but hid in their familiar mountains and used the jungle like a weapon. As a result, neither side could win. . . . The Viets would raid suddenly, rob and get away fast, so that just as our army obtained its supplies from the home base, the Viets obtained theirs from our army.

—Chinese general, c. 200 B.C.

In A.D. 40 two Vietnamese sisters called Trung, clad in armor and riding atop elephants, led a successful revolt against the Chinese. For two years Vietnam was independent of China. Then the Chinese returned in greater numbers and defeated the Vietnamese. Rather than surrender to the Chinese, the Trung sisters are said to have drowned themselves in a river.

During the confusion after the overthrow of the Tang dynasty, the Vietnamese took advantage of China's disunity to revolt again. The Chinese sent a fleet of warships to Vietnam to try to subdue the rebels. In A.D. 938, however, under the leadership of Ngo Quyen (noo chu

FOOTNOTES TO HISTORY
SHADOW PUPPETS

Could you watch a puppet show from 9:00 P.M. until 6:00 A.M.? The Southeast Asian islanders in Java and Bali do just that. In fact, the ancient art of shadow puppetry is popular throughout the Indonesian archipelago.

During a shadow puppet show, the puppeteer sits behind a white screen and acts out stories with flat leather or wooden puppets. A palm-oil lamp between the puppeteer and the puppets throws the shadows of the puppets onto the white screen. These shadows are all the audience sees. At the same time, the audience hears the puppeteer telling the stories and speaking the part of each puppet.

yen), the Vietnamese defeated the warships in the battle of the Bach Dang River. Although Emperor Tai Cong countered this defeat by launching an invasion of Vietnam, the Vietnamese date their independence from the battle, because Tai Cong's invasion failed.

After the Song dynasty gained control of China, the Song emperor threatened the Vietnamese with invasion. To keep peace with China, the Vietnamese agreed to send tribute—gifts—to the Chinese emperor. In return, China agreed not to invade Vietnam. From then on, the Vietnamese ruler called himself emperor at home, but in his messages to the Chinese court he referred to himself merely as a king.

SECTION 2 REVIEW

Recall
1. **Define:** archipelago, animism
2. **Identify:** King Suryavarman II, Trung sisters, Ngo Quyen
3. **Locate:** Find mainland Southeast Asia on the map on page 311. Why would the mainland, and not the Indonesian and Philippine archipelagos, be more likely to come under the influence of India and China?

4. **Explain:** To build Angkor Wat, the Cambodians needed wealth and skill. Where did they get their wealth? Where did they get their architectural skill and techniques?

Critical Thinking
5. **Synthesize:** How might Buddhism or Confucianism complement a belief in animism?

6. **Hypothesize:** Why did the Vietnamese have their own spoken language, which differed from Chinese, but use Chinese characters to write that language?

Applying Concepts
7. **Cultural diffusion:** List some of the ways in which China and India influenced Southeast Asia.

Korea and Japan

Like the nations of Southeast Asia, Korea and Japan adopted elements of Chinese culture. But also like these other nations, they retained their own rich traditions.

Korea

A glance at Korea on the map will reveal why a Korean proverb describes the country as "a shrimp between whales." Korea forms a peninsula on the east coast of Asia, extending southward toward the western tip of Japan. Thus, it acts as a bridge between its two powerful neighbors, China and Japan.

Early History   By legend, the Koreans claim descent from Tangun, the son of a bear and a god who supposedly founded the first Korean kingdom 5,000 years ago. Historians believe that the first Korean people were immigrants from northern Asia. These settlers lived in villages, grew rice, and made tools and other implements of bronze. They were animists who practiced **shamanism**, a belief that good and evil spirits inhabit both living and nonliving things. Shamans, or priests, interceded between the spirit world and humans.

In 200 B.C. China first invaded Korea, putting Korea under the control of the Han dynasty. From 200 B.C. until the fall of the Han dynasty in A.D. 220, Korea was dominated by China. But after the fall of the Han dynasty, Koreans regained control of their peninsula and eventually formed three kingdoms—Silla, Paekche (pah ek chee), and Koguryo. During the Three Kingdoms period, from 57 B.C. to A.D. 668, the Koreans adopted many elements of Chinese culture. Among these were Confucianism, Buddhism, calligraphy, and ideas about government.

Koreans also used Chinese knowledge of arts and sciences to make their own unique creations. For example, in the A.D. 300s, the Koguryo produced mammoth cave art murals. In Silla, Queen Sondok built an astronomical observatory that still stands today and is the oldest observatory in Asia.

In A.D. 668 the kingdom of Silla conquered all of Korea, ushering in a period of peace, prosperity, and creativity. Korean potters produced superb porcelain decorated with flower designs. Koreans also created a unique mask dance that expressed sentiments of shamanism and Buddhism, which was adopted as the state religion in A.D. 845. Over a 16-year period, Korean scholars compiled the *Tripitaka Koreana*, the largest collection of Buddhist scriptures in the world today. The *Tripitaka* has 81,258 large wooden printing plates.

The Yi Dynasty   In A.D. 1392 a dynasty called the Yi came to power in Korea. The Yi called their kingdom Choson and built

Learning from Artifacts   *After the Silla rulers united Korea, the arts flourished. These gold vessels were found in a Silla tomb.* **What arts besides metalworking appeared at this time?**

Hanyang—today the city of Seoul—as their capital. They opened schools to teach Chinese classics to civil service candidates and made neo-Confucianism the state doctrine.

The adoption of Korean neo-Confucianism deeply affected people's roles and relationships. According to Korean Confucian doctrine, the eldest son in each family was bound by duty to serve his parents until their death. Korean women—who had been accorded high status under shamanism and Buddhism—were given much lower standing under Korean Confucianism. In fact, women from the higher ranks of society had to stay indoors until nightfall, when a great bell signaled the closing of the city gates. Even then, to go out they had to obtain permission from their husbands.

One of the greatest Yi rulers, King Sejong, had two significant accomplishments. He ordered bronze instruments to be used in measuring rain. As a result, Korea now has the oldest record of rainfall in the world. He and his advisers made a greater contribution by creating simplified writing to spread literacy. Together they devised *hangul*, an alphabet that uses 28 consonants and 11 vowels to represent Korean sounds. Although scholars continued to write with Chinese characters after the invention of *hangul*, writers began using *hangul* to transcribe folk tales and popular literature.

Although the Japanese tried to capture Korea in A.D. 1592, the Yi dynasty managed to successfully rebuff the Japanese invaders, mainly because of an invention created by Korean Admiral Yi-Sun-shin. The admiral's ironclad warships, or "turtle ships," devastated the Japanese fleet. Although the Koreans won the war, they did not escape unscathed. In the years that followed, Koreans increasingly avoided contact with the outside world and eventually isolated themselves so thoroughly that Korea became known as the Hermit Kingdom.

Japan

Just 110 miles east of Korea lies the Japanese archipelago. It consists of four large islands—Honshu, Shikoku, Kyushu, and Hokkaido—and many smaller ones.

Island Geography   Because of its island geography, Japanese culture formed mostly in isolation from mainland Asian cultures, except for that of China. Although the Japanese borrowed from Chinese civilization, their customs and traditions were different from those of most other Asian peoples.

The geography of these islands influenced the formation of Japanese culture in other ways too. Because much of the land is mountainous—less than 20 percent of it is suitable for farming—the Japanese learned to get most of their food from the sea. They also learned to rely on the sea for protection from invaders—being a natural barrier to invasion from the mainland—and yet to regard it as a route of transport between the islands. The physical beauty of the land inspired deep reverence for nature in works by many Japanese painters and poets. Because these islands are located in an area where earthquakes, typhoons, floods, and volcanic eruptions are frequent, the Japanese long ago created a myth that helped to explain the stormy weather there.

Creation Myth   An ancient Japanese creation myth is the oldest explanation for the origins of Japan, its turbulent weather, and its first emperor. According to the myth, brother and sister gods Izanagi and Izanami dipped a spear into the churning sea. When they pulled it out, the drops of brine that fell upon the water's surface became the islands of Japan. The two gods then created the sun goddess Amaterasu, and because they loved her best of all their children, they sent her to heaven to rule over the world. Next they created Tsuki-yumi, the moon god, and Susanowo, the storm god, to be her companions.

Amaterasu gave life to everything around her. But Susanowo, who had a fierce temper, ruined his sister's rice crop and so frightened her that she hid in a cave. Without her in heaven, the world became dark. The other gods placed a jewel and a mirror on a tree outside the cave to coax Amaterasu back outside. When she came out and told them why she had hidden, the other gods banished Susanowo to the earth.

According to the myth, Susanowo's descendants were the first inhabitants of Japan. Amaterasu sent her grandson, Ninigi, to govern these

Learning from Photographs *A masked Shinto priest performs a traditional dance. Each dance tells a story about such things as human courage in war, animal hunts, or the gods' delight in the Japanese people.* **In early Japanese society, who served as Shinto priests?**

descendants on the island of Honshu. So that all would acknowledge his divine power, she sent with him her mirror, her jewel, and a great sword. According to legend, Ninigi's grandson, Jimmu, conquered the rest of Susanowo's descendants in 660 B.C., becoming the first emperor of Japan.

By tradition, each successive emperor has received Amaterasu's three gifts: a mirror, a jewel, and a sword. Also by tradition, each emperor—until Hirohito—has claimed to be Amaterasu's descendant. In 1945, after the Japanese defeat in World War II, Emperor Hirohito announced that he did not possess divine status.

Early Inhabitants   Among the first people to inhabit the Japanese islands were hunter-gatherers who came there from the mainland more than 10,000 years ago. These people had developed the technology to make pottery but not to make bronze or iron. When Koreans and others from mainland Asia invaded Japan during the 200s and 100s B.C., they were easily able to defeat the early inhabitants by using iron and bronze weapons.

The invaders introduced the islanders to agricultural methods, such as how to grow rice in flooded paddies. Heavy summer rains in Japan made it the ideal place to grow rice, which soon became Japan's most important crop.

Between A.D. 200 and 300, another influx of mainlanders came to Japan. According to schol-ars, these armor-clad warriors who fought on horseback were probably the ancestors of the aristocratic warriors and imperial family of Japan referred to in the creation myth.

In early Japan, though, even before there was an emperor or an imperial family, separate clans ruled their own regions. Clan members practiced a form of animism called Shinto, meaning "the way of the gods." Each clan included a group of families descended from a common ancestor, often said to have been an animal or a god. The clan worshiped this ancestor as its special *kami*, or spirit. Practitioners of Shinto believed that *kami* dwelled within people, animals, and even nonliving objects such as rocks and streams. To honor this *kami*—and the *kami* of their ancestors—they held festivals and rituals. Often these ceremonies were conducted by the chief of the clan, who acted as both military leader and priest.

The Yamato Clan   By about A.D. 400, the military skill and prestige of the Yamato clan, which claimed descent from Amaterasu, enabled it to extend a loose rule over most of Japan. Although other clans continued to rule their own lands, they owed their loyalty to the Yamato chief. In effect, he became the emperor.

Initially, the emperor had a great deal of political power. By the A.D. mid-500s, however, the emperor had become more of a ceremonial figure who carried out religious rituals. The real political power was held by the members of the Soga family. The emperors kept their position as heads of Japan because people believed that only they could intercede with the gods. But the Soga family controlled the country.

Chinese Influences

In A.D. 552 a Korean king sent a statue of Buddha and some Buddhist texts to the Japanese court. The king wrote, "This religion is the most excellent of all teachings" and suggested that the emperor make Buddhism the national religion. Buddhism had come to Korea from China, and its introduction to Japan made the Japanese open to Chinese culture. This curiosity about China was especially strong among Japan's nobles and scholars.

Through a kind of cultural exchange program that lasted four centuries, the Japanese learned much from the Chinese. Not only did they learn about the teachings of Buddha, they also learned a great deal about Chinese art, medicine, astronomy, and philosophy. And they incorporated a good deal of this knowledge into Japanese culture. For instance, the Japanese adopted the Chinese characters for writing to create their own writing system.

Prince Shotoku was responsible for much of this cultural exchange. When he became the leading court official in A.D. 592, he instituted programs that encouraged further learning from Chinese civilization. He ordered the construction of Buddhist monasteries and temples and sent officials and students to China to study. When Shotoku heard about the Chinese Confucian ideas of government, he wrote a constitution for Japan in which he set forth general principles that explained how government officials should act.

After Shotoku's death, the Fujiwara family seized power in the name of the emperor and began to urge him to pattern the government more closely on that of China. China had a strong central government.

In A.D. 645 government officials instituted the Taika reforms, or "Great Change." These reforms attempted to do what the Fujiwara family had begun. They proclaimed that all the land was the property of the emperor rather than clan leaders. Clan leaders could oversee the peasants working the land, but they could no longer assign them land or collect taxes from them. Instead, government officials were to allocate plots to peasants and collect part of their harvest in taxes for the emperor.

Although these reforms were somewhat effective at increasing the central government's control over the clans, most clan leaders refused to give up their land. Even after the Taika reforms, Japan remained much divided under the control of regional clan leaders.

The Nara Period

Greater government centralization did not take place until A.D. 710, when Japan built its first permanent capital at Nara. A smaller version of China's Chang-an, Nara had an imperial palace, broad streets, large public squares, rows of Chinese-style homes, and Buddhist temples.

With the completion of the colossal Todaiji Temple at Nara in A.D. 752, Buddhist fervor in Japan reached its peak. Buddhism, however, did not replace Shinto, for each religion met different needs. Shinto linked the Japanese to nature and their homeland, and Buddhism promised spiritual rewards to the good. Therefore, many people practiced both.

During the Nara period, the Japanese also produced their first written literature. Scribes wrote histories of ancient Japan that combined the creation myths with actual events. Other writers compiled collections of Japanese poems.

The Heian Period

In A.D. 794 the Japanese established a new capital, Heian Kyo, "the City of Peace and Tranquillity," later called Kyoto. For more than 1,000 years, this city remained the capital of Japan.

A century after the city was founded, Japan stopped sending cultural missions to China. In the period that followed, a small group of about 3,000 Japanese aristocrats, calling themselves "dwellers among the clouds," created Heian culture.

The focus of Heian court life was the pursuit of beauty. It pervaded all of life's activities, from wrapping presents to mixing perfumes and colors. People devoted hours each day to writing letters in the form of poems. Calligraphy was as important as the poem itself, for a person's handwriting was taken to be an indication of his or her character. People were even said to fall in love upon seeing each other's handwriting.

During the Heian period, women were the creators of Japan's first great prose literature. Lady Murasaki Shikibu wrote *The Tale of Genji*, which some believe to be the world's first novel. The novelist chronicles the life and loves of a fictional prince named Genji. Filled with poems about the beauty of nature, it quickly became very popular.

The Heian aristocrats were so deeply involved in their search for beauty, however, that they neglected tasks of government. Order began breaking down in the provinces. Warlike provincial leaders started running their estates as independent territories, ignoring the emperor's officials and refusing to pay taxes. Thus the Heian aristocrats eventually lost control of the empire completely.

The Way of the Warrior   As Heian power faded, two powerful court families, the Taira and the Minamoto, struggled for control. The families fought a decisive battle in A.D. 1185 in which the Taira were defeated. To Yoritomo, head of the Minamoto family, the emperor then gave the title **shogun,** or great general, and delegated to him most of the real political and military power. While the emperor remained with his court in the capital of Kyoto carrying on ritual

---

CONNECTIONS: HISTORY AND THE ENVIRONMENT

Natural Protection

Both China and Japan were able to develop in relative peace and isolation from outsiders because the landforms surrounding these countries acted as physical barriers to large-scale invasion.

China was protected on the east by the Pacific Ocean, on the northwest by the Tianjin Mountains, and on the southwest by the highest mountains in the world, the Himalayas. The only direction from which the Chinese lacked a natural barrier to invasion was the north. The Chinese therefore built the Great Wall to keep out the nomadic peoples who wanted to enter the country from that direction. When this wall failed to protect the Chinese from large-scale invasion by the nomadic Jurchen, the Chinese retreated south of the Chang Jiang. This river then acted as a natural defense against the Jurchen invaders from the north.

For Japan even more than for China, water was a barrier to invasion. The Japanese islands were separated from Asia on the west by the Sea of Japan and from other peoples to the east by the Pacific Ocean. Thus, for hundreds of years the only way to invade Japan in large numbers was with a navy that had the ships and technical knowledge to sail against strong currents and unfavorable winds. Not until the A.D. 1200s did any one have such a navy. And even this, the Mongol navy led by Kublai Khan, was no match for the typhoon that arose during its crossing.

Making the Connection
1. Identify the landforms that enabled China and Japan to evolve in relative isolation from outsiders.
2. Do you think that oceans and mountains are still significant barriers to invasion today?

The Art of Feudal Japan

In A.D. 1185, when the Minamoto family came to power in Japan, it not only established military rule but also ushered in a new period in the arts. For these new military patrons of the arts wanted to hear and see literature and artworks that reflected and glorified their military values. Thus, rather than glamorizing beauty—which artists had been encouraged to do when the Fujiwara clan was in power—artists began glamorizing warriors and war. Poets and writers created stories about conquests in which they highlighted the prowess of warriors. Artists portrayed military subjects that were infused with a great sense of action and immediacy.

The painting reprinted here, which was created during this period of military rule, celebrates the samurai. One knows instantly that this rider is a samurai from the man's richly patterned clothing, the beautiful horse he rides, and the sword he wields. These were the privileges of the samurai alone. The resplendence of the samurai's vibrantly colored costume is accentuated by the painting's dark background.

The painting also conveys the sense of action and immediacy, or drama, that artists of the day strove to instill into their works. The artist achieved this effect by several noticeable means. The expressions chosen for the rider and his horse communicate wild, but disciplined, emotions evoked in the moment just before charging into battle. And by posing the figures as if on the verge of battle—rather than at rest—the artist gives the painting an active quality. He further heightens this active impression by showing the water stirred into turbulent waves.

Finally, the warrior's splendor coupled with the dramatic intensity of the moment lends glamor to doing battle. This aura would have appealed greatly to a military patron of the arts.

Responding to the Arts
1. What three things identify the subject of this painting as a samurai warrior?
2. Choose one military value reflected in this painting. Explain how the artist has managed to convey this value.

Much like his European counterpart–the knight–an armored samurai astride his horse could strike courage and fear into the hearts of friend and foe.

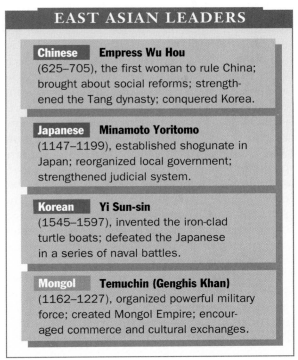

EAST ASIAN LEADERS

Chinese   **Empress Wu Hou**
(625–705), the first woman to rule China; brought about social reforms; strengthened the Tang dynasty; conquered Korea.

Japanese   **Minamoto Yoritomo**
(1147–1199), established shogunate in Japan; reorganized local government; strengthened judicial system.

Korean   **Yi Sun-sin**
(1545–1597), invented the iron-clad turtle boats; defeated the Japanese in a series of naval battles.

Mongol   **Temuchin (Genghis Khan)**
(1162–1227), organized powerful military force; created Mongol Empire; encouraged commerce and cultural exchanges.

Learning from Charts *Although each of the Asian leaders listed on the chart represents a different civilization, some features of political and military leadership are common to all.* **What are these basic characteristics?**

tasks, Yoritomo and his soldiers ran a military government, or **shogunate,** from Kamakura near present-day Tokyo.

The shogunate proved to be quite strong. In fact, although Kublai Khan tried twice to invade Japan—once in A.D. 1274 and again in A.D. 1281—he did not succeed. On the first occasion, Japanese warriors on the beaches forced the Mongols to withdraw. On the second occasion, 150,000 Mongol warriors came by ship, but a typhoon arose and destroyed the fleet. The Japanese thought of the storm as the kamikaze, or "divine wind," and took it to be confirmation that their islands were indeed sacred.

In A.D. 1336 the Ashikaga family gained control of the shogunate. But the family failed to get control of regional warriors. So Japan soon broke into individual warring states, leaving the shogun and the emperor as mere figureheads.

The powerful landowner-warriors in the countryside were called **samurai.** The most powerful samurai became **daimyo** (DY mee oh), or lords. Like the medieval knights of feudal Europe who pledged their loyalty to lords, samurai pledged their loyalty and military service to their daimyo. There were many samurai and many daimyo. Poor rice farmers paid high taxes for the right to farm a daimyo's lands. In return, that daimyo provided the farmers with protection. The system in which large landholders give protection to people in exchange for their services is called feudalism. Japanese feudalism was similar to European feudalism as described in Chapter 11.

The samurai fought on horseback with bows, arrows, and steel swords. They dressed in loose-fitting armor. And they followed a strict code of honor called Bushido, meaning "the way of the warrior." Bushido stressed bravery, self-discipline, and loyalty. It demanded that the samurai endure suffering and defend his honor at all costs. If a samurai was dishonored or defeated, he was expected to commit suicide.

Japanese women too could be warriors. This passage from *The Tale of the Heike* describes a female Minamoto samurai:

*T*omoe *had long black hair and a fair complexion, and her face was very lovely; moreover she was a fearless rider whom neither the fiercest horse nor the roughest ground could dismay, and so dexterously did she handle sword and bow that she was a match for a thousand warriors and fit to meet either god or devil. Many times had she . . . won matchless renown in encounters with the bravest captains, and so in this last fight, when all the others had been slain or had fled, among the last seven there rode Tomoe.*

—*Tale of the Heike*, A.D. 1100s

Growth of a Merchant Class   Despite the political turmoil during its feudal period, Japan developed economically at this time. Workshops on daimyo estates produced arms, armor, and iron tools. Each region began to specialize in goods such as pottery, paper, textiles, and lacquerware. Trade increased between regions.

The increasing trade led to the growth of towns around the castles of the daimyos. Merchants and artisans formed guilds to promote their interests—just as they did in medieval Europe. These guilds, called *za* in Japan, benefited their members in many ways. A *za* might pay a fee to exempt its members from paying tolls for shipping their goods. Over a long period of time, this assumption would save the members quite a bit of money.

Japanese merchants began to trade with Chinese and Korean merchants. Chinese copper coins became the chief means of exchange. The Japanese exported raw materials such as lumber, pearls, and gold, as well as finished goods such as swords and painted fans. The Japanese imported items such as medicines, books, and pictures.

Religion and the Arts   The opening words of *The Tale of the Heike* describe the Buddhist sentiments that were prevalent in Japan during its feudal period:

In the sound of the bell of the Gion Temple echoes the impermanence of all things. The pale hue of the flowers of the teak tree show the truth that they who prosper must fall. The proud do not last long, but vanish like a spring-night's dream. And the mighty ones too will perish in the end, like dust before the wind.

The samurai followed a form of Buddhism called Zen, which the Japanese scholar Eisai had brought from China late in the A.D. 1100s. Zen taught that the individual had to live in harmony with nature and that this harmony could be achieved through a deep religious understanding called enlightenment. The followers of Zen rejected book learning and logical thought, embracing instead bodily discipline and meditation. They believed that by meditation a student could free his mind and arrive at enlightenment.

Zen was particularly useful for warriors because it taught them to act instinctively, and thinking was a hindrance to action. Samurai could improve skills such as archery by freeing their minds from distractions to better concentrate on the object or target.

Zen also created new art forms and rituals such as ikebana, or flower arranging, meditation gardens, and the tea ceremony. Ikebana grew out of the religious custom of placing flowers before images of Buddha. The Zen practice of meditation gave rise to meditation gardens, which consisted of carefully placed rocks surrounded by neatly raked sand.

Meditation also sparked the tea ceremony, an elegant, studied ritual for serving tea. One tea master said of the ceremony that it was intended to "cleanse the senses . . . so that the mind itself is cleansed from defilements." These and other arts and rituals derived from Buddhism are still popular in Japan today.

SECTION 3 REVIEW

Recall
1. **Define:** shamanism, shogun, shogunate, samurai, daimyo
2. **Identify:** King Sejong, Admiral Yi-Sun-shin, Amaterasu, Jimmu, Shinto, Prince Shotoku, Taika reforms, Lady Murasaki Shikibu, Minamoto, Yoritomo, Bushido
3. **Locate:** Find the islands of Japan on the map on page 311. Why might the early Japanese have found that boats were the quickest and easiest way to travel from place to place?
4. **Explain:** What is traditionally given to each new emperor of Japan? Why?

Critical Thinking
5. **Decide:** In which society do you think women enjoyed more privileges, the neo-Confucian Korean society or the Japanese feudal society? Why?

6. **Evaluate:** Which would you prefer to follow, the ideals of the Heian court or the samurai code of Bushido? Why? What effects might each have had on the people of Japan?

Applying Concepts
7. **Innovation:** Identify one Chinese innovation that the Koreans or Japanese borrowed and describe how they made it their own.

MAKING GENERALIZATIONS

How many times have you heard people make statements such as "Bob is a great athlete," "Mary is a good student," or "Kristen is the most popular girl in school"? Has it ever occurred to you to question the validity of such statements or do you just accept them at face value?

These types of statements are called *generalizations,* or broad statements about a topic—and they may not be valid. If the generalization is based on individual facts that can be verified objectively, that are related, and that support the statement, then it is valid. For example, how do we know that Mary is a good student? One possible supporting statement might be that Mary received all A's on her report card.

Here we began with a generalization and then looked for supporting facts. In other cases you will make a generalization from a group of individual facts.

Explanation

Use the following steps to make a generalization about a topic:

- Collect information relevant to the topic. Remember that the information must be factual, not merely an opinion.
- Classify the information into categories. The same piece of information may suggest several categories.

- Look for ways in which the categories are related to one another and consider what conclusion you might draw from these relationships.
- Make a generalization that identifies one or more of the relationships and is consistent with most of the information.

Example

Suppose you were asked for a generalization based on the text, concerning literature during the Tang dynasty. You would begin by listing the following facts:

1. Two of China's greatest poets, Duo Fu and Li Bo, produced their works in Xuanzong's court.
2. Scholars produced encyclopedias, dictionaries, and official histories of China.
3. Writers popularized stories about ghosts, crime, and love.
4. Block printing was invented in China.

Next, consider possible categories into which the information above falls. The first statement relates to poetry, the second and third to prose, and the fourth to the means of spreading literature.

Then, consider how the categories relate to one another and what conclusion you might draw. The fact that Xuanzong allowed China's greatest poets to produce their work at his court provides evidence of the importance of poetry

under the Tang. The wide range of prose suggests that people were eager to read all types of literature. The fact that Chinese Buddhist monks gave their time and their energy to the invention of printing indicates that there was a wide demand for written materials. In each case there is evidence that literature was highly regarded. Therefore, the following generalization can be made: During the Tang dynasty, literature flourished.

Application

Use the outlined steps to make a generalization about the Khmer from the following statements:

1. Indian traders and scholars introduced both Hinduism and Buddhism to Southeast Asia.
2. Borrowing from the Indian idea of kingship, Khmer rulers presented themselves as incarnations of the Hindu god or as future Buddhas.
3. The Khmer built hundreds of temples that glorified Hindu and Buddhist religious figures.
4. King Suryavarman II built Angkor Wat to glorify both the Hindu god Vishnu and himself.

Practice

Turn to Practicing Skills on page 329 of the Chapter Review for further practice in making generalizations.

Four Poems
by Li Bo

Li Bo was born in A.D. 701 in western China. People began praising his beautiful poems even before he reached adulthood. Throughout his life he traveled extensively in China, amazing people with his ability to compose insightful, touching poems. He usually wrote about the world around him, the people he met, and the emotions he felt. By the time of his death in A.D. 762, he was regarded as one of China's greatest poets, a distinction he still holds today.

In the following poem, Li Bo comments on an experience everyone faces at some time: parting with a close companion.

Taking Leave of a Friend

Blue mountains to the north of the walls,
White river winding about them;
Here we must make separation
And go out through a thousand miles
  of dead grass.

Mind like a floating wide cloud,
Sunset like the parting of old acquaintances
Who bow over their clasped hands at a distance.
Our horses neigh to each other
  as we are departing.

The following poem is a favorite of many Chinese citizens who have left their homeland and settled in the United States or elsewhere.

On a Quiet Night

I saw the moonlight before my couch,
And wondered if it were not the frost
    on the ground.
I raised my head and looked out on the
    mountain moon;
I bowed my head and thought of my
    far-off home.

Li Bo used extensive symbolism in his writing. In the following poem, he compares life to a traveler on a journey

Hard Is the Journey

Gold vessels of fine wines,
    thousands a gallon,
Jade dishes of rare meats,
    costing more thousands,

I lay my chopsticks down,
    no more can banquet,
And draw my sword and stare
    wildly about me:

Ice bars my way to cross
    the Yellow River,
Snows from dark skies to climb
    the T'ai-hang Mountains!

At peace I drop a hook
    into a brooklet,
At once I'm in a boat
    but sailing sunward . . .

    (Hard is the Journey,
    Hard is the Journey,
    So many turnings,
    And now where am I?)

So when a breeze breaks waves,
    bringing fair weather,
I set a cloud for sails,
    cross the blue oceans!

Since Li Bo spent much of his time traveling, he was often separated from his family. He wrote and sent the following poem to his children.

Letter to His Two Small Children Staying in Eastern Lu at Wen Yang Village Under Turtle Mountain

Here in Wu Land mulberry leaves are green,
Silkworms in Wu have now had three sleeps:

My family, left in Eastern Lu,
Oh, to sow now Turtle-shaded fields,
Do the Spring things I can never join,
Sailing Yangste always on my own—

Let the South Wind blow you back my heart,
Fly and land it in the Tavern court
Where, to the East, there are sprays and leaves
Of one peach-tree, sweeping the blue mist;

This is the tree I myself put in
When I left you, nearly three years past;
A peach-tree now, level with the eaves,
And I sailing cannot yet turn home!

Art and Literature *After leaving government service, Tang Yin became one of the masters of Chinese art in the 1500s. His* Voyage to the South *gave a romantic quality to the landscape.*

Art and Literature *The Qing dynasty emphasized personal expression, as in this luminous silk painting, c.1851-62.*

Pretty daughter, P'ing-yang is your name,
Breaking blossom, there beside my tree,
Breaking blossom, you cannot see me
And your tears flow like the running stream;

And little son, Po-ch'in you are called,
Your big sister's shoulder you must reach
When you come there underneath my peach,
Oh, to pat and pet you too, my child!

I dreamt like this till my wits went wild,
By such yearning daily burned within;
So tore some silk, wrote this distant pang
From me to you living at Wen Yang . . .

RESPONDING TO LITERATURE

1. **Comprehending:** In "On a Quiet Night," why is the person unhappy?
2. **Analyzing:** In "Hard Is the Journey," what do the gold vessels and jade dishes symbolize?
3. **Synthesizing:** What types of images did Li Bo use in each of his poems included here?
4. **Thinking critically:** Which poem do you like best? Explain why.

CHAPTER 13 REVIEW

HISTORICAL SIGNIFICANCE

As civilizations of East and Southeast Asia met, they benefited from the other's knowledge. For example, the Chinese acquired tea and faster-growing rice plants from the Southeast Asians, which boosted southern China's economy. The Mongols became an even more powerful fighting force once they learned to use Chinese gunpowder. The Khmer people of Cambodia acquired architectural techniques from the Indians. These techniques enabled the Khmer to build huge temples. In addition, the Khmer kings were able to use Indian religious beliefs to increase their own power. Japan and Korea experienced economic growth by adopting Chinese Confucianism and the Chinese system of civil service examinations. The Japanese and Vietnamese both learned calligraphy from the Chinese, which enabled them to develop their own literature.

Today, cultural diffusion occurs on a global scale. Thus, Westerners learn a great deal from the peoples of East and South Asia, and they, likewise, benefit from their encounters with people from the West.

SUMMARY

For a summary of Chapter 13, see the Unit 3 synopsis on pages 354–357.

USING KEY TERMS

Write the key term that best completes each analogy below.

a. animism
b. archipelago
c. daimyo
d. meritocracy
e. samurai
f. shamanism
g. *shogun*
h. shogunate

1. Indochina : Korea :: ___ : peninsula
2. Kamakura : Kyoto :: ___ : royal court
3. Buddhism : Zen :: ___ : Shinto
4. military : royalty :: ___ : emperor
5. Japan : Europe :: ___ : lord
6. qualify : inherit :: ___ : aristocracy

REVIEWING FACTS

1. **Identify:** Who was Tai Cong? What important things did he achieve?
2. **List:** What important scientific and artistic achievements were made during the Song dynasty?

3. **Name:** What powerful ruler established the Yuan dynasty?
4. **Identify:** What is Angkor Wat? Who built it?
5. **Explain:** Of what significance was the Battle of the Bach Dang River to the Vietnamese?
6. **Identify:** What three clans were most powerful in Japan between A.D. 400 and 1336?
7. **Define:** What is *Bushido?*

THINKING CRITICALLY

1. **Apply:** How did civil service exams aid in the development of a strong central government in China?
2. **Analyze:** Explain why China's economic growth increased during Song rule.
3. **Synthesize:** Do you think the strengths of Mongol society would benefit a nation today? Why or why not?
4. **Evaluate:** In what ways did Chinese innovations change the cultures of Korea and Japan?

ANALYZING CONCEPTS

1. **Cultural diffusion:** What are some of the similarities between Chinese culture and the cultures of other East and Southeast Asian nations?

2. **Uniformity:** What elements of Chinese society remained the same during the Tang, Song, and Yuan dynasties? What effect did this stability have on China's culture?

3. **Movement:** The Mongols were able to conquer a vast territory, but their empire survived for a relatively short time. Provide a hypothesis that might explain this situation.

4. **Regionalism:** Compare the social and governmental structure of feudal Europe to that of feudal Japan.

5. **Innovation:** Identify one Chinese discovery and explain some of the ways in which it has been used by the Chinese and others. Name things in our culture that derive from this innovation?

PRACTICING SKILLS

1. Review information in the chapter about religion in China, India, Cambodia, Vietnam, Korea, and Japan. Write a generalization about religion in East and Southeast Asia. Then support your generalization with facts.

2. The Japanese believed that their islands were protected by the gods. They supported this generalization with the historical fact that a typhoon—which the Japanese believed to have been sent by the gods—prevented a fleet of Mongol ships from invading Japan in A.D. 1281. Do you think this fact adequately supports the generalization?

GEOGRAPHY IN HISTORY

1. **Location:** Refer to the map on page 308. What is the global address of Chang-an?

2. **Place:** What characteristics of the region in which the Japanese islands lie might have prompted the Japanese to believe in a fierce storm god?

3. **Relationships Within Places:** Why did Koreans see Korea as "a shrimp between whales"?

4. **Movement:** What role did the Silk Road play in the exchange of goods and ideas between China and other cultures?

TRACING CHRONOLOGY

Refer to the time line below to answer these questions.

1. Who was ruling China when the Fujiwara family took control of Japan? Why might the Fujiwaras have wanted to pattern their government after China's?

2. Which Chinese dynasty had the shortest life: Tang, Song, or Yuan? Why?

LINKING PAST AND PRESENT

1. How has Japan's possession of Heian and samurai values helped it to become a world leader in industry today?

2. Confucianism spread to many East and South Asian countries. How do Confucian values benefit these countries today?

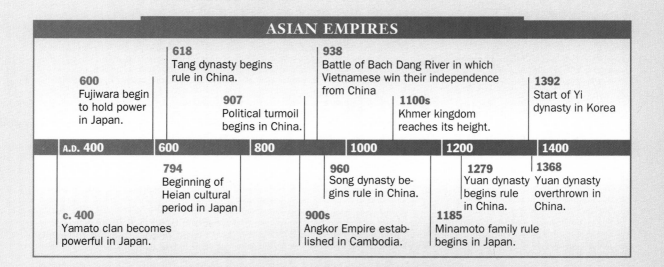

ASIAN EMPIRES

600 Fujiwara begin to hold power in Japan.

618 Tang dynasty begins rule in China.

907 Political turmoil begins in China.

938 Battle of Bach Dang River in which Vietnamese win their independence from China

1100s Khmer kingdom reaches its height.

1392 Start of Yi dynasty in Korea

A.D. 400 | **600** | **800** | **1000** | **1200** | **1400**

c. 400 Yamato clan becomes powerful in Japan.

794 Beginning of Heian cultural period in Japan

960 Song dynasty begins rule in China.

900s Angkor Empire established in Cambodia.

1185 Minamoto family rule begins in Japan.

1279 Yuan dynasty begins rule in China.

1368 Yuan dynasty overthrown in China.

Africa and the Americas

*T*he Yoruba—West Africans living by the Niger River—gather each winter to hear storytellers recount a legend that tells of how their ancestors struggled to clear their land with tools made of wood and soft metal. Even *orishas*, or gods, could not cut through vines or trees with those tools until the god Ogun appeared, carrying his bush knife.

"He slashed through the heavy vines, felled the trees and cleared the forest from the land. . . . So [the people] made [Ogun] their ruler. . . . He built forges for them and showed them how to make spears, knives, hoes, and swords."

Legends such as this describe experiences that early people valued most. Early Africans and Americans built civilizations that have left rich traditions for today's peoples.

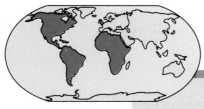

CHAPTER PREVIEW

Key Terms to Define: plateau, savanna, matrilineal, age set, maize, cultural differentiation

People to Meet: Ezana, Mansa Musa, Askia Muhammad, Pueblo, Mayan, Aztec, Cortés, Inca

Places to Discover: Kush, Axum, Ghana, Mali, Songhai, Zimbabwe, Mexico, Tikal, Tenochtitlán, Cuzco

Objectives to Learn
1. What natural resources did early African civilizations use?
2. How did trade develop among early African civilizations?
3. Why did people migrate to North and South America?
4. How did environment affect early cultures of the Americas?

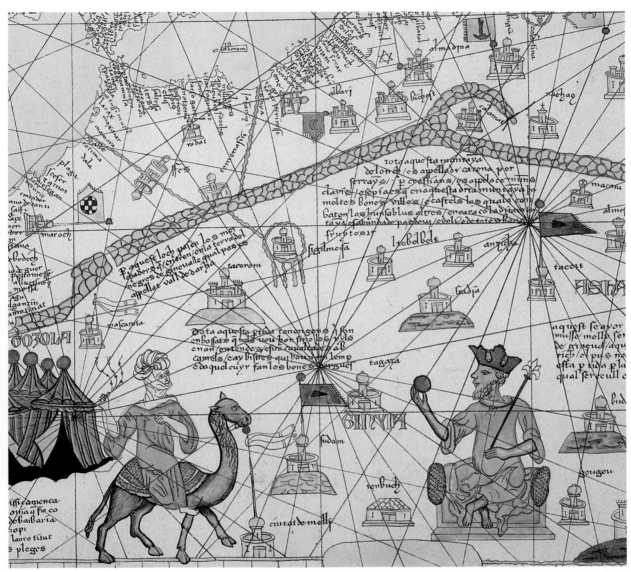

Mansa Musa, King of Mali, is enthroned between Timbuktu and Gao on a map from about A.D. 1375.

5. What caused the decline of early American empires?

Concepts to Understand:
- Movement—Bantu and Native American migrations influenced the cultural development of Africa and the Americas. Sections 1,3
- Cultural diffusion—The Nok metal-working technology spread to other African cultures; Africa's trade con-tacts with Europe and Asia changed African cultures. Section 2
- Relation to environment—Native Americans adapted to a variety of North and South American environ-ments. Sections 3,4
- Change—Powerful empires devel-op in Mexico, Central America, and South America. Section 4

331

Early Africa

Africa's earliest civilizations left few written records of their existence. It was through oral traditions—legends and history passed by word of mouth from one generation to another—that early African peoples communicated knowledge about their culture. Thus, archaeologists and historians have had to rely on legends and artifacts to learn about the culture of African civilizations between 1100 B.C. and A.D. 1500.

Archaeologists have discovered that early African cultures developed technologies and trade based on regional natural resources. Civilizations rose and declined, and were influenced by the movement of people and by the way in which natural resources were developed.

Geography and Environment

Africa's geography and climate are a study in contrasts. Africa, the world's second-largest continent, is three times larger than the United States. Within its huge expanse lie desolate deserts, lofty mountains, rolling grasslands, and fertile river valleys.

The African continent can be divided into two large regions—North Africa, the region along the Mediterranean Sea; and sub-Saharan Africa, the vast area south of the Sahara. North Africa, the region of the continent along the Mediterranean Sea, has mild temperatures and frequent rainfall. In contrast, the area south of this thin green belt is a vast expanse of sand: the Sahara, the world's largest desert. Extending across the continent, the Sahara is a region of shifting dunes and jagged rock piles.

The sub-Saharan region, which embraces all of the continent that lies south of the Sahara, features a great central **plateau**—a relatively high, flat area known as the Sahel. This region receives moderate rainfall to sustain the **savannas,** or treeless grasslands, that cover the plateau. The sub-Saharan savannas constitute about 40 percent of Africa's land area.

On the eastern edge of the Sahel, the land splits into a deep crack known as the Great Rift Valley. It extends 40 miles (64.4 kilometers) in width and 2,000 feet (610 meters) in depth. The Great Rift Valley runs 3,000 miles (4,827 kilometers) from the Red Sea in the north all the way to South Africa. Rising above the plateau east of the valley are two mountain peaks—Mount Kenya and Mount Kilimanjaro. Kilimanjaro is Africa's highest mountain, with an elevation of 17,564 feet (5,354 meters).

In West Africa, the Sahel rises above a narrow coastal plain that has a relatively unbroken coastline. The major rivers that do flow through the coastal plain—the Niger and the Zaire (Congo)—are navigable only for short distances. The few natural harbors and limited river travel isolated early African civilizations and made foreign invasions difficult in some areas.

Near the equator is a lush tropical rain forest so thick that sunlight cannot penetrate to the forest floor. Although the climate of the rain forest is hot and humid, 1,500 miles (2,413 kilometers) farther south the land again turns into a desert. Farther south, the desert gives way to a cool, fertile highland in today's South Africa.

The African continent has provided rich resources for its people. Early cultures developed where rainfall was plentiful, or near lakes or along rivers like the Nile.

Kush and Axum

One African river civilization known to exist in 2000 B.C. was the kingdom of Kush, which used its location along the Upper Nile River to

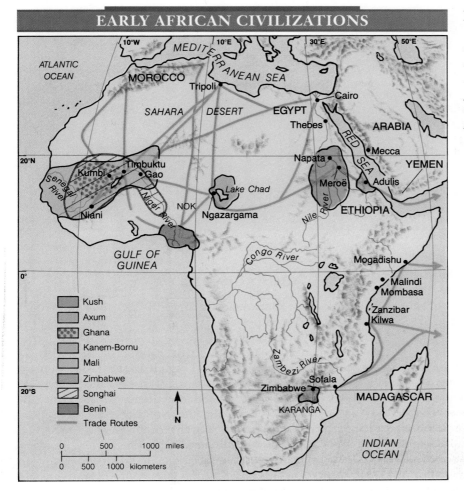

EARLY AFRICAN CIVILIZATIONS

Learning from Maps
The Nile River and the Red Sea provided a trade corridor for the kingdoms of Kush and Axum. **What geographic features might have served West Africans as a way to transport goods?**

Map labels: ATLANTIC OCEAN, MOROCCO, Tripoli, SAHARA DESERT, EGYPT, Thebes, Cairo, MEDITERRANEAN SEA, ARABIA, RED SEA, Mecca, YEMEN, Napata, Meroë, Adulis, ETHIOPIA, Kumbi, Timbuktu, Gao, Senegal River, Niger River, Lake Chad, NOK, Ngazargama, Niani, GULF OF GUINEA, Congo River, Mogadishu, Malindi, Mombasa, Zanzibar, Kilwa, Zambezi River, Sofala, Zimbabwe, KARANGA, MADAGASCAR, INDIAN OCEAN

Legend:
- Kush
- Axum
- Ghana
- Kanem-Bornu
- Mali
- Zimbabwe
- Songhai
- Benin
- Trade Routes

0 500 1000 miles
0 500 1000 kilometers

develop a strong trade economy. Kush had been under Egyptian rule for 500 years. As early as 1450 B.C., Egyptian pharaohs had stationed soldiers in Kush to collect duties on goods moving through the region. The Kushite cities of Napata and Meroë stood where trade caravans crossed the Nile, bringing gold, elephant tusks, and timber from the African interior. This strategic location brought wealth to the merchants and kings of Kush.

Around 1000 B.C. Kush broke away from Egypt and became politically and culturally independent. By the 700s B.C., Kush kings ruled over both Egypt and Kush, establishing their capital at Napata. The city boasted white sandstone temples, monuments, and pyramids fashioned in the Egyptian style.

But in 671 B.C., the Assyrians invaded Egypt, easily defeating the Kushites, whose bronze weapons were no match against Assyrian iron swords. The Kushites were forced to leave Egypt and return to their home territory at the bend of the Upper Nile. In spite of their defeat, the Kushites learned from their enemies the technology of making iron. They built a new capital at Meroë that became a major center for iron production. Kush merchants traded iron, leopard skins, and ebony for goods from the Mediterranean and the Red Sea regions. They also conducted business throughout the Indian Ocean area. Meroë's merchants used their wealth to construct fine houses built around a central courtyard and public baths modeled after ones they had seen in Rome.

Learning from Photographs *The Kush pyramids resemble those of the ancient Egyptians.* **Do you think the Kushites used their pyramids for the same purposes as the Egyptians?**

For about 150 years, the Kushite kingdom thrived. Then a new power—Axum, a kingdom located near the Red Sea—invaded Kush and ended Kushite domination of northeastern Africa.

A Christian Kingdom Because of its location along the Red Sea, Axum also emerged as a trading power. During the 200s B.C., merchants from Egypt, Greece, Rome, Persia, and India sent ships laden with cotton cloth, brass, copper, and olive oil to Axum's main seaport at Adulis. Traders exchanged their goods for cargoes of ivory that the people of Axum hauled from Africa's interior.

Through trade Axum absorbed many elements of Roman culture, including a new religion: Christianity. A remarkable event led to the conversion of Axum's King Ezana to Christianity. Shipwrecked off the coast of Ethiopia, two Christians from Syria were picked up and brought to King Ezana's court, where they lived for several years. The young men convinced Ezana that he should become a Christian. About A.D. 330 the king made Christianity the official religion in Axum.

Axum began its decline when Muslim merchants and soldiers from Arabia raided Axum's trading ships and ports in the A.D. 600s. As a result, Axum lost much of its coastal territory and trade. Confined to the remote interior of East Africa, the rulers of Axum set up a Christian kingdom that became known as Ethiopia.

Sub-Saharan Africa

Between 700 and 200 B.C., during Axum's rise to power, a West African culture called the Nok had already established itself in the fertile Niger and Benue river valleys. In the 1940s archaeologists working in present-day central Nigeria found terra cotta, or baked clay, figurines that provided evidence of the Nok culture. Working in the Nok sites and other areas of West Africa, archaeologists also unearthed iron hoes and axe-heads. This latter discovery provided evidence that metal production had enabled sub-Saharan cultures to farm their land more effectively.

As West African farmers used their iron tools to produce more food, the population increased. In time, arable land became scarce, causing widespread food shortages. Small groups of black Africans began to migrate from West Africa to less populated areas. Other groups followed. Over about a thousand years a great migration took place.

Bantu Migrations Historians call this mass movement the Bantu migrations because descendants of the people who migrated into central, eastern, and southern parts of the continent share elements of a language known as Bantu.

The Bantu migrations did not follow a single pattern. Some villagers followed the Niger or other rivers, settling in one spot to farm for a few years and moving on as the soil became less fertile. Other groups penetrated the rain forests and grew crops along the riverbanks. Still others moved to the highland savannas of East Africa and raised cattle. Groups that settled on the eastern coastal plain grew new crops, such as bananas and yams that had been brought to East Africa by traders from Southeast Asia.

As people pushed into new areas, they met other African groups that joined the migrants and adopted their ways of life. In time, Bantu-speaking peoples became the dominant group of sub-Saharan Africa.

Village Life   Africans who spoke Bantu languages became divided into thousands of ethnic groups, each with its own religious beliefs, marriage and family customs, and traditions. Ethnic groups living around A.D. 1000 formed close-knit communities where most families were organized into large households that included descendants of one set of grandparents.

Many villages were **matrilineal** societies in which villagers traced their descent through mothers rather than through fathers. However, when a girl married, she became a member of her husband's family. To compensate the bride's family for the loss of a member, the husband's family gave the bride's family gifts of iron tools, goats, or cloth.

Even before marriage, specific jobs were assigned to groups of males and females of a similar age, called **age sets**. Boys younger than 10 or 12 herded cattle; girls of the same age helped their mothers plant as well as tend and harvest crops. At about 12 years old, boys and girls took part in ceremonies initiating them into adulthood. A boy remained with his age set throughout his life. After marriage, a girl joined an age set in her husband's village.

Religious Beliefs   To most Africans, marriage customs and all other social laws and traditions were made by a single supreme god who created and ruled an orderly universe. The god rewarded those who followed social rules with abundant harvests and the birth of healthy children, and punished those who violated tradition with accidents, crop failures, or illness.

Beneath the supreme god were many lesser deities who influenced the daily affairs of men and women. These deities were present in natural phenomena such as storms, mountains, and trees. Many Africans also believed that spirits of dead ancestors lived among the people of the village and guided their destiny.

The religious beliefs and family loyalties of most Africans maintained stability and support within villages. Most communities expected their members to obey the social rules they believed to have come from the supreme god.

Although African communities relied heavily on religious and family traditions to maintain a stable social structure, outside influences through trade and learning still managed to affect them. North Africans absorbed influences from the Arab world, whereas sub-Saharan people adapted to Persian, Indian, and later, European influences. From these outsiders, African communities adopted many new customs, ideas, and languages.

SECTION 1 REVIEW

Recall
1. **Define:** plateau, savanna, matrilineal, age set
2. **Identify:** Sahel, Kush, Axum, Ezana, Nok, Bantu
3. **Locate:** Find the Nile River Valley on the map on page 333. Why did the early people of the kingdom of Kush settle in the Upper Nile valley?
4. **Explain:** What was the importance of iron technology to the development of early West African cultures?

Critical Thinking
5. **Apply:** Explain how Mediterranean trade influenced the economy of the Kingdom of Axum.

6. **Evaluate:** The Bantu language changed as people moved into central, eastern, and southern Africa. Why do you think this happened?

Applying Concepts
7. **Movement:** Contrast the Bantu migration with that of the Aryan migration.

African Kingdoms and Empires

Sub-Saharan Africa provided rich natural resources for the early kingdoms of West Africa and to civilizations located in Central Africa. Africans living in these areas between A.D. 300 and 1600 mined the resources they found in their regions—gold, copper, and iron ore. An active trade developed between Islamic peoples from outside sub-Saharan Africa and the African kingdoms based on the rich supplies of gold and other resources. Trade contacts brought power and wealth to the West African kingdoms of Ghana, Mali, and Songhai and to city-states that developed along the east African coast. There Arab traders brought cotton, silk, and Chinese porcelain from India and Southeast Asia to exchange for ivory and metals from Africa's interior. Through their trade contacts with the Muslim world, African cultures gradually adopted Islamic cultural elements such as language and religion.

Kingdom of Ghana

The kingdom of Ghana became one of the richest trading civilizations in sub-Saharan Africa due to its location midway between Saharan salt mines and tropical gold mines. Between A.D. 300 and 1200 the kings of Ghana built and controlled a trading empire that stretched more than 100,000 square miles (260,000 square kilometers). They prospered from the taxes they imposed on goods that entered or left their kingdom. Because the king, or ghana, ruled such a vast region, the land became known by the name of its ruler—Ghana.

There was two-way traffic by caravan between cities in North Africa and Ghana. Muslim traders from North Africa sent caravans loaded with cloth, metalware, swords, and salt across the western Sahara to northern settlements in Ghana. Large caravans from Ghana traveled north to Morocco, bringing kola nuts and agricultural produce. Ghanaian gold was traded for Saharan salt brought by Islamic traders.

Salt was an important trade item for the people of Ghana. They needed salt to preserve and flavor their foods. Using plentiful supplies of gold as a medium of exchange, Ghanaian merchants traded the precious metal for salt and other goods from Morocco and Spain.

Masudi, an Arab traveler, writing about A.D. 950, described how trade was conducted.

The merchants . . . place their wares and cloth on the ground and then depart, and so the people of [Ghana] *come bearing gold which they leave beside the merchandise and then depart. The owners of the merchandise then return, and if they are satisfied with what they have found, they take it. If not, they go away again, and the people of* [Ghana] *return and add to the price until the bargain is concluded.*

Ghana reached the height of its economic and political power as a trading kingdom in the A.D. 800s and 900s. The salt and gold trade moving through Ghana brought Islamic ideas and customs to the kingdom. Muslims held court positions, and many Ghanaians converted to Islam. Archaeologists digging at the site of an ancient city have found Islamic objects such as glass weights for weighing gold and verses from the Quran, painted on stone tablets.

At the end of the A.D. 1000s, an attack on the Ghanaian trade centers by the Almoravids, a group of Islamic people from North Africa, led to the eventual decline of Ghana. Groups of Ghanaians broke away to form Islamic communities that developed into many small independent states.

Learning from Photographs *In the early 1000s caravans from North Africa crossed the western Sahara loaded with goods to trade in Ghana.* **What was more dangerous to these traders—the desert environment or attacks by nomadic tribes?**

Kingdom of Mali

Mali, one of the small states to break away from Ghana, became a powerful kingdom that eventually controlled much of West Africa. The word *Mali* means "where the king resides" and is an appropriate name for a kingdom that gained much of its power and influence from its kings. Sundiata Keita, one of Mali's early kings, defeated his leading rival in A.D. 1235 and began to conquer surrounding territories. By the late 1200s, Mali's territory included the old kingdom of Ghana.

Sundiata worked to bring prosperity to his new empire. He sought to improve agricultural production, and he restored the trans-Saharan trade routes that had been interrupted by the Almoravid attacks. Sundiata ordered soldiers to clear large expanses of savanna and burn the grass that had been cleared to provide fertilizer for crops of peanuts, rice, sorghum, yams, beans, onions, and grains. With the benefit of adequate rainfall, agriculture flourished in Mali. With larger tracts of land under cultivation, farmers produced surplus crops that Mali's kings then collected as taxes.

Mali's greatest king was Mansa Musa, who ruled from A.D. 1312 to 1332. A scholar living in the A.D. 1300s described Mansa as "the most powerful, the richest, the most fortunate, the most feared by his enemies, and the most able to do good to those around him." By opening trade routes and protecting trade caravans with a powerful standing army, Musa maintained the economic prosperity begun by Sundiata. He also introduced Islamic culture to Mali.

A Muslim himself, Musa enhanced the prestige and power of Mali through a famous pilgrimage to Mecca in A.D. 1324. Arab writers report that Musa traveled in grand style. He took with him 12,000 slaves, each dressed in silk or brocade and carrying bars of gold. Musa gave away so much gold on his journey that the world price of gold fell. At Mecca, Musa persuaded a Spanish architect to return with him to Mali. There the skilled architect built great mosques —Moslem houses of worship—and other fine buildings, including a palace for Musa in the capital of Timbuktu (tihm buk TOO). Timbuktu became an important center of Moslem art and learning mainly through the efforts of Mansa Musa, who encouraged Muslim scholars to teach at his court.

After Mansa Musa died in A.D. 1332, the empire came under attack by Berber tribesmen from the Sahara region to the north. They raided Mali and captured Timbuktu. From the south, warriors from the rain forest also attacked Mali. Inside the kingdom, the Songhai people living in the Niger River valley had long resented losing control over their region and were rebelling against the empire. By the middle of the A.D. 1500s, the empire of Mali split up into several independent states.

Learning from Photographs *Because metalworking required considerable skill and knowledge, these West African metalworkers had special status among their people. The metal trade brought wealth to villagers.* **What metals were traded in West Africa?**

Kingdom of Songhai

The rebellious Songhai, who were skilled traders as well as farmers and fishermen living along the Niger River, were led by strong leaders. During the late A.D. 1400s, their ruler, Sunni Ali, fought many territorial wars and managed to conquer the cities of Timbuktu and Jenne, expanding his empire to include most of the West African savanna. Sunni Ali was a Muslim ruler, but when he died, rule fell to his son, a non-Muslim. The Muslim population of Songhai overthrew Ali's son and brought a Muslim ruler to the throne.

Under the new ruler, Askia Muhammad, the Songhai Empire reached the height of its glory. Ruling from A.D. 1493 to 1528, Askia Muhammad divided Songhai into five huge provinces, each with a governor, a tax collector, a court of judges, and a trade inspector—very much like the government structure of China in the A.D. 1400s. The king maintained the peace and security of his realm with a cavalry and a navy.

Devoted to Islam, Muhammad introduced laws that reflected Islamic philosophy based on the teachings of the Quran. Lesser crimes were sometimes overlooked, but those who committed major crimes such as robbery or idolatry received harsh punishments. Askia Muhammad appointed Muslim judges to larger districts of his empire, assuring that Islamic laws would be upheld.

In A.D. 1528 Askia Muhammad was overthrown by his son. A series of struggles for the throne followed, leading to a weakened central government. By A.D. 1589 the rulers of Morocco sent an army across the Sahara to attack Songhai gold-trading centers. Moroccan soldiers, armed with guns and cannons, easily defeated the Songhai forces fighting with only swords, spears, and bows and arrows. By A.D. 1600 the Songhai Empire had come to an end.

East Africa During the same time that West African kings ruled their empires, important trading communities developed along the coast of East Africa. As early as 200 B.C., the Arabs had developed a trade network between East African and Indian Ocean ports in Ceylon and India. East Africans used monsoon winds to sail across the 2,500-mile (4,023-kilometer) stretch of Indian Ocean that separates Africa from India. By the A.D. 900s Arab and Persian merchants had settled on the East African coast and controlled the trade there. Traders from the interior of Africa brought ivory, gold, iron, and rhinoceros horn to the east coast to trade for Indian cotton and silk and for Chinese porcelain.

By A.D. 1200 small East African trading settlements, such as the gold port of Kilwa, had become thriving city-states. Within each city-state, Islamic and African cultures blended. For the most part, Arab and Persian merchants ruled the trading states. They converted many Africans to Islam.

Arab merchants married local women who had converted to Islam. Families having members with African and Islamic cultural backgrounds began speaking Swahili, a Bantu language that included Arabic and Persian words. The people of the East African coastal city-states also developed an Arabic form of writing that enabled them to write about their history.

The East African trading states reached the height of their prosperity during the A.D. 1300s, but when Portuguese merchants and soldiers

CONNECTIONS: HISTORY AND THE ENVIRONMENT

African Farmers Adapt to the Land

The African continent is so huge that it encompasses diverse landscapes and climates. Within each region, groups of people adapted to the local climate and landforms and developed an agricultural life that suited their particular environment.

On the central plateau of the Sahel, farmers felled trees and cleared grasses to make fields. Because the soil of the savannas lacked nutrients and because rainfall in the region was scarce, after a few growing seasons the fields no longer produced adequate crops. When this happened, the whole farming village moved a few miles away to more fertile land and began the process again.

In the tropical rain forests of Central Africa, along the banks of the Zaire River, farmers expended enormous energy to cut and clear the tall, tangled trees and vines from the land. In small clearings in the midst of towering trees, farmers planted gardens with yams, cassava, taro, and other root crops.

Bantu villages in the southern African highlands were built in river valleys and among rocky hills. Bantu farmers grew grains such as millet and sorghum and raised chickens and goats. To protect themselves and their domestic animals from lions and other predators, Bantu villagers built stone walls from outcroppings of rock scattered around their villages and land.

Making the Connection

1. How did farmers living in the Sahel adapt to their environment?
2. Where else in today's world are rain forests threatened by human development? What steps are being taken to remedy the problem?

attacked the city-states in the 1500s, prosperity declined. Europeans then took over the economy and trade of the region.

The Bantu Kingdoms   The Indian Ocean trade was not limited to the coastal trading states. It reached far inland, contributing to the rise of wealthy Bantu kingdoms in Central and South Africa. The inland kingdoms mined rich deposits of copper and gold. During the A.D. 900s, traders from the East African coast made their way to the inland mining communities in Central Africa and began an active trade among the people living there. The traders brought Chinese silk and porcelain, Indian glass beads, carpets from Middle Eastern Arab lands, and fine Persian pottery.

The people of Karanga, a Bantu kingdom located on a high plateau between the Zambezi and Limpopo (or Crocodile) rivers, built nearly 300 stone-walled fortresses throughout their territory between A.D. 1000 and 1500. The largest was called the Great Zimbabwe—meaning "stone house"—and served as the political and religious center of the kingdom. The oval stone wall of the Zimbabwe enclosure was 30 feet (9.15 meters) high and was made from 900,000 stones fitted together without mortar. Within the wall was a maze of interior walls and hidden passages that protected the circular house of the Zimbabwe chief. Near the house, archaeologists have uncovered a platform with several upright stones that may have been the place where the chief held court.

FOOTNOTES TO HISTORY

GOLDEN EMPERORS

Ghana's emperors became very wealthy from the taxes they imposed on the gold and salt trade. One emperor—Kinissai—owned a thousand horses. An Arab chronicler states that each horse "slept only on a carpet, with silken rope for a halter." Another wealthy ruler, according to an Arab traveler, tethered his horse to an enormous gold nugget weighing thirty pounds. Ghana's prosperity enabled its rulers to wear gold headdresses and adorn themselves with jewelry. One ruler's dogs even wore collars and bells made of silver and gold.

For nearly five centuries, Karanga and the other Bantu states grew wealthy from their control of the chief routes between the gold mines and the sea. However, during the A.D. 1500s, Bantu states in South Africa struggled in civil wars that brought disorder to the kingdoms and disrupted trade. The empire was split between two rival forces. The northern territory was called Monomutapa. The southern territory was taken over by the Changamire dynasty. At the same time, the Portuguese explorers arrived along the East African coast. Eager to control the sources of gold, ivory, and copper, the Europeans attacked the Monomutapa empire, threatening the survival of the interior African civilizations.

SECTION 2 REVIEW

Recall

1. **Identify:** Almoravids, Sundiata Keita, Mansa Musa, Askia Muhammad
2. **Locate:** Find Timbuktu on the map on page 333. How did Timbuktu become an important center of Islamic art and learning during the A.D. 1300s?
3. **Explain:** How did ruler Askia Muhammad keep order and control over his huge empire of Songhai?

Critical Thinking

4. **Analyze:** Determine why trade was vital to the economies of Ghana and Mali.
5. **Synthesize:** Imagine that you are an Arab merchant visiting an East African coastal city-state in the A.D. 1300s. What aspects of the people's culture would be familiar to you? What parts might seem strange?

Applying Concepts

6. **Cultural diffusion:** Explain how trade between African regions and the Islamic world influenced the development of African cultures between A.D. 900 and 1500.

The Early Americas

In Chapter 1 you read about the first people to inhabit the Americas—early people who migrated to North America from Asia, following herds of bison and other game across the land bridge called Beringia. The continents to which the migrating groups came make up the world's longest landmass. North and South America stretch over 9,000 miles (14,400 kilometers) from the northern edge of Canada to the southern tip of South America.

Isolated from other continents by the Atlantic and Pacific oceans, the Americas were among the last areas of the earth to be settled, but by about 10,000 B.C. bands of hunters ranged over a wide area of North and South America. Eventually groups of people settled in regions throughout the two continents, adapting to the environments of those regions.

The First Americans

The hunters and gatherers who migrated to the Americas used the resources of their particular environment for basic needs of food, clothing, and shelter. If they lived near the ocean, people collected mussels and snails. Some groups fished in rivers and streams, while others hunted. Archaeologists have found evidence of this life in artifacts found in coastal regions throughout the Americas. They found rounded stones for grinding seeds, bone hooks for fishing, and heaps of snail and mussel shells at campsites.

By about 5000 B.C., a group of hunting and gathering people in a highland area of what is now Mexico had discovered that the seeds of **maize**, or corn, and other native plants could be planted and harvested, providing a reliable source of food. As this discovery spread from Mexico into the southwestern United States,

groups of early people began to settle in permanent villages. About 3000 B.C. farmers made use of stone axes to clear their fields and pointed digging sticks to plant improved varieties of maize, beans, and squash.

As the food supply improved, the population of the Americas grew. By the time Europeans arrived in North America around A.D. 1500, about 20 million Native Americans belonging to more than 2,000 different groups of people were inhabiting the two continents. About 1 million of these early inhabitants lived in what is now the United States and parts of Canada.

North Americans

Much of what we know about the early people of northern North America comes from the work of archaeologists. Archaeological digs have uncovered homes, burial mounds, pottery, baskets, stone tools, and the bones of people and animals in the Arctic and Northwest, California and the Great Basin, the Southwest, the Great Plains, and the Eastern Woodlands. By studying these artifacts, archaeologists discovered that there were distinct regional differences. People who settled in a particular region developed a common culture. Gradually the arts and crafts and religious customs of each region grew to be distinct from those of other regions, a pattern historians call **cultural differentiation.** In each region, culture reflected the local geography and natural resources.

The Arctic and Northwest The early people of the Arctic lived in the cold northern regions of present-day Canada and Alaska. The severe climate of this region prohibited farming. Thus, small bands of extended families moved about, hunting and fishing. By 6500 B.C. some

Arctic people were living in small villages of pit houses, covered with dome-shaped roofs of whalebone and driftwood. Villagers hunted whales, sea lions, seals, and water birds. They ate the meat and used the skins to make warm, protective clothing.

In contrast to the cold and snow of the Arctic, the thickly forested seacoast of the Pacific Northwest had a milder climate. Rainfall was plentiful, and mild winters and warm ocean currents kept rivers and bays free of ice. Like the people of the Arctic, those who settled along the Pacific Coast—the Kwakiutl, for example—hunted whales, fish, and other sea animals as their main source of food. Forests of the Northwest provided additional sources of food—small forest animals and acorns. After about A.D. 500 the people of the Northwest used other resources from the surrounding forests and rivers. With stone and copper woodworking tools they split cedar, fir, and redwood trees into planks to make houses and large canoes. They also developed ways to harvest salmon with fiber nets, stone-tipped spears, and elaborate wooden traps called weirs.

Society among the Kwakiutl and other Northwest peoples was organized into lineages, each of which claimed to be descended from a mythical ancestor. A lineage group lived together in a single large house and owned the right to use or display special designs, songs, ceremonies, or prized possessions, such as patterned sheets of copper. A lineage maintained exclusive use of its own fishing area and berry-picking grounds. The wealth of each lineage was displayed and given away as gifts at festive gatherings called potlatches. At a potlatch a chief might give away canoes, blankets, and other goods. In turn, guests might bring the chief deerskins and food.

IMAGES
OF THE TIME

Native Americans

Many cultures inhabited North America before European settlers arrived. The diversity of the land meant each group had its own way of life.

The Anasazi people built these cliff dwellings in Mesa Verde (Colorado) 800 years ago.

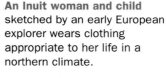

An Inuit woman and child sketched by an early European explorer wears clothing appropriate to her life in a northern climate.

To obtain items they could not make themselves, some people of the Northwest developed trading networks with people living farther south. Traders paddled redwood canoes along the coast, stopping at shore villages to exchange goods. Trade networks stretched from southern Alaska to northern California.

California–Great Basin   Native Americans living along the California coast enjoyed a warm climate and an abundance of food resources. Many communities lived on diets of abalone and mussels. Near San Francisco Bay, archaeologists have found evidence of this diet in heaps of discarded shells that date from 2000 B.C. In addition to shellfish, the first Californians fished for sea bass, hunted seals, and gathered berries and nuts. Having such abundant resources made food gathering easier for the people living in this region.

Like other Native Americans, they developed elaborate religious ceremonies designed to worship nature spirits that inhabited all of the natural world, but especially those spirits related to animals or plants used for food. The Chumash, who lived in what is today southern California, would gather together at harvest festivals to celebrate the goodness of the earth. Villagers participated in dances and games.

Compared with those living along the coast, people living farther inland scratched their living from a harsh desert and mountain environment. Great Basin people moved about in small bands, living in windbreak shelters and eating seeds, grasshoppers, and small animals.

Southwest   People who settled in the high desert regions of Arizona, New Mexico, southern Colorado and Utah, and northern Mexico had fewer resources than those who settled

A huge serpent mound (left) was made by Hopewell or Adena peoples about 2,000 years ago. It may have had religious significance. Below, a Pueblo bowl from the Southwest is decorated with geometric designs.

Reflecting on the Times
From the images shown here, how would you say Native Americans adapted to the different environments of North America?

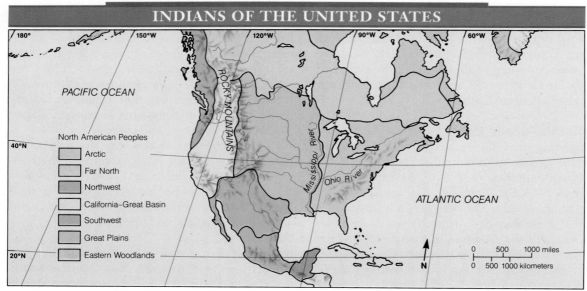

INDIANS OF THE UNITED STATES

North American Peoples
- Arctic
- Far North
- Northwest
- California–Great Basin
- Southwest
- Great Plains
- Eastern Woodlands

PACIFIC OCEAN

ROCKY MOUNTAINS

Mississippi River

Ohio River

ATLANTIC OCEAN

0   500   1000 miles
0   500 1000 kilometers

N

Learning from Maps *Many of the first people to inhabit North America lived near the seacoast or made their homes in river valleys.* **Why did North Americans choose to settle in those locations?**

along the Pacific Coast. Nevertheless, the people of the Southwest adapted to their harsh environment by inventing techniques of irrigation to farm the land. For example, around 300 B.C. a Hohokam community in southern Arizona dug an irrigation canal 3 miles (4.8 kilometers) long to draw the river's waters onto fields planted with maize, kidney beans, and squash.

Farther north, a group of Southwest people known as the Pueblo grew maize in fields terraced like a series of stair steps to check the erosion of topsoil caused by heavy late summer rains. The Pueblo employed a style of building that used adobe, a sun-dried brick easy to produce under desert conditions. The Pueblo often built their villages under ledges on the sides of cliffs to shade residents from the desert sun and to make the village easier to defend.

Religious leaders governed Pueblo villages. They led religious ceremonies to ensure the harmony between humans and the spiritual world. The Pueblo believed that if harmony existed, the spirits would provide rain for crops and small game for food.

Another Southwest group known as the Apache lived in areas that were unsuitable for

farming. They hunted and gathered wild birds, rabbits, and plants. Sometimes they raided Pueblo fields; other times they traded meat and hides with Pueblo villagers for maize and other food supplies. A neighboring people, the Navajo, did manage to raise a breed of sheep that could live on the sparse desert vegetation.

Great Plains   In contrast to the sparse southwestern environment, vast grasslands covered the Great Plains, stretching from the Rocky Mountains to the Mississippi River. This environment provided a different challenge for the early people who inhabited the region. Native Americans adapting to life on the plains needed a reliable source of food. Farming in the region was difficult, as the thick plains sod was hard to plow. Moreover, maize needs more water than is naturally available on most parts of the Great Plains.

Although some farming was done along streams, most Native Americans of the plains depended on one abundant resource—the great herds of bison, or buffalo, that roamed the plains. From earliest times, the Kiowa, Crow, Blackfoot, and other people of the plains

Learning from Art
The Sioux in this picture play a game that later became the popular sport of lacrosse. **How did the geography of the Great Plains support the people who lived there?**

followed the herds from one grazing ground to another. They used every part of the bison for their food, clothing, shelter, and tools.

Eastern Woodlands   Unlike the Plains people who depended on the bison, Native Americans of the woodlands east of the Mississippi River hunted a large variety of animals. Deer, turkeys, geese, and squirrels were common in eastern forests. Like the Plains people, Woodland people made use of every part of the animals they killed. They ate deer meat, wore deerskin clothing, and made tools out of animal bones and antlers. Since summers were warm, rainfall abundant, and soil fertile throughout most of the Eastern Woodlands, the people of

this region lived in farming villages and grew crops such as corn, squash, beans, and tobacco.

Native Americans living in the northeastern part of the present-day United States had a high level of political organization compared with the peoples of the plains and the Southwest. Around A.D. 1400 the Cayuga, Mohawk, Oneida, Onondaga, and Seneca formed a confederation—the League of the Iroquois. A council of representatives from each group met to discuss and resolve disputes among its members. The Iroquois League predated the formation of United States representative government by more than 300 years. When Europeans invaded Native American land, they met strong resistance from the Iroquois League.

SECTION 3 REVIEW

Recall

1. **Define:** maize, cultural differentiation
2. **Identify:** Kwakiutl, Hohokam, Pueblo, Plains people, Iroquois League
3. **Locate:** Using the map on page 344, find the region where the Blackfoot and the Crow lived. How does the physical relief of this region differ from that of the Northwest?

4. **Describe:** How did new methods of farming help people of the Southwest adapt to living in a dry climate?

Critical Thinking

5. **Analyze:** Compare the early cultures that lived along the California coast with the early people of the Great Basin. What factors led to the differences in culture?

6. **Analyze:** Compare the organization of the Iroquois League with the structure of the United States government. What is similar?

Applying Concepts

7. **Relation to environment:** Explain how cultures within the seven regions of North America depended on their environment and natural resources.

American Empires

Around A.D. 1500 to 1450 B.C., sophisticated civilizations grew throughout Mexico, Central America, and South America. Farmers living in Mexico and Central America learned how to produce enough maize to support large populations. Because food was plentiful, others not involved in the production of food could develop trade and attend to religious activities. Cities grew up around market centers. Religious leaders supervised the religious life of the people, while political rulers introduced centralized governments and maintained armies to manage and protect their large empires.

The Olmec

Between 1500 and 600 B.C., a people scientists have named the Olmec developed one of the earliest agricultural societies to live along the Gulf Coast of Mexico. Olmec farmers grew maize in raised fields along swampy coastal areas. Much of what is known about the Olmec comes from archaeological discoveries made in the late 1930s at La Venta near the Gulf of Mexico. Until then, Olmec culture had been buried beneath the soil of southern Mexico for thousands of years. Archaeologists unearthed several enormous stone heads, some more than 9 feet (2.7 meters) tall and weighing as much as 40 tons. They believe that the sculptures are portraits of Olmec rulers used as protective symbols on Olmec temples.

The stone heads were carved from volcanic rock. Without the use of wheels or pack animals, the Olmec moved the enormous heads from mountainous areas more than 60 miles away from the place where archaeologists unearthed them.

From jade carvings found at Olmec sites, archaeologists infer that religion played an important role in the lives of the Olmec. Many carvings show the Olmec god, a being with a human body and the catlike face of a jaguar. The Olmec believed the jaguar-god controlled their harvests. Similar images have been found among artifacts of other Central American civilizations.

The Maya

Southeast of the Olmec ruins, located in the steamy lowland forests of modern Guatemala, are the remains of several Mayan cities. These ruins are evidence of a civilization that rose to power and reached its cultural height between A.D. 300 and 800.

Mayan life centered on religion. Cities were really religious centers, with houses, courtyards, and plazas built around enormous stepped temple-pyramids. Surrounding the largest Mayan city, Tikal, stood six temple-pyramids, the tallest 212 feet (65 meters) high. Priests and rulers lived at Tikal, as did artisans and merchants.

On the day of a religious festival, the great cities drew crowds of people. Some came to pray at the shrines; others watched priests conduct elaborate rituals to the gods at the temple-pyramids. The plazas filled with people who watched masked dancers twirl to the rhythms of drums and flutes.

Some festivals included a ceremonial ball game, called *pok-a-tok*. Players wearing protective padding batted a solid rubber ball back and forth across a court. Archaeologists who study Mayan drawings believe that the game had religious meaning. Players may have represented gods.

Sciences   Like the ancient Greeks, the Maya believed that the movements of the sun, moon, and planets were the journeys of gods across the sky. Since these gods controlled nature—including harvests—charting the movements of the sun and moon was an essential religious duty. Thus the religious leaders developed an understanding of astronomy and mathematics. Mayan astronomers observed and carefully recorded these movements on large calendar stones, using a type of hieroglyphic writing. The calendars helped priests predict eclipses, schedule religious ceremonies, and determine times to plant and harvest.

Economy   Although much of Mayan life centered on religion, trade was also important to the imperial economy. Perhaps as often as every five days, farmers brought surplus crops to open-air markets in the major cities. There they could trade maize and other produce for cotton cloth, jade ornaments, pottery, fish, deer meat, and salt brought by merchants from surrounding districts.

Mayan merchants exported surplus goods on routes throughout Mexico and Central America. Traders traveled by sea, by river, and by a well-constructed road system. Wheeled vehicles and beasts of burden, such as horses and oxen, were unknown. So goods moving overland had to be carried on human backs.

By about A.D. 800 the Mayan civilization began to decline. All construction ceased, people abandoned many of their cities, and they moved to other areas. Historians do not know the reason for this collapse. Some think it may have been caused by food shortages, weather changes, or epidemic diseases. Others theorize that farmers revolted against their rulers, bringing about a cultural decline.

Teotihuacános and Toltec

At the same time that the Maya were developing their religious culture, another civilization known as the Teotihuacános (tay oh tee wah KAHN ohs) established itself in a high valley 30 miles (48 kilometers) northeast of today's Mexico City. Today, only the ruins of this civilization remain. The fire that destroyed the city of Teotihuacán in about A.D. 750 was probably set by the Toltec—invaders from the north.

After the destruction of Teotihuacán, the Toltec people controlled central Mexico. Using a powerful army, they conquered land as far south as the Yucatán peninsula. They built beautiful houses decorated with mosaic tiles. The Toltec capital of Tula was the center of a powerful mining and trading empire. Traders carried their goods from Tula to markets as far away as Colombia. When invaders destroyed Tula in A.D. 1170, the empire collapsed.

The Aztec Empire

During the last years of Toltec rule, a band of wandering hunters moved from the north into central Mexico. The Aztec, as they were called, settled on a small uninhabited island near the western shore of Lake Texcoco, today the site of Mexico City. In A.D. 1325, the Aztec established their capital city of Tenochtitlán (tay nohch tee TLAHN).

Tenochtitlán   The Aztec turned Tenochtitlán into an agricultural center and marketplace. Since land for farming was scarce on the island, the Aztec devised a way of making *chinampas*, or artificial islands, by piling mud from the bottom of the lake onto rafts secured by stakes. These became floating gardens where farmers grew a variety of crops, including corn and beans. With a plentiful food supply, the population grew and people moved outside the boundaries of the city to the mainland. The Aztec built a network of canals, bridges, and three stone causeways to connect the mainland with the capital city.

Empire   Tenochtitlán continued to grow, and the Aztec civilization flourished under the leadership of powerful emperors. The Aztec army conquered all of central and southern Mexico by A.D. 1500. Conquered people were forced to pay tribute to the emperor in the form of maize, cotton cloth, rubber, copper, and weapons. Prisoners captured during war served as slaves in Aztec communities.

Government and Society   The Aztec civilization was based on a sophisticated political and social hierarchy. The emperor topped both

Mayan Monuments

The pyramids of Central America form an intriguing document of Mayan civilization. At several sites throughout Central America, Mayan stone temple-pyramids still remain. The temple-pyramids, along with palaces, plazas, observatories, and ball courts, made up the religious and political centers of Mayan cities. The centers were often the only permanent structures in a Mayan city.

Archaeologists have estimated that some cities may have had as many as 50,000 inhabitants who were ruled by a privileged class of warriors and priests. From the evidence that survives, archaeologists know that as early as 2000 B.C. some form of organized religious or ceremonial center existed in Mayan cities.

The temple-pyramids dating from the Classic period (A.D. 300 to 900), like the one at Palenque, were vast stepped structures built of stone. Essentially they were platforms for religious ceremonies. In early periods, wooden temples were built on top of the stone pyramids; in later years, more permanent stone temples replaced the wooden structures. In many cases, these temples were built to memorialize dead rulers by associating them with the gods. In addition to inscriptions and pictorial carvings, the temple-pyramids seem to have been coated with plaster and painted with bright, symbolic colors. Religious ceremonies and sacrifices conducted by priests took place outside the temple on top of the pyramid platform.

Archaeologists believe the stepped levels of the pyramids may have represented the harmonious layers of the cosmos, or universe. Mayan astronomers and priests held high positions in the Mayan culture. Much of a priest's power resided in his ability to predict the movements of the stars and planets. Thus, a priest would consult with astronomers before major battles or projects were undertaken to see when the heavens would favor such actions.

Further evidence of the Mayan concern with astronomy and proper timing appears in the pyramid inscriptions. Carvings found on Mayan pyramids and official buildings often record important dates in the lives of rulers—for example, a ruler's birth date, the date he began his reign, the date of his marriage, and dates of military victories.

Responding to the Arts

1. What purpose did the Mayan pyramids serve?
2. How might you compare the Mayan religious and political centers discussed here with the buildings and organization of cities today?

Learning from Photographs *The ruins of Machu Picchu, an early Inca city, lie on top of a high ridge of mountains.* **What other geographic features are visible in the photograph?**

the political and social structures. His power came from his control of the army. Emperors were aided by a chief deputy whose job was to communicate with the gods and relay their wishes back to the emperor. Ranked below these officials was a council of four noble princes and three honored classes of warriors who managed the day-to-day affairs of the empire.

In addition to the empire's political hierarchy, Aztec society consisted of four social classes—nobles, commoners, serfs, and slaves. Nobles owned private plots of land or land held in common with other families. Serfs farmed the nobles' land. Commoners made up the largest segment of Aztec society. This group included priests, merchants, artisans, and farmers who held land in common with a nobleman's family. The lowest class included criminals and people who could not pay their debts, as well as women

and children prisoners of war who worked as slaves for nobles. Male prisoners of war were sacrificed on the altar of the Aztec sun god.

Religion The Aztec worshiped many gods and goddesses and forced conquered peoples to worship the Aztec deities as well. As in the Mayan culture, Aztec priests conducted ceremonies and performed sacrifices to gods and goddesses believed powerful enough to bring good harvests. Aztec priests considered the sun god particularly important and honored the god with human sacrifices to ensure that the sun would rise each morning. Records show that as many as 20,000 prisoners were sacrificed at the dedication of a great temple-pyramid.

Much of Aztec art reflected religious themes or had a religious function. The walls of temple-pyramids displayed decorated scenes of gods or battles. Poets and writers also glorified Aztec gods and narrated the legendary history of the Aztec people. One poem ends with the proud question: "Who could conquer Tenochtitlán?" Despite the poet's confidence, Tenochtitlán faced rebellions from its outlying territories that weakened the empire. Then in 1521 Spanish explorers, led by Hernando Cortés, invaded and destroyed Aztec villages and cities.

Inca Civilization

Rivaling the Aztec in power and influence, the Inca civilization developed in the Andes Mountains of South America. Like the Aztec, the Inca began as one of a number of small tribes competing for fertile farmland that was scarce in the Andes highlands. Rival tribes battled for the right to settle in warm highland valleys or near the rivers. Around A.D. 1200 the Inca had settled at Cuzco (KOO skoh), in what is now southern Peru. They raided other villages and slowly established a powerful empire.

Government and Society   Like the Maya and the Aztec, Inca emperors also developed strong central governments to rule their people. The first great Inca emperor, Pachacuti, came to power in A.D. 1438. Pachacuti expanded the Inca Empire to include the whole Andes region. He incorporated newly conquered territory into the empire by appointing loyal governors. He also instituted a complex system of tribute collections, courts, military posts, trade inspections, and local work regulations to bind outlying lands closely to the central government. To further unify the diverse people of the empire, the Inca established an imperial language: Quechua (KEHCH hwah).

The Inca emperor and his officials closely regulated the lives of the common people. As a divine ruler, the emperor owned all land and property. Each year, to prevent uprisings, government officials redistributed land among the farmers within a province. Farmers and other commoners had to earn the right to own luxury goods by doing extra work for the government—which included repairing bridges, constructing public buildings, cultivating lands owned by religious leaders, and serving in the army. Women were expected to weave one garment a year for the government.

On November 15, 1533, the Spanish conqueror Francisco Pizarro and his troops entered the Peruvian city where Inca emperor Atahualpa resided. Having requested a meeting with the Inca leader, Pizarro and a priest met with Atahualpa. The emperor arrived at the meeting flanked with 3,000 of his soldiers. Pizarro's troops surrounded the Inca forces and captured their leader. Pizarro held Atahualpa hostage, and after receiving a ransom in silver and gold, executed him. Then, Spanish troops advanced to the Inca capital of Cuzco.

The Inca civilization declined after Pizarro, and later other Spanish governors slew those Inca who threatened their authority or challenged their rules—actions that would be repeated in many parts of the Americas.

SECTION 4 REVIEW

Recall
1. **Identify:** Olmec, Maya, Aztec, Toltec, Pachacuti, Atahualpa
2. **Locate:** Use the maps in the Atlas to describe the physical geography of Central America and the country of Peru. How did geography affect the Maya and Inca civilizations located in these two areas?
3. **Describe:** What were the major cultural elements of the Maya civilization?

Critical Thinking
4. **Analyze:** Contrast the religious beliefs of the Maya and Aztec. How did religion contribute to social order in each culture?
5. **Synthesize:** What do modern nations take as tribute after a war? How is this the same as or different from the tribute paid by Aztec people?

Applying Concepts
6. **Change:** Contrast the methods used by the Maya, Aztec, and Inca to expand and administer their empires.

HYPOTHESIZING

Half your history class failed a chapter test. The rest of the students, with one exception, received a grade of D. This general reversal may have had more than one cause. Can you think of any? One cause might be that your class had a substitute teacher all week, and the teacher spent only 30 minutes reviewing the chapter with the class.

Explanation

This *hypothesis,* or logical guess, is a possible explanation for a cause and can serve as a basis for further investigation. A hypothesis can usually be proved or disproved by further research and is revised as new information becomes available. For example, you could interview each student for information that might confirm or revise your hypothesis.

To improve your skill in hypothesizing, follow these steps:

- State the fact or topic for which you wish to make a hypothesis and formulate questions that will help focus your research.
- Gather all the information you think may contribute to an explanation by recalling pertinent facts.
- Brainstorm all possible hypotheses.
- Test each hypothesis. See if the explanation fits with every known fact and is reasonable. Sometimes several explana-

tions fit the facts and seem reasonable.

- Using your best judgment, decide which hypothesis provides the best explanation.
- If new information becomes available, retest and, if necessary, revise your hypothesis.

Example

Here is how the formulating and testing of hypotheses has been applied to sculptures discovered in the ruins of Monte Alban, a city of Zapotec culture in Mexico. The sculptures found there resemble distorted human figures.

First, archaeologists focused their research by asking questions such as these: "Of what kind of building was the sculpted stone a part? Why was the figure on that type of building? Does the figure have a meaning?"

The archaeologists recalled available facts. The carved stones once formed the wall of a building facing a large open court believed to be a ball court. Researchers considered all that was known about activities that usually took place in a court; the types of buildings usually found around ball courts in other Mexican ruins; the social, religious, and medical practices of the time; Olmec influence on the Zapotecs; and other facts known about the Zapotecs.

Various hypotheses were formulated. The figures have been

interpreted as dancers, ball players, victims being sacrificed, or medical case studies. Although the carvings are widely called "The Dancers" (los Danzantes), most archaeologists have rejected this hypothesis because the explanation does not fit with one fact— the pained expression on many of the figures' faces. This consistent characteristic led researchers to favor the last two hypotheses (sacrificed victims and medical case studies). Neither explanation, however, has convinced a majority of scientists.

Archaeologists hope to uncover more evidence that will confirm one of the two popular hypotheses or improve on them.

Application

In Chapter 14 you read about the decline of Ghana. "At the end of the A.D. 1000s, an attack by the Almoravids, a group of Islamic people from North Africa, on the Ghanian trade centers led to the eventual decline of Ghana." Form a hypothesis to explain why Ghana broke into separate states. Explain why you consider it to be the best explanation.

Practice

Turn to Practicing Skills on page 353 of the Chapter Review for further practice in hypothesizing.

CHAPTER 14 REVIEW

HISTORICAL SIGNIFICANCE

Throughout the early history of Africa and the Americas, civilizations developed religious beliefs, agriculture, and trade networks in harmony with their environment. Africans and Native Americans regarded the earth as sacred. Their religions expected people to respect and honor nature gods who were thought to control phenomena such as the amount of rainfall, the rising and setting of sun and moon, and the annual flooding of rivers.

Early Africans and Americans used the natural resources of their environment to develop trade networks. Some groups mined gold, silver, and other minerals from the land and then turned the raw ores into trade items. Others, adapting to the climate and growing conditions of their environment, grew surplus crops to sell at local markets. The environment gave early civilizations in Africa and the Americas spiritual strength and economic support.

SUMMARY

For a summary of Chapter 14, see Unit 3 Synopsis on pages 356-357.

USING KEY TERMS

Write the definition of each key term. Then list a geographical place name or a people to which the term relates:

1. age set
2. matrilineal
3. cultural differentiation
4. maize
5. plateau
6. savanna

REVIEWING FACTS

1. **List:** What are the two major geographical regions of Africa?
2. **Explain:** How did Ghana become a wealthy nation?
3. **List:** What are the regions of North America?
4. **Describe:** How did the people of southwestern North America adapt to their desert?
5. **Explain:** In what scientific fields did the Mayans excel?
6. **Locate:** Where was Tenochtitlán, and what was unique about its geography?

7. **Identify:** Who were the Nok?
8. **Describe:** Who was the emperor of the Inca Empire?

THINKING CRITICALLY

1. **Apply:** How do climate and geography affect the development of a civilization?
2. **Analyze:** Contrast the rise and decline of North and South American civilizations in the 1400s.
3. **Synthesize:** Imagine the daily activities of people living in the northwestern part of North America in about A.D. 1500. Describe some typical activities.
4. **Evaluate:** Find evidence from Section 3 that supports a cause for the decline of the Mayan civilization.

ANALYZING CONCEPTS

1. **Movement:** How did movement affect the development of sub-Saharan Africa?
2. **Cultural diffusion:** Explain how trade affected cultural diffusion in sub-Saharan Africa. From what areas did sub-Saharan Africans receive new ideas and practices?
3. **Relation to environment:** Give two examples of how early inhabitants of North America used the natural resources of their region. How do people use them today?

4. Change: How did Spanish conquests of Mexico and Peru change the Aztec and Inca cultures?

PRACTICING SKILLS

1. On Tuesday morning you find a note in your pocket in your own handwriting that says "Hamburger—after noon Tues—3 or so." You can't remember writing it or what it means. Explain how you can use hypothesizing and your knowledge of your own habits to figure out the note.
2. Stelae are vertical shafts of stone, about the height of a human being. Many stelae found in Mayan ruins were sculpted with portraits and carved with hieroglyphics; archaeologists believe that each stela commemorates a ruler. The Maya monuments were destroyed, leaving only fragments that archaeologists have put together. Suggest as many hypotheses as you can for this destruction.
3. About 25 years ago sub-Saharan civilizations were rarely discussed in U.S. history texts. Make a hypothesis to explain that gap and a way to test it.

GEOGRAPHY IN HISTORY

1. **Location:** Using the maps on pages 333 and 994 in the Atlas, compare the ancient kingdom of Ghana with its modern counterpart.

2. **Movement:** Explain where the migration of people to North America originated. How far did the migration spread?
3. **Place:** What archaeological artifacts did the Olmec leave, and what is the geographic significance of the artifacts?

TRACING CHRONOLOGY

Refer to the time line below to answer these questions.

1. How long after the origin of Olmec civilization did the Maya reach the height of their civilization?
2. How many years separate the height of the gold-salt trade and the decline of Ghana?
3. Name the civilizations that existed between A.D. 1250 and 1500.
4. Name the civilizations that existed before A.D. 500, and contrast their economies.

LINKING PAST AND PRESENT

1. Gold helped make Ghana a powerful empire. Name another natural resource that has made African countries wealthy today.
2. Ancient peoples adapted to their environments in order to survive. Explain some ways we adapt today.
3. How do strong central governments affect a nation's economic and social structures? What factors often lead to a weakening of central governments?

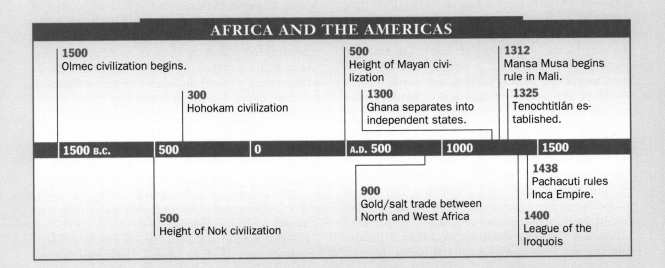

AFRICA AND THE AMERICAS

1500	Olmec civilization begins.
300	Hohokam civilization
500	Height of Mayan civilization
1300	Ghana separates into independent states.
1312	Mansa Musa begins rule in Mali.
1325	Tenochtitlán established.
1500 B.C. — 500 — 0 — A.D. 500 — 1000 — 1500	
500	Height of Nok civilization
900	Gold/salt trade between North and West Africa
1438	Pachacuti rules Inca Empire.
1400	League of the Iroquois

UNIT 3 SYNOPSIS

The period from A.D. 500 to 1500 was one of growth in many areas of the world. Expanded trade routes and missionaries' journeys spread intellectual, cultural, and religious beliefs from one people to another. Such contact between cultures caused conflict that lasted for decades, even centuries, but at other times, ideas and ideals were peacefully assimilated.

CHAPTER 9
Byzantines and Slavs

When the Roman Empire was divided in A.D. 395, the eastern half became known as the Byzantine Empire. One of the most advanced civilizations of its time, Byzantine culture blended Greek teachings, Christianity, and influences from eastern cultures. Emperor Justinian, seeking to restore the Roman Empire, reconquered lands that had been taken by Germanic invaders. He also created great architectural masterpieces in the capital city of Constantinople. But his greatest contribution to posterity was his revision of Roman law known as the Justinian Code.

Following its founding, the Byzantine Empire was repeatedly attacked. In A.D. 1054 after centuries of conflict, the Church, divided over papal rule, split into two separate bodies: the Roman Catholic Church in the west and the Eastern Orthodox Church in the east. The empire, weakened by this schism, was further pressured in the west by Christian Crusaders who had conquered part of Italy, and in the east by attacking Seljuk Turks.

Byzantine culture was spread north by traders and missionaries, who converted the Slavic peoples to Christianity. Schools, churches, and monasteries were constructed in towns and villages throughout the countryside, attracting many Christian converts. Kiev, a fortress-village on the Dnieper River, was first Lithuanian, second Polish, and finally Russian. In A.D. 911, Kiev made a trade agreement with the Byzantines, establishing the city as an important trade link between Europe and Asia. But in A.D. 1240, Kiev was destroyed by Mongol invaders in an invasion that isolated the eastern Slavs from western influence. The Mongols did, however, allow Russians to continue to practice their Christian religion and to govern themselves.

Mongols did not succeed in capturing the northern region called Muscovy or its capital, Moscow. Muscovy became the center of the Eastern Orthodox Church after Constantinople fell in A.D. 1453. The Russian tsar Ivan III, "The Great," proclaimed Russia the "Third Rome," the protector of the eastern church.

CHAPTER 10
Islam

While the Byzantine influence was spreading Christianity, another religion was emerging on the Arabian Peninsula. In A.D. 610 Muhammad, a businessman in Mecca, experienced a revelation from Allah (the Arabic name for God), and established a new religion called Islam. Muhammad's religion called for devotion to the one God, Allah, and preparation for the judgment day. Suffering persecution, Muhammad and his followers (known as Muslims) fled Mecca and settled in the town of Medina. Muhammad created an Islamic state in Medina, putting Islamic law above tribal law.

Muslims eventually conquered Mecca and extended their influence throughout the Arabian peninsula. The holy book of Islam, the Quran, relates the revelation of Allah to Muhammad. It outlines moral values and guidelines for daily life and presents the five pillars of Islam: faith, prayer, almsgiving, fasting, and pilgrimage to Mecca.

Islam spread through the efforts of caliphs, the successors of Muhammad. Their military expeditions carried Islam throughout the weakened Byzantine and Persian empires in conquests that were looked on as *jihads*, or holy wars.

While Islam's cultural influence widened abroad, it also suffered from internal strife. Following years of struggle, Islam split into two factions, the Sunnis and the Shiites.

The Umayyad dynasty (A.D. 661–750) ruled the Muslim world during a period of tremendous change. Umayyad conquerors carried Islam eastward to India and China, as well as to North Africa and Europe. The Umayyads were later overthrown by the Abbasids, who established the city of Baghdad.

Through all the profound modification in Islam's formative centuries, Muslim scholars preserved Greek philosophy and made advances in mathematics, astronomy, geometry, and medicine. Islamic art, architecture, and literature were also deeply influenced by religion. In later centuries western Europe would reflect all these advances.

Learning from Art *This is a French illuminated manuscript from the 1200s.* **Who created these works?**

CHAPTER 11
The Rise of Medieval Europe

Compared with the Byzantine and Islamic societies of this period, western European culture was extraordinarily backward. This period in western European history has, in fact, been referred to as the Dark Ages. Yet many forces were combining to create a new civilization in Europe.

Charlemagne, king of the Franks (843–877) and Holy Roman emperor (875–877), united most of Europe for the first time since the fall of Rome. Charlemagne also strengthened the ties between the pope and the monarchy. However, within 50 years of his death, Charlemagne's empire was destroyed by internal strife and external invasion.

The feudal system evolved in Europe as a means of protection against such invaders as Muslims and Vikings. Feudalism joined loyalty between lord and vassals to ownership of land and military service for mutual protection in an

age of conflict. Individual fiefs had their own political and legal rules but bore no fealty to and got no support from a central government. Because the fiefdoms and their knights spent much of their time warring among themselves, trade was limited. The manorial system, onto which feudalism was grafted, formed a self-sustaining unit. Each lord, in his castle on his manor, could in theory dispense with tradings.

The Church exerted strong influence, both religious and political, over daily life in the Middle Ages. In A.D. 520 a Roman Catholic monk named Benedict established the first monastery at Monte Cassino in Italy. Benedict's monks lived simply, prayed and meditated, and worked in the monastery. Although apart from society, they influenced it by preserving religious writings, establishing schools, and teaching various skills to peasants. Missionaries began spreading the Gospel throughout Europe.

Although medieval kings were generally weak rulers, William the Conqueror and his successors began to strengthen the English monarchy. In A.D. 1215 the Magna Carta, the great charter of English political and civil liberties, placed some limits on the king's growing power. A council called Parliament was formed to advise the monarch and pass laws. In France, too, the monarchy was strengthened under Philip II and his grandson, Louis IX. Louis's grandson, Philip IV, established the Estates-General.

While England and France were strengthening their monarchies, the Holy Roman Empire continued to struggle with the papacy. A compromise was reached at Worms, but power struggles between popes and emperors continued.

Chapter 12
Medieval Europe at Its Height

When the Seljuk Turks conquered Jerusalem, Christian pilgrimages were forbidden. The Byzantine emperor's call to Pope Urban II for help resulted in a series of Christian pilgrimages to the Holy Land known as crusades. In A.D. 1099 warriors of the First Crusade recaptured Jerusalem. Other crusades followed, but none were as successful as the first. The crusades did, however, open Europe to new ways of life.

Around A.D. 1000 the European economy began to revive. Innovations in agriculture increased food production. As trade expanded through annual fairs, a money economy was established. Towns soon grew up along trade routes. Merchants and artisans founded guilds to regulate commerce and protect their interests. Merchants' guilds could buy materials cheaply and keep prices up. Craft guilds set standards for membership, training, quality, and prices.

The money economy created a new wealthy middle class, the *bourgeoisie*. This class gained political power that led to the decline of the feudal system. They also influenced the growth of art, literature, and the universities. Intellectual movements such as scholasticism flourished.

The Hundred Years' War between England and France grew out of a feudal dispute over control of France. England won the major battles, including Crécy, Poitiers, and Agincourt, but in the end was driven out of France and off the Continent. After the long off-and-on war, the French monarchy was firmly established. King Louis XI strengthened the French bureaucracy and created a unified state in France. In Spain, Christians were engaged in reconquering lands taken by Muslim invaders, nearly all of today's Spain. Meanwhile, the Holy Roman Empire continued its struggle with the Church, which was experiencing its own problems.

The Babylonian Captivity, as it was called, during which French popes lived in France under the king's influence, weakened the Church. Later the Great Schism split the Church for 40 years, supporting a rival pope in Avignon and thus further undermining the authority of the pope in Rome.

Chapter 13
East and South Asia

The Tang dynasty ruled in China from A.D. 618 to 907. It expanded Chinese frontiers and created a stable government. Trade with Japan, India, and the Middle East increased, as well as overland trade to Syria along the "Silk Road." The Tang capital, Chang-an, became the largest city in the world. Later weakened by rebellion and invasion, the Tang Dynasty declined.

The Northern Song dynasty then came to power, and with it a golden age of achievement in the arts, literature, science, and technology. Confucianism continued to exert influence on the culture, resulting in social reforms. Great strides were made in economic growth as well as science and technology before China fell to Mongol hordes.

The Mongols established peace in China. Under their rule, trade increased with Europe, Arabia, and Russia. But by A.D. 1300, Mongol society had begun to decline.

China's influence extended to Vietnam and nearby Cambodia in southeast Asia, and to Korea and Japan to the northeast. The Koreans had been influenced by Chinese religion, government, and science. Japan, isolated from mainland Asia because of its island geography, developed traditions different from other Asian countries. Yet it too adopted certain Chinese customs.

Japan developed a feudal system of government that lasted 450 years. Samurai, or warrior landowners, similar to European knights, protected their lands from other samurai. Trade increased and towns were established, complete with guilds similar to those of medieval Europe.

Learning from Art   *The second emperor of the Tang dynasty, Tai Cong, ruled a Chinese empire that included Korea and central Asia.* **What reforms endeared him to his people?**

CHAPTER 14
Africa and the Americas

The vast African continent has varied geographic regions that have influenced the development of civilizations. In a land where rainfall is scarce, cultures grew up near lakes or rivers, such as the Nile. Trading cultures, like the people of Axum in eastern Africa, imported new ideas and religions along with goods. Movement of people, such as the Bantu migrations, spread culture to other areas in Africa. Family traditions and customs were built around religious beliefs in many African villages.

Ghana was one of the wealthiest nations, trading its own rich resource of gold for salt brought by Muslim traders. Mali, a nation that broke away from Ghana, also became a powerful kingdom. Its Muslim king, Mansa Musa, created a rich trading empire through his contacts with Muslims. Islamic culture spread throughout Africa—an example of cultural diffusion.

The earliest inhabitants on the North American continent came from Asia by way of the Beringia land bridge. They eventually set-

tled as far as the southern tip of South America. As in Africa, geography and climate determined the way of life for various cultures.

Central and South American cultures were more advanced than those in North America. The creation of centralized governments enabled sophisticated civilizations to flourish. Religion also played a large part in the Mayan and Aztec cultures in Mexico. The Mayans developed an understanding of science and mathematics and created calendars to calculate the agricultural cycles of planting and harvesting. The Inca of South America unified their culture with a strong central government and an official business language.

SURVEYING THE UNIT

1. **Making Comparisons** Compare the development of civilizations in Africa with those in North and South America. How did geography and climate affect the people?

2. **Relating Ideas** How did the spread of Christianity affect various cultures?

3. **Analyzing Trends** Why was trade so important to medieval Europe?

UNIT 3 REVIEW

REVIEWING THE MAIN IDEAS

1. **Identify:** What were some of the major forces that helped shape civilizations in western European countries during the Middle Ages? What effect did these forces have on politics, society, and economics?
2. **Explain:** What brought about the Crusades, and how did they affect Western European history?
3. **Describe:** Why was Confucianism so important to Chinese civilization?
4. **List:** Name the various cultures of South America, and their geographic locations.

THINKING CRITICALLY

1. **Apply:** How did European monarchies change during the Middle Ages? Explain the consequences of this change. How did this growth affect culture, religion, and politics in European societies?
2. **Analyze:** Compare the growth of civilizations in North America and South America. What were the consequences of this growth?
3. **Synthesize:** Imagine you are the curator of a Chinese museum. What objects might you collect that would tell the story of the growth of Chinese civilization? Explain your choices.
4. **Compare:** How does Islam's expansion through the centuries compare with that of Christianity? How does the expansion of these religions compare today? What is the extent of their influence today?

A GLOBAL PERSPECTIVE

Refer to the time line on page 210–211 to answer these questions.

1. How long after the Islamic year 1 did the crusades begin?
2. How many years after the start of the crusades did the Black Death begin?

3. How long after the Magna Carta was signed did Marco Polo start his travels in China?
4. How many years elapsed between China's invention of block printing and the advent of the Gutenberg Bible?
5. How soon after Justinian became Byzantine emperor did Arabs perfect the astrolab?
6. How long after Muhammed left Mecca did the Northern Song Dynasty begin in China?

LINKING PAST AND PRESENT

1. Compare the conflicts between Islam and Christianity today with those during medieval times. Make a list of the similarities and the differences.
2. The growth of trade completely changed the world of the Middle Ages. It encouraged the growth of towns and the exchange of goods and ideas. What evidence is there that trade is as important today?
3. What evidence can be seen today of the Byzantine Empire's effect on history? How has Byzantine influence affected everyday life?

ANALYZING VISUALS

The mosaic of the Byzantine emperor Justinian, shown on page 359, dates from the A.D. 500s and is in the church of San Vitale in Ravenna, Italy. During Justinian's reign, Ravenna was the Byzantine emperor's most important center in Italy. Accompanied by officials and members of the clergy, Justinian appears as though taking part in a church procession. He wears a purple robe, indicating his imperial status. Since antiquity, the color purple had been associated with royalty. Known as Tyrian purple, true purple dye was extracted from shellfish in the eastern Mediterranean at great expense. Justinian is depicted with both a halo and a crown, indicating his authority over both church and state.

A Byzantine mosaic of Emperor Justinian in the church of San Vitale in Ravenna, Italy.

1. Which elements of this mosaic tell you that Justinian is the most important figure in the procession?
2. You learned about Justinian's interest in the arts when you read about the church of Hagia Sophia in Constantinople. How does this mosaic in Ravenna further reflect that interest?
3. In the Byzantine Empire, Justinian had authority over both church and state. In the United States, there is a separation of church and state. Make a chart that describes the advantages and disadvantages of these different forms of government.

USING LITERATURE

1. What mood does the poem "Taking Leave of a Friend" bring to mind? Make a list of the words and the images that create this mood.
2. What does the sunset represent in this poem?
3. Why does the moon in "On Quiet Night" make the speaker think of his home? Explain your answer.
4. Choose a person or group of people from the unit who might identify with these two poems.

WRITING ABOUT HISTORY

1. Compare the attitudes of the Buddhist, Christian, and Muslim religions toward monotheism. How did the change from polytheism to Monotheism affect each of these societies? Make a list for each religion. Have attitudes changed?
2. You are an archaeologist exploring the ruins of an ancient North or South American civilization. Choose one of the cultures described in Chapter 14, and write a report on the results of your "dig." What artifacts did you discover? What do they tell you about the people of the culture? How were these artifacts used? Describe the typical daily life in the culture and the significance of the artifacts to that culture.
3. Choose a trade from medieval times that is still being practiced today (such as shoemaker, silversmith, baker). Research the modern version of the trade and report on (1) how one learns the trade, (2) what organizations represent or influence the trade, and (3) how the product is marketed today. How is the trade both different from and similar to its medieval counterpart? Is it possible that current or developing technology will change this trade?

UNIT 4

Emergence of the Modern World

1400–1800

"I have taken all knowledge to be my province."

Chapter 15
Renaissance and Reformation

Chapter 16
Exploration and Empire

Chapter 17
Royal Power and Conflict

Chapter 18
Empires of Asia

So wrote the English philosopher Francis Bacon, expressing the spirit of the age in which Europeans took first steps into the modern world. Renaissance artists proclaimed the glories of the human spirit. Voyagers set out on uncharted seas. A humble monk boldly challenged the power of the Church. Reigning over this age were the greatest monarchs Europe had ever known. As Europeans explored, traded, and exerted influence around the world, civilizations in Asia reached pinnacles of cultural achievement.

A GLOBAL CHRONOLOGY

	1400	1480	1560
Political Sphere	**1469** Lorenzo de' Medici begins rule of Florence.		**1581** Dutch rebels fight for independence from Spain.
Scientific Sphere	**1492** Columbus reaches the Bahamas.		
Cultural & Social Sphere	**1517** Martin Luther nails the 95 Theses to the door of the Wittenberg Church.		**1600** English East India Company established.

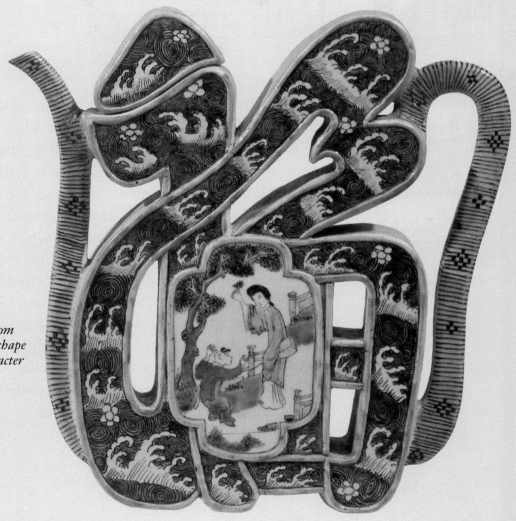

A wine pitcher from the 1600s in the shape of a Chinese character

1640	1720	1800
1642 Beginning of English Civil War	**1763** Peace of Paris ends the Seven Years' War.	**1795** Russia, Prussia, and Austria divide Poland among themselves.
1717 Lady Mary Wortley Montagu introduces inoculation against smallpox.		
1608 First checks used to replace cash in Netherlands.		**1764** Mozart writes his first symphony at age eight.

Renaissance and Reformation

*I*sabella d'Este, married in 1490 at the age of 16 to the Marquis of Mantua, played a vital role in ruling the Italian city-state of Mantua. A brilliant and well-educated young woman who loved Latin literature, Isabella gathered a fashionable assemblage of artists and statesmen in her sparkling court. In a room decorated with ornately carved woodwork and paintings that illustrated Greek myths, Isabella entertained her guests to her own lute recitals and poetry readings. Isabella was one of the many Italians of her time who rediscovered and repopularized Greek and Roman classics, educating their contemporaries to the glories of their classical past after a thousand years of neglect. The word *Renaissance*, coming from the French word meaning "rebirth," was coined to refer to this rebirth of interest in classical ideas and culture.

CHAPTER PREVIEW

Key Terms to Define: humanism, sonnet, doge, justification by faith, indulgence, vocation, predestination, seminary, baroque

People to Meet: Lorenzo de' Medici, Machiavelli, Pope Leo X, Leonardo da Vinci, Michelangelo, Montaigne, Erasmus, Martin Luther, John Calvin, King Henry VIII, Ignatius Loyola

Places to Discover: Florence, Rome, Venice, Zurich, Geneva, Trent

Objectives to Learn:
1. What inspired the Renaissance?
2. How did the Renaissance reach northern Europe?
3. How did Luther's religious reforms lead to Protestantism?
4. How and why did the Church of England separate from Rome?

This painting depicts a banquet during the early Renaissance.

5. How did the Catholic Church try to halt the spread of Protestantism?

Concepts to Understand:
- Innovation—The Renaissance leads to an artistic and intellectual awakening in Europe. Section 1
- Cultural diffusion—Renaissance ideas and artistic styles spread from Italy to northern Europe. Section 2
- Conflict—Martin Luther's protests against the Catholic Church result in Protestantism. Section 3
- Cultural diffusion—Other reformers in Europe separate from the Catholic Church. Section 4
- Reaction—The Catholic Church enacts its own reform, the Catholic Reformation. Section 5

The Italian Renaissance

The Renaissance—that period from about 1350 until 1600 during which western Europeans experienced a profound cultural awakening—was in many ways a continuation of the Middle Ages, but it also signaled the beginning of modern times. The Renaissance caused educated Europeans to develop new attitudes about themselves and the world around them.

The Renaissance first began in the city-states of Italy. Unlike other areas of Europe, Italy had largely avoided the economic crisis of the late Middle Ages. Italian towns remained important centers of Mediterranean trade and boosted their production of textiles and luxury goods.

More than other Europeans, Italians were attached to classical traditions. The ruins of ancient Roman buildings, arches, and amphitheaters constantly reminded them of their heritage. In addition, through trade, Italian towns remained in close contact with the Byzantine Empire, where scholars preserved the learning of ancient Greece.

Humanism

As newly discovered works came to their attention, Italian scholars developed a strong interest in classical writings. This interest in the classics was called **humanism.** Humanists—the scholars who promoted humanism—improved their understanding of Greek and Latin, studied old manuscripts, and tried to copy the classical writing style.

As they studied, humanists came to admire classical culture but also adopted many Greek and Roman beliefs. For example, humanists found the classical idea of seeking fulfillment in daily life more appealing than the medieval belief that people should expect little comfort from life on earth. Humanists also embraced the Greco-Roman belief that each individual has dignity and worth. Humanists also renewed the Greek idea of an ideal person—one who participates in a variety of activities: politics, sports, art, literature, and music.

To help others gain fulfillment and achieve the Greek ideal, humanists opened schools to teach subjects related to the study of humanity—history, philosophy, Latin, and Greek. These schools soon became so popular that humanists began to replace the clergy as teachers of the sons of wealthy merchants and artisans.

Humanism also inspired new forms of writing—in particular, writing about the daily life and feelings of people. Among the most noted works of humanist Francesco Petrarca, or Petrarch, were 36 **sonnets,** or short poems, that express his love for a woman named Laura who had died during the Black Death. Benvenuto Cellini (chuh LEE nee), a goldsmith and sculptor by trade, wrote the first modern autobiography. He encouraged anyone who had done anything of excellence "to describe their life with their own hand," as he had.

Another literary achievement was in political science. In the early 1500s, Florentine diplomat Niccolò Machiavelli (mak ee uh VEHL ee) wrote *The Prince*, a treatise in which he analyzed the politics of Renaissance Italy. Although embraced by power-hungry rulers, the book was attacked by many for the methods Machiavelli advocated. In his analysis he advised rulers to be prepared to use force and deceit to maintain power.

Humanism affected literature in another significant respect. Some humanists broke free of the tradition of writing in Latin, the language of the clergy. By writing in the language of everyday speech, humanists provided literature that was accessible to more people and inspired civic pride in those who read it.

Humanist scholars influenced more than just literature. With their independent thinking, they began to challenge long-accepted traditions, assumptions, and institutions. As they made all sorts of unsettling discoveries, it further validated their desire to challenge and question just about everything—even Church traditions. For example, in an exciting piece of Renaissance detective work, Lorenzo Valla determined that a document that supposedly provided the legal basis for the pope's supremacy over kings was actually a forgery.

Through their teaching and writing—and by their example—humanists reawakened the educated public to classical culture and values. They also encouraged a ferment of new ideas that eventually spread throughout Europe and reshaped its civilization.

City Life

Town life was stronger in Italy than in other parts of Europe. As a result, Italians could easily discard feudalism and other medieval institutions that had their origins in the rural north. Italy did not become unified as did France and England. Wealthy and successful, most Italian communes resisted the efforts of emperors, kings, and nobles to control them. They became independent city-states, each of which included a walled urban center and the surrounding countryside.

Social Groups The Italian city-states fashioned a new social order in which wealth and ability mattered more than aristocratic titles and ownership of land. Wealthy merchants and bankers replaced the landed nobility as the most powerful social and political group—the upper class. Shopkeepers and artisans ranked below the wealthy merchants, forming a moderately prosperous middle class that employed large numbers of poor workers. Most of these workers—who were the majority of town dwellers—came to urban areas from the countryside. At the bottom of the social order were the peasants who worked on the country estates of the upper class.

RENAISSANCE ITALY 1400s

Learning from Maps *Notice the locations of the Italian city-states during the 1400s.* **Which city-state was in the best position to trade by land as well as by sea with the Byzantine Empire to the east?**

Government During the Renaissance, Italy was not under one government, but consisted of individual city-states, each ruled by a wealthy family whose fortunes came from commercial trading or banking. Peasants often rebelled against the upper classes. Their demands for equal rights and lower taxes, however, were suppressed.

During the 1400s, social conflicts created upheaval so often that certain city-states felt it necessary to turn over all political authority to a single powerful leader to restore peace. These powerful political leaders were called *signori* (seen YOHR ee). Some *signori* ruled as dictators, using violence to maintain control. Others won popular loyalty by improving city services, supporting the arts, and providing festivals and parades for the lower classes.

While dealing with internal unrest, city-states also fought with each other in territorial disputes. But the prosperous merchants and bankers, unlike the nobility they had supplanted, did not want to fight in these battles. Since military service would interfere with conducting business and trade, the signori replaced citizen-soldiers with hired soldiers known as *condottieri* (kahn duh TYEHR ee).

Hiring *condottieri* made wars very costly. To avoid this expense, *signori* began to seek territorial gain through negotiated agreements. To carry out this policy, they assembled the first modern diplomatic services. Permanent ambassadors were appointed to represent their city-states at foreign courts. The city-states also worked out an agreement among all the city-states that no one city-state would be allowed enough power to threaten the others. During the 1500s, other European states adopted similar agreements with one another and also began to practice diplomacy.

Although the Italian city-states had much in common, each developed its own individual life. Three cities in particular played leading roles in the Renaissance: Florence, Rome, and Venice.

Florence   Originally a republic, Florence in the 1400s came under the rule of a prominent banking family known as the Medici (MEHD uh chee). Medici rulers helped to foster the spirit of humanism among the city-state's scholars and artists. With this spirit alive throughout the city, Florence became the birthplace of the Italian Renaissance.

Cosimo de' Medici was the first Medici to rule Florence. He worked to end peasant uprisings by introducing an income tax that placed a heavier burden on wealthier citizens. He used the tax revenues to make city improvements, such as sewers and paved streets, that benefited everyone. Cosimo also worked to establish peaceful relations between the city and its neighbors.

Cosimo's grandson Lorenzo ruled Florence from 1469 to 1492, and he continued policies like those of his grandfather. He used his wealth to support artists, philosophers, and writers and to sponsor public festivals. As a result of the city's prosperity and fame, Lorenzo was known as "the Magnificent."

During the 1490s, Florence's economic prosperity, based mostly on the banking and textile industries, began to decline with increasing competition from English and Flemish clothmakers. Tired of the Medici rule, discontented citizens rallied in support of a Dominican friar named Girolamo Savonarola. In fiery sermons before hundreds of people, Savonarola attacked the Medici for promoting ideas that he claimed were causing the downfall of Florence:

In the mansions of the great prelates and great lords there is no concern save for poetry and the oratorical art. Go . . . and see; [you] shall find them all with books of the humanities in their hands. . . . Arise and come to deliver [your] Church from the hands of the devils!

So many people were won over by Savonarola that the Medici family was forced to turn over the rule of Florence to his supporters. On Savonarola's advice, the city's new leaders imposed strict regulations on public behavior. Parties, gambling, swearing, and horse racing were banned. Savonarola had crowds make bonfires to burn paintings, fancy clothes, and musical instruments.

Savonarola soon aroused a great deal of opposition. His criticism of Church officials angered the pope. Many people in Florence disliked his strict ways. In 1498 Savonarola was hanged for heresy, and the Medici family returned to power. By this time, however, Florence's greatness had passed.

Rome   By 1500 Rome had replaced Florence as the leading Renaissance city. In Rome, the pope and the cardinals living in the Vatican made up the wealthiest and most powerful class.

Eager to increase their prestige, Renaissance popes rebuilt the ancient city. They commissioned architects to construct ornate churches and palaces. They had artists create magnificent paintings and sculptures glorifying religious themes to decorate these buildings. One of their most notable projects was rebuilding St. Peter's Basilica, the largest Christian church in the world. They amassed so many manuscripts and books in the Vatican Library that it attracted scholars from all over Europe.

Renaissance popes lived and behaved more like signori than religious leaders. They often

Learning from Photographs *Filippo Brunelleschi's dome for the cathedral of Florence was probably the greatest engineering feat of the Renaissance period. The dome still dominates the skyline of Florence, rising over the cathedral's bell tower and the spire of the town hall clock.* **Under which ruler did Florence become a famous center of art and learning?**

overlooked their religious duties to handle political affairs. They relied on political ambassadors to direct negotiations between their city-state and other city-states in Italy. The popes also collected taxes. In fact, the fortunes they spent on architecture and arts were financed mostly by taxes.

Many Renaissance popes were greedy and corrupt. Pope Alexander VI was elected to office in 1492 because he bribed the College of Cardinals to vote for him. Once in office, he used the Church's wealth to support his family, the Borgias. Other popes spent lavishly on entertainment. In the early 1500s, Pope Leo X had his forests and ponds stocked with exotic animals so that he could entertain thousands of hunters for weeks. In an even greater display of wealth, he had his servants ceremoniously toss out his dinner guests' silver plates after each course.

Although Rome possessed enormous wealth and beauty, by the late 1500s the city of Venice in northeastern Italy rivaled it. Furthermore, as Venetian wealth and power grew, so too did its power to lure artists and scholars away from Rome. By the late 1500s the focus of the Italian Renaissance had shifted from Rome to Venice.

Venice   Perched on a hundred islands at the north end of the Adriatic Sea, Venice was ideally situated to maintain a trade monopoly with Asia.

Because it served as the link between western Europe and Asia, this bustling port city also attracted traders from all over the world. These advantages made Venice the wealthiest and most powerful city-state in Italy during the late Renaissance. At the height of its power, Venice stretched from the Adriatic Sea in the east to Milan in the west.

A tremendous variety of cultures converged in Venice, each making its unique contribution to art and architecture. For example, the Cathedral of St. Mark possessed the intricate mosaics and domed architecture characteristic of the Byzantine Empire while the palace of the **doge** (dohj), or ruling duke, was a reflection of European Gothic architecture.

Unlike Florence and Rome, Venice had a republican form of government headed by the elected doge. Although the doge administered the city, the wealthiest merchants held the real power. In fact, by law the doge could not answer important political correspondence or speak to foreign envoys unless an executive committee of wealthy merchants known as the Council of Ten was present. This council passed laws, elected the doge, and even had to be consulted should the doge's son want to marry.

The city's merchants collected money on all products that passed through their port. And, because Venice teemed with commercial activity, this income kept them rich enough to afford *palazzos*, or palaces, overlooking the Grand Canal and luxuries such as Flemish tapestries to hang on their walls.

Meanwhile, Venice's reputation as the jewel of the Renaissance was growing. Shipyards grew famous producing huge galleys and graceful gondolas. Venetian printing houses earned a solid reputation for publishing works of high quality, and paintings by Venetian artists came to be in great demand.

Artistic Achievements

What were the unique characteristics of Renaissance art? The humanists' emphasis on cultivating individual talent inspired Italian artists to express their own values, emotions, and attitudes. No longer content with creating symbolic representations of their subjects, artists made their subjects as lifelike and captivating as possible. Although much of the art was still devoted to religious subjects, it had more secular, or worldly, overtones. Interest in ancient Greece and Rome moved artists to include classical mythology as well as biblical themes in their works.

To make their creations lifelike and captivating, artists experimented with new techniques. For example, they learned to create a sense of perspective, which gave their paintings depth.

They studied anatomy so they could portray human figures more accurately and naturally. They also learned to depict subtleties of gesture and expression to convey human emotions.

The public in Renaissance Italy appreciated works of art and hailed great artists as geniuses. Nobles and townspeople used art to decorate homes as well as churches. They lavishly rewarded artists and gave them a prominent place in society.

Architecture   During the Middle Ages, cathedral architects had pointed soaring arches and spires heavenward for the glory of God. During the Renaissance, however, Italian architects returned to the classical style. On churches, palaces, and villas they substituted domes and columns from classical Greek and Roman architecture for the medieval arches and spires. They sought both comfort and beauty in their buildings, adorning them with tapestries, paintings, statues, finely made furniture, and glass windows. Unlike the anonymous architects of the Middle Ages, Renaissance architects took credit for their fine buildings.

The most famous Italian Renaissance architect was Filippo Brunelleschi (broon uhl EHS kee), best known for the dome he designed and completed in 1436 for the Cathedral of Florence. Until Brunelleschi submitted his design, no one had been able to come up with a way to construct a dome large or strong enough to

Learning from Art
Masaccio's painting of Jesus and his disciples, Tribute Money, *looks like a scene from real life.* **What techniques did Masaccio use to help give this painted scene depth?**

Learning from Art *Michelangelo carved human expression and physical detail into this statue of Moses.* **In what city did Michelangelo begin his career and under whose patronage?**

cover the cathedral without the dome collapsing from its own weight. Brunelleschi's design—based on his own study of the domes, columns, and arches of ancient Rome—was considered to be the greatest engineering feat of the time.

Sculpture Renaissance sculpture reflected a return to classical ideals. In fact, the free-standing statues of nude figures sculpted in bronze or marble during the Renaissance resembled ancient Greek and Roman sculptures of nude figures more than they did medieval sculptures. Human figures in medieval sculptures had usually been portrayed only as they appeared when clothed—in a stiff, stylized manner.

Some of the best-known Renaissance sculptors—Donatello, Michelangelo, and Ghiberti—came from Florence. There the Medici family opened a school for sculptors. Donatello was the first sculptor since ancient times to cast a statue in bronze. Although the brilliant sculptor Michelangelo Buonarroti later moved to Rome to sculpt works for the pope, he learned his craft in Florence. Florentine sculptor Lorenzo Ghiberti took 21 years to create 10 magnificent New Testament scenes on bronze doors for Florence's cathedral baptistry.

Painting Italian Renaissance painters departed from the flat, symbolic style of medieval painting to begin a more realistic style. This change first appeared in the early 1300s when the Florentine artist-sculptor-architect Giotto effectively captured human emotions in a series of frescoes portraying the life of Francis of Assisi. In the 1400s Florentine artist Masaccio (muh SAH chee oh) employed lighting and perspective in his paintings to give depth to the human body and to set off his figures from the background. He thus created an even greater sense of realism than Giotto had.

One of the greatest Renaissance artists was Leonardo da Vinci (VIHN chee). A citizen of Florence, he did much of his work in Milan and Rome. Da Vinci is best known for the Mona Lisa, a portrait of a strangely smiling young woman of Florence, and the *Last Supper*, a wall painting of Jesus' last meal with his disciples. In both works, da Vinci skillfully portrayed the subjects' personalities, thoughts, and feelings.

Leonardo da Vinci was also a scientist. He wrote books on astronomy, mathematics, and anatomy. His illustrations of inventions—far ahead of his time—included designs for parachutes, flying machines, mechanical diggers, and artillery.

Another outstanding Renaissance artist—Michelangelo Buonarroti—began his career as a sculptor in Florence. There he did a famous marble statue of David, after the heroic biblical king. Later, in Rome he sculpted *La Pietà*, which shows the dead Jesus in the arms of his mother, Mary. Most of Michelangelo's sculptures were awesome in size and suggested controlled but intense emotions.

In 1505 Pope Julius II hired Michelangelo to work at the Vatican, painting the ceiling of the Sistine Chapel with scenes from the Bible. The Renaissance biographer Giorgio Vasari described the completion of Michelangelo's masterwork: "When the work was thrown open, the whole world came running to see what Michelangelo had done; and certainly it was

Renaissance Sculpture

During the Middle Ages, most sculpture was placed in the architectural framework of either a castle or a church. During the Renaissance, artists in the Italian city-states began to create lifelike sculpted monuments that were freestanding, intending them to be viewed from all angles. They chose this style partly because of a renewed appreciation for the classical sculptures typical of ancient Greek and Roman artists.

Equestrian statues—that is, statues depicting a person on horseback—were a Renaissance innovation in the creation of these freestanding sculptures. The bronze equestrian monument to Venetian military commander and condottiere Bartolomeo Colleoni shown here is a superb example of Renaissance sculpture.

In his will, Colleoni left a fortune to the Republic of Venice and requested that city officials commission a sculpture to honor him and his military exploits on behalf of the city. According to the diary of a monk who was traveling in Venice at the time, at least three artists exhibited models of equestrian statues to compete for the city's commission. Florentine sculptor Andrea del Verrocchio (vuh RAWK ee oh) won the commission, creating the sculpture seen here which stands in one of Venice's many piazzas, or squares.

Although Verrocchio is probably best remembered as one of Leonardo da Vinci's teachers, he was an accomplished artist, having created magnificent works of art such as this equestrian monument. Here Verrocchio depicts Bartolomeo Colleoni's powerful horse stepping forward with its head turned and muscles straining while Colleoni stands straight and masterful in the stirrups. In skillfully emphasizing these precise details, Verrocchio imparts to his sculpture an almost frightening and overwhelming power. Verrocchio further intensifies the power and drama by portraying in the expression on Colleoni's face the tension and excitement of a general riding into battle.

Responding to the Arts

1. In what ways was the sculpture of Renaissance Italy different from the sculpture of the Middle Ages?
2. What specific aspects of Verrocchio's equestrian monument to Colleoni convey a sense of Colleoni's personality?

Learning from Art
Michelangelo painted figures such as St. Zacharias on the ceiling of the Sistine Chapel while lying on his back on scaffolding raised 70 feet (21 meters) above the floor. In this position he was unable to step back periodically to view his work as most artists need to do in order to see the broader effect of their painting. **How does Michelangelo's art compare with that of the ancient Greeks?**

such as to make everyone speechless with astonishment."

All of Michelangelo's painted figures resembled sculptures. They had well-formed muscular bodies that expressed vitality and power. Michelangelo ended his career by designing the dome of the new Saint Peter's Basilica.

The Renaissance produced many other artists who overwhelmed the world with their fabulous works. The period's great outpouring of creative genius could not be contained within Italy's boundaries. The ideas of the Renaissance soon filtered northward into France, England, and the Netherlands.

SECTION 1 REVIEW

Recall

1. **Define:** humanism, sonnet, doge
2. **Identify:** Machiavelli, Lorenzo de' Medici, Savonarola, Leonardo da Vinci, Michelangelo
3. **Locate:** Find Florence, Rome, and Venice on the map on page 365. How did Venice's location affect its affluence?

Critical Thinking

4. **Analyze:** Think about the Greek concept of what constitutes an ideal person. Do you think Leonardo da Vinci was such a person? Why or why not?
5. **Synthesize:** Imagine you were present to hear one of Savonarola's sermons. How might you have reacted?

Applying Concepts

6. **Innovation:** Identify one thing in literature or art (painting, sculpture, or architecture) that was developed during the Renaissance, and explain how it was an innovative elaboration on some aspect of Greek or Roman culture rather than just an imitation.

SECTION 2

The Northern Renaissance

During the late 1400s, Renaissance art and humanist ideas—characterized by a revival of interest in classical antiquity—began to filter northward from Italy to France, England, the Netherlands, and other European countries. War, trade, travel, and a newly invented method of printing helped to promote the cultural diffusion. The people of the Northern Renaissance adapted ideas of the Italian Renaissance to their own individual tastes, values, and needs.

Spreading Ideas

War, as usual, helped disseminate ideas by furthering contact between people of different cultures. When France invaded Italy in 1494, for example, King Francis I and his warrior-nobles became fascinated by Italian Renaissance art and fashions. They brought Leonardo da Vinci and other Italian artists and scholars to their court in France, thus promoting the entry of Renaissance ideas into northern Europe.

IMAGES OF THE TIME

Life in Northern Europe

During the Renaissance, society began placing greater emphasis on the importance of the individual. In northern Europe, this emphasis was reflected in various forms.

Each panel of this object shows a drawing that can be read straight or upside down, showing a different face each way. It shows off the artist's cleverness.

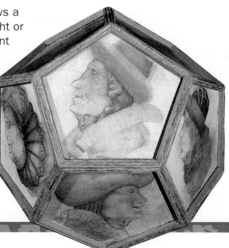

In this self-portrait, the German artist Albrecht Dürer painted himself wearing the clothes typical of a refined gentleman in 1498—unlike the traditional view of painters as lower-class craftsmen.

Other monarchs soon followed suit. In fact, kings and queens so eagerly supported scholars and artists that the number of humanists in the north grew rapidly. And, as they proliferated, so too did the popularity of humanist ideas.

At the same time, Italian traders living in the north set an example for northern European merchants, who began to appreciate wealth, beauty, personal improvement, and other Renaissance values. These northern merchants—having only recently become successful enough to afford life-styles based upon such values—began to spend their wealth on education, fine houses, and material goods. Some northerners began travel to Italy to study with Italian masters. Thus began the emergence of a privileged and newly educated middle class.

This spread of knowledge among the middle class was aided by the invention of the printing press. About 1440 a German metalworker named Johannes Gutenberg discovered a revolutionary printing technique using movable metal type. As a result, books were published more quickly and less expensively. Production of humanist texts could now begin to match the newfound desire for such works.

Although Italian Renaissance ideas became quite popular in the north, they were not merely transplanted there. Rather, northern scholars interpreted them according to their own individual styles of thought. Furthermore, the people of each northern culture adapted them slightly to suit their own needs and traditions.

The French Renaissance

The French Renaissance had a character all its own. French architects blended medieval Gothic towers and windows with the classical

Peter Brueghel the Elder painted many scenes of peasant life, like *The Peasant Wedding*. Much of his work portrays daily life of the lower class.

Reflecting on the Times How do the subjects of these images show the new importance placed on the individual in Northern Europe?

Learning from Photographs *French architects blended elements of classical and Gothic architecture to create châteaus such as this one at Chambord.* **Where did the French erect most of these châteaux?**

columns used by Italian architects to create châteaux (sha TOZ), or castles, for Francis I and his nobles. These large country estates were erected primarily in the Loire River Valley. The château of Chambord is a fine example.

Many French Renaissance writers, on the other hand, borrowed extensively from the new literary forms of the Italian Renaissance. Inspired by Petrarch's sonnets, Pierre Ronsard wrote his own sonnets with common humanist themes such as love, the passing of youth, and the poet's immortality. Michel de Montaigne (mahn TAYN) may have modeled his informal and direct style on Italian autobiography. He cultivated the literary form called the personal essay, a short prose composition written to express clearly the personal view of a writer on a subject. In his essay "Of the Disadvantages of Greatness," Montaigne analyzed the authority of royalty:

> *The most difficult occupation in the world, in my opinion, is to play the part of a king worthily. I excuse more of their faults than people commonly do, in consideration of the dreadful weight of their burden, which dazes me. It is difficult for a power so immoderate to observe moderation . . .*

Physician-monk François Rabelais (RAB uh lay), France's most popular Renaissance author, wrote comic tales, satires, and parodies on a broad spectrum of contemporary life. Exceptionally knowledgeable and gifted as a writer, he also wrote on such subjects as law, medicine, politics, theology, botany, and navigation.

Northern Europe

The Italian Renaissance was enthusiastically accepted by the wealthy towns of Germany and the Low Countries (today, Belgium, Luxembourg, and the Netherlands). Universities and schools promoted humanist learning, and printers produced a large quantity of books. Latin was still the main scholarly language, but writers increased their use of German and Dutch.

Christian Humanism   Unlike in Italy, the Renaissance in northern Europe had a more religious tone. Groups of scholars, known as Christian humanists, wanted reforms in Catholicism that would eliminate abuses and restore the simple piety of the early Church. They believed that humanist learning and Bible study were the best ways to promote these goals.

The most famous Christian humanist, Erasmus of Rotterdam, inspired his colleagues to study Greek and Hebrew so that they could understand older versions of the Bible written in these languages. Erasmus also prompted people to take a more critical view of the Catholic Church. He specifically attacked the extravagance of Renaissance popes. In his noted work, *In Praise of Folly*, he describes these popes, claiming that they were so corrupt they no longer practiced Christianity.

> *Scarce any kind of men live more* [devoted to pleasure] *or with less trouble. . . . To work miracles is . . . not in fashion now; to instruct the people, troublesome; to interpret the Scripture,* [too bookish]; *to pray, a sign one has little else to do . . . and lastly, to die, uncouth; and to be stretched on a cross, infamous.*

Northern European Painters   Artists in northern Europe developed a style of painting that relied more on medieval than classical models. In the early 1400s, a group of Flemish painters, led by the brothers Jan and Hubert van Eyck (eyek), painted scenes from the Bible and daily life in sharp, realistic detail. They developed the technique of painting in oils. Oils provided artists with richer colors and allowed them to make changes on the painted canvas. Painting in oils soon spread to Italy. Meanwhile, Italian Renaissance art reached northern Europe. Dutch artists such as Peter Brueghel (BROY guhl) combined Italian technique with the artistic traditions of their homeland. They began painting realistic portraits, landscapes, and scenes of peasant life.

The English Renaissance

Renaissance ideas did not spread to England until 1485, when the Wars of the Roses—bloody conflicts over who was the rightful heir to the throne—ended. Ultimately, the Tudor family defeated the York family, bringing the Tudor king Henry VII to power. Henry invited Italian Renaissance scholars to England, where they taught humanist ideas and encouraged the study of classical texts.

English humanists expressed deep interest in social issues. Thomas More, a statesman and a friend of Erasmus, wrote a book that criticized the society of his day by comparing it with an ideal society in which all citizens are equal and prosperous. The book, written in Latin, was called *Utopia*.

The English Renaissance was especially known for drama. The best-known English playwrights were William Shakespeare and Christopher Marlowe. They drew ideas for their works from medieval legends, classical mythology, and the histories of England, Denmark, and ancient Rome. Shakespeare dealt with universal human qualities such as jealousy, ambition, love, and despair so effectively that his plays are still relevant to audiences today.

SECTION 2 REVIEW

Recall
1. **Identify** François Rabelais, Michel de Montaigne, Erasmus, Peter Brueghel, Jan Van Eyck, King Henry VII, Thomas More, William Shakespeare
2. **Explain:** How did the spread of Renaissance ideas from Italy change ways of thinking and living in northern Europe?
3. **Describe:** What were some elements of Italian Renaissance architecture that French architects incorporated? Describe the features of French Renaissance architecture.

Critical Thinking
4. **Analyze:** How did the Renaissance in northern Europe differ from the Renaissance in Italy?
5. **Apply:** Choose one writer or artist from the northern Renaissance and explain how the works of this writer or artist exemplified Renaissance ideas.

Applying Concepts
6. **Cultural diffusion:** How did Italian Renaissance ideas and fashions spread to northern Europe?

The Protestant Reformation

The Renaissance values of humanism and secularism stimulated widespread criticism of the Catholic Church's extravagance. By about 1500, educated Europeans began calling for a reformation—that is, a change in the Church's ways of teaching and practicing Christianity. In Germany the movement for church reform eventually led to a split in the Church that produced a new form of Christianity known as Protestantism. The series of events that gave birth to Protestantism is known as the Protestant Reformation.

Martin Luther

The Protestant Reformation was begun by a German named Martin Luther, born in 1483, the son of peasants. His father wanted him to become a lawyer, but Luther was interested in religion. In 1505, he was nearly struck by lightning in a thunderstorm. Terrified that the storm was God's way of punishing him, the law student knelt and prayed to Saint Anne. In return for protection, he promised to become a monk. Shortly thereafter, Luther entered a monastery.

As a young monk, Luther struggled to ensure his soul's salvation. He would confess his sins for hours at a time. But still he worried that God might not find him acceptable.

Then he read Saint Paul's Epistle to the Romans: "He who through faith is righteous shall live"—and Luther's worries dissolved. He interpreted this to mean that a person could be made just, or good, simply by faith in God. Luther's idea became known as **justification by faith.**

Protesting Against Church Abuses
While Luther was shaping his new ideas, Pope Leo X was trying to raise money to rebuild St. Peter's Basilica in Rome. To this end, the pope sold church offices, or positions, to his friends and also authorized sales of **indulgences.**

Indulgences were certificates issued by the pope that were said to reduce or even cancel punishment for a person's sins—as long as one also truly repented. People purchased indulgences believing that the document would assure them admission to heaven. John Tetzel, the Church's agent for selling indulgences in northern Germany, even went so far as to promise peasants that indulgences would relieve them of guilt for *future* sins. He also encouraged people to buy indulgences for the salvation of their dead relatives. Tetzel's sale of indulgences inspired a popular jingle: "Once you hear the money's ring, the soul from purgatory is free to spring." (Purgatory is a place in the afterlife where people are made fit for heaven).

Luther, then a professor and priest in the town of Wittenberg, preached against the sale of indulgences. And he lectured against other Church practices he believed were corrupt.

Then, on October 31, 1517, Luther nailed on the door of the Wittenberg Church a placard with 95 theses, or statements, criticizing the sale of indulgences and attacking other Church policies. This bold act had dramatic consequences.

Breaking with Rome   Printed copies of Luther's theses spread quickly all over Germany. Sales of indulgences declined sharply. Encouraged by this reaction, Luther wrote and published hundreds of essays advocating justification by faith and attacking Church abuses.

Pope Leo X responded to the decline in indulgence sales by sending envoys to Germany to persuade Luther to withdraw his criticisms. But Luther refused. In 1520 the pope issued a statement in which he formally condemned Luther and banned his works. In 1521 Pope Leo X excommunicated Luther from the Church.

CONNECTIONS: SCIENCE AND TECHNOLOGY

Movable Metal Type and Printing

Before the 1400s, books had to be copied by hand, which was a laborious and time-consuming method. Books were rare, and only wealthy people or scholars had access to them or could even learn how to read. Johannes Gutenberg's invention of movable metal type in the 1440s changed all that: books could be reproduced much faster and much less expensively than ever before. Consequently, more people were able to obtain books and to learn about new ideas and practices. This, in turn, caused them to question age-old traditions and to yearn for change.

German printers quickly adopted Gutenberg's invention and set up similar printing presses in other European countries. In less than 50 years after Gutenberg produced his first book, almost 20 million books had been printed in Europe.

The German religious reformer Martin Luther was one of the first authors to reap the benefit of this new technology. Since his books could be reproduced inexpensively and in large quantities, they could be easily obtained throughout Europe shortly after Luther completed them. Thus, Martin Luther was able to spread his religious ideas and call for reformation quickly throughout Europe, gaining widespread support for them before the Catholic Church could even formulate a proper response.

Making the Connection

1. Explain why only scholars and wealthy people could obtain books in Europe before Johannes Gutenberg invented a printing press based on movable type.
2. How did Martin Luther benefit from Gutenberg's invention of movable type?

Shortly after Luther's excommunication, a diet, or council, of German princes convened in Worms, Germany, to try to bring Luther back into the Church. They decided that Luther should take back his criticisms of the papacy. Meanwhile, Luther traveled to Worms in an apparently triumphant parade—because crowds of cheering people lined the road. Luther strode into the assembly hall and, when asked to take back his teachings, gave this reply: "I am bound by the Sacred Scriptures I have cited . . . and my conscience is captive to the Word of God. I cannot and will not recant [take back] anything. . . . God help me." Luther, condemned as a heretic and outlaw, was rushed out of Worms and hid-den at a castle in Wartburg by a friend, Prince Frederick of Saxony.

While in hiding, Luther translated the New Testament into German. Earlier German translations of the Bible were so rare and costly that only priests and teachers had them. With Luther's more affordable translation, the common people could now read the Bible.

Lutheranism

After Worms, Luther made his final break with Rome and formed the first Protestant faith: Lutheranism. Although Lutheranism and

Learning from Art *After hearing Luther's defense at the Diet of Worms, Emperor Charles V said, "A single friar who goes counter to all Christianity for 1,000 years must be wrong."* **Where did Luther hide after the Diet of Worms and what did he do while in hiding?**

Catholicism had many of the same beliefs, Luther stressed several teachings that distinguished his form of Christianity from that of Catholicism. Luther's most important teaching was salvation by faith alone—that no amount of good works can win God's approval for salvation, that only trust in God's love and mercy will win salvation.

Luther's second important teaching was that religious truth and authority lie only in the Bible. As a result, Luther and other Protestant reformers simplified church doctrine and rituals. Protestant leaders, called ministers, preached the Bible, and Protestant worship services were held in the local language instead of Latin.

Luther also emphasized that the Church was not a hierarchy of clergy, but a community of believers. All useful occupations, not just the priesthood or ministry, were important. They were **vocations,** or callings, in which people could serve God and their neighbors. This view appealed especially to merchants and artisans. Business people were glad to find a religious belief that gave respect to their occupations.

By the mid-1500s, Lutheranism had swept across Germany, especially in the north where princes made Lutheranism the state religion. In addition, German merchants carried Luther's ideas to France, England, the Netherlands, and the Scandinavian countries.

SECTION 3 REVIEW

Recall

1. **Define:** justification by faith, indulgences, vocation
2. **Identify:** Protestant Reformation, Martin Luther, Pope Leo X
3. **List:** What were some of the purposes for which John Tetzel claimed indulgences could be used?

4. **Explain:** Why was Luther's translation of the Bible into German so influential?

Critical Thinking

5. **Synthesize:** If you wanted to protest against something today, what medium would you use? Why?

6. **Evaluate:** What might have happened if Luther had recanted his beliefs in Worms?

Applying Concepts

7. **Conflict:** Explain why the pope asked Luther to recant his beliefs and excommunicated him when Luther would not do so.

The Spread of Protestantism

Although the Protestant Reformation continued to gain the support of Europeans throughout the 1500s, divisions began to appear within the movement soon after it had started. Not only did the Protestant reformers not believe in the same methods; they did not even agree on the same goals.

Swiss Reformers

After the rise of Lutheranism, preachers and merchants in Switzerland separated from Rome and set up churches known as Reformed. Huldreich Zwingli, a Swiss priest who lived from 1484 to 1531, led the Protestant movement in Switzerland. Like Luther, Zwingli stressed salvation by faith alone and denounced many Catholic beliefs and practices, such as purgatory and the sale of indulgences. Unlike Luther, though, Zwingli wanted to break completely from Catholic tradition. He wanted to establish a theocracy, or church-run state, in the Swiss city of Zurich. By 1525 Zwingli had achieved this goal. But in 1531 war broke out over Protestant missionary activity in the Catholic areas of Switzerland. Zwingli and his force of 1,500 followers were defeated by an army of 8,000 Catholics.

In the mid-1500s, John Calvin, another reformer, established the most powerful and influential Reformed group in the Swiss city of Geneva. Here Calvin set up a theocracy similar to Zwingli's rule in Zurich.

Born in 1509, Calvin grew up in Catholic France during the beginning of the Reformation. He received an education in theology, law, and humanism that prompted him to study the Bible very carefully and to formulate his own Protestant theology. In 1536 Calvin published his theology in *The Institutes of the Christian Religion*, soon one of the most popular books of its day, influencing religious reformers in Europe and eventually in North America.

The cornerstone of Calvin's theology was the belief that God possessed all-encompassing power and knowledge. Calvin contended that God alone directed everything that happens in the past, present, and future. Thus, he argued, God determines the fate of every person—a doctrine he called **predestination.**

To advance his views, Calvin tried to turn the corrupt city of Geneva into a model religious community. He began this project in 1536 by establishing the Consistory, a church council of 12 elders that was given the power to control almost every aspect of people's daily lives. All citizens were required to attend Reformed church services several times each week. The Consistory inspected homes annually to make sure that no one was disobeying the laws that forbade fighting, swearing, drunkenness, gambling, card playing, and dancing. It dispensed harsh punishments to people who disobeyed any of these laws. People convicted of holding Catholic beliefs or of practicing witchcraft might even be executed. This strict atmosphere earned Geneva the title "City of the Saints" and attracted reformers from all parts of Europe.

Visitors to Geneva helped to spread Calvinism, or John Calvin's teaching, throughout Europe. Because the Calvinist church was led by local councils of ministers and elected church members, it was easy to establish in most countries. Furthermore, the somewhat democratic structure of this organization gave its participants a stake in its welfare and inspired their intense loyalty.

The people of the Netherlands and Scotland became some of Calvin's most ardent supporters. John Knox, a leader of the Reformation in Scotland, and other reformers used Calvin's

Learning from Art *Zwingli preached that unless a practice of the Church could be supported literally by the Bible, it should be abandoned.* **What was one Church practice that Zwingli forbade?**

teachings to encourage moral people to overthrow tyrannical rulers. They preached, as Calvin had, "We must obey princes and others who are in authority, but only insofar as they do not deny to God, the supreme King, Father, and Lord, what is due Him." Calvinism thus became a dynamic social force in western Europe in the 1500s and contributed to the rise of revolutionary movements later in the 1600s and 1700s.

Radical Reformers

Several new Protestant sects in western Europe, called Anabaptists, initiated the practice of baptizing, or admitting into their groups, only adult members. They based this practice on the belief that only people who could make a free and informed choice to become Christians should be allowed to do so. Catholic and established Protestant churches, on the other hand, baptized infants, making them church members.

Many Anabaptists denied the authority of local governments to direct their lives. They refused to hold office, bear arms, or swear oaths, and many lived separate from a society they saw as sinful. Consequently, they were often persecuted by government officials, forcing many Anabaptists to wander from country to country seeking refuge.

Although most Anabaptists were peaceful, others were fanatical in their beliefs. These zealots brought about the downfall of the rest. When, in 1534, radical Anabaptists seized power in the German city of Münster and proceeded to burn books, seize private property, and practice polygamy, Lutherans and Catholics united to crush them. Together they killed the Anabaptist leaders and persecuted any surviving Anabaptist believers.

As a result, many Anabaptist groups left Europe for North America during the 1600s. In the Americas, the Anabaptists promoted two ideas that would become crucial in forming the United States of America: religious liberty and separation of church and state.

England's Church

Reformation ideas filtered into England during the 1500s. A serious quarrel between King Henry VIII and the pope, however, brought these ideas to the forefront.

The quarrel arose over succession to the throne. Although Henry's wife Catherine of Aragon had born five children, only one child, Mary, survived. Henry wanted to leave a male heir to the throne so that England might not be plunged into another civil war like the Wars of the Roses. Believing that Catherine was too old to have more children, the king decided to marry Anne Boleyn. In 1527 Henry asked the pope to agree to a divorce between himself and Catherine. But Catherine's nephew was the powerful Holy Roman Emperor Charles V, upon whom the pope depended for protection. And Charles wanted Catherine to remain as queen of England in order to influence the country's policies in favor of his own interests. The pope refused Henry's request.

Henry would not be thwarted. Gradually, and with Parliament's backing, he succeeded in breaking England's ties with the Catholic Church. The English Parliament granted Henry more authority over the English clergy. By rallying Parliament's support, Henry was trying to show that breaking with the Catholic Church was the will of the English people, not merely a whim of his own. In 1534 Parliament finally passed the law that separated the Church of England from Rome and declared Henry head of the English Church.

Henry had the new church grant him his divorce and then married Anne Boleyn. But Anne did not give him the heir he wanted. Instead she gave birth to a daughter, Elizabeth. A few years after Elizabeth's birth, Henry had Anne beheaded for treason. Henry's third wife, Jane Seymour, finally gave birth to a son, Edward, but she herself died 12 days later. The king married three more times before his death in 1547, but none of these marriages produced male heirs.

The sickly 9-year-old Edward VI succeeded his father. Because Edward was too young to rule, a council of lords governed England for him. Since most of the council members were Protestants, they brought Protestant doctrines into the English Church.

Upon Edward's death in 1553, Henry's Catholic daughter Mary became queen. Mary tried to restore Catholicism in England by burning hundreds of Protestants at the stake. These atrocities earned her the nickname "Bloody

FOOTNOTES TO HISTORY

KING HENRY VIII AS A YOUNG MAN

Henry VIII was typical of Renaissance rulers— a king who tried to excel in many areas. As a youth he had a lean, athletic physique and a keen mind. He enjoyed tennis, jousting, music, and discussions about astronomy and geometry. Leg injuries sustained in a jousting accident eventually kept him from the sports he loved. He composed several pieces of music and may even have written the song "Greensleeves." He also wrote a book called *Assertions of the Seven Sacraments,* in which as a devout Catholic he attacked the views of Martin Luther.

Mary," and only served to strengthen people's support for Protestantism.

Mary's Protestant half sister took the throne in 1558, becoming Queen Elizabeth I. To unite her people, she made the English Church Protestant with Catholic features. Anglicanism, as this blend of Protestant belief and Catholic practice was called, pleased most churchgoers. But some Protestants insisted on removing all Catholic rituals. Because they strove to purge these remnants of Catholicism, or "purify" the Church, these Protestants became known as Puritans. Although at first in the minority, Puritans gradually became influential both in the Church of England and in the English Parliament.

SECTION 4 REVIEW

Recall
1. **Define:** predestination
2. **Identify:** Huldreich Zwingli, John Calvin, Henry VIII, Catherine of Aragon, Anne Boleyn, Edward VI, Mary, Elizabeth I
3. **Explain:** Why did divisions appear among the different reformers within the Protestant movement?

4. **Describe:** What was Church government like in John Calvin's Geneva?

Critical Thinking
5. **Analyze:** Contrast Anabaptist and Calvinist attitudes toward participating in government.
6. **Synthesize:** Imagine that Catherine of Aragon had pro-

duced a male heir to the English throne. Do you think England would have become Protestant? Why or why not?

Applying Concepts
7. **Cultural diffusion:** Explain why the Catholic Church wanted to stop the spread of Protestant ideas.

The Catholic Reformation

Most of the people in Spain, France, Italy, Portugal, Hungary, Poland, and southern Germany remained Catholic during the Protestant Reformation. Nevertheless, Catholicism's power was threatened by Protestantism's increasing popularity in northern Europe. To counter the Protestant challenge, Catholics decided to reform Church practices. The Catholic Church had had a history of periodic reform since the Middle Ages. Thus, in the movement that came to be known as the Counter-Reformation, or Catholic Reformation, the Catholic Church eliminated many abuses, clarified its theology, and reestablished the pope's authority over Church members.

Redefining Catholicism

In 1536 Pope Paul III established a distinguished commission of cardinals and bishops to prepare a report on the need for reform and how such reform might be undertaken. The completed report blamed church leaders, including popes, for many abuses. It also called for reforms that would convince Protestants to rejoin the Church.

The reforms undertaken as a result of this report were only partially carried out. The Church's financial problems had increased, and the Church was unable to respond quickly and effectively to the Protestant threat.

By the 1540s Catholic Church leaders, sensing the importance of checking the spread of Protestantism, finally decided to embark on an ambitious reform program. The goals were to introduce a rebirth of faith among its followers, reassess the Church's principles, and halt the spread of Protestantism.

The Inquisition   In 1542 the Church gave full powers to an Inquisition, a church court based in Italy, to find, try, and judge heretics—especially Protestants. The purpose of this Inquisition, however, was not merely to rid Italy of non-Catholics. The purge was also intended to

Learning from Art *The decisions of the Council of Trent brought needed reforms to the Catholic Church. The Council's influence was so strong that more than 300 years passed before the Church deemed it necessary to hold another Church council.* **How did the Council of Trent result in an enthusiasm for baroque art and music?**

restore the pope's authority over church members. With the imposition of rigid repression, the pope succeeded in restoring his authority over the entire Italian peninsula. The Church also introduced censorship to curtail the humanist thinking that had fueled Italy's Renaissance. In 1543 the Inquisition published the first Index of Prohibited Books.

The Council of Trent One of the needs of the Church was to clearly state and defend Catholic teaching. In 1545 Pope Paul III called a council of bishops at Trent, Italy, to define official doctrine. The Council of Trent met in several sessions from 1545 to 1563.

The Council strictly and clearly defined Catholic doctrine, especially teachings that the Protestants had challenged. Salvation, the Council declared, could not be achieved by faith alone, but only by faith and works together. The Latin Vulgate translation of the Bible was made the only acceptable version of scripture. In addition, the Church hierarchy alone was to decide the interpretation of the Bible.

The Council of Trent also put an end to many Church abuses that had been practiced for

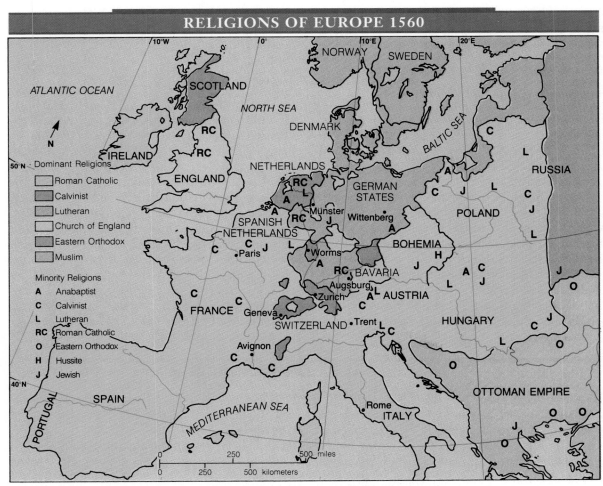

RELIGIONS OF EUROPE 1560

Dominant Religions
- Roman Catholic
- Calvinist
- Lutheran
- Church of England
- Eastern Orthodox
- Muslim

Minority Religions
- A Anabaptist
- C Calvinist
- L Lutheran
- RC Roman Catholic
- O Eastern Orthodox
- H Hussite
- J Jewish

Learning from Maps *By 1560 many northern Europeans had become Protestants. Most southern Europeans, however—including those in two of the most powerful countries, Spain and France—remained Catholic.* **What were the results of this religious division?**

centuries. It forbade the selling of indulgences. Clergy were ordered to follow strict rules of behavior. The Council decided that each diocese had to establish a **seminary,** or training school, for the proper education of priests.

The Council decided to maintain the elaborate art and ritual of the Church, and it declared that Mass should be said only in Latin. The Church's art and its Latin ritual were to serve as necessary sources of inspiration for less educated Catholics, who had difficulty understanding church teachings by other means. Thus, the Catholic Reformation renewed religious enthusiasm in the arts, sparking a new style of art and music called **baroque** (buh ROHK). Renaissance art had demonstrated symmetry, order, and restraint, but baroque art employed asymmetry and exaggeration for dramatic effect.

Spreading Catholicism

The Church planned to halt Protestantism in two phases. The first was to reform the Church. The second was to launch a missionary offensive against Protestants to reclaim formerly Catholic lands that were now Protestant.

Many religious orders and individuals in the Catholic Church became involved in this missionary effort. One priest named Ignatius Loyola played a particularly significant role. In 1540 Loyola and his followers founded the Society of Jesus, later known as the Jesuits. The Jesuits pledged absolute obedience to the pope, wore the black robes of monks, and lived simple lives but did not withdraw from the world. They be-

lieved, as Loyola said, "The more universal your work, the more divine it becomes." Jesuits taught throughout Europe and in countries as far away as India, China, Japan, Brazil, and Ethiopia to strengthen the faith of Catholics and bring Protestants back to the Church.

The Jesuits' missionary efforts helped the Catholic Church to retain the loyalty of people in southern Germany, Bohemia, Poland, and Hungary. The Jesuits also established many schools and universities, which remained prominent centers of education in Europe for the next 200 years. At these centers Jesuits not only taught Roman Catholic theology and philosophy but also advanced the study of physics, astronomy, mathematics, archaeology, linguistics, biology, chemistry, and genetics.

Results of Reformation

By the mid-1500s, the Roman Catholic Church had strengthened its following and reclaimed some territories that had previously been won over by Protestants. Large areas of Europe, however, were still Protestant—especially in the northern countries. Although the Catholic Reformation had helped correct many Church abuses, it did not eliminate Protestantism but only stopped the spread of Protestantism in Europe. By 1545 Europe was roughly divided into a Protestant north and a Catholic south, with each side wanting to prove that its faith was the true one. These religious tensions soon erupted into full-scale religious wars, which ravaged Europe from 1545 to 1600.

SECTION 5 REVIEW

Recall

1. **Define:** seminary, baroque
2. **Identify:** Pope Paul III, Ignatius Loyola
3. **List:** What educational opportunities did the Jesuits provide?
4. **Describe:** What new style of art and music was sparked by the Catholic Reformation?

Critical Thinking

5. **Analyze:** List any three of the reforms proposed by the Council of Trent. Beside each, give the Protestant viewpoint to which it responded.
6. **Evaluate:** Were the Jesuits effective in maintaining the power of Catholicism through-

out Europe? Explain specifically why or why not.

Applying Concepts

7. **Reaction:** Evaluate the actions the Church took to halt the spread of Protestantism and their effects. Which were successful and which were not?

IDENTIFYING EVIDENCE

Your answer in a sports trivia game doesn't match the one that came with the game materials. Your friends insist that the game developers knew the correct answer, but you are sure you are right. What do you do?

Explanation

You must *identify evidence* that will establish your claim. *Evidence* is any information that proves a claim or conclusion. For example, the best evidence for the claim that your school football team is the greatest is a scorecard listing all 10 wins and no losses.

There are basically four kinds of evidence, including oral accounts (eyewitness testimony), written documents (diaries, letters), objects (items, artifacts), and visual items (photographs, videos, art objects). These four types of evidence fall into one of two categories—primary evidence and secondary evidence.

Primary evidence is obtained first hand, while *secondary evidence* is obtained after the fact. For example, an eyewitness account of an event is primary evidence, while an account written by someone who was not there is secondary evidence. Use the following steps to help you identify evidence and prove a claim:
- Define the claim.
- Identify the evidence that should exist if the claim is true

and the evidence that should exist if the claim is false.
- Search available information for evidence that either supports or disproves the claim.
- Rank your evidence according to its objectivity. Evidence that is interpreted the same way by all observers must be given more consideration than evidence that is less definite.

Example

The text asserts that Florence was a great city-state during the Italian Renaissance. To check this claim we need to clarify the meaning of the word "great." For our purposes, we can assume that great means politically powerful, economically strong, and culturally advanced.

If the claim is true, then, there should be evidence of a well-managed government, a thriving economy, and achievements in the arts or public works projects. If it is false, the evidence should point to a government dominated by other city-states and plagued by internal rebellion, a poor economy reflected by poverty, and a lack of achievement in the arts and public works.

The following primary source—part of a letter to Cosmo de' Medici—can serve as a source of evidence on some early achievements in education. Six-year-old Piero de' Medici wrote the follow-

ing in a letter addressed to his father: "I have already learned many verses of Virgil and I know nearly the whole of the first book of Theodoro [a Greek grammar] by heart; I think I understand it."

Although the primary source letter reflects the experiences of only one young boy, it remains a strong piece of evidence supporting the claim because the boy is the son of Florence's ruler.

The text reports the stability of rule by the Medicis, their civic improvements, and their generous support for the arts. Works of art produced in Florence include Giotti's works and Michelangelo's statue of David. The major evidence against the claim is the text's description of Florence's decline. This piece of evidence, however, does not negate the fact that Florence was indeed great for a long period of time.

Application

Identify evidence from this chapter that proves or disproves the following statement: The Renaissance affected the visual arts in England more than in any other country, except Italy.

Practice

Turn to Practicing Skills on page 391 of the Chapter Review for further practice in identifying evidence.

from The Prince
by Niccolò Machiavelli

*Like many other Renaissance thinkers, Niccolò Machiavelli (1469–1527)
analyzed human actions rather than spiritual issues. Unlike many of his contemporaries,
however, he focused on the selfish side of human nature more than on humanity's potential for
progress. Machiavelli observed how successful politicians won and secured power. He sent his
thoughts to an Italian prince, hoping to win a job as an advisor. His ruthlessly honest look at
how politicians act challenges the view many of us have toward our leaders.*

It is the custom of those who are anxious to find favor in the eyes of a prince to present him with such things as they value most highly or in which they see him take delight. Hence offerings are made of horses, arms, golden cloth, precious stones and such ornaments, worthy of the greatness of the Prince. Since therefore I am desirous of presenting myself to Your Magnificence with some token of my eagerness to serve you, I have been able to find nothing in what I possess which I hold more dear or in greater esteem than the knowledge of the actions of great men which has come to me through a long experience of presentday affairs and continual study of ancient times. And having pondered long and diligently on this knowledge and tested it well, I have reduced it to a little volume which I now send to Your Magnificence. Though I consider this work unworthy of your presence, nonetheless I have much hope that your kindness may find it acceptable, if it be considered that I could offer you no better gift than to give you occasion to learn in a very short space of time all that I have come to have knowledge and understanding of over many years and through many hardships and dangers. I have not adorned the work nor inflated it with lengthy clauses nor pompous or magnificent words, nor added any other refinement or extrinsic ornament wherewith many are wont to advertise or embellish their work, for it has been my wish either that no honor should be given it or that simply the truth of the material and the gravity of the subject should make it acceptable. . . .

As for the exercise of the mind, the prince should read the histories of all peoples and ponder on the actions of the wise men therein recorded, note how they governed themselves in time of war, examine the reasons for their victories or defeats in order to imitate the former and avoid the latter, and above all conduct himself in accordance with the example of some great man of the past. . . .

We now have left to consider what should be the manners and attitudes of a prince toward his subjects and his friends. As I know that many have written on this subject I feel that I may be held presumptuous in what I have to say, if in my comments I do not follow the lines laid down by others. Since, however, it has been my intention to write something which may be of use to the understanding reader, it has seemed wiser to me to follow the real truth of the matter rather than what we imagine it to be. For imagination has created many principalities and republics that have never been seen or known to have any real existence, for how we live is so different from how we ought to live that he who studies what ought to be done rather than what is done will learn the way to his downfall rather than to his preservation. A man striving in every way to be good will meet his ruin among the great number who are not good. Hence it is necessary for a prince, if he wishes to remain in power, to learn how not to be good and to use his knowledge or refrain from using it as he may need. . . .

Here the question arises; whether it is better to be loved than feared or feared than loved. The answer is that it would be desirable to be both but, since that is difficult, it is much safer to be feared than to be loved, if one must choose. For on men in general this observation may be made: they are ungrateful, fickle, and deceitful, eager to avoid dangers, and avid for gain, and while you are useful to them they are all with you, offering you their blood, their property, their lives, and their sons so long as danger is remote, as we noted above, but when it approaches they turn on you. Any prince, trusting only in their words and having no other preparations made, will fall to his ruin, for friendships that are bought at a price and not by greatness and nobility of soul are paid for indeed, but they are not owned and cannot be called upon in time of need. Men have less hesitation in offending a man who is loved than one who is feared, for love is held by a bond of obligation which, as men are wicked, is broken whenever personal advantage suggests it, but fear is accompanied by the dread of punishment which never relaxes. . . .

CAES·BORGIA·VALENTINV

Art and Literature *This portrait of Cesare Borgia embodies the pride and confidence of the prince to whom Machiavelli wrote his political commentary. Borgia was the son of the controversial Pope Alexander VI. Using his power as duke of Romagna and captain of the armies, Borgia enhanced papal political power.*

Hence a wise leader cannot and should not keep his word when keeping it is not to his advantage or when the reasons that made him give it are no longer valid. If men were good, this would not be a good precept, but since they are wicked and will not keep faith with you, you are not bound to keep faith with them. . . .

So a prince need not have all the aforementioned good qualities, but it is most essential that he appear to have them. Indeed, I should go so far as to say that having them and always practising them is harmful, while seeming to have them is useful. It is good to appear clement [merciful], trustworthy, humane, religious, and honest, and also to be so, but always with the mind so disposed that, when the occasion arises not to be so, you can become the opposite. It must be understood that a prince and particularly a new prince cannot practise all the virtues for which men are accounted good, for the necessity of preserving the state often compels him to take actions which are opposed to loyalty, charity, humanity, and religion. Hence he must have a spirit ready to adapt itself as the varying winds of fortune command him. As I have said, so far as he is able, a prince should stick to the path of good but, if the necessity arises, he should know how to follow evil.

A prince must take great care that no word ever passes his lips that is not full of the above mentioned five good qualities, and he must seem to all who see and hear him a model of piety, loyalty, integrity, humanity, and religion. Nothing is more necessary than to seem to possess this last quality, for men in general judge more by the eye than the hand; as all can see but few can feel. Everyone sees what you seem to be, few experience what you really are and these few do not dare to set themselves up against the opinion of the majority supported by the majesty of the state. In the actions of all men and especially princes, where there is no court of appeal, the end is all that counts. Let a prince then concern himself with the acquisition or the maintenance of a state; the means employed will always be considered honorable and praised by all, for the mass of mankind is always swayed by the appearances and by the outcome of an enterprise. . . .

I am not ignorant of the fact that many have held and hold the opinion that the things of this world are so ordered by fortune and God that the prudence of mankind may effect little change in them, indeed is of no avail at all. On this basis it could be argued that there is no point in making any effort, but we should rather abandon ourselves to destiny. This opinion has been the more widely held in our day on account of the great variations in things that we have seen and are still witnessing and which are entirely beyond human conjecture. Sometimes indeed, thinking on such matters, I am minded to share that opinion myself. Nevertheless I believe, if we are to keep our free will, that it may be true that fortune controls half of our actions indeed but allows us the direction of the other half, or almost half. . .

RESPONDING TO LITERATURE

1. **Comprehending:** Describe in your own words Machiavelli's view of human nature.

2. **Applying:** Write a brief essay giving an example that explains whether contemporary politicians follow Machiavelli's advice.

3. **Synthesizing:** Propose an alternative principle to Machiavelli's view that "the end is all that counts."

4. **Thinking critically:** Do you think individuals should follow Machiavelli's advice in dealing with their family, friends, and classmates? Why or why not?

CHAPTER 15 REVIEW

HISTORICAL SIGNIFICANCE

During the Renaissance, people began to focus on more worldly and individualistic concerns than they had in medieval times. These more secular interests and values, in turn, shaped the way in which they—and their descendants—lived and thought about themselves, their world, and their religion.

People began focusing their time, energy, and money on things that would improve their homes and cities. They bought more luxury items and increased their patronage of the arts. As a result, painting, sculpture, architecture, music, and literature flourished, leading to innovations in these and associated fields.

People also sought better education for self-improvement. They began to invest in books and to interpret texts themselves. No longer were they content to settle for a priest's interpretation of the Bible.

As people began to study the Bible for themselves, they constructed their own interpretations of religious doctrine and began to question some of Catholicism's beliefs and practices. Many demanded church reforms and, when these were not forthcoming, they established their own forms of Christianity. Protestantism, with its many branches, is the legacy of these reformers.

SUMMARY

For a summary of Chapter 15, see the Unit 4 Synopsis on pages 458–461.

USING KEY TERMS

A. Write a sentence or two about each pair of words below, showing how the words are related.

1. indulgences, justification by faith
2. humanism, predestination
3. vocation, seminary

B. Write the key term that best completes each sentences below.

    a. baroque   d. seminary
    b. doge   e. sonnet
    c. indulgences

4. ____ reduced punishment for sins.
5. The Catholic Reformation established ____ to educate and train priests.
6. Petrarch invented the ____ , a new poetic form.
7. The ____ administered the city of Venice.
8. The new style of art and music in the Catholic Church was called ____.

REVIEWING FACTS

1. **List:** What were the three social classes present in most Italian city-states during the Renaissance, and who were their members?
2. **Describe:** How did the art and architecture of Renaissance Italy differ from that of the Middle Ages?
3. **Explain:** How did Renaissance ideas spread northward from Italy?
4. **Describe:** Briefly state the main events that led to the Protestant Reformation.
5. **Explain:** Why did Henry VIII separate from the Catholic Church and create the Church of England?
6. **Tell:** What did the Council of Trent do to reform Catholicism?

THINKING CRITICALLY

1. **Apply:** Why did the Medici place a heavy tax burden on the wealthy and use tax revenues to fund public works projects that benefited all the citizens of Florence?
2. **Analyze:** Examine the effects of humanism on literature, architecture, sculpture, and painting during the Renaissance.

3. **Synthesize:** If you had been a supporter of Martin Luther, how might you have suggested he reform the Church?

4. **Evaluate:** What might Europe be like today if Martin Luther had become a lawyer instead of a priest and had never formulated or promoted the ideas that inspired the Protestant Reformation?

ANALYZING CONCEPTS

1. **Innovation:** Why do you suppose Renaissance artists and scholars did not merely imitate Greco-Roman culture?

2. **Cultural diffusion:** How did the people of northern Europe adapt Italian Renaissance ideas?

3. **Conflict:** Do you think Luther really wanted to create a rift in the Catholic Church? Why or why not?

4. **Cultural diffusion:** What factors helped Protestantism to spread so rapidly?

5. **Reaction:** In what ways could the Catholic Reformation be called the Counter-Reformation?

PRACTICING SKILLS

Was Luther a rebel intent on splitting the Church or a sincere believer desiring to reform the Church? Use the four steps to identify evidence in Section 3 and come to a decision.

GEOGRAPHY IN HISTORY

1. **Regions:** How did the division of Italy into independent city-states affect the rise and development of the Renaissance as a cultural movement?

2. **Movement:** On the map on page 383, pinpoint where the Protestant Reformation began. How did this point of origin affect the spread of Protestant ideas and practices throughout Europe?

TRACING CHRONOLOGY

Refer to the time line below to answer these questions.

1. Which two events in the time line were part of the Italian Renaissance?

2. Which two events in the time line could be considered part of the religious ferment caused by the spread of Lutheranism?

3. Approximately how long did it take after the Renaissance began in Italy in the mid-1300s for Renaissance ideas to spread north?

LINKING PAST AND PRESENT

1. Do you think ancient Greek and Roman culture influence artists, architects, and writers as much today as they did during the Renaissance? Why or why not?

2. Do you think the Inquisition could happen today in the United States? Why or why not?

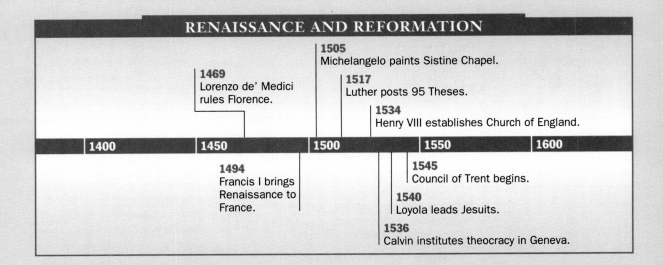

RENAISSANCE AND REFORMATION

1469 Lorenzo de' Medici rules Florence.

1505 Michelangelo paints Sistine Chapel.

1517 Luther posts 95 Theses.

1534 Henry VIII establishes Church of England.

1400	1450	1500	1550	1600

1494 Francis I brings Renaissance to France.

1545 Council of Trent begins.

1540 Loyola leads Jesuits.

1536 Calvin institutes theocracy in Geneva.

CHAPTER 16
1400–1750

1 Early Explorations

2 Overseas Empires

3 Expanding Horizons

Exploration and Empire

*O*n the night of October 11, 1492, Christopher Columbus scanned the horizon, praying that landfall was near. "About 10 o'clock at night, while standing on the sterncastle, I thought I saw a light to the west. It looked like a little wax candle bobbing up and down. It had the same appearance as a light or torch belonging to fishermen or travellers. . . . "

The light flickered out, though, and the ships sailed on. The moon rose, but no land appeared. Two hours later, the boom of a cannon roared across the water. A sailor aboard the *Pinta*, the fastest of the expedition's three ships, had sighted land. For Spain and other nations of Europe, the land that appeared in the darkness was part of a far greater treasure. Columbus's voyage opened the way for Europeans to explore and take for themselves two continents in the New World.

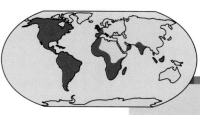

CHAPTER PREVIEW

Key Terms to Define: cartographer, line of demarcation, circumnavigation, conquistador, triangular trade, middle passage, joint-stock company, entrepreneur, mercantilism, bullion, balance of trade

People to Meet: Henry the Navigator, Vasco da Gama, Christopher Columbus, Ferdinand Magellan, Hernán Cortés, Montezuma II,

Francisco Pizarro, Atahualpa, John Cabot

Places to Discover: Cape of Good Hope, Straits of Magellan, Brazil, Peru, Jamestown, Plymouth

Objectives to Learn:
1. Why did Europeans risk dangerous ocean voyages to discover sea routes to new lands?

Spectators offer their prayers as a European explorer prepares to depart in search of new lands.

2. How did Europeans exploit the lands and people they found?

3. What was the impact of the overseas empires?

Concepts to Understand:

• Innovation—European sailors borrowed Asian travel ideas. Section 1

• Movement—European nations established colonies in the lands they explored. Section 2

• Change—The wealth of overseas colonies caused Europe to experience a Commercial Revolution. Section 3

• Cultural diffusion—Increased trade and contacts among Europe, Asia, and the Americas spread ideas and products worldwide. Section 3

Early Explorations

In the late 1400s, Europeans forever changed the world as they tested uncharted oceans in search of a trade route to Asia. Explorers left Europe filled with a desire for gold and glory and for spreading Christianity. In just over 250 years, many new empires were created and old ones were destroyed. Europeans reaped the treasures of their discoveries—spices, silk, silver, and gold.

The Quest for Spices

Europe in the 1300s had depended on spices from Asia and India. Such spices as pepper, cinnamon, nutmeg, mace, and cloves were in great demand. Used chiefly to flavor and preserve meat, spices were also used for perfumes, cosmetics, and medicine.

The spice trade was controlled in Asia and Europe by Islamic and Venetian merchants. Chinese and Indian merchants sold spices to Arab merchants, who then shipped the cargoes overland to Europe and reaped huge profits in the sale of the spices to Venetian merchants. Europeans, eager to amass quick fortunes through direct trade with Asians, began to look for quicker routes to Asia. Because the Mongols—by the mid-1300s—could no longer guarantee safe passage for traders on overland routes, Europeans were forced to consider the sea as a possible route to Asia.

Several motivations led Europeans into an era of exploration and expansion. Not only did merchants seek a profitable trade with Asia, but also Christian religious leaders sought to halt the expansion of Islamic empires and to spread Christian teachings. Learning and imagination also played a part. Renaissance thinkers had expanded the European world view to include new possibilities for exploration and discovery.

Technology of Exploration Open-water ocean sailing—necessary to find a water route to Asia—requires sailors trained in navigation, accurate maps, and oceangoing ships. For exploration to succeed, ships had to be able both to leave the coastal waters and sight of land and to return home. Ancient navigators stayed close to the coast, using landmarks to determine their position. Later, sailors who traveled beyond sight of land used the positions of stars and the sun to determine in which direction they were traveling. Hourglasses told them how long they had traveled. Keeping track of speed, direction, and time theoretically enabled a captain to tell where the ship was. But these calculations were very inaccurate.

The compass, of Chinese origin, enabled sailors to determine geographical direction. By 1100, sailors used the astrolabe—perfected by the Arabs—to determine the altitude of the sun or other heavenly bodies. But in practice, standing on the deck of a heaving ship, few ship captains had the skill and patience that the astrolabe required.

Maps were another problem for early navigators. Most maps were wildly inaccurate, drawn from scattered impressions of travelers and traders. **Cartographers**, or mapmakers, filled their parchments with lands found only in rumor or legend.

Cartographers' skills gradually improved. About 1300, coastal charts showed the Mediterranean coastline with a great degree of accuracy. During the Renaissance, works by the Egyptian Ptolemy reappeared in Europe. His maps, improved over the centuries by Byzantine and Arab scholars, gave Europeans a new picture of the world. Ptolemy also introduced the grid system of map references based on the coordinates of latitude and longitude that is still in use today all over the world.

Innovations were also made in the construction of ships. Late in the 1400s, shipwrights began to outfit ships with triangle-shaped lateen sails perfected by Islamic traders. These sails made it possible for ships to sail against the wind, not simply with it. Shipwrights also abandoned using a single mast with one large sail. Multiple masts, with several smaller sails hoisted one above the other, made ships travel much faster. And moving the rudder from the ship's side to the stern made ships more maneuverable.

In the 1200s a European ship called a caravel incorporated all these improvements. Because a caravel drew little water, it allowed explorers to venture up shallow inlets and to beach the ship to make repairs. A Venetian mariner

EUROPEAN KNOWLEDGE OF THE WORLD

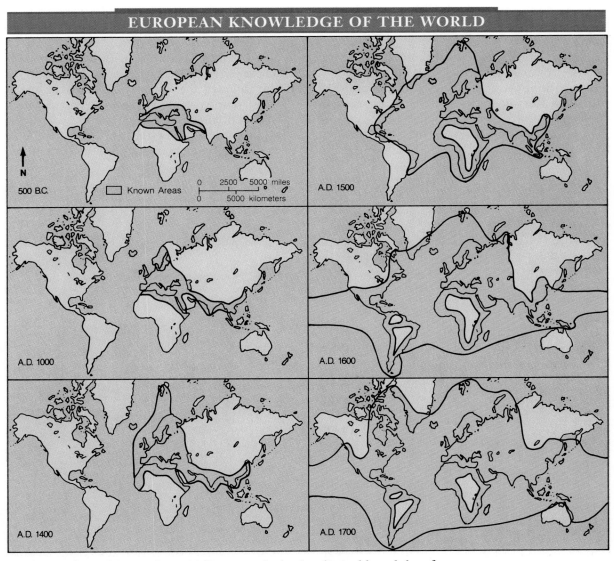

Learning from Maps   *In 1400 Europeans had only a limited knowledge of the globe. Geographers believed that the world was round, but they disagreed on its size. Their notions of the relationship of Asia, Africa, and Europe were vague.* **How did European knowledge of the world change by 1600?**

called the caravels "the best ships that sailed the seas." The caravels also carried new types of weapons—both rifles and cannons.

Portugal Leads the Way

Portugal was the first European country to venture out on the Atlantic Ocean in search of spices and gold. Between 1420 and 1580, Portuguese captains pushed farther and farther down the west coast of Africa in search of a sea route to Asia.

Although Prince Henry the Navigator, son of King John I of Portugal, was not a sailor—never making an ocean voyage—he established the first European school for navigators in Sagres, Portugal. He also sponsored many Portuguese exploratory voyages westward into the Atlantic and southward down Africa's west coast.

Henry's explorers discovered the Azores in 1427, which the Portuguese settled in 1439, the Senegal River, the Madeira Islands, and the Cape Verde Islands. These discoveries were the foundation of what in the 1500s became the Portuguese empire.

In August 1487 Bartholomeu Dias left Portugal, intent upon finding the southern tip of Africa. In 1488 his expedition of three ships discovered the southern tip of Africa, which was later renamed the Cape of Good Hope. Dias's voyage proved that ships could reach East Asia by sailing around Africa.

In June 1497 four ships led by Vasco da Gama sailed from Portugal for India. The expedition rounded the Cape of Good Hope, made stops at trading centers along the east coast of Africa, and landed at Calicut on the southwest coast of India in 23 days. There Da Gama found Hindus and Muslims trading fine silk, porcelain,

IMAGES OF THE TIME

The Dutch Republic

With no monarchy or aristocracy, the tastes and ideals of Dutch society in the 1600s were determined largely by the Protestant middle classes.

Paintings of home life, like this one by Jan Steen, show typical middle-class life of the time.

Dutch artists used food and everyday objects as subjects of their still-life paintings. Many showed luxury items imported from foreign lands.

The town of Delft was famous for its blue pottery. Delft plates graced the cupboards of middle-class families.

and spices that made the glass beads and trinkets of the Portuguese appear shoddy.

Da Gama tried to persuade the ruler of Calicut and Muslim merchants in India to trade with the Portuguese. He had little success and returned home. In Portugal, however, Da Gama was regarded as a national hero. He had pioneered a water route to India, and he had provided a glimpse of the riches that could come from direct trade with the East.

Spain's Quest for Riches

In the late 1400s, Spain ended a long period of internal turmoil and wars against the Moors, and, under King Ferdinand and Queen Isabella, entered the race for Asian riches by backing the expeditions of an Italian navigator named Christopher Columbus.

Columbus Crosses the Atlantic In 1492 Christopher Columbus approached Queen Isabella with an intriguing plan—to reach India by sailing west across the Atlantic. For years Columbus had tried unsuccessfully to persuade other European rulers to finance his voyage. With Queen Isabella his persistence paid off.

In August 1492 Columbus sailed from Spain with three small ships. He calculated the distance to India to be 700 leagues, about 2,200 nautical miles; he knew that the actual distance might be greater. To calm the crews' fears, he showed them a log that understated the distance they had sailed from home.

But the days out of sight of land wore on and on, and the sailors begged Columbus to turn back. After a false sighting of land, the crews began to talk of mutiny. Columbus reluctantly agreed to turn back if they did not reach land in three days.

Rembrandt's group portrait of *The Syndics* shows a group of wealthy businessmen, members of the cloth guild, at work.

Reflecting on the Times
From the images shown here, what do you think were the ideals of Dutch society in the 1600s?

Learning from Art *The development of navigational devices led to many advances in astronomy, physics, and geography and opened the door for extended sea voyages.* **What other factors contributed to European exploration?**

After midnight on the second day, the expedition sighted land. In the morning Columbus and his men went ashore, becoming the first Europeans to set foot on one of the islands of the Bahamas. Columbus wrote of the inhabitants:

The islanders came to the ships' boats, swimming and bringing us parrots and balls of cotton thread . . . which they exchanged for . . . glass beads and hawk bells . . . they took and gave of what they had very willingly, but it seemed to me that they were poor in every way. They bore no weapons, nor were they acquainted with them, because when I showed them swords they seized them by the edge and so cut themselves from ignorance.

Believing he was off the coast of India, Columbus called the islanders "Indians." Columbus spent the next three months exploring the islands of Hispaniola—present-day Haiti and the Dominican Republic—and Cuba in search of gold. Although he found enough gold to raise Spanish hopes, he saw no evidence of the great civilizations of Asia.

When Columbus returned to Spain, Ferdinand and Isabella gave him the title "Admiral of the Ocean Sea, Viceroy and Governor of the Islands he hath discovered in the Indies." Before he died in 1506, Columbus made three more voyages to the Caribbean islands and South America seeking proof that he had discovered a new route to Asia. He died certain that he had.

Even without sure proof, it was difficult for anyone to dispute Columbus's claim. Maps of the time did not show any landmass between Europe and Asia. It was not until 1507 that another Italian explorer, Amerigo Vespucci (veh SPOO chee), suggested that Columbus had discovered a "New World." In honor of Vespucci, the name *America* began to appear on maps that included the new lands.

Dividing the World Both Spain and Portugal wanted to protect their claims in the New World and turned to the pope for help. In 1493 the pope drew a **line of demarcation**, an imaginary line running down the middle of the Atlantic from the North Pole to the South Pole. Spain was to have control of all lands to the west of the line, while Portugal was to have control of all lands to the east of the line.

The Portuguese, however, feared that their line was so far to the east that Spain might take over their Asian trade. As a result, in 1494, Spain and Portugal signed the Treaty of Tordesillas (tawd uh SEE yuhs), an agreement to move the line of demarcation farther west. The treaty divided the entire unexplored world between just two powers, Spain and Portugal.

Voyage of Magellan

In 1519 an expedition led by Ferdinand Magellan, a Portuguese soldier of fortune, set sail from Seville under the Spanish flag to find a western route to Asia. The five ships and 270-man crew sailed across the Atlantic and made their way along the eastern coast of South America, searching every bay and inlet for this route.

Along the coast of Argentina, crews of three of the ships attempted a mutiny because Magellan had decided to halt the expedition until spring. Magellan executed the captain who had instigated the mutiny, took control of the fleet, and renamed the expedition. Finally, near the southern tip of South America, the ships reached the straits that now bear Magellan's name. The ships threaded their way through the maze of rocky islands in the 300-mile (480-kilometer) long straits. Strong currents and unpredictable gales, separated one ship from the others, and its crew forced its return to Spain. Another was shipwrecked.

Magellan's ship and two others finally passed through the straits into the South Sea, which had been discovered and named six years earlier by Núñez de Balboa. Because the water was so calm, Magellan renamed it the Pacific Ocean. The fleet then sailed nearly four months before reaching land. Water and food ran out, and some sailors died. One of the crew wrote in his journal, "We ate biscuit, which was no longer biscuit, but powder of biscuits swarming with worms, for they had eaten the good."

At last the ships reached the island of Guam. There, caught in a skirmish between a local chief and his enemy, Magellan was killed. The surviving crew escaped and sailed for Spain.

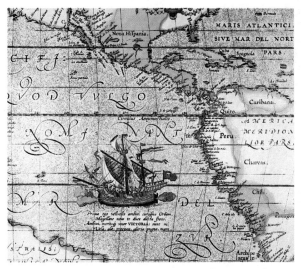

Learning from Maps *This map of the Pacific Ocean drawn in 1590 shows Magellan's surviving ship, the* Victoria *under full sail.* **What problems did Magellan encounter on his trip around the tip of South America?**

In 1522, after three years at sea, the last ship with its 18 survivors arrived at Seville, completing the first **circumnavigation**, or circling of the globe. The spices they brought home with them barely covered the cost of the voyage, but the expedition had a value far beyond money. It proved that the world was round and much larger than anyone had believed, that the oceans of the world were connected, and that the lands discovered by Columbus were not part of Asia.

SECTION 1 REVIEW

Recall
1. **Define:** cartographer, line of demarcation, circumnavigation
2. **Identify:** Henry the Navigator, Bartholomeu Dias, Vasco da Gama, Christopher Columbus, Ferdinand Magellan
3. **Locate:** Look at the map on page 395. Interpret the changes in European knowledge of the world.

4. **Explain:** Why did Portugal and Spain want to find a sea route to Asia?

Critical Thinking
5. **Synthesize:** Using the text as a resource, write a journal entry describing your experiences as a sailor on an expedition of Dias, Columbus, Magellan, or Da Gama.

6. **Evaluate:** Predict what would have happened to Columbus if there had been no land between Spain and Asia.

Applying Concepts
7. **Innovation:** What sciences and new technologies helped sailors to venture into the open ocean and led to European voyages of exploration?

SECTION 2

Overseas Empires

The Treaty of Tordesillas divided the unexplored world between Spain and Portugal. Only Spain and Portugal, however, recognized the treaty. The Dutch, the French, and the English soon joined them in a race to exploit wealth from the lands and peoples of unexplored and newly explored areas.

Portugal and Spain

Portugal's main interest lay in Africa and Asia, and in trade rather than colonization. Eager to monopolize the spice trade, the Portuguese reacted quickly to Vasco da Gama's voyage to India. In 1500, less than six months after da Gama's return, 13 ships were dispatched to Calicut. Led by Pedro Alvares Cabral, the Portuguese won a bloody trade war with Muslim merchants and defeated a large Arab fleet to establish Portuguese control of the Indian Ocean.

The Portuguese then built naval bases along the Indian Ocean—in the Persian Gulf and in Southeast Asia. They soon controlled shipping in the Indian Ocean. Next, they expanded eastward toward the Moluccas or the "Spice Islands." From the Spice Islands, the Portuguese established trading ports in China and Japan.

Portugal also colonized the area that is now Brazil. Cabral claimed this territory as he swung west across the Atlantic to India in 1500. Because this area of South America juts east of the line of demarcation set by the Treaty of Tordesillas, it became Portuguese. The rest of South America had been claimed by Spain.

Settlers in Brazil grew income-producing crops such as sugarcane, tobacco, coffee, and cotton. Because the local population did not supply enough labor, slaves were imported from Africa. By the late 1500s, Brazil was one of Portugal's three remaining colonies.

Spain Spanish **conquistadors,** meaning conquerors, came to the Americas "to serve God and his Majesty, to give light to those who were in darkness and to grow rich as all men desire to do."

One conquistador, Hernán Cortés, left Cuba for Mexico in 1519. Two earlier expeditions brought back enough gold and stories to convince Cortés that more gold would be found there than on any island. He sailed with 11 ships and more than 500 men.

Cortés landed and marched toward Tenochtitlán, the Aztec capital. Messengers described the approaching army to the Aztec ruler Montezuma II as "supernatural creatures riding on hornless deer, preceded by wild animals on leashes, dressed in iron." Believing that the Spaniards had come to fulfill a legendary prophecy, Montezuma offered gifts of gold.

The city's riches were beyond anything the Spaniards had seen. Soon fighting broke out. With the advantage of horses and guns, the Spanish force ultimately slaughtered 50,000 Aztecs. European diseases killed hundreds of thousands more. Within three years Cortés ruled Mexico.

A decade after Mexico's conquest, another conquistador, Francisco Pizarro, invaded the Inca Empire in what is now Peru. He captured the Inca leader Atahualpa (aht uh WAHL puh) and slaughtered his 6,000 bodyguards. After accepting a ransom in silver and gold for Atahualpa's release, Pizarro executed him. With their leader gone, Inca resistance evaporated, and the Spanish controlled an area covering 375,000 square miles (975,000 square kilometers) with 32 million inhabitants.

Spain also claimed territory in North America. In 1539 Hernando de Soto reached the Mississippi River. Later, Francisco Vásquez de Coronado explored the Grand Canyon.

Las Meninas

Diego Velásquez's (vuh LAS kuhs) painting *Las Meninas* (the Maids of Honor) is among the Spanish painter's most famous works. Painted in 1656, the canvas is about twelve feet high and ten feet wide. Velásquez (1599-1660) was a court painter for Philip IV, who ruled Spain beginning in 1621.

Las Meninas shows several members of the royal family. The young girl at the center is the Infanta Margarita, Philip IV's daughter. Gathered around the young princess are her court attendants. Another servant appears in a doorway across the room. To the left of the doorway, a mirror reflects an image of Philip IV and his wife. At the left, Velásquez stands working.

Las Meninas was unusual for its time. Velásquez showed members of the royal court, but not in a formal portrait or at an official ceremony. Instead, he showed an informal view of life at court. Servants are included in the painting, and there is a sense that someone (probably the king and queen whose reflection appears in the mirror) has just interrupted this group.

By including a self-portrait in this painting of the royal family, and by making the painting so large, Velásquez may have been commenting on his own status as court painter. At this time in Spain, there was disagreement about the social status of artists. By showing himself as a member of the royal household, Velásquez may have been saying that he should be given noble status.

Responding to the Arts

1. Why was the scene shown in *Las Meninas* unusual for its time?
2. What might Velásquez have been saying with this painting about his status as an artist?

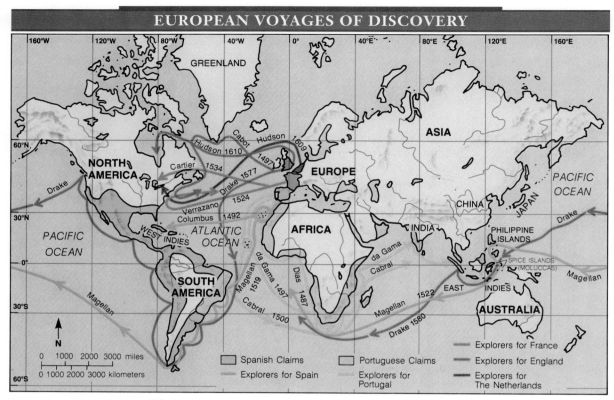

EUROPEAN VOYAGES OF DISCOVERY

GREENLAND

NORTH AMERICA

Drake

Cabot 1497

Hudson 1610

Cartier 1534

Drake 1577

Verrazano 1524

Columbus 1492

WEST INDIES

ATLANTIC OCEAN

PACIFIC OCEAN

SOUTH AMERICA

Magellan 1519

Cabral 1500

da Gama

Dias 1487

Magellan

EUROPE

AFRICA

ASIA

CHINA

INDIA

JAPAN

PACIFIC OCEAN

PHILIPPINE ISLANDS

Drake

SPICE ISLANDS (MOLUCCAS)

da Gama 1497

Cabral

Magellan 1522

EAST INDIES

AUSTRALIA

Drake 1580

Magellan

N

0 1000 2000 3000 miles
0 1000 2000 3000 kilometers

Spanish Claims
Explorers for Spain

Portuguese Claims
Explorers for Portugal

Explorers for France
Explorers for England
Explorers for The Netherlands

Learning from Maps *This map shows nearly 150 years of European voyages.* **How did the destinations change over time?**

Building an Empire By the early 1600s, Spain's empire in the Americas included many islands in the West Indies, Central America, much of South America, and parts of the United States. Spain established colonies rather than trading settlements as the Portuguese had. Spanish viceroys ruled the colonies.

The Spanish had two goals for its American empire—to exploit its wealth and to convert the native people to Christianity. There was conflict, however, over how to treat the inhabitants. In theory the Spanish considered the native people their subjects. They were free and could retain their lands; however, they had to abide by Spanish law and accept Christianity. In reality Spanish plantation owners forced the people to work for them, took their lands, and abused them. Spanish priests destroyed temples and banned native religious rituals. One priest, Bartolomé de Las Casas, tried to protect the natives from such abuses.

Disease was an enemy worse than the Spanish state or church. Isolated for thousands of years, the natives lacked immunity to European diseases such as smallpox, measles, and influenza. In the first 50 years under Spanish control, the Inca population fell from 10 million to just over 1 million. This decline led the Spanish to import more and more African slave laborers.

Animal hides, sugar, and tobacco were the heart of the colonial economy. The most valuable exports, however, were silver and gold. The crown made efforts to retain its one-fifth share of the minerals. Official corruption and pirated shipments nevertheless cut into Spanish profits.

Colonies of the Netherlands

The Netherlands was also interested in expansion. In the late 1500s, the Dutch won their independence from Spain. This small country on the North Sea had few natural resources and limited farmland. A large Dutch middle class saw commerce as the key to survival.

The period of the 1600s was the golden age of the Netherlands. Dutch ships were efficient, carrying more cargo and smaller crews than other ships. Amsterdam became the world's largest commercial city, and the Dutch enjoyed the world's highest standard of living.

The first Dutch expedition to the Far East returned in 1599. Three years later the Dutch chartered the Dutch East India Company to expand trade and ensure close relations between the government and enterprises in Asia.

In 1619 the company set up headquarters at Batavia on the island of Java in what is now Indonesia. Soon the Dutch controlled island trade in sugar, spices, coffee, and tea. Using Batavia as a base, the Dutch pushed the Portuguese and English out of Asian outposts. After taking Malacca from the Portuguese in 1641, the Netherlands controlled all trade with the Spice Islands.

At the same time, the Dutch set out for North America. An English navigator, Henry Hudson, claimed territory for the Dutch along the Atlantic coast of North America, and in 1621 the government chartered the Dutch West India Company to establish colonies in the New World. The company founded New Amsterdam on Manhattan Island at the north of the Hudson River. This settlement was soon a major center for European and colonial trade.

The Dutch established a colony in Africa too. In 1652 Dutch farmers known as Boers settled at the Cape of Good Hope to provide fresh food and water for sailing ships. By the 1700s, however, Dutch power was declining.

French and English Colonies

The French and English played only a small part in the early voyages of explorations. Religious conflicts and civil wars kept their interests focused at home. During the 1500s, however, France and England searched for overseas trading colonies.

Thwarted by the Portuguese and later the Dutch control of Asian markets, England and

Learning from Art *Montezuma II reluctantly welcomed Cortés to Tenochtitlán. He thought Cortés might be the legendary god, Quetzalcoatl.* **What was Cortés's real mission?**

France turned toward North America and the Caribbean. In general, the French companies sought quick profits from trade rather than the long-term investment of farming. For the English, colonies could provide the raw materials—lumber, fish, sugarcane, rice, and wheat—they would otherwise have to purchase from other countries.

France In 1524 the French hired an Italian captain, Giovanni da Verrazano, to find a Northwest Passage through America to Asia. Da Verrazano explored the North American coast from North Carolina to Maine without success. Ten years later the French navigator Jacques Cartier continued the search and sailed up the St. Lawrence River to the present-day city of Montreal. He claimed much of eastern Canada for France.

In 1608 Samuel de Champlain, a French mapmaker, founded Quebec, the first permanent settlement in the New World. In 1673 missionaries Jacques Marquette and Louis Joliet explored the Mississippi Valley. Later, Robert Cavelier, also known as Sieur de la Salle, claimed the entire inland region surrounding the Mississippi River for France.

Like the Spanish, the French sent Jesuit missionaries to convert the native people to Christianity. French explorers traded the people blankets, guns, and wine for animal skins. Trapping, fishing, and lumbering were also profitable.

Some French settlers went to the West Indies, where they claimed the islands of St. Kitts, Martinique, and Guadeloupe. The French brought African slaves to work on sugar and tobacco plantations on the islands. Although most of their interests were in North America, the French also established colonial ports in India.

England   As early as 1497, England began to show an interest in overseas trade. In that year, Henry VII commissioned the Italian navigator John Cabot to find a northern route to the area discovered by Columbus. Cabot explored the coasts of Newfoundland, Nova Scotia, and New England, giving England a claim in the New World. Because of internal conflict, however, it was 100 years before England established colonies there.

During the 1500s the English harassed their Spanish and Portuguese competitors. Sea captains turned pirates raided Spanish ships for gold and silver. In 1580 the most daring of these captains, Francis Drake, became the first Englishman to circumnavigate the globe. Six years later he sacked Spanish seaports in the Caribbean.

The English first settled in the West Indies, claiming Jamaica, the Bahamas, and Barbados. In 1640 English planters introduced sugarcane. Sugar plantations worked by slave labor made three times as much profit as tobacco plantations did. In the 1600s sugar from sugar plantations made Barbados the most profitable English colony.

English merchants also began sending expeditions to North America. In 1606 the Virginia Company of London sent an expedition to America to search for gold and silver. The following year, the company founded the first permanent English settlement at Jamestown in what is now Virginia. Later, a group of religious

Learning from Art
Canadian native people traded with French fishermen during the 1500s. They exchanged beaver, fox, otter, and mink pelts for European fishhooks, kettles, and knives. By the early 1600s, the French-Indian fur trade was firmly established in Canada. ***Where else did the French settle?***

dissenters calling themselves Pilgrims founded a second colony, Plymouth, in present-day Massachusetts.

Slave Trade

In the 1600s the colonies in the Americas based their economies on agricultural products that required intensive labor. Slaves planted and harvested sugar, tobacco, and coffee crops. They also worked silver mines.

Triangular Trade   The slave trade was part of what was called the **triangular trade**. Ships sailed the legs of a triangle formed by Europe, Africa, and the New World. Typically, European ships left their home ports carrying manufactured goods. In West Africa the ship captains traded their goods for slaves. During the second leg of the journey, the ships brought the slaves across the Atlantic to Caribbean islands or to the North American mainland. The slaves were sold, and the money was used to buy sugar or tobacco. Finally, the ships returned to Europe to sell the goods purchased in the New World.

Middle Passage   A slave's journey from Africa to the New World was a ghastly ordeal called the **middle passage**. This second or middle leg of the triangular trade originated from ports along a 3,000-mile (4,800-kilometer) stretch on the west coast of Africa. Often captured by other Africans, slaves were sold to European slave traders at outposts along the coast for transport to New World plantations.

Because large cargoes brought large profits, the slave traders packed the captives as tightly as possible. Below deck, each slave occupied a space only four or five feet (152.40 centimeters) long and two or three feet high (91.44 centimeters). Chained together, they could neither stand nor lie at full length. In the darkness and stifling heat, many slaves suffocated or died of disease.

Estimates of the number of African slaves brought to America range from 10 to 24 million. One in five who began the trip did not survive it. Because of the enormous value of their "cargo," however, slave traders made some effort to keep the slaves alive. Psychological torment may have been worse than physical conditions. Some Africans committed suicide by jumping overboard. Others simply lost the will to live and refused to eat. Slaves on hunger strikes were fed forcibly.

A Slave's Life   Slaves who survived the long middle passage faced another terror when they arrived in New World ports: the slave auction. Examined and prodded by plantation owners, most slaves were sold to work as laborers—clearing land, hoeing, planting, weeding, and harvesting. The work was hard, the hours long, and life expectancy short. Because many Europeans believed that Africans were physically suited to hard labor, especially in hot, humid climates, slaves were viewed as nothing more than a unit of labor to exploit for profit.

SECTION 2 REVIEW

Recall

1. **Define:** conquistador, triangular trade, middle passage
2. **Identify:** Pedro Alvares Cabral, Henry Hudson, Hernán Cortés, Montezuma II, Francisco Pizarro, Atahualpa, Hernando de Soto, Francisco Vásquez de Coronado, Giovanni da Verrazano, Jacques Cartier, Samuel de Champlain, Jacques Marquette, Louis Joliet, John Cabot
3. **List:** Where did the Portuguese and Dutch establish empires?
4. **Name:** What goals had the Spanish for an American empire?

Critical Thinking

5. **Analyze:** Compare and contrast the treatment of the native people in the colonies of Spain, France, and England.
6. **Evaluate:** What impact did the slave trade have on Europeans who had large amounts of property?

Applying Concepts

7. **Movement:** What motivated Europeans to move from the Old World to the New?

Expanding Horizons

The age of exploration brought far-reaching changes to European society and culture. Overseas trade and colonial ventures stimulated and expanded the European economy. Business methods and banking practices became more sophisticated in order to facilitate profit from the flourishing world trade.

Commercial Revolution

By the 1600s the nation had replaced the city and village as the basic economic unit. Nations competed for both markets and trade goods. New business methods were instituted for investing money, speeding the flow of wealth, and reducing risks in commercial ventures. These changes, which came to be known as the Commercial Revolution, formed the roots of modern business life.

New Business Methods Launching an overseas trading venture was a major financial undertaking. The financial backer of the voyage had to raise money to pay for goods and supplies and to hire a captain and crew. Often several years passed as a fleet traveled from port to port, buying and selling, then embarked for the trip home. Only then could the initial investment be recovered. Governments and rich merchants alone had enough money to back such trading voyages, and even they needed financial assistance.

At first merchants turned to bankers for the capital, or money, to finance their ventures. Families like the Medici of Florence and the Fuggers of Augsburg loaned money as part of their commercial operations. By the 1500s these families were so wealthy that they accepted deposits, made loans, and transferred funds over long distances. Both banking families had

branches in several European cities and also made loans to European monarchs.

By the 1600s, however, these banking families were beginning to be replaced by government-chartered banks. The banks accepted deposits of money and charged interest on loans. Before long the banks began to provide other services to simplify trade transactions. They issued bank notes and checks, making large payments in heavy coins a thing of the past. They acted as money changers, exchanging currencies from other countries. The banks even provided official exchange rates for foreign currency.

Individual merchants who wanted to invest in exploration often raised money by combining their resources in **joint-stock companies**, organizations that sold stock, or shares, in the venture, enabling large and small investors to share the profits and risks of a trading voyage. If a loss occurred, investors would lose only the amount they had invested in shares. This sharing of risk provided a stable way of raising funds for voyages.

A few joint-stock companies became rich and powerful through government support. The Dutch government gave the Dutch East India Company a monopoly in trade with Africa and the East Indies. It also gave the company the power to make war, to seize foreign ships, to coin money, and to establish colonies and forts. In return the government received customs duties, or taxes on imported goods, from the company's trade.

Increase in Money Coins remained the usual means of exchange, so that the gold and silver that flowed into Europe from colonies around the world caused the supply of money to increase. As money became more widely available for large enterprises, ideas changed about the nature and goals of business. Gradually, a

Learning from Art *In the late 1400s, increased trade demanded changes in the organization and operation of commercial activities. Advanced banking methods were adopted at small exchange banks such as this one in Florence.* **What other economic innovations were made during the Commercial Revolution?**

system based on the belief that the goal of business was to make profits took shape. Individuals known as **entrepreneurs** combined money, ideas, raw materials, and labor to make goods and profits.

An entrepreneur in the cloth industry, for example, would buy wool and employ spinners to make the wool into yarn. Weavers and dyers would also be hired to turn the yarn into cloth. The entrepreneur would then sell the cloth on the open market for a price that brought a profit. Of course, entrepreneurs took risks when they put up capital for businesses. They could lose their investment if prices fell or workers could not produce goods at a specified time or for a specific market.

In the 1600s the greatest increase in business activity took place in the countries bordering the Atlantic Ocean—Portugal, Spain, England, and the Netherlands—in large part because these countries had the largest colonial empires. Italian cities such as Venice and Genoa, formerly the leading trade centers in Europe, found themselves cut out of overseas trade as trade routes and trade fortunes gradually moved westward toward the Atlantic Ocean and the New World.

Mercantilism

A new theory of national economic policy called **mercantilism** also appeared. This theory held that a state's power depended on its wealth. Accordingly, the goal of every nation was to become as wealthy as possible.

Europeans believed that the measure of a nation's wealth was the amount of **bullion**, or gold and silver, it owned. One Venetian summed up the general feeling about bullion: "[It is] the sinews of all government, it gives it its pulse, its movement, its mind, soul, and it is its essence and its very life. It overcomes all impossibilities, for it is the master. . . without it all is weak and without movement."

Nations could gain wealth by mining gold and silver at home or overseas. Thus, Spain sent conquistadors to the Americas to seize the silver and gold mines of the Aztec and Inca empires. Governments could also gain wealth through trade. Nations sought to create a favorable **balance of trade** by exporting more goods than they imported. The gold and silver received for exports would exceed that paid for imports. This greater wealth meant greater national power and influence in the world.

Las Casas and the Colonial System

"All the peoples of the world are men," stated Dominican friar Bartolomé de Las Casas in a proclamation in 1519. It touched off a controversy that endures today. What Las Casas meant was that Spanish conquistadores should stop viewing New World inhabitants as "beasts" or "natural" slaves or childlike. For Las Casas, the people in the New World needed to be respected.

To convince his fellow Spaniards of his ideas, Las Casas published pamphlets and treatises documenting the inhumanity of the Spanish colonial system. His writings were so passionate and horrific that they were used as propaganda against Spain for hundreds of years, long after Las Casas' death. This has made Las Casas controversial.

Despite his notoriety in the Spanish government, there are no known paintings of Las Casas made during his lifetime or any accounts that describe him. He was born in Spain, and became a priest. In 1502, at the age of 28, Las Casas journeyed to Haiti in the New World. Despite being a priest, Las Casas was a landowner and slave owner until 1514. At that time he renounced his material ambitions and dedicated the rest of his life to securing Indian rights.

The ideas of Las Casas did not dramatically change the Spanish conquest in the New World. However, it is significant that he was the first European to protest the injustices of the colonial system.

Reflecting on the Person
1. How did Spaniards of the 1400s view New World inhabitants?
2. Why was Las Casas such a controversial figure?

Colonies served a definite purpose in the mercantilist system. They were both the sources of raw materials as well as vital markets for finished goods provided by the parent country. The primary reason for having colonies was to help make the parent country self-sufficient.

Businesses that produced export goods also helped a nation to prosper. For instance, the Dutch exported wool cloth throughout Europe. Governments encouraged manufacturing by setting tariffs, or taxes, on imports and exports. One reason Spain and Portugal went into decline was that they did not build extensive manufacturing industries within their countries. Gold and silver from the Americas flowed to the Far East to pay for spices and silk and to northern Europe to pay for manufactured goods and weapons to send to their colonies. On the other hand, mercantilism helped European countries like England amass enormous national wealth that it used to build a colonial empire.

Social and Religious Trends

From the time of the Black Death in the mid-1300s, European populations grew. Towns outgrew their fortifications as more and more people left the countryside to be closer to trade centers where goods and services were in high demand. Europe's population was about 55 million in 1450. By 1650 it was 100 million.

During the years of this population growth, European contact with the rest of the world also increased. New ideas and new products flooded into Europe. New foods, such as corn, chocolate, and potatoes, and new drinks like coffee and tea were introduced. Sugar became widely available. Some people enjoyed the luxuries of African ivory or perfumes, silk, and jewels from East Asia.

Coffee houses became social gathering places where these new products were tasted and discussed. A Spaniard described a coffee house in Amsterdam in 1688:

[They] are of great usefulness in winter, with their welcoming stoves and tempting pastimes; some offer books to read, others gaming-tables and all have people ready to converse with one; one man drinks chocolate, another coffee, one milk, another tea and practically all of them smoke tobacco. . . . In this way they can keep warm, be refreshed and entertained for little expense, listening to the news.

—Joseph de la Vega, from *The Wheels of Commerce*, 1817

At first some people rejected foods from the New World. For example, many believed that

CONNECTIONS: GEOGRAPHY IN HISTORY

Language, Customs, and Culture

During the age of exploration, Europeans spread their customs and languages to the lands they explored and settled. Today, the world has distinct cultural regions that reflect European influences.

Spain at one time controlled all of South America except Brazil, as well as the southern half of North America. "Latin" America is so called because the people there still speak Spanish, Portuguese, or French— each a language derived from Latin. Many Latin Americans today practice Roman Catholicism, brought by Christian missionaries in the 1500s.

When Portuguese explorers first landed on the eastern shores of South America, they called certain trees they saw brazilwoods. The trees had the color of a glowing ember, called *brasa* in Portuguese. They named the country Brazil, after the trees. Today the Portuguese language and culture are still strongly felt in what is now the largest and most populous country in South America.

During the 1700s and 1800s, on the other side of the world, the British Empire controlled India and the island of Hong Kong in China. The English language is still spoken in both places, along with the native languages. In turn, the English language has been enriched by Indian words such as *pajama* and *jodhpur* and by Chinese words such as *kowtow* and *kumquat*.

Making the Connection
1. What evidence of Spanish colonization remains in the United States?
2. How do language and customs spread culture from one people to another? Which of these do you think is adopted first and why?

potatoes caused leprosy. Eventually new foods and beverages became accepted at European tables. New dress materials, such as calico and muslin, arrived from Asia, and spun cotton clothing came into general use.

Merchants prospered most from the trade and colonial expansion of the Commercial Revolution. Living better than the princes of a few centuries earlier, they began to surpass the nobility in both wealth and power. Hereditary nobles had to rely on rents from their lands for wealth, but rents did not rise as fast as prices. The newly rich entrepreneurs used their influence to change European society.

In the countryside, however, peasants lived as meagerly as they ever had. The French writer Jean de La Bruyère (lah broo YAYR) remarked that European peasants worked like animals, lived in hovels, and survived on a diet of water, black bread, and roots.

During the Middle Ages, street beggars were pitied, not scorned, but mercantilist ideas held that those who were idle were a burden to society. Changing religious attitudes also greatly emphasized the value of work. New laws made it a crime not to work. Governments provided some relief to the "worthy poor," not out of charity but because a strong nation needed healthy workers and soldiers.

Later, overseas colonies became an outlet for some of Europe's surplus population. Governments used colonies as a dumping ground for the poor, criminals, and other outcasts. Some people went voluntarily, drawn by tales of wealth and unlimited free land.

FOOTNOTES TO HISTORY

SPANISH DOUBLOONS AND PIECES OF EIGHT

While Spain dominated New World trade during the sixteenth century, Spanish ships called galleons sailed the seas loaded with gold doubloons and silver pieces of eight. Minted from the plunder of Central and South American mines, the coins were a favorite target for pirates from other nations. By raiding Spanish galleons, English, Dutch, and French pirates acquired the gold and silver bullion so important to their balance of trade. Today, marine archaeologists working in the Caribbean have explored a number of sunken galleons and recovered hundreds of doubloons and pieces of eight—still worth a fortune.

Economic pressure, wars, and religious persecution led many people to venture to the Americas. Most went to Dutch and English colonies because the Spanish barred non-Spaniards and the French banned Huguenots, or French Protestants. With land of their own and economic freedom, colonists prospered and enriched the countries that had cast them out.

Exploration and empires spread European civilization. Christian missionaries brought European culture to Africa, Asia, and the Americas. Traders in colonial ports spread their customs and language to native populations.

SECTION 3 REVIEW

Recall
1. **Define:** joint-stock company, entrepreneur, mercantilism, bullion, balance of trade
2. **Identify:** Who were some of the first banking families to begin to finance trading ventures?
3. **Explain:** Why did a trade voyage overseas require large sums of money?

Critical Thinking
4. **Analyze:** How important were European governments to the operation of the Commercial Revolution?
5. **Synthesize:** Imagine that you are an entrepreneur living during the 1700s. Invent a way in which you can make profits by using your capital and talents.

Appraise the potential risks and profits in your venture.

Applying Concepts
6. **Change:** Decide which class of European society benefited most from the Commercial Revolution. Explain its effects on two social groups living at that time.

COMPARING THEMATIC MAPS

Have you ever gone to a theme party? A theme is a central idea, and a theme party is structured around it.

Explanation

Maps also can have a theme. A thematic map is a map that shows information about a specialized subject. By comparing thematic maps, you can uncover new information. Use the following steps to *compare thematic maps*:

- Read titles to determine the theme or subject.
- Interpret symbols, dates, and map keys to clarify meaning.
- Draw conclusions about the relationships that exist between two maps.

Example

Comparing the thematic maps on this page, you realize from the title that the maps compare European land claims in North America at different times. The colors indicate the land area individual nations claimed. In 1650 Spain claimed the most land in North America. By 1753, however, France and England had extended their claims. You can conclude that Spain's New World claims were challenged by other nations between 1650 and 1753.

Application

Study the maps on page 395 of Section 1, and answer the questions:
1. What is the theme or themes?
2. What conclusions can be drawn by comparing these maps?

Practice

Turn to Practicing Skills on page 413 of the Chapter Review for further practice comparing thematic maps.

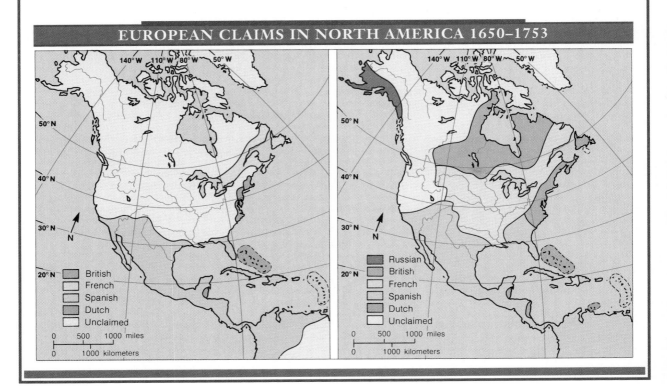

EUROPEAN CLAIMS IN NORTH AMERICA 1650–1753

CHAPTER 16 REVIEW

HISTORICAL SIGNIFICANCE

The age of exploration brought the people of Europe, Asia, the Americas, and sub-Saharan Africa into direct contact for the first time. Through exploration, the size and dimensions of the world and of the world's oceans became known. Europeans established control over the Americas, beginning a process of colonization that would leave a permanent—and often negative—imprint on the cultures they conquered.

Western civilization spread throughout the world by means of competitive trade networks, devastating many older cultures and empires and bringing economic stability and prosperity to a few European nations. Thus began the modern era, in which all peoples of the world are linked—if not equally, then at least economically—which contributes to a borrowing and blending of ideas from many cultures.

SUMMARY

For a Summary of Chapter 16, see Unit 4 Synopsis on pages 458-461.

USING KEY TERMS

A. Write a sentence or two about each set of terms. The sentences should show how the words are related.
1. triangular trade, middle passage
2. mercantilism, bullion, balance of trade

B. Write a definition for each key term below. Then write one or two sentences that show how the terms are related to the European exploration of the world.
3. cartographer
4. circumnavigation
5. conquistador
6. entrepreneur
7. joint-stock company
8. line of demarcation

REVIEWING FACTS

1. **Identify:** How did Prince Henry the Navigator inspire early Portuguese expeditions along the west coast of Africa?
2. **Describe:** What improvements were incorporated in the European caravel?
3. **Explain:** Why did the Dutch turn to commerce instead of agriculture in the late 1500s?

4. **List:** What European countries showed the biggest increase in business activity in the 1600s?
5. **Describe:** What was the middle passage like for African slaves?
6. **Explain:** What was the chief difference between French and English aims for their colonies?
7. **List:** What factors motivated European settlers who went to the New World?
8. **Explain:** How did a joint-stock company enable small investors to profit from a major voyage?

THINKING CRITICALLY

1. **Apply:** Why did Columbus's plan to reach Asia by a western route appeal to Spain?
2. **Analyze:** Were the English and the Spanish justified in colonizing the Americas? Why or why not?
3. **Evaluate:** How would the colonies have been different if Europeans had not used slave labor?
4. **Synthesize:** Would the Portuguese have tried to colonize North and South America if the line of demarcation had not been drawn?
5. **Evaluate:** How did the influx of wealth from the colonies help bring about the Commercial Revolution?
6. **Analyze:** What were the results of Magellan's circumnavigation?

7. Apply: Why were the Dutch eager to establish overseas colonies?

ANALYZING CONCEPTS

1. Innovation: How did discoveries by non-Europeans help Europeans begin their voyages of exploration?

2. Movement: How did European exploration and colonization affect changes in world populations?

3. Change: How did the Commercial Revolution encourage more voyages of exploration and colonization?

PRACTICING SKILLS

1. Imagine that you are viewing three maps of Florida that appear together. One map shows the average rainfall in the state, another shows the average temperature, and the third shows the natural vegetation. What kind of conclusion might you draw by comparing these three maps?

2. Imagine that you are looking at a map that shows the climate of a certain area. You also have information that shows a dramatic rise in automobile emissions since 1900. What other maps would you need to consult if you wanted to determine whether the increased automobile emissions had any effect on average temperatures?

GEOGRAPHY IN HISTORY

1. Location: Refer to the map on page 402. What is the global address of Columbus's first landfall in the New World?

2. Place: What are the present-day names for much of what used to be the Aztec and Inca empires?

3. Movement: Refer to the map on page 402. Which way did Europeans first sail to reach the Indies? Who first reached the Indies by going east?

TRACING CHRONOLOGY

Refer to the time line below to answer these questions.

1. Which European nation dominated exploration in the 1400s? in the 1500s?

2. How long did Portugal's control of the spice trade last? Who replaced the Portuguese?

3. How long after England's first exploration of North America was the first permanent English colony established?

LINKING PAST AND PRESENT

1. History books used to say that Columbus "discovered" America. What did they mean, and why do we no longer see his voyage in this way?

2. Making profits was the force behind early entrepreneurs' efforts. Is this still their goal?

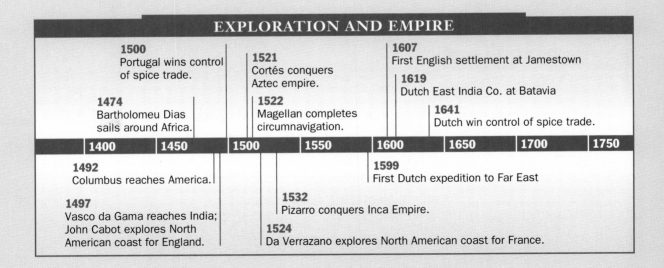

EXPLORATION AND EMPIRE

1500 Portugal wins control of spice trade.

1521 Cortés conquers Aztec empire.

1607 First English settlement at Jamestown

1619 Dutch East India Co. at Batavia

1474 Bartholomeu Dias sails around Africa.

1522 Magellan completes circumnavigation.

1641 Dutch win control of spice trade.

| 1400 | 1450 | 1500 | 1550 | 1600 | 1650 | 1700 | 1750 |

1492 Columbus reaches America.

1599 First Dutch expedition to Far East

1497 Vasco da Gama reaches India; John Cabot explores North American coast for England.

1532 Pizarro conquers Inca Empire.

1524 Da Verrazano explores North American coast for France.

Royal Power and Conflict

*W*e hunted all morning, got back around 3 o'clock in the afternoon, changed, went up to gamble until 7 o'clock, then to the play, which never ended before 10:30, then on to the ball until 3 o'clock in the morning. . . . So you see how much time I had for writing."

Princess Elizabeth-Charlotte, sister-in-law of France's King Louis XIV, described court life at the Palace of Versailles in a letter to a friend as an endless round of social activities. A man of tremendous energy and drive, Louis routinely devoted eight or nine hours daily to matters of state, regularly rode and hunted, ate with great enthusiasm, and expected courtiers, or members of his court, to do the same as well.

CHAPTER PREVIEW

Key Terms to Define: absolutism, balance of power, intendant

People to Meet: Philip II, Henry VIII, Mary I, Elizabeth I, William Shakespeare, Huguenots, Henry of Navarre, Henry IV, Louis XIII, Cardinal Richelieu, Louis XIV, Maria Theresa, Frederick the Great, Ivan the Terrible, Peter the Great, Catherine the Great

Places to Discover: Versailles, Silesia, Moscow, St. Petersburg, Siberia

Objectives to Learn:
1. Why did Philip II have difficulty ruling the Spanish Empire?
2. How did Elizabeth I affect the balance of power in Europe?
3. How was the Thirty Years' War different from wars prior to it?

Royal court life in Europe reflected the great wealth and power of monarchs.

4. What is absolute monarchy and why did monarchs demand complete loyalty to the crown?

Concepts to Understand:
- Conflict—Spanish and English monarchs engage in a dynastic struggle. Section 1
- Change—Tudor monarchs bring stability to England. Section 2
- Uniformity—France's Louis XIV strengthens absolute monarchy in France and limits rights of religious dissenters. Section 3
- Conflict—Dynastic and religious conflicts divide the German states. Section 4
- Innovation—Peter the Great attempts to modernize Russian society. Section 5

Spain

In the 1500s and 1600s, the monarchs of Europe worked to end the independence of cities and feudal territories. They sought to create powerful kingdoms in which the loyalties of all their subjects would be directed to the Crown. The authority of such rule was based on **absolutism,** a form of government with unlimited power held by one individual or a group (such as a monarch and his or her advisers). Its strength came from the political theory popular in the 1500s and 1600s that a king or queen ruled by divine right—that is, he or she derived absolute, or complete, authority to govern directly from God and was responsible to God alone for his or her actions. Centralized rule, it was reasoned, would serve as a unifying force and bring about greater efficiency and control.

For most of this period, the Hapsburgs of Spain were the leading power of western Europe. They drew their strength from their possessions in the New World and Europe, which included Spain, the Netherlands, Milan, Burgundy, and after 1580, Portugal. The Spanish Hapsburgs tried to increase their empire's prestige and wealth but faced unrest and opposition to their absolute rule.

Philip II

Philip II, who ruled from 1556 to 1598, was the most powerful monarch in Spanish history. A devout Catholic, Philip saw himself as the leading defender of the faith. His efforts to end Protestantism in his domains made him the enemy of all Protestants. Son of the Holy Roman Emperor Charles V and Isabella of Portugal, Philip worked to increase the Hapsburg family's power throughout Europe. This effort led Philip to involve Spain in a number of costly European wars.

Known as the Prudent King, Philip II was cautious, hardworking, and suspicious of others. He built a granite palace called El Escorial, which served as royal court, art gallery, monastery, and tomb for Spanish royalty. There Philip spent most of his time at his desk, carefully reading and responding to hundreds of documents that poured in from all over the empire. He used councils of bureaucrats to advise him and to handle routine matters, but he made all decisions and signed all papers.

Unrest Philip II faced many difficulties in ruling Spain and his vast European and overseas empire. The provinces of Spain had been officially united when Ferdinand of Aragon married Isabella of Castile in 1469. A uniform system of government for the country had not been established, however. Separate laws and provincial authorities were allowed to remain. Gradually the ways of the Castile region came to dominate Spanish life. In the 1500s Castile had the most territory, the largest population, and the greatest wealth of all the Spanish territories.

Philip II made Castile the center of Spain and the empire. Madrid, located in Castile, became the capital. The Castilian, or literary, form of Spanish was spoken at the royal court. Most of Philip's advisers came from Castile. Trade from the overseas empire was controlled by the Castilian city of Seville, and Castilian merchants benefited most from trade. Leaders in Aragon and other Spanish provinces resented the dominance of Castile, and in the 1590s, Aragon revolted. The revolt was put down, but discontent continued into the 1600s.

Religious Policy Philip had to deal with a number of troubling religious issues in his European domains. He was concerned about the loyalty of large religious minorities in Spain. These minorities included Protestants, Marranos (Jews who had converted to Christianity), and Moriscos (Muslims who had become Christians). Philip supported the Inquisition's efforts to uproot the heresies believed to exist among these groups. The Inquisition was so thorough that Protestantism never took hold in Spain. Its actions, however, led to a revolt by the Moriscos in 1569. The revolt was brutally crushed two years later.

In 1566, when Philip had sought to impose Catholicism on the Netherlands, Dutch Protestants rebelled against his rule. This conflict proved to be long, bloody, and complex. The Dutch declared their independence in 1581, but the fighting continued. England gave support to the Dutch and to the English "sea dogs" who raided Spanish ships in their ports.

Spanish Armada In the early years of his reign, Philip had supported Elizabeth I as queen of England, in spite of the pope's opposition. When Elizabeth helped Protestant rebels in the Netherlands, Philip decided that to solve his problems with the Netherlands, he had to rid himself of Elizabeth first.

In 1586 Philip laid plans to invade England. For two years the wealth and talent of his empire went toward that effort. On May 30, 1588, a force of 130 ships and 33,000 men, known as the Spanish Armada, sailed for England.

In late July the Armada entered the English Channel in crescent formation. The English had faster, more maneuverable ships and longer-range cannons than did the Spanish. But they were unable at first to block the Spanish formation. English fire ships, however, were able to separate the Spanish ships. Running out of shot and desperately short of water, the Spanish fleet was forced to retreat to the stormy North Sea. About 40 Spanish ships sank near the rocky coasts of Scotland and Ireland. As many as 15,000 Spanish soldiers died.

Last of the Spanish Hapsburgs

The defeat of the Armada marked the beginning of Spain's decline as a European power. Costly wars drained the country's treasury, and the government was forced to borrow from foreign bankers. The Spanish economy suffered inflation; industry and agriculture deteriorated; and twice Philip's government had to declare bankruptcy.

Philip II's successors were not prepared to deal with Spain's decline. Philip's son and grandson, Philip III and Philip IV, lacked his intelligence, enthusiasm, and interest in politics. They turned over most of the affairs of the government to nobles. Government mismanagement led to widespread corruption. The royal family and nobles retreated from national problems by building extravagant homes, holding lavish parties, and wearing expensive clothes.

The war with the Dutch was renewed under Philip IV. Spain then became involved in a series

Learning from Art *For more than 25 years, the Dutch rebelled against Spanish rule under Philip II. Eventually the Dutch were successful in this first major challenge to western European absolutism.* **What other country opposed Philip?**

Learning from Maps
The Spanish and Austrian Hapsburgs sought to gain territories throughout Europe during the 1500s and 1600s. **What area won independence from Spanish Hapsburg rule in 1581?**

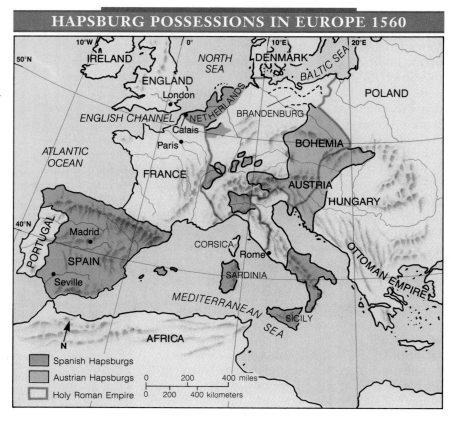

HAPSBURG POSSESSIONS IN EUROPE 1560

Spanish Hapsburgs
Austrian Hapsburgs
Holy Roman Empire

of conflicts involving Germany and France. A decade of famine in the 1640s ended with the plague of 1648–1649, resulting in the death of thousands of Spaniards. Overburdened and overtaxed, citizens in parts of the country began to rebel. Portugal, a part of Spain since 1580, was one of those areas. The Portuguese struggle continued until 1668, when Spain finally recognized Portugal's independence.

Philip IV's son Charles II was the last of the Spanish Hapsburgs. He became king in 1665 at the age of four, ruling under the regency of his mother. No one expected him to rule long, since he was physically and mentally weak. Although Charles later married, he did not have any children. With no heirs to the throne of Spain, European monarchs plotted to control the succession to the Spanish throne.

SECTION 1 REVIEW

Recall

1. **Define:** absolutism
2. **Identify:** Philip II, El Escorial, Marranos, Moriscos, Spanish Armada
3. **Locate:** Milan, Burgundy, Castile, Madrid, the Netherlands, Portugal

Critical Thinking

4. **Explain:** What were the reasons for internal conflict under Philip II's rule?
5. **Analyze:** Why did Philip II send the Spanish Armada against England? What was the outcome of this effort?

6. **Analyze:** What happened to Spain and its European empire under Philip II's successors?

Applying Concepts

7. **Conflict:** How did Philip II's successors respond to the Spanish Empire's decline?

England

England, like Spain, developed a strong monarchy. Its Tudor dynasty, which ruled from 1485 to 1603, brought unity to the country after a long period of decline and disorder. Tudor monarchs were hardworking, able, and popular. They greatly expanded the power and authority of the Crown. They were not, however, as absolute in their rule as other European monarchs. Instead, institutions such as Parliament and the courts of law set bounds to their authority.

Early Tudors

Henry VII, the first Tudor monarch, became king in 1485 after the Wars of the Roses. He used shrewd maneuvering to disarm his rivals and to increase the prestige of his family. Most of Henry's close advisers came from the gentry and merchant classes. Titles were given to these officials, who formed a new aristocracy dependent on the king.

Henry VII helped rebuild England's commercial prosperity. He encouraged the expansion of foreign trade, especially the export of finished woolens to the Netherlands, Germany, and Venice. He promoted the improved collection of taxes as well as careful government spending. In foreign policy Henry avoided war, using diplomacy and royal marriages to strengthen England's interests abroad.

The second Tudor to rule was Henry VIII, son of Henry VII and the most powerful of all Tudor monarchs. Unlike his father, Henry VIII fought wars on the European continent and began to make England a great naval power. His personal life, however, would have a lasting effect on English history. In his pursuit of a male heir and a happy marriage, Henry married six times. Although he was the most powerful of the Tudor monarchs, Henry VIII worked with Parliament to obtain his personal goals and to break with the Catholic Church. As a result of this cooperation, the House of Commons increased its power during Henry's reign.

After Henry VIII's death in 1547, England entered a brief period of turmoil. Edward VI, Henry's son and successor, was only 10 years old when he became king. He died in 1553 after a short reign. Protestant nobles then plotted to prevent Edward's Catholic half-sister, Mary, from becoming queen. The English people, however, supported Mary's claim to the Tudor throne.

Mary's Catholic policies soon offended the English. Despite strong opposition, Mary married Philip II of Spain in 1554. The next year, she restored Catholicism and burned more than 300 Protestants at the stake for heresy. At Philip's urging, Mary involved England in a war with France. As a result, England lost the port of Calais, its final foothold on the European continent. Many English people feared that England would be controlled by Spain. Before this fear could be realized, Mary died childless, and the throne then passed to her Protestant half-sister, Elizabeth.

Elizabeth I

Elizabeth I became queen in 1558, when she was 25 years old. She was shrewd, highly educated, and had a forceful personality. With a sharp tongue she asserted her iron will, causing sparks to fly in exchanges with Parliament. However, Elizabeth used her authority for the common good of her people. On frequent journeys throughout the kingdom Elizabeth earned the loyalty and confidence of her subjects. During her travels, Elizabeth stayed at the homes of nobles who entertained her with banquets, parades, and dances.

Elizabeth's reign was one of England's great cultural periods. Poets and writers praised Elizabeth in their works. The theater flourished under playwrights such as William Shakespeare. During Elizabeth's reign, English was transformed into a language of beauty, grace, vigor, and clarity.

People fully expected that Elizabeth would marry and that her husband would rule. The common attitude of the time was that only men were fit to rule and that government matters were beyond a woman's ability. Elizabeth, however, was slow in seeking a husband. She had learned from the lesson of her sister Mary: to marry a foreign prince would endanger England. At the same time, marrying an Englishman would cause jealousies among the English nobility. In the end, Elizabeth refused to give up her powers as monarch for the sake of marriage. To one of her suitors she stormed, "God's death! My lord, I will have but one mistress [England] and no master." Elizabeth's refusal to marry caused a great deal of speculation as to who would succeed her.

Domestic Policy In matters of government, Elizabeth was assisted by a council made up of 12 to 15 nobles. With her approval they drafted proclamations, handled foreign relations, and supervised such matters as the administration of justice and the regulation of prices and wages. These royal advisers were assisted by small staffs of professional but poorly paid bureaucrats.

Although Parliament did not have the power to initiate legislation, it could plead, urge, advise, and withhold approval. These powers gave Parliament some influence, especially when it was asked to consider tax laws.

IMAGES
OF THE TIME

Tudor England

Under Tudor monarchs, England enjoyed a period of stability and relative prosperity.

William Shakespeare (1564–1616) was the author of many plays—tragedies, comedies, and histories—that were performed at London's Globe Theatre.

Henry VIII, Elizabeth I's father, commissioned several palaces, among them Hampton Court (above). A map c. 1574 (right) provides a detailed view of London's streets, buildings, and surrounding countryside.

Elizabeth believed in the importance of social rank. During the late 1500s, English society was led by the queen and her court. Next were prominent nobles from the great landed families and a middle group of gentry, merchants, lawyers, and clergy. This group provided the source of Tudor strength and stability. The lowst social rank was comprised of yeomen, or farmers with small landholdings, and laborers.

Government laws and policies closely regulated the lives of the common people. The Statute of Apprentices of 1563 declared work to be a social and moral duty. It required people to live and work where they were born, controlled the movement of labor, fixed wages, and regulated apprenticeships. The Poor Laws of 1597 and 1601 made local areas responsible for their own homeless and unemployed. These laws included means to raise money for charity and to provide work for vagabonds.

Elizabeth inherited a monarchy that was badly in debt. Royal revenues barely covered annual expenses. The queen, however, spent lavishly on court ceremonies to show the power and dignity of the monarchy. In other matters, she showed the greatest financial restraint, leading many to call her a "pinchpenny."

To raise funds without relying on Parliament, Elizabeth sold off royal lands, offices, licenses, monopolies, and the right to collect customs. These measures helped but could not solve the problem. England faced the costs of war and mounting inflation. Elizabeth was therefore forced to turn to Parliament for funds. When she ended her reign, England remained badly in debt.

Foreign Policy By Elizabeth's time, England had lost all of its possessions on the European continent. France was too powerful for

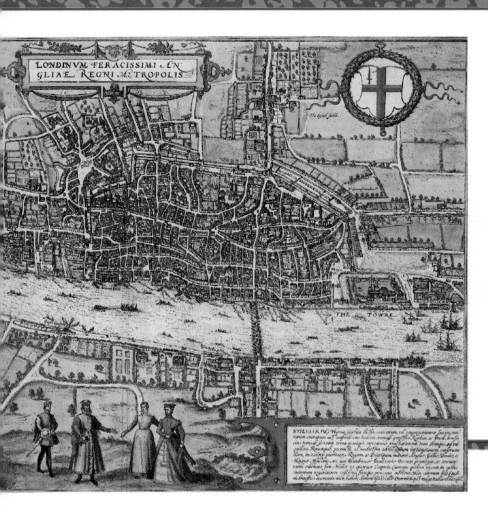

Miniature portraits were often given by Elizabeth I to members of the court. Nicholas Hilliard, the queen's official miniaturist, painted this one.

Reflecting on the Times
What can you learn about life in London from the map at the left?

England to defeat in order to regain territories. Although England could not completely withdraw from continental affairs, it developed a foreign policy suitable for a small island nation with limited resources.

For security, the English relied on the English Channel to protect their island from European invaders. Building and maintaining a strong navy was therefore important in defending the nation. For that reason, Elizabeth continued the efforts begun by her Tudor predecessors to build such a navy.

Spain and France posed the greatest naval threats to England. The attack of the Spanish Armada made England realize the dangers of an alliance between Spain and France. England might be able to defeat one power, but certainly not both. As a result, the English relied on diplomacy as well as sea power to protect their interests.

During Elizabeth's reign, England worked to balance the power of European nations. In international affairs, **balance of power** refers to the system in which each nation helps to keep peace and order by maintaining power that is equal to, or in balance with, rival nations. One nation cannot overpower another. If one nation becomes more powerful than the other, a third nation can reestablish the balance by supporting the second nation.

CONNECTIONS: SCIENCE AND TECHNOLOGY

Fountains

In Rome, water pours from this fountain, created by Bernini in the 1600s.

Fountains have existed for thousands of years in many parts of the world. During the 1600s, French and English monarchs admired Rome's magnificent fountains and decided to make fountains an integral part of their palace grounds.

The ancient Romans, copying earlier Greek models, built hundreds of fountains throughout their city. Eleven aqueducts carried a continuous torrent of water to the sprawling metropolis. The water flowed constantly, feeding 1,200 fountains and 1,000 public baths. The flow ended in A.D. 537, when the Goths destroyed the aqueducts and many of the fountains.

It was not until the 1600s—nearly a thousand years later—that the Romans began restoring the pipes. The popes commissioned artists to design and build beautiful new fountains where citizens could gather water and restore their spirits.

The fountain builders constructed the flow of water over exquisite sculptures. Gigantic marble statues of ancient gods and goddesses spouted water from their mouths, ears, feet, and fingers.

Roman sculptor Giovanni Bernini's Fountain of the Four Rivers (1651) featured not only deities, but also marble lions, horses, crocodiles, and armadillos. Several beautiful fountains (begun in 1661) on the palace grounds at Versailles, near Paris, featured elaborate pumping systems.

Making the Connection
1. What technological feature of the fountains at Versailles replaced the ancient Roman use of aqueducts?
2. Why are fountains a special feature in many of today's malls and city centers?

Learning from Art
Although Elizabeth I always appeared to be an extravagant monarch, the queen actually had many financial worries. Throughout her reign, she relied increasingly on Parliament for funds. **How did Elizabeth raise additional money?**

Under Elizabeth's rule, England operated as the third balancing nation. In the early part of Elizabeth's reign, England and Spain feared the power of the French. England cooperated with Spain in order to keep France out of the Netherlands. Later, when the Netherlands revolted against Philip II, the English supported the rebels and allied with the weaker power against the stronger one.

Scotland was largely Catholic and hostile toward England during the 1550s. Although part of Ireland was under English rule, the rest of the country resisted English armies. To protect English interests, Elizabeth sought to solidify her ties with Scotland and Ireland so they could not be used as bases for Spanish and French attacks on England.

In the 1560s, with Elizabeth's help, Scotland became Protestant and an ally of England. Thirty years later, England carried out military campaigns in Ireland to conquer the Irish. With Scotland and Ireland allied with England, a period of temporary peace came to the British Isles.

Elizabeth died in 1603 at the age of 69. With her death came the end of the Tudor dynasty. King James VI of Scotland, the Protestant son of Mary, Queen of Scots, became the new monarch of England. As James I, he founded the Stuart dynasty and united Scotland and England under a common ruler.

SECTION 2 REVIEW

Recall
1. **Define:** balance of power
2. **Identify:** Henry VII, Henry VIII, Edward VI, Elizabeth I, William Shakespeare, Poor Laws, James I
3. **Locate:** English Channel, Calais, Scotland, Ireland

Critical Thinking
4. **Explain:** How did Tudor monarchs restore order and respect for their throne?
5. **Analyze:** What was Elizabeth I's foreign policy?
6. **Evaluate:** Contrast the effect on English history of Henry's VIII's many marriages with the effect of his daughter's refusal to marry.

Applying Concepts
7. **Change:** Explain how the rule of Elizabeth I and the Tudor monarchy affected England.

France

After a period of religious conflict, peace was restored to France when Henry of Navarre became King Henry IV in 1589. He founded the Bourbon dynasty, which ruled France with some interruptions until the early 1800s. During most of that time, Bourbon kings maintained an absolute monarchy that was imitated by monarchs throughout Europe.

Henry IV

Henry IV was a Huguenot, but he converted to Catholicism to quiet his Catholic opponents. Believing that people's religious beliefs need not interfere with their loyalty to the government, Henry issued the Edict of Nantes in 1598 to reassure the Huguenots. The edict allowed Protestant worship to continue in areas where the Protestants were a majority, but barred Protestant worship in Paris and other Catholic strongholds. The edict granted Huguenots the same civil rights as Catholics.

These actions ended religious strife and enabled France to rebuild itself. With the help of his minister of finance, Henry restored the Crown's treasury, repaired roads and bridges, and supported trade and industry. He also tried to restore discipline in the army and bring order to the government bureaucracy. All of these royal policies were put into effect without the approval of the Estates-General and thus laid the foundation for the absolute rule of later Bourbon rulers.

Cardinal Richelieu

Henry's son Louis XIII inherited the throne in 1610 at the age of eight. Louis's mother, Marie de Medici, was regent for the next seven years. In 1617 Louis gained the throne by force and exiled his mother from court. A few years later he recalled Marie, and she convinced him to give power to one of her advisers, Cardinal Richelieu.

Gradually Louis gave complete control of the government to the cardinal, who set out to build an absolute monarchy in France. To realize this goal, he had to reduce the power of the nobles and the Huguenots.

When Louis XIII came to the throne, the nobility was in control of the provinces. Nobles collected taxes, administered justice, appointed local officials, and even made alliances with foreign governments. To end the nobles' power, Richelieu destroyed their fortified castles and stripped them of their local administrative functions. The nobility retained social prestige, while authority in local government affairs was given to special agents of the Crown known as **intendants.**

Richelieu also sought to take away the military and territorial rights given to the Huguenots by the Edict of Nantes. After radical Huguenots revolted against Louis XIII, Richelieu took away their right to independent fortified towns. However, they were allowed to keep their religious freedom.

Having weakened the monarchy's internal enemies, Richelieu sought to make France the supreme power in Europe. He strengthened the French army and took steps to build up the economy and to foster national unity.

Richelieu's support of French culture led to the French Academy, which received a royal charter to establish "fixed rules for the language . . . and render the French language not only elegant but also capable of treating all arts and sciences." In the following century, French became the preferred language of European diplomacy and culture.

Learning from Art *A formal portrait of Louis XIV captures the grandeur and majesty of the period's most renowned monarch.* **How did French culture reflect the glory of Louis XIV?**

Louis XIV

Louis XIV is recognized as the most powerful Bourbon monarch. He became king in 1643 at the age of five. At first, France was ruled by his two regents—his mother, Anne of Austria, and Cardinal Mazarin, Richelieu's successor. When Mazarin died in 1661, Louis announced that he would run his own government. He was then 23 years old.

Absolute Rule   The 72-year reign of Louis XIV was the longest in European history. It set the style for European monarchies during the 1600s and 1700s. During his own lifetime, Louis was known as the Sun King, around whom the royalty and nobility of Europe revolved. He set up a lavish court and surrounded himself with pomp and pageantry. Louis's monarchy had power as well as style. Although Louis relied on a bureaucracy, he was the source of all political authority in France. In one of his audiences, he is said to have boasted *"L'état, c'est moi!"* (I am the state!).

Louis emphasized a strong monarchy because of his fear of disorder without it. As a child, he had lived through the Fronde, a series of uprisings by nobles and peasants that occurred between 1648 and 1652. During the Fronde, royal troops lost control of Paris and mobs rioted in the streets. The young Louis and his regents were called to give an account of their actions before the Parliament, or supreme court of law. The Fronde was crushed, but Louis never forgot this attempt to limit royal power. As king, he intended never to let it happen again.

Court Life   Refusing to live in Paris, Louis moved his court and government to a new palace he built at Versailles. The palace was a vast, splendid structure. No expense was spared, for Versailles was to demonstrate the wealth, power, and glory of France.

The palace had elegant royal apartments, sweeping staircases, mirrored halls, priceless tapestries, and lavish formal salons and dining rooms. There were offices for government bureaucrats as well as tiny, cramped rooms where officials lived. As many as 10,000 people lived at Versailles. Outside the palace were acres of formal gardens, filled with marble sculptures and fountains.

In this setting Louis felt secure from the danger of Parisian mobs. Here he had the nobility attend his court so that he could control them.

Government Policies   Although Louis was an absolute monarch, he was not able simply to change the traditions of his country's feudal past. Changing these practices would have disrupted the kingdom and endangered his throne. Instead, the king kept the traditional ways, but added to them new administrative offices and practices.

Johann Sebastian Bach

Bach's signature appears on this manuscript for one of his cantatas.

Born in Eisenach, Germany, in 1685, Johann Sebastian Bach was one of the world's most talented composers. During his lifetime, however, he was best known for his abilities as an organist and harpsichordist.

The baroque style of music, which reached its height during the early 1700s, was characterized by lively, dramatic compositions. Often using complex rhythms and melodies, baroque music—like baroque painting and architecture—appealed to the audience's emotions.

Bach is especially known for his work with counterpoint and the fugue. In counterpoint, two or more melodies are combined. In the fugue, several instruments or voices play together, each playing the same melodies but with variations. Both techniques of composition produce complex and elaborate music. While exploring these compositional techniques, Bach drew upon various musical traditions from northern and southern Europe.

Bach's jobs included serving as musical director for Lutheran churches, which involved writing and playing music as well as directing other musicians and singers. During this period, "professional" music was found in only a few places—concert hall performances would come in the future.

Music—aside from folk music, of course—was played in basically three places: at churches for religious ceremonies; in wealthy or aristocratic homes, where chamber music was featured; and in the theaters, accompanying performances. Bach wrote works for the Lutheran Church and accepted commissions from wealthy aristocrats.

In addition, Bach wrote a number of works that seem to address not so much a listening audience as the musicians who would play the music. One example of such a work is the *Well-Tempered Clavier*, a collection of pieces that covers virtually every technique and key of the time to be played on the clavier, a keyboard instrument. The collection functioned not only as a guide in tuning the instrument but also as an exercise for the musician. The performance of this work requires a great deal of skill from the player.

Although the quantity of work Bach produced is impressive, very few of his compositions were published during his lifetime. It was only years after his death that he was recognized as a masterful composer of baroque music.

Responding to the Arts

1. How were Johann Sebastian Bach's musical compositions perceived during his lifetime? How were they viewed in later times?
2. For what types of compositions is J. S. Bach most noted?

While reforming some aspects of government practice, Louis failed to adjust the complicated and unjust tax system. The poor carried most of the tax burden, while nobles, clergy, and government officials were exempt from many payments.

Louis, however, carried out drastic changes in France's religious life. He regarded the Huguenots as a threat to his rule and believed that by accepting Catholicism, the Huguenots could prove their loyalty to the throne. In 1685 the Edict of Nantes was repealed. Huguenots could no longer practice their religion, and their children had to be educated in the Catholic faith. Many Huguenots who were diplomats, artisans, and merchants fled France to settle in the Netherlands, England, and England's American colonies. The loss of Huguenot skills seriously weakened France's economy.

Expansion Louis XIV pursued a bold and active foreign policy. His goal was to expand the glory and power of France. Other European rulers were fearful of Louis's desire for expansion, and as a result, allied in opposition to France.

Concern about the succession to the Spanish throne led both France and Austria to assert claims to it. Other nations were alarmed that the balance of power would be disrupted if France inherited Spain's vast empire. Prior to Spanish king Charles II's death, the European powers worked out a plan to divide the Spanish Empire. The will of Charles II upset this plan by stating that the entire empire should remain intact and pass to Louis XIV's grandson, Philip of Anjou.

Louis XIV accepted the provisions of the will. When Charles II died in 1700, Philip of Anjou became King Philip V of Spain. As a result, Europe was plunged into the War of the Spanish Succession.

Conflict The War of the Spanish Succession lasted from 1702 to 1713. During the conflict England, the Dutch Netherlands, and Austria led a Grand Alliance of European nations against France and Spain.

Peace was finally restored with the Treaty of Utrecht in 1713 in which England and the Dutch Netherlands recognized Philip V as king of Spain, on the condition that France and Spain never be united under one crown. France gained trade advantages with the Spanish colonial empire. However, France was forced to surrender the North American provinces of Nova Scotia and Newfoundland to England.

The War of the Spanish Succession drained the French treasury, brought increased poverty, and created opposition to Louis's rule.

Louis XIV's Legacy France enjoyed one of its most brilliant cultural periods under Louis XIV. Yet the Sun King's extravagances left the country near financial ruin. His rule weakened the nobility considerably. The peasants and the middle class resented the social privileges and wealth of the nobles. After Louis XIV's death in 1715, the nobility sought to expand its power under Louis's great-grandson, Louis XV. Continued conflict between the nobles and the middle and lower classes would bring France to the brink of revolution.

SECTION 3 REVIEW

Recall

1. **Define:** intendant
2. **Identify:** Henry IV, Edict of Nantes, Richelieu, Treaty of Utrecht
3. **Locate:** Versailles

Critical Thinking

4. **Explain:** How did Henry IV try to bring religious peace to France?
5. **Analyze:** What were Richelieu's goals? How did Richelieu reduce the power of the nobility? of the Huguenots?
6. **Synthesize:** What were the successes and failures of Louis XIV's reign?
7. **Analyze:** Why was the Edict of Nantes repealed, and what effect did this have on religious freedom in France?

Applying Concepts

8. **Uniformity:** How and why did Louis XIV seek to strengthen his rule in France?

The German States

While the Bourbons were building the strongest monarchy in Europe, the Hapsburgs of Austria were trying to set up their own absolute monarchy in the Holy Roman Empire. Their efforts renewed tensions between Europe's Catholics and Protestants. This eventually led to yet another conflict—the Thirty Years' War. Though most of the fighting took place in Germany, all the major European powers except England became involved.

Thirty Years' War

Conflicts between Catholics and Protestants had continued in Germany after the Peace of Augsburg in 1555. These disputes were complicated by the spread of Calvinism, a religion that had not been recognized by the peace settlement. Furthermore, the Protestant princes of Germany resisted the rule of Catholic Hapsburg monarchs.

In 1618 the Thirty Years' War began in Bohemia, where Ferdinand of Styria had become king a year earlier. An enemy of Protestantism who wanted to strengthen Hapsburg authority, Ferdinand began his rule by curtailing the freedom of Bohemian Protestants, most of whom were Czechs. In 1618 the Czechs rebelled and took over Prague. Soon the rebellion developed into a full-scale civil war—Ferdinand and the Catholic princes against the German Protestant princes. Philip III of Spain, a Hapsburg, sent aid to Ferdinand.

The Czech revolt was crushed by 1622 and, over the next 10 years, the Czechs were forcefully reconverted to Catholicism. However, instead of ending, the war continued. Protestant Denmark now fought against the Hapsburgs, hoping to gain German territory. The Danes were soon defeated and forced to withdraw.

Then Sweden entered the war to defend the Protestant cause. By this time the war had been going on for 17 years, and religious issues were taking second place to political ones. In 1639, under Cardinal Richelieu, Roman Catholic France took up arms against the Roman Catholic Hapsburgs to keep them from becoming too powerful.

Finally, after another 13 years, the Thirty Years' War ended in 1648. The outcome was the further weakening of Germany and the emergence of France as Europe's leading power. An international peace conference met at Westphalia in Germany to work out a peace agreement. The Treaty of Westphalia extended the Peace of Augsburg by adding Calvinism to the list of recognized religions. The Holy Roman Empire remained divided into more than 300 separate states. Although the Hapsburgs still

---

FOOTNOTES TO HISTORY
TULIP MANIA

In the midst of the brutal Thirty Years' War, the people of the Netherlands fell in love with tulips. Traders brought tulip bulbs into Europe from Turkey beginning in the 1500s, and gardeners in England and the Netherlands took a particular liking to the flowers. Soon their appreciation led to a public craze for tulips that reached a peak in the 1630s.

Frenzied buyers bid increasingly large sums for the flowers. Investing in tulips became big business, and tulip growers were forced to hire guards to protect their precious flower beds. Some investors lost fortunes when the mania abruptly ended three years after it had begun. One person had even gone so far as to trade his house for tulip bulbs.

controlled Austria and Bohemia, they ruled the other German states in name only, thus ending their hope of establishing an absolute monarchy over all of Germany.

Austria

After the Thirty Years' War, the Austrian Hapsburgs concentrated on building a strong monarchy in Austria, Hungary, and Bohemia. Austria was still the most powerful of the German states. As a result of the War of the Spanish Succession, the Austrians received the Spanish Netherlands and acquired lands in Italy.

In 1740, 23-year-old Maria Theresa inherited the throne of Austria from her father, Holy Roman Emperor Charles VI. According to law and custom, women were not permitted to rule Austria. In 1713 Charles convinced the monarchs of Europe to sign the Pragmatic Sanction, by which Europe's rulers promised not to divide the Hapsburg lands and to accept female succession to the Austrian throne.

Maria Theresa had not received any training in political matters, yet she proved to be a clever and resourceful leader. Overcoming the opposition of the nobility and most of her ministers, Maria Theresa greatly strengthened the Austrian central government. Under her direction, the central government accepted responsibility for such services as public health, prisons, and roads. Understanding that the unity of her empire depended on a strong economy, Maria Theresa ended trade barriers between Austria and Bohemia and used government funds to encourage the production of textiles and glass.

Prussia

In the 1700s a new European power rose to prominence in northeastern Germany. Brandenburg-Prussia was ruled by the Hohenzollern

EUROPE AFTER TREATY OF WESTPHALIA

Learning from Maps
The Treaty of Westphalia confirmed the division of central Europe into Roman Catholic and Protestant territories and maintained the Holy Roman Empire as a unit of more than 300 states. **What was the result of this confirmation?**

Learning from Art *Frederick II inspects his troops, standing at attention. His disciplined and skilled army soon brought Prussia to Europe's attention.* **In which two wars did Frederick's army fight?**

family, which had governed the territory of Brandenburg since the 1400s. During the Thirty Years' War, they gained control of Prussia and other widely scattered lands in Germany.

Prussia's most powerful ruler, Frederick II, became king in 1740 and set out to expand Prussian territory. Frederick the Great, as he became known, rejected the Pragmatic Sanction and seized the Austrian province of Silesia.

The Prussian attack of Silesia began a conflict called the War of the Austrian Succession. Prussia's army was the most efficient fighting force in Europe at that time. To avoid conflict, Maria Theresa's ministers advised her to give up Silesia in return for Frederick's promise not to attack her other territories. Instead, the Austrian ruler turned to her Hungarian subjects and persuaded them to send her military aid. Spain and

France then backed Prussia. To preserve the balance of power, England and the Dutch Netherlands supported Austria.

After seven years of fighting, in 1748 the European powers signed the Treaty of Aix-la-Chapelle, which officially recognized Prussia's rise as an important nation. Frederick was allowed to keep Silesia; Maria Theresa was able to hold the rest of her domain: Austria, Hungary, and Bohemia.

However, the Austrian ruler was not satisfied with the treaty and was determined to recover Silesia. To this end, Maria Theresa changed her alliance from Great Britain to France. She also gained the support of Russia since Prussia's Frederick II was an archenemy of Tsarina Elizabeth of Russia. These alliances set the stage for further conflict.

Learning from Art *When the Protestant city of Magdeburg fell to Catholic forces in 1631, the city was burned and most of its people perished.* **Why was the Thirty Years' War such a devastating event for Germany?**

The Seven Years' War—from 1756 to 1763—was a worldwide conflict in which Great Britain was in competition with France for an overseas empire, and Prussia opposed Austria, Russia, France, and other nations. The war between Austria and Prussia erupted in 1756. After victories in Saxony—a German state and an ally of Austria—and after a later victory over the Austrians in Silesia, Frederick II signed a peace agreement that enabled him to retain most of Silesia.

The struggle between Great Britain and France in North America was known as the French and Indian War. The British and French also fought in India. At the Treaty of Paris in 1763, France gave up most of French Canada, its lands east of the Mississippi River, and part of Florida to Great Britain. Great Britain also replaced France as the leading power in India. As a result of the Seven Years' War, Great Britain emerged as the strongest colonial empire and Prussia retained the province of Silesia.

SECTION 4 REVIEW

Recall

1. **Identify:** Ferdinand of Styria, Treaty of Westphalia, Maria Theresa, Frederick II, Silesia
2. **Locate:** Prussia, Austria

Critical Thinking

3. **Explain:** What factor caused the Thirty Years' War? What was the result of this conflict?
4. **Analyze:** How did Maria Theresa strengthen the central government in Austria and in her other domains?
5. **Analyze:** What were the results of the Seven Years' War?

6. **Synthesize:** How did the many conflicts among German states affect the balance of power?

Applying Concepts

7. **Conflict:** What political issues changed during the course of the Thirty Years' War?

Russia

Isolated from Western developments, Russia created its own civilization based on the values of the Eastern Orthodox Church and the Byzantine Empire. All-powerful, the Russian monarchy easily crushed its opponents. The Church, the nobility, the towns—all of which repeatedly opposed royal authority in western Europe—never posed the same challenge to Russian rulers.

Ivan IV

The most powerful of the early tsars was Ivan IV, who ruled from 1533 to 1584. Known as Ivan the Terrible, he was at once learned, pious, and cruel. Ivan assumed the throne at the age of three, and while growing up, was caught between rival groups of nobles vying for power. As an adult, he saw treason everywhere and regarded the nobles as a threat to his throne.

Russian Expansion Under Ivan IV, Russia increased its trade and contacts with western Europe. Ties to the West further expanded after English traders found a northern sea route to Russia in 1553.

Ivan used his armies to expand Russia's borders in all directions. Despite Russia's vast size, it had few seaports, none of which were free of ice throughout the year. Gaining access to the sea for trade was a long-standing goal of Russian rulers.

Peter the Great

In 1689 Peter I, known as Peter the Great, after ruling Russia jointly with his brother for seven years, assumed the throne alone as tsar. A towering man, nearly seven feet (2 meters) tall,

Peter was a mountain of boundless energy and volcanic emotions. During his reign, he sought to modernize Russia.

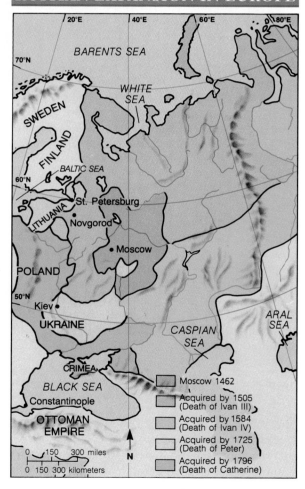

RUSSIAN EXPANSION IN EUROPE

Moscow 1462

Acquired by 1505
(Death of Ivan III)

Acquired by 1584
(Death of Ivan IV)

Acquired by 1725
(Death of Peter)

Acquired by 1796
(Death of Catherine)

Learning from Maps *Both Peter the Great and Catherine the Great looked westward to increase the power and influence of Russia.* **What areas came under Russian control during their reigns?**

Encounter with the West   Peter discovered that Russian knowledge of the outside world was quite limited. Most Russians were illiterate peasants; only a few members of the nobility were well educated. After he became tsar, Peter took an 18-month study tour of England and the Netherlands.

When he returned home, Peter forced Russians to adopt the ways of western Europe. He also sent Russians abroad to study shipbuilding, naval warfare, foreign languages, and mathematics. He invited foreign experts to train Russians. His greatest effort to open Russia to Europe was the building of a new capital called Saint Petersburg. Located near the Baltic Sea in northwestern Russia, Saint Petersburg was considered the "window to the West."

Foreign Policy   With the goal of making Russia a European power, Peter expanded Russia's boundaries to the south, east, and northwest. In 1689 Russia forced China to recognize Russian claims to Siberia.

In 1721 the Russians defeated the Swedes in a long war for control of the Baltic coastline. The fight against Turkey for a warm-water port on the Black Sea failed, however. This defeat convinced Peter of the need to create a professional army and navy. Raising the money and developing the essential training and resources made widespread changes necessary.

Government Service   To provide needed leadership, Peter created a new class of loyal nobles called *dvorianie*, who, in return for government service, would be allowed to own hereditary landed estates. A noble's duty to the tsar started at age 15 and continued until death.

Peter used privileges and force to make the established nobility accept government service. Nobles were given full control over the peasants who worked on their estates. While freedom for peasants had gradually increased in western Europe, the opposite was true in Russia.

Administration   In setting out to reform the Russian government, Peter borrowed ideas from France with the goal of bringing more order to his administration. A central bureaucracy was established, and local government was placed

Learning from Art   *A caricature shows Peter the Great taking his scissors to a noble's beard. Peter wanted to cut Russia's ties to centuries-old traditions.* **In what ways did Peter modernize Russia?**

completely under the tsar's control. Peter also brought the Church under his direct authority. When the patriarch (the head of the Eastern Orthodox Church) of Moscow died in 1700, a successor was never named. Instead, Peter established the Holy Synod, a council of bishops responsible to a secular government official appointed by the tsar.

Economy   Tax policies were also changed to increase government income and efficiency. Under the new plan, the nobility did not have to pay. As in France, the burden of taxes fell on the poorest social groups.

Effects   Peter's reforms strengthened Russia's role in foreign affairs. In his own country, however, Peter had only limited success. His domestic policies destroyed the Eastern Orthodox culture that had united nobles and peasants.

Learning from Art *A successful foreign policy earned Catherine the Great recognition as an able leader and administrator.* **What goal was finally achieved during her rule?**

Beginning in Peter's reign, a split occurred between the few who accepted European ways and the many who clung to traditional values. An observer noted: "The tsar pulls uphill alone with the strength of ten, but millions push downhill." Many of Peter's reforms were incomplete and hasty. Yet his changes brought Russia into contact with developments in the West and into the mainstream of western European civilization.

Catherine the Great

In 1762 the German-born Catherine II seized the throne from her husband, Peter III, and ruled as empress of Russia until 1796.

Catherine was greatly influenced by leading western European thinkers. For a time, she came to believe that all people were born equal and that it was "contrary to the Christian faith and to justice to make slaves of them."

Early in her reign, Catherine considered freeing the serfs. However, a peasant rebellion that threatened her rule changed her mind. Catherine allowed the nobles to treat their serfs as they pleased. During her rule, more peasants were forced into serfdom than ever before, and their status worsened. The common people of Russia had fewer rights than those in any other part of Europe. When groups revolted, Catherine brutally crushed the uprisings.

A successful foreign policy earned her the name Catherine the Great. She significantly expanded Russia's borders to the south and achieved Peter the Great's goal of securing a warm-water port on the Black Sea. In the west, Catherine acquired territory from Poland.

Catherine was the last of the great absolute monarchs of the 1700s. By the time of her death in 1796, new ideas of liberty and equality had spread throughout western Europe. They directly challenged the age-old institution of monarchy.

SECTION 5 REVIEW

Recall

1. **Identify:** Ivan IV, Peter the Great, Catherine the Great
2. **Locate:** Moscow, Saint Petersburg, Siberia

Critical Thinking

3. **Explain:** How did Russia's isolation affect its monarchy?
4. **Analyze:** Why did Ivan IV want to gain a seaport that was free of ice throughout the year?
5. **Synthesize:** How did the reigns of Peter the Great and Catherine the Great affect the people of Russia?
6. **Analyze:** How did Peter the Great's government reforms affect the nobility?

Applying Concepts

7. **Innovation:** How and why did Peter the Great try to modernize Russia?

RECOGNIZING A STEREOTYPE

A student asks her friend if she plans to try out for the cheerleading squad. The friend responds, "No way! All cheerleaders are snobs." This person may have other reasons for not going out for cheerleading, but she is using a *stereotype* to justify her conduct.

Explanation

A stereotype is a simplified, overgeneralized description of members of a group. The group may be a sex, a race, a religion, a country, a region, a city, a neighborhood, or a profession. A stereotype can blur or ignore characteristics of the group's individual members. Stereotypes may have positive, neutral, or negative connotations. Negative stereotypes usually are the least accurate but the most harmful.

Stereotyping can influence not only one's conception of a group's members, but one's behavior toward the group. You will encounter stereotypes in materials you read as well as elsewhere in your daily life. Recognizing stereotypes can matter greatly when you examine descriptions of groups or individuals, especially if you have reason to believe a source is slanted for or against a group.

To recognize a stereotype, follow these steps:
- Skim the material to identify characteristics given to a subject or a group.
- Search for exaggeration or over-generalization, often indicated by such words as *all, none, every, always,* and *never.*
- Look for "loaded" emotional words such as *dumb, lazy, dirty, sneaky, cruel,* and *corrupt* when applied to a group or a member of a group.
- Look for the use of vague words such as *changeable* and *interesting.*
- Note a consistently positive or negative tone.
- State what stereotype, if any, is presented in the account.
- Determine to what extent the stereotype represents individuals in the group by recalling what you already know or finding additional data to expose the stereotype.

Example

The following lines from plays by William Shakespeare include stereotypes that are identified in parentheses.
- "Frailty, thy name is woman!" (The "loaded," emotional word is *frailty,* the stereotype is the generalization that all women are emotionally or physically weak.)
- "These Moors are changeable in their moods." (The vague words are *these* and *changeable,* and the stereotype is that the Moors are moody or unreliable people.)

Application

Use the outlined steps to help you identify the stereotypes in the following ideas held by people living in the 1500s through the 1700s. Then, tell whether the stereotype has a positive, neutral, or negative connotation:
- No papist can be a good subject for England. (England, 1572)
- England is an isle fouled by heretics and barbarians. (Spain, 1554)
- It is against the law, human and divine, that a woman should reign and have empire above men. (England, 1560)
- The Italians are so jovial and addicted to music that nearly every countryman plays on the guitar, and will commonly go into the field with a fiddle. (England, 1600)
- Do not put such unlimited power into the hands of husbands. Remember all men would be tyrants if they could. [We ladies] will not hold ourselves bound by any laws in which we have no voice, or representation. (United States, 1776)

Practice

Turn to Practicing Skills on page 437 of the Chapter Review for further practice in recognizing stereotypes.

CHAPTER 17 REVIEW

HISTORICAL SIGNIFICANCE

One of the results of the Age of Monarchy in Europe during the 1500s and 1600s was the emergence of strong national states. These powerful nations helped to create and define a new European order. Absolute monarchs centralized their governments and established powerful armies and navies both to protect and to expand their countries' natural borders.

Monarchs engulfed the continent in devastating wars over territorial, religious, and economic issues. By forcefully asserting their power and authority, monarchs created the national boundaries that would form modern Europe. The result of these conflicts was to define the political and cultural boundaries that exist in the world today.

SUMMARY

For a summary of Chapter 17, see the Unit 4 Synopsis on pages 458–461.

USING KEY TERMS

Write the key term that best completes the following sentences.

   a. absolutism
   b. balance of power
   c. intendant

1. The form of government with unlimited power held by one person or a group is known as ____.
2. During her reign, Elizabeth I sought to maintain the ____ among the European nations.
3. Under Louis XIII, in an effort to limit the power of nobles, the authority to direct local government affairs was given to agents of the crown known as ____.

REVIEWING FACTS

1. **List:** Name at least four major European royal families discussed in this chapter.
2. **Identify:** What were the two main European religious groups during the 1500s?
3. **Explain:** What were Henry VIII's reasons for establishing the Church of England?
4. **Explain:** Who was called the Sun King?

5. **Recall:** What circumstances and events led to the War of the Austrian Succession?
6. **Identify:** What changes did Peter the Great bring to Russia?
7. **Recall:** How did England become the strongest European empire?

THINKING CRITICALLY

1. **Analyze:** Compare and contrast the Hapsburg and Tudor monarchies of the 1500s. Which one do you think was more successful?
2. **Synthesize:** Imagine you are a soldier during the Thirty Years' War. Describe how you joined the army and what conditions were like during the war. What hopes do you have for the future?
3. **Evaluate:** Why do you think Richelieu believed in absolute monarchy, even though he wasn't a king?
4. **Analyze:** Consider Louis XIV's activities. Which ones benefited France? Which did not? Would France have been better off without him? Why or why not?
5. **Evaluate:** Which of the monarchs described in this chapter do you most admire? Which one do you least admire? Explain your reasons.
6. **Evaluate:** Consider the leadership style of Maria Theresa of Austria, who had no training in political matters. Can a person today be a successful political leader with no prior training or experience?

ANALYZING CONCEPTS

1. **Change:** How do you think changes in power affected Europe between 1500 and 1750?
2. **Conflict:** Which groups of people benefited from the European conflicts of the 1600s? Which groups suffered?
3. **Uniformity:** Why do you think people believed in absolute monarchs between 1500 and 1750?
4. **Innovation:** Did absolute monarchy improve people's lives or merely bring unproductive change? Support your answer by examples from the reigns of at least two monarchs.
5. **Change:** How did German-born Catherine the Great adjust to her role as a Russian ruler?

PRACTICING SKILLS

1. Why is it important that we recognize stereotyping in today's world?
2. List the ways in which stereotyping can affect people's lives—for instance, employment opportunities.
3. Situation comedies on television often present stereotyped characters. One example is the Pushy News Reporter. He or she is loud, abrasive, ambitious, and cares only about the story, not the people concerned. Give titles to three such characters and explain why they fit the description "stereotype."

GEOGRAPHY IN HISTORY

1. **Place:** Refer to the map on page 988. Why was England able to avoid involvement in the wars of the 1500s and 1600s?
2. **Location:** Refer to the map on page 989. Which countries are near the center of Europe? Which countries are located on Europe's edges?
3. **Movement:** Refer to the map on page 988. Why did the Huguenots leave France during the 1600s? Where did they go?
4. **Regions:** Refer to the maps on pages 988 and 989. How do the geographic regions of Europe compare with the national boundaries of the 1700s?

TRACING CHRONOLOGY

Refer to the time line below to answer these questions.
1. Which royal families dominated Europe during the 1500s?
2. Which two monarchs began their rule within two years of each other?

LINKING PAST AND PRESENT

European monarchs in the 1600s and 1700s resolved their territorial disputes and ambitions through war. How do present-day leaders resolve disputes? Explain the similarities and the differences.

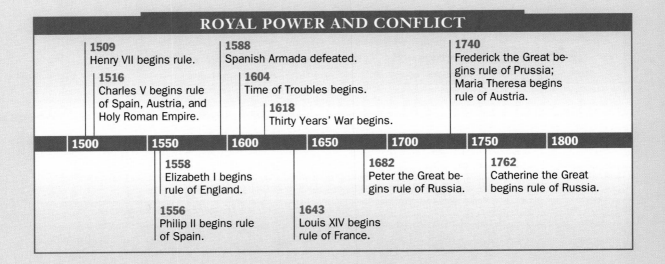

ROYAL POWER AND CONFLICT

1509 Henry VII begins rule.

1516 Charles V begins rule of Spain, Austria, and Holy Roman Empire.

1588 Spanish Armada defeated.

1604 Time of Troubles begins.

1618 Thirty Years' War begins.

1740 Frederick the Great begins rule of Prussia; Maria Theresa begins rule of Austria.

| 1500 | 1550 | 1600 | 1650 | 1700 | 1750 | 1800 |

1558 Elizabeth I begins rule of England.

1556 Philip II begins rule of Spain.

1682 Peter the Great begins rule of Russia.

1643 Louis XIV begins rule of France.

1762 Catherine the Great begins rule of Russia.

Empires of Asia

Within the Vienna city walls, people quaked as the sounds of the Muslim siege began on September 18, 1529. The Viennese heard the warlike sounds of Turkish flutes, drums, and cymbals. Cannonballs thundered over the ancient walls.

Outside the walls, hundreds of white tents covered the hills. Suleiman, commander of the Turkish forces, had left Istanbul in May with an army of 100,000. Thousands of camels had carried supplies of powder, shot, and cannon. By October 9, Turkish troops broke through part of the walls. Desperately, Viennese troops plugged the breach. Vienna would not fall that day.

The Turks poured forces into one last assault on the city in mid-October, but it failed. This clash between European and Asian armies was one of many encounters between different civilizations during this period.

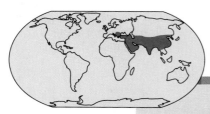

CHAPTER PREVIEW

Key Terms to Define: sultan, grand vizier, queue, janissaries, labor-intensive farming, *sankin-kotai,* geisha, haiku

People to Meet: Suleiman I, Shah Abbas, Tamerlane, Babur, Akbar, Hong Wu, Zheng He, Oda Nobunaga, Toyotomi Hideyoshi, Tokugawa Ieyasu, Francis Xavier, Matsuo Basho

Places to Discover: Istanbul, Isfahan, Taj Mahal, Beijing, Edo, Nagasaki

Objectives to Learn:
1. How did Muslim emperors conquer and rule much of the Middle East and India between 1500 and 1800?

The Ottoman fleet blocking the entrance to the harbor of Marseille, France

2. Why did China flourish and then decline during the Ming and Qing dynasties?

3. Why was Japan more adaptable than China before the 1800s?

Concepts to Understand:

• Movement—Muslim armies invaded India, and Chinese voyagers explored lands to the west as far as Africa. Sections 1,2

• Cultural diffusion—East Asia was directly challenged by European cultures. Sections 2,3

• Reaction—Japan enforced isolationist policies. Section 3

• Change—The center of Japanese society shifted from rural to urban areas; merchants challenged the position of the samurai. Section 3

Muslim Empires

Between the 1400s and the 1800s, three Muslim empires—the Ottoman Empire, the Persian Empire, and the Mogul Empire—conquered and controlled much of eastern Europe, central Asia, and India respectively. Strong leaders used powerful armies to amass territory that gave them economic control over major trade routes. As these empires added new geographic areas, Muslim culture also expanded.

The Ottoman Empire

During the late 1200s, Turkish clans—calling themselves Ottoman Turks after their first leader, Osman—settled part of Asia Minor and began conquests to build an empire. They conquered much of Byzantine territory, making Constantinople their capital in 1453. Extending their Muslim empire even farther, by the 1600s the Ottomans controlled the Balkan Peninsula and parts of eastern Europe. By the end of their reign, they had acquired most of the Middle East, North Africa, and Asian parts of today's Soviet Union.

The Ottoman Empire maintained a strong navy in the Mediterranean to protect the lucrative trade they controlled there. Alarmed by the threat to their trade and to Christianity, Europeans under Philip II of Spain fought and defeated the Ottoman fleet at the Battle of Lepanto in 1571. But the Ottomans rebuilt their navy and remained a significant seapower until the 1700s.

Suleiman I   Suleiman I was one of the early Ottoman rulers who strengthened Muslim forces prior to the Battle of Lepanto. He was a multitalented man—a heroic military commander, a skillful administrator, and a patron of the arts. Ruling from 1520 to 1566, Suleiman re-ceived the name "the Codifier" for his work in organizing Ottoman laws. Suleiman boastfully described himself to the French king Francis I: "I, who am the sultan of sultans, the sovereign of sovereigns, the dispenser of crowns to the monarchs on the face of the earth."

Suleiman acted as both the **sultan,** or political ruler, and the caliph, or religious leader; he enjoyed absolute authority. But to rule effectively, he needed support from his personal advisers, the bureaucracy, a group of religious advisers known as the Ulema, and a well-trained army. A **grand vizier,** or prime minister, headed the bureaucracy that enforced the sultan's decisions throughout the empire. The Ulema made rulings on questions of Islamic law, and the army held much control within the empire by conquering and controlling new territories. The sultan maintained an elite corps of soldiers called **janissaries.** Rigorous military and religious training made these troops a fierce and loyal fighting force.

Islamic Influence   Because the empire was so large, Ottoman Muslims ruled diverse peoples, including Arabs, Greeks, Albanians, Slavs, and Armenians. The population was divided into several classes: a ruling class made up of the sultan's family and high government officials; the nobility, which administered agricultural estates; and the largest class, the peasants who worked on those estates.

To accommodate the diverse populations of people, the government made special laws affecting those who did not practice Islam, the empire's official religion. Non-Muslims were allowed to practice their faith in return for payment of a tax. Ottoman law also permitted religious groups to run affairs in their own *millets,* or communities, and choose their own leaders to present their views to the Ottoman government.

The Ottoman Islamic civilization borrowed many elements from the Byzantine, Persian, and Arab cultures they had absorbed. Mosques, bridges, and aqueducts reflected this blend of styles. The Christian city of Constantinople was transformed into a Muslim one and then called Istanbul. Islamic architects renovated Hagia Sophia into a mosque and then planned new mosques and palaces that added to Istanbul's beauty.

Decline of the Ottomans   By 1600 the Ottoman Empire had reached the peak of its power; thereafter it slowly declined. Even at its zenith, however, the empire faced enemies on its borders. Conquests ended as the Ottomans tried to fight both Persians and Europeans. Military might had brought the empire wealth from booty, slaves, and control of trade routes. When military conquests ceased, the wealth also dried up. Though population increased, production of food and goods did not, leaving massive poverty and civil discontent.

During the 1800s, influenced by Western ideas, the government attempted to reform the social and economic ills of the empire. Under the Hatt-I Humayun decree, people from all cultures and religions were allowed to hold public office. Tax reform, property rights, and military reforms followed. The reforms, however, did not prevent parts of the empire from breaking away to form their own independent states.

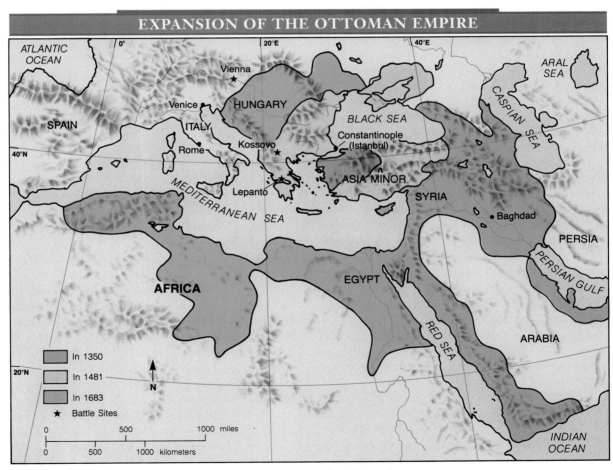

EXPANSION OF THE OTTOMAN EMPIRE

In 1350
In 1481
In 1683
★ Battle Sites

Learning from Maps *This map includes topographic relief.* **How do you think the geography of the Ottoman Empire in 1481 affected conquests?**

Safavid Persia

To the east of the Ottoman Empire lay Persia, a land that had once been part of the Islamic Empire, but which had broken away because of religious differences. In the 1500s Shiite Muslims, bitter enemies of the Ottoman Turks, conquered the land of present-day Iran. The Shiite leader, Ismail (ihs MAH eel), conquered and unified the numerous people living there, declaring himself to be the founder of the Safavid (sah FAH weed) dynasty.

Safavid rulers required all Persians to accept the Shiite form of Islam. Belief in Shiite Islam distinguished people living in Persia from neighboring Sunni Muslim peoples—the Arabs and Turks.

The Glory of Persia   The Safavid leader Shah Abbas came to the throne in 1588. His army regained some western territory lost to the Ottomans in previous years. Then the Shah sought allies against the Ottomans even among such Christian states as Great Britain. The British used their alliance with Persia to seize the strategic Persian Gulf port of Hormuz in 1622, gaining control of the Persian silk and East Indian spice trade.

With his empire secure against the Ottoman forces, Shah Abbas set up his court in Isfahan, which became one of the most magnificent cities in the entire Muslim world. Towering above the city was the blue dome of the Royal Mosque, which was covered with lacy white decorations. Near the mosque, Abbas had a three-story palace built for his personal use. He also ordered beautiful streets and parks constructed throughout the city.

During the reign of Abbas, Persian spread as the language of culture, diplomacy, and trade in most of the Muslim world. Later the language spread to India. Urdu, spoken in Pakistan today, is partly based on Persian.

After the death of Shah Abbas in 1629, inept Safavid rulers weakened the empire, bringing on its decline. In 1736, after the Safavid decline, Nader Shah came to power. He expanded the Persian Empire to its greatest height since Darius. But after his assassination in 1747, territory was lost and the country was divided. In the late

Learning from Paintings   *This miniature painting shows Akbar greeting a court official. It blends Persian and Indian art.* **How does this painting differ from the portrait of Louis XIV on page 425?**

1700s, another Turkic group, the Qajar dynasty, seized the Persian throne and established a new dynasty in Tehran.

The Mogul Empire

Even before the Ottomans and the Safavids built their empires, Islamic invaders from central Asia had conquered much of northern India in the 1100s. The invaders set up a sultanate, or Muslim kingdom, in Delhi in 1200. The Muslim rulers taxed Hindus who would not convert to Islam, and Muslim armies destroyed Hindu temples and shrines.

By the late 1300s, a Muslim Mongol known as Tamerlane—who claimed descent from Genghis Khan—had conquered much of central Asia and made Samarkand the capital of his empire. Although a devout Muslim, Tamerlane was also a ruthless leader. His forces sacked Delhi in

1398, killing thousands and leaving the city in rubble. After Tamerlane's death, his Islamic empire disintegrated; yet northern India would face other Muslim invasions.

Akbar the Great

In the early 1500s, Babur, who was a descendant of Tamerlane, led another attack on northern India. Using artillery and with cavalry riding elephants and horses, Babur conquered Delhi at the Battle of Panipat in 1526. Then he set up the Mogul dynasty, the Persian name for Mongol, which lasted three centuries in India. Unlike Tamerlane, the Moguls encouraged orderly government, and they expanded the arts.

Babur's grandson, Akbar, was a benevolent ruler who brought peace and order to northern India. Recognizing that most of the people he ruled were Hindus, Akbar encouraged religious tolerance to end quarrels between Hindus and Muslims. Whereas Muslims believed in one god, Hindus worshiped many deities. Hindus and Muslims differed about sacred foods, social organization, and religious customs. To reduce tension among his people, Akbar repealed a tax on Hindus.

Extremely curious about all religions, Akbar invited religious scholars of other faiths to his court to learn about other religions. He concluded that all religions revealed the same divine truth, whatever their external practices were. He tried to set up a new religion that he called Divine Faith. The new religion included features of many of the world's religions.

Mogul Civilization

Under Akbar's rule music, painting, and literature flourished in Mogul India. Mogul rulers made their lavish courts centers of art and learning. Although Akbar could not read, he understood the value of learning and set up a large library, employing more than 100 court painters to illustrate the books.

Another Mogul ruler, Shah Jahan, created one of the world's most beautiful buildings—the Taj Mahal at Agra—a magnificent example of Muslim architecture. Muslim architects introduced the arch and dome to India, and in trading contacts with China, Muslim merchants brought gunpowder, paper, and Chinese porcelain to Mogul India.

Decline of the Mogul Dynasty

In spite of its cultural achievements, Mogul influence in India was weakened at the end of the 1600s by Hindu rebellions and by a new religion, Sikhism (SEEK ih zuhm). Led by Nanak, the first of their 10 religious teachers, the Sikhs tried to unite Hinduism with Islam. Most Indians still held onto their Hindu traditions and Hindu customs, and they rebelled against later Mogul rulers, who abandoned the religious tolerance that had been practiced by earlier leaders. Shah Aurangzeb destroyed many Hindu temples and persecuted the Hindus. Local rulers began to grow more independent as the central government lost much of its control over them. Mogul rule continued in a weakened state, with reduced territory, until 1858.

SECTION 1 REVIEW

Recall

1. **Define:** sultan, grand vizier, janissaries
2. **Identify:** Suleiman I, Ulema, Ismail, Shah Abbas, Tamerlane, Akbar
3. **Locate:** Use the map on page 441 to compare the Ottoman Empire's boundaries in 1481 to those in 1683. How did its growth lead to decline?

4. **Define:** What was the relationship between Sunni Muslims and Shiite Muslims living in the Ottoman Empire and Persian Empire?
5. **Explain:** What was the Moguls' religion and why did it bring them into conflict with the majority of India's people? Describe how Mogul rulers dealt with this conflict.

Critical Thinking

6. **Synthesize:** Compare Shah Abbas's patronage of the arts to that of a contemporary European monarch.

Applying Concepts

7. **Movement:** Evaluate the movement of Islamic invaders into northern India. How did the invaders affect people there?

Chinese Dynasties

In 1368, after the Yuan dynasty fell, a new era of reform began. The Ming and the Qing dynasties built strong central governments that implemented agricultural and public works projects. As food production and trade increased, so did China's population. At the same time, China looked to earlier achievements to invigorate its culture. After years of prosperity, Chinese emperors isolated themselves from their people and the outside, resulting in government corruption, rebellions, and decline.

The Ming Dynasty

After 89 years of Mongol rule, a military officer named Zhu Yuanzhang (joo yoo ahn jahng) led a rebellion that overthrew the Yuan dynasty. Born into a poor peasant family, Zhu had been a Buddhist monk before entering the army. In 1368 he became emperor, taking the name Hong Wu and establishing his capital at Nanjing. For the first time in more than 1,000 years, the Son of Heaven was of peasant origin. Hong

IMAGES OF THE TIME

Chinese Life

Under the stable, centralized rule of the Ming and Qing dynasties, crafts, industry, and agriculture flourished with government support.

Cloisonné was a craft developed during the Ming dynasty. The dragon-boat contest shown on this plaque was a popular sporting event.

Rice cultivation became a major industry in many parts of China. Above, men and children work in flooded rice paddies.

Wu gave the name Ming ("brilliant") to his dynasty, which would rule China for nearly 300 years.

Peace and Stability   The Ming dynasty brought peace and stability to China. Hong Wu and the early Ming rulers imposed new law codes, reorganized the tax system, and reformed local government.

The new law codes were harsher than those of previous Chinese dynasties. Scholars, traditionally exempt from corporal punishment, had to endure public whippings if they displeased the emperor. Formerly, the saying was that "a gentleman could be ordered to die but should never be humiliated."

Chinese persons replaced Mongols in all civil service posts, and Confucianism again became the empire's official doctrine after its decline under the Yuan. The Ming dynasty restored the old examination system, making the tests even stricter than in earlier dynasties.

Strong rulers at the beginning of the dynasty enforced peace throughout the land. With peace and additional revenues from a reformed tax system, economic prosperity came to China. But northern China had been devastated by barbarians. To encourage farmers to move there, the government offered free land, tools, seeds, and farm animals. Farmers reclaimed and restored much of the land in the north, and the policy helped secure the northern frontier from invaders.

With more land under cultivation, farmers could sell their surplus produce at local markets. Government workers repaired and maintained the canal system that connected local markets, an efficient way for bringing farm goods to market. Northern China began to regain its strength and status as a rich farming region.

Beijing's Forbidden City was built around 1700. The immense complex includes imperial palaces, audience halls, and temples.

Porcelain ware was decorated with colorful, elaborate patterns, unlike the much simpler designs of earlier dynasties.

Reflecting on the Times
Compare these images with images in earlier chapters on Chinese history. How are they alike or different?

Increased agricultural productivity also freed workers for nonfarming tasks. Artisans increased in number, expanding production of crafts, silk, tea, porcelain, and cotton cloth. Thus, trade within China expanded, and port cities like Guangzhou (gwong joh) and Shanghai continued to grow. Merchants sold food, textiles, and luxury goods to the growing urban populations.

As city merchants and artisans grew wealthier, they demanded more popular entertainments and learning. The third Ming emperor, Yong Le, ordered 2,000 scholars to compile a treasury of Chinese histories and literature. This massive library included neo-Confucian writings from the Song dynasty and also many Buddhist scriptures.

Ming writers preferred the novel to other forms of fiction. Many novelists were students who had failed examinations; thus, many of their works such as *The Scholars* satirize scholars and officials. Novelists ended many chapters on a suspenseful note. However, these tales could hardly rival the real adventures at sea that some sailors lived.

Exploration   The early Ming emperors spent government money on a navy that could sail to foreign ports and collect tribute for the emperor. The ships, known as junks, usually traveled

CONNECTIONS: HISTORY AND THE ENVIRONMENT

Feeding the Empire

Terrace farming, encouraged in the Ming dynasty, is still used today in modern China.

Both the Ming and the Qing dynasties encouraged agricultural development in China. Rapid population growth, particularly in the Chinese heartland in the eastern part of the empire, made it necessary for farmers to produce more food. The Chinese also had to develop new ways of distributing food to the growing population.

New crops from the Americas arrived in China on Chinese trade ships that traveled regularly to the Philippines and other areas of Southeast Asia. During the mid-1500s, Spanish ships brought sweet potatoes, maize (corn), and peanuts as well as silver and gold from the Americas to the Philippines. There Chinese merchants exchanged silk or porcelain for the precious metals and exotic foods. Farmers found that the foreign plants grew well in poor soil. Thus, land that had not been productive in earlier times became a valuable economic resource.

The government continued its efforts to build canals and irrigation systems to help farmers water their crops and transport them to market. Terracing—the flat steplike areas that farmers dug out of the sides of hills—helped them make full use of their lands. All these factors helped make China's population the largest in the world.

Making the Connection

1. How did Chinese farmers change their environment to provide opportunity for agricultural development?
2. How have modern farming practices affected the environment in various parts of the world?

along the coastline, but they could also venture into open water.

From 1405 to 1433, Emperor Yong Le sent out seven seagoing expeditions. Their purpose was "glorifying Chinese arms in the remote regions and showing off the wealth and power of the [Middle] Kingdom." The leader of the voyages was a Chinese Muslim named Zheng He.

Zheng He took his first fleet to the nations of Southeast Asia. In later voyages he reached India, sailed up the Persian Gulf to Arabia, and even visited kingdoms on the east coast of Africa. Everywhere he went, he demanded that the people submit to the emperor's authority. If they refused, he applied force; rulers who accepted were rewarded with gold or silk.

Zheng He brought back trade goods and tribute from many lands. But later Ming emperors did not follow through: ocean voyages were costly, and in the early 1400s, China concentrated its funds on military forces to combat threats from nomadic tribes to the north. The emperor's officials saw no great benefit in exploring expeditions and halted them. The government discouraged trade with foreign countries partly because Confucian philosophy regarded trade as the lowest of occupations. The emperor even forbade construction of seagoing vessels.

Inside the Forbidden City   To help defend the northern border, Yong Le shifted his capital from Nanjing to Cambaluc, renaming it Beijing. He ordered the city completely rebuilt, modeled after the great Tang capital of Chang-an. For 16 years, from 1404 to 1420, workers labored on its construction. On the Chinese New Year's Day in 1421, the government moved to Beijing.

A visitor entering Beijing walked through the great gate in the 30-foot-high (9-meter) southern wall. If you had government business, you passed through the Gate of Heavenly Peace. There stood the government offices and parks of the Imperial City.

Farther north, across a moat and through the Meridian Gate, stood the Forbidden City, where the emperor and his family lived. The Forbidden City had two main sections: one for the emperor's personal use and another for state occasions. The main courtyard outside the gate held 90,000 people. The emperor sometimes ap-

peared before guests here, but ordinary people stayed out or faced a penalty of death.

The residential section of the Forbidden City consisted of many palaces with thousands of rooms. Pavilions and gardens gave comfort to the imperial family, who spent their days in fabulous splendor. In fact, later Ming emperors devoted much of their time to pleasure. In the last 30 years of one emperor's reign, he met with his closest officials only five times.

Corrupt officials, eager to enrich themselves, took over. As law and order collapsed, Manchu invaders from Manchuria attacked the northern frontier settlements. Revenues for military spending were limited by the expenses of the lavish court. The Manchus managed to conquer a weakened China.

The Qing Dynasty

In 1644 the Manchus set up a new dynasty, called the Qing, or "pure." For only the second time in history, foreigners controlled all of China. The Manchus slowly extended their empire to the north and west, taking in Manchuria, Mongolia, Xinjiang (SHIN shee ahng), and Tibet. The offshore island of Taiwan became part of the empire in 1683. For almost 300 years the Qing dynasty ruled over the largest Chinese empire that ever existed.

Adapting Chinese Culture   The Manchus had already accepted Confucian values before invading China. Their leaders understood that these precepts benefited the ruling class. Ruling over an empire in which Chinese outnumbered Manchus by at least thirty to one, the Manchu rulers controlled their empire by making every effort to adopt many of the native Chinese customs and traditions.

Manchus kept control by naming Manchus to the officer corps and by ensuring that most of the soldiers were Manchus. To control the Chinese civil service, Manchus reserved the top jobs in the government hierarchy for their people. Even Chinese officials in lower positions had a Manchu monitoring their work. Critical army and government positions thus remained loyal to the Manchu leadership.

Learning from Paintings *This Chinese painting from the 1600s shows the Qing conquest of China.* ***From what region did the invaders originate?***

In 1645, the Manchu emperor ordered all Chinese men to shave their heads and to grow a **queue,** or braid, at the back of their head—or be executed. Among the people, this order was known as "Keep your hair and lose your head" or "Lose your hair and keep your head." The upper classes had to adopt the Manchu tight, high-collared jacket and abandon their customary loose robes. But in spite of the many-layered controls, the Manchu rulers took on more elements of Chinese culture.

The Qing were fortunate in having able emperors in the first years of their rule. Emperor Kang Xi, who ruled from 1661 to 1722, reduced taxes and undertook public works projects, such as flood control. Kang Xi, himself a poet, also sponsored Chinese art. Other emperors secured new territory, extending the Qing Empire.

Daily Life   The Manchus made few changes in China's economy. The government-sponsored work projects and internal peace contributed to economic prosperity in the 1700s. Agricultural improvements increased food production, whereupon China's population exploded, from about 150 million in 1600 to 350 million in 1800. China was the most populous country in the world.

More than three-fourths of the Chinese people lived in rural areas. In the south where Chinese farmers worked as tenants, each family farmed its plot and paid rent to a landlord. In the north, more families owned their land. But because the family divided its land among its sons, over the generations the average peasant's share of land shrank.

As population increased, every inch of land had to be made productive. Although the Chinese had invented such simple machines as the wheelbarrow and paddlewheel pumps, farmers depended on human labor for most farm tasks. In hill country, farm workers dug flat terraces into the hillsides where rice and other crops could be grown. Workers carried pails of water to fill the rice paddies. This **labor-intensive farming,** in which work is performed by human effort, contrasts with agriculture, in which the hard work is done by animals or machinery.

Subsistence farming was not a year-round occupation during the Qing dynasty. Many farmers grew cash crops such as cotton, rather than just their own food. A writer in the 1700s described the life of farm families in one district:

The country folk only live off their fields for the three winter months. . . . During the spring months, they . . . spin or weave, eating by exchanging their cloth for rice. . . . The autumn is somewhat rainy, and the noise of the looms' shuttles is once again to be heard everywhere in the villages. . . . Thus, even if there is a bad harvest . . . our country people are not in distress so long as the other counties have a crop of cotton [for them to weave].

Silk production provided extra income for farm families. They grew mulberry trees, whose leaves provided food for silkworms. From the leaves women and girls plucked the cocoons and carefully unwound them. Then the silk was ready for those who spun it into thread and others who wove it into silk cloth.

Internal trade flourished during the Qing period. Great merchant families made fortunes trading rice, silk, fish, timber, cloth, and luxury goods. The growth of trade prompted specialization. Some regions were famous for textiles; others for cotton, porcelain, tea, or silk. At Jingdezhen, the emperor's porcelain factory employed thousands of workers. Artists painted delicate patterns or scenes on vases, bowls, and plates. Others made chemical glazes that formed a hard, shiny surface on the pottery after it was fired in a hot kiln.

Contacts with Europeans   European demand for Chinese goods such as silk and porcelain was high, attracting European ships to China's coast. The first Europeans arrived in China during the Ming dynasty. In 1514, Portuguese caravels landed near Guangzhou. The Chinese called Portuguese sailors ocean devils, and local officials refused to deal with them. Nonetheless, by 1557 the Portuguese had built a trading base at Macao.

Jesuit missionaries followed the Portuguese traders with the dream of converting China's huge population to Christianity. Although most Chinese officials were not interested in Christianity, the Jesuits' scientific knowledge impressed them. In 1611 the emperor placed a Jesuit astronomer in charge of the Imperial Calendar, and in years to come Jesuits gained other government positions. They also converted some court officials to Christianity. By the 1700s, however, Qing rulers worried that Jesuits were too involved in government affairs and forced the missionaries to leave. The Jesuits had failed to make China a Christian nation.

Qing Decline   During the 1700s government corruption and internal rebellions forced the Qing dynasty into a slow decline. As the population grew, the government raised taxes to support public services it routinely provided. But the government received little of the tax revenue: high-ranking officials took much of it for themselves. Peasant rebellions followed.

By 1850 the Qing, weakened by internal corruption, also faced the Taiping Rebellion. The leader of this revolt came in contact with Christian missionaries and developed his version of Christianity. He organized many Chinese into a political movement that attempted to start a new dynasty. He wanted to replace the Qing dynasty with a "Heavenly Kingdom of Great Peace." Lasting 14 years, the rebellion left much of southern China destroyed and the central government weakened. Thus undermined, the Qing faced new threats from foreign imperialistic powers.

SECTION 2 REVIEW

Recall

1. **Define:** queue, labor-intensive farming
2. **Identify:** Hong Wu, Yong Le, Zheng He, Forbidden City
3. **Locate:** Use the world map on pages 984–985 in the Atlas to determine the distance Chinese explorers traveled to reach the east coast of Africa. How does this record compare to Prince Henry's expeditions?

4. **Describe:** Explain the reasons for the Qing dynasty's decline and how the Taiping Rebellion affected that decline.

Critical Thinking

5. **Analyze:** Examine the reasons for China's growth in both population and land area during this period. How did government policies contribute to this growth?

6. **Evaluate:** Contrast the achievements of the Ming and Qing dynasties. Did the Qing build on the successes of the Ming, or create a new civilization?

Applying Concepts

7. **Movement:** What might have happened if the Chinese had continued moving westward? Would China have taken on colonization as Europeans did?

The Japanese Empire

While China enjoyed stability in the 1400s and 1500s, Japan experienced a period of turmoil. The shogun was a mere figurehead, and the emperor performed only religious functions. Daimyos, who controlled their own lands, waged war against their neighbors as feudal lords had done in Europe in the 1400s. "The strongest eat and the weak become the meat" was a Japanese expression of the time. Warriors showed no chivalry or loyalty. This time of local wars left Japan with a political system known as the Tokugawa shogunate that combined a central government with a system of feudalism.

Tokugawa Shogunate

Oda Nobunaga was the first military leader to begin uniting the warring daimyos. He announced his ambition on his personal seal: "to bring the nation under one sword." After winning control of a large part of central Japan, Nobunaga led his army against Kyoto in 1568. Five years later, amid the chaos caused by the weak Ashikaga family, Nobunaga deposed the Ashikaga shogun. Meanwhile, his forces had moved against Buddhist military strongholds around Kyoto. After a 10-year siege, he won and so became the most powerful man in the country. In 1582, however, a treacherous soldier murdered him.

Power then shifted to Nobunaga's best general, Toyotomi Hideyoshi, who rose from a peasant family to his high position in the military. By 1590 Hideyoshi had forced Japan's daimyos to pledge their loyalty to him. Acting as a military dictator, Hideyoshi furthered his goal of unity by disarming the peasants to prevent them from becoming warriors. In 1588 he ordered the "great sword hunt," demanding that all peasants turn in their weapons. To stabilize the daimyo realms he controlled, he imposed laws that prevented warriors from leaving their daimyo's service to become merchants or farmers. The laws also prevented farmers and merchants from becoming warriors.

Hideyoshi, planning to expand Japan's power abroad, invaded Korea as a step toward conquering China. The invasion had another purpose—to rid the country of warriors who could start rebellions at home. However, as you learned in Chapter 13, Admiral Yi's Korean turtle ships thwarted Hideyoshi's conquest.

After Hideyoshi's death in 1598, a third leader, Tokugawa Ieyasu, completed the work of unification that Nobunaga and Hideyoshi had begun. At the Battle of Sekigahara in 1600, Ieyasu defeated the last of his opponents. Three years later, Ieyasu asked the emperor to make him shogun. The Tokugawa family retained the shogunate for 250 years.

Political System Ieyasu established his government headquarters at the fishing village of Edo, today's Tokyo. There he built a stone fortress protected by high walls and moats. Today, the fortress is the Imperial Palace, but during the Tokugawa shogunate, the Japanese emperor continued to live in Kyoto. Although the emperor remained the official leader of Japan, the shogun exercised the real power.

After taking control, Ieyasu reassigned the daimyos' lands. He divided the daimyos into three groups: Tokugawa relatives, longtime supporters of the Tokugawa family, and those who came to the Tokugawa side only after the Battle of Sekigahara. He issued the most productive lands near Edo to the Tokugawa relatives. The others—potential enemies—received less desirable lands in outlying areas of Japan.

To ensure daimyo loyalty, Ieyasu set up a system called *sankin-kotai*, or attendance by turn. Each daimyo had to travel to Edo every other year, bringing tribute and remaining in the shogun's service for a full year. Thus, half the daimyos were directly under the shogun's control at any one time. Even when the daimyos returned to their estates, they had to leave their families at Edo as hostages.

The daimyos spent much of their income traveling to and from Edo and maintaining several households. They also had to get the shogun's permission to marry and to repair or build their castles. *Sankin-kotai* kept them weak, obedient to the shogun, and less able to rebel against the government. Much like Louis XIV of France, the shogun turned his aristocracy into courtiers.

Social Classes   The Tokugawa rulers officially divided the Japanese people into four classes. At the top were the samurai, including the daimyos. They alone could wear as symbols of authority a sword and a distinctive topknot in their hair. The farmers, as major food producers, were the second-highest class. They were followed by artisans who made goods. Merchants were at the bottom of society, because they only exchanged goods and thus were not productive.

No one could change his social class or perform tasks that belonged to another class. One samurai recalled that his father took him out of school because he was taught arithmetic—a subject fit only for merchants. A character in a popular puppet play, written by the author Chikamatsu, described the proper order of society:

A samurai's child is reared by samurai parents and becomes a samurai himself because they teach him the warrior's code. A merchant's child is reared by merchant parents and becomes a merchant because they teach him the way of commerce. A samurai seeks a fair name in disregard for profit, but a merchant, with no thought to his reputation, gathers profit and amasses a fortune. This is the way of life proper to each. This strict social order helped maintain peace and stability throughout Japan.

Learning from Photographs   *Toyotomi Hideyoshi built the magnificent White Heron castle in 1577.* **What features do you think helped make it a strong military fortress?**

Contacts with the West

The peace and order of the Tokugawa shogunate were interrupted when the first Europeans—the Portugese—arrived in Japan in 1543. Although the Japanese looked upon Europeans as barbarians, the warrior society saw that European weapons meant power. They purchased muskets and cannon to defeat their opponents.

Roman Catholic missionaries soon followed the Portuguese merchants. Francis Xavier, the earliest of the Jesuit priests who came to Japan, admired the Japanese people. To convert them, the Jesuits adopted their customs. Jesuit missionaries learned the subtleties of conversing in polite Japanese and set up a tea room in their houses so that they could receive their visitors properly.

After Xavier won the support of some local daimyos, Christianity spread rapidly. Oda Nobunaga himself lent support to the Christians, for during this time he was moving against the Buddhist monasteries that were serving as military strongholds. Jesuits trained Japanese priests to create a strong Japanese Christian church. By 1614 the Jesuits had converted 300,000 Japanese.

Many Japanese welcomed the first contact with Westerners, whose customs and styles became widespread in Japanese society. Even for Japanese who had not converted to Christianity, Christian symbols became fashionable. A missionary described non-Christian daimyos who would wear "rosaries of driftwood on their breasts, hang a crucifix from their shoulder or waist. . . . they think it good and effective in bringing success in daily life."

Hideyoshi began to suspect that Christian influence could be harmful to Japan. He had heard of Spanish missionaries in the Philippines who had helped establish Spain's control over the islands. In 1591 Hideyoshi outlawed Christianity. Despite crucifying some priests, his ban on the religion was not generally enforced.

Tokugawa Ieyasu and his successors also feared that Christianity threatened their power and thus continued to persecute Christians, killing them or forcing them to leave Japan. When Japanese Christians in Nagasaki defied authorities and refused to disband, the government attacked their community in 1637 and finally wiped them out in 1639.

Seclusion Policy   The Tokugawa rulers, deciding that contact with outsiders posed too many dangers, laid down edicts. Their seclusion policy lasted 200 years. The Act of Seclusion of 1636 forbade any Japanese to leave the country and added, "All Japanese residing abroad shall be put to death when they return home." As the Chinese had done at an earlier time, the government banned construction of ships large enough for ocean voyages.

Japan barred all Europeans except the Dutch. Unlike the Spanish and Portuguese, the Dutch were interested only in trade, not conquest or religious conversion of the Japanese. For this reason, after 1641 the Tokugawa government confined the Dutch to a tiny island in Nagasaki Harbor where they and a few Chinese carried on a tightly regulated trade. Through the Dutch traders, a trickle of information about the West continued to flow into Japan.

FOOTNOTES TO HISTORY

SHOGUN: THE TRUE STORY

In James Clavell's best-selling novel *Shogun*, a shipwrecked English sailor named Blackthorne helps a Japanese general both to win control of Japan and to become shogun. Though *Shogun* is fiction, its hero is based on a real person. In 1598, William Adams led five English ships across the Pacific, bound for the East Indies. Adams's ship was lost in a storm, and he landed in Japan in 1600.

Adams did not become shogun, but his knowledge of shipbuilding and navigation impressed Ieyasu, who gave him an estate and forbade him to leave Japan. Today, a street in Tokyo is named *Anjin-cho* in honor of Adams, whom the Japanese called *anjin,* or "the pilot."

Changes in Japanese Society   Despite Japan's geographic isolation and the Tokugawa policy of isolation, Japan's society and economy continued to change internally. During the early Tokugawa period, agriculture brought wealth to daimyos and samurai, who profited from the rice produced on their lands. Merchants, in turn, grew wealthy by lending money to daimyos and samurai. As the daimyos became a debtor class, the merchant class became more powerful.

The system of *sankin-kotai* also helped merchants to prosper and trade to increase, because merchants provided the goods and services that the daimyos needed on their twice-yearly trips to Edo. To smooth the daimyos' journey, the government built roads, which also made it easier for traders to take their goods to distant regions. Rest stations along the roads often grew into towns of considerable size.

At the same time, the demands for increased taxes led the daimyos to invent better farming methods that would increase agricultural yields. As agriculture became more efficient, farming required fewer people. Unemployed farm workers moved to the towns and cities, seeking work as artisans. In urban centers such as Edo, Kyoto, and Osaka, social order began to break down and class distinctions became less rigid.

Social life converged on amusement centers—bathhouses, restaurants, and theaters—

Kabuki Theater

Over the centuries, Japan's Kabuki theater tradition has grown and flourished. Continuing a tradition that historians have traced back to the 1600s, Kabuki plays are still performed today in Japan to large audiences. Kabuki theater seems to have originated as a new form of drama to satisfy the lavish and melodramatic tastes of a new social class in Tokugawa Japan.

When the lower and middle classes of society began to increase in the urban centers, they sought new forms of entertainment. The name *kabuki* means "to lean in the direction of fashion," reflecting Kabuki theater's popular origins. Amid a tradition of theater that catered to the tastes of the ruling class, Kabuki theater sought to appeal to the tastes of the middle class and lower class in Japanese society.

Kabuki concentrates on various subjects: historical dramas, daily life, tales of tragedy and loyalty, and sometimes stories making fun of political figures. During the 1600s, there were times when government officials banned performances they felt were too controversial. If anything, this censorship by the government seems to have made Kabuki all the more popular. Controversy stirred up interest, ensuring good attendance.

With elaborate, colorful costumes, movable stage decorations, and amazing special effects (including snowstorms and fires), Kabuki melodramas are spectacular events. In the early days of Kabuki theater, some plays lasted almost all day. Audiences delighted in the splendor of the shows themselves but also came to enjoy the other attractions available in the theaters. Many theaters included souvenir shops and restaurants.

In 1629 the government banned women from performing in Kabuki plays. With elaborate makeup and costumes, *onnagata,* or female impersonators, played all female roles. The best Kabuki actors became quite famous and had many fans. Painters produced actor portraits and sold them just as posters of modern movie stars are available today. Shown here is a print of two Kabuki actors performing on stage. In the foreground, the actors, in elaborately embroidered robes, converse. In the background, two chorus members and a musician appear, ready to accompany the drama with music.

Responding to the Arts

1. How does the name *kabuki* reflect the origins of Kabuki theater?
2. What are some characteristics of Kabuki performances?

where people could enjoy themselves. Japanese merchants and samurai could relax in the company of **geishas**, women who were professional entertainers. Geishas were trained in the arts of singing, dancing, and conversation.

Cities became the leading centers of Japanese culture. The arts flourished because townspeople had money to spend on leisure activities. The amusement centers provided employment for playwrights, artists, and poets. At this time the Kabuki theater developed, along with the elaborate Japanese puppet theater called **Bunraku,** in which three-man teams manipulated each puppet as a backstage chorus sang a story.

A popular form of art called ukiyo-e developed from the demand for prints of famous actors and scenes from their plays. At first, ukiyo-e prints were black-and-white, but soon ornate, brightly colored prints appeared in street stalls. Printed on delicate rice paper, they were easily damaged and today are highly prized collectors' items.

A new form of poetry called **haiku** also became popular among city people. In only 17 syllables, the haiku was to express a thought that would surprise the reader. Matsuo Basho, one of the great haiku masters, wrote this haiku:

In my new clothing
I feel so different
I must
Look like someone else.

FOOTNOTES TO HISTORY

KARATE

Karate is a Japanese word that means "empty hand" or "China hand." It is a martial art, or form of unarmed combat in which a person uses primarily hands or feet to strike a blow at an opponent.

During the 1600s, a Japanese clan had conquered the population of the island of Okinawa. The new Japanese rulers passed laws against owning weapons. As a result, many Okinawans learned how to make their hands and feet into weapons that were strong enough to smash through bamboo armor or break the arm of an attacker. The art of karate was passed down from one generation to another and spread to the main islands of Japan soon after Okinawa became a province of Japan in 1879.

As cities grew in size and population during the 1700s and 1800s, the ban on foreign contacts was gradually relaxed. Some Japanese began to study Western medicine in books that the Dutch brought to Nagasaki. Their interest in the so-called Dutch learning spread to Western gunnery, smelting, engineering, shipbuilding, mapmaking, and astronomy. However, it would not be until the Europeans arrived in the 1800s that Japan would begin to absorb other Western ideas.

SECTION 3 REVIEW

Recall

1. **Define:** *sankin-kotai,* geisha, haiku
2. **Identify:** Oda Nobunaga, Toyotomi Hideyoshi, Tokugawa Ieyasu, Francis Xavier, Matsuo Basho
3. **Describe:** How did the *sankin-kotai* system affect the daimyos? How did shoguns benefit from the system? How was the emperor affected?

4. **List:** What were the four classes of Japanese society? Explain why each class was thought to be more important than the one below it.

Critical Thinking

5. **Synthesize:** Imagine that you lived in Japan during the Tokugawa shogunate. Which social class would you have wanted to belong to? Explain.

6. **Analyze:** How did the new urban centers influence growth in the arts?

Applying Concepts

7. **Reaction:** Explain why Japan reacted to Western ideas by adopting a policy of isolation. How did this reaction to outside influences affect Japan's development over the next few centuries?

ANALYZING PRIMARY AND SECONDARY SOURCES

On the day of an earthquake, you see a television interview with an excited eyewitness to the event. Two weeks later, you see a televised interview with a scientist who studies earthquakes but who was not an eyewitness to this particular earthquake. Is one account more accurate than the other?

Explanation

To determine the accuracy of an account, you must analyze the source. *Primary sources* include oral or written accounts from eyewitnesses as well as objects or visual evidence. Diaries, autobiographies, first-person news accounts, interviews, artifacts, and paintings are primary sources. *Secondary sources* are accounts made by someone using information from something or someone else. Textbooks and biographies are secondary sources.

To determine whether a primary or secondary source is reliable, use the following steps:

- Briefly review the source.
- Determine if the source is primary or secondary.
- If it is a primary source, ask when it was written—at the time of the event or afterwards. If the account was written years after the event, the chances for accuracy lessen.
- Look for good documentation or factual evidence and correlation with other sources.

- Evaluate the author. Did the author understand the topic? Would he or she allow personal interest to color the account?

Example

Read the following excerpt from page 451:

> *"No one could change his social class or perform tasks that belonged to another class. One samurai recalled that his father took him out of school because he was taught arithmetic—a subject fit only for merchants. A character in a popular puppet play, written by Chikamatsu, described the proper order of society:*
>
> *A samurai's child is reared by samurai parents and becomes a samurai himself because they teach him the warrior's code. A merchant's child is reared by merchant parents and becomes a merchant because they teach him the way of commerce. A samurai seeks a fair name in disregard for profit, but a merchant, with no thought to his reputation, gathers profit and amasses a fortune. This is the way of life proper to each.*

The narrative leading to the quote is from a textbook and is therefore a secondary source. The samurai's recollection, however, and the quotation that follows are primary sources.

Since Chikamatsu lived and wrote at the time, the chances for account's accuracy increase. He understood the society he described, and there is no evidence that he favored or disapproved of the samurai or merchant.

The information in the quotation agrees with the samurai's account—the other first-hand report in the passage. Thus, we have no reason to doubt the reliability of the source.

Application

Use the outlined steps to evaluate the reliability of this primary source from page 448.

> *The country folk only live off their fields for the three winter months. . . During the spring months, they . . . spin or weave, eating by exchanging their cloth for rice. . . . The autumn is somewhat rainy, and the noise of the looms' shuttles is once again to be heard. . . . Thus, even if there is a bad harvest . . . our country people are not in distress so long as the other countries have a crop of cotton [for them to weave].*

Practice

Turn to Practicing Skills on page 457 of the Chapter Review for further practice in evaluating primary and secondary resources.

CHAPTER 18 REVIEW

From 1350 to 1850 social and political change in the Middle East and in Asia shaped the relationships among many cultures today. Europeans successfully halted the spread of Islam into Europe in the 1500s. Since that time, religious and political differences between predominantly Christian Europe and Islamic Middle East have remained.

Within the Middle East, dynastic and religious rivalries continued between Sunnis and Shiites. Those differences still exist and affect the political alliances of the region.

The Mogul invasion of India altered the religious composition of the subcontinent through the introduction of Islam to the Hindu country. Despite some Mogul rulers' attempts to show tolerance for the Hindu religion, the two faiths have remained fundamentally opposed to each other. Conflicts between Hindus and Muslims continue in the region today.

Although China's culture blossomed during this 500-year period, it did not change to meet the challenges brought by Westerners in the late 1800s and early 1900s. The rigid Confucian values that promoted cultural achievements in the 1600s worked against the country in later centuries. China turned inward and fought Western political and economic ideas.

Japan, ruled by military samurai rather than the educated elite, withstood the advances of Western nations. While China faced civil unrest during the early 1900s, Japan attended to economic and military growth, which enabled its leaders to challenge the West.

SUMMARY

For a summary of Chapter 18, see the Unit 4 Synopsis on pages 460–461.

USING KEY TERMS

A. Write the key term that best completes each sentence.

- a. geisha
- b. grand vizier
- c. haiku
- d. janissaries
- e. labor-intensive farming
- f. queue
- g. *sankin-kotai*
- h. sultan

1. ____ kept the daimyos weak and obedient to the shogun.
2. Suleiman served as a ____, or political ruler of the Ottoman Empire.
3. Agriculture in which people do most of the hard work is called ____ .
4. Manchus made Chinese men wear a ____ .
5. The ____ were the Ottoman sultan's elite corps of soldiers who maintained order throughout the palace.

B. Write the key term that best completes each analogy.

6. caliph : religious: ____ : political
7. sonnet : English: ____ : Japanese

REVIEWING FACTS

1. **Name:** What were the three great Muslim empires in eastern Europe, central Asia, and India?
2. **Explain:** What was the purpose of the voyages of Zheng He?
3. **List:** What steps did the Manchus take to maintain their control over China?
4. **Name:** Who were the generals that unified Japan?
5. **Describe:** Why did the Tokugawas enforce the policy of *sankin-kotai?*

THINKING CRITICALLY

1. **Apply:** How did religious differences cause strife between Muslim empires?
2. **Analyze:** Contrast Akbar's religious tolerance with that of the Manchus.
3. **Evaluate:** Which government described in this chapter was most successful in meeting its people's needs? Why?

ANALYZING CONCEPTS

1. **Movement:** How did the Chinese voyages of exploration differ from those of Columbus and other Europeans?
2. **Cultural diffusion:** Compare the spread of Islam into India with the spread of Christianity to China and Japan.
3. **Reaction:** What good and bad effects resulted from Japan's policy of isolation?
4. **Change:** What factors caused Japanese society to shift from rural to urban centers?

PRACTICING SKILLS

Which of the following is the most accurate source of information about the personality of Suleiman I? Explain your reasons.

a. diary of a foot soldier who defended Vienna during Suleiman's siege of the city
b. memoirs of one of Suleiman's officials after his dismissal for accepting bribes
c. a modern psychologist's essay on Suleiman, based on a selection of records, including Suleiman's speeches

GEOGRAPHY IN HISTORY

1. **Location:** Refer to the map on page 995. What is the global address (latitude and longitude) of Delhi?
2. **Movement:** Refer to the map on page 441. How far did Muslim empires spread through Europe and Asia?

TRACING CHRONOLOGY

Refer to the time line below to answer these questions.

1. What happened in China during Zheng He's voyages that indicated China cared more about security than expansion?
2. What indicates that Christianity was a powerful force in Japan for a short time?
3. When did the power of the great Muslim empires in Asia reach their height?

LINKING PAST AND PRESENT

1. Do you think it is possible for today's nations to follow a policy of isolation like Japan's? Have any tried to?
2. Conflict between Muslims and Hindus continues in India today. In what other nations do people fight over religion?

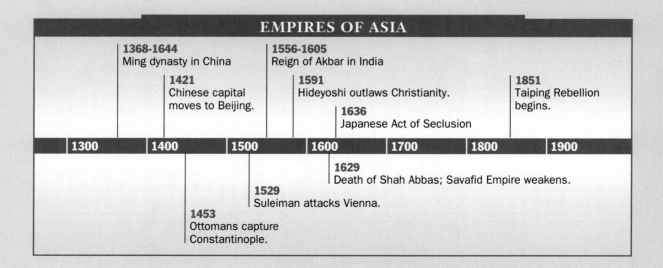

EMPIRES OF ASIA

- **1368-1644** Ming dynasty in China
- **1421** Chinese capital moves to Beijing.
- **1556-1605** Reign of Akbar in India
- **1591** Hideyoshi outlaws Christianity.
- **1636** Japanese Act of Seclusion
- **1851** Taiping Rebellion begins.

1300 **1400** **1500** **1600** **1700** **1800** **1900**

- **1453** Ottomans capture Constantinople.
- **1529** Suleiman attacks Vienna.
- **1629** Death of Shah Abbas; Savafid Empire weakens.

UNIT 4 SYNOPSIS

Throughout the world from 1400 to the mid-1700s, strong rulers solidified the power of their nations. In Europe two major movements—the Renaissance and the Protestant Reformation—resulted in a new European culture and powerful political alliances. Religion was likewise a force in Asia. There, Muslim empires extended control over a vast area between the Mediterranean Sea and India. A foreign dynasty took control of China, significantly changing its culture, and Japan united its warring daimyos under a new shogunate.

CHAPTER 15
Renaissance and Reformation

In the 1300s Italian scholars revived the ancient Greek ideal of individual achievement. This movement, called humanism, spurred a rebirth of European thought and art known as the Renaissance. For the first time since the fall of Rome, artists and writers expressed personal values and emotions in their works. Multitalented people like Michelangelo and Leonardo da Vinci created paintings, sculptures, and build-

ings that have been admired and studied through the centuries for their technical skill and beauty. The Renaissance spread north into France, Germany, the Low Countries, and England. After Johannes Gutenberg discovered how to use movable type in printing, books became widely available. Because many books were published in the everyday languages of the people, humanist ideas spread rapidly.

The Protestant Reformation   Religious reformers began to protest against Church abuses. Martin Luther, a young German monk, led the opposition when he nailed 95 statements to the door of Wittenberg Church on October 31, 1517. Refusing to withdraw his criticisms, Luther was imprisoned. Nonetheless, his ideas spread throughout Europe. He believed people could be saved by faith alone, rather than by good works. His beliefs became known as justification by faith. By the mid-1500s, many Germans had accepted Lutheranism. Other Protestant reformers soon put forth their own ideas. John Calvin, a reformer from Switzerland, preached predestination—the idea that God alone controlled all past, present, and future

Learning from Photographs *Filippo Brunelleschi, the first great Renaissance architect, designed this ingenious dome to top Santa Maria del Fiore Cathedral in Florence. Rising 270 feet above the paved stone street, the dome faces the Tuscan hills outside the city.* **What motivated Brunelleschi to design the dome?**

events. Calvinism spread from Switzerland to the Netherlands, Scotland, and England.

The English king, Henry VIII, broke his country's ties with the Catholic Church when the pope refused to allow him to divorce his wife. Henry assumed the position of head of the English church, but retained most of the Catholic Church's rituals.

In a Counter-Reformation, the Catholic Church began its own internal reform. Between 1545 and 1568, the Council of Trent defined Catholic doctrine and put an end to many Church abuses. The Catholic Church attempted to stop the spread of Protestantism by empowering an Inquisition to find heretics and execute them. A new Catholic religious order, the Jesuits, were sent as missionaries to areas dominated by Protestants in Europe as well as Asia. Much of northern Europe remained Protestant, however, but southern sections were mostly Catholic.

CHAPTER 16
Exploration and Empire

Because the city-state of Venice controlled the rich overland spice trade from Asia, other European powers looked for a sea route to the islands in Southeast Asia, where spices grew. Advances in nautical science made oceangoing voyages possible. The Portuguese prince Henry the Navigator organized exploring expeditions and began to send ships along the west coast of Africa. By the 1500s, Portugal had set up trading centers in Asia and the East Indies.

Portugal's rival, Spain, sent Christopher Columbus to reach the Indies by sailing west. In 1492, Columbus arrived in America—the "New World." News of his voyage prompted further expeditions to find a water route to Asia. Ferdinand Magellan left Spain in 1519; four years later, only 17 of his crew completed the first circumnavigation of the world.

Spanish conquistadors defeated native empires in the New World. Using native and African slave labor, Spanish colonists mined gold and silver, grew sugar and tobacco, and raised cattle—bringing great wealth to Spain. The Netherlands, France, and England, however, outstripped Spain in the next phase of overseas exploration.

The Dutch took over much of Portugal's spice trade in the Indies. France began trading with the natives of North America and explored its interior lands. England moved into India, the East Indies, and the West Indies in the Caribbean Sea. Like Spain, England brought slaves from Africa to work its plantations. The slave trade became part of a triangular trade that linked Europe, Africa, and America.

As a result of European colonial expansion, a commercial revolution occurred. Europeans started to use new business methods to handle the upsurge in wealth from their overseas trade. Joint-stock companies enabled groups of investors to share both risks and profits. The idea of mercantilism, that a nation's strength depended on wealth, spurred new trade and business.

CHAPTER 17
Royal Power and Conflict

In the early 1500s, strong monarchs arose in Europe. One of the most powerful was Charles V of the Hapsburg family. He inherited rule of Austria, the Netherlands, and Spain in 1519. A year later he became Holy Roman Emperor as well. As a Catholic, Charles faced rebellions among the Protestant German princes. He finally agreed to the Peace of Augsburg (1555), which allowed the princes to choose the religion for their own domains.

After Charles retired, his son Philip ruled Spain and the Netherlands. Philip supported the efforts of the Spanish Inquisition to wipe out Protestants, Jews, and Muslims. The Netherlands, however, revolted and won independence in 1581. Philip prepared to invade Protestant England, but his mighty fleet of ships, the Armada, suffered a terrible defeat by the British navy in 1588. Spain would never recover its old power.

In England, Elizabeth I, Henry VIII's Protestant daughter, negotiated a religious

Learning from Art *Catherine II became the Russian tsarina after seizing her husband's throne.* ***How did she earn the title Catherine the Great?***

compromise between English Catholics and Protestants that brought an era of stability to England. Her foreign policy followed the principle of a balance of power—seeking to keep the power of opposing nations equal, or in balance, so that one could not overcome another. Elsewhere, though, the new divisions within Christianity broke into warfare.

In France, years of bloody strife between Catholics and Huguenots (French Calvinists) ended when King Henry IV came to the throne. In 1598 he issued the Edict of Nantes, which granted religious freedom to his subjects. When the new Holy Roman emperor, Ferdinand, tried to curtail Protestants' freedoms, war erupted between Protestant and Catholic princes. Other European nations entered the conflict, called the

Thirty Years' War. The Peace of Westphalia finally ended the war in 1648.

Absolute Monarchy   From 1600 to 1780, European monarchs wielded great power. They believed in the theory of absolute monarchy, which held that kings and queens ruled as representatives of God. Louis XIV, an outstanding example of an absolute monarch, occupied the French throne for 72 years (1643–1715). Louis built a magnificent palace at Versailles, where he surrounded himself with courtiers, composers, and writers.

In 1685 Louis XIV revoked the Edict of Nantes, causing thousands of Huguenots to flee France. Louis also sought to expand his territory in a series of wars that cost France thousands of lives and much wealth.

In the 1700s a clash between two other absolute rulers exploded into a major war. Frederick the Great of Prussia forced Maria Theresa, ruler of Austria, to yield part of her domains. She formed an alliance with France and Russia to regain the territory. Prussia allied with Great Britain. The resulting Seven Years' War (1756–1763) spread to Europe's colonies. Prussia kept its territory, but France lost much of its overseas empire to Great Britain.

Russia, isolated for centuries, had neither expanded trade nor advanced in technologies as the European nations had during the early 1600s. Peter Romanov, who became tsar at a young age, expanded the state, enhanced its military power, modernized its technology, and even changed its name. But he enforced his reforms violently and left most of Russia's population, the serfs, bound as tightly as ever to their masters, the nobles.

CHAPTER 18
Empires of Asia

From the late 1400s to the early 1700s, three Muslim empires—the Ottoman, the Persian, and the Mogul—conquered and controlled much of eastern Europe, central Asia, and India. The multinational Ottoman Empire controlled not only the Middle East, but also much of southeastern Europe. Military defeats at Vienna and Lepanto halted the Ottoman conquests in Europe.

The Safavids established a dynasty in Persia, the geographic area today named Iran. Because the Safavids followed the Shiite branch of Islam, they were bitter enemies of the Ottomans, whose rulers were Sunni Muslims. Under the leadership of Shah Abbas, Persia reached the height of its cultural achievements.

Muslims from central Asia conquered northern India and set up a Mogul dynasty. Akbar, a Muslim ruler of the 1500s, fostered religious tolerance between Muslims and the Hindu people of India. The Moguls encouraged the arts—music, painting, and literature, and Shah Jahan created the Taj Mahal, a mausoleum dedicated to his favorite wife, and one of the world's most beautiful buildings.

Chinese Dynasties

The Ming dynasty ruled China from 1368 to 1644. Early Ming rulers encouraged farmers to move back into northern China, which had been devastated during the preceding dynasty. The Ming built oceangoing ships and sailed them as far as Africa and Arabia. Seven large expeditions under the command of Admiral Zheng He brought back rich tribute from foreign rulers. The Chinese did not continue their voyages of discovery. In 1644, new invaders from the north, the Manchus, conquered China and set up the Qing dynasty. The Manchus named their own people to high army and government posts, and forced Chinese to adopt some Manchu customs. In spite of changes brought by Manchu rule, Confucianism continued to be the leading philosophy during the Qing dynasty. Internal peace and

Learning from Photographs *The Forbidden City, in the city of Beijing, includes palaces of former Chinese emperors.* **Who was forbidden to enter the palace complex?**

government-sponsored improvements brought prosperity and increased population. By 1800, China was the world's most populous country.

Military Government Unites Japan

In the 1500s three powerful generals brought all of Japan's daimyos, or lords, under their control. After Tokugawa Ieyasu won the Battle of Sekigahara in 1600, he became the shogun, or military leader. From the capital at Edo, the Tokugawa shoguns would rule Japan for the next 250 years. They maintained control by forcing the daimyos to live in Edo for one year out of every two, a system called *sankin-kotai.*

Portuguese traders brought Christianity to Japan in 1543. Jesuit missionaries made many converts, but Japan's military rulers feared the influence of foreigners and stamped out Japanese Christianity in 1639. The Tokugawas decreed an Act of Seclusion, which closed Japan's borders to all except a few Dutch traders.

SURVEYING THE UNIT

1. **Examining Facts:** Recount the significance to Europe of the invention of moveable type.
2. **Making Comparisons:** Compare the political power of the European absolute monarchs to the political power of the Ottomans, Moguls, or Ming dynasty.
3. **Analyzing Ideas:** Would the world be different if there had not been a Counter-Reformation?

UNIT 4 REVIEW

REVIEWING THE MAIN IDEAS

1. **Comprehend:** What ideas and philosophy produced the flowering of art and thought called the Renaissance?
2. **Explain:** What were the causes of the Protestant Reformation, and how did the Catholic Church respond to it?
3. **Describe:** What goals did European nations have as they explored the world in the 1400s and 1500s?
4. **Explain:** How did European monarchs increase their power in the 1600s and 1700s?
5. **List:** Which Muslim empires controlled parts of Europe and Asia in the 1500s and 1600s?
6. **Explain:** Why did China's population grow so rapidly between 1600 and 1800?
7. **Describe:** How did the Tokugawa shogunate gain and maintain power in Japan?

THINKING CRITICALLY

1. **Apply:** How did the Renaissance help to create the Protestant Reformation?
2. **Explain:** How did humanism influence Martin Luther's ideas?
3. **Analyze:** Contrast the goals of European voyages of exploration with the purposes of the Chinese voyages made by Admiral Zheng He. What significance did the voyages have for both Europe and China?
4. **Analyze:** Contrast the actions of Louis XIV of France with those of Akbar in Mogul India. How did their actions reflect the character of each ruler?
5. **Synthesize:** Imagine that you are an adviser to one of the absolute monarchs described in this unit. What advice would you give him or her about domestic and foreign policies?
6. **Synthesize:** Suppose Columbus had not persuaded Queen Isabella to sponsor his voyage. Would European nations have sailed to the Americas anyway? Explain.

A GLOBAL PERSPECTIVE

Refer to the time line on pages 360–361 to answer these questions.

1. How long had Europeans known about the Americas before the English East India Company was established?
2. How many years after Columbus reached the Americas did a European discover a way to prevent smallpox?
3. What Renaissance leader was known as "the Magnificent"?
4. What significant event in Dutch history took place about 40 years after Martin Luther began the Protestant Reformation?
5. How was Dutch rebellion against Spanish rule related to the issuing of the first checks used to replace cash in the Netherlands?
6. During the time that Mozart was composing, what was happening in Europe?

LINKING PAST AND PRESENT

1. Religious differences between Catholics and Protestants, Shiites and Sunnis, and Muslims and Hindus caused conflicts in the 1500s and 1600s. What religious conflicts exist today? Trace their origins. Why do religious differences create such anger?
2. The explorations of the 1500s brought Europeans to all parts of the globe. The colonies they established have had a lasting influence on cultures today. Make a list of countries other than Spain, Portugal, the Netherlands, France, and England in which these languages are spoken today.
3. The Ottoman Empire included most of the nations of today's Middle East. Some modern leaders in this area wish to recreate a new united Muslim nation. How would this change affect the balance of power among world nations? What important resource would such a nation control, and how large would it be in population and area?

ANALYZING VISUALS

Under Mogul rule, the arts flourished in India. Akbar, who came to the throne in 1556, was especially supportive of art, culture, and intellectual pursuits. Although he was illiterate himself, he encouraged discussion among scholars at his court, and set up court workshops for artists. Because of his support for the arts, the time of his rule was a "golden age" for Indian culture.

In the painting shown here, Akbar, dressed in a golden robe, receives a court official. The audience hall shown is an elaborately decorated space, with gardens outside, finely carved doors, and richly decorated carpets. The visitor, seated at Akbar's feet, extends his hands in a gesture of respect and polite greeting toward the ruler.

1. How did Akbar's support for artists and intellectuals at his court influence the art produced during his reign?
2. Compare this image of Akbar with other images of rulers you have seen in this unit. How are these ruler portraits similar or dissimilar?
3. This painting shows Akbar greeting a court official. How would you compare the atmosphere in this painting to the way world rulers greet visitors today?
4. How would you compare Akbar's support of the arts to the United States government's support of the arts?

USING LITERATURE

Refer to the excerpt from The Prince *on pages 386–389 to answer these questions.*

1. Today in Eastern Europe, some Communist countries are attempting to form new systems of government. What does Machiavelli say about such a process? Do you agree or disagree with his explanation? Why?
2. What practice does Machiavelli say was the beginning of the downfall of the Roman Empire? Compare this reaction to the reason why the Ottoman Turks were able to conquer Constantinople.
3. What does Machiavelli say about the need for a prince to "stick to the path of good"? Which of the rulers in Chapter 17 followed this advice? Explain your answer.

WRITING ABOUT HISTORY

1. Choose one of the rulers mentioned in Chapter 18 and write a report about the effects of the ruler's political and social actions. Include the reaction of the subjects to the actions.
2. Find out more about Luther's trial at the Diet of Worms. Write a dialogue in which Luther and a Catholic debate the wisdom of Luther's stand against the Church. Include Luther's personal reasons for taking a step that could have caused him to be burned at the stake.
3. Choose one of the Renaissance city-states, Florence, Venice, or Rome. Research daily life in the city you select, and write a description contrasting the life of a noble and a craftsperson.

UNIT 5

Age of Revolution

1500–1830

"Dare to know! . . .
Have the courage to use your intelligence."

Chapter 19
Scientific Revolution

Chapter 20
British and American
Revolutions

Chapter 21
The French Revolution

With these words, the German philosopher Immanuel Kant voiced the spirit of the 1700s. Philosophers, writers, scientists, and inventors discarded traditions and looked at the world in new ways. Their discoveries and writings ignited a fuse of knowledge that spread from the elite salons of the learned to become the bonfire of the masses. But before the flames of change would be tempered, England would face a turbulent succession of kings, a new nation would be born in America, and France would be ripped apart by violence.

A GLOBAL CHRONOLOGY

	1500	1570	1640
Political Sphere	1521 Cortéz conquers the Aztec Empire.		1660 Charles II restored to the English throne
Scientific Sphere		1600 Dutch optician invents the telescope.	
Cultural & Social Sphere	1520 Michelangelo finishes work on Medici chapel in Florence.		

Military drum from the French Revolution

1710	1780	1850
	1789 French Revolution begins.	**1832** Parliament passes the Reform Bill in Great Britain.
1687 Newton states laws of motion and theory of gravity.	**1799** Rosetta Stone found in Egypt makes deciphering hieroglyphics possible.	
1740 Frederick the Great introduces freedom of press and freedom of worship in Prussia.		**1804** Ludwig van Beethoven composes his Third Symphony, the *Eroica*.

Scientific Revolution

*A*nton van Leeuwenhoek, a Dutch cloth merchant in the late 1600s, found that his odd hobby unlocked the door to an unknown world. By carefully grinding very small lenses out of clear glass, van Leeuwenhoek discovered that he could make things look much bigger than they appeared to the naked eye.

Soon the Dutch merchant turned his lenses to everything he could find—from the cloth he had just bought to the scales of his own skin. His most remarkable find was tiny microorganisms, which he described as "wretched beasties" with "incredibly thin feet" swimming through a tiny universe.

New technology such as van Leeuwenhoek's microscope and scientific study in general captured the imagination of many European people in the 1600s. A scientific revolution would lead to a new era in Western thought.

CHAPTER PREVIEW

Key Terms to Define: hypothesis, scientific method, natural law, philosophe, salon, enlightened despot

People to Meet: Nicolaus Copernicus, Johannes Kepler, Galileo Galilei, Francis Bacon, Isaac Newton, Andreas Vesalius, Robert Boyle, Joseph Priestley, Antoine Lavoisier, Thomas Hobbes, John Locke, Hugo Grotius, William Penn, Montesquieu, Voltaire, Frederick the Great, Maria Theresa, Jean-Jacques Rousseau

Places to Discover: Great Britain, France, Paris

Objectives to Learn:
1. How did scientific thought change in the 1600s?

Scholars examine age-old institutions with the tools of reason and observation.

2. What effects did changes in scientific thought have on thinking in other fields?

3. What factors helped Enlightenment ideas to spread throughout Europe?

4. How and why did many European people react to the ideas of the Enlightenment?

Concepts to Understand:

• Innovation—Interest in science leads to discoveries and ideas based on reason. Section 1

• Conflict—Changing views based on science and reason conflict with traditional beliefs. Section 2

• Reaction—Reason and order are applied to many human endeavors. Section 3

New Scientific Ideas

Magic, mysticism, and ancient writings ruled scientific thought throughout the Middle Ages. Scholars based their ideas on theories proposed almost a thousand years before by ancient Greek thinkers such as Aristotle, Ptolemy, and Galen. During the Middle Ages, most people believed that the earth was flat, and they accepted the Catholic Church's view that the earth was the center of the universe. According to Church doctrine, God created the universe to serve people. Therefore, the Church reasoned, the people's home—the earth—must be at the center of the universe.

In the 1600s, however, such ideas would topple as a scientific revolution spread throughout Europe. New technology, combined with innovative approaches to seeking knowledge, led to a breakthrough in Western thought. At the forefront of this scientific revolution was a Polish astronomer named Nicolaus Copernicus.

A Scientific Revolution

Copernicus started his scientific career at the University of Cracow in Poland in 1492—the same year in which Christopher Columbus reached the New World. Like Columbus, Copernicus began his questioning in a time when few people dared to question age-old beliefs and superstitions.

As Copernicus delved into his studies, he became convinced that ideas commonly accepted about the universe were wrong. Copernicus believed that the earth was round and that it rotated on its axis around the sun, which stayed still at the center of the universe.

Copernicus realized, however, that his ideas were revolutionary and even dangerous. Disputing or even questioning the Church's views about the universe could mean persecution, ex-

communication, or even burning at the stake. To avoid this risk, Copernicus worked in privacy, without publishing his ideas. The Polish scientist spent more than 30 years writing his treatise. Friends who realized the significance of his ideas helped publish Copernicus's work just before his death.

New Thinking About the Universe   Two other scientists took the Polish astronomer's ideas and ventured even further into a scientific understanding of the universe. The German astronomer Johannes Kepler and the Italian mathematician Galileo Galilei ignited a true revolution in astronomy in the early 1600s.

Early in his studies, Kepler believed in Copernicus's theory. But by the end of his career, Kepler had refuted all but two of Copernicus's **hypotheses,** or theories that attempt to explain a set of assumptions. Copernicus's hypothesis that the earth revolved around the sun was based on study and observations. But Copernicus could not prove his hypothesis, since the necessary mathematics was not available to him.

A skilled mathematician, Kepler used mathematical formulas to prove that although the sun stays in its place, the planets move in oval paths called ellipses, not in circles, as Copernicus had believed. Kepler also found that planets do not always travel at the same speed, but move faster as they approach the sun and slower as they move away from it.

Challenging the Church   Kepler challenged the teachings of many academics and religious leaders. Because Kepler was a Protestant, however, he did not have to fear the Catholic Church. But his Catholic contemporary, Galileo, did face considerable opposition from Church leaders.

In 1609 Galileo built his own telescope and observed the night skies. His discovery of moons circling a planet convinced him that the Copernican theory about the earth revolving around the sun was correct. Because these moons revolved around Jupiter, Galileo reasoned, not all heavenly bodies revolved around the earth. It was possible that some planets did move around the sun.

In 1632 Galileo published his ideas. Soon afterward, the Catholic Church banned the book. The Church would not tolerate Galileo's spreading ideas that contradicted its own position. An outraged Pope Urban VIII demanded that Galileo come to Rome and stand trial.

Urban's threats of torture and possible death forced Galileo to recant many of his statements and publicly state that he had gone too far in some of his writing:

> *I*, *Galileo Galilei, . . . swear that with honest heart and in good faith I curse . . . the said heresies and errors as to the movement of the earth around the sun and all other heresies and ideas opposed to the Holy Church; and I swear that I will never assert or say anything either orally or in writing, that could put me under such suspicion.*

Galileo continued his work after the trial. As he experimented with the motion of objects on earth, he helped to establish the universal laws of physics. Among these discoveries was the law of inertia, which specifies that an object remains at rest or in straight-line motion unless acted upon by an external force. Other investigations into the workings of the pendulum helped to advance its application as a time controller in clocks.

New Ways of Thinking

As scientists revolutionized the world of astronomy, philosophers such as Francis Bacon and René Descartes incorporated scientific thought into philosophy. Bacon, an English philosopher, claimed that ideas based solely on tradition or unproven facts should be discarded completely.

Learning from Art *Using new technology such as the telescope, Galileo discovered mountains on the moon and the satellites of Jupiter.* **Why was the Church upset by Galileo's work?**

To Bacon, truth resulted only from using the **scientific method.** The scientific method is made up of several steps. The scientist begins with careful observations of facts or things. Then the scientist tries to find a hypothesis to explain the observations. By experimenting, the scientist then tests the hypothesis under all possible conditions and in every possible way to see whether it is true. Finally, if careful and repeated experiments show that the hypothesis does prove true under all conditions, it is considered a scientific law. In other words, a scientific truth is not assumed—it is deduced from observations and a series of thorough experiments.

Like Bacon, French philosopher and mathematician René Descartes believed that truth must be reached through reason. The inventor of analytic geometry, Descartes saw mathematics as the perfect model for clear and certain knowledge. In 1637 he published *Discourse on Method*

The Development of the Telescope

This replica of Sir Isaac Newton's reflection telescope of 1691 is an enhancement of Galileo's first telescope.

In the early 1600s, the Italian mathematician Galileo learned of a new invention—the telescope. The telescope allowed its Dutch inventor to see the stars and the planets in the night sky more clearly.

Excited by the invention, Galileo proceeded to build a telescope of his own. Eventually, he built an instrument that would enlarge the image of distant objects more than 30 times. Using his telescope, Galileo discovered mountains on the moon, the stars of the Milky Way, the satellites of Jupiter, the rings of Saturn, and spots on the sun. Throughout the centuries, scientists continued to perfect Galileo's telescope.

Today, American astronomers are hoping the Hubble telescope will unlock many mysteries of the universe. The 43-foot-high telescope was launched into space in 1990 on a 15-year mission to search for other solar systems and the very origin of the universe.

The Hubble sends signals to a satellite 22,000 miles above the earth. Then, by a series of transmissions to ground receivers in New Mexico and Maryland, a computer finally reconstructs the Hubble's "pictures" of objects in outer space.

But like the inventions of the 1600s, even today's sophisticated Hubble needs refinement. Already astronomers are planning a mission into space to fix flawed mirrors and to replace lenses for a clearer image of the exciting discoveries they hope to make with the Hubble.

Making the Connection

1. What were some of the discoveries Galileo made with his telescope in the 1600s?
2. What are scientists hoping to find out from the Hubble telescope?

---

to explain his philosophy. In the book, Descartes began his search for knowledge by doubting everything except his own existence. He believed he had found one unshakable and self-evident truth in the statement "I think, therefore I am."

New Theories in Physics In 1642, as Bacon and Descartes transformed European thinking, one of the most influential figures in modern science was born in England. His name was Isaac Newton. Newton took full advantage of the scientific method as he studied science and mathematics. He once commented, "Asking the correct question is half the problem. Once the question is formulated there remains to be found only proof. . . ."

At Cambridge University, Newton was a below-average student with few friends. He almost left school without realizing his mathematical genius. But one of his teachers recognized his ability and began tutoring him. With this help Newton quickly became an eager and successful student. He explored the most complicated mathematics of his day, reading the writings of Copernicus and Galileo.

In 1665 an outbreak of the plague closed the university and forced Newton to return to his family's farm. During two years at home, Newton laid the foundation for his ground-breaking theories in mathematics and physics. The legend of Newton's apple originated during these years. Newton wrote that while sitting in his garden one day, he watched an apple fall to the ground. The apple's fall led him to the idea of gravity.

Nearly 20 years later, in 1687, Newton published his theories about gravity and other scientific concepts in his book *Mathematical Principles of Natural Philosophy*, often called *Principia*. Newton offered in *Principia* a new understanding of the universe, explaining and expanding the work of Copernicus, Galileo, and Kepler.

The book stated Newton's theory of universal gravitation, explaining why the planets move as they do. According to this theory, the force of gravity not only prevents objects from flying off the revolving earth, it also holds the entire solar system together by keeping the sun and the planets in proper orbits. To prove his theory, Newton developed calculus, an entirely new system of mathematics.

Newton's work greatly influenced the thinking of his own age and all later scientific thought. It suggested that precise mathematical formulas could be used to describe an orderly world and universe.

Studying the Natural World

As astronomy, philosophy, and mathematics advanced at an incredible pace, so too did the sciences of anatomy and chemistry. Like astronomy and physics, anatomy had been based on ancient works. Most knowledge of anatomy had come from the work of Claudius Galen, an ancient Roman.

Because Roman law forbade the dissection of human corpses, Galen formulated his theories of human anatomy by dissecting dogs and apes. Galen did make many anatomical discoveries, such as the existence of blood within the arteries, but he also held many mistaken views. Galen wrote that human beings have 13 pairs of ribs (they have 12), and he believed that the liver digested food and processed it into blood. A thousand years would pass before anyone began to question the accuracy of his findings.

Investigating the Human Body   French lawmakers in the 1500s also considered dissecting human bodies illegal. But this limitation did not stop a young medical student from making great advances in anatomy. Self-assured and outspoken, Andreas Vesalius made it clear to his professors that because Galen's views were based on dissected apes and dogs, his beliefs about human anatomy could not be accepted as truth.

Determined to learn more, Vesalius set out to find human corpses to dissect. Ignoring the laws, he roamed the countryside around Paris looking for the bodies of people who had been hanged. When Vesalius found a corpse hanging from a tree, he promptly cut the dead person down and hoisted the body over his shoulders.

By dissecting human bodies, Vesalius made ground-breaking discoveries in anatomy. In 1543 he published his findings in *The Working of the Human Body*. The book challenged and refuted many of Galen's ideas and opened the doors to modern medical research.

Almost 100 years later, English physician William Harvey made a discovery that also disproved many of Galen's hypotheses. From his first-hand observations of human bodies, Harvey announced that blood circulates throughout the body. His findings astonished a medical world that had based their beliefs about circulation on Galen's work.

As Vesalius and Harvey explained the workings of the human body, still another English

---

FOOTNOTES TO HISTORY

THE CIRCUS

The origins of the modern circus stem from the use of centripetal force, a property of motion identified by Newton in *Principia*. Centripetal force pulls an object traveling in a circular path toward the center of the circle.

Peter Astley, an English performer, relied on centripetal force to perform breathtaking stunts on horseback while the horse ran in a large circle at full gallop. Astley first performed for delighted crowds in 1768. He took his horse show to Paris in 1772, beginning the "traveling circus troupe." (*Circus* is the Latin word for circle.) Circuses quickly became very popular in England and France. They soon featured a variety of acts, such as jugglers and acrobats.

scientist, Robert Hooke, made a more fundamental biological discovery—the cell. Using the newly invented microscope, Hooke recognized cells in vegetable tissue. Hooke decided to call them "cells" because they reminded him of the cells in a honeycomb.

Experimenting with Chemistry   Scientists working in the field of chemistry joined their peers in astronomy, mathematics, and medicine in challenging ideas that had firmly prevailed for hundreds of years. By careful scientific experimentation, Robert Boyle was primarily responsible for taking chemistry from its mystical and unscientific origins and establishing it as a pure science.

When Boyle was born into an Irish noble family in 1627, the chemistry of the day was alchemy. People who practiced alchemy, called alchemists, spent much of their time trying to transform base metals into precious metals such as gold. They also held to the age-old belief that all matter was made of four elements: earth, fire, water, and air.

Boyle criticized alchemists and attacked the theory of the four elements in his book *The Skeptical Chemist*, published in 1661. Boyle proved that air could not be a basic element because it was a mixture of several gases. He also defined an element as a material that cannot be broken down into simpler parts by chemical means. As one scientist said about Boyle, "To him we owe the secrets of fire, air, water, animals, vegetables, and fossils. . . ." Today, Boyle is often called the founder of modern chemistry.

A century later, in 1775, an English chemist and clergyman named Joseph Priestley conducted further experiments into the properties of air and discovered the existence of oxygen. His study of the properties of carbon dioxide resulted in his invention of carbonated drinks. Toward the end of his career, Priestley wrote, "Every year of the last twenty or thirty has been of more importance to science . . . than any ten in the preceding century."

Across the English Channel in France, Antoine Lavoisier contributed still more to knowledge about oxygen. Lavoisier conducted scientific experiments that probed the nature of air and discovered that materials do not throw off a substance called phlogiston when burned, as commonly believed, but rather they consume oxygen. Lavoisier discovered the nature of combustion, which results from the chemical union of a flammable material with oxygen.

Marie Lavoisier contributed significantly to her husband's work. She learned English and Latin so that she could translate scientific essays and books for him. She also read numerous articles and condensed them so that he could be informed on many scientific subjects. Madame Lavoisier also helped to make the illustrations that accompanied her husband's writing.

Perhaps more significant than any single discovery in the 1700s was the application of the scientific view to an understanding of the world. Influenced by the discoveries in science, philosophers in the 1700s began to apply the scientific method to all human ideas, customs, and institutions.

SECTION 1 REVIEW

Recall
1. **Define:** hypothesis, scientific method
2. **Identify:** Nicolaus Copernicus, Francis Bacon, Isaac Newton, William Harvey, Robert Boyle
3. **Explain:** Why did the Catholic Church oppose Galileo's work?
4. **List:** Name three discoveries of the 1500s, 1600s, and 1700s.

Critical Thinking
5. **Analyze:** Examine how people viewed the universe and the workings of the human body before the scientific revolution of the 1600s.
6. **Imagine:** Imagine you are Galileo on trial, facing the possibility of a long imprisonment or even death unless you re-nounce the ideas you have worked a lifetime to prove. Write a short paragraph describing your feelings about the choice you have to make.

Applying Concepts
7. **Innovation:** How did Boyle revolutionize chemistry by applying the scientific method?

Impact of Science

As scientists made revolutionary discoveries about people, nature, and the universe, popular interest in science spread throughout Europe. Using new technology such as the microscope, scientists and amateurs alike looked with wonder at the world inside a drop of pond water. Others tinkered and prodded in their home laboratories, studying gases and other substances. At social gatherings across Europe, people discussed the latest findings with lively interest.

Monarchs helped the new sciences by supporting scientific academies, observatories, and museums. In England Charles II established the Royal Society of London in 1666. The group included Isaac Newton and Robert Boyle among its members. In the same year, Louis XIV of France supported the founding of the French Academy of Science. These societies provided financial support to scientists and published scientific books and journals.

Exploring Political Ideas

The advances in science led philosophers and other thinkers to believe that if systematic laws governed the workings of nature and the universe, it followed that political, economic, and social relationships could also be understood through reasoned analysis. Scientific thought and method profoundly influenced political theory. Political philosophers believed in the idea of **natural law,** or a universal moral law that, like physical laws, could be understood by applying reason.

Two English philosophers, Thomas Hobbes and John Locke, grappled with their ideas of natural law and government during the mid-1600s, as England struggled with the political tensions of a civil war. The country was torn between people who wanted the king to have absolute power and those who thought the people should govern themselves.

Hobbes Explores Government   Thomas Hobbes used the idea of natural law to argue that absolute monarchy was the best form of government. He believed that violence and disorder came naturally to human beings and that without an absolute government, chaos would ensue. In his book *Leviathan*, published in 1651, Hobbes wrote about a state in which people lived without government. The book showed how "nasty, brutish, and short" life in such a world would be.

Hobbes believed that people should form a contract or agreement to give up their freedom and live obediently under a ruler. In this way, they would be governed and ruled by a monarch who would protect them by keeping their world peaceful and orderly. According to Hobbes, people do not have the right to rebel against their government, no matter how unjust it might be.

Locke Offers a Different View   Another English philosopher, John Locke, also based his theories on the idea of natural law. But he came to an entirely different conclusion. Like Hobbes, Locke said that government was based on a contract and that it was necessary to establish order. Unlike Hobbes, he believed that people in a state of nature are reasonable and moral, and that they have natural rights to life, liberty, and property.

Locke believed that these rights exist apart from any government, and people have the right to break their contract if their government fails to uphold their natural rights. According to Locke, if people employed reason, they would arrive at a cooperative and workable form of government.

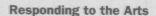
Rembrandt

Rembrandt Harmensz van Rijn (1609–1669) was one of the most prominent Dutch artists of the 1600s. Born in the university city of Leiden, Rembrandt moved to the Dutch capital of Amsterdam in the early 1630s. In this active, commercial city, the aspiring young artist earned a reputation for being one of the best European painters of his time. Many of his Dutch commissions were for portraits—either of individuals or of groups (often of businessmen or merchants, or of a husband and wife together).

**Self-portrait
by Rembrandt**

In the portrait painting shown here, Rembrandt—with muted colors and subtle lighting and shading—created a quiet, domestic scene of simple elegance. Executed around 1660, nine years before Rembrandt's death, this famous painting is one of about 100 self-portraits that Rembrandt painted in his career.

In each of his many self-portraits, Rembrandt showed his personality in a different way. In his earlier paintings, Rembrandt portrayed himself in a variety of costumes and manners—as a confident young man, as a medieval knight, and once even dressed in Asian clothing with a turban on his head.

In this late portrait of himself, Rembrandt seems to have stepped away from some of the fanciful ideas that were behind his earlier self-portraits. Here is a very honest portrait, showing Rembrandt as a thoughtful, weary artist, holding his palette and brushes in his hand. The serious, tired expression on the artist's face betrays the hard times he had known in his life—Rembrandt had gone bankrupt in 1656. Nevertheless, his dignity as a talented artist still remains to inspire later generations of artistic admirers.

Besides painting, Rembrandt was an accomplished printmaker. In his studio, he produced many famous etchings of Dutch landscapes and of biblical subjects. Like his paintings, Rembrandt's prints display fine, subtle tones of light and dark. Few European artists have ever achieved a similar refinement in etching.

Responding to the Arts

1. What are some of the major characteristics of Rembrandt's painting style?
2. What does Rembrandt's self-portrait shown here reveal about the life or personality of one of the Netherland's most famous artists?

Locke published his ideas in 1690 in *Two Treatises of Government*. His writings became widely read and were tremendously influential throughout Europe and in England's American colonies. Ironically, the ideas that the American colonists used to justify their independence from Great Britain were formulated by British thinkers. Thomas Jefferson based much of the Declaration of Independence on Locke's ideas about the social contract between government and individuals.

Reason Influences Thought

As Europeans searched for new principles that would meet the standards of reason, great changes were made in the practice of law. Incorporating scientific or reasoned thought in applying the law helped to end unjust trials. Lawmakers placed less value on hearsay and on confessions made under torture in determining the guilt or innocence of suspected criminals.

In the 1600s several people made the first attempts to create a body of international law. A Dutch jurist named Hugo Grotius called for an international code based on natural law. He believed that one body of rules could reduce the dealings of governments to a system of reason and order.

In the American colonies, William Penn, founder of the Quaker colony of Pennsylvania, believed in pacifism and advocated an assembly of nations committed to world peace.

Viewing the Past   The new emphasis on science also heightened interest in gathering information and learning about the past. Using microscopes and other new equipment, scientists examined manuscripts for evidence of possible forgery, studied old coins, and analyzed inscriptions on buildings. Interest awakened in chronology and in relating the different calendar systems of civilizations throughout history.

Examining Religion   Many Europeans also applied reason to religious beliefs. Although most maintained an active faith in God, many acknowledged that no one faith should be claimed as the one true religion. Increasingly, people became tolerant of other religions and viewpoints. As members of the upper and middle classes turned away from strict religious views, Europe became a more secular society. Many people looked to reason, morality, and justice in determining codes for their behavior and for the government of society.

In the 1700s a new religious philosophy called deism swept through Europe and America. Deists often denounced organized religion, declaring that it exploited people's ignorance and superstitions. Deism was intended to construct a simpler and more natural religion based on reason and natural law. In *An Essay on Man*, Alexander Pope, an English poet of the 1700s and a Deist, asserted the rightness of humanity's place in an orderly universe.

Say first, of God above, or man below,
What can we reason, but from what
* we know?*
Of man, what see we but his station here,
From which to reason, or to which refer?
Through words unnumbered through the God
* be known,*
'Tis ours to trace him only in our own.

SECTION 2 REVIEW

Recall
1. **Define:** natural law
2. **Identify:** Thomas Hobbes, John Locke, deism
3. **Explain:** What was John Locke's theory of the contract of government?

Critical Thinking
4. **Analyze:** Contrast Hobbes's views of government with Locke's views.
5. **Analyze:** How did the scientific revolution of the 1600s influence the idea of natural law?

Applying Concepts
6. **Conflict:** What was the purpose of the new religious philosophy known as deism, and how did deism conflict with the beliefs of established religions?

Triumph of Reason

Compared to their ancestors, who lived in a world that seemed to be run by inexplicable forces and filled with magic, Europe's new thinkers believed that their scientific approach helped illuminate and clarify both the natural world and the study of human behavior. As a result, the late 1600s through the 1700s came to be called the Age of Enlightenment.

Men and women of the Enlightenment studied the world as though they were looking at it for the first time. No longer held back by tradition, they defined the world in their own way, using science as their base. Natural scientists analyzed and classified thousands of animals, insects, and plants. Geologists drew maps of the earth's surface. Astronomers continued to make discoveries about the universe.

Largely due to reading Newton's *Principia*, Enlightenment thinkers perceived the universe as a machine governed by fixed laws. They saw God as the master mechanic of the universe—the builder of a machine who provided laws and then allowed it to run on its own, according to these orderly principles. They also believed in progress, or the idea that the world and its people could be improved.

Such radically new perceptions and ideas started a philosophical revolution. Jean Lerond d'Alembert, a French mathematician, claimed that the new method of thinking and the enthusiasm that accompanied it had "brought about a lively fermentation of minds, spreading through nature in all directions like a river which has burst at its dams."

Spreading Ideas

The thinkers of the Enlightenment who spread these exciting new ideas came to be called **philosophes** (fee luh ZAWFSZ), the French word for philosopher. Most philosophes passionately believed in Locke's political philosophy and Newton's scientific theories. Most disapproved of superstition and religious opposition to new scientific endeavors. They believed in both freedom of speech and the individual's right to liberty. Many philosophes were talented writers whose essays and books helped to spread and popularize ideas and beliefs of the Enlightenment.

Activity in Paris   France was the most active center of ideas. In Paris especially, the new intellectuals delighted in gatherings called **salons** held in the homes of wealthy patrons. In a salon, writers, artists, and educated people of the growing middle class mingled with men and women of the nobility. Besides discussing the philosophies of the day, salon guests prized the art of conversation and often engaged in contests to see who had the sharpest wit.

Wealthy and influential women ran many of the popular salons. Madame de Pompadour was perhaps the most celebrated. A mistress to Louis XV, Pompadour's intelligence and courtly charm won the admiration of many philosophes.

A remarkable achievement compiled by some of the most prominent philosophes of the Enlightenment was the *Encyclopédie*. First published in 1751, these 28 volumes covered everything then known about the sciences, technology, and history in more than 3,000 pages crammed with illustrations.

The *Encyclopédie* was initially conceived to be simply a French translation of a two-volume English encyclopedia, but its editor, Denis Diderot, had a work of much greater scope in mind. Diderot devoted much of his life to this project. Among other things, the *Encyclopédie* criticized the Church and government and praised religious tolerance.

The Catholic Church banned the *Encyclopédie*. When Diderot discovered that the printer, frightened by the controversial material in the volumes, had omitted passages that might offend Church leaders, he became enraged and screamed at the printer:

*Y*ou have massacred . . . the work of twenty good men who have devoted to you their time, their vigils, their talents, from a love of truth and justice, with the simple hope of seeing their ideas given to the public. . . .

For their writings, Diderot and several others went to prison. Still, the *Encyclopédie* was widely read and its ideas spread all through Europe.

Montesquieu A contributor to the *Encyclopédie* and one of the most learned of the philosophes in political matters was Charles-Louis de Secondat, Baron de Montesquieu (mahn tuhs KYOO). His master work, *The Spirit of Laws*, appeared in two volumes in 1748.

After studying existing governments, Montesquieu wrote about his admiration for the English government and promoted the idea of separating governmental powers. Montesquieu believed that power should be equally divided among the branches of government: the legislative branch, which made the laws; the executive branch, which enforced them; and the judicial branch, which interpreted the laws and judged when they were violated.

Montesquieu strongly believed in the rights of individuals. His work powerfully influenced the writing of the constitutions in many countries, including the United States.

Voltaire Perhaps the most celebrated of the philosophes was François Marie Arouet, known to the world by his pen name, Voltaire. A French author and Deist, Voltaire wrote poetry, plays, essays, and books in a style that was entertaining and often satirical. *Candide*, his most celebrated satire, challenged the notion that everything that happens is for the best in "the best of all possible worlds."

In his youth, Voltaire twice served time in the Bastille, the famed prison in Paris. His satirical works that mocked the Church and the royal court of France earned him one prison term; he received the other term when he was accused of claiming to be a nobleman. After his second offense, Voltaire was given a choice between further imprisonment and exile from France. He chose the latter. When Voltaire moved to England, he felt unfettered in an atmosphere of political and religious freedom.

During the three years he spent in England, Voltaire wrote books promoting Bacon's philosophy and Newton's science. Voltaire deeply admired the English ideal of religious liberty and its relative freedom of the press. Voltaire is credited with the famous statement in defense of free speech, "I disapprove of what you say, but I will defend to the death your right to say it."

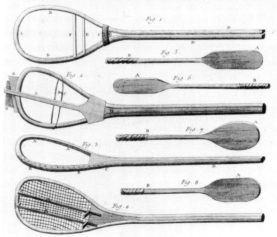

Learning from Art *Diderot's* Encyclopédie *featured detailed illustrations, such as this tennis court and the steps in a tennis racket's construction.* **Why was the** Encyclopédie *such a valuable work?*

Impact of Enlightenment

The ideas introduced by the philosophes and other enlightened thinkers spread into the realm of politics. Philosophes asserted the right of people to speak freely and to disagree with their rulers, and advocated reforms such as ending the use of torture in prisons. Their work influenced rulers in such countries as Prussia, Austria, Spain, Portugal, Denmark, and Sweden. These leaders began to implement humanitarian reforms to help their people.

Some Leaders Initiate Reform Monarchs who attempted to practice some of the political ideas of the Enlightenment were called **enlightened despots**. In other words, these leaders aimed to rule according to the principles of the Enlightenment while maintaining their traditional royal powers. They worked hard to improve the performance of government in their countries and promoted agriculture, industry, culture, and education.

Frederick II of Prussia, the most famous of the enlightened despots, played the flute, wrote poems and essays, and earned a reputation as a minor philosophe. Frederick believed that as king, he was the "first servant of the state." He corresponded with Voltaire for many years, and both men greatly admired each other. In fact, it was Voltaire who first honored Frederick with the title "the Great." In one letter, Frederick wrote to Voltaire:

My chief occupation is to fight the ignorances and the prejudices in this country. . . . I must enlighten my people, cultivate their manners and morals, and make them as happy as human beings can be; as happy as the means at my disposal permit me to make them.

IMAGES OF THE TIME

Salon Society

During the Enlightenment, Europe's high society often gathered in the salons of wealthy patrons to discuss the ideas and events of the day.

Salon gatherings like the one depicted on this painted fan were often hosted by wealthy women. As a result, the status of women in high society rose.

Frederick's reforms included abolishing the use of torture except for treason and murder, establishing elementary schools, and promoting industry and agriculture. After the Seven Years' War, Frederick tried to help the peasants by giving them seeds to plant and money to rebuild houses and barns.

Another ruler who introduced several humanitarian reforms was Maria Theresa of Austria. She bore the titles of Holy Roman Empress, Queen of Hungary and Bohemia, and Archduchess of Austria. She was one of Austria's most able rulers. Although as a Catholic she disagreed with much of Enlightenment philosophy, Maria Theresa tried to protect the rights of serfs by issuing codes governing the relationship between them and their lords. She also freed all peasants who lived on land owned by the crown. In 1774 she set up elementary schools supported by local and national funds.

Maria Theresa's son, Joseph II, also admired and followed the ideas of the Enlightenment. After the Empress's death in 1780, Joseph II quickly implemented stronger reforms in the kingdom. He abolished serfdom, made land taxes equal for peasants and nobles, and gave freedom to the press. He also took property from the Church and used the money to support hospitals.

Most of Joseph's reforms failed, however. His abrupt changes antagonized too many people. Rebellion by the nobles forced him to repeal many of his reforms. Joseph's brother and successor, Leopold II, revoked most of Joseph's remaining laws, but did allow the peasants to keep their freedom.

Throughout Europe, nobles and church leaders, afraid of losing too much political power to the common people, frustrated many reform efforts made by enlightened despots. In

Literature was a favorite topic for discussion in the salon. Note the elaborate decoration and costumes in the salon scene below.

The decorative arts flourished during this period. Finely painted French porcelain was especially popular.

Reflecting on the Times
How did the salon gatherings in Europe during the 1700s reflect Enlightenment ideas?

Learning from Art Gulliver's Travels *by Jonathan Swift was one of the major novels written in 1726. Though it contains some of Swift's most savage satire, it has become a children's favorite.* **Who were some of the other writers of the period?**

addition, many monarchs backed away from Enlightenment ideals when they realized that their own positions would be threatened by giving too much power to their subjects. In doing so, they struck down many of the political reforms that might have stopped the violent revolutions that were to come.

Classical Movements The worlds of art, music, and literature also shared in the Enlightenment beliefs. Writers, artists, and architects strove to achieve the ideals of Greek and Roman classicism, which to them represented ultimate order and reason. Using classical titles and imitating classical themes and styles, they attempted to capture the refined and simplified spirit of the ancients.

Architects built palaces, opera houses, and museums based on the architecture of ancient Rome. They used simple forms, such as squares and circles, rather than the elaborate swirls of the baroque style.

Sculptors and painters also emulated the ideals and forms of antiquity. Whereas artists following the baroque and rococo styles tended to appeal to their viewers with elegant, swirling forms, these artists sought a return to a calm, rational style of art that would appeal to the mind through the logic and geometry of its forms.

Sculptors such as Antonio Canova created works based on subjects from classical mythology. Jean-Antoine Houdon carved sculptures of contemporary figures in poses that recall ancient portraits of philosophers and political leaders.

In the field of painting, Jacques-Louis David also drew from classical subjects and forms. His paintings show a concern with geometry and simplicity of form that results in powerful, monumental images. He used clear and uncomplicated primary colors. These reds, yellows, and blues created powerful contrasts and accented the clarity of his forms.

Writers worked to achieve the classical ideal while maintaining their devotion to the concept of reason. Often, imitation of a classical model resulted in an ornate and affected style that was focused more on form than on content. French dramatists Moliere, Jean Baptiste Racine, and Pierre Corneille and English poets John Dryden, Alexander Pope, and John Milton mastered the classical tradition.

Musical composers of the Enlightenment also stressed classical elements such as balance, contrast, and refined expression of emotion. At the same time, they witnessed a great evolution in music. Music made the transition from merely supporting religious services and dance and opera companies, to being an "art" in its own right. For the first time, people began going to concerts for the pleasure of listening to the music itself.

The piano, evolving in the late 1600s, allowed musicians to produce much greater ranges of loudness and softness. The violin was

Learning from Art *Following the trend to a return to nature, it became popular for nobles to dress and act in an idealized version of happy peasants enjoying country life.* **How does this painting reflect these ideals?**

perfected at the same time, changing the sound of music. As composers grouped similar instruments, they laid the foundations for chamber music and the modern orchestra. Germany's Johann Sebastian Bach and George Frideric Handel and Austria's Joseph Haydn and Wolfgang Amadeus Mozart were among the great musicians composing during this era.

Other Views

Not everyone agreed with the ideas of the Enlightenment. Some saw the structured and ordered view of the universe as overly rational and devoid of emotion and feeling. English poet William Blake exclaimed, "God is not a mathematical diagram!"

In the 1700s the French philosopher Jean-Jacques Rousseau criticized what he saw as ex-cessive reliance on reason and claimed that people should rely more on instinct and emotion. Born in Geneva to French Huguenot parents, Rousseau led an unhappy life. He suffered from chronic physical ailments and possibly from mental illness. Nevertheless, he became a leading thinker and one of the most profound writers of his day. In Paris in the 1740s, his associates included Diderot and the Encyclopedists, and he continued to stay in touch with his Parisian intellectual circle.

Rousseau's unhappy life convinced him that human beings were naturally good but that civilization and institutions made them evil. The inspiration for this philosophy came to him in 1750, when he entered a contest that offered a prize for the answer to the question: Have science and the arts done more to corrupt morals or improve them? Rousseau won the contest with his essay *Discourse on the Effect of the Arts* and *Sciences on Morals*; his reply that science and the arts did corrupt morals made him famous. Ten years later he published *La Nouvelle Héloise*, a novel describing the beauties of nature and the pleasures of a simple country life. The popular book influenced people from every level of society to live humbler lives, closer to nature. The fashion spread as far as the French palace of Versailles, where Marie Antoinette, Queen of France, constructed a rural village on royal grounds and pretended to be a milkmaid.

Rousseau also believed that the power to rule belonged to the people, and governments should receive their authority from the people. He wrote that people had the right to rise up against their government and carry out needed change.

Rousseau's writings influenced German philosopher Immanuel Kant. Kant believed that reason could not explain the problems of metaphysics—the aspects of philosophy that deal with universal, spiritual, and eternal questions, such as the existence of God and the limits of knowledge. In his major work, *The Critique of Pure Reason* (1781), Kant asserted that human feelings about religion, beauty, and morality were real even though science and reason could not explain them.

Kant divided the universe into the realm of physical nature and the realm of ultimate reality. He claimed that the methods for knowing varied greatly in these two worlds. In the physical world, people attained knowledge through the senses such as sight, hearing, and touch, as well as through reason. In the second realm, however, Kant believed that faith, intuition, and conviction were valid instruments for attaining knowledge. For example, the natural sciences, which belonged to the first realm, could not provide a guide for morality, which rested in the second realm.

Religious Movements   Not only philosophers, but ordinary men and women found something wanting in the rationalism of the Enlightenment. Many rejected deism, the religion of reason, and searched for a religion that was more emotionally satisfying.

In Germany, Count von Zinzendorf established the Moravian Brethren, which emphasized the emotional and mystical side of Christianity. In England, a movement called Methodism, led by John Wesley, also stressed the value of personal religious experience. Methodism was a reaction to the cold formality of the Church of England. In Eastern Europe, Hasidism, which promoted mysticism and religious zeal—as opposed to an emphasis on external ritual—spread among Jews. All of these religious movements rejected reason in favor of an enthusiastic faith.

As people questioned the philosophies of the Enlightenment, classicism in the arts gave way to romanticism, which was a movement that celebrated emotion and the individual. These developments marked the ending of the Age of Enlightenment. Tired of the privileged ruling classes and inspired by new ideas such as the writings of Rousseau, lower classes began to demand more rights. The sun set on the tranquil world of the Enlightenment as history moved on to a period of tumult and revolution.

SECTION 3 REVIEW

Recall
1. **Define:** philosophe, salon, enlightened despot
2. **Identify:** Enlightenment, Montesquieu, Voltaire, Rousseau, Kant, Wesley
3. **Explain:** Describe some of the main ideas of Enlightenment thinkers.

4. **List:** Name some of the reforms implemented by enlightened despots.

Critical Thinking
5. **Evaluate:** How did Rousseau's philosophies influence the work of the German philosopher Immanuel Kant?

6. **Analyze:** Compare John Locke's ideas about government with those of Rousseau's.

Applying Concepts
7. **Reaction:** In what ways did people react to Enlightenment ideas?

INTERPRETING POINTS OF VIEW

Suppose you are interested in seeing a new science fiction movie, but you are getting mixed reviews from your friends. Opinions range from "terrific" to "awful." Some of your friends liked the stars of the film, while others dislike them. People often have different opinions about the same people, events, or issues because they look at these things from different *points of view*.

Explanation

A person's point of view is the way in which he or she interprets topics or events. There are a number of factors that affect a person's point of view, including age, sex, ethnic background, and religion. The ability to interpret points of view will help you determine the objectivity of an argument or the accuracy of a description.

Use the following steps to help you interpret points of view in written material:

- Read the material and identify the main idea.
- Gather background information on the topic and the author.
- Identify aspects of the topics that the author has emphasized or excluded.
- Identify any words or phrases that suggest a personal opinion. Pay special attention to emotionally-charged words such as *cruel, drastic, heartrending, vicious.*

- Look for metaphors and analogies that indirectly give an opinion: "The mayor's announcement was a slap in the face." "If this budget can work, then dogs can fly."
- Identify the author's point of view on the topic.

If you have difficulty identifying the point of view in a work, compare it to another work on the same subject by an author with a different background.

Example

Read the following excerpt from Jean-Jacques Rousseau's book *Emile* and determine the author's point of view:

Men are not made to be crowded together in ant-hills, but scattered over the earth to till it. The more they are massed together, the more corrupt they become. . . . Huddled together like sheep, men would very soon die. Man's breath is fatal to his fellows. . . . Send your children to renew themselves, so to speak, send them to regain in the open fields the strength lost in the foul air of our crowded cities.

The main idea of this selection is that cities are unhealthy places in which to live. Only negative aspects of city life have been emphasized. Rousseau's position as the leader of a movement urging

people to abandon degenerate civilization (crowded cities) and go back to nature (open fields) is clearly stated.

Words such as *corrupt, fatal,* and *foul* suggest his negative attitude toward cities. The metaphors comparing men to *sheep* and cities to *ant-hills* add to this negative view.

The passage contains the unstated opinions that crowding causes corruption. It also excludes the fact that cities often offer greater employment opportunities, culture, and trade than rural areas.

Application

Read the following passage by Denis Diderot, the French philosophe and editor of the *Encyclopédie*. Use the outlined steps to interpret the point of view of the passage:

You have massacred . . . the work of twenty good men who have devoted to you their time, their vigils, their talents, from a love of truth and justice, with the simple hope of seeing their ideas given to the public. . . .

Practice

Turn to Practicing Skills on page 485 of the Chapter Review for further practice in interpreting point of view.

CHAPTER 19 REVIEW

HISTORICAL SIGNIFICANCE

The scientific revolution and the Enlightenment marked a turning point in the history of human thought. A new philosophy about knowledge was being constructed, emphasizing observation, experiment, and reason rather than faith and tradition. One of the most influential aspects of this new interest in science was a changed view of the solar system. Men such as Copernicus and Galileo held that the sun, not the earth, was the center of the universe. These ideas culminated in the work of Isaac Newton, who unified the discoveries of his predecessors by formulating the law of universal gravitation.

As scientific knowledge advanced, the nature of political systems and the rights of individuals were also questioned and explored. Philosophers tried to apply reason to every field of knowledge. Locke and Montesquieu investigated government; Voltaire and Rousseau analyzed religion and morality.

The Age of Enlightenment continues to shape our lives and still arouses debate, particularly on religious issues. The United States Constitution incorporates many of Locke's and Montesquieu's beliefs, and scientists continue to use the scientific method in research today.

SUMMARY

For a summary of Chapter 19, see the Unit 5 Synopsis on pages 542–545.

USING KEY TERMS

Write a sentence or two about each pair of words to show how the words are related.

1. hypothesis, scientific method
2. philosophe, salon
3. enlightened despot, natural law

REVIEWING FACTS

1. **Explain:** Copernicus, Galileo, Kepler, and Newton all worked on problems in astronomy. Explain how each added something new to our understanding of the solar system.
2. **Describe:** In what ways did people's thoughts about the universe, the human body, and philosophy change during the Enlightenment?
3. **Explain:** How was the field of history affected by the philosophical developments of the scientific revolution?

4. **Explain:** What political idea advocated by Montesquieu can be found in the U.S. Constitution?
5. **Identify:** Name two philosophers in the 1700s who disagreed with Enlightenment ideas. What were their views?

THINKING CRITICALLY

1. **Apply:** How did neoclassical art reflect the values of the Enlightenment? Give examples to support your answer.
2. **Synthesize:** Why do you suppose witch hunts became a thing of the past after the Enlightenment?
3. **Evaluate:** Were the 1700s an era of optimism or pessimism? Explain.
4. **Synthesize:** Do scientific laws apply to society in the way that they apply to the physical universe? Why or why not?
5. **Analyze:** What prevented the enlightened despots from carrying out thorough reforms in their governments? Why?
6. **Evaluate:** Has science fulfilled the promise of progress it seemed to hold in the 1700s? Why or why not? Give examples to support your answer.

ANALYZING CONCEPTS

1. **Innovation:** How did the scientific revolution change the ways in which people investigated the natural world?
2. **Conflict:** Catholic Bishop Bossuet said that the skepticism of the philosophes was an "unending error, a risk-all boldness, a deliberate dizziness, in a word, a pride that cannot accept its proper cure, which is legitimate authority." Explain the bishop's view in your own words. What does he mean by "legitimate authority"?
3. **Reaction:** What religious movements formed as a reaction to the ideas of the Enlightenment? Why?

PRACTICING SKILLS

1. Read the editorial page of a newspaper and choose an editorial, column, or letter to the editor with a point of view that conflicts with your own. Analyze the author's view, and write a brief paragraph comparing his or her view with your own.
2. Think about a topic on which you and your parents or teachers disagree. Topics might include curfews or dress codes. Analyze each point of view. Then, in a brief paragraph, describe the compromises each side might make to resolve your differences.

GEOGRAPHY IN HISTORY

Location: Refer to the map of Europe on page 988. Give the global address of London, England, and Cracow, Poland.

TRACING CHRONOLOGY

Refer to the time line below to answer these questions.
1. In which years were Enlightenment ideas published that influenced the writing of democratic constitutions?
2. Were the 1600s and the 1700s truly an age of enlightenment? Use examples from the time line to support your answer.

LINKING PAST AND PRESENT

1. William Penn envisioned an assembly of nations working for world peace. What modern organization reflects Penn's idea?
2. Classical movements in music, art, and literature reflected the spirit of the Enlightenment. Does popular music, art, and literature reflect how people feel about society today? Why or why not? Give examples.
3. Do you agree or disagree with Rousseau's philosophy that people are naturally good but that civilization and institutions make them evil? Give examples from modern life to support your viewpoint.

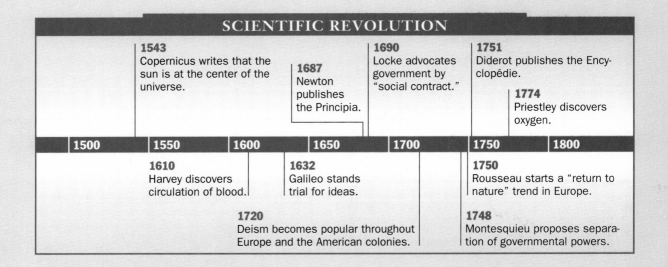

SCIENTIFIC REVOLUTION

1543 Copernicus writes that the sun is at the center of the universe.

1687 Newton publishes the Principia.

1690 Locke advocates government by "social contract."

1751 Diderot publishes the Encyclopédie.

1774 Priestley discovers oxygen.

| 1500 | 1550 | 1600 | 1650 | 1700 | 1750 | 1800 |

1610 Harvey discovers circulation of blood.

1632 Galileo stands trial for ideas.

1750 Rousseau starts a "return to nature" trend in Europe.

1720 Deism becomes popular throughout Europe and the American colonies.

1748 Montesquieu proposes separation of governmental powers.

British and American Revolutions

*I*n 1649, seventeen-year old Philip Henry stood near the back of the crowd gathered around a public platform near Whitehall Palace in London. There he watched Charles I, the king of England, prepare to die. The king made a short speech, prayed silently, and then lay down with his neck on the block.

Silence hung over the crowd. The king resolutely raised his arm, giving the executioner a clear sign. With just one blow, the executioner severed the king's head from his body. At that moment, the crowd uttered "such a groan as I never heard before, and desire I may never hear again," Henry wrote in his diary.

By the late 1600s, England would undergo two revolutions limiting the power of the monarch. A new political age was dawning in England and throughout the world.

CHAPTER PREVIEW

Key Terms to Define: divine right of kings, royalist, commonwealth, constitutional monarchy, habeas corpus, prime minister, revolution, federal system

People to Meet: James I, Charles I, William Laud, Oliver Cromwell, Charles II, James II, William and Mary, Sir Robert Walpole, George Grenville, George Washington, Thomas Paine, Thomas Jefferson

Places to Discover: Great Britain, the American colonies

Objectives to Learn:
1. What caused the English Civil War?
2. Why was the monarchy restored?
3. How did England establish a representative government?

Onlookers gather for the execution of King Charles I in England in 1649.

4. What caused the American Revolution?

5. How did the experience of the English Civil War and the American Revolution influence the U.S. Constitution?

Concepts to Understand:

• Conflict—Civil war divides England. Section 1

• Change—The English Parliament restores the monarchy but limits its powers. Section 2

• Conflict—The American colonies resist British control. Section 3

• Revolution—The American colonies revolt against Great Britain and form the United States of America. Section 4

487

Civil War

Elizabeth I, daughter of King Henry VIII and Anne Boleyn, ruled England from 1558 to 1603. She was a strong monarch, but she did not have absolute power. Elizabeth took into consideration the views of Parliament, which grew more politically involved during her reign.

An able leader, Elizabeth recognized the importance of the good will of the people—and of Parliament. She once said, "Though God has raised me high, yet this I account the glory of the crown, that I have reigned with your loves." For its part, Parliament was willing to defer to the popular queen. But after Elizabeth died in 1603, Parliament, especially the House of Commons, was determined to increase its control over national policy. This move by Parliament resulted in a conflict with the Crown that would eventually tear the nation apart.

Opposition to the Crown

Because Elizabeth died without leaving any children to inherit the throne, James I, the son of Elizabeth's cousin, Mary, Queen of Scots, became king in 1603. James, a member of the Stuart family, was the king of Scotland when he assumed the English throne.

King and Parliament   Soon after James became king, problems arose with the English Parliament. Although James was an educated man, he was a poor judge of people and political situations. His experience in dealing with the weak Scots parliament had not prepared him for dealing with the English Parliament.

The rift between Parliament and the king grew even deeper when James professed his belief in the **divine right of kings**—that is, his belief that a king derives his power directly from God and that such power is absolute. He lectured the Parliament:

Kings are not only God's lieutenants upon earth and sit upon God's throne, but even by God himself they are called Gods. . . . I will not be content that my power be disputed on.

Such statements only increased the resentment among the members of Parliament.

Problems with Parliament   James I's greatest political weakness in these conflicts was his constant need to ask Parliament for money. He spent huge sums of money on the government as well as on himself and his advisers. After one of James's parties, a member of Parliament remarked that James had "given away more plate [money] than Queen Elizabeth did in her whole reign." When Parliament refused to vote him enough funds, James resorted to other means of raising money, such as selling titles of nobility.

Parliament also criticized the king's foreign policy. James's decision to end a war with Spain created outrage in Parliament. The war repayments that were part of the peace treaty put England deep into debt. Opposition to James's policies grew even stronger when James tried to arrange the marriage of his son, Charles, to a Spanish Catholic princess. Fearing the return of Catholics to power, the people celebrated when James's marriage plans for his son failed.

Religion and the Monarchy   England's complicated and unsettled religious issues only added to the tension between Parliament and the Crown. In the 1600s, most English people were members of the Church of England, but they had differences of opinion about the doctrine and rituals of the Church. One powerful group of dissenters, or opponents, within the Church was the Puritans. They wanted the Church to be "purified" of remaining Catholic rituals and symbols. Many Puritans in Parliament called for these reforms.

When James had become king, the Puritans presented him with a petition asking for reforms to be made in the Church of England. Not only did James reject the suggested changes; he warned the Puritans that if they did not conform to the Church of England, he would "harry [force] them out of the land."

Charles Inherits the Throne

When James I died in 1625, his son Charles became king. Charles I inherited the country's religious conflicts and political divisions. Like his father, Charles opposed the Puritans and believed in the divine right of kings. Adding to the tension, Charles eventually married a Catholic woman—Henrietta Maria, sister of France's King Louis XIII.

Early in his reign, Charles asked Parliament for money to fight a war against Spain and France. When it gave him only a fraction of the sum he had requested, the king dissolved Parliament immediately and tried to raise money without its consent. Charles then forced landowners to give "loans" to the government. When they refused, he put them in jail. People were outraged by the king's behavior.

People were also angered by Charles's demand to billet, or board and lodge, his troops in private homes. The king also declared martial, or military, law in some areas. During times of martial law, the military was given temporary rule and individual rights were limited. Thus, people's discontent was high when Charles again called Parliament into session in 1628.

By this time England was at war with both France and Spain. But now Parliament was ready to press changes on the king. In return for its approval of additional taxes to support the war, Parliament forced Charles to sign the Petition of Right. The petition severely limited Charles's power in four ways. First, the king was forbidden to collect taxes or force loans without Parliament's consent. Second, the king could not

Learning from Art *Charles I is pictured here as the model gentleman. But his abrasive style with the Parliament was not well received.* **How did the king anger Parliament?**

imprison anyone without just cause. Third, troops could not be housed in a private home against the will of the owner. Fourth, the king could not declare martial law unless the country was at war.

But Charles's desire to maintain his power was not checked by the Petition of Right. Nearly a year after Parliament had authorized funds in return for his signature on the document, Charles dissolved Parliament and vowed never to call it again. For the next 11 years, Charles ruled without the advice or consent of the Parliament. He continued to collect taxes and imprison opponents—ignoring the Petition of Right he had signed.

At the same time, Charles deepened the religious divisions within England. He named

William Laud to be Archbishop of Canterbury, the leading official of the Church of England. Laud and Charles persecuted the Puritans. They denied them the right to preach or publish. They burned their writings, and punished some with public whippings.

As a result, thousands of Puritans sought religious freedom in the English colonies in America. Their exodus from England from 1630 through 1643 is known as the Great Migration. But most Puritans remained in their homeland, determined to fight Charles and others who opposed them.

Charles and Archbishop Laud then turned their attention to Scotland. In an effort to establish the Church of England in Scotland, the king and the archbishop tried to force the Calvinist Church of Scotland to accept the Church of England's prayer book. The Scots rejected the new prayer book and formed a National Covenant, or agreement, in which they pledged to preserve their religious freedom. Outraged by the king's actions, they were prepared to go to war to do so.

Learning from Art *Oliver Cromwell was noted for his military skill and intense religious beliefs. In all that he did, he was convinced he was doing God's work.* **How does this portrait suggest these qualities in contrast to the portrait of Charles I ?**

Beginnings of the Civil War

By 1640 the Scots had invaded England. In dire need of money, Charles was forced to recall a Parliament that he had ignored for 11 years. The members of Parliament, however, refused to discuss anything without first venting their complaints about Charles's handling of religious and governmental issues. As a result, Charles dissolved this Parliament, known as the Short Parliament, after only three weeks.

But Charles became so desperate for money that he had no choice but to summon Parliament once again. By this time members of Parliament were seething with anger and demanded to voice their complaints to the King. Controlled by Puritans, this session of Parliament, called the Long Parliament, would meet for almost 20 years.

The Long Parliament was determined to decrease Charles's power. The members abolished the special courts used to imprison Charles's opponents and passed a law requiring Parliament to be called every three years. They

ended all forms of illegal taxation and jailed and later executed the hated Archbishop Laud.

While Parliament convened, trouble erupted in Ireland. Relations between England and Ireland had been strained since the 1100s. The Irish people remained Roman Catholic and refused to accept the Church of England. What angered the Irish most was the continuing English practice of seizing land from Irish owners and giving it to English and Scots settlers. In 1641, the Irish rebelled. Faced with rebellion in both Scotland and Ireland, Charles was at the mercy of the Puritan-controlled Parliament.

As the Puritans grew stronger, a **royalist,** or pro-monarchy, group formed in Parliament. It was made up of people who supported the king and opposed Puritan control of the Church of England. As time went on, debates between Puritans and royalists became more heated.

Despite resistance by the royalists, Parliament in June 1642 sent Charles "Nineteen Propositions" that made Parliament the supreme power in England. Charles, however, refused to agree to its demands. With a dramatic personal appearance, Charles led troops into the House of Commons and attempted to arrest five of its leaders. The five were hidden and protected from capture. The king's use of force meant there could be no compromise. Both Charles and Parliament prepared for war.

The English Civil War

Charles gathered an army that included nobles and landowners in the north and west of the country. They were called Cavaliers because many belonged to the king's cavalry, or armed horsemen. Supporters of Parliament and Puritans drew their strength from the south and east of England. They were called Roundheads because many of them had close-cropped hair.

Parliament organized its military forces under the leadership of Oliver Cromwell. Cromwell was a very religious man and a brilliant military leader. His rigorous training and firm discipline of the parliamentary forces led to several decisive victories. After nearly four years of conflict, the royalist armies surrendered in May 1646. Parliament had won complete control of the English government. The Puritans removed their remaining opponents from Parliament, leaving behind what was known as the Rump Parliament.

After a failed attempt to escape from his enemies, Charles surrendered in 1647. The army then tried, sentenced, and executed the king. It was a shocking moment for many English people, however they had felt about Charles.

A New Government

With the monarchy abolished, Parliament faced the difficult task of constructing a new republican form of government. England was declared a **commonwealth,** a state governed by elected representatives. Yet Parliament quarreled about reforming the government and refused to hold new elections. Meanwhile, Cromwell continued to gain power by brutally crushing the revolts in Scotland and Ireland.

Cromwell and his army grew tired of waiting for Parliament's reforms and took Parliament by force in 1653. Named Lord Protector, Cromwell dismissed the Rump Parliament and ruled England for five years as a military dictator. Cromwell enforced strict Puritan rules during this time. Drinking, dancing, and gambling were forbidden; swearing and missing church services were punished with fines.

When Cromwell died in 1658, his son Richard assumed power. But Richard lacked his father's leadership. The army forced Richard to resign after less than a year.

Many English people were tired of the constant changes in government. They were dissatisfied with military rule, tired of civil wars, and unhappy with Puritan restrictions. The army finally recalled the Long Parliament, which searched for a stable government by negotiating with Charles I's son, who had been living in Europe during the upheavals.

At last, Parliament prepared to reestablish the monarchy. But the idea of representative government and many individual rights would survive. A king would soon rule England, but no king would ever claim absolute power again.

SECTION 1 REVIEW

Recall

1. **Define:** divine right of kings, royalist, commonwealth
2. **Identify:** James I, Charles I, Petition of Right, William Laud, Puritans, Oliver Cromwell, Cavaliers, Roundheads
3. **Explain:** Why did the Puritans oppose the beliefs of Church of England?

Critical Thinking

4. **Analyze:** Contrast the methods of Elizabeth I and the Stuart monarchs in getting what they wanted from Parliament.

Whose methods were more effective? Why?

Applying Concepts

5. **Conflict:** Contrast the problems of Parliament before and after the Civil War. Did Parliament achieve what it wanted?

A King Returns to the Throne

As the king's son, Charles II had faced danger throughout the Civil War and Cromwell's rule. He risked death on the battlefield as he joined the royalist forces in their fight and in their defeat. He saw his father imprisoned and put to death. He narrowly escaped his own capture and execution by disguising himself as a servant and fleeing to Europe.

In Europe, Charles wandered from country to country. While some European rulers received him as royalty, others threatened him with arrest as a fugitive. In his own country, the Puritans kept a steady eye on Charles. Since he was the direct heir to the English throne, Charles posed a threat to their political power. By the time Parliament had restored the monarchy, Charles had learned a good deal about pleasing people he needed for support and safety. Charles willingly accepted a change from the absolute power of his ancestors.

The Merry Monarch

When Charles II returned to London on May 29, 1660, the English people celebrated wildly. They felt released from a violent, unstable period followed by harsh Puritan rule. A court member described the happiness of the English people as they rejoiced in a lavish parade marking the king's return:

A triumph of above 20,000 horse and foot, brandishing their swords and shouting with inexpressible joy; the ways strawed with flowers, the bells ringing, the streets hung with tapestry, fountains running with wine. . . . I stood and beheld it, and blessed God.

This period, in which the House of Stuart was returned to the throne, is called the Restoration. In contrast to the severe and religious rule of Cromwell, Charles II was known as the Merry Monarch. He loved social life—parties, games, and witty conversation. He supported the arts, science, and entertainment. People once again danced and enjoyed sports and theater. Charles married a Portuguese princess; and though they had no children, he fathered several illegitimate children by his mistresses.

Dealing with Religious Questions When Charles accepted the monarchy, he agreed to let Parliament settle the country's raging religious debates. Outwardly, Charles accepted the Church of England. Secretly, however, he leaned toward Catholicism, his mother's religion. Although he hoped for a policy of religious toleration, he realized that the decision depended on Parliament.

In 1661 a new Parliament was elected. It was known as the Cavalier Parliament because it contained a majority of royalists. During the next few years, this Parliament passed a series of acts known as the Clarendon Code. These laws made the Church of England once again the state religion. Only Anglicans, or members of the Church of England, could attend the universities, serve in Parliament, or hold religious services. Hundreds of Puritan clergy were driven from their churches.

Limiting the Power of the King The Parliament also maintained its limits on the power of the king. All the acts of Parliament to which Charles I had agreed, such as the Petition of Right, were still in effect. The restoration thus gave England a **constitutional monarchy**—a monarchy limited by a constitution. However, rather than being a single document, England's constitution was made up of many—such as the Magna Carta and the Petition of Right—plus

Rebuilding London

On September 2, 1666, a small fire broke out in a bakery shop on Pudding Lane in east London. Since most of the buildings at the time were made of wood and many were separated only by narrow streets and alleyways, the fire spread very quickly. The blaze lasted five days—destroying about 13,000 houses, 100 churches, four prisons, and most of the government buildings in London. Miraculously, fewer than 20 Londoners died in the fire, although 80,000 were left homeless. Over the next decades, a royal commission worked to rebuild the city and to make it a beautiful capital.

One of the men chosen to work on the commission was Christopher Wren. Although he was a well-respected mathematician and astronomer at Oxford University, Wren is best remembered as the architect of St. Paul's Cathedral, an outstanding London landmark begun in 1675.

The new St. Paul's Cathedral was to be the first cathedral constructed for the Church of England. As the "mother church" of the Church of England, St. Paul's had to be an impressive, monumental structure that

dominated the city. At the same time, Wren needed to use a style of architecture that was clearly different from the styles of existing churches on the European continent. St. Paul's had to be more austere and serious than the ornate Catholic cathedrals in France, Germany, Italy, and Spain.

In his design, Wren combined the classical and baroque styles of architecture to produce a dramatic, original monument. The classical tradition used simple, geometric forms, such as columns, to give a sense of logic, proportion, and order to buildings. The baroque tradition tended to use more elaborate decoration, dramatic lighting, and visual effects. The final form of St. Paul's Cathedral combined these traditions into an architectural style quite different from any of its individual sources.

Wren's work had an enormous impact on the buildings constructed in central London in the late 1600s. In the end, he designed a total of 51 Anglican churches for the city in the period following the fire and was eventually knighted by Charles II for his work as an architect.

Responding to the Arts
1. Why was London's St. Paul's Cathedral an important building for the Church of England?
2. What architectural sources did Wren use in his design of St. Paul's Cathedral?

Learning from Art *A revolution without violence or bloodshed occurred when Parliament presented the Crown of England to William and Mary.* **Why did Parliament decide to give the crown to William and Mary?**

other laws and customs. Although Charles II disagreed with some of the reforms that limited royal power, he never fought Parliament forcefully. Charles was determined to avoid his father's fate.

The French ambassador to England was astonished at the mood of the country. In France, the king had absolute power. The ambassador commented on the changes in England in a letter to the French king, Louis XIV:

> *This Government has a monarchical appearance because there is a King, but at bottom it is far from being a monarchy. . . . The members of Parliament are . . . allowed to speak their mind freely. . . .*

While the English people celebrated their freedom from harsh Puritan rule, they were struck by two disasters in 1665. The plague returned to London for the last time, killing as many as 125,000 people. Later, a terrible raging fire destroyed much of London. Some people falsely blamed Catholics for setting the fire as part of a plan to gain control of the country.

Establishing Political Parties Opposition to Catholicism helped to spark the growth of England's first political parties. The parties grew out of a debate over who would succeed Charles as the king of England. Because Charles

had no legitimate children, James II, Charles's brother, was next in line to the king. James, who was a practicing Catholic, ignited the fears of a revival of Catholic power in England.

In 1679 Parliament tried to pass the Exclusion Bill, which would have kept James from becoming king. During this conflict, those members of Parliament who wanted to exclude James from the throne were known as Whigs. Those who defended the hereditary monarchy were called Tories.

In a compromise, the Tories were able to defeat the Exclusion Bill by accepting another bill supported by the Whigs. This bill established the principle of **habeas corpus** as law. According to habeas corpus, a person could not be held in prison by the king (or anyone else) without just cause or without a trial. It was another step that increased individual rights and reduced those of the Crown.

A Bloodless Revolt

When Charles II died in 1685, his Catholic brother, James II, did become king, effectively ending the peaceful relations between Parliament and the Crown. James wanted absolute power and claimed he had the power to suspend the law. Ignoring Parliament's religious laws, James appointed Catholics to government and university positions. He also allowed all Christian religions to worship freely.

Glorious Revolution These actions alarmed the members of Parliament, but they tried to be patient. They were waiting for James to die and for the throne to pass to his Protestant daughter Mary, who was married to William of Orange, ruler of the Netherlands.

But in 1688, a birth prompted Parliament to take action. James's second wife bore a son, who would be raised a Catholic. He would inherit the throne, rather than the Protestant Mary. Both Whig and Tory leaders united against James and invited Mary's husband William to invade England and take over the Crown. James fled to France when he realized he had little support in England. William and Mary gained the English throne without battles or bloodshed. This peaceful transfer of power was so welcome and so different from previous struggles that the English called it the Glorious Revolution.

New Limits on Royal Power At previous coronations, kings and queens had sworn to observe laws and customs established by their royal ancestors. But in 1689, William and Mary swore that they would govern the people of England "according to the statutes in Parliament agreed upon, and the laws and customs of the same."

In that same year, Parliament strengthened its power by passing the Bill of Rights. According to the Bill of Rights, the king could not raise taxes or maintain an army without the consent of Parliament and could not suspend laws. Further, it declared that Parliament should be held often and that there should be freedom of debate in Parliament.

The Bill of Rights also guaranteed certain individual rights. It guaranteed the right to a trial by jury, outlawed cruel and unusual punishment for a crime, and limited the amount of bail that could be required for a person awaiting trial. Citizens were given the right to appeal to the king and to speak freely in Parliament.

A failed revolt led by James II to recapture the Crown led Parliament to pass even more legislation limiting the Crown's power. In the Act of Settlement, Parliament excluded any Catholic from inheriting the English throne.

Since James had led Irish Catholics in the revolt, Parliament also passed laws that excluded the Catholic majority in Ireland from government and business. A Protestant minority ruled Ireland, only deepening the hatred Irish Catholics had for English policies.

Parliament and the Crown

The Bill of Rights and the Act of Settlement made it clear that Parliament had won the long battle with the Crown. England was still a monarchy, but a king or queen could not rule without Parliament's consent.

England was not yet a true democracy, however. Although members of the House of Commons were elected, only male property owners—250,000 people out of 6 million, or 4 percent of the population—had the right to vote. Members of the House of Commons were not paid, so only the wealthy could afford to run for office. Parliament was controlled by people of property—nobles, gentry, wealthy merchants, and clergy.

Succession and Union The power of Parliament further increased when Mary's sister Anne succeeded William in 1702. At the same time, Parliament had to establish a new order of succession to the throne. Since Anne had no living children to succeed her, she would be succeeded by the children of Sophia, a Protestant granddaughter of James I. Sophia was married to the German elector of Hanover. In short, the English throne would pass to heirs from the House of Hanover.

Yet there still remained a danger that the Scots might prefer a Stuart monarch to a member of the House of Hanover. Parliament also feared that the Scots would form an alliance with France against England. After negotiations with the Scots, who were militarily and economically weak, the two governments signed the Act of Union in 1707. It united the two countries into a new nation called Great Britain. Both the English and the Scots would now be "British." Although the Scots gave up their own parliament, they were given representation in the English Parliament. Scotland also retained its

Learning from Art *George I and George II relied upon Robert Walpole's expertise in finance and diplomacy.* **How did Walpole increase the powers of the British prime minister?**

own Calvinist religion, and its laws, courts, and educational system as well.

Political Parties and the Cabinet During Anne's reign (1665–1714), Parliament's political powers continued to increase. Anne was unskilled in British politics and sought guidance from a cabinet, a small group of advisers selected from the House of Commons. Because a cabinet made up of both Whigs and Tories often quarreled, it became the custom to choose cabinet members only from the majority party.

Anne died in 1714 and Sophia's son George I took the throne according to the Act of Settlement. George had been raised in Germany, however, and did not speak English very well.

George I relied on the cabinet even more than Anne had. Eventually, Sir Robert Walpole, the leader of the Whigs, gained control of the cabinet. Although he spoke no German, Walpole advised the king. Walpole's position as head of the cabinet was later called **prime minister**, the chief executive of a parliamentary government. Walpole remained prime minister when a new king, George II, took the throne in 1727. With the king's encouragement, Walpole gradually took over many responsibilities: managing finances, appointing government officials, and requesting the passage of laws. He helped avoid wars and allowed the American colonies to grow without interference from Great Britain.

In 1760, George III, grandson of George II, became king at the age of 22. George III greatly expanded the British Empire through victory in a war against France. Great Britain gained Canada and all of France's territory east of the Mississippi River. But the cost of waging the war—and the ways in which George III and his government ministers tried to deal with that cost—would lead to rebellion in Great Britain's American colonies.

SECTION 2 REVIEW

Recall
1. **Define:** constitutional monarchy, habeas corpus, prime minister
2. **Identify:** Restoration, Charles II, William and Mary, Bill of Rights, Sir Robert Walpole
3. **Explain:** Why was Charles II called the Merry Monarch?

How was his reign different from his father's reign?
4. **Describe:** What was the Glorious Revolution?

Critical Thinking
5. **Analyze:** Compare the royal power of William and Mary with the power of Charles II. How

had Parliament's powers expanded by the time William and Mary came to the throne?

Applying Concepts
6. **Change:** Briefly describe how England evolved into a constitutional monarchy. What rights did individuals gain?

Road to Revolt

While Great Britain struggled through civil war and a changing government, its colonies in America changed, too. By the mid-1700s, 13 colonies thrived on the eastern coast of North America. As more people migrated to North America to escape religious persecution or to gain a new start in life, the population of the colonies grew to more than 1.5 million by 1763.

Since most of the colonists were British, they shared a common language and political background. Although many radical political ideas—ideas about universal suffrage, liberty, and equality—had died out in Great Britain, many political radicals had fled to the colonies and here the old ideas stayed alive. In the colonies there was no aristocracy. The hardships of life on the frontier and the easy availability of land tended to blur class divisions. Each colony had a representative assembly, and the colonists were used to governing themselves.

Britain's American Empire

Except for regulating trade, the British government generally left the colonies alone. In the British mercantilist view, the American colonies were valuable to Great Britain only to the extent that they benefited British trade. The role of the colonies was to produce goods—mostly raw materials—that could not be produced in Great Britain, and to provide markets for British manufactured goods.

By the early 1700s, the colonies pulsated with economic activity. In the South, plantations produced tobacco, rice, and indigo with the labor of thousands of slaves from Africa. Settlers in the rich farming land of the Middle Colonies grew enough grains to feed their families and trade throughout the year. New England colonists turned to the sea because of their poor soil and harsh climate. In 1673 a sea captain described busy Boston harbor, reporting that "ships arrive dayly from Spain, France, Holland & Canarys bringing all sorts of wines, linens, silks and fruits, which they transport to all the other plantations. . . ."

To protect this profitable trade with its colonies, Parliament passed a series of Navigation Acts in the 1600s. According to the Navigation Acts, the colonists were required to export certain products only to Britain or other British colonies. In addition, all goods going to the colonies had to first pass through Great Britain, where they could be taxed before they were eventually shipped to the colonies. Finally, all goods going to or coming from the colonies were to be carried by ships built in Great Britain or in the colonies.

The colonists did not suffer as much as one might imagine from the effects these laws had on trade. Actually, the Navigation Acts helped some colonies. Some colonies developed a strong shipping industry, and some businesses grew prosperous in the absence of foreign competition. Moreover, the British government was never able to enforce these laws. Smuggling goods in and out of ports along the coast became a major part of the colonial trade.

Colonial Political Power

As people in the colonies grew more settled and economically secure, they also became more involved in their government. Most of the colonies were managed by a governor appointed by the king. The royal governor then appointed judges and other officials. But each colony had an elected assembly as well, similar to the House of Commons in Great Britain. Voting in the colonies was restricted to men who owned property or paid taxes, as it was in England. But in the colonies it was much easier to acquire land. A much greater percentage of the population, therefore, could vote for their government.

The assemblies often struggled with the royal governors for power in the same way that Parliament and the Crown struggled in Great Britain. These power struggles were often over money. In the early 1700s, assemblies won the right to limit the salaries of governors and judges. If a governor would not do as colonists pleased, the assembly would reduce or withhold his salary for the next year. In 1731 the New Hampshire assembly refused to pay the governor any salary for five years.

The assemblies also held tight to their right to approve any taxes requested by the Crown or governors. This issue would become a central point of conflict between the colonies and Great Britain. Just as the British Parliament had fought hard for its right to approve or refuse any taxes, so too would the American colonists.

Tightening Colonial Controls

A bitter rivalry between Great Britain and France for territory in North America would eventually lead the British government to interfere more actively in the colonial economy. A dispute over French and British land claims in North America as well as rights to the rich North American fur trade led France and Great Britain to war in 1754. The conflict, called the French and Indian War, brought French troops and French Canadian colonists against British forces and the American colonists. Some Native Americans fought on behalf of the British, while others supported the French.

IMAGES OF THE TIME

Colonial America

European settlers came to America for many reasons, among them trade, religious freedom, and to get a new start in life.

England's monarch controlled the colonies. A colonial coin from 1773 bore a portrait of King George III.

William Penn founded the colony "Sylvania," which means woodlands. Penn promoted religious tolerance and was well received by Native Americans.

After six years of war, the British-led forces finally defeated the French in 1760. Three years later, a treaty was signed in Paris. Under the treaty's terms, Great Britain acquired nearly all of France's possessions in North America, including Canada and land in the area west of the Appalachian Mountains.

Great Britain's empire had grown both in size and in power, but at a considerable cost. The war strained the British economy, and defending the huge new lands they had gained would cost even more.

George Grenville, whom George III appointed First Lord of the Treasury in 1763, took the first steps to solve these problems. Grenville issued a proclamation that said the colonists could not, for the time being, settle in the lands west of the Appalachians. This move, he hoped, would avoid wars with Native Americans until Great Britain had the area under control and could gradually open the land to settlers. But the American colonists were eager to build new settlements in the west, and they were outraged by this attempt to stop them.

Grenville also believed that colonists should help pay the costs of their own defense. He began raising money by enforcing the Navigation Acts with the British navy. British warships hunted down smugglers, who were then tried in British military courts rather than in colonial courts. Another new law allowed British troops to be housed in colonists' homes.

But it was the Stamp Act that most infuriated the colonists. The Stamp Act declared that all printed materials, from newspapers and shipping documents to playing cards, must bear a stamp to show that a tax had been paid to Great Britain. Colonial lawyers, tavern owners, merchants, and printers were most affected by the Stamp Act.

Baltimore was still a fairly small coastal settlement in 1752 (left). A German immigrant's plate (below) portrays figures dancing and playing music.

Reflecting on the Times
What conclusions can you draw about life in colonial Baltimore from the image pictured above?

Learning from Art *In protest against the Stamp Act, American colonists hung British stamp agents upon posts, subjecting them to public harassment.* **Why do you think colonists reacted so strongly to the Stamp Act?**

Colonial Protests

Colonists reacted to these measures quickly. They refused to buy British goods, attacked stamp agents, and burned stamps in the streets. In 1765, they sent nine representatives to a colonial Stamp Act Congress in New York City. The Congress resolved that Parliament could not tax the colonies because the colonies did not have representatives in Parliament. They rallied under the cry "No taxation without representation!" and insisted that only their own colonial assemblies had the right to tax them. The British Parliament repealed the Stamp Act in 1766. The struggle for control of the colonies,

however, had begun in earnest. Colonial leader John Adams wrote in his diary:

The people have become more attentive to their liberties, . . . and more determined to defend them. . . . Our presses have groaned, our pulpits have thundered, our legislatures have resolved, our towns have voted; the crown officers have everywhere trembled, and all their little tools and creatures been afraid to speak and ashamed to be seen.

Unrest in Boston The British Parliament reasserted its right to pass laws governing the colonies in the Declaratory Act of 1766. The next year, Great Britain placed new taxes on glass, lead, paper, and tea coming into the colonies. Royal agents trying to enforce these laws pleaded for British soldiers to protect them from the angry colonists.

In 1770 the first clash between the Americans and British troops took place. Two regiments of British troops had been sent to Boston to support the governor. One evening, a squad of soldiers was harassed by a Boston crowd throwing snowballs and rotten eggs. Gunfire erupted, and five people died in what became known in the colonies as the Boston Massacre.

Because of the unrest in Boston, Parliament repealed most of the taxes but kept the tax on tea. In an effort to keep the British East India Company from going bankrupt, a special law was passed that allowed it to sell tea in the colonies without paying the tax. Because their tea could be sold more cheaply, it hurt the business of colonial tea merchants. The Boston colonists decided to retaliate. Disguised as Native Americans, the colonists dumped wooden chests of British tea into Boston harbor.

The British quickly punished the Massachusetts colonists for the Boston Tea Party by passing what the colonists called the Intolerable Acts. These acts closed the harbor until the tea had been paid for and required colonists to feed and house British soldiers in their homes. The acts also greatly reduced the colonists' right of self-government. Town meetings, for example, could not be held more than once a year without special permission from the royal governor. Parliament also passed the Quebec Act, placing

Canada and territories north of the Ohio River under a separate government, thus closing the area to the colonists.

The First Continental Congress The latest repressive measures of the British convinced the 13 colonies to form a union of resistance. On September 5, 1774, 56 colonial delegates met at Philadelphia at the First Continental Congress. The Congress marked an important event in colonial affairs. This was the first time that leaders from different colonies had met face to face. Previously, most colonies had considered their differences with Great Britain individually. Now they were united as a group. Patrick Henry, a leading statesman from Virginia, commented: "There are no differences between Virginians, Pennsylvanians, New Yorkers, and New Englanders. I am not a Virginian but an American." George Washington of Virginia and Sam Adams of Massachusetts were among the leading members of Congress.

The Congress, which met for more than seven weeks, resolved that the "English colonists . . . are entitled to a free and exclusive power of legislation in their several provincial legislatures." In other words, only the colonial assemblies should have the right to make laws in the colonies. Although the Congress recognized Parliament's right to regulate trade, the Congress agreed that the colonies would not import goods from Great Britain after December 1774. After September 1775, they resolved not to send colonial goods to Great Britain.

JOIN, or DIE.

Learning from Political Cartoons *Benjamin Franklin is credited with designing this colonial political cartoon urging the colonists to unite.* **Why might Franklin use an image of a rattlesnake to represent the colonies?**

Many colonists, however, were determined to take more radical measures to rid themselves of Great Britain's political control. In every colony a volunteer army was being organized and weapons collected. In New England, minutemen (so named because they could be ready for battle on a minute's notice) assembled to drill on village greens, while the town officials stored ammunition, weapons, and food. In the southern colonies, wealthy planters undertook to recruit and equip companies of men at their own expense. It began to appear that the dispute between Great Britain and the American colonies would be settled only by force.

SECTION 3 REVIEW

Recall

1. **Define:** What was Great Britain's mercantile policy toward the American colonies

2. **Identify:** Navigation Acts, French and Indian War, Stamp Act, First Continental Congress

3. **Explain:** Why did relations between Great Britain and the colonies worsen after the end of the French and Indian War?

4. **Explain:** How did Great Britain punish the Massachusetts colonists after the Boston Tea Party?

Critical Thinking

5. **Evaluate:** Do you think that the British were right in expecting the colonists to shoulder the burden of defending the American colonies? What other approaches might Grenville have taken?

Applying Concepts

6. **Conflict:** Compare and contrast Parliament's struggles for power with the king and the colonists' later struggle for control of their own affairs. What were the key issues for Parliament? For the colonists?

A War for Independence

Hostilities between the American colonists and the British broke out near Boston in 1775. People there were outraged by the British government. Their seaport was still closed because of the Tea Party, causing many Bostonians to lose their jobs. As British troops filled the city, rumors accusing the "redcoats" of robberies and murders swept through shops, inns, and other meeting places.

Sensing the tension in the city, the British Parliament ordered the governor of Massachusetts, General Thomas Gage, to seize the colonists' military supplies. Before dawn on April 19, 1775, Gage sent a troop of 700 British soldiers to destroy weapons collected in the town of Concord, about 18 miles from Boston.

Colonists Paul Revere and William Dawes learned of the British plan and rode to warn the colonial minutemen. As the British marched into Lexington on their way to Concord, they found about 70 farmers and villagers blocking their path. When the colonists refused to put down their guns, a shot was fired, though no one knows which side fired first. In the skirmish, British soldiers killed eight colonists; later at Concord, the "redcoats" held off a sharp attack by more colonial minutemen.

As the British troops marched back toward Boston, colonists fired at them from behind buildings, trees, and stone walls. The next day, almost 300 British soldiers and nearly 100 colonists lay dead. The British were humiliated. No one expected the colonists to be any match for the professional British soldiers.

Moving Toward Separation

News of the colonial attack on the British troops spread throughout the American colonies. When the Second Continental Congress gathered in Philadelphia one month after the battles at Lexington and Concord, it immediately organized an army and named George Washington as commander.

However, many colonists still resisted the idea of declaring war on Great Britain. The Congress tried one last time to arrange a peaceful compromise with Parliament and the king. They sent a proposal, called the Olive Branch Petition, to King George III. When the British government refused the petition, chances of a peaceful settlement between Great Britain and the American colonies grew dimmer. To more and more colonists, independence seemed the only answer.

A Call to Part   The most stirring arguments in favor of independence came from the pen of colonist Thomas Paine. Paine, who recently had come to the American colonies from Great Britain, wrote a pamphlet called *Common Sense* in January 1776. In it he called upon the colonists to break away from Great Britain. Paine promoted independence for economic, social, and moral reasons.

> *E*very thing that is right begs for separation from Britain. The Americans who have been killed seem to say, 'TIS TIME TO PART. England and America are located a great distance apart. That is itself strong and natural proof that God never expected one to rule over the other.
>
> —Thomas Paine, *Common Sense*, 1776

Common Sense circulated widely and helped to convince thousands of American colonists that it was "time to part." The delegates to the Congress sensed the changing mood in the colonies and assigned five of their best thinkers and writers to prepare a declaration of independence that would clearly state their resolve.

The Declaration of Independence Thomas Jefferson, a young Virginian, was the principal author of the colonists' declaration of independence. The document set forth the colonists' reasons for separation from Great Britain. Jefferson, like many other colonial leaders, knew and valued the works of John Locke and other Enlightenment thinkers. He incorporated many of their ideas into the declaration.

The declaration stated that individuals have certain basic rights that cannot be taken away by any government. Focusing on John Locke's concept of the "social contract," the declaration announced that governments are created by an agreement, or contract, between the rulers and those ruled. If a ruler loses the support of the people by taking away basic rights, the people have a right to change the government through rebellion. The beginning of the declaration reads:

> *We hold these truths to be self-evident, that all men are created equal, that they are endowed by their Creator with certain unalienable Rights, that among these are Life, Liberty and the pursuit of Happiness. That to secure these rights, Governments are instituted among Men, deriving their just powers from the consent of the governed; that whenever any Form of Government becomes destructive of those ends, it is the Right of the People to alter or to abolish it. . . .*

The declaration continued with a long list of the ways in which Great Britain and George III had abused their power and concludes that "these United Colonies are and of Right ought to be Free and Independent States."

On July 4, 1776, the Congress adopted the Declaration of Independence. A few days later, George Washington had the declaration read to his troops to inspire them and give them hope as war loomed ahead. Cheers went up from the ranks when the reading was done. That night, some of the troops joined a crowd of townspeople who pulled down a statue of George III and broke off the head.

Learning from Art *Benjamin Franklin, Thomas Jefferson, Roger Sherman, John Adams, and Robert Livingston (left to right) were the authors of the Declaration of Independence.* **How did the Declaration reflect Enlightenment thought?**

The War for Independence

The signing of the Declaration of Independence made war a certainty. The Americans had taken a step that made a peaceful reconciliation impossible. The only course that remained for the colonists was **revolution,** the violent overthrow of a government. For the leaders of the revolution, now seen as traitors to the British king, failure would mean disgrace and even death. As colonist Benjamin Franklin said, "We must all hang together now, or assuredly we shall hang separately."

The first battles of the American Revolution were concentrated in the states of New York and New Jersey. The British hoped to gain control of the middle states and separate New England from the southern states. Great Britain devised plans from a position of military strength. Its

Loyalists Migrate to Canada

Loyalists draw lots for land in Canada

They were tarred and feathered and hung in effigy. Their windows were broken, books burned, and houses destroyed. It was dangerous for colonists to remain loyal to King George III during the Revolution.

Some colonists, called Loyalists or Tories, were British government officers; some were clergy of the Church of England. Others were artisans or shopkeepers who believed that it was wrong to oppose the king.

Once war broke out, it was not safe to be a Loyalist in an area unprotected by British troops. While many Loyalists joined the British, others moved to the Canadian border or farther into Canada. As many as 50,000 Loyalists migrated to Nova Scotia and what is now Ontario by the end of the Revolutionary War.

With land and tools given to them by the British, the Loyalists began to settle the sparsely populated Canadi-an lands. The Loyalists also pledged loyalty to the king, and their territory remained a British colony with a British form of government.

However, this migration only added to the tension between British and French people in Canada. Canada had begun as a French colony but was taken over by the British in 1763 after the French and Indian War.

Some of the divisions between the French and British settlers remain in Canada today. Canada has two official languages: English and French. Some descendants of French settlers in Quebec are dedicated to forming their own separate nation.

Making the Connection

1. Why did the Loyalists migrate to Canada?
2. How was the Loyalists' migration to Canada similar to the Puritans' migration to America?

---

troops were well led, well trained, and well equipped. Its navy, the most powerful in the world, controlled the seacoast; and the British government had enough money to pay 30,000 German mercenaries, or hired soldiers, to fight with them. After decades of fighting around the world, the British forces were prepared for war.

The American colonists, on the other hand, had no navy, little battle experience, and lacked money, clothing, guns, ammunition, and food. Officers identified themselves with colored ribbon on their hats because they had no uniforms. However, the Americans did find ways to match the seasoned British forces. Washington was a skillful general who mustered the support of the colonial forces. The Americans also eventually received help from the French in the form of arms and ammunition. The French were eager for an American victory, hoping to revenge the losses of the French and Indian War.

Fighting the War Volleys from British muskets scattered the colonial army in the first battles waged in the war. But the colonists began to surprise the British with their ability and tactics. They would ambush British troops, then disappear into the countryside with the help of neighbors and friends. The British also had the disadvantage of having to wait weeks or months for supplies to cross the Atlantic Ocean.

The turning point of the war came in October 1777, with a decisive victory against the British at Saratoga in New York. Over 6,000 British soldiers surrendered. The French—anxious to strike back at the British—decided that the Americans were a good political risk and entered the war on the American side. French troops helped win several colonial victories.

In 1779 Spain declared war on Great Britain, and both Spain and France sent strong naval forces to fight the British in the West Indies. The Netherlands also joined Spain and France against Great Britain in 1780. Soon the British found themselves not only fighting for their American colonies but for their empire.

Finally, in October 1781, with the aid of the French, the Americans defeated the British army. George Washington accepted the surrender of the commander of the British troops, Lord Charles Cornwallis, at Yorktown, Virginia.

FOOTNOTES TO HISTORY

"YANKEE DOODLE"

The British loved to make fun of the colonists, who cared little about the fashions of the times. "Yankee Doodle" began as a song that mocked the colonists:

> *Yankee Doodle came to town,*
> *Riding on a pony;*
> *He stuck a feather in his cap*
> *And called it macaroni.*

"Macaroni" was a term used for British men who thought they were dressed in the latest styles but who actually looked ridiculous. Although British troops sang it as an expression of ridicule, the colonists loved the tune and added many verses. It became a song of defiance. Ironically, it was to this tune that the British surrendered at Yorktown.

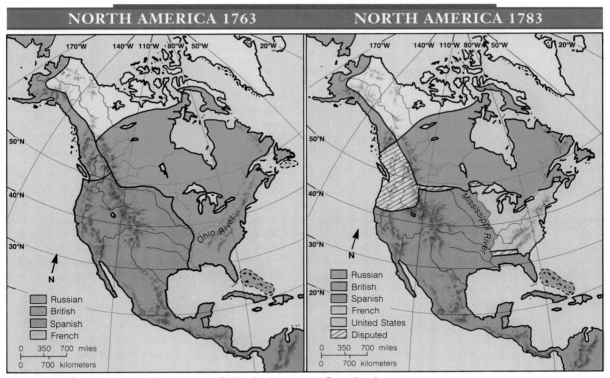

NORTH AMERICA 1763

NORTH AMERICA 1783

Learning from Maps *These maps of North America reflect the changes in European territorial control before and after the American Revolution.* **What portion of North America did Great Britain control after the American Revolution?**

Forming a New Government

In 1783 Great Britain recognized its former colonies as an independent nation, the United States of America. Now the Americans faced the same problem Parliament had following the execution of Charles I. What type of government should take the place of the old government?

America needed a workable government that would unite the separate states. But the states were reluctant to give up control to a central government. Instead, they formed a confederation, or league of independent states, under an agreement called the Articles of Confederation.

The Articles of Confederation The Confederation, however, was very weak. It could not collect taxes or establish a currency. It also could not force the states to pay national debts from the war or to raise armies.

Another of the Confederation's major problems was its failure to regulate the states' economic activities. Soon states began competing against each other economically. New York charged Connecticut and New Jersey merchants high fees for using the harbor at New York City. Some Connecticut merchants then refused to buy New York goods, and New Jersey officials charged New Yorkers huge fees for using a New Jersey lighthouse. At a time when the United States needed to establish its economy and gain recognition from the world as a stable government, the states only quarreled while the country accumulated more debt.

A New Constitution The Confederation's weaknesses led to calls for a stronger central government that would unite the country. In 1787 the Congress called a convention to revise the Articles. After much discussion and debate, the delegates decided to abandon the Articles and create a new constitution.

After further debates, the states finally ratified the United States Constitution in 1789. The new constitution set up a **federal system**, or a government in which power is divided between a central government and regional, or state, governments. Following the recommendations in Montesquieu's *The Spirit of the Laws* (1748), central political power was divided among the executive, legislative, and judicial branches of government, and careful checks and balances were arranged. For example, the president, as head of the executive branch, can appoint judges for the judicial branch, but the legislators in the legislative branch must approve them.

Under the new constitution, the United States was a republic. Elections were held in 1788, and George Washington became the first president of the United States. One of the first steps taken by the U.S. Congress was the development of a Bill of Rights, which was added to the Constitution in the form of ten amendments. The Bill of Rights protected personal liberties such as freedom of religion, freedom of speech, and trial by jury. It also protected the rights of the individual states that made up the new nation.

SECTION 4 REVIEW

Recall

1. **Define:** revolution, federal system
2. **Identify:** Thomas Paine, Thomas Jefferson, the Declaration of Independence
3. **Explain:** What was the basic message of the Declaration of Independence? Why did the colonists believe the Declaration was necessary?

Critical Thinking

4. **Apply:** Describe the weaknesses of the Articles of Confederation. Why did the colonists first choose such a weak form of central government? Why did the Articles fail?
5. **Evaluate:** Do you think that if Great Britain had treated the colonists differently, they would have been content to remain under British control? Support your answer.

Applying Concepts

6. **Revolution:** Compare the Americans' attempts to organize a new form of government with those of the British after executing King Charles I. Did both governments ensure representation and individual rights?

OUTLINING

Often, it's easier to recall events from a movie plot than it is to remember events and ideas you just read in a textbook. Why? In a nonfiction account such as a textbook, connections sometimes seem less obvious than they are in imaginative stories. Readers often pay so much attention to identifying major events that they forget to look for connections between them.

Focusing on these connections can help you see the pattern holding written material together. Once this pattern is clear, remembering the main ideas—and even the details supporting them—becomes easier.

Explanation

The process of finding and examining the pattern in written materials is called *outlining*. Outlining can be informal or formal. An informal outline is much like taking notes. It does not have a strict pattern, and you write only the words or phrases you need to remember ideas. An informal outline indents subheads under main heads to show related but less important ideas. Dashes or numerals usually set off related details.

A formal outline, however, follows a more standard format. In a formal outline, main heads are identified with Roman numerals, subheads with capital letters, and details with Arabic numerals. Each level should have at least two entries, and all entries use the same grammatical form.

Use the following steps to prepare your outline:
- Define your purpose, and decide what kind of outline you will need.
- Scan the heading structure to give you a quick overview of the material. Heads in a textbook provide clues to main topics and can sometimes be used as part of the formal outline.
- Read the material carefully, and identify the principal head under which all the other material falls.
- Identify the subheads that relate to the main head.
- Look for statements that supply details supporting, defining, or explaining these subheads. Be alert to maps, charts, and other graphics; sometimes information from these should be included in your outline.
- Place these details under the appropriate head in logical order.

Example

Let's assume you decide you need a formal outline for the first section of Chapter 20. There are many ways to outline this section. One way would be to use the actual heads listed in the section and fill in the details. Another way would be to select "Government in England" as the principal head. After scanning the material in the section, it becomes clear that the three main subheads are "Monarchy," "Commonwealth," and "Military Dictatorship."

Government in England
I. Monarchy
  A. James I
    1. Believed in the divine right of kings
    2. Fought with Parliament over money and religion
  B. Charles I
    1. Continued to believe in divine right
    2. Tried to rule without Parliament
    3. Lost the Civil War and was beheaded
II. Commonwealth
  A. England ruled by Parliament
  B. Army led by Cromwell
III. Military dictatorship
  A. Headed by Oliver Cromwell
  B. Enforced Puritan rules

Application

Use these steps to outline Section 2, "A King Returns to the Throne," on pages 492–496. Use a formal outline format .

Practice

Turn to Practicing Skills on page 509 of the Chapter Review for further practice in outlining written material.

CHAPTER 20 REVIEW

HISTORICAL SIGNIFICANCE

The British and American revolutions helped to establish the rights of the people within a representative government. In Great Britain, after the civil war, Parliament eventually established a constitutional monarchy that limited royal power to actions agreed upon by the people. It also guaranteed certain individual rights.

In the United States, the Americans developed a strong belief in written constitutions and the principle of the separation of powers. Moreover, the Bill of Rights clearly spelled out the rights of individual citizens. The American republic would become a source of inspiration to people seeking freedom throughout the world.

SUMMARY

For a summary of Chapter 20, see the Unit 5 Synopsis on pages 542–545.

USING KEY TERMS

Match the following terms from this chapter with their definitions below.

   a. commonwealth
   b. constitutional monarchy
   c. divine right of kings
   d. federal system
   e. habeas corpus
   f. prime minister
   g. revolution
   h. royalist

1. belief that a king derives his power directly from God
2. supporters of the monarchy
3. a state governed by elected representatives of the people
4. monarchy whose powers are limited by a constitution
5. belief that a person cannot be held in prison without just cause or a trial
6. the chief executive of a parliamentary government
7. the violent overthrow of a government by its opponents
8. arrangements in which power is divided between a central government and regional, or state, governments

REVIEWING FACTS

1. **Describe:** How did the Petition of Right limit the powers of the Crown?
2. **Explain:** How did the military rule of Oliver Cromwell help to set the stage for the Restoration?
3. **Name:** Who was the English monarch at the time of the English Civil War? the American Revolution?
4. **Identify:** What was the significance of the First Continental Congress?
5. **Explain:** Why did Great Britain believe it could easily defeat the colonists at the beginning of the American Revolution?

THINKING CRITICALLY

1. **Apply:** How did James I and Charles I try to impose the divine right of kings on the English Parliament?
2. **Analyze:** How did religious issues affect the conflict between Parliament and the Crown in England?
3. **Evaluate:** Was it unfair of the British government to tax the American colonies? Why or why not?
4. How was the influence of the Enlightenment reflected in the American Revolution?

ANALYZING CONCEPTS

1. **Conflict:** What caused the conflict between Parliament and the Stuart monarchs?

2. **Change:** Why do you think the English people chose to restore the monarchy after the Commonwealth? What changes came to the monarchy after 1660?
3. **Revolution:** Why did the American Revolution lead to a stable republican government, whereas the English Civil War did not?

PRACTICING SKILLS

1. Using an informal outline, outline the passage "Forming a New Government" on page 506 in Section 4 of this chapter.
2. Use an outline to plan and write a research paper about the activities and accomplishments of Thomas Jefferson and George Washington before, during, and after the American Revolution. Your formal outline should include these elements:
   - a title for your paper
   - all of the main topics labeled by Roman numerals
   - under a main topic, all the subtopics labeled by capital letters
   - under a subtopic, at least two additional details

GEOGRAPHY IN HISTORY

1. **Movement:** How did the American Revolution affect the development of Canada?

2. **Place:** How did the colonial resources affect Great Britain's relationship with the American colonies?
3. **Location:** How did the location of the colonies affect the events and the outcome of the American Revolution?

TRACING CHRONOLOGY

Refer to the time line below to answer these questions.
1. Which decisions made by Great Britain prior to 1776 do you think were most influential in leading the colonists to seek independence?
2. How many years after the signing of the Declaration of Independence did the British surrender at Yorktown?

LINKING PAST AND PRESENT

1. Some of the quarrels that led to the Revolutionary War concerned taxes. In what ways does the United States continue to struggle with the issue of fair taxes?
2. Religious differences helped fuel the English Civil War. Where do religious differences cause political problems today?
3. The United States and Great Britain are both democracies. How are their governments similar? How are they different? To what extent do they base their political principals on the events of the 1600s and 1700s?

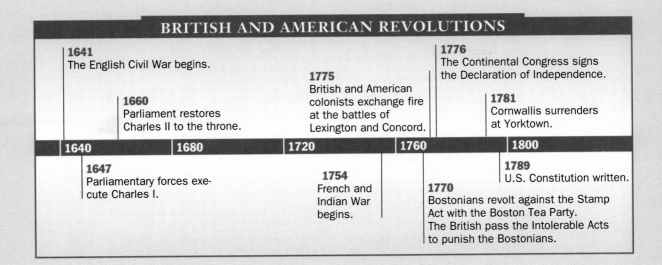

BRITISH AND AMERICAN REVOLUTIONS

1641
The English Civil War begins.

1660
Parliament restores Charles II to the throne.

1775
British and American colonists exchange fire at the battles of Lexington and Concord.

1776
The Continental Congress signs the Declaration of Independence.

1781
Cornwallis surrenders at Yorktown.

| 1640 | 1680 | 1720 | 1760 | 1800 |

1647
Parliamentary forces execute Charles I.

1754
French and Indian War begins.

1770
Bostonians revolt against the Stamp Act with the Boston Tea Party. The British pass the Intolerable Acts to punish the Bostonians.

1789
U.S. Constitution written.

The French Revolution

*I*n 1791 the violence of the French Revolution filled the streets of Paris, where a young seamstress named Marie-Victoire Monnard lived and worked. Walking back to her workshop one afternoon, Marie-Victoire saw six large carts coming toward her. The 13-year-old girl later wrote in her diary, "The carts were full of men and women who had just been slaughtered . . . legs and arms and heads nodded and dangled on either side of the carts."

The next year she wrote again about the carts, "People just went on working in the shops when they passed by, often not even bothering to raise their heads to watch or to turn their backs to avoid the grisly sight."

What happened during the French Revolution that allowed people to become accustomed to the bloodied bodies? What events led to such bloodshed in the first place?

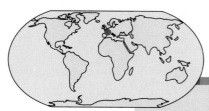

CHAPTER PREVIEW

Terms to Define: estate, tithe, bourgeoisie, unicameral legislature, émigré, conscription, coup d'état, dictatorship, plebiscite, nationalism, buffer state, reactionary, liberalism

People to Meet: Louis XVI, Marie Antoinette, the Jacobins, Robespierre, the Girondists, the Directory, Napoleon Bonaparte, Prince von Metternich

Places to Discover: Paris, Versailles, the Bastille, Elba, Waterloo, Moscow, Vienna

Objectives to Learn:
1. What led to the storming of the Bastille?
2. Why was the French monarchy overthrown?
3. Who tried to control France during the First Republic?

On August 10, 1792, insurgent forces stormed the Tuileries palace.

4. What did Napoleon accomplish?
5. How was peace eventually restored to Europe?

Concepts to Understand:
• Revolution—The French overthrow their absolute monarchy. Section 1
• Change—The National Assembly establishes a constitutional government. Section 2

• Conflict—The new French Republic faces enemies at home and abroad. Section 3
• Movement—Napoleon becomes France's emperor and conquers much of Europe. Section 4
• Reaction—European leaders try to re-establish the old order. Section 5

511

The Old Order

While the American colonies struggled to gain independence from Great Britain and to establish a republic, the absolute monarchy in France was at its height. During this time France enjoyed its role as the richest and possibly the most powerful state in Europe. The French aristocracy set European trends in literature, clothing, art, and ideas for change.

Yet the majority of the people in France did not share the wealth or power of the aristocracy. Working men and women who had few rights yearned for a better way of life. The Americans' success only fueled their desires for change.

French Society Divided

The source of the unhappiness lay within France's class system, which fostered great inequalities among the French people. All French people belonged to one of three **estates**, or orders of society. The estates determined a person's legal rights and status. The Catholic clergy formed the First Estate. The nobility formed the Second Estate. Everyone else, 97 percent of the French people, were members of the Third Estate.

Members of the Third Estate deeply resented the privileges that members of the First and Second estates enjoyed. For example, neither the First Estate nor the Second Estate was required to pay taxes. The nobilities received high positions in the Church, in the government, and in the army, and they could also hunt and carry swords. Third Estate members enjoyed none of these social and political privileges. However successful and well educated Third Estate members became, they were always excluded from the First and Second estates—simply because of the families into which they were born.

The First Estate The First Estate consisted of Roman Catholic clergy and made up about 1 percent of the population. The First Estate comprised two groups: the higher clergy and the lower clergy.

Bishops and abbots, noblemen by birth, made up the higher clergy. These powerful men controlled between 5 and 10 percent of the land in France and enjoyed many privileges. At their disposal were the revenues from their land as well as a **tithe**, or a 10 percent tax on income, from each church member. Although this money was used to support schools, aid poor people, and maintain church property, it also paid for the grand life-styles the higher clergy enjoyed, often at the expense of their religious duties.

The lower clergy, made up of parish priests, came from poorer backgrounds and were socially more a part of the Third Estate. Many lower clergy members who carried out religious duties, ran schools, and cared for the poor resented the luxurious life-styles of the higher clergy.

The Second Estate The nobility, the Second Estate, formed about 2 percent of the population and owned about 25 percent of the land in France. Like the upper clergy, the members of the Second Estate enjoyed many privileges and lived in great style.

The nobility held high posts in the government and the military. Some resided in the palace at Versailles. Others lived in lavish homes on inherited land, some of which they rented to peasants to farm. The Second Estate's main income came from the feudal dues they collected from the peasants who lived on and worked their land.

The Third Estate The Third Estate made up the largest social group. Peasants and artisans, as well as members of the **bourgeoisie**

(boor zhwah ZEE), or middle class, belonged to the Third Estate. Yet they had almost no political rights.

The doctors, lawyers, merchants, and business managers of the bourgeoisie generally lived in the towns and cities. Educated and well-to-do, they had read Enlightenment works and believed in freedom and social justice.

Other members of the Third Estate, such as thousands of poor artisans and their families, also lived in the cities. Artisans worked for low wages and in poor working conditions in places such as dockyards or in government-owned carpet factories. Many lived in Paris' slums.

The peasants, the Third Estate's largest group, lived in rural areas. Although they owned 40 percent of the land, they were very poor because of the payments they had to make to the other estates. These payments included a tithe to the clergy; feudal dues, fees, and fines to the nobles; and a taille, or land tax, to the king. Although members of the Third Estate worked hard, they had no voice in the government.

Learning from Cartoons *A member of France's Third Estate is shown bearing the costs of fees and taxes during the Old Regime.* **What is the message of the cartoon?**

Growing Unrest

Unhappy with this unfair social structure, the people of the Third Estate began to call for change. An Englishman traveling in France saw this growing unrest reflected in a conversation he had with a peasant woman:

Walking up a long hill . . . I was joined by a poor woman who complained of the times, and that it was a sad country; . . . she said her husband had but a morsel of land, one cow, and a poor little horse, yet they had [42 lbs.] of wheat and three chickens to pay as rent to one [lord], and [four lbs.] of oats, one chicken and 1s. [shilling] to pay to another, besides very heavy tailles and other taxes.

—Arthur Young, from *Travels*, 1789

As a growing population put increasing demands on resources, and the cost of living in France increased, the peasants' anger rose. Nobles also charged the peasants higher fees for the use of such equipment as mills and wine presses.

At the same time, artisans in the cities faced higher prices while their wages stayed the same. Members of the bourgeoisie also wanted change. Although they were prosperous, they wanted more political power. Nobles, too, were unhappy. They resented the king's absolute power and wanted to increase their political influence in the government.

A growing financial crisis in government only added to the country's problems. The 1700s had begun with debts from the wars waged by Louis XIV. The extravagant court of Louis XV had further increased this debt.

In 1774 Louis XV's 19-year-old grandson followed his grandfather to the throne as Louis XVI. His wife, Marie Antoinette, was a year younger. In spite of his inexperience, the young king recognized the growing financial crisis. Supporting the American revolution had only increased his debt. After initiating government cost-cutting measures, Louis decided that he had no choice but to begin taxing the nobility and the clergy. But both groups refused to be taxed.

By 1786 banks began to refuse to lend money to the ailing government. The economy suffered a further blow when crop failures caused bread shortages in 1787 and 1788. When the privileged classes refused to aid the government, Louis made a bold choice. He summoned the Estates-General to meet in May 1789 in Versailles. Only in this way could he get additional taxes.

Calling the Estates Together

The Estates-General, which had not met since 1614, was made up of delegates representing each estate. Although the king had hoped that the Estates-General would agree to new taxes on the First and Second estates, the nobles had different ideas. They intended to use the power of the Estates-General to protect their privileges, weaken the king's power, and ultimately gain control of the government. Because each estate in the Estates-General had a single vote, the nobles hoped that the First and Second estates together could easily dominate the Third Estate.

Members of the Third Estate, excited by the prospect of gaining more political power, refused this plan. Claiming that they had more right to represent the nation than either the clergy or the nobles, Third Estate delegates called for a meeting of the three estates, with each delegate voting as an individual. The Third Estate was almost as large as the other two combined, and several reform-minded nobles and clergymen supported their views. A mass meeting would give the Third Estate a majority vote. A clergy member who supported the Third Estate, the Abbé Siéyés (syay EHS), wrote:

Therefore, what is the Third Estate? Everything; but an everything shackled and oppressed. What would it be without the privileged order? Everything, but an everything free and flourishing. Nothing can succeed without it, everything would be infinitely better without the others.

The king, however, turned down the Third Estate's request for a mass meeting and insisted that the estates meet separately. Refusing the king's demands, the representatives of the Third Estate, most of whom were members of the bourgeoisie, were eventually locked out of the Estates-General. In response, they named themselves the National Assembly and demanded a constitution for France.

The National Assembly gathered at a nearby indoor tennis court with deputies from the other estates who supported their cause. Here they took an oath, known as the Tennis Court Oath, promising not to disband until they had written a French constitution.

The king recognized the power of the National Assembly and saw the danger of letting the Third Estate alone draw up a constitution. He ordered the first two estates to join the Third Estate in the National Assembly. Fearing trouble, he also called for troops to concentrate in areas around Paris.

A Call to Revolt

In the meeting of the National Assembly, estate delegates loudly voiced their overwhelming unhappiness with the rigid French social order and the government. While the upper clergy and nobility fought to keep their privileges, some members of the Third Estate called for complete social equality and the abolition of titles. Between the two extremes, other deputies called for a limited, constitutional monarchy like that of Great Britain.

While members of the National Assembly boldly expressed their ideals, the spirit of rebellion against the government spread. Debates raged on streets and in cafes. Some members of the Third Estate even physically attacked people who would not support their cause.

The king only added to the anxiety by gathering more troops at his palace in Versailles. Fearing that he planned to dissolve the National Assembly and halt reforms, the citizens reacted. They focused their action on a Paris prison called the Bastille (bas TEEL).

The Fall of the Bastille   The Bastille symbolized the power and the unfairness the French people detested about the monarchy. On July

Learning from Art *In an indoor tennis court at Versailles, members of the Third Estate and a few clergy and nobles pledged never to adjourn until they had given France a new constitution.* **How did the nobles' demands for change differ from those expressed by the Third Estate?**

14, 1789, a huge mob surrounded the Bastille in an attempt to steal weapons needed to defend the National Assembly from royal troops. Tensions grew as the angry crowd tried to force open two closed drawbridges leading into the fortress. The enraged mob chanted, "We want the Bastille!"

Finally the prison commander lowered a bridge, hoping to calm the crowd. But it was too late. The mob angrily pressed forward into the main courtyard. Armed with axes, they freed the seven prisoners held in the Bastille. The soldiers opened fire, and 98 rioters were killed. Several soldiers were also massacred as the rioters took over the prison. This outbreak led to the formation of a revolutionary city government in Paris, while people committed violent acts against the government in other regions of France as well.

Violence in the Countryside   The storming of the Bastille released a wave of violence in France called the "Great Fear." When rumors spread wildly that nobles had hired robbers to kill peasants and seize their property, the peasants armed themselves.

No robbers came. But fear fanned the peasants' anxiety into violence. Peasants broke into manor houses, robbed granaries, and destroyed feudal records showing the dues they owed. Swearing never again to pay feudal dues, they drove some landlords off their property. The first wave of the French Revolution had struck.

SECTION 1 REVIEW

Recall
1. **Define:** estate, tithe, bourgeoisie
2. **Identify:** Louis XVI, Marie Antoinette, National Assembly, Tennis Court Oath
3. **Describe:** Use a chart to describe France's class system under the Old Regime. What conflicts set the nobility against the members of the Third Estate?

Critical Thinking
4. **Analyze:** July 14, Bastille Day, is celebrated in France like an independence day. Why is it an important national event?

5. **Synthesize:** Which individuals or groups in France were most responsible for beginning the French Revolution?

Applying Concepts
6. **Revolution:** When did events in France become a revolution? Give specific evidence.

Constitutional Government

While violence swept the countryside, the National Assembly worked to create a new French government. Many delegates hoped to establish a constitutional system in which the king and a new legislature would work together. Others, however, supported Louis XVI's belief that he had a God-given right to rule alone. Adding to this tension-filled atmosphere was the nobility's refusal to give up their privileges. Still, the Third Estate demanded reform.

End of the Old Order

The continuing violence of the "Great Fear" in the countryside finally convinced the nobles that they could no longer hold back demands for reform. On August 4, 1789, the nobles announced they were ready to give up their privileges. In a session that lasted until 2 A.M., deputies wept and cheered as the National Assembly passed reform after reform, destroying the last remnants of feudalism in France. The

IMAGES OF THE TIME

Revolutionary Life

Although the causes of the French Revolution had existed for years, the events of 1789 sparked the beginning of the Revolution.

Shouting, "We want the Bastille," an angry mob stormed the prison on July 14, 1789.

National Guard divisions had identifiying flags. This banner proclaims "Our unity gives us our strength."

reforms included abolition of feudal dues and tithes owed by the peasants. The nobles also agreed to be taxed, and all male citizens could hold government, army, or church office.

Declaration of Rights

With the old order of estates abolished, the deputies turned to another critical issue—the basic rights due each French citizen. Inspired by the American Declaration of Independence and the United States Constitution, as well as the English Bill of Rights, the National Assembly composed the Declaration of the Rights of Man in late August 1789. It is in the French Constitution of today.

The Declaration, which incorporated the ideas of Enlightenment writers Locke, Montesquieu, and Rousseau, stated that all people are equal before the law. It also guaranteed freedom of speech, press, and religion, and protected against arbitrary arrest and punishment.

These principles, however, did not include women. When a group of French women created their own declaration of rights, revolutionary leaders rejected it. They did not believe that women were equal to men.

March to Versailles

When the king refused to accept the new reforms and the Declaration of Rights, the citizens of Paris feared that he would take action against the National Assembly. The people wanted Louis to move to Paris from his countryside palace in Versailles to show his support for the Assembly.

In October 1789 thousands of women demanding bread marched in the rain to the king's palace in Versailles. Wielding sticks and pitchforks, the angry mob surrounded the palace, shouting for the king and queen. As the cries grew louder and armed guards were not able to hold back the surging crowd, the king declared

Marie Antoinette, shown in prison mourning her husband's death, was herself executed in October 1793.

Reflecting on the Times
How do these images reflect the basic changes in French society caused by the Revolution?

at last, "My friends, I will go to Paris with my wife and children."

That afternoon, women waving banners and loaves of bread on bayonets surrounded the king's carriage as it drove to Paris. In Paris, revolutionaries watched the king, Marie Antoinette, and their two children. A few days later, the National Assembly also moved to Paris.

A New France

With the king and the National Assembly settled in Paris, government affairs began to move forward again. The delegates could turn their attention to political reforms.

Political Reforms   The National Assembly also faced the practical problem of paying for the government and paying off the national debt. To solve its financial problems and to weaken the power of the Catholic Church, the Assembly decided to confiscate church lands and sell them. In return for the land, the Assembly agreed to assume church expenses such as supporting the clergy and aiding the poor.

In 1790 the Assembly also passed the Civil Constitution of the Clergy, which stated that each parish should elect its own priest. As a result Pope Pius VI condemned the revolution. The National Assembly then required clergy to take a loyalty oath to the government; about half of them refused. There were now two Catholic churches in France—one loyal to the government, the other loyal to the pope.

The Constitution of 1791   In 1791 the National Assembly presented a new constitution to the people. The constitution kept the monarchy but limited royal powers. It set up a **unicameral legislature**, or one-house assembly, whose members were to be chosen by voters. Although equal rights were declared for all, only males who paid a minimum tax could vote.

Many French people were not happy with the Constitution of 1791. For some, the reforms went too far; for others, not far enough. Delegates in the National Assembly were seated according to their political beliefs. The royalists, who supported the king, were seated on the right. Moderates, who favored a limited monarchy, sat in the middle. The radicals, who wanted a republic, sat on the left. Among the radicals were the extremists, who demanded a republic in which all males could vote, whether or not they owned property.

Defending the Revolution

As political groups became more divided, France entered one of the most tumultuous periods in its history. Disagreements led to unrest and violence throughout the country.

Living in Paris, Louis XVI and Marie Antoinette could see the angry people in the streets and hear the calls for revolution. In June 1791 they decided to flee to Austrian-ruled territory, where the French queen's brother was emperor. Disguised as ordinary French people, the royal family left Paris in a carriage late at night.

Learning from Art
In 1788 a failed harvest caused a 50 percent rise in the price of bread. Nearly one-fourth of Parisians were out of work by the summer of 1789. By that fall, these conditions, as well as the fear of royal interference with the National Assembly, caused 7,000 Parisian women to march on Versailles. **What did the march accomplish?**

PENDULUM OF POLITICAL OPINION

LEFT		MIDDLE	RIGHT	
Radical	**Liberal**	**Moderate**	**Conservative**	**Reactionary**
Favors making extreme changes, strongly opposed to the status quo	Favors making changes, reluctant to accept the status quo	Favors the status quo, but open to changes	Favors maintaining the status quo, reluctant to make changes	Favors a return to the past, strongly opposed to changes

Learning from Charts   *Locate the radicals, the moderates, and the conservatives and their political views on the chart above.* **Which group held the most political power in France by the summer of 1792?**

A bystander who recognized the king at a road stop in Varennes, a town west of Paris, foiled the escape plan. Soldiers immediately arrested the royal family, returning them to Paris. A virtual prisoner, Louis reluctantly accepted the limited monarchy established by the National Assembly. The limited monarchy, though, had little chance of success, for the people distrusted the king and were leaning toward a republic.

As news of the revolt against the French monarchy spread to neighboring countries, monarchs in the German states and the Austrian Empire began to worry about the stability of their own governments. French **émigrés** (ehm i GRAYS), nobles who had fled France, hoped to restore Louis XVI to full power. The émigrés tried to convince the leaders of these governments that their own rule would be threatened unless they smashed the revolution before it spread.

Meanwhile French revolutionary leaders, fearing that Austria would try to reinstate Louis, declared war on Austria in 1792. Austria was soon supported by other monarchies, including Prussia and Sardinia.

War threw France into total upheaval. It pushed the revolution into a more dangerous phase, as fears grew about opposition to the revolt. During the summer of 1792, citizens and troops, frustrated by food shortages caused by the war, attacked the palace where the king and his family were being kept and killed many of the king's guards. The king had fled moments before to the National Assembly for protection. Yet the National Assembly offered him no safety. The radicals suspended the king's powers and voted to imprison the royal family. Then they dissolved the National Assembly. The radicals wanted to replace the limited monarchy established by the National Assembly with a republic. The king was clearly in danger.

SECTION 2 REVIEW

Recall
1. **Define:** unicameral legislature, émigré
2. **Identify:** Declaration of the Rights of Man, Civil Constitution of the Clergy
3. **List:** What reforms did the National Assembly make?

4. **Explain:** Why did the mob of women march on Versailles? What was the result of their protest?

Critical Thinking
5. **Analyze:** Contrast the views of French moderates and extreme radicals. What type of government did each political group advocate?

Applying Concepts
6. **Conflict:** Why might absolute rulers in other countries fear the French Revolution?

Dawn of a New Era

In September 1792 the French revolutionary leaders faced the result of their declared war on Austria and Prussia. Prussian troops had taken the major French fort of Verdun and the road to Paris was now open for them. As fear gripped the country, Georges-Jacques Danton, a revolutionary orator, exclaimed to the people: "All are burning with a desire to fight! We need boldness . . . and France will be saved."

In response to Danton's stirring words, thousands of volunteers came forward to defend the revolution. A week later, thoughts of defeat vanished when the French army won an astonishing victory at Valmy, less than 100 miles (161 kilometers) from Paris. After the battle, the French commander wrote in his diary:

> *Our soldiers were badly clothed, they had no straw to sleep on, no blankets, they sometimes went two days without bread. I never once saw them complain. . . . The tiredness and hardship they have suffered have been rewarded. The enemy has* [yielded] *to the season, misery, and illness. Its formidable army is in flight, its numbers halved. . . .*

—Commander Dumouriez, 1792

The victory at Valmy boosted the spirits of the revolutionaries. French forces had halted the powerful armies of Europe's monarchs, and had saved the revolution for the time being.

Birth of a Republic

As cannons thundered at Valmy, members of the National Convention gathered in Paris to create a new government for France. Shouts of "Long Live the Nation!" echoed through the chamber as the delegates ended the monarchy and made France a republic.

The National Convention met from 1792 to 1795. Its members, who were all male—and mostly lawyers, doctors, and other middle-class professionals—passed into law a number of democratic reforms. The Convention wrote the country's first democratic constitution. The constitution placed political power in a single national legislature based on universal manhood suffrage, meaning that every man could vote, whether or not he owned property. Convention members also replaced the monarchy's confusing system of weights and measures with the metric system that is still used throughout the world today.

The National Convention also adopted a new calendar, naming September 22, 1792—the date of the republic's creation—the first day of the Year I of Liberty. Although this revolutionary calendar did not last, it and the other democratic reforms expressed the French people's hope that the republic would be the dawn of a new era of freedom.

Death of a King

Before it could forge ahead into the republican era, the Convention had to deal with the legacy of the past. Its first task was to decide Louis XVI's fate. In November 1792 a large iron box holding Louis's secret correspondence with foreign monarchs was found in the royal palace. Although the letters provided little evidence against the ex-king, the radicals successfully used them to discredit the royal family.

In December 1792 Louis was tried before the Convention and sentenced to die as an enemy of the people. He was beheaded on the guillotine—a killing machine the revolutionaries had adopted as a humane means of execution. As he faced execution, the king reportedly said:

I forgive my enemies; I trust that my death will be for the happiness of my people, but I grieve for France and I fear that she may suffer the anger of the Lord.

Parisian crowds joyously celebrated the king's death. For them, it meant that there was no turning back; the republic would remain.

Toward the Future   In the days that followed, republican enthusiasm swept the country. Parisians were the most fervent. The *sans-culottes*—Paris's shopkeepers, artisans, and workers—saw themselves as heroes and heroines and demanded respect from the upper classes.

Soon even wealthy Parisians addressed each other as "citizen" or "citizeness" rather than "mister" or "madame." They rejected elaborate clothes and powdered wigs in favor of simple styles. Men wore long trousers instead of knee-length breeches (hence the name *sans-culottes*, meaning "without breeches"); women wore long dresses in the style of ancient Rome.

While the nation celebrated the republic, debate over the revolution's future erupted in the Convention. There, supporters of the *sans-culottes* and extreme radicals called the Jacobins (JAK uh bins) formed the Mountain, so called because its members sat on high benches at the rear of the hall. Under leaders such as Maximilien Robespierre, Georges-Jacques Danton, and Jean-Paul Marat, the Mountain saw itself as the defender of the people's will.

Across the aisle was a group of moderates known as Girondists (juh RAHN duhsts), because many of them came from the Gironde, a region in southwestern France. The Girondists felt that the revolution had gone far enough and wanted to protect the wealthy middle class from radical attacks. They organized support to resist the growing strength of the Mountain in Paris.

Seated between these two rivals on the main floor was a group called the Plain. It was made up of undecided deputies, who were a majority of the Convention. As the influence of the *sans-culottes* increased during 1793, members of the Plain came to support the Mountain. Together, they helped make the revolution more radical, more open to extreme and violent change.

Spreading the Revolution

Meanwhile Europe's monarchs viewed events in France with horror. After Louis's execution, they feared democratic revolutions could spread from France and endanger their thrones and their lives. In January 1793 the monarchs of Great Britain, the Netherlands, Spain, and Sardinia joined those of Austria and Prussia in an alliance against revolutionary France.

At the same time, France's leaders were determined to overthrow royalty everywhere. In early 1793 Danton declared that "the kings in alliance try to frighten us, [but] we hurl at their feet, as a gage of battle, the French king's head." He then called upon French forces to expand

Learning from Art *The revolutionaries executed the king under the sharp blade of the guillotine, a beheading machine. The guillotine was the official instrument of execution in France by 1792.* **What course did the revolution take immediately after Louis's death?**

Revolutionary Music

Revolutionaries throughout the world have often used music to spread their message and unite people around their cause. Just as the sound of the charge played at a football game rallies sports fans, revolutionary music can appeal to people's emotions and stir them to action. By vocalizing ideals and aims, songs of revolution can inspire people to become part of a larger group, persuading them to devote their efforts—and perhaps their lives—to a cause they believe is important.

The French Revolution found its voice in a rousing military march that inspired the rebels in their cause. Written in 1792 by Joseph Rouget de Lisle, a young captain in the army engineers, the march became the symbol of the French Revolution. Later known as "The Marseillaise," the message and emotion of the song rallied the patriotism and courage of French citizens by sounding the call to battle:

To arms, citizens!
Form your battalions,
Let us march, let us march!

An allegorical figure of Liberty leads the people in this painting of the French Revolution.

"The Marseillaise" became the French national anthem in 1795. Because of its revolutionary character, it was banned under the regimes of Napoleon, Louis XVIII, and Napoleon III. It once again became the national anthem in 1879.

The best-known and most enduring song of the American Revolution was "Yankee Doodle." The British had originally used the term "yankee" as an insult. Singing "Yankee Doodle" as they marched, they showed their scorn for American soldiers. But the colonists turned the insult into a battle cry for freedom.

Today, revolutionary and protest groups continue to use music to gain public support for their causes. In the United States, for example, "We Shall Overcome" became a unifying force in the civil rights movement of the 1960s. This song is sung throughout the world today by people fighting for freedom.

Responding to the Arts

1. How can revolutionary music be used to motivate people?
2. Can you think of cases today where music is used to unite people around a cause?

France's territories to their natural frontiers: the Alps, the Pyrenees, the Rhine River, and the Mediterranean Sea.

In response to this call, an army made up of volunteers poured outward from France, eager to seize the natural frontiers and to bring "liberty, equality, and fraternity" to Europe's people. Although poorly trained, the French forces often caught the enemy off guard and won many battles. But the enemy's professional soldiers soon inflicted on the French a string of defeats. In despair, the French commander-in-chief abandoned his troops and surrendered.

As French forces retreated, the National Convention took steps to repel the foreign invasion. It formed the Committee of Public Safety to direct the entire war effort. In summer 1793 when the French army needed more troops, the Committee adopted **conscription**, or the draft, calling up all men between the ages of 18 and 45 for military service. It also called upon the skills and resources of all civilians, both men and women. The Committee turned the conflict into what has been called the world's first "people's war," one that involved the entire population.

While waging war, France's revolutionaries had to struggle with problems at home. A fierce civil war raged in western France as royalist peasants revolted against the revolutionaries. They were angered by the drafting of their sons

---

FOOTNOTES TO HISTORY

THE WAX MUSEUM

A young Swiss woman skilled in modeling wax figures found herself in the middle of Paris during the Reign of Terror. When the revolutionary leaders heard about her artistic skill, they ordered the woman to immortalize the revolution's leaders and many of their victims by making wax models of them.

At last the woman escaped to London. Here, too, she used her wax-modeling skill and opened a museum, Madame Tussaud's Exhibition. Today, millions of people marvel at the life-like wax figures in Tussaud's museum in London, run by her descendants.

---

to fight a war they opposed. Elsewhere in France, economic hardships weakened support for the revolution. Mobs in French cities rioted to protest rising food prices and food shortages.

Meanwhile, the government itself was embroiled in a political crisis. After a long power struggle, the Jacobins in the Mountain won control of the Convention and arrested Girondist delegates who disagreed with their policies.

In retaliation Girondist supporters rebelled against the Jacobins in the Convention. During the uprising Charlotte Corday, a loyal Girondist supporter, killed the Jacobin leader Marat and was sent to the guillotine. Within a few months, other Girondists suffered the same fate.

Reign of Terror

Overwhelmed by enemies at home and abroad, the Jacobins set out to crush all opposition within France. This effort, known as the Reign of Terror, lasted from September 1793 to July 1794.

During the Terror, neighborhood watch committees hunted down suspected traitors and turned them over to the courts. Pressured by mobs, the courts carried out swift trials and handed down harsh sentences. Innocent people often suffered—many of them sentenced because of false statements made by hostile neighbors. Among the victims of the Terror was Marie Antoinette, Louis XVI's wife. Royalty and aristocrats, however, were only a few of those killed. Historians estimate that about 85 percent of the 40,000 people executed were probably commoners—merchants, laborers, and peasants.

In spring 1794 Danton finally decided to call an end to the killings. Robespierre, however, disagreed and accused Danton of betraying the cause. He had Danton and his followers put to death for disloyalty.

With fanatical zeal Robespierre tried to increase the Terror during the next four months. However, his followers—fearing for their lives—had Robespierre arrested and executed on the guillotine. The day after the execution, a Paris newspaper expressed the relief that everyone felt: "We are all throwing ourselves into each other's arms."

The Directory

After Robespierre's fall the Convention briefly carried on as France's government. In 1795 it wrote a new constitution. Universal manhood suffrage was ended; only citizens who owned property could vote. This constitution, in effect, brought the government under the control of the wealthy middle class. The constitution also set up an executive council of five men called directors. The Directory, as the council was called, ruled with a two-house legislature.

Once in power the Directory faced many enemies. Despite the Terror enough royalists remained to threaten a takeover. Even more alarming was the growing discontent of the radical *sans-culottes*, angered by food shortages and rising prices. During its rule from 1795 to 1799, the Directory used the army to put down uprisings by both groups.

Meanwhile, the Directory made little effort to resolve a growing gap between the rich and the poor people of France. It was having its own problems: the revolutionary government was on the brink of bankruptcy, and the directors were beset by financial and moral scandals in their personal lives. As the Directory appeared more and more inept, French people of all classes looked to the power of the army to save France from ruin.

PERSONAL PROFILES

Marie Antoinette, the Tragic Queen

Austrian Princess Marie Antoinette was just 15 years old when she married the crown prince of France, Louis, who soon would be king of the richest and most splendid monarchy in Europe.

Unprepared for her role as queen and unhappy with her new husband, who was interested mainly in eating and hunting, Marie Antoinette spent money extravagantly, buying as many as 170 dresses in one year. Her excessive spending earned her the nickname "Madame Deficit"among the French people.

When the fires of Revolution ignited, however, the seemingly frivolous Marie Antoinette displayed strength and courage. In the face of Louis's indecisiveness, she sought support for the French monarchy from other European rulers. She especially sought the assistance of her brother, the emperor of Austria.

This help was not to come, however. In January 1793 Louis went to his death. Thinking of Marie Antoinette to the last, he had decided to spare his beloved wife the pain of a final parting. Only the cannon booming in the distance told the imprisoned Marie Antoinette that Louis was dead.

Nine months later, head held high, the proud Queen rode to her death in a rubbish cart with shouts of "Death to the Austrian!" ringing in her ears. For Marie Antoinette the decade of revolutionary horror was over. She was just 37years of age.

Reflecting on the Person

1. Why did the French people resent Marie Antoinette?
2. How did Marie Antoinette think she might save the French monarchy from the revolution?

Napoleon Takes Over

As the Directory faced growing unpopularity at home, the French army won victories in the continuing war with the European monarchies. One of the many able French military leaders who attracted public attention was a young general named Napoleon Bonaparte. During the French Revolution, Bonaparte's great military skills won him quick promotion to the rank of general. In 1795 at age 24, he crushed a royalist uprising against the Directory.

A year later Bonaparte married Josephine de Beauharnais, a leader of Paris society. Using Josephine's connections, he won command of the French army that was fighting the Austrians in Italy. Upon arriving Napoleon improved the soldiers' conditions and mustered their support.

He also created a plan to defeat the enemy by rapidly moving and massing French forces at weak points on the enemy's line. With this strategy Napoleon defeated the Austrians and forced them to sign a peace treaty giving France control over most of northern Italy. These victories made Napoleon France's leading general. He was now ready to influence events at home.

In 1799 Napoleon seized his opportunity. For more than a year, he had been fighting the British in Egypt, hoping to cut off Britain's trade with the Middle East and India. Although Napoleon won victories on land, the British navy destroyed his fleet, leaving French forces stranded among the pyramids. Hearing of the troubled political situation back home,

Learning from Art *This unfinished portrait of the young Napoleon suggests his intelligence and determination. French army life fueled his ambition: by age 28 he was a national hero.* **For what accomplishment did Napoleon first earn his fame?**

Napoleon abandoned his army in Egypt and returned to France.

When Napoleon entered Paris in October 1799, he was greeted by cheering crowds. Realizing that people were tired of war and revolution, he joined leaders in a **coup d' état**, or a quick seizure of power from the Directory.

SECTION 3 REVIEW

Recall
1. **Define:** conscription, coup d'état
2. **Identify:** Jacobins, Girondists, Reign of Terror, Napoleon Bonaparte
3. **Locate:** Where are France's "natural frontiers" according to Danton? Why do you think Danton called for expansion to the "natural frontiers"?

Critical Thinking
4. **Apply:** Select a revolutionary leader such as Robespierre and show how he or she succeeded—or failed—in carrying out the ideals of "liberty, equality, and fraternity."
5. **Synthesize:** Compare and contrast the Directory government of 1796 with the National Assembly government of 1794.

Which was more democratic? Why? Give examples to support your answer.

Applying Concepts
6. **Revolution:** What conditions led to the Reign of Terror? Why might the French revolutionaries use such violent and drastic measures to advance their cause?

Napoleon's Empire

By 1804, only ten years after Louis XVI's execution, Napoleon named himself Emperor of the French. The people attending his coronation had lived through the bloody, tumultuous days of the revolution. Now they were to witness a grand ceremony.

Pope Pius VII had been summoned from Rome to crown the emperor. Napoleon wore a purple velvet cape embroidered with gold bees and lined with ermine. He dressed in a white silk tunic, white silk pants, white stockings, and white shoes, all embroidered in gold. The Empress Josephine wore a white gown and had a purple cape to match Napoleon's.

After Napoleon had taken his oath as Emperor, the people witnessed an astonishing act. Napoleon took the crown from the pope's hands and placed it on his own head. Napoleon's actions spoke loudly. How had the French government been transformed from a democracy to an empire in five short years?

The Consulate

After his successful overthrow of the Directory in 1799, Napoleon had proclaimed the new constitution, which theoretically established a republic. The constitution actually set up a **dictatorship**, a government headed by an absolute ruler. The executive branch was a committee of three members, called consuls, who took their title from ancient Rome. But Napoleon became First Consul and quickly concentrated power in his own hands.

Having studied the writers and ideas of the Enlightenment, Napoleon saw himself as a great reformer and bearer of the republican traditions of the revolution. His one-man rule, however, would eventually place severe limits on individual rights.

Restoring Order   Napoleon wanted to bring order to the country. One of his first goals was to restructure the government. Although he tried to keep many of the revolutionary reforms, Napoleon replaced elected local officials with men he appointed himself. He also placed education under the control of the national government, creating technical schools, universities, and secondary schools. The secondary schools, called lycées (lee SAY), were designed to provide well-educated, patriotic government workers. Although students who attended the lycées came mostly from wealthy families, some poorer students received scholarships. In this way the French schools were a step toward a public system open to all children.

Napoleon also changed the country's financial system. He created the Bank of France and required that every citizen pay taxes. The collected taxes were deposited in the bank and used by the government to make loans to businesses. These changes gradually brought inflation and high prices under control.

Napoleon's many supporters welcomed his strong government and the peace and order it brought. In 1802 Napoleon named himself Consul for life. This move was overwhelmingly approved by a **plebiscite**, or popular vote.

The Napoleonic Code   Many historians say that Napoleon made his greatest impact on French law. Old feudal and royal laws were often contradictory and confusing. Napoleon combined these into a unified system. With his knowledge of the Enlightenment, he rewrote the laws to follow the principles of natural law.

The Napoleonic Code made French law clear and consistent. Although it put the state above the individual, the new code preserved some revolutionary reforms, such as making all men equal before the law. The code did, however, curtail freedom of speech and press, including the censorship of books, plays, and pamphlets. Women, too, found that their rights were curtailed under the Napoleonic Code.

The Church   Napoleon also made peace with the Catholic Church. Realizing that French Catholics had objected to the Civil Constitution of the Clergy, he negotiated an agreement called the Concordat of 1801 with Pope Pius VI. In this agreement Napoleon acknowledged that Catholicism was the religion of the majority of French people but affirmed religious toleration for all. Napoleon did, however, retain the right to name all bishops, who had to swear allegiance to the state. The Pope agreed to accept the loss of church lands; in return the state agreed to pay salaries to the Catholic clergy.

Building an Empire

Although Napoleon proved that he was an able administrator, he was more interested in building an empire. Soon after becoming First Consul, Napoleon commanded the French forces that defeated both Italy and Austria. He also persuaded Russia to withdraw from the war. Though Napoleon was not able to defeat the British navy, the British were ready for peace because their commerce had suffered during the war. The two powers signed the Treaty of Amiens in March 1802.

In one of the battles in Italy, Napoleon had bravely led his soldiers across a bridge under heavy fire. He later wrote,

It was not till that evening that I knew I was superior to other men, and actually planned to put into practice the great ideas that, till then had filled my thoughts only as a dream.

Over the next few years Napoleon combined his talents as a masterful military leader and brilliant diplomat to build an empire. In 1804 he named himself Emperor of the French and soon set his armies on the road to conquest.

Yet despite his successes on the continent of Europe, Great Britain remained Napoleon's most tenacious enemy. By 1805 Napoleon felt he was ready to invade Great Britain's shores from the English Channel; his fleet never made it that far, however. In October 1805 at the battle of Trafalgar, off the southern coast of Spain, the British admiral Lord Nelson soundly defeated the French navy, removing once and for all the possibility of a French invasion of Great Britain.

After Trafalgar Napoleon decided to use economic warfare against the British. He believed he could defeat Great Britain by destroying its economic lifeline—trade. In a plan called the Continental System, Napoleon ordered all European nations he had conquered to stop trade with the British. In another decree he forbade British imports entry to the European ports that he controlled. Napoleon also required Russia and Prussia to go along with the blockade of British goods.

Meanwhile, Great Britain responded to the trade blockade with a counterthreat: any ship on its way to a continental port had to stop first at a British port. Napoleon responded that he would seize any ship that did so.

This conflict put the United States and other neutral nations in a difficult position. The United States relied heavily on its trade with both Great Britain and France. If the United States ignored the British threat, American ships would be seized by the British navy. If it obeyed the British, the French navy would seize its ships. This conflict on the seas was one of the causes that eventually led to the War of 1812 between the United States and Great Britain.

Despite the blockades, the aggressive British navy did maintain control of the seas; and Napoleon's Continental System failed. French trade suffered, and the French economy worsened. But Napoleon's empire kept growing as he continued to win battles on land.

Napoleonic Europe

By 1812 Napoleon controlled most of Europe. France's boundaries now extended to the Russian border. Through successful French military conquests, Napoleon became king of Italy, his brother Joseph became king of Naples and later, Spain, and his other brother, Louis, became king of Holland. Napoleon then abolished the Holy Roman Empire and created the Federation of the Rhine, a loose organization of the German states, and named himself its "Protector." This move led Prussia to declare war on France, but the French easily crushed the weak Prussian army.

Countries such as Spain and Italy, and members of the Confederation of the Rhine, came under the control of France. Their leaders followed Napoleon's dictates. Unrest in these countries soon developed, though.

The people who lived in the countries under Napoleon's rule resented paying taxes to France and sending soldiers to serve in Napoleon's armies. This resentment ignited in the conquered people a feeling of **nationalism**, the yearning for self-rule and restoration of their customs and traditions. Nationalism helped to stir revolts against French rule throughout Europe.

The first sign of trouble appeared in Spain. Spaniards were tired of French rule. In an attempt to return their king to the throne, Spanish nationalists attacked French soldiers stationed in Spain. In 1812, aided by British troops under the command of Arthur Wellesley (later named Duke of Wellington), the Spaniards finally overthrew their hated enemy Napoleon. They reinstated their old king under a system of limited monarchy. Prussia also joined the revolt against Napoleon, as nationalist leaders rebuilt its army and amassed political support in the hope of ridding themselves of French rule.

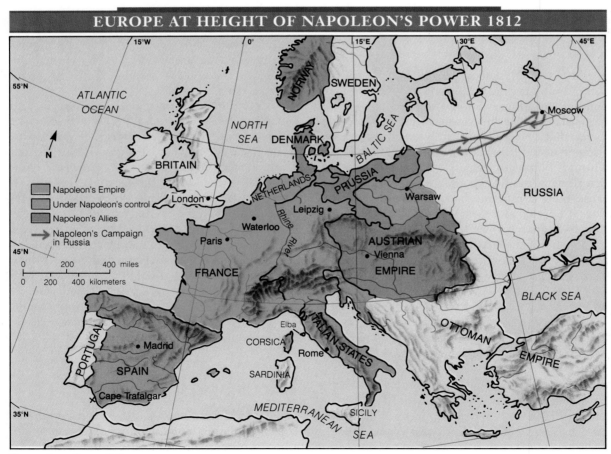

EUROPE AT HEIGHT OF NAPOLEON'S POWER 1812

Learning from Maps *Napoleon dominated most of the European continent in 1812.* **What geographic factors helped to protect Great Britain and Russia from Napoleon's armies?**

Downfall of the Empire

When Russia joined the movement against Napoleon, it signaled the end of the empire. Alexander I of Russia viewed Napoleon's control of Europe as a threat to Russia. Additionally, Napoleon's Continental System had hurt the Russian economy. In 1812 Alexander withdrew from the Continental System and resumed trade with Great Britain.

This withdrawal outraged Napoleon, leading him to invade Russia. He assembled a massive army of 600,000 soldiers from countries throughout Europe. The long French march toward Moscow began in May 1812. But the Russians refused to yield to Napoleon's threat. They retreated to central Russia, adopting a "scorched-earth policy" in which they burned everything as they went. On September 14, one of Napoleon's men finally saw the city of Moscow from a nearby hill. But the day after the French entered Moscow, a giant fire, probably started by Russian patriots, destroyed most of the city. In a letter to Alexander I, Napoleon wrote, "The beautiful and magnificent city of Moscow no longer exists."

Shortly afterward the harsh Russian winter began to set in, and the French army could not remain in Russia without shelter. But Napoleon delayed before ordering a retreat. When the

CONNECTIONS: SCIENCE AND TECHNOLOGY

Bubbling Waters

Have you ever sipped a fizzy soft drink to settle an upset stomach? People have long believed that bubbling waters contain healing properties. For centuries royalty and wealthy Europeans sought the health benefits of the mineral-rich, bubbling springs scattered throughout Europe.

Scientists in Europe and in the United States attempted to reproduce these effervescent waters. In 1775 the French chemist Antoine Lavoisier identified the gaseous element as carbon dioxide. In 1782 the English chemist Thomas Henry described how to make artificial carbonated waters commercially. Factories and bottling plants soon began operating in London, Paris, Dublin, and Geneva. Today "bubbling waters" are as close to us as our refrigerator or the nearest market.

"Soft drinks" were originally sold at drugstores in the United States as syrupy tonics used for medicinal purposes. In the early 1800s, it became popular to combine these tonics with carbonated water. Advances in manufacturing in the 1820s greatly increased the output of bottled waters. Bottled colas appeared on the market in the late 1800s.

Today mineral waters and carbonated beverages are popular around the world. People like the tangy, sparkling taste provided by carbonization, which also prevents spoilage. In the United States alone, soft-drink sales total about $30 billion a year.

Making the Connection

1. Do you think carbonated soda has a positive or a negative effect on your health?
2. Can you think of any inventions or technologies that have been produced by the soft-drink industry?

French troops finally did retreat in the midst of a bitterly cold winter, the Russians relentlessly attacked them. The retreat became a rout. About four-fifths of Napoleon's army—500,000 men—died in battles or blizzards.

Defeat The Russian blow to Napoleon's power ruined him. From all directions his enemies—Russians, Prussians, Spaniards, English, Austrians, Italians—sent armies against Napoleon's forces. Russia and Prussia announced a War of Liberation, and joined by Austria, they defeated Napoleon at Leipzig, Germany, in October 1813. Napoleon fatalistically described his defeat: "I foresaw the outcome, and that was my agony; my star was setting, the reins slipped from my hands, and I could do nothing about it."

By March 1814 the allies were in Paris, forcing Napoleon to surrender and abdicate as emperor. The victors restored the French throne to Louis XVIII, a member of the Bourbon family and the brother of Louis XVI. Napoleon was exiled to Elba, an island off the coast of Italy. The boundaries of France were reduced to those of 1792.

Although thousands of young French soldiers had died all over Europe, many French people still hoped that Napoleon could return to power. He appealed to their national pride and to their desire for order.

Still determined to rule, Napoleon returned to France on March 1, 1815, and easily won widespread popular support. The troops of the restored Bourbon king, Louis XVIII, deserted to their former commander when Napoleon announced, "Your general, summoned to the throne by the prayer of the people and raised upon your shields, is now restored to you; come and join him." In a period known as the Hundred Days, Napoleon again reigned as emperor. To avoid war he announced that France wanted no more territory.

The European governments, however, feared that he might regain his former strength. Determined to stop Napoleon, the armies of Prussia, Great Britain, and the Netherlands advanced toward France under the command of the Duke of Wellington. Napoleon met them at Waterloo in the Austrian Netherlands in June 1815; the French troops were decisively defeated. Napoleon was then placed under house arrest on the island of St. Helena in the South Atlantic. He died there in 1821.

Napoleon's Legacy Throughout his rule Napoleon helped spread the ideas and reforms of the French Revolution throughout Europe. In all the countries he conquered, constitutions were established and the Napoleonic codes, with their basic principles of freedom of religion and equality before the law, were enforced. Remnants of feudalism were destroyed as taxes and the manorial systems were reformed.

These reforms helped to modernize the conquered governments, and when Napoleon's empire did eventually collapse, many Europeans wanted to hold onto the changes that he had introduced—especially the abolition of an absolute monarchy. And monarchs, nobles, and clergy throughout Europe would find that they were no longer strong enough to restore the way of life that had existed before the French Revolution.

SECTION 4 REVIEW

Recall
1. **Define:** dictatorship, plebiscite, nationalism
2. **Identify:** the Napoleonic Code, the Continental System, Waterloo
3. **List:** Outline three reforms that Napoleon introduced in France.

Critical Thinking
4. **Synthesize:** Compare Napoleon's rule after the French Revolution to Cromwell's rule after the English Civil War.
5. **Analyze:** Tell why you think Napoleon Bonaparte proved to be such a popular leader following the French Revolution.

Applying Concepts
6. **Conflict:** How did the rise of nationalism in conquered nations contribute to the downfall of Napoleon's empire?

SECTION 5

Peace in Europe

Walking along the streets of Vienna, Austria, in the fall of 1814 were the kings, princes, and diplomats who had gathered for a peace conference known as the Congress of Vienna. With Napoleon in exile, the delegates had come to Vienna to achieve two chief goals: to restore the political balance in Europe and to provide a means of settling disputes among the great powers.

Although almost every European nation sent representatives, delegations from the great powers of Europe—Great Britain, Prussia, Russia, and Austria—dominated the Congress, which met in September 1814 and lasted nearly eight months.

The Congress of Vienna

Austria's chief minister, Prince Klemens von Metternich, served as host to the Congress and presided over it. Metternich believed that in order to establish European stability, Europe should be restored to the way it was before the French Revolution. To achieve his goal, Metternich maintained that settlements reached at Vienna would be guided by three principles: compensation, legitimacy, and balance of power. Compensation meant that all countries should be repaid for the expenses they incurred while fighting the French. By legitimacy, Metternich meant restoring to power the royal families who had ruled before Napoleon. And balance of power meant that no country should ever again dominate continental Europe.

Redrawing the Map As the victors of the war claimed their rewards, they redrew the map of Europe. France was forced to give up its recently gained territory and to pay a large indemnity, or compensation, to other countries for war damages. Although Great Britain did not gain land in continental Europe, it took from France most of its remaining islands in the West Indies.

Learning from Art
As host to the Congress of Vienna, Metternich was obliged to entertain large groups of royal consorts, family members, and delegates' aides. Plays, musicals, and balls helped to make Vienna the center of European society at the time.
What was the chief purpose of the Congress of Vienna?

EUROPE AFTER CONGRESS OF VIENNA 1815

Learning from Maps *The territory France held under Napoleon was divided among the great European powers at the Congress of Vienna. Compare this map with the map on page 528 showing Europe at the height of Napoleon's power.* **What country ruled Poland after the Congress of Vienna?**

Austria gained the Italian provinces of Lombardy and Venetia as well as territory on the eastern coast of the Adriatic Sea.

At the conference Prussia and Russia also made it known that they wanted to expand their borders by seizing formerly French-held lands. Yet Britain and Austria feared that increased Prussian and Russian influence in central Europe would lead to an imbalance of power on the continent. To put pressure on Prussia and Russia, Great Britain and Austria made an agreement with France. The agreement bound the three powers—Great Britain, Austria, and France—to resist any further Prussian or Russian territorial expansion in Europe by armed force if it was necessary.

In the end a compromise was reached. Prussia received extensive territories along the Rhine River and almost half the kingdom of Saxony for its compensation. Russia received most of the Polish territory formerly held by Prussia and Austria. This increased the Polish territory held by Russia. A new kingdom of Poland was then formed under the rule of the tsar.

Restoring the Monarchies Once the territorial compensation was settled, delegates at the Congress of Vienna turned to stabilizing European governments. Believing that divine-right monarchy was necessary for proper order, the delegates made settlements based on legitimate claims to the throne and restored the absolute monarchs who ruled Europe before Napoleon. The Congress reestablished royal dynasties in France, Spain, Portugal, Naples, Sardinia, and Sicily. In France the Congress officially recognized the Bourbon heir Louis XVIII as the legitimate, or legal, ruler.

To safeguard other ruling dynasties, the Congress placed further controls on France. It reduced French borders to those of 1790 and established **buffer states**, or neutral territories, around French territory. To the north of France, the Austrian Netherlands and the Dutch Netherlands became one country under the Dutch ruler. Thirty-nine independent German states formed the German Confederation, headed by Austria. Switzerland regained its neutrality and independence as a federal league of states. The Italian kingdom of Piedmont united with the Mediterranean island of Sardinia.

Forces Changing Europe

The diplomats responsible for most of the agreements made at the Congress of Vienna were **reactionaries**, that is they opposed change and wanted to return things to the way they had been in earlier times. They strongly felt that Europe could maintain peace only by returning to the tradition of strong monarchies in effect before the French Revolution.

The reactionaries hoped that their plans would thwart the spread of **liberalism**, a political philosophy influencing European people in the 1800s. The liberals accepted the ideas of the Enlightenment and the democratic reforms of the French Revolution. Believing in individual freedom, liberals supported ideas such as freedom of speech, freedom of the press, and religious freedom—which had led to revolution.

The reactionaries also hoped to crush the rise of nationalism throughout Europe. When they redrew national boundaries, the delegates reflected the wishes of the rulers rather than those of the people they governed. The new boundaries thwarted the nationalistic hopes of many groups. For example, the boundaries crushed the Polish peoples' hopes for a united nation. Instead, their land was parceled out among Austria, Prussia, and Russia.

Alliances   The statesmen knew that nationalistic desires for independence, democratic rule, and national unity could well lead to revolution, and revolution threatened everything they believed in. To prevent democratic revolutions, they agreed to form new alliances. Great Britain, Austria, Prussia, and Russia joined in the Quadruple Alliance to maintain the settlements of Vienna. The four powers concluded the alliance in November 1815. France was admitted three years later, when the members of the alliance met for the first time at Aix-la-Chapelle.

According to the alliance agreement, representatives of the great powers were to meet periodically to discuss the security of Europe. Their goals included preservation of territorial boundaries set at the Congress of Vienna, exclusion of Napoleon Bonaparte and his heirs from French rule, and prevention of any revolutionary movements from taking hold in Europe.

With the goal of securing international order based on "Justice, Christian Charity, and

Learning from Art *Prince von Metternich pushed for the creation of the Quadruple Alliance.* ***What was the Alliance's major role?***

Peace," Tsar Alexander I of Russia created the Holy Alliance. Issued in the name of the tsar, the Prussian king, and the Austrian emperor, the Holy Alliance called for Christian rulers in Europe to cooperate as a union of monarchs. Metternich dismissed the idea as "a loud-sounding nothing." Nevertheless, all the invited rulers joined the Holy Alliance except Pope Pius VII and the British government. The Pope had said that "from time immemorial the papacy had been in possession of Christian truth and needed no new interpretation of it." The British government excused itself on the grounds that, without approval by Parliament, such an alliance would violate the British constitution.

Concert of Europe

The two alliances encouraged European nations to work together to preserve the peace. The members decided to have regular meetings to settle international problems. These meetings became known as the Concert of Europe. This system helped to maintain the balance of power and to avoid major European conflicts by resolving local problems peaceably.

For almost 30 years, Metternich used the system set up by the Congress of Vienna to achieve his own political goals: to oppose liberalism and nationalism and to defend absolute monarchies in Europe. His system of beliefs came to be known as the Metternich system.

Metternich's political goals and the Concert of Europe did not go unchallenged, however. In Germany university students demonstrated for liberal reforms and national unity. Alarmed by this revolutionary activity, Metternich persuaded King Frederick William III of Prussia to pass a series of repressive measures in 1819. These so-called Carlsbad Decrees imposed strict censorship on all publications and suppressed freedom of speech. Metternich, with the support of the Prussian king, managed to end student agitation in Germany, but new challenges to the status quo arose in other areas.

Liberal reformers in Spain, for example, forced their monarch to agree to constitutional governments in 1820. Metternich pressured members of the Quadruple Alliance to intervene in those countries to prevent the spread of liberalism. Great Britain, with a tradition of liberalism in government, opposed the action and broke from the alliance. Metternich's system did prevail, however, as French troops restored the Spanish king to full power. But the spirit of revolt did not die, for Spanish colonies in Latin America successfully revolted against Spanish control during the 1820s.

The Greeks also fought for their independence in 1821 when Greek nationalists revolted against Turkish rule. Metternich intervened by attempting to stop other countries from aiding the rebellion. But the British and the French provided assistance to the Greek nationalists despite Metternich's threats. Greek independence from the Ottoman Empire was achieved in 1829.

The stable political system Metternich envisioned throughout Europe would soon be under attack. The nationalistic spirit fostered by the French Revolution would not die in Europe.

SECTION 5 REVIEW

Recall
1. **Define:** buffer state, reactionary, liberalism
2. **Identify:** Congress of Vienna, Quadruple Alliance, Prince Klemens von Metternich
3. **List:** What were the three guiding principles Metternich used at the Congress of Vienna?

Critical Thinking
4. **Analyze:** Contrast the political philosophies of a liberal and a reactionary in the 1800s.
5. **Synthesize:** Create a dialogue between diplomats from Prussia and Austria about territorial compensation to Prussia at the Congress of Vienna.

Applying Concepts
6. **Reaction:** Why were the countries at the Congress of Vienna mostly represented by reactionaries? What effect did the views and policies of the reactionaries have on the spread of liberalism and nationalism throughout Europe?

INTERPRETING DIAGRAMS

If you ever tried to hook up a stereo receiver, you probably noticed that written directions are easier to follow when accompanied by a *diagram,* a drawing that explains a process, an idea, or concept. Learning how to interpret a diagram will help you understand the information it presents.

Explanation

Diagrams use a variety of visual elements to organize information. Time lines sequence events along a line. Circles indicate a repetitive process. Arrows clarify cause-and-effect relationships or a sequence of events. Pyramids show size and proportion.

Most diagrams also use verbal elements—words to identify or label information within the visual elements. These steps will help you interpret diagrams:
- Read the title
- Read captions and text.
- Determine how visual elements organize information and show relationships

Example

This diagram shows France's estate system. The cubes show the relative size and proportion of population among the estates. The diagram's verbal elements also provide information by telling how the first two estates controlled the wealth, while the third estate remained poor and powerless in French society.

Application

Analyze the diagram on page 519. First, identify the diagram's visual and verbal elements. Then explain the purpose of the visual and verbal elements.

Practice

Turn to the Chapter Review on page 541 for further practice interpreting diagrams.

FRENCH ESTATES

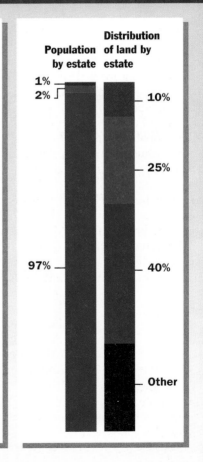

The First Estate
Clergy of the Roman Catholic church
- received income from land plus 10% of churchgoers' income
- paid no taxes

The Second Estate
Nobility
- held key positions in government and army
- lived in splendor paid for by peasants who lived on and worked on their land
- paid no taxes

The Third Estate
Bourgeoisie (Doctors, lawyers, and merchants)
- earned large incomes but resented lack of political power

Artisans (skilled workers)
- suffered from low wages and rising prices

Peasants
- bore heaviest taxes, titles, and fees

Population by estate

Distribution of land by estate

1%
2%
97%

10%
25%
40%
Other

from Les Misérables
by Victor Hugo

As we have seen, literature can be a bridge to the past, transporting us to a world that may seem strange or obscure at first, but that has much in common with our own. Across the gap between then and now we can see faces that we recognize, situations that are familiar, hopes that we share. The selection that appears below was written by one of France's most celebrated writers, Victor Hugo. Hugo lived from 1802 to 1885, a time of dramatic and violent change for France. In this scene, Monsieur Gillenormand is snooping through the belongings of his grandson, Marius. Assisting the grandfather is Marius's aunt. Marius's father has recently died.

The box opened by pressing a spring. They found nothing in it but a piece of paper carefully folded.

"More and more predictable," said M. Gillenormand, bursting with laughter. "I know what it is. A love letter!"

"Ah! Then let's read it!" said the aunt.

And she put on her spectacles. They unfolded the paper and read this:

"For my Son.—The emperor made me a baron on the battlefield of Waterloo. Since the Restoration contests this title I have bought with my blood, my son will take it and bear it. I need not say that he will be worthy of it."

The feelings of the father and daughter are beyond description. They felt chilled as by the breath of a death's head [skull]. They did not exchange a word. M. Gillenormand, however, said in a low voice, and as if talking to himself, "It is the handwriting of that bandit."

The aunt examined the paper, turned it over every which way, then put it back in the box.

At that very moment, a little rectangular package wrapped in blue paper fell out of the coat pocket. Mademoiselle Gillenormand picked it up and unwrapped the blue paper. It was Marius' hundred [calling] cards. She passed one of them to M. Gillenormand, who read: *Baron Marius Pontmercy.*

The old man rang. Nicolette [the chambermaid] came. M. Gillenormand took the ribbon, the box, and the coat, threw them all on the floor in the middle of the drawing room [room for receiving guests], and said:

"Take those things away."

A full hour passed in complete silence. The old man and the old maid sat with their backs turned to one another, and were probably each individually thinking over the same things. At the end of that hour, Aunt Gillenormand said, "Pretty!"

A few minutes later, Marius appeared. He was just coming home. Even before crossing the threshold of the drawing room, he saw his grandfather holding one of his cards in his hand; the old man, on seeing him, exclaimed with his crushing air of sneering bourgeois superiority, "Well! Well! Well! Well! Well! So you are a baron now. My compliments. What does this mean?"

Marius blushed slightly, and answered, "It means I am my father's son."

Art and Literature *The people in this painting are shown rejoicing in Louis XVIII's return to Paris after the final defeat of Napoleon. Other French people opposed the restoration of the Bourbons. In this selection, a grandfather and grandson argue about the French monarchy.*

Art and Literature *This painting celebrates the French Declaration of the Rights of Man. Inspired by the English Bill of Rights and the U.S. Constitution, French revolutionaries created this document to guarantee French people basic rights such as freedom of speech and trial by jury.*

M. Gillenormand stopped laughing, and said harshly, "Your father; I am your father."

"My father," resumed Marius with downcast eyes and stern manner, "was a humble and heroic man, who served the Republic and France gloriously, who was great in the greatest history that men have ever made, who lived a quarter of a century in the camps, under fire by day, and by night in the snow, in the mud, and the rain, who captured colors [flags], who was twenty times wounded, who died forgotten and abandoned, and who had but one fault; that was to have too dearly loved two ingrates [ungrateful persons], his country and me."

This was more than M. Gillenormand could bear. At the word, "Republic," he rose, or rather, sprang to his feet. Every one of the words Marius had just spoken, produced on the old royalist's face the effect of a blast from a bellows on a burning coal. From dark he had turned red, from red to purple, and from purple to flaming.

"Marius!" he exclaimed, "abominable child! I don't know what your father was! I don't want to know! I know nothing about him and I don't know him! But what I do know is that there was never anything but miserable wretches among them! That they were all beggars, assassins, thieves, rabble in their red bonnets! I say all of them! I say all of them! I don't know anybody! I say all of them! Do you hear, Marius? Look here, you are as much a baron as my slipper! They were all bandits, those who served Robespierre! All brigands who served Bu-o-na-parté! All traitors who betrayed, betrayed, betrayed! Their legitimate king! All cowards who ran from the Prussians and English at Waterloo! That's what I know. If your father is among them I don't know him, I'm sorry, so much the worse. Your humble servant, sir!"

In turn, it was Marius who now became the coal, and M. Gillenormand the bellows. Marius shuddered in every limb, he had no idea what to do, his head was burning. He was the priest who sees all his wafers thrown to the winds, the fakir [member of a Muslim religious order] seeing a passerby spit on his idol. He could not allow such things to be said before him. But what could he do? His father had just been trodden underfoot and stamped on in his presence, but by whom? By his grandfather. How could he avenge the one without outraging the other? It was impossible for him to insult his grandfather, and it was equally impossible for him not to avenge his father. On one hand a sacred tomb, on the other a white head. For a few moments he felt dizzy and staggering with all this whirlwind in his head; then he raised his eyes, looked straight at his grandfather, and cried in a thundering voice: "Down with the Bourbons, and that great hog Louis XVIII!"

Louis XVIII had been dead for four years; but that made no difference to him.

Scarlet as he was, the old man suddenly turned whiter than his hair. He turned toward a bust of the Duc de Berry that stood on the mantel and bowed to it profoundly with a sort of peculiar majesty. Then he walked twice, slowly and in silence, from the fireplace to the window and from the window to the fireplace, covering the whole length of the room and making the parquet creak as if an image of stone were walking over it. The second time, he bent toward his daughter, who was enduring the shock with the stupor of an aged sheep, and said to her with a smile that was almost calm, "A baron like Monsieur and a bourgeois like myself cannot remain under the same roof."

And all at once straightening up, pallid, trembling, terrible, his forehead swelling with the fearful radiance of anger, he stretched his arm towards Marius and cried out, "Be off!"

Marius left the house.

The next day, M. Gillenormand said to his daughter, "You will send sixty pistoles [old gold coins] every six months to that blood drinker, and never speak of him to me again."

RESPONDING TO LITERATURE

1. **Identifying:** What political conflict of the period does the clash between Marius and his grandfather represent?
2. **Analyzing:** What sort of person is Monsieur Gillenormand?
3. **Synthesizing:** If Marius's father had not been a hero at Waterloo, do you think that Marius still would have become a revolutionary? Explain.
4. **Thinking critically:** Was the era of the French Revolution and Napoleon "the greatest history that men have ever made," as Marius claims? Support your answer.

CHAPTER 21 REVIEW

HISTORICAL SIGNIFICANCE

Today, the ideals of liberty and equality continue to inspire people around the world. In Eastern Europe and the Soviet Union, and in South Africa, China, and South America, people of diverse backgrounds struggle for political freedom from oppressive governments.

Many of these struggles have been ignited by feelings of nationalism, as people yearn for self-rule and the return of their traditions. As Napoleon learned in the collapse of his empire, even the strictest military control cannot suppress the power of nationalism.

SUMMARY

For a summary of Chapter 21, see the Unit 5 Synopsis on pages 544–545.

USING KEY TERMS

A. *Write the definition for each key term below. Then write one or two sentences that show how the term is related to the concept of revolution.*

1. bourgeoisie
2. tithe
3. estate
4. coup d'état
5. émigré

B. *Write the key term that completes each sentence.*

a. bourgeoisie	h. liberalism
b. buffer state	i. nationalism
c. conscription	j. plebiscite
d. coup d'état	k. reactionary
e. émigré	l. tithe
f. estate	m. unicameral legislature
g. dictatorship	

6. Supporters of the political philosophy of ___ believed in democratic reforms for France.
7. Napoleon's move to become Consul for life was supported by a ___ , or popular vote.
8. Many ___ tried to persuade European leaders to oppose the French Revolution.
9. Feelings of ___ caused people to fight for self-rule and a return to their traditional customs.
10. The Congress of Vienna established ___ , or neutral areas, around France.
11. In the limited monarchy set up by the Constitution of 1791, a ___ made the laws.
12. French revolutionaries resorted to ___ , or drafting civilians, in their fight against European powers.
13. ___ wanted to return absolute monarchs to Europe after the collapse of Napoleon's empire in 1814.
14. When he first gained power, Napoleon established a government based on consuls, but it was a ___ in reality.

REVIEWING FACTS

1. **Identify:** Who made up the three estates?
2. **Explain:** Why did the revolutionaries execute Louis XVI?
3. **List:** What were three accomplishments of the National Assembly?
4. **Name:** What group was responsible for the Reign of Terror? What did they hope to gain?
5. **Explain:** What was the Concert of Europe?

THINKING CRITICALLY

1. **Apply:** How did France's class structure contribute to the French Revolution?
2. **Analyze:** Contrast the ideas of Metternich with those of one of the Enlightenment thinkers.
3. **Synthesize:** What circumstances justify a violent revolution, if any? What other means

could be used to change an unfair system of government?

4. **Evaluate:** In your opinion, did Napoleon's thirst for power hurt or help France?

ANALYZING CONCEPTS

1. **Revolution:** What similarities and differences do you see between the American and the French revolutions?
2. **Conflict:** Before the French Revolution, the Third Estate wanted a fairer system of government. Do you feel that the reforms established between 1789 and 1814 achieved this goal? Why or why not?
3. **Conflict:** Describe the conflict between the Jacobins and the Girondists. What was the result of this conflict?
4. **Movement:** How did the desire to expand help to bring about the downfall of Napoleon's empire?
5. **Reaction:** How was the Congress of Vienna a reaction to revolutionary ideals?

PRACTICING SKILLS

1. Imagine you wanted to illustrate how the French government was organized under the Constitution of 1791. Describe the type of diagram you might use.
2. Suppose you are viewing a diagram in which a number of items are connected by arrows.

The item and arrows are all joined in the shape of a circle. What is the significance of the circle in this diagram?

3. What conclusion would you draw about two pieces of information in a diagram that were presented in different sizes?

GEOGRAPHY IN HISTORY

1. **Location:** Refer to the map on page 988. What is the global address of Paris?
2. **Place:** What role did agriculture play in starting the French Revolution?
3. **Movement:** Why did Napoleon want to prevent British ships from trading at European ports?

TRACING CHRONOLOGY

Refer to the time line below to answer these questions.

1. How soon after the beginning of the French Revolution was Louis XVI executed?
2. How many years did it take Napoleon to establish himself as the French emperor?
3. What event was a leading cause of the collapse of Napoleon's empire?

LINKING PAST AND PRESENT

1. Napoleon tried to use military force to unite Europe under his rule. What recent efforts are uniting the countries of Europe?

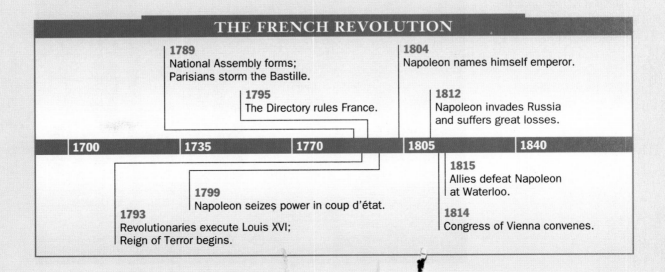

THE FRENCH REVOLUTION

1789
National Assembly forms; Parisians storm the Bastille.

1795
The Directory rules France.

1804
Napoleon names himself emperor.

1812
Napoleon invades Russia and suffers great losses.

| 1700 | 1735 | 1770 | 1805 | 1840 |

1793
Revolutionaries execute Louis XVI; Reign of Terror begins.

1799
Napoleon seizes power in coup d'état.

1815
Allies defeat Napoleon at Waterloo.

1814
Congress of Vienna convenes.

UNIT 5 SYNOPSIS

From about 1600 to the early 1800s, people in the Western world lived through a time of revolution, or swift and far-reaching change. During this period, Western thinkers laid the foundation of modern science and developed new ideas about society and politics. The two most powerful ideas were democracy—the right of people to take a part in government—and nationalism—the right of people who shared a common culture to have their own nation. In some areas, people influenced by the new ideas rebelled against monarchs in the hope of creating better societies.

CHAPTER 19
Scientific Revolution

During the 1500s and 1600s, European thinkers began relying on their own reasoning rather than automatically accepting traditional beliefs. In their investigations of nature, they gradually developed the scientific method. They also developed new instruments, such as the telescope and microscope, to help them in their work. Over time, one discovery or invention led to others, creating an explosion of knowledge known as the Scientific Revolution.

The advance of science transformed the European understanding of the natural world. The work of scientists such as Galileo and Isaac Newton enabled Europeans to view the universe as a huge, orderly machine that worked according to definite laws that could be stated mathematically.

Triumph of Reason Impressed by scientific findings in the natural world, many European thinkers came to believe that reason could also discover the natural laws governing human behavior. They claimed that once these laws were known, people could use the laws to guide their

Learning from Art
This French painting from the early 1700s is titled The Reading from Molière. ***How does this painting reflect Enlightenment ideals?***

lives and to improve society. England was an early leader in this effort. There, philosophers such as Thomas Hobbes and John Locke applied scientific reasoning to the study of government. Locke's basic conclusions—that government's authority rested on the people, and that the people had the right to overthrow an unjust government—later were important in the development of democracy in Europe and North America.

During the 1700s Europeans boasted that they had entered an Age of Enlightenment, when the light of reason would free all people from the darkness of ignorance and superstition. They looked to France as the leading center of Enlightenment thought. Through the printed word and at public gatherings, French thinkers called philosophes claimed that science and reason could be used to promote progress in all areas of human life.

CHAPTER 20
British and American Revolutions

While Europe experienced a revolution in science and ideas, its monarchs faced mounting opposition to their methods of rule. The first successful challenge to the power of monarchy came in England. There, during the early 1600s, a bitter quarrel divided the Stuart kings—James I and Charles I—and Parliament.

Monarch and Parliament   The monarchs were determined to impose their absolute rule on the country, while Parliament, under the control of Puritan landowners, wanted to bind royal authority to its will.

During the 1640s, a violent civil war was fought between the supporters of the monarchy and the supporters of Parliament. The conflict finally ended in 1649 with the monarchy's defeat and Charles I's execution—events that shocked the rest of Europe. A republic was then proclaimed under the leading parliamentary general, Oliver Cromwell. Although Cromwell brought reforms and efficient government, most English people grew to resent his strict Puritan rule. Cromwell's death in 1658 was followed two years later by the restoration of the monarchy under Charles II, the son of Charles I.

During Charles II's reign, the monarch and Parliament shared political power in an often uneasy relationship. When Charles died in 1685, his brother, James II, ascended the throne. James, a Roman Catholic, angered the English with his desire to restore Catholicism and absolute monarchy. In 1688, Protestant nobles in Parliament invited Mary, James's Protestant daughter, and William of Orange, her husband and ruler of the Netherlands, to invade England with Dutch troops.

In return for the English throne, William and Mary agreed to accept a Bill of Rights. This document assured the English people basic civil rights and made the monarch subject to the laws of Parliament. During the next 100 years, England developed into a constitutional monarchy. Under this political system, the monarch's powers were gradually reduced, and Parliament became the major power in the government of England.

The American Republic   By the mid-1700s, Great Britain was trying to tighten its control over its recently acquired overseas empire, especially North America. Enjoying a large measure of self-government, the North American colonies opposed Parliament's efforts to enforce trade laws and impose taxes on them. They began to press for even more freedom from the home country.

During the 1770s, relations between Great Britain and the North American colonies steadily worsened. The arrival of British troops in North America to put down colonial protests signaled the beginning of what became known as the Revolutionary War. In 1776, 13 of the colonies declared their freedom from British rule and became a new nation—the United States of America. Five years later, an American victory at Yorktown ended the war, and the British officially recognized the independence of their former colonies. From the 1700s to the present century, the success of the American Revolution has inspired colonial peoples struggling to escape from the hold of empires.

Following the Revolutionary War, the United States briefly functioned as a loose union of states with republican governments. In 1788, the nation adopted the U.S. Constitution. With its blend of European Enlightenment philosophy and American democratic ideals, the U.S. Constitution served as a model for people in other countries who wanted republican governments.

CHAPTER 21
The French Revolution

The formation of the American republic had a profound impact on the French, who were becoming increasingly critical of their absolute monarchy. Under this sytem, France's few no-

bles and clergy—the First and Second Estates—enjoyed power and privilege, while the majority of the people—the Third Estate—paid most of the taxes and had almost no voice in running the nation's government. During the late 1780s, an explosive combination of social injustice, economic distress, and Enlightenment ideas led to the French Revolution.

The Revolution began in 1789 when King Louis XVI called a meeting of the Estates General to solve the government's deepening financial problems. When the monarch refused to reform voting methods, Third Estate delegates took the revolutionary step of meeting separately as the National Assembly. As the government of France from 1789 to 1791, the National Assembly ended the privileges of nobles and clergy, guaranteed basic human rights for all citizens, and established a constitutional monarchy. Louis XVI, however, was not content to rule

Learning from Art *This 1752 print shows Baltimore as a sparsely populated colony, but it would soon grow to become a thriving American port.* **How did colonial economic interests help to spur the American Revolution?**

under a constitution. He plotted with nobles and foreign monarchs to regain his absolute authority. In the summer of 1792, Austria and Prussia responded to Louis's appeals for help and invaded France. In response, angry revolutionaries in Paris arrested the king and called for a democratic government.

Afer the king's removal, a National Convention elected by all adult males proclaimed France a democratic republic and executed the king. The Convention then drafted a large army to push back the foreign invaders and to spread the revolution throughout Europe. To crush opposition at home, the leaders of the Convention put aside democratic practices and carried out a Reign of Terror, executing thousands of people. The Terror ended in 1794, and the wealthy middle class came to power a year later under a new republican government called the Directory. Plagued by scandal and opposed by both conservatives and radicals, the Directory was overthrown by Napoleon Bonaparte in 1799.

Napoleon and Europe   Although Napoleon professed loyalty to the revolutionary ideals, he made himself emperor and imposed strict rule on France. With a powerful army, he deposed many foreign monarchs and brought a large part of Europe under French rule. However, by 1814, Napoleon's empire was falling apart as a result of the combined military might of France's enemies and the growth of anti-French nationalism in the conquered lands.

After Napoleon's defeat, European leaders met in 1814 and 1815 at the Congress of Vienna to determine Europe's future. Opposed to democracy and nationalism, they sought to re-

Learning from Art   *Napoleon Bonaparte is shown here at the beginning of his military career.* **How did Napoleon's military success allow him to assume control of France?**

turn to the political and social system that had existed before 1789. They restored monarchs ousted by Napoleon to their thrones and adjusted political boundaries so that France would no longer be able to dominate the Continent. Although France never again ruled a European empire, the Congress failed in its efforts to restore absolute monarchy. Democracy and nationalism became powerful forces in the years after the Congress of Vienna and swept aside Europe's traditional social and political order.

SURVEYING THE UNIT

1. **Identifying Trends:** How did the European view of the natural world change from the 1500s to the early 1800s?
2. **Relating Ideas:** How was Enlightenment thought reflected in the political events and the political changes that took place in North America and in France during the 1700s?
3. **Making Comparisons:** Compare the political revolutions in England, North America, and France? Which revolution was the most conservative? Which was the most radical? Explain your answers.

UNIT 5 REVIEW

REVIEWING THE MAIN IDEAS

1. **Explain:** What brought about the Age of Enlightenment? Why was it called the Age of Enlightenment?
2. **Comprehend:** In what ways did European art, literature, and music change in the 1600s and 1700s?
3. **Describe:** What were some of the philosophies that developed during the Age of Enlightenment? Identify the thinkers associated with these philosophies.

THINKING CRITICALLY

1. **Apply:** What effect did the Enlightenment have on the monarchies of Europe? on the common people?
2. **Analyze:** How did the balance-of-power principle affect European political relations between the 1600s and 1815?
3. **Evaluate:** How did Oliver Cromwell both succeed and fail in advancing the growth of political liberties in England?
4. **Synthesize:** Create a chart comparing the consequences of the Glorious Revolution, the American Revolution, and the French Revolution.
5. **Analyze:** How did the constitutional monarchy of Great Britain differ from the presidential democracy of the United States?

A GLOBAL PERSPECTIVE

Refer to the time line on pages 464–465 to answer these questions.

1. What type of government existed in Great Britain as Sir Isaac Newton developed his laws of gravity?
2. Could people in the early 1700s decipher Egyptian hieroglyphics?
3. How many years after the development of the first telescope did Newton publish his theories about gravity?

4. What was happening in the Americas as Michelangelo worked on the Medici chapel?

LINKING PAST AND PRESENT

1. Although the French received inspiration for their revolution from the Americans, the results were not the same. Why did the American Revolution lead to a stable government, whereas the French Revolution did not? What "revolutions," if any, are occurring today that have American freedoms as their goal? Are the current "revolutions" peaceful or violent? Why?
2. The scientific discoveries of the 1600s transformed Europe and the world. What scientific discoveries are changing the world today? How will these discoveries affect your future?
3. Compare and contrast the Congress of Vienna and meetings of world leaders today in terms of (a) the leaders participating, (b) the issues discussed, and (c) the principles influencing final decisions.

ANALYZING VISUALS

Thomas Gainsborough (1727–1788) was one of Great Britain's most revered painters during the late 1700s. In the early years of his career, Gainsborough studied with a French artist in London, learning much about the ornate French rococo style. Thus, despite his British roots, Gainsborough's work exhibits a style similar to that of the great French painters of the 1700s.

Gainsborough supported himself by producing formal portraits of wealthy British patrons. His well-known painting *The Honorable Mrs. Graham* (shown opposite) is an elegant portrait of a high-society figure. The painting was exhibited at London's Royal Academy in 1777. As Mrs. Graham stands in front of a landscape background with her arm resting on the base of

lic, red bonnets, Robespierre, Prussians, Waterloo, the Bourbons.

2. What does the phrase "on one hand a sacred tomb, on the other a white head" mean, and what effect does it have on your feelings toward Marius?

3. Based on what the passage reveals, do you think Marius and Monsieur Gillenormand will resolve their differences at a later time? Explain.

4. Compare and contrast the relationship between the two men in the excerpt with the "generation gap" that may exist between a young person and his or her grandparent today.

WRITING ABOUT HISTORY

1. Describe the best system of government according to the writings of one of the following: Thomas Hobbes, John Locke, Charles Montesquieu, and Jean-Jacques Rousseau. Then take the role of that philosopher, and write an essay on whether or not the United States has the "best" system of government.

2. Research and write a report about the religious life in the country of France during the late 1700s. Discuss the following questions: What role did religion play under the French monarchy? Why did many French thinkers and revolutionaries criticize traditional religion and its values? What kind of religion did they promote and why? How was religious life affected by the coming of the republic?

3. Turn to the introduction to Chapter 21 on page 510 in your book. Read the excerpt from Marie-Victoire Monnard's diary, in which she describes the reactions of the French people to the violence and bloodshed that is surrounding them. Then write either an argument for or an argument against the following statement: "The French people's complacent view of mutilated bodies during the Revolution is similar to my reaction upon viewing violence and war on televised news."

a classical column, she is bathed in light, giving a delicate effect of fine satin and lace.

1. Look at the other paintings from the 1700s shown in Chapter 19. In what ways are they similar to this painting by Gainsborough?

2. How does Gainsborough's portrait of Mrs. Graham reflect the ideals of "enlightened" British society in the late 1700s?

3. Are wealthy people today similarly portrayed in paintings? Why or why not?

USING LITERATURE

Refer to the excerpt from Les Misérables on pages 536–539 to answer the following questions.

1. Define or identify the following terms and people used in the passage: bourgeois, Repub-

UNIT 6

Age of Industry and Nationalism

1750–1914

"Change is inevitable in a progressive society. Change is constant."

These words of British Prime Minister Benjamin Disraeli describe not just a country but the world between 1750 and 1914. New industries sprang up in nearly every country and restructured the way societies worked. Battles for democracy and independence raged as revolutionaries fought to win reform. New technologies changed the ways in which people lived and thought. Around the world, inspired and forward-thinking scientists, philosophers, and political leaders laid the groundwork to lead civilization into the 1900s.

A GLOBAL CHRONOLOGY

	1750	1783	1816
Political Sphere	**1756** Great Britain ousts France from India.		**1803** The United States purchases the Louisiana Territory from France.
Scientific Sphere		**1793** Eli Whitney invents the cotton gin.	**1825** World's first public railroad opens in Great Britain.
Cultural & Social Sphere		**1776** Adam Smith publishes *The Wealth of Nations*.	**1800** Robert Owen founds utopian community in Scotland.

Peugeot automobile manufactured in 1896 in France.

1849	1882	1915
1871 Bismarck unifies Germany.	**1911** Revolution topples Qing dynasty in China.	
	1876 Alexander Graham Bell invents telephone.	**1914** Panama Canal opens.
1848 Karl Marx publishes *The Communist Manifesto*.	**1874** French impressionists hold first major exhibition in Paris.	**1915** Chinese students found reform journal called *New Youth*.

Age of Industry

*C*hange swept across Europe and North America as new coal mines and iron works began to dominate rural landscapes. Susan Pitchforth, an 11-year-old British girl, was just one of the millions of men, women, and children who left farming villages to find work in these growing industries.

Like countless others, Susan suffered difficult and dangerous industrial working conditions. When the British Parliament investigated horrible conditions in coal mines, young Susan told them her story:

"I have worked at this pit going on two years . . . I walk a mile and a half to my work, both in winter and summer. I get porridge for breakfast before I come, and bring my dinner with me—a muffin. When I have done about twelve loads, I eat it while at work. I run 24 [loads] a day; I cannot come up till I have done them all."

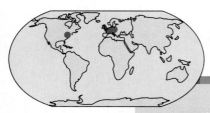

CHAPTER PREVIEW

Key Terms to Define: domestic system, enclosure movement, capital, entrepreneur, factory system, industrial capitalism, division of labor, assembly line, partnership, corporation, business cycle, depression, labor union, collective bargaining

People to Meet: John Kay, Richard Arkwright, Eli Whitney, James Watt, Henry Cort, Robert Fulton, Samuel Slater, Henry Ford, Samuel Morse, Alexander Graham Bell, Henry Bessemer, Thomas Edison, Rudolf Diesel, Wilbur and Orville Wright

Places to Discover: Western Europe and the United States from the 1700s to the early 1900s.

Railway travel transformed daily life in the late 1800s.

Objectives to Learn:
1. What was the nature of life in preindustrial times?
2. Why did the Industrial Revolution begin in Great Britain?
3. How did the technology spur industrial growth?
4. How did the Industrial Revolution affect people's lives?

Concepts to Understand:
- Innovation—Changes in technology spur the Industrial Revolution. Sections 2,3
- Change—Farming communities become factory towns. New social classes emerge. Sections 1,2,3,4
- Conflict—Workers form unions to gain better wages and better working conditions. Section 4

551

SECTION 1

Living from the Land

During the 1700s and 1800s, a series of innovations in agriculture and industry led to profound economic and social change throughout Europe and the United States. Urban industrial economies emerged in these areas and eventually spread around the world. This transformation, known as the Industrial Revolution, began when power-driven machinery in factories replaced work done in homes—revolutionizing the way people had lived and worked for hundreds of years.

Cloth making provides a dramatic example of the far-reaching effects of the Industrial Revolution. In the 1700s a home weaver worked many hours to produce a yard of cloth. A century later, a worker operating machines in a textile mill could make 50 times more cloth.

As adventurous businesspeople brought machines and workers together in factories, industries produced mass quantities. Millions of people in search of new opportunities to make a living left rural villages to find factory work in growing towns and cities. A new era of mechanization had arrived.

A Harsh Way of Life

Before the dawn of the Industrial Revolution in the 1700s, people lived in much the same way their ancestors had lived for hundreds of years. Nature's seasons and religious traditions measured time, and social change was rare. Relying almost solely on farming to make a living, people planted and harvested fields, hoped for good weather, and lived always under the threat of disease.

Families, both rich and poor, remained relatively small because of a very high infant death rate. One baby in three died in his or her first year of life, and only one in two people reached

age 21. Life expectancy hovered around age 40. People expected life to be short and harsh. As one mother in the 1770s said after her baby's death, "One cannot grieve after her much, and I have just now other things to think of."

Only 25 percent of Europeans lived in towns or cities in the 1700s. London was the largest city in Europe in 1750 with 750,000 people. Yet it too had a rural character. British novelist Charles Dickens described the sights of a London morning in the early 1800s:

> *B*y degrees, other shops began to be unclosed, and a few scattered people were met with. Then, came straggling groups of labourers going to their work; then men and women with fish baskets on their heads; donkey carts laden with vegetables; chaise carts filled with live-stock or whole carcasses of meat, milk women with pails; an unbroken concourse of people. . . .
>
> —Charles Dickens,
> from his novel *Oliver Twist*, 1837

Most people in preindustrial times lived in small country villages consisting of a few hundred people. Many never ventured beyond the village borders. When braver sorts traveled to other cities and towns, their tales delighted their less-worldly neighbors.

Village Life

Virtually all rural villagers were farmers. Wealthy landowners controlled the majority of the village land, renting most of it to small farming families. Families owned or rented small strips of land in several areas of the village. This practice ensured both fair land distribution and

Learning from Art *This engraving from the 1700s shows a British family spinning flax into linen.* **What benefits did this domestic system provide farming families?**

economic protection should disaster strike any one field. Farmers worked the land cooperatively, jointly deciding what crops to grow and when to plant and harvest.

In most of the villages, private and public lands were not separated or fenced off. The public lands, called the village commons, consisted of woodlands, pastures, and less fertile land near the village. For centuries, farmers could gather wood and graze their livestock on the commons. Poorer farmers even used these public lands for raising crops.

Village economies were limited largely to the local area because transporting goods to other areas was difficult and unprofitable. Rain turned the few roads into muddy rivers. For this reason, villages had to be nearly self-sufficient. People grew enough food for their families and perhaps a small amount to sell to nearby towns. They made their own homes, clothes, and tools from products raised in the fields or gathered from the land.

The richest rural landowners lived on sprawling country estates with a huge main house, cottages, several barns, and extensive fields. Landowners and their families lived lavishly. Servants ran the households and catered to the families' needs.

People who rented land from the landowners lived quite differently. Most lived in small, smoky, poorly lighted cottages with dirt floors. Since the poorest farming families often did not have barns, they sometimes shared their cramped living quarters with farm animals.

All daily activities revolved around farming, an occupation dominated by tradition. Farmers used the same simple methods and tools of their ancestors and relied on nature to provide good growing seasons. But nature was never predictable, and harvests ranged from plentiful to disastrously small.

Everyone in the farming family worked hard. From morning to night, husband, wife, and children worked together. Boys helped their fathers in the fields or at the workbench. Girls helped their mothers with chores such as milking cows and household duties such as churning butter and preparing meals.

Early Industries

In addition to farming, many people worked in small industries or in coal mines. These industries met local needs for goods such as coal, glass, iron, and clothing and employed a small number of workers. Since many workers were also farm workers, work schedules were coordinated with the agricultural cycle.

During harvest time, nail makers, glassblowers, ironworkers, and miners helped farmers with the crops; likewise, in the winter, farmworkers worked in the mines and in the workshops. This close relationship between farming and industry provided a steadier income to workers than either farming or industry alone.

Making Wool In Great Britain, the woolen industry had for centuries been second only to farming in the numbers of people it employed and in the volume of trade it created. In the 1700s the demand for wool grew so great that merchants hired workers to produce woolens in their own homes. This system of labor, called the **domestic system**, spread to other industries such as leatherworking and lacemaking and was widespread throughout Europe in the 1700s.

The domestic system depended on a network of workers. In the case of wool, a merchant first bought the raw fiber and divided it among several families. Women and children usually cleaned, sorted, and spun the fiber into thread or yarn. Men usually did the actual weaving. Then the merchant collected the yarn, paid the spinner a fee, and took the yarn to a weaver. The material next went to a fuller, who shaped and cleaned the material, and at last to the dyer for coloring. Finally, the merchant took the finished products to market and sold them for the highest possible price.

The domestic system had many benefits. Workers set their own hours and could tend to duties at home during work breaks. Women cared for children, tended vegetable gardens, and cooked meals while they earned money at home. Men carried on farming tasks, such as plowing and planting fields. Children also helped their parents. In one British region, children attended special schools to learn the art of lacemaking. With this skill they contributed to the family income. The domestic system provided work and income during hard times, saving many families from starvation.

Mining Coal The domestic system also had its place in coal mining. Coal fields often lay under farmland. The people who worked the mines often became farm laborers during the harvest, and farm horses pulled coal wagons from the pits. In some coal fields, women and children even hauled baskets of coal from the pits. One observer described these loaded baskets, saying it was "frequently more than one man could do to lift the burden."

With the money earned from mining or farm work, country people might buy in nearby towns the few things they could not manufacture for themselves. Craftspeople sold handmade guns, furniture, and clothing in their shops. Some craftspeople sent their goods abroad to pay for imported goods and traded the rest for food from nearby farmers and products from other local craftspeople.

Yet changes to this way of life were on the horizon. The development of new machinery and sources of power would upset the domestic system, transforming forever the way people lived and worked.

SECTION 1 REVIEW

Recall

1. **Define:** domestic system
2. **Identify:** Industrial Revolution
3. **Describe:** Where did most people live during preindustrial times?
4. **Explain:** What was the main occupation of a preindustrial community?

Critical Thinking

5. **Predict:** During the Industrial Revolution, many traditions were abandoned. How could abandoning tradition help the small farming villages? How might it hurt them?
6. **Analyze:** What were the advantages of coordinating small industries' work schedules with farming cycles?

Using Concepts

7. **Change:** During the Industrial Revolution, work shifted from home to factory. What effects do you think this movement had on people's lives?

The Beginnings of Change

For hundreds of years, British farmers had planted crops and kept livestock on unfenced private and public lands. Village society depended on this age-old system of farming and grazing. By the late 1700s, however, wealthy British landowners would end this open field system, which had been slowly giving way to private ownership since the 1100s.

The landowners felt that larger farms with enclosed fields would increase farming efficiency and productivity. When Parliament endorsed this **enclosure movement**, new laws allowed landowners to enclose private and common lands, combining them into their estates.

The enclosure movement transformed rural areas throughout Great Britain. Many small farmers who had depended on village lands were forced to move to larger towns and cities to find work. At the same time, landowners began to practice new, more effective farming methods.

To achieve the greatest output from their land, these large-scale farmers improved traditional farming methods such as crop rotation systems. Many also experimented with breeding—using larger and stronger animals to produce fatter cattle and more powerful horses. New tools, such as the seed drill, enabled farmers to plant seeds in orderly rows instead of scattering them over the fields. As innovation and competition replaced traditional methods, British agriculture was soon a successful profit-making business, not just a way of life.

Great Britain Leads the Way

This "agricultural revolution" helped Great Britain to lead the Industrial Revolution. Successful farming businesses provided landowners with money to invest in growing industries. Many displaced farmers became industrial workers. These factors added to the key elements for industrial success that Great Britain already possessed—capital, natural resources, and labor supply.

Money and Industry   **Capital**, or money to invest in labor, machines, and raw materials, is essential for the growth of industry. Many British people became very wealthy during the 1700s. Landowners and other members of the aristocracy not only profited from new large-scale farming, but also from overseas commerce and the slave trade, as you learned in Chapter 16. At the same time, an emerging middle class of British merchants and shopkeepers had grown more prosperous from trade.

Industry provided the aristocracy and the middle class with new opportunities to invest their money. By investing in growing industries, they stood a good chance of making a profit. Parliament encouraged investment by passing laws that helped the growing businesses.

Natural Resources   Great Britain's wealth also included its rich supply of natural resources. The country had fine harbors and a large network of rivers that flowed year round. Water provided power for developing industries and transported raw materials and finished goods.

Great Britain also had huge supplies of iron and coal, the principal raw materials of the Industrial Revolution. Iron and the steel made from it proved to be the ideal materials for building industrial machinery. Coal also helped to fuel industry.

Large Labor Supply   Perhaps the country's greatest "natural resource" was its growing population of workers. Improvements in farming led to an increased availability of food. Better, more nutritious food allowed people to enjoy longer,

Learning from Art *The development of machinery such as the power loom helped to speed textile production.* ***Why did such machinery lead to the factory system?***

healthier lives. In just one century, England's population nearly doubled, growing from 6 million in 1700 to 11 million in 1800.

The changes in farming also helped to increase the supply of industrial workers. With the introduction of machinery such as the steel plow, farms needed fewer workers. Former farm workers left their homes to find jobs in more populated and industrialized areas.

Ambitious British people in the middle and upper classes organized and managed the country's growing industries. These risk-taking businesspeople, or **entrepreneurs** (on truh pruh NYERS), set up industries by bringing together capital, labor, and new industrial inventions.

By the mid-1700s, the British domestic system was ready for change. One observer wrote, "The age is running after innovation. All the business in the world is to be done in a new way." The textile industry led the way.

Growing Textile Industries

In the 1700s, people in Britain and overseas were eager to buy cool, colorful cotton cloth. Since the domestic system could not meet the demand, cotton merchants looked for new ways to expand production. A series of technological advances would revolutionize cloth production.

Advances in Machinery One of the first innovations in cloth making occurred at the dawn of the Industrial Revolution. Weaving cloth was difficult and time-consuming work. Weavers had to push a shuttle back and forth across a loom by hand. Then they had to beat the woof—the threads that run crosswise—down tightly against the previous row. The width of the fabric was limited by the distance a weaver could "throw" the shuttle.

In 1733 British clock maker John Kay improved the loom with his "flying shuttle." Instead of pushing the shuttle by hand, the weaver simply pulled sharply on a cord, and the shuttle "flew" across the loom. Wider fabrics could be woven at a faster pace.

Using the flying shuttle, weavers could produce two to three times more material; thus they needed more yarn than ever from the spinners. To answer this need, James Hargreaves, a weaver-carpenter, invented in the 1760s a more efficient spinning machine that he called the "spinning jenny." Early models of the spinning jenny enabled one person to spin 6 to 7 threads at a time; later refinements increased this number to 80 threads at a time.

While the spinning jenny revolutionized spinning in the home, another invention revolutionized spinning in industrial settings. In 1768 Richard Arkwright, a struggling barber with a great interest in machines, developed the water frame, a huge spinning machine that ran continually on water power.

By 1769 spinner Samuel Crompton combined the best features of the spinning jenny and the water frame into a new machine called the "cotton mule." It produced strong thread that could be woven into high-quality cloth.

Producing More Cloth The new spinning machines produced more yarn or thread than there were weavers to use it. In 1784 Edmund Cartwright, a British poet and minister, answered this shortage of weavers with the development of a power loom. Running on horse, water, or steam power, the mechanical loom made it possible for weavers to keep up with the amount of yarn produced.

These new inventions created a growing need for raw cotton. Yet raw cotton was expensive because cleaning the seeds out of it was a slow and tedious job. In 1793 Eli Whitney, an American inventor, developed a machine that cleaned cotton 50 times more quickly than a person could. The cotton "gin" helped the booming British textile industry to overcome its last major hurdle on its journey toward full mechanization.

The Factory System

Since the new textile machinery was too large and costly for most workers to use in their homes, industrialists gradually moved cloth pro-duction out of workers' cottages and into the large buildings they built near major waterways. This marked the beginning of the **factory system**, an organized method of production that brought workers and machines together under the control of managers. The waterways powered the machines and provided transportation for raw materials and finished cloth.

As the factory system spread, manufacturers required more power than horses and water could provide. Steam power answered these growing needs. In 1785 a Scottish mathematician named James Watt designed an efficient steam engine. Watt's steam engine helped to set the Industrial Revolution in full gear. Factories

---

Development of Industrial Cities

The growth of industrial cities depended on geographic factors such as the availability of raw materials and accessible routes. The city of Manchester in northern England had many geographic advantages. It lies within 25 miles of two coal fields and at the meeting point of three rivers—the Irwell, the Medlock, and the Irk. A canal connects the city to the Irish Sea, making it an inland port.

Despite being a wool trade center, Manchester retained a rural atmosphere in the early 1700s. Merchants lived in city townhouses, and people enjoyed sailing on the Irwell.

These scenes changed during the 1800s, when Manchester grew into one of the world's centers for the production of cotton textiles. Mills and warehouses replaced private homes in many areas. The Irwell became so badly polluted that it was described as "a flood of liquid manure."

Although many saw Manchester's transformation as the result of the evils of industrialization, others saw change as a symbol of progress. In 1858, editors of the *Edinburgh Journal* wrote:

Manchester streets may be irregular, its smoke may be dense, and its mud ultra-muddy, but not any or all of these things can prevent the image of a great city rising before us as the very symbol of civilization, foremost in the march of improvement, a grand incarnation [embodiment] of progress.

Making the Connection

1. What factors caused Manchester to become a large industrial city?
2. Do you think that what happened to Manchester can be called "progress"? Why, or why not?

---

that had once closed down when the river froze or flowed too low could now run continuously on steam power. The steam engine also enabled industrialists to build factories in more convenient locations, not just beside waterways.

Industrial Developments

The invention of more factory machinery produced a great demand for iron and steel. Accordingly, the iron industry developed new technologies to keep up with the demand.

In 1783 Henry Cort, a British navy agent, revolutionized the iron industry by freeing it from its dependence on wood to fuel its furnaces. Cort's iron-making method used coal to produce a higher-quality iron. This technique enabled iron refineries and foundries to move away from woodlands and set up near coal fields.

Progress continued in the mid-1800s as William Kelly, an American ironworker, and Sir Henry Bessemer, a British engineer, developed methods to inexpensively produce steel from iron. Steel answered industry's need for a sturdy, workable metal that could withstand the stresses of the new industrial machines. Engineers would design and build bridges and buildings larger than people had ever dreamed possible.

Improvements in Transportation At the same time, people worked to advance transportation systems throughout Europe and the United States. Improvements to the slow, often impassable, roadways began when private companies began building and paving roads. Two Scottish engineers, Thomas Telford and John McAdam, further advanced road making with better drainage systems and the use of layers of crushed rock for construction.

Water transportation also improved. In 1761 British workers dug one of the first modern canals to link coal fields with the industrial city of Manchester. When the price of coal dropped 80 percent because of this efficient transportation system, a canal building craze began both in Europe and the United States.

Harnessing Steam Power A combination of steam power and steel would soon revolutionize both water and land transportation. Robert Fulton, an American inventor, designed the first practical steamboat in 1807. Fulton's *Clermont* set a record by traveling on its own power from Albany to New York City in five days. Steampowered ocean travel followed later. In 1838 the first steamships plowed across the Atlantic.

In 1801 British engineer Richard Trevithick first brought steam-powered travel to land. He devised a steam-powered carriage that ran on wheels, and three years later, a steam locomotive that ran on rails. Later design improvements started a railroad boom throughout the world.

Steamships and railroads helped to transport increasing quantities of goods faster and farther away. The growth of transportation laid the foundations for a world economy and opened up new forms of investment.

SECTION 2 REVIEW

Recall

1. **Define:** enclosure movement, capital, entrepreneurs, factory system
2. **Identify:** James Hargreaves, Richard Arkwright, Edmund Cartwright, Eli Whitney, Henry Bessemer
3. **Describe:** What factors favored rapid industrialization in Great Britain?

Critical Thinking

4. **Imagine:** Write a diary entry describing the thoughts of a British farmer who had been forced off his land because of the enclosure movement.
5. **Analyze:** Each advance in textile machinery created a need for further technological progress. Name two modern-day inventions that have grown day inventions that have grown out of previous technological advances.

Applying Concepts

6. **Innovation:** Is an Industrial Revolution still happening today? If so, name some of today's revolutionary inventions or technological developments. How have they changed modern life?

The Growth of Industry

In 1789 a tall, ruddy young British worker boarded a ship bound for New York, listing his occupation in the ship's record as farmer. Although he looked like the farmer he claimed to be, Samuel Slater was actually a smuggler. Slater was stealing a valuable British commodity—industrial know-how. The 21-year-old spinner headed for the United States with the knowledge of how to build an industrial spinning wheel. When he arrived two months later, Slater introduced spinning technology to the United States.

By keeping spinning and other technologies secret, Great Britain had become the most productive country in the world. To maintain its position, Parliament passed laws restricting the flow of machines and skilled workers to other countries. Until 1824 the law that Samuel Slater had ignored prohibited craftworkers from moving to other countries. Another law made it illegal to export machinery. Nonetheless, by the late 1820s, many mechanics and technicians had left Great Britain, carrying industrial knowledge with them.

Spread of Industry

As British workers left the country, Great Britain gave up trying to guard its industrial monopoly. Wealthy British industrialists saw that they could make money by spreading the Industrial Revolution to other countries.

In the mid-1800s, financiers funded railroad construction in India, Latin America, and North America. In Europe, British industrialists set up factories, supplying capital, equipment, and technical staff. The industrialists earned Great Britain the nickname "the workshop of the world." In most of these areas, however, large-scale manufacturing based on the factory system did not really take hold until 1870 or later. The major exceptions were France, Germany, and the United States.

Because the French government encouraged industrialization, France developed a large pool of outstanding scientists. In spite of this, France's industrialization was slow-paced. The Napoleonic Wars had strained the economy and depleted the work force. For a long time, the French economy depended more on farming and small businesses than on new industries. Yet with the growth of mining and railway construction, a major network of railway lines radiated in every direction from Paris by 1870.

Germany's efforts to industrialize proved more successful. Before 1830 Germans brought in some machinery from Britain and set up a few factories. In 1839 German industrialists used British capital to build the country's first major railway. In the following decade, strong coal, iron, and textile industries emerged. Even before the German states united in 1871, government funding had helped industry to grow.

At the same time, industrialization gained momentum in the United States, especially in the Northeast. British capital and machinery, combined with American mechanical invention, promoted new industry. In time, shoe and textile factories flourished along rivers in New England. Coal mines and ironworks expanded in Pennsylvania. By 1870 the United States was becoming as industrialized as Britain and Germany.

Growth of Big Business

The spread of industry strengthened capitalism, the economic system in which individuals and private firms, not the government, own the means of production—that is, land, machinery, and the workplace. In a capitalist system, individuals decide how they can make a profit and determine business practices accordingly.

Industrialists practiced **industrial capitalism**, which involved continually expanding factories or investing in new businesses. After investing in a factory, industrial capitalists used profits to hire more workers and buy raw materials and new machines.

Mass Production   Looking to increase their profits, manufacturers invested in machines to replace more costly human labor. Fast-working, precise machines enabled industrialists to mass-produce, or to produce huge quantities of identical goods.

In the early 1800s, Eli Whitney, inventor of the cotton gin, contributed the concept of **interchangeable parts**, resulting in increased production in the factories. Whitney's system involved machine-made parts that were exactly alike and easily assembled. In the past, parts made by hand were not uniform—each differed from the next to some degree.

By the 1890s industrial efficiency had become a science. Frederick Taylor encouraged manufacturers to divide tasks into detailed and specific segments of a step-by-step procedure.

Learning from Art   *Manufacturing became more important to the American economy with the building of Samuel Slater's textile mill in Rhode Island.* ***What advantages did building mills near waterways give early industrialists?***

Using Taylor's plan, industrialists devised a **division of labor** in their factories. Each worker performed a specialized task on a product as it moved by on a conveyor belt. The worker then returned the product to the belt where it continued down the line to the next worker. Because products were assembled in a moving line, this method was called the **assembly line**.

American automobile manufacturer Henry Ford used assembly-line methods in 1908 to mass-produce his Model T automobiles. Ford described the assembly line this way:

> *The man who places a part does not fasten it. The man who puts in a bolt does not put in a nut; the man who puts on the nut does not tighten it. Every piece of work in the shop moves; it may move on hooks, on overhead chains. . . . No workman has anything to do with moving or lifting anything. Save ten steps a day for each of the 12,000 employees, and you will have saved fifty miles of wasted motion and misspent energy.*

> —Henry Ford, from his autobiography, *Ford*, 1913

As Ford produced greater quantities of his cars, the cost of producing each car fell, allowing him to drop the price. Millions of people could then buy what earlier only a few could afford.

Organizing Business   As mass production increased, industry leaders strove to manage the growing business world. In addition to individual and family businesses, many people formed **partnerships.** A partnership is a business organization involving two or more entrepreneurs who can raise more capital and take on more business than if each had gone into business alone. Partners share management responsibility and debt liability.

Corporations take the idea of partnership many steps further. Corporations are business organizations owned by stockholders who buy shares in a company. Stockholders vote on major decisions concerning the corporations. Each vote carries weight according to the number of shares owned. Shares decrease or increase in value depending on the profits earned by the company. In the late 1800s, as industries grew larger, corporations became one of the best ways to manage new businesses.

Business Cycles   The growing industries came to be dependent on each other. When one industry did well, other related industries also flourished. A great demand for cars, for example, led to expansion in the petroleum industry. Likewise, bad conditions in one industry often spread rapidly to other related industries.

The economic fate of an entire country came to rest on these **business cycles**, or alternating periods of business expansion and decline. Business cycles follow a certain sequence, beginning with expansion. In this "boom" phase, buying, selling, production, and employment rates are high. When expansion ends, a "bust" period of decreased business activity follows. The lowest point in the business cycle is a **depression**, which is characterized by bank failures and widespread unemployment.

In the age of industrialization, more people suffered during "bust" periods. As industry grew, millions of people made their living in manufacturing. Workers and business owners depended solely on the money they earned to buy what they needed. Unlike in earlier days, they did not grow or make what their families needed to eat, wear, or use.

Science and Industry

Amateur inventors relying heavily on trial and error produced most industrial advances at the beginning of the Industrial Revolution. By the late 1800s, manufacturers began to apply more scientific findings to their businesses.

Communications   Science played an important role in the development of communications. In the 1830s Samuel Morse, an American inventor, assembled a working model of the telegraph. Using a system of dots and dashes, the telegraph carried information at high speeds. Soon telegraph lines linked most European and U.S. cities.

Other advances in communications included the development of the radio. Although British

Scenes of Modern Life

As technology transformed the way people worked and lived, artists began painting modern subjects and developing styles that reflected modern life. The painting shown here, Claude Monet's *Gare St. Lazare* (1877), is an example of this trend in European paintings of the late 1800s. Here the French painter shows the atmosphere of a Parisian train station.

In the early 1800s, the subject of a painting helped determine how important the painting was. Historical paintings showing important events or stories were considered to be the most important paintings. Landscape paintings—paintings without a story to tell—were considered the least important paintings.

During the 1800s, a number of artists began to reject these standards for determining a painting's importance. Landscape painting rose in popularity and importance. Among the subjects artists chose to paint were modern landscapes, scenes of contemporary cities. This subject matter is evident in Monet's *Gare St. Lazare*. The view of the train station is fleeting. Steam and smoke rise from the locomotives, and sunlight filters through the glass-and-iron roof of the building. People walk to and fro, in the hurried fashion of modern urban life.

The development of photography in the nineteeth century may have influenced Monet and his colleagues in their painting style. Photographs froze time, catching a split-second view of a scene. As photography became more and more widespread and sophisticated, it became a challenge of sorts for painters to record in painting their fleeting impressions of everyday scenes.

Responding to the Arts

1. How did the importance of landscape painting change in the 1800s?
2. How does what Monet captured in this painting differ from what a photograph might have captured?

physicist James Clark Maxwell in 1864 promoted the idea that electromagnetic waves travel through space at the speed of light, it took 30 years to apply this idea to technology. Italian inventor Guglielmo Marconi devised the wireless telegraph in 1895. This machine was later modified into the radio.

Development of the telephone in 1876 is credited to Alexander Graham Bell, a Scottish-born American teacher of the deaf. Tiny electrical wires carrying sound allowed people to speak to each other over long distances.

Electricity By the early 1900s, scientists had devised ways to harness electrical power. As a result, electricity replaced coal as the major source of industrial fuel. In 1833 Michael Faraday, a British chemist and physicist, had discovered that moving a magnet through a coil in a copper wire would produce an electric current. Over 40 years later, in the 1870s, an electric motor was based on this principle.

An American inventor made great strides in the development of electricity. In 1877 Thomas Edison invented the phonograph, which reproduced sound. Two years later, he made electric lighting cheap and accessible by inventing incandescent light bulbs.

Energy and Engines The Industrial Revolution surged forward with further advances in engines. In the late 1880s, Gottlieb Daimler, a German engineer, redesigned the internal-combustion engine to run on gasoline.

The small portable engine produced enough power to propel vehicles and boats. Another German engineer, Rudolf Diesel, developed an oil-burning internal-combustion engine that could run industrial plants, ocean liners, and locomotives. These inventions ushered in a whole new era in transportation. France, Germany, Britain, and the United States developed and introduced motor cars.

Gasoline engines carried aviation technology to new levels of achievement. In the 1890s Ferdinand von Zeppelin streamlined the dirigible, a 40-year-old balloonlike invention that could carry passengers. Meanwhile, other scientists experimented with flying heavier aircraft. Wilbur and Orville Wright achieved success in 1903 with the first flight of a motorized airplane. Although the first flight covered a distance of only 120 feet, the brothers flew their wooden airplane a distance of 100 miles (160 kilometers) only five years later.

The new airplanes and other vehicles needed a steady supply of fuel for power and rubber for tires and other parts. As a result, the petroleum and rubber industries skyrocketed. In 1860 the world produced half a million barrels of crude oil; by 1910 annual production had risen to 325 million barrels. Similarly, in about the same period, rubber production increased sevenfold.

Innovations in transportation, communications, and electricity changed life at an amazing rate. The world sped forward into an era of ever-increasing mechanization.

SECTION 3 REVIEW

Recall

1. **Define:** industrial capitalism, interchangeable parts, division of labor, assembly line, partnerships, corporations, business cycles, depression
2. **Identify:** Samuel Slater, Henry Ford, Samuel Morse, Frederick Taylor, James Clark Maxwell, Rudolf Diesel, Alexander Graham Bell, the Wright brothers
3. **Describe:** What are the major advantages of assembly-line production?

Critical Thinking

4. **Predict:** How do you think advances in communications would affect the development of business and industry.
5. **Synthesize:** Imagine you are a teenager living in the early 1900s. Choose one invention mentioned in this section and describe how it changed your life.

Applying Concepts

6. **Change:** What effects do you think that industrial advancements such as mass production and the assembly line have had on workers' lives?

A New Society

Before the Industrial Age, a person's position in life was determined at birth, and most people had little chance of rising beyond that level. Few managed to rise above their inherited place in the rigid European society.

As the Industrial Revolution progressed throughout the 1700s and 1800s, however, new opportunities made the existing social structure more flexible. Many people, such as inventor Richard Arkwright, used their talents and the opportunities presented by the Industrial Age to rise from humble beginnings to material success.

The youngest of 13 children of poor parents, Arkwright trained to become a barber. Yet machines, not his barbershop, occupied his time and energy. Spurred by the developments in the textile industry, Arkwright developed the huge water-frame spinning wheel that was powered by water and spun continuously. Arkwright persuaded investors to join him in establishing textile mills throughout Great Britain.

Soon Arkwright's mills employed more than 5,000 people. He amassed a great fortune, became active in politics, and was eventually knighted by Great Britain's King George III.

The Rise of the Middle Class

Although few businesspeople in Europe and America prospered as Arkwright had, industrialization did expand the power and wealth of the middle class. Once made up of a small number of bankers, lawyers, doctors, and merchants, the middle class now also included successful owners of factories, mines, and railroads. Professional workers such as clerks, managers, and teachers added to the growing numbers.

Many wealthy manufacturers and other members of the middle class strongly believed in education as the key to business success.

Politically active, they became involved in many reform efforts, including education, health care, and sanitation.

Middle-Class Lifestyles   As European and American middle-class men rose in society and assumed the role of sole provider for families, home life began to change. Men centered their energy on the workplace, while women concentrated their efforts on maintaining the home and bringing up children.

As soon as the family could afford it, a middle-class woman would hire domestic help. The number of her servants increased with her wealth. In 1870 an English guidebook listed the sequence in which women hired new help. First she "hires a washerwoman occasionally, then a charwoman, then a cook and housemaid, a nurse or two, a governess, a lady's maid, a housekeeper. . . ." Servants, usually women, did the more difficult and unpleasant household chores, such as carrying loads of wood and coal, washing laundry, and cleaning house.

FOOTNOTES TO HISTORY

SHAMPOO

In the early 1900s, the onset of premature baldness prompted 25-year-old Joseph Breck to embark on a search for a cure to his receding hairline. He tried in vain to develop a product that would bring back his once thick head of hair. Breck's efforts were not completely wasted, however, for he succeeded in developing a full line of improved hair care products, replacing the harsh soaps most people had used on their hair at the time. Soon Breck's businesses led the United States in shampoo production.

As middle-class women freed themselves from more tedious labor, they devoted their time to other occupations, such as educating their children, hand-sewing and embroidering, and planning meals. Magazines for women proliferated at this time, instructing housewives in everything from cooking and housekeeping to geography and natural science.

A typical day for one middle-class woman in the early 1800s began at 6:00 A.M. and lasted until after 10:00 P.M. After waking up the family, the woman breastfed her infant son and then sat down to breakfast with her family. She read the Bible to her other three children, prayed with the servants, and then ordered the meals for the day. During the day she wrote letters, took one child to the park, and supervised the older daughters in feeding the younger children and folding up the laundry. The woman's schedule continued after nightfall. "After tea," she wrote, "read to [the children] till bedtime. . . ."

Middle-class parents sent their boys to school to receive training for employment or preparation for higher education. Sons often inherited their fathers' positions or worked in the family business. Most daughters were expected to learn to cook, sew, and attend to all the workings of the household so that they would be well prepared for marriage.

Lives of the Working Class

As the middle class in Europe and America grew, so too did the working class in even greater numbers. The members of this class enjoyed few of the new luxuries that the upper middle classes could now afford. Most people in the working classes had once labored on rural farms and now made up the majority of workers in the new industries.

At the Mercy of Machinery When British and American industrialists first established mill towns such as Lowell, Manchester, Sheffield, and Fall River, work conditions were tolerable. But as industrial competition increased, work became harder and increasingly more dangerous. Managers assigned workers more machines to operate and insisted that

Learning from Photographs *Loneliness and despair etch the face of this homeless woman holding her child.* **What were some of the social problems created by industrialization?**

workers speed up and perform their tasks as fast as possible throughout the day.

Under the system of division of labor, workers did the same tasks over and over again, and did not have the satisfaction of seeing the completed work. The combination of monotonous work and heavy, noisy, repetitive machinery made the slightest interruption in the work potentially dangerous. Many workers—often children—lost fingers and limbs, and even their lives, to factory machinery.

Time ruled the lives of the industry workers down to the second. On the farms, workers' days had followed the sun and the weather. Now rigid schedules clocked by ringing bells commanded their every minute. One woman who worked in a Lowell, Massachusetts, textile mill wrote about her frustration in 1841:

I am going home, where I shall not be obliged to rise so early in the morning, nor be dragged about by the factory bell, nor confined in a close noisy room from morning to night. I shall not stay here. . . . Up before day, at the clang of the bell—and out of the mill by the clang of the bell—into the mill, and at work in obedience to that ding-dong of a bell—just as though we were so many living machines.

—Anonymous worker,
from the workers magazine,
The Lowell Offering, 1841

In the textile mills, workers spent 10 to 14 hours a day in unventilated rooms filled with lint and dust. Diseases such as pneumonia and tuberculosis spread throughout the factories, killing many workers. In coal mines, workers faced the danger of working with heavy machinery and of breathing in coal dust in the mines.

For these long hours at dangerous work, employees earned little. Factory owners kept workers' wages low so that their businesses could make profits. Women often made half the salary as men for the same job. Children were paid even less.

Workers' Lives   To earn enough money, whole families worked in the factories and mines, including small children as young as six years old. Children often worked 12-hour shifts, sometimes longer and through the night, with only a short break to eat a small meal.

Working-class children did not usually go to school, spending most of the day working instead. Many became crippled or ill from working under unhealthful and dangerous conditions.

IMAGES OF THE TIME

The Industrial Age

Industrialization had a major impact on the living and working conditions of most people. New social problems, and some solutions, arose as a result.

Inventions such as the typewriter helped companies keep up with the increase in paperwork as the pace of production quickened.

To improve working conditions and increase wages, workers organized labor groups such as the Associated Shipwright's Society.

In 1843 an observer wrote that a child worker in the brick-fields "works from 6 in the morning till 8 or 9 at night . . . Finds her legs swell sometimes . . . and [suffers] pains and aches between the shoulders, and her hands swell."

For many women, the industries offered new opportunities for independence. For centuries, women's choices were limited almost entirely either to marriage or to life in a convent. Now they could earn a living. Textile mills in New England, for example, provided young single women an opportunity to make money while making new friends. These "mill girls" lived together in mill boardinghouses where they often gathered in study groups devoted to reading and discussing literature.

Yet for the majority of working-class women and their families, life consisted of a difficult working life and an uncomfortable home life. Workers often lived in crowded, cold apartments in poorly constructed tenement housing near factories. Sometimes whole families lived in one or two rooms.

Because the mill owners often owned the workers' housing, they controlled the rent and decided when and whether to improve living conditions. New urban problems complicated life. Human and industrial waste contaminated water supplies and spread diseases such as cholera and typhoid. In the late 1800s, Holyoke, a Massachusetts mill town, had the highest infant mortality rate in the United States.

Creating a Better Life   In the mid-1800s, factory workers throughout Europe and the United States began to protest the dangerous and unsanitary conditions under which they were forced to live and work. In 1845 American mill workers signed a petition addressed to the Massachusetts legislature:

Unlike children of middle–class families, those from poor families were forced to take jobs, working long hours for low wages.

Urban populations grew quickly in the industrial age, leading to crowded, unsanitary living conditions.

Reflecting on the Times
How are the problems of the early industrial age shown here similar to the problems of today's society? How are they different?

We the undersigned, peaceable, industrious, hard-working men and women of Lowell . . . in view of our condition—the evils already come upon us by toiling thirteen to fourteen hours per day, confined in unhealthy apartments, exposed to the poisonous contagion of air, vegetable, animal and mineral properties, debarred from proper Physical exercise, . . . seek a redress to those evils. . . .

—Lowell workers' petition, 1845

Workers Unite Although governments in Great Britain, Germany, and France began to recognize the workers' complaints and initiate industrial reforms such as better lighting and safety equipment, workers still labored under harsh conditions. Only through forming organized labor groups were workers able to begin to improve their working conditions in the late 1800s and early 1900s.

Workers knew that they could not fight successfully as individuals against the factory owners. They had to join together into groups to make their problems heard. In Great Britain, many workers joined to form worker associations, which were groups dedicated to representing the interests of workers in a specific industry. The associations hoped to improve the wages and working conditions of their members. Eventually these worker associations developed into **labor unions** both in Europe and in the United States in the 1800s.

Union Tactics Workers in labor unions protested in many ways. They organized strikes, in which every worker refused to work. Other times, in sit-down strikes, workers stopped working but refused to leave their work area.

Despite these efforts, unions faced great opposition. Manufacturers complained that the shorter hours and higher wages would add to production costs, increase the price of goods, and hurt business. To discourage workers from joining unions, factory owners added the names of suspected union members to a "blacklist" to prevent them from getting jobs throughout the industry. British Parliament even banned unions in the Combination Acts of 1799 and 1800.

Yet British workers kept their cause alive. They finally won their cause in the 1820s when Parliament agreed that workers could meet to discuss working hours and wages. In the following years, skilled British workers formed unions based on a specific trade or craft, such as woodworking. Because they had valuable skills, these trade union members were able to bargain with employers. When union leaders and an employer meet together to discuss problems and reach an agreement they practice **collective bargaining**. The British unions' power increased in the 1870s after Parliament legalized strikes.

Following the skilled trade unions' success, unskilled workers such as textile workers and coal miners formed unions in the late 1880s. By the beginning of the 1900s, union membership grew steadily in Great Britain, Western Europe, and the United States.

SECTION 4 REVIEW

Recall
1. **Define:** labor unions, collective bargaining
2. **Identify:** Combination Acts
3. **Explain:** How did the Industrial Revolution begin to dissolve rigid class distinctions? How did it create new class distinctions? How were the new class distinctions different from the old ones?
4. **Describe:** What were some of the problems that factory workers faced? Why did they form labor unions to solve them?

Critical Thinking
5. **Analyze:** Why were industrialists often able to subject workers to poor working conditions?
6. **Contrast:** In preindustrial times, families were considered an economic and social unit. How did this notion of family change for the middle class during the Industrial Revolution?

Applying Concepts
7. **Conflict:** What effect did the separation of home and work have on middle-class and working-class people?

DETECTING BIAS

Have you ever read two critical reviews of the same movie and thought that the critics described different films? The viewpoint or set opinion that a writer brings to a subject is called *bias.* A writer's bias is revealed in part by his or her choice of words.

Because most people have pre-conceived feelings and attitudes, their writing often reflects their opinions and preferences. Thus, an idea that sometimes professes to be fact is only opinion.

Recognizing bias in writing will help one to evaluate a writer's viewpoint and to compare the writing with passages by those expressing different viewpoints.

Explanation

When trying to detect bias in writing, follow these steps:

- Identify the writer's purpose for the written material and the writer's position or role in history. For example, if a wealthy landowner in 1790 were to write about enclosure, you might expect a bias in favor of it.
- Examine the writing for loaded language. Emotionally charged words such as **exploit, lambaste, provocative,** and **terrorize** are indicators of opinion.
- Look for words that reflect over-generalizations such as **unique, the greatest,** and **everybody**

- Notice punctuation, underlining, or italicized words that emphasize specific ideas.
- Identify opinions stated as facts.
- Examine the writing for imbalanced presentation—leaning to one viewpoint and failing to provide equal coverage of other viewpoints.
- Assess the evidence of bias and draw conclusions.

Example

Read this quotation from Henry Ford's description of the assembly line: "Save ten steps a day for each of the 12,000 employees, and you will have saved fifty miles of wasted motion and misspent energy."

You know that Ford designed the assembly line, and so you could assume that he will favor it. Ford shows a bias when he uses the emotionally charged words **wasted** and **misspent** contrasted with **save** and **saved**. The words show Ford's bias for the time-saving qualities of the assembly line. If you read the full excerpt on page 561, you will see an imbalance of information. The excerpt mentions no ill effects of the assembly line on workers lives. You could conclude that while Ford's statement can be accepted as moderately factual, it is also somewhat biased.

Application

As industry changed society, some observers suggested alternative courses of action for dealing with industrialization. In the *Manifesto of the Communist Party* of 1888, Karl Marx and Friedrich Engels presented the following point of view. Analyze this excerpt for bias using the steps above.

The bourgeoisie [the class of factory owners and employers] . . . has put an end to all feudal, patriarchal, idyllic relations. It has pitilessly torn asunder the motley feudal ties that bound man to his "natural superiors," and has left remaining no other nexus [link] between man and man than naked self-interest, than callous "cash payment." It has drowned the most heavenly of ecstasies of religious fervor, of chivalrous enthusiasm, . . . in the icy water of egotistical calculation. . . . In one word, for exploitation, veiled by religious and political illusions, it has substituted naked, shameless, direct, brutal exploitation.

Practice

Turn to Practicing Skills on page 571 of the Chapter Review for practice in detecting bias.

CHAPTER 22 REVIEW

HISTORICAL SIGNIFICANCE

The new industries, technologies, and business practices of the Industrial Revolution resulted in seemingly limitless possibilities for people living in modern times. Many of the cities created by the early factories and mills have grown and prospered. International business is carried on with the aid of computer technology.

At the same time, the Industrial Age has carried with it a host of new social and environmental problems and a depletion of natural resources. Today, people face the challenge of successfully integrating industrial development with preservation of their fragile and threatened environment.

SUMMARY

For a summary of Chapter 22, see the Unit 6 Synopsis on pages 682-685.

USING KEY TERMS

A. *Write one or two sentences that explain how the words in each pair are related.*
1. factory system, domestic system
2. division of labor, assembly line
3. partnerships, corporations
4. collective bargaining, labor union
5. business cycle, depression

B. *Write the key term that best completes each sentence.*

a. assembly line	f. entrepreneurs
b. business cycle	g. factory system
c. capital	h. industrial capitalism
d. domestic system	i. labor unions
e. enclosure movement	j. partnerships

6. Small farmers and peasants lost the right to farm public land after the ___.
7. Business leaders who practiced ___ used profits to continually expand their industries, hiring more workers and buying more raw materials and machinery.
8. The money used to invest in labor, machines, and raw materials is called ___ .
9. Risk-taking businesspeople, or ___ , brought capital, labor, and industrial inventions together in business ventures.
10. As workers could no longer afford to buy their own textile machinery, the ___ developed in Great Britain.

REVIEWING FACTS

1. **Describe:** What was life like for a family working under the domestic system?
2. **Name:** Who were three inventors who helped revolutionize the textile industry?
3. **List:** What are some reasons that workers organized into labor unions?
4. **Explain:** Why did Great Britain pass laws prohibiting skilled craftspeople from leaving the country?
5. **Identify:** What were three important technological inventions of the late 1800s? How did they affect peoples' lives?

THINKING CRITICALLY

1. **Apply:** How did the Industrial Revolution affect Great Britain's social structure?
2. **Analyze:** Contrast the life of a farm laborer with the life of a factory worker.
3. **Synthesize:** Great Britain had several key elements that led it to industrialize before other nations. Which element do you think was the most critical?
4. **Evaluate:** What do you see as the positive and negative effects of the Industrial Revolution?
5. **Evaluate:** How can consumer demand influence technological development?

ANALYZING CONCEPTS

1. **Innovation:** It is often said that "necessity is the mother of invention." Using one invention in this chapter, illustrate this statement.
2. **Change:** Do you think that progress is a necessary result of change?
3. **Conflict:** How has conflict between employers and workers produced positive effects for workers in the modern world?

PRACTICING SKILLS

Read this excerpt from "The Gospel of Wealth," an 1889 essay by Andrew Carnegie. Then answer the questions below about bias in the selection.

Carnegie came to the United States in 1848 as a poor boy from Scotland but eventually became a millionaire through work in the U.S. steel industry.

The contrast between the palace of the millionaire and the cottage of the laborer with us today measures the changes which had come with civilization. This change, however, is not to be deplored, but welcomed as highly beneficial. It is well, nay, essential for the progress of the race that the houses of some should be homes for all that is highest and best in literature and the arts, and for all the refinements of civilization, rather than that none should be so. Much better this great irregularity than universal squalor.

1. Is the term cottage positively charged, negatively charged, or neutral? Does its use coincide with the description of workers' living conditions described on page 567?
2. What other evidence of bias do you find in this excerpt?

GEOGRAPHY IN HISTORY

1. **Place:** What geographical feature prompted industrialists to build factories in places such as Manchester, England?
2. **Movement:** What factors influenced British laborers to leave farms and move to cities?
3. **Place:** Why did Great Britain's natural resources help the country lead the way in industry?

TRACING CHRONOLOGY

Refer to the time line below to answer this question.
Using the time line below, trace the development in the textile industry. Why was the cotton gin a major milestone in the industrialization of textile production?

LINKING PAST AND PRESENT

1. What effects do you see of the Industrial Revolution in your everyday life?
2. What changes and challenges has industry presented society in recent years?

AGE OF INDUSTRY

1733 John Kay invents flying shuttle.

1767 James Hargreaves invents spinning jenny.

1785 James Watt perfects steam engine.

1844 First telegraph is sent.

1876 Alexander Bell patents telephone.

1903 Wright Brothers fly in first airplane flight.

1740	1780	1820	1860	1900	1940

1768 Richard Arkwright invents water frame spinner.

1793 Eli Whitney develops cotton gin.

1855 Henry Bessemer obtains patent for mass-producing steel from iron.

1908 Henry Ford develops assembly line.

Cultural Revolution

A new world was in the making. Factories boomed. Cities grew. By the late 1800s, steamships and trains allowed people to move in search of better lives. It was the late 1700s and the 1800s, and rapid change was occurring everywhere. American novelist Theodore Dreiser described the excitement that attracted people to Chicago:

"Its many and growing commercial opportunities gave it widespread fame, which made of it a giant magnet, drawing to itself, from all quarters, the hopeful and the hopeless. . . . It was a city of over 500,000 with the ambition, the daring, the activity of a metropolis of a million."

The Industrial Revolution presented opportunities and difficulties to people and governments in western Europe and North America. Cities became overcrowded. The gap between rich and poor widened. People struggled to make sense of an increasingly complex society.

CHAPTER PREVIEW

Key Terms to Define: laissez-faire, socialism, utopia, communism, cell theory, evolution, atomic theory, emigration, immigration, urbanization, romanticism, realism, symbolism, impressionist, post-impressionist

People to Meet: Adam Smith, Karl Marx, Friedrich Engels, Louis Pasteur, Charles Darwin, Edward Jenner, Auguste Comte, Sigmund Freud, Eugène Delacroix, Gustave Courbet, Leo Tolstoy, Claude Monet, Vincent van Gogh

Places to Discover: London, New Lanark, Central Park

Objectives to Learn:
1. Why did Karl Marx advocate doing away with the existing economic system?

This drawing depicts a typical business district in New York City in 1880.

2. What advances made in science between 1750 and 1914 have improved life today?

3. Why did the population grow dramatically during the 1800s?

4. What did artists say about society between 1750 and 1914?

Concepts to Understand:

•Change—Political and economic philosophies attempt to make sense of a changing industrial world. Sections 1,2

•Movement—People move from rural to urban areas and from continent to continent in search of better lives. Section 3

•Innovation—Scientists give people longer, better lives, and artists reflect the good and the bad in a changing society. Section 4

573

SECTION 1

New Ideas

English essayist William Hazlitt, writing in the early 1800s, described Europe in the critical years after the French Revolution:

There was a mighty ferment in the heads of statesmen and poets, kings and people. According to the prevailing notions, all was to be natural and new. Nothing that was established was to be tolerated. . . . The world was to be turned topsy-turvy.

The Western world did appear to be turning upside down, as society underwent a transformation. In little more than 100 years, the Industrial Revolution converted Europe from a farming economy centered in the country to an industrial economy based in urban areas.

Industry produced great wealth for the middle class. However, workers lived in grim, crowded cities and worked in noisy, dirty mills and factories. Many reformers decried a society of "haves" and "have nots." They argued that the government should regulate working conditions and distribute wealth fairly.

Let Them Be!

The leaders of the Industrial Revolution—owners of railroads, factories, and mines—did not agree with those who called for reform. They believed people should be able to buy and sell, hire and fire, free from government interference. Only then, they said, was material progress possible. Government interference would threaten their growth.

These leaders believed in **laissez-faire** (leh say FAYR) economics. *Laissez-faire* is a French term that means "let do," or more loosely, "let them alone." In the 1700s and early 1800s, well-known economists were promoting this idea.

Adam Smith   Adam Smith, a Scots professor, was the first to explain capitalism and laissez-faire economics. In *The Wealth of Nations*, published in 1776, he justified a change from mercantilism and government restriction on business. He argued that labor, not money, was the primary source of wealth, and that a person's motive for labor was self-interest. Allowing people to act in their own self-interest would bring economic progress and social harmony.

According to Smith, the economy follows the principle of supply and demand. People buy what they need or want, and businesses produce what people are willing to buy. Without government interference, businesses compete to produce goods as inexpensively as possible. Consumers buy the best goods at the lowest prices. Efficient producers make more profit, hire more workers, and continue to expand—benefiting everyone. Competition and free market pricing would work as "an invisible hand" to guide resources to the most productive use.

Smith's ideas were adopted by merchants and business leaders. Great Britain, in the early years of the Industrial Revolution, was so much more advanced than other nations that it flourished under free trade.

A Gloomy View   By the end of the 1700s, some economists began taking a more pessimistic view of the workings of the economy. In 1798 Thomas Malthus, an English clergyman and economist, published *An Essay on the Principles of Population*. Malthus believed that a growing population caused poverty. In his view, because population grew faster than food supply, nothing could be done to prevent a looming disaster. Misery and poverty were unavoidable.

Twenty years later David Ricardo, an English banker and economist, linked the persistence of poverty to what he called the "iron law of wages." According to Ricardo, as the population increased, so did the labor supply. This in turn increased competition for jobs and kept wages low. If the labor supply declined and wages rose, workers had more children, glutting the labor market. Government interference would only increase the competition for jobs, making workers' lives worse. Thus—like Malthus—Ricardo believed poverty was unavoidable.

Looking for a Better Way

Others refused to believe that poverty was unavoidable. As more people became aware of working conditions in factories and mines, criticism of laissez-faire economics mounted.

Early Reformers Humanitarians and religious leaders believed that society should be improved. In the late 1700s and early 1800s, William Wilberforce led a reform movement in England. A member of Parliament, he spoke out on behalf of reforms for workers and the abolition of slavery. Another devoutly religious political leader, Lord Shaftesbury, organized activities to support factory workers. He promoted legislation to limit hours for women and children working in mines and factories.

The work of these early reformers spurred Parliament to establish commissions to investigate conditions in factories and mines. The commission reports raised a public outcry. As a result, Parliament passed the first factory legislation of the industrial era, an 1833 act regulating the employment of children in factories. An 1842 act prohibited women and children from working in underground mines. The Ten Hours Act of 1847 established a 10-hour working day in textile factories for children under 18 and women.

Other Voices of Reform Another reformer, British philosopher Jeremy Bentham, developed the doctrine of utilitarianism. He held that the true test of any action or institution was its usefulness to society: did it promote the greatest happiness for the greatest number? Bentham crusaded for universal public educa-

Learning from Art *Jeremy Bentham's philosophy of utilitarianism led him to work for many vital reforms. He advocated annual elections, equal electoral districts, expanded voting rights, and use of the secret ballot.* **How did these reforms support Bentham's belief in utilitarianism?**

tion, legal reforms, public health service, and improved prisons.

John Stuart Mill, Bentham's pupil, rejected laissez-faire economics. He argued that the distribution "depended on the laws and customs of society." Governments could influence the distribution of wealth by taxing income. He argued for legislation against monopolies and that protected individual liberties. With free thought and free discussion, progress was possible.

Popular English writers also took up the workers' cause. Charles Dickens attacked the misery of industrialization in several novels. In *Hard Times* he described workers' lives:

It contained . . . people equally like one another, who all went in and out at the same hours, with the same sound upon the same pavements, to do the same work, and to whom every day was the same as yesterday and tomorrow, and every year the counterpart of the last and the next.

Socialist Alternatives

Some reformers felt that the capitalist economic system was the cause of human suffering. They argued that the struggle for profits led to misery, not to a better society. Some advocated **socialism**—a society in which the workers own, manage, and control production. Some Socialists believed that production should be controlled by governments, not workers.

Early Socialists   Early Socialists, known as utopian Socialists, wanted to create a **utopia**, or ideal society. They called for a society in which everyone would share equally in society's abundance.

The first to establish a working utopia was Robert Owen, a wealthy Scots manufacturer. Owen believed that competition caused society's problems. Thus, he reasoned that if cooperation replaced competition, life would improve.

In 1800 Owen set out to prove his point in New Lanark, a dreary Scottish mill town. In time he reconstructed it into a model industrial community. Although he did not turn the textile mill completely over to the workers, he greatly improved their living and working conditions. In 1826 Owen sold New Lanark and bought New Harmony, Indiana, where he established a cooperative community. New Harmony became famous, but like other communities established by the utopian Socialists, it failed.

Marxism

German philosopher Karl Marx dismissed utopian socialism as impractical. The son of a prosperous German lawyer, Marx received a doctorate in history and philosophy. When his radical views got him into trouble with the Prus-

sian government, he fled to Paris. There in 1844 he met Friedrich Engels. Engels was on his way to work at one of his father's factories in Manchester, England. Horrified by what he saw there, he wrote a classic book called *The Condition of the Working Class in England.*

Marx and Engels later settled in London and became lifelong friends and collaborators. Engels, a successful businessman, supported Marx, who devoted his life to writing about economics and the rise of the working class.

Marx's Theories   Basic to Marx's thinking were his views of history, economics, and historical change. Marx believed that history advanced through conflict. But, in his view, economics was the major force. Production was at the base of every social order. Laws, social systems, customs, religion, and art all developed in accord with a society's economic base.

The most important aspect of the economic base was the division of society into classes. The class that controlled production became the ruling class. No ruling class would willingly give up its control of production. The only way to make the ruling class give it up was through revolution. Therefore, conflict between classes was inevitable. This conflict, which Marx called "class struggle," was what pushed history forward.

Marx argued that Europe had moved through four stages of economic life—primitive, slave, feudal, and capitalist. During the primitive stage, people produced only what they needed to live. There was no exploitation, or unfair use, of a person for one's own advantage. But once tools were developed and people could produce a surplus, they became exploitable. From then on, history was a class struggle. One class was pitted against another—master against slave, lord against serf, capitalist against worker. It was the "haves" against the "have-nots."

Marx believed that capitalism was only a temporary phase. A crisis in one of the advanced industrial countries would cause the workers, or the proletariat, to seize control from the bourgeoisie, or middle class. The proletariat would build a society in which the people owned everything. Without private property, class distinctions would vanish, and the government would wither away. This last stage would be genuine

communism, with each individual finding true fulfillment. The governing principle would be "from each according to his ability, to each according to his need."

Marx and Engels published their views in *The Communist Manifesto* in 1848. In it, they appealed to the world's workers:

> *Let the ruling classes tremble at a Communist revolution. The proletarians have nothing to lose but their chains. They have a world to win. Working men of all countries unite!"*

Marx expanded his views in *Das Kapital*. The first volume was published in 1867. Before the work was finished, he died, and Engels completed the work.

The Socialist Legacy History did not proceed the way Marx and Engels had envisioned. When they were writing, workers' poverty contrasted sharply with industrialists' wealth. By 1900 conditions had changed in western Europe. Workers could buy more with their wages than they could 50 years earlier. Rather than overthrow their governments, workers gained the right to vote and used it to correct the worst social ills. Workers saw that gradual reform would allow them to share the wealth.

In time, democratic socialism developed in western European nations. Today, democratic Socialists urge public control of some means of production, but they gain that control by democratic means, and they respect individual values.

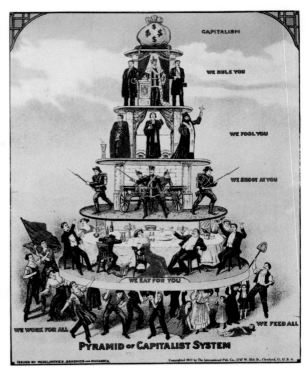

Learning from Cartoons *This pyramid illustrates Marx's theories on class struggle that he believed would lead to a workers' revolution.* ***According to Marx, when did the class struggle begin?***

However, in the early 1900s, revolution swept Russia. Modern communism grew out of Marx's ideas but was imposed by a small elite. Its leaders shunned liberal democratic values and practiced extreme centralized control.

SECTION 1 REVIEW

Recall

1. **Define:** laissez-faire, socialism, utopia, communism
2. **Identify:** Adam Smith, Jeremy Bentham, John Stuart Mill, Robert Owen, Karl Marx, Friedrich Engels
3. **Explain:** According to Adam Smith, why would a laissez-faire policy promote economic progress and social harmony?

4. **Outline:** According to Karl Marx, what steps would societies follow in moving toward communism?

Critical Thinking

5. **Synthesize:** How did social reforms grow out of the beliefs of such leaders as Wilberforce, Lord Shaftesbury, Bentham, and Mill?

6. **Analyze:** Compare and contrast the viewpoints of Robert Owen and Karl Marx.

Applying Concepts

7. **Change:** Why did industrialization make people think about the causes and cures of poverty? Can poverty be changed? Which thinkers of the period fit your views?

The New Science

The scientist Albert Einstein wrote: "The most beautiful thing we can experience is the mysterious. It is the source for all true art and science." Einstein might have been thinking of the 1800s and early 1900s, a time in which scientific discoveries were beginning to unravel some intriguing mysteries. Not only did discoveries help our understanding of the nature of life and structure of the universe, but they also led to advances in medical techniques, longer life spans, and cures for deadly diseases.

New Look at Living Things

In the 1600s scientists had observed under a microscope the cells that make up living things, but they did not understand what they saw. It was not until 1858 that German botanist Mathias Schleiden and biologist Theodor Schwann formulated the **cell theory**: all living things are made up of tiny units of matter called cells. They also discovered that living cells can come only from other living cells, not from nonliving matter as previously thought, and that cells have a life of their own independent of the life of the organism. Cell theory helped explain how living things grow, and it changed people's ideas of what a living organism is.

Understanding the Diversity of Life Cell theory could not explain why the world has so many kinds of plants and animals. In the mid-1800s, scientists proposed the theory that all plants and animals descended from a common ancestor by **evolution** over millions of years. During that time, they said, plants and animals had evolved from simple to complex forms.

In France, the scientist Jean-Baptiste de Lamarck observed similarities between fossils and living organisms. He found that an animal's parts—its legs, for example—might grow larger or smaller depending on how much it used them. He suggested that living things adapt to their environment and then pass the changes on to the next generation. Lamarck's theory, though later disproved, influenced Charles Darwin, a British naturalist who would build his own theory of evolution.

In December 1831, Charles Darwin set off on a world voyage on HMS *Beagle*, a British naval ship. While traveling he became curious about the great variety of plants and animals. He also wondered why some kinds had become extinct while others lived on.

Darwin reasoned thus: Because most animal groups increase faster than the food supply, they are constantly struggling for survival. The plants and animals that survive are better adapted to their environment, so that they alone live on, producing offspring that have the same characteristics. Darwin called this process of struggle natural selection.

In 1859 Darwin published *The Origin of Species by Means of Natural Selection*, a book that startled the world with radical new ideas. Its theories challenged the beliefs of many scientists who believed that species arose spontaneously.

Many religious leaders believed Darwin's theories contradicted the Biblical account of creation. The controversy grew in 1871 when Darwin published *The Descent of Man*, in which he theorized that humans and apes might have descended from a common ancestor. Darwin's theories transformed people's understanding about living things and their origin.

Development of Genetics In the 1860s Gregor Mendel wondered how plants and animals pass characteristics from one generation to another. Mendel, an Austrian monk, experimented with pea plants. He concluded that characteristics are passed from one generation to the next by tiny particles. The particles were later called genes, and Mendel's work became the basis for **genetics,** the science of heredity.

Medical Advances

Through most of history, diseases have killed more people than famines, natural disasters, and wars. In the 1800s knowledge of living organisms brought medical advances that would give people longer, healthier lives.

Understanding and Fighting Disease

Edward Jenner, an English doctor, wrote about his despair in treating disease: "I hate this bluff that my medical practice is. . . . it is not that I do not want to save babies from diphtheria . . . but mothers come to me crying—asking me to save their babies—what can I do? Grope . . . fumble . . . reassure them when I know there is no hope. . . . How can I cure diphtheria when the wisest doctor in Germany doesn't know?" Jenner's sense of helplessness motivated him to begin research on disease.

Smallpox, which killed millions of people over the centuries, was one of the most dreaded diseases. In 1796 Jenner noticed that dairy workers who had contracted cowpox, a mild disease, never caught smallpox. Jenner hypothesized that he could prevent smallpox by injecting people with cowpox. To prove his theory, Jenner injected a boy with cowpox serum and later with smallpox serum. As Jenner expected, the boy contracted cowpox but not smallpox. Jenner had given the world's first vaccination.

More than 50 years later, Louis Pasteur, a French chemist, learned why Jenner's vaccination had worked. In the 1850s he discovered bacteria, or germs, and proved that they cause infectious diseases. He also discovered that bacteria do not appear spontaneously, but instead reproduce like other living things. He knew then that they could be killed and the diseases they cause could be prevented.

In the 1870s Pasteur joined German physician Robert Koch in studying anthrax, a disease deadly to humans and animals. Koch isolated the organism that causes anthrax and later those that cause tuberculosis, cholera, and other diseases. Discovering these organisms paved the way for finding cures for these diseases and led to modern disease prevention.

New Approaches to Surgery

Surgery benefited from advances in chemistry. Until the mid-1800s, surgeons could operate only when their patients were forcibly held down. The experience was gruesome and often fatal. In the

Learning from Art
The momentous medical advances of the 1800s and early 1900s started in science labs like this one.
What advances in the biological sciences do you think made the greatest improvements in people's lives?

1840s a Boston dentist demonstrated surgery using ether. When ether was administered, patients slept through their operations, feeling no pain. Sir James Simpson, a professor at the University of Edinburgh, investigated the use of another sleep-producing chemical, chloroform. Using the anesthetic ether and chloroform led to painless surgery.

Still, many people died after surgery because of infection introduced during the procedure. Joseph Lister, an English surgeon, searched for a way to destroy bacteria and make surgery safe. He found that carbolic acid could be used to sterilize medical instruments. Lister's use of an antiseptic moved surgery into a new era.

Breakthroughs in Physics

The explosion of ideas also advanced the physical sciences. Expanding ideas of Galileo and Newton, scientists created our modern theories of atomic energy.

Understanding the Atom Atomic theory is the idea that all matter is made up of tiny particles called atoms. Although scientists had long believed this theory, it had never been proved.

An English schoolteacher and chemist named John Dalton provided the proof. Dalton discovered that elements are composed of atoms, and that all atoms of an element are

---

CONNECTIONS: SCIENCE AND TECHNOLOGY

Triumph over an Ancient Enemy

Louis Pasteur is shown in his laboratory.

When a wine maker asked his friend French scientist Louis Pasteur to find out why some wines turned sour as they fermented, science and medicine vaulted into a new era. Pasteur discovered that the wines would not sour if they were heated to a specific temperature and bottled without contact with the air.

With his microscope, Pasteur saw that tiny microbes were destroyed in this heating, later called pasteurization. He had proved that the germs that caused contamination came from an outside source. Pasteur worked to show that bacteria were carried in the air, on hands or clothes, and in other ways. He developed the theory that bacteria can cause disease, and he argued that bacteria could be killed only by heat or other means.

Pasteur then applied his knowledge of bacteria to diseases in animals. He injected chickens with a weakened form of chicken cholera to protect them against the disease. For the first time, a vaccine carried bacteria from the very disease it was meant to prevent. When Robert Koch had isolated two forms of the germ that caused anthrax, Pasteur used this information to produce an anthrax vaccine.

Understanding human diseases occupied the later years of Pasteur. On Pasteur's seventieth birthday, scientist Joseph Lister praised Pasteur, saying, "You have raised the veil which for centuries had covered infectious diseases. . . ."

Making the Connection
1. How did Pasteur come to express the germ theory of disease?
2. How did Pasteur change people's understanding of disease?

---

identical and unlike the atoms of any other element. From this theory, Dalton determined chemical formulas showing which atoms make up specific elements. After Dalton, Dmitri Mendeleev discovered that two elements with similar atomic structures have similar properties.

Until the 1890s scientists accepted the notion that atoms were solid and indivisible; then came the theory of the X ray. In 1895 German physicist Wilhelm K. Roentgen (RENT guhn) saw that high-energy electromagnetic waves could penetrate solid matter, including human skin and tissue. He did not know why, and so he named the emissions X (for "unknown") rays.

Excitedly, scientists took up the challenge to understand why X rays could penetrate atoms. They proved that X rays are made up of particles of electricity called electrons, which are part of every atom. Atoms are *not* solid and indivisible as Dalton thought; instead, they consist of three particles: protons, electrons, and neutrons.

These beginnings led scientists to frame modern physics. In 1900 German physicist Max Planck theorized that energy is not continuous, but is released in separate units called quanta. Planck's quantum theory eventually helped Albert Einstein develop his theory of relativity, leading us to the nuclear age.

Social Sciences

While natural scientists investigated the natural world, others explored the workings of society, bringing advances in the new social sciences.

Sociology In the mid-1800s Auguste Comte (kawnt), a French philosopher, helped originate sociology, the study of human behavior in society. He believed that human behavior operates according to discoverable laws. He urged people to apply scientific methods to human behavior.

In the late 1800s, some people used Darwin's theories to explain social, economic, and political realities. Led by British philosopher Herbert Spencer, they thought that in the human struggle, only the strongest survive. They concluded that people such as the poor should be allowed to die off "naturally." This theory, Social Darwinism, was later rejected.

Psychology During this time psychology, the science of human behavior, also developed. In the 1890s Ivan Pavlov, a Russian researcher, advanced the idea that human behavior is based on responses to outside stimuli. In one experiment, he gave food to a dog while ringing a bell. The dog associated the food and the bell so that it drooled when the bell rang, even without food. Pavlov's experiments influenced scientists, who came to believe that human actions were not governed by reason but were unconscious reactions to stimuli. Pavlov reasoned that a person's actions could be changed by training.

No scientist had more influence on psychology than Sigmund Freud (froid). Freud discovered that mentally ill patients under hypnosis remembered things long forgotten. He argued that people's actions grew out of unknown needs. Freud's theories led to psychiatry and psychoanalysis, a method of treatment.

SECTION 2 REVIEW

Recall
1. **Define:** cell theory, evolution, atomic theory
2. **Identify:** Jean-Baptiste de Lamarck, Charles Darwin, Gregor Mendel, Edward Jenner, Louis Pasteur, John Dalton, Ivan Pavlov, Sigmund Freud
3. **Describe:** Explain Darwin's theory of natural selection.
4. **Identify:** What major discoveries were made in physics in the 1800s and early 1900s?

Critical Thinking
5. **Apply:** Explain in writing how a scientist discussed in Section 2 helped to change the ideas of the day.
6. **Analyze:** How did the discovery of bacteria change health care?

Applying Concepts
7. **Change:** How are the scientific understandings of the 1800s and early 1900s being expanded today? What impact are scientific discoveries having on your life?

Popular Culture

As the 1900s began, the new science and technology were making a difference throughout Europe and North America. Most people could now expect a longer and healthier life. The rate of infant mortality dropped in the late 1800s, and life expectancy climbed. In 1850 the average person lived about 40 years; by 1900 most people could expect to live beyond 50.

Thus, as industrialization grew, so did world population. At the beginning of the Industrial Revolution, 140 million people lived in Europe. By 1850, about 100 years later, Europe's population had soared to 266 million. In Europe and the United States, the first industrialized places, the rate of population growth was highest.

Improved Living Conditions

The medical advances of the 1800s were partly responsible for this dramatic growth in population. So too was the availability of more and better food. Before 1740 many people died of starvation and of diseases caused by vitamin deficiency such as rickets. At that time a person's entire daily diet might have consisted of three pounds of bread.

In the 1800s, however, bread ceased to be the staple it had been for centuries. With new machinery and scientific methods, farmers could produce many kinds of foods. Potatoes, nutritious and easy to grow, became popular. Methods for preserving foods, including canning and eventually refrigeration, enabled people to take advantage of the greater variety of food that was available.

One observer of working-class life in London during the late 1890s wrote: "A good deal of bread is eaten and tea is drunk especially by the women and children, but . . . bacon, eggs and fish appear regularly in the budgets. A piece of meat cooked on Sundays serves also for dinner on Monday and Tuesday." Some Europeans imported corn from the United States and fruit and frozen meat from Australia and New Zealand.

Seeking a Better Life As the population grew, people became more mobile. Railroads revolutionized not only the food people ate, but also the way they lived. In 1860 London's Victoria Station opened, making it easier for Londoners to leave their crowded city. Steamships carried people to other countries and continents in search of a better life. Between 1870 and 1900, more than 25 million people left Europe for the United States; others moved to South America, South Africa, and Australia.

For a number of reasons, some Europeans chose **emigration**, leaving their homelands to settle elsewhere. Some looked for higher-paying jobs and better working conditions. Others sought to escape discrimination and persecution by oppressive governments. Still others hoped to escape famine.

Advertisements of steamship companies, along with low fares, lured many immigrants to the United States. Industries looking for cheap labor offered additional encouragement. Some U.S. industrialists sent recruiters whose task was to urge people to leave Europe and move to the United States.

Twelve-year-old Mary Antin joined thousands of Russian Jews fleeing persecution in 1894. Many years earlier Mary's father had **immigrated**, or moved permanently, to the United States. Mary, her mother, and her brothers and sisters endured a harrowing journey across Europe and the Atlantic Ocean to join him in Boston, Massachusetts. Mary wrote of her experiences: "And so suffering, fearing, brooding, and rejoicing, we crept nearer and nearer to the coveted shore until on a glorious May morning . . . our eyes beheld the Promised Land and my father received us in his arms."

Most immigrants left their homes knowing they would never see their parents or their birthplace again. The ocean voyage often proved a frightening experience. One youngster remembered "the howling darkness, the white rims of the mountain-high waves speeding like maddened dragons toward the tumbling ship."

When the immigrants reached their new homes, many learned that their troubles had only begun. Now they had to find housing and jobs in strange surroundings where they did not know the culture or the language and were unfamiliar with the monetary system. Some people took advantage of the European immigrants, who seemed to them strange "foreigners."

From Country to City   Some moved within their own country. Cities around the world were absorbing newcomers who were moving from rural villages to find new opportunities. As farms grew larger and more mechanized, they needed fewer workers. The growing industries in or near the cities offered new and challenging ways to make a living.

Although the new city dwellers faced no language barriers, some of their problems were similar to those of the European immigrants. Their old life was gone, with its known boundaries, familiar people, and established routines. Although work was plentiful, living quarters in the cities were often cramped, and neighbors might be less friendly than people they had known. British poet Lord Byron summed up the feelings of many newcomers to the city:

> *I live not in myself, but I become a*
> *Portion of that around me: and to me*
> *High mountains are a feeling, but the hum*
> *Of human cities torture.*

Growth of Cities

The movement of people into the cities resulted in the **urbanization,** or the spread of city life, of the industrialized countries. A country is

Learning from Photographs *This photo was taken in New York around 1900.* **What can you discern from it about city life at the time?**

urbanized when more people live in the cities than in the country. Great Britain is a prime example. In 1800 London was its only city with a population of more than 100,000. By 1851 Britain had nine such cities. In the same year, and for the first time, slightly more than half of the British people lived in cities. By 1914 that figure had reached 80 percent.

Urbanization was taking place elsewhere as well. In 1914, 60 percent of the Germans, 50 percent of the Americans, and 45 percent of the French were city dwellers.

As people moved to cities, they began to marry earlier. Children could increase a family's income by working in factories. As a result, people had more children, adding to the population.

The cities' growth soon outpaced their ability to provide needed housing and sanitation. Few cities had building codes that mandated adequate housing. Houses were built together in long rows, one against another. The workers crowded together in damp, cold, unsanitary rooms, with fire a constant danger.

The factories added to the unpleasant city environment. Here is a report on the working conditions of British miners in 1843: "Sheffield is one of the dirtiest and most smoky towns I ever saw. The town is also very hilly, and the smoke ascends the streets, instead of leaving them. . . . One cannot be long in the town without experiencing the necessary inhalation of soot."

City Services   City governments in Europe and the United States began to look for solutions to the overwhelming troubles. They saw that one of the most pressing problems was sanitation. An observer in the British city of Leeds reported, "The ashes, garbage, and filth of all kinds are thrown from the doors and windows of the houses upon the surface of the streets and courts." Ditches and open sewers carried waste from public toilets. Polluted water encouraged epidemics of cholera and other diseases, especially in the crowded slums.

In the late 1800s, the germ theory and the newly invented iron pipe spurred city leaders to clean up their cities. They installed closed sewer lines and improved garbage collection. Police and fire protection created safer cities.

As city planning progressed, a number of city governments set aside areas as parks. In New York City, landscape architect Frederick Law Olmsted saw the need for "a simple, broad, open space of clean greensward [grassy turf]" enclosed by a large enough green space to "completely shut out the city." With the architect and landscape designer Calvert Vaux, Olmstead designed Central Park in 1858.

IMAGES OF THE TIME

Changing Times

As urban populations grew in number during the Industrial Age, people began to spend their leisure time in new ways.

The bicycle became popular in the late 1800s. A family in New York poses with their bicycles, ready for an outing.

This biscuit tin with colorful scenes from popular folklore brightened up the home of a middle-class English family.

With advances in railway and bus transportation, more and more people could live outside the city in areas called suburbs. Yet until the late 1800s, the advantages of living in the suburbs and working in the city were available only to people in the middle class. Working-class people, who were far more numerous, could seldom afford to travel between their home and their work.

Leisure Time   Leisure time activities expanded for the middle classes and for the working classes. Men and women took more outings and enjoyed more cultural activities. Newspapers helped to make people interested in places and events outside of their own neighborhoods and communities.

In the 1700s the fine arts were available only to the wealthy upper classes. Concerts were performed in palaces and grand homes, or they were performed in churches. Wealthy aristocrats, prosperous merchants, and religious leaders commissioned cultural events and artworks, such as concerts and paintings, to commemorate special events or to honor special people.

In the 1800s, however, fine art and music became available to middle- and working-class people in the city. City governments in Europe and North America built concert halls and opera houses, such as London's vast Albert Hall, erected in 1871. Cities sponsored the opening of art museums, such as the great Louvre (loov) Museum in Paris.

When people were not visiting libraries and museums, they went to amusement parks, which provided shows, rides, games, and food. Sports such as soccer and rugby began to be organized between cities and around the nation. Many people also enjoyed archery, lawn tennis, and cricket.

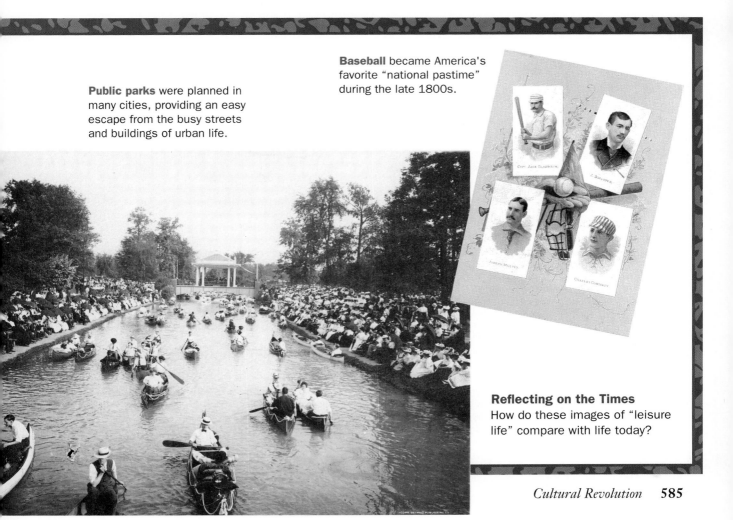

Public parks were planned in many cities, providing an easy escape from the busy streets and buildings of urban life.

Baseball became America's favorite "national pastime" during the late 1800s.

Reflecting on the Times
How do these images of "leisure life" compare with life today?

New Interest in Education

In the early 1800s, when governments began to support public schools, their reasons were political. For example, the Prussian government established public schools to train its people in citizenship and in devotion to the monarcy and the army. In the United States, government support for public schools grew out of a desire to foster national unity after the Revolutionary War.

By the late 1800s, as people grew more and more interested in improving their lives, they became more actively involved in promoting education. Both in Europe and the United States, they supported education that was funded by the government and available to everyone. Believing education would improve their children's chances for a better life, they voted for increased educational opportunities. Schools and colleges were also established to provide better training for teachers.

The new kind of society—urbanized and industrialized—also benefited from the cause of public education. Industrialists needed employees who could read and write. Advanced technologies based on science depended on workers who had scientific training. Many people came to see that an ever more complex society would demand a well-educated populace. People were needed who could participate intelligently in public affairs.

Education for Women Education for women was a hotly debated topic in the 1800s. Some felt that women's roles as wives and homemakers did not require education. Others believed women should be given the same educational opportunities as men. Girls were included in the laws providing education to all. Still, they could usually attend only elementary schools. Access to secondary education was limited only to the wealthy few.

Determined to offer higher education to women, some people began to open secondary schools and colleges especially for them. In 1837, American educator Mary Lyon opened the first women's college, the Mount Holyoke Female Seminary, which later became Mount Holyoke College in Massachusetts. In 1874 the London School of Medicine was opened, and after two years of bitter debate, the British Parliament finally allowed women to be registered as doctors.

Results of Education The advances in education created a growing demand for accessible reading materials. Magazines and books became popular. Libraries with large collections opened as early as the 1840s in major cities such as Paris and London. Lending libraries loaned books for small fees.

Mass-circulation newspapers were first printed at this time, and by the mid-1800s, more than 500 newspapers were published in the United States. Newspaper publishers benefited from the combination of rapid communication provided by the telegraph, cheaper printing methods, and improved distribution by railroad and steamship.

SECTION 3 REVIEW

Recall
1 **Define:** emigration, immigration, urbanization
2. **Identify:** Frederick Law Olmsted, Mary Lyon
3. **Explain:** What caused the increases and shifts in population in the late 1800s?
4. **Describe:** List three improvements in city life that were made in the 1800s and the early 1900s.

Critical Thinking
5. **Synthesize:** Compare the experience of emigrating to another country with that of moving from the country to the city.
6. **Analyze:** Contrast attitudes about women's education now with attitudes in the late 1800s. Explain reasons for the differences.

Applying Concepts
7. **Movement:** Why did many people in Europe and North America move in the late 1800s and early 1900s? Do the same reasons apply today?

Revolution in the Arts

European and American artists in the 1800s mirrored society's mixed feelings about the rapid disappearance of the old order and the uncertainty of the new. A growing middle class created a larger audience for music, literature, and poetry. Formerly, artists had depended on patronage by the wealthy. Now, although some artists sought support in the new industrial society, others rebelled against middle-class values and shunned patronage of any kind, preferring to work independently. In fact, those who rebelled would dominate the arts in the late 1700s and early 1800s.

The Romantic Movement

By the late 1700s, artists had begun to react to the emphasis on order and reason that spread during the Enlightenment. The French philosopher Jean-Jacques Rousseau taught that people were naturally good and needed only to be free. In rejecting society's formal structures and rules, Rousseau anticipated **romanticism**, a movement in which artists would emphasize human emotion and imagination over reason.

Romantic artists tried to free themselves from the rigid forms and structures of neoclassical art. Rejecting the mechanization and ugliness of industrialized society, many turned to nature, glorifying its awesome power and quiet beauty.

Many romantic artists looked to the past, admiring the mythical heroes of old. They felt compassion for the weak and oppressed, and they celebrated the lives of "simple peasants." The struggle for personal freedom and heroic rebellion against society's established rules are frequent themes in their works. The French poet Charles Baudelaire described the movement: "Romanticism is precisely situated neither in choice of subject nor in exact truth, but in a way of feeling."

Romantic Music The composers of the Enlightenment had emphasized form and order, but romantic composers departed from traditional forms and styles. They often fused music

Learning from Art *Romantic artists made the past—with its great castles and dashing heroes—and nature—in all its freedom and beauty—the subjects of fiction, poetry, and painting.* **How does the image above differ from a realistic picture of the same setting?**

with imaginative literature, creating operas—dramas set to music—and *lieder* (LEED uhr)—art songs, or poems set to music.

Even in purely instrumental music, they tried to evoke images and moods. Short piano pieces called "character pieces" or "songs without words" had such titles as "March of the Dwarves," "Venetian Gondola Song," and "Nocturne" ("night piece"). Music was meant to stir the emotions—whether in large works, such as symphonies by German composer Ludwig van Beethoven (BAY toh vuhn) or Russian composer Peter Tchaikovsky (chy KAHF skee), or in smaller, more intimate works, such as piano pieces by Poland's Frédéric Chopin (SHOH pan) or the *lieder* of Austria's Franz Schubert. Romantic music expressed a broad range of emotion—from utter sadness to glorious triumph. Melodies from folk music added emotional power to romantic music, as in works by Czech composer Antonín Dvořák (DVAWR zhahk), whose symphony *From the New World* echoes American spirituals.

At the same time, instrument builders were increasing the range and power of instruments, particularly the piano. In fact, pianos found a place not only in concert halls but also in many households. Orchestras grew until they reached the nearly 200 players needed to perform Hector Berlioz's (BEHR lee ohz) *Symphonie Fantastique*. This elaboration led to the building of large public concert halls in many large cities. Going to concerts or operas and making music at home became favorite middle-class pastimes.

Romantic Literature

Like romantic composers, romantic writers created emotion-filled, imaginative works. Early leaders of the romantic movement in literature include German writers Friedrich von Schiller and Johann Wolfgang von Goethe (GUHR tuh). Schiller glorified freedom fighters, such as the legendary hero William Tell. His drama with that title is about the medieval Swiss struggle for freedom. Goethe is best known for *Faust*, a drama about human striving and the need for redemption.

France produced some of the most popular romantic writers. Alexandre Dumas's novel *The Three Musketeers* recounts the exploits of three dashing adventurers in the 1600s. Aurore Dupin, better known as George Sand, made peasants and workers heroes in her fiction. The novels of Victor Hugo, the foremost French romanticist, include *The Hunchback of Notre Dame* and *Les Misérables*, tales portraying human suffering with compassion and power.

Romanticism was also influential in Great Britain. Scots writer Sir Walter Scott won a huge following with his historical novels *Ivanhoe*, *Quentin Durward*, and *The Talisman*. Another Scot, Robert Burns, showed deep feeling for nature and romantic love in his poetry. English poet and painter William Blake attacked the growing results of industrialization in *Songs of Innocence* and *Songs of Experience*.

Similar themes fill the works of English poets Samuel Taylor Coleridge and William Wordsworth. Together they published *Lyrical Ballads* in 1798. The first significant work of romantic poetry, it expressed their belief that nature embodied a universal spirit uniting all things. Wordsworth especially blamed industrialization for the decline in religious faith and the loss of traditional values.

Other English romantic poets were John Keats, Percy Bysshe Shelley, and Lord Byron. In "Ode on a Grecian Urn," Keats expressed the romantic philosophy: "Beauty is truth, truth beauty,—that is all Ye know on earth, and all ye need to know."

Romantic Painting

Painters, like writers, reflected romantic ideals. Turning from the order, clarity, and balance of the neoclassical style, painters began to portray exotic, powerful subjects in a dramatic and colorful way. They sought to explore the extremes of human emotion.

One of romanticism's most famous paintings is Antoine-Jean Gros's *Napoleon in the Plague House at Jaffa*, which shows Napoleon as a godlike ruler visiting his plague-stricken soldiers. The lighting is dramatic, the architecture exotic, and the victims' suffering intense.

Eugène Delacroix's *Liberty Leading the People* shows the figure of Liberty as a brave woman carrying a flag and leading patriots through the streets of Paris. Like many other romantic works, the painting was meant to stir the emotions, not appeal to the intellect.

Learning from Art The Gleaners, *by Jean-François Millet, depicts French peasant women picking up leftover grain after a harvest. When the painting was first exhibited in Paris in 1857, it was criticized by some as supporting revolution.* **Why do you think realist painters chose to call attention to society's problems?**

The Turn Toward Realism

In the mid-1800s, some artists began to reject the sentimentality of romanticism. They sought to portray life in a realistic manner. In France, painter Gustave Courbet (koor BEH) expressed the idea behind this style, known as **realism:** "Painting. . . does not consist of anything but the presentation of real and concrete things." Realist painters and writers wished to portray life as it was, not to escape from it.

Courbet's own large, somber canvases presented images from French life. He called attention to the less fortunate members of society and their difficult circumstances. *Burial at Ornans* portrayed peasants from his hometown standing around the grave of a loved one. He portrayed the peasants honestly rather than sentimentally, explaining to his friends that the work's real title was *The Burial of Romanticism.* By the end of the 1850s, other artists had joined Courbet in painting realistically. Among the most notable were Honoré Daumier (doh MYAY) and Jean-François Millet (mee LAY).

Realism in Literature Realism also flourished in literature. French writer Honoré de Balzac grouped about 90 of his novels and short stories of French life in the 1800s into a collection he called *The Human Comedy.* Many described frankly the greed and stupidity that Balzac saw in the growing middle class.

Gustave Flaubert (floh BEHR), another French writer, portrayed the conflict between dreary realities and romantic dreams in *Madame Bovary,* the story of a young woman married to a dull provincial doctor. The novel created such a stir among the middle class that the French government sued Flaubert for committing an "outrage to public morals and religion."

In *Vanity Fair,* English novelist William Makepeace Thackeray poked fun at the middle and upper classes with their showy displays of wealth. Another English writer, Mary Ann Evans, wrote under the pen name George Eliot. Her novels portrayed the rigidity and senselessness of the British social order.

Charles Dickens, the foremost English realistic writer, spoke out on behalf of the poor.

Dickens focused on the deplorable conditions in the prisons, hospitals, and poorhouses of London. In his novel *Hard Times,* he attacked the materialism of Coketown, a fictional city.

Russian writers came to be known for their penetrating novels about the human spirit. In 1852 Ivan Turgenev wrote *A Sportsman's Sketches,* describing walks through the woods near his home and conversations with the peasants he met along the way. Turgenev pictured the peasants as wise and intelligent, and he drew attention to their plight.

The novels of Russian writer Leo Tolstoy also reflected his compassion for the peasants and gave his analysis of social customs. *War and Peace* is a family novel in which Tolstoy takes five families through the stages of life. It is also a historical novel about Napoleon's invasion of Russia in 1812. *Anna Karenina,* Tolstoy's second masterpiece, tells how a woman's faith in romantic love leads to her downfall.

The works of American novelist Theodore Dreiser belong to a pessimistic style of realism called naturalism, in which writers tried to apply scientific methods to imaginative writing. In Dreiser's novel *An American Tragedy*, a young man is executed for killing his pregnant girlfriend. To Dreiser, the man is a victim whose tragedy results from circumstances over which he has no control.

Symbolism   Some writers became disgusted with what they viewed as the ugly and brutal realities of European industrial civilization. To escape, they created a world of shadowy images evoked by symbols. This movement, called **symbolism,** began in France and was led by the poet Stéphane Mallarmé (mah lahr MAY), who believed that "to name an object is to destroy three quarters of the enjoyment of a poem, which is made up of the pleasure of guessing little by little." He and his followers, Paul Verlaine and Arthur Rimbaud, gave impressions by suggestion rather than by direct statement.

Symbolism spread to the other arts and to other countries. The symbolists focused on the exotic, using imagery to suggest the world of the spirit. Intellectuals applauded this effort, but the average reader found symbolism difficult to understand.

New Trends in Painting

Intense competition and rigid, traditional standards characterized the artistic world in the 1800s. An artist's works had to be considered "correct" and the subject matter "proper" by judges at London's Royal Academy of Art or Paris's École des Beaux-Arts (School of Fine Arts). Acceptance by those schools and a place in their yearly exhibitions were crucial to a beginning artist's success.

In 1863 the Ecole turned down more than 3,000 of the 5,000 works that were submitted for its approval—the highest proportion of rejections that anyone could remember. Napoleon III, the French emperor at the time, decided to hold an exhibit to let the public see the paintings that had been rejected by the Ecole. Those paintings delighted many people and gave the painters renewed hope that their works would win recognition.

Impressionism   Among the rejected paintings were many by painters who came to be known by the name of **impressionists.** They abandoned many of the rules on which earlier painters had based their art—rules about proper subject matter and traditional techniques of line, perspective, and studio lighting. Fascinated by color and light, the impressionists sought to capture the impression a subject made on their senses. Their figures were most generally distorted, for they sought to represent an entire object by showing only a few of its more significant details. They rejected the use of black to represent shadows, relying instead on deeper shades of the same hue and creating paintings of "pure color."

The impressionists tried to capture the essence of the fleeting moment—the sparkle of sunlight on a river, for example. They moved out of the studio and into the real world, choosing to work outdoors, in theaters, and in cafes.

Pierre-Auguste Renoir (rehn WAHR) painted idealized portraits of women and children and outdoor scenes. Claude Monet (mo NEH), one of the most famous impressionists, painted series of paintings on the same subject to show variations in light and color during various times of the day and seasons of the year.

Henri Matisse

Henri Matisse's painting *The Red Room* reflects the ideas of a group of artists who worked in France around 1905. Known as the *fauves* (meaning "wild beasts"), they worked together for about three years. They sought to interpret and communicate their experience of nature with intense, vivid colors. At times they painted objects in colors that were entirely different from the objects' real colors— tree trunks in green or purple or red, for example. Although the fauves exhibited their paintings together and shared enthusiasm for color as an expressive tool, each had his own style. Henri Matisse was probably the most important artist in the group.

Matisse's The Red Room *is an example of fauvist painting.*

From the time of the Renaissance, artists had generally thought of the surface of a painting as a kind of window through which the viewer looked. Painters tried to create in their paintings the illusion of three-dimensional space receding into the distance. To do so, they used converging lines and lighting effects to create perspective, a sense of depth or distance.

In *The Red Room,* as in many of his fauvist paintings, Matisse rejects this Renaissance idea of the picture as a window. Instead, he emphasizes the painting's two-dimensional surface. He uses large, flat areas of color with no shading. In doing so, Matisse focuses the viewer's attention on the bright, pure colors and bold patterns. He makes it almost impossible for the viewer to "read" this image as a three-dimensional world. The nearly identical patterns and colors on the wallpaper and tablecloth in *The Red Room* blend, as if they were on the same surface.

In the real world, of course, the subject of Matisse's painting is three-dimensional. The room has a woman, a table and chairs, and a window overlooking a lush, green garden. All of these require a three-dimensional space if they are to be seen realistically. But Matisse uses a style that denies the three-dimensional quality of his subject. With intense color and bold patterns, he makes the image appear decorative and two-dimensional.

Notice the kinds of choices that the artist has made. Matisse chooses not to depict this scene as a photographer would, with precise scientific accuracy. Like other fauvists, he believes a scientific approach will not communicate his own subjective, nonscientific experience. Essentially, Matisse uses colors and patterns to express his own personal experience of the scene.

Responding to the Arts

1. What Renaissance concept did the fauves reject?
2. How does Matisse's *The Red Room* sum up the aims of the fauves?

Learning from Art *This impressionist painting,* Child with a Whip, *was created by Pierre-Auguste Renoir.* **How does it idealize childhood and the outdoors?**

Post-Impressionism In the late 1880s, some artists turned away from impressionism. Known as **post-impressionists,** they formed their styles independently to express in different ways the chaos and complexity around them. One of their leaders was Paul Cézanne (say ZAN). Earlier, he had identified with romanticism and impressionism. By the 1880s he had laid the foundation for post-impressionism when he declared, "I do not want to reproduce nature, I want to re-create it."

Georges Seurat (suh RAH), another post-impressionist, applied science to his paintings. He developed a method called pointillism, placing small dabs of color close together to produce a three-dimensional effect. His painting *A Sunday Afternoon on the Island of La Grande Jatte* consists of thousands of different-colored dots.

Paul Gauguin (goh GAN) moved to the Pacific island of Tahiti, where he painted *Where do we come from? What are we? Where are we going?* It was an attempt to find universal truths in the symbols of a nonindustrial culture.

The son of a Dutch minister, Vincent van Gogh (van GOH) led an unhappy life. After failing at the ministry, he turned to painting. Within two years, he produced most of the paintings for which he is known, using brilliant colors and distorted forms to make intense statements.

Henri de Toulouse-Lautrec (too LOOZ loh TREHK) used Paris night life as a major subject. He painted with vivid detail, using bright colors to catch the reality of lives he portrayed. His use of line and color in posters of Paris's Moulin Rouge attracted worldwide attention.

The work of the post-impressionists pointed toward the present, when artists would explore techniques to create personal visions of reality.

SECTION 4 REVIEW

Recall

1. **Define:** romanticism, realism, symbolism, impressionist, post-impressionist
2. **Identify:** Jean-Jacques Rousseau, Franz Schubert, George Sand, Gustave Courbet, Gustave Flaubert, Leo Tolstoy, Claude Monet, Paul Cézanne, Vincent van Gogh

3. **Explain:** Which events and movements of the time resulted in the rise of realism?

Critical Thinking

4. **Analyze:** How might Antoine-Jean Gros's depiction of Napoleon have influenced people's feelings and attitudes about Napoleon?

5. **Synthesize:** Select a movement from Section 4, and explain how it reflected the way people felt about the 1800s.

Applying Concepts

6. **Innovation:** How was nature significant in romantic music, poetry, and painting? Why was this so?

PARAPHRASING INFORMATION

Like millions of people in the United States, you may have watched the President deliver a State of the Union address. After the speech, suppose a friend should ask, "What did the President say?" How would you respond?

Explanation

To answer the question, you would probably *paraphrase*, or put into your own words, what the President said. Later, if more detail is needed, you could refer to a written account of the speech.

When you take notes while reading or listening, paraphrasing helps you to think about the information and to understand better what the author or speaker meant. It makes the content more meaningful to you.

Use the following steps to help you paraphrase information:

- Note the source of the information. For example, with a book write the title, author, publishing company, date of publication, and the page number of the passage to be paraphrased. If you use just one book, such as your textbook, the page number is enough.
- Read the passage carefully for understanding. Identify the main ideas and important details.
- Write the main idea and important details in your own words. Usually, leaving out minor de-

tails will shorten the passage; but sometimes your version will be longer because you define terms or explain relationships.

- Compare your version to the the original to make sure the ideas you recorded match those in the original. If you added definitions or explanations not in the original, you can set them off by using brackets.

Example

To paraphrase information in Chapter 23, Section 1, "Looking for a Better Way," on page 575, begin by writing the title of the text, *World History: The Human Experience*, and the page number. Then, read the passage.

Paragraphs 1 to 3 describe the beginnings of reform and list specific reform laws whose provisions must be noted fairly precisely. Paragraphs 4 to 8 summarize the contributions of the British novelist Charles Dickens and philosophers Jeremy Bentham and John Stuart Mill.

You might write the following paraphrase of the passage:

Appalling factory conditions provoked a reform movement led by William Wilberforce and Lord Shaftesbury. Parliament investigated factory conditions and passed laws to (1) regulate employment of children in factories, (2) prohibit women and children

from working in underground mines, and (3) limit the working day to ten hours. Charles Dickens wrote about the misery of industrialization. Jeremy Bentham and John Stuart Mill preached utilitarianism (an institution had to be useful to society) and proposed government reform in education, public health, law, and prisons.

Application

Paraphrase the information in the following passage:

German philosopher Karl Marx dismissed utopian socialism as totally impractical. Instead, Marx advocated what he called scientific socialism. Changes in history, he believed, came about because of changes in economic conditions. The son of a prosperous German lawyer, Marx developed his radical political views in the 1840s when Europe was embroiled in a series of political revolts. When his views got him into trouble with the German government, he fled to France, where he met Friederich Engels, the son of a textile manufacturer.

Practice

Turn to Practicing Skills on page 599 of the Chapter Review for further practice in paraphrasing information.

from The Beggar
by Anton Chekhov

Anton Chekhov, who died in 1904 at age 44 , wrote several plays and short stories that became classics of Russian literature. The issue he confronts in the following excerpt—how to help those in need—remains a vital issue today. A wealthy lawyer, Skvortsoff, is angered by the lies a beggar tells to win sympathy and money from passersby. Skvortsoff complains to the beggar that "you could always find work if you only wanted to, but you're lazy and spoiled and drunken!"

By God, you judge harshly!" cried the beggar with a bitter laugh. "Where can I find manual labor? It's too late for me to be a clerk because in trade one has to begin as a boy; no one would ever take me for a porter because they couldn't order me about; no factory would have me because for that one has to know a trade, and I know none."

"Nonsense! You always find some excuse! How would you like to chop wood for me?"

"I wouldn't refuse to do that, but in these days even skilled wood-cutters find themselves sitting without bread."

"Huh! You loafers all talk that way. As soon as an offer is made you, you refuse it. Will you come and chop wood for me?"

"Yes, sir; I will."

"Very well; we'll soon find out. Splendid—we'll see—"

Skvortsoff hastened along, rubbing his hands, not without a feeling of malice, and called his cook out of the kitchen.

"Here, Olga," he said, "take this gentleman into the wood-shed and let him chop wood."

The tatterdemalion [clothed in ragged garments] scarecrow shrugged his shoulders, as if in perplexity, and went irresolutely after the cook. It was obvious from his gait that he had not consented to go and chop wood because he was hungry and wanted work, but simply from pride and shame, because he had been trapped by his own words. It was obvious, too, that his strength had been undermined by vodka and that he was unhealthy and did not feel the slightest inclination for toil.

Skvortsoff hurried into the dining room. From its windows one could see the wood-shed and everything that went on in the yard. Standing at the window, Skvortsoff saw the cook and the beggar come out into the yard by the back door and make their way across the dirty snow to the shed. Olga glared wrathfully at her companion, shoved him aside with her elbow, unlocked the shed, and angrily banged the door.

"We probably interrupted the woman over her coffee," thought Skvortsoff. "What an ill-tempered creature!"

Next he saw the pseudo-teacher, pseudo-student seat himself on a log and become lost in thought with his red cheeks resting on his fists. The woman flung down an ax at his feet, spat angrily, and, judging from the expression of her lips, began to scold him. The beggar irresolutely pulled a billet [log] of wood toward him, set it up between his feet, and tapped it feebly with the ax. The billet wavered and fell down. The beggar again pulled it to him, blew on his freezing hands, and tapped it with his ax cautiously, as if afraid of hitting his overshoe or of cutting off his finger. The stick of wood again fell to the ground.

Skvortsoff's anger had vanished and he now began to feel a little sorry and ashamed of himself for having set a spoiled, drunken, perchance sick man to work at menial labor in the cold.

"Well, never mind," he thought, going into his study from the dining room. "I did it for his own good."

An hour later Olga came in and announced that the wood had all been chopped.

"Good! Give him half a ruble [the Russian unit of currency]," said Skvortsoff. "If he wants to he can come back and cut wood on the first day of each month. We can always find work for him."

On the first of the month the waif made his appearance and again earned half a ruble, although he could barely stand on his legs. From that day on he often appeared in the yard and every time work was found for him. Now he would shovel snow, now put the wood-shed in order, now beat the dust out of rugs and mattresses. Every time he received from twenty to forty kopecks [one kopeck equals one-hundredth of a ruble], and once, even a pair of old trousers were sent out to him.

When Skvortsoff moved into another house he hired him to help in the packing and hauling of the furniture. This time the waif was sober, gloomy, and silent. He hardly touched the furniture, and walked behind the wagons hanging his head, not even making a pretense of appearing busy. He only shivered in the cold and be-

Art and Literature *In this 1976 painting, Russian-born artist Marc Chagall captures the spirit of a simple Russian village, the type of setting where Chekhov's story takes place.*

came embarrassed when the carters jeered at him for his idleness, his feebleness, and his tattered, fancy overcoat. After the moving was over Skvortsoff sent for him.

"Well, I see that my words have taken effect," he said, handing him a ruble. "Here's for your pains. I see you are sober and have no objection to work. What is your name?"

"Lushkoff."

"Well, Lushkoff, I can now offer you some other, cleaner employment. Can you write?"

"I can."

"Then take this letter to a friend of mine tomorrow and you will be given some copying to do. Work hard, don't drink, and remember what I have said to you. Good-bye!"

Pleased at having put a man on the right path, Skvortsoff tapped Lushkoff kindly on the shoulder and even gave him his hand at parting. Lushkoff took the letter, and from that day forth came no more to the yard for work.

Two years went by. Then one evening, as Skvortsoff was standing at the ticket window of a theater paying for his seat, he noticed a little man beside him with a coat collar of curly fur and a worn sealskin cap. This little individual timidly asked the ticket seller for a seat in the gallery and paid for it in copper coins.

"Lushkoff, is that you?" cried Skvortsoff, recognizing in the little man his former wood-chopper. "How are you? What are you doing? How is everything with you?"

"All right. I am a notary [a clerk who certifies legal documents] now and get thirty-five rubles a month."

"Thank Heaven! That's fine! I am delighted for your sake. I am very, very glad, Lushkoff. You see, you are my godson, in a sense. I gave you a push along the right path, you know. Do you remember what a roasting I gave you, eh? I nearly had you sinking into the ground at my feet that day. Thank you, old man, for not forgetting my words."

"Thank you, too," said Lushkoff. "If I hadn't come to you then I might still have been calling myself a teacher or a student to this day. Yes, by flying to your protection I dragged myself out of a pit."

"I am very glad, indeed."

"Thank you for your kind words and deeds. You talked splendidly to me then. I am very grateful to you and to your cook. God bless that good and noble woman! You spoke finely then, and I shall be indebted to you to my dying day; but, strictly speaking, it was your cook, Olga, who saved me."

"How is that?"

"Like this. When I used to come to your house to chop wood she used to begin: 'Oh, you sot [drunkard], you! Oh, you miserable creature! There's nothing for you but ruin.' And then she would sit down opposite me and grow sad, look into my face and weep. 'Oh you unlucky man! There is no pleasure for you in this world and there will be none in the world to come. You drunkard! You will burn in hell. Oh, you unhappy one!' And so she would carry on, you know, in that strain. I can't tell you how much misery she suffered, how many tears she shed for my sake. But the chief thing was—she used to chop the wood for me. Do you know, sir, that I did not chop one single stick of wood for you? She did it all. Why this saved me, why I changed, why I stopped drinking at the sight of her I cannot explain. I only know that, owing to her words and noble deeds a change took place in my heart; she set me right and I shall never forget it. However, it is time to go now; there goes the bell."

Lushkoff bowed and departed to the gallery.

RESPONDING TO LITERATURE

1. **Comprehending:** Explain how Lushkoff's character and behavior change between the beginning of Chekhov's story and the end.

2. **Analyzing:** Contrast Skvortsoff's plan for helping Lushkoff and what actually helped Lushkoff.

3. **Synthesizing:** What advice do you think Chekhov would give to people today who want to help the poor?

4. **Thinking critically:** Predict what would have happened if Skvortsoff had found out immediately that Olga was chopping the wood for Lushkoff.

CHAPTER 23 REVIEW

HISTORICAL SIGNIFICANCE

The Industrial Revolution created such fundamental changes that where it spread, little remained untouched. It forced new ways of thinking and experimentation in economics, social policy, medicine, city planning, arts, and leisure activities. Improved nutrition, sanitation, and medical practices resulted in healthier, longer-lived, growing populations.

But were these changes for the better? At the time people were unsure. The rosy optimism of laissez-faire capitalism was later challenged, as urban crowding increased and dismal working conditions and poverty became more and more recognized.

Out of this period developed the contemporary world—now even more rapidly changing. Today, government intervention to restrict working hours, regulate working conditions, and redistribute wealth through taxation has become widely accepted.

A democratic form of socialism has been introduced in Western Europe that seems lasting, while the authoritarian brand of Marxist socialism in Eastern Europe has been challenged.

SUMMARY

For a summary of Chapter 23, see the Unit 6 Synopsis on pages 682-685.

USING KEY TERMS

Show how these sets of words are related by comparing and contrasting the concepts that the words represent.

1. atomic theory, cell theory
2. cell theory, evolution
3. communism, laissez-faire
4. emigration, immigration, urbanization
5. impressionist, post-impressionist
6. realism, romanticism, symbolism
7. socialism, utopia

REVIEWING FACTS

1. **Explain:** Why did business leaders promote laissez-faire economics?
2. **Explain:** What did Joseph Lister contribute to science? Upon whose ideas did he base his work?
3. **Describe:** How did Auguste Comte's ideas change social science in the 1800s?
4. **Define:** What is atomic theory?

5. **List:** What were three reasons people left Europe in the late 1800s?
6. **Identify:** With what movement do you associate each artist: Jean-Jacques Rousseau, Claude Monet, Vincent van Gogh?
7. **Describe:** What was one work by: Gustave Courbet, Victor Hugo, Theodore Dreiser?

THINKING CRITICALLY

1. **Apply:** What are three examples of the romantics' emphasis on emotion?
2. **Analyze:** How did Charles Darwin's theories answer his question about the variety of living things?
3. **Synthesize:** Imagine that you have decided to create a self-sufficient utopian community near your town or city. Would you advocate public or private ownership of the means of production? Why?
4. **Evaluate:** Write a letter to the editor of an imaginary newspaper of the 1800s, expressing your views on the need for secondary-school and college education for women.

ANALYZING CONCEPTS

1. **Change:** Explain how changes brought about by industrialization created a need for labor

laws. How were people's lives changed by these laws? How did recent changes create a need for laws regulating the number of hours that teenagers could work in places such as fast-food chains?

2. **Innovation:** Describe one innovation of the 1800s in each of these sciences: biology, physics, psychology. Explain how each affected people's lives.

3. **Movement:** How did improved methods of transportation affect immigration and urbanization in the 1800s and early 1900s?

PRACTICING SKILLS

1. Refer to the review at the end of Section 2 (page 581). Which of the questions require answers that call for paraphrasing? Explain the reasons for your answer.

2. Identify one or more situations in which word-for-word reproduction of the original passage would be more valuable than paraphrasing.

GEOGRAPHY IN HISTORY

1. **Place:** In the 1800s cities coped with a rapid increase in population. Describe problems rural communities might have faced as their populations decreased.

2. **Relation to environment:** How did industrialization affect people's diets?

3. **Movement:** How many people left Europe between 1870 and 1900? Where did they go?

TRACING CHRONOLOGY

Refer to the time line below to answer these questions.

1. How many years passed between Jenner's discovery of a vaccine for smallpox and Pasteur's discovery of bacteria and their relation to disease? How does this gap relate to the quotation on page 579?

2. How soon after passage of the Ten Hours Act was compulsory education made a requirement? How were these laws significant to industrialists?

3. When was *The Communist Manifesto* published?

4. How long after Dalton's atomic theory did Planck's quantum theory follow?

LINKING PAST AND PRESENT

1. Explain why some countries in Eastern Europe today have turned away from the radical Socialist movement that had its origins in the social unrest accompanying the Industrial Revolution.

2. Choose a writer from Section 4, and tell how his or her work reflected the broad changes of the day. Compare the writer you have chosen with a modern writer, and explain how both reflect their eras.

THE CULTURAL REVOLUTION

1776 Adam Smith writes *The Wealth of Nations.*

1796 Edward Jenner invents smallpox vaccine.

1848 Karl Marx and Friedrich Engels publish *The Communist Manifesto.*

1858 Frederick Law Olmsted designs Central Park.

1876 Elementary education is made compulsory in Great Britain.

1775	1800	1825	1850	1875	1900

1800 Robert Owen begins to set up New Lanark.

1804 John Dalton develops atomic theory.

1847 Parliament passes the Ten Hours Act.

1850 Louis Pasteur discovers that bacteria cause disease.

1863 Napoleon III exhibits works of impressionist painters.

1859 Charles Darwin publishes *The Origin of Species.*

1900 Max Planck creates quantum theory.

Democracy and Reform

*B*ritish politician Richard Cobden stood before the House of Commons in 1845. In a loud voice, he demanded that the middle and working classes be given more representation in a government that unfairly favored the landed aristocracy. Cobden declared:

"I say without being revolutionary . . . that the sooner the power of this country is transferred from the landed ruling class, which has so misused it, and is placed absolutely . . . in the hands of the intelligent middle and industrious classes, the better for the condition and destinies of this country."

While Cobden worked within the British political system, people across Europe and in Latin America faced fiercer struggles for democratic reform. Often the fight was brutal and bloody. But by the end of the 1800s, democracy was spreading to many parts of the world.

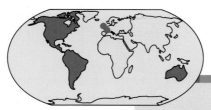

CHAPTER PREVIEW

Key Terms to Define: disenfranchised, suffragette, home rule, dominion, ultraroyalist, sectionalism, secede, ratify, *peninsulares,* Creole, mestizo, mulatto

People to Meet: William Gladstone, Benjamin Disraeli, Louis XVIII, Charles X, Louis Philippe, Louis Napoleon, Abraham Lincoln, Toussaint L'Ouverture, Simón Bolívar, José San Martín

Places to Discover: Great Britain, Ireland, France, the Ottoman Empire, the United States, Haiti, Mexico, Venezuela, Chile, Peru, Brazil

Objectives to Learn:
1. How did political change come to Great Britain during the 1800s?
2. What led to the revolutions in France and the rest of Europe?

A politician rouses support during a British political rally.

601

Reform in Great Britain

Political change in Great Britain took place gradually and peacefully. The British government moved toward greater democracy through evolution rather than revolution. By the 1800s Great Britain was a limited constitutional monarchy. The monarch's authority consisted only of the rights to encourage, to warn, and to be consulted by those who really governed Britain. Real executive power belonged to the Cabinet led by the prime minister, while Parliament maintained legislative control.

Although all British people were theoretically represented in the House of Commons, the British government was not a true democracy in the early 1800s. Political power remained with the landed aristocracy, while the industrial and commercial classes had no voting rights.

Electoral Reforms

By the mid-1800s, industrial workers, farm laborers, and the middle class began to demand social and electoral change. They were determined to gain a greater political voice. The liberal minority party, the Whigs, continually introduced bills to give voting rights to more people and to apportion election districts more fairly. But the Whigs were repeatedly defeated by the Tory party, which opposed such bills.

When the Whigs came to political power in 1830, however, their demands could no longer be ignored. In 1832 the Whigs forced the king to announce that he would create as many new lords as necessary to give the reform bill a majority in the House of Lords. To avoid this action, the lords gave in and passed the bill.

The Reform Act of 1832

The Reform Act of 1832 lowered the property qualifications for voting and gave most middle-class males the right to vote. The proportion of voters increased from 1 in 100 to 1 in 32 men. The act also took representation rights away from areas that had declined in population. With 143 seats freed in the House of Commons, the heavily populated cities finally increased their representation. One observer recalled the moments after the passing of the reform bill:

We shook hands and clapped each other on the back, and went out laughing, crying . . . into the lobby. And no sooner were the outer doors opened than another shout answered that within the House. All the passages . . . were thronged by people who had waited till four in the morning to know the issue.

Reform Movements

While the Reform Act gave middle-class men the right to vote, it only frustrated the industrial and farm workers, who remained **disenfranchised,** or deprived of their right to vote. These disenfranchised citizens banded together to demand further reforms. In a document called *A People's Charter,* the Chartists, an important reform group of the working class, proposed political changes. The Chartists' demands included voting rights for all adult men, no property qualifications for voting, a secret ballot, salaries for representatives so that the middle and lower classes could take seats, and equal electoral districts.

The Chartists submitted two petitions to Parliament, one with over a million signatures and the other with over 3 million. Parliament rejected both petitions. After the defeat, the Chartists had little success and their movement faded by the 1840s. Parliament did, however, eventually pass many of their reforms.

Another reform movement, the Anti-Corn Law League, was supported by the middle class. The aim of the League was to repeal the Corn

Learning from Art *The intense rivalry between Gladstone (left) and Disraeli (right) led to a consolidation of many small political interest groups into two unified parties.* **Which parties did Gladstone and Disraeli lead?**

Law, which since 1815 had severely limited and taxed the importation of foreign grain. Wealthy landowners benefited from the law, as it ensured them a profitable hold on the grain market. Middle-class industrialists fought the Corn Law because it forced them to pay higher wages to workers to enable them to buy bread.

The League—the first major political pressure group in Great Britain—captured public attention with lectures, pamphlets, books, and meetings. When a crop failure forced Britain to import much grain, Parliament responded to the pressure and repealed the law.

Political Parties   One result of electoral reform was more elaborate organization of political parties. Before 1800 both parties—the Tories and the Whigs—represented wealthy landowners. They had no formal organization. They were, in fact, loose groups of politicians with common interests. As more middle-class men gained voting rights, the old parties reorganized to win support from the new voters. After 1832 the Tory and Whig parties began to change into the modern Conservative and Liberal parties.

Support for the Conservative party came from the aristocracy and members of the old

Tory party. The industrial and commercial classes and members of the old Whig party supported the Liberal party. Both parties competed for middle- and working-class votes.

Political Leadership

This era of political reform took place during the reign of Queen Victoria. She came to the throne in 1837 at age 18 and reigned for 64 years. Two brilliant prime ministers—William Gladstone and Benjamin Disraeli—served during Victoria's reign. Both men offered dynamic leadership for the emerging Liberal and Conservative parties. Through their efforts Great Britain continued toward full democracy.

Gladstone   William Gladstone of the Liberal party was prime minister between 1868 and 1894. His first term, from 1868 to 1874, became known as the Great Ministry because of his many social changes. Deeply religious, Gladstone always sought to apply morality to politics.

Gladstone directed reforms in such areas as civil administration, education, and elections. A civil service reform of 1870 made appointments to most civil service positions dependent on competitive examinations. The Education Act of 1870 divided the country into school districts, which were maintained by local control. With the Ballot Act of 1872, Gladstone satisfied the old Chartist demand for the secret ballot. He also changed election districts. The Redistribution Act of 1885 divided Britain into electoral districts almost equal in population.

Disraeli   Benjamin Disraeli of the Conservative party first gained fame in Great Britain as a novelist and later as a politician. He served two terms as prime minister—his first term in 1868 and his second term from 1874 to 1880.

Disraeli believed that the Conservative party could save aristocratic traditions while cautiously adopting democratic reforms. He realized that blocking change would be damaging to the Conservative party, which began to base its primary support among the upper middle class.

In 1867, Disraeli introduced a Conservative-backed reform bill. By lowering property qualifications for voters, the Reform Bill of 1867 extended the vote to all male homeowners and most men who rented property. The bill increased the electorate by about 1 million men.

Growth of Democracy

The British government changed in the last quarter of the 1800s. As steps were taken toward democracy, the working class, women, and Irish Catholics tried to influence political life.

Rise of Labor   Political reforms inspired many groups to fight for increased rights. Labor unions had been steadily growing and gaining political strength since the mid-1700s. By the time of Gladstone's Great Ministry, unions had become a way of life among the working classes. Laborers from nearly every trade organized into unions, which achieved great gains by staging strikes and demonstrations.

At the same time that labor unions were growing stronger, socialism was also gaining followers. In 1884 a group of middle-class intellectuals formed the Fabian Society, an organization whose aim was to establish a Socialist govern-ment. Through education, they promoted social justice such as improved conditions and fair wages for workers. Unlike labor unions, the Fabians favored parliamentary action over strikes and demonstrations.

Gradually, trade unionists and Socialists formed a new political party—the Labour party—to speak for the working class. The Labour party backed the reform-minded Liberal government elected in 1906. Together the Liberal and Labour parties promoted government reform to improve workers' lives. Between 1906 and 1914, new legislation provided the working classes with old-age pensions, a minimum wage, unemployment assistance, and health and unemployment insurance.

A Constitutional Crisis   To finance these measures, the Liberal government called for higher taxes in the budget of 1909. The largely Conservative House of Lords vehemently opposed the proposed taxation, as it directly threatened the wealth of the aristocracy.

The contest ended in victory for the House of Commons when the 1911 Parliament Act narrowed the powers of the House of Lords by removing money bills from their control. This symbolized the aristocracy's political decline.

Women Demand Greater Rights   Women also sought to benefit from Great Britain's move toward fuller democracy. British women, mostly from the middle class, spoke out for political and social equality in the mid-1800s. In the 1850s women's rights activist Barbara Leigh Smith fought to win property rights for married women. Her efforts led to the passage of the Married Women's Property Acts of 1870 and 1882, which gave women increased legal control over a family's earnings and property.

Achieving women's voting rights came more slowly. Although women had gained the right to vote in local elections in 1867, they still could not vote on a national level. In 1903 Emmeline Pankhurst and her two daughters, Christabel and Sylvia, founded the Women's Social Political Union (WSPU). They led a voting rights campaign on behalf of all British women and became known as **suffragettes.** The WSPU attracted attention to its cause by staging street

British Political Cartoons

Although the history of cartoons can be traced back to antiquity, it was not until the 1700s and early 1800s that cartoons reached wide popularity. At that time, artists began printing and selling individual cartoons with political and social themes. By the mid-1800s, political cartoons began appearing in weekly magazines. By the late 1800s, they were a regular feature in daily newspapers.

In this political cartoon of the period, Disraeli leads the race.

The rising popularity of British political cartoons was clearly related to Great Britain's movement toward greater democracy in the mid-1800s. As the number of British voters expanded, politicians were forced to seek public support, and voters wanted to know more about current issues. As a result, daily news publications flourished, and the popular press became an influential force in British politics. Editorial cartoons especially rose in popularity as they communicated opinions about important current events, issues, and personalities.

The cartoon shown here is by Sir John Tenniel (1820–1914), a well-known British illustrator. Here Tenniel portrayed the competition between Benjamin Disraeli and William Gladstone in their efforts to institute democratic reforms. To convey the idea of the close competition between the two politicians, Tenniel showed the two men riding in a horse race. Leading the race is Disraeli (nicknamed "Dizzy"), with Gladstone trailing just behind.

Cartoon artists use a style of drawing that communicates their ideas quickly and clearly. For example, instead of using detailed, realistic images, they emphasize a few elements of a person's appearance to make the person instantly recognizable. This style of drawing is called caricature, from an Italian word meaning "to exaggerate." Just as newspaper writers try to convey their message quickly and concisely, without too much detail, cartoon artists use a style that makes their image immediately understood.

With their concise, clear style, political cartoons have continued to be an important forum for political commentary. By simplifying the positions on a political or social issue, cartoons can sway public opinion and influence political action.

Responding to the Arts

1. Why did political cartoons become popular in Britain in the late 1800s?
2. Compare this cartoon with a contemporary political cartoon. How are the two similar? different?

demonstrations and hunger strikes. The violence cost the cause much political support. Nevertheless, the movement grew. In 1918, after World War I, Parliament finally granted British women over 30 the right to vote; 10 years later, in 1928, it gave the vote to all women over 21.

Ireland

Unlike others in the British Isles, Irish Catholics did not seek greater participation in the government. Most of them wanted the right to govern themselves. The Irish question—whether to grant the Irish self-government—dominated Parliament in the late 1800s.

For centuries, English and Scots Protestants in Ireland enjoyed almost total political and economic control. This privileged minority owned large amounts of land. They rented it at high prices to Irish Catholic peasants, who were prohibited from purchasing land. Most Irish people lived in poverty. Ireland was predominantly Catholic, and a law requiring Catholics to pay taxes to the Protestant Church only intensified anti-British feeling.

As you read in Chapter 20, in 1801 the Act of Union joined Ireland and Great Britain. This union entitled Ireland to representation in Parliament. Not until 1829 did Catholics win the right to hold office in Ireland. Although these acts increased their rights, most Irish people still demanded to rule themselves.

Irish hatred of British rule heightened when a disastrous potato famine hit the country in the 1840s. Because peasants were forced to export the grain they grew in order pay their high rents, they came to rely on the potato as their main source of food. But in 1845 a deadly fungus destroyed much of the potato crop. The British government failed to send aid to Ireland during the famine. Thousands of people died of starvation; over a million more, weakened by malnutrition, died of disease. Roughly a million others fled Ireland altogether; many people fled to the United States.

Various groups fought for Irish rights. Elected to Parliament in 1875, Charles Stewart Parnell—Irish-born member of a Protestant family—led Irish nationalists who sought to have the question of **home rule,** or self-government, heard in Parliament. The Irish nationalists also worked for land reform. But Parliament chose to protect Ireland's Protestant minority by refusing to give Catholics political and economic control.

Liberal Prime Minister Gladstone fought to pass legislation granting Irish home rule. In 1886 he introduced a home rule bill in spite of opposition from Conservatives and even many Liberals. The bill would have given Ireland control of its domestic matters, while Britain retained control of foreign policy, defense, trade, and coining money. Gladstone's action split the Liberal party, but the bill was defeated.

In 1893 Gladstone tried again to pass Irish home rule legislation. Again the bill failed. In 1914 Parliament finally passed a home rule bill, but it never went into effect. Irish Protestants threatened to fight British troops if Parliament enforced it.

SECTION 1 REVIEW

Recall

1. **Define:** disenfranchised, suffragette, home rule
2. **Identify:** Chartists, Anti-Corn Law League, William Gladstone, Benjamin Disraeli, Emmeline Pankhurst
3. **List:** Name at least three democratic reforms that occurred in Great Britain during the 1800s.
4. **Explain:** What was the Irish question?

Critical Thinking

5. **Synthesize:** Imagine that you are an Irish Catholic peasant living in Ireland in the 1800s. Express your feelings and attitudes about the British government.

Applying Concepts

6. **Change:** What might have happened if Parliament had not responded to the demand for democracy?

The Dominions

As Great Britain moved toward greater democracy, the British Empire reached its height. With its colonies making up one-quarter of the world's land and people, Great Britain became the richest and most powerful country in the world. Political changes also took place in the empire, especially in territories largely inhabited by British settlers. Colonies such as Canada, Australia, and New Zealand sought self-government.

Canada

By the mid-1800s, Canada consisted of a number of British colonies dependent on the British government. The colonial population was ethnically divided. One part was French, another immigrant British, and a third part descendants of the Loyalists—Americans loyal to Great Britain during the American Revolution. Most Britons and Loyalists lived in Nova Scotia, New Brunswick, and near the Great Lakes. The French lived in the Saint Lawrence River Valley.

In 1763 as a prize in their victory in the French and Indian War, the British gained control of Quebec, which included most of French Canada. From that time, the French in Quebec firmly resisted British rule. The predominantly Catholic French were irritated by the influx of British immigrants, English-speaking and Protestant, that began about 1760.

To solve the growing English and French problem, the British government passed the Constitutional Act of 1791. This law divided Quebec into two colonies: Lower Canada and Upper Canada. Lower Canada remained French-speaking, but Upper Canada became English. Each colony had an assembly whose laws were subject to veto by a governor-general appointed by the British government. This ar-

rangement worked until political differences brought rebellion in each colony.

By the late 1830s, the French began to feel threatened by the growing English-speaking minority. Meanwhile, a division over political authority occurred between the ruling group of United Empire Loyalists and more recent British immigrants. In 1837 unrest triggered rebellions in both colonies.

Canadian Self-Government   Uprisings in both Upper and Lower Canada convinced the British that they had a serious problem. In 1838 the British Parliament ordered Lord Durham to Canada to investigate. Durham urged granting virtual self-government to Canada. Durham insisted that the real authority should be an elected assembly, not a British-appointed governor-general or the British government in London. With acceptance of the Durham report by the British Parliament, self-government developed in Canada. This pattern was later adopted by other territories of the British Empire.

Creation of the Dominion   In 1867 Parliament passed the British North America Act. This law established Canada as a **dominion,** or a self-governing territory owing allegiance to the British king or queen. The British North America Act joined Upper Canada (Ontario), Lower Canada (Quebec), and Nova Scotia and New Brunswick in a federation called the Dominion of Canada. This act became the basis of the modern nation of Canada. In that same year, Canadian voters elected their first parliament and their first prime minister.

Expanding Canadian Territory   At first, the Dominion of Canada consisted of four provinces in the southeast, from the Great Lakes to the Atlantic Ocean. However, in 1869

Learning from Art *Growth of the wool industry was a vital factor in the development of Australia.* The Golden Fleece, *a painting by Tom Roberts, illustrates the importance of wool to the Australian economy.* **What other resources attracted people to Australia?**

the Dominion acquired the vast Northwest Territory, which extended to the Pacific. From this territory, the province of Manitoba was formed in 1870. In 1871, British Columbia, including Vancouver Island, became a province. In 1873 Prince Edward Island joined the Dominion of Canada.

To link the eastern provinces with the western provinces, the Canadian Pacific Railway was completed in 1885. This made possible the development of the Canadian prairies. In 1905 the prairie provinces of Saskatchewan and Alberta were added to the dominion.

Australia and New Zealand

On the other side of the world—in the south and southwest Pacific—the British colonies of Australia and New Zealand also

sought greater self-government. British claims to both Australia and New Zealand were based on the expeditions of Captain James Cook. Cook first explored the South Pacific in 1769. As a result of Cook's explorations, Australia and New Zealand became British domains.

Australia   Initially, Great Britain established Australia as a penal colony to relieve overcrowded British jails. But by 1860, after a gold rush lured new immigrants, the population reached 1 million, and this practice was abolished.

The increase in population called for a better administration of colonial Australia. By the late 1800s, Australia was made up of six British colonies—New South Wales, Victoria, Queensland, Tasmania, Western Australia, and South Australia. In 1901 Parliament made Australia a dominion, thereby approving its constitution and creating the Commonwealth of Australia.

The commonwealth included the former colonies plus a region known as the Northern Territory.

Conflicts of settlement that the British had experienced elsewhere were avoided in Australia because the early settlers had little resistance from the local people. With the gradual advance of British settlement from the coast, the aboriginals, as the original Australians are called, were forced into the dry, harsh interior.

New Zealand   The first Europeans to settle in New Zealand were from James Cook's expedition in 1770. Hunters from Great Britain and the United States set up whaling stations during the 1790s. New Zealand also attracted timber traders.

Foreigners brought many problems to the local Maori people. Firearms, for example, increased warfare among the Maori tribes. Foreigners also brought diseases to which the Maori had no immunity, causing an almost 50 percent reduction in the Maori population in 20 years.

In an effort to provide law for the Maori and the settlers, British naval officers and Maori chiefs concluded the Treaty of Waitangi in 1840. The treaty protected Maori rights, including property rights, while the Maori gave the British sovereignty over New Zealand. In 1840 the first permanent British settlements were founded at Wellington and Wanganui. Their economies were based on wool exports to British markets.

As with Australia, New Zealand's British population was small until the discovery of gold.

FOOTNOTES TO HISTORY

AUSTRALIAN LANGUAGE

When the first convicts arrived in Australia, the people had to adjust to their new environment as well as to the aboriginals, the native Australians. "Waltzing Matilda," Australia's best-known song, shows how aboriginal language flavored Australian speech:

*Once a jolly swagman camped by a
    billabong
Under the shade of a coolibah tree,
And he sang as he watched and waited till
    his billy boiled
Who'll come a-waltzing Matilda with me?*
Swagman was the convicts' term for "hobo," while *billabong and billy* are aboriginal words meaning "waterhole" and "milkpail."

The gold discovery also brought conflict between the newcomers and the Maori.

Prospectors unsuccessful in finding gold in New Zealand remained to farm. To gain more land, they violated those Maori land rights guaranteed by the treaty with the British. During the Maori Wars in the mid-1800s, the New Zealand government sided with the newcomers and seized some Maori land for public use.

The colonial government of New Zealand exercised much self-rule throughout the late 1800s. Great Britain had granted it a constitution in 1852. In 1907 New Zealand became a dominion within the British Empire.

SECTION 2 REVIEW

Recall

1. **Define:** dominion
2. **Identify:** Lower Canada, Upper Canada, Lord Durham, British North America Act, Treaty of Waitangi
3. **Locate:** Find Canada, Australia, and New Zealand on the world map on pages 984–985. What was the original purpose of British settlement of Australia?
4. **Explain:** What was accomplished by the Constitutional Act of 1791?

Critical Thinking

5. **Evaluate:** The Canadians originally decided to call their union "the Kingdom of Canada." The British government, however, suggested the term *dominion* because they felt *kingdom* would be offensive to the United States. Why might Americans find *kingdom* an offensive title?

Applying Concepts

6. **Change:** How did the development of self-government in Canada, Australia, and New Zealand reflect political change in Great Britain?

Political Struggles in France

When the Congress of Vienna placed Louis XVIII on the throne in 1815, the Bourbon monarchy once again ruled France. In the beginning of Louis XVIII's reign, the French enjoyed relative calm under the constitutional monarchy. But calm did not last long as conservative aristocrats tried to reestablish the old order. Called **ultraroyalists,** these aristocrats even sought to create courts to punish radicals. The ultraroyalists grew even stronger when their leader, Charles X, became king after Louis's death in 1824.

After a splendid coronation reminiscent of earlier times, Charles X set out to restore absolute royal authority to France. When he passed a bill to repay the aristocrats for the property they had lost during the Revolution, he set in motion a storm of rebellion.

Revolt in France

The legislative assembly passed a vote of no-confidence in the government after this unpopular act. Undaunted, the king dissolved the assembly and held new elections. But this proved fruitless when voters elected more liberals who rejected Charles's policies.

In response, Charles issued the July Ordinances. The ordinances proposed to dissolve the newly elected assembly, abolish freedom of the press, and restrict voting rights. Several journalists, however, ignored the restrictions and wrote fiery tracts urging rebellion.

On July 27, 1830, angry Parisian workers and students thundered through the streets, as they had done in 1789. By July 29, after *Les Trois Glorieuses* (three glorious days), triumphant revolutionaries forced Charles X to give up his right as monarch and abdicate the throne. The fallen king fled to Great Britain.

The "Citizen-King" Takes the Throne

After the chaos had subsided, revolutionary leaders set up a new constitutional monarchy that did not have close ties to the old aristocracy. Louis Philippe, a cousin of Charles, accepted the throne. Because he dressed and behaved like a middle-class person, Louis Philippe became known as the "Citizen-King" and won the support of the growing middle class.

From 1830 to 1848, however, many French people became discontented with Louis Philippe's government. At heart, the "Citizen-King" favored the wealthy, and many working-class citizens began to demand political reforms, especially voting rights.

Louis Philippe refused their demands. When they appealed to Prime Minister François Guizot, he too refused. Frustrated, leaders organized political banquets, where they called for an extended vote and Guizot's resignation.

Revolution of 1848 In 1848 Guizot canceled a banquet, fearing a demonstration. But the order came too late. On February 22, crowds flooded the streets, singing "The Marseillaise" and shouting protests against Guizot. Louis Philippe called in troops, but the soldiers sympathized with the rebels and joined them. Over the next days, at least 52 civilians were killed or wounded. The disturbances forced Louis Philippe to abdicate and flee to Great Britain. The Revolution of 1848 ended with the rebels proclaiming France a republic.

Inspired by events in France, revolutionaries in other European countries also fought for greater political rights. Political discontent in Austria, Italy, and Prussia was particularly significant in the changing political climate on the Continent. In these areas, however, the political status quo was more or less maintained despite the uprisings.

Learning from Art
The Revolution of 1848 in France triggered a wave of revolution throughout Europe. **What was the revolutionaries' primary demand?**

The Second Empire

When the political turmoil in France had finally subsided, the revolutionary leaders proclaimed the Second Republic of France and set out to create a new constitution. The French constitution featured many democratic reforms, including a legislative branch called the National Assembly, the election of a president, and an extension of voting rights to all adult men. Eight million men eagerly set off to the polls to elect a new French government in the spring of 1848. Only briefly, however, would the French enjoy the freedoms of the Second Republic.

The Rise of Louis Napoleon   Choosing from four presidential candidates, voters gave Louis Napoleon Bonaparte, the nephew of Napoleon Bonaparte, an overwhelming victory. Louis Napoleon's popularity came more from his name than from his political skills. The name *Napoleon* reminded the French people of the greatness their nation had once enjoyed.

Although Louis Napoleon presented himself as a democratic reformer, the charismatic president hoped to take advantage of his popularity to make himself a dictator. To guarantee victory, Louis Napoleon worked to win the support of powerful groups in France—the army, the Church, the middle class, and the peasants. For

example, in 1849 he won the confidence of the predominantly Catholic French population by ordering French troops to help the pope suppress an attempt by Italian nationalists to set up a republic in Rome. He also gave the Church more control over French education.

This support for the Catholics, however, created an uproar in Paris. Demonstrators opposing support for the pope filled the streets. Alarmed by the mob action, the National Assembly restricted people's rights in order to keep law and order. They also revoked voting rights for about a third of the voters.

Louis Napoleon used this uproar to his advantage by convincing the French people that the republic was a failure. Deciding to take control of the French government, Louis Napoleon directed a coup d'etat on December 2, 1851. He dissolved the National Assembly and arrested 70 of his opponents. With shrewd planning, he won popular support by reestablishing voting rights for all French men.

Louis Napoleon then called for a plebiscite, or national vote, asking the people to give him the power to create a new French constitution. The people enthusiastically gave him their support. Now Louis Napoleon had complete legislative and executive control, and the people appeared happy with the order and stability he provided. In a second plebiscite, 95 percent of the people approved the transformation of the French republic into a hereditary empire. In 1852 Louis Napoleon became Napoleon III, Emperor of France.

Although Napoleon restricted the press and limited civil liberties, he had a successful economic program. During the 1850s French industrial growth doubled and foreign trade tripled. France built new railroads and roads, including Paris's famous wide boulevards.

The Crimean War In 1854 Louis Napoleon led France into the Crimean War. The war pitted France and Great Britain against Russia. All three countries had interests in the Ottoman Empire. When a dispute arose over whether France or Russia had the right to protect Christians in the empire or visiting the Holy Land, the Ottoman emperor sided with the French.

Angered by the decision, Russian tsar Nicholas I decided to try to extend the Russian Empire by encroaching upon Ottoman land. Nicholas's aggression and invasion of Ottoman territory in the Balkans upset both Great Britain and France, who wanted to protect their trade and financial interests in the Middle East. When the Ottoman Empire declared war on Russia in 1854, Great Britain, France, and the tiny Italian kingdom of Sardinia joined the battle.

French and British armies invaded Russia, setting up posts on the Crimean Peninsula, where most of the fighting took place. This peninsula juts into the Black Sea from southern Russia. During the winter of 1854 to 1855, little fighting took place as armies battled cold, violent storms, and especially disease. Frostbite, cholera, and other diseases weakened and depleted the ranks on both sides and caused more deaths than war-related injuries. Finally, in the early fall of 1855, weakened British troops captured the Russian port of Sebastopol, forcing the Russian government to make peace. In early 1856 the Crimean War came to an end.

End of the Empire

In 1870, conflict with Prussia ended Napoleon's empire. Alarmed by Prussia's growing power in Europe, Napoleon made his most costly error in judgment: he declared war on the Prussians on July 19, 1870.

Few French or foreign observers anticipated the quick and relatively easy defeat of France in the Franco-Prussian War. The French armies were slow to mobilize, and German forces crossed into France with little armed resistance. The Prussians defeated the French in just over six weeks. On September 2, after winning a decisive victory at Sedan, the Prussians took Napoleon III as prisoner.

When the news of the emperor's capture reached Paris on September 4, crowds filled the streets and forced the collapse of the Second Empire. The people of Paris endured a Prussian siege for four months before a truce was signed.

Making Peace with Prussia The French people elected a new National Assembly, dominated by royalists, to make peace with Prussia. The Assembly surrendered the provinces of Alsace and Lorraine and agreed to pay 5 billion francs—the equivalent of 1 billion dollars—to Prussia. Prussian forces further humiliated France by staging a victory march through Paris. The people of Paris, strong republicans who wanted a renewal of the war with Prussia instead of peace, were angered by the peace terms. They sank into despair after their loss.

In March, the National Assembly set about restoring order in France, particularly in Paris. The provisional government inspired an angry outcry when it demanded that Parisians pay the rents and the debts that had been suspended during the siege. At the same time, the Assembly stopped payments to the National Guard, which many Parisian workers had joined during the Prussian siege. These drastic measures led to unrest and to an uprising in Paris.

Revolt in the Streets During the revolt, the workers established a Socialist government known as the Commune of Paris. The leaders of the Commune refused to recognize the National Assembly and called for the conversion of France into a decentralized federation of independent cities. The Commune declared war on the propertied classes and the Church.

In a bitter civil war, the National Assembly reasserted its control over Paris. Armies pushed past the Commune's barricades throughout the strife-ridden city. During the "Bloody Week" in May 1871, the Assembly's powerful military forces arrested nearly 40,000 people and killed more than 20,000. The horror of rebellion set back the political and social advances made by workers and caused distrust between the middle and working classes.

The Third Republic

After the fall of the Commune, the dispirited country again tried to rebuild its government. But this proved to be a difficult task, as royalists and republicans alike fought bitterly over the form the government should take. It took four years for members to agree on the form of the new government.

Finally, in 1875 a new constitution gave France a republican government. The Third Republic's constitution provided for a two-house legislature. The two houses elected a president, who served for four years and who had little real power. Every official act needed to receive the full support of both houses of the legislature to be signed into power. A cabinet of ministers was responsible for government policy, and the post of premier was created to handle all executive business.

CONNECTIONS: HISTORY AND THE ENVIRONMENT

The Development of Photography

An early Eastman camera

People experimented with photography long ago. In ancient Greece, Aristotle noticed that light shining through a small hole produced an upside-down image of an object. In the early 1500s, Italian innovators built the "camera obscura" based on this idea. The camera obscura, which means "dark room" in Latin, was large enough for a person to walk into. It projected an image onto a wall. Artists then traced the outline of the image and colored the picture.

For centuries, scientists tried to record the projected images in a lasting way. In 1826 Joseph Niépce, a French inventor, produced the world's first photograph—a blurry farmyard view—by coating a metal plate with a light-sensitive chemical. In 1837 French inventor Louis Daguerre perfected Niépce's techniques. Daguerre invented a method to fix an image on silver-coated copper. Daguerreotypes,

as these images were called, produced detailed pictures.

Photography progressed rapidly throughout the 1800s. Some photographers took portraits of kings and queens and wealthy families. Others risked their lives photographing the horrors of war.

In 1888 George Eastman developed the box camera. Small and lightweight, the camera was easy to use and relatively inexpensive. The mass-produced box cameras put photography into the hands of millions. The slogan for Eastman's camera company read, "You Press the Button, We Do the Rest."

Making the Connection

1. How did photography help people record their lives in the 1800s?
2. In what ways does photography affect events today? Think about the power of the media.

Threats to the Republic Although France had finally established itself as a republic, the new government was particularly vulnerable to attack. The 1880s and 1890s were filled with crises for the young government. One of its greatest threats came from General George Boulanger, who was a popular war hero. Boulanger urged the French people to seek revenge against Prussia, and the people met his ideas with great enthusiasm. Boulanger launched a campaign to demand the election of a new legislature in 1888.

Boulanger won great support from royalists and other antirepublicans. In 1889 his supporters urged him to overthrow the Third Republic with a coup d'état. When the government ordered him arrested for treason, Boulanger fled the country to Belgium. Without the direction of its popular leader, the Boulanger movement collapsed .

A second threat to the republic in the early 1890s centered around the construction of a canal through Panama. The canal would provide France with a waterway connecting the Atlantic and Pacific oceans.

When the Panama Company collapsed and the Panama project failed, thousands of French stockholders lost all of the money they had invested. Charges of dishonesty and poor managerial practices erupted. The scandal spread to the highest government offices, as members of both houses were accused of accepting bribes to get more funding for the troubled project. During the trials, the public learned that the government had knowingly tried to hide the scandal from the people.

The Panama scandal partly benefited France's growing Socialist movement. In 1893 nearly 50 Socialists won seats in the legislature.

The Dreyfus Affair The 1890s saw the Third Republic's greatest crisis—the Dreyfus affair. Alfred Dreyfus, a Jewish army officer, was arrested and charged with selling military secrets to the Germans. A military court convicted Dreyfus and sentenced him to a life term on Devil's Island, off the coast of South America.

Yet Dreyfus's family and many supporters maintained his innocence. In 1897 growing evidence pointed to the fact that much of the original evidence against Dreyfus had been forged. Dreyfus's supporters demanded a retrial, but army officials refused, arguing that to do so would undermine military authority.

The Dreyfus affair became a national issue that divided France, because the honor of the military, the security of the country against Germany, the reputation of the republic, as well as Dreyfus's life, seemed to be at stake. While the media popularized the issue, republicans, Socialists, writers, and artists rallied to support Dreyfus. In 1906 pro-Republic forces finally prevailed. A civil court pardoned Dreyfus on all charges and reinstated him into the army.

The Dreyfus affair was an important event in modern French history. Although it deeply split a generation of French people, it also proved that the republican form of government was able to survive in France. After the Dreyfus affair, republicans directed their attention to other reforms, among them the separation of church and state in 1905.

SECTION 3 REVIEW

Recall

1. **Define:** ultraroyalist
2. **Identify:** Louis Philippe, Louis Napoleon, Paris Commune, Alfred Dreyfus
3. **Explain:** What political and social effects did the 1848 revolution in France have on other nations in Europe?

4. **Explain:** How did the French government change under the rule of Louis Napoleon?

Critical Thinking

5. **Analyze:** Why was the government of the Third Republic especially vulnerable to political opposition?

Applying Concepts

6. **Revolution:** Trace France's turbulent political history during the 1800s. What events led the French people to revolt against their government in 1830? What events led the French people to revolt in 1848?

Expansion of the United States

While political upheavals shook Europe during the 1800s, the United States grew in size, wealth, and power. The rich and sparsely populated areas west of the original colonies lured American settlers by the thousands, and no European powers with colonial interests blocked their westward drive. In fact, the conflicts in the European countries during the early years of the nation created opportunities for the United States to acquire more territory.

The Young Nation Grows

The United States gained its biggest territorial prize as a result of Napoleon I's desire to conquer his most hated enemy, Great Britain. In 1803 Napoleon was preparing to go to battle against Great Britain and needed money to finance it. Desperate for money, Napoleon offered to sell the French-owned Louisiana territory to the United States. With a quick stroke of the pen and a payment of $15 million, U.S. President Thomas Jefferson acquired the Louisiana Purchase—all the land between the Mississippi River and the Rocky Mountains. The area eventually formed 13 states.

The United States also gained land as a result of Spain's internal conflicts. Weakened by political and financial problems, Spain ceded, or gave up, Florida in 1819.

Later acquisitions of new land from other nations proved to be not so easy or peaceful. In 1845 President James K. Polk annexed the Republic of Texas to the United States. By 1846 this territorial acquisition resulted in a conflict between the United States and Mexico that escalated into war. The United States defeated the Mexicans in 1848, and in the resulting treaty, Mexico gave up a vast area that later formed all of California, Utah, and Nevada and parts of Colorado, Arizona, Wyoming, and New Mexico.

Farther north, the United States argued with Great Britain over the exact borders of the Oregon Country. In a treaty with Great Britain, the United States gained this vast region. Oregon, Washington, and Idaho, as well as parts of Wyoming and Montana, were created.

By the mid-1800s, the young country had grown to 3 million square miles (8 million square kilometers). Only one step remained in the country's move across the continent. In 1853 James Gadsden, the American minister in Mexico, offered Mexico $10 million for 45,000 square miles (116,550 square kilometers) of land in southern New Mexico and Arizona, south of the Rio Grande. Mexican officials agreed to the deal, and with the Gadsden Purchase, the United States stretched from "sea to shining sea."

Rise of the United States

As settlers forged new communities and established new states in these new lands, democratic rights in the United States expanded. When the nation was first founded, the right to vote and hold public office was generally restricted to white male property owners.

The people of the West sought to extend these voting rights. All of the new states adopted constitutions that granted the right to vote to all men. These new states gradually gained power in Congress, and, over time, their liberal policies influenced the country. By 1856 every state had granted all white men the vote.

An Expanding Economy Many factors contributed to the rapid growth of the U.S. economy. The Industrial Revolution, which began in Great Britain, spread to the United

States. Busy commercial regions filled with factories and heavily populated cities characterized the North. Immigrants joined the Northern work force, settling in cities and farmlands. Northern workers received pay for their labor, as well as the right to leave their jobs for better ones. This system of work was called free labor.

On the other hand, the South became the chief producer of raw cotton for the booming British textile industry. The South's economy remained primarily agricultural and depended on slave labor. Most white Southerners, even those who owned no slaves, believed in slave labor. As the United States expanded, it was clear that the different economic interests of the two U.S. regions would cause conflict.

A Nation Divided The differences in their economies led the two regions, North and South, to take widely different positions on many political and economic issues. The result was **sectionalism,** the devotion to the political and economic interest of a region or a section of the country. The most divisive issue, however, was slave labor. The South wanted to expand slavery into the territories gained during the Mexican War. The North wanted these new western areas to remain territories employing free labor.

By 1860 the United States consisted of 18 free states and 15 slave states. In the presidential election of 1860, proslavery and antislavery forces vied for power. When Abraham Lincoln won the presidency, the South feared he would abolish slavery.

To protest the election, South Carolina decided to **secede,** or withdraw, from the Union. Other Southern states followed suit. By February 8, 1861, seven states had joined to form their own nation, the Confederate States of America.

IMAGES
OF THE TIME

The Civil War

There had always been economic and cultural differences between the North and South. In 1861 those differences led to the War Between the States.

Frock coats decorated with elaborate embroidery were part of a Confederate general's military uniform.

New technology introduced during the Civil War marked the beginning of modern warfare. Rotating cannons, such as the one pictured here at Fort Pulaski, Georgia, led to massive destruction and thousands of deaths.

In Washington, Congress worked on a compromise, but to no avail. When Lincoln was sworn in as president in March, he declared that "no state, upon its own mere motion, can lawfully get out of the union." By April the divided nation was at war. The Civil War, lasting from 1861 to 1865, was one of the bloodiest struggles of the 1800s.

Although the North had a population of 22 million people and the South had only 9 million, of which nearly a third were slaves, Northern forces had a difficult time defeating the Confederacy. In brutal warfare, the two sides sent volleys of shells as soldiers advanced within yards of each other.

After four years of war that claimed the lives of over 500,000 Americans, the Northern forces defeated the Confederate forces. After the war, Congress passed three amendments to the Constitution of the United States. These amendments abolished slavery and gave former slaves citizenship and equal protection under the law, as well as the right to vote. The nation set about to rebuild itself.

A New Society

After the Civil War, the United States underwent a period of incredible growth. Across the country textile mills, lumberyards, and steelworks had increased their output to keep up with the high production needs of the war. They kept up the pace after the war.

In this postwar spirit of progress and competition, industry flourished. In 1900 oil fields drilled 900 times more oil than they had in 1860, ironworks produced 160 times more iron, and steelworks smelted a phenomenal 1,000 times more steel. The "captains of industry"

Northern troops often wrote home complaining about unpleasant conditions in the camps. This photo shows their more privileged officers.

Reconstruction followed the Civil War. Eventually, African-Americans were allowed to hold office in the U.S. Senate.

PLANTATION SENATE.

Reflecting on the Times
What problems did the United States work to resolve at the end of the Civil War?

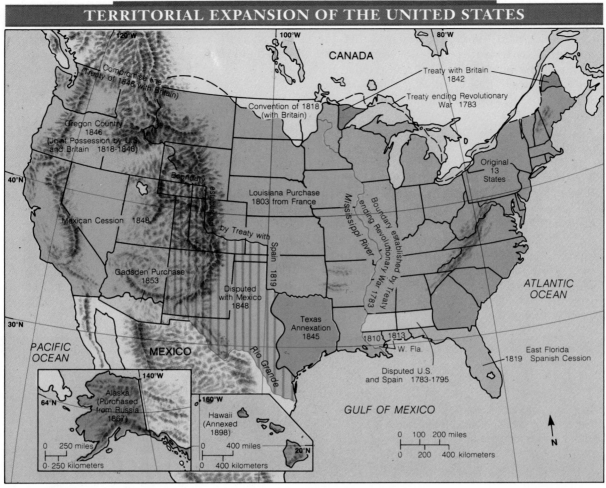

TERRITORIAL EXPANSION OF THE UNITED STATES

Learning from Maps *Trace the development of the United States on the map above.* ***From what nation did the United States receive the largest area of land?***

who developed and invested in these thriving industries amassed great fortunes.

Immigration As industry grew, so did the nation's population. Between 1870 and 1900, the population of the United States doubled, rising from 38 million to 76 million. Immigrants contributed a great deal to this growth.

In the years before the Civil War, most immigrants to the United States had come from Great Britain, Ireland, and Germany. The Irish Potato Famine had caused nearly 350,000 Irish people to immigrate to the United States. The failed German revolution of 1848 had prompted

many disappointed liberals and intellectuals to leave their homeland. They carried with them their knowledge in the fields of science, medicine, agriculture, music, and crafts.

After the Civil War, the flow of immigrants from northern European countries decreased. Immigrants from eastern and southern Europe, especially from Italy, Russia, and Austria-Hungary, began to arrive in the United States in increasing numbers. By 1900, immigrants from these three countries made up more than three-fourths of the country's immigrant population.

After landing at Ellis Island in New York, most immigrants headed for urban areas to

Learning from Photographs *Women and children march in this 1912 parade aimed at getting women the vote, a goal they eventually achieved in 1920.* **Why did women argue that women's voting rights were vital for a true democracy?**

work. Cities pulsed with the energy of different nationalities. By 1900 one in four city dwellers had been born outside of the United States.

Women's Rights The thriving U.S. industries employed a large number of the nation's women. As women gained economic opportunities, they also demanded political equality.

Like the women in Great Britain, U.S. women fought hard for the vote and became known as suffragettes. Led by Elizabeth Cady Stanton, suffragettes formed the National American Women's Suffrage Association. They traveled across the land, speaking in cities, towns, and farm areas for women's right to vote.

They stood before members of state legislatures, wrote books, and tried to convince the nation that female suffrage was vital.

Slowly women achieved the right to vote at the state level, beginning with Wyoming, Colorado, and Utah. By 1918 women had gained full suffrage in every western state, Michigan, and New York. Finally, it became impossible for politicians to ignore women's demands. In September 1918 President Woodrow Wilson asked Congress to pass a constitutional amendment guaranteeing all U.S. citizens 21 years of age and older the vote regardless of their sex. In 1920 Congress decided to **ratify,** or approve, the Nineteenth Amendment.

SECTION 4 REVIEW

Recall

1. **Define:** sectionalism, secede, ratify
2. **Identify:** Louisiana Purchase, the Civil War, Elizabeth Cady Stanton
3. **Explain:** Briefly outline how the United States acquired territory to achieve its present-day continental borders.
4. **Explain:** How did U.S. voting rights expand in the 1800s?

Critical Thinking

5. **Analyze:** How did the Industrial Revolution in the North contribute to the cause of the Civil War?

Applying Concepts

6. **Change:** Describe the changes to the economy of the United States in the late 1800s. What caused these changes?

Latin American Independence

For 300 years Spain and Portugal held colonies in the Americas without facing serious threats to their rule. In the early 1800s, however, the situation changed. Inspired by the American and French revolutions, Latin Americans sought an end to colonial rule and joined independence movements.

Ruling the Colonies

Like other European nations, Spain and Portugal regarded their Latin American colonies with a mercantilist view—that is, the colonies existed chiefly to increase the home countries' wealth. Mexico, Peru, and Brazil contained large deposits of gold and silver as well as apparently endless forests that yielded valuable, exotic woods such as mahogany and ebony.

Farming provided another major source of colonial income. Spanish and Portuguese monarchs granted huge tracts of land to explorers and nobles for the growing of cash crops, such as corn, sugar, and cocoa. The landowners then forced the Indians to work the farms. When the Indians died from forced labor and diseases that the Europeans had introduced to the Americas, the Spanish and the Portuguese imported large numbers of slaves from Africa.

The Catholic Church also played a critical role in the colonial economies, strengthening Spanish and Portuguese rule in Latin America. Both the Spaniards and the Portuguese brought the Catholic religion with them to the New World. Priests and monks converted the Indians who worked on the farms to Catholicism and taught them loyalty to the Crown.

The colonial governments and the clergy worked very closely together. Clergymen held high government offices. The government, in turn, supported the Church. By 1800 the Catholic Church controlled almost half the wealth of Latin America.

Over the years, colonists became increasingly unhappy with colonial rule. They resented the trade restrictions and high taxes Spain and Portugal imposed upon them. Most of all, they resented the rigid colonial social structure.

A Rigid Social Order Social classes based on privilege divided colonial Latin America. Colonial leaders, called *peninsulares,* were born in Spain or Portugal and stood at the top level of the social order. Appointed by the Spanish and Portuguese governments, the *peninsulares* held all important military and political positions. Below them were the colonial-born, white aristocrats, called the **Creoles.** Although they controlled most of the land and business in the colonies, Creoles were regarded as second-class citizens by the *peninsulares.* The Creoles envied the privileged leadership positions that were held exclusively by the *peninsulares.*

At the bottom of the colonial social pyramid were the majority of Latin Americans. **Mestizos** (meh STEE zohz) were of Indian and white ancestry. **Mulattoes** were of African and white ancestry. Spurned by the ruling white classes, mestizos and mulattoes faced social and racial barriers in colonial society. They worked as servants for *peninsulares* and Creoles, and as unskilled laborers and carpenters. Some worked as plantation overseers and farmhands.

Growing Discontent In the 1800s Latin Americans began to challenge the rigid social order and its controls in revolts throughout Latin America. The Creoles played the largest leadership roles in these conflicts. Wealthy and well educated, many were well versed in the liberal political philosophies of the Enlightenment, but their colonial birth prevented them from holding the highest government positions. The Creoles were eager to take control of Latin American affairs.

Uprising in Haiti

Although the Spanish and Portuguese colonies were ripe for revolt, the first successful uprising in the Latin American colonies took place in the French colony of Haiti, on the island of Hispaniola in the Caribbean Sea. Huge plantations of sugar, cotton, and coffee spread across the mountains and valleys of the lush tropical land. France and many other countries depended on the tiny colony for their supply of sugar and coffee.

The plantations were owned by white French planters and worked by the island's huge slave population. More than 450,000 of the 500,000 people living in Haiti in the late 1700s were slaves or freed slaves. The few white French planters who controlled the island often went to severe and brutal extremes to control the black majority.

Unrest erupted in the summer of 1794 when black slaves led by a former slave named François Toussaint L'Ouverture (too san LOO vuhr tyoor) revolted, setting fire to plantation homes and fields of sugar cane. One observer described the horrifying scene:

Picture to yourself the whole horizon a wall of fire, from which continually rose thick vortices of smoke, whose huge black volumes could be likened only to those frightful storm-clouds . . . for nearly three weeks we could barely distinguish between day and night, for so long as the rebels found anything to feed the flames, they never ceased to burn. . . .

In 1802 Napoleon sent forces to overthrow L'Ouverture and take back control of the island. Captured by French officers, L'Ouverture was imprisoned in France, where he died in 1803. Then a wave of yellow fever aided the revolutionaries. The epidemic swept across the island, killing thousands of French soldiers. The rebel army defeated the French, and in 1804 Haiti proclaimed its independence.

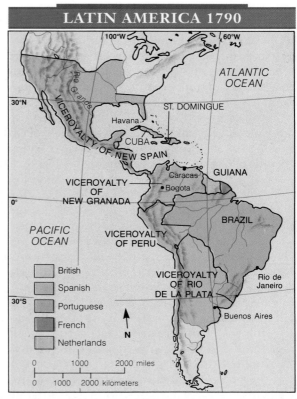

LATIN AMERICA 1790

Learning from Maps *Simón Bolívar began his revolutionary march throughout South America in the Viceroyalty of New Granada.* **Which South American colony did the Portuguese control in 1790?**

Mexico Struggles for Freedom

One of the earliest uprisings against Spanish rule occurred in Mexico, which at the time was part of New Spain. In 1810 Father Miguel Hidalgo led the fight against the Spanish government in Mexico, a colony which he described as made up of "those who have everything and those who have nothing." The Catholic priest cared deeply for the poverty-stricken native Americans and mestizos in his Mexican parish. To Hidalgo, revolt was the only way to bring humanitarian and democratic reform to Mexico.

In September 1810 Hidalgo led native Americans and mestizos on a freedom march. They headed to Mexico City, gathering recruits along the way. The army plundered cities and killed those who defended Spain. Finally, they landed in Guadalajara (gwahd uh leh HAHR uh), where Hidalgo based his government.

In January Spanish forces attacked the rebels. The 80,000 Native Americans and mestizos greatly outnumbered the 6,000-man Spanish army. However, when a wild shot hit the rebels' store of ammunition, the well-trained Spanish army quickly overtook the confused rebels in the ensuing fire. Spanish authorities charged Hidalgo with heresy and executed him in 1811.

Another priest, Father José María Morelos, took charge of the revolution after Hidalgo died. Morelos captured Acapulco in 1813 and then controlled a large portion of southern Mexico. In 1813 he called a conference that declared Mexico's independence from Spain. Morelos's forces fought the Spanish but were defeated in 1815.

Despite many battles, Mexico did not gain full independence until 1821. That year, a liberal revolt in Spain threatened to overthrow the monarchy and establish a constitution, abolish the Inquisition, and grant freedom of speech and the press. These liberal reforms frightened wealthy Mexican Creoles, who feared such changes might infringe on their own privileges. To make sure this did not happen, they declared independence from Spain in 1821.

Ironically, their leader was Agustín de Iturbide (ee tur BEE thay), the army officer who had crushed Morelos's movement. Iturbide made himself emperor in 1822. But opposition to his oppressive rule developed. The Mexican people soon deposed Iturbide and declared their country a republic in 1824.

When Mexico became a republic, the Central American provinces in New Spain declared their independence. In Guatemala, representatives established the United Provinces of Central America. In the 1830s leaders divided the region into the countries of Costa Rica, El Salvador, Guatemala, Honduras, and Nicaragua.

Spanish South America

Creoles in the Spanish colonies of South America gained an opportunity for independence in 1808 when Napoleon seized control of the Spanish government. The refusal of the Spanish-American colonists to acknowledge Napoleon's government resulted in revolts throughout the empire. In addition, Spain's fight against France, together with the colonies' isolation from their home country, left the Spanish weak and vulnerable to attack. Three outstanding leaders—Simón Bolívar, José de San Martín, and Bernardo O'Higgins—led South American colonies in their fight against Spanish rule.

Simón Bolívar, a young Creole from Venezuela, led many colonies to independence. Bolívar believed in equality and saw liberty as "the only object worth a man's life." Bolívar witnessed the reforms of the French Revolution. Called "the Liberator" by Latin Americans, Bolívar devoted his life to liberation.

In 1810 Bolívar started a revolt against the Spanish in Caracas. After nearly 9 years of fighting, Bolívar finally succeeded in crushing Spain's power in Venezuela in 1819. After a series of battles over the next 20 years, Bolívar and his revolutionary forces won freedom for countries known today as Venezuela, Colombia, Panama, Bolivia, and Ecuador.

While Bolívar fought in Venezuela, another revolutionary leader, José de San Martín of Argentina, led Latin American armies over the Andes Mountains and into Chile. In Chile, San Martín joined Bernardo O'Higgins. Together, their forces successfully achieved independence for Chile in 1818. San Martín then set off to free Peru in 1820. Within a year, he captured Lima and declared Peru independent.

In July 1822 San Martín and Bolívar met in the Ecuadorian port of Guayaquil (gwy uh KEEL) to discuss the future of the Latin American independence movement. Though they shared a common goal, they could not agree on strategy and policy. San Martín finally decided to withdraw from the revolt and allowed Bolívar to take command. By 1826 Bolívar and his armies had liberated all of South America.

Brazil Gains Independence

Brazil achieved its independence without the bloodshed that accompanied the liberation of Spanish America. In 1808 Napoleon's French

Learning from Art
In his address to the Venezuelan congress in 1819, Bolívar pleaded for unity. His dream was to unite the liberated states of South America under one government. **What factors kept Bolívar's dream from becoming a reality?**

army had invaded Portugal, causing the Portuguese royal family to flee to Brazil.

King João transferred his monarchy to Brazil, declaring Rio de Janeiro capital of the Portuguese Empire. João immediately introduced governmental reforms in Brazil. He reinstated more favorable trade laws by opening Brazil's ports to the world. João also worked to make the agriculture and mining industries more profitable. Soon both industry and commerce flourished.

The liberal ruler brought Brazilians increasing opportunities by funding public education, including military academies, an art school, and medical schools. With these reforms Brazil moved quickly toward independence, and in 1815 João made Brazil a self-governing kingdom within the Portuguese Empire.

King João came to love the semitropical land of mountains and endless forests; he chose to remain there after Napoleon was defeated in 1815. But in 1820 liberals took over the Portuguese government. Determined to save his throne, he returned to Portugal. He left Brazil in the hands of his 23-year-old son, Pedro.

The new Portuguese government fought to make Brazil a colony again. Leaders ended free trade and many of the other advantages Brazil had enjoyed under João's monarchy. They also demanded that Pedro abandon his rule and immediately return to Portugal. Supported by his father, Pedro declared that he would remain. Pedro defied Portuguese leaders by calling a constitutional convention and answered their angry response with a cry of "Independence or death!"

In September 1822 Brazil won full independence from Portugal. Three months later Pedro was crowned Emperor Pedro I of Brazil. With Pedro ruling the empire under a constitution, Brazil became the only independent country in South America to choose a constitutional monarchy as its form of government.

Meanwhile, João maintained his support of his beloved Brazil by refusing to allow the Portuguese government to send new forces to fight the rebels. Great Britain also pressured Portugal to end its battle. In 1825 Portugal finally recognized Brazil's independence.

Challenges to Growth

By the mid-1820s, most Latin American countries had won their independence. Their next task was to achieve national unity and a stable government. These goals, however, were difficult to reach. Simón Bolívar, who had dreamed of uniting all of northern South America into one large and powerful state, became so disappointed and disillusioned that he wrote, "Those who have toiled for liberty in South America have plowed the sea."

Common Problems In trying to build stable and prosperous nations, Latin Americans faced a number of challenges. One obstacle was the geography of Central and South America. High mountains and thick jungles made transportation and communication difficult, hindering trade and economic growth. Vast areas of fertile land remained undeveloped. Population centers, separated by physical barriers, became rivals instead of allies.

Other problems were part of Latin America's colonial heritage. Spanish and Portuguese rule had given the Latin Americans little practice in self-government. Instead, they were used to authoritarian government, which was not responsible to the people and demanded obedience from them.

In the colonial system, political power was in the hands of the executive branch of government. The judicial branch was weak and limited, and the legislative branch was practically nonexistent. Latin Americans had strong, well-educated leaders, but they had no experience in the legislative process. Simón Bolívar complained that the colonial system had kept his people in a state of "permanent childhood" with regard to knowledge of running a government. "If we could have at least managed our domestic affairs and our internal administration, we could have acquainted ourselves with the process and machinery of government," he wrote.

Independence did not bring about much change in Latin American social conditions. Catholicism remained the official religion, and Church and government continued to be closely tied. The new countries also continued to divide upper and lower classes. The dominant group was now the Creoles instead of the *peninsulares*. Creoles now owned the best land and controlled business and government. The conservative, wealthy Creoles fought to keep power in the hands of an educated, landed class allied to the Church. Their privileged position was resented, especially by the mestizos.

Continuing Political Conflicts Soon after independence, political conflicts increased. Liberals called for separation of Church and state, the breakup of large estates, higher taxes on land, public social services, and civilian control of the government. Most of the liberals were mestizos, intellectuals, or merchants who wanted free trade. Opposed to this group were the Creoles, who drew most of their support from the creole aristocracy, rich landowners, Church leaders, and military officers.

The decades that followed the wars for independence saw Latin America in an ongoing struggle for economic strength and social justice. People fought bitterly to control the policies of the republics. One government often succeeded another, not by election but by revolution or military coup. Although many South American governments were republics in appearance, many actually were military dictatorships. Today, there still remains in many Latin American countries a sharp line between the ruling rich and the underprivileged poor.

SECTION 5 REVIEW

Recall

1. **Define:** *peninsulare,* Creole, mestizo, mulatto
2. **Identify:** François Toussaint L'Ouverture, Simón Bolívar, José de San Martín
3. **Explain:** How did Haiti win its independence from France?

4. **Explain:** Why were the Creoles at the forefront of the Latin American revolutions?

Critical Thinking

5. **Analyze:** Contrast the revolution in Mexico with the revolution in Brazil.

6. **Evaluate:** If Bolívar had not fought for freedom, how might Latin America be different?

Applying Concepts

7. **Nationalism:** Did independence bring social advances in Latin America? Why or why not?

IDENTIFYING UNSTATED ASSUMPTIONS

It's Friday night after a football game, and you and your friends decide to go to a local restaurant before the dance. The restaurant you chose has had problems with teenagers and the waitress refuses to seat you.

Explanation

The waitress's behavior was based on an *unstated assumption*, or an idea that is taken for granted as true but that is not directly expressed. In the case above, the waitress assumed that since one group of teenagers had caused trouble, all teenagers would.

You need to be able to identify unstated assumptions to determine the validity of statements and arguments. Investigation may show that a certain assumption is based on fact, is reasonable, and is therefore valid. Or, it may show that there is no basis in fact for the assumption.

To identify an unstated assumption in written material, use the following steps:
- Read the information to get a general idea of its meaning.
- Look for a conclusion or claim, sometimes indicated by signal words, such as thus, therefore, so, consequently, as a result, if . . . then.
- Search immediately before and after a conclusion to find a stated reason that supports it.
- Identify any missing links between a conclusion and the reason for the conclusion. Ask, "What else must be true if I am to believe this conclusion?"

Example

Note the unstated assumptions in the following statements:
- "The common people are not fit to govern themselves and must be guided by a ruler's hand." (Unstated assumption: a ruler is superior to common people.)
- "Louis XVIII tried to find a middle road, one that would please both those who favored monarchy and those who wanted a republic." (Unstated assumption: Louis XVIII would do anything to retain the throne of France.)
- "Women, who are supported and protected by men, should accept male domination and give up this ungrateful demand for suffrage." (Unstated assumption: Women's ability to vote posed a threat to men.)
- "Great Britain refused to pass a home rule (self-government) bill for Ireland until 1914. (Unstated assumption: British people thought that the Irish were unfit to govern themselves.)

Application

Identify the unstated assumptions in the following quotations and statements:

- The Tories and Whigs were two major political parties in Great Britain before 1800, and both were made up of wealthy, male landowners.
- In 1847, Louis Philippe, then at the head of France's constitutional monarchy made it clear how he felt about reforms: "There will be no reform; I do not wish it. . . "
- "Man for the field and woman for the hearth:
Man for the sword and for the needle she:
Man with the head and woman with the heart:
Man to command and woman to obey.
—"The Princess," Alfred Lord Tennyson
- "The English workingmen are the first-born sons of modern industry. They will then, certainly, not be the last in aiding the social revolution produced by that industry, a revolution which means the emancipation of their own class all over the world." [Karl Marx, 1856]
- "We are perhaps too educated to put up with a constitution— we are too critical." [Otto von Bismarck, 1862]

Practice

Turn to Practicing Skills on page 627 of the Chapter Review for further practice in identifying unstated assumptions.

CHAPTER 24 REVIEW

HISTORICAL SIGNIFICANCE

The 1800s marked an important turning point in the growth of world democracy as people throughout Europe, the United States, and Latin American colonies began to demand social and political reform. In some countries such as Great Britain, people achieved their aims through legislation. In other countries such as France and the Latin American nations, violent revolts led to greater rights.

Although many of the revolts of the 1800s were initially unsuccessful, they sowed the seeds of self-government that reached fruition in the twentieth century. Today, a large portion of the world's countries are republics under a democratic form of government. Constitutions theoretically provide people with representation in their governments and protect them from injustice.

SUMMARY

For a summary of Chapter 24, see the Unit 6 Synopses on pages 684–685.

USING KEY TERMS

A. Write the key term that best completes each sentence below.

a. Creole	g. *peninsulares*
b. disenfranchised	h. ratify
c. dominion	i. secede
d. home rule	j. sectionalism
e. mestizo	k. suffragette
f. mulatto	l. ultraroyalist

1. An ___ returned to France years after the revolution to reestablish the old order.
2. Although Parliament passed several political reforms, Ireland still fought for ___.
3. Canada achieved self-government when its status was changed from a colony to a ___.
4. The U.S. Congress can formally approve or ___ changes to the Constitution.

B. Write a sentence or two about each pair of words. The sentences should show how the words are related.

5. suffragette, disenfranchised
6. *peninsulares*, Creole
7. sectionalism, secede
8. mestizo, mulatto

REVIEWING FACTS

1. **List:** What social groups in Great Britain gained the right to vote in national elections under the Reform Act of 1832? What social groups were still excluded from voting?
2. **Explain:** Why did the French feel frustrated under the constitutional monarchy of Louis Philippe, the "Citizen King"? How did they respond to Louis Philippe's rule?
3. **Explain:** Why did Napoleon lead France into war with Prussia? What was the result of the war?
4. **Identify:** Name three land acquisitions that expanded the territorial borders of the United States in the 1800s.
5. **Name:** Who were three Latin American leaders who helped win independence?

THINKING CRITICALLY

1. **Apply:** Compare the movement toward democratic reform in Great Britain with similar movements in France under Louis Philippe. How were they alike? How did they differ?
2. **Synthesize:** What factors in French society enabled Napoleon III to name himself emperor of France?
3. **Evaluate:** How did conflict in Europe in the 1800s contribute to the development of the United States?

ANALYZING CONCEPTS

1. **Change:** From your reading, what would you say is the best way to go about achieving long-lasting political reform?
2. **Revolution:** Why do you suppose revolutions are often followed by governments led by dictators?
3. **Change:** How did immigration affect the economic development of the United States in the 1800s?
4. **Nationalism:** How has conflict among social classes affected the political stability of Latin American countries?

PRACTICING SKILLS

Identify the unstated assumptions in the following excerpt from an 1898 speech by U.S. politician Albert Beveridge (Beveridge was a U.S. Senator from Indiana.):

America's factories are making more than American people can use; American soil is producing more than they can consume. Fate has written our policy for us; we must get an ever-increasing portion of foreign trade. . . . Great colonies, flying our flag and trading with us, will follow our flag on the wings of commerce. And American law, American order, American civilization, and the American flag will plant themselves on shores . . . to be made beautiful and bright.

GEOGRAPHY IN HISTORY

Location: Look at the relief map of South America on page 987. Name some geographic features that would make trade and communication between South American countries difficult in the 1800s.

TRACING CHRONOLOGY

Using the time line below, briefly outline France's evolution from a constitutional monarchy to the democracy of the Third Republic.

LINKING PAST AND PRESENT

1. British and American women fought for many years to win the right to vote. What rights do women continue to seek today? Are their methods today similar to or different from past methods?
2. After slavery was abolished in the United States, many people still had to fight for fair employment and educational practices. One active period was the civil rights movement of the 1960s. What educational and employment opportunities do some American people seek today?
3. The Irish were granted home rule in 1914, but it never went into effect. How does this relate to the disturbances that are occurring in Ireland today?

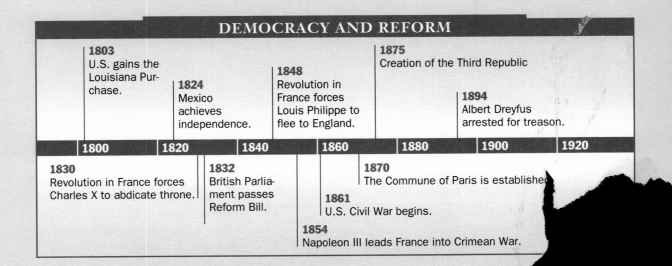

DEMOCRACY AND REFORM

1803 U.S. gains the Louisiana Purchase.

1824 Mexico achieves independence.

1848 Revolution in France forces Louis Philippe to flee to England.

1875 Creation of the Third Republic

1894 Albert Dreyfus arrested for treason.

| 1800 | 1820 | 1840 | 1860 | 1880 | 1900 | 1920 |

1830 Revolution in France forces Charles X to abdicate throne.

1832 British Parliament passes Reform Bill.

1870 The Commune of Paris is established

1861 U.S. Civil War begins.

1854 Napoleon III leads France into Crimean War.

Reaction and Nationalism

*O*ne Sunday in 1821, 16-year-old Giuseppe Mazzini walked along a street in Genoa, Italy. Suddenly a tall, black-bearded stranger of rough appearance approached them. With a piercing look, he held out his hand for money and spoke the words, "for the refugees of Italy." Everyone in Genoa knew that the refugees were those who had taken part in a recent revolt to end Austrian control of the Italian peninsula and establish a unified nation there.

Forty years later, Mazzini—now a leader of the Italian nationalist movement—wrote of this incident: "That day was the first in which a confused idea presented itself to my mind . . . an idea that we Italians could and therefore ought to struggle for the liberty of our country." During the early 1800s feelings of nationalism similar to Mazzini's began to stir all across Europe.

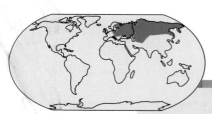

CHAPTER PREVIEW

Key Terms to Define: nation-state, guerrilla warfare, kaiser, chancellor, papal infallibility, autocracy, emancipation, zemstvo, anarchy, nihilist, russification, pogrom, soviet, duma, dual monarchy, jingoism

People to Meet: Giuseppe Mazzini, Giuseppe Garibaldi, Count Camillo di Cavour, Otto von Bismarck,

Alexander II, Nicholas II, Francis Joseph

Places to Discover: Lombardy, Sardinia, Schleswig, Holstein, Main River, St. Petersburg, Serbia

Objectives to Learn:
1. How did nationalism contribute to the unification movements in Italy and Germany?

A massive celebration was held in Turin on March 18, 1861, to mark the unification of I

2. How did Bismarck's antiliberal sentiments affect Germany?

3. Why did revolutionary movements develop in Russia?

4. How did the growth of nationalist feelings affect Austria-Hungary?

Concepts to Understand:

• Nationalism—The rise of nationalism contributes to the unification of Italy and Germany. Sections 1,2

• Reaction—Monarchs in Germany, Austria-Hungary, and Russia fight the forces of nationalism and liberalism in the 1800s. Sections 3,4,5

• Diversity—The large empires of Russia and Austria-Hungary contain many different nationalities. Sections 4,5

The Unification of Italy

From the Middle Ages to the nineteenth century, central Europe was made up of numerous kingdoms, principalities, and free cities. Stimulated by the desire for economic growth, by the success of the American Revolution, and by the experience of the Napoleonic Wars, a small but dedicated group of Italians and Germans worked to unify these territories into nations in the 1800s. The desire for national independence that inspired them, known as nationalism, became one of the most powerful forces at work in Europe during the nineteenth century.

In 1815 the modern nation of "Italy" did not yet exist. At that time the Italian peninsula was divided into a number of independent states, many of which had foreign rulers. A French Bourbon monarch ruled the Kingdom of the Two Sicilies, for instance, while Austria controlled Lombardy and Venetia and the pope controlled the Papal States.

In addition to political divisions, cultural and economic differences divided the regions of the Italian peninsula. Not only did people speak different dialects of the Italian language, but trade barriers and poor transportation discouraged the flow of goods and people. To move goods the 200 miles (320 kilometers) from ____ to Milan often took eight weeks.

____ cultural and economic divisions con ____ the twentieth century, a growing ____ vement eventually swept aside the ____ ons on the Italian peninsula. By ____ had become a single country.

____ empts

____ given to the movement for Italian ____ orgimento, meaning the "resur- ____ revival." Giuseppe Mazzini was its most effective speaker. A native of Genoa and a bold and active leader in the fight for Italian independence, Mazzini founded in 1831 a secret society called "Young Italy." The goal of this society was to transform Italy into an independent sovereign nation. According to Mazzini, the **nation-state**, a political organization consisting of one nationality rather than several nationalities, was very important. Through it, people in one unified country with common ideals could best contribute their efforts to the well-being of all its citizens.

In January 1848, Mazzini-inspired nationalists led a republican revolution in Sicily. Some weeks later, news of larger revolutions in France and Austria sparked uprisings throughout the Italian peninsula. When fighting began against Austrian forces in Lombardy and Venetia, King Charles Albert of the Kingdom of Sardinia joined the war to expel the foreigners. Nationalists pressured the rulers of Naples, Tuscany, and the Papal States to send troops against the Austrians.

By April 1848 the united Italian forces had almost succeeded in driving the Austrians from the peninsula. Then, saying that he opposed a war with another Catholic country, Pope Pius IX suddenly withdrew his troops. Naples followed suit. Their withdrawal enabled Austria to defeat the army of Charles Albert and reestablish its control over Lombardy and Venetia.

The pope's decision infuriated Italian nationalists. In November 1848 angry mobs forced the pope to flee the city. Nationalists proclaimed Rome a republic and summoned Mazzini to the capital to head the government. The expulsion of the pope, however, aroused the Catholic governments of Naples, Spain, and France. As a result, Louis Napoleon sent a French army to Rome. His troops occupied the city and restored the pope to power.

The events of 1848 caused Italian nationalists to lose faith in Mazzini. Charles Albert, on the other hand, earned their respect with his brave stand against the Austrians. Consequently, nationalists now looked to Sardinia to lead the struggle for unification.

Count Cavour's Diplomacy

In 1849 Victor Emmanuel II, Charles Albert's son, became king of Sardinia. During the next few years Victor Emmanuel toiled to keep popular support for the unity movement alive. He was greatly helped in his efforts by a shrewd and determined adviser named Count Camillo di Cavour.

Physically, Cavour was not impressive, as the following description by one of his contemporaries illustrates:

The squat . . . pot-bellied form; the small, stumpy legs; the short, round arms, with the hands stuck constantly in the trousers' pockets . . . and the sharp grey eyes, covered by the goggle spectacles . . . The dress itself seemed a part and property of the man.

But Cavour's looks were deceptive. Hidden behind the rumpled clothes and strange appearance was a bold, intelligent man of great personal charm. By the time of the Crimean War in 1854, Cavour dominated Sardinia's council of ministers. The program he supported included the promotion of rapid industrial growth, the reduction of the Roman Catholic Church's influence, and a continual focus on the advancement of Sardinia's national interests in all matters of foreign policy.

The defeat of Sardinia in 1848 convinced Cavour that the kingdom needed the aid of a foreign power to expel Austria and achieve Italian unity. To win such aid, Cavour decided to support France and Britain in the Crimean War. One historian later called this action "one of the most brilliant strokes of statecraft in the nineteenth century."

By sending an army to the Crimea in 1854, Sardinia established a claim to equality with the other warring nations. Participating in the war

Learning from Art *After leading revolts in Naples and Turin in 1820 and 1821, many Italian nationalists were imprisoned or exiled.* **What was the major goal of these Italian nationalists?**

also won Sardinia admittance to the Congress of Paris, which settled treaty matters after the war.

War with Austria Not long after the Crimean War, in the summer of 1858, Cavour met secretly with Napoleon III at Plombiéres-les-Bains in France. There Napoleon III promised to aid Sardinia in expelling Austria if Sardinia found itself at war. In return, Sardinia agreed that it would give the provinces of Savoy and Nice to France in the event of an Italian-French victory over Austria. Cavour next forced Austria to declare war against Sardinia. He did this by encouraging nationalist groups in Lombardy to revolt. When Austria demanded that Sardinia withdraw its support of the rebels, Sardinia refused. Austria declared war in April 1859. As he had promised, Napoleon III led a force of 120,000 soldiers to aid Sardinia.

The combined forces of France and Sardinia defeated the Austrians at Magenta and Soferino in June 1859. Austria was on the run. The French suffered heavy losses, however, and

Napoleon III feared the loss of public support at home if fighting continued.

Without consulting Cavour, Napoleon III withdrew from the fighting in July and signed a treaty with Emperor Francis Joseph of Austria. By the terms of the treaty, Austria gave Lombardy to Sardinia but retained control of Venetia. When Cavour read these terms, he became furious. He insisted that Victor Emmanuel II continue to fight. Believing that victory was impossible without France, the king refused.

The fighting, however, did not stop. People in Tuscany, Parma, Modena, and the papal province of Romagna overthrew their rulers in late 1859 and early 1860. Their new governments demanded the right to unite with Sardinia. To gain Napoleon III's consent for this unification, Cavour gave Savoy and Nice to France. In April 1860, Victor Emmanuel II accepted the territories into his kingdom.

Garibaldi Seizes the South

Southern Italy remained isolated from the revolutionary fever sweeping the peninsula. But at the death of Ferdinand II, ruler of the Kingdom of the Two Sicilies, Italian nationalists prepared for a revolution. Their leader was a charismatic military commander named Giuseppe Garibaldi.

As a young man, Garibaldi had joined Young Italy. Forced into exile after taking part in the 1830 uprisings, he went to South America, where he fought in several revolutionary wars. As a result of this experience, Garibaldi became an expert in **guerrilla warfare**, a method of warfare using hit-and-run tactics. Garibaldi returned to Italy in 1847 and took part in Mazzini's short-lived Roman Republic. When the republic fell in 1848, he again fled his homeland, this time to the United States.

IMAGES
OF THE TIME

A United Italy

The unification of Italy was a long, complicated process. Political, economic, and cultural differences among various regions had to be resolved.

Southern Italy and Sicily were still largely agricultural areas. Although feudalism had technically ended, the peasants of the south were generally quite poor, unable to afford land of their own.

In the south, which was predominantly rural, traditional customs were strong and fine craftsmanship continued.

Sensing that the people of the Kingdom of the Two Sicilies were ready to revolt, Garibaldi returned to Italy in 1860. After collecting a thousand volunteers in Genoa, he set out for Sicily. When his troops faltered in the midst of the first battle of the Sicilian campaign, Garibaldi rallied them to victory. In a few weeks, he gained total control of the island.

He then crossed to the mainland and advanced toward Naples. The army of the Kingdom of the Two Sicilies proved no match for the guerrilla tactics of Garibaldi's "Red Shirts," so called because of the color of their uniforms. Naples fell, and the king of the Two Sicilies fled.

Garibaldi's successes in the south made Cavour nervous. He worried about his fellow countryman's political ambitions. To prevent Garibaldi from further victories, Cavour sent an army into the Papal States. On September 18 the forces of Sardinia defeated the papal army at Castelfidaro. The victory kept Cavour in control of the campaign for national unity.

When voters in southern Italy supported union with Sardinia in October 1860, Garibaldi surrendered his conquests to Victor Emmanuel II. By February 1861 the whole peninsula, with the exception of Rome and Venetia, was united under one government. Victor Emmanuel II was now king of the newly created constitutional monarchy of Italy.

Building a New Nation

Three months after the unification of Italy, Count Cavour died. His last words were "Italy is made. All is safe."

Despite Cavour's optimism, many difficult problems faced the new nation. For example,

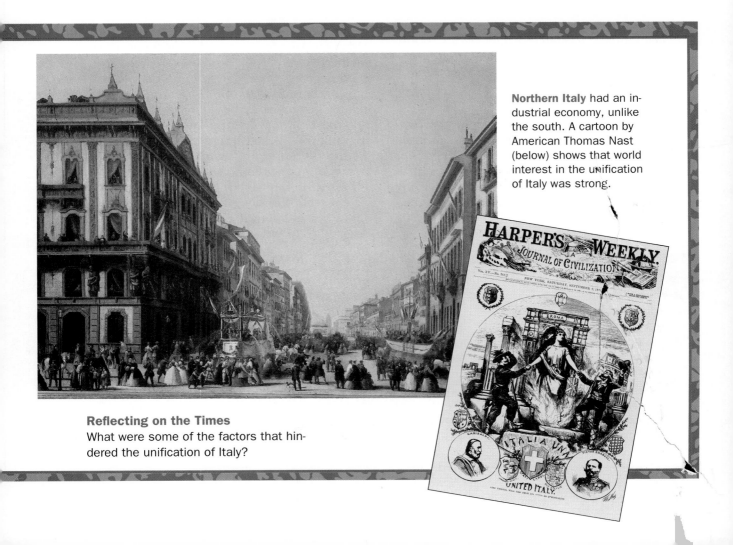

Northern Italy had an industrial economy, unlike the south. A cartoon by American Thomas Nast (below) shows that world interest in the unification of Italy was strong.

Reflecting on the Times
What were some of the factors that hindered the unification of Italy?

ITALIAN UNIFICATION 1872

Learning from Maps *The unification of Italy was largely accomplished between 1859 and 1870.* **During which year was the largest amount of new territory added?**

Map legend:
- Sardinia Before 1859
- Territory Added 1859
- Territory Added 1860
- Territory Added 1866
- Territory Added 1870

national unification had not erased the profound cultural and economic divisions that separated the south and north of Italy. The south was poor and agricultural while the north had begun to industrialize. The gap in the standard of living between the two regions fueled discontent and hampered unification efforts.

In the name of national unity, Sardinia often tried to force its laws and customs onto the other Italian states. This tactic only fanned resentment. Former rulers also encouraged discontent. When some of these rulers tried to regain their thrones, bloody civil wars erupted.

Gradually the Italian government developed a unified military force and a national educational system. It built railroads, linking not only the south with the north but also Italy with the rest of Europe. While these developments were important steps in the process of unification, cultural and economic barriers remained.

Another problem concerned the location of the nation's capital. Most Italians thought that Rome should be the capital of the new nation. During the 1860s, however, the pope still ruled the city. In addition, the Austrians continued to control Venetia.

Italy again sought foreign help to solve a political problem. In 1866 Italy allied itself with Prussia in a war against Austria. In return, Prussia promised to give Venetia to Italy. Although Austria defeated Italian forces in the conflict, the Prussian victory was so overwhelming that Prussia gave Venetia to Italy anyway.

Foreign intervention also played a role in helping Italy win Rome. When war broke out between France and Prussia in 1870, Napoleon III withdrew French troops that had been protecting the pope. Italian troops then entered Rome and conquered the Pope's territory. In 1872 Victor Emmanuel II moved the national capital from Florence to Rome. The political unification of Italy was finally complete.

SECTION 1 REVIEW

Recall

1. **Define:** nation-state, guerrilla warfare
2. **Identify:** Giuseppe Mazzini, Count Cavour, Charles Albert, Victor Emmanuel II, Giuseppe Garibaldi
3. **Locate:** Find Sardinia on the map above. What was unusual about this nation?
4. **List:** Name three problems Italy faced after unification.

Critical Thinking

5. **Apply:** Select a leader in the movement for Italian unification and show how that leader furthered the aims of the movement.
6. **Evaluate:** Predict what might have happened if Victor Emmanuel had bowed to Cavour's wishes and continued the war against the Austrians.

Applying Concepts

7. **Nationalism:** Explain how the spirit of nationalism contributed to the eventual unification of Italy.

The Unification of Germany

Germany was the last of the great European powers to achieve political unity. In 1815, 39 independent German states stretched north and south from the Baltic Sea to the Alps, and east and west from the Rhine River to Russia. Political rivals Austria and Prussia were the most powerful of these German states.

While Great Britain and France were developing as strong industrial nations, Germany remained divided and economically disadvantaged. The Reformation and the Thirty Years War contributed to Germany's social and political divisions. Antagonisms between Protestant and Catholic states ran deep. By 1871, however, the German states—excluding Austria and Switzerland—had united into a single nation.

Steps Toward Unity

The Congress of Vienna had created the German Confederation in 1815 as a buffer against possible future French expansion. This first major step toward German unity established closer economic ties between the German states and helped pave the way for greater political union.

The German Confederation loosely tied together the numerous German states with a diet sitting at Frankfurt. Austria dominated the confederation. Its position as head of the diet eventually brought it into conflict with Prussia. Neither Austria nor the smaller German states wanted to see a united Germany. Austria feared the economic competition, while the smaller states feared domination by Prussia.

The largest of the German states, Prussia had a well-organized government and a strong economy. Political power in Prussia lay in the hands of aristocratic landowners called Junkers,

but rising business classes demanded a share of political power. To reduce trade barriers among German lands, the Prussian Junkers called for a Zollverein, or economic union. Formed in 1834, the Zollverein reduced tariffs and other trade barriers between most of the 39 states, resulting in lower and more uniform prices of goods throughout the confederation. The Zollverein also standardized systems of currency, weights, and measures and strengthened the business classes.

By forming this close economic union, Prussia won an important political victory over

GERMAN CONFEDERATION 1815

Learning from Maps *The German Confederation consisted of dozens of small independent states in 1815.* **Which was the largest and most important of these states?**

Learning from Cartoons *This cartoon from* Kladderadatsch, *a German satirical journal, depicts Germany as it would have been if the Zollverein had been discontinued.* **In what ways did member states benefit by joining the Zollverein?**

Austria. Just as Sardinia led Italy toward unification, Prussia now directed events that would eventually unite Germany.

Rise of Bismarck

In January 1861 William I became king of Prussia, succeeding his brother Frederick William IV. Believing that Prussia could establish its position of leadership in Germany only with a powerful military force, William planned to expand the army. But liberal German nationalists feared the Junkers' control of the army. As a result, their representatives in the Prussian assembly overwhelmingly defeated new taxes to support a larger army.

Frustrated by the defeat, the king appointed as his new prime minister a man who shared his views on army reconstruction. That man was Otto von Bismarck. A Junker himself, Bismarck had served in the Prussian assembly and as ambassador to Russia and France. A brilliant negotiator, Bismarck embraced the policy of realpolitik, the right of the state to pursue its own advantage by any means, including war and the repudiation of treaties.

On September 30, 1862, Bismarck defied the finance committee of the Prussian assembly. He declared that the great issues of the times would not be decided "by speeches and majority decisions . . . but by blood and iron."

When the lower house again refused to approve the new army budget, Bismarck pushed the program through by simply collecting the necessary taxes without authorization.

Three Wars

Bismarck once said, "Show me an objective worthy of war and I will go along with you." As prime minister, he found several worthy objectives. His initial goal was to raise money for army expansion. Then he wanted Prussia to use its military and economic power to reduce Austrian influence among the German states. Finally, he arranged the unification of all German states except Austria and Switzerland under Prussian domination. To accomplish these objectives, Bismarck went to war three times.

Danish War By inheritance, the Danish king ruled the territories of Schleswig and Holstein. Schleswig's population was part German and part Danish; Holstein's was entirely German. When King Christian IX proclaimed Schleswig a Danish province in 1863, Germans in both territories appealed to the larger German states for support.

To prevent Danish annexation of Schleswig, Bismarck persuaded Austria to join Prussia in declaring war against Denmark in 1864. Prussia and Austria soon won this war and forced Denmark out of the disputed provinces. By mutual agreement, Prussia took control of Schleswig, and Austria took over the administration of Holstein. This arrangement strained the relationship between these rival powers.

The war accomplished two of Bismarck's objectives. First, it made Europe aware of Prussia's military might and influence. Second, the tension resulting from the war settlement gave Bismarck the excuse he wanted for going to war with Austria.

Seven Weeks' War   One month before the Austro-Prussian invasion of Schleswig, Bismarck wrote to his envoy in Paris:

Y̶ou do not trust Austria. Neither do I. But I consider it the correct policy at present to have Austria with us. Whether the moment of parting will come, and on whose initiative, we shall see. . . . I am not in the least afraid of war, on the contrary . . . you may very soon be able to convince yourself that war also is included in my program.

Bismarck prepared for war by stripping Austria of possible allies. He gained Russia's goodwill by offering the tsar aid against Polish rebels in 1863. He offered France possible "compensations" for its neutrality in case of an Austro-Prussian war. And he forged an alliance with Italy by supporting its claim to Venetia in return for military support against Austria.

Bismarck gained public support for his actions when Austria sided with the duke of

---

CONNECTIONS:
GEOGRAPHY
IN
HISTORY

A Divided Land

Various physical features contributed to German sectionalism. While mountains and valleys isolated people, rivers drew them in different directions. The north-flowing Weser and Oder rivers connect the peoples of these valleys with those of the northern plains. To the south, however, rivers flow in different directions. The southern highlands are drained by the Danube, which orients the people of that region to the southeast, and the Rhine, which flows in the other direction to the southwest.

Within these regions are many physical barriers that have isolated populations from outsiders and strengthened local dialects, traditions, and allegiances. For example speakers of Low German dialects of the northern plains had trouble understanding Swabians; Rhinelanders could not communicate easily with Saxons.

Past revolutions, civil wars, and religious strife have aggravated hostile attitudes between the people of various regions, so that Swabians considered Westphalians as foreigners, and Bavarians regarded Prussians as archrivals.

This spirit of regional allegiance led the Germans to resist political centralization to a much greater extent than the separatists of Spain, France, or England. In Germany, power remained largely in the hands of the many territorial princes until the mid-1800s.

Making the Connection

1. What geographical factors contributed most to the growth of separatism in Germany?
2. How did the natural physical barriers that existed in the region delay the growth of nationalism in Germany?

Augustenburg, who claimed title to Schleswig and Holstein. To prevent an alliance between Austria and the duke, Bismarck ordered Prussian troops into Austrian-occupied Holstein. When Austria then asked the German Confederation to take military action against Prussia for this invasion, Bismarck responded by declaring war against Austria.

The war between Austria and Prussia began on June 15, 1866, and ended in a Prussian victory just seven weeks later. The treaty ending the war gave Holstein to Prussia and Venetia to Italy. The treaty also called for "a new organization of Germany without the participation of Austria."

This "new organization" became the North German Confederation in 1867. Its constitution gave each state the right to manage its domestic affairs but put foreign policy and national defense in the hands of Prussia. The establishment of this confederation did not, however, end Bismarck's work of uniting Germany.

GERMAN UNIFICATION 1871

Learning from Maps *Bismarck succeeded in unifying Germany in just 15 years.* **Why do you think it was important to Prussia to add northern Germany to its territory?**

Franco-Prussian War The southern German states, which were largely Catholic, remained outside the new German confederation. Most of them feared Protestant Prussia's military strength and its control of Germany.

But it was France that posed the most serious obstacle to a united Germany. Napoleon III would not accept German unification unless France received some territory—its "compensation" for not joining Austria in the Seven Weeks' War. To resolve the situation, Bismarck again chose war. Bismarck knew that he could not invade France without public support. Instead, he had to lure France into war. His chance came in 1870.

A revolution in 1868 had deposed Queen Isabella of Spain. The Spanish government offered the throne to Prince Leopold of Hohenzollern, a Catholic cousin of William I of Prussia. Fearing a Spanish-German alliance against France, Napoleon protested the offer. William brushed aside this protest, but Leopold later voluntarily declined the throne.

In July 1870, France demanded a promise from William that a Hohenzollern would never sit on the Spanish throne. William, who was vacationing at the German resort of Ems, refused. In a telegram to Bismarck, he described the details of his meeting with the French ambassador. To make it appear that William had deliberately insulted the French envoy, Bismarck altered the Ems telegram and released it to the press. Newspaper coverage of the supposed insult enraged the French, leading Napoleon to declare war on Prussia.

The fighting began on July 19, 1870. Because they were more anti-French than anti-Prussian, the southern German states allied with Prussia. With the easy defeat of the French, Bismarck gained support from all the German states for the unification of Germany under Prussian rule.

Formation of an Empire

On January 18, 1871, William I assumed the title of **kaiser**, or emperor, of a united Germany. Bismarck became the German **chancellor**, or chief minister. The new empire united 25

Learning from Art *On January 18, 1871, King William I of Prussia was proclaimed emperor of Germany in the Hall of Mirrors at Versailles.* **Why do you think this ceremony took place at Versailles, a French palace?**

German states into one federal union. Although each state had its own ruler, and some had their own armies and diplomatic staffs, the kaiser headed the national government. He had authority to make appointments, command the military in time of war, and determine foreign policy. Prussian Junkers now shared power with wealthy industrialists. Unification did not make Germany a model democratic state.

William's son, Crown Prince Frederick of Prussia, deplored the means Bismarck used to bring about the unification of Germany. In his diary, he wrote of his despair: "We are no longer looked upon as the innocent victims of wrong, but rather as arrogant victors." While he foresaw many of the consequences of Bismarck's policies, however, Frederick did nothing to change them.

SECTION 2 REVIEW

Recall

1. **Define:** kaiser, chancellor
2. **Identify:** William I, Otto von Bismarck, Prince Leopold
3. **Locate:** Find Schleswig and Holstein on the map on page 638. Why do you think the Danish king claimed Schleswig and not Holstein as a Danish province?
4. **Explain:** Why did some German states oppose the unification of Germany under Prussian control?

Critical Thinking

5. **Synthesize:** Imagine that you are a member of the Prussian assembly. How would you have tried to persuade William I to adopt more liberal principles as a means of gaining support for unification from other German states?

6. **Analyze:** Bismarck altered the Ems telegram he had received from William I. What does this act reveal about Bismarck's methods?

Applying Concepts

7. **Nationalism:** Compare Cavour's methods for bringing about the unification of Italy with the methods employed by Bismarck.

Bismarck's Realm

Victory on the battlefield brought about German political unification, but the German people were not united. Religious, economic, social, and political divisions remained. German leaders now had to encourage a spirit of unity in their people.

Bismarck became the key figure in early German nation building. With the support of Kaiser William I, Bismarck took charge of policy in the German Empire. Over the years, he faced several direct challenges to the German nation-state and his own political authority.

Bismarck and the Church

One of the first challenges Bismarck faced was with the Catholic Church in the so-called *Kulturkampf*, or cultural struggle, between church and state. After German unification, Catholics in Germany organized the Center party to represent their interests in opposition to the predominantly Protestant Prussians.

Bismarck viewed Catholicism as an antinationalist force and consequently supported the Protestants in political affairs. In part, he was annoyed at the popularity of the Center party. But he was also worried about an 1870 proclamation by Catholic bishops in Rome declaring the doctrine of **papal infallibility**—meaning that the pope, when speaking on matters of faith and morals, is infallible, or free from error.

Since the Jesuits, in Bismarck's eyes, were papal agents working to destroy the German Empire, the chancellor launched his campaign against the Church by expelling the Jesuits from Germany in 1872. One year later, the German legislature began passing a series of laws aimed at destroying Catholic influence in Germany. These so-called May Laws deprived bishops of much of their authority and even required that

weddings be performed by secular officials. In response, Pope Pius IX declared the laws invalid and broke diplomatic ties with Germany.

Bismarck soon realized that he was fighting a losing battle. Instead of weakening the Center party, Bismarck's repressive measures strengthened it. In the legislative elections of 1877, the Center party gained even more seats. Even the Junker-controlled Conservative party began to oppose Bismarck's policies. Knowing that he needed the support of the Center party to defeat a serious challenge from the socialists, Bismarck sought to make peace with the Catholics.

When Pope Pius IX died in 1878, his successor, Leo XIII, made an effort to heal the rift with Germany. Eventually, the German legislature repealed most laws directed against Catholics. By 1881 the *Kulturkampf* was over.

Industry and Socialism

Prior to unification, Germany was not a great industrial nation. Primarily agricultural, the German states lagged far behind Great Britain in the production of textiles, coal, iron, and steel. Knowing that Germany's position as a major political and military power depended on a strong economy, Bismarck encouraged efforts to expand the nation's industry. By the mid-1800s, advances in many areas began to transform Germany's economy. The establishment of the Zollverein had already encouraged economic growth and spurred efforts to improve transportation. After unification, investment capital from Great Britain, France, and Belgium helped to modernize production and establish a mechanized factory system.

The development of deep-pit coal mining in the provinces along the Rhine and the opening of new coal mines in the Saar made available large reserves of cheap fuel for the new plants. Cities grew rapidly. Many young men and women streamed in from the villages to work in the new factories. As a result, at the end of the 1800s, Germany finally became a major industrial power. The economic changes sweeping Germany conferred on at least some of its people the highest standard of living in Europe. The middle class and the business leaders benefited enormously from the rapid industrialization of the country. But every improvement in factory machinery resulted in lower wages and higher unemployment for many German workers. They lived in crowded, filthy tenements and toiled long hours under dangerous conditions.

Poor wages, long workdays, and job uncertainty made German workers receptive to a more hopeful vision of the future. They looked forward to a democratic social order in which they would no longer be exploited. To help bring about this new order in Germany, Ferdinand Lassalle, a writer and labor leader, founded the German Working Men's Association in 1863. Although he called himself a socialist and a disciple of Karl Marx, Lassalle did not preach revolution. Whereas Marx called for the workers of the world to revolt against capitalism, Lassalle advocated mass political action to change the system.

Lassalle was a national celebrity who knew Bismarck and lectured him on the workers' plight. However, he did not live long enough to finish the fight, for he was killed in a duel in 1864. The party he founded grew slowly until it merged with the Social Democratic party in 1875 and became a major political force.

Bismarck and the Socialists

Despite his association with Lassalle, Bismarck believed that any socialist party was out to change the government and that it therefore posed a serious threat to the German Empire. To destroy the socialist movement in Germany, he set out to crush its organization. After a former socialist attempted to assassinate William I, Bismarck saw his opportunity and introduced a bill to ban all socialist activities in Germany.

When the German legislature failed to pass the bill, Bismarck then dissolved the legislature, called for elections, and appealed directly to the voters for support. The newly elected legislature passed Bismarck's antisocialist bill in 1878. Although the bill did not outlaw the party itself, it banned all socialist meetings and publications that supported "social democratic, socialist, or communist activities designed to subvert the existing political and social order. . . . "

Bismarck's efforts to suppress the socialists met with only temporary success. Consequently, Bismarck changed his tactics. He tried to show the workers that the government, and not the socialists, had their true interests at heart. He directed the passage of several bills that gave workers some measure of comfort and security. In 1883, for example, the Sickness Insurance Law gave limited compensation to those who missed work because of illness. And in 1889 the Old Age Insurance Law protected industrial workers in retirement.

But Bismarck's reform efforts did not go far enough to end the popularity of the socialists. In 1890 the Social Democratic party won 35 seats in the legislature. With strong socialist backing, the legislature refused to renew Bismarck's antisocialist law. This vote was the beginning of the end of Bismarck's political career.

The Fall of Bismarck

In 1888 Kaiser William I died at the age of 91. Crown Prince Frederick, his son, succeeded him as Frederick III. He was a liberal and no friend of Bismarck. In fact, on the night his father had appointed Bismarck chancellor, Frederick wrote in his diary that he was "an opponent of Bismarck and his disastrous theories."

With Frederick on the throne, liberals in Germany looked forward to a new progressive era. Unfortunately, Frederick III died only 91 days after his coronation. William II, his son, succeeded him as emperor in 1888.

Only 29 years old at the time of his coronation, William II was a man of great energy and strong conservative opinions. Like his grandfather, William I, he favored a powerful military. But his belief in the absolute authority of the

DROPPING THE PILOT.

Learning from Cartoons *After steering the German ship of state for 30 years, Bismarck resigned in 1890. This cartoon was published upon Bismarck's departure from office.* **What is the cartoon saying about Bismarck's relationship with Kaiser William II?**

emperor and the divine right of his Hohenzollern family to rule Germany immediately brought him into conflict with Bismarck. Bismarck wanted the kaiser to leave political affairs to him.

The first major clash between William II and Bismarck came over a disagreement on antisocialist laws. Bismarck demanded continuing restrictions on the socialists. The kaiser proposed a milder approach. A more serious disagreement erupted when William demanded that cabinet officials report directly to him and not to Bismarck.

Under William I, Bismarck often got his way by threatening to resign. When Bismarck offered his resignation in 1890, the kaiser accepted it. Much to Bismarck's surprise, William II "sent the veteran pilot over the side," as the cartoon this page illustrates.

Bismarck's policies had left Germany strong, but they frustrated the German people. His strict rule prevented the development of a parliamentary democracy. The growing middle class and working class were never permitted effective participation in political affairs.

With Bismarck gone, William II was free to pursue his own policies. During his reign Germany became one of the world's major industrial and military powers. Production in coal and iron eventually exceeded that of all other European countries, including Great Britain. By 1913 Germany's standing army numbered over 800,000 soldiers. Bismarck's achievements were the cornerstone for what had become a mighty empire.

SECTION 3 REVIEW

Recall

1. **Define:** papal infallibility
2. **Identify:** Pius IX, Ferdinand Lassalle, Frederick III, William II
3. **List:** Name the advances that contributed to the growth of industry in Germany.
4. **Describe:** What tactics did Bismarck use in his attempt to destroy socialism in Germany?

Critical Thinking

5. **Analyze:** Why did the usually conservative Bismarck begin a program of social reforms in the 1880s?
6. **Evaluate:** Predict what might have happened if Frederick III had not died so soon after his coronation.

Applying Concepts

7. **Reaction:** Explain how Bismarck's domestic and foreign policies promoted conflict with the German government's enemies both at home and abroad.

Empire of the Tsars

In the early 1800s, the Russian Empire stretched from Europe to the Pacific Ocean. More than 60 nationalities, speaking over 100 different languages, populated this vast territory. Although Slavs, including Russians, comprised nearly two-thirds of the population, many other European, Middle Eastern, and Asiatic peoples lived within the empire.

The economy of the Russian Empire was more oppressive but not much more effective than it had been during the Middle Ages. A system of serfdom, long in decline in western Europe, still governed the agricultural economy. As a result of this entrenched agricultural system, Russia's level of industrialization remained lower than that of western Europe.

As an **autocracy**, a government in which one person rules with unlimited authority, the political structure of the Russian Empire had also remained much as it was in the days of Peter the Great. But the forces of reform, already at work in Europe in the early 1800s, soon threatened the traditional economic and political order of the Russian Empire as well.

Autocracy on the Defensive

Alexander I, who ruled from 1801 to 1825, dreamed of improving Russia's system of government and even granted a constitution to Russian-ruled Poland for a brief period of time. However, convinced by the Napoleonic Wars that he was the savior of Europe, Alexander soon lost his desire to improve social and political conditions within his country.

The Russian officers who fought in the Napoleonic Wars were impressed by the reforms they saw in western Europe. Many of these officers joined secret societies to discuss the need in their country for economic reform, for a constitutional government, and for freeing the serfs. In December 1825, some of these officers took advantage of the uncertainty about the transfer of power after Alexander I's death and staged a military revolt.

Although the government quickly crushed the so-called Decembrist Revolt, the uprising had two very different effects. Its leaders were seen as martyrs and inspired later generations of revolutionaries. In the short term, however, the uprising hardened the determination of Alexander I's successor, Nicholas I, to strengthen the autocracy and suppress all opposition.

Under Nicholas I, the secret police had unlimited power to arrest and imprison people

Learning from Photographs *Peasants made up roughly 90 percent of Russia's population in 1861, the year they received their freedom.* ***Why were so many peasants dissatisfied with the terms of their emancipation?***

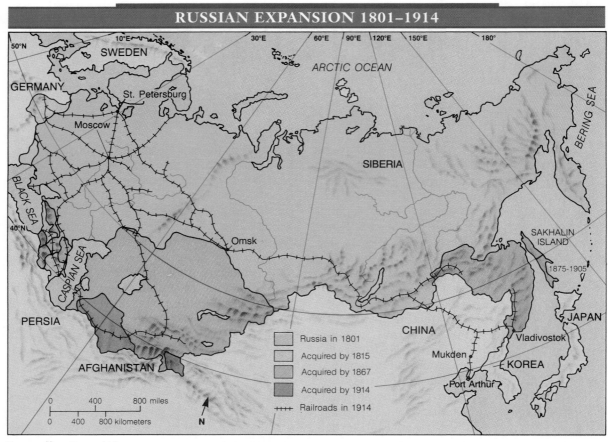

RUSSIAN EXPANSION 1801–1914

Learning from Maps *Russia expanded its borders in every direction between 1801 and 1914.* **To what nation did Russia lose Sakhalin Island in 1905?**

without trial and to censor the press. Yet despite Nicholas I's efforts to resist change, demands for reform persisted during the 1830s and 1840s. Following Nicholas I's death in 1855, his son Alexander II undertook the task of saving the autocracy and preventing a revolution.

Alexander II and Reforms

Russia's humiliating defeat in the Crimean War revealed the extent to which the nation lagged behind the other European powers militarily and economically. One major reason for Russia's backwardness was its system of serf labor. To progress, Russia needed to industrialize, but to industrialize, the factories needed a steady source of cheap labor. Only the serfs could provide this labor force, but they were not free to leave the land.

On March 3, 1861, Alexander II decreed the **emancipation**, or freeing, of the serfs. Although the serfs attained legal freedom, they received no land individually. Their village communities, called mirs, were granted half of the landlords' holdings, for which they had to pay a 50-year mortgage. Peasants could not leave the mirs without paying their share, so they were still bound to the worst land and had an additional tax to pay. The landlords kept the best land and received compensation from the government for their losses.

Many peasants gave up farming rather than return to bondage. Landless peasants moved from the farms to the cities, adding to the growing numbers of unskilled urban workers. Their discontent revealed itself in occasional minor uprisings and produced new stirrings of revolutionary activity in Russia.

Because the emancipation decree took control of the provinces away from the landowners, it also created the need for a new system of local government. An 1864 law created this new system. Locally elected assemblies called **zemstvos** took charge of provincial matters such as schools and health care. Three groups could vote in zemstvo elections: the nobility, the wealthy townspeople, and the peasants. However, the vote was weighted so that noblemen and rich taxpayers dominated both types of assemblies.

Tsar Alexander II became known as the Tsar Liberator for freeing the serfs and for his many reforms. In addition to those already mentioned, he limited the use and authority of the secret police, eased restrictions on the press, modernized the judicial system, and expanded the educational system. Alexander also reorganized the Russian army, reducing the period of active military service from 25 to 6 years.

Unfortunately, the reforms of Alexander II satisfied few Russians. The landowners had lost both land and power. The peasantry had made few economic gains. Conservatives feared weakening the autocracy, while reformers pushed for even greater changes. Designed to stem discontent, the reforms failed to halt the growth of revolutionary movements.

Terror and Reaction

Among the most vocal critics of the Russian government during Alexander II's reign were intellectuals and students from the upper and middle classes. Although these reformers had strong ideals, they had little practical political experience and almost no direct contact with the Russian people. Some radical reformers, such as Michael Bakunin, advocated **anarchy**, or the absence of government, and called for the complete destruction of the state, the family, law, property, and other institutions. **Nihilists** (from

Learning from Photographs *Nicholas II poses here with the Empress Alexandra and their four daughters: Marie, Tatiana, Olga, and Anastasia. Their son, Alexis, is seated at his mother's knee. Nicholas had little sympathy for his people's demands for change.* **Why did Nicholas have so little understanding of Russia's problems?**

the Latin nihil, meaning "nothing") also rejected all traditions, believing that Russia would have to build a completely new society.

Beginning in the early 1870s, many reformers became active in a new movement known as Populism. The Populists believed that the peasants would eventually lead a revolution, overthrow the tsar, and establish a socialist society. To further their cause, groups of students and intellectuals went to the villages to prepare the peasants for revolution. The peasants, however, often grew suspicious of the young revolutionaries and sometimes even turned them over to the police. Frustrated by their lack of success, many Populists turned to violent tactics.

The most radical faction of the revolutionaries plotted the assassinations of key officials in order to frighten the government into making radical reforms. Beginning in 1866, revolutionaries made several attempts to assassinate Alexander II. Although Alexander insisted that these radicals be crushed, he eventually responded to popular pressure by drafting a plan to establish a national assembly. Before the plan could be enacted, however, a young revolutionary killed the tsar with a bomb in 1881.

Alexander III, who succeeded his father, vowed to maintain the old order and crush revolutionaries. He warned that he would not tolerate a constitution and reduced the powers of the zemstvos. Reversing his father's reforms, he abolished autonomy in the schools, restored censorship of the press, and extended the powers of the secret police. To protect the autocracy, Alexander III used a resurgence of nationalism to promote a policy of **russification**. Designed as an attempt to unite the empire's many provinces, russification instead became an official policy of intolerance and persecution of non-Russian peoples. Anyone who questioned the tsar's authority, who spoke a language other than Russian, or who followed a religion other than Eastern Orthodoxy risked prosecution.

Russification singled out the Jews in particular for persecution. Government decrees deprived Jews of the right to own land and forced them to live in a certain area of the empire called the Pale. The government also encouraged bloody **pogroms,** or organized massacres of a minority group, in Jewish communities.

The Revolution of 1905

When Alexander III died in 1894, most Russians expected his son, Nicholas II, to pursue more liberal policies. Nicholas, however, continued his father's rigid defense of the autocracy. But Nicholas lacked the strong will needed to make absolute rule effective. He was easily influenced by those around him, particularly his wife, Alexandra, whose chief aim was for her son to inherit an undiminished autocracy.

During the reign of Nicholas II, a revolutionary mood swept over Russia. Peasants grew increasingly dissatisfied; national minorities called for an end to persecution; and middle-class reformers pushed for a constitutional monarchy. At the same time, the emancipation of the serfs and rapid industrialization had resulted in a marked increase in the size of the urban working class. Russian factories at the turn of the century lacked proper lighting, ventilation, and sanitation. Workers toiled long hours for little pay and lived in terrible, overcrowded housing. Not surprisingly, then, urban workers joined the ranks of the dissatisfied.

By the early 1900s several revolutionary groups in Russia followed the teachings of Karl

FOOTNOTES TO HISTORY
A SICKLY PRINCE

When Nicholas II and Empress Alexandra finally had a son after four girls, it turned out that Tsarevich Alexis suffered from hemophilia. Hemophilia is an inherited disease, mainly afflicting males, in which the blood does not clot normally. For hemophiliacs, the slightest fall may cause internal bleeding, resulting in excruciating pain, paralysis, and even death. His son's hemophilia was not only a personal tragedy for Nicholas II but a political disaster as well. In a desperate attempt to ease her son's agonies, Alexandra turned to a mystic healer named Grigori Rasputin. Rasputin's apparent success in healing the tsarevich gave him great political influence over the tsar, which in turn increased Nicholas's isolation and fanned the anger of the Russian people.

Jewels for a Tsar

Sometime around 1886, the first of many jeweled Easter eggs was presented at the imperial court of Tsar Alexander III of Russia. From that time until the abdication of Tsar Nicholas II in 1917, these jeweled "surprise" Easter eggs were a tradition of the imperial family of Russia. Each egg was made of carefully worked jewels and precious metals native to Russia, and each revealed a "surprise" when it was opened. All were exceptional for the detail and precision of their workmanship.

The jeweled egg shown here is the Spring Flowers Egg, given by Tsar

Alexander III to his wife, Maria Feodorovna, probably in 1890. Only three and one-half inches high, the egg is formed of red enameled gold with gold and diamond detail work around it. It sits on a finely carved and adorned base. Once the egg is opened, a jeweled basket of spring flowers (only one and one-half inches high) is revealed.

The man who was ultimately responsible for these masterpieces was Peter Carl Fabergé (1846–1920). After studying in Germany and traveling throughout Europe seeing the objects in royal treasuries, the young Fabergé returned home to St. Petersburg. There, at the age of 24, he took over the family jewelry shop. He quickly ex-

panded the business and brought it to international fame, opening new shops in Kiev, Moscow, and Odessa. In 1884 the Russian government appointed Peter Carl Fabergé imperial jeweler.

The Fabergé workshops produced many distinctive objects in addition to the imperial Easter eggs. Among them were cigarette cases, miniature jeweled animals and flowers, ornate clocks and picture frames, and other luxury items. It is interesting, however, that none of the objects bearing the Fabergé stamp is believed to be by Peter Carl Fabergé himself. Instead, Fabergé seems to have excelled at managing his jewelry business and attracting the most talented jewelers to work in his shops. The egg shown here bears the initials "MP," standing for Michael Perchin, one of the two men in the Fabergé firm responsible for creating the imperial Easter eggs.

In 1917, after the Bolshevik Revolution, the new government took over the Fabergé business. Peter Carl Fabergé fled the country and moved to Switzerland, where he died three years later. The beautiful objects produced by his shops are still known throughout the world for their exquisite workmanship.

Responding to the Arts

1. For whom were the famous Fabergé Easter eggs made?
2. How did Peter Carl Fabergé transform the business he inherited from his father?

Marx. Their members believed that the working class, not the peasants, would lead the revolution. The Mensheviks believed that Russia needed to develop into an industrial state with a sizable working class before a socialist revolution could occur. The more radical Bolsheviks, led by Vladimir Ilyich Ulyanov—commonly known as Lenin—believed that a small party of professional revolutionaries could use force to bring about a socialist society in the near future.

War between Russia and Japan in 1904 over control of Manchuria furthered the socialists' cause. The Russian government already faced opposition from peasants, urban workers, and middle-class thinkers. Russia's quick and disastrous defeat only increased this criticism and tension. The Russo-Japanese War strained the Russian economy, raising food prices while keeping wages low.

Spontaneous strikes began to break out in many cities throughout the empire. On Sunday, January 22, 1905, about 200,000 workers marched in a peaceful procession to the tsar's palace in St. Petersburg to present a petition for reform. Palace soldiers opened fire on the crowd, killing hundreds of workers. Bloody Sunday, as the demonstration was called, sparked riots and strikes in most industrial centers and set off a wave of political protests.

Middle-class organizations drew up programs for political reform. The zemstvos issued lists of demands. In the spring of 1905, the first **soviets**, or workers' councils, formed to voice workers' grievances. From all reformist and revolutionary groups came the cry for the establishment of a representative government elected by universal suffrage.

In October 1905, angry workers seized control of the major cities in a general strike. As disorder and violence in the cities and rural areas continued, Nicholas II announced a law providing for the election of a national **duma**, or legislature. However, the tsar proposed that the Duma serve as an advisory council rather than a genuine legislative body. Instead of appeasing the Russian people, the measure set off a series of nationwide strikes.

The events of October forced Nicholas to yield reluctantly to the demands of his people. The tsar issued the October Manifesto, granting civil rights to citizens and allowing the Duma to make laws. In theory, Russia had become a constitutional monarchy; however, in practice, Nicholas continued to act like a despot. Stern measures to restore order, including pogroms against the Jews and the arrest of peasant and labor leaders, remained in place. When the Duma tried to act independently of the tsar, Nicholas quickly dissolved it.

Nicholas II's ability to silence opposition was only temporary. Russia's many serious troubles had not been resolved. On the eve of World War I, growing numbers of peasants, workers, national minorities, and middle-class reformers supported revolutionary activity and the immediate overthrow of the autocracy. Their demands and the stress of war would soon bring revolution to Russia.

SECTION 4 REVIEW

Recall

1. **Define:** autocracy, emancipation, zemstvo, anarchy, nihilist, russification, pogrom, soviet, duma
2. **Identify:** Nicholas I, Alexander II, Nicholas II, Empress Alexandra, Vladimir I. Lenin
3. **List:** Name three reforms that took place under Alexander II.
4. **Explain:** Name the two major Russian revolutionary groups that followed the teachings of Karl Marx and explain the differences between the two.

Critical Thinking

5. **Apply:** Select one of the Russian tsars and tell how the policies of his reign contributed to the downfall of the Russian Empire.

6. **Evaluate:** Predict what might have happened if Nicholas II had given the Duma full legislative powers.

Applying Concepts

7. **Reaction:** Why do you think effective and meaningful reform was so difficult to achieve in Russia during the reign of Nicholas II?

Austria-Hungary's Decline

In the early 1800s, there was, in addition to Russia and the Ottoman Empire, a third dominant power in eastern Europe: Austria. The Austrian Empire at this time contained more than 12 different nationalities, including the Germans of Austria and the Magyars of Hungary.

Like Russia, Austria lacked national and geographical unity. As in Russia also, life in Austria remained almost feudal at the beginning of the 1800s. A powerful landed nobility controlled a large peasant population and resisted any change in the old agricultural system. Through strict censorship and the arrest and intimidation of protesters, the government sought to stem the forces of nationalism and revolution sweeping through the rest of Europe.

The Revolution of 1848

As you learned in Chapter 21, the principal political figure in Austria during the early 1800s was Prince Klemens von Metternich, who held the office of minister of foreign affairs from 1809 to 1848. Metternich believed that democratic and nationalist movements would destroy the Austrian Empire and threaten peace in Europe. As a result, Metternich worked to crush all revolutionary activity, both within and outside the empire.

Despite Metternich's conservative policies, however, the revolutionary movement that had begun in France in 1848 spread to Austria the same year. Throughout the empire, nationalist groups demanded freedom of speech and press, peasant relief from feudal dues, and a representative government. The Austrian Empire seemed on the verge of dissolution.

The tide of revolutionary activity was to turn once more, however. Infighting among na-

tionalist groups and within radical factions with different political ideas enabled conservative forces to strike back. In Vienna, for example, conflict between middle-class moderates who wanted to reform the political system and radical workers who wanted to overthrow it weakened the revolutionary movement. By October 1848, the government once more occupied the capital. When Emperor Francis Ferdinand resigned his throne, his nephew, Francis Joseph, became emperor at the age of 18.

Francis Joseph moved quickly to restore the conservative order. He dissolved the revolutionary assembly and rejected the new constitution. Although threatened, the old regime had managed to withstand revolutionary change by playing one nationalist faction against another.

Throughout his 68-year reign, Francis Joseph struggled to maintain a unified empire. But neither repressive measures nor reforms helped ease the nationalist tensions that threatened Austria. At the same time, a series of foreign crises further weakened the empire. In 1859, for example, Austria was forced to give up the Italian province of Lombardy. Then in 1866, during the Seven Weeks' War with Prussia, Austria lost its influence over its German states as well.

The Dual Monarchy

Francis Joseph's efforts to strengthen his authority were most effectively challenged by the Magyars of Hungary. After Austria's defeat in the Seven Weeks' War, Francis Joseph sought a compromise with Hungary. Hungary agreed to this compromise because it seemed the only way to preserve its own national existence.

Soon after the Seven Weeks' War, Francis Joseph sent for Francis Deak, the Hungarian

Learning from Art
Francis Joseph ruled Austria for 68 years. When he came to the throne in 1848, Europe was in the midst of revolutions. When he died in 1916, Europe was in the midst of World War I. **To what change did Francis Joseph agree in order to preserve his empire?**

leader, and asked him what the people of Hungary wanted. When Deak answered that they wanted their rights, the emperor is said to have replied, "I suppose it must be as you insist."

After months of negotiations, Austria and Hungary finally reached an agreement in 1867. The *Ausgleich*, or Compromise, restored Hungary's independence and divided the Austrian Empire into a **dual monarchy**: the empire of Austria and the kingdom of Hungary. Francis Joseph remained ruler of both areas. He kept his title as emperor of Austria, and the Hungarians crowned him king of Hungary.

In addition to sharing a monarch, the two states had common ministries of foreign affairs, war, and finance. A system of committees handled other matters of mutual concern. In internal affairs, however, Austria and Hungary were completely independent of each other. Each had its own constitution, prime minister, and parliament.

While Austria and Hungary were independent politically, they were dependent on each other economically. Industrialized Austria supplied manufactured goods for the dual monarchy. Agricultural Hungary supplied food products. Their cooperation, however, was not without conflict. Disputes inevitably developed between the two countries over foreign trade, tariffs, and currency.

During the mid-1800s, Austrian industrial growth had been slow. But after the creation of the dual monarchy, the empire's production of coal, iron, steel, and manufactured goods grew rapidly. Bohemia and Moravia became the leading industrial centers, producing machine tools, textiles, armaments, shoes, and chemicals. The concentration of industry in Bohemia and Moravia meant more rapid urbanization in those areas.

The dual monarchy satisfied both the Austrian-Germans, who maintained power in Austria, and the Magyars, who controlled Hungary. Other nationalities remained discontented. Three-fifths of the population of Austria-Hungary were Slavs—Poles, Czechs, Slovaks, Serbs, Bosnians, and Montenegrins—who had no voice in the government. Many dissatisfied Slavic nationalist groups dreamed of breaking free from the Austro-Hungarian Empire and forming a pan-Slav kingdom. Their discontent became a serious threat to the unity of the empire.

Powder Keg in the Balkans

By the mid-1800s, the Ottoman Empire had declined to a weakened and diminished state. In 1829 Greece won its independence. By 1850 the Ottomans had lost the provinces of Moldavia and Wallachia to Russia and Algeria to France. In addition, Egypt, Arabia, and the Balkan states of Serbia and Montenegro had gained their autonomy.

Foreign powers watched the decline of the Ottoman Empire closely. Austria hoped to expand into the Balkan region. France sought to protect persecuted Roman Catholics within the empire. Great Britain feared disruption of its Mediterranean trade. The primary objective of these foreign powers, though, was to prevent Russian expansion into the region. "We have a sick man on our hands," declared Tsar Nicholas I, referring to Turkey, and Russia stood ready to contribute to its demise.

During the Crimean War, from 1854 to 1856, France, Great Britain, and Sardinia helped defend the Ottoman Empire against Russia's advances. Although the Ottoman allies defeated Russia in this war, the empire continued to lose power and territory. In 1875 nationalists in the Balkan states of Serbia, Bulgaria, and Romania rose up in revolt, demanding independence from Turkey. The Turks brutally suppressed these revolts with widespread massacres.

Congress of Berlin In 1876 Russia went to war on behalf of the Slavic people in the Balkans. Publicly embracing the pan-Slav movement because it suited the government's imperial ambitions, Russia used the conflict

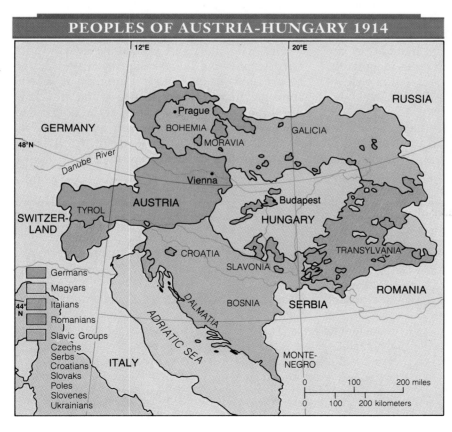

PEOPLES OF AUSTRIA-HUNGARY 1914

Learning from Maps
Although Germans held the dominant position in Austria-Hungary in 1914, they still made up less than one half of the total population. **What was the social and political status of the many Slavic peoples who lived in Austria-Hungary?**

known as the Russo-Turkish War to justify its expansion into the Balkans. The Treaty of San Stefano (1878), which ended the war, created a large Russian-controlled Bulgarian state.

As news of Russian victories reached Great Britain, the public cried out for war. A popular slogan in Great Britain at the time captured the public sentiment: "We don't want to fight, but by jingo, if we do, we've got the men, we've got the ships, we've got the money, too." From this slogan came the term **jingoism**, used to describe extreme patriotism, usually provoked by a perceived foreign threat.

The great European powers protested the Treaty of San Stefano. In the end a congress of European leaders met in Berlin to revise it. At the meeting, which began in June 1878, representatives of the European powers divided Bulgaria into three parts, one of which remained under Ottoman rule. Serbia, Montenegro, and Romania, on the other hand, won their complete independence. Britain gained control of Cyprus, and Austria-Hungary won the Balkan provinces of Bosnia and Herzegovina.

The Congress of Berlin satisfied few. Russia lost its war gains, and the Ottoman Empire lost much of its European territory. In addition, the congress dealt with the Balkan states inequitably, granting independence for some, but not all, of the people of any given nationality.

Balkan Conflict   By 1912 the Balkan states had joined forces and moved to free members of their respective nationalities from Ottoman rule. Encouraged by Italy's easy victory over the Turks in North Africa, the Balkan League—consisting of Bulgaria, Greece, Montenegro, and Serbia—declared war on Turkey in 1912. As a result of the war, the empire lost all of its European territory with the exception of Istanbul and a small surrounding area.

Unity among members of the Balkan League was short-lived. No sooner had the Balkan states won the war than they began to fight among themselves over the lands they had gained. Before the war, Serbia and Bulgaria had secretly arranged for land distribution in case of victory. After the war, however, they disputed the treaty of partition. In June 1913 the Bulgarians attacked the Greeks and Serbs in the disputed area. By July Romania, Turkey, and Montenegro had joined forces against Bulgaria. In the Treaty of Bucharest, Bulgaria surrendered much of the land it had won from the Ottomans in the previous war.

The Treaty of Bucharest did not bring lasting peace to the Balkans. Serbia's increased power encouraged nationalism among Slavs and threatened Austria-Hungary. Russia, in supporting the pan-Slavic movement, sought to extend its own influence in the Balkans. The French, British, and German governments tried to preserve the existing balance of power to prevent either Austria-Hungary or Russia from gaining greater influence in the area. It is not difficult to see why writers of the time called the Balkans "the powder keg of Europe." It seemed inevitable that events in the Balkans would sooner or later explode into a major European war.

SECTION 5 REVIEW

Recall
1. **Define:** dual monarchy, jingoism
2. **Identify:** Prince Klemens von Metternich, Francis Joseph
3. **List:** Name two ways in which the Austrian and Hungarian states were dependent upon one another in the dual monarchy. Name two ways they were independent of each other.
4. **Outline:** List three key events that led to the dissolution of the Ottoman Empire.

Critical Thinking
5. **Analyze:** Contrast Austria-Hungary's and Russia's reasons for intervening in the Ottoman Empire's problems with the Balkan states.
6. **Evaluate:** Predict what might have happened if the European powers had not intervened in the Ottoman Empire's internal problems.

Applying Concepts
7. **Diversity:** Explain how ethnic diversity contributed to the decline of the Austrian and the Ottoman empires. Could this decline have been avoided? Why or why not?

SELECTING AND USING RESEARCH SOURCES

When you have to do a report or simply want to find out more about something, you probably turn to the school or local library to find research resources. Becoming familiar with sources can help you select the most appropriate ones to use when researching a topic.

Explanation

There are many research sources available in a library—reference books, card catalogs, periodical guides, and computer data bases. But before you can effectively use any research source, you must determine its contents.

Reference Books

Some of the most useful and widely available reference books are general encyclopedias, biographical dictionaries, atlases, almanacs, and books of quotations.

A *general encyclopedia* is a set of books with short articles on many subjects. The articles are arranged alphabetically in one or more volumes. Most multi-volume encyclopedias include an index volume listing all the topics contained in the encyclopedia. A general encyclopedia is a good choice to begin a research report because it covers a wide range of topics, some in detail. A one-volume *biographical dictionary* usually provides brief biographies listed alphabetically by last names. Each biography gives such data as the

person's place and date of birth, occupation, and achievements.

An *atlas*, which is a collection of maps and charts, is helpful when you need to locate geographical features or places. It contains an alphabetical index of place names that directs you to a map on which the place name appears. A historical atlas shows various regions of the world as they were in times past.

An *almanac* is an annually updated reference that provides current statistics and data together with historical information on a wide range of topics.

A *book of quotations* provides the exact wording of many quotations, citing the originator along with each quotation.

Card Catalog

The library's catalog, on computer or cards, can help in locating a variety of books on a topic. Books are listed by author, title, and subject. Each card or entry notes the book's call number and indicates its location.

Periodical Guides

A periodical guide is a book or set of books that list current topics covered in magazine and newspaper articles.

Computer Data Bases

Computer data bases provide collections of information organized for rapid search and retrieval.

To evaluate the selection of sources, follow these steps:

- Determine what information you need—broad overview, historical, biographical, geographical, or current data.
- Select needed resources.
- Skim resources to be sure each provides the information you seek.

Example

Suppose you needed to write a report to answer this question:

What was Grigori Rasputin's influence over Tsar Nicholas II and his family?

You could use a general encyclopedia. Start with an article on Rasputin and then read articles on Tsar Nicholas II. For further details about Rasputin's life and influence, you could use a biographical dictionary and card catalog.

Application

Utilize research resources from your school or local library to research the following topic:

What medical treatment was given to Tsarevich Alexis, son of Nicholas II and Alexandra? How has medical care of hemophiliacs improved since 1910?

Practice

Turn to Practicing Skills on page 655 of the Chapter Review for further practice in selecting and using research sources.

CHAPTER 25 REVIEW

HISTORICAL SIGNIFICANCE

The forces of nationalism changed the map of Europe dramatically in the 1800s. A scattering of independent states on the Italian peninsula had united into the nation of Italy by the 1860s. And by 1871, a loose confederation of states in the European heartland had become the modern nation of Germany.

But nationalism could pull empires apart as well as put nations together. A growing nationalist fervor in the Austrian and the Ottoman empires, for example, led minority groups to declare their independence and break away. Nationalism gradually weakened the power of these once mighty empires to the point that they began to break apart.

Another side effect of nationalism was to create a strong sense of national pride that often led to increased national ambitions. During the late 1800s, as nations vied for more territory and influence, tensions in Europe grew. By the early 1900s, the peace in Europe had degenerated into a kind of cold war between rival power blocs of nations. One international crisis followed another in rapid succession. Each of these crises brought Europe one step closer to all-out war.

SUMMARY

For a summary of Chapter 25, see the Unit 6 Synopsis on pages 686-689.

USING KEY TERMS

A. Write the definition of each key term below. Then write one or two sentences that show how the terms are related to the concept of revolution.

1. anarchy
2. duma
3. emancipation
4. nation-state
5. nihilist
6. soviet
7. zemstvo
8. russification

B. Write the key term that completes each sentence.

a. autocracy
b. chancellor
c. dual monarchy
d. guerrilla warfare
e. jingoism
f. kaiser
g. papal infallibility
h. pogrom

9. Garibaldi was an expert at ___ .
10. Catholic bishops proclaimed the doctrine of ___ at the First Vatican Council.
11. In the 1800s, Russia was an ___ .
12. In 1971, William I assumed the title of ___ of a united Germany.

13. ___ were responsible for the deaths of thousands of Jews in Russia.
14. In 1867, a compromise between Austria and Hungary established the ___ .
15. The term ___ came from a slogan popular in Great Britain after the Crimean War.

REVIEWING FACTS

1. **Explain:** How did Sardinia gain control of the Italian struggle for unification?
2. **Identify:** Who were the leaders of Italy's unification movement?
3. **Describe:** What was the Zollverein? How did it help Prussia gain leadership of the German Confederation?
4. **List:** What were the challenges that faced the new German state?
5. **Explain:** Why did the reforms of Alexander II satisfy no one?
6. **State:** What interests did foreign powers have in the Balkans?

THINKING CRITICALLY

1. **Apply:** How did foreign powers help Italians achieve independence?

2. **Analyze:** Contrast the problems Italy faced after unification with the problems Germany faced.
3. **Synthesize:** Why do you think Austria agreed to the compromise that established the dual monarchy?

ANALYZING CONCEPTS

1. **Nationalism:** How did the rise of nationalism spur unification movements in Italy and Germany?
2. **Reaction:** Why do you think the restoration of monarchies in Italy and Germany was important in bringing about unification?
3. **Diversity:** How did the great diversity of nationalities in the Austrian Empire lead to the establishment of the dual monarchy in the mid-1800s?

PRACTICING SKILLS

1. Which reference book discussed in the skills lesson is most likely to show how the borders of the countries discussed in Chapter 25 have changed since World War I ? To which part of the book would you turn first? For what purpose?
2. How would you find the latest figures on the size of Germany's standing army? Identify three sources that might have up-to-date figures.

3. List the reference books discussed on the skills page in the order you would buy them for a new library. Explain your priorities.

GEOGRAPHY IN HISTORY

1. **Place:** Refer to the map on page 639. What landforms and water bodies marked the borders of Germany?
2. **Region:** Refer to the map on page 65. How many nationalities lived in eastern Europe?

TRACING CHRONOLOGY

Refer to the time line below to answer these questions.
1. How long after the Revolutions of 1848 was the Kingdom of Italy established?
2. How long after the Congress of Vienna was German unification completed?
3. How long was Bismarck in power?

LINKING PAST AND PRESENT

1. Bismarck had the difficult task of forging a strong union. What problems did he face? What problems confront German leaders today in uniting East and West Germany?
2. Alexander III instituted "russification," which became an official policy of intolerance and persecution of non-Russian peoples. Are similar policies carried out in the Soviet Union today? Explain your answer.

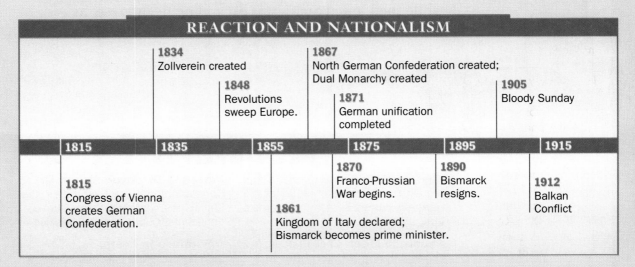

REACTION AND NATIONALISM

1834 Zollverein created

1848 Revolutions sweep Europe.

1867 North German Confederation created; Dual Monarchy created

1871 German unification completed

1905 Bloody Sunday

| 1815 | 1835 | 1855 | 1875 | 1895 | 1915 |

1815 Congress of Vienna creates German Confederation.

1861 Kingdom of Italy declared; Bismarck becomes prime minister.

1870 Franco-Prussian War begins.

1890 Bismarck resigns.

1912 Balkan Conflict

The Age of Imperialism

*N*o one knows how the rumor started, but it spread quickly. The bullets for the new rifles, the story went, were greased with the fat of cows and pigs. The sepoys, Indian soldiers in the service of the British army, were outraged. Because Hindus regarded the cow as sacred and Muslims could not touch pork, using these bullets violated the beliefs of both groups. As a result, the sepoys started a rebellion in May 1857 that soon engulfed the entire sub-continent of India.

The Sepoy Rebellion was not an isolated incident. As European powers began to acquire new territories in the 1800s, conflicts between colonial rulers and colonial peoples became a common occurrence. By the early 1900s European nations controlled large parts of Africa and Asia, while the United States was expanding its interests in Latin America.

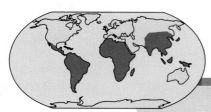

CHAPTER PREVIEW

Key Terms to Define: imperialism, protectorate, sphere of influence, partition, culture system, westernization, arbitration

People to Meet: Cecil Rhodes, Leopold II, Abd al-Qadir, Ferdinand de Lesseps, Menelik, Sun Yat-sen, the Meiji Emperor, Matthew C. Perry, James Monroe, Theodore Roosevelt

Places to Discover: Algiers, The Congo, Ethiopia, the East Indies, the Philippines, Vietnam, Siam, Burma, Venezuela, Cuba, Panama, Mexico

Objectives to Learn:
1. What were the political, economic, and social causes of imperialism?
2. What effects did imperialism have on the continent of Africa?

The British often negotiated treaties with individual Indian princes.

3. How did the countries of Asia respond to imperialism?

4. Why was the Monroe Doctrine so important to American imperialism?

Concepts to Understand:

• Movement— Political, economic, and social factors lead to a new period of expansion know as the Age of Imperialism. Sections 1,2,3,4

• Change— Imperialism produces significant economic and social changes in Africa and Asia. Sections 2,3

• Nationalism— The first stirrings of nationalist movements occur in Asia and Latin America. Sections 3,4

• Revolution— Revolutions occur in China and Latin America. Sections 3,4

657

Pressures for Expansion

The term **imperialism** is a Latin word from the days of the Roman Empire. It means one country's domination of the political, economic, and social life of another country. Two thousand years ago, imperial Rome controlled most of the Mediterranean. By the end of the 1800s, a handful of European countries, together with the United States, controlled nearly the entire world. Not surprisingly, the era between 1800 and 1914 has come to be known as the Age of Imperialism.

Nineteenth-century imperialism resulted from three key factors. First, nationalism prompted rival European nations to build empires in their competitive quests for power. Second, the Industrial Revolution created a tremendous demand for raw materials and expanded markets, which prompted industrialized nations to seek new territories. Finally, both religious fervor and feelings of racial and cultural superiority inspired Europeans to introduce their culture to distant lands.

IMAGES OF THE TIME

British India

In the 1800s India was Great Britain's most valuable possession—the Jewel in the Crown. The British presence influenced both British and Indian culture.

This Sikh painting shows a *durbar*, a traditional Indian court celebration adopted by the British to cultivate the loyalty of Indian princes.

Political Rivalries

In the mid-1800s, European countries saw themselves as actors on the world stage, and each country wanted to play a starring role. If Great Britain started a small colony in distant Asia or Africa, France had to start one too—and so did Belgium, Germany, Italy, Holland, Spain, Portugal, and Russia.

Once begun, the quest for colonies became a continuing enterprise that seemed to have no limits. Slow and difficult communication between remote territories and European capitals often enabled colonial governors and generals to take matters into their own hands. If a colony's borders did not provide military security, for instance, military officials based in the colony used their armies to expand the colony's borders. This strategy worked well enough until colonial governments started claiming the same territories. Then new conflicts arose, and European troops found themselves facing off on remote battlefields in Africa and Asia.

Desire for New Markets

The Industrial Revolution of the 1800s knew no borders. Factories in Europe and the United States consumed tons of raw materials and churned out thousands of manufactured goods. The owners and operators of these factories searched constantly for new sources of raw materials and new markets for their products. They hoped to find both in foreign lands.

Rubber, copper, and gold came from Africa, cotton and jute from India, and tin from Southeast Asia. These raw materials spurred the growth of European and American industries and financial markets, but they represented only

Queen Victoria became empress of India in 1876. Indian princes still ruled much of India, but they were required to swear allegiance to the British crown.

British tradeships carried goods to and from India (left). British and Indian architectural styles merged in Bombay's Prince of Wales Museum (above).

Reflecting on the Times
How do these pictures show the tolerance or intolerance of the British toward Indian culture?

Learning from Cartoons *Cecil Rhodes, a British administrator and financier, proposed building a railroad linking northern and southern Africa.* **Why might someone like Rhodes have wanted to see such a railroad built?**

the tip of the iceberg. Bananas, oranges, melons, and other exotic fruits made their way to European markets. People in Paris, London, and Berlin drank colonial tea, coffee, and cocoa with their meals and washed themselves with soap made from African palm oil.

The colonies also provided new markets for the finished products of the Industrial Revolution. Tools, weapons, and clothing flowed out of the factories and back to the colonies whose raw materials had made them possible.

Seeking New Opportunities

Imperialism involved more than just guns, battles, raw materials, and manufactured goods. Colonies needed people who were loyal to the imperialist country. Great Britain, France, and Germany needed British, French, and German citizens to run their newly acquired territories and keep them productive.

Throughout the 1800s European leaders urged their citizens to move to far-off colonies. Many of them responded. In the 1840s, for example, thousands of French citizens sailed across the Mediterranean Sea to Algeria, where they started farms and estates on lands seized from local Algerian farmers.

The British, meanwhile, emigrated to the far corners of the globe, hoping to find opportunities not available at home. Many rushed to Australia and New Zealand in the 1850s in search of gold. As the British government continued to acquire vast tracts of land in Africa, Asia, and the Pacific, the phrase "the sun never sets on the British Empire" became a popular way of describing Great Britain's vast holdings.

Strong-minded individuals saw emigration as a chance to strike it rich or make a name for themselves. Perhaps the most spectacular success story of the era belonged to Cecil Rhodes, a British adventurer who made a fortune from gold and diamond mining in southern Africa. Rhodes went on to found a colony that bore his name: Rhodesia (now Zimbabwe).

"Civilizing" Mission

Some emigrants had motives that went beyond mere personal glory and profit. Religious and humanitarian impulses inspired many individuals to leave their secure lives at home and head for the distant colonies. The desire to spread Western customs and traditions also fueled colonial expansion.

During the Age of Imperialism, growing numbers of Catholic and Protestant missionaries decided to bring the Christian message to the most remote corners of Africa and Asia. Over the decades they set up hundreds of Christian missions and preached to thousands of Africans and Asians throughout these two continents. Like many other Europeans and Americans of this period, these missionaries believed that Christianity and Western civilization together could transform the world.

The missionaries were not military conquerors, but they did try to change people's beliefs and practices. They believed that, in order to become "civilized," the people of Africa and Asia would have to reject their old religions and convert to Christianity. To achieve this goal, missionaries built churches and taught Christian doctrine. Missionaries often set up schools and hospitals as well.

Other Europeans also believed that Western civilization was superior to the civilizations of colonial peoples. As a result, colonial officials tried to impose Western customs and traditions on the people they conquered. These officials insisted that their colonial subjects learn European languages, and they encouraged Western life-styles as well. They also discouraged colonial peoples from practicing traditional customs and rituals.

Some Europeans seized on the theory of Social Darwinism as proof of their cultural superiority. This theory adapted Darwin's ideas about the evolution of animals—particularly his notion of "the survival of the fittest"—to explain differences between human beings. Social Darwinists believed that white Europeans were the "fittest" people in the world and that Western nations had a duty to spread Western ideas and traditions to "backward" peoples.

In 1897 the British poet Rudyard Kipling captured the essence of the imperialist attitude in his famous poem "The White Man's Burden." Kipling addressed the poem to the United States, which at this time had just begun to establish colonies of its own.

Take up the White Man's burden—
Send forth the best ye breed—
Go bind your sons to exile
To serve your captives' need;
To wait in heavy harness
On fluttered folk and wild—
Your new-caught, sullen peoples,
Half-devil and half-child.

Forms of Imperialism

Imperialist nations used a variety of means to gain new land. Sometimes they made treaties with the people who lived there. Sometimes they bought the land from another imperialist country. More often than not, however, they simply conquered the area with military force.

Imperialists used several types of territorial control. The first of these, a colony, was a territory that an imperialist power ruled directly. A **protectorate** had its own government, but officials of a foreign power guided its policies, particularly in foreign affairs. A **sphere of influence** was a region of a country in which an imperialist power held exclusive investment or trading rights.

The type of government an imperialist power chose for a region depended on the size of the area and the number of people living there. But the main idea behind all three forms of imperialism was to give the imperialists firm control of a conquered territory.

SECTION 1 REVIEW

Recall

1. **Define:** imperialism, protectorate, sphere of influence
2. **Identify:** Cecil Rhodes, Rudyard Kipling
3. **Explain:** How did rivalries lead to the growth of imperialism? Who were the main rivals?
4. **List:** Name at least five raw materials that imperialists took from their colonies. What did they send to these colonies?

Critical Thinking

5. **Synthesis:** Imagine you have been hired to write a brochure to recruit people to live in the colonies. What arguments would you use in the brochure to attract people to move?

Why? Write a few paragraphs for the brochure.
6. **Evaluate:** What does the Kipling poem reveal about his attitude toward Africans and Asians?

Applying Concepts

7. **Movement:** Explain the main reasons for the growth of imperialism in the 1800s.

The Scramble for Africa

Until the 1800s Europeans knew little of Africa beyond its northern, western, and southern coasts. Then, in the mid-1800s, a few brave explorers began to venture into the African interior. The most famous of these was Scottish doctor and missionary David Livingstone, who first went to Africa in 1840. For the next 30 years, Livingstone explored wide tracts of central Africa, setting up Christian missions and sending back to Great Britain detailed reports of his discoveries.

When Europeans temporarily lost touch with Livingstone late in the 1860s, the *New York Herald* hired a journalist named Henry M. Stanley to track him down. Their famous meeting in 1871 is best remembered for Stanley's understated greeting, "Dr. Livingstone, I presume?" With help from European financial backers, Stanley went on to lead several major expeditions through central Africa himself.

The publicity surrounding the explorations of Livingstone and Stanley generated new interest in Africa throughout Europe. This interest swelled when subsequent explorers sent back excited reports about the continent's abundance of resources. Reports such as these helped set off a mad European scramble for Africa between 1880 and 1914. One European country after another laid claim to parts of Africa. In 1885 fourteen nations met in Berlin, Germany, and agreed to **partition**, or divide, the prize King Leopold II of Belgium called "this magnificent African cake." By 1914 European nations controlled 90 percent of the continent.

The Conquest of North Africa

The world's largest desert—the Sahara—stretches across North Africa from the Atlantic Ocean to the Red Sea. Most of the people in North Africa live on a thin strip of land located to the north of the Sahara along the Mediterranean coast. Here the land is fertile and the climate mild. In the early 1800s, Muslim Arabs (technically under the authority of the Ottoman sultan) ruled the large territories west of Egypt, which at that time were called Tripoli, Tunis, Algiers, and Morocco.

The French Conquer North Africa In 1830 King Charles X of France ordered an invasion of Algiers with the aim of colonizing that country. French troops encountered stiff resistance from the native Algerians, whose leader was Abd al-Qadir.

In the end it took the French 10 years and an army of 100,000 soldiers to subdue the determined Abd al-Qadir. They went on to seize neighboring Tunis in 1881 and secured special rights in Morocco by 1905. About one million French people settled in North Africa during these years of struggle.

Britain Invades Egypt In 1869 a French company headed by Ferdinand de Lesseps completed the Suez Canal after ten years of work. Cutting through Egyptian territory to connect the Mediterranean and Red seas, the canal was a vital shortcut between Europe and Asia. During the next ten years, Egypt sold some of its holdings in the canal company to Great Britain to pay off its debts. When Egyptian nationalists rebelled in 1882 against the westernized *khedive*, or governor, British forces invaded to protect their government's interests in the canal. British influence was to remain strong in Egypt until the 1950s.

Having subdued Egypt, the British looked southward to the Sudan. In 1898 British forces defeated the Sudanese at the battle of Omdurman. No sooner was the battle over than the

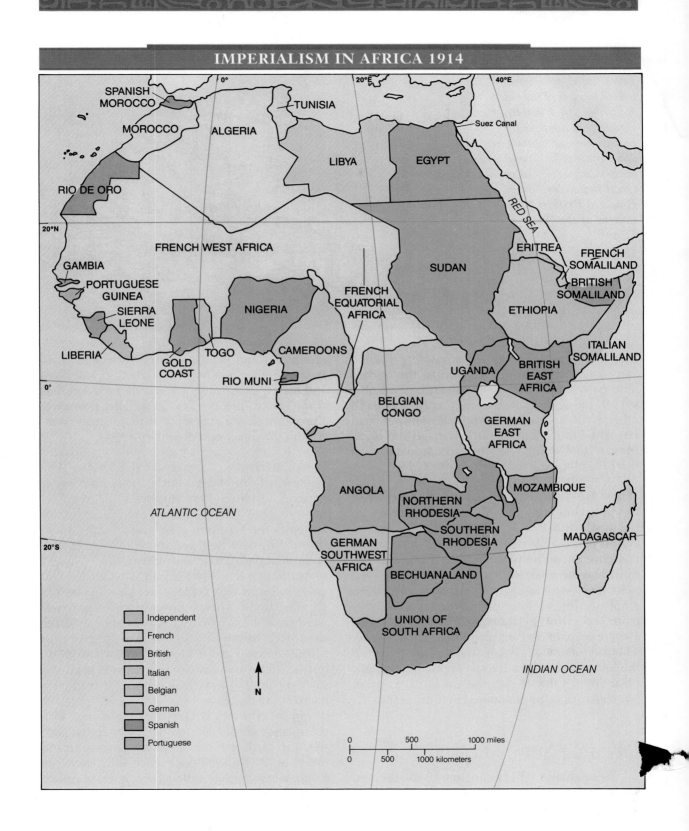

IMPERIALISM IN AFRICA 1914

SPANISH MOROCCO
TUNISIA
MOROCCO
ALGERIA
Suez Canal
LIBYA
EGYPT
RIO DE ORO
RED SEA
20°N
FRENCH WEST AFRICA
ERITREA
FRENCH SOMALILAND
GAMBIA
SUDAN
PORTUGUESE GUINEA
BRITISH SOMALILAND
SIERRA LEONE
NIGERIA
FRENCH EQUATORIAL AFRICA
ETHIOPIA
LIBERIA
TOGO
ITALIAN SOMALILAND
GOLD COAST
CAMEROONS
RIO MUNI
UGANDA
BRITISH EAST AFRICA
0°
BELGIAN CONGO
GERMAN EAST AFRICA
ANGOLA
MOZAMBIQUE
ATLANTIC OCEAN
NORTHERN RHODESIA
SOUTHERN RHODESIA
MADAGASCAR
20°S
GERMAN SOUTHWEST AFRICA
BECHUANALAND
UNION OF SOUTH AFRICA
INDIAN OCEAN

Independent
French
British
Italian
Belgian
German
Spanish
Portuguese

N

0   500   1000 miles
0   500   1000 kilometers

Learning from Art *The Suez Canal opened in 1869 with a lavish ceremony attended by most of the rulers of Europe. After initially opposing the canal, the British realized that a more direct route to India and points east was crucial to Great Britain's economy.* **How did Britain gain control of the Suez Canal?**

British learned of a rapidly advancing French force that was also laying claim to the Sudan. The two armies met at the town of Fashoda, where for several weeks they stared at each other across the Nile. An imperialist dispute had brought France and Great Britain to the brink of war. The French finally backed down when the British recognized their claim to Morocco.

Italy Seizes Libya Libya lies between Egypt on the east and Algeria and Tunisia on the west. Known as Tripoli in the late 1800s, the country had almost no economic value but it was coveted by Italy, the nearest European nation. Having entered the imperialist race late, however, Italy was eager to establish an African empire. After seeking guarantees of neutrality from several other European nations, Italy in 1911 declared war on the Ottoman Empire, which controlled Tripoli. Italy easily defeated the Ottoman Turks and took Tripoli as a colony, renaming it Libya. Libya was the last country in North Africa to be conquered by Europeans.

Dividing Sub-Saharan Africa

Sub-Saharan Africa consists of all the land between the Sahara and the southern tip of the continent. It is an immensely varied land of mountains and plains, deserts and rain forests. In the 1800s it was home to dozens of kingdoms and states, each of which had its own rich and complicated history. The imperialist powers of Europe swallowed up most of these small countries in the final decades of the 1800s.

West Africa As early as the 1400s, Portuguese sailors had explored the west coast of Africa. During the next hundred years, the Portuguese, Dutch, British, and French set up trading posts and forts along the coast. By the 1600s these outposts had become the center of a booming transatlantic slave trade.

Although the West African states traded salt, gold, and iron wares, they were also involved in the slave trade. Their economies declined rapidly when key European countries abolished the slave trade in the early 1800s. They then began to rely on cash crops such as cotton and cacao beans. They also exchanged natural products such as palm oil, ivory, and rubber for European manufactured goods.

In an effort to control this trade, and with the further aim of expanding their coastal possessions, European nations began to push inland in the 1870s. By 1900 the French had conquered a vast territory they called French West Africa. During this same period, the British acquired the Gold Coast, the kingdom of Ashanti, and parts of Nigeria. And while Spain and Portugal expanded older claims, Germany staked out new colonies in the region.

By the early 1900s, Liberia was the only remaining independent state in West Africa. Established in 1822 by freed American slaves, Liberia had become an independent republic in 1847. The support Liberia received from the United States discouraged European powers from attempting to seize it as a colony.

Central and East Africa   After a grueling three-year journey that began on the east coast of Africa, Henry M. Stanley arrived at the mouth of the Congo River on the west coast of Africa in 1877. Stanley sang the praises of the Congo to all who would listen. "The [European] Power possessing the Congo," he wrote, "would absorb in itself the trade of the whole enormous basin behind. The river is and will be the grand highway of commerce to . . . Central Africa."

King Leopold II of Belgium liked what he heard. An ambitious man, Leopold wanted to make a name for himself and his small country. Consequently, he formed a private company called the International African Association in 1878 to promote Belgian colonization in Africa. As a result of Stanley's explorations, Leopold claimed the entire Congo Basin and named it the Congo Free State.

CONNECTIONS:
GEOGRAPHY
IN
HISTORY

Coastal Trading Centers

"The king of the white people wishes to find out a way by which we may bring our own merchandise to you and sell everything at a much cheaper rate," said British explorer Mungo Park to a West African king in 1805. "For this purpose, I propose sailing down the Joliba [the Niger River] to the place where it mixes with the salt water, and if I find no rocks or danger in the way, the white man's small vessels will come up to trade."

Park was interested in the possibilities of trade on the Niger River. Like the other great rivers of Africa—the Congo, the Nile, and the Zambezi—the Niger flows to the sea. To the imperialist traders of the nineteenth century, few places were more important than the mouth of a river. These were the places where the large trading ships exchanged their manufactured goods for the raw materials of Africa.

At the mouth of the Niger in the late 1800s, exchange centered on palm oil. The English used the oil for manufacturing soap. Barrels of the precious oil were floated down the Niger and collected at depots, or port towns, with names like Calabar and Port Harcourt.

In time these depots grew into cities. People from all across Nigeria have come to these ports in search of jobs. Calabar is now home to 100,000 people, and Port Harcourt to a quarter million. These ports still provide oil to the world, but today it is crude oil, the lifeblood of the world's industries and transportation.

Making the Connection
1. What was Mungo Park interested in doing in Africa?
2. Why did the mouths of African rivers become centers for trade with Europeans?

Leopold soon transformed the Congo Free State into his own private plantation. Like a plantation, the Congo had an owner—Leopold II—and an enormous source of slave labor—the people of the Congo. Leopold forced these people to cut down entire forests for rubber trees and to kill herds of elephants for their ivory tusks. His rule stripped large parts of the Congo of both its people and its raw materials.

Leopold's brutal control of the Congo lasted about 20 years, despite the world's outrage. A year before his death, he finally agreed to give his plantation to the Belgian government in return for a large loan. Thus, in 1908, the Congo Free State became the Belgian Congo.

While the Belgians were claiming the Congo Basin, the British, the Germans, and the Italians were doing the same in East Africa. In fact, the only country in East Africa to remain independent during this period was Ethiopia, located in a remote region known as the Horn of Africa. Beginning in the 1880s, Italy tried to conquer this country, but the Italians underestimated the determination of their opponent, Ethiopia's Emperor Menelik II.

When the Italians attacked Ethiopia in 1896, Menelik's well-trained forces crushed the invaders at the battle of Adowa. His victory was so devastating that no Europeans dared invade his country again during his lifetime. Ethiopia

PERSONAL PROFILES

Menelik II: King of Kings

Menelik II

Menelik II was born a prince in the Ethiopian province of Shoa in 1844. Eleven years later, when his father died, Menelik was taken prisoner by Tewodros, a rival king. In nine years of house arrest, Menelik learned how to rule by watching Tewodros strive to create a modern, unified Ethiopia. When he was 20, Menelik escaped and returned to Shoa to be named *negus*, or king, of the province.

In less than 25 years, Menelik became the most powerful king in Ethiopia and took the title of *negus neghest*, or king of kings. His policies echoed the lessons of his youth. He unified and expanded his empire while firmly committing himself to European-style modernization. Modernization was the empire's best hope, but it also posed the greatest threat to the empire. Modernization—better roads, communication systems, and weaponry—strengthened the empire

against outside attack. But it also meant trading and dealings with European powers when those nations were literally dividing up the continent of Africa into colonies.

In 1896 the European threat to Ethiopia became a reality when the Italians deceived Menelik into signing a treaty that made Ethiopia a protectorate of Italy. Declaring the treaty null and void, Menelik rallied his army to meet the Italians in battle. At Adowa the Ethiopians crushed a stunned Italian army. The victory sent a clear message to the rest of Europe: Ethiopia was a free nation. No other power attempted to colonize Ethiopia for 40 years.

Reflecting on the Person
1. What role did Tewodros play in Menelik's development?
2. Why was modernization important to Menelik?

and Liberia were the only two African nations to escape European domination completely during the Age of Imperialism.

Southern Africa   Dutch settlers came to southern Africa in 1652 and established the port of Cape Town. For the next 150 years, the Afrikaners, as these settlers came to be called, conquered the lands around the port. The lands they eventually acquired became Cape Colony.

Before construction of the Suez Canal, the quickest sea route to Asia from Europe was around the Cape of Good Hope at the southern tip of Africa. Sensing the strategic value of Cape Colony, the British seized it during the Napoleonic Wars in the early 1800s. The Afrikaners resented British rule, particularly laws that forbade the owning of black slaves. The white Afrikaners believed that they were superior to black Africans and that God had ordained slavery.

In the 1830s about 10,000 Afrikaners, whom the British called Boers (the Dutch word for farmers), decided to leave Cape Colony rather than live under British rule. In a move known as the Great Trek, the Afrikaners migrated northeast into the interior. Here they established two independent republics, the Transvaal and the Orange Free State. The constitution of the Transvaal stated, "There shall be no equality in State or Church between white and black."

The Afrikaners fought constantly with their neighbors. First they battled the powerful Zulu nation for control of the land. Then they fought British settlers who came to the Transvaal in search of gold and diamonds. These conflicts erupted in 1899 into the Boer War, which the British finally won three years later.

In 1910 Great Britain united the Transvaal, the Orange Free State, the Cape Colony, and Natal into the Union of South Africa. The constitution of this British dominion made it all but impossible for nonwhites to win the right to vote. As one black African writer of the time said, "The Union is to be a Union of two races, namely the British and the Afrikaners—the African is to be excluded."

Effects of Imperialism

Imperialism had profound and lasting effects on the African continent. These effects varied from colony to colony, but they centered mainly on economic and social life.

The imperialists profited from the colonies by digging mines, starting plantations, and building factories. They hired Africans at extremely low wages and imposed taxes that had to be paid in cash. Men were often housed in dormitories away from their families and subjected to brutal discipline.

Although schools were few, they taught Africans that European ways were best. Missionaries taught them to reject African customs and beliefs. Africans learned to read European books and to wear European clothes. Under some colonial governments, entire villages broke up, families came apart, and ancient traditions withered and disappeared.

SECTION 2 REVIEW

Recall

1. **Define:** partition
2. **Identify:** David Livingstone, Henry Stanley, Leopold II, Abd al-Qadir, Ferdinand de Lesseps, Menelik II
3. **Locate:** Find the countries of North Africa on the map on page 663. What geographical feature separates these countries from the rest of the African continent?
4. **Describe:** What were the advantages of the Suez Canal? Why was it so valuable to Europe?

Critical Thinking

5. **Evaluate:** How did King Leopold II's personal management of the Congo affect that region?

6. **Analysis:** Explain how British attitudes toward black Africans differed from those of the Afrikaners. Find evidence to support your answers.

Applying Concepts

7. **Change:** What were the main causes and effects of the European partition of Africa?

The Division of Asia

In his book *Description of the World*, written in 1298, Italian explorer Marco Polo relates the many stories he heard about Zipangu, an East Asian island with a supposedly inexhaustible supply of gold. Polo never did visit Zipangu, now called Japan, but his description of its treasures, and of the Asian riches he did see, inspired generations of Europeans. They looked eastward to Asia, dreaming of wealth.

The British in India

European trade with Asia opened up in the 1500s as sea routes began to replace the difficult overland route Marco Polo had taken. British involvement in India dates back to this period, when English traders first sailed along India's coast. In 1600 some of these traders banded together and formed the East India Company. It later became one of the richest and most powerful trading companies the world has ever known.

FOOTNOTES TO HISTORY
THE TAJ MAHAL

Today the Taj Mahal is considered one of the wonders of the world. But in British India of the late 1800s, it was a monument to robbery and neglect. The British rulers held many parties and dances there. Partygoers soon discovered how easy it was to pull the beautiful carvings and other objects out of the walls. Some even arrived at the parties with hammers and chisels, ready to go to work. Eventually the British government put an end to the thievery, but the damage was considerable. The British and Indians worked together throughout the 1900s to restore the beautiful building.

After its founding the East India Company built trading posts and forts in strategic locations throughout India. The French East India Company did the same and challenged the British for control of the India trade. In 1757 the British defeated French-trained Indian forces at the Battle of Plassey. During the next hundred years, the British expanded their territory in India through wars and commerce.

The Sepoy Rebellion As a result of steady expansion, the East India Company came to control most of India by 1857. But their power was tested that year when the sepoys rebelled against their British commanders. Long before the greased bullet rumor discussed at the beginning of this chapter triggered the Sepoy Rebellion, sepoy resentment had been growing over British attempts to impose Christianity and European customs on them.

The Sepoy Rebellion lasted six long months. Although the uprising failed, it forced the British government to tighten its control of India. In 1858 the British Parliament dissolved the East India Company and sent a viceroy, or governor, to take over the company's territory. A viceroy soon won the loyalty of the few remaining independent Indian states by signing agreements with the maharajahs who ruled them. In 1877 Prime Minister Disraeli conferred upon Queen Victoria the title of "Empress of India."

Indian Nationalism The British government tried to quell further unrest in India by spending vast amounts of money on India's economic development. It built paved roads and an extensive railway system; it installed telegraph lines and dug irrigation canals; and it established schools and universities.

At the same time, British colonial officials discriminated against Indians and forced them to change their ancient ways, often with tragic results. Indian farmers, for example, were told to grow cotton instead of wheat, because British textile mills needed cotton. But the lack of wheat led to food shortages that killed millions of Indians during the 1800s.

Outraged by the food shortages and other problems, many Indians demanded more power for Indian leaders. In 1885 some of them formed the Indian National Congress, a political group that eventually led the long struggle for Indian independence. Continued protests and scattered violence led to a few reforms, but at the beginning of the 1900s Great Britain still held India firmly in its grasp.

China Faces the West

While the British were establishing an empire in India, they and other Europeans also developed trade with China. During the 1500s Chinese civilization had been highly advanced, and the Chinese at that time showed little interest in acquiring European products. In fact, there was only limited trade between China and Europe during the next 300 years. During this period, however, China's political, military, and economic position weakened under the rule of the Qing dynasty. Qing emperors ruled the country from 1644 to 1911.

The Unequal Treaties In the early 1800s, British merchants found a way to break China's trade barriers and earn huge profits. In exchange for Chinese tea, silk, and porcelain—and to avoid paying cash—the merchants smuggled a drug called opium, which they obtained from India and Turkey, into China. In 1839 Chinese troops tried to stop the smuggling. When the British resisted, war broke out.

Great Britain won the Opium War in 1842 and signed the first of many foreign treaties with the Qing dynasty. Because the treaties took advantage of China's weakness, the Chinese called them the unequal treaties. Over the next 60 years, Great Britain, France, Germany, Japan, Russia, and the United States all signed unequal treaties with China. In general, these treaties increased foreign power in China and weakened

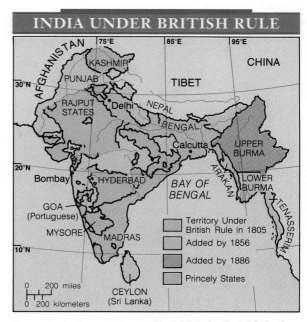

Learning from Maps *By 1886 the British had gained control of most of India.* **What areas remained free of British rule?**

the Qing dynasty. Civil wars such as the Taiping Rebellion (1850–1864) did even more to erode the dynasty's control of the country.

By the end of the century, the imperialist nations had won their struggle for power in China. Great Britain, France, Germany, Russia, and Japan claimed large sections of China as spheres of influence—areas where they had exclusive trading rights. Because it came late to the imperialist scramble, the United States did not claim a sphere of influence. Instead, it tried to open China to the trade of all nations through the Open Door Policy. Deadlocked by their own intense rivalries, the European nations reluctantly agreed to this policy in 1899.

By 1900 foreign power in China was at a high point. This influence infuriated Empress Ci Xi (TSUH see), the domineering mother of the Qing emperor, who opposed all foreigners and modernization. She wrote her thoughts on China's dilemma in her diary: "The various Powers cast upon us looks of tiger-like voracity [intense hunger], hustling each other in their endeavors to be the first to seize upon our innermost territories."

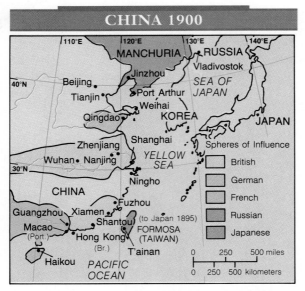

CHINA 1900

Spheres of Influence
- British
- German
- French
- Russian
- Japanese

Learning from Maps *The European powers divided China into spheres of influence in the late 1800s.* **Which of these powers controlled Manchuria in 1900?**

The Boxer Rebellion   Ci Xi prevented the emperor from ruling in his own right and encouraged Chinese antiforeign groups that gathered in secret to plot ways of driving out the imperialists. One such group called itself the Society of Righteous and Harmonious Fists because it also practiced a Chinese form of boxing. Its members became known as the Boxers.

The Boxers gained strength from their belief in Chinese rituals and traditions and their hatred of foreigners. In June 1900 they launched a series of attacks that killed several hundred foreigners and thousands of Chinese Christians. They besieged the foreigners in Beijing, the capital of China.

The foreign powers responded quickly and decisively. Their governments formed a combined army of 25,000 troops, which marched on Beijing and quelled the rebellion with a hail of bullets. When the fighting was over, thousands of Chinese lay dead in the streets. The empress, who had praised the "patriotic Boxers" and ordered them to kill foreign officials, fled the city.

Foreign troops crushed the Boxers in a few weeks. But a greater revolt was already brewing, one that took aim at the Qing dynasty.

The Revolution of 1911   After the Boxer Rebellion, Ci Xi struggled to hold on to power. She agreed to allow foreign troops to remain in China and gave in to some of her people's demands for change. For example, she established schools and reorganized the government. But it was too little, too late. Many Chinese believed that a modern republic should replace the Qing dynasty. In their view, the only way to achieve this goal was through revolution.

The revolutionaries wanted China to regain its former power and influence. One of them, a doctor named Sun Yat-sen, wrote in the early 1900s, "Today we are the poorest and weakest nation in the world and occupy the lowest position in international affairs. Other men are the carving knife and serving dish; we are the fish and the meat."

The revolutionaries came together to form the United League (later called the Kuomintang, or "Nationalist Party") in 1905, choosing Sun Yat-sen as their leader. They soon attacked troops loyal to the Qing dynasty, but without success. Then the empress died, in 1908, and by law two-year-old Prince Pu Yi became the new emperor of China. The resulting confusion further weakened the dynasty.

Three years later Sun Yat-sen was raising money in the United States when the emperor's own troops joined in a successful revolt against the dynasty. Sun hurried back home and became the first president of the new Republic of China in 1911. His country had finally entered the modern age.

Modernization of Japan

Japan's dealings with the European powers began in much the same way as China's, but they ended differently. European traders first came to the island country in the 1500s. Like the Chinese, the Japanese were uninterested in European products, and they cut off almost all trade with Europe in the early 1600s. At the time a military commander called a shogun ruled Japan. Although the country also had an emperor, he had no real power.

Japan did not trade again with the outside world until 1853, when four American warships commanded by Commodore Matthew C. Perry sailed into the bay at Edo (later called Tokyo). Perry wanted Japan to begin trading with the United States. The shogun, knowing what had happened to China in the recent Opium War, decided early in 1854 to sign a treaty with Perry.

The Meiji Leaders

In the first five years after Perry's arrival, the shogun signed trade treaties with Britain, France, Holland, Russia, and the United States. Since the treaties favored the imperialist powers, the Japanese people called them unequal treaties, just as the Chinese had. Unhappiness with the treaties led to the overthrow of the shogun in 1868. A group of samurai put a new emperor, Mutsuhito, on the Japanese throne, but kept the real power to themselves. Because Mutsuhito was known as the Meiji, or "Enlightened" emperor, Japan's new rulers were called the Meiji leaders.

The Meiji leaders tried to make Japan a great power capable of competing with Western nations. Adopting the slogan "Rich country, strong military" they brought the forms of parliamentary government to Japan, strengthened the military, and worked to transform the nation into an industrial society. The Meiji leaders established a system of universal education designed to produce loyal, skilled citizens who were ready to work for Japan's modernization. In this way, the Japanese hoped to create a new ruling class based on talent rather than birth.

Industrialization

In the 1870s Japan began to industrialize in an effort to strengthen its economy. The Japanese carried out this task with little outside assistance. They were reluctant to borrow money from the West, fearing foreign takeovers if loans could not be repaid. In any case, most Western banks were not interested in making loans to Japan, because they considered the country a poor financial risk.

The Japanese government laid the groundwork for industrial expansion. It revised the tax structure to raise money for investment. It also developed a modern currency system and supported the building of postal and telegraph networks, railroads, and port facilities.

Beginning in the late 1880s, Japan's economy grew rapidly. A growing population provided a continuing supply of cheap labor. The combination of new methods and cheap labor allowed Japan to produce low-priced goods. Wars at the turn of the century further stimulated Japan's economy and helped it enter new markets. By 1914 Japan had become one of the world's leading industrial nations.

Japan as a World Power

By the 1890s the Meiji leaders had taken great strides toward creating a modern nation. Japan had acquired an efficient government, a vigorous economy, and a strong army and navy. Needing more natural resources to increase its strength, the Japanese government began to establish its own overseas empire. Its first prize was Korea.

When the people of Korea revolted against their Chinese rulers in 1894, Japan decided to intervene. Japanese troops easily defeated the Chinese army in the Sino-Japanese War.

Learning from Art *This nineteenth-century Japanese portrait of Commodore Matthew Perry shows how foreigners appeared to the Japanese.* **What demands did Perry make on the Japanese after his arrival?**

Although Korea officially became an independent country, Japan gained partial control of its trade. Over the next few years, thousands of Japanese settled in Korea.

Korea also figured in Japan's next war. The Russian Empire had interests in Korea as well, and its interests began to clash with Japan's. Even more important was neighboring Manchuria, where the Russians kept troops and had a naval base at Port Arthur. In 1904 the Japanese navy launched a surprise attack on Port Arthur. Few people expected Japan to win the Russo-Japanese War, but they piled up victory after victory. The conflict ended in 1905, when Russia signed a treaty granting Japan control over Korea and other nearby areas.

Japan's victory over Russia inspired non-Western nationalist leaders throughout the world. It proved that the European empires could be defeated if one had the will. On the other hand, Japan had now become an imperialist country itself. It annexed Korea as a colony in 1910 and continued to expand its empire for the next 35 years.

Southeast Asia and the Pacific

Southeast Asia and the islands of the Pacific Ocean are two distinct geographic areas. Southeast Asia consists of a large peninsula south of China and a group of islands near the peninsula. The Islands of the Pacific consist of thousands of islands scattered all across the Pacific Ocean between Asia and the Americas.

The growth of imperialism in these areas followed a familiar pattern. Beginning in the 1500s, imperialist powers came, saw, and conquered. Over the next 400 years, Great Britain, France, Germany, Holland, Portugal, Spain, and the United States all set up colonies, both large and small, in the region. They ranged in size from the huge Dutch East Indies in Southeast Asia to the tiny British settlement on Pitcairn Island in the Pacific.

The Islands of Southeast Asia The island region of Southeast Asia forms two main groups: the East Indies and the Philippines. At the beginning of the 1800s, the Dutch controlled most of the East Indies, and Spain controlled the Philippines.

The Dutch East Indies (now called Indonesia) had many natural resources, including rich soil. Farmers grew coffee, pepper, cinnamon, sugar, indigo, and tea; miners dug for tin and copper; loggers cut down ebony, teak, and other hardwood trees. The Dutch government used a method of forced labor called the **culture system** to gather all these raw materials. The Dutch also discouraged **westernization**, or the spread of European civilization. The enormous profits the Dutch received from the East Indies made the colony the envy of the imperialist powers.

Diponegoro, a native prince from the East Indian island of Java, started a revolt against the Dutch in 1825. Although it lasted 10 years, this revolt eventually ended in failure, and the Dutch encountered little real opposition for the next 80 years. One of the Dutch governors put it this way: "We have ruled here for 300 years with the whip and the club and we shall still be doing it in another 300 years."

The Spanish rule of the Philippines resembled the Dutch rule of the Dutch East Indies. Native Filipinos worked for very low wages, if any, on tobacco and sugar plantations owned by wealthy Spaniards. During the 1800s the Filipinos' resentment grew until it finally exploded into revolution in 1896.

When the United States declared war on Spain in 1898, the American government promised to make the Philippines an independent country in return for the rebels' help against the Spanish. But when the United States won the Spanish-American War later that year, it broke its promise and instead ruled the Philippines as a colony. The Filipinos then arose against American rule, but United States troops defeated them two years later.

The Southeast Asian Peninsula The peninsula region of Southeast Asia consisted of several territories in the early 1800s, including Burma and Malaya in the west, Vietnam in the east, and Siam, Cambodia, and Laos in the middle. All through the 1800s, the British and French struggled for control of the area, more for military than for economic reasons.

Japanese Woodblock Prints

Katsushika Hokusai (1760–1849) is one of the most famous painters and printmakers in the long history of Japanese art. He began drawing from nature at age six. Later he studied under professional artists to learn various techniques and styles. His work includes Kabuki theater portraits, book illustrations, and studies of people, plants, landscapes, and animals. His images are lively and colorful, with an immediacy and power that only the best artists can achieve.

Hokusai was one of the last masters of ukiyo-e prints. The word *ukiyo-e* means "picture of the floating world." Ukiyo-e images became an important form of Japanese art as early as the 1600s. The "floating world" referred to fashionable or fleeting subjects and events—for example, images of daily life or popular actors as opposed to formal portraits or epic events. The ukiyo-e print began as a form of popular art for the lower classes of Japanese society. Over the years, however, it became an important and vital art form.

The image here, *Fuji Seen from Nakahara*, is one of Hokusai's many woodblock prints of Mount Fuji. In this print, Hokusai included several people in the landscape. One man fishes in the river with a basket net, while a woman with a child carries a hoe in one hand and a basket atop her head. Other figures pass by, each going about his or her business. In the distance looms Mount Fuji.

Hokusai portrays the mountain and the surrounding landscape in a schematic, abstract way. The mountain is hardly more than a triangle, with a touch of color to indicate trees on the lower portions and snow at the peak. Distance is suggested by deeper colors and less detail in the more distant parts of the landscape. Hokusai's schematic, or simplified, way of depicting this image helps to make it vibrant and immediate. Because no intense detail is included, the viewer of the print is not drawn to study each portion carefully to determine what is happening. The landscape and activities portrayed are immediately understandable.

Responding to the Arts

1. What were ukiyo-e prints?
2. What were some of the artistic techniques Hokusai used in this image of Mount Fuji?

The British swept into Burma from India in the 1820s. Over the next 60 years, they took full control of Burma and neighboring Malaya. Meanwhile, the French were slowly conquering Indochina (what is now Vietnam, Cambodia, and Laos). They, too, established complete control in the 1880s.

Squeezed between the two growing blocks of British and French territory lay the kingdom of Siam (now called Thailand). In 1893 the French invaded Siam, sending forces into Bangkok, the capital city. Great Britain and France avoided armed conflict, however, when they agreed to define their spheres of influence in Southeast Asia. As a result of the agreement, Siam remained independent.

Struggles between Europeans for control of economic resources brought much destruction and disturbance to the peninsula region of Southeast Asia. Western products and business practices also changed the traditional ways of life of the people who lived there. Colonial landowners and trading companies forced local farmers and workers to grow cash crops, usually rice. They also hired them to mine coal and teak trees. These were the raw materials and cash crops that interested Western capitalists.

Pacific Islands American writer Herman Melville first saw the Pacific island of Nuku Hiva from the deck of a whaling ship in 1842. It is just one of thousands of tropical islands scattered across the Pacific. When his ship approached the island in search of food and water, this is the sight that greeted Melville's eyes:

Towards noon we . . . entered the bay of Nukuheva. No description can do justice to its beauty; but that beauty was lost to me then, and I saw nothing but the tri-colored flag of France trailing over the stern of six vessels, whose black hulls and bristling broadsides proclaimed their warlike character. . . . To my eye, nothing could be more out of keeping than the presence of these vessels; but we soon learnt what brought them there. The whole group of islands had just been taken possession of by Rear Admiral Du Petit Thouars, in the name of the invincible French nation.

Melville's description captures many of the elements of imperialism in the South Pacific region. Sailing ships depended upon refitting and resupply stations; navies depended upon strategic ports; the islands were there for the taking. Throughout the 1800s the imperialist powers grabbed as many islands as they could, often meeting with little resistance from the startled islanders.

The new masters behaved in predictable ways. They exported the islands' few raw materials, mostly copra (dried coconut meat), and they started plantations where local workers harvested coffee, sugar, pineapples, and other cash crops. By 1910 the British, French, Germans, and Americans had divided the islands among themselves, and their conquest seemed complete. But the peoples of the region had other ideas. Like their counterparts around the world, they dreamed of independence.

SECTION 3 REVIEW

Recall

1. **Define:** culture system, westernization
2. **Identify:** Ci Xi, Sun Yat-sen, Matthew C. Perry, Meiji Emperor, Diponegoro
3. **Explain:** Why did the British government dissolve the East India Company?
4. **Identify:** Why did China refuse to import European products before the Opium War?

Critical Thinking

5. **Synthesis:** How did the forms of imperial domination differ in India, China, Southeast Asia, and the Pacific?
6. **Evaluate:** How did the Japanese succeed in avoiding imperialist takeover by European powers and the United States when the Chinese could not?

Applying Concepts

7. **Change:** What were the Europeans' main goals in conquering Asia and the Pacific? How did they compare to Japan's imperialist goals?

SECTION 4

Imperialism in the Americas

On the floor of the Senate in 1898, United States Senator Albert J. Beveridge delivered a stirring speech on America's growing role as a world power:

Fate has written our policy for us; the trade of the world must and shall be ours. We will establish trading-posts throughout the world as distributing-points for American products. . . . Great colonies governing themselves, flying our flag and trading with us, will grow about our posts of trade.

Beveridge's grand ambition capped a half-century of growing American influence in world affairs. The imperialist powers of Europe had already laid claim to much of the world. Now American expansionists seemed ready to go after what was left. The United States government was also determined to use the Monroe Doctrine to block the revival of European brands of imperialism in neighboring Latin America, an area that includes the Caribbean islands, Central America, and South America.

The Monroe Doctrine

The United States was the only independent country in the Americas in 1800. European powers such as Great Britain, France, Holland, Portugal, and, particularly, Spain ruled the rest of the hemisphere. Over the next two decades, however, many Latin American colonies revolted against their distant European rulers.

First Haiti and then Paraguay, Chile, Colombia, Mexico, and Peru broke free from Spain. At about the same time, Brazil escaped Portugal's rule. Spain gave signs in 1823 of trying to regain its colonial empire, but the United States would have none of it. In an address to

Congress late in 1823, President James Monroe set forth the policy that is now called the Monroe Doctrine. It contained two major points:

1. *The American continents, by the free and independent condition which they have assured and maintain, are henceforth not to be considered as subjects for future colonization by any European powers.*
2. *We should consider any attempt on their part to extend their system to any portion of this hemisphere as dangerous to our peace and safety.*

Seven years after Monroe uttered his famous doctrine, Bolivia, Uruguay, Ecuador, and Venezuela had added their names to the list of independent countries in Latin America. By 1890 Cuba, Puerto Rico, and other Caribbean islands were the only territories in the region still in European hands.

Throughout the 1800s the European powers mounted few serious challenges to the Monroe Doctrine. France did send troops to Mexico in 1863, during the American Civil War, but they withdrew four years later rather than risk war with the United States. Another challenge occurred in 1895, when Great Britain threatened to invade Venezuela over a border dispute with British Guiana. But after receiving a warning from the American secretary of state, Great Britain backed down. The United States government's dislike of European influence in Latin America, however, led to a war with Spain.

The Spanish-American War

Cuba and Puerto Rico were still Spanish colonies in the late 1800s. Cuba was particularly important to Spain, which reaped huge profits from the island's many sugar plantations.

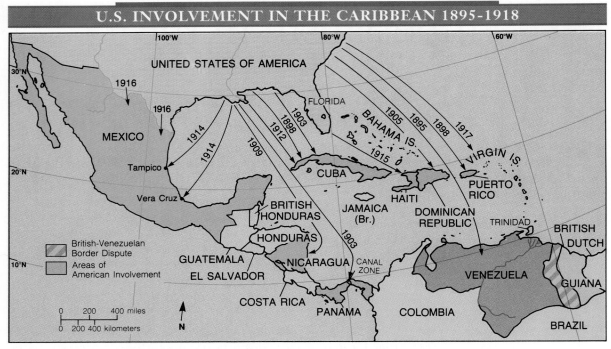

Learning from Maps *The United States intervened in the affairs of Latin American nations in the early 1900s.* **How did Latin Americans view American intervention in their affairs?**

When Cubans revolted against Spain in 1895, Spanish leaders embarked on a bloody purge of the rebel forces and the Cuban people. Spanish troops rounded up thousands of Cubans and sent them to prison camps where conditions were brutal. Disease and starvation soon claimed more than 200,000 Cuban lives.

Remember the *Maine!* American newspapers printed vivid stories describing Spain's brutal treatment of the Cubans. Soon, prominent American politicians began clamoring for war with Spain. Business persons who had invested in Cuba also joined in. Finally, in January 1898, President William McKinley ordered the battleship *Maine* to Havana, the capital of Cuba, to demonstrate growing American interest in Cuban affairs. A few weeks later, an explosion ripped through the *Maine* while it was still anchored in Havana harbor, sinking the ship and killing 260 American sailors.

The cry "Remember the *Maine!*" swept across the United States. American newspapers left little doubt that Spain was responsible for the disaster. Under pressure from all sides, McKinley asked Congress to declare war on Spain in April 1898.

In four short months, Spain lost Cuba, Puerto Rico, the Philippines, and the Pacific island of Guam to the United States. The Spanish official who signed the peace treaty in December 1898 noted that the loss "strips us of the very last memory of a glorious past, and expels us . . . from the Western Hemisphere, which became peopled and civilized through the proud deeds of our ancestors."

A Nation of Warriors

As a result of the Spanish-American War, the United States found itself the ruler of four island colonies. Debate raged throughout the nation on what to do with them. The debate ended in a draw. The United States kept Puerto Rico, Guam, and the Philippines. Cuba, on the other hand, did receive its independence, but under certain special conditions. The United States government forced the new nation to accept an agreement called the Platt Amendment in 1900. Under this agreement the United States would not annex Cuba but would have the right to send its troops to Cuba "for the protection of life, property, and individual liberty." The amendment also allowed the United States to build two naval bases in Cuba.

In 1898 the United States also took over Hawaii, a country in which American business had valuable holdings. Like the European powers, the United States government appeared to be harboring dreams of building an empire. A newspaper editorial that appeared in 1898 captured the country's new mood: "From a nation of shopkeepers we become a nation of warriors. . . . From a provincial huddle. . .we rise to the dignity and prowess of an imperial republic incomparably greater than Rome."

Statements such as these sent shivers through Latin America. After all, the Monroe Doctrine protected Latin America only from "colonization by any European powers." It said nothing about colonization by the power that the Latin American countries called "the Colossus of the North."

The Roosevelt Corollary

By the end of the Spanish-American War, former Assistant Secretary of the Navy Theodore Roosevelt had become an American hero, known to one and all for leading the "Rough Rider" Cavalry Regiment in a brave charge up Cuba's San Juan Hill. Within months he was elected governor of New York; three years later, in 1901, he became President of the United States.

During his eight years in office, Roosevelt contributed to the growth of American imperialism by expanding the Monroe Doctrine, building the Panama Canal, and intervening in the affairs of Latin American nations. His motto was "Speak softly, and carry a big stick."

In 1902 European powers again tested the Monroe Doctrine, when Venezuela failed to repay debts to Great Britain, Germany, and Italy. The three powers sent warships, intending to blockade Venezuela until it agreed to pay. Citing the Monroe Doctrine, Roosevelt urged the Europeans to settle the dispute by **arbitration**, a process in which an impartial third party settles a dispute between two other parties. After an uneasy standoff, the Europeans agreed to Roosevelt's diplomatic solution.

In 1904 Roosevelt announced a corollary, or addition, to the Monroe Doctrine. He said that a country's failure to pay debts may "require intervention by some civilized nation, and in the Western Hemisphere the adherence of the United States to the Monroe Doctrine may force the United States, however reluctantly. . . to the exercise of an international police power."

A former police commissioner for New York City, Roosevelt got his chance to be an international police officer the next year when the Dominican Republic failed to pay its debts. Backed by U.S. troops, American accountants took charge of the government's finances and found a way of paying the debt. The United States government intervened in a similar manner in such countries as Haiti, Honduras, and Nicaragua during the next three decades.

American military intervention provoked a storm of protest in other Latin American countries. Understandably, anti-American feeling in the region continued to grow long after Roosevelt had left office.

The Panama Canal

For several centuries, Europeans and Americans dreamed of building a canal across Central America. Such a canal would allow ships to sail between the Atlantic and Pacific oceans without having to go all the way around the southern tip of South America. In the 1880s the Frenchman Ferdinand de Lesseps, who had built the Suez Canal, tried to build a Central American canal in Panama. He failed. Twenty years later, Theodore Roosevelt found a way to succeed.

The best route for the canal lay through Panama, which in 1903 was still part of Colombia. Roosevelt tried to negotiate a treaty with Colombia that year that would allow the United States to build a canal through Panama. When

Colombia refused to sign the treaty, Roosevelt and the American public were outraged.

Roosevelt soon developed a plan, however. With his approval, American agents encouraged the people of Panama to revolt against the government of Colombia. They did so on the night of November 3, 1903, with the help of the United States Navy, which prevented Colombian troops from landing. The rebellion was over by the next day, and the new Republic of Panama quickly signed a treaty granting the United States the right to build the Panama Canal.

Construction of the canal took 10 years. More than 40,000 workers cut through hills, built dams, and drained swamps until the two mighty oceans were connected. Many of these workers died of malaria and yellow fever. When the first ship finally steamed through the canal in August 1914, Roosevelt had long since retired from office. But with the Panama Canal and his aggressive foreign policy, Theodore Roosevelt had left his mark on the Americas.

Intervention in Mexico

By 1913 repeated United States interventions in the region had angered the countries of Latin America. The new American President, Woodrow Wilson, tried to calm their fears by promising that the United States would "never again seek one additional foot of territory by conquest."

Wilson broke that promise the following year. At the time, Mexico was in the midst of a bloody revolution that had started in 1910 with the overthrow of dictator Porfirio Díaz. In 1913 one of Díaz's former generals, Victoriano Huerta, assassinated Mexico's new leader and seized the reins of power himself.

Wilson despised Huerta and immediately began looking for a way to topple him from power. After the Mexican police arrested some disorderly American soldiers visiting Mexico in 1914, Wilson saw his chance. He ordered U.S. Marines to seize the Mexican port of Veracruz and shut off Huerta's flow of guns and supplies.

Although uprisings by the Mexican people did soon topple Huerta from power, no strong leader emerged to take his place. Instead, Venustiano Carranza, Francisco "Pancho" Villa, and Emiliano Zapata competed for power. When the United States recognized the Carranza government in 1916, Villa launched a series of anti-American raids. He not only removed 17 American citizens from a Mexican train and had them shot but killed 19 more Americans in a raid on a New Mexican border town as well. In response, President Wilson sent American troops into Mexico in 1916 to capture Villa.

The entry of the United States into World War I in 1917 led to the withdrawal of these troops, and a probable war with Mexico was avoided. That same year, Carranza consolidated his power, adopted a new constitution, and launched a series of liberal reforms. Although tension between Mexico and the United States decreased sharply after these events, the memory of U.S. intervention lingered in the minds of Latin Americans for years to come.

SECTION 4 REVIEW

Recall

1. **Define:** arbitration
2. **Identify:** James Monroe, Theodore Roosevelt, Venustiano Carranza
3. **Explain:** What were the two main points presented in the Monroe Doctrine?
4. **Define:** What was the purpose of the Roosevelt Corollary?

Critical Thinking

5. **Analysis:** Why do you think the United States government was so concerned about maintaining its influence in Latin America in the late 1800s and early 1900s?
6. **Evaluation:** Do you think U.S. President Theodore Roosevelt was justified in announcing the Roosevelt Corollary to the Monroe Doctrine? Explain.

Applying Concepts

7. **Nationalism:** What factors motivated the United States' expansion into Latin America and the Pacific? What resistance did the United States encounter in these regions?

ANALYZING POLITICAL CARTOONS

Do you turn to the comics section of the newspaper first? Most people enjoy reading comic strips, but newspapers have another type of cartoon known as the *political cartoon*—a drawing that gives visual commentary on current events.

Explanation

A cartoonist relies mostly on images to communicate a message. Using caricatures and symbols, political cartoons help readers see relationships and draw conclusions about an event.

A caricature is a drawing that exaggerates a subjects' distinctive features. The cartoonist uses caricature to create a favorable or a negative impression of that person. For example, if a figure is drawn three times the size of another, the cartoonist may be suggesting that one figure is more powerful than the other.

A symbol is an idea, image, or object that stands for something else. For instance, a crown is commonly used as a symbol for monarchy. Symbols give visual power to the opinion presented.

To analyze a political cartoon, follow these steps:
- Identify the main idea and principal characters.
- Read words for messages.
- State the action, if any.
- Note relationships and connections between any caricatures or symbols.

- Recall recent events or read about related issues to help you understand any visual elements that are unclear.
- Summarize the cartoon's message.

Example

Look at the political cartoon on this page. The cartoon, published in 1900, shows China after the Boxer Rebellion. The cartoonist used both caricatures and symbols. Exaggerated Asian features on the face of the dragon and the word *China* printed on the dragon's back makes its identity clear. The dragon's position on the ground indicates that China has been defeated by the other animals. The animals are symbols for nations: the bear—Russia, the eagle—the United States, and the leopard—Japan. In summary, China has been defeated by the imperialist nations, each of whom wants to expand its sphere of influence.

Application

Look at the cartoon on page 660 and answer these questions:
1. What is the main idea?
2. How does the cartoonist use caricature and symbol?

Practice

Turn to Practicing Skills on page 681 of the Chapter Review for further practice in analyzing political cartoons.

CHAPTER 26 REVIEW

HISTORICAL SIGNIFICANCE

The Age of Imperialism profoundly influenced subsequent world history. It brought together and produced extensive interactions between different cultures. The people of Western Europe ate new foods and became familiar with new forms of art and music from Africa, India, China, and the Americas. In turn, many Africans and Asians were introduced to Western traditions and technologies for the first time—sometimes against their will. These interactions left the world more closely linked politically, economically, and culturally.

Imperialism also led to sharper rivalries and tensions among Western powers. Many small wars and a major world conflict—World War I—resulted in part from these rivalries. As the United States grew in political and economic importance, it became a global power and began interfering in Latin America, creating new tensions in that region. Finally, imperialism inspired the rise of nationalist movements that ultimately brought independence to the peoples of Africa and Asia and helped shape the world as we know it today.

SUMMARY

For a summary of Chapter 26, see the Unit 6 Synopsis on pages 682-685.

USING KEY TERMS

For each key term below, write a definition that explains how the term relates to imperialism.
1. sphere of influence
2. protectorate
3. partition
4. culture system
5. westernization
6. arbitration

REVIEWING FACTS

1. **Define:** What is "Social Darwinism" and how does it relate to imperialism?
2. **Explain:** In what parts of the world did Great Britain use the strategy of "divide and conquer" with great success?
3. **List:** Name at least four European powers that participated in the scramble for Africa and, for each European power, name at least one African country that it conquered.
4. **List:** What land did the United States gain as a result of the Spanish-American War?

5. **Identify:** Name three policies the Meiji leaders implemented to promote industrial expansion in Japan.

THINKING CRITICALLY

1. **Apply:** How did the Industrial Revolution stimulate imperialism?
2. **Evaluate:** Why was Japan able to establish itself as an imperial power, unlike other Asian countries?
3. **Synthesize:** Imagine that your country is under the control of an imperialist power. What steps might the imperialists take to make your country profitable?
4. **Analyze:** Contrast the ways in which the Age of Imperialism has contributed to unity in the world with the ways in which it has contributed to disunity.

ANALYZING CONCEPTS

1. **Movement:** What factors stimulated outward expansion by the European powers in the Age of Imperialism?
2. **Change:** Imperialism is a form of international competition that provokes change in the affected countries. What were some of the effects of imperialism in Africa?

3. **Nationalism:** Describe the nationalist response to imperialism in India. Where are nationalist resistance movements active in the world today?

4. **Revolution:** Describe the relationship between imperialism and revolution in China.

PRACTICING SKILLS

1. Turn to page 662. What analogy does Belgium's King Leopold use to describe the imperialist nations' view of Africa? List two other elements that might appear in a cartoon about King Leopold's comments.

2. Read about Theodore Roosevelt on pages 677-678. What does Roosevelt's "big stick" symbolize? How might a political cartoon illustrate this episode?

3. Suppose you were planning to draw a cartoon featuring a political leader you regarded as very wise. What features might you include in your caricature to communicate your opinion of this leader?

GEOGRAPHY IN HISTORY

1. **Movement:** Refer to the map on pages 984-985. How much shorter is the route from Britain to India via the Suez Canal than the route around Africa?

2. **Place:** What geographical considerations made South Africa so attractive?

3. **Location:** Refer to the map on page 994. What is the global address of Port Harcourt in West Africa?

4. **Movement:** Refer to the map on pages 984-985 and speculate about why the United States continues to maintain military bases in the Philippines.

TRACING CHRONOLOGY

Refer to the time line below to answer these questions.

1. How many years passed between the opening of Japan by Perry and the Russo-Japanese War?

2. How many years passed between the Opium War and the fall of the Qing dynasty?

3. How soon after the Spanish-American War did Theodore Roosevelt announce the Roosevelt Corollary?

LINKING PAST AND PRESENT

1. During the twentieth century, colonial peoples around the world won their independence. What remains of the empires created during the Age of Imperialism?

2. The United States has continued to intervene in Latin America. Investigate and explain three of these interventions.

3. Have attitudes about the morality of imperialism changed from the 1800s to the present time? Explain.

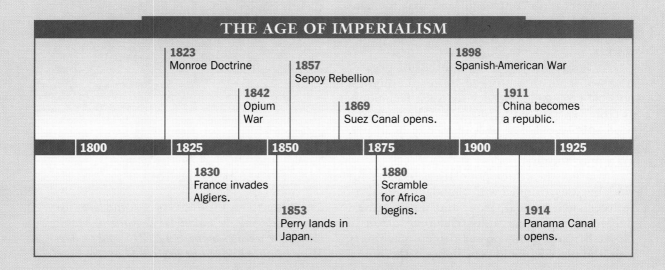

THE AGE OF IMPERIALISM

1823 Monroe Doctrine
1857 Sepoy Rebellion
1898 Spanish-American War
1842 Opium War
1869 Suez Canal opens.
1911 China becomes a republic.

1800 | 1825 | 1850 | 1875 | 1900 | 1925

1830 France invades Algiers.
1853 Perry lands in Japan.
1880 Scramble for Africa begins.
1914 Panama Canal opens.

UNIT 6 SYNOPSIS

In the 1800s a new and vigorous spirit of change and progress enveloped the world. Great Britain led the way in the late 1700s, as inventors and industrialists helped to transform primarily rural, agricultural economies to industrial economies based on manufactured goods and products. This swift advance of industrialism throughout western Europe and the United States was accompanied by discoveries in science and medicine, as well as changing cultural and political attitudes. In many countries people were inspired to fight for political reform. At the same time, increasingly industrialized nations competed to establish themselves as world powers.

As industry spread throughout the world, inventors helped industrialists speed production. New technologies soon allowed factories to produce goods at an unlimited rate.

Expanding and increasingly complex industries led to a changing social order in the mid-1800s. As factory owners and managers gained wealth, a sizable middle class grew. Women were given new opportunities to earn a living and support themselves independently. At the same time, however, workers endured crowded and unsanitary living quarters and poor working conditions. In the late 1800s, workers joined to form labor unions in the hope of improving their lives.

CHAPTER 22
Age of Industry

Before the 1700s, age-old tradition ruled daily living in Europe, and change was rare. Most people lived in rural villages and farmed small tracts of land. They were generally self-sufficient people who grew the food or made the things their families needed. In the late 1700s, however, great changes began to occur. Wealthy landowners took control of land that for centuries had been open to all villagers, forcing many small farmers to move to the cities to find work.

As landowners gained control of greater tracts of land, they worked to get the highest possible crop yield and devised such techniques as crop rotation and fertilization. The increased food supply enabled people to live healthier, longer lives. As a result, Europe's population grew dramatically.

A larger, healthier population looking for work in cities, coupled with abundant natural resources such as coal, iron, and water power, helped to ignite an industrial revolution in Great Britain. Now, power-driven machinery took the place of handwork done in the home.

Learning from Photographs *Child labor was common during the Industrial Revolution. Many children worked as many as 12 to 15 hours a day.* **Why might children be preferred as workers?**

CHAPTER 23
Cultural Revolution

As the Industrial Revolution spread throughout the world, people grappled with the challenges a new industrialized society presented. Throughout the 1700s and 1800s, several economists and other political thinkers proposed ideas for dealing with an industrialized society. Some, such as economists Adam Smith and David Ricardo, felt that government should let industry run as owners saw fit. Others, including British philosophers Jeremy Bentham and John Stuart Mill, called for government supervision and regulation of industry and for labor reform. Still others, such as German philosopher Karl Marx, supported socialism, which held that workers should control government and industry.

Scientific Discoveries Just as innovative thinkers had opened the door to the Industrial Age, they also contributed many exciting scientific discoveries. In the 1850s, British naturalist Charles Darwin proposed a theory of evolution to explain the origins of life. At roughly the same time, medical pioneers such as Louis Pasteur and Robert Koch used new scientific knowledge to conquer diseases such as smallpox and rabies that had plagued humankind for thousands of years.

New advances meant a better quality of life. With growing confidence, people ventured from their native lands and emigrated to other countries to take advantage of increased opportunities. At the same time, increased interest in education led to the spread of literacy as public schools and libraries were established throughout Europe and the United States.

The rapidly changing society was also reflected in the arts. Painters, influenced by the birth of photography, experimented with new techniques. Romantics wrote nostalgic poems about the beauties of nature that industry was so rapidly destroying, and about the traditions of the past that were quickly disappearing. Realistic writers, such as Charles Dickens, captured the gritty realities of the industrialized world.

CHAPTER 24
Democracy and Reform

The spirit of change inspired people around the world to speak out for democratic reform. In Great Britain the transformation to a more democratic society proved peaceful. Liberal leaders fought to pass political reform into parliamentary law. Slowly, the government responded to this pressure. By 1900 nearly all British men could vote, women had gained new rights, and laws had been implemented to help and protect workers. Overseas colonies such as Canada, Australia, and New Zealand also benefited from this era of reform and were awarded self-rule by the British government.

In France political reform did not come so easily. The 1800s was a century of turmoil, as revolution against monarchy tore through the country in 1830 and 1848. In the years following, the government tottered between an empire and a republic. After a shaky beginning, the government finally stabilized as a republic in the late 1800s.

As the countries of Europe struggled with demands for reform, the United States expanded its borders. In 50 years, between 1803 and 1853, the country grew to 3 million square miles.

All was not peaceful, however, in the thriving young country. As new states entered the union, the slavery issue became heated. The South fought to allow slavery in these states, while the North argued for freedom. The debate drew the country into a bloody civil war in 1861. President Abraham Lincoln led the United States through this bitter conflict as he strove to save the Union.

Farther south, in the Spanish and Portuguese colonies of Mexico, Central America and South America, colonists fought for independence. Led by such men as Simón Bolívar and Jose de San Martín, Latin Americans fought to elevate their countries from colonial status to that of an independent country. By the mid-1820s, they had achieved this goal. The newly independent people soon found that establishing working, stable governments was not an easy achievement.

CHAPTER 25
Reaction and Nationalism

The desire for national independence, known as nationalism, became one of the most powerful forces at work in Europe during the 1800s. In some areas people struggled to unify small, individual states into one nation. In others people fought to break free from large empires and establish their own countries.

In the early 1800s, Italy still consisted of a number of kingdoms and principalities. People in the various regions of the Italian peninsula spoke different dialects and practiced their own customs and traditions. Trade barriers and poor transportation discouraged the flow of goods and people from one region to another.

Following the Congress of Vienna in 1815, a movement for Italian unity grew and spread across Italy. Nationalist leader Giuseppe Mazzini was an early promoter of unification to make the Italian peninsula one nation. Count Camillo di Cavour of Sardinia used shrewd politics and help from other European nations to make Italian unification a reality. By 1861, after numerous battles and treaties, the entire peninsula was united under one government.

A similar quest for unification took place in the much larger area of central Europe known as Germany. In 1815, this entity encompassed 39 independent German states, including the large states of Austria and Prussia. Under forceful leadership by Prime Minister Otto von Bismarck, Prussia fought three wars and engaged in complicated diplomatic efforts to bring about German unification. By 1871 the German states, except for Austria, had joined to form a unified Germany under the rule of Kaiser William I.

After unification, Germany—like Italy before it—struggled with the problems of a young nation. Divisions in language, culture, and economy did not disappear overnight. But Bismarck, now William I's chancellor, controlled the government with an iron fist to ensure that Germany would remain strong and unified.

The Russian tsars struggled with their own internal problems. As reform swept the European continent during the 1800s, these autocratic rulers strove to withstand social and political change.

After 25 years of repressive rule by Nicholas I, Alexander II undertook major reforms, including the emancipation of serfs in 1861. For many liberals these reforms did not go far enough. When radicals assassinated Alexander II in 1881, they touched off another wave of political repression, but revolutionary groups continued to grow. As strikes and protests broke out, after Russia's defeat in the Russo-Japanese War, a bloody revolt won some political concessions from Tsar Nicholas II.

The Austrian Empire also tried to maintain its repressive monarchy. But censorship and other restrictive measures fanned political dissent. As states rallied for independence and reform in 1848, Emperor Francis Joseph was able to retain power only by playing one nationalist faction against another. In 1866, after Austria's defeat in the Seven Weeks' War, Francis Joseph was forced to accept the dual monarchy of Austria and Hungary to satisfy the nationalist desires of the Hungarians. The Slavic peoples of the dual monarchy continued to push for greater political rights and independence in the decades that followed.

CHAPTER 26
The Age of Imperialism

Three key factors led to the rise of imperialism in the 1800s. First, European nationalism prompted rival countries to engage in competition for territory. Second, the Industrial Revolution created a great demand for raw materials and new markets. Finally, feelings of cultural and racial superiority also inspired Europeans to introduce their culture in distant lands.

Imperialism in Africa and Asia Africa was especially affected by the European zeal to found new colonies. Beginning around 1870, the major European powers began a mad scramble to divide up the continent, establish colonies, and exploit the wealth of natural resources they found there. By 1914 only two African nations—

Liberia and Ethiopia—had managed to escape European control.

In India the British-based East India Company established a strong hold over the subcontinent and its abundant resources in the 1700s. Following the Sepoy Rebellion in 1857, the British government took over management of India directly and extended its control. The British attempted to quell further unrest in India by spending vast amounts of money on the country's economic development; still, most Indians resented British rule. In 1885 the Indian National Congress was formed, signaling the start of the long struggle for independence.

Also during the 1800s, the major European powers established their control over China. Using military power or the threat of it, they forced China to accept trade agreements that favored the imperialist powers. These pacts allowed the Europeans to carve out economically valuable spheres of influence in China. When the Chinese fought back in the Boxer Rebellion of 1900, the Europeans quickly crushed the revolt. Eleven years later, Chinese revolutionaries overthrew the Qing dynasty and established a republic in China. This revolution was followed by years of civil war and political chaos.

The United States forced Japanese leaders to open their doors to trade when it sent Commodore Matthew C. Perry to Japan in 1853. As a result, the Meiji leaders who took control of Japan in the late 1860s decided to make Japan a great power capable of competing with the imperialists. They reformed Japan's government and began a program to modernize and industrialize the nation. Partly as a result of this program, Japan defeated Russia in 1905 in the Russo-Japanese War. By 1914, Japan was well on

Learning from Art *This 1846 Sikh painting shows a meeting between British officials and Indian leaders.* **What event led the British government to become more involved in the management of India?**

its way to becoming a modern industrial nation and world power.

American Imperialism Like the rulers of European powers, leaders in the U.S. government began to dream of empire building in the late 1800s. During these decades the United States invoked the Monroe Doctrine on several occasions to block European involvement in Latin America. At the same time, the U.S. government and American businesses were becoming more and more involved in the affairs of Latin American nations. This trend increased following the Spanish-American War and construction of the Panama Canal. Tension between Latin American nations and the United States grew as a result of the U.S. government's repeated interventions in the region during the first two decades of the 1900s.

SURVEYING THE UNIT

1. **Relating Ideas:** In what sense were the democratic reforms of the 1800s a response to the Industrial Revolution?
2. **Making Comparisons:** How did the influence of nationalism on Italy in the mid-1800s differ from its influence on Austria-Hungary during this period?
3. **Identifying Trends:** What factors led to the growth of imperialism as a significant force in the world in the 1800s?

UNIT 6 REVIEW

REVIEWING THE MAIN IDEAS

1. **Identify:** What were Malthus's views on population growth?
2. **Explain:** How did the colonial system of government in Latin America contribute to the rise of independence movements there?
3. **Explain:** What contribution did Garibaldi make to the cause of Italian unification?
4. **Identify:** What two African nations did not experience European colonial rule?
5. **Explain:** What was Commodore Perry's purpose in visiting Japan in 1853?

THINKING CRITICALLY

1. **Synthesize:** How did Karl Marx's views on economic issues differ from those of Adam Smith?
2. **Analyze:** What does the Dreyfus Affair reveal about French society in the late 1800s?
3. **Evaluate:** Why did revolutionary activity in Russia increase in spite of Alexander II's many reforms?
4. **Apply:** How were political rivalries, the desire for new markets, and a sense of cultural superiority all evident in the European scramble for Africa in the late 1800s?
5. **Analyze:** Do you think the United States was justified in announcing the Monroe Doctrine in the early 1800s? Why or why not?

A GLOBAL PERSPECTIVE

Refer to the time line on pages 548-549 to answer these questions.

1. How long after the opening of the world's first railroad in Great Britain did the Panama Canal open?
2. What significant event occurred in the United States at about the same time as Robert Owen founded his utopian community in Scotland?

3. What political event made possible the founding of New Youth in China?
4. Could the French impressionists have telephoned their friends to invite them to the first major exhibit of impressionist works in Paris?
5. Did German unification occur before or after the Qing dynasty was toppled in China?

LINKING PAST AND PRESENT

1. How is the technological revolution that began in the 1960s similar to the Industrial Revolution in the early 1800s?
2. How might Thomas Malthus respond to the population problems in Third World countries today?
3. What nations today are experiencing problems as a result of multinational populations that are similar to those of Austria-Hungary in the mid-1800s?
4. In what sense did the 1910 constitution of the Union of South Africa lay the groundwork for the apartheid policy that the Afrikaner government put into effect in 1948?

ANALYZING VISUALS

As Great Britain became more and more industrialized in the 1800s, new problems erupted in British cities. The growth of the urban labor force meant that more housing was needed for workers. With many people moving to cities looking for factory jobs, new buildings had to be erected quickly and cheaply to accommodate these new residents. The result of this quick expansion overcrowded cities and slums. This print of row houses from around 1900 gives a sense of the problems caused by urban overcrowding.

This engraving depicts rows of houses packed together near an overhead railroad bridge.

1. What factors might have led to the spread of disease during the Industrial Revolution?
2. Using this print as a starting point, imagine that you live in one of the houses pictured here. Based on the image and on what you've read, write a diary entry about life in London during the Industrial Revolution.
3. Find out about the housing problems faced by low-income families today. What are the problems? What are some possible solutions to these problems?

USING LITERATURE

Refer to the short story "The Beggar" on pages 594-597 to answer these questions.

1. A wide gulf divided the poor and the wealthy in Russia in the late 1800s. Taking this gap into account, would you have expected the privileged Skvortsoff to react in the way that he did to the beggar Lushkoff? Why or why not?
2. Were Skvortsoff's motives for helping Lushkoff geniunely compassionate or were they self-serving? Use evidence from the selection to explain your answer.
3. Is Lushkoff's explanation for his turnaround believable? Why or why not?
4. Put yourself in Lushkoff's place. How would you have responded to Skvortskoff's behavior toward you? Explain.

WRITING ABOUT HISTORY

1. Industry in the late 1700s and early 1800s depended upon such practices as child labor, 15-hour workdays, and dangerous and unhealthy working conditions. Imagine you are a newspaper editor during this time, and write an editorial expressing your point of view about the labor practices of your day.
2. What is your idea of a utopian society? Could your society be successful in today's world? Why or why not?
3. Write a brief essay on the following topic: How did European attitudes toward colonial peoples affect European nations' way of managing their colonies?

World in Conflict

"More than an end to war, we want an end to the beginnings of all war."

*I*n an address written for a Jefferson Day broadcast on April 13, 1945, Franklin Delano Roosevelt, the thirty-second president of the United States, expressed the desire of a war-weary people for a lasting peace. In the three decades that preceded Roosevelt's remarks, two world wars had convulsed the globe. Never before in the history of civilization had the world endured devastation on such a massive scale.

A GLOBAL CHRONOLOGY

		1915		1921		1927
Political Sphere		**1914** World War I begins.	**1917** The Russian Revolution occurs; women in Russia win right to vote.			
Scientific Sphere						**1926** Robert Goddard launches first liquid-propellant rocket.
Cultural & Social Sphere			**1922** James Joyce publishes *Ulysses;* T. S. Eliot publishes *The Waste Land.*		**1925** Diego Rivera works on famous murals in Mexico City.	

*An American Army
Air Service poster
from World War I*

	1933		1939		1945
	1933 Hitler comes to power in Germany.		**1939** World War II begins.		**1945** United States drops atomic bomb on Hiroshima.
1928 Alexander Fleming discovers penicillin.				**1942** Enrico Fermi produces first controlled nuclear chain reaction.	
		1935 Jews lose rights of citizenship in Germany.		**1940** Charlie Chaplin makes *The Great Dictator*.	

World War I

*T*o survive days of bombardment on the Western Front during World War I, men crouched down in deep ditches. During these times there was nothing to do but wait and watch. Finally, they would receive orders to attack:

"Suddenly the nearer explosions cease. The shelling continues but it has lifted and falls behind us, our trench is free. We seize the hand-grenades, pitch them out in front of the dug-out and jump after them. The bombardment has stopped and a heavy barrage now falls behind us. The attack has come."

In this passage from *All Quiet on the Western Front*, Erich Maria Remarque captures the chaos and horror of what is now called World War I. When this war broke out in the summer of 1914, most Europeans thought it would be over by Christmas. Instead, it lasted four long years and changed Europe and the world forever.

CHAPTER PREVIEW

Key Terms to Define: militarism, entente, alliance system, ultimatum, mobilization, propaganda, trench, contraband, provisional government, convoy, armistice, reparation, mandate

People to Meet: Tsar Nicholas II, Archduke Francis Ferdinand, President Woodrow Wilson, Grigori Rasputin, Alexander Kerensky, Vladimir Ilyich Lenin, T. E. Lawrence

Places to Discover: Morocco, the Balkans, Serbia, Bosnia and Herzegovina, Tannenberg, Ypres, Verdun, the Dardanelles, Gallipoli, Petrograd, Czechoslovakia, Yugoslavia

Objectives to Learn:
1. What were the underlying causes of World War I?
2. What events led to the Russian Revolution?

C.R.W. Nevinson captured the horror of World War I in his painting Harvest of Battle.

3. Why was the Treaty of Versailles ultimately unsuccessful?

Concepts to Understand:
• Cooperation—European powers form a series of alliances before World War I. Section 1
• Conflict—Tensions between the European powers erupt into first a European-wide and then a world-wide war. Sections 2, 3

• Revolution—Revolution in Russia overthrows the tsar and brings Lenin and the Bolsheviks to power. Section 4
• Internationalism—The Treaty of Versailles provides for the creation of a League of Nations to mediate international disputes. Section 5

The Seeds of War

The outbreak of World War I shattered almost a century of relative peace that had followed the Congress of Vienna. The absence of a major war for so long a period had lulled many Europeans into believing that such a war would not ever happen again.

Major social reforms and important scientific advances during the 1800s reinforced a widespread belief that as time passed the world was improving steadily and that people had outgrown the need for war to solve their problems.

In the late 1800s, however, ominous signs began to threaten the extended period of peace and progress in Europe.

The growth of nationalism and imperialism created intense rivalries among European powers. In addition, militarism and the growth of complex alliances made even the smallest of disagreements between these rivals increasingly dangerous. By 1914 Europe had become a tinderbox waiting for the spark that would cause it to explode.

IMAGES
OF THE TIME

End of an Era

World War I marked the end of an era of British history that had been dominated by the personalities of Queen Victoria and Edward VII.

Edward's death in 1910 caused great sadness. Edward, who placed great importance on fashion and social events, had been an extremely popular king. His funeral in London (at right) was attended by thousands of mourners.

IN MEMORIAM

Nationalism and Imperialism

Nationalism was the source of many tensions among European nations in the late 1800s and early 1900s. By glorifying the idea that no personal sacrifice for one's homeland was too great, nationalism motivated people to fight even when the objectives were vague.

Nationalism also caused internal divisions in countries that contained several ethnic groups. The Slavs in Austria-Hungary and the Irish in Great Britain threatened the unity of these nations by demanding independence. Some nations tried to create unrest in neighboring countries by stirring ethnic discontent.

By setting neighbors against one another and by dividing nations internally, nationalism became a destabilizing force in Europe during the 1800s. It helped to create the atmosphere that led to a major European war.

Like nationalism, imperialism created hostility between European powers. As Germany, Belgium, and Italy joined France and Great Britain in the scramble for overseas territories, disputes often erupted between these nations.

Morocco was the scene of two major crises between imperialist powers. In 1905 France took steps to add Morocco to its list of colonies. Germany, which had commercial interests there, opposed France's actions and called for an international conference to discuss the issue. With Great Britain acting as mediator, this conference ruled that Morocco would be under French influence but remain independent. Thus a war was averted between France and Germany.

Similar crises occurred in Sub-Saharan Africa, Asia, and the Pacific Islands. Although a peaceful solution was found in each case, the already strained relations between European powers worsened with every dispute.

Hunting parties were a favorite activity of the English aristocracy during the Edwardian era. At right is a painting of a fox hunt in the English countryside.

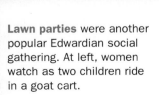

Lawn parties were another popular Edwardian social gathering. At left, women watch as two children ride in a goat cart.

Reflecting on the Times
What do the images shown here convey about life in Edwardian England?

Militarism and New Alliances

The leading European powers believed that the only way to back up their imperialistic goals was to build strong and effective military systems. Governments increasingly let the military play a major role in deciding matters of state. Military expenditures in Europe tripled between 1870 and 1914.

Nowhere was this policy of **militarism**—the enthusiastic support of military strength—more evident before World War I than in Germany. By 1900 Germany had the most powerful weapons and the best army in Europe. Determined to end Great Britain's naval supremacy, Germany also launched a massive program of naval expansion in the late 1890s. As a result, the British felt compelled to match the German naval buildup, increasing tensions between the two nations.

Other nations joined in the arms race. After its disastrous defeat in the Franco-Prussian War, France began its own campaign of militarism based on the German model. Russia also increased the size of its army and navy. Although few people saw its dangers at the time, the military buildup in Europe made a major war much more likely.

In addition to winning colonies and expanding their armed forces, European powers established new alliances to protect themselves in the event of war. For example, in 1879, German Chancellor Otto von Bismarck established the Dual Alliance, a mutual defense pact between Germany and Austria-Hungary. Three years later, in 1882, Bismarck brought Italy into this alliance. Each member of what was now called the Triple Alliance agreed to attack any country that attacked one of its members.

Bismarck's main motives for forming these alliances were to avoid a two-front war and to keep France isolated so it could not seek revenge for the Franco-Prussian War. As a result, France went to great lengths to find new allies. Finally, in 1894, France entered an alliance with Russia. Each country agreed to help the other if attacked by a member of the Triple Alliance.

Ten years later, in 1904, Great Britain and France ended their ancient rivalry and signed an **entente**, or friendly agreement, settling key colonial disputes. More than any other factor, fear of Germany's military buildup brought the two countries together. In 1907 Great Britain and Russia also signed an entente that divided up disputed colonial lands in the Middle East. With this diplomatic agreement, the Triple Entente of France, Great Britain, and Russia eventually emerged to counterbalance the Triple Alliance.

By 1907, then, two clear sides had taken shape in Europe. Instead of making their members more secure, however, these **alliance systems**, or defense agreements between nations, threatened the peace of the continent. Given the conditions of the Triple Alliance and the Triple Entente, a minor conflict between rival nations had the potential to involve all major European powers in war.

SECTION 1 REVIEW

Recall

1. **Define:** militarism, entente, alliance system
2. **Identify:** Otto von Bismarck, Triple Alliance, Triple Entente
3. **Locate:** Find Western Europe and Eastern Europe on the maps on pages 988–989. In what sense was Germany at a disadvantage, in fighting a European-wide war?

4. **Explain:** What were the causes of the Moroccan crisis of 1905 between France and Germany?

Critical Thinking

5. **Apply:** Choose one European power and discuss the ways in which nationalism, imperialism, militarism, and the alliance systems pushed it toward war before 1914.

6. **Evaluate:** What were the factors that led to alliances between nations prior to World War I?

Applying Concepts

7. **Cooperation:** Given the conditions that existed in Europe before 1914, could the nations of that continent have avoided a major war? How?

The Spark

SECTION 2

Nationalist stirrings in the Balkans eventually created the spark that set off World War I. Years of minor wars and political unrest had given the region a reputation as the "powder keg" of Europe. That reputation proved to be true when an assassination in Bosnia in the summer of 1914 ignited the deadliest war the continent had yet seen.

Trouble in the Balkans

By 1910 a variety of ethnic minority groups, the largest and most dissatisfied of which was the Slavs, represented a majority of the population in Austria-Hungary. Despite their numbers, however, the Slavs (including the Czechs, Slovaks, Serbs, Croats, Poles, and Ukrainians) did not enjoy the same rights as the Austrians and the Hungarians.

Slavic nationalism was especially strong in the Austro-Hungarian provinces of Bosnia and Herzegovina in the Balkans. The goal of the Slavs in these provinces was not to win full political rights in Austria-Hungary but to join the Balkan nation of Serbia.

Tsar Nicholas II of Russia supported Serbia's desire to absorb the Slavic territories of Bosnia and Herzegovina. But because it was not yet prepared for military action against the Triple Alliance, the Russian government persuaded Serbia to accept the situation for the time being. In spite of Russia's advice, however, radical Serbian nationalist groups—many of whose members were willing to die for the cause—sprang up throughout the region.

On June 28, 1914, Archduke Francis Ferdinand, nephew and heir to Austro-Hungarian Emperor Francis Joseph, paid a visit to Sarajevo, the capital of Bosnia. Francis Ferdinand planned, upon becoming emperor, to give the Slavs of Bosnia and other parts of the empire a voice in the government equal to that of the Austrians and Hungarians. This political action might have defused the movement for Slavic independence.

Before the archduke and his wife, Sophie, began their ride through the streets of Sarajevo in an open car, seven young assassins had already taken their places along the route. All were members of a secret Serbian nationalist group

Learning from Art *Within a month of the assassination of Archduke Ferdinand and his wife, the continent of Europe was ablaze with war.* **How did Austria-Hungary react to the royal deaths?**

CENTRAL POWERS
ALLIED POWERS
NEUTRAL NATIONS

Learning from Maps *World War I split Europe into two armed camps.*
Which side do you think had the better strategic position: the Triple Alliance countries or the Triple Entente countries?

known as the Black Hand, or Union of Death. Although the archduke and Sophie survived the first assassin's attempt, their luck did not hold. When the couple's car took a wrong turn, 19-year-old Gavrilo Princip fired his gun, fatally wounding them both.

Although the assassination had not occurred in Serbia, Austro-Hungarian leaders held the Serbians responsible. Austria-Hungary was determined to punish the Serbs, but it wanted to receive assurance of German support in case Russia entered the conflict. When the Austro-Hungarian foreign minister, Count Leopold Berchtold, contacted German Emperor William II, William assured him that Germany would give its full support to any actions Austria-Hungary might take against Serbia.

On July 23, Austria-Hungary gave Serbia an **ultimatum**, a set of final conditions that must be accepted to avoid severe consequences. The ultimatum demanded that Serbia allow Austro-Hungarian officials into the country to suppress all subversive movements there and to lead an investigation into the archduke's murder. Austria-Hungary gave Serbia 48 hours to agree to these terms or face war. Berchtold knew, however, that the ultimatum "would be wholly impossible for the Serbs to accept."

Although the ultimatum outraged Serbian leaders, they knew that their nation was not ready for war with Austria-Hungary. Therefore, on July 25, they answered the ultimatum in a conciliatory manner. However, they rejected the demand that Austro-Hungarian officials take

Dada

The founders of Dada, an artistic movement that arose in Switzerland during World War I, were anarchists—that is, they were opposed to all forms of authority or order. Dadaists rebelled against established systems of European art. They sought to make their opposition to tradition known through the practice of "non-art."

Dadaists were completely negative in their attitudes about European culture and society. They opposed all established ideas but did not propose any new alternatives to replace the traditions they sought to destroy. Their interest was solely in pointing out the meaninglessness of these traditions. The very name, Dada, was chosen because it was a completely meaningless, nonsense word that would cause public comment and controversy.

One of Dada's most important proponents was the French painter Marcel Duchamp (1887–1968). The works which he called "ready-mades" were perhaps the clearest expression of the Dada attitude toward traditions. To deny artistic customs and norms, Duchamp began exhibiting "non-art." His "ready-mades" were familiar, manufactured objects taken out of their normal context and placed on display, as one might display a painting. One of Duchamp's "ready-mades," a freestanding door called "Door, II rue Larrey, Paris," is shown here. Others included a bottle, a rack, and a snow shovel.

In the past, art had been valued largely for the workmanship, genius, or creativity of its creator, the artist. By displaying "ready-mades," Duchamp essentially proclaimed that the workmanship and creativity of the artist were meaningless. Duchamp claimed that his selection of an object made it "art," and that his selection was not based on traditional European artistic values but was completely arbitrary.

By declaring that an artist's workmanship and ingenuity play no important role in the designation of an object as "art," Duchamp and the Dadaists called into question the standards by which European art had been judged for centuries. Despite their rejection of the traditional arts, however, the Dadaists have, over time, come to be thought of as artists in their own right.

Responding to the Arts

1. What aspects of European society did the Dadaists oppose?
2. In what sense is Marcel Duchamp's door a challenge to traditional art values?

part in the investigation and trial of those involved in the archduke's assassination.

The Serbian answer did not satisfy Austria-Hungary. Consequently, on July 28, 1914, exactly one month after the assassination of Archduke Ferdinand, Austria-Hungary declared war on Serbia. Both countries immediately issued general orders for **mobilization,** the gathering and transport of military troops and fighting equipment in preparation for war. News of these mobilizations spread quickly across Europe.

A European War

Many Europeans still believed war could be avoided. In fact, the major European powers pushed each other to the brink of war believing that the other side would back down at the last minute. They were tragically mistaken.

Russia was the first to act once Austria-Hungary declared war. Knowing it had lost face often in the past, the Russian government had to support Serbia now or risk the bitter hatred of all the Slavs in the Balkan region. Although the tsar was convinced that Germany would fight, he had also been assured through diplomatic channels that France would support Russia.

Consequently, on July 30, Tsar Nicholas II ordered a general mobilization of his armed forces against both Austria-Hungary and Germany. Austria-Hungary mobilized against Russia the following day. Once Russia's intentions were clear, the other members of the Triple Entente, France and Great Britain, showed their hands.

On July 31, Germany issued Russia an ultimatum to cancel its mobilization order or face war. On the same day, Germany also delivered an ultimatum to France. France had 18 hours to decide whether or not it would remain neutral if Germany went to war with Russia. When Tsar Nicholas did not even reply to Germany's ultimatum, Germany declared war on Russia on August 1. Two days later, Germany declared war on France as well.

The British still hoped to avoid war by negotiating. The same day that Germany declared war on Russia, however, the German army marched into Luxembourg. The Germans then demanded passage across Belgium, claiming that France intended to invade that country at any moment. At the time, Belgium was a neutral country, whose borders and neutrality had been guaranteed in an 1839 treaty.

The Belgians refused the Germans entry and appealed to Great Britain for help. When the Germans went ahead and invaded Belgium on August 3, Britain protested and sent an ultimatum to Germany that demanded withdrawal of German forces from Belgium. The German chancellor responded by calling the 1839 treaty "a scrap of paper." This left the British little choice. On August 4, Britain declared war on Germany.

Designed to protect nations against their enemies, the European alliance systems dragged a whole continent into war. What should have remained a local dispute between Austria-Hungary and Serbia soon escalated into a global conflict that had no clear, limited objective.

SECTION 2 REVIEW

Recall

1. **Define:** ultimatum, mobilization
2. **Identify:** Francis Joseph, Nicholas II, Francis Ferdinand, Gavrilo Princip, Leopold Berchtold, William II
3. **Locate:** Find Serbia on the map on page 696. How did its location affect its relations with Austria-Hungary?

Critical Thinking

4. **Analyze:** Contrast the task of an Austro-Hungarian diplomat with that of a Russian diplomat in the period just before the declarations of war in 1914. What did each hope to gain?
5. **Evaluate:** Historians have long argued over which European nation was most responsible for the start of World War I. Using examples to support your statements, explain which country you think was most responsible for the war.

Applying Concepts

6. **Conflict:** Why do you think World War I came as a surprise to many people?

The War

By August 1914 the major powers of Europe had lined up against each other. Germany and Austria-Hungary, joined by the Ottoman Empire and Bulgaria, became known as the Central Powers. Great Britain, France, Russia, Serbia, Belgium, and, later, Japan and Montenegro, became known as the Allied Powers, or Allies. Claiming that Austria-Hungary and Germany had acted aggressively rather than defensively, Italy remained neutral.

In spite of their military buildups, none of the European powers was fully prepared for what lay ahead. For example, cavalry and horse-drawn vehicles still played an important role in each nation's army—traditions that were quickly discarded. Nations from both sides also seriously underestimated the length of the war. No country had stockpiled enough war materials or ammunition to last more than six months. The widespread feeling among Europeans was that the war would be over by Christmas.

The Schlieffen Plan

Germany's invasion of Belgium on August 3 had been part of the Schlieffen Plan, a war strategy that German General Alfred von Schlieffen drew up in 1905. Germany's main problem was that it had enemies in both the east and the west. Schlieffen assumed, however, that Russia would be slow to mobilize. As a result, Schlieffen believed that the Germans could reach Paris and defeat the French in six weeks and then move on to the Eastern Front and fight against Russia.

Schlieffen's plan ran into problems from the beginning. First, German Commander Helmuth von Moltke led his troops through an area of Belgium that proved to be heavily fortified. Second, Moltke encountered far stronger resistance than anyone had expected; the German advance was delayed until August 20. Third, the Russian army mobilized far more quickly than Schlieffen had estimated, necessitating the movement of two German divisions to the Eastern Front.

The Germans were held up further when they met British forces in the north of France. British troops eventually had to retreat, but they

Learning from Art *Many nations used propaganda during the war. In Great Britain this poster urged men to join the army.* **Why was it necessary for nations to encourage enlistment in the armed forces?**

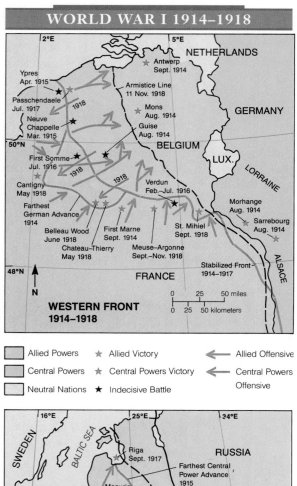

WORLD WAR I 1914–1918

WESTERN FRONT 1914–1918

NETHERLANDS
GERMANY
BELGIUM
LUX.
LORRAINE
FRANCE
ALSACE

Antwerp Sept. 1914
Ypres Apr. 1915
Passchendaele Jul. 1917
Neuve Chappelle Mar. 1915
Armistice Line 11 Nov. 1918
Mons Aug. 1914
Guise Aug. 1914
First Somme Jul. 1916
Cantigny May 1918
Farthest German Advance 1914
Belleau Wood June 1918
Chateau-Thierry May 1918
First Marne Sept. 1914
Verdun Feb.–Jul. 1916
Meuse-Argonne Sept.–Nov. 1918
St. Mihiel Sept. 1918
Morhange Aug. 1914
Sarrebourg Aug. 1914
Stabilized Front 1914–1917

0   25   50 miles
0   25   50 kilometers

☐ Allied Powers	★ Allied Victory	← Allied Offensive
☐ Central Powers	★ Central Powers Victory	← Central Powers Offensive
☐ Neutral Nations	★ Indecisive Battle	

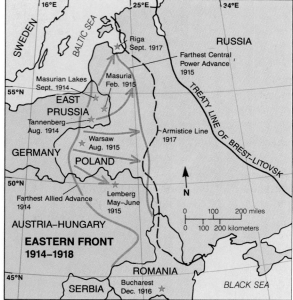

EASTERN FRONT 1914–1918

SWEDEN
BALTIC SEA
RUSSIA
EAST PRUSSIA
GERMANY
POLAND
AUSTRIA–HUNGARY
ROMANIA
SERBIA
BLACK SEA

Riga Sept. 1917
Farthest Central Power Advance 1915
Masurian Lakes Sept. 1914
Masuria Feb. 1915
TREATY LINE OF BREST-LITOVSK
Tannenberg Aug. 1914
Warsaw Aug. 1915
Armistice Line 1917
Farthest Allied Advance 1914
Lemberg May–June 1915
Bucharest Dec. 1916

0   100   200 miles
0   100   200 kilometers

Learning from Maps *World War I was fought on two major European fronts.* ***Which member of the Allied Powers fought exclusively on the Eastern Front?***

---

fought expertly and inflicted heavy losses on the Germans. At the same time, the French attacked another wing of the German army in Alsace-Lorraine. The French offensive eventually collapsed but not before delaying the German advance yet again.

France struggled to recover after the defeat at Alsace-Lorraine. The French chief of command, General Joseph Jacques Joffre, pulled back his troops to protect Paris. While many Parisians fled the city, General Joseph Simon Gallieni strengthened the army in Paris to the point that it was able to launch a counterattack. To speed troops into position, the French army requisitioned several hundred Parisian taxis.

On September 5 the French and German armies collided in northeastern France in the Battle of the Marne. After four days of shelling, the French finally pushed back the Germans. The German retreat at the Marne signified the abandonment of the Schlieffen Plan. It also made it clear that neither side was capable of defeating the other quickly or easily.

Russia, meanwhile, kept its word to the French and sent troops into battle even before its military was fully mobilized. The speed with which the Russians moved surprised Germany and Austria-Hungary. By August 13 the Russians had invaded East Prussia from the south and from the east. This attack diverted German troops from the attack against the French and British during the first critical weeks of the war.

Russia's success did not last long. At the end of August, Russian and German troops met at Tannenberg in present-day Poland. There the Russians suffered a disastrous defeat from which they never fully recovered. At Tannenberg, the Germans were able to encircle and destroy the Russian army. They killed more than 30,000 Russian soldiers and took 92,000 prisoners. German casualties numbered only about 13,000.

Years of Deadlock

After the Battle of the Marne, the Germans and the Allies began a series of battles known as "the race to the sea," with each attempting to reach the North Sea first and outflank the other. As the Germans advanced toward the ports of

Dunkirk and Calais, they ran into British troops at Ypres, a town in southwestern Belgium. The battle that followed cost the Germans 130,000 men, but the victorious British lost nearly 60,000 themselves. At this point the war in the west settled into a stable front from the Swiss border to the North Sea. By November 1914, the war had already reached a stalemate.

All of the belligerent nations now had to adjust their plans. To produce the needed ships, guns, food, ammunition, and medicines, large numbers of civilians had to enter the war effort. To raise morale, newspapers gave even the smallest victories big headlines. In addition, governments used **propaganda**—ideas or rumors used to harm an opposing cause—to portray the enemy as beastly and inhuman. Making peace with such an enemy seemed unthinkable.

Trench Warfare   By early 1915 the war on the western front had turned into a deadly war of attrition. To protect themselves, soldiers on both sides dug **trenches**, or ditches. Eventually, two parallel trenches stretched for approximately 500 miles in an unbroken line from Switzerland to the North Sea. Land mines and barbed wire protected the area in front of each trench. The desolate area that separated the two sides, which could vary from a half a mile to a few yards, was known as "no man's land."

CONNECTIONS: SCIENCE AND TECHNOLOGY

Flaming Coffins

American flying ace Eddie Rickenbacker shot down 22 enemy planes during World War I.

Aviation technology opened up a third dimension to the war. For the first time, combat took place not only on land and at sea but also in the air. Airplanes flown in World War I were crude but operational. These noisy, pitching, and bucking machines were not built with the pilot's safety foremost in mind. The main structural pieces were made of thin wood reinforced by steel wire. The body and wings were covered by cloth coated with a highly flammable liquid. The pilot sat on a seat directly over the fuel tank. Fire was such a constant danger that airplanes were often referred to as "flaming coffins."

Brakes did not exist on World War I era planes. On takeoff, the crew had to hold the plane back while the pilot revved the engine. On landing, the pilot had to turn the engine off and on to slow the approach. Once the pilot was airborne, there was no way to make contact with the ground unless an unwieldy Morse code transmitter was on board. Sometimes, pilots would release carrier pigeons to convey emergency messages or to effect a rescue.

Although the pilot's life was glamorized in posters and in the public imagination, the statistics were grim. The average life expectancy of a new pilot was from three to six weeks. During the war, 77 percent of French combat pilots were killed. The first groups of British airmen sent to France were told that only 1 in 20 would return. Such high losses resulted from accident and malfunction, as well as to enemy action.

Making the Connection

1. In what sense were World War I airplanes "crude" vehicles?
2. How dangerous was the life of a World War I pilot? Explain.

Soldiers lived in the trenches for weeks at a time, fighting boredom and terror. They endured cold, mud, rats, and disease. To attack, the soldiers charged "over the top" of their own trenches and ran across "no man's land" to the enemy's trenches. As attackers struggled through the barbed wire, their opponents mowed them down with heavy artillery and machine guns.

Throughout 1915, battle followed battle—Neuve-Chapelle, St. Mihiel, Ypres, Artois, and Champagne—and the casualties mounted. At Ypres, the Germans introduced a new weapon—poison gas. From cylinders in their trenches, they released yellow-green chlorine gas. The wind carried the gas into French trenches, causing blindness, choking, vomiting, torn lungs, and death. Wilfred Owen, an English poet and soldier, described the horrors of poison gas in his poem "Dulce et Decorum Est" (1916):

Gas! Gas! Quick, boys!—An ecstasy of
*   fumbling,*
Fitting the clumsy helmets just in time;
But someone still was yelling out and
*   stumbling*

FOOTNOTES TO HISTORY

HOLIDAY CHEER

At the outset of the war, most people thought the fighting would be over by Christmas. But after the Battle of the Marne, such hopes became less realistic. The entrenchment and deadlock that followed would characterize the rest of the war. However, the Christmas holidays, traditionally a time of peace and good will, had a powerful effect on British and German soldiers at the front. On Christmas Day, 1914, the firing at the front line in France stopped. British and German soldiers met in "no man's land" to trade cigarettes and chat. Some even played soccer. They met again on December 26. Enemy officers posed together for photographs. When Allied headquarters found out about the fraternization, it issued a strong reprimand. Eventually, the men returned to their positions and took up firing at one another again.

And flound'ring like a man in fire or lime. . .
Dim, through the misty panes and thick green
*   light,*
As under a green sea, I saw him drowning.

The year 1916 opened with the war on the Western Front still stalemated. Although Italy had denounced the Central Powers six months earlier and entered the war on the side of the Allies, it had gained little ground after four battles against the Austro-Hungarians. Then in February 1916, the Germans made a move. They staged a surprise attack against French forces at Verdun, a massive fortress in northeastern France on the Meuse River. The French, under General Henri Petain, rallied to the cry "They shall not pass." More than 2 million soldiers took part in this battle, one of the longest and bloodiest of the war. Before it was over, more than 750,000 French and German soldiers had lost their lives. When the fighting stopped, the Western Front had moved less than 10 miles (16 kilometers).

Later that year the British, aided by a small French force, launched a similar offensive against the Germans in the valley of the Somme River in northern France. The Battle of the Somme turned out to be as terrible and inconclusive as the one at Verdun. Although the British introduced another new weapon during this battle—an armored vehicle called the tank—it made little difference to the outcome of the struggle. Tanks were still too clumsy and slow to be an effective weapon, and the generals on both sides did not yet understand how best to use them.

Eastern Front   The Eastern Front in Russia was less entrenched than the Western Front in France; the war there was far more mobile, involving constant changes in battlefield positions. However, neither side was able to achieve a complete victory.

By mid-1915, the Russians had been forced to give up territory greater than the whole of France. In addition to suffering a staggering number of casualties, they had lost ammunition and guns equal to the amount they had possessed when the war began. Russia was doing so badly at this point that the Allies feared

Nicholas II would make a separate peace with the Central Powers. As a result they promised the Russian government that if the Allies won the war, they would give Russia Constantinople and control of the Dardanelles straits, which connect the Mediterranean and Black seas.

Inspired by this agreement, the Russians went to work rebuilding their army. In March 1916 they launched an offensive against the Germans but made little headway. A few months later, however, they fared much better against Austria-Hungary. In addition to capturing many cities, they took several hundred thousand prisoners. But they paid a heavy toll in the process, losing more than a million men and most of their supplies.

Although morale in the Russian army suffered greatly as a result of the 1916 offenses, their efforts helped the Allies on the Western Front. The Germans had to transfer several divisions from the west to the east, hampering the effectiveness of their attack at Verdun.

Gallipoli Campaign   As the war dragged on and casualties soared, each side tried to find ways to turn the war in its favor. In Britain, First Lord of the Admiralty Winston Churchill—head of the British navy—favored opening an offensive on the Dardanelles straits, which Turkey controlled. These straits were the only practical means of supplying Russia and of strengthening Serbia. From there, the Allies could take Constantinople and possibly put the Ottoman Empire out of the war. This offensive, Churchill believed, might also lead to the collapse of Austria-Hungary.

Churchill's idea had merit. In fact, the Allies' initial offensive in early 1915 nearly succeeded. But a lack of coordination, planning, and reinforcements gave the Turks time to rearm. When the Allies followed up in April with a land attack on the peninsula of Gallipoli, the Turks drove them back. On January 9, 1916, the Allies finally gave up the effort and withdrew the last of their troops from the area.

On the Seas   The British, meanwhile, had been using their naval superiority to dominate the seas. They were determined to keep the Germans from invading Great Britain and to keep war materials from reaching the Central Powers by sea. The Germans were just as determined to disrupt Allied shipping. Both Britain and Germany depended heavily on the seas for their food and war materials.

Britain blockaded all ports under German control at the start of the war. The blockade was so effective that Germany had to receive most of its supplies through the neutral countries of Holland, Denmark, Sweden, and Norway. The Germans protested that the blockade violated international law and called it "the hunger

Learning from Art
World War I gave rise to the development of new and more deadly means of warfare. Submarines, regarded until 1914 as solely defensive, were developed by Germany into long-range vessels of aggression.
Where did Germany first use submarines in World War I?

blockade." Ignoring these protests, the British also stopped ships they suspected of carrying **contraband**, or prohibited goods. They escorted these ships into port and seized their cargoes.

The Germans eventually found a new way to counter the British blockade and to wear down British sea power. They instituted a policy of submarine warfare. At first, German submarines, or U-boats, struck only warships. But in 1915 they began to strike civilian and commercial ships without warning, disregarding all rules of naval warfare. The Allies were particularly enraged when the Germans sank the British passenger liner *Lusitania* in May 1915, killing over 1,000 people.

At this time the naval code stated that enemy ships had to give warning before attacking a non-military target so the passengers and crew could be evacuated. The attacking ship was expected to take the evacuees on board. But the Germans said that their submarines would be easy targets if they surfaced to give warning. In addition, they had no space for passengers or contraband cargo. By April 1917, German U-boats had sunk dozens of British ships.

United States Enters War

One of the most important events of 1917 was the decision of the United States to enter the war. Until this point, Americans had mixed feelings about the conflict in Europe. Many Irish-Americans were staunchly anti-British, while many German-Americans sided with the Central Powers. Many other Americans favored the Allies. The majority of Americans, however, agreed with President Woodrow Wilson that the war was strictly a European conflict. While incidents such as the sinking of the *Lusitania* in 1915 angered them, Americans were not ready to take an active part in the war.

The Germans did not want the Americans to enter the war. At the same time, they were determined to break British control of the seas. They believed that the way to do this was a policy of unrestricted submarine warfare. As a result, Germany announced that beginning February 1, 1917, it would sink any merchant ships heading to British or western European ports. President Wilson responded to the announcement by breaking off relations with Germany.

Tensions between the two countries grew worse in March 1917 when American newspapers published the Zimmermann telegram, a message sent to the Mexican government by Arthur Zimmermann, the German foreign minister. The British had found and passed on the note to the Americans. In this telegram, Zimmermann proposed a deal with Mexico. He promised that if Mexico joined Germany in the war, Mexico would receive New Mexico, Texas, and Arizona after a German victory.

That same month the Germans sank four American merchant ships. For the the United States, this was the final provocation. On April 2, 1917, President Wilson asked Congress for a declaration of war. Wilson also called upon Americans to help "make the world safe for democracy."

SECTION 3 REVIEW

Recall

1. **Define:** propaganda, trench, contraband
2. **Identify:** Alfred von Schlieffen, Helmuth von Moltke, Joseph Jacques Joffre, Henri Petain, Winston Churchill, Woodrow Wilson
3. **List:** Name the nations that made up the Central Powers and the Allied Powers during World War I.

Critical Thinking

4. **Analysis:** Why did the Germans eventually abandon the Schlieffen Plan?
5. **Synthesis:** Create your own strategy for avoiding a stalemate in trench warfare. Determine the main factors working against a breakthrough in this type of warfare.

Applying Concepts

6. **Conflict:** Explain how World War I was a new kind of war. Consider objectives, strategy, and technology in the course of your explanation.

The Russian Revolution

World War I proved to be the breaking point for tsarist rule in Russia. By 1917, morale in the Russian army had reached bottom. As many as one-fourth of the Russian soldiers, having no weapons of their own, had to pick up the guns of dead soldiers. Inadequate transport made grave food shortages even worse. Almost all of the country's resources went to supply the army, making the human and financial costs of war increasingly unbearable.

A nurse at the Russian front in 1917 described the situation that helped bring about the collapse of the autocracy and the establishment of a Communist state:

> *Discontent among the masses in Russia is daily becoming more marked. Disparaging statements concerning the Government are being voiced. . . . "Bring the men home!" "Conclude peace!" "Finish this interminable war once and for all!" Cries such as these penetrate to the cold and hungry soldiers in their bleak earthworks, and begin to echo among them. Now that food has grown scarce in Petrograd and Moscow, disorder takes the shape of riots and insurrections. We are told that mobs of the lower classes parade the streets shouting 'Peace and Bread!'*

Fall of the Tsar

Events leading to the fall of the tsar began to accelerate in the last half of 1916. When Russia's legislative body, the Duma, criticized the government's conduct of the war in the fall of 1916, Tsar Nicholas II closed it down. By this time the tsar and his wife, Alexandra, had already become extremely unpopular with the Russian people. One of the reasons for their lack of popularity was the tsar's increasingly incompetent handling of both the war and governmental affairs. Another reason was the royal couple's strange relationship with a disreputable monk named Grigori Rasputin.

Nicholas and Alexandra's only son and heir, Alexis, had an incurable blood disease called hemophilia. His condition forced the royal couple to rely more and more on Rasputin's alleged healing powers. When the tsar took command of Russian troops on the Eastern Front, he left the country in the hands of his wife, who relied almost completely on the advice of Rasputin.

Nicholas's political incompetence—and his reliance on Rasputin—alarmed many conservatives, who feared that he was endangering the monarchy. In December 1916 two relatives of the tsar decided that the only solution was to rid Russia of Rasputin's influence. On the night of December 29, they invited the monk to dine with them. Although they both poisoned and shot him, Rasputin still did not die. Finally, his assassins dragged Rasputin to a bridge in Petrograd (formerly Saint Petersburg) and threw his body into the Neva River.

Rasputin's death did not solve the monarchy's problems. Public anger against the government mounted as a result of food and fuel shortages, and strikes erupted across the country. On March 8, 1917, and for the next few days, hundreds of thousands of men and women gathered in the streets of Petrograd. Demanding food and an end to the war, the crowds shouted, "Down with the tsar!" On March 11 and 12, the troops the government ordered to put down the riots refused to fire on the crowds. Many soldiers joined the protesters.

When the tsar ordered his generals at the front to crush the rebellion, they told him that any troops they might send to the capital would also join the rioters. With the country sinking into chaos, the tsar finally abdicated on March

15, ending the 300-year-old Romanov dynasty. The March revolution was a spontaneous rebellion of the people. It caused the loss of relatively few lives and took place, surprisingly, without the leadership of its revolutionary intellectuals, most of whom were living in exile abroad.

The Provisional Government

After Tsar Nicholas II's abdication, political authority in Russia passed into the hands of a temporary central government known as the **provisional government**. This new regime called for elections later in the year to choose a constituent, or constitutional, assembly. The constituent assembly would then establish a permanent government.

The provisional government consisted largely of moderate, Duma representatives who supported Russia's involvement in World War I. It soon became clear, however, that the government could not make any serious moves without the support of a rival group, the Petrograd Soviet of Workers' and Soldiers' Deputies. Most of the members of the Petrograd Soviet were workers and soldiers who belonged to a variety of socialist groups. The majority of these members were either Mensheviks or Social Revolutionaries, the political heirs of the populists. A more radical minority were Bolsheviks.

One man who moved easily between the provisional government and the Petrograd Soviet was Alexander Kerensky. A moderate socialist, Kerensky served first as the provisional government's minister of justice and then as its prime minister. He also belonged to the executive committee of the Petrograd Soviet.

The Petrograd Soviet became a model for the founding of other soviets throughout Russia. Together, the soviets called for an immediate peace, the transfer of land to the peasants, and the control of factories by workers. As the Russian economy continued to collapse under the war effort, this three-point program gained great popularity among the Russian masses.

In spite of the suffering and anger of the Russian people, however, the provisional government did not withdraw from the war. As a result of intense pressure from the Allies, it decided to remain in the conflict. But desertion, worsening transportation problems, and a drop in already low armament production plagued the Russian army.

Preoccupied with war policy, the provisional government could not carry out the social reforms proposed by the soviets. In the countryside, peasants drove landlords from their estates and seized their land. In cities, workers went on strike or took over the operation of their factories. The provisional government took little constructive action. As a result, the government lost much of its popular support, a factor that contributed to its eventual downfall.

Lenin

As the provisional government struggled to maintain order, a variety of revolutionary groups vied to fill the power vacuum. Since their split into two factions in 1903, the Mensheviks and the Bolsheviks had competed for control of Russia's revolutionary movement. By 1917 the Mensheviks far outnumbered the Bolsheviks. Because they believed that a socialist revolution would be the work of the masses, however, the Mensheviks did not make concrete plans to seize control of the government.

The more radical Bolsheviks, on the other hand, believed that a socialist society could be introduced immediately by force. They claimed that a small group of dedicated revolutionaries could carry out the revolution with the help of a relatively small working class and the peasants. They also believed that Russia's revolution would spread worldwide. Their leader, Vladimir Ilyich Lenin, urged them to make plans to topple the provisional government from power.

Born in 1870 Lenin came from a middle-class provincial background. When Lenin was in high school, his older brother, Alexander, became involved in a plot to assassinate Tsar Alexander III, the father of Nicholas II. The attempt failed, however, and the government hanged Lenin's brother and four fellow conspirators in 1887. Alexander's death made a powerful impression on Lenin, who dedicated his life to promoting a revolution.

In 1895 the Russian government arrested Lenin for his activities and exiled him to Siberia. After his release, he went to Germany, Great Britain, and Switzerland, where he wrote revolutionary articles and kept a close eye on the political situation in Russia. After hearing the news of the March 1917 revolution, he wanted to return to Russia as soon as possible. Since Germany wanted Russia out of the war and knew that Lenin would promote a withdrawal, it provided him with a special "sealed" train that allowed no one to enter or exit during the trip. Lenin's goal upon his arrival in Russia was to organize the Bolsheviks and seize power from the provisional government.

Lenin realized that the provisional government could not maintain the support of the soldiers, peasants, and workers. His slogan, "Peace, Land, and Bread," promised the Russian people that Russia would withdraw from the war, that the peasants would be given land, and that everyone would have enough to eat. Another point in Lenin's program was that the soviets should become the nation's only government. This goal was summed up in the slogan "All power to the soviets!"

The Bolshevik Revolution

During the summer of 1917, a number of demonstrations against the provisional government broke out across Russia. Blaming these demonstrations on the Bolsheviks and calling Lenin a German agent, the government issued arrest warrants for all Bolshevik leaders, forcing Lenin into hiding. By late August, however, the Bolsheviks started to show new strength in local elections, and by mid-September they had gained control of the Petrograd Soviet.

Two months later, in November 1917, the Bolsheviks staged a coup d'etat in Petrograd, overthrowing the provisional government in the name of the soviets. Bolshevik soldiers, workers, and sailors took over the main post office, the telephone system, electrical generating plants, and train stations. When the Bolsheviks turned the guns of the warship *Aurora* against the Winter Palace, the former home of the tsar, the ministers of the provisional government quickly

ТОВ. Ленин ОЧИЩАЕТ
ЗЕМЛЮ ОТ НЕЧИСТИ.

Learning from Art   *Lenin uses a revolutionary broom to sweep aside kings, capitalists, and clergy in a propaganda poster issued after the Bolshevik takeover.* **What impression does this poster convey of the people Lenin is sweeping away?**

surrendered. As a result, the revolution was relatively bloodless.

In spite of the Bolshevik coup, the election for the constituent assembly still took place in late November. Of those elected, 420 seats went to the Social Revolutionaries and only 225 to the Bolsheviks. When the assembly met in Petrograd in January 1918, however, the Bolsheviks dissolved it after only one day.

Lenin's first goal after seizing power was to end Russian involvement in World War I. But after the Allies rejected the Bolshevik proposal for a general armistice, Lenin realized that Russia would have to negotiate a separate peace with Germany. Russia eventually signed the Treaty of Brest-Litovsk in March 1918, in which the Bolsheviks gave up the Baltic provinces, the Ukraine, and Poland to Germany. Lenin was not worried about these losses; he believed that a revolution would soon sweep Germany, too.

Civil War

After dissolving the constituent assembly, the Bolsheviks faced challenges from many different groups within Russia. Royalists favored the restoration of the tsar, middle-class liberals supported a capitalist democracy, and moderate socialists wanted both democracy and a state-controlled economy. During the early months of 1918, Russia slipped into a devastating civil war between the Bolsheviks and their opponents.

Reds and Whites   The various groups opposed to the Bolsheviks came to be called the Whites. The Bolsheviks at this time began to call themselves Communists. Because they favored the red flag of revolution, they were also called the Reds. The Bolsheviks and their supporters throughout the world founded an international revolutionary movement. Their political ideology, based on the ideas of Marx and Lenin, became known as communism.

The Allies wanted to overthrow the Bolsheviks and get Russia back into the war against the Central Powers. As a result, they sent soldiers and military aid to help the Whites, who promised to defeat the Reds quickly and then to begin helping with the war effort again. Lenin's government, however, was determined not to yield power. Under the Communist leader Leon Trotsky, the Red Army was organized to defend the Communist state. Trotsky restored discipline to Russian military ranks and fostered loyalty to communism by teaching soldiers, many of whom were illiterate, how to read and write.

Although the Whites had many soldiers and arms, they suffered from a lack of unity. Royalists were suspicious of middle-class liberals. Both royalists and liberals thought that moderate Socialists were as dangerous as the Communists. As a result, the Whites were not able to work together to inflict a quick defeat on the Reds as they had planned.

For three grim years, the fighting raged across the vast landscape of Russia. Both sides burned villages and slaughtered civilians. When the Whites captured an area, they killed all suspected Bolsheviks. The Reds did the same to "counter-revolutionaries," or those believed to be opposed to communism. In the meantime, workers and peasants were starving and the nation's economy was disintegrating.

During the upheaval, Lenin used terror as a political weapon against his opponents. In July 1918, acting on Lenin's orders, Communist soldiers killed the imprisoned tsar and his family.

Learning from Art
When the Germans threatened Petrograd, Lenin (seated at right) moved the government to Moscow. There he worked tirelessly to build the Red Army and to establish state control of all food supplies and industries. **What settlement did Lenin make with Germany?**

RUSSIAN CIVIL WAR 1918–1922

Soviet Territory
Denikin Forces
Yudenitch Forces
Kolchak Forces
Allied Forces
Trans-Siberian Railroad

Learning from Maps *The leaders of the White forces during the Russian Civil War included General Anthony Denikin, General Nicholas Yudenitch, and Admiral Alexander Kolchak.* **Why do you think Kolchak chose the strategy indicated by the map to attack Moscow?**

To further strengthen his control, Lenin set up the Cheka, a secret police force that arrested anyone considered an "enemy of the revolution." In keeping with communism's anti-religious viewpoint, Lenin also placed severe restrictions on the Russian Orthodox Church.

Many Socialists who had backed Lenin's revolution now withdrew their support and fled Russia. By 1921 Lenin had extended Communist control throughout the country. Outnumbered, disorganized, and poorly equipped, the White armies finally admitted defeat.

SECTION 4 REVIEW

Recall

1. **Define:** provisional government
2. **Identify:** Tsar Nicholas II, Grigori Rasputin, Alexander Kerensky, Vladimir Ilyich Lenin, Leon Trotsky
3. **Outline:** What were the main differences that separated the Mensheviks and the Bolsheviks?

Critical Thinking

4. **Synthesize:** Imagine that you are a member of the working class in Russia. How would you have proposed to solve Russia's most pressing problems in March 1917?
5. **Evaluate:** Do you think Lenin was justified in closing down the democratically elected constituent assembly in January 1918? Why or why not?

Applying Concepts

6. **Revolution:** Analyze the reasons for Russia's withdrawal from the war. How did the war lead to the collapse of tsarist autocracy and the birth of a radical Socialist state?

Peace at Last

Russia's withdrawal from the war in 1918 might have proved a disaster for the Allied cause if it had not been offset by the entry of the United States into the war. American intervention took some of the pressure off the British navy and strengthened French positions along the Western Front. Although no single decisive victory turned the war around, what had seemed like a permanently stalemated war eventually gave way in 1918 to an Allied victory.

The American Contribution

The U.S. declaration of war in 1917 did much to raise Allied morale. It also gave the Allies much needed resources, both industrial and human. The Americans threw themselves into the war effort. A Selective Service System was instituted to draft soldiers into the army. Although it took time to train this army, the American navy was of immediate help.

The German U-boat campaign had been increasingly effective in late 1916 and early 1917. As a result, American Admiral William S. Sims went to London to discuss with the British how to deal with the German submarines. In London, Sims introduced the idea of the **convoy**. Under this system, merchant ships crossed the Atlantic in clusters surrounded by a small number of warships for protection. Before long, the Allies were using the convoy system for all ships crossing the Atlantic.

The hopes of many people, in both Europe and America, were focused on the President of the United States, Woodrow Wilson. Even before the war ended, Wilson put forth his Fourteen Points, a peace plan whose terms included international recognition of freedom of the seas and of trade, limitations on arms, and an end to all secret alliances. Wilson's plan also called for just settlements of colonial claims, the right of self-determination for all nations, and the establishment of a "general assembly of nations" to settle future problems peacefully.

Defeat of the Central Powers

In the spring of 1918, the Allies created their first unified command under the direction of French General Ferdinand Foch. At about the same time, the Germans mounted their last series of offensives in France. The Germans came to within 37 miles (59.2 kilometers) of Paris before the Allies finally stopped them.

By that time, the Germans had lost enormous numbers of men and were out of reserves. The Allies, however, had strong reserves, and each month 25,000 fresh American troops arrived in France. Sensing that the tide was turning, General Foch ordered a counterattack in July that pushed the Germans back to the border of Germany. With the British advancing in the north, and the Americans and French attacking through the Argonne region of France, the offensive continued into September.

Meanwhile, the Allies were advancing in the Middle East. British efforts in that region were aided by Arab fighters who sought independence from the Ottoman Empire. Led by a young British officer named T. E. Lawrence, Arab guerrilla raiders harassed the Turks and gave the British valuable information about important Turkish locations. On October 30, 1918, the Turkish army finally surrendered and the Ottoman Empire crumbled. Less than a week later, following an impressive Italian victory, Austria-Hungary surrendered as well.

At about the same time, the German army began to disintegrate. Thousands of German soldiers surrendered in October—in many cases, without a fight. Defeatism among the troops and low morale at home finally forced Germany to give way. On November 9, 1918, Emperor William II abdicated and fled to the Netherlands. On November 11, the Germans signed an **armistice**, or agreement to end the fighting.

Effects of the War

The fury of the war had shattered Europe. Nearly 9 million soldiers died in the fighting, and another 21 million were wounded. Europe had lost nearly an entire generation of young men. In addition, approximately 20 million civilians died of disease and starvation.

The war also shook the old political and social order. A once wealthy and thriving continent lay in economic ruin. The old aristocratic political order was dead. Four mighty empires—the German, Austro-Hungarian, Russian, and Ottoman empires—had fallen, and revolution threatened much of eastern Europe.

As a result of the war, human misery had become commonplace. Atrocities on a grand scale, such as the Turkish genocide of the Armenians in 1915, added to the list of horrors. Angry at Armenian support for the Allies and fearful of Armenian nationalism, the Turkish government decided to use the war as an excuse to end the long history of animosity between Turks and Armenians. The Turkish army first removed all Armenian soldiers from its ranks and deported them to labor camps. Then they rounded up Armenian civilians, roped them together, and drove them into the desert to starve. In other cases they destroyed whole Armenian villages and shot the inhabitants. Some historians have estimated that more than 1 million Armenians lost their lives in this slaughter.

Restoring the Peace

President Wilson of the United States had presented his Fourteen Points peace plan to the American Congress as early as January 1918. At first the victorious nations seemed to agree that Wilson's points should be the framework for the peace settlement. Only two countries had major

Learning from Art *T. E. Lawrence led bands of Arab guerrillas against the Turks in the Middle East. Lawrence's soldiers wrecked ammunition trains, blew up bridges, and dynamited railroads.* ***In what other ways did they help the British?***

reservations. Since control of the seas had been a British war aim, Great Britain opposed the idea of "open" seas. France, on the other hand, rejected Wilson's belief that "no annexations, no contributions, and no punitive damages" should occur as a result of the war. France believed that a clause demanding **reparations**, or payments for damages, should be included in any peace settlement.

In January 1919, delegates from 27 nations gathered in Paris to work out 5 separate peace treaties known as the Peace of Paris. The Allies did not invite representatives from the defeated Central Powers or Russia. In a break with tradition, heads of state attended the conference. President Wilson represented the United States; Prime Minister Georges Clemenceau, France; Prime Minister David Lloyd George, Britain; and Prime Minister Vittorio Orlando, Italy. These men were known as the Big Four.

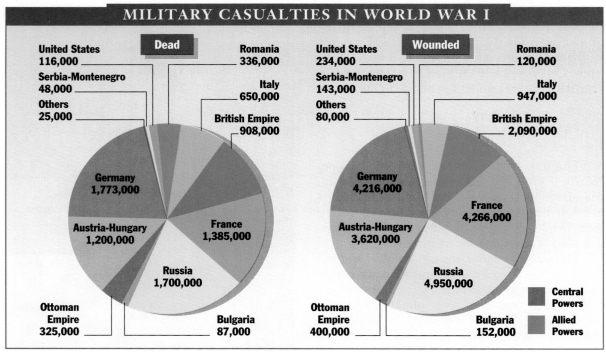

MILITARY CASUALTIES IN WORLD WAR I

Dead

United States 116,000
Serbia-Montenegro 48,000
Others 25,000
Germany 1,773,000
Austria-Hungary 1,200,000
Ottoman Empire 325,000
Russia 1,700,000
Bulgaria 87,000
France 1,385,000
British Empire 908,000
Italy 650,000
Romania 336,000

Wounded

United States 234,000
Serbia-Montenegro 143,000
Others 80,000
Germany 4,216,000
Austria-Hungary 3,620,000
Ottoman Empire 400,000
Russia 4,950,000
Bulgaria 152,000
France 4,266,000
British Empire 2,090,000
Italy 947,000
Romania 120,000

Central Powers
Allied Powers

Learning from Charts *The casualties resulting from World War I were worse than those of any other war before that time.* **Which major power suffered the worst combined casualties? Which suffered the least combined casualties?**

It soon became clear that there was a large gap between the idealistic goals of Wilson and the nationalistic goals of the French, British, and Italian leaders. Lloyd George and Clemenceau were determined to make Germany pay for the war. Wilson's chief aim was to win acceptance for his idea of an international assembly of nations. The League of Nations, as Wilson called it, became a bargaining point. Again and again, Wilson gave in on other issues to ensure that the League was included in the treaties.

The Treaty of Versailles was the most important treaty of the Peace of Paris, for it spelled out the details of the Allied peace settlement with Germany. Lloyd George and Clemenceau prevailed in their goal to punish Germany. Militarily, the treaty reduced the German army and prohibited both conscription and the manufacture of major weapons of aggression.

The treaty reduced and restricted Germany territorially as well. Germany had to return Alsace-Lorraine, seized in the Franco-Prussian War of 1870, to France. France also received

control for 15 years of the coal-rich Saar Basin. In addition, Allied troops would occupy the Rhineland region of Germany for 15 years.

In the east, Germany had to renounce the Treaty of Brest-Litovsk. The Allies also reestablished an independent Poland out of lands held by Germany, Austria-Hungary, and Russia. So that it had access to the Baltic Sea, Poland received the Polish Corridor, a strip of land separating East Prussia from the rest of Germany.

The Treaty of Versailles stripped Germany of all of its overseas colonies as well. The Allies received all of Germany's overseas possessions as **mandates**, territories administered by other countries. Great Britain and France divided Germany's African colonies, Australia and New Zealand split the German Pacific islands south of the equator, and Japan took the German Pacific islands north of the equator.

Although the above terms were harsh, France and Great Britain were still not satisfied. The Allies also demanded that Germany pay reparations for the property damage it caused during the war and for the costs to the Allies of fighting the war.

The Allies signed the treaty at the palace of Versailles on June 28, 1919. Only four of Wilson's Fourteen Points and nine supplementary principles emerged intact in the treaty. The most important of these was the Covenant of the League of Nations.

The Allied powers signed separate peace agreements with Austria, Bulgaria, Hungary, and Turkey. The most important provisions of these treaties concerned territorial matters. New nations emerged in eastern Europe from the ashes of the old Russian and Austro-Hungarian empires. These included Finland, Estonia, Latvia, Lithuania, Poland, Czechoslovakia, and Yugoslavia. The Allies, particularly France, regarded these countries as a *cordon sanitaire*, or quarantine line, that would serve as a buffer against any potential threat from Russia or Germany. In creating Yugoslavia, the Serbs achieved their goal of forming a nation of South Slavic peoples. Hungary lost territory to Yugoslavia, Czechoslovakia, and Romania, while Bulgaria lost land to Yugoslavia, Greece, and Romania.

In the Middle East, the Allies divided what was left of the Ottoman Empire. The Arabs did not receive the independence that Great Britain had promised them. Instead, Palestine, Transjordan, and Iraq became British mandates. At the same time, Lebanon and Syria became French mandates.

EUROPE IN 1919

Learning from Maps *The map of Europe changed considerably after four years of war. Some countries disappeared, while several new ones emerged.*
Which major power lost the most territory as a result of World War I?

FULL TERMS OF THE PEACE TREATY.

Learning from Art
Newspapers gave full coverage to the peace conference and resulting peace agreements. **Which two countries insisted that the Treaty of Versailles punish Germany for its role in the war?**

Bitter Fruits

A general disillusionment set in after World War I. Slogans such as "the war to end all wars" and "to make the world safe for democracy" rang hollow after years of slaughter. In addition to killing millions of people, the war destroyed the homes and lives of millions more. Many people suddenly found themselves to be minorities within newly formed nations. Others who believed they would become the citizens of independent nations found their hopes dashed by the settlements. Those whose lands were defeated were embittered by the loss of territory and prestige.

The Germans felt an especially deep sense of resentment about their loss in World War I. Because they had fought mostly on foreign territory and used resources from other countries to supplement their own, German economic strength remained largely intact. But the harsh provisions of the Treaty of Versailles left Germany weakened and humiliated as well as deprived of great-power status. The Germans' festering resentment burst forth upon the world with an even greater violence two decades later in the form of Nazism. In analyzing Germany's postwar situation, one historian has noted:

The Versailles Treaty had failed in its essential task: to settle the problem of Germany. The peace was neither stern enough to eradicate the danger of German nationalism nor generous enough to permit reconciliation. By saddling the German democrats with the odium of capitulation and the burden of being treated as a pariah nation, the Atlantic powers paved the way for Hitler.

SECTION 5 REVIEW

Recall

1. **Define:** convoy, armistice, mandate, reparation
2. **Identify:** William S. Sims, Woodrow Wilson, Ferdinand Foch, T. E. Lawrence, Georges Clemenceau, David Lloyd George, Vittorio Orlando
3. **Describe:** What were the main goals of Wilson's Fourteen Points?
4. **Outline:** What were the terms of the Treaty of Versailles?

Critical Thinking

5. **Synthesize:** Create your own Treaty of Versailles. What would you have done the same? What would you have done differently?
6. **Analyze:** How do you think a German citizen in 1919 would have felt about the provisions of the Treaty of Versailles?

Applying Concepts

7. **Internationalism:** Explain some of the problems created by the Treaty of Versailles. How did this treaty lay the foundation for another international conflict? How could it have been written to prevent this?

INTERPRETING MILITARY MOVEMENTS ON MAPS

A television documentary about a major war can be a dramatic and chilling event. Producers draw on many sources to make war real for viewers. In recreating a war, maps can be particularly useful. Maps can show military movements and can clarify events. *Interpreting military movements on a map* will help you form a clearer picture of the complexities of war.

Explanation

Use the following steps to interpret a military map:

- Determine how symbols are used. Symbols can be used to indicate battle victories. They can also help clarify whether an action took place on land, air, or sea.
- Decide how arrows are used. Arrows typically indicate an army's advance or offensive action. The size of the arrows indicate the extent and direction of the offensive.
- Determine how color has been used. Nations or alliances are often assigned a color to differentiate them. The map symbols may appear in those colors, indicating which nation won a battle or engaged in an offensive. Color may also indicate which force controls a particular territory.
- Determine how words in titles, labels, keys, and captions are used. Words help clarify the images on the map. For example, the map's title describes the main topic of the map while events may be labeled with dates to show the order in which they took place.

Example

This map shows the Middle Eastern front in World War I. Stars indicate battles, and arrows indicate offensives. The stars and arrows are coded with colors to indicate which force conducted an offensive and which force was victorious. The Allied Powers, the Central Powers, and the neutral nations have each been assigned a color. This color is used to indicate which force controlled a particular territory when the war began.

This map also relies on words to communicate information. Labels indicate battle names and the dates on which they occurred. The dates aid in seeing the pattern of Allied victories toward the end of the war.

Application

Turn to the two maps on page 700 and answer these questions:

1. Did most fighting on the Western Front take place in territory controlled by the Allied Powers or by the Central Powers?
2. What three battles were fought in the Allied Powers' territory on the Eastern Front? What force was victorious in each of these battles?

Practice

Turn to Practicing Skills on page 717 in the Chapter Review for further practice in interpreting military movements on maps.

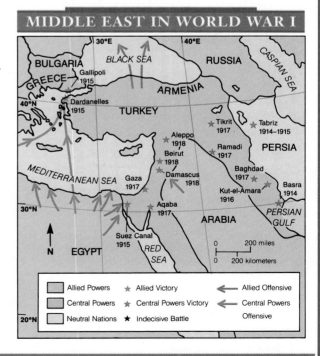

MIDDLE EAST IN WORLD WAR I

▢ Allied Powers	★ Allied Victory	◀━ Allied Offensive
▢ Central Powers	★ Central Powers Victory	◀━ Central Powers Offensive
▢ Neutral Nations	★ Indecisive Battle	

CHAPTER 27 REVIEW

HISTORICAL SIGNIFICANCE

The outbreak of World War I followed an extraordinary century of scientific and technological advances. At the beginning of the 1900s, people in western Europe and the United States had great faith in Western civilization. They shared a belief in progress and a sense that large wars were a thing of the past. World War I shattered their illusions and changed the way people looked at the world.

World War I transformed the nature of warfare. It introduced weapons of mass destruction, such as the machine gun, that made traditional military strategy obsolete. The stalemate and slaughter that characterized much of the fighting destroyed the image of war as a glorious and heroic enterprise. The nature of the fighting also left many people disillusioned about the goals of the war.

By changing the way people looked at the world, World War I gave rise to new artistic movements. The writers, composers, and painters who emerged following the war rejected old traditions and introduced radical new styles. Their work was often darker and more pessimistic than that of an earlier generation. World War I also swept away the old political and social order in Europe. It brought down mighty empires and redrew the map of the continent. Finally, by leaving much of the continent in economic ruin, and many Europeans angry and bitter at the peace settlement, World War I laid the foundation for another, even more destructive, war.

SUMMARY

For a summary of Chapter 27, see the Unit 7 Synopsis on pages 802-805.

USING KEY TERMS

A. Define the key terms below, and then write one or two sentences relating each term to the conduct of World War I.

1. armistice
2. contraband
3. convoy
4. entente
5. propaganda
6. provisional government
7. trench

B. Define each term in the pairs below, and then write two or three sentences describing how the terms in each pair were related during World War I.

8. militarism, alliance system
9. mobilization, ultimatum
10. reparation, mandate

REVIEWING FACTS

1. **Identify:** Which nations formed the Triple Alliance? Which nations formed the Triple Entente?
2. **Explain:** How did Germany's war strategy change after the Battle of the Marne?
3. **Tell:** How many soldiers were killed or wounded in World War I? How many civilians died of disease or starvation?
4. **Explain:** Explain the social changes promised by the Bolshevik slogans.
5. **List:** List at least five of the points President Wilson supported at the Paris peace conference in 1919.
6. **Identify:** Name seven new European nations that emerged as a result of World War I.

THINKING CRITICALLY

1. **Analyze:** In what sense were the European alliance systems more responsible for setting off World War I than any specific event?
2. **Apply:** How did sea power have a major effect on the outcome of World War I?

3. Analyze: How were technological advances in weaponry most responsible for the military stalemate during much of World War I?

ANALYZING CONCEPTS

1. Cooperation: Compare the Triple Alliance and the Triple Entente with NATO and the Warsaw Pact today. Which pair provided better deterrence to war? Why?

2. Conflict: Identify one war goal for each of these countries: Serbia, Austria-Hungary, Russia, and France. Discuss a situation today where a conflict between the goals of different nations might lead to war.

3. Revolution: Name the main causes of the Russian Revolution of 1917. Compare these causes with the causes of recent radical changes in the Soviet Union.

4. Internationalism: Do you think the peace settlement following World War I was conducive to the success of the newly created League of Nations? Explain.

PRACTICING SKILLS

1. World War I saw the introduction of many innovations in the way war is fought. Based on your reading about World War I, think of two examples of innovations first used in this war and explain how these innovations might be shown on a military map.

2. Imagine you were studying a war in which no side emerged as the clear victor. What might you expect to see on a military map of such a war?

GEOGRAPHY IN HISTORY

1. Regions: Refer to the map on page 696. Which territories did Serbia want to unite?

2. Movement: Refer to the maps on page 700. How did location contribute to Germany's defensive weaknesses?

3. Movement: Refer to the map on page 709. Who controlled the Trans-Siberian Railroad during the Russian Civil War?

TRACING CHRONOLOGY

Refer to the time line below to answer these questions.

1. How soon after the assassination of Archduke Ferdinand were most of the major powers of Europe at war?

2. In what sense was 1917 the pivotal year of the war?

LINKING PAST AND PRESENT

1. Where in Europe today would you find nationalist tensions that might spark conflict?

2. The postwar ideal of self-determination was not granted to colonies. Where do struggles for self-determination continue today?

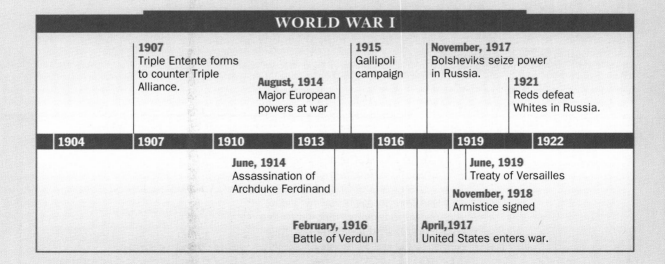

WORLD WAR I

1907 Triple Entente forms to counter Triple Alliance.

August, 1914 Major European powers at war

1915 Gallipoli campaign

November, 1917 Bolsheviks seize power in Russia.

1921 Reds defeat Whites in Russia.

1904 — 1907 — 1910 — 1913 — 1916 — 1919 — 1922

June, 1914 Assassination of Archduke Ferdinand

February, 1916 Battle of Verdun

April, 1917 United States enters war.

November, 1918 Armistice signed

June, 1919 Treaty of Versailles

Between Two Fires

*F*rom early evening until far past midnight, Nazi stormtroopers and youth groups marched in disciplined columns through Berlin. Joachim, now a priest and medical missionary, participated in that torchlight parade in the early 1930s:

"When I marched in that parade, I thought it was only the beginning. I had been privileged to be an important person in helping to create the Thousand Year Reich, the great new Germany that Hitler would bring forth out of the chaos and trouble around us."

Looking back on that night, Joachim is appalled at how little he really knew about the movement to which he had intended to devote his life. But the economic and political chaos caused by World War I and the Great Depression led many Europeans to throw their support behind powerful dictators in the 1920s and 1930s.

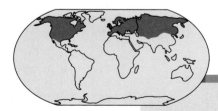

German dictator Adolf Hitler mesmerized his followers with fiery speeches.

2. What led to the rise of Fascist dictatorships in Italy and Germany after World War I?

3. How did Stalin's rule transform the Soviet Union?

Concepts to Understand:

• Innovation—The period after World War I witnesses revolutionary changes in culture, style, science, and the arts. Section 1

• Change—As a result of the Great Depression, governments in Europe and North America increase their involvement in economic affairs. Section 2

• Uniformity—Italy, Germany, and the Soviet Union develop regimented, totalitarian societies and suppress dissidents and minorities. Sections 3,4

The Postwar World

"ARMISTICE SIGNED, END OF THE WAR!" proclaimed *The New York Times* headline on November 11, 1918. In the United States and Europe, people exploded in a frenzy of celebration. The critic and author Malcolm Cowley wrote later of the feeling of euphoria that marked the end of the war: "We danced in the streets, embraced old women and pretty girls, swore blood brotherhood with soldiers in little bars. . ." But the excitement did not last. "On the next day," continued Cowley, ". . . we didn't know what to do."

World War I marked the great divide between the old and the new. The war changed the way many people looked at the world, and the disillusionment it caused led artists and intellectuals on a restless search for something new. The postwar period was a time for breaking with tradition and experimenting with new styles in politics and culture.

Changing Patterns of Life

Warren Harding became president of the United States in 1920, promising a "return to normalcy." But there was no going back to the past. The war had changed the world too much for that to be possible. Instead, people in both North America and Europe began to experiment with new customs and ways of life.

New Trends in Culture and Style In the postwar era, women gained a new level of independence. With the ratification of the Nineteenth Amendment in 1920, women in the United States won the right to vote at last. Women also won the vote in most other Western countries following the war.

Many women now demanded other freedoms as well. Throwing off the inhibitions of the prewar era, some women in the United States and western Europe began to use rouge and lipstick openly. Their skirts rose from a few inches above the ankle to an inch above the knee. They cropped their hair to a shingle bob and aimed for a carefree, little-boy look. Thus attired, the "flapper" created a revolution in manners and morals.

In the postwar era, not only the flapper but people in general disdained the familiar and the commonplace. They wanted heroes who were larger than life. Babe Ruth, the "Sultan of Swat," was the darling of baseball. Tennis champions Big Bill Tilden and Helen Wills Moody became national heroes. When Gertrude Ederle swam the English Channel and Charles Lindbergh flew nonstop from Long Island to Paris, the public saluted them with tumultuous ticker-tape parades on Broadway.

Amid all the hoopla, bankers and business leaders were having a heyday. The war had

---

FOOTNOTES TO HISTORY

FADS

Sitting on top of flagpoles for days at a time was just one of many fads that swept the United States in the "Roaring Twenties." The public craved anything new. Mahjong, a Chinese version of rummy played with tiles, became a national obsession. In 1924 a publisher issued the first book of crossword puzzles. Soon everyone was systematically filling in blank squares. Marathon dancers would drag themselves around the dance floor for hours until they dropped from utter exhaustion. Most of the fads were harmless, but people embraced these fashions with an enthusiasm that bordered on the irrational.

opened new prospects for economic development. President Calvin Coolidge neatly summed up the nation's focus in the 1920s when he said, "The business of America is business."

The Impact of Technology   New forms of technology altered people's life-styles and brought people closer together in the 1920s. The decade following the war witnessed a revolution in transportation and communication.

The automobile had perhaps the greatest impact on European and American society. A network of highways began to crisscross Europe and the United States. People could now move easily from place to place, and move they did. The United States, in particular, became an increasingly mobile society. Americans traveled farther afield on vacations and moved from rural areas to cities.

Radio also brought about dramatic changes. By exposing millions of people to the same news and entertainment shows, radio helped to produce a more homogeneous, or uniform, culture. Through its advertisements, radio also stimulated the public's desire for consumer goods. Advertisers learned the art of motivation, and ads now played on people's insecurities and self-doubts. "Why had he changed so in his attentions?" queried a forlorn-looking woman in an ad for a leading mouthwash.

Many products of the new technology eased the burden of the homemaker. With the advent of packaged foods, refrigerators, vacuum cleaners, and electric irons, people had more leisure time. Instead of working at home, they could take a drive, listen to the radio, or go out dancing. Millions spent their idle moments with another new product of technology: the movies.

A Revolution in Ideas

New inventions had an enormous impact on people's daily lives in the postwar period. At the same time, exciting new ideas in physics and psychology transformed the way people looked at themselves and the world.

Physics   In 1905 German physicist Albert Einstein published three papers in a German

Learning from Photographs *The radio brought a wide variety of information and entertainment to millions of people at the same time.* **How did radio change people's lives in the 1920s and 1930s?**

scientific periodical that became the basis of a new branch of physics. His theories radically altered scientific thought with new conceptions of time, space, mass, and motion. The theory of relativity provided the groundwork for controlling the release of energy from the atom. With this theory, Einstein launched the Atomic Age.

Einstein started a revolution that has now affected almost every branch of science and technology. Since he first advanced his theories, scientists have harnessed the atom in nuclear bombs. They have also used atomic energy to generate electricity and improve agricultural and industrial techniques.

Psychology   The Austrian physician Sigmund Freud revolutionized people's ideas about how the human mind works. After observing many patients, Freud concluded that the unconscious mind plays a major role in shaping behavior. The unconscious, he said, is full of memories of events from early childhood. If the memories are especially painful, people sometimes suppress them. Such suppression may lead to a variety of mental disorders.

When Freud first introduced his theories in the late 1800s, many people ridiculed or attacked them. By the 1920s, however, his ideas about human psychology had become more accepted and influential. Freud's theories eventually led to new approaches in the treatment of mental illness, in child rearing, and in education.

Upheaval in the Arts

The break between old and new following World War I was perhaps most sharply defined in the arts. In painting, music, literature, and dance, artists abandoned long-accepted traditions. The avant-garde experimented with new styles, media, and subject matter. Often the public greeted their pioneering efforts with cries of shock and protest.

Literature   Many of the period's most thoughtful writers had been disillusioned by World War I and its aftermath. The war had destroyed their belief in the traditional values of middle-class society. In expressing that disillusionment, they broke new literary ground.

In his poems *The Waste Land* and "The Hollow Men," for example, American-born poet T. S. Eliot used a patchwork style that juxtaposed different literary, religious, and historical references to convey a sense of despair about life. German novelist Thomas Mann, Austrian novelist Franz Kafka, and British novelist Virginia Woolf also experimented with new literary techniques. Both in terms of their style and content, all of these writers represented a sharp break with the literature of the past.

While they echoed Eliot's sense of disenchantment, American writers such as Ernest Hemingway and F. Scott Fitzgerald developed markedly different literary styles. For instance, in his 1926 novel *The Sun Also Rises,* Hemingway used a lean, straightforward style to tell the tale of American and English expatriates who roamed France and Spain, living for the moment while trying to find meaning in their lives. In contrast, Fitzgerald used a more elaborate poetic style in his 1925 novel *The Great Gatsby* to explore the atmosphere and excesses of the Roaring Twenties.

Several years earlier, in 1922, Irish novelist James Joyce had published *Ulysses,* an in-depth account of a day in the lives of three ordinary people in Dublin. *Ulysses* was a landmark in the development of the modern novel. Influenced by Freud's theories, Joyce developed a style known as "stream of consciousness" in which he presented the inner thoughts—rather than just the external actions—of his characters. Joyce's psychological emphasis and his earthy language caused a storm of protest, which led to a number of court battles over the publication of his novel.

In the late 1920s and the 1930s, many writers became interested in important social issues of the day. Langston Hughes, Claude McKay, and Zora Neale Hurston, who belonged to a black literary movement known as the Harlem Renaissance, explored the black experience in America. In *The Grapes of Wrath*, John Steinbeck described the plight of Oklahoma farmers who, in the midst of a severe drought, abandoned their farms and moved to California. John Dos Passos's *U.S.A.* trilogy was a broader social criticism of conditions in American society during the postwar period.

Painting   The postwar period also witnessed a revolution in the visual arts. Artists no longer tried to be realistic or tell a story in their paintings. Instead, they developed radical new styles and redefined the nature of painting.

Pablo Picasso, a Spanish painter, was one of the most influential artists of the period. Picasso constantly experimented with new styles, new techniques, and new media. In 1907 he created a commotion in the art world when he painted *Les Demoiselles d'Avignon.* The painting was the earliest example of **cubism**, an abstract art form that employs intersecting geometric shapes. Cubist painters transformed their subjects by flattening them, cutting them up, rearranging different portions of them, and altering their shapes and colors to fit their own vision. As Picasso explained: "Art is a lie that makes us realize the truth."

Another startling artistic development was **surrealism**, an art form that used dream-like images and unnatural combinations of objects. Influenced by Freud, surrealist painters tried to find a new reality by exploring the unconscious mind. The Spanish painter Salvador Dali created such realistically impossible images as limp watches set in bleak landscapes. The bizarre, often haunting quality of these paintings shocked the public.

In the tradition of Steinbeck and Dos Passos, other artists used their talents to attack social problems. Ben Shahn, Moses Sayer, Peter Blume, and Dorothea Lange made a name for themselves as social realists. In their paintings and photographs, they showed the human suffering caused by the Depression of the 1930s.

Music and Dance   Composers also broke new ground after the war. Several eastern European composers transformed the classical form. Sergei Prokofiev, a Russian, composed driving and dissonant music that lacked the familiar harmonies of traditional forms. Critics dubbed him the "age of steel" composer.

Arnold Schönberg, a self-taught Austrian composer, made radical changes in music theory. Instead of harmonies based on the traditional eight-note scale, he proposed new musical arrangements based on 12 equally valued notes. In his groundbreaking composition, *Pierrot Lunaire* (1912), Schönberg used harsh, dissonant music to express what he regarded as the decay of civilization. His composition outraged conservative audiences.

Meanwhile, in the United States, musicians were creating their own distinctive sound. The 1920s was "the golden age of jazz." What some have called the only art form to originate in the United States, jazz is a mixture of American folk songs, West African rhythms, harmonies from European classical music, and work songs from the days of slavery. Trumpet player Louis Armstrong, blues singer Bessie Smith, and pianist Jelly Roll Morton popularized the new music.

The postwar era also saw a transformation in the art of dance. Performing barefoot in a loose tunic, the American dancer Isadora Duncan changed people's ideas about dance. Another American, Martha Graham, expanded on Duncan's style and turned modern dance into a striking new art form.

Sergei Diaghilev, the Russian impresario, or sponsor, developed modern ballet, which blended modern dance with classical ballet. When

Russian composer Igor Stravinsky wrote *The Rite of Spring* (1913) for Diaghilev and his company of dancers, the Ballets Russes, it was a turning point for ballet. The leaping dance steps that ballet star Vaslav Nijinsky performed to Stravinsky's music created a sensation. George Balanchine, who had been a **choreographer**, or dance arranger, with the Ballets Russes, expanded on Diaghilev's work after moving from the Soviet Union to the United States.

Architecture   The 1920s and 1930s saw striking new designs in buildings and furnishings. Walter Gropius founded the Bauhaus school of design in Weimar, Germany. He and his followers created a simple, unornamented

Learning from Art *The 1920s produced a number of new kinds of entertainment for Americans.* **What does this painting indicate about the mood in the United States during this period?**

Charlie Chaplin

Although American companies began making entertainment films early in the 1900s, it was not until the 1920s that motion pictures became a major American industry. In the early years, film companies used anonymous actors and actresses, counting on a movie's story rather than the individual performers to draw an audience. By the 1920s, however, favorite stars began to emerge. Hollywood was quick to realize that a performer's popularity could determine the success or failure of a movie.

One of the earliest stars of American film was a British comedian named Charlie Chaplin. Born in London in 1889, Chaplin had worked on stage in vaudeville shows from the time he was a child. In 1913 he was discovered by an American movie producer, and in 1914 he made his first film. Within two years, Charlie Chaplin became one of the most popular comedians in the United States. Before long, he began producing his own films. His success was so great that he had no need for financial backing from the established movie studios.

Charlie Chaplin is shown in his 1936 film Modern Times.

In many ways, Chaplin's films commented on the social issues and concerns of American society in the 1920s and 1930s. His most famed character, a tramp, was featured in many of his films. His tramp costume consisted of baggy pants, big shoes, a cane, a derby hat, and a moustache. In years of silent films, with his costume and funny walk, Chaplin's misfit provided comic relief from his audience's everyday problems. At the same time, the themes behind many of his films addressed social issues. His tramp was often cast opposite a character who represented big business or high society. Inevitably Chaplin's tramp would turn out to be the more human and endearing character of the two. Chaplin mocked the values of American society—but always with humor.

In an era when few Americans could afford lavish entertainment, motion pictures provided a pleasant diversion for the nation. Radio broadcasting was still in its earliest years, and television was yet to come. For many people of the time, motion pictures were the primary form of "modern" entertainment available to them. Stars like Charlie Chaplin became national heroes, loved for their ability to make people laugh.

Responding to the Arts

1. What did movie companies soon realize about the main reason for a film's success or failure?
2. For what role was Charlie Chaplin most famous?

style of design. Linking beauty to practicality, Gropius pioneered geometric concrete and glass structures in both Germany and the United States.

In the United States, Frank Lloyd Wright blended his structures with their natural surroundings. Because of their low horizontal form, his houses seem to grow out of the ground. Instead of creating boxlike rooms, Wright reduced the number of walls so that one room flowed into another.

Popular Culture While the revolutionary developments taking place in art and music may not have had an immediate effect on the lives of ordinary people, films and big bands did. In the postwar era, Hollywood productions dominated the movie screens of the world. The movies reflected the new morality of the "Jazz Age" and the doctrine of living for the moment. During the 1930s the public flocked to movie theaters, where for 10 cents they could escape the harsh realities of hard economic times.

In the early part of the century, the creative use of the camera elevated the motion picture to an art form. In *The Last Laugh*, a silent film directed by German filmmaker F. W. Murnau, the camera work is so expressive that the story is told entirely without subtitles. British actor and director Charlie Chaplin also broke new ground in his films while delighting millions of moviegoers with his humor.

But in 1927 motion pictures found their voice. *The Jazz Singer*, starring American actor Al Jolson, changed motion pictures overnight and signaled the beginning of the end of the era of silent films. During the early 1930s, American musicals, gangster movies, and horror movies were popular. But some filmmakers tried to educate as well as entertain their audience. *I Am a Fugitive from a Chain Gang* (1932) was a forceful indictment of the southern penal system, while *Mr. Smith Goes to Washington* (1939) showed the effects of political corruption.

The public also sought escape from their troubles on the ballroom floor. In the 1930s and 1940s, dance bands reached their greatest popularity. Tommy Dorsey, Count Basie, Benny Goodman, Duke Ellington, Artie Shaw and their swing bands performed in ballrooms and hotels all across America. Swing was the new word for music played with a happy, relaxed jazz beat. But if swing was not everyone's cup of tea, there were alternatives. The bands of Guy Lombardo and Sammy Kaye played traditional waltzes and fox-trots.

Obviously the social upheavals and economic hardships that World War I created did not dampen the creative spirit following the war. During this era artists introduced new styles in every major art form. At times it seemed as if they were transforming the world with their radical new visions of life. But the euphoria did not last. The stock market crash that took place on Wall Street in late October of 1929 plunged the United States and much of the world into an economic depression that had devastating and deadly consequences.

SECTION 1 REVIEW

Recall
1. **Define:** cubism, surrealism, choreographer
2. **Identify:** Albert Einstein, Sigmund Freud, T. S. Eliot, Pablo Picasso, Sergei Prokofiev, Walter Gropius
3. **Explain:** How did the events and aftermath of World War I affect the way many people looked at the world?

4. **Identify:** Name three artists who produced revolutionary changes in literature, art, music, or architecture and describe the contributions each made.

Critical Thinking
5. **Illustrate:** How did Freud's theories affect the work of James Joyce and Salvador Dali?

6. **Analyze:** What effect did new technological advances have on American culture in the 1920s?

Applying Concepts
7. **Innovation:** The postwar era was a time for breaking with tradition. How could abandoning traditions help a society? How might it harm a society?

The Western Democracies

Peace brought neither stability nor lasting prosperity to the Western democracies, which paid a heavy price for their victory in World War I. Although the United States suffered comparatively low financial losses, huge war debts threatened the economic and political stability of Great Britain and France. The West did enjoy a brief period of prosperity in the 1920s, but a global economic depression soon followed. This depression further weakened the Western democracies in the 1930s, making it difficult for them to counter the rising totalitarian threat in Italy and Germany.

The United States

The United States emerged from World War I in better shape than its allies. No battles were fought on American soil, and because of its late entry into the conflict, America suffered far fewer casualties than the other nations. Moreover, unlike the economies of many European countries, the American economy remained strong until 1929.

Cutting Foreign Ties   President Woodrow Wilson wanted the United States to assume a greater role in world affairs following the war. But Americans were weary of war and of the foreign entanglements that had dragged the nation into war. They wanted to return to a life of isolation, free from international problems.

An idealistic man, Wilson had seized on the notion of a League of Nations as the cornerstone of a lasting peace. But the newly elected Republican majorities in both the Senate and the House of Representatives had no wish to accommodate the Democratic president. When Congress failed to ratify the Treaty of Versailles in 1919, it also rejected American membership in the League. The absence of the United States significantly weakened the League's effectiveness as a strong international peacekeeping organization.

Economic Boom   Unlike Europe, the United States had come out of World War I with a dynamic industrial economy. In addition, the Allies owed the United States huge sums of money, and these loans more than canceled out America's prewar debt of $4 billion. The war had transformed the United States from a debtor nation, which owed money, into a creditor nation, to which money was owed.

The 1920s were boom years for many American industries. Factories turned out millions of automobiles, radios, vacuum cleaners, and refrigerators. The United States was soon producing 40 percent of the world's manufactured goods. Employment was rising, and many workers' wages reached the highest levels ever paid in the history of the nation.

As a result of this economic prosperity, more and more people entered the stock market. In the hope of doubling and tripling their money in a rising market, schoolteachers, cabdrivers, shoe clerks, doctors, and lawyers gambled their life savings. But despite the soaring "bull market," the economy was shaky.

Crash and Depression   On Tuesday morning, October 29, 1929, the crash came. In that one day, the value of stocks listed on the New York Stock Exchange dropped $14 billion. In the next three years, as prices continued to fall, thousands of businesses and banks closed. Sales dropped off, forcing a curtailment of production. Salaries and wages also fell, and many workers lost their jobs. By 1933 more than 13 million American workers were unemployed—nearly one-fourth of the nation's work force.

As property owners defaulted on taxes, hundreds of small towns found themselves unable to pay their teachers or sanitation workers. Schools shut down, garbage rotted in the streets, and people went hungry. Since state and local governments could provide little relief, private businesses and organizations sometimes stepped in to help care for the needy.

In the opinion of many political leaders, direct relief was not the responsibility of the national government but of the individual, the family, and the local community. Government-funded relief, they believed, would destroy American self-reliance and would lead to socialism. Not everyone agreed.

The New Deal   In 1932 voters elected a new president, former New York governor Franklin Delano Roosevelt. Roosevelt had campaigned on the promise of "a new deal" for the American people. He believed that the federal government had to aid the stricken economy and provide relief for the unemployed.

In the first 100 days of his administration, in the spring and early summer of 1933, Roosevelt sent a number of bills to Congress that quickly became laws. These measures regulated the banks and stock market and established production guidelines for industry and agriculture. To put people back to work, the government established public works projects to build roads,

CONNECTIONS: HISTORY AND THE ENVIRONMENT

The Dust Bowl

By 1937 the drought had forced farmers from this property in Oklahoma.

Although American farmers in the 1930s suffered greatly, their suffering was not solely the result of the Great Depression. Nature itself seemed to conspire against them during this decade.

The most devastating of all the natural phenomena farmers experienced was the drought that afflicted the central part of the nation from 1933 to 1937. As the land of the Great Plains became powder-dry, winds lifted vital topsoil into the air in clouds of dust that turned day into night. Dust storms had swept over the area before but never on such a large and destructive scale.

The roots of this disaster lay well in the past. Cattle barons overgrazed an area that experienced scant rainfall. In the wake of these ranchers came farmers, who tore up the soil with their plows and planted wheat. These early settlers farmed land that

should never have been cultivated, and they farmed it badly. They did not use contour plowing to check erosion, rotate their crops, or plant trees as windbreaks to hold the soil.

Ruined by the drought, many farmers packed up their belongings and headed West.

The 200,000 people who left the Dust Bowl found little relief in the West. Low-paying seasonal jobs awaited the migrants in California, and local townspeople and farmers resented the intrusion. It took many years of normal rainfall and improved farming techniques to transform the Great Plains from a Dust Bowl into productive land again.

Making the Connection
1. What factors created the Dust Bowl?
2. What did many Dust Bowl farmers do in the 1930s?

dams, bridges, homes, and parks. Later New Deal legislation provided for social security and unemployment insurance. Although Roosevelt's New Deal policies were not entirely successful in ending the Depression, they did much to restore the confidence of the nation.

Foreign Affairs   The American government was concerned with more than just domestic affairs during the 1920s and 1930s. Despite its rejection of the League of Nations and binding alliances, the United States did take steps to prevent a future world war. In 1921 it played host in Washington, D.C., to an international conference on **disarmament**, the reduction of military weapons. At this conference, the United States signed a treaty with Japan and Great Britain limiting the number of naval warships each could stockpile. The leading powers at the conference also agreed to seek peaceful rather than military solutions to disagreements.

In 1928 the United States and France signed the Kellogg-Briand Pact, which denounced war as a means of settling disputes. Eventually, nearly all the nations of the world signed this agreement. Unfortunately, it was nothing more than a statement of intentions and had no powers of enforcement.

Great Britain

Although World War I increased the United States' economic and political influence, it cost Great Britain its position as a leading economic power in the world. Before the war British banks lent money to nations all over the globe. But the war was costly, and Britain was forced to borrow heavily from the United States. As a result, Great Britain became a debtor instead of a creditor nation.

The war also cost Great Britain its privileged position in world trade. American and Japanese companies captured many of Britain's overseas markets during the war. In addition, Britain's factories were old and the equipment outdated. Countries like the United States and Japan, which had industrialized later, had newer factories and more modern equipment. Consequently they could produce goods at a lower cost. Many factories in Britain closed or cut back production after the war. By 1921 more than 2 million workers had lost their jobs.

General Strike   Britain's economic woes reached a crisis point in 1926. Coal miners were engaged in a bitter strike for higher wages that year. For months the coal companies had refused to give in to their demands. In an effort to end the stalemate, the coal miners convinced many other trade union workers to join in a **general strike**, a strike involving all or a large number of a nation's workers. On May 4 all transport workers, dockers, public utility employees, and workers in the building trades and heavy industry walked off their jobs. The government declared a state of emergency and called out the troops to run essential services.

In the end, the General Strike was a failure. By December 1926 the coal strike had also collapsed. And in 1927 Parliament passed the Trade Disputes Act, which made general strikes illegal.

Rise of the Labour Party   Despite the failure of the General Strike, British workers gained political strength during the 1920s. During this decade the Labour party became the second leading party in the country after the Conservatives. In 1924 and again in 1929, Labour governments were elected to office. Each time, King George V named Scottish Labour leader Ramsay MacDonald prime minister. Because the Labour party supported Socialist causes, its rise to power alarmed the Conservatives and their wealthy supporters. However, once in power, MacDonald and other Labour leaders tempered many of their radical demands.

From Empire to Commonwealth   In the 1920s and 1930s, Great Britain retained control of its colonial territories. However, the dominions, like Canada and Australia, became completely independent states. In 1931 Parliament passed the Statute of Westminster, which established the Commonwealth of Nations, a voluntary association linking Great Britain and its former colonies on an equal basis.

One of Great Britain's major postwar problems was its relationship with Ireland. After an unsuccessful rebellion by Irish nationalists, the

Learning from Photographs *The General Strike of 1926 in Great Britain involved almost 3 million trade union members.* **Which political party came to represent the British working class during the 1920s?**

British government and the Irish agreed to a compromise that moved Ireland toward independence.

A treaty signed in 1921 granted dominion status to the 26 counties of southern Ireland, known as the Irish Free State. The largely Protestant northern counties remained part of Great Britain. Because the treaty retained British control in the north, a radical group, led by Eamon de Valera, revolted against the new Irish Free State. The Irish government suppressed this rebellion, but economic distress brought de Valera to power in 1932. Five years later, the Irish Free State received a new constitution and changed its name to Eire.

France

World War I had an even more devastating effect on France than on Great Britain. In the four years of fighting, the combatants had destroyed thousands of square miles of farmland and forests and reduced villages and cities to rubble. French casualties were enormous. Half of the males between the ages of 18 and 32 were killed in the fighting.

Troubled Years Like Great Britain, France faced severe economic problems after the war. High unemployment and soaring inflation caused terrible hardships. The French government was nearly bankrupt, and its war debts were staggering. As a result of these financial problems, France's factories, railways, and canals could not be quickly rebuilt.

The political picture was as bleak as the economic one. Many political parties competed for votes. Since each party received seats in the national legislature according to its percentage of the vote, no party ever won a majority of seats. In order to form a government, several parties had to band together into a **coalition**, or alliance of factions, but the coalition governments often fell apart soon after they were formed.

Extremist groups on both the left and the right also threatened the political stability of the nation. Communists and Socialists struggled for power against Fascists, and outbreaks of violence were common.

Popular Front In 1934 the political crisis reached a head. Fascist groups rioted in Paris, killing several people. Fearing a Fascist takeover, the Communists appealed to leaders of the Socialist party for "a broad Popular Front to combat fascism and for work, liberty, and peace."

The new coalition won enough votes in a 1936 election to form a government. Leon Blum, the Socialist leader, became prime minister. The Popular Front was in power for less than a year, but in that short time it passed many new laws that benefited workers and farmers.

Foreign Policy Exhausted and drained by World War I, France wanted, above all else, to prevent another war. Consequently, the French government strongly supported the League of Nations in the postwar years and worked to create a series of alliances to contain Germany. But it also sought friendly ties with Germany's new democratic Weimar Republic. In 1928 France signed the Locarno Agreements with Germany,

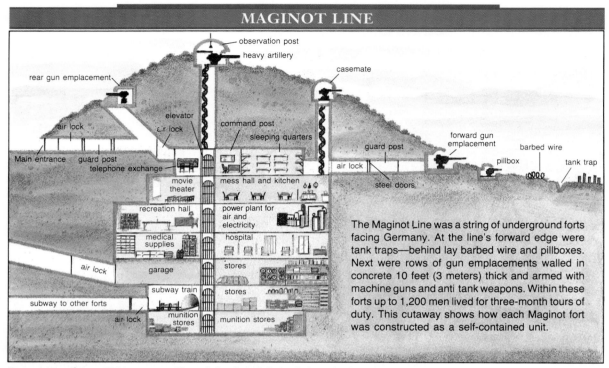

MAGINOT LINE

The Maginot Line was a string of underground forts facing Germany. At the line's forward edge were tank traps—behind lay barbed wire and pillboxes. Next were rows of gun emplacements walled in concrete 10 feet (3 meters) thick and armed with machine guns and anti tank weapons. Within these forts up to 1,200 men lived for three-month tours of duty. This cutaway shows how each Maginot fort was constructed as a self-contained unit.

Learning from Diagrams *French leaders believed that the Maginot Line would repel any attempted German invasion of their nation.* **What important historical evidence did these leaders fail to consider?**

Italy, Belgium, and Great Britain that appeared to ensure a lasting peace.

As added insurance against a future German invasion, France built a series of fortifications 200 miles (320 kilometers) long called the Maginot Line. This stretch of concrete bunkers and trenches extended along France's border with Germany. French military leaders boasted that the Maginot Line could never be crossed. What they failed to consider was that past German invasions had come through Belgium, whose border with France remained virtually undefended.

SECTION 2 REVIEW

Recall
1. **Define:** disarmament, general strike, coalition
2. **Identify:** Franklin Roosevelt, Ramsay MacDonald, Commonwealth of Nations, Eamon de Valera, Leon Blum
3. **Explain:** How did World War I affect the economies of the United States, Great Britain, and France?
4. **Explain:** Why did the United States retreat into a period of isolationism in the postwar years?

Critical Thinking
5. **Analyze:** What steps did Americans and Europeans take to prevent another world war?
6. **Evaluate:** Why do you think the democracies of the United States, Great Britain, and France survived despite postwar political, economic, and social problems?

Applying Concepts
7. **Change:** How did President Franklin Roosevelt's New Deal change the role the federal government played in American society after 1933?

Fascist Dictatorships

World War I shattered the economic and political stability of many European nations. For example, it caused staggering inflation in Germany in the early 1920s. The situation in Italy during this period was equally serious, causing workers there to stage lengthy nationwide strikes. When the United States stock market crashed in October 1929, the resulting worldwide economic depression wreaked havoc on the already weakened German economy. The economic and social chaos created by war and depression made both Italy and Germany ripe for revolution in the postwar period.

Rise of Fascism in Italy

A general mood of dissatisfaction permeated Italy after the war. Although it had fought on the side of the Allies, Italy did not gain all that the Allies had promised. It had expected to receive huge portions of territory from the Central Powers. Instead, it only gained a small piece of Austrian territory, leaving many Italians with bitter feelings.

The war had also aggravated Italy's economic woes. War debts were staggering. When millions of Italian soldiers returned home, they found no work. The nation's industries lacked raw materials. But even if it had possessed the materials, Italy had no market for its products. Its best customers, Germany and Austria, had no money to buy anything.

Conditions were perfect for an opportunistic leader, and one soon emerged on the political horizon. His name was Benito Mussolini (moo seh LEE nee). Born in 1883, Mussolini came from a working-class family. As a young man, he worked as a journalist and was active in Socialist politics. But after the war, he attacked the So-

cialists for failing to put forward a policy of social reform. He eventually abandoned socialism and become an ardent nationalist.

Mussolini formed a new political party in 1919 called the *Fasci di Combattimento*, or Fascist party. **Fascism** (FASH ihz uhm) is a political philosophy that advocates the glorification of the state, a single-party system with a strong ruler, and an aggressive form of nationalism. Like communism, fascism was a totalitarian system of government, meaning that it gave the state absolute authority. But fascism defended private property and the class structure. According to its principles, the cause of the nation was to be advanced at all cost. War and conquest were glorified to achieve national goals.

Learning from Art *Fascists adopted the* fasces, *the ancient Roman symbol of strength through unity, and greeted each other with the Roman salute.* ***What did this poster intend to convey about Mussolini to the Italian people?***

Mussolini's Road to Power

Conditions in Italy continued to deteriorate in the months following the war. The value of the lira declined steadily, the price of bread rose, and a shortage of coal hampered industrial production. To express their dissatisfaction, workers staged a series of strikes that paralyzed the country. In September 1920, workers in Lombardy and Piedmont took over the factories. Mussolini showed his support for the strikers in a speech at Trieste:

I demand that the factories increase their production. If this is guaranteed to me by the workers in place of the industrialists, I shall declare without hesitation that the former have the right to substitute themselves . . . [for] the latter.

The unrest spread to rural Italy. Peasants seized land from wealthy landowners, and tenant farmers refused to pay their rents. The situation was so chaotic that the middle and upper classes feared a Communist revolution. Ever the politician, Mussolini offered "a little something to everyone." To appease the landowners, he vowed to end the unrest and protect private property. To woo the workers, he promised full employment and workers' benefits. He pleased nationalists by pledging to restore Italy to its former greatness.

By 1921 fascism had become a major political force in Italy. But the Blackshirts, as Mussolini's followers were called, did not rely on verbal assaults alone to achieve their goals. They physically attacked political opponents in the streets and drove elected officials from office.

Believing that fascism was a useful way of controlling the Socialists and workers, the democratic government did nothing to stop the Blackshirts. As a result, Mussolini grew bolder. In October 1922 the Fascists staged a march on Rome. Mussolini waited in Milan to see how the government would react. Believing that the Fascists were planning to seize power, the cabinet asked King Victor Emmanuel III to declare martial law. The king refused, and the cabinet resigned. Instead of calling for new elections, the monarch named Mussolini prime minister.

Mussolini's Dictatorship

Mussolini quickly put an end to democratic rule in Italy. In a 1924 election, Blackshirts used their now familiar brutal tactics to make sure that Italians voted for Fascist candidates. As a result, Fascists won a majority of seats in the Italian parliament. The Fascist-controlled parliament gave Mussolini sweeping new powers. After this election Mussolini began calling himself *Il Duce*, "The Leader."

To consolidate his power, Mussolini reorganized the Italian government and established a **corporate state.** Under the corporate state, Mussolini hoped to bring workers and employers together and consequently to end the political quarreling that he associated with a democratic, multiparty system. To this end, he banned non-Fascist parties and ordered that **syndicates**, or corporations of workers and employers, be formed in each industry. Each syndicate sent representatives to a legislature in Rome that set policies on wages, production, and distribution. In theory, the corporate state was a new form of democracy; in practice, it was a political tool expressly designed for strengthening Mussolini's power.

Many Italians bitterly opposed fascism. They mourned the loss of democracy and individual freedoms. The Fascists arrested, assaulted, and murdered any who dared speak out against the abuses. "The masses must obey," thundered Mussolini. "They cannot afford to waste time searching for truth."

A majority of Italians, however, supported Mussolini. They believed he had done Italy a great service by preventing a Communist revolution and had brought order to the nation. After all, they said, he "made the trains run on time."

By building up Italy's armed forces, Mussolini did solve the unemployment problem. But considerably more important, he rekindled the feelings of patriotism and nationalism that had lain dormant in the Italian people. He made it clear to Italians that it was in their destiny to recapture all the greatness that made the glory of ancient Rome. He would use all the economic and human resources available to make Italy a "great power" again.

Learning from Photographs *Nazis perfected the art of propaganda and used it to persecute Jews. Anti-Semitic posters described Jews as money-grubbing capitalists and moneylenders.* **How did the Nuremberg laws reflect anti-Semitic policies?**

Weimar Republic

While Mussolini was founding the Fascist party in Italy, the Allies were preoccupied with making sure that Germany would never again threaten the peace in Europe. As a result, the Versailles Treaty limited the size of Germany's armed forces and required the Germans to form a democratic government. While many Germans believed that democracy had become inevitable after the breakdown of the monarchy, few really believed in it.

In early 1919 Germans went to the polls and elected delegates to a national assembly. Meeting in Weimar, the assembly drafted a constitution for Germany that established a democratic republic. The republic, which lasted from 1919 to 1933, was called the Weimar Republic.

Soon after the Weimar Republic became a reality, political instability and violence threatened to overwhelm it. In 1920 nationalist army officers tried to overthrow the government in a coup d'état. Like many other Germans, they claimed that Weimar leaders had betrayed the nation by accepting the Versailles Treaty. Although the revolt was suppressed, the government failed to overcome widespread opposition to its policies.

Reparations More than just political problems threatened Germany. Great Britain and France promised their citizens that the German government would pay reparations for the full cost of the war. The Allies set this cost at $35 billion. Already beset by serious economic problems, the German government in 1922 announced that it could not meet its obligations.

France, however, insisted that Germany pay its debt. To ensure this result, French troops marched into Germany's industrial Ruhr Valley in 1923 and took control of the coal mines and steel mills. Angered at the French invasion, German workers went on strike while their government paid them. With income from Ruhr industries going to France, Germany had lost an important asset.

Inflation To meet its growing expenses, the German government printed more and more paper money. As a result, inflation soared. Before the war, four marks equaled one American dollar. By the end of 1923, it took four trillion marks to equal one dollar. For members of the middle class, inflation was a disaster. It wiped out all their savings.

In the mid-1920s, Germany finally saw ahead some relief from its troubles. The French reached a compromise with the Germans that eased payments, and they left the Ruhr. Freed of debt and strengthened by American loans, Germany entered a five-year period of relative prosperity. But the seeds of discontent had already been sown.

Rise of Nazism

Among the many new political parties challenging the Weimar Republic's authority was the National Socialist Workers' party, or Nazi party. One of the first recruits to this new party was a World War I veteran named Adolf Hitler. Born in Austria in 1889, Hitler failed in his efforts to become a successful artist. After the war, he settled in Munich and joined the Nazi party.

Hitler soon formed the Brownshirts, a private army of young veterans and street thugs.

During the inflationary crisis of 1923, Hitler made an attempt to seize power. With armed Brownshirts outside, Hitler jumped on a table in a Munich beer hall and announced, "The revolution has begun!" When the police intervened and arrested Hitler, however, the revolt quickly collapsed.

While in prison, Hitler wrote his autobiography, *Mein Kampf* (*My Struggle*). In Hitler's view, the Germans were not responsible for losing the war. He blamed the Jews and the Communists for the German defeat. He also declared that the Germans were a "master race" whose destiny was to rule the world.

During the economic boom of the mid-1920s, the Nazis' influence declined. But when the worldwide depression struck in 1929, the fortunes of the Nazi party revived. After listening to Hitler blame the depression on the Jews for three years, many Germans began to believe

Between the Wars

After World War I, Germany's economy was hard hit. In the 1930s the National Socialist party came into power. Many Germans believed Hitler would solve the nation's problems.

Inflation in Germany after World War I made the currency almost worthless. One woman used paper money to light her stove.

him. In 1932 the Nazis won 207 seats and became the largest party in the Reichstag (RYKS tahg), the German parliament. On January 30, 1933, German President Paul von Hindenburg asked Hitler to become chancellor. Through entirely legal means, the Nazis had come to power.

Hitler in Power

Hitler's goal all along was the creation of a totalitarian state. Because the Nazis were still a minority in the Reichstag, however, he planned to hold a new election. But a week before it was to be held, the Reichstag building mysteriously caught fire and burned to the ground. Hoping to reduce Communist support among the workers, Hitler blamed the Communists for the fire. In the election, the Brownshirts forced German voters to back the Nazis. When the Nazi-dominated Reichstag met after the election, it voted Hitler emergency powers to deal with the "Communist threat."

Hitler used his new powers to crush his opponents and consolidate his rule. He banned all political parties except the Nazi party. He discarded constitutional guarantees of freedom of speech, assembly, religion, and press. He placed labor unions under Nazi control.

But Hitler directed his most bitter attacks against the Jews. In 1935 the Nuremberg Laws stripped Jews of their citizenship and their right to hold public office. The laws barred Jewish students from schools and destroyed Jewish businesses. They forced Jews to wear a yellow star on their clothing. Members of the Nazi party attacked Jews on the streets and vandalized their businesses, homes, and synagogues. Hitler's secret police, the Gestapo, arrested Jews and other opponents of the government by the

Under the Nazis, Jewish citizens were terrorized. At right, Jewish shopowners find their stores vandalized and looted. Below, a Nazi poster portrays the "perfect" Aryan youth.

DER DEUTSCHE STUDENT

KÄMPFT FÜR FÜHRER UND VOLK IN DER MANNSCHAFT DES NSD-STUDENTENBUNDES

Reflecting on the Times
Why do you think Hitler and the Nazi party gained public support in Germany during the 1930s?

Learning from Photographs *After becoming dictator of Germany in 1933, Adolf Hitler often held large rallies to inspire the loyalty of the German people. Hitler also adopted the slogan Ein Volk, Ein Reich, Ein Führer (One People, One Empire, One Leader).* **What ambitions did Adolf Hitler have for Germany?**

thousands. Many of these opponents were shot. Others were sent to **concentration camps,** large prison camps where political prisoners or refugees were confined.

Hitler was suspicious of even his closest supporters. He particularly feared radical members among the Brown Shirts and set out to purge their ranks. In 1934 Hitler had hundreds of Brown Shirts and their leaders shot.

Assured of absolute power, Hitler took the title of *Der Führer*, "the Leader." He called his government the Third Reich, or Third Empire, and boasted it would last 1,000 years. To this end, he set about restoring Germany's military might. He ignored the provisions of the Versailles Treaty, which limited the size of the German army, and ordered German factories to begin turning out guns, ammunition, airplanes, tanks, and other weapons. He made no secret of his ambitions to expand Germany's territory: "Today Germany; tomorrow, the world!"

Hitler also brought all intellectual and artistic activity in Germany under his control and imposed his own ideas on the arts. To glorify nazism, he made plans to rebuild Berlin in the style of monumental classical architecture. He discouraged the artistic experimentation that had flourished during the 1920s. As a result, many of Germany's most talented artists and scientists—among whom were Sigmund Freud, Albert Einstein, Walter Gropius, and Arnold Schönberg—fled the country.

SECTION 3 REVIEW

Recall

1. **Define:** fascism, corporate state, syndicate, concentration camp
2. **Identify:** Benito Mussolini, Adolf Hitler
3. **Explain:** How did World War I affect Italy economically?
4. **List:** What problems did the Weimar Republic face after World War I?

Critical Thinking

5. **Analyze:** Explain the appeal of fascism and nazism to Italians and Germans in the decade following World War I.
6. **Examine:** How did Mussolini and Hitler consolidate their power?

Applying Concepts

7. **Uniformity:** Why did democratic governments fail in Italy and Germany in the 1920s and 1930s?

The Soviet Union

By 1921 Russia had endured the horrors of world war, revolution, and civil war. In the course of seven years of conflict, 27 million Russians had perished. Most had died on the battlefields and in countless guerrilla engagements, but millions had died of disease and starvation as well. In addition, the nation's transport system was in ruins, the peasants were in open revolt, and the economy was plunging toward collapse. At the Tenth Party Congress, Red Army director Leon Trotsky proclaimed: "We have destroyed the country in order to defeat the Whites."

Lenin in Power

In their struggle for survival during the civil war, Lenin and the Bolsheviks had introduced an economic policy called war communism in 1918. Under war communism, the government carried out a policy of **nationalization,** in which it brought under state control all major industries. Applying the principle that those who would eat must work, the government required everyone between the ages of 16 and 50 to hold a job. It also erected a huge bureaucratic administration that wielded tremendous power but was extremely inefficient.

In 1921 Lenin tried to bring order out of the chaos that both war and government policy had caused. He announced a plan called the New Economic Policy, or NEP. Major industries such as steel, railroads, and large-scale manufacturing remained under government control. But in an attempt to stimulate the economy, Lenin allowed some private businesses to operate. In a startling departure from Marxist theory, NEP permitted small manufacturers and farmers to own their own businesses and to sell what they produced for a profit.

In 1922 the Communists changed the official name of the country from Russia to the Union of Soviet Socialist Republics (U.S.S.R.), or the Soviet Union. During this time, Lenin and other Communist leaders also completed a new constitution. This constitution stated that the U.S.S.R. was a Socialist state, meaning that the government controlled the means of production.

In theory this state, called the **dictatorship of the proletariat,** was controlled by workers. But in practice the leadership of the Communist party controlled the workers. It was, as German

Learning from Photographs *Lenin's New Economic Policy (NEP) helped put the Soviet Union's economy back on its feet in the early 1920s.* ***What power struggle followed Lenin's death?***

Communist party member Rosa Luxemburg observed: ". . . a dictatorship, to be sure, not the dictatorship of the proletariat, however, but only the dictatorship of a handful of politicians." The classless society envisioned by Marx was, in the Soviet Union, a pyramid, with the party boss at the top and the peasants at the bottom.

The non-Russian nationalities in the U.S.S.R. did not fare much better than the peasants. Because Lenin did not want to break up the old Russian Empire into independent states, he gave each major nationality its own republic with its own bureaucracy. In reality, however, the central government in Moscow still made the important decisions for these republics. In spite of the government's talk about equality for all nationalities, the Russians remained the dominant group in the Soviet Union and largely determined its policies.

RUSSIA 1914-1922

Russian Border 1914
Area Lost at Brest-Litovsk 1918
Area Regained 1922

Learning from Maps *Russia gave up a vast amount of territory in the 1918 Treaty of Brest-Litovsk.* **Why was the land Russia regained by 1922 particularly valuable to the nation?**

Trotsky and Stalin

In 1922 Lenin suffered two strokes that left him permanently disabled. He died two years later at the age of 54.

The struggle to succeed Lenin began during his final illness. The two main contenders for the position were Leon Trotsky and Joseph Stalin. Next to Lenin, Trotsky had been the most important person in the Communist party. He had played a key role in the Bolshevik Revolution and had built the Red Army into a powerful fighting force. Trotsky came from a middle-class background and was a scholar who contributed many new ideas to the Marxist movement. He was also a speaker of great power and eloquence.

Born in Georgia, a territory south of Russia, Stalin was the son of artisans. A seminary student in his youth, Stalin was punished repeatedly for reading books about revolution and social conditions, including novels such as *Les Miserables*. Stalin later renounced Russian Orthodoxy and became a Marxist revolutionary. Unlike Trotsky, Stalin was a skilled administrator. In 1922 he rose to the important post of secretary general of the Communist party.

Trotsky and Stalin held fundamentally different views about the path the Soviet Union should follow. Like Lenin, Trotsky believed in the theory of a "permanent revolution." In other words, he believed that only when the Russian Revolution had touched off uprisings all over the world could socialists build an ideal society in the Soviet Union. Stalin, on the other hand, declared it possible and necessary to "build socialism in a single country."

Trotsky was better known than Stalin, both at home and in the Comintern (Communist International), an organization of Communist parties from all over the world. Trotsky had been closer to Lenin as well. Nevertheless, Stalin managed to outmaneuver Trotsky politically. Using his post as secretary general, Stalin gradually gained control of the party bureaucracy. As soon as he was securely in power, Stalin exiled Trotsky to Siberia and then expelled him from the Soviet Union. Trotsky eventually settled in Mexico City, where he continued to write about communism and the Soviet Union. An assassin acting on Stalin's orders murdered him in 1940.

The Five-Year Plan

Fearing war with the Western democracies, Stalin wanted to rapidly transform the Soviet Union into a leading industrial power. In 1928 he declared an end to NEP and announced the first of his Five-Year Plans, a program that set economic goals for a five-year period. The plan brought all industrial and agricultural production under government control. It also provided for housing, health care, and other services.

While promising a better future, Stalin demanded sacrifices from Soviet people. The first Five-Year Plan concentrated on building heavy industry. Consumer goods were produced in small amounts and were of inferior quality.

Responsibility for administering the plan lay in the hands of bureaucrats in Moscow. Theirs was a difficult task requiring tight control and careful planning. Not surprisingly, they made plenty of mistakes. For example, one Soviet enterprise purchased its nail supply from a nail factory 1,500 miles away, while a nail factory across the street was shipping its goods a similar distance. Despite the mistakes, the first Five-Year Plan was a success in spurring industrial growth.

Collective Farms In agriculture, Stalin's plan called for **collectivization,** a system of farming in which the government owned the land and used peasants to farm it. Stalin believed that collective farms would be more efficient. They would not only produce food for the Soviet people but produce it for export as well. By increasing agricultural exports, Stalin hoped to pay for Soviet industrialization without borrowing from the capitalist West.

Stalin also planned to use collectivization to intimidate the Soviet Union's peasant majority, most of whom were fiercely anti-Communist. **Kulaks,** or the most prosperous peasants, especially opposed collectivization. They had prospered under NEP and did not want to give up their land, livestock, and machinery. Fighting broke out in the countryside when the government tried to impose its plans. Thousands of peasants and their families were killed or arrested and sent to labor camps in Siberia. Stalin also took measures to crush anti-Communist resistance in the Ukraine. By seizing the region's

Learning from Photographs *Joseph Stalin was a master of political infighting. By the mid-1920s he had eliminated his rivals and consolidated his position as leader of the Communist party.* **What, according to Stalin, was the purpose of the Communist movement?**

grain during the terrible winter of 1932, Stalin promoted a "terror famine," causing the deaths of more than 5 million Ukrainian peasants.

Results The first Five-Year Plan transformed the Soviet Union into an industrial power, but the human cost of the plan was enormous. Industrial workers received low wages, or none at all, and food was often limited in quantity. Millions of people died because of rural unrest, and collective farms were often unable to provide enough grain to feed the nation's population.

Stalin's Dictatorship

Stalin ruled the Soviet Union from the mid-1920s until his death in 1953. During this period he established one of the most brutal dictatorships the world has ever seen.

Secret Police   Stalin demanded complete obedience from the people he ruled and got it through an effective use of terror. He granted the secret police immense power, which they used to scrutinize every aspect of the nation's social and political life. Agents of the secret police encouraged workers to spy on each other and children to spy on their parents. Those accused of disloyalty were either shot or sent to labor camps in Siberia. The secret police and their activities helped to create a climate of fear in Soviet society.

Purges   In the 1930s Stalin began a methodical attack upon his potential enemies in every sphere of public life. Even members of the Communist party did not escape the reach of Stalin and his secret police. In 1934 an unknown assailant, probably acting on Stalin's orders, assassinated a high party official. Stalin used the event to rid himself of opponents and strengthen his hold on the party. He had millions of Communist party members expelled from the party, arrested and put in labor camps, or shot.

Stalin then turned against the Old Bolsheviks. These officials had been associates of Lenin and Stalin in the early days of the movement. Because some of them had sided with Trotsky, Stalin moved in 1936 to **purge,** or remove, them from any position where they could threaten his leadership. He had them arrested and put on trial. In open court in Moscow, with foreign reporters looking on, they pleaded guilty to false charges of treason, murder, and other crimes. Although these prisoners showed no signs of mistreatment, many Western experts have since concluded that the secret police used psychological torture to break their wills.

The Arts   Stalin also set out to put all artistic and cultural activities under the Communist party's control. In 1934 he put Maxim Gorky, one of the Soviet Union's leading writers, in charge of all Soviet culture. Gorky promoted a new literary style that soon became obligatory in all the arts: **Socialist realism.** Writers and artists created a "new reality" by glorifying Soviet heroes and achievements, while denouncing the rumors about forced labor and terror. Artists who violated these dictates faced exile or imprisonment in labor camps. The Soviet government also banned foreign publications and jammed foreign radio broadcasts.

Stalin's restrictions had a chilling effect on Soviet artists. Although talented writers and artists struggled to survive, most official artistic works were predictable and uninspiring.

Comintern   In 1919 Lenin had established the Communist International, or Comintern. The goal of the Comintern was to encourage Communist parties in other countries to overthrow their governments by legal or illegal means and to establish Soviet-style regimes. While Stalin at first gave low priority to Comintern affairs, he later took more seriously the relations of the Soviet Union to the Communist parties in other countries. Stalin eventually dissolved the Comintern in 1944, to win the favor of the Western Allies during World War II.

SECTION 4 REVIEW

Recall
1. **Define:** nationalization, dictatorship of the proletariat, collectivization, kulak, purge, Socialist realism
2. **Identify:** Vladimir Lenin, Leon Trotsky, Joseph Stalin, Maxim Gorky
3. **Explain:** Why did Lenin begin the New Economic Policy?

4. **Describe:** How did Stalin transform the Soviet economy? What effects did Stalin's economic policies have on the Soviet people? Are these effects still felt today? Explain.

Critical Thinking
5. **Contrast:** How did Lenin and Stalin's new Socialist order differ from the society envisioned by Karl Marx?
6. **Evaluate:** Predict what might have happened if Trotsky—and not Stalin—had succeeded Lenin.

Applying Concepts
7. **Uniformity:** How does fascism differ from communism?

WRITING A RESEARCH REPORT

Think about a nonfiction book you have enjoyed reading. The content probably interested you because the author had researched the information carefully and presented it in a clear manner. When you *write research papers,* you can use the techniques that many published writers use.

Explanation

These steps can guide you through a research project:

- **Select a topic.** If one is assigned, you must find an aspect that interests you. Brainstorming, skimming books and magazines, and talking with classmates are ways of getting topic ideas.

  Then, do preliminary research to discover whether your idea is too broad or too specific. For example, the topic "Italy Between the World Wars" is too broad. This topic might be narrowed to "The Rise of Mussolini." As early as possible, write a statement of what you will prove or illustrate, such as, "Radio aided Mussolini's rise to power." The statement will help focus your research.

- **Prepare to do research.** Consider what sources—books, newspapers, interviews, news videos—may be useful and how you can obtain them. Then, formulate questions to guide your research: "When did

Mussolini decide to take a leadership role? What means did he use to gain attention? How did he raise funds?"

- **Research your topic and organize your information.** Early in your research, you may need to take pages of notes. As you become more focused, record individual facts on index cards. Remember to use your own words or to use quotation marks. For each note, record information that identifies the source.

  To organize your information, sort your note cards by topics. Then, select a pattern of organization, such as comparison and contrast, or order of importance, and draw up a graphic organizer or write an informal outline.

- **Write a rough draft.** Follow your outline or organizer to develop your points. As you write, you may need to do more research or revise your outline. After you complete your rough draft, review the introduction to make sure it agrees with your final thoughts.

- **Revise and finish you report.** Reread your draft, preferably aloud, for sense and organization. Ask a friend to read it, too. Rearrange sentences or paragraphs if needed. If necessary, write a second draft and revise that also. After you have completed your revisions,

proofread your report. Check for errors in grammar, spelling, capitalization, and punctuation. You are now ready to make a clean copy of your report. Remember the bibliography.

Example

You are assigned a research paper, and you choose "Environmental Problems" as a topic. You narrow the topic to "Recycling" and then narrow it down again to "Recycling of Bottles: What It Accomplishes." You write a list of questions, such as, "How is the recycled material used?" You research your topic in the library and visit a recycling plant and a waste dump site. You record information on note cards and then use your card to make an outline. After writing a draft, you read it aloud and ask a friend to evaluate it. You then proofread your report and make a final copy.

Application

Read "Changing Patterns of Life" on page 720. List six topics to research. Select one topic, and use the steps to write a report.

Practice

Turn to Practicing Skills on page 743 of the Chapter Review for further practice in writing research reports.

CHAPTER 28 REVIEW

HISTORICAL SIGNIFICANCE

World War I was a watershed event in the history of the twentieth century. It marked the end of one era and the beginning of another. Scientists and artists broke with old traditions and sought a "new reality." They experimented with new ideas, styles, and customs and introduced revolutionary changes in both technology and the arts.

The war also shattered the economies and political stability of many countries in Europe.

Political, economic, and social chaos ultimately led to the rise of totalitarian regimes in Italy, Germany, and the Soviet Union. The onset of a worldwide depression in the late 1920s also threatened the Western democracies with social unrest and weakened their ability to counter the rise of the dictatorships. As a result, tensions between the totalitarian and the democratic nations increased, and war would once again engulf the world.

SUMMARY

For a summary of Chapter 28, see Unit 7 Synopsis on pages 802–805.

USING KEY TERMS

A. Compare and contrast each pair of words. Begin by describing the similarities and then the differences.

1. cubism, surrealism
2. corporate state, syndicate
3. nationalization, collectivization

B. Write the letter of the key term that matches each definition below.

a. coalition
b. concentration camp
c. dictatorship of the proletariat
d. disarmament
e. fascism
f. general strike
g. kulak
h. nationalization
i. purge
j. Socialist realism

4. large prison camp in which political prisoners and refugees are confined
5. a totalitarian system of government that gave the state absolute authority
6. remove
7. landowning peasants
8. the reduction of military weapons
9. control of the state by the workers
10. a strike in which all or a large number of workers participate
11. government control of industry
12. literary style that involved glorifying Soviet heroes and achievements
13. alliance of factions

REVIEWING FACTS

1. **List:** What technological advances in the 1920s and 1930s had an important impact on people's lives?
2. **Explain:** What led to the rise of fascism in Italy?
3. **Explain:** What led to the rise of fascism in Germany?
4. **Identify:** What was Lenin's New Economic Policy (NEP)?
5. **Describe:** How did Stalin manage to defeat Trotsky in their struggle for power?

THINKING CRITICALLY

1. **Apply:** Why was World War I a watershed event in the twentieth century?
2. **Analyze:** How did fascism and communism differ?
3. **Synthesize:** To aid Germany's economic recovery after the First World War, how

might the Allies have structured the peace settlements?

ANALYZING CONCEPTS

1. **Innovation:** How did new movements in literature, art, and music reflect the change in the way many people viewed the world following World War I?
2. **Change:** How was Roosevelt's New Deal similar to Stalin's Five-Year Plan?
3. **Uniformity:** How and why did the leaders of Nazi Germany and Communist Soviet Union suppress dissidents and minorities?

PRACTICING SKILLS

1. Write a topic for a research report related to Section 4. Then write questions focusing your search for information.
2. Write a note based on the passage below, and record the bibliographic information.

   Frances Perkins, the first woman member of the U.S. Cabinet in history, was appointed Secretary of Labor in 1933 by . . . Franklin Delano Roosevelt. She served in this post for twelve years, longer . . . than any other person. A graduate of Mount Holyoke . . ., she had a long record in the field of labor.
   —from *An Album of Women in American History*, by Claire R. and Leonard W. Ingraham (Franklin Watts, 1972, p. 47)

GEOGRAPHY IN HISTORY

1. **Place:** Why is the area east of the Rocky Mountains a semiarid region?
2. **Place:** What is the primary economic activity of the Ruhr Valley?

TRACING CHRONOLOGY

Refer to the time line below to answer these questions.
1. How long after Mussolini became prime minister of Italy did Hitler become chancellor of Germany?
2. When did the stock market crash take place? When did Hitler's rise to power occur? How were these two separate events related?

LINKING PAST AND PRESENT

1. During the 1920s and 1930s, the automobile, motion pictures, and the radio transformed the way Americans lived. What technological advances shape our lives today? Do they have a negative or a positive impact on society? Explain.
2. Totalitarian regimes came to power in Italy and Germany primarily because of political weakness and economic chaos. Name a country that is today ruled by a dictator or a one-party system. How did this person or party come to power?

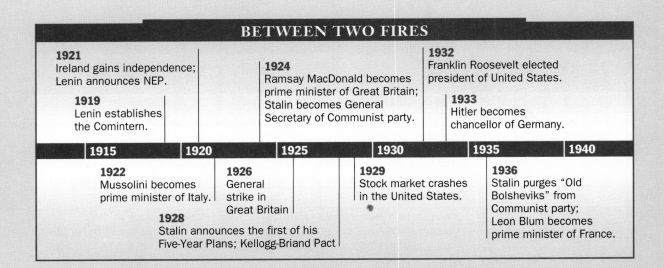

BETWEEN TWO FIRES

1921 Ireland gains independence; Lenin announces NEP.

1919 Lenin establishes the Comintern.

1924 Ramsay MacDonald becomes prime minister of Great Britain; Stalin becomes General Secretary of Communist party.

1932 Franklin Roosevelt elected president of United States.

1933 Hitler becomes chancellor of Germany.

1915 | 1920 | 1925 | 1930 | 1935 | 1940

1922 Mussolini becomes prime minister of Italy.

1926 General strike in Great Britain

1928 Stalin announces the first of his Five-Year Plans; Kellogg-Briand Pact

1929 Stock market crashes in the United States.

1936 Stalin purges "Old Bolsheviks" from Communist party; Leon Blum becomes prime minister of France.

CHAPTER 29

Nationalism in Asia, Africa, and Latin America

1919–1939

I swear before country and history that my sword will defend our nation's dignity, that it will be a sword for the oppressed. I accept the invitation to fight. . . . The last of my soldiers, the soldiers of freedom for Nicaragua, may die; but before that, more than a battalion of your blond invaders will have bitten the dust of my wild mountains."

With these fighting words, General Augustino César Sandino challenged the United States Marines in 1927. Sandino was trying to drive out the "blond invaders" who had occupied Nicaragua for 15 years. In the years following World War I, nationalist leaders such as Sandino struggled to end foreign control and win independence for their countries around the globe.

This mural shows the many diverse peoples of Mexico united in the struggle for independence.

3. What divided and what united nationalist forces in China?

4. How did militarism shape Japan?

5. Why did nationalism in Latin America bring conflict with the United States?

Concepts to Understand:

• Nationalism—Hope for a new world order after World War I leads to nationalism. Sections 1,2,3,4,5

• Conflict—Struggles between nationalists and European powers, and among nationalists with different views bring about continuing violence and conflict. Sections 1,2,3,4,5

• Change—Industrial growth in developing nations transforms their economies and ways of life. Sections 1,2,3,4,5

New Forces in the Middle East and Africa

At the end of World War I, European powers continued to control most of the Middle East and Africa. Many colonies had assisted the Allies during the war, hoping to gain their independence as a reward. President Woodrow Wilson of the United States raised their hopes in 1918 by endorsing the concept of **self-determination:** the right of regional peoples to set up independent nations.

But instead of relaxing their grip, the European powers tightened it. Nationalists prepared to fight for independence. They were eager to establish modern countries where their own cultures could flourish.

Learning from Photographs *Kemal Ataturk is shown wearing a fez, the traditional hat that he later banned.* **How does the photo reveal his efforts to blend Western and Turkish cultures?**

Turkey

For nearly 500 years, Turkish emperors called sultans ruled the vast Ottoman Empire, which at one time included parts of Eastern Europe, the Middle East, and North Africa. But during the 1800s, large sections of this empire broke away or were conquered. When World War I began, the Ottomans joined forces with Germany, hoping to save their remaining lands.

War with Greece The Allied victory in World War I dashed Ottoman hopes. The Ottoman emperor lost all of his lands except what is now Turkey. In 1919 the Greeks invaded Turkey in an attempt to complete the destruction of the Ottoman Empire. But Turkish general Mustafa Kemal rallied forces to his country's defense. Kemal led a political group known as the Young Turks who wanted reforms to modernize Turkey. Turkish armies under Kemal counterattacked and defeated the Greeks in 1922.

The Turkish victory led to dramatic changes. The sultan gave up his throne, and the Turks formed a new country, the Republic of Turkey. Kemal became its first president. The new government moved the capital from Istanbul to Ankara, a city near the center of the country. Believing that Turkey needed to industrialize in order to assert its role in world affairs, Kemal's government established industries and planned their growth. Tariffs on imports were raised to protect the new industries from foreign competition and to reduce dependence on foreign countries.

Kemal's Reforms Kemal carried out a number of radical reforms in Turkish society. As a result of Kemal's policies, Turkey adopted a

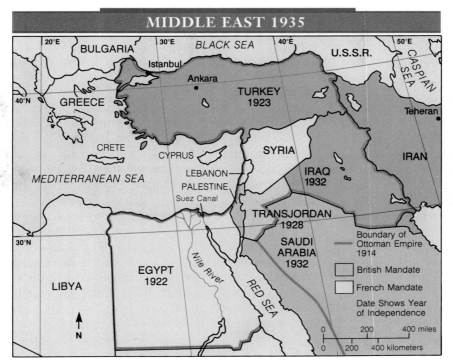

MIDDLE EAST 1935

BULGARIA
BLACK SEA
U.S.S.R.
CASPIAN SEA
Istanbul
Ankara
TURKEY 1923
GREECE
Teheran
CRETE
CYPRUS
SYRIA
IRAN
MEDITERRANEAN SEA
LEBANON
PALESTINE
Suez Canal
IRAQ 1932
TRANSJORDAN 1928
SAUDI ARABIA 1932
EGYPT 1922
Nile River
RED SEA
LIBYA

Boundary of Ottoman Empire 1914
British Mandate
French Mandate
Date Shows Year of Independence

0   200   400 miles
0   200   400 kilometers

N

Learning from Maps
The destruction of the Ottoman Empire was part of a global trend away from large empires. Nationalism disrupted imperial rule in eastern Europe, Africa, and southern Asia in the decades following World War I. ***Based on this map, how many countries contain territory that was part of the Ottoman Empire in 1914?***

Western way of life. The Turks began using the Western calendar, the Latin alphabet, and the metric system. Kemal ordered men to stop wearing the fez, a traditional hat, and he allowed women to remove their veils. He also urged Turks to use Western-style last names. To modernize the government along Western lines, he reformed the legal code and separated government and religion.

In defense of these reforms, Kemal said: "We have suffered much. This is because we have failed to understand the world. Our thoughts and our mentality will become civilized from head to toe."

Some of Kemal's changes were designed to promote national pride among the Turks. For example, he urged Turks to "purify" their language by ridding it of all words that had Persian or Arabic origins. He also changed his own name to Kemal Ataturk (ke MAHL AT uh terk), which means "father of the Turks."

Kemal ruled Turkey with an iron fist until his death in 1938. His policies were not always popular, but he changed Turkey from an ancient empire into a modern nation.

Iran

Located between Turkey and Pakistan, Iran is a land of mountains, deserts, and oil. At the end of World War I, this land, known by its historic name of Persia, was ruled by a shah, or king. However, Great Britain and the Soviet Union each had controlling interests in Persia's oil fields and consequently limited the shah's power.

In 1921 nationalist forces led by Reza Khan wanted to cut back the foreign influence on their government and economy. The nationalists overthrew the shah and set up a new government. Like Ataturk, Reza Khan built schools, roads, and hospitals, and he allowed women more freedom. Improved communications helped unite the diverse groups in the country. Although adopting many Western ways, he tried to reduce Western political influence in Persia.

Reza wanted to change the Persian monarchy into a republic. However, traditional Muslim leaders opposed this change, so Reza ruled as a dictator. Later, in 1925, he declared himself shah and changed his name to Reza Shah. He earned money from Persia's oil fields and factories and from his vast royal estates.

During the 1930s, Reza Shah aligned his country with Germany. He admired Hitler, in part because he believed that Germans and Persians shared a common ancestry in the ancient Aryan people. In 1935 he changed the name of the country from Persia to Iran, a variation of the word *Aryan*. In 1941, when Great Britain and the Soviet Union were at war with Germany, British and Soviet forces deposed Reza Shah and replaced him with his son, Mohammed Reza Pahlavi (rih ZAH PAL uh vee). The new government permitted British and Soviet troops to remain in Iran.

Palestine

While Iran was trying to free itself from European control, another Middle Eastern region was just coming under British domination. After World War I, the newly formed League of Nations gave Great Britain a mandate, or authorization, to control Palestine. This region had previously belonged to the Ottoman Empire. Britain was eager to benefit from control of Palestine's fine ports and strategic location at the eastern end of the Mediterranean Sea.

In Palestine, the nationalism of two groups —Jewish and Arab—came into conflict. Jews recalled that nearly 3,000 years before, the ancient state of Israel had been located there. Arabs pointed out that the region had been inhabited by Muslim and Christian Palestinians whose ancestors had lived there for thousands of years also. During this period, the small number of Jews and the large number of Arabs living in Palestine coexisted most of the time.

Beginning in the late 1800s, the number of Jews in Palestine began increasing. European Jews, facing harsh anti-Semitism in Russia and influenced by the growth of nationalism throughout Europe, believed they should reestablish a Jewish national homeland in the Middle East. This movement was known as Zionism. By World War I, about 500,000 Arabs and 50,000 Jews lived in Palestine.

During World War I, the British government promised independence to the Arabs and a homeland to the Jews in return for their help against the Ottoman Turks. The Balfour Declaration—a letter from British Foreign Secretary Arthur Balfour in 1917 to the British Zionist Federation—promised Great Britain's help in establishing "a national home for the Jewish people" in Palestine. Great Britain's pledge of support, however, was on the condition that the civil and religious rights of non-Jewish Palestinians be protected. To the Arab majority, Great Britain promised the establishment of a government authorized by the dominant group in the region.

Under the British mandate, tensions heightened between Arabs and Jews. As the persecution of Jews in Nazi Germany increased, so did Jewish immigration to Palestine. As more Jews moved into a region long inhabited by Arabs, the two groups clashed. Riots broke out, resulting in hundreds of casualties. When Great Britain tried to limit Jewish immigration, Zionists responded in anger. By the end of the 1930s, Great Britain had failed to keep its promise to both Jews and Arabs, and the conflict in Palestine was worsening.

Egypt

Palestine's neighbor Egypt also confronted troubles after World War I. A protectorate of Great Britain since 1882, Egypt was beginning to feel the power of nationalism. Saad Zaghlul (zag LOOL) led the nationalist forces in Egypt demanding independence. The British tried to weaken the nationalist cause by arresting Zaghlul, but their action only sparked riots and violence. Finally, in 1922, Great Britain granted Egypt limited independence. However, the British still kept troops in the country and retained control of the Suez Canal.

Egypt moved slowly toward independence from Great Britain. But when Italy invaded Ethiopia in 1936, the British decided they needed Egypt's help to prevent further Italian aggression. As a result, the British government granted Egypt its complete independence in 1936 and helped it become a member of the League of Nations the following year. Britain, however, retained military control of the Suez Canal.

The Influence of African Art

Until the early 1900s, Europeans did not think that the carvings, masks, sculptures, paintings, or other forms of art from African cultures had artistic value. In the 1800s, missionaries and explorers—not art collectors—brought African art to Europe. Much of this art was displayed in ethnological museums, not as works of art, but as artifacts of exotic cultures. Other pieces were sold to second-hand shops or novelty stores.

However, in the first decade of the 1900s, European artists began to scour museums and shops in search of these African creations. Artists such as Georges Braque, Henri Matisse, André Derain, and Pablo Picasso were beginning to value African art for its highly expressive style and its direct and spontaneous approach to its subjects.

These European artists, mostly French, felt that traditional European art overemphasized realistic portrayal at the expense of emotion and power. African art, they believed, expressed the spiritual reality of a person or an animal more effectively than did European art. In short, they felt that African art captured the essential qualities of a subject more accurately than did European art.

The influence of African art can be seen throughout Western art. For example, the long, angular faces on people that characterize much of the Western art of the early 1900s reflect the influence of African art. One of the most famous paintings that shows this use of faces is Pablo Picasso's *Les Demoiselles d'Avignon*, a painting of five French women. Many of Picasso's works show the sharp angles and exaggerated features that often appear in African art.

More broadly, European and American artists began to produce more and more abstract art after recognizing the strength of African art. Abstract art takes the important qualities of a subject and portrays them, but not necessarily as they appear visually. A feature is abstracted, or portrayed in a more general way, to highlight something about the feature. In developing abstract art, European artists hoped they might achieve the spirit and vitality that they saw in African art.

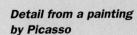

Detail from a painting by Picasso

Responding to the Arts

1. How did European collectors in the 1800s consider African art?
2. What elements of African art appealed to European artists at the beginning of the 1900s?

Kenya

South of Egypt, in central East Africa, lay another part of Great Britain's empire: Kenya. During World War II, about 45,000 Kenyans died while helping the British fight the Germans in East Africa. The survivors returned home after the war with dreams of independence and a new life. However, instead of granting Kenya its independence, the British allowed European settlers to seize the land of many Kenyans in order to start large coffee plantations and other agricultural operations. The settlers hired Kenyans at low wages and made them work under harsh conditions. Resentment of British rule in Kenya gave rise to a protest movement in 1921 led by Harry Thuku (THOO koo). The protesters complained about high colonial taxes and strict British labor laws. Colonial officials promptly arrested Thuku, and in the riot that followed, British troops killed 25 Kenyans. The British government then exiled Thuku from Kenya.

In Thuku's absence, Jomo Kenyatta took over the growing nationalist movement. Instead of fighting the British in Kenya for independence, Kenyatta took his struggle to the center of British power in London. By meeting with government officials in the 1920s and 1930s, he succeeded in making progress—but at a very slow pace. He later recalled his frustrations:

**CONNECTIONS:
GEOGRAPHY
IN
HISTORY**

Imperialist Boundaries

Kenyan leader Jomo Kenyatta

During the scramble for Africa, Europe carved up the continent without respect to historic boundaries. The lines split groups of people and forced unwanted confrontations. Nowhere were these problems more evident than in Nigeria.

Nigeria is home to more than 250 separate ethnic groups. The three largest are the Hausa, the Yoruba, and the Ibo. In the days before colonization, each group controlled its own territory.

When the British united the region in 1914, Hausa, Yoruba, and Ibo people were part of the same country for the first time. They eyed each other with suspicion. One of Nigeria's leaders put the matter bluntly:

> Since 1914 the British Government has been trying to make Nigeria into one country, but the Nigerian people them-

selves are historically different in their backgrounds, in their religious beliefs and customs and do not show themselves any sign of willingness to unite.

After independence arrived in 1960, the struggle for unity continued. However, hostilities flared into warfare in 1967. Eastern Nigeria seceded and established Biafra. The Nigerian government eventually won the war and reclaimed Biafra, but the country remains haunted by the prophetic words that nationalist leader Obafemi Awolowo spoke in 1947: "Nigeria is not a nation. It is a mere geographical expression."

Making the Connection
1. How did colonial boundaries cause dissension among groups?
2. Why were Nigerians reluctant to unite?

By driving [the African] *off his ancestral lands, the Europeans have robbed him of the material foundations of his culture, and reduced him to a state of serfdom incompatible with human happiness. . . . It is not in his nature to accept serfdom forever. He realizes that he must fight unceasingly for his own complete emancipation; for without this he is doomed to remain the prey of rival imperialisms.*

—Jomo Kenyatta, *Facing Mount Kenya, 1938*

In spite of Kenyatta's efforts, when World War II began in 1939, Kenya remained firmly in British hands.

Nigeria

Across the continent from Kenya, on the west coast of Africa, lies Nigeria. The British controlled this region of Africa as well, and they made large fortunes from Nigeria's rubber, oil, and tin. As in Kenya, the British imposed heavy taxes on men and strict labor laws.

In 1929 Nigerian women learned that they too would be taxed. When a group of unarmed women protested by attacking British goods and property, police fired on them, killing 50.

The violent ending of the women's uprising drove many Nigerians to adopt nonviolent methods in their struggle for independence. One of these was Nmandi Azikiwe (noo MAHN dee ahzee KEE WEE), who started the newspaper *The West African Pilot* in 1937. He wrote

Learning from Photographs *Nmandi Azikiwe used his newspapers and leadership in the Nigerian Youth Movement to promote independence in West Africa.* **How were his efforts like those of Kemal Ataturk, Reza Shah, and Jomo Kenyatta?**

many articles in favor of independence, not only for Nigeria but for all of Africa. "Africa needs a pilot," he wrote once. "Those who follow the true pilot, believing they are on the right track, will find their way to their destination."

SECTION 1 REVIEW

Recall
1. **Define:** self-determination
2. **Identify:** Kemal Ataturk, Reza Shah, Saad Zaghlul, Jomo Kenyatta
3. **List:** Identify at least three of Ataturk's reforms.
4. **Explain:** Why was Reza Shah forced out of office in 1941?

Critical Thinking
5. **Apply:** How did Nmandi Azikiwe apply the concept of self-determination to Africa?
6. **Analyze:** How could conflict between Arabs and Jews in Palestine have been avoided?
7. **Evaluate:** The British in Kenya said they were "exercising a trust on behalf of the African population." What does that phrase imply about Britain's attitude toward Africans?

Applying Concepts
8. **Nationalism:** What were the reasons for the rise of nationalism in the Middle East and Africa?

India's Struggle for Independence

When World War I began, the most important colony in the British Empire was India. As in the Middle East and Africa, nationalism was spreading in India. Some Indians wanted independence. Many were willing to remain in the British Empire but demanded home rule. Two of the largest nationalist organizations were the Indian National Congress and the Muslim League.

During World War I, Indian nationalists supported Great Britain and its allies. More than a million Indian soldiers fought on the battlefields of the Middle East and Africa. Indian wheat fed the Allied troops, and Indian cotton kept them clothed. In return for this aid, Great Britain promised in 1917 to support "the gradual development of self-governing institutions."

The Amritsar Massacre

Independence did not came easily to India. The nationalist movement was divided by religion. The Hindu majority and the Muslim minority did not trust each other. The British encouraged that distrust.

A second difficulty was British opposition. Many Britons were unwilling to see their empire's power reduced and staunchly opposed granting India its independence. In 1919 Great Britain imposed on India harsh laws intended to stifle dissent. British officials could arrest Indians without cause and jail them without trial.

British repression reached an extreme in the northern city of Amritsar in April 1919. The British had outlawed all large gatherings and declared that they would respond to any violation with force. When 10,000 unarmed Indians assembled in a walled garden in Amritsar for a political meeting, the local commander decided that the British needed to demonstrate their authority. Without warning, British troops blocked the only entrance to the garden and began firing into the trapped crowd. When the firing ceased, nearly 400 people, including many children, lay dead. Another 1,200 people were wounded. Criticized for his action, the British commander declared:

I fired and continued to fire until the crowd dispersed, and I consider this is the least amount of firing which would produce the necessary moral effect. . . . If more troops had been at hand, the casualties would have been greater.

Indians across the country were shocked by the brutal massacre and the general's justification of it. In large numbers, they came together in meeting after meeting, more determined than ever to drive the British out of their land. However, they needed a strong leader to spearhead their struggle.

FOOTNOTES TO HISTORY

GANDHI AND THE WEST

Gandhi rejected many aspects of Western civilization, but he owed much to many Westerners. Among these were three writers of the 1800s: John Ruskin of England, Henry David Thoreau of the United States, and Leo Tolstoy of Russia.

In turn, Gandhi influenced Western civilization. He served as a model for Martin Luther King, Jr., who led the African-American struggle for civil rights until his assassination in 1968. Like Gandhi, King protested with nonviolent boycotts, court challenges, and other peaceful means.

Gandhi and Satyagraha

Mohandas Gandhi

Someone once observed that Mohandas Gandhi was "the catalyst if not the initiator of three of the major revolutions of the twentieth century: the revolutions against colonialism, racism, and violence." This statement makes it easier to understand the legacy of Gandhi because it focuses on the universality and timeliness of his struggles rather than on the specifics of his reform movements in South Africa and later in India. By the same token, it may be easier to understand Gandhi the man by first understanding the term that was at the very heart of his moral and spiritual life: satyagraha.

Satyagraha was coined by Gandhi to describe his struggle against the British in South Africa. It is a combination of the words *satya*, meaning "truth," and *agraha*, meaning "holding firm to." In other words, satyagraha is the force born of truth.

Gandhi distinguished satyagraha from passive resistance; he saw satyagraha as a means to directly confront injustice. This is what Gandhi meant in saying that "the idea underlying satyagraha is to convert the wrongdoer, to awaken a sense of justice in him, to show him also that without the cooperation direct or indirect of the wronged, the wrongdoer cannot do the wrong intended by him."

For Gandhi, satyagraha was a way to face injustice without bitterness or violence. Satyagraha also depends on individual will. Gandhi wrote that "satyagraha depends but little upon help from the outside, and it is only internal remedies that are effective."

Reflecting on the Person
1. What two words make up the term *satyagraha*?
2. How might satyagraha be applied today?

Gandhi

In the months following the Amritsar massacre, a civil rights lawyer, Mohandas Gandhi, became a leader in the Indian National Congress. Gandhi was a **pacifist**, a person opposed to using war and other violence to settle disputes, and he believed that India could win its independence with quiet actions instead of guns.

Gandhi had spent his life struggling for justice. After studying law in England, he worked as a lawyer in South Africa for 21 years. During that time, he helped Indians in South Africa gain rights by strikes, sit-ins, and other forms of **civil disobedience**. They tried these and the use of nonviolent resistance, to challenge laws considered unjust. Gandhi returned to India from South Africa in 1915 a hero and soon began working with the Indian National Congress. Gandhi urged Indians to reject much of Western civilization for its use of brute force, its worship of money, and its prejudicial attitudes toward non-Western peoples.

Gandhi believed that one could force an evil person or government to change by challenging it directly, but without violence. He used the term *satyagraha*, which means "truth force," to describe the nonviolent protests he led after the Amritsar massacre. One effective form of protest was the boycott, in which Indians refused to buy

British cloth and other manufactured goods. As a step toward independence, Gandhi urged Indians to begin spinning their own cloth.

Gandhi practiced what he preached by spinning cloth for a half-hour every day. He made the spinning wheel the symbol of the National Congress, and he wore nothing but simple homespun clothes for the rest of his life.

Gandhi's courage inspired millions of Indians to join in protests. They called him *Mahatma*, which means "great soul." In 1922, however, the British arrested Gandhi, and he disappeared from active protest for the rest of the decade. Undaunted, the Indian National Congress continued to protest, but it had little success until Gandhi's return in 1930.

Toward Independence

Gandhi planned his next major protest around salt. In India's hot climate, the millions of people who worked in fields and factories needed salt to replace what they lost daily in sweat. The British controlled the salt mines and the ocean salt fields. They taxed every grain of salt they sold and jailed Indians who gathered salt on their own.

In 1930 Gandhi protested the salt tax. First he led thousands of his followers on a 200-mile march from Ahmadabad to the sea, where they made salt from sea water. One month later, Gandhi openly defied British authority by wading into the sea and picking up a lump of salt. The British did not dare arrest him, but they did arrest thousands who followed his example. To quell the mounting protests, they arrested him a month later, but the protests only increased. Webb Miller, a British journalist, described one such protest, in which a group of Indians marched on a heavily guarded salt mine: "Although every one knew that within a few minutes he would be beaten down, perhaps killed, I could detect no signs of wavering or fear. . . . There was no fight, no struggle; the marchers simply walked forward until struck down."

And so it went throughout the 1930s. As Indians protested, the British responded with guns and clubs. Their violence could not stop the millions of people motivated by nationalism.

Hindu–Muslim Relations   Even as India fought for its independence in the 1930s, conflicts among Indians increased. For every Muslim, India had three Hindus. As independence approached, the Muslim minority began worrying about its future treatment by the Hindus, and many joined the Muslim League.

In 1935 the British Parliament passed the Government of India Act, which allowed Indians to elect representatives with limited powers and promised eventual independence. Hindus won in 8 of 11 provinces, prompting Muslim leader Muhammad Ali Jinnah to declare that India was for the Hindus.

Gandhi—a Hindu—tried to make peace with Jinnah, saying, "We are friends, not strangers." But Muslim Indians called for their own state. As 1939 ended, India continued its long struggle for freedom. But now the nationalist movement had split in two, and not even Gandhi could put it together again.

SECTION 2 REVIEW

Recall

1. **Define:** pacifist, civil disobedience
2. **Identify:** Mohandas Gandhi, Muhammad Ali Jinnah
3. **Locate:** In what three countries did Gandhi spend most of his life? Locate these countries on the map on pages 984–985.

Critical Thinking

4. **Synthesize:** What could Hindus have done to keep Muslims united with them against the British?
5. **Analyze:** What factors caused the Indian independence struggle to split in two?
6. **Synthesize:** Imagine you are a British soldier in Amritsar. Your commander has just ordered you to fire. What would you do? What would happen then?

Applying Concepts

7. **Change:** What nonviolent methods did Gandhi use to bring about change?

China's Drive for Modernization

Unlike India, China was never entirely controlled by a European country. However, despite its independence and size, China did not have the military power to demand respect. That they lacked the respect of Europeans was shown by the final terms of the Versailles peace conference that followed World War I. The Versailles Treaty had a provision granting Japan economic control of the Shandong (shahn doong) peninsula of northeastern China. This provision was a humiliating and surprising blow to the Chinese. During and after World War I, China was torn apart by internal divisions, and the foreign powers took advantage of China's weakness.

The Chinese Republic

As you read in Chapter 26, the revolutionary leader Sun Yat-sen (sun yaht sehn) formally declared China a republic in January 1912. Sun dreamed of a free, democratic society. However, just two months after taking office, he was ousted by a military strongman, Yuan Shikai (yoo ahn shur gy). Yuan quickly turned the new republic into a dictatorship. Meanwhile, Sun formed the nationalist Guomindang (kwoh min tang) party, tried and failed to overthrow Yuan, and then fled to Japan.

When Yuan died in 1916, China slipped into chaos. Local military leaders called **warlords** divided the vast country among themselves. An almost continual state of civil war followed.

Sun Yat-sen returned to China in 1917 and tried in vain to restore strong central government to China and rebuild the Guomindang party. Then in 1923, with aid from the Soviet Union and an ambitious young officer named Chiang Kai-shek (jee ahn ky shehk), the Guomindang army grew rapidly in strength. Three years after Sun's death in 1925, Chiang led the army to victory over the warlords and established a government in the city of Nanjing (Nanking).

Though undemocratic, government under the Guomindang promoted economic development by building schools, roads, and railways. However, the Guomindang did very little to raise the living standards of the peasants who comprised the vast majority of the population of China.

FOOTNOTES TO HISTORY
THE MAY 4th MOVEMENT

When the Versailles peace conference awarded the Shandong peninsula to the Japanese, Chinese students were furious. On May 4, 1919, students in Beijing (Peking) came together for a mass demonstration, urging the Chinese government not to sign the Versailles Treaty. Similar demonstrations throughout the country culminated in a general strike in Shanghai. Under intense pressure from the students, the government at last yielded to their demands.

The demonstrations provided visible evidence of a student movement that had been building since 1915. In that year, students founded the magazine *New Youth,* which advocated revolutionary changes throughout Chinese society.

In the coming years, China's students continued to play a significant role in the nation's long struggle for justice. As recently as 1989, thousands of students demonstrated in Tiananmen Square in Beijing, calling for democratic reforms.

Rivalry with the Communists

Many peasants, along with intellectuals and urban workers, supported another party that opposed the warlords: the Communists. During Chiang's drive against the warlords, Communist soldiers provided him with crucial military support. But in 1927 the Communists attempted to take over the Guomindang party and failed. Chiang turned against the Communists and tried to wipe them out in a bloody purge. In the city of Guangzhou (gwong joh), Guomindang soldiers killed 6,000 suspected Communists in just three days.

As Chiang began his purge, tens of thousands of Communists fled to the mountains in the southern province of Jiangxi (jee ong shee). Here they gathered their strength and formed the Red Army, led by the son of a prosperous peasant family, Mao Zedong (mow dzu doong). Mao believed that the Communists could still triumph with the help of China's millions of peasants:

Learning from Photographs *In 1927 Guomindang leader Chiang Kai-shek married Soong Mei-ling, Sun Yat-sen's sister-in-law. Chiang pledged to fulfill Sun's dream of a united, republican government over all of China.* **How successful was Chiang at fulfilling his pledge?**

In a very short time, in China's central, southern, and northern provinces, several hundred million peasants will rise like a mighty storm, like a hurricane, a force so swift and violent that no power, however great, will be able to hold it back.

—Mao Zedong,
Report on an Investigation, 1926

Living conditions for China's peasants had changed little over the centuries. They worked small plots of land and turned over most of their crops to wealthy landlords. The Red Army gained popular support in rural areas of the country by overthrowing local landlords and distributing their land to the peasants. Before long, the Red Army included nearly 250,000 peasant troops.

The success of the Red Army worried Chiang. In the early 1930s, he ordered a series of "extermination campaigns" in an attempt to destroy this rival army. Mao fought back, however, using his own strategies: "The enemy advances, we retreat; the enemy camps, we harass; the enemy tires, we attack; the enemy retreats, we pursue."

Mao's military plans worked at times, but by October 1934, the Guomindang had nearly surrounded the Communists with a million troops. Mao decided to retreat once again, leading 90,000 followers out of Jiangxi province in a desperate gamble for survival.

The Long March

Mao's retreat from Jiangxi lasted for one year and covered over 5,000 miles (8,000 kilometers). During that time the Red Army marched an average of 16 miles (26 kilometers) a day, across rivers and mountains, and defeated 10 provincial armies—all the while being chased by Guomindang military forces. The Chinese Communists called the arduous undertaking the Long March.

At times the line of marching Communist soldiers stretched out for nearly 50 miles (80 kilometers). One of these soldiers later recalled the march:

If it was a black night and the enemy far away, we made torches from pine branches or frayed bamboo, and then it was truly beautiful. At the foot of a mountain, we could look up and see a long column of lights coiling like a fiery dragon up the mountainside. From the summit we could look in both directions and see miles of torches moving forward like a wave of fire. A rosy glow hung over the whole route of the march.

Conditions on the Long March were far from rosy, however. Thousands of soldiers froze or starved to death, and others died in battle. As it marched forward, the army continued to seize landlords and distribute their property to local peasants, thereby winning many new recruits to replace some of those who died. Of the original 90,000 troops, fewer than 10,000 remained at the end of the march in 1935. Yet Mao was too proud to give up. "Let us ask, has history ever known a long march to equal ours? No, never."

Learning from Art *Young Mao rallies his army during a pause in the Long March. Portraits of Lenin and Marx on the wall inspire Mao's followers.* **Why was the Long March important to Chinese Communists?**

Threat from Japan

While Chiang and Mao battled each other in 1931, the Japanese had conquered the large section of northeast China known as Manchuria. Now it appeared that Japan wanted even more land, and Chiang's advisers urged him to confront the Japanese. Mao offered "to join forces against attacks from without in the spirit of brothers quarreling at home [and] to discuss specific measures for resisting Japan and saving the nation." Chiang at first rejected Mao's pro-posal, but then members of the Guomindang kidnapped Chiang and held him prisoner until he agreed to end his war with the Communists. Nationalism overcame, at least temporarily, the ideological war dividing the Chinese.

However, neither Chiang nor Mao could stop the Japanese invasion that came eight months later. By 1939 Japan controlled most of eastern China. Chiang withdrew to the interior of the country, where Mao was awaiting the proper moment to strike back. Before that moment arrived, the entire world was at war.

SECTION 3 REVIEW

Recall
1. **Define:** warlord
2. **Identify:** Sun Yat-sen, Yuan Shikai, Chiang Kai-shek, Mao Zedong
3. **List:** Which groups of people supported the Communists most strongly?

Critical Thinking
4. **Analyze:** How did the Chinese people suffer under the rule of warlords?
5. **Analyze:** Why do you think Mao decided to undertake the Long March? What other choices did he have?

6. **Evaluate:** Do you think Mao and Chiang were wise to join forces against Japan? Explain.

Applying Concepts
7. **Conflict:** What conflicts kept China in turmoil after World War I?

Militarism in Japan

Like China, Japan, an independent country, had fought on the side of the Allies in World War I. During the conflict, the Japanese supplied weapons to their European partners, particularly to Russia. At the same time, they took advantage of the war to expand their economic and political influence in East Asia. In addition to ruling Korea and Taiwan, Japan pressed for an enlargement of its role in China. In 1915 Japanese diplomats forced the Chinese government to accept a list of terms known as the Twenty-one Demands. The Twenty-one Demands, in effect, made China a Japanese protectorate.

Japan and the West

When World War I ended, Japan received Germany's Pacific islands north of the equator as mandates from the League of Nations. The Japanese also entered into a series of military

Japanese women did not benefit from the military's increased power. They did not receive the right to vote until 1945.

Militaristic Japan

As a result of the economic woes of the 1930s, many Japanese withdrew their support for democracy and gave it to Japan's military forces.

Military conquest seemed to many Japanese to be the solution to the nation's problems. Military dress included items such as the samurai sword, which appealed to nationalist sentiments.

and commercial agreements with the Western powers. Yet, in spite of these gains, the Japanese were bitter toward the West.

First, Japan felt that the West did not accept it as an equal. In 1919 the League of Nations, dominated by Western powers, refused to accept Japan's demand for a statement on racial equality in the League's charter. The Japanese regarded this rejection as a humiliation. In 1924 the United States banned further Japanese immigration to its shores. In response, the Japanese staged demonstrations and boycotted American goods.

The Japanese were angered further by the West's refusal to support Japanese policy in China. Japan wanted to tie China closer to itself; the West wanted to retain the Open Door policy. As a result of Western pressure, Japan had to abandon the Twenty-one Demands and recognize Western interests in China.

Social and Political Tensions

After World War I, Japan faced social and economic problems at home. Of major concern was a **population explosion.** Japan's population had increased from nearly 35 million in 1872 to about 60 million in 1925. This rate of increase was a problem because of the already high density of population on the Japanese islands. Since emigration was cut off to such places as the United States, the Japanese looked for other ways to cope. They placed new emphasis on manufacturing and foreign trade. It was hoped that new factories and markets would provide employment for large numbers of people.

During the 1920s and 1930s, Japan's industry grew rapidly, and Japanese manufactured goods began to flood world markets. Increased manufacturing, however, stimulated the desire for raw materials. Since Japan had few mineral

Militarism pervaded all aspects of Japanese society in the 1930s—from foreign policy to education. Children dressed as officers take part in a parade. Japan's flag (below) was adopted in 1854.

Reflecting on the Times
How would a parade like the one shown above provide support for the military?

resources of its own, it was forced to look overseas for them.

Meanwhile, Japan's working class increased in importance. Labor unions became more powerful and increased their membership to a third of a million members by the end of the 1920s. At the same time, steps were taken toward greater democracy. In 1925 the Japanese parliament granted universal male suffrage; voters increased from 3 million to 14 million.

In spite of these gains, democracy remained very limited in Japan. Political power was in the hands of nobles and urban industrialists. The emperor, Hirohito, was a constitutional monarch. However, he was a powerful symbol of traditional authority. Behind the emperor was an influential group of military leaders, who were opposed to democratic reforms.

The appeal of antidemocratic nationalist groups increased as the economy deteriorated in the 1930s. A worldwide fall in prices caused by the Great Depression devastated Japan's silk factories and other industries. Millions of workers lost their jobs and could not find new ones. Some began to starve, and children went begging in the streets. In November 1930 an assassin from a secret society shot Prime Minister Osachi Hamaguchi. Teetering on the brink of economic and political chaos, many impoverished farmers and workers in Japan looked to strong-minded military leaders such as Hashimoto Kingoro for answers:

We are like a great crowd of people packed into a small and narrow room, and there are only three doors through which we might es-

cape, namely emigration, advance into world markets, and expansion of territory. The first door . . . has been barred to us by the anti-Japanese immigration policies of other countries. The second door . . . is being pushed shut by tariff barriers. . . . Japan should rush upon the last door [expansion of territory].

—Hashimoto Kingoro,
Addresses to Young Men

Influence of the Military

In September 1931 the Japanese military demonstrated just how powerful it had become. Without seeking approval from the government, army leaders decided to invade the northeastern region of China known as Manchuria. In short order, they launched an invasion. It was clear that the Japanese government could no longer control its own army. In five months the powerful Japanese army had conquered Manchuria.

The conquest of Manchuria was a clear sign of the plans of the military to dominate the Japanese government at home and expand Japanese influence abroad. In 1932 army officers assassinated a prime minister who dared to oppose their views. Then, in 1936, officers led an armed revolt against the government. Although the revolt failed, by early 1937 the army and the government had become one and the same. Japan's military leaders looked forward to conquering all of Asia. Their dreams of a mighty Japanese empire—like the dreams of German and Italian rulers—brought the world to war.

SECTION 4 REVIEW

Recall
1. **Define:** population explosion
2. **Identify:** Osachi Hamaguchi, Hashimoto Kingoro
3. **Locate:** On the map on pages 990–991, find Manchuria. Explain why the location of this region made it valuable to the Japanese.

Critical Thinking
4. **Analyze:** How did Japan get the money to pay for its food and other imports?
5. **Synthesize:** Imagine you are an unemployed worker in Japan in the 1930s. Would you support the military's new powers? Why or why not?

6. **Analyze:** Reread and think about Hashimoto Kingoro's arguments in the quotation on this page. Explain why they are or are not persuasive.

Applying Concepts
7. **Change:** What factors led to the rise of militarism in Japan?

Nationalism in Latin America

After World War I, economic change and nationalism swept Latin America. Although the region's economy remained basically agricultural, the oil and mineral industries became increasingly important. Much of the investment that developed these resources was from the United States, Great Britain, France, Germany, and Italy. Anger at foreign influence led to growing nationalism among Latin Americans. Rubén Darío, a noted Nicaraguan writer, expressed the view of many Latin Americans:

> *The United States is grand and powerful.*
> *Whenever it trembles, a profound shudder*
> *runs down the enormous backbone of the*
>   *Andes.*
> *If it shouts, the sound is like the roar of a*
>   *lion. . . .*
> *But our own America, which has had poets*
>   *since the ancient times . . .*
> *and has lived, since the earliest moments*
>   *of its life,*
> *in light, in fire, in fragrance, and in love—*
> *the America of Moctezuma and Atahualpa,*
> *the aromatic America of Columbus,*
> *Catholic America, Spanish America. . . .*
> *our America lives. And dreams. And loves.*
> *And it is the daughter of the Sun. Be careful.*
> *Long live Spanish America!*

—Rubén Darío, *"To Roosevelt,"* 1903

Economic Changes

In the twenty years following World War I, Latin Americans continued to grow coffee, bananas, wheat, corn, beans, sugar cane, and other crops in large amounts. However, industrial growth—particularly in the United States and Europe—increased the demand for tin, copper, silver, oil, and other raw materials from Latin America. As mineral exports increased, Latin Americans had more cash with which to buy imports. More and more of the Latin American economy became tied to global markets.

When world prices for raw materials increased, Latin American economies improved. However, in the 1920s, prices for coffee, sugar, and other raw materials plunged. The price declines foretold the global economic depression that was soon to occur. Like much of the world, Latin America suffered high unemployment and low prices for its products in the decade of the Great Depression, 1929–1939.

Mexico's Oil Economy Oil was one of the vital resources for growing industries, and Mexico was an important source of oil. Mexico entered the postwar era, still reeling from its own bloody and divisive revolution that had begun in 1910. However, a stable, one-party system was evolving that seemed able to maintain order and unity. Mexico's constitution, ratified in 1917, authorized the government to protect workers from exploitation and to require private property owners to act in the public interest.

Despite the constitution, reforms came slowly until 1934. In that year, Lázaro Cárdenas (KAHR thai nahs) was elected to the presidency. Over the next six years, the government helped Mexicans regain control of the economy. For example, the government actively pushed land reform. By 1940 more than half of all Mexicans farmed land they could finally call their own.

More important, Cárdenas supported an oil workers' strike in 1937. About 17,000 Mexican workers went on strike against their British and American employers, demanding higher wages and better working conditions. Cárdenas urged the oil companies to meet their demands, but the companies refused. After a year of futile

Learning from Art
Mexican mural artist José Orozco in 1931 painted these armed soldiers of the 1910 revolution, named Zapatistas after their leader, Emiliano Zapata. The government invited Orozco and other artists to decorate the walls of public buildings. **What reforms of the 1930s reflected the spirit of the 1910 revolution?**

negotiations, Cárdenas seized the oil wells on March 18, 1938, and declared them the property of the government. He explained his actions by reaching all the way back to a law written by the Spanish king in 1783, which had been retained in the new constitution: "The Mines are the property of My Royal Crown, [including] all bitumens and [minerals] juices of the earth."

The British and American companies were furious, but the Mexican people were ecstatic. They celebrated March 18 as the day of their "Declaration of Economic Independence." Cárdenas, meanwhile, defused the crisis by offering to pay a fair price for the oil wells. With World War II looming on the horizon, Great Britain and the United States soon accepted this offer. They did not want an angry Mexico to sell its oil to Japan and Germany.

The nationalization of Mexico's oil fields signaled the arrival of economic nationalism in Latin America. For Mexico it was a clean break from the economic dependence of the past.

Changes in Venezuela Another oil-rich country, Venezuela, followed a course unlike that of Mexico, but more like that of other Latin American countries that had a single source of wealth. Between 1908 and 1935, President Juan Vicente Gómez ruled Venezuela as a dictator. During this period, engineers discovered oil along Venezuela's Caribbean coast. By the late 1930s, Venezuela was the third-largest oil-producing country in the world. However, British, Dutch, and American oil companies controlled the Venezuelan oil industry. Gómez, instead of nationalizing the oil companies, worked closely with them. He, his political allies, and oil companies prospered, but most Venezuelans did not.

Gómez used the oil profits to strengthen his government. He paid off his country's huge national debt to European bankers and created a strong army. He also used some of the profits for his personal benefit.

After Gómez died in 1935, workers and students around the country rioted to protest the domination of their country by foreign oil companies and their Venezuelan partners. The army intervened to stop the protests and remained in charge of the country for the next several decades.

Democracy and the Military

Venezuela was one of many Latin American countries in which a small group of people prospered from the natural wealth found in the country. It was also typical in that the military intervened to put down protests that threatened business interests. Argentina and Brazil are two of the other countries in which democracy failed to take hold.

Argentina Becomes Fascist In 1916, Argentina held its first open presidential election in which every male could vote. The winner, Hipólito Irigoyen (ee PAW lee toh ihr ih GOH yehn), advocated democratic reforms and efforts to help the poor. After serving six years as president, Irigoyen proudly claimed:

*W*e have held public office in obedience to the popular mandate and inspired by the duty to make reparation . . . for all the injustices, moral and political, collective and individual, that have long dishonored the country.

In 1928 Irigoyen was again elected president, but he did not complete his term in office. Although he was popular, his government had often been ineffective. He was slow to make decisions, so that official documents needing his attention piled up on his desk awaiting action. More important, corrupt aides stole money from the national treasury. In addition, few Argentinians believed in the democratic process by which Irigoyen had won office.

Angered by inefficiency and corruption and opposed to democracy, General José F. Uriburu led a successful coup against Irigoyen in 1930. Uriburu canceled elections and tried to abolish the congress. Uriburu, like Italy's Mussolini, believed in fascism. For the remainder of the 1930s, military men and their sympathizers ruled Argentina. They faked elections, suppressed their opponents, and consolidated their power. Democracy was dead in Argentina, destroyed by the military.

Brazil's Popular Dictator Brazil, like Argentina, fell under an authoritarian government. In 1930 President Getúlio Vargas took power.

Seven years later, Vargas proclaimed a new constitution that made him a virtual dictator. He strengthened the government by transferring powers from the cities and states to the national government. He won support from many Brazilians for his willingness to oppose the interests of large businesses. His adminisration increased wages, shortened working hours, and gave unions the right to organize. Vargas's supporters called him "father of the poor" for these efforts.

Vargas, with the support of the military, was able to keep Brazil united and stable until 1945. In that year, a democratic revolt threw him out of power. When Vargas refused to leave office, military leaders stepped in and forced Vargas out of office. Although the military did not actually rule in Brazil, their support was crucial in deciding who did.

Learning from Photographs *During President Herbert Hoover's tour of Latin America in 1928, he called the visit that of "one good neighbor to another." This phrase inspired Franklin D. Roosevelt's Latin American policy.* **What changes in policy did Roosevelt make?**

Ties with the United States

Before World War I, the United States often intervened in Central American and Caribbean affairs. Under Presidents William McKinley and Theodore Roosevelt, several acts of U.S. intervention took place. For example, by encouraging a 1903 revolution in Panama against the Colombian government, the United States won the right to build a canal through Panama. The United States had also made Cuba an independent republic under U.S. protection and had annexed Puerto Rico.

Increasing U.S. Intervention   In 1904 Theodore Roosevelt declared his corollary to the Monroe Doctrine: the United States intended to intervene as needed to maintain stability. Over the next two decades, U.S. troops and warships were very active in Central America and the Caribbean to assert the interests of the U.S. government. In 1912 U.S. Marines invaded Nicaragua when the country failed to pay its debts. They stayed for 21 years, fighting off the repeated attacks of General Augustino Sandino and protecting American businesses. The persistent presence of U.S. troops heightened nationalist fervor in Latin America.

By 1922 U.S. troops occupied Haiti and the Dominican Republic as well as Nicaragua. José Ingenieros, a sociologist from Argentina, said what many Latin Americans felt:

The United States is to be feared because it is great, rich, and enterprising. What concerns us is to find out whether there is a possibility of balancing its power to the extent necessary to save our political independence and the sovereignty of our countries.

Under President Herbert Hoover, who took office in 1929, the United States began to change its policy. Hoover was reluctant to use military power to force repayment of debts. He began bringing U.S. troops home from Nicaragua, Haiti, and elsewhere. Franklin D. Roosevelt, Hoover's successor, expanded the policy. Roosevelt declared, "I would dedicate this nation to the policy of the good neighbor—the neighbor who resolutely respects himself, and because he does so, respects the rights of others."

The Good Neighbor Policy meant that the United States would rely on economic pressure—not military force—to influence Latin America. Roosevelt continued withdrawing U.S. troops from Latin America and watched revolutionary changes in Cuba without directly intervening.

In 1933 the United States took another step toward improving its relationship with Latin America. Diplomats from the United States joined with their Latin American counterparts at the Pan American conference in Montevideo, Uruguay. After much discussion, all parties signed an agreement stating "No state has the right to intervene in the internal or external affairs of another." For the remainder of the 1930s, the United States avoided military involvement in Latin America.

SECTION 5 REVIEW

Recall

1. **Identify:** Lázaro Cárdenas, Juan Vicente Gómez, Hipólito Irigoyen, José Uriburu, Getúlio Vargas, Augustino Sandino, Good Neighbor Policy
2. **List:** Identify three of the Latin American countries into which the United States sent troops between 1890 and 1940.

Critical Thinking

3. **Analyze:** Compare how Mexico and Venezuela responded to foreign control of their oil industries.
4. **Synthesize:** Based on the experience of Brazil, what advice would you give a ruler who wished to avoid a military takeover?

5. **Evaluate:** Does the United States have the right to intervene in the affairs of other countries? Explain, using recent examples.

Applying Concepts

6. **Change:** How did nationalism change Latin America following World War I?

IDENTIFYING AN ARGUMENT

If you have ever had an argument with someone about a political or social issue, you may have had difficulty expressing your views because your emotions overpowered clear thinking.

Explanation

In everyday conversation, the word *argument* refers to a conflict between two (or more) opinions. In writing, however, as in debate, an argument is the full presentation of a single opinion. The main idea of an argument is its *thesis*. The thesis is the stated position or proposition in an argument. In some arguments the thesis is stated explicitly. In others, you must read carefully to determine what the writer is attempting to prove.

The thesis of an argument is supported with reasons, and the reasons are supported by examples or other information. You can accept or reject any argument. However, before you decide how to respond to or evaluate an argument, you must first recognize its thesis and determine how the reasons and/or examples support the thesis.

To identify an argument use the following steps:
- Determine the main point the writer is making.
- Look for any of three types of reasons the writer uses to support the thesis—generalizations, rules (accepted laws), and specific facts.
- Identify the examples or other information that support each reason.
- Evaluate the relevance of the argument, looking for bias or weaknesses in reasoning, and decide whether to accept or reject the argument.

Example

If you wanted to identify an argument presented in the "Kenya" discussion in Section 1 on pages 750–751, begin by reading the entire discussion, including this quote from Jomo Kenyatta:

By driving [the African] *off his ancestral lands, the Europeans have robbed him of the material foundations of his culture, and reduced him to a state of serfdom incompatible with human happiness. . . . It is not in his nature to accept serfdom forever. He realizes that he must fight unceasingly for his own complete emancipation; for without this he is doomed to remain the prey of rival imperialisms.*

The main idea of this portion of text is that Africans had been driven from their lands, and in the process, lost not only their homes, but also their way of life. To verify that this is the thesis, review the text for examples that support the thesis. The text describes how the British took Kenyans' land to build coffee plantations and other agricultural projects. The British hired African laborers who worked for low wages and under harsh conditions. These specific examples of European interference and suppression of local desires confirms that the first sentence of the quote is the thesis of the argument.

The quotation expresses Kenyatta's anti-European bias. He uses emotionally-charged words, such as *robbed, serfdom, emancipation,* and *prey* to support his argument that Africans should fight for their independence. Despite Kenyatta's bias, you could accept the argument because enough facts support it.

Application

Refer to the quotation made by Hashimoto Kingoro on page 760 of Section 4, "Militarism in Japan." Identify Kingoro's argument. State both the thesis and at least two reasons or examples given in the quotation to support that thesis. What type of reason did Kingoro use in the argument?

Practice

Turn to Practicing Skills on page 771 of the Chapter Review for further practice in identifying arguments.

from Gifts of Passage
by Santha Rama Rau

Santha Rama Rau, born in Madras, India, in 1923, spent her childhood in India, England, and South Africa. In each place, she closely watched the way people from different backgrounds related with one another. Advances in transportation and communication have sharply increased the interactions of people from different cultures. Today these interactions shape the world more than ever before. In the following excerpt, Rau recalls her early experiences at a school for English and Indian children in India.

At the Anglo-Indian day school in Zorinabad to which my sister and I were sent when she was eight and I was five and a half, they changed our names. On the first day of school, a hot, windless morning of a north Indian September, we stood in the headmistress's study and she said, "Now you're the *new* girls. What are your names?"

My sister answered for us. "I am Premila, and she"—nodding in my direction—"is Santha."

The headmistress had been in India, I suppose, fifteen years or so, but she still smiled her helpless inability to cope with Indian names. Her rimless half-glasses glittered, and the precarious bun on the top of her head trembled as she shook her head. "Oh, my dears, those are much too hard for me. Suppose we give you pretty English names. Wouldn't that be more jolly? Let's see, now— Pamela for you, I think." She shrugged in a baffled way at my sister. "That's as close as I can get. And for *you*," she said to me, "how about Cynthia? Isn't that nice?"

My sister was always less easily intimidated than I was, and while she kept a stubborn silence, I said, "Thank you," in a very tiny voice. . . .

That first day at school is still, when I think of it, a remarkable one. At that age, if one's name is changed, one develops a curious form of dual personality. I remember having a certain detached and disbelieving concern in the actions of "Cynthia," but certainly no responsibility. Accordingly, I followed the thin, erect back of the headmistress down the veranda [porch] to my classroom feeling, at most, a passing interest in what was going to happen to me in this strange, new atmosphere of School. . . .

I can't remember too much about the proceedings in class that day, except for the beginning. The teacher pointed to me and asked me to stand up. "Now, dear, tell the class your name."

I said nothing.

"Come along," she said, frowning slightly. "What's your name, dear?"

"I don't know," I said, finally.

The English children in the front of the class—there were about eight or ten of them—giggled and twisted around in their chairs to look at me. I sat down quickly and opened my eyes very wide, hoping in that way to dry them off. The little girl with the braids put out her hand and very lightly touched my arm. She still didn't smile.

Most of the morning I was rather bored. I looked briefly at the children's drawings pinned to the wall, and then concentrated on a lizard clinging to the ledge of the high, barred window behind the teacher's head. Occasionally it would shoot out its long yellow tongue for a fly, and then it would rest, with its eyes closed and its belly palpitating, as though it were swallowing several times quickly. The lessons were mostly concerned with reading and writing and simple numbers—things that my mother had already taught me—and I paid very little attention. The teacher wrote on the easel blackboard words like "bat" and "cat," which seemed babyish to me; only "apple" was new and incomprehensible.

When it was time for the lunch recess, I followed the girl with braids out onto the veranda. There the children from the other classes were assembled. I saw Premila at once and ran over to her, as she had charge of our lunchbox. The children were all opening packages and sitting down to eat sandwiches. Premila and I were the only ones who had Indian food—thin wheat chapatties [a type of bread], some vegetable curry, and a bottle of buttermilk. Premila thrust half of it into my hand and whispered fiercely that I should go and sit with my class, because that was what the others seemed to be doing. . . .

I had never really grasped the system of competitive games. At home, whenever we played tag or guessing games, I was always allowed to "win"—"because," Mother used to tell Premila, "she is the youngest, and we have to allow for that." I had often heard her say it, and it seemed quite reasonable to me, but the result was that I had no clear idea of what "winning" meant.

Art and Literature *Misunderstandings arising from cultural differences were common in Anglo-Indian schools. Indian children in these schools also experienced prejudice and discrimination on a regular basis at the hands of both teachers and students.*

When we played twos-and-threes that afternoon at school, in accordance with my training, I let one of the small English boys catch me, but was naturally rather puzzled when the other children did not return the courtesy. I ran about for what seemed like hours without ever catching anyone, until it was time for school to close. Much later I learned that my attitude was called "not being a good sport," and I stopped allowing myself to be caught, but it was not for years that I really learned the spirit of the thing. . . .

It was a week later, the day of Premila's first test, that our lives changed rather abruptly. I was sitting at the back of my class, in my usual inattentive way, only half listening to the teacher. I had started a rather guarded friendship with the girl with the braids, whose name turned out to be Nalini (Nancy, in school). The three other Indian children were already fast friends. Even at that age it was apparent to all of us that friendship with the English or Anglo-Indian children was out of the question. Occasionally, during the class, my new friend and I would draw pictures and show them to each other secretly.

The door opened sharply and Premila marched in. At first, the teacher smiled at her in a kindly and encouraging way and said, "Now, you're little Cynthia's sister?"

Premila didn't even look at her. She stood with her feet planted firmly apart and her shoulders rigid, and addressed herself directly to me. "Get up," she said. "We're going home."

I didn't know what had happened, but I was aware that it was a crisis of some sort. I rose obediently and started to walk toward my sister.

"Bring your pencils and your notebook," she said.

I went back for them, and together we left the room. The teacher started to say something just as Premila closed the door, but we didn't wait to hear what it was.

In complete silence we left the school grounds and started to walk home. Then I asked Premila what the matter was. All she would say was "We're going home for good.". . .

When we got to our house the ayah [maid] was just taking a tray of lunch into Mother's room. She immediately started a long, worried questioning about what are you children doing back here at this hour of the day.

Mother looked very startled and very concerned, and asked Premila what had happened.

Premila said, "We had our test today, and she made me and the other Indians sit at the back of the room, with a desk between each one."

Mother said, "Why was that, darling?"

"She said it was because Indians cheat," Premila added. "So I don't think we should go back to that school."

Mother looked very distant, and was silent a long time. At last she said, "Of course not, darling." She sounded displeased.

We all shared the curry she was having for lunch, and afterward I was sent off to the beautifully familiar bedroom for my siesta. I could hear Mother and Premila talking through the open door.

Mother said, "Do you suppose she understood all that?"

Premila said, "I shouldn't think so. She's a baby."

Mother said, "Well, I hope it won't bother her."

Of course, they were both wrong. I understood it perfectly, and I remember it all very clearly. But I put it happily away, because it had all happened to a girl called Cynthia, and I never was really particularly interested in her.

RESPONDING TO LITERATURE

1. **Identifying:** Why did Santha and her sister leave school?
2. **Applying:** Explain why Santha was unable to tell the class her name.
3. **Synthesizing:** When the headmistress gives Santha and her sister new names, what can you determine about her attitude toward Indian culture?
4. **Thinking critically:** Explain why Santha's mother would or would not keep her children home permanently from the Anglo-Indian school.

CHAPTER 29 REVIEW

HISTORICAL SIGNIFICANCE

World War I shattered the old order in Europe and stirred nationalist feelings in Western-dominated countries around the world. With Europe weakened and preoccupied, people in Africa, Asia, and Latin America had reason to hope that their lands would gain greater freedom from foreign control. As a result, these people were bitterly disappointed when they learned that the principles of self-determination discussed at the Versailles peace conference did not apply to them.

The upsurge of nationalism and the rise of independence movements that followed shaped the future of Africa, Asia, and Latin America. During the 50 years following the end of World War I, dozens of new nations emerged from the wreckage of old empires. In addition, countries began to follow nationalistic policies in economics, taking over industries and limiting foreign investment to free themselves of foreign domination and to reclaim control over their economic futures.

SUMMARY

For a summary of Chapter 29, see the Unit 7 Synopsis on pages 802–805.

USING KEY TERMS

1. Why is *civil disobedience* a strategy pacifists might use to change a law they oppose?
2. Define the term *self-determination*. Illustrate your definition with two examples from the chapter.
3. How is the term *warlord* used in Chinese history?
4. What effect might a *population explosion* have on the politics and economics of a country?
5. Use *pacifist* in a sentence.

REVIEWING FACTS

1. **Name:** What were three major contributions India made to the British war effort in World War I? What did Great Britain promise India in return?
2. **Identify:** Name three nationalist leaders who would probably agree with the statement "Political power grows out of the barrel of a gun."
3. **Describe:** What were two nonviolent tactics for social change used by Gandhi?

4. **List:** What were five modernization reforms ordered by Ataturk?
5. **Describe:** What problems did colonial boundaries create in Africa? Discuss Nigeria as an example.
6. **Identify:** What major event in 1938 marked the arrival of economic nationalism in Latin America?

THINKING CRITICALLY

1. **Apply:** How does political control relate to economic control? Give examples from Egypt or India.
2. **Apply:** How did religious differences hamper the Indian independence movement? Give examples to support your opinion.
3. **Analyze:** In 1939 most of Africa and much of Asia were European colonies. What needed to change before self-determination could be achieved by all countries? Give examples to support your answer.
4. **Synthesize:** Instead of warlords, imagine "peacelords." How would they acquire their power? How would they use it? What would they accomplish?
5. **Evaluate:** Did Western influence become more or less widespread in the two decades after World War I? Give examples to support your opinion.

ANALYZING CONCEPTS

1. **Nationalism:** Explain how nationalism is related to self-determination and militarism.
2. **Conflict:** Describe three different ways that the people of a country might express their desire for self-determination.
3. **Change:** What forces contributed to the dramatic changes that occurred in Japan during the 1920s?

PRACTICING SKILLS

1. What is the thesis of "Footnote to History: The May 4th Movement" on page 755? Identify one specific example and one generalization in support of the thesis.
2. Which of the following thesis statements is best supported by the information in the section "Democracy and the Military" on page 763?
   a. Misguided U.S. foreign policy has caused many problems in South America.
   b. Many South American countries will never be democracies.
   c. Many South Americans prefer authoritarian government to democracy.
3. Find an article in a recent newspaper or magazine that states an argument about a political or historical issue. Identify the thesis of the argument and the major reasons supporting it.

GEOGRAPHY IN HISTORY

1. **Place:** Refer to the map on page 747. List the five countries that bordered Palestine in 1935.
2. **Place:** Refer to the map on pages 990–991. Identify three important geographic differences between China and Japan.
3. **Movement:** How was Mao Zedong able to use the Long March to his advantage?

TRACING CHRONOLOGY

Refer to the time line below to answer these questions.
1. Which country suffered nearly constant warfare during this time span?
2. Compare and contrast the two events listed for 1930.
3. Compare this time line with those in the first chapters of the book. How is the time span different on this one?

LINKING PAST AND PRESENT

1. Review Gandhi's major criticisms of Western civilization. Were they accurate? Do they apply today? What other ideals do Gandhi's statements imply?
2. Do you think nationalism is stronger or weaker today than it was in the 1920s and 1930s? Give examples from current events that support your opinion.

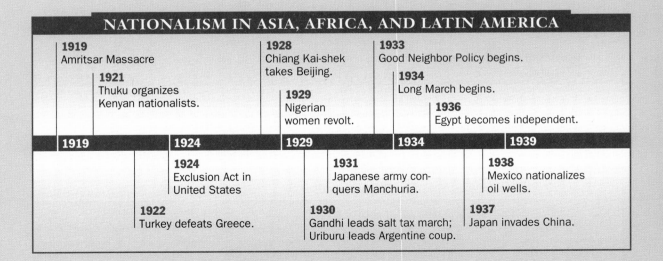

NATIONALISM IN ASIA, AFRICA, AND LATIN AMERICA

1919 Amritsar Massacre

1921 Thuku organizes Kenyan nationalists.

1928 Chiang Kai-shek takes Beijing.

1929 Nigerian women revolt.

1933 Good Neighbor Policy begins.

1934 Long March begins.

1936 Egypt becomes independent.

1919　**1924**　**1929**　**1934**　**1939**

1924 Exclusion Act in United States

1922 Turkey defeats Greece.

1931 Japanese army conquers Manchuria.

1930 Gandhi leads salt tax march; Uriburu leads Argentine coup.

1938 Mexico nationalizes oil wells.

1937 Japan invades China.

World War II

*O*n June 6, 1944, the Allies opened the long-promised second front when they mounted an all-out attack against German forces in Normandy, France. The invasion began with the greatest amphibious operation in history. Years later an American infantryman named Elliott Johnson could still vividly recall the events of the day:

"I remember going up to the highest part of that ship and watching the panorama around me unfold. In my mind's eye, I see one of our ships take a direct hit and go up in a huge ball of flames. There were big geysers coming up where the shells were landing and there were bodies floating, face down, face up."

The invasion of Normandy was one of the key military events of World War II, a conflict that engulfed the entire world. Although the war began in 1939, it had its roots in the peace treaties that settled World War I.

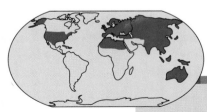

CHAPTER PREVIEW

Key Terms to Define: collective security, sanctions, appeasement, blitzkrieg, blitz, cash-and-carry policy, lend-lease, scorched-earth policy, kamikaze

People to Meet: Haile Selassie, Francisco Franco, Neville Chamberlain, Winston Churchill, Emperor Hirohito, Dwight Eisenhower, Charles de Gaulle, Harry Truman

Places to Discover: Manchuria, The Rhineland, Dunkirk, Pearl Harbor, Normandy, Midway, Hiroshima

Objectives to Learn:
1. In what sense was World War II a product of World War I?
2. Why and how did the major powers form alliances?
3. How did Hitler take over most of Europe?

The Allied invasion of Normandy in June 1944 signaled the decline of Hitler's power.

4. How did the Japanese pursue their goals of empire?

Concepts to Understand:

• Movement—Japan, Italy, and Germany win significant territorial gains in a number of expansionist moves. Section 1

• Cooperation—The major powers form alliances to protect their national interests. Sections 1,2,3

• Conflict—Two separate and opposing alliances, the Allies and the Axis, wage a worldwide war. Sections 2,3,4,5

• Innovation—Advances in military technology change the conduct of war and create a state of total war that involves millions of civilians. Sections 3,4,5

773

The Path to War

In the 1930s the Western democracies watched uneasily as totalitarian regimes came to power in Europe and Asia. Despite their fears, Britain, France, and the United States could not agree on what steps to take to ensure their **collective security**, or what was needed to defend their common interests against enemy attack. Much of the unrest in Europe and Asia can be traced to the peace settlements made at the end of World War I. Great Britain, France, and the United States were substantially satisfied with these settlements; however, Japan, Italy, and Germany were not.

Japan's Expansion in Asia

Japan was the first of the nondemocratic powers to reveal its territorial ambitions in the interwar period. With limited natural resources of its own, Japan depended heavily on foreign sources for raw materials and on foreign markets for finished goods. To acquire more of these materials and markets, Japan sought new territories for conquest.

As you read in Chapter 29, the Japanese military used a bomb explosion on the South Manchurian Railway in September 1931 as an excuse to overrun Manchuria. The following year Japan established Manchuria as an independent state, renamed it Manchukuo, and set up former Chinese emperor Pu Yi as puppet ruler.

When China protested in the League of Nations about Japan's actions, the League ordered a commission under British statesman Lord Lytton to investigate the affair. Lytton's commission laid the blame squarely on Japan and ordered the Japanese government to return Manchuria to China. The League voted overwhelmingly in favor of this recommendation, to which Japan responded in May 1933 by withdrawing from the League. The Manchurian incident not only revealed that the League of Nations was powerless, but also boosted the expansionist ambitions of Mussolini and Hitler.

In the early 1930s, the Japanese military hoped to gain control of the East Indies and its oil reserves, which would supply Japan's ships and airplanes. But to control the East Indies, Japan needed ports on the South China coast.

Consequently, during the summer of 1937, the Japanese launched a full-scale invasion of China. In August Japanese armies attacked Shanghai and began a bold drive up the Chang Jiang to Nanjing, the Chinese capital. After seizing Nanjing, Japan went on to invade South China, but the Japanese soon lost their momentum in the struggle against the Chinese nationalist forces under Chiang Kai

Italy's Conquest of Ethiopia

The relative ease with which Japan acquired Manchuria encouraged Italy to make a similar move. In 1934 Italian and Ethiopian forces clashed in a disputed zone on the frontier of Italian Somaliland in Africa. When the Italian dictator, Mussolini, demanded an apology and reparations, the Ethiopians responded by asking the League of Nations to investigate the matter. The League decided that because each side viewed the area where the incident took place as its own territory, neither side was to blame.

The League's decision did not satisfy Mussolini, who thought an Ethiopian colony would enhance Italy's image as a world power. Consequently, in October 1935, Mussolini ordered the Italian army to invade Ethiopia. In a dramatic appearance at the League of Nations, Ethiopian Emperor Haile Selassie appealed for help. This time the League condemned the action and voted economic **sanctions**, measures designed to stop trade and other economic contacts, against Italy. The League forbade its members to sell Italy arms and certain raw materials. But the sanctions did not include oil, coal, and iron, all vital to Italy's war efforts.

Once again the League's actions were ineffective. Mussolini completed his conquest of Ethiopia, and in May 1936 he formally annexed the African nation.

Spanish Civil War

A civil war in Spain further inflamed the international situation in the 1930s. After presiding over years of social and economic chaos, King Alfonso XIII abdicated in 1931, and Spain became a republic. The new republican government immediately began a program of social reforms. It ended the Catholic Church's role in educating Spanish youth and redistributed land from nobles to peasants.

As a result of these and other reforms, many right-wing groups in Spain opposed the republic and wished to restore the old order. In July 1936 right-wing army chiefs staged an uprising in Spanish Morocco that soon spread to Spain. For three years the conservative Spanish Nationalists, led by General Francisco Franco, and the left-wing Loyalists, or Spanish Republicans, battled for control of Spain.

Early in the fighting several foreign powers intervened in the Spanish war. The Soviets supported the Loyalists, while the Germans and Italians aided the Nationalists. Volunteers from Britain, France, the United States, and other countries around the world flocked to Spain to join the International Brigade and fight for the Republican cause against fascism. The governments of the Western democracies, however, refused to intervene because they feared a general European war.

Hitler viewed German participation in the Spanish Civil War as a way to strengthen ties with Italy and to secure a vital supply of Spanish iron ore and magnesium. Hermann Goering, head of the Luftwaffe—or German air force—saw an opportunity "firstly, to prevent the further spread of Communism; secondly, to test my

young Luftwaffe in this or that technical aspect." To accomplish these goals, Goering formed the Condor Legion, an all-German air and ground force. They used Spanish towns and cities as testing grounds for new weapons and tactics, such as the combined use of fire and high-explosive bombs.

By the summer of 1936, the Nationalists had taken most of western Spain. When the Soviets stopped sending aid to the Loyalists in 1938, Franco launched his final offensive. In March 1939 Franco entered Madrid, the last of the Loyalist strongholds. The civil war had ended, but more than half a million Spaniards had died, and much of the country lay in ruins. Although Spain joined Italy and Germany as countries headed by Fascist dictators, Franco did not ally himself with Italy and Germany.

Hitler on the Offensive

The same year the Spanish Civil War broke out, Hitler made his move in Germany. The

Learning from Photographs *Haile Selassie appealed to the League of Nations for decisive action against Italian aggression in Ethiopia. The League's inaction led to its downfall.* **Why were the League's sanctions against Italy ineffective?**

German dictator was convinced that Germany needed more *lebensraum*, or living space, for its expanding population. In *Mein Kampf* (my struggle), he stated:

> *Only an adequate large space on this earth assures a nation freedom of existence. . . . We must hold unflinchingly to our aim . . . to secure for the German people the land and soil to which they are entitled. . . .*

Occupying the Rhineland   To protect French security, the signers of the Treaty of Versailles had created a demilitarized zone in the Rhineland and forbidden German troops from entering the area. But Hitler gambled that if he violated the treaty, France and Great Britain would do nothing to stop him. In March 1936, therefore, Hitler sent troops into the Rhineland. France had the right to take military action if German troops entered the demilitarized zone, and Britain had the obligation to back France with its own armed forces. But neither country acted, because politically and militarily neither was willing to risk a war.

FOOTNOTES TO HISTORY
WRITERS AT WAR

The Spanish Civil War became a crusade for many famous writers. Ernest Hemingway covered the war as a war correspondent, and his novel *For Whom the Bell Tolls* describes the adventures of an idealistic American fighting the Fascist forces in Spain. English novelist and social critic George Orwell also went to Spain to report on the civil war but ended up joining the fight against the Fascists. Orwell drew on his experiences to write *Homage to Catalonia,* in which he describes trench warfare on the Aragon front and his nearly fatal gunshot wound. André Malraux, the French author of such world-renowned works as *Man's Fate, The Royal Road,* and *Man's Hope,* was the organizer of the first International Air Squadron in Spain. The squadron flew against the best units of the Italian Air Force and the German Condor Legion.

In October 1936 Hitler signed a political and military pact with Mussolini called the Rome–Berlin Axis. As a result of this treaty, Italy and Germany became known as the Axis powers. The next month Hitler signed the Anti-Comintern Pact, an anti-Communist alliance that included Germany, Italy, and Japan. Stalin was afraid that the new alliance would threaten Soviet security and urged the Western powers to unite against Germany and its allies. But the West, fearing that such a union would lead to war, refused.

Seizing Austria   Hitler, meanwhile, grew bolder. For a long time he had dreamed of *Anschluss*—the annexation of Austria to Germany. "German-Austria must return to the great mother country," he wrote. "One blood demands one Reich."

In 1934 Hitler had tried to take over Austria but backed down when Mussolini responded by mobilizing Italy's troops. In 1938, now that Germany and Italy were allies, Hitler tried again. The Austrian chancellor appealed to Britain and France for help, but once more the two major democracies in Europe did nothing. In March 1938 Hitler sent German troops into Austria and then annexed it.

Tension Builds in Europe

Austria was the first victim of Hitler's policy of expansion. Czechoslovakia was the next. In the late 1930s, Czechoslovakia was the only democratic nation in central Europe. It held the key strategic position in the region. Its standard of living was second only to that of Germany, and it had a strong army and alliances with France and the Soviet Union.

Czechoslovakia was created by treaty at the end of World War I. In addition to Czechs and Slovaks, it had 1 million Hungarians, half a million Ruthenians, and more than 3 million Germans. During the 1930s these minorities began to demand more autonomy than they had received under the terms of the treaties, creating serious problems for the Czechoslovak government. Hitler took advantage of Czechoslovakia's ethnic problems to destroy the country.

Learning from Photographs
Upon his return from Munich, Neville Chamberlain waves the Anglo–German agreement that he signed with Hitler. Chamberlain believed that the Munich Agreement and this "no war" guarantee promised "peace in our time." **Why was Chamberlain's policy of appeasement criticized?**

Sudeten Crisis On September 12, 1938, Hitler demanded that the Germans of the Sudetenland, a heavily fortified region in northwestern Czechoslovakia, be given the right of self-determination. The Czechoslovak government responded by proclaiming martial law. In an effort to avert an international crisis, British Prime Minister Neville Chamberlain suggested to Hitler that they meet to discuss the matter. France supported his request.

Chamberlain met with Hitler in Germany on September 15, 1938. There Hitler demanded the return of the Sudetenland to Germany. At a second meeting a week later, Chamberlain accepted Hitler's demands. He thought that a policy of **appeasement**, granting concessions to maintain peace, would stabilize Europe. But Hitler responded by saying that the "plan is no longer of any use" and upped his demands. After further talks the two failed to reach any accord. Czechoslovakia, meanwhile, called for the full mobilization of its troops.

The Munich Conference On September 29, Chamberlain met with Hitler a third time at the Munich Conference. Mussolini and French Premier Édouard Daladier were also present at this meeting, but no representative was there from the Czechoslovak government.

Mussolini offered a "compromise" that gave Germany control over the Sudetenland. In return, Hitler promised to respect Czechoslovakia's sovereignty. He also promised not to take any more European territory and to settle future disputes by peaceful negotiation. Still hoping to avoid war, Britain and France accepted the terms. On September 30, Czechoslovakia reluctantly accepted the agreement.

Chamberlain returned home to cheering crowds, proclaiming that the Munich Agreement had ensured "peace in our time." He trusted Hitler and believed that the Nazis would cause no more trouble. Events soon proved him wrong. On March 15, 1939, Hitler sent his armies into Czechoslovakia and took control of the western part of the country. The eastern part, Slovakia, became a German puppet state. After the takeover the Western democracies could no longer maintain their illusions about Hitler's plans and began to prepare for war.

The Nazi–Soviet Pact

In March 1939 Hitler turned his attention to eastern Europe. He threatened to take over the Baltic port of Danzig and the Polish Corridor. Britain and France promised to help Poland defend its borders if it became necessary.

To defend Poland, the democracies had to consider the Soviet Union, Poland's neighbor but also its traditional enemy. During the late 1930s, Stalin had urged the Western powers to do something about Hitler. He suspected that the Munich Agreement was an attempt by the British and the French to turn Hitler's attention away from the West and toward the Soviet Union. Chamberlain, on the other hand, did not trust Stalin. He suspected that the Soviet leader wanted to extend his influence in eastern Europe. This confusion as to whether the Fascists or the Communists were the greater enemy contributed to the coolness of the British and the French toward Stalin.

Despite Chamberlain's suspicions and his lack of faith in the fighting ability of the Soviet army, he asked the Soviets to join Britain and France in an alliance to contain nazism. Stalin agreed on the condition that the Western powers acknowledge the Soviet right to occupy a broad zone stretching from Finland to Bulgaria. Chamberlain refused Stalin's request, deepening Stalin's suspicion that the West would like nothing better than to see Germany and the Soviet Union destroy each other.

Stalin believed that Hitler's desire for "living space" would eventually lead the German dictator to move into the rich agricultural areas of eastern Europe. Because he doubted that the West would come to his country's aid if Germany threatened it, he began secret talks with the Germans. On August 23, 1939, the Soviet Union and Germany signed the Nazi–Soviet Nonaggression Pact. According to the agreement, the two nations pledged that they would never attack each other. Moreover, each would remain neutral if the other became involved in a war. Stalin and Hitler also secretly agreed to create spheres of influence in eastern Europe. Germany would occupy the western part of Poland, while the Soviet Union would govern the eastern part. They agreed to include Finland, part of Romania, and the Baltic republics of Estonia, Latvia, and Lithuania in the Soviet sphere of influence.

Neither Stalin nor Hitler had any illusions about their agreement. Stalin still believed that war with Germany was inevitable. But he thought that the pact would improve Soviet security. If nothing else, it would buy the Soviets time to prepare for war. Hitler saw the pact as a means of securing Germany's eastern border. If he did not have to worry about fighting the Soviets, he would be free to act as he wanted.

The pact shocked and outraged Western leaders, who realized that it destroyed the last barrier to war. The West had also lost a potential ally, and Hitler had won a pledge of neutrality that freed him to pursue his military objectives regarding Poland. Hitler remained convinced, however, that the West would do nothing if he moved against Poland. "The men of Munich," he said, "will not take the risk." With this thought in mind, Hitler sent his armies across the Polish frontier on September 1, 1939. However, he had finally misjudged what the Western leaders would do. Two days after Hitler's invasion of Poland, Great Britain and France declared war on Germany. World War II had begun.

SECTION 1 REVIEW

Recall

1. **Define:** collective security, sanctions, appeasement
2. **Identify:** Chiang Kai-shek, Benito Mussolini, Haile Selassie, Francisco Franco, Adolf Hitler, Neville Chamberlain
3. **Locate:** Find Czechoslovakia on the map on page 988. What about this country's location gave it such strategic value in Hitler's eyes?
4. **Describe:** How did the League of Nations respond to the Japanese takeover of Manchuria and the Italian invasion of Ethiopia? Why did it respond this way?

Critical Thinking

5. **Evaluate:** How did the West's policy of appeasement contribute to the start of World War II?

6. **Examine:** In what sense was the Spanish Civil War a "rehearsal" for World War II?

Applying Concepts

7. **Movement:** How was the response by the League of Nations to Japanese aggression in 1933 similar to the response by the Western democracies to German aggression in 1938?

War in Europe

On September 1, 1939, the German Luftwaffe roared toward its targets in Poland, spreading panic and confusion with its bombs. At the same time, armored tank divisions known as panzers swept across the Polish border. Next came the infantry, a million and a half strong, in motorized vehicles. This was **blitzkrieg**, or "lightning war," a new German strategy aimed at taking the enemy by surprise.

The blitzkrieg worked with speed and efficiency, devastating Poland in a few weeks. Great Britain and France could not move fast enough to send troops to Poland. Stalin, meanwhile, moved quickly to occupy the eastern half of that nation.

Stalin also forced the Baltic republics of Latvia, Lithuania, and Estonia to accept Soviet military bases. When he tried to do the same with Finland, war broke out. The Finns held out heroically until March before the Soviets forced them to surrender. As a result of their victory, the Soviets moved their frontier 70 miles (112 kilometers) to the west, making the city of Leningrad less vulnerable to German attack.

Hitler Looks to the West

All through the winter and spring of 1939–1940, the western front was quiet. The Germans called this period the "sit-down war," or *Sitzkrieg*, while the West dubbed it the "phony war." Many hoped that an all-out war could still be avoided.

When Finland capitulated to the Soviets, however, the British took steps to ensure that the same fate would not befall Norway. In early April 1940, they mined Norwegian waters to block any ships trading with Germany. Hitler used the mining to support his claim that the Allies were about to invade Scandinavia. He delivered an ultimatum to Norway and Denmark, demanding that they accept the "protection of the Reich." The Danes accepted his demands; the Norwegians did not.

The Invasion of Scandinavia   In the early morning hours of April 9, three small German transports steamed into the harbor of Copenhagen, and after meeting only token resistance, took control of Denmark.

That same morning German forces landed all along the Norwegian coast. Within hours Germans had seized the ports of Narvik and Trondheim. Bergen, the second-largest city, put up more resistance, but it too fell, as did Oslo.

Although Germany now controlled Norway, the Norwegian invasion had proved costly. Germany lost 10 of 20 destroyers and 3 of 8 cruisers—a large segment of its navy. On the other hand, Hitler had won the outlet to the Atlantic that he needed to ensure that the German navy would not be bottled up in the Baltic Sea.

News of the fall of Norway and Denmark caused an uproar in the House of Commons. The Labour and Liberal opposition strongly attacked Prime Minister Neville Chamberlain and his policies. Knowing that he had lost the confidence of his own Conservative party as well, Chamberlain stepped down. On May 10, 1940, King George VI summoned Winston Churchill to Buckingham Palace and asked him to form a new government. Churchill, one of the few politicians to warn of the Nazi danger in the 1930s, was now prime minister.

The Fall of France   On that same momentous date, the war began in earnest on the western front. Along the Maginot Line, the British and French watched and waited. The Maginot Line was impressive, but it had one major flaw. It had a 50-mile (80-kilometer) gap in the

Ardennes. Although the Germans had invaded through Belgium and the Ardennes during World War I, the French still believed that the forests, swamps, and hills of that region were a sufficient barrier. A French tank commander, Charles de Gaulle, pleaded for more tanks and planes, but the French command insisted that the Maginot Line was impenetrable.

Hitler, meanwhile, carried out a massive attack on the Low Countries—Luxembourg, the Netherlands, and Belgium. Before dawn on May 10, 1940, German troops parachuted into the Netherlands. It was the first large-scale airborne attack in the history of warfare and caught the Dutch completely by surprise. Five days after the start of the invasion, the Dutch capitulated.

On the same day that Germany invaded the Netherlands, Britain and France moved their best troops into Belgium. German panzers swept into the Ardennes and began to encircle them. Other panzer divisions drove through Luxembourg and raced toward France.

Learning from Photographs *Paris fell quickly to the Nazis. Perhaps the French feared the Luftwaffe would destroy the city's beautiful architecture.* **What were the terms of the armistice France signed with Germany?**

Although the Belgian forces fought valiantly, they did not hold out as long as had been expected. The Germans were now rolling through undefended open country. They pushed westward toward the English Channel, trapping the Belgian, British, and French forces in the northwest corner of France. The only hope for the Allies was an evacuation by sea from the French port of Dunkirk. With German forces within sight of the coast, the rescue of 300,000 Allied soldiers seemed impossible. But for reasons never entirely understood, Hitler ordered his forces to halt.

The British Admiralty began a desperate rescue operation at Dunkirk on May 26. A ragtag armada of 850 vessels, ranging from destroyers and cruisers to trawlers, tugs, yachts, and fishing boats, left England and set sail for Dunkirk. Civilians operated many of the smaller boats. Over the next nine days, under fierce air and ground attack, this hastily assembled fleet rescued the Allied armies.

The evacuation of Dunkirk was a stunning military achievement, but as Churchill said, "wars are not won by evacuations." Faced with an unprepared French army and a confused French government, the Germans continued their sweep into France and on June 14 entered Paris. A week later France signed an armistice with Germany.

By the terms of this armistice, the Germans occupied all of northern France and the Atlantic coastline to the Spanish border. In southern France, the Nazis set up a puppet government in the city of Vichy under French Marshal Henri Pétain. Pétain and other officials in the so-called Vichy government collaborated with the Germans. Many French citizens, on the other hand, continued to fight for freedom. In Britain, de Gaulle organized a Free French government, while in France many joined the French Resistance, an underground movement that opposed the German occupation.

Battle of Britain

All that stood between Hitler and German domination of western Europe was Winston Churchill and the determined British people.

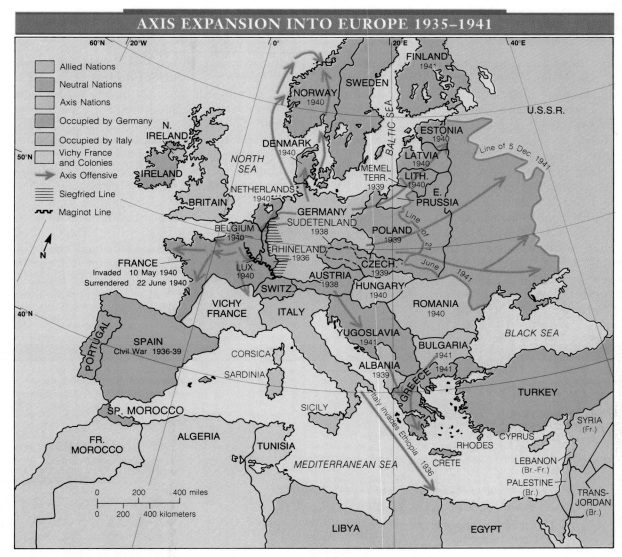

AXIS EXPANSION INTO EUROPE 1935–1941

Legend:
- Allied Nations
- Neutral Nations
- Axis Nations
- Occupied by Germany
- Occupied by Italy
- Vichy France and Colonies
- Axis Offensive
- Siegfried Line
- Maginot Line

N. IRELAND
IRELAND
BRITAIN
NORTH SEA
NORWAY 1940
SWEDEN
FINLAND 1941
U.S.S.R.
Line of 5 Dec. 1941
DENMARK 1940
ESTONIA 1940
LATVIA 1940
MEMEL TERR. 1939
LITH. 1940
E. PRUSSIA
NETHERLANDS 1940
GERMANY
SUDETENLAND 1938
POLAND 1939
BELGIUM 1940
RHINELAND 1936
CZECH. 1939
AUSTRIA 1938
LUX. 1940
HUNGARY 1940
FRANCE
Invaded 10 May 1940
Surrendered 22 June 1940
SWITZ.
VICHY FRANCE
ITALY
YUGOSLAVIA 1941
ROMANIA 1940
BULGARIA 1941
BLACK SEA
ALBANIA 1939
GREECE 1941
TURKEY
PORTUGAL
SPAIN
Civil War 1936-39
CORSICA
SARDINIA
SICILY
SP. MOROCCO
FR. MOROCCO
ALGERIA
TUNISIA
MEDITERRANEAN SEA
RHODES
CRETE
CYPRUS
SYRIA (Fr.)
LEBANON (Br.-Fr.)
PALESTINE (Br.)
TRANS-JORDAN (Br.)
LIBYA
EGYPT
Italy invades Ethiopia 1936
BALTIC SEA
Line of 21 June 1941

0   200   400 miles
0   200   400 kilometers

Learning from Maps *By the end of 1941, Germany had seized control of much of Europe.* **Which European nations chose to remain neutral during the war?**

Hitler expected that Britain would seek peace with Germany, but he misjudged the resolve of the British. Alone and only partially prepared, Britain faced the mightiest military machine the world had ever seen.

On May 13, 1940, Churchill delivered his first speech before the House of Commons. He told the Commons that he had "nothing to offer but blood, toil, tears, and sweat." He ended the speech with these words:

You ask, what is our policy? I will say: it is to wage war, by sea, land, and air, with all our might and with all the strength that God can give us: to wage war against a monstrous tyranny, never surpassed in the dark, lamentable catalogue of human crime. That is our policy. You ask, what is our aim? I can answer in one word: Victory—victory at all costs, victory in spite of all terror, victory, however hard and long the road may be; for without victory, there is no survival.

Immediately after France fell, Hitler began making plans to invade Great Britain. Hitler and the German High Command soon realized that this invasion depended on winning air supremacy over the English Channel and destroying British airfields and vital industries. To accomplish this goal, the Luftwaffe began bombing the southern coast of Britain in early August 1940. The bombings damaged four aircraft factories and five Royal Air Force (RAF) airfields, but British fighter planes known as Hurricanes and Spitfires shot down 75 German planes. From then on, Goering focused his attacks on the RAF. From August 24 to September 6, Goering sent over 1,000 planes a day. The RAF lost 466 fighters and 103 pilots, but it inflicted even heavier losses on the Germans.

Seeking to do better, the Luftwaffe changed tactics once again, switching its attack to massive night bombings of London. For 57 consecutive nights, from September 7 to November 3, German bombers pounded London in its great **blitz,** or series of air raids. In one night alone, the Luftwaffe dropped 70,000 fire bombs on Britain's capital. The devastation was enormous, killing and injuring thousands of civilians, damaging light, power, and gas lines and destroying buildings, roads, and railways. But the bombings did not break the British people's morale.

The Luftwaffe never did gain air supremacy over Britain. While incurring heavy losses of its own, the RAF downed more than 1,700 German aircraft during the Battle of Britain, and in so doing, blocked Hitler's invasion. Churchill spoke for all Britons when he said of the RAF pilots: "Never in the field of human conflict was so much owed by so many to so few."

IMAGES OF THE TIME

The Blitz

During the Battle of Britain, German bombers blitzed London and strategic targets in an attempt to knock out all of Great Britain's defenses.

German bombers destroyed buildings all over London. Below, two women survey the damage done to their neighborhood.

Public shelters were set up throughout London in underground tunnels and other protected areas. At the height of the blitz, one out of seven Londoners slept in a shelter.

Anglo–American Cooperation

Throughout the early phase of the war, the United States expressed its determination to remain neutral. Public opinion was divided about the war, with some Americans believing the United States should enter the conflict to help defeat fascism and others wanting the nation to stay out of the war at all costs. Even before the fighting began, isolationists in the U.S. Congress had enacted laws designed to prevent American involvement in the war. The Neutrality Acts, passed in 1937 after Mussolini attacked Ethiopia, prohibited arms shipments, loans, and credit to belligerent nations. After the Spanish Civil War began, Congress also banned the export of munitions, or armaments, "for the use of either of the opposing forces in Spain."

President Roosevelt disagreed with the isolationists. He became convinced that Germany's expansion endangered American security and had to be stopped. He also realized that Britain and France could not stop Hitler without aid. Throughout his campaign for the presidency in 1940, Roosevelt tried to rally national opinion. And as they listened to news reports of German aggression, Americans became more sympathetic to Britain's plight.

After Dunkirk, Churchill appealed to the United States for help. Roosevelt gave the British 50 old American naval destroyers in return for the right to maintain American bases in Newfoundland, Bermuda, and the British West Indies. Churchill recognized the significance of this gesture. He wrote: "It marked the passage of the United States from being neutral to being non-belligerent."

Roosevelt also convinced Congress that a **cash-and-carry policy**—a program in which Great Britain traded cash for desperately needed

Londoners carried on with their lives, to some extent. At right, men browse in a library, seemingly oblivious to the destruction in their midst. German bombs like the one below were designed to set their targets on fire.

Reflecting on the Times
What did the Germans achieve by bombing London during the blitz?

supplies—would allow the United States to supply the British without risking the loss of American neutrality. Throughout 1940 this policy enabled the British to import U.S. food and armaments. They paid cash and transported the goods in their own ships.

But the cost of the war drained the British treasury. Britain ordered 12,000 airplanes from the United States in 1940 but could not pay for them. On Roosevelt's urging, Congress approved a policy of **lend-lease.** It authorized the President to lend war equipment to any country whose defense he deemed vital to the national security of the United States.

On August 9, 1941, Churchill met with Roosevelt on a British battleship off the Newfoundland coast to discuss war aims. The leaders issued a joint declaration that came to be called the Atlantic Charter. The declaration laid down certain principles, such as freedom of trade and the right of people to choose their own government. But it also called for the "final destruction of Nazi tyranny." Thus, although the United States was still a "neutral" country, the charter minced no words in delivering to Germany a challenge the Nazis could not ignore.

Eastern Europe and Africa

While Hitler was conquering much of western Europe, Mussolini was dreaming of building a Mediterranean empire for Italy. On June 10, 1940, four days before Paris surrendered to the Germans, Mussolini declared war on France and Britain. Italy's armies in Libya and Italian East Africa were poised for an attack on the British forces guarding Egypt and the Sudan, but all through the summer Mussolini waited.

The British, however, were not so cautious. Although vastly outnumbered, they attacked the Italians on December 7. In the following weeks they scored victory after victory against the Italians stationed along Libya's north coast. By mid–February 1941, the British had only to take Tripoli to remove the Italians' last foothold in North Africa. At this point Churchill directed the commander of the Western Desert Force to halt the advance. Leaving this commander with only a minimal force, Churchill sent the rest of the British troops to Greece to stop a German advance in southeast Europe that had already claimed Romania, Bulgaria, and Hungary.

It was a fatal decision. German forces swept through Yugoslavia and invaded Greece in April 1941, forcing the British into a second Dunkirk. Although most British troops escaped by sea, they left behind their tanks and 12,000 men. Meanwhile, Hitler sent Erwin Rommel, a brilliant general who had led the 7th Panzer Division in France, to take command of a tank force in Libya and rescue the Italians. By April 11, Rommel had pushed the British out of northern Libya, except for a small force at Tobruk.

The British fared better in Italian East Africa. In February 1941 the British left Kenya to invade Italian Somaliland. At the same time British forces from the Sudan invaded Ethiopia. By May the British had prevailed in both places, and Mussolini had lost his African empire.

SECTION 2 REVIEW

Recall

1. **Define:** blitzkrieg, blitz, cash-and-carry policy, lend-lease
2. **Identify:** Winston Churchill, Charles de Gaulle, Franklin Roosevelt
3. **Locate:** Find Libya on the map on page 781. Why was it important for Great Britain to gain control of Libya?

4. **Explain:** Why did Chamberlain step down as British prime minister in 1940?

Critical Thinking

5. **Evaluate:** What effect do you think Germany's losses in the Norwegian campaign had on German plans to invade Great Britain?

6. **Analyze:** What mistakes did French military leaders make that led to the fall of France?

Applying Concepts

7. **Cooperation:** How did the United States move from a policy of isolationism to a policy of openly assisting the British war effort?

A Global Conflict

I n the spring of 1941, Great Britain stood alone against Germany. As a result of its aggression, Germany now controlled almost all of western Europe. The countries under its control included Austria, Norway, Denmark, Belgium, the Netherlands, France, Romania, Bulgaria, Hungary, Yugoslavia, and Greece. In Africa, Rommel had succeeded in pushing the British back and had taken control of most of Libya. But in East Africa, the British had defeated the Italians and seized both Italian Somaliland and Ethiopia.

In Asia, meanwhile, the Japanese held Manchuria and controlled much of China. The Philippines, Australia, and the countries of Southeast Asia were bracing themselves for a Japanese invasion most felt was imminent.

By the end of 1941, the expansive war would grow even larger. Events since July drew two more major powers into the conflict: the Soviet Union and the United States.

Invasion of the Soviet Union

Having failed in his attempt to defeat Britain, Hitler now turned his attention to the Soviet Union. Only by conquering the vast Soviet steppe could Hitler gain the "living space" he felt was crucial to Germany's future. He also wanted the wheat of the Ukraine and the oil reserves of the Caucasus.

On June 22, 1941, Hitler launched a massive attack on the Soviet Union. Despite British warnings and the massing of German troops along the border, the invasion took the Soviets by surprise. In the first few days of fighting, the Germans destroyed the greater part of the Soviet air force, disabled thousands of Soviet tanks, and captured almost a million Soviet soldiers. As German divisions advanced deeper into Soviet

territory, Stalin appealed to his people to resist the invasion and issued his famous **scorched-earth policy**. If the Germans forced the Red Army to retreat, Stalin ordered, Soviet citizens should destroy everything that could be of use to the invaders.

By November 1941 German armies had pushed 600 miles (960 kilometers) inside the Soviet Union to the outskirts of Moscow. In addition to controlling 40 percent of the Soviet population, the Germans had captured Kiev and begun the siege of Leningrad. Yet the Soviets

Learning from Photographs *The powerful German panzers were no match for the harsh Soviet winter of 1941. The intense cold froze lubricating oil and cracked engine blocks.* **What other problems did the German divisions encounter during that winter?**

refused to surrender. Young Soviet soldiers rallied to the cry, "Behind us is Moscow—there is no room left for retreat!" The Germans faced not only a steely Soviet resistance but another equally formidable foe—the Russian winter. A German soldier described the conditions:

> *We had no gloves. We had no winter shoes. We had no equipment whatsoever to fight or withstand the cold. . . . We lost a considerable part of our equipment. . . . Due to the cold we lost a lot of people who got frost-bitten, and we had not even the necessary amount of ointments, or the most simple and primitive things to fight in. . . . Guns didn't fire anymore. Even our wireless equipment didn't work properly anymore because the batteries were frozen hard. . . .*

On December 1, 1941, German troops began an assault on Moscow, and in just one day they drew within sight of the Kremlin. It was as far as they ever got. When all seemed lost, the Soviets staged a powerful counteroffensive and forced the Germans to retreat.

The Nazi Order

Hitler wanted to conquer the Soviet Union as part of his plan to create a "New Order" in Europe. In the new world that Hitler envisioned, the Nazis would rule Europe and exploit its resources. In addition to enslaving the conquered peoples and forcing them to work for the German "master race," the Nazis would simultaneously exterminate "undesirable elements" such as the Jews and the Slavic peoples. Conquest would make Hitler's dream a reality.

The Nazis began to implement Hitler's plan by plundering the occupied countries. Goering instructed his subordinates: "Whenever you come across anything that may be needed by the German people, you must be after it like a bloodhound. It must be taken out . . . and brought to Germany." The Nazis confiscated art treasures, gold, food, cattle, raw materials, and factory equipment. At the same time, the Nazis drove millions into forced labor and concentration camps and massacred millions more.

Between 1939 and 1944, the Nazis deported more than seven and a half million people to Germany and put them to work in factories, fields, and mines. In flagrant violation of the Geneva Convention and international law, they put prisoners of war to work in armament factories and fed them only enough to enable them to work. Of the Russian prisoners of war, two million died from starvation and disease.

There were even worse horrors. In July 1941, Goering instructed Reinhard Heydrich, head of the German Security Service (S.S.), "to carry out all preparations with regard to . . . a total solution of the Jewish question." By "solution" he meant the complete extermination of all Jews in Europe.

During the next four years, the S.S. rounded up Jews by the hundreds of thousands and sent them to concentration camps such as Dachau and Auschwitz in Germany and eastern Europe. Those who did not work as slave laborers were shot or were poisoned in gas chambers.

Altogether, the Nazis murdered more than 6 million Jews during the war. This mass destruction of the Jewish people has become known as the **Holocaust.** Another 6 million people, including gypsies and Slavs, also perished in the Holocaust.

Even though the Nazis exercised almost total control over life in the conquered nations of Europe, they did encounter opposition. Many people in these countries joined underground resistance movements to commit acts of sabotage and combat the Nazis in any way possible.

Japanese Expansion

After seizing much of China in the 1930s, Japan shifted its attention to the European colonies in East and Southeast Asia and their store of raw materials. Taking advantage of Hitler's offensive in Europe, the Japanese acquired many of these territories. The collapse of France and the Low Countries left French Indochina and the Dutch East Indies virtually defenseless. And when the Germans threatened to invade Britain, the British withdrew their fleet from Singapore, leaving that colony open to attack as well.

Images of War

Margaret Bourke-White (1904–1971) was one of the premier photojournalists in the United States by the 1920s. Early in her career she concentrated on the clear, logical beauty of simple industrial forms. She composed photographs carefully, including only the elements essential to her story or idea. She often used contrasts in her photographs to help convey a message.

During the Depression, Bourke-White began to work on more human stories. She photographed the victims of the Dust Bowl and documented American farm life for the Farm Security Administration in the 1930s. At the end of World War II, she traveled to Buchenwald concentration camp and photographed the survivors there.

The photograph shown here is one of many she took at Buchenwald.

Bourke-White's attention to careful, clear compositions makes this picture all the more dramatic. The prisoners stand close together in front of a barbed-wire fence. Bourke-White composed the photograph so that the entire picture space is taken up by the figures of the prisoners, instead of using a more distant view that would have shown the setting of the camp. As a result, the viewer is confronted by these figures. By composing the photograph in this way, Bourke-White challenges the viewer of this image to recognize the suffering of the concentration-camp victims. It is this unavoidable challenge that makes the photograph such a powerful image.

Responding to the Arts
1. What subject did Bourke-White concentrate on early in her career?
2. How does this photograph challenge the viewer?

In July 1940 the Japanese government announced its plan to create a "new order in greater East Asia." Proclaiming "Asia for the Asiatics," Japan moved to establish the "Greater East Asia Co-prosperity Sphere," an appeal to Asians who wanted to rid their lands of European rule. First, it asked France for the right to build airfields and station troops in northern Indochina. After gaining this foothold, Japan invaded Tonkin Province in southern Indochina.

The United States retaliated by placing an embargo, or ban, on the sale of scrap iron to Japan. In response, Japan signed the Tripartite Pact with Germany and Italy on September 27, 1940. Under this pact, the three powers affirmed the right of every nation to "receive the space to which it is entitled" and pledged to cooperate to reach that goal as well as to come to one another's aid if attacked.

Pearl Harbor

When the Japanese invaded southern Indochina on July 24, 1941, President Roosevelt demanded that they withdraw—not only from Indochina but also from China. To back up his demands, Congress placed an embargo on oil

Learning from Photographs *Ships lined up neatly at Pearl Harbor made easy Sunday-morning targets. Here rescuers approach the damaged battleship U.S.S.* West Virginia. **Why did the Japanese attack Pearl Harbor?**

and froze all Japanese assets in the United States. Negotiations with the Japanese government continued during the summer and fall.

The Japanese government decided to go to war with the United States because it believed the United States stood in the way of its plans for expansion in the East. But to defeat America's military forces, Japanese leaders knew they had to destroy its Pacific fleet based at Pearl Harbor in Hawaii. Although most U.S. and Japanese leaders believed that Pearl Harbor was safe from attack, Admiral Isoroku Yamamoto, the commander of the Japanese navy, did not agree. He convinced Japanese leaders that bombers taking off from aircraft carriers and equipped with newly designed torpedos for use in shallow water could effect a successful surprise attack on Pearl Harbor.

In November 1941 the Japanese emperor, Hirohito, gave the go-ahead for war. He feared that if he refused, Japan would be plunged into a civil war. Yamamoto's plan now went into effect. The Japanese fleet came together in Saiki Bay, off the northeast coast of Kyushu, and set sail for Hawaii on November 26.

Meanwhile, the U.S. negotiations with Japan had all but broken down. By now Roosevelt and his advisers knew that the Japanese were "poised for attack," but they were convinced that Japan would move "against either the Philippines, Thai or Kra Peninsula [in Malaya], or possibly Borneo." As a precaution, U.S. military leaders sent all aircraft carriers and half the army's planes from Pearl Harbor.

On the morning of December 7, the Japanese attack squadron took off from their carrier decks and headed for Pearl Harbor. Within the first 25 minutes of the attack, they sank or damaged the battleships *Arizona, Utah, Oklahoma, West Virginia*, and *California*. The Japanese success was even greater than they had hoped. In all, they sank or disabled 19 American ships and destroyed 188 airplanes. They also killed more than 2,400 people and wounded 1,100. Fortunately for the United States, its aircraft carriers were at sea and escaped the attack. Calling December 7 "a date which will live in infamy," President Roosevelt, in an appearance before Congress the next day, asked for and received a declaration of war against Japan.

The Allies

The United States was now officially at war. On December 11, 1941, Germany and Italy honored the pledge they had made to Japan in the Tripartite Pact by declaring war on the United States. Britain, in support of the United States, declared war on Japan.

Although mistrust still lingered between the Western democracies and the Soviet Union, they put aside their differences in their resolve to defeat their common enemy. Stalin subscribed to the aims of the Atlantic Charter and agreed with Churchill and Roosevelt not to make separate peace agreements with any of the Axis powers. Churchill and Roosevelt further agreed that the defeat of Japan was secondary to the defeat of Germany.

Meanwhile, the fighting in the Soviet Union remained fierce. Vast areas of the country were under German occupation. The Germans had completely surrounded Leningrad, trapping 3 million people. When the Germans cut the main railway line and supplies could no longer get through to Leningrad, many starved.

Stalin urged the Allies to open a "second front" in Europe as quickly as possible. In a speech in June 1942, Vyacheslav Molotov, the People's Commissar for Foreign Affairs, explained the need for this front:

A second front in Europe would create insuperable difficulties for the Hitlerite armies at our front. Let us hope that our common enemy will soon feel on his own back the results of the ever-growing military co-operation between the three Great Powers.

Learning from Photographs *The demand for arms created thousands of jobs in munitions factories. As most young men left for war, women filled the gap in the work force.* **What impact do you think the war had on unemployment?**

Although President Roosevelt was open to the idea of creating a second front, Winston Churchill was opposed to it. He knew that Britain would have to bear the brunt of any second-front operation. Consequently, the two Allied leaders postponed plans for an invasion of Europe. Instead, they laid plans for military campaigns in North Africa, the Middle East, and the Mediterranean.

SECTION 3 REVIEW

Recall

1. **Define:** scorched-earth policy
2. **Identify:** Joseph Stalin, Isoroku Yamamoto, Emperor Hirohito, Vyacheslav Molotov
3. **Explain:** What were Hitler's reasons for attacking the Soviet Union?

Critical Thinking

4. **Examine:** How did the "New Order" that Adolf Hitler wanted to create in Europe affect the people living on that continent?
5. **Hypothesize:** Should U.S. leaders have foreseen the Japanese attack on Pearl Harbor? Give reasons to support your answer.

Applying Concepts

6. **Conflict:** How did World War II turn into a large-scale global conflict?

Turning Points

In the early months of 1942, the war was going badly for the Allies. By destroying much of the American fleet at Pearl Harbor, Japan had gained control of the Pacific Ocean and cleared the way for a seaborne invasion of American, British, and Dutch territories in that region. In December 1941 Japanese forces had captured Hong Kong and invaded Malaya. In the West, meanwhile, Rommel controlled a large area of North Africa, and German forces held the upper hand in the Soviet Union as well.

Despite these successes, the Axis powers would never again enjoy such a strong position. By the end of 1942, the tide of the war had begun to turn in favor of the Allies.

Sea and Air Battles

Even before the United States entered the war, it was shipping food and war supplies to Britain under the Lend-Lease Act. But German submarines, or U-boats, threatened this vital lifeline across the Atlantic. By the end of 1939, U-boats had already sunk 114 Allied and neutral ships. German air attacks also took their toll.

To make matters worse for the Allies, the new German battleship *Bismarck*, accompanied by the new cruiser *Prinz Eugen*, entered the fight in May 1941. With 11 Allied convoys either at sea or about to sail, the British hastily dispatched several ships to intercept the Nazis. On May 23 they sighted the two German ships in the Denmark Strait between Iceland and Greenland and opened fire. In the battle that followed, the *Bismarck* sank the British battle cruiser *Hood* and damaged a new British battleship before slipping away to safety.

Three days later, on May 26, a British patrol plane spotted the *Bismarck* 400 miles (644 kilometers) off the French coast. In the battle that

followed, the *Bismarck* sustained at least eight torpedo hits before it finally sank. With this crucial victory, the British put an end to German efforts to win the Battle of the Atlantic with surface ships. Gradually, the Allies devised new methods for protecting their convoys against U-boats as well.

As they fought for control of the Atlantic, the Allies launched a sustained air offensive against Germany in May 1940. A few months later, in August, the RAF bombed Berlin for the first time. During the next five years, the Allies flew mission after mission against Germany, destroying factories, oil refineries, and railways and leveling entire cities.

The Soviet Offensive

In July 1942 the military situation in the Soviet Union looked desperate. With the Soviet army in full retreat, the Germans were approaching Stalingrad, a major industrial center on the Volga River. In angry exchanges with Churchill, Stalin continued to press for a second front in the West to take some of the military pressure off his nation. But in August Churchill went to Moscow to tell Stalin that there would be no second front in 1942.

On August 22 the Germans attacked Stalingrad. Because it was named after Stalin, losing the city would have been a severe blow to Soviet morale. Just as determined to protect Stalingrad as Hitler was to take it, Stalin ordered that the city be held at all costs.

The Soviets launched a counterattack in September and encircled the German troops threatening the city. They cut off German supply lines and gradually tightened their trap. Although the Soviets and the frigid winter weather were closing in on the Germans, Hitler refused to allow his troops to retreat. By the time German officers finally surrendered in February 1943, the German army had lost the best of its troops. Many historians now view the Soviet victory at Stalingrad as the major turning point of World War II. By killing 200,000 German soldiers, capturing 80,000 more, and seizing large quantities of German military equipment, the Soviet Union broke the back of the Nazi military machine.

War in the Desert

In January 1942 Allied forces in North Africa were struggling to regain ground lost to the Germans. They faced a formidable foe. Erwin Rommel, commander of the Afrika Korps, applied blitzkrieg tactics to warfare in the desert. His exploits earned him the nickname "the Desert Fox."

In the spring of 1942, Rommel pushed the British two-thirds of the way back to the Egyptian frontier. He struck again at the end of May, but the British, under General Bernard Montgomery, stopped him at El Alamein, a railway junction about 70 miles (112 kilometers) from Alexandria. In October Montgomery launched a counterattack that forced the Germans back across the Egyptian–Libyan frontier and ended with the British capture of Tripoli, the capital of Libya, in January 1943.

As Montgomery was advancing westward, the Allies were landing troops in Morocco and Algeria. The landings were part of a planned offensive against Rommel. By advancing from the east and from the west, the Allies hoped to trap Rommel in "the pincers." But the Allied landings met with heavy resistance from the Vichy French, who governed French North Africa. To end the fighting, Allied commander Dwight D. Eisenhower struck a deal with Admiral François Darlan, a Vichy official. In return for Allied support of his claim to French North Africa, Darlan ordered an end to the resistance. With the armistice concluded in November 1942, the Free French, under Charles de Gaulle, joined the Allies in Africa. Meanwhile, in a series of powerful attacks, the Allies began closing the jaws of the pincers. When Rommel flew to

EASTERN FRONT 1941–1944

Learning from Maps *Some of the fiercest battles of World War II took place on the eastern front in the Soviet Union.* **Which battle proved a major turning point of the war?**

Berlin to tell Hitler that the situation was hopeless, the Nazi dictator rejected his general's assessment and barred Rommel from returning to Africa. But Rommel was right. In May 1943, General von Vaerst, the new commander of the German forces in Tunisia, surrendered. The Allies now controlled all of North Africa.

Invasion of Italy

In early 1943, the American and British chiefs of staff and political leaders met in Casablanca to discuss their next move. Because they wanted to secure communications in the Mediterranean and intensify the pressure on Italy, they decided to invade Sicily.

Under the command of General Eisenhower, the Allies began a combined air and sea attack on Sicily in July 1943. The seaborne landings met little resistance at first, but when the Allies approached Messina, on the extreme northeastern tip of the island, the Germans put up a stronger fight to cover their withdrawal across the Strait of Messina. In six days nearly 40,000 German and 70,000 Italian troops escaped to Italy.

The conquest of Sicily led quickly to Mussolini's downfall. On July 25, King Victor Emmanuel III, pressed into action by antiwar factions, fired Mussolini and had him arrested. The new prime minister, Marshal Pietro Badoglio, soon dissolved the Fascist party and on September 3 signed a secret act of surrender.

That same day, Allied forces crossed the Strait of Messina and landed in Calabria on the Italian mainland. The broadcast announcement of Badoglio's unconditional surrender caught the Germans by surprise, but they recovered in time to occupy Rome two days later, forcing the king and Badoglio to withdraw to the south. The Germans later rescued Mussolini and put him in control of northern Italy.

For the remaining months of 1943 and early months of 1944, the Allies fought their way up the Italian peninsula. Although Allied troops made some progress, they could not penetrate the German defenses at Monte Cassino, a sixth-century monastery located on a mountaintop that dominated the road to Rome. In the end it took a massive artillery bombardment and almost five months for the Allies to dislodge the Germans in May 1944. One month later, on June 4, Allied forces entered Rome.

War in the Pacific

While the war raged in Europe, the Japanese were having great success in Asia. In the months following Pearl Harbor, they captured Malaya, Singapore, and Burma. In the Pacific, they seized the Dutch East Indies, Guam, Wake Island, and the Philippines.

Only at sea had the Allies been able to make any gains. In May 1942, in the Battle of the

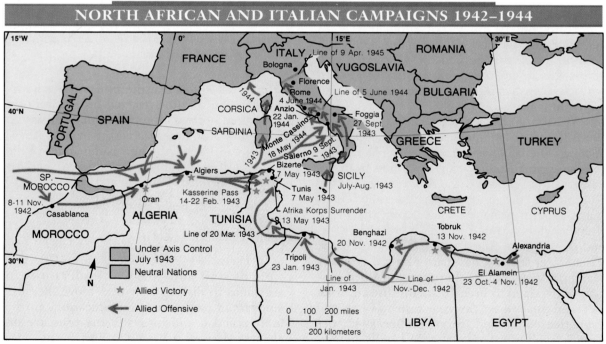

NORTH AFRICAN AND ITALIAN CAMPAIGNS 1942–1944

Learning from Maps *Before the Allies could invade Italy, they had to defeat the Italians and Germans for control of North Africa.* **From which country in this region did the Allies eventually launch their invasion and why?**

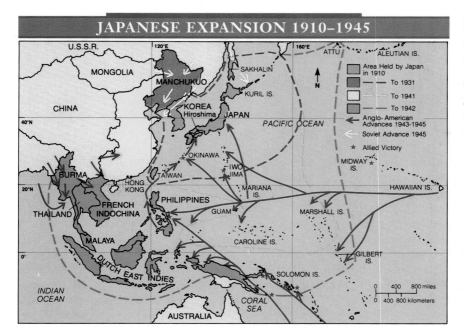

JAPANESE EXPANSION 1910–1945

	Area Held by Japan in 1910
	To 1931
	To 1941
	To 1942
←	Anglo-American Advances 1943–1945
	Soviet Advance 1945
★	Allied Victory

Learning from Maps *Between 1931 and 1942, Japan took over large areas of Southeast Asia and the Pacific.* **Why were the Japanese able to seize the European colonies in this region so easily in 1941 and 1942?**

Coral Sea, neither side had been able to claim victory. But in June, at the Battle of Midway, the Americans defeated the Japanese navy and ended Japanese naval superiority in the Pacific.

To follow up this victory, the Americans launched an attack against Guadalcanal in early August. While troops under General Douglas MacArthur attacked the Japanese on land, naval forces under Admiral Chester W. Nimitz confronted them at sea. The six-month land, sea, and air battle for control of the island ended in victory for the Allies. Guadalcanal was the first in a series of island battles the Americans fought as they leapfrogged their way north to Japan. Their strategy was to capture some islands and bypass others. Those bypassed would be cut off from supplies and made to "wither on the vine."

After Guadalcanal, a lengthy lull in the hostilities ensued as the Americans built up their forces in the Pacific. When the American advance resumed in November 1943, Japanese military leaders called upon their soldiers to die for their homeland. Japanese pilots known as **kamikazes** volunteered for suicide missions, crashing their bomb-laden aircraft into Allied bases and ships. The Japanese were far from ready to surrender.

SECTION 4 REVIEW

Recall
1. **Define:** kamikaze
2. **Identify:** Erwin Rommel, Bernard Montgomery, Dwight Eisenhower, Pietro Badoglio, Douglas MacArthur
3. **Locate:** Find Stalingrad on the map on page 791. Why was the Battle of Stalingrad a major turning point in World War II?

Critical Thinking
4. **Examine:** Why did Stalin press the Allies to establish a second front in Europe?
5. **Analyze:** How did Hitler's decisions contribute to Germany's defeats in both Stalingrad and North Africa?

Applying Concepts
6. **Conflict:** Why did the Allies decide to "leapfrog" their way to Japan rather than launch a direct attack against the Japanese islands?

Allied Victories

At a conference in Washington, D.C., in May 1943, Roosevelt and Churchill decided that the Allies would invade Normandy, a province of northwestern France on the English Channel, the following spring. When Stalin, Churchill, and Roosevelt met in Tehran, Iran, in November of that year, the Soviet leader learned that the Allies would finally be opening a second front in Europe. He promised to start a Soviet offensive on the eastern front at the same time as the invasion of France occurred.

D-Day

No other offensive in history was as large and carefully planned as Operation Overlord, the Allied plan to land troops in France. Under the direction of General Eisenhower, the Allies assembled a force of 150,000 soldiers, 5,300 ships, and 12,000 planes in southern England in early 1944 in preparation for the invasion. Although the Germans expected an invasion, they did not know when or where it would occur. As a result, they spread their forces thinly along the Channel coast of France.

The Allies set the day of attack, or D-Day, for June 5, but bad weather forced a 24-hour postponement. Finally, in the early morning of June 6, large convoys sailed from the Isle of Wight to the Normandy coast. Royal Air Force bombers attacked the German coast-defense guns, and at midnight three airborne divisions parachuted into France to assist the seaborne assault. At dawn, landing craft with infantry, tanks, and other weapons moved toward the coast as destroyers and battleships pounded the beaches. Then the infantry waded ashore.

Despite the confusion of the fighting and the heavy German resistance, the invasion was a great success. The Allies now had a foothold in western Europe from which they could launch an effective drive against Germany. By the beginning of July 1944, more than 1 million troops and massive amounts of supplies poured into northern France.

On July 25 the Americans broke through the German line. By early August, American tank commander General George Patton and his forces were racing across northern France through open countryside. At the same time, General de Gaulle ordered his Free French forces to advance on Paris, where 10 days earlier members of the French Resistance had risen up against their German occupiers. On August 25, 1944, de Gaulle entered Paris, a free city for the first time in four years.

Victory over Germany

Months before the Allies invaded Normandy, the Red Army was advancing steadily toward Germany from the east, recovering one Soviet city after another. In January 1944, it finally broke the siege of Leningrad. During the 890-day siege, more than 800,000 of the city's inhabitants had died from cold, starvation, or German bombs. By the spring of 1944 the Soviets had liberated the Crimea and the Ukraine as well. In July they crossed the Polish frontier and soon stood on the outskirts of Poland's capital city, Warsaw.

With Soviet troops approaching the city, the Polish Resistance rose up against the Germans on August 1 and fought them in the streets of the capital. In retaliation, the Germans destroyed much of the city and killed more than 250,000 Poles. Because the Polish resisters were anti-Communist, Stalin did nothing to help them, nor would he allow the British to airlift in

Learning from Photographs *Landing craft and supply ships crowd the Normandy coast in northern France in this colored photograph of D-Day. In three days more than 4,000 landing craft put ashore 185,000 troops and 20,000 vehicles.* **What was the Allied invasion of France called?**

supplies. This action embittered the Poles and renewed the West's suspicions that Stalin wanted to extend his control over eastern Europe.

On August 23 Romania surrendered to the Soviets. This victory opened the Balkans to the advancing Soviet forces. Shortly thereafter, Bulgaria sued for peace and joined the war on the Soviet side. By October 1944, the Soviets controlled almost all of east-central Europe.

While the Soviets advanced through eastern Europe, the Allies attacked Germany itself in September 1944. Despite the Allied gains and the devastating bombing of Germany, Hitler insisted that Germany would never surrender. Although most of the German people remained loyal to Hitler, resistance to his leadership had grown among his top military leaders. Two months earlier, several of his generals had even plotted to take his life. Colonel Klaus von Stauffenberg placed a bomb under a conference table in the "Wolf's Lair," Hitler's headquarters in East Prussia. Although the bomb exploded just a few feet away, the *Führer* escaped serious injury.

Despite the increasing inevitability of an Allied victory, Hitler was convinced that a surprise offensive might still reverse the Allied advance. Over his generals' objections, he ordered a last, desperate offensive in mid-December 1944. In the famous Battle of the Bulge, the Germans cut through the center of the American forces, creating a great bulge in the Allied line of troops. The Allies finally checked the German drive at Bastogne, Belgium, and in January 1945 they stormed across the Rhine River, Germany's historic defensive barrier. By April they reached the Elbe River and met Soviet troops at Torgau.

On May 8, 1945, V-E (victory in Europe) Day, the Germans surrendered unconditionally. The war in Europe had formally come to an end. The end had also come for the Fascist dictators. Italian partisans had shot Mussolini, and Hitler had committed suicide in his bunker, a fortified underground chamber, in Berlin.

Yalta and Potsdam

In February 1945 Roosevelt, Churchill, Stalin, and their chief advisers had met at Yalta, a resort on the Black Sea in Crimea. Because it was clear that the end of the war was at hand, the participants discussed issues affecting postwar Europe. The Allied leaders agreed to divide Germany, as well as the capital city of Berlin, into four zones that Britain, France, the United States, and the Soviet Union would occupy and

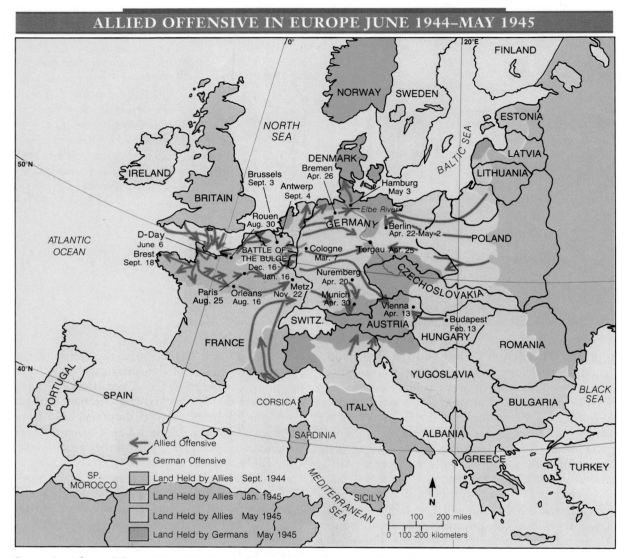

Learning from Maps *From D-Day in June 1944 to its surrender in May 1945, Germany was in full retreat on both the western and eastern fronts.* **Where did the one German offensive occur during this period?**

administer. They also agreed "to disarm and disband all German armed forces . . . to remove or destroy all German military equipment . . . to bring all war criminals to just and swift punishment and . . . wipe out the Nazi party."

Because Winston Churchill and Franklin Roosevelt feared that Stalin intended to establish Communist governments in eastern Europe, they pressured him to hold free elections in the Soviet-occupied countries. In return, they gave Stalin the eastern part of Poland. The Western leaders were also eager to get Stalin to declare war on Japan. They feared that unless Russia joined the Japanese war, the war in the Pacific would last another two years. Stalin agreed to join the war, but in return he asked for and got the Kurile Islands and the southern part of Sakhalin Island.

Six months later the Allied leaders met again at Potsdam in Germany, but by this time some of the key participants had changed. After Franklin Roosevelt died in April, Harry Truman succeeded him as president. And though Churchill was there at the opening, his Conservative party lost the general election, and Clement Attlee of the Labour party replaced him as prime minister halfway through the conference. The atmosphere at Potsdam was also quite different from that at Yalta. Although the Allies made plans for the occupation of Germany and issued an ultimatum to Japan demanding unconditional surrender, more issues were raised than were settled. New tensions over the future of the European continent were beginning to pull apart the wartime alliance.

Victory over Japan

By the early summer of 1945, it was clear that an Allied victory over Japan was inevitable. American planes had been bombing Japanese cities since the end of 1944. In October, at the Battle of Leyte Gulf in the Philippines, Japan lost most of what remained of its naval power.

Still the Japanese fought on. In early 1945 Japanese and American troops engaged in two of the fiercest battles of the Pacific campaign for

CONNECTIONS: SCIENCE AND TECHNOLOGY

The Atomic Bomb

The atomic bomb dropped on Hiroshima completely destroyed large parts of the city.

At 9:15 on the morning of August 6, 1945, the United States dropped the "Little Boy" on Hiroshima, Japan. The bomb was the first atomic weapon ever used in actual warfare. The massive destruction this bomb caused shocked the world and changed the course of modern history.

The first atomic bomb had its roots in scientific discoveries made in the late 1800s and early 1900s. Especially important to its development was the work of physicist Albert Einstein.

In early 1939 scientists succeeded in splitting atoms for the first time. Three years later, in 1942, the United States government set up the Manhattan Project, a top-secret research and development program to build an atomic bomb. A team of scientists worked around the clock to devise the complicated system needed to set off an atomic explosion.

Knowing it was crucial that they beat the Germans in this deadly race spurred the efforts of these scientists.

In the early morning hours of July 16, 1945, scientists watched from a safe distance as the first atomic bomb was detonated in a remote part of New Mexico. But many of the scientists who witnessed this historic event were as sobered as they were cheered by the results. They knew they had created the most terrible weapon in the history of warfare. And they knew that the world would never be the same again.

Making the Connection

1. Whose scientific work made the development of the atomic bomb possible?
2. Why did the scientists working to create the atomic bomb feel so much pressure to succeed?

control of two islands: Iwo Jima and Okinawa. Despite putting up fierce resistance, the Japanese lost both battles. The victories were extremely important to the Allies because they now controlled air bases within reach of Japan.

On July 26, 1945, the United States issued another ultimatum to Japan demanding unconditional surrender. When the Japanese refused to accept defeat, the United States decided to use a new secret weapon—the atomic bomb—to swiftly end the war. Earlier, President Truman had written his family about the fateful decision:

I certainly regret the necessity of wiping out whole populations because of the 'pigheadedness' of the leaders of a nation and, for your information, I am not going to [use the atomic bomb] unless it becomes absolutely necessary. My object is to save as many American lives as possible. . . .

On August 6, 1945, the Americans dropped the first atomic bomb used in warfare on Hiroshima, a center of the Japanese munitions industry. The blast leveled more than 60 percent of the city. When the Japanese still refused to surrender, the Americans dropped another atomic bomb on the port city of Nagasaki. The destruction there was even greater than in Hiroshima. Altogether, nearly 200,000 Japanese lost their lives in three days.

After the bombings, Japan's Emperor Hirohito proclaimed that "the unendurable must be endured," and on August 14, 1945, Japan surrendered. Truman declared August 15 V-J (Victory in Japan) Day. On September 2, Japan officially surrendered. The war was over.

Effects of the War

World War II left large parts of Europe and Asia in ruins. The use of deadly new weapons made World War II the most destructive war in history. The Allies dropped thousands of tons of incendiary and explosive bombs in Japan and Germany. The effects were devastating. In Tokyo alone, a quarter of the city's total area, nearly 16 square miles, was burned out and more than 267,000 buildings were destroyed.

In Germany, too, the bombings caused enormous destruction. By war's end the Allies had reduced Mannheim, Frankfurt, Hanover, Kassel, Dresden, and Berlin to rubble. England did not escape the destruction. The Germans targeted almost every major city in the country for bombing, but the hardest hit areas were London, the port cities along the south coast, and the manufacturing towns in the Midlands.

More than 70 million people fought in World War II. The casualties among the military and civilian populations were staggering. The Soviet Union lost 22 million people, Germany almost 8 million, and Japan 2 million. In addition, 6 million Jews died in concentration camps. Altogether, some 55 million people died.

Because of the widespread destruction, as many as 12 million people were left homeless after the war. Food, medicine, and clothing were in short supply. One Japanese student recalls life after the war: "When winter came we were really miserable. We had neither food nor clothing. . . . We were told to go to the countryside and find food wherever we could. There was nothing in Tokyo." For millions of people the suffering and hardships lasted long after the war's end.

SECTION 5 REVIEW

Recall
1. **Identify:** Harry Truman
2. **Explain:** In what sense was Operation Overlord "unmatched in history"?

Critical Thinking
3. **Examine:** Why was the war so difficult for the Germans to fight following the invasion of Normandy?
4. **Analyze:** Why do you think the Allies made the decision to divide Germany and Berlin into four sectors after the war was over?

Applying Concepts
5. **Innovation:** World War II was even more costly in the destruction of human life and property than World War I. What factors made World War II the most destructive war in the history of the world?

EVALUATING AMBIGUOUS STATEMENTS

What would your first reaction be if someone said to you, "In that outfit, you're really going to attract attention." Initially, you might be flattered, thinking the person meant to compliment you. On second thought, however, you might think that the statement was a criticism.

Explanation

Situations such as the one above happen because someone made an *ambiguous or equivocal statement.* An ambiguous statement is one that is unclear or misleading by accident. An equivocal statement is one that is unclear or misleading on purpose.

Sometimes an ambiguous statement is unclear because of poor use of grammar. Consider this sentence: "The League of Nations suggested to the Allies that they meet to discuss the matter." The two meanings in the sentence are not intended. The confusion is due to the unclear use of the pronoun *they.*

An equivocal statement often represents an attempt to avoid a clear position on an issue. Consider this statement that might have been given by a member of the French Underground during World War II: "The Underground is composed of a large network of citizens." The phrase *large network* is not specific, leading the listener to determine the size of the

French force without a sense of how large the network really is.

Sometimes, the effect of an equivocal statement is to disguise the truth, as in this statement made by Adolf Hitler during the mid-1930s when he was trying to expand Germany's control over Europe: "German-Austria must return to the great mother country. . . . One blood demands one Reich."

To identify an ambiguous or equivocal statement use the following steps:

- Examine the statement carefully and determine whether it can have more than one meaning.
- Look for pronouns that do not have clear antecedents.
- Identify vague words or phrases, such as *large*, or *with the usual methods.*
- Identify who is speaking or writing, and determine his or her personal viewpoint.
- Identify the audience intended to hear or see the statement.
- Look for a motive to mislead readers or listeners.
- Determine what statements are ambiguous or equivocal.

Example

Before taking power in Germany, Hitler called for *lebensraum,* the German word for "living space." To determine whether this term is ambiguous or equivocal, first decide whether the word can have more than one meaning.

How much space is needed for living? Is there an amount generally agreed upon to be the fair share of every human or nation? Clearly, Hitler's term *living space* is so vague that it can be called ambiguous language.

Next, consider who is speaking. The speaker was Hitler, whose view was that Germany deserved to rule all of its neighbors and, indeed, the world. The audience included neighboring countries that did not want to be ruled by Germany. Keeping the other countries unaware of their danger was to Hitler's advantage. The term *lebensraum,* then, can be considered ambiguous as well as equivocal.

Application

Using the outlined steps, analyze the use and meaning of each term below. Determine if the term is ambiguous or equivocal, or both.

1. a cash-and-carry policy (Chapter 30, Section 2, pages 783-784)
2. a total solution to the Jewish question (Chapter 30, Section 3, page 786)

Practice

Turn to Practicing Skills on page 801 of the Chapter Review for further practice in recognizing ambiguous and equivocal statements.

CHAPTER 30 REVIEW

HISTORICAL SIGNIFICANCE

In addition to inflicting greater suffering and physical devastation than any other war in history, World War II dramatically shifted the world balance of power. European nations lost their empires and much of their preeminence in world affairs after the war. The United States and the Soviet Union, on the other hand, emerged as superpowers and rivals. Tension between the two nations grew rapidly as the Soviet Union extended its sphere of influence over most of Eastern Europe, and the United States funneled in millions of dollars to help rebuild Western Europe. Mistrust and hostility clouded Soviet–American relations for the next 40 years, and the tension of these decades was made worse by the threat of nuclear war that now hovered in the background of any political crisis involving the two superpowers.

Although tension between the two superpowers cast a chill over the world, one hopeful development after the second world war was the establishment of the United Nations, a new international organization dedicated to preserving and protecting world peace. Despite their rivalry, the United States and the Soviet Union both joined the United Nations, assuring the two nations of a neutral forum in which to discuss their differences.

SUMMARY

For a summary of Chapter 30, see the Unit 7 Synopsis on pages 802-805.

USING KEY TERMS

A. Write the definition of each key term below. Then write one or two sentences showing how the terms are related to the concept of cooperation.

1. cash-and-carry policy
2. collective security
3. Lend-Lease Act

B. Write the key term that best completes each sentence.

a. appeasement	d. kamikaze
b. blitz	e. sanctions
c. blitzkrieg	f. scorched-earth policy

4. After the invasion of Ethiopia, the League of Nations imposed economic ___ against Italy.
5. German bombers pounded London and other industrial cities in the ___ .
6. Stalin tried to thwart the German invasion with his ___ .
7. The German ___ devastated Poland in a few weeks.
8. Chamberlain's policy of ___ led to his fall from power.
9. Japanese military leaders ordered ___ to fly their planes into Allied ships.

REVIEWING FACTS

1. **Explain:** Why was the League of Nations ineffective in stopping Japanese a nd Italian aggression?
2. **List:** What countries did Germany occupy before the outbreak of war?
3. **Identify:** What was the immediate cause of World War II?
4. **Explain:** Why did Japan attack Pearl Harbor?
5. **Describe:** What was the "New Order" that Hitler set out to create?

THINKING CRITICALLY

1. **Apply:** Why did the Western democracies let Hitler overrun much of Europe before trying to stop him?

2. **Analyze:** Why did the Allies wait until 1944 to open a second front?
3. **Synthesize:** If the Japanese had not bombed Pearl Harbor, would the United States have entered the war?

ANALYZING CONCEPTS

1. **Movement:** What were Hitler's objectives in Europe? What were Japan's objectives in Asia?
2. **Cooperation:** What did the Allies hope to accomplish at Yalta and Potsdam?
3. **Conflict:** What were the long-range causes of World War II?
4. **Innovation:** What effect did new technology have on the war?

PRACTICING SKILLS

1. Refer to the first two paragraphs of "Hitler Looks to the West" on page 779. Decide whether the phrase *protection of the Reich* was ambiguous or equivocal. Explain your answer.
2. Find in a news report or advertisement at least one example of each of the following: simple ambiguous language; equivocal language. State at least two interpretations for each example of simple ambiguity. Suggest the motivation for each example of equivocation.

GEOGRAPHY IN HISTORY

1. **Movement:** Refer to the map on page 793. Judging from the directions of their advances, what were the main objectives of the Japanese?
2. **Movement:** Refer to the map on page 781. In what order did European countries fall to Germany?

TRACING CHRONOLOGY

Refer to the time line below to answer these questions.
1. How long after Italy invaded Ethiopia did World War II begin?
2. In what sense did events in 1941 greatly expand the scope of the war?

LINKING PAST AND PRESENT

1. To avert war with Germany, the European democracies allowed Hitler to occupy Czechoslovakia. How did the United Nations react to Iraq's occupation of Kuwait in 1990? Do you think the United Nations made the correct decision, or do you think the situation is different from that in the 1930s? Explain.
2. After World War II, several historians and publications bestowed on Churchill the title "Man of the Century." Do you think he still deserves the title? Explain.

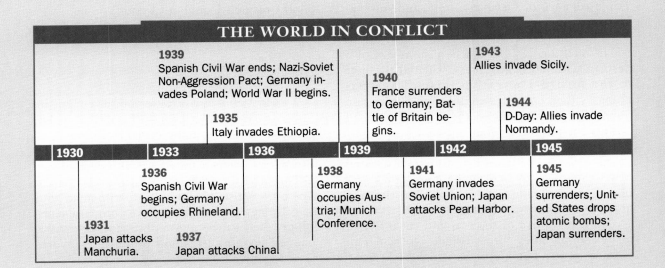

THE WORLD IN CONFLICT

1939 Spanish Civil War ends; Nazi-Soviet Non-Aggression Pact; Germany invades Poland; World War II begins.

1935 Italy invades Ethiopia.

1943 Allies invade Sicily.

1940 France surrenders to Germany; Battle of Britain begins.

1944 D-Day: Allies invade Normandy.

| 1930 | 1933 | 1936 | 1939 | 1942 | 1945 |

1936 Spanish Civil War begins; Germany occupies Rhineland.

1931 Japan attacks Manchuria.

1937 Japan attacks China

1938 Germany occupies Austria; Munich Conference.

1941 Germany invades Soviet Union; Japan attacks Pearl Harbor.

1945 Germany surrenders; United States drops atomic bombs; Japan surrenders.

UNIT 7 SYNOPSIS

After a century of relative peace in Europe, two great wars engulfed the world in the first half of the 1900s. World War I brought about the collapse of once mighty empires, triggered a revolution in Russia, and left much of Europe in chaos. This disarray, the bitterness created by the peace treaties that ended the war, and the worldwide depression that started in 1929 contributed to the rise of totalitarian dictatorships in Germany and Italy and once again set the nations of Europe on a course toward war. When it arrived, World War II proved to be the most destructive in history and ended with two superpowers in the world: the United States and the Soviet Union.

CHAPTER 27
World War I

In the late 1800s, nationalism and imperialism created intense rivalries between European powers. Aware that their policies could lead to war, the nations of Europe built powerful military machines and established new alliances. France, Britain, and Russia together formed the Triple Entente in the early 1900s to offset the Triple Alliance of Germany, Italy, and Austria-Hungary.

The conflict between the two armed camps began on June 28, 1914, when members of a Serbian nationalist group assassinated the heir to the Austro-Hungarian throne. Austria-Hungary thereupon declared war on Serbia, and bound by their alliances, the other European powers entered the conflict.

For four years war raged on land, at sea, and in the air. The belligerents used sophisticated new weapons, such as machine guns, tanks, airplanes, and poison gas. In the west the war quickly settled into a stalemate.

To win control of the seas and cut off Germany's supply lines, Great Britain blockaded all German ports. The Germans struck back, however, with U-boats, or submarines. After German U-boats sank four American merchant ships in 1917, President Woodrow Wilson asked Congress for a declaration of war. It was America's intervention that proved to be the turning point of the war, as the United States gave the Allies much-needed human and material resources. In November 1918, Germany finally surrendered.

The war changed the map of Europe. The Ottoman and the Austro-Hungarian empires ceased to exist and new nations rose from the breakup. The peace settlements signed at Versailles, moreover, weakened Germany and imposed a heavy financial burden on its people.

The Russian Revolution   In Russia, the war brought about the fall of the tsarist autocracy. The Russian people endured great hardships in the war, and public anger against the government mounted. In early 1917 spontaneous riots and protests forced Tsar Nicholas II to abdicate. Later that year the Bolsheviks, a Marxist political party led by Vladimir Ilyich Lenin, overthrew the provisional government that had replaced the tsar. The Bolsheviks were eventually victorious in the civil war that followed, and Russia became a Communist state.

CHAPTER 28
Between Two Fires

World War I was a watershed event in the 1900s. It carried away the old political order, shattered traditions, and ushered in an era of experimentation in culture and customs. In the postwar era, women found a new independence and adopted new fashions and morals. At the same time, artists of all kinds experimented with radically new styles. Innovative forms of technology, such as the automobile and the radio, changed people's lives and brought the world closer together.

The United States came out of the war in far better shape than its allies. The 1920s were boom years for the American economy, and an atmosphere of exuberance and frivolity earned the decade the name "Roaring Twenties." But when the stock market crashed in 1929, the nation fell into a major depression that had worldwide repercussions.

The Western Democracies   Although the war and the depression also had a terrible effect on Britain and France, democratic traditions there were firmly entrenched. Thus, unlike Germany and Italy, these nations were able to survive assaults from the left and right. Great Britain, however, lost its privileged position in world trade and was no longer a leading economic power. France, too, faced severe economic problems after the war, and Communist, Fascist, and Socialist parties vied for power. In 1934, however, the Communists joined forces with the Socialists to thwart a Fascist takeover. While in power, the Popular Front, as it was called, instituted many social reforms.

The Rise of Dictators   World War I shattered the economies of Germany and Italy. Amid political and economic chaos in Italy, Benito Mussolini seized power and in 1922 established a Fascist dictatorship. In Germany Adolf Hitler and the Nazi party gained an audience by blaming the Communists and Jews for Germany's economic woes. In 1933 the Nazi party won control of the German parliament, and Hitler moved quickly to crush his opponents and establish a dictatorship.

Dramatic changes were also occurring in Russia. Seven years of world and civil war had devastated the country. In 1921 Lenin moved to consolidate Communist control. After Lenin's death in 1924, Joseph Stalin won a political struggle with his rival, Leon Trotsky, and established a brutal dictatorship in the Soviet Union. Beginning in the late 1920s, Stalin set about putting Russian industries and agriculture under state control. In a succession of purges in the 1930s, Stalin also eliminated his opponents from positions of leadership.

CHAPTER 29

Nationalism in Asia, Africa, and Latin America

In spite of the turmoil created by the World War I, the European powers retained control of their colonial territories in the Middle East and Africa. But in the years following World War I, nationalist forces in these Middle Eastern and African territories began the long struggle for independence.

Learning from Art   *This painting shows well-known characters from one of the most popular new forms of entertainment during the 1920s—the movies.* **What other technological advances changed daily life in industrialized nations during this decade?**

The Middle East, Africa, and India The old Ottoman Empire of Turkey, weakened by discord and external threats, crumbled during the war. After General Mustafa Kemal repulsed a Greek invasion in 1922, the Turks deposed the Ottoman sultan and formed a new government with Kemal as president. Persians, too, won independence and renamed the country Iran.

Although Great Britain granted Egypt complete independence in 1936, it secured its control of Palestine and continued to exploit Kenya and Nigeria. And despite India's contributions to its war effort, Britain moved to quash dissent in that country. As a result, nationalist leader Mohandas Gandhi organized nonviolent protests against British rule.

East Asia In China the nationalist Guomindang army led by Chiang Kai-shek joined with Chinese Communists to overthrow the warlords who had ruled the country since 1916. Then Chiang turned on his Communist allies and drove them into a remote part of China. When the Japanese threatened to invade in the 1930s, however, Chiang again joined with the Communists to repulse the invaders.

In Japan military leaders became a powerful force in the 1920s. Believing that Japan could solve the problems of an expanding population and limited resources by acquiring new territories, these leaders launched the invasion of China without their government's approval.

Latin America Although most Latin American countries had achieved political independence long before the 1920s, they remained economically dependent on the United States and other countries. In 1933 President Franklin Roosevelt proclaimed a "good neighbor" policy and withdrew American troops from Nicaragua and Haiti, where they were protecting American business interests. This policy eased Latin America's fears of the United States, but tensions increased again in 1938 when Mexico began the move toward economic nationalism.

CHAPTER 30
World War II

The aggressive policies and imperialist aims of the totalitarian regimes that came to power in the 1920s and 1930s increasingly threatened world peace. The League of Nations, which the Western democracies had formed to prevent aggression, proved powerless to stop it.

Learning from Photographs *Nazi dictator Adolf Hitler salutes columns of German storm troopers at a Nazi party rally.* **How did Hitler rise to power in Germany?**

Hitler set about to bring all of Europe under Nazi control. When he threatened to invade Czechoslovakia, British Prime Minister Neville Chamberlain negotiated a compromise that gave Germany control of the Sudetenland. But appeasement only whetted Hitler's appetite. Six months later, he seized all of Czechoslovakia. Convinced that the West would do nothing to stop him, Hitler negotiated a Nonaggression Pact with the Soviet Union and then attacked Poland on September 1, 1939. Two days later, Britain and France declared war on Germany.

Waging War   After taking control of Norway and Denmark, German troops invaded the Netherlands in May, raced through Belgium and northern France, and pushed the British and French forces to the English Channel.

In the summer and fall of 1940, Great Britain won a crucial victory over Germany in the Battle of Britain. Although Britain now stood alone against Hitler, isolationists in the United States kept the nation out of the war. The American government did, however, supply Britain with war equipment. By 1941 German forces had overrun all of Eastern Europe, and in June, invaded the Soviet Union.

To prevent the United States from interfering with its expansionist aims in East Asia and the Pacific, Japan attacked the U.S. fleet at Pearl Harbor. The attack brought the United States into the war.

Not until 1942 did the tide begin to turn in favor of the Allies. Americans defeated the Japanese navy at the Battle of Midway. In 1943, Soviet forces repulsed a German attack on Stalingrad, and British and American forces defeated the Germans in North Africa. From there,

Learning from Photographs *Many Londoners sought shelter in underground, or subway, stations to escape the German blitz in the fall of 1940.* **During what famous battle did the blitz take place?**

the Allies launched an invasion of Sicily and the Italian peninsula.

On June 6, 1944, Allied forces invaded Normandy in France and pushed toward Germany as Soviet troops advanced in Eastern Europe. In April 1945 the Allies met at the Elbe River, and the following month Germany surrendered. When Japanese leaders refused to surrender, the United States dropped its new secret weapon, the atomic bomb, on Hiroshima and Nagasaki in August. Days later Japan surrendered.

The war was over, but much of Europe and Asia lay in ruins and tens of millions of people had died. The Allies divided Germany and its capital into four sections, each of which was occupied by one of the powers. But tensions between the Soviet Union and its allies increased, and the wartime alliance began to unravel.

SURVEYING THE UNIT

1. **Explain:** Why was World War I a watershed event in the 1900s?
2. **Illustrate:** How did nationalist movements in Europe, Asia, Africa, and Latin America contribute to world tensions during the 1920s and 1930s?
3. **Making Comparisons:** Compare and contrast the causes of World Wars I and II.

UNIT 7 REVIEW

REVIEWING THE MAIN IDEAS

1. **Identify:** What events and ideas influenced art, music, and literature in the 1920s and 1930s?
2. **List:** What problems confronted the countries of Western Europe after World War I?
3. **Explain:** What events contributed to global tensions in the 1920s and 1930s?

THINKING CRITICALLY

1. **Apply:** What steps did the European powers take to prevent a second world war? Why were their efforts unsuccessful?
2. **Analyze:** Why did democracy survive in Britain and France after World War I, but not in Italy and Germany?
3. **Synthesize:** Create a chart comparing the peace settlements made after World War I with those made after World War II. How did the peace settlements contribute to global tensions?
4. **Evaluate:** Compare the methods Gandhi used to shape the independence movement in India with the methods nationalist leaders employed in Kenya. Which method do you think had the greater chance of success? Explain your answer.
5. **Evaluate:** Compare Great Britain's attitude toward its territories in the 1920s and 1930s with Germany's expansionist policy during this period. How were their goals similar? How did they differ?

A GLOBAL PERSPECTIVE

Refer to the time line on pages 688–689 to answer these questions.

1. Why did women in Russia probably win the right to vote in 1917?
2. How long before the outbreak of World War II did Robert Goddard launch the first liquid-propelled rocket?

3. How many years passed between the outbreak of World War I and the outbreak of World War II?
4. How long after Hitler came to power did Jews lose their citizenship rights?
5. How long after Enrico Fermi produced the first controlled nuclear chain reaction did the United States drop the first atomic bomb on Hiroshima?
6. What two influential literary works appeared on the scene not long after the conclusion of World War I?
7. What was happening in the world when Charlie Chaplin made *The Great Dictator*?

LINKING PAST AND PRESENT

1. In the 1920s and 1930s, the League of Nations failed to stop Japanese and Italian aggression. How has the United Nations reacted to Soviet aggression in Afghanistan and Iraqi aggression in Kuwait? Were these actions more successful? Why or why not?
2. In 1933 President Roosevelt proclaimed a "good neighbor" policy for Latin America. Is this policy still in effect? Describe current relations between some Latin American countries and the United States.
3. In the years after World War I, isolationists kept the United States from joining the League of Nations and delayed America's entrance into World War II. Is there any evidence of isolationism in the United States today?
4. In 1920 women in the United States won the right to vote. How has the role of women changed since that time? What issues concern women today?
5. In 1929 the stock market crashed in the United States, setting off a worldwide depression. What caused the crash? What is the state of today's economy? Do you think a crash could happen again? Explain your answer.

ANALYZING VISUALS

One method by which Adolf Hitler rose to power and maintained the support of the German people was through the use of propaganda. As leader of the Nazi party, Hitler organized massive rallies and published books and pamphlets promoting Nazi ideals. Among the many items distributed and used to sway popular opinion were, of course, posters. The poster shown here, from the 1930s, praises a German students' league connected with the Nazi party. The slogan reads: "The German student fights for the Führer and the people." The artist who made the poster depicted a strong Aryan youth holding a German flag with the Nazi swastika. The student shown here, held up as the ideal of the "pure" German race, is the picture of health, strength, and goodness.

1. Why would a poster like this one have appealed to some German citizens around 1930?
2. What were the consequences of Hitler's promotion of the so-called Aryan race?
3. What visual characteristics of this poster make it a successful piece of propaganda?
4. Are you familiar with any forms of political propaganda in today's world? Explain.

USING LITERATURE

Refer to the excerpt from By Any Other Name *on pages 766–769 to answer these questions.*

1. Premila and Santha's mother refused to send her children to a British-run school because ". . . you can take a Britisher away from his home for a lifetime and he still remains insular." What did she mean? Did the girls' experiences at the Anglo-Indian school support her statement? Use examples to support your answer.
2. What does this excerpt reveal about the attitude of the British toward the Indians?
3. Santha stated, "Even at that age it was apparent to all of us that friendship with the English or Anglo-Indian children was out of the question." Why was this attitude so

apparent? In light of this statement, why do you think the Indians' struggle for independence was so long and difficult?

WRITING ABOUT HISTORY

1. Choose what you think is the most important event in the period 1919 to 1945. Then explain your choice in writing.
2. The convictions for murder of Italian-born anarchists Nicola Sacco and Bartolomeo Vanzetti in 1921 stirred a worldwide protest. Write a report about the trial and the reasons for these men's convictions. Explain what this event revealed about attitudes in the United States in the postwar era.
3. Choose one of the leaders you read about in this chapter. Write a biography of the person. Include information about the person's training and experience that prepared him or her for a leadership role.

UNIT 8
The Contemporary World

1945–Present

"The problems of victory are more agreeable than those of defeat, but they are no less difficult."

*W*inston Churchill accurately summarized the problem of the post–World War II world. The victors had to rebuild not only their own countries but also the defeated nations, caring for the victims of war, redrawing national boundaries, and forming new governments—in effect redesigning the modern world. Ironically, Churchill's words also prophesied the fate of the European colonies, which, a decade later, would launch wars of independence against Great Britain and the other imperial powers.

A GLOBAL CHRONOLOGY

	1945	1955	1965
Political Sphere	**1950** Korean War begins.	**1962** Cuban missile crisis	**1967** Six-Day War
Scientific Sphere		**1954** Salk vaccine ends polio.	**1969** U.S. lands first astronauts on the moon.
Cultural & Social Sphere	**1945** *Animal Farm*, by George Orwell	**1951** Jackie Robinson becomes first black in major-league baseball.	

Family Group, *1944*
bronze sculpture by
Henry Moore

1975

1973 U.S.
leaves Vietnam;
Arab oil embargo

1971 Invention of
microprocessor starts
computer revolution.

1985

1989
Berlin
Wall falls.

1991
Gulf War
ends.

1986 Disaster at U.S.S.R.'s Chernobyl
nuclear power plant leaks radiation into
the atmosphere.

1995

1978 John Paul II becomes
first pope from Poland.

The Cold War

*I*n 1948 the city of West Berlin was an island in the middle of a hostile sea. The Soviets had cut off all land routes into the German city in the hope of driving out the Western Allies. For 11 months the United States airlifted food to 2 million stranded residents in West Berlin.

One day while his plane was on the ground in West Berlin, an American pilot, Lieutenant Gale S. Halvorsen, met a group of German children. Although they had had few sweets to eat during the blockade, they did not beg. He told them to wait for his plane at the end of the runway at Tempelhof Airport the next day. The children appeared, and, to their delight, packets of gum and chocolate showered down from Halvorsen's plane.

Soon other pilots joined "Operation Little Vittles," and the crowds of children grew. The children named Halvorsen *Der Shokolade Flieger*—the Chocolate Pilot.

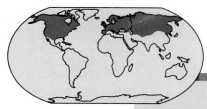

CHAPTER PREVIEW

Key Terms to Define: cold war, satellites, iron curtain, containment, peaceful coexistence, intercontinental ballistic missiles, dissidents, welfare state

People to Meet: George C. Marshall, Nikita S. Khrushchev, Leonid I. Brezhnev, Josip Broz Tito, Clement Attlee, Charles de Gaulle, Konrad Adenauer, Joseph McCarthy, Dwight D. Eisenhower, John F. Kennedy, Lyndon B. Johnson

Places to Discover: Berlin, Federal Republic of Germany, German Democratic Republic, Berlin Wall, Camp David

Brandenburg Gate at the Berlin Wall

Objectives to Learn:
1. What key events caused and aggravated the cold war?
2. How did postwar recovery in Eastern Europe differ from that in Western Europe?
3. What effects did the cold war have on politics in the United States?

Concepts to Understand:
- Conflict—Democratic and Communist regimes compete for influence in Europe. Sections 1,2
- Cooperation—New alliances form among democratic nations and among Communist nations in Europe. Sections 2,3,4

811

Increasing Tensions

World War II had weakened the nations of Europe to the point where their influence in world affairs was greatly diminished. The United States and the Soviet Union emerged as the most powerful nations in the world. Differences in political beliefs and policies soon pulled the two countries apart and led to a struggle between them known as the **cold war**. In the cold war, each superpower sought world influence by means short of total war, such as the threat of force, the use of propaganda, and the sending of military and economic aid to weaker nations.

Planning for Peacetime

At the end of World War II, the Allies looked forward to an era of tranquillity in foreign affairs. To handle future global problems, they created the United Nations, a permanent international organization to replace the League of Nations. The purpose of the United Nations was to maintain peace by guaranteeing the security of member nations. It would foster good relations among nations based on the principles of equal rights and self-determination. It would also encourage cooperation in economic, cultural, and humanitarian problems.

The United Nations As planned at the Yalta Conference, representatives from 50 nations met in San Francisco on April 25, 1945, to draft the Charter of the United Nations (UN). The Charter was completed and signed in June.

The organization, headquartered in New York, held its first sessions 4 months later. Although the Charter provided for 6 major bodies, it assigned the bulk of power to only 2 of them—the Security Council and the General Assembly. The Security Council, which decided

diplomatic, political, and military disputes, was made up of 11 members. The 5 permanent members were Great Britain, China, France, the United States, and the Soviet Union. Each was given the right to veto any Security Council decision. The other 6 members served 2-year terms. The General Assembly, the policy-making body, was made up of representatives from all the member nations of the organization. Each nation had 1 vote.

The third body, the Economic and Social Council, was created to oversee the fights against poverty, ignorance, and disease. The fourth, the International Court of Justice, was established to deal with international legal disputes. The fifth, the Trusteeship Council, was created to promote the welfare of people in colonial territories and to help them toward self-government. The sixth, the Secretariat, was created to handle the administrative work of the United Nations.

During the postwar period, the UN effectively resolved many crises. However, the right of veto granted the Security Council's permanent members rendered the UN powerless to resolve any dispute involving the two superpowers: the United States and the Soviet Union. The United Nations became deadlocked. It was criticized as being a "debating society"—far from what the signers of the Charter had hoped it would be.

Cracks in the Alliance While the United Nations became paralyzed, the wartime alliance of nations also began to disintegrate. Tensions began to develop even before the end of the war, as the Allies met to discuss the future distribution of power in peacetime Europe.

It was clear that the United States would assume the leading role in postwar politics. Unlike the other Allies, the United States had survived the war with its military and industrial capacity intact. Presidents Roosevelt and Truman brought this new political power to the conferences at Yalta and Potsdam in 1945, as discussed in Chapter 30.

Although Great Britain now took a secondary role to the United States, it still had an important part in the conferences—first under Prime Minister Winston Churchill, then under his successor, Clement Attlee. The Soviet Union had suffered extreme losses during the war, but because of the Soviet army's large role in liberating much of Eastern Europe, there was no doubt that Joseph Stalin would have a strong hand in reshaping the region.

The three powers came to the conferences with differing goals—goals that rapidly opened cracks in the wartime alliance. The United States and Great Britain were concerned with building democratic governments and economies in Europe. In Germany, the Western Allies saw their occupying role as temporary. They would remain only long enough to help stabilize the country; then they would withdraw,

EUROPE 1945–1955

Warsaw Pact Member
Communist Nation Outside Soviet Bloc
Neutral
NATO Member

Learning from Maps *As distrust among the Allies grew, Europe became sharply divided between the Soviet and Western spheres of influence.* **Why did the alliance disintegrate after World War II?**

Learning from Photographs *The cold war quickly paralyzed the United Nations in its early years.* **Do you think the UN could have helped prevent the establishment of Soviet satellites? Why or why not?**

leaving Germany free to determine its own political future.

The Soviets had different priorities. Historically, they had well-justified fears of invasion. In World War II alone they lost 20 million people. Stalin was determined to establish a buffer zone of friendly governments in Eastern Europe to prevent future attacks.

The Iron Curtain

Eastern Europe became the first region where Soviet and Western interests came into conflict. During the closing months of World War II, Soviet troops had captured Europe. In Albania and Yugoslavia, local Communist parties, which had led the resistance against Axis forces in their countries, took control with little help from the Soviets. In Poland, Romania, and Bulgaria, where Soviet troops were in full command, the Soviet Union aided in the formation of coalition governments that included Communists. Soon the Soviets further tightened their grip. They refused to allow free elections and eliminated freedoms of speech, religion, and the press in Bulgaria and Poland. In the next few years, the same tactics were used in other countries of Eastern Europe. Non-Communists were ousted from governments, and the Communists gained control. These nations became Soviet **satellites**, controlled by the Soviet Union.

President Roosevelt had believed that postwar cooperation with the Soviets was possible. But a few weeks before his death in April 1945, he realized that Soviet policies in Eastern Europe were undermining the spirit of the wartime alliance. During this time, a major shift in U.S.–Soviet relations was taking place, as Western perceptions of Stalin changed radically.

New Views of Stalin Although there had long been considerable mistrust of Joseph Stalin in the West, his true goals—and his brutal methods of achieving them—were not widely understood until after World War II. Gradually, "Uncle Joe"—the man that FDR had felt he could "handle"—was revealed to the West as a ruthless dictator.

Stalin was able to maintain his relatively benign image by tightly controlling information about Soviet internal affairs. Even within his own country, Stalin created an almost godlike image of himself. For example, as the Soviet Union faced serious economic problems, the government newspaper advised readers:

> *If you meet with difficulties in your work, or suddenly doubt your abilities, think of him—of Stalin—and you will find the confidence you need. If you feel tired in an hour when you should not, think of him—of Stalin—and your work will go well. If you are seeking a correct decision, think of him—of Stalin—and you will find that decision.*
>
> —From *Pravda*, February 17, 1950

However, people throughout the Soviet bloc—and eventually in the West—came to know the cold-blooded realities of Stalin's rule that stretched back to the purges of the 1930s.

Reports reached the West of prison camps and executions for those who questioned Stalin's actions. Stalin murdered many of his critics and even some supporters simply to maintain terror and ensure obedience. Scholars estimate that Stalin's holocaust against his own people resulted in the deaths of up to 20 million citizens—as many Soviets as had been killed in World War II. Since few foreigners were allowed inside the iron curtain, word of these atrocities leaked out slowly.

A Tougher Stand   While Roosevelt may have underestimated Stalin, FDR's successor, Harry Truman, took a harder line toward the Soviets. When Truman, a longtime anti-Communist, bluntly protested the Soviet Union's violation of the Yalta accords to the Soviet ambassador, Vyacheslav Molotov, Molotov replied, "I have never been talked to like that." "Carry out your agreement," Truman said, "and you won't get talked to like that."

In his tough stance toward the Soviets, Truman received the backing of British statesman Winston Churchill. In March 1946, Churchill, in a speech given in Fulton, Missouri, said: "From Stettin in the Baltic to Trieste in the Adriatic an iron curtain has descended across the

OCCUPATION OF GERMANY AND AUSTRIA 1945

Learning from Maps
The Soviets and the West had different priorities for rebuilding their occupied zones. **What were the differences?**

continent of Europe." Thereafter the phrase **iron curtain** referred to the Soviet-made barrier that split Europe into two distinct parts: non-Communist Western Europe and Communist Eastern Europe. Alarmed by Soviet moves, the Western democracies began to take steps to prevent further Soviet expansion.

Containing Communism

To counter any expansionist threat from the Soviet Union, the Truman Administration developed a new American foreign policy in 1947. The policy, known as **containment,** was intended to contain, or hold back, the spread of communism.

Through a display of firmness, President Truman hoped to keep communism inside its existing borders. He planned to carry out the containment policy by increasing U.S. military strength, sending military aid to countries threatened by communism, and giving economic aid to needy areas overseas.

The idea of containment was first presented in early 1947 by George Kennan, a State Department expert on the Soviet Union. In an article in the *Journal of Foreign Affairs*, Kennan said that the Soviets believed that communism would triumph over capitalism throughout the world. He noted that the Soviets sought to expand their territory, but that they did not want to risk war in order to do so.

Kennan therefore proposed that the United States pursue a "policy of firm containment, designed to confront the [Soviets] . . . at every point where they show signs of encroaching upon the interests" of the West. Kennan's ideas became the basis of the United States government's foreign policy for the following 30 years.

IMAGES OF THE TIME

Rebuilding Warsaw

In October 1944, the city of Warsaw, Poland, surrendered to Nazi troops. The Germans evacuated the city and methodically destroyed its remaining buildings.

Seventy-four percent of Warsaw's buildings and bridges were destroyed during World War II.

After the war, workers had to clean out the debris of the bombed-out buildings before reconstruction could begin.

The Truman Doctrine In the spring of 1947, President Truman applied the containment policy for the first time in the eastern Mediterranean. In Greece, local Communists were fighting a guerrilla war against the pro-Western monarchy. The West feared that the fall of Greece to communism would endanger Western influence in the eastern Mediterranean region. British troops had checked the Communist advance in 1946 and continued to assist the Greek monarchy afterward. But aid flowed to the Greek Communists from neighboring Yugoslavia, Bulgaria, and Albania.

Meanwhile, economic weakness at home prevented Great Britain from continuing its commitment in Greece. In February 1947, Great Britain informed Truman of this fact and asked the United States to assume British responsibilities in the area. Truman and Secretary of State George Marshall decided that the United States would take Britain's place in defending the eastern Mediterranean. In March, Truman asked Congress for a $400 million aid program for Greece and Turkey. In asking Congress for support, Truman made a new statement of foreign policy that became known as the Truman Doctrine. He stated:

> *I believe that it must be the policy of the United States to support free peoples who are resisting attempted subjugation by armed minorities or by outside pressures. . . . [W]e must assist free peoples to work out their own destinies in their own way.*

Congress approved Truman's aid request. With the acceptance of the Truman Doctrine, the United States took on international responsibilities as the leader of the Western world. American military aid would now be

Almost 20 years after the war, buildings on Warsaw's main street were still being rebuilt (left). Bricks from destroyed buildings were saved and used in the reconstruction (below).

Reflecting on the Times
When the people of Warsaw began to reconstruct their city, what kinds of problems do you think they faced?

available to any nation threatened by communism. As a result of American assistance, Greece was able to defeat the Communist guerrillas.

The Marshall Plan   The Truman Doctrine effectively stopped the spread of communism in the eastern Mediterranean, but the future of Western Europe remained in doubt. World War II had weakened Europe's economy. The United States feared that a European economic collapse would open the area to communism. It believed that its own military and economic security depended on a strong and free Europe.

Therefore, the U.S. government devised a new approach to provide aid to Europe. Speaking at Harvard University on June 5, Secretary of State Marshall proposed a European aid program that became known as the Marshall Plan. Its purpose, he said, was to restore "the confidence of European people in the economic future of their own countries." For the plan to work, Marshall urged a united European effort to determine where Europe's economic needs lay and how the United States could help.

Western European countries responded enthusiastically to the Marshall Plan. However, the Soviet Union turned down the chance to participate in the plan and forced its satellites to do the same. Despite their great need for economic aid, the Soviets felt they could not afford to give out information about their economy. They also opposed linking their socialist economy with the largely capitalist ones of Western Europe.

The Marshall Plan was a great success. Western European nations worked together to boost productivity, reduce trade barriers, and use resources efficiently. They received about $13 billion in aid from the United States during the next four years. By 1951, Western European economies were prospering, and Communist interest in these nations had declined.

The Marshall Plan extended American influence in Western Europe and helped unite the region into a single economic bloc to counter the Soviets. In reaction to the Marshall Plan, in 1949 the Soviet Union set up a rival plan known as the Council of Mutual Economic Assistance, or COMECON. Eastern Europe was thus formed into a single economic bloc under the leadership of the Soviet Union.

A Divided Germany

As part of its containment policy, the United States wanted to incorporate Germany into the

Learning from Photographs *During the Soviet blockade of Berlin, American and British planes airlifted tons of medicine and food into the western sector of the city for 11 months.* **Name two ways in which the episode was a victory for the United States.**

Marshall Plan. But Germany was still divided into zones of foreign occupation. As tension increased between the Soviet Union and the West, it was becoming obvious that no final peace agreement would be reached about Germany.

The Germans in the Western zones, with assistance from the Western Allies, moved quickly to rebuild their area. The British, French, and Americans believed that a strong democratic western Germany would be an asset in any confrontation with the Soviet Union. Free elections for local governments were held in the Western zones. In Berlin, the Americans, British, and French zones of the city were joined into what became known as West Berlin.

The three Western powers also planned to set up a West German state by joining their zones of occupation. The Soviets, fearful of a strong, reunited Germany, were determined to prevent this step. In June 1948, the Soviets acted to force the West to give up its merger plan. They blocked land routes from the West into West Berlin, which lay well within the Soviet zone of occupation.

The West's response was to launch a massive airlift to supply the city's needs. Several thousand tons of food, fuel, and other necessities were flown in every day for 11 months, with planes landing and taking off every 3 minutes in West Berlin's 2 airports. The morale of the 2 million West Berliners was boosted by this show of support. The success of the airlift finally forced the Soviets to lift the blockade in May 1949.

Following the Berlin blockade, the Western Allies carried out their plans for the formation of an independent West German state. In May 1949, a constitution was approved that set up a federal system of 11 states. In the fall of that year, the Federal Republic of Germany, or West Germany, was proclaimed, with its capital at Bonn. The Soviets then set up the German Democratic Republic, or East Germany, with its capital at East Berlin. Thus, Germany was divided into 2 different countries.

New Alliances

Just before the Berlin blockade, another crisis had occurred in Europe. In February 1948, Czechoslovakia was taken over by Communists and became a Soviet satellite. The Czechoslovak and Berlin crises increased Western concerns about military defense. In April 1949, shortly before the end of the Berlin blockade, the North Atlantic Treaty Organization (NATO) was formed by Belgium, Great Britain, Canada, Denmark, Norway, France, Iceland, Italy, Luxembourg, the Netherlands, and the United States. NATO expanded to include Greece and Turkey in 1952 and West Germany in 1955. Members of this military alliance agreed that an attack on one would be considered an attack on all. In response to NATO, the Soviet Union and its Eastern European satellites signed a military alliance in 1955 known as the Warsaw Pact.

Later events suggested that the purpose of the Warsaw Pact was as much to strengthen the Soviet hold on its satellites as to defend them. Soviet troops stationed in Hungary under the terms of the Warsaw Pact were used to suppress a 1956 uprising there. In 1968 the Soviet Union invoked the treaty to justify its invasion of Czechoslovakia, which had introduced a liberal form of communism.

SECTION 1 REVIEW

Recall
1. **Define:** cold war, satellites, iron curtain, containment
2. **Identify:** Marshall Plan, Truman Doctrine, NATO, Warsaw Pact
3. **Locate:** Find the Soviet satellites on a map of Europe.

Critical Thinking
4. **Analyze:** Why did the Soviet Union seek to control Eastern Europe?
5. **Evaluate:** Why do you think Stalin risked a war with the West by blockading Berlin?

Applying Concepts
6. **Conflict:** What were some of the political and economic "weapons" of the cold war? What goals did the superpowers hope to accomplish using these varying strategies?

The Communist Bloc

The cold war affected the internal policies of the Soviet Union and its Eastern European allies. Stalin believed that a full-scale conflict with the West was inevitable. To guard against the West, the Soviet ruler increased his control over the Soviet Union and Eastern Europe. He purged Communist parties of officials suspected of disloyalty. He also forbade writers and artists to use Western ideas in their works.

The Soviet Union

After World War II, Stalin worked to reconstruct heavy industry and boost the military might of his country. The Soviet Union surpassed its prewar rates of production in several major products, including coal, steel, and oil. It continued a high level of military spending and exploded its first nuclear bomb. To aid Soviet citizens, the government rebuilt the many towns and villages that were destroyed during the war. However, the needs of consumers for better food, clothing, and housing were not met.

Stalin died on March 5, 1953. He was succeeded by a collective leadership of top Communist officials. Among the new Soviet leaders was Nikita Khrushchev (who served as Communist party secretary). After a struggle for power, Khrushchev emerged as the dominant leader in 1955.

Removing Stalin's Legacy   In the following year, the 20th Congress of the Soviet Communist Party was held in Moscow. At a secret session, Khrushchev delivered a controversial speech. He denounced Stalin for the purges of the 1930s, in which thousands of loyal party members had been tortured and condemned to

Learning from Photographs *To celebrate Soviet Navy Day in 1950, sailors formed a star around this banner, which reads "Glory to Great Stalin." Only three years after Stalin's death, Khrushchev denounced Stalin's "cult of personality."* **What major changes did Khrushchev's de-Stalinization program bring about?**

death or sent to labor camps. Stalin was also accused of creating a "cult of personality," in which he boosted his own honor at the expense of the Communist party.

In attacking Stalin, Khrushchev ignored his own role in assisting Stalin in the purges. His anti-Stalin speech was primarily designed to strengthen his own power and to appease a growing restlessness among the Soviet people. Now that Stalin was gone, many Soviets wanted a relaxation of government controls and a better standard of living.

From 1956 to 1964, Khrushchev carried out a program of de-Stalinization, or a reversal of some of Stalin's policies. While keeping Stalin's program of Five-Year Plans and collective farming, Khrushchev ended certain restrictions. He gave artists and intellectuals more freedom. He also reduced the terror of the secret police and freed many political prisoners from labor camps. Soviet citizens were promised better wages and more consumer goods.

Cold War Thaw By the mid-1950s, the terrible threat of nuclear war led Soviet and American leaders to seek ways of relaxing cold-war tensions. Under Khrushchev, the Soviets adopted a new policy toward the West known as **peaceful coexistence**. This meant that they would compete with the West but would avoid

CONNECTIONS: SCIENCE AND TECHNOLOGY

The Space Race

On October 5, 1957, the Soviets announced that they had launched the first orbiting satellite, *Sputnik I*, into space. A month later *Sputnik II* sent the first living creature, a dog named Laika, into space.

These events shocked the United States. Since World War II, it had been assumed that the United States had technological superiority. Now, U.S. institutions reexamined their priorities. Schools reorganized their curricula to include more math and science, so students could "catch up" with their Soviet counterparts.

Within months after *Sputnik*, Congress created the National Aeronautics and Space Administration (NASA). The first U.S. satellite, *Explorer I*, followed about four months after *Sputnik I*.

Thereafter, the superpowers competed to claim accomplishments in space. For a time the Soviets continued to score big successes. In April 1961, Soviet cosmonaut Yuri Gagarin became the first human to orbit the earth. The next month Alan Shepard became the first American astronaut in space. Not until 1962 did the United States send an astronaut, John Glenn, into orbit. The next year cosmonaut Valentina Tereshkova became the first woman to orbit Earth.

The two countries experimented with unmanned moon probes, weather and communications satellites, and extended manned orbits. But the grand prize of the space race remained: putting a human on the moon. U.S. astronaut Neil Armstrong won that honor on July 20, 1969.

Making the Connection:
1. How did the United States react to the launch of *Sputnik I*?
2. How did the cold war influence the superpowers' space programs?

FOOTNOTES TO HISTORY

THE KITCHEN DEBATE

In July 1959 the United States sponsored a national exhibition of American products in Moscow to help promote East–West cultural ties. Vice President Richard M. Nixon represented the United States government. While Nixon was touring the exhibition with Soviet leader Nikita Khrushchev, their conversation erupted into a heated argument on the merits of capitalism versus communism.

Standing in front of a model kitchen display, Nixon shook his finger in Khrushchev's face, to the delight of the American photographers recording the scene. The photographs appeared on the front page of every U.S. newspaper, and the argument was nicknamed "the Kitchen Debate." The episode illustrated the desire of American leaders to take a tough stand with the Soviets.

war. In carrying out this policy, Khrushchev stated that the Soviet Union would surpass the United States economically, encouraging other nations to follow the Communist model.

To make the Soviet Union more economically competitive, Khrushchev embarked on a program to boost industrial and agricultural production. For example, he sought to improve the working conditions of laborers to encourage better productivity.

Khrushchev also placed a new emphasis on technological research, hoping to modernize industry and close the technology gap with the United States. That effort triumphed in 1957 with the launch of *Sputnik I*, the world's first space satellite. *Sputnik* added to the prestige of the Soviet Union and its leader.

Despite the cold-war thaw, both superpowers engaged in a massive military buildup as their technological abilities increased. In the late 1950s, the Soviets successfully tested long-range rockets known as **intercontinental ballistic missiles**, or ICBMs, which for the first time could target locations in the United States. Likewise, U.S. missiles were pointed at Soviet targets. A nuclear war would result in what was

known as mutual assured destruction—that is, the certain destruction of both nations.

Meanwhile, contacts increased between Soviet and American leaders in an effort to maintain peace. In 1959 Soviet Premier Nikita Khrushchev made a historic visit to the United States, meeting with President Dwight D. Eisenhower at Camp David in Maryland. The leaders renounced the use of force and agreed on the need to end the arms race. Another meeting between the two leaders was to be held in Paris in May 1960. Eisenhower planned to visit the Soviet Union during that year also. But shortly before the conference, the Soviets shot down an American U-2 spy plane over their territory and captured its pilot. Khrushchev used the occasion to launch a propaganda attack on the United States. He also canceled Eisenhower's planned visit to the Soviet Union.

The next two years were possibly the most dangerous and volatile period of the cold war. In 1961 Eisenhower was succeeded by John F. Kennedy, who wanted to have a dynamic foreign policy that would impress the Soviets with American strength and boost American prestige abroad. Testing the resolve of the new American leader, in 1961 Khrushchev pressured the Western Allies to get out of Berlin. A year later, he tried to install Soviet missiles on the Communist-ruled island of Cuba, which was 90 miles from American shores. In both cases, Khrushchev was unsuccessful, but his actions heightened world tensions and brought the superpowers to the brink of nuclear war.

Not willing to face again the prospect of a nuclear conflict, the superpowers worked to establish a better relationship after the Cuban missile crisis. In 1963, a telephone "hot line" linked Washington and Moscow for the first time, so that the leaders of both nations could instantly communicate with each other.

In the same year, the Soviet Union and the Western Allies signed a treaty banning the testing of nuclear weapons in the atmosphere. For the next few years, the superpowers, although disagreeing sharply on many issues, avoided crises and confrontations. Meanwhile, Khrushchev's policies had suffered a number of setbacks at home as well as overseas. His agricultural reforms failed, as an increasing portion of Soviet government funds went into defense and technology instead of into farm programs. Investment in heavy industry also diverted money from the production of consumer goods, causing shortages that were highly unpopular with the Soviet people. These difficulties, along with Khrushchev's handling of the Cuban missile crisis, badly damaged his image, and the Soviet leader was forced from power in 1964.

New Leaders The Soviet Communist party made another attempt at collective leadership with Aleksei Kosygin as premier and Leonid I. Brezhnev as general secretary. Brezhnev emerged as the dominant figure to lead the Soviet Union for the next 18 years.

Brezhnev not only slowed Khrushchev's program of de-Stalinization; he actually reversed it. He reinstituted measures against intellectuals and **dissidents**—those who criticized the party or the regime. One prominent dissident was Alexander Solzhenitsyn, the author of many works, including *The Gulag Archipelago*, an account of the horrors of Soviet prison camps. He was eventually deported and settled in the United States. Another dissident whose case received worldwide attention was Dr. Andrei Sakharov, a prominent scientist and developer of the Soviet hydrogen bomb, who later denounced the arms race. Sakharov was finally sentenced to internal exile in Siberia.

In foreign policy, Brezhnev made it clear that he would not hesitate to use force to keep the satellite nations within the bounds set for them by the Soviet Union. Brezhnev also launched a Soviet arms buildup. He felt that the military power of the Soviet Union gave it a stronger hand in world diplomacy.

By the end of the 1960s, the Soviet Union faced enormous problems. Brezhnev's military buildup diverted even more funds from the sluggish Soviet economy. Farm workers in the U.S.S.R. were only one-sixth as productive as their U.S. counterparts. Technologically, many industries were at least 20 years behind the times. The failure of Soviet domestic programs undermined Soviet military and diplomatic programs abroad. Far from luring jealous capitalist countries toward communism, as Khrushchev had predicted, the failures of the Soviet system made it even more difficult for the Soviets to secure the loyalty of their satellite countries.

Soviet Satellites

During the height of the cold war, the Soviet Union maintained tight control over its satellites in Eastern Europe. The peoples of these nations resented Soviet domination, but were largely powerless to change their situation.

Yugoslavia After World War II, Yugoslavia became the only large Communist state in Eastern Europe to resist Soviet domination. Its popular leader, Josip Broz Tito, had led the resistance against the Nazis and was as much a Yugoslav nationalist as a Communist. Despite Yugoslavia's close ties to the Soviet Union, Tito went his own way in making policies for his country. Angered by Tito's independent attitude, the Soviets expelled Yugoslavia from the international Communist movement. Throughout Eastern Europe, they waged a propaganda war against what they called Titoism, or the tendency of some Communists to place their national interests above those of the Soviet Union. With the support of his people, Tito was able to resist Soviet pressures. He developed his own brand of communism and received economic and diplomatic aid from the West.

East Germany During the 1950s and early 1960s, industrial East Germany was the most prosperous of the Soviet satellites. However, its people were deeply dissatisfied with Soviet controls. After Stalin's death in 1953, they let loose their frustrations. In 1953, a workers' uprising occurred in East Berlin. Soviet troops stationed in East Germany put down the rebellion with little difficulty.

In the years that followed, many East Germans fled to West Berlin, which was easily accessible to them. The population of East Germany declined by about 2 million during the 1950s as a result of this migration. This was an embarrassment to the government and an economic blow to the nation, since those who left were among the best-trained workers.

Learning from Photographs *Armed Hungarian freedom fighters were no match for Soviet troops and tanks that moved in to crush the rebellion of 1956.* **What caused the Soviet Union to intervene in Hungary?**

East Germany's problems contributed to a new cold-war crisis in 1958. By then, West Germany had recovered from the war and was fully re-armed—not only with conventional weapons, such as tanks, bombs, and guns, but also with nuclear weapons under the control of NATO command. Alarmed at this prospect, Khrushchev called for negotiations on European security and on a nuclear-free Germany. He also demanded that the Western powers withdraw from Berlin.

The negotiations failed to reach agreement on the major issues. New talks were scheduled but were abruptly canceled as a result of the U-2 incident in 1960. Shortly thereafter Khrushchev ordered the construction of the notorious Berlin Wall to divide the eastern and western sections of the city.

East German soldiers went to work building the wall, a massive concrete structure 26 miles (42 kilometers) long and up to 15 feet (4.6 meters) high and topped with electrified wire. The stated purpose of the wall was to keep Westerners out, but in fact it halted the exodus of East Germans from East Berlin. To escape to West Berlin, people had to survive mined trenches, guard dogs, and self-activating guns. Then they had to scale the wall itself. Stories reached the West of heroic escapes, but scores of East Germans died trying to run to freedom.

Although the Berlin Wall effectively stopped the migration, it also became a rallying point for the opponents of communism. Moreover, it became a powerful physical symbol of the iron curtain.

Poland Under Communist rule, Poland became industrialized. Like East Germany, it was restless under tight Soviet controls. Khrushchev's program of de-Stalinization raised hope in Poland for greater freedom. However, the Communist government of Poland did not make changes fast enough to suit the Polish people. In June 1956, workers rioted in the industrial city of Poznan. Their action was followed by upheavals throughout the country. Poland's Communist leaders decided that some concessions had to be made. Polish supporters of Stalin were removed from office. The popular Communist leader Wladyslaw Gomulka, who under Stalin had been accused of anti-Soviet activities and jailed, came to power.

In the late 1950s, the Soviets allowed Poland greater freedom to run its affairs. Many political prisoners were freed, and farmers were allowed to own land. The Roman Catholic Church, which had the loyalty of most Poles, was able to carry out its activities. However, the Communist party kept its hold over the country and maintained close ties to the Soviet Union. By the mid-1960s, the party had eliminated many of the Polish freedoms that had been won a decade earlier.

Hungary Hungary, a largely agricultural nation, experienced harsh Communist rule after 1947. Large estates were broken up and given to poor farmers. But the Communist government forced the farmers to combine their new properties into collective farms. Great stress was placed on industrialization, often at the expense of workers' living standards. Communist opposition to religion led to restrictions on the Roman Catholic Church, Hungary's largest religious group. By 1950, even many Communist leaders were accused of disloyalty to the Soviet Union and were executed.

When de-Stalinization was introduced in Hungary, it led to a full-scale revolt in the fall of 1956. As in Poland, worker uprisings brought a liberal Communist government to power. However, Imre Nagy, the new Hungarian prime minister, went further than the Polish leaders. He supported Hungary's withdrawal from the Soviet bloc and its declaration of neutrality. The Soviets at first seemed willing to accept this change. However, too much was at stake for them to let Hungary go on its own. A neutral Hungary would eventually mean the breakup of Soviet control in Eastern Europe.

In November 1956, Soviet troops and tanks poured into Hungary, crushing the revolt. Realizing that intervention could cause World War III, the Western powers sympathized with the Hungarians, but did nothing to help. Order in Hungary was restored under a Soviet-controlled government led by János Kádár. More than 150,000 refugees fled the country to the West.

Czechoslovakia   Czechoslovakia, with its developed industry and democratic traditions, was the last Eastern European country to become Communist. After the 1948 Communist takeover, Czechoslovakia based its industrial economy on the Soviet model. The Communist government crushed political opposition and acted to destroy the influence of the Roman Catholic Church. At the same time, it carried out purges against its own officials. These were the bloodiest purges outside of the Soviet Union. After Stalin's death, Czechoslovakia refused to promote de-Stalinization. Under President Antonin Novotny, it had one of the most rigid Communist regimes in Eastern Europe.

In 1968, Alexander Dubček became the leader of the Communist party in Czechoslovakia. He began to "democratize" the country by introducing more liberal reforms than were allowed in any other Communist state. He eased press censorship and began to allow some political groups to meet freely. He also cut back restrictions on intellectuals and educators.

Dubček assured the Soviets that Czechoslovakia was still loyal to the Warsaw Pact and to communism. Before long, however, many Czech intellectuals demanded more freedom. There were hints that opposition parties might be allowed to operate and that Czechoslovakia might withdraw from the Warsaw Pact. This alarmed the Soviet Union. The Soviets saw the liberal Czech policies as a threat to their security.

On August 20, 1968, about 500,000 troops from the Soviet Union and its Warsaw Pact allies invaded Czechoslovakia. They seized Prague and sent Dubček and other Czech leaders to Moscow. Most of Dubček's reforms were withdrawn and a new constitution put into effect. In April 1969, Dubček was replaced as party leader. In 1970, he was expelled from the party entirely.

In the Soviet newspaper *Pravda*, the government justified the invasion by declaring the Soviets' right to intervene in Communist states to counter anti-Communist uprisings. This principle, known as the Brezhnev Doctrine, was the basis for relations between the Soviet Union and its satellites for the next 20 years.

SECTION 2 REVIEW

Recall

1. **Define:** peaceful coexistence, intercontinental ballistic missiles, dissidents
2. **Identify:** de-Stalinization, Josip Broz Tito, Alexander Dubček, Brezhnev Doctrine
3. **Explain:** Why did East Germany build the Berlin Wall?

Critical Thinking

4. **Analyze:** Contrast the purpose of Khrushchev's 1956 de-Stalinization speech with the effects of the speech in Eastern Europe.
5. **Synthesize:** Hypothesize what would have happened if the Soviet Union had not used force to keep its Eastern-bloc allies under control.

Applying Concepts

6. **Conflict:** Analyze whether the death of Stalin substantively affected the cold war between the United States and the Soviet Union.

Western Europe

After World War II, the non-Communist nations of Western Europe were concerned about two major issues: economic development and military security. They came to realize that only through united action would they be able to improve their economies, strengthen the Western Alliance, and contribute to world affairs.

Great Britain

In the postwar period, Great Britain's position as a world power further declined. Many of its important Asian and African colonies became independent. With the loss of empire, Great Britain no longer had easy access to markets and sources of raw materials. British industries, often inefficient and outdated, had difficulty competing in world markets that were increasingly dominated by the United States, Japan, and by other Western European nations. Because of its economic weakness, Great Britain had to pass on many of its international obligations to the United States. However, it maintained a strong military role in the Western Alliance, developing its own nuclear force.

In internal affairs, Great Britain underwent many changes. In 1945 Churchill and the Conservatives were voted out of office. They were replaced by the Labour party, which appealed to many Britons who wanted greater social equality. Under Prime Minister Clement Attlee, the Labour government continued wartime restrictions to improve the economy. However, it also promised a better standard of living for all British citizens.

Carrying out a moderate Socialist program, the Labour government nationalized the coal, steel, and transportation industries. Greater freedom was given to labor unions to strike and to participate in political activities. The Labour government also created a **welfare state,** a system in which the government provides programs for the well-being of its citizens. Social security was expanded to provide lifetime benefits for the needy. Free education was provided to all children up to the age of 16. The government also introduced a national health service that provided free medical care for everyone.

As the economic situation improved in the early 1950s, the Conservatives returned to power and ruled until 1964. Although they ended many government controls over the economy, Conservative prime ministers such as Winston Churchill, Anthony Eden, and Harold Macmillan did not eliminate the social welfare programs introduced by the Labour party.

In 1952 the popular wartime monarch, George VI, died and was succeeded by his daughter Elizabeth. As queen, Elizabeth II had little, if any, power. However, for many Britons, she became a reassuring symbol of traditional British values during a period of rapid, and sometimes discouraging, change.

France

German occupation of France during World War II had ended the Third French Republic established in 1870. Following the war, a new constitution was approved establishing the Fourth French Republic. It closely resembled that of the Third French Republic, having a strong legislature and a weak presidency.

In spite of economic growth, France in the 1950s was plagued with domestic and international problems. The existence of many political parties undermined hopes for stable government. No single political party was strong enough to obtain a working majority in the National Assembly. Cabinets were formed by coalitions of several parties. When one of the parties disagreed with established policy, the cabinet members had to resign and form a new government.

Overseas, demands for independence swept French colonies in Africa and Asia. Unlike Great Britain, however, France clung to its empire. It fought, and lost, expensive and bloody wars in Indochina and Algeria.

The threat of civil war in Algeria in 1958 resulted in the downfall of France's ineffective Fourth Republic. Charles de Gaulle, leader of the French Resistance during World War II, was called from retirement to head an emergency government. De Gaulle asked the French people to approve the creation of a strong presidency elected directly by the people. French voters responded overwhelmingly to de Gaulle's appeal. Thus, the Fifth French Republic was born.

De Gaulle was chosen the first president of the Fifth Republic. His political party, the Gaullist Union, formed a working majority in the National Assembly. As president, de Gaulle recognized that France could not stubbornly hold on to its empire against strong nationalistic opposition. In the early 1960s, he allowed France's African colonies, including Algeria, to become independent.

With the loss of France's empire, de Gaulle worked to strengthen French cultural and economic influence throughout the world. His strongly nationalistic policies angered France's allies, especially the United States and Great Britain. In the mid-1960s, de Gaulle withdrew France from NATO's military command, while maintaining political ties with the Western Alliance. Under de Gaulle, France built its own nuclear strike force. It also sought to compete with the United States and the Soviet Union by giving economic aid to poorer nations.

West Germany

During the postwar years, West Germany rebuilt its economy and became Western Europe's leading industrial nation. New industries used the latest in modern equipment, and industrial production more than tripled in the 1950s. Prosperity enabled West Germany to absorb more than 10 million workers from the rest of Europe.

West Germany's democratic political system was dominated by two parties: the Christian Democrats and the Social Democrats. The

Learning from Photographs *On a visit to Cologne in 1962, Charles de Gaulle tried to restore friendly relations with West Germany. De Gaulle became a close ally of Adenauer, and they worked together for a Franco-German treaty of economic cooperation.* **What were de Gaulle's goals as the leader of France?**

Abstract Sculpture

From the beginning of her artistic career in the 1930s, Dame Barbara Hepworth, a sculptor, had a big part in the evolution of abstract art in Great Britain. Abstract art is art that does not depict a recognizable place, person, or thing. Instead, pure form—that is, form that does not represent anything—makes up the work of art.

Although European artists had been exploring abstract art for decades, little abstract art had been produced in England. In 1932, Hepworth joined a group of artists in Paris who were exploring abstraction in art. Until then, her works had been figurative—depicting the human figure.

In the sculpture shown here, *Pelagos,* Hepworth used a geometric form to display the physical qualities of tension and balance. The activity and tension of this piece are contained in a sphere, a perfect geometric form. Hepworth hollowed out parts of the sphere to form a spiral. The spiral form within the sphere gives a sense of movement—the viewer's eye is drawn around the spiral, toward the center of the piece. With this spiral,

Hepworth created the sense that this form is under tension. At the center of the piece, Hepworth placed the strongest tension. Here, strings are pulled taut, as though they are holding the spiraled form in, keeping it from breaking out of the sphere.

Although *Pelagos* is abstract, Hepworth seems to have made some allusions to music and nature in the sculpture. The taut strings at the center remind the viewer of the strings of a musical instrument. The materials used in the sculpture may refer to nature. The polished wood is clearly a material from nature, and Hepworth took the reference to nature further by making the interior of the sphere pure white. The dark surface of the sphere and the white interior recall the skin and pulp of a piece of fruit.

With the coming of abstract art, artists began exploring qualities of form that had until then been used as aspects of the human form: tension, movement, balance. In *Pelagos,* Barbara Hepworth shows that these physical forces can be shown effectively in an abstract form.

In later years Hepworth continued to explore the expressive possibilities of abstract forms. Some of her works of the 1950s seem to suggest the human figure.

Responding to the Arts

1. What was Barbara Hepworth's role in British art?
2. What qualities of form did Barbara Hepworth explore in her famous sculpture, *Pelagos*?

Christian Democrats, under the leadership of Konrad Adenauer (AH duh now ur), formed the first West German government, in 1949. They established a capitalist economy and close ties to the West. In 1955 West Germany joined NATO and began to establish its armed forces.

As chancellor, Adenauer was known as a strong leader devoted to the Western Alliance, European unity, and the reunification of Germany. During his tenure, West Germany became one of the world's stablest democracies. Adenauer retired in 1963.

During the 1960s the Christian Democrats lost support to the Social Democrats, a moderate Socialist party led by West Berlin's mayor, Willy Brandt. The Social Democrats maintained strong support for NATO while seeking improved relations with the Soviet bloc.

European Unity

Throughout Europe's history, local disputes between two or more nations often drew the entire continent into war. In the twentieth century, advances in technology, such as nuclear weapons, made it clear that future wars could lead to global catastrophe. This possibility prompted leaders to seek regional solutions to European issues.

As World War II neared its end, leaders discussed plans for the postwar unification of European countries. These plans included organizations for economic cooperation and the resolution of disputes. Some even raised the idea of a united Europe. Others proposed that each nation retain its national identity but hand over control of powers, such as defense and foreign policy, to a European government. This arrangement, it was felt, would prevent nations from waging war on each other.

To coordinate economic policies, six nations—France, Italy, West Germany, Belgium, the Netherlands, and Luxembourg—established the European Coal and Steel Community (ECSC) in 1951. The purpose of the organization was to create a tariff-free market for European coal and steel products. By ending trade barriers and developing uniform standards, the European Coal and Steel Community would further European industrial growth.

The Community was so successful that the same countries decided to bring together the rest of their economies. In 1957 the six nations signed the Treaty of Rome, creating the European Economic Community (the EEC), also known as the Common Market. They planned to abolish all tariffs among themselves and form a single economic market by 1970. During the 1960s and 1970s, Great Britain, attracted by the Common Market's success, ended its traditional aloofness from European affairs and sought membership in the European organization.

The Common Market has benefited Europe in several ways. By promoting economic cooperation, it has reduced the threat of conflict and has contributed to European prosperity. It has also enabled Europe to pursue cooperative technological programs such as space research and nuclear energy, both of which would be too expensive for any one nation to pursue. Finally, it has enabled Europe to compete with North America and Asia in world markets.

SECTION 3 REVIEW

Recall
1. **Define:** welfare state
2. **Identify:** Clement Attlee, Charles de Gaulle, Konrad Adenauer, Common Market
3. **Explain:** Why was de Gaulle considered an independent leader?

Critical Thinking
4. **Analyze:** Contrast the steps taken by European nations to rebuild their economies.
5. **Synthesize:** What do you think would be the advantages and disadvantages of a United States of Europe?

Applying Concepts
6. **Cooperation:** Explain why a strong European economy was vital to world peace in the period after World War II. What factors contributed to the rebuilding of European economies?

SECTION 4

The United States and Canada

Because they were spared the destruction of their territory in World War II, the United States and Canada emerged from the war with healthy economies. The United States experienced stunning technological progress that raised standards of living during the 1950s. But the cold war left its mark on American life and foreign policy.

The United States

After World War II, the United States entered an era of economic growth that brought material wealth to a larger group of Americans. Businesses boosted production, and new industries appeared. Higher wages and better benefits gave Americans more money to spend on goods.

The desire to make up for wartime shortages increased market demand. A soaring birthrate added to the number of consumers.

During the late 1940s and the 1950s, the United States played a leading role in science and technology. Americans in greater numbers received a university education, contributing to a "knowledge explosion." American technical skills brought the United States into competition with the Soviet Union in space exploration.

The Cold War at Home   During this time of prosperity, the cold war created deep divisions in the United States. Conservatives blamed government leaders for allowing communism to make gains overseas. They also charged that Communists were serving in high government positions. The growing fear of the

Learning from Photographs *Eisenhower and Kennedy had different presidential styles, but both supported the idea of containing Communist expansion.* **Compare and contrast the two leaders' ideologies.**

"enemy within"—of subversion within the U.S. government—helped to launch a controversial anti-Communist crusade to discover and expose suspected Communists. The search was concentrated on diplomats, intellectuals, liberals, and other opinion leaders whose views could be interpreted as sympathetic toward, or even tolerant of, communism.

Both houses of Congress set up panels to investigate suspected Communists. In 1947 the House Committee on Un-American Activities conducted hearings on suspected Communist influence in the entertainment industry and in labor unions. As a result, several well-known writers were jailed or found their careers ruined.

The Senate Committee on Investigation was headed by Senator Joseph McCarthy of Wisconsin. In 1950 McCarthy began voicing charges of a vast Communist conspiracy within the State Department and calling government employees before the committee to defend themselves. He never proved a single case. But the climate of opinion in the country was such that the accusation alone was enough to label someone a Communist, and many lost their jobs. The term *McCarthyism* came to mean the leveling of public accusations of political subversion without regard to evidence.

During the 1950s and 1960s, fear of communism would influence most major foreign policy decisions by the United States. In relations with Eastern Europe, Africa, the Middle East, Latin America, and Asia, diplomacy was perceived as an extension of the struggle against Soviet communism. The next three chapters in this unit will explore the effects of cold-war politics on these changing regions.

In the 1950s the effort to contain communism, strongly supported by the American public, caused the United States to send troops to fight Communist forces in Korea and Vietnam. The United States engaged in an unprecedented military buildup during this time, even during the cold war "thaw" in the late 1950s.

By the end of his presidency, Dwight D. Eisenhower, though a proponent of a strong military, was deeply concerned about the global arms race. On leaving office in 1960, he warned of a growing "military-industrial complex" in the United States. The American fear of com-

Learning from Photographs *In August 1963, more than 200,000 people marched on Washington, D.C. They gathered at the Lincoln Memorial and heard Martin Luther King, Jr., deliver his powerful "I have a dream" speech, which outlined his hopes for equal rights for all Americans.* **How did King work to achieve that goal?**

munism, the armed services' enthusiasm for new and better weapons, and the large profits earned by weapons manufacturers had created a built-in incentive to increase military expenditures and build more machines of war.

Another World War II veteran followed Eisenhower in 1960. President John F. Kennedy had campaigned on a theme of restoring the strength and prestige America had lost after the embarrassments of the U-2 spying incident and *Sputnik*.

Kennedy engaged in cold-war maneuvering on several fronts. He acted quickly to create the Peace Corps, a program to help impoverished countries and correct the conditions that would make them vulnerable to Communist influence. Kennedy's cold-war views influenced his actions in several major foreign policy crises, including the building of the Berlin Wall and the Cuban missile crisis.

Kennedy's assassination in 1963 brought Lyndon Johnson to the White House. The consuming issue during Johnson's five years in office was the Vietnam War, in which the United States assisted South Vietnam in resisting a Communist takeover. American involvement in the war, described in Chapter 32, began with Eisenhower and Kennedy and grew out of their cold-war strategies.

Domestic Unrest   Despite general economic prosperity in the United States after World War II, issues of poverty, unemployment, and racism caused growing political upheaval. Many minority groups faced discrimination in jobs, housing, and education.

During the late 1940s and 1950s, blacks—joined by whites and other ethnic groups—began a movement for civil rights. This effort resulted in several United States Supreme Court decisions that attacked discrimination. In the best-known case, *Brown v. Board of Education of Topeka, Kansas* (1954), the Supreme Court ruled that racial segregation, or separation of the races, in public schools was illegal. President Eisenhower ordered federal agencies to enforce the Supreme Court decision.

Civil rights became the leading domestic issue in the United States. In 1955, Martin Luther King, Jr., a Baptist minister, used nonviolent means to protest against discrimination in housing, public facilities, and voting. In spite of opposition, he was able to convince many Americans of the injustice of racial discrimination.

President Kennedy urged Congress to pass laws outlawing discrimination.

After Kennedy's assassination in 1963, President Johnson persuaded Congress to pass many major civil rights laws. He also supported reforms in education and social welfare to achieve what he called the Great Society.

Canada

Canada's politics and economy changed significantly as British influence declined after World War II. As Great Britain sought new economic ties with Europe, its ties to Canada grew weaker. At the same time, Canada developed much stronger ties with the United States.

During the postwar period, Canada worked to define its status as a global power. Suspicious of a world dominated by the superpowers, Canada instead advanced a role for itself as a "middle power"—that is, one that is strong economically, if not militarily.

Nevertheless, as a principal founder of the United Nations, Canada fulfilled its obligation to contribute to UN peacekeeping forces. Like other Atlantic nations, Canada was fearful of Soviet aggression after World War II. This concern prompted Canada to sign the NATO agreement in 1949. In 1950 Canada sent troops to Korea under NATO, but in 1969, it withdrew some of its troops from Europe. Yet, it remained loyal to the alliance.

Since World War II, the United States and Canada have increased trade in manufactured goods. They also have engaged in joint ventures to develop Canada's natural resources.

SECTION 4 REVIEW

Recall

1. **Identify:** McCarthyism, Dwight D. Eisenhower, John F. Kennedy, Lyndon Johnson, Great Society
2. **Describe:** How did the court rule in *Brown v. Board of Education of Topeka, Kansas*?

Critical Thinking

3. **Analyze:** Why did President Eisenhower believe that the military-industrial complex was dangerous? Why do you think his warning shocked people?
4. **Synthesize:** Speculate on why significant poverty continued in the United States in the midst of postwar prosperity.

Applying Concepts

5. **Cooperation:** Compare the foreign policy of Canada with that of France under President de Gaulle.

RECOGNIZING FALLACIES IN A LINE OF REASONING

Your best friend has been absent from school for a week. After he or she returns, your history teacher decides to give a test. Your friend borrows your notes but fails the test anyway. Your friend says the reason for the failure was that your notes were inadequate. Is this a fallacy in reasoning?

Explanation

If you analyze your friend's line of *reasoning*, or a thought process that uses reason to arrive at conclusions, you would see that it contained a *fallacy*, or an erroneous idea. Although your friend blamed your notes, it is likely that he or she failed for other reasons, such as not studying enough.

Use these steps to recognize a fallacy in a line of reasoning:
• Identify the conclusion that is presented.
• Determine the line of reasoning used (see chart).
• Determine if the reasoning flows logically or if the statement reveals a fallacy.

Example

Consider this statement: Because the Marshall Plan was designed to bolster the weak European economy and prevent the spread of communism, it will receive universal support in the United States. This line of reasoning involves either–or thinking—that

is, people who abhor communism will support the Plan. The conclusion is faulty because although most Americans supported the Marshall Plan, some opposed it.

Application

Read the following statement and use the outlined steps to determine if there is a fallacy in the line of reasoning:

• Because the United Nations was created by the Allies to maintain peace, the Allies will always support all United Nations' policies.

Practice

Turn to Practicing Skills on page 835 of the Chapter Review for further practice in recognizing fallacies in a line of reasoning.

LOGICAL FALLACIES

Type of fallacy	Description	Example
Cause-effect	Assumes a cause-effect relationship	Both Lincoln and Kennedy had vice-presidents named Johnson. Presidents with vice-presidents named Johnson will be shot.
Only reason	Assumes only one cause	World War II ended after the Soviet Union entered the war. The Soviet Union ended the war.
Either-or thinking	Ignores more than two possibilities	Any European nation that does not join NATO must be in the Warsaw Pact.
Circular reasoning	Repeats a statement in different terms	Stalin was a dangerous person because nobody was safe around him.
Overgeneralization	Makes a statement too broad to be true	De Gaulle's stands inspired every French citizen.
Stereotyping and name calling	Makes unjustified assumptions about a group	Every Communist wants to rule the world. Never trust Yankee imperialists.

CHAPTER 31 REVIEW

HISTORICAL SIGNIFICANCE

The cold war between the United States and the Soviet Union not only crushed hopes for European unity after World War II, but it also forced nations to choose sides between the superpowers. The development of long-range nuclear weapons made the superpowers' quarrel even more frightening and introduced the possibility of a total nuclear catastrophe that would destroy civilization.

Gradually, this realization compelled the superpower leaders to seek methods for reducing the tensions. Ultimately, Western Europe's rapid economic development undermined the ideology of communism and stimulated demands for change within Communist systems. Many of these changes are being played out in the Soviet Union and Eastern Europe today.

SUMMARY

For a summary of Chapter 31, see the Unit 8 Synopsis on pages 980–981.

USING KEY TERMS

Write the key term that best completes each sentence.

a. cold war
b. containment
c. dissidents
d. ICBMs
e. iron curtain
f. peaceful coexistence
g. satellite country
h. welfare state

1. Czechoslovakia became a ___ of the Soviet Union.
2. The United States adopted a policy of ___ to block Communist expansion in Europe and in other areas of the world.
3. The weapons of the ___ were espionage, propaganda, diplomacy, economic aid, and military aid.
4. The ___ was a physical barrier as well as a psychological one.
5. Great Britain created a ___ to raise its citizens' standards of living.
6. Brezhnev launched a crackdown on suspected ___ in the Soviet Union.
7. Khrushchev developed a new policy toward the West known as ___.
8. The invention of ___ greatly enhanced the superpowers' ability to threaten each other.

REVIEWING FACTS

1. **Explain:** What was the purpose of the Marshall Plan? In what ways was the plan effective?
2. **Explain:** Why did Stalin order the Berlin blockade?
3. **List:** Name the Soviet satellite countries.
4. **Identify:** What reforms did Dubček introduce in Czechoslovakia?
5. **Explain:** What is McCarthyism?

THINKING CRITICALLY

1. **Apply:** What postwar developments launched the cold war?
2. **Analyze:** In your view, why did the United States government assume global responsibility for containing communism?
3. **Synthesize:** The Western Allies saw the Soviet takeover of Eastern Europe as brutal aggression. Did the Soviets have any justification for their actions?
4. **Evaluate:** Was Americans' fear of communism during the 1950s justified? Do you think the actions that Congress took to counter communism were appropriate? Explain your reasoning.
5. **Apply:** How do you think the cold war affected politics in Western European countries?

6. **Analyze:** Are communism and capitalism compatible? Explain your reasoning.
7. **Synthesize:** What steps might have been taken to make the United Nations more effective in its early years?
8. **Evaluate:** Some analysts of the cold war believe the United States should have exploited the Soviet Union's weakness right after World War II, when only the United States had the atomic bomb. How might Truman have taken advantage of this imbalance? Do you think he should have done so? Why or why not?

ANALYZING CONCEPTS

1. **Conflict:** By the 1950s the superpowers had enough nuclear weapons to eliminate each other. What effect did this power have on superpower relations during the cold war?
2. **Cooperation:** How has the Common Market benefited Western European economies?

PRACTICING SKILLS

1. Identify the type of logical fallacy you find in this statement and explain the error: "If the U-2 incident hadn't happened, the cold war might have ended in the early 1960s."
2. Choose an issue in the news. State the issue and the arguments on one side of the issue. Identify fallacies in the arguments.

GEOGRAPHY IN HISTORY

1. **Location:** In his "iron curtain" speech, Churchill stated that the iron curtain stretched from Stettin on the Baltic Sea to Trieste on the Adriatic Sea. Locate these bodies of water on the map on page 813.
2. **Region:** Using the same map, explain why Truman applied the Truman Doctrine in Greece and Turkey.

TRACING CHRONOLOGY

Refer to the time line below to answer these questions.
1. What events mark the beginning and ending of the cold war "thaw"?
2. List the dates of episodes of Soviet intervention in Eastern Europe.
3. List the dates on which new alliances among nations were formed.

LINKING PAST AND PRESENT

1. Key cold war issues continued until 1989, when they reached a dramatic conclusion. Name these issues and explain their link to recent events.
2. Name a previous period in history when Europe was united. When did the continent become fragmented again?
3. Is containment an issue in U.S. foreign policy today? Explain your reasoning.

THE COLD WAR

1945 United Nations formed.

1947 Truman Doctrine and Marshall Plan initiated.

1949 NATO formed.

1955 Warsaw Pact formed.

1961 Berlin Wall erected.

1964 Khrushchev ousted.

1945	1950	1955	1960	1965	1970

1946 Churchill delivers his "iron curtain" speech.

1948 Soviets blockade Berlin; United States launches airlift.

1956 Khrushchev delivers de-Stalinization speech; Soviets crush uprising in Hungary.

1960 U-2 incident heightens cold war tensions.

1968 Soviets invade Czechoslovakia.

Asia and the Pacific

My methods are old," declares Japanese artist Kako Muriguchi, "but my designs are new." Muriguchi designs innovative patterns for kimonos, the traditional Japanese garment for women. The people of Japan have such respect for his contributions to their heritage that they have declared him a *ninguen kokuma*, or "living national treasure." As a result of this designation, Muriguchi is entitled to lifetime national support for his art. Like Muriguchi, Japan and other countries in Asia have found success by combining old and new. Traditional values that encourage education and hard work, combined with modern developments such as computer technology, have brought prosperity to many countries in Asia since the end of World War II.

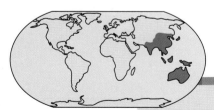

CHAPTER PREVIEW

Key Terms to Define: gross national product, trade deficit, pragmatists, stalemate, nonaligned, domino theory, boat people, developing country, developed country, protectionism

People to Meet: Mao Zedong, Kim Il Sung, Roh Tae Woo, Jawaharlal Nehru, Indira Gandhi, Ho Chi Minh, Ferdinand Marcos

Places to Discover: Tiananmen Square, Taipei, Korea's 38th parallel, Vietnam's 17th parallel, Gulf of Tonkin, Saigon, Manila, the Pacific Rim

Objectives to Learn:
1. What problems did Asian countries face after colonial rule?
2. How did the cold war affect countries in Asia and the Pacific?

Communist rally in Beijing, China

3. In what ways have Asian nations assumed new roles in world politics since World War II?

4. What factors have contributed to the economic success of Japan and other Asian countries?

Concepts to Understand:
- Change—Communists make gains in Asia; democracies form along the Pacific Rim. Sections 1, 2, 3
- Conflict—Independence movements and cold war political struggles cause violence. Sections 4, 5
- Nationalism—Nations in South Asia and Southeast Asia emerge from colonial status. Sections 4, 5
- Cultural diffusion—Changing political and economic roles open cultural exchange between Asia and the rest of the world. Section 6

837

SECTION 1

Japan's Economic Rise

The end of World War II brought dramatic changes to Asia. Japan lost much of the territory it had acquired. Great Britain, France, and other European powers lost or relinquished their Asian colonial possessions and withdrew from the region. National boundaries were redrawn and independent countries emerged. Despite this turmoil some countries—most notably Japan—experienced dramatic economic growth. Japan's rise to world economic power was one of the most important changes in post-World War II history.

Occupation and Reform

Japan, a proud nation with a long history of self-reliance, ended World War II with its pride crushed, its economy wrecked, and its people demoralized by the humiliating defeat. The victorious countries established an occupation government, the Supreme Command of the Allied Powers (SCAP), to govern Japan after the war. Although planned as a coalition of the Allies, the occupation government became entirely a U.S. enterprise, headed by General Douglas MacArthur. The general was determined not to plant the seeds of future war by imposing an unjust and unworkable system on the Japanese. MacArthur's reform policies fell into three major categories: political, economic, and educational.

A New Constitution SCAP required Japan to adopt a new constitution in 1947. The constitution stripped the imperial family of its political power and gave it to the Japanese citizens. No longer could Japanese emperors rule by their claim to divine authority. Instead, the constitution allowed Emperor Hirohito to remain in office as "a symbol of the state." Moreover, he was encouraged to renounce any claims to divine origins. The constitution established a cabinet based on the British model. Both houses of the

Learning from Photographs *This photo was taken a few hours after the atomic bomb exploded in Hiroshima.* **What problems did the Japanese have to deal with in the aftermath of nuclear destruction?**

Learning from Photographs *After the war, MacArthur (left) directed Emperor Hirohito to command the imperial forces to submit to the Allied occupation. In this way, the Japanese and their government accepted MacArthur's authority over Japan more readily.* **What statement did MacArthur require of the emperor?**

Diet, or legislature, were made elective, and citizens over the age of 20 could vote. A bill of rights guaranteed basic freedoms.

The new constitution included one unusual provision. Article Nine prohibited all warfare except for defense. SCAP hoped that Article Nine would prevent Japan from ever threatening its neighbors again. Article Nine had additional significance, however. It enabled Japan to focus all of its resources on producing better consumer goods, such as cars and televisions, rather than military goods.

Economic Reform   The second great area of reform was in economic reorganization. SCAP attempted to break up the giant industrial and banking organizations, called *zaibatzu*, which monopolized the Japanese economy and hindered the development of small enterprise. However, efforts to decentralize economic power in manufacturing and finance achieved only limited success. Large corporations remained powerful.

Decentralization was more successful in agriculture than in industry. Absentee landholders could own only 2.5 acres of land. The law required them to sell off holdings beyond this figure at very low prices. Those who actually farmed the soil were permitted to own up to 7.5 acres. Decentralization changed the face of Japanese agriculture, resulting in the transfer of ownership of more than 3 million acres. As a result of transferring land from absentee owners to farmers, agricultural production increased sharply. Japan's rural population, though small, prospered.

Reshaping Education   SCAP's third major reform was to improve education. Educational opportunity was extended to a much greater proportion of the Japanese. Local school boards gained greater control over the schools. Parents and teachers organized associations to improve their schools. Publishers revised textbooks to reflect more democratic views. Everyone encouraged students to study long and hard. For example, today the standard school year in Japan is 243 days, 63 days longer than in the United States.

Japan's Dramatic Recovery   The war-weary Japanese people, hoping to end the occupation quickly, cooperated with MacArthur. In 1951 Japan signed a formal peace treaty, and occupation ended.

Japan still faced enormous obstacles in regaining its prosperity. In addition to the destruction caused by the war, the country was small and possessed few natural resources needed by an industrial country. Japan had to import most of the oil, coal, copper, and other raw materials its factories needed.

Despite these obstacles, Japan began to grow rapidly. The talented engineers, skillful managers, and hard-working laborers who graduated from Japanese schools were willing to work hard to make their country prosperous. And because of Article Nine of the constitution, the government and the people directed their efforts to building a strong economy rather than a strong military. The government worked closely with large corporations to plan and promote industrial growth. For example, government and industry leaders agreed to invest heavily in the home electronics industry. Japanese radios, televisions, stereos, and other items soon dominated the world market.

Similarly, the Japanese government and industrial leaders targeted the automobile industry as one they thought could help bring prosperity to Japan. The government helped fund researchers who developed dependable, high-mileage engines. Managers and laborers worked together to develop newer and more efficient production techniques. As a result of these innovations, Japan began producing high-quality cars at competitive prices, and sales of Japanese autos around the world soared. Japan increased its share of world automobile production from 3 percent in 1960 to 29 percent in 1980.

By 1980 Japan had one of the most successful economies in the world. Although only as big

CONNECTIONS: HISTORY AND THE ENVIRONMENT

A Warning From Animals

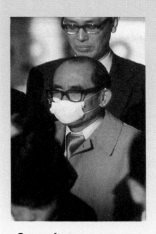

Some Japanese wear protection against the effects of air pollutiion.

Japan's spectacular economic growth after 1945 raised the standard of living for most of its citizens. However, the Japanese found a price tag attached to this success: environmental damage.

The country's developing industries clustered along a narrow coastal belt between the city of Tokyo and the southernmost island, Kyushu. Along with industry came a dense concentration of people and automobiles and the pollution of air, water, and food supplies so familiar to other industrialized regions.

In 1953 people in the fishing villages outside of the community of Minamata noticed strange behavior in birds and pets. Birds flew into buildings and trees or fell from their perches; cats walked with a strange gait, frequently stumbling or falling. Often they went mad, foaming at the mouth, and had to be destroyed.

Soon the affliction spread to humans. The problem was blamed on poor sanitation by the villagers, and stricken families were shunned. Eventually, however, the cause was found to be mercury poisoning. The source of the mercury discharge was a nearby chemical plant.

The victims filed lawsuits, and the publicity that followed forced the Japanese government to consider the hidden costs of rapid economic development. The need to balance industrial growth with environmental protection has become a pressing issue not only in Japan but throughout the world.

Making the Connection
1. What made Japan's pollution problem so severe?
2. What steps can governments take to curb pollution and maintain growth?

as California, Japan's **gross national product** (GNP)—the sum value of all goods and services it produced—was half that of the United States. Its per capita GNP, the amount of production per individual, surpassed that of any other industrialized country.

Japan in World Affairs

As a result of this economic growth, once self-reliant and isolated Japan became tightly interwoven into the world economy. It became a leading buyer of raw materials such as minerals and oil. It became a leading seller of manufactured goods, particularly cars, stereos, televisions, and computers. Its banks invested money around the world. And as a result of this economic power, Japan became a world political power as well.

Japan's economic growth occurred during the U.S.–Soviet cold war. The United States was eager to build up allies against the Soviets. Hence, the United States encouraged economic growth in Japan. However, Japan's prosperity eventually brought it into conflict with several countries, particularly the United States.

One cause of conflict was Japan's trade imbalance with other countries. A **trade deficit** occurs when a country imports more than it exports. Because Japan sold far more goods to other countries than it purchased, many countries, including the United States, had trade deficits with Japan.

Several reasons help explain why many countries imported more goods from Japan than they exported to it. Japan's complex set of government regulations limited foreign companies' ability to sell goods in Japan. Japanese retailers had long-standing ties with local producers that they wanted to maintain. Japanese consumers preferred to purchase goods made in their own country, in part because the goods were well made and in part because they wished to protect the jobs of Japanese citizens. But the flow of Japanese goods to the United States and the flow of U.S. dollars into Japan upset many Americans.

Japan's growing affluence also brought demands that it spread its wealth to other countries. For example, in 1990 one African nationalist leader, Nelson Mandela, stated bluntly that Japan's financial aid to African countries trying to overcome poverty was insignificant.

And that same year, when Iraq invaded its tiny neighbor Kuwait, the United States called upon Japan to help force Iraq out of Kuwait. After considerable debate, Japan responded with financial help to countries affected by the conflict. However, Japan did not send troops, in part because of Article Nine of its constitution. Referring to World War II, one member of Parliament said, "After that experience, we should never again aim a gun at foreign peoples—even the people of Iraq."

In recent years, Japan has begun to transform itself into a service economy, using its wealth to provide banking and insurance in addition to producing durable goods. Four of the world's largest banks are already located in Japan. The political, economic, and educational systems that brought recovery after World War II probably will continue to fuel the nation's prosperity in the future.

SECTION 1 REVIEW

Recall
1. **Define:** gross national product, trade deficit
2. **Identify:** Douglas MacArthur, Emperor Hirohito
3. **Describe:** What are some of the reforms instituted during the Allied occupation of Japan?

Critical Thinking
4. **Synthesize:** Imagine how Japan's modern history might have been different if General MacArthur had wanted to punish Japan for its actions in World War II.
5. **Evaluate:** Explain whether you think the United States was wise in helping Japan rebuild after World War II.

Applying Concepts
6. **Change:** What economic policies have promoted Japan's prosperity?

China in Revolution

The Allied defeat of Japan in World War II effectively removed the last foreign power from China. Relieved of their common enemy, the Soviet-backed Communists and the Western-backed Nationalist forces then engaged in a bitter civil war, which the Communists won in 1949. The defeated Nationalist leader, Chiang Kai-shek, and nearly 2 million of his followers retreated to the island of Taiwan, where they set up the new capital of the Republic of China at Taipei. On October 1, 1949, Mao Zedong proclaimed mainland China as the People's Republic of China, with its capital at Beijing. Over the next two decades, the Communists radically transformed China.

The People's Republic

In spite of some opposition, the new Communist government enjoyed wide support in China. Internationally, the People's Republic of China was immediately recognized by the Soviet Union and its satellites. Burma, India, and Great Britain soon followed. In 1950 the Chinese signed a treaty of "friendship, alliance, and mutual assistance" with the Soviet Union. It was followed by a series of economic agreements between the two countries.

In 1953 the Chinese began receiving considerable aid from the Soviet Union to build up their industry. That year, the Chinese launched an ambitious program of economic development known as the first Five-Year Plan. Mao wanted this program to promote China's "transition to socialism." His goal was to replace private ownership of factories, banks, and other businesses with public ownership. Mao believed that all businesses should be owned jointly by the people of China through the government. As the economy changed, Mao expected the entire cul-

ture to change. His goal was to completely replace traditional Chinese values with Communist ones.

Building a New Society The Five-Year Plan stressed the development of heavy industry, such as steelmaking, and of agriculture. Industrial output increased an average of 15 percent a year, a phenomenal rate. The rural economy changed less rapidly. At first, farmers joined cooperatives in which individual small landowners shared machinery and other resources and cooperated in managing their land. This program's success encouraged further reforms.

In 1958 China began the second Five-Year Plan, known as the "Great Leap Forward." It called for the full-scale collectivization, or public ownership and management, of all agricultural production. This was done through a system of communes. The commune was to be the basic element of socialist society, combining production of goods, administration of laws, and allocation of social welfare in one self-sustaining unit. Communes included about 5,000 households, which were divided into production teams of about 30 families each.

By 1959 it was clear that the Great Leap Forward was failing. Poor weather caused the crops to fail, and local officials—fearing punishment—turned in false reports of crop production. Industrial production declined. The result was suffering on a massive scale. Eventually the government restored some private control in an effort to boost production. Price controls were dropped, and farmers were allowed to sell some of their crops for profit. However, as many as 20 million people died of starvation.

Promoting Revolution During the 1949 revolution, Mao announced that China would "lean to one side" in foreign affairs, meaning that it would follow the Soviet example and oppose capitalist countries, such as the United States, where it could. In 1950 China and the Soviet Union both supported the Communist government of North Korea, which fought against U.S.-backed South Korea. In 1954 Chinese Prime Minister Zhou Enlai took part in the Geneva peace conference that ended the French role in Vietnam and opened the door for United States involvement in the region a few years later.

During the 1950s, however, China increasingly criticized the Soviet Union, under Nikita Khrushchev, as being too willing to compromise with the capitalist West. China broke with the Soviets and began to develop its own model Communist state. "The east wind," Mao proclaimed, "will prevail over the west wind." In response, the Soviet Union withdrew all its technological advisers from China, who took with them plans for many vital projects.

The open split between China and the Soviet Union awakened many people in the United States and around the world to the different forms of communism. Many who once assumed that all Communist governments would follow closely the policies of the Soviet Union began to realize they were wrong. Communism would vary in each country depending on that country's history and culture.

Learning from Art *This Chinese wall poster celebrates Communist forces entering Beijing in January 1949, marking the victory of Mao Zedong's revolution.* **How long did Mao rule China?**

The Cultural Revolution

Mao's revolutionary zeal made him impatient with the slow pace of the social and economic progress in China. The people, he feared, had lost their revolutionary spirit. He charged that the government and Communist party bureaucracies were too bloated and self-serving to conquer rural poverty, the disparity of wealth among regions, and other problems plaguing China.

Mao decided that China needed a new revolution, not to overthrow the government, but to radicalize it once more. The result was the Cultural Revolution of the 1960s, one of the most dramatic experiments in social change in modern history. The goal was to revolutionize Chinese society by bringing greater equality. The government sent medical doctors and other professionals to work in the fields, while members of the working classes were assigned to high government positions or appointed to revolutionary committees to oversee the work of the intellectual and professional classes. The mission of these workers was to root out and punish any suspected deviations from Communist thought.

Local politicians, teachers, and other leaders were persecuted and removed from office by groups of students and young adults. These young people were known as Red Guards. They agreed with Mao that China must punish all those suspected of being too sympathetic to Western cultural ideas or of "taking the capitalist road." Education, especially, was paralyzed, as street demonstrations disrupted classes and Red Guards arrested professors. Universities virtually shut down for four years. Eventually, Mao decided that the efforts of the Red Guards to root out non-Communists were too vigorous, and he

Learning from Photographs *Industrial centers, such as this gas refinery in Yumen, were built during the first Five-Year Plan. In the "Great Leap Forward," the government pressed for more industrial production, instead of improving other sectors of the economy. The result was economic failure.* **What other factor hindered economic growth in China?**

restrained them. By the time Mao acted, however, the education and careers of thousands of people had been permanently disrupted.

Reform and Reaction

In the early 1970s, several moderate leaders emerged as possible replacements for the aging Mao Zedong. These leaders were less interested in promoting revolutionary fervor than in pragmatic, or practical, solutions to problems. For example, they were more willing than was Mao to tolerate the growth of an elite, wealthy group of citizens if doing so would increase economic production. And they wanted China to worry less about confronting capitalist countries and more about developing ties with them in order to acquire their technology.

Desire for improved technology was one reason China began to reach out to other countries. In addition, China's growing conflict with the Soviet Union prompted it to search for allies. In the 1960s China and the Soviet Union disagreed over their respective roles in the Vietnam War. By 1969 Chinese–Soviet relations had deteriorated so much that a border incident erupted between the two countries. The former allies were now shooting at one another.

The split between China and the Soviets gave the United States an opportunity to reestablish relations with China. In 1971 U.S. Secretary of State Henry Kissinger made a secret trip to China, which was followed by the historic visit of President Richard Nixon in 1972. The events marked the beginning of a new era in global politics. China, long viewed by the United States as an ally of the Soviet Union against the United States, had begun to side with the United States against the Soviets.

When Mao and Zhou each died in 1976, the Chinese Communist party split over who should become the next leader. Mao's widow, Jiang Jing, led a group of radicals who wanted to return to the fervor of the Cultural Revolution. Opposing the radicals were the **pragmatists**, those who advocated modernization through increasing China's world trade, learning new technology from the West, and interpreting communism less strictly. One of the leaders of the pragmatists was Deng Xiaoping (duhng syow ping), a longtime leader in the Communist party who was expelled from government during the Cultural Revolution. Deng and his allies emerged victorious. Once in power they imprisoned Jiang Jing and three of her top allies, a group known as the Gang of Four.

Four Modernizations The pragmatists put into practice a plan developed by Zhou Enlai for the economic renewal of China known as "the Four Modernizations." It covered agriculture, industry, national defense, and science and technology and was supported by Hua Guofeng, who had assumed the dual roles of Communist party chairman and premier.

The essence of the plan was to abandon long-held Chinese notions of self-reliance and economic independence. It sought instead to build on the growing relationship with the West. Under the pragmatists light industry prospered, led by the textile and food-processing groups. Today China produces significant quantities of consumer goods, many of which were not produced at all before 1950, including televisions, tape recorders, sewing machines, cameras, washing machines, and refrigerators.

In that same spirit of expanding relations, the government allowed more students to study in foreign countries. By the late 1980s, there were 60,000 Chinese students studying in American universities.

Crackdown The pragmatists were less successful in the sphere of government. Under the pragmatists, government corruption increased. Citizen anger at dishonest government officials, combined with growing demands for free speech and popular participation in government, led to large demonstrations. In 1989 thousands of Chinese students gathered in Beijing's Tiananmen Square to protest corruption in government and to demand greater civil liberties and an improvement in conditions at Chinese universities. The government's tolerance of these demonstrations appeared to signal that China was allowing greater freedom of speech.

However, after six weeks of student protest, government hard-liners, led by Deng, sent in tanks and troops to break up the demonstrations, killing and wounding many students. Hundreds of other protesting Chinese citizens, mostly workers rather than students, were killed along the roads leading to the square. The government then launched a campaign of retribution against those advocating free speech, creating an atmosphere of fear and stifling political thought and discussion.

The crackdown on students and workers set back Chinese economic development. Fearing political instability, foreign investors backed away, severely damaging the economy and China's prestige abroad. By late 1990 a new prime minister, Li Peng, was again appealing to the West for investment to build the Chinese economy.

Taiwan One issue that China has faced since the 1949 revolution is the status of Taiwan. Under the dictatorial rule of Chiang Kai-shek, Taiwan's export of manufactured goods grew rapidly. After Chiang died in 1975, his son became the most powerful leader in the country. He continued the pro-business policies of the government. The Communists claim Taiwan as part of China, while Taiwan claims to be an independent republic. The future of Taiwan remains uncertain.

SECTION 2 REVIEW

Recall
1. **Define:** pragmatists
2. **Identify:** Chiang Kai-shek, Mao Zedong, Zhou Enlai, Cultural Revolution, Jiang Jing, Deng Xiaoping, Tiananmen Square
3. **Describe:** What changes occurred in China's relations with the United States and with the Soviet Union between 1949 and 1973?

Critical Thinking
4. **Analyze:** Examine how the "four modernizations" affected China's international relations.
5. **Evaluate:** Explain whether you think Deng Xiaoping was a good leader for China.
6. **Analyze:** Compare and contrast Mao's policies for the redevelopment of China with those of MacArthur in Japan.
7. **Analyze:** Describe how the Cultural Revolution differed from other revolutions you have studied.

Applying Concepts
8. **Change;** Can political struggles within a country always be viewed as a battle between pragmatists and radicals? In your answer use other historical examples of change through political struggle.

A Divided Korea

Korea's modern history has been heavily shaped by international politics. In 1910 the Korean peninsula was annexed by the Japanese, who ruled it as a colony until the end of World War II, when Japan was stripped of its territorial possessions.

After the war the United States occupied southern Korea, and the Soviet Union occupied the north. Thereafter Korea became the scene of a major cold war struggle. Koreans expected that the division of their country would be tem-porary, lasting only until UN-supervised elections could be held and a new government established. However, with the coming of the cold war, the Soviets refused to cooperate with the UN elections procedures. Korea remained divided along the 38th parallel.

North Korea, officially called the Democratic People's Republic of Korea, allied with the Soviet Union and China. South Korea, called the Republic of Korea, allied itself with the United States.

IMAGES OF THE TIME

The Korean War

The war between North and South Korea was devastating for both troops and civilians. Although fighting ended in 1953, no permanent peace treaty was ever signed.

The North Korean flag, adopted in 1948, bears a red star symbolizing communism.

The United Nations sent troops to South Korea in 1950 to force Communist troops to withdraw.

The Korean War

On June 25, 1950, North Korea, hoping to unify the country under a Communist government, invaded South Korea. The United Nations Security Council immediately condemned the invasion and organized an army to counter it. While 16 countries contributed troops to the UN force, over 90 percent of the soldiers came from the United States.

In the first months of the war, the North Koreans swept southward, conquering almost all of South Korea. However, on September 15, 1950, the UN troops counterattacked, led by General Douglas MacArthur of the United States. MacArthur launched a surprise invasion at Inchon, along Korea's west coast and far behind the North Korean front lines. The daring move gave the UN forces the offensive they needed. Within six weeks, MacArthur's troops had retaken all of South Korea and had conquered most of North Korea.

The Chinese then came to the aid of their ally, North Korea. Chinese troops forced the UN army to retreat southward. By the middle of 1951, after one year of fighting, each army dug in along a line not far from the 38th parallel. There the fighting reached a **stalemate**, a situation in which two opponents are unable to move significantly or make further gains. Truce talks began on July 10, 1951. The armies continued to attack one another, but neither side advanced very far.

On July 27, 1953, the two sides agreed to stop fighting and accept a temporary armistice line that divided Korea along the existing battlefront. After the deaths of nearly 5 million people and the devastation of much of Korea, the war ended with Korea still divided not far from where it had been divided three years earlier.

Many civilian homes were demolished by the fighting and had to be rebuilt (left). U.S. combat engineers sweep mountain trails for mines and booby traps (below).

Reflecting on the Times
How did the Korean War reflect world political tensions of the 1950s?

Korea Today

The stalemate in the Korean War has been matched by a stalemate in diplomacy. The two Koreas continue to draw economic and military aid from their respective sponsors, the United States and China.

North Korea, under the dictatorial rule of Kim Il Sung since 1948, has rebuilt since the end of the Korean War. It exports large amounts of fish and grain and has a growing manufacturing economy. The standard of living is comfortable but allows for very little disposable income. Health care is effective, and life expectancy is more than 70 years. Education focuses on science and technology. Economic growth, though, has been limited by North Korea's heavy investment in its military. North Korea devotes about 20 percent of the country's gross national product to military expenditures.

South Korea, far wealthier than North Korea, has enjoyed sustained economic growth since the mid-1960s. Between 1983 and 1987, the South Korean economy grew 10 percent per year, a remarkably high rate. To promote prosperity the South Korean government has strongly encouraged exports. In recent years Korean electronic products, cars, and other goods have begun to compete with those made in Japan.

The economic growth of South Korea has occurred under a repressive and corrupt government. However, since 1979 massive student protests have demanded greater democracy. In 1987 Koreans elected Roh Tae Woo as president, the first peaceful transfer of power in South Korea's short history. South Korean students have also called for uniting North and South Korea. In October 1990 reunification talks began. The end of the cold war may prepare the way for the two Koreas to once again become one country.

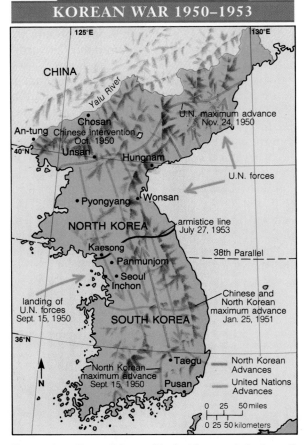

KOREAN WAR 1950–1953

Learning from Maps *Each side occupied virtually the entire Korean peninsula at various times.* **Why was MacArthur's Inchon landing so effective?**

SECTION 3 REVIEW

Recall
1. **Define:** stalemate
2. **Identify:** Kim Il Sung, Roh Tae Woo, Inchon
3. **Explain:** What is the political significance of the 38th parallel?

Thinking Critically
4. **Evaluate:** What do you think might be the costs and the benefits of reunifying Korea?
5. **Analyze:** How are North and South Korea similar, and how are they different?

6. **Evaluate:** Compare South Korea's growth with Japan's.

Applying Concepts
7. **Conflict:** How might Korea's future be influenced by the end of the cold war?

SECTION 4

Turmoil in South Asia

Citizens of British-ruled India had been agitating for independence since the 1870s. Finally, during World War II, Great Britain agreed to end its colonial domination of the region. After almost 200 years of British rule, South Asia would be free. However, the creation of five independent countries in South Asia has been marred by bloody conflicts between religious and ethnic groups.

Dividing the Subcontinent

Even before Great Britain agreed to grant India independence, the people of the region began dividing along religious lines. India's Muslim minority feared domination by the Hindu majority. In 1946, with independence looming, violent riots between Hindus and Muslims erupted throughout India. Thousands were killed in the bloody confrontation.

Afterwards, leaders of the two religious groups agreed that British India should be divided into two separate independent countries. They hoped that dividing the Hindu-dominated regions from the Muslim-dominated regions would bring peace.

In August 1947 Great Britain granted independence to two countries formed out of its Indian territory. Heavily Muslim areas in the far west and the far east formed the nation of Pakistan. The vast area in between, where most people were Hindus, became the new nation of India. One Indian leader, Jawaharlal Nehru, delivered a moving radio address in which he expressed the hope that independence gave him:

A moment comes, which comes but rarely in history, when we step out of the old to the new, when one age ends, and when the soul of a nation, long suppressed, finds utterance.

Independence did not bring religious harmony, however. Fighting continued between Hindus and Muslims. Before the killing had subsided, hundreds of thousands of people were dead. Another 10 to 12 million people had fled their homes, hoping to escape persecution as a religious minority. Hindus in Pakistan moved to India, while Muslims in India headed to Pakistan. This movement of people was one of the largest single mass dislocations of people in history. Tragically, another casualty of the conflict was Hindu leader Mohandas Gandhi. A Hindu extremist, angered at Gandhi's demands that

Learning from Photographs *Whereas Gandhi had appealed to the Indian masses, Nehru, a wealthy intellectual, gained the support of the upper-class members of the Indian National Congress party that ruled independent India.* **What political movement did Nehru lead?**

Learning from Photographs *Indira Gandhi speaks at a political rally. The daughter of Jawaharlal Nehru, she followed in her father's footsteps and became prime minister in 1966.* **Why was her rule marked by violence?**

Muslims be treated fairly, assassinated him on January 30, 1948.

The migrations and the killings did not end the conflicts between Hindus and Muslims. More than 60 million Muslims remained in their homes in India, and the tension between them and the Hindu majority remained high.

India

The first prime minister of the new country of India was Jawaharlal Nehru. Along with Gandhi, Nehru had led the fight for independence. He headed the Indian government from independence until his death in 1964.

Under Nehru's leadership, India became a leader in world affairs. Nehru argued that countries such as India should not align themselves with either superpower and get caught up in the cold war. By remaining **nonaligned**—that is, tied to neither superpower—the smaller countries of the world could then provide an alternative to the United States and the Soviet Union.

In domestic affairs Nehru believed in following a democratic path to socialism. He thought that the government should actively promote economic development and equality. India's new constitution aimed to unite the diverse groups that made up the country. It established the equality of all people under the law and granted universal suffrage. Caste distinctions were banned and discrimination against untouchables and outcastes became illegal. By making Hindi the official national language, the government hoped to further national unity.

The reforms, however, conflicted with the traditional Hindu practices followed by a majority of Indians. For example, women traditionally could not inherit property on an equal basis with men. Under Nehru's leadership, the Indian government passed a law giving women equal rights to inherit property. But even with the support of the law, many women were reluctant to break with tradition. Similarly, the constitutional provisions that banned discrimination did little to change the attitudes of most Indians.

In 1950 the Indian government introduced a series of five-year plans for economic development. The plans set up a mixed economy, one in which some businesses are privately owned, while others are under the control of the government. The Indian government backed large projects, such as road building, factories, irrigation systems, and energy plants. India, however, remained largely a nation of farmers who worked their own small plots of land.

Two years after Nehru died, his daughter, Indira Gandhi, was elected prime minister. Gandhi was the first woman to lead the Indian government. Before becoming prime minister, she had been a leader in the Congress party, the dominant political party in India, and had been minister of information and broadcasting.

In her seventh year in office, Gandhi greatly strengthened her popular support with her handling of a major crisis. In 1971 East Pakistan declared its independence from West Pakistan. Civil war broke out, and 10 million refugees from East Pakistan poured into India, looking for safety. With the diplomatic and military support of India, East Pakistan won its independence and, in 1971, became the country of Bangladesh.

India's successful intervention in the war enhanced Gandhi's popularity. "India is Indira, Indira is India," people shouted. India, the largest country in South Asia, had demonstrated its willingness to use its military and political might to influence events in other countries in the region.

In 1975 Gandhi's political opposition attempted to oust her on charges of corruption. She met this crisis by suspending the constitution and placing thousands of opposition leaders under arrest. The state of emergency lasted two years. In 1977 she called for new elections. Unexpectedly, Gandhi lost and was briefly jailed by the new prime minister, Moraji Desai, leader of the Janata party. In 1980 Gandhi regained the position of prime minister.

During the 1980s India was beset by increasing religious and ethnic conflicts. In 1983 over 2,000 people died in clashes between Hindus and Muslims in Bengal in eastern India. Conflicts between the two religious groups also continued in Kashmir, the region along India's western border with Pakistan.

A third area of conflict was northern India. In 1984 Gandhi sent troops into the holiest shrine of the Sikhs, a religious minority group, to put down a Sikh rebellion. The Sikhs wanted greater autonomy in their state of Punjab. In retaliation for violating the shrine, two of Gandhi's personal bodyguards, themselves Sikhs, assassinated her.

POSTWAR INDEPENDENCE IN ASIA

Learning from Maps *With the crumbling of the European colonial empires after World War II, a large portion of the world's population came under self-rule.* **How do you think Asia's geography affected its postwar politics?**

Learning from Photographs *Nehru sent Sikh soldiers to defend Kashmir's Hindu ruler when neighboring Pakistanis crossed the border to aid a Muslim revolt.* ***In what other Indian region did a great deal of violence occur?***

In the six years following Indira Gandhi's death, four different people served as prime minister, including her son, Rajiv. Chandra Sekar took power in 1990. Under him, India continues to face the difficult task of uniting its diverse ethnic and religious groups.

Pakistan and Bangladesh

Pakistan confronted severe problems soon after gaining independence from Great Britain. First, the gap between the rich and the poor was very wide. A group of 22 families controlled 60 to 70 percent of the country's financial assets. Second, Pakistan lacked leadership. The most popular national leader during the independence movement, Ali Jinnah, died a year after the establishment of Pakistan.

Third, and most important, Pakistan consisted of two dissimilar regions separated by over 1,000 miles (1,609 kilometers). West Pakistan was a dry, mountainous region in which most people spoke Urdu. East Pakistan was a wet lowlands region in which most people spoke Bengali. The two regions vied for government positions and funds for economic development. By 1971, the tension between the west and the east had reached the breaking point. Although the Bengalis constituted a majority of the population of Pakistan before independence, only 36 percent of the national budget and 20 percent of foreign aid were spent in East Pakistan. The country's government was dominated by West Pakistanis, who attempted to impose the Urdu language on East Pakistan.

The Bengalis, led by Sheikh Muriban Rahman, organized the Awami League to oppose West Pakistani rule. In 1970 the league won a majority of the seats in the National Assembly. The government then postponed the assembly, which the Bengalis interpreted as a denial of their rights, and declared a strike. The crisis escalated into violence, causing as many as 10 million people to flee into India and leading to the war that ended in the creation of a new country—Bangladesh.

Bangladesh   Although only the size of the state of New York, Bangladesh has a population about six times larger. It is one of the most densely populated countries in the world, with about 2,000 people per square mile (760 people per square kilometer). Its population, already over 100 million, continues to grow rapidly.

Bangladesh has been plagued by political, economic, and natural disasters. In spite of some economic growth, the per capita GNP in Bangladesh is one of the lowest in the world, only one-hundredth that of the United States. The country is vulnerable to periods of extreme drought and floods that have caused destruction and hunger on a disastrous scale. Although the country's economy is 80 percent agricultural, much of the land is submerged during the monsoon season. Bangladesh's political history since 1971 has been marked by factional strife, martial law, and transfer of power by assassination.

Pakistan Since 1971   The loss of Bangladesh in 1971 demoralized the Pakistanis and brought a new leader, Zulfikar Ali Bhutto, to power. Bhutto attempted many reforms, but his harsh methods provoked bitter opposition. In 1977 he was ousted and was later tried and executed for the murder of a political opponent.

Bhutto's successor, General Mohammed Zia ul-Haq, was a skilled foreign policy strategist. Often during the Soviet Union's occupation of neighboring Afghanistan in 1979, Zia permitted Afghan rebels to use Pakistan as a base for operations against Afghanistan's Communist government. He also assisted in distributing American economic and military aid to the rebels. Zia's government also took in 3 million refugees from the Afghan war. These policies increased the danger to Pakistan from the Soviet Union but won Zia the friendship and massive foreign aid of the United States.

Within Pakistan, Zia ruled strictly. A devout Muslim, Zia supported legal changes to make laws conform to the Islamic legal code. He kept Pakistan under martial law from 1977 to 1985.

In 1988 Zia was killed in an airplane crash, which was widely thought to be an assassination. In the elections following Zia's death, the popular and reform-minded Benazir Ali Bhutto, daughter of the former prime minister, became Pakistan's new leader. She was the first woman to lead a Muslim state. Although her election was perhaps the first truly democratic transfer of power since independence, her narrow victory limited her ability to implement reforms.

In August 1990 Bhutto's government was "dismissed" by Pakistan President Ghulam Ishak Khan on the charges of corruption. Although this was a legal move under the Pakistani consti-tution, Bhutto charged that it was in fact a plot by the military to again seize control. Bhutto sought reelection in October 1990 but was defeated. She was succeeded by Nawaz Sharif, leader of the military-backed Muslim League.

Burma and Sri Lanka

In 1948, the year after Great Britain granted independence to India and Pakistan, it also freed two other countries. One was Burma, which recently changed its name to Myanmar. This densely populated, agricultural country just west of India and Bangladesh has been under military rule for much of its history. The government has emphasized development of a self-reliant economy, so its trade with other countries has been limited. This policy has slowed the country's economic development, but it has kept Myanmar out of political conflicts.

The other country created by Great Britain in 1948 was Ceylon, known since 1972 as Sri Lanka. This beautiful island off the southeast coast of India has been the site of a recurring conflict between two ethnic groups. The Sinhalese, who make up about three-fourths of the population, are Buddhists. The Tamils, who make up about one-fifth of the population, are Hindus. In recent years the Tamils, complaining of discrimination against them by the Sinhalese, have demanded their own state within Sri Lanka. Hundreds of people have died in conflicts between government troops, who are Sinhalese, and Tamil guerrillas. The conflict seems likely to continue.

SECTION 4 REVIEW

Recall
1. **Define:** nonaligned
2. **Identify:** Jawaharlal Nehru, Indira Gandhi, Zulfikar Ali Bhutto, Mohammed Zia ul-Haq, Benazir Ali Bhutto
3. **Explain:** What were the consequences of Great Britain's withdrawal from India?

Critical Thinking
4. **Analyze:** What do you think is the underlying cause of continuing political strife in India?
5. **Synthesize:** Form a hypothesis to explain why India and Pakistan have had female heads of state while the United States has not.

6. **Evaluate:** How do you think India's nonaligned policy affected the cold war?

Applying Concepts
7. **Conflict:** Was the division of India into two separate countries beneficial? Explain your answer.

Southeast Asia and the Pacific

U nlike India, which remained nonaligned during much of the cold war, Southeast Asia was thrust into the middle of the superpower contest and suffered because of regional war. The competition between Communists and anti-Communists brought war and instability to much of the region of Asia known as Indochina. Only in recent years have countries such as Vietnam and Cambodia begun to recover from earlier conflicts.

Struggle for Indochina

Before Japan conquered Southeast Asia in World War II, France ruled the region as a colony. When Japanese forces withdrew following the war, France attempted to reestablish its authority. By then, however, nationalist movements demanding independence had grown strong. Vietnamese nationalists in the Indochinese Communist party, later known as the Vietminh, declared the existence of the independent Democratic Republic of Vietnam in 1945. The Vietminh were supported by the Soviet Union and the Chinese.

The Vietminh, under the leadership of Ho Chi Minh, and the French could not reach an agreement on how to share power. In 1947 the two sides went to war. The United States, fearing Ho's Communist ties and wanting to support its ally France, provided military and financial aid to France to subdue the Vietminh. Despite U.S. aid, the French could not win a military victory. In May 1954 the Vietminh defeated the French in the decisive battle at Dien Bien Phu. After their loss, the French agreed to a cease-fire and decided to pull out of Vietnam completely.

A month before the battle, the Vietminh, the French, the United States, and several other countries had agreed to meet in Geneva, Switzerland, to negotiate a settlement to the Vietnam conflict. Negotiators divided Vietnam along the 17th parallel, creating a Communist North Vietnam and a pro-Western South Vietnam. This arrangement was to last only until elections could be held in 1956. But the elections never took place. They were scuttled by the new leader in South Vietnam, Ngo Dinh Diem, a staunch anti-Communist who feared that elections would demonstrate Ho's popularity. Guerrillas in South Vietnam, known as Viet Cong, continued to fight against the Diem government, hoping to unify the country under Ho. The United States government sent financial aid and several hundred military advisers to bolster Diem.

However, Diem was a weak and unpopular leader. In 1963 the South Vietnamese military, despairing of Diem's leadership and fearing that the South would fall to the Communists, staged a coup in which Diem was killed. This was done with the quiet approval of the U.S. government and President John F. Kennedy.

Reflecting on France's earlier troubles in Vietnam, French President Charles de Gaulle urged Kennedy to withdraw. "I predict you will sink step by step into a bottomless quagmire," he warned.

War in Southeast Asia   In its zeal to contain the spread of communism, the United States ignored de Gaulle's advice and moved deeper into the conflict. The growing U.S. role in Vietnam was justified by those who accepted the **domino theory**—the belief that if one country in a region fell to communism, its neighbors would fall as well. American military and political advisers since the early 1950s had believed in this theory. By the end of 1963, the number of U.S. advisers in Vietnam rose to 16,000.

In August 1964, U.S. President Lyndon Johnson announced that North Vietnam had fired on two American destroyers in the Gulf of Tonkin off the coast of Vietnam. Johnson seized on this incident to increase U.S. involvement in the war. He ordered air strikes on North Vietnam. At his request Congress passed the Gulf of Tonkin Resolution, which gave him broad powers to conduct war. In March 1965 Johnson sent the first ground troops to South Vietnam. By the middle of the year, the United States had 60,000 troops in Vietnam.

Over the next three years, the war escalated sharply. By 1968 U.S. troops numbered over 500,000, and U.S. planes were bombing Vietnam heavily. The South Vietnamese army numbered about 800,000. The number of Viet Cong and their North Vietnamese allies was about 300,000. Despite numerical superiority, the U.S. and South Vietnamese forces did not seem close to victory. And as the U.S. role in Vietnam increased, so did opposition to the war within the United States.

The turning point in the war came in early 1968. The Viet Cong launched a major military offensive during the Vietnamese New Year holiday, Tet. Although they failed to capture any major cities, the bitter fighting made more and more Americans realize that several years of U.S. involvement had failed to significantly weaken the Viet Cong. Opposition to Johnson's war policy became so fierce that Johnson decided not to seek reelection in 1968.

Ending the War   As the antiwar movement grew stronger, the United States began withdrawing its troops. In 1973 the last U.S. combat troops left Vietnam. However, the war continued until 1975, when the Viet Cong successfully defeated the South Vietnamese army.

After more than 20 years of fighting, Vietnam was unified under a Communist government. However, at least 2 million people, including 58,000 Americans, had died in the conflict. Half of South Vietnam's population, 10 million people, were refugees.

In recent years, relations between the United States and Vietnam have begun to improve. The Vietnamese government has helped locate and return the bodies of American soldiers killed

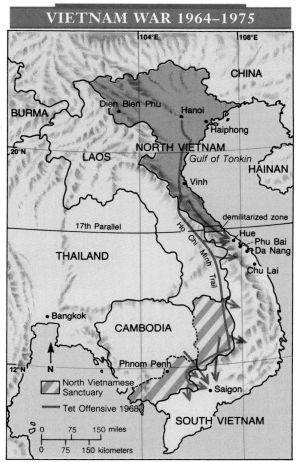

VIETNAM WAR 1964–1975

Learning from Maps *The negotiated division of Vietnam, unlike the partitioning of Korea, did not hold.* **What were some reasons for the different outcomes of the Korean and Vietnam conflicts?**

in Vietnam. Some former American soldiers have returned to Vietnam to help disarm land mines they planted during the war.

A Legacy of Violence

The Vietnam war affected all of Southeast Asia. Cambodia, Laos, and Thailand suffered from their closeness to the conflict between Communists and anti-Communists in Vietnam.

Cambodia   In 1953, the year before the Geneva talks, Cambodia won its independence

Learning from Photographs *Helicopters were used in the Vietnam war to spot enemy positions, transfer troops and supplies, and transport the wounded.* **How successful were U.S. tactics in Vietnam?**

from France. The country became a constitutional monarchy led by King Norodom Sihanouk, a member of Cambodia's historic ruling family. In 1955 he abdicated the throne in order to become prime minister.

Like Nehru in India, Sihanouk tried to follow a policy of nonalignment. However, as war intensified in Vietnam, Cambodia was drawn in. In 1969 and 1970, American planes bombed Viet Cong camps in Cambodia. As a result of this bombing, the conflict between Communist rebels and the Cambodian government increased. In 1970 an American-backed army officer, Lon Nol, ousted Sihanouk. Lon Nol charged that Sihanouk was not battling the Communists aggressively enough.

The combination of the bombing and the overthrow of Sihanouk led to civil war in Cambodia. Cambodian Communists, known as the Khmer Rouge, battled and finally defeated Lon Nol's forces. In April 1975, Khmer Rouge troops, under the leadership of Pol Pot, took control of Cambodia's capital, Phnom Penh.

The Khmer Rouge hoped to rapidly undo all of the corruption, elitism, and oppression that had built up under colonial and capitalist rule. They wanted Cambodia, which they renamed Kampuchea, to once again become an independent, self-sufficient agricultural country. To reach this goal, the Khmer Rouge devastated the country. They destroyed all money and books. Soldiers forced city dwellers into the countryside to perform grueling work on farms. Troops slaughtered civil servants, teachers, and students who may have supported the old system. Starvation, torture, and widespread executions by the brutal regime killed up to 3 million people—possibly one-third of the entire population of Cambodia.

In 1979, after a series of border incidents, Vietnam invaded Cambodia and ousted Pol Pot. Vietnamese forces established a new government under Heng Samrin. Vietnamese troops were withdrawn under UN pressure in 1989. Various factions of the Khmer Rouge continued their guerrilla warfare against the government. The fate of Cambodia remains uncertain.

Laos Laos won its independence from France at the Geneva meeting in 1954. While the war raged in neighboring Vietnam, Laos had its own civil war between Communist forces and the American-backed government.

The withdrawal of the United States from the region left Laos without adequate defenses, and it soon fell under the total domination of Vietnam. Under the Communist puppet regime, the country has made little economic progress and relies heavily on Soviet aid. Black marketing and the opium trade supplement the economy.

Thailand   Thailand's postwar history has been less violent than that of its neighbors, possibly because it is the only Southeast Asian country that escaped European colonial occupation. Therefore, it has been spared many of the problems faced by other countries in the region, such as reestablishing a national identity and creating new forms of government. The monarchy continues as a stabilizing force in Thai society, but real power is now held by the military.

After World War II, Thailand pursued a firm anti-Communist policy, aligning itself decisively with the United States in the Vietnam War. In recent years Thailand has adopted a more relaxed policy toward China, partly as a means of resisting threats from Vietnam. The country remains an ally of the United States.

In 1967 Thailand led the formation of the Association of Southeast Asian Countries (ASEAN). This regional alliance, like the European Economic Community, was designed to promote political stability, economic growth, and cooperation. Other members of ASEAN include Indonesia, Malaysia, the Philippines, and Singapore.

The Boat People   The turmoil in Southeast Asia from 1975 to 1979 forced thousands of Vietnamese, Cambodians, Laotians, and ethnic Chinese living in the region to flee their homes. Some settled in refugee camps near Thailand's borders with Laos and Cambodia. Others, known as **boat people**, took to the sea in anything that would float, leaving behind their homes and possessions and hoping to make their way to safe ports such as Hong Kong. Some of the most fortunate eventually made connections with family and friends in the United States and elsewhere.

Unfortunately, many boats—bought from unscrupulous people—proved unseaworthy, and many people drowned. The boat people who survived endured terrible hardships—malnutrition, the death of loved ones, and the perils of a sea escape. Some were assaulted and robbed by pirates. One refugee describes his experience:

We left Cam Ranh Bay [in Vietnam] *on . . . September 16, 1977, without any provisions. There were storms on the high seas.*

Without the navigation equipment we could not manage the tiny boat. We threw off all five of our fuel-filled tanks and all our possessions to lighten the boat. We starved for fourteen days. My mother-in-law was the first one who died. Then all four of my children, and other children, too. Altogether we lost eighteen children and two adults. . . . Several ships passed by. None of them responded to our cry for help. We were once given some food by a passing Taiwanese merchant ship.

—From *The Boat People and Achievement in America*, by Nathan S. Caplan, 1989

Many of the boat people eventually settled in the United States. Others scattered throughout Asia. The process of reuniting war-torn families continues today.

Rim of Southeast Asia

The former colonies of Great Britain, of the United States, and of the Netherlands—like the former French colonies—also suffered great turmoil. Many of these problems continue to remain today.

Indonesia   Indonesia won its independence in 1949, ending almost 350 years of Dutch rule. Under the leadership of the first president, Achmed Sukarno, efforts were made to unite the many peoples of the 13,000-island country. A national language was chosen that put all the people on an equal footing. Although it is 90 percent Muslim, women took an important role in developing the country. Progress was set back in 1965 when Communists tried to seize control. In a bloody rampage, about 300,000 suspected Communists were killed. Sukarno was forced out of office, and General Suharto, a staunch anti-Communist, took control of the country.

Today Suharto continues to lead Indonesia. Indonesia has a population of about 180 million, making it the fifth largest country in the world. It is also the most populous Muslim nation in the world.

Learning from Photographs *Philippine President Corazon Aquino responds to cheering admirers. Her rule ended years of repressive government under Ferdinand Marcos.* ***Who supported Aquino in her effort to replace Marcos?***

Malaysia   Malaysia was formed in 1963 by the merger of several former British colonies on the Malay Peninsula and on the neighboring island of Borneo. Malaysia's brief history has been marked by conflict between the two largest ethnic groups, the Malays and the Chinese. In 1965 the Malays forced Singapore, a heavily Chinese region, to leave Malaysia. Four years later riots between the Malays and the Chinese exploded in the capital, Kuala Lumpur. Since 1971 Malaysia has enjoyed relative political stability and economic growth.

Singapore   Singapore, a country of 55 islands, has been a commercial center for centuries because of its excellent port and its strategic location on international shipping routes in the Strait of Malacca. Many residents of Singapore are highly skilled in shipping, banking, storage, insurance, and telecommunications. Singapore also produces petroleum products, ships, electronic equipment, and chemical and food products. It also has a thriving publishing industry.

Singapore's government was dominated until recent years by Prime Minister Lee Kuan Yew. Although his government had strict curbs on the press, labor unions, and academic freedom, it was popular because it provided housing, health care, and education and because it encouraged private businesses.

The Philippines   When the Philippines declared their independence from the United States in 1946, they faced severe problems. The country had suffered over a million casualties in World War II, and Manila, its capital and largest city, had been virtually destroyed. However, the country began to rebuild between 1954 and 1957, under the leadership of the popular president Ramón Magsaysay.

Eight years later the Philippines had another strong president, Ferdinand Marcos, who governed from 1965 to 1986. Initially, Marcos was popular because he tried to improve the schools and transportation facilities. But growing evidence of his corruption fueled bitter protests against him. For example, U.S. foreign aid poured into the Philippines in return for the right to maintain military bases in the country. However, much of the aid money was apparently appropriated by Marcos for his personal use.

The incident that finally ended the Marcos era began with the assassination of Marcos's longtime opposition leader, Benigno Aquino, Jr. In 1983 Aquino was granted permission to return to Manila from exile in the United States. As he arrived under Philippine government guard, he was shot and killed, perhaps by one of the guards.

President Marcos was widely suspected to have ordered the killing. A massive public outcry forced new elections, which Marcos "won" mainly through fraud. Nevertheless, popular anger forced him to flee the country. Aquino's widow, Corazon, who had run against Marcos, claimed victory. Filipinos looked forward to a new era of political reform.

However, Aquino failed to move quickly to push reforms such as redistributing land from the wealthy to the peasants. She soon faced strong opposition from Marcos loyalists, Communists, the Muslim minority, and corrupt bureaucrats. Meanwhile, Filipinos increasingly

Tradition in Cloth

Part of a long heritage, the art of making *tapa* cloths, or bark cloths, is still practiced in several cultures of the Pacific region. The craft, passed down for generations, continues as a tradition in central Polynesia—on Samoa, Tonga, Futuna, Rotuma, and other Pacific islands. In different cultures, *tapa* cloths are used for different functions. Made in various sizes and thicknesses, the cloths are used for clothing, decorations, and household items such as tablecloths and blankets. In some cultures, *tapa* cloths are also used for ceremonial and symbolic functions.

Tapa cloth is made from the bark of the mulberry tree. The bark is pulled from young, straight branches in long strips. The soft bendable inside layer of the bark is peeled away. After being soaked in water, a strip of this inner bark is placed on a flat hardwood log and is pounded with a wooden mallet. The fibers of the bark gradually spread out, creating sheets of cloth. By the time the pounding is complete, a single strip of bark is often twice its original length. Long strips of cloth can then be pieced together, using glues made from plants, to form large sheets of *tapa* cloth.

Once the *tapa* cloth is pieced together,

Tapa Cloth from Western Samoa

decoration is applied. There are two common techniques of applying decoration to *tapa* cloth. In one method, the artist uses a finely carved wooden board to apply a design to the cloth. The wood is carved so that the raised areas of the board create a pattern. The *tapa* cloth is placed on top of the carved board, and then a piece of cloth soaked with dye is pressed against the cloth, picking up the impression of the carved design beneath the cloth (in much the same way that a printing press works). The other method commonly used to decorate *tapa* cloth is to paint a design directly onto the cloth. These methods are often used together, with the painted design emphasizing details of the printed design in deeper colors and a bolder design.

The designs on *tapa* cloths vary among different Oceanic cultures. Many are geometric, abstract designs; others depict animals or plants as well. Although some designs have been influenced by increasing contact with industrial products, most designs still reflect the traditional forms of specific cultures. Through the continued production of *tapa* cloths, the artists of Samoa and other Pacific islands are keeping alive an age-old tradition of their oceanic culture.

Responding to the Arts

1. How are *tapa* cloths used in the Pacific region?
2. How are designs applied to *tapa* cloths?

Learning from Photographs *Sydney, Australia, known for its beautiful harbor and skyline, is a major shipping center in the Pacific.* **How have Australia's trade relationships changed since World War II?**

resented the presence of American bases and troops in their country. As a result, the United States agreed in 1990 to scale back its forces in the Philippines. In order to maintain its military presence in the western Pacific Ocean, the United States will open new bases in Singapore.

Brunei Brunei is a small independent country on the north coast of the island of Borneo, which it shares with the Malaysian states of Sarawak and Sabah, and Kalimanzan, which is a part of Indonesia. The borders of all these states were readjusted when the region began to move toward independence.

Occupied by the Japanese during World War II, Brunei was returned to British control after the war and remained a British protectorate until 1984, when it gained independence. The country is technically a constitutional democracy, but power remains in the hands of the sultan.

Although there is no effective democracy in Brunei, its people, mostly Malays and Chinese, enjoy one of the highest standards of living in Southeast Asia, thanks to the discovery of oil in the early 20th century. About 70 percent of its oil exports go to Japan.

Australia and New Zealand

Although Australia is not part of Asia, occasional Japanese bombing raids on Australian cities during World War II, reminded Australians of their proximity to Asia. Once Great Britain withdrew from its former colonies in Asia, Australians realized that they could no longer depend solely on Great Britain for military and economic support. The new Australia would have to become more independent and self-reliant. It would also need to develop closer ties to its Pacific neighbors and to the United States.

After the war Australia began a rapid changeover from a primarily agricultural to an industrial economy. It built its first automobiles in 1948, with the aid of the American-owned General Motors Corporation. In 1952 it signed the Australia, New Zealand, United States Defense Treaty (ANZUS), a Pacific regional defense alliance.

In 1973 Prime Minister Gough Whitlam traveled to China for a visit with Mao Zedong, thus underscoring the shift to the east in the Pacific Basin diplomacy. In addition, Australia began a new immigration policy that opened the doors to non-British European immigrants and to Asians for the first time. In the early 1970s, less than 50 percent of Australians were of British stock; this was down from 75 percent in 1949.

Under Prime Minister Robert J. L. Hawke, who took office in 1983, Australia has enjoyed a growing prosperity that is more equally distributed than it is in many industrialized countries. Today, Australia is one of the world's most affluent countries. Even as it developed closer relationships with its Asian neighbors, Australia has retained its ties to Great Britain and the United States and has emerged as a strong figure in world affairs.

Like Australia, New Zealand in the postwar period began changing its role in regional and world affairs. Traditionally New Zealand had

FOOTNOTES TO HISTORY

NO NUKES IN NEW ZEALAND

In 1985 New Zealand Prime Minister David Lange announced that ships carrying nuclear weapons, including those from the United States, could no longer enter New Zealand ports. The move strained relations among the signers of the Australia, New Zealand, United States Defense Treaty (ANZUS).

When U.S. Vice President Daniel Quayle visited New Zealand in early 1989, Lange announced his intention of abrogating the treaty agreement. Lange, however, resigned later that year. In October 1990 the new government announced that it would seek closer ties with the United States. But it was not clear whether nuclear ships would again sail in New Zealand waters.

been closely tied through trade and politics with the Commonwealth countries of Great Britain and Australia. While these links remain, New Zealand has increased its trade with other countries. For example, as Japan prospered economically, it purchased more goods from New Zealand. The ANZUS pact further cemented New Zealand's military ties to Australia and the United States.

These steps were intended to help resist Communist influence from Asia. They also acknowledged Asia's growing importance in world affairs, which was to become more significant as time passed.

SECTION 5 REVIEW

Recall
1. **Define:** domino theory, boat people
2. **Identify:** Ho Chi Minh, Ngo Dinh Diem, Pol Pot, Ferdinand Marcos, Corazon Aquino
3. **Locate:** What country was the chief colonial power in Southeast Asia until World War II?

Critical Thinking
4. **Apply:** Relate the domino theory in Southeast Asia to the policy of containment in Europe.
5. **Synthesize:** How did the geographic location of Singapore contribute to its economic development?

6. **Analyze:** How has the economy of Australia changed since World War II?

Applying Concepts
7. **Conflict:** Evaluate whether the domino theory was proven correct by events in Southeast Asia. Explain your reasoning.

Asia and the Pacific in a Global Society

Since the end of World War II, Asia—home to almost 60 percent of the world's people—has transformed itself and its role in the world. In 1945 most of eastern and southern Asia was devastated by war, wracked by revolution, or struggling to become independent. During the next half-century, many of these nations were concerned with drawing new boundaries; choosing a form of government; and resolving conflicts among ethnic, religious, and social classes.

Today, parts of Asia have strong economies, influential cultures, and optimism about their future. But whether through wars or through economic prosperity, Asia has had a tremendous influence on the rest of the world since 1945. One historian has called the second half of the 1900s the "Asian Century."

Building Stable Governments

In the years immediately following World War II, few nations in Asia and the Pacific had a strong government with wide popular support. Most nations had to rebuild their political system. Japan was under occupation by the United States. China was in a civil war. India, Pakistan, Southeast Asia, and Indonesia were throwing off colonial rule. Australia was the only major country in this region to begin the postwar period with a stable government.

In many nations the instability reflected profound conflicts among their people about the basic ideas that should guide their government. In China, Korea, Vietnam, Cambodia, Indonesia, the Philippines, and elsewhere, Communists and anti-Communists fought fierce and bloody battles in which millions of people died.

In other nations the disputes were over religious and ethnic differences. India, Sri Lanka, Malaysia, and Indonesia are the clearest examples of countries disrupted by diversity. Ethnic or religious conflicts continue in almost every Asian country.

Because of the diversity of beliefs and backgrounds, political power is fragmented into a variety of political groups. Coalitions of groups are able to unite against a common enemy, but their basic differences reemerge once peace comes and they reach their goal. For example, in the Philippines, Corazon Aquino led an anti-Marcos coalition into power. Once in power, however, she disappointed many of her supporters who had hoped she would overturn more of the Marcos legacy than she has.

Despite these hurdles, a number of nations have developed stable governments. Japan, South Korea, North Korea, India, Pakistan, Thailand, and Myanmar (Burma) each has had a fairly stable government. China, despite experiencing tremendous upheavals such as the Great Leap Forward and the Cultural Revolution, was ruled by one man, Mao Zedong, for almost three decades.

This stability was often achieved by authoritarian regimes that used force and other oppressive measures to keep their people silent. China, both Koreas, Pakistan, and some other nations cared little for freedom of speech, freedom of the press, freedom of religion, or other basic human rights. Elections, if held at all, were meaningless. Anyone protesting government policy risked going to jail.

Yet stability did have benefits in many places. South Korea, Taiwan, and Singapore had stable but repressive governments. However, by keeping wages low and restricting the rights of workers to protest, these nations attracted investments from overseas. Factories and assembly plants built in these nations provided jobs needed by the people who lived there.

Economic Development

Asia includes great extremes in wealth. Japan is one of the wealthiest countries in the world, while Bangladesh is one of the poorest. Most of the people in the heavily populated nations such as China, India, and Indonesia are poor. Therefore the overall per capita GNP in Asia is about one-third of the world average.

The continent also includes extremes in economic development. A nation with a high level of industrialization, such as Japan or Australia, is called a **developed country**. A nation such as India or Thailand, which is primarily agricultural and is working to build new industries, is called a **developing country**. South Korea is an example of a country that is moving from developing to developed status.

Along the coasts and in river valleys of the Asian continent, large industrial cities have risen. These cities include the most prosperous communities in Asia. The fertile areas of Indochina and eastern China are rural but heavily populated. The dry, mountainous region in western China is rural and less populated. The people in this region are generally poor.

Many countries have had to overcome agricultural problems. In Pakistan and the Philippines, land ownership is highly concentrated in the hands of a few wealthy families. In Bangladesh, farmers rely so heavily on the production and sale of one crop, jute, that they are at the mercy of the world market for their crop. If prices decline, the entire economy suffers.

Many countries had to develop educated and skilled work forces. After a promising start, industry in China failed to grow rapidly because of a shortage of skilled workers. Countries such as Japan, which have invested in education and have developed a skilled work force, have prospered. However, finding the money to invest in education is difficult for poor countries.

Industrial growth, while bringing jobs, also brought problems. In 1984 poisonous gas leaking out of a Union Carbide chemical plant near the city of Bhopal, India, killed 2,000 people and injured 200,000 others. The Bhopal incident was one of the worst industrial disasters ever.

Yet despite these problems, Asia is making economic progress overall. It was the only continent in the world that made significant improvements in its standard of living during the 1980s.

Asia in the World

Asian economic growth has been intertwined with that of other countries. In 1948 an American scientist invented the transistor, a

POPULATION GROWTH

	1990	2000 *	2025 *
Afghanistan	19.3	24.2	35.9
Bangladesh	115.2	145.8	219.4
Burma	44.5	55.2	82.2
Cambodia	8.4	9.9	12.5
China	1,119.6	1,255.7	1,460.1
Hong Kong	6.1	6.9	7.9
India	831.9	961.5	1,188.5
Indonesia	178.4	204.5	255.3
Japan	122.7	127.7	127.6
Korea (PDR)	22.4	27.3	37.6
Korea (ROK)	43.8	49.5	58.6
Laos	5.0	6.2	9.2
Malaysia	17.3	20.6	26.9
Nepal	18.5	23.0	33.9
Pakistan	113.3	142.6	212.8
Philippines	61.4	74.8	102.3
Singapore	2.7	3.0	3.2
Sri Lanka	18.0	20.8	26.2
Thailand	56.2	66.1	86.3
Vietnam	65.4	78.1	105.1

Population in Millions   ***Projection**

Learning from Charts *One of China's biggest challenges is population growth.* **Compare the 5 most-populated nations in 1990 and 2025. Speculate on the reason for the changes.**

small electronic device. Four years later a Japanese firm introduced the transistor radio, and at once they found a market in Europe and the United States. The radios marked the beginning of a new era in world trade. Exports from Asia would win an increasing share of the world market.

In the 1950s and 1960s, Japan, South Korea, Taiwan, and other Asian producers entered the international market, producing low-cost items such as inexpensive radios, clothing, and toys. Formerly, consumers in the United States and elsewhere had looked down upon many goods carrying the label "Made in Japan." Over time, however, Japan and other Asian countries began producing high-quality products, from radios to automobiles to computers, and trade increased dramatically.

In 1980, for the first time, U.S. trade with Asia surpassed U.S. trade with Western Europe. The majority of the Asian trade was with the "Pacific Rim" countries: Japan, South Korea, China, Taiwan, the Philippines, Thailand, Malaysia, Singapore, Indonesia, Australia, and New Zealand. In 1990 exports from Japan to the United States were about $100 billion a year, about $400 per U.S. citizen.

As Asian countries have prospered, they—and most especially Japan—have begun to invest their wealth overseas. For example, Japanese banks and corporations have purchased movie studios in California and several U. S. skyscrapers (including Rockefeller Center in New York); they have set up automobile factories in Tennessee and loaned billions of dollars to the U.S. government.

The success of Japan has also stimulated calls for **protectionism** in the United States and elsewhere. Protectionism is the use of trade quotas, tariffs, or other methods of restricting trade for the purpose of helping industries in the home country. An example of protectionism is the restrictions imposed by Congress on the number of cars that can be imported from Japan.

Because of their economic growth, Japan and Taiwan have become models for the rest of the world. Writers of numerous books have analyzed Japanese manufacturing techniques, management methods, labor relations, and governmental activities, pointing out how other industrialized countries can emulate Japan's success. Students of developing countries have analyzed the economy of Taiwan, hoping to find a model for other countries struggling to overcome poverty.

Asians have also been influential as individuals. Mohandas Gandhi's teachings about nonviolence inspired Martin Luther King, Jr., and the civil rights movement in the United States. The theories of revolution developed by Mao Zedong guided rebels in Africa and South America. Jawaharlal Nehru's nonalignment doctrine provided developing countries around the world a political strategy for avoiding being drawn into the cold war.

The influence of Asia goes far beyond politics and economics. Japanese movies, Korean musicians, and Indian religions are among the many other aspects of Asian cultures that have left a strong imprint on culture in other countries. As a former United States Secretary of State, George Shultz, said, "The Pacific region has rapidly emerged as a leading force on the world stage." It is expected to remain there for years to come.

SECTION 6 REVIEW

Recall

1. **Define:** developed country, developing country, protectionism
2. **Identify:** Pacific Rim
3. **Name:** What country in East Asia has become a world economic power?

Critical Thinking

4. **Analyze:** Explain how the economic and political systems of Japan and China differ.
5. **Predict:** Do you think democracy will dominate Asia during your lifetime? Why or why not?

Applying Concepts

6. **Cultural diffusion:** Is protectionism a good policy for a country to follow in order to stimulate its economic growth? Devise an alternative policy to achieve the same goal.

UNDERSTANDING WORLD TIME ZONES

When clocks say 2:00 P.M. in Boston, they say 7:00 P.M. in London. The clocks differ because the world is divided into time zones. By *understanding a time zone map*, you can calculate the time in various parts of the world.

Explanation

In 1884 an international conference established standard time zones around the world. The Prime Meridian, 0° longitude, running through Greenwich, England, became the reference point from which all time would be measured. The conference divided the world into 24 time zones, each 15° of longitude apart. If you travel east from Greenwich, the time is one hour later in each time zone. To the west, the time is one hour earlier.

The conference also agreed to establish the International Date Line at 180° longitude. When crossing this line, a day is gained or lost depending on travel direction.

To read a time zone map, use the following steps:

- Locate the reference point.
- Locate the place for which you wish to know the time.
- Determine if the place lies east or west of the reference point.
- Calculate the time.

Example

If it is 3:00 P.M. in Greenwich, England, and you want to know the time in Moscow, first locate the reference point, Greenwich, on the time zone map. Then locate Moscow, which is two time zones away. By adding two hours to Greenwich time, you calculate that it is 5:00 P.M. in Moscow. If it is 7:00 A.M., Sunday, in Los Angeles and you want to know the time in Tokyo, locate the reference points, calculate the time zones, and add a day. It is 9:00 P.M., Monday, in Tokyo.

Application

Study the map to answer this question.
1. If it is 6:00 P.M. in Beijing, what time is it in New York?

Practice

Turn to page 867 in the Chapter Review for further practice.

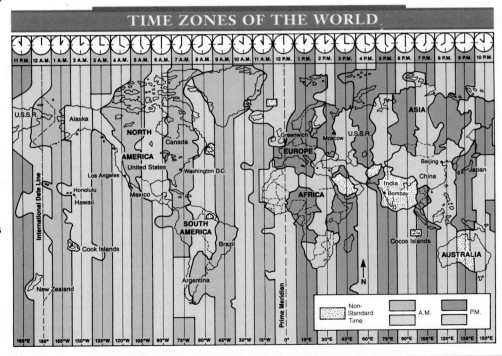

TIME ZONES OF THE WORLD

CHAPTER 32 REVIEW

HISTORICAL SIGNIFICANCE

The most dramatic change in Asia since the end of World War II is the dazzling economic achievements of Japan, and, to a lesser extent, of Taiwan, Singapore, and South Korea. In these countries strong, stable governments worked with private companies to foster economic growth. Many regions of Asia, including these countries, that were once isolated and poor or exported only raw materials now prosper through exports. For many Asians, the poverty of their childhood has been replaced by prosperity.

Along with economic recovery has come a new respect for Asian ideas. In the early 1900s, many Asians went abroad to attend school, to study foreign governments, and to analyze businesses, but few foreigners looked to Asia for ideas. In recent years, the flow has changed. While Asian students continue to study overseas, now experts from around the world study Japan and other Asian countries to learn the reasons for their success. In a global age, Asia has much to teach as well as to learn.

SUMMARY

For a summary of Chapter 32, see the Unit 8 Synopsis on pages 980–981.

USING KEY TERMS

Write the key term that best completes each sentence below.

a. boat people
b. developed country
c. developing country
d. domino theory
e. gross national product
f. nonaligned
g. pragmatists
h. protectionism
i. stalemate
j. trade deficit

1. Countries that did not take sides in the cold war were ___ .
2. ___ is a name for the practice of keeping foreign goods out of a country by means of tariffs, quotas, and other restrictions.
3. The sum value of all goods and services produced by a country in a year is its ___.
4. A ___ is one that is highly industrialized, such as Japan or Australia.
5. The Korean war reached a ___ that left the country divided at its pre-war boundary.
6. Vietnam's ___ suffered terribly because of the political upheaval in their country.
7. The ___ is the belief that if one country becomes Communist so will its neighbors.
8. A country that imports more goods than it exports has a ___ .
9. Bangladesh, Indonesia, and China could each be considered a ___ .
10. Chinese leaders who advocated modernization through increased trade and mechanization were known as ___ .

REVIEWING FACTS

1. **List:** What were the major areas of reform in Japan under MacArthur's occupation?
2. **Identify:** Who was the leader of the Gang of Four in China?
3. **List:** U.S. military involvement in Vietnam occurred primarily during the terms of three U.S. presidents. Name them.
4. **Explain:** What is meant by the term *Pacific Rim nations*?
5. **Identify:** Who were the boat people?
6. **Explain:** What were the goals of the Red Guards?

THINKING CRITICALLY

1. **Apply:** Using examples from Asia, explain whether a country's economic progress is related to its form of government.
2. **Analyze:** Why was MacArthur's occupation of Japan so successful?

3. **Synthesize:** Explain how events in Asia since 1945 have influenced the demographic make-up of the people in the United States.
4. **Analyze:** Why did the British colony of India divide into four separate countries?

ANALYZING CONCEPTS

1. **Nationalism:** How did nationalism bring both independence and political crisis to India?
2. **Change:** What event led to the downfall of the Marcos government?
3. **Conflict:** Explain why you think Asia will have more or less violence in the next 50 years than it has had in the last 50 years.
4. **Cultural diffusion:** Identify examples from your experience that suggest the influence of Asian countries in your life.

PRACTICING SKILLS

1. Assume you are in New York and you want to call someone in Tokyo on Friday at 8:00 A.M., Tokyo time. What time would you call?
2. Find New Guinea on the map on page 865. Explain why the line dividing the time zones on the island is not straight.
3. Assume that flying from Chicago to Beijing requires 26 hours. When would a flight leaving Chicago at 11:00 A.M. on a Wednesday arrive in Beijing?

GEOGRAPHY IN HISTORY

1. **Location:** Describe the location of Singapore.
2. **Place:** What geographic traits make Japan an unlikely site for industrial development?
3. **Movement:** What motivated the migration of 10 to 12 million people between India and Pakistan in the late 1940s?

TRACING CHRONOLOGY

Refer to the time line below to answer these questions:
1. How many years passed between the first U.S. financial aid to Vietnam and the beginning of rapid escalation of U.S. involvement in the war?
2. How long were the Communists in control of China before President Nixon's visit?
3. When did Mao take power in China?

LINKING PAST AND PRESENT

1. The second half of the twentieth century has been called the Asian Century. Explain what name you would give to the first half of the century.
2. The involvement by the United States in Vietnam was based on the Truman Doctrine, which declared the U.S. policy of containing communism. What earlier presidential doctrine justified overseas intervention by the United States?

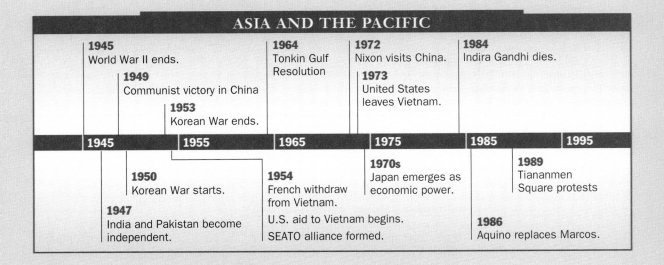

ASIA AND THE PACIFIC

1945 World War II ends.

1949 Communist victory in China

1953 Korean War ends.

1964 Tonkin Gulf Resolution

1972 Nixon visits China.

1973 United States leaves Vietnam.

1984 Indira Gandhi dies.

| 1945 | 1955 | 1965 | 1975 | 1985 | 1995 |

1950 Korean War starts.

1947 India and Pakistan become independent.

1954 French withdraw from Vietnam.

U.S. aid to Vietnam begins.

SEATO alliance formed.

1970s Japan emerges as economic power.

1989 Tiananmen Square protests

1986 Aquino replaces Marcos.

Africa and the Middle East

*D*uring the winter of 1961, more than 20,000 black Rhodesians gathered in the country's capital, Salisbury, to protest the rule of a powerful white minority in their country. All of them had taken off their shoes, symbolizing their shedding of European customs.

The rally began as nationalist leader Robert Mugabe declared, "Today you removed your shoes. Tomorrow you may be called upon to destroy them altogether or to perform other acts of self-denial. If European industries are used to buy guns which are aimed against us, we must . . . destroy those industries." It would be another 20 years of struggle before Mugabe's country, now named Zimbabwe, became free.

By 1990 nearly 1 billion people in more than 60 African and Middle Eastern nations had thrown off colonial rule, but political, ethnic, and other struggles continued.

CHAPTER PREVIEW

Key Terms to Define: apartheid, negritude, kibbutzim, cartel, *intifada,* fundamentalism

People to Meet: Mobutu Sese Seko, Jomo Kenyatta, Nelson Mandela, Gamal Abdel Nasser, Reza Shah Pahlavi, Yasir Arafat, Menachem Begin, Anwar al-Sadat, Ayatollah Ruhollah Khomeini, Saddam Hussein

Places to Discover: Soweto, South Africa, Suez Canal, Palestine, Aswan High Dam, Golan Heights, the West Bank, Beirut

Objectives to Learn:
1. What caused the rise of nationalism in Africa and the Middle East?
2. How did these regions change after independence?

Independence celebration in Swaziland

3. Why have these regions suffered so much violence?

4. What role do traditional values play in Middle East politics?

Concepts to Understand:

• Nationalism—European empires crumble, and independent nations come into being in Africa and the Middle East. Sections 1,2,3,4

• Conflict—Civil wars plague Africa, and Arab–Israeli strife dominates the Middle East. Sections 1,2,3,4

• Diversity—Ethnic and cultural diversity characterizes the continent of Africa. Sections 1,2

• Change—Economic and political development occurs unevenly in Africa and the Middle East. Sections 1,2,3,4,5

A New Africa

After World War II, the desire for liberation that found expression in Europe's Asian colonies spread to colonial Africa. On that vast continent only Egypt, Ethiopia, Liberia, and South Africa were independent. Great Britain, France, Portugal, and Belgium ruled the rest of Africa—skillfully in some areas, ineptly in others.

The path to independence was often bloody, and once free, the new nations faced the massive task of building modern societies. Civil wars and economic and political crises plagued Africa for decades. Today the struggle continues.

Winds of Change

Since the beginning of colonial rule, nationalist groups in Africa had resisted European control, often violently. But following World War II, these relatively small efforts for freedom swelled into powerful mass movements.

African Nationalism The democratic ideals for which the Allies fought in the war—self-rule and freedom from tyranny—inspired Africans, many of whom had fought in the Allied armies. "[We] overseas soldiers are coming back home with new ideas," wrote Nigerian Theo Ayoola, stationed with British troops in India. "We have been told what we fought for. That is freedom! We want freedom, nothing but freedom!"

For the colonial powers, the hypocrisy of continuing to rule African populations while upholding democratic ideals became unjustifiable in the eyes of the world. But besides the moral questions, imperial nations faced political and economic changes that made it impractical to retain their African possessions. Europe itself was devastated after World War II, and debt-ridden Europeans could scarcely afford to sus-

tain empires abroad. The price of colonization had already become clear in Asia, where France had lost Indochina in a costly war. Even so, imperial nations clung stubbornly and steadfastly to the idea of empire, making the inevitable changes more painful.

What the imperial nations did not recognize, or perhaps ignored, were the changes occurring throughout Africa. In many countries, nationalism was growing among the European-educated African elite who worked in colonial governments and in businesses. In the late 1940s, leaders emerged among this group. In speeches and at conferences, they rallied support for African independence.

Nationalist leaders found a ready audience for their ideas among workers in the fields, mines, and factories owned by overseas investors. World demand for African minerals and crops boomed after World War II, but Africa's European-owned industries absorbed the profits. Africans saw little change in their conditions, and their resentment of foreign rule grew.

Ghana Leads the Way Great Britain's richest colony, the Gold Coast, traveled a relatively easy road to independence, raising the hopes of other African nations for just such a smooth transition. Before World War II ended, the British had begun to give Gold Coast colonists more political rights. By then, well-educated African leaders had also begun to organize an independence movement. This group was made up of traditional African chiefs, a few professionals, and rich planters. In 1947 the group asked Kwame Nkrumah (KWAH may ehn KROO muh) to lead them.

Nkrumah had long been involved in continent-wide efforts to end colonialism. The pattern he established in freeing his own country would be followed by his fellow nationalists throughout Africa during the next decades. Starting in 1947, Nkrumah organized mass meetings and spoke on radio and television, calling on blacks to demand change. He led a series of strikes that culminated in a general strike in 1950. For his role in the strike, Nkrumah was jailed, but his efforts were effective. Great Britain relinquished political control beginning in 1951. Nkrumah moved from a jail cell to the highest office when he was elected in 1952 to head a new government and lead the country to freedom. In 1957 the Gold Coast, now renamed Ghana, became the first sub-Saharan nation to gain full independence after World War II.

The Nkrumah years came to represent the best and the worst in African leadership after independence. The young nation got off to a strong start. Ghana exported cocoa, gold, and diamonds. The people were literate; many were highly trained. But the government of the one-time hero became corrupt; it mismanaged the economy and wasted the country's resources. Western nations, alarmed by Nkrumah's socialist leanings, encouraged efforts to depose him. Ever since he was ousted by the army in 1966, one regime after another has ruled Ghana, forcing the nation into a slow decline.

French Colonies

Other countries, inspired by Ghana's independence, found their own freedom struggles more difficult. Although the British had not

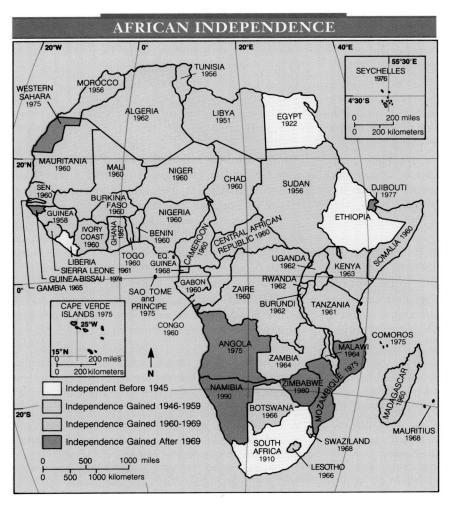

AFRICAN INDEPENDENCE

Learning from Maps *Between 1951 and 1982, more than 50 African colonies achieved independence.* **Speculate on why some countries were freed sooner than others.**

tried to make colonial peoples Britons, the French had attempted to spread French civilization throughout their holdings. Because of this cultural relationship to its colonies, France clung proudly and desperately to its empire.

Algeria   Freedom for the North African country of Algeria came only after one of the most costly wars on the continent. France's refusal to relinquish Algeria reflected the long history of French involvement in its large Mediterranean colony. French settlers, called *colons*, had been coming to Algeria since the 1830s. By 1940 nearly 1 million *colons* had taken the best land and jobs in Algeria, ignoring the needs of 9 million Muslim Algerians.

Backed by Egypt, Morocco, and Tunisia, 15,000 Algerian guerrillas launched a war for independence in 1954. In response to guerrilla raids, 200,000 French troops destroyed Algerian property, herded thousands of people into concentration camps, and used helicopters and heavy artillery to hunt down rebels.

Despite French firepower, the guerrillas fought on. The controversial war forced the collapse of France's government, the Fourth Republic. After General Charles de Gaulle became president in May 1958, he promised self-determination for Algeria. Despite fierce resistance from the *colons*, de Gaulle arranged talks with the rebels that led to independence on July 1, 1962. The price of freedom had been eight years of warfare and more than 1 million deaths.

Nationalism Spreads   While France was becoming mired in the Algerian war, nationalist movements were taking hold in other French colonies. France decided to give up its other North African holdings, Morocco and Tunisia, in 1956 because the Algerian war was draining its resources. These two countries had never been officially part of France, as was Algeria.

Throughout the French colonies in western and central Africa, demands for change came slowly. Many Africans held high-paying jobs, and some even received French citizenship. Although political resistance was not allowed, few leaders felt the need to demand change.

In 1958, however, President de Gaulle, seeking to head off future "Algerias," decided to reorganize the French empire into the French Community. Under this plan, the colonies could choose to remain linked to France, with their foreign and economic policies under French control. Or they could choose independence—with no economic support from France.

Only Guinea (GIH nee) chose freedom, supporting Ahmed Sekou Touré, the future president, who declared he would choose "poverty in freedom over riches in slavery." De Gaulle swiftly ordered all 4,000 French out of Guinea. Administrators carried away colonial records, development plans—even light bulbs and plates from the governor's palace. De Gaulle vowed to abandon Guinea and urged other nations not to help the new nation. However, newly independent Ghana and the Soviet Union promised aid.

In a postwar world dominated by the cold war, Sekou Touré's appeal to the Soviets angered de Gaulle, who feared that other sub-Saharan colonies would follow suit. To prevent this, France gave the remaining colonies freedom in 1960, this time with French help.

The Belgian Congo

By the late 1950s the vast Belgian Congo was ready for change. To avoid a war like France's in Algeria, Belgium began planning a staged withdrawal.

Belgian authorities imprisoned nationalist leaders in the Congo. But following riots in 1959, Belgium hastily freed the Congo in June 1960. Nationalist leader Patrice Lumumba became prime minister.

The new nation, unprepared to govern itself, erupted in civil war. The copper-mining province of Katanga, under local leader Moise Tshombe, seceded from the Congo in July 1960. UN peacekeeping forces were sent to the Congo to prevent the superpowers from becoming involved. Katanga was returned to the Congo, and UN forces withdrew in 1964. However, revolts soon broke out again among rival interests. Not until General Joseph D. Mobutu became dictator in 1965 was order restored.

Ruling with a strong arm, Mobutu held the Congo's 200 ethnic groups together. He also en-

Nationalistic Art

In addition to political and economic changes, many African nations have undergone rapid cultural changes in recent decades. Traditionally, African art was produced by artists from different ethnic groups. Sculpture was the primary art form. As African nations have changed, however, many artists have moved away from traditional techniques and begun experimenting with new materials and methods. Painting has grown in popularity and now rivals sculpture as a major art form.

In Chapter 29, you saw how European artists like Picasso were influenced by traditional African art early in the early 1900s. As contact between European and African cultures has increased over the years, the artists of African nations have begun to adopt techniques and subjects from the art of Europe and other regions for use in their own work. The increased popularity of painting and the subject matter of much modern African art reflect this interest in the art of other cultures.

Among African ethnic groups, traditional art often served religious functions. In contrast, today's artists have begun to use their work to explore the many facets of modern life. Some create paintings or sculptures that celebrate cultural traditions by focusing on African heritage. Others use their art to examine modern Africa—for example, the impact of industrialization and city life.

Although there are many styles in modern African art, a number of stylistic elements are common to much of African painting and use traditional designs and images from a number of African cultures. For example, many painters use bright colors and strong, decorative patterns similar to the colors and patterns of traditional sculpture and textiles.

Many new African nations have sought to establish a sense of community and national identity. Some have found that government support for the arts reinforces national pride. Governments have purchased art works and set up schools, museums, and art organizations to maintain Africa's artistic heritage.

Responding to the Arts

1. How has African art changed in recent decades?
2. Why do many governments in Africa choose to support the arts?

couraged people to honor their heritage by taking African names. He himself took the name Mobutu Sese Seko (SAY say SAY koh). In 1971 Mobutu changed the name of the country to Zaire (zah IHR).

During the early 1970s, high copper prices produced an economic boom in Zaire. But Mobutu, like Nkrumah, took advantage of his political power. He built monuments to himself and made his close friends millionaires. He also expelled foreign businesses and seized their property.

When copper prices plunged in the 1980s, Zaire's economy declined sharply. Mobutu then asked European businesses to return to Zaire to help steady the country's development.

Portuguese Africa

Portugal ruled the neighboring countries of Angola and Mozambique much as Belgium had governed the Congo. The Portuguese kept order through military force. Unwilling to hear requests for peaceful change, Portugal created conditions for a brutal revolt.

Starting in 1961 in Angola and 1964 in Mozambique, rebel groups waged guerrilla wars against Portugal. For over a decade, Portuguese troops were able to suppress the guerrillas. In 1974, however, Portugal itself underwent a revolution. The new government, facing many problems at home, freed Angola and Mozambique in 1975.

Both countries eventually came under Marxist governments. Mozambique's transition to self-rule was smooth initially, but the new government quickly developed troubles with its neighbors. In 1976 Mozambique closed its border with Rhodesia to protest white minority rule there. It also aided black rebel groups fighting the white minority government of South Africa. South Africa in return helped anticommunist guerrillas working to overthrow Mozambique's Marxist rulers. But by the 1980s, Mozambique had begun to introduce reforms such as private enterprise that helped to ease political tensions.

In Angola, civil war broke out in 1975 between pro-communist and pro-Western rebel groups. Cuba sent 20,000 Cuban troops to An-gola; the Soviet Union sent equipment and advisers. Demoralized by the Vietnam war, the United States supported the opposition groups but sent no aid. In 1976 the pro-communist forces prevailed and formed a Marxist regime.

Opposition groups, operating from bases in neighboring countries, continued the war throughout the 1980s. The violence ravaged Angola, disrupting the economy. In 1990, however, hopes for peace began to rise as new negotiations were held. The United States and the Soviet Union joined in urging the rival groups to compromise.

British Colonies

Despite the example for quiet change set when Ghana was freed from British rule in 1957, many of Great Britain's other colonies suffered violence during and after their battles for independence. In Kenya, a leading ethnic group led a bloody fight for freedom. And in Nigeria, civil war tarnished hopes for successful self-rule, as it did in Angola and the Congo.

Nigeria   Unlike Portuguese and Belgian colonies with thousands of settlers, the enormous colony of Nigeria had few Europeans. With little resistance, the Nigerians won independence from Great Britain in 1960. Creating a modern, stable nation was far more difficult, however.

Because the new nation followed old colonial boundaries, Nigeria's population consisted of 250 ethnic groups speaking 395 languages, as well as 3 major religious groups. Muslims dominated the north, followers of traditional African religions the east, and Christians the west. From 1960 to 1965, first one group, then another seized control.

In 1966 a Christian, Yakubu Gowon, tried to create a single nation of 12 states, hoping to calm tensions. But ethnic conflict and persecution caused a Christian group from the north, the Ibo, to flee to the east, where they tried to set up an independent Republic of Biafra.

Civil war ravaged Nigeria for three years, killing more than 600,000. About 2 million Biafrans died of hunger as a result of the fighting.

Learning from Photographs *These Ibo soldiers fought for the independence of Biafra during Nigeria's civil war.* **What caused Nigeria to split temporarily apart so soon after it was freed from British colonial rule?**

Biafra surrendered in January 1970. The Nigerian government then turned to rebuilding the country, developing the nation's rich oil reserves. In the early 1970s, Nigeria forced foreign oil companies to sell 40 to 80 percent of their holdings to Nigerians. As oil prices rose, Nigeria grew wealthy. However, world oil surpluses in the late 1970s and in the 1980s dealt crippling blows to the Nigerian economy.

Kenya As you read in Chapter 29, Kenya suffered for decades under British rule. European settlers held land in the temperate, fertile highlands of central Kenya, which the Kikuyu (kih KOO yoo) people regarded as their homeland. At the same time, Africans were banned from owning land.

Prior to World War II, Kenyan nationalist Jomo Kenyatta, a Kikuyu, spent years in Great Britain pushing unsuccessfully for political change in Kenya. After the war, Kenyatta brought his battle back home. By this time, nationalism in Kenya had become intense. A political movement—the Kenya African Union—was formed, and it chose Kenyatta as its president in 1947. Kenyatta began organizing groups who wanted Great Britain to leave: educators, religious and political leaders, and workers.

In the meantime, some Kikuyus formed an underground freedom movement, which the Europeans called the Mau Mau. In the early 1950s, the movement began a bloody campaign of guerrilla attacks on European settlers. The widespread uprising became known as the Mau Mau rebellion. Although he denied any role in the violence, Kenyatta was accused of leading the rebellion and was jailed from 1953 to 1961.

With troops and heavy bombers, Great Britain set out to crush the nationalists. Within three years Great Britain had smashed the uprising, but not the calls for freedom. To avoid more bloodshed, the British finally granted Kenya its freedom in 1963.

Kenyatta, nicknamed "Wise Old Man" by the Kenyans, was elected president in 1964 and ruled until 1978. He maintained a free market

FOOTNOTES TO HISTORY

THE GREAT ZIMBABWE

Once they won their freedom, many African nations took new names with great meaning for their people. Zimbabwe, for instance, refers to the 1,000-year-old royal city of Great Zimbabwe. Massive, protective stone walls gave the city its name—*zimbabwe*—which means "stone enclosure." Inside the walls the city of 20,000 contained palaces, religious buildings, markets, and the clay houses of Zimbabwe's citizens. Some think the city declined because fields outside the walls became less fertile and food was scarce. Whatever the reason, the kings of Zimbabwe left the city about 1450.

economy and made Kenya a popular spot for tourists and international businesses.

Central Africa Throughout the late 1950s and early 1960s, Great Britain slowly gave up control of its other African colonies. In 1964, Nyasaland became Malawi, and Northern Rhodesia became Zambia. But the future remained uncertain for one colony: Southern Rhodesia, with 7.5 million Africans and 250,000 Europeans.

As European Rhodesians saw new African nations coming into existence in the 1960s, they formed a party called the Rhodesian Front. Two years later, the Front took control of Rhodesian politics to keep Africans from gaining power.

The Front sought independence from British rule, but Great Britain refused to grant independence until Rhodesia gave Africans a share of political power. White Rhodesians were enraged. In 1965 Rhodesian Prime Minister Ian Smith declared Rhodesia independent. Although most of the world refused to recognize or trade with Rhodesia, the country did get support from South Africa, where a white minority also ruled.

In the 1970s, bands of guerrilla fighters began attacking Rhodesia's European settlers. The hit-and-run attacks increased in number and grew deadlier. European settlers began to flee, and the nation's economy was disrupted.

Finally, in 1979 Smith, agreed to negotiate with the African majority, and in 1980, Rhodesia—renamed Zimbabwe—won its freedom. Freedom fighter Robert Mugabe became prime minister. Once in control, Mugabe worked hard to keep European settlers, rather than lose their skills. During the 1980s, Zimbabwe prospered, but struggled with a soaring population.

South Africa

The fight for black freedom in South Africa began nearly from the moment the nation was created in 1910. Following the British victory over the Dutch Afrikaners in the Boer War, Great Britain united Afrikaner and British holdings in the southern part of the continent. This new British dominion—the Union of South Africa—firmly shut the door on black participation in government. The African National Congress (ANC) was formed in 1912 to oppose white domination. But generations would pass without a return to freedom.

A gradual political shift in South Africa brought the Afrikaners to power by 1948. The Afrikaners were strongly nationalistic and believed they had divine authority to rule South Africa. Their belief in white superiority was enacted into law in 1948, with the imposition of a policy of racial separation called **apartheid.**

Under apartheid—meaning "apartness"—white, black, and mixed races were strictly segregated. Black South Africans suffered the worst. Apartheid laws defined whom blacks could marry and where they could travel, eat, and go to school. Blacks could not vote or own property. To enforce separation of the races, the government moved thousands of blacks to desolate rural areas that it called "homelands," where jobs and food were scarce. Those who were able to get low-paying jobs in the cities were forced to live in wretched, fenced-in townships like Soweto, on the outskirts of Johannesburg. Blacks had to carry identity cards at all times. Under the repressive police state, blacks could be jailed indefinitely without cause.

The ANC and other groups staged strikes and demonstrations to press for reforms, but the government repeatedly crushed the resistance.

By the 1960s ANC leader Nelson Mandela had formed a military operation to press for change. In 1962 officials charged Mandela with treason and sabotage, and jailed him for life. From his prison cell, Mandela became a world-renowned symbol of the fight for freedom in South Africa.

In the face of strong criticism from Great Britain, South Africa angrily withdrew from the Commonwealth of Nations in 1961, increasing its political isolation. World condemnation grew, especially after police fired on a student protest march in the black township of Soweto in 1976, provoking riots. South African athletes were banned from the Olympics. In 1974 South Africa was barred from the United Nations. In the 1980s, the United States and other nations halted investment in South Africa until the government freed political prisoners and planned an end to apartheid. These economic sanctions crippled the nation's once-booming economy.

Some easing of apartheid began during the 11-year tenure of President P. W. Botha. The ban on interracial marriage was lifted, and the nation's large segment of Asians and mixed-race people won voting rights. But in 1985, outbreaks of guerrilla warfare in South African cities prompted Botha to declare a state of emergency, enlarging his police powers. Meanwhile, conservative whites continued to block efforts toward majority rule, keeping South Africa's 5 million whites firmly in control over the 26 million blacks.

In 1989, faced with continuing violence and economic pressure, South Africa's new president, F. W. de Klerk, began rolling back apartheid. On February 18, 1990, de Klerk re-

Learning from Photographs *In the early 1960s a young lawyer named Nelson Mandela led an anti-apartheid campaign that landed him in prison, sentenced to life.* **What changes brought about Mandela's release in 1990?**

leased 71-year-old Nelson Mandela from prison. By the early 1990s, it seemed that South Africa was heeding Mandela's warning that "there will never be peace and stability in this country until the principle of majority rule is accepted." De Klerk invited white and black groups to discuss a new constitution that would end apartheid and begin an era of black voting rights.

In the early 1990s, South Africa's new challenges became clear. Several black ethnic groups began vying for power, and new clashes among blacks broke out. As his negotiations with de Klerk continued, Mandela urged blacks to work in unity and with patience.

SECTION 1 REVIEW

Recall

1. **Define:** apartheid
2. **Identify:** Kwame Nkrumah, Jomo Kenyatta, Robert Mugabe, Nelson Mandela, F. W. de Klerk
3. **Explain:** How did Nkrumah's movement serve as a model for other Africans?

Critical Thinking

4. **Apply:** Show how the presence of large European populations in Algeria, Kenya, and Rhodesia contributed to long wars of independence.
5. **Synthesize:** If you were a white government leader in South Africa today and aware of other African struggles for freedom, how would you respond to the demand for black rule?

Applying Concepts

6. **Nationalism:** Explain the reasons why African nationalist movements gained appeal after World War II.

Africa's Challenges

African civilization has seen enormous changes in less than half a century. In that short time, a largely rural continent has become increasingly urban, with ties to all parts of the globe. In 44 young nations, the number of children in school soared from 18 million to 38 million in just 12 years. Africa also has become an international force, wielding more than a third of the votes in the United Nations General Assembly.

Yet huge challenges remain. "Africa has its feet in the neolithic age and its head in the thermonuclear age," wrote African expert Elliott Skinner. "Where is the body? It is managing as best it can."

Search for Unity

After the excitement of independence celebrations had passed, Africa's new nations entered a difficult period. Many of them adopted the political borders that had been drawn by the colonial powers. These boundaries divided people with similar customs and faiths. Old ruling families and ethnic groups began to struggle for power, and civil wars often erupted.

Politicians and parliaments were unable to stop the violence. At first, many African leaders governed through political systems inherited from their colonial predecessors—systems that were unfamiliar to most Africans. Often these systems did not work for African countries in the post-independence years. All too often, a nation's most powerful group, the military, stepped in to restore order.

By the 1970s, military leaders ruled about half of Africa's newly freed nations. In some, like Nigeria, dividing strong regional groups into smaller states helped to break down some regional rivalry. Even so, by the mid-1980s, well over half of all African nations lived under one-party or military regimes—often the only kind of government that could keep order.

Besides the problem of national unity, leaders had long worried about harmony among African nations. Through a movement called Pan-Africanism, they sought to promote a feeling of oneness and cooperation among all the nations on the continent. In 1963 Kwame Nkrumah of Ghana and Ahmed Sekou Touré of Guinea took the idea of unity a step further and invited 32 countries to form the Organization of African Unity (OAU). Nkrumah hoped the organization would be the first step in creating a United States of Africa. That idea failed, but the OAU did dedicate itself to building a strong African identity and coordinating national defense, health, and other policies. Member nations also agreed to respect one another's borders and to remain neutral in cold war politics.

Economic Development

Building strong economies proved as difficult as building a united continent. To move Africa's rural economies into the world of mining, manufacturing, and service industries, millions of people had to learn to read and write. Workers who made a living with their hands had to learn to operate machines in factories. Governments had to repair aging phone lines, railroads, and highways. "While the great powers are trying to get to the moon," President Julius Nyerere of Tanzania observed, "we are trying to get to the village."

When the colonial powers withdrew, they often left the new nations with fragile, if not ruined, economies. Most had a poor balance between farming and industry. Many were rich in one or two key resources or crops but had not yet developed economies that could provide the countries' basic needs. One-product economies, such as Ghana with cocoa and Nigeria with oil, were constantly at the mercy of changing prices for products on world markets. In addition, war had left some countries with scorched land and heavy war debts.

During the early years of independence, leaders organized various kinds of government-controlled economies to bring some order to the confusion. This turn to socialism pleased many nationalists, who equated capitalism with colonialism. No matter how they organized their economies, however, many countries failed to develop agriculture in their push to modernize.

Soon food crops began to suffer and thousands of unskilled rural people moved to the cities, searching in vain for jobs. With millions out of work and unable to buy the products of African industry, business suffered.

This poor balance between farming and industry left most nations with few products to export and too little food for their soaring populations. Governments had to borrow from foreign sources, often to buy food, and their debts grew. Severe droughts in Africa in the 1970s and 1980s made matters worse, causing tragic food shortages in 24 countries.

By the 1980s, Africa was a continent in crisis. A World Bank study showed that 21 of the

CONNECTIONS:
HISTORY
AND THE
ENVIRONMENT

The Moving Sahara

Deep in the Sahara, ancient rock paintings show grazing cattle and grasses where now there is only rock and sand. In recent times, farmers also grazed cattle in areas bordering the Sahara. But now those grasslands too are giving way to desert. Droughts are part of the problem. But so are people. "The Sahara isn't moving south; we're pulling it south," said a forestry official in Niger.

Before Africa was colonized, people lived in harmony with the land. Farmers cultivated fields until the soil was exhausted. When they moved to new plots of land, they let the old ones lie fallow, replenishing the soil.

Colonization changed life in Africa. Better medical care caused a population boom and a growing demand for food. Europeans pushed Africans to grow big cash crops for export.

Destruction of the land increased. Farmers cut trees to open up new

fields. Huge demands for food and cash crops also forced farmers to farm land year after year, never letting fields lie fallow. Droughts in the 1980s brought disaster. People had to use grains for food instead of for seed. Without plants to anchor the soil, tons of topsoil disappeared. The mixture of overfarming, overgrazing, cutting trees, and drought pushed the Sahara south as fast as 90 miles (145 kilometers) a year.

The solution to this problem lies with individual farmers. By planting trees, terracing fields, and fertilizing the soil, they may be able to slow the shifting of the Sahara.

Making the Connection

1. What is causing the Sahara to spread south?
2. Why do you think it is difficult to get individual farmers to change their practices?

world's 34 poorest countries were in Africa. More than 60 percent of all Africans received too little food each day, and more than 5 million children died every year. To cope with these problems, many African nations continued to rely on foreign help. By the mid-1980s, sub-Saharan Africa was $130 billion in debt.

Today the problems of inadequate food, growing populations, and foreign debt still plague Africa, but some hopeful signs exist. For example, 8 drought-ravaged countries formed a group to teach farmers how to preserve precious topsoil. A group of 16 West African nations agreed to barter among themselves, trading products for oil instead of for scarce cash. David Lamb, a journalist who spent years covering Africa, recalled with hope what Africans repeatedly told him. "Give us time," they said. "We are young."

African Identity

I love a world,
This priceless world,
Sweet home of haunting melodies
And roll of tom-toms—
My Africa.

> —Michael Dei-Anang,
> from the poem "My Africa"

In 1963 American poet Langston Hughes gathered nearly 100 African poems into a collection called *Poems from Black Africa*. It included this one by Dei-Anang, a poet and government official in Ghana.

"Usually," Hughes wrote in the foreword, "poets have their fingers on the emotional pulse of their peoples." The poet Dei-Anang, like other Africans, had begun to rekindle a deep pride in his heritage.

During the colonial era, Africans had learned much, both good and bad, from Europeans. There remained the idea, although not accepted by all Africans, that European culture was superior to African culture in art, music, literature, and technology.

As free nations emerged, many leaders stressed the need to take pride in Africa. In Senegal, a former French colony, President Léopold Sédar Senghor published poems that expressed his love of Africa. Because Africans had never lost touch with nature, he thought, they could help restore "a world that has died of machines and cannons." Senghor helped found a poetry movement called **negritude**, an effort to recapture black Africa's past dignity.

During the decades since independence, African artists and writers have built on this foundation of pride. Theater groups, filmmakers, novelists, painters, and others have explored the pain of colonialism as well as the modern problems of corruption and hunger. Music, in particular, continues to be a form of social protest in countries such as South Africa.

Open now to influences from around the globe, Africans have also created exciting new art forms. Congolese music, for instance, a mix of African, Latin American, and Caribbean styles, brings pleasure and delight to people in all of Africa and around the world.

SECTION 2 REVIEW

Recall
1. **Define:** negritude
2. **Identify:** Pan-Africanism, OAU
3. **Explain:** Why did many African nations come under military or one-party rule?
4. **Identify:** What changes are occurring in African culture?

Critical Thinking
5. **Apply:** Explain the sentence "[Africa's] feet are in the neolithic age and its head is in the thermonuclear age."
6. **Evaluate:** What might have happened if African nations had spent funds producing more food for their people instead of growing cash crops and industrializing their economies?

Applying Concepts
7. **Diversity:** Illustrate the benefits and drawbacks of Africa's cultural and ethnic diversity.

Nationalism in the Middle East

In the decades after World War II, nationalist movements took hold in the Middle East. For more than 20 years, Great Britain and France had governed much of the area under the terms of post–World War I agreements. Gradually the presence of foreign officials and troops on Middle Eastern soil revived the desire for independence, as it did in Asia and Africa.

While most Middle Eastern countries shook off European control in the postwar years, foreign influence in the region remained strong. With its valuable waterways and oil reserves, the Middle East became the scene of superpower maneuvering for influence during the cold war.

Arab Independence

Several Arab countries achieved independence before World War II ended, although Western powers still retained control over their affairs. Egypt, for example, had won its freedom in 1922, but Great Britain stationed troops there to control the Suez Canal. Likewise, although Iraq became free in 1932, Great Britain controlled its economy and military.

By the end of World War II, Arabs in French- and British-ruled areas of the Middle East began to demand freedom. In 1943, France granted independence to Lebanon, where Christian and Muslim leaders agreed to share power under a new constitution. Syria's independence came three years later, after France delayed approval of a new constitution and riots erupted. When the French finally relinquished control in 1946, the Syrians elected their first parliamentary government. In 1946, the British also withdrew from the Transjordan.

As independent states emerged, the Pan-Arab movement grew stronger. Pan-Arabism sought to build close cultural and political ties among Arab states. In 1945, leaders of Egypt, Iraq, Transjordan, Syria, Lebanon, Saudi Arabia, and Yemen formed the Arab League. Its mission was to unify the Arab world.

Formation of Israel

By 1947 only one European-ruled territory remained in the Middle East: British-occupied Palestine. Palestinian Arabs wanted the freedom from British control that had been promised them in the early 1900s. Zionist settlers, meanwhile, wanted to build a Jewish state on that same land—land that the Jews had claimed since biblical times.

Competing Claims The flow of immigrants into Palestine had swelled to a torrent during World War II, as Jews fled the Holocaust in Europe. Many settlers joined **kibbutzim,** or collective farms. On the kibbutzim, thousands of Jews struggled to turn swamps and thorny, boulder-strewn hillsides into productive farms.

Fearful of the growing Jewish population, Arabs began to attack settlers, hoping to slow the Jewish influx. To defend themselves, Jewish leaders formed a secret military force called the Haganah. By the end of World War II, guerrilla raids were common in Palestine. Unable to keep the peace, Great Britain turned Palestine over to the United Nations in 1947.

Israel Is Born For months, world leaders debated the future of Palestine. The United States and much of the West wanted to divide Palestine into a Jewish and an Arab state. Arab nations, along with several European and Pacific nations, rejected the idea. At a meeting of the General Assembly on November 29, 1947, the United Nations voted to partition Palestine.

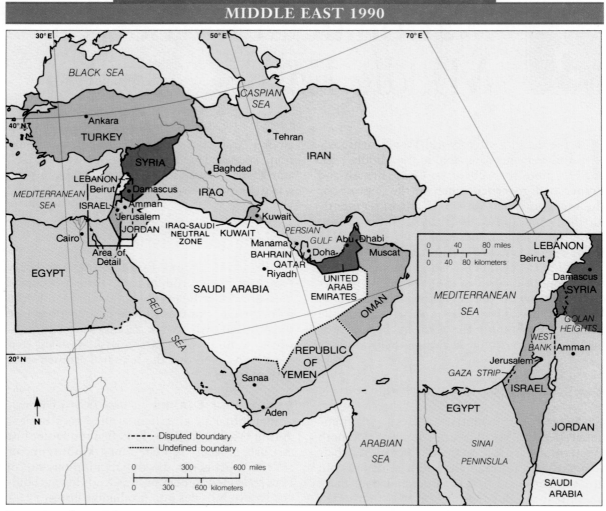

Learning from Maps *The geographic location of the Middle East complicates the politics of the region.* **Why do you think the Soviet Union and the West are so interested in protecting their interests in this strategic area?**

Jerusalem was to become an international city under UN administration. Jews took to the streets in celebration. Throughout Palestine, however, Arabs mourned the loss of territory they considered their own.

Jewish leaders were quick to accept the UN partition plan, while embittered Arab leaders rejected it. When Great Britain announced it would relinquish Palestine on May 14, 1948, Jewish settlers and leaders prepared to defend their territory from Arab attack. Mournful bagpipes sounded the British withdrawal on May

14, as soon-to-be Prime Minister David Ben-Gurion proclaimed the new state of Israel. Within 24 hours, the armies of Syria, Lebanon, Iraq, Egypt, and Transjordan attacked. Ready to fight and helped by a flood of immigrants and arms, the Israelis defeated the Arab forces in nine months.

When the fighting ended in early 1949, Israel held 77 percent of Palestine, almost 20 percent more than it had been granted by the United Nations. Jerusalem emerged divided, with the holy sites of the Old City in Arab hands.

Transjordan annexed the rest of Arab Palestine and changed its name to Jordan.

The war was a resounding victory for the new nation of Israel. To the Arabs, the war spelled disaster. As a result of partition, more than 700,000 Palestinians became homeless. Many fled to neighboring Arab lands, expecting eventually to return home.

Arab Unity

The 1948–1949 war had other serious consequences for the Arab world. In Egypt, many people blamed rich, corrupt King Farouk for the Arab defeat and the British presence in Egypt. In 1952 army officers seized control of the government and proclaimed a republic. Within a year, Colonel Gamal Abdel Nasser, a leader of the coup, took over as president.

Nasser profoundly disliked Western influence in the Middle East, and quickly launched new policies through which he hoped Egypt would lead the Arab world to greatness. In an extremely popular move, Nasser broke up the estates of wealthy Egyptian landowners and gave plots of land to the peasants. Then he negotiated the British withdrawal from the Suez Canal. Finally, he set out to modernize Egypt and build up its military muscle to confront Israel.

Suez Crisis   Nasser wanted to help modernize Egypt by building a dam at Aswan in the Upper Nile Valley. Known as the Aswan High Dam, the massive structure—36 stories high and more than 2 miles (3 kilometers) wide—would end flooding, increase irrigation, and give farmers two extra harvests a year. Electricity generated by the dam would power new industries.

Seeking political influence in the economic development of Egypt, the United States offered Egypt a $270 million loan to build the dam. However, Nasser's growing Soviet leanings, including a major arms deal with the Soviet Union, caused the United States to angrily withdraw its offer. In July 1956 Nasser retaliated by nationalizing the Suez Canal, vowing to use millions of dollars in canal fees to finance the dam.

Throughout the summer and fall, President Dwight D. Eisenhower tried to negotiate an end to the crisis. In October, however, Great Britain, France, and Israel invaded Egypt, hoping to overthrow Nasser and seize the canal, Europe's lifeline to Middle Eastern oil. The United States, the Soviet Union, and the United Nations denounced the invasion and demanded a cease-fire. In the face of this pressure, the three powers pulled out of Egypt. Nasser then accepted the Soviet offer to build the Aswan High Dam.

Middle East Crises   Nasser emerged from the Suez crisis as a powerful Arab leader. He had embarrassed Great Britain and France, won control of the Suez Canal, and had stopped Israel from taking more territory. Pro-Nasser parties began forming throughout the Arab world. It seemed that Nasser might rise to lead a unified Arab world.

In early 1958 Syria and Egypt merged to form a Nasser-led state called the United Arab Republic (UAR). The union lasted about three years. At that point, Syrian leaders had grown resentful of the loss of their power, and Syria withdrew from the UAR.

That same year, Nasser's brand of Arab nationalism seemed to be taking hold in Iraq. There, King Faisal II, Nasser's strongest Arab opponent and a friend of the West, was killed by pro-Nasser military forces in his country. They set up a one-party regime like Nasser's and broke ties with the West.

In the face of pro-Nasser pressure, some Arab leaders turned to the West for support. Jordan's King Hussein asked for British and U.S. help when pro-Nasser forces threatened his government. In Lebanon, violence broke out between the Christians, who dominated the nation, and a huge Muslim population that sympathized with Nasser and the UAR. Christian President Camille Chamoun, a supporter of the West, sought reelection to a new term. Anti-Western elements revolted, and a civil war followed. Chamoun asked for Western help to stop the violence. Concerned about the loss of Iraq, Eisenhower sent 15,000 marines to Lebanon in July 1958. When order was restored that fall, the troops pulled out.

By 1960 Arab nationalism had made gains, but the Middle East was in a state of uncertainty.

A fragile peace held between Arabs and Jews; competing Arab groups were at an impasse; and neither superpower had managed to achieve dominance in the region.

Pro-Western Tier

Two other important Middle Eastern countries, Turkey and Iran, also suffered from tensions that swept the region. During the 1950s and early 1960s, they experienced the upheaval of nationalism and rapid modernization. Both countries also bordered the Soviet Union, making them pawns in cold-war struggles.

Turkey   At the end of World War II, Soviet leaders began pressuring Turkey for territorial concessions and control of shipping lanes with access to the Black Sea. Afraid of a Soviet takeover, the Turkish government turned to the United States for political and military assistance. In keeping with the Truman Doctrine and the Marshall Plan, the United States gave Turkey economic and military aid in order to block Soviet advances. The funds also helped Turkey to modernize.

Following a period of authoritarian rule, Turkey made new strides toward democracy in the early 1950s, under the administration of Prime Minister Adnan Menderes. Menderes favored a capitalist economy and encouraged foreign investment. Under Menderes, Turkey was admitted to NATO in 1952. It also joined Great Britain, Iraq, Pakistan, and Iran in the Baghdad Pact, an alliance aimed at blocking Soviet expansion in the Middle East.

By the late 1950s, however, the Menderes regime had become corrupt, and inflation and a huge international debt plagued the economy. A group of military officers seized the government in 1960. Within a year, free elections were held, but the military still wielded a strong influence over Turkish politics. The new government continued its ties with the West.

Iran   By contrast, Western influence in oil-rich Iran was shaken after World War II. Throughout the war, Great Britain and the United States had supported the young shah, Mohammed Reza Pahlavi. After the war the shah continued to rely on Western help to block Soviet influence. The Iranian people, however, resented the West. For decades, the British had grown rich on Iranian oil at Iran's expense.

In 1951, a wealthy politician, Mohammed Mossadegh, became prime minister. A strong nationalist, Mossadegh nationalized the British-owned oil industry and declared that all oil money would be used for social and economic reforms. Great Britain called for a world boycott of Iranian oil. As Iranians began to suffer, their hatred of the West and the shah grew.

Events climaxed in 1953, when growing support for Mossadegh forced the shah to flee the country briefly. He returned after a military coup—promoted by the United States—deposed Mossadegh. Once in control, the shah increased his ties to the United States and signed the Baghdad Pact. He also signed an agreement with Western oil companies to buy and sell Iranian oil and share profits. Backed by the army and Western powers who wanted Iranian oil, the shah was firmly in control by the 1960s.

SECTION 3 REVIEW

Recall

1. **Define:** kibbutz
2. **Identify:** Pan-Arabism, Gamal Abdel Nasser, Arab League, Mohammed Reza Pahlavi
3. **Explain:** Why did the United Nations divide Palestine into an Arab and a Jewish state?

Critical Thinking

4. **Apply:** Show how the Holocaust in Europe contributed to the development of the Jewish state in Palestine.
5. **Synthesize:** If you were an Arab leader after the 1948 war with Israel, how would you have reacted to Nasser's emerging popularity in your country?

Applying Concepts

6. **Change:** Explain why the United States gave money and political support to Turkey and to Iran after World War II.

War and Peace in the Middle East

From the 1960s to the 1990s, many violent changes rocked the Middle East. Wars broke out repeatedly between Israel and its Arab neighbors, with rival countries and factions getting support from the superpowers.

Within Israel, angry Palestinians turned to strong resistance to achieve nationhood. In 1964 the Palestinian Liberation Organization (PLO) was formed to press for an independent Palestinian homeland. For the next 30 years, the Palestinian question would affect the politics of nearly every country in the Middle East.

Arab-Israeli Conflict

The uneasy cease-fire between Israel and its Arab neighbors disintegrated during the 1960s. A radical new regime in Syria sought the elimination of Israel and the restoration of Palestine to Arab control. Supplied with Soviet weapons, Syria engaged Israeli troops in border clashes in early 1967. Egyptian leader Gamal Abdel Nasser aided Syria by closing the Gulf of Aqaba to Israel, cutting off Israel's oil supplies.

Six-Day War   Israel responded with decisive force on June 5, 1967. At 8:45 A.M., Israeli fighter jets bore down on 17 Egyptian airfields, destroying 300 of Egypt's 350 warplanes. Hundreds of miles away, Israeli jets also demolished the air forces of Iraq, Jordan, and Syria.

In the so-called Six-Day War, Israeli forces tripled Israel's land holdings, seizing the Sinai Peninsula and the Gaza Strip from Egypt, and the Golan Heights from Syria. Israeli troops also took the Old City of Jerusalem.

In a move that spawned decades of upheaval, Israel occupied the West Bank of the Jordan River. The West Bank was land that had been designated as part of Arab Palestine when the United Nations partitioned Palestine in 1947. Palestinian Arabs had never achieved self-rule, however; they had been under Jordanian rule ever since 1949, when Jordan annexed the West Bank. Now, as a result of the Six-Day War, the area's more than one million Palestinians found themselves under Israeli military occupation.

Thousands more Palestinians fled to neighboring countries such as Lebanon. They turned more than ever to the PLO and its militant leader, Yasir Arafat, who vowed to use armed struggle to establish a Palestinian state.

The United Nations asked Israel to pull out of the occupied territories and asked Arab nations to recognize Israel's right to exist. Both sides refused. Terrorist attacks and border raids continued for several years.

Oil and Conflict   Nasser died in 1970. His successor, President Anwar al-Sadat, led Arab forces in a new war against Israel. On October 6, 1973, Egyptian and Syrian forces launched a surprise attack on Israel on the Jewish holy day of Yom Kippur and during the Muslim holy month of Ramadan. The Arabs destroyed much of Israel's air force. Egyptian troops invaded the Sinai, and Syria moved into the Golan Heights. With a U.S. airlift of weapons, Israel struck back. Israeli troops crossed the Suez Canal and occupied Egyptian territory. The fighting raged until the UN negotiated a cease-fire. Secretary of State Henry Kissinger negotiated a disengagement agreement in late 1973.

American support of Israel during the 1973 war angered Arab countries. Attempting to halt Western support, Arab oil countries imposed an embargo on oil sales to Israel's allies in 1973. Additional pressure came from the Organization of Petroleum Exporting Countries (OPEC), a **cartel**, or group of businesses formed to regulate production and prices among its members.

OPEC, which included Arab and non-Arab oil producers, quadrupled the price of oil. However, the embargo threatened such dire economic problems for the world, including Arab countries, that it was lifted in 1974.

A Separate Peace   In 1977, Egypt's President Sadat acted independently to break the deadlock. He accepted an invitation to visit Israel, becoming the first Arab leader to step in peace on Israeli soil. In a speech before Israel's parliament, the Knesset, Sadat called for Arab acceptance of Israel, a just solution to the Palestinian problem, and an end to hostilities.

The next year Sadat accepted an invitation from President Jimmy Carter to meet with Israeli Prime Minister Menachem Begin (BAY gihn). The 13 days of meetings at Camp David in Maryland resulted in the Camp David Accords, the basis for an Arab-Israeli peace treaty.

Sadat and Begin signed the treaty in March 1979—the first time an Arab nation recognized Israel's right to exist. Many nations applauded Sadat's actions, but Syria, Iraq, and the PLO broke ties with Egypt. Sadat's separate peace with Israel, they said, threatened Arab unity. They accused Sadat of treason.

In 1981 Muslim extremists assassinated Sadat, and Hosni Mubarak succeeded him as president. Mubarak has supported Egypt's peace with Israel, but it has often been a tense peace.

The Palestinian Uprising

For 20 years after the Six-Day War in 1967, Palestinians in the Israeli-held West Bank and the Gaza Strip lived in a smoldering rage. They had to carry identity cards; most could get only low-paying jobs. Those who protested could be

IMAGES OF THE TIME

Beirut

In the 1950s and 1960s, Beirut, Lebanon, was one of the most popular resorts in the Mediterranean. Today, civil war has ruined much of the city.

Lebanon's economic system favored foreign trade and investment, making Beirut an important commercial and financial center.

Called the "Lebanese Riviera," Beirut had beaches, shopping, and luxury hotels that attracted tourists from around the world.

arrested and see their homes bulldozed. The PLO fought back with hijackings and bombings.

In December 1987, Israeli soldiers in the Gaza Strip were surrounded by a group of angry Palestinians. In the confusion, one soldier fired, killing a 17-year-old boy. The incident sparked an uprising called the *intifada*. Palestinian workers went on strike throughout the occupied lands. Thousands of youths took to the streets, hurling stones at Israeli soldiers. After a year of riots and harsh Israeli responses, the *intifada* focused world sympathy on the Palestinians.

In late 1988 the PLO's Arafat made a surprise move. He agreed to give up terrorism and accept Israel's right to exist. Still, Israel refused to recognize or negotiate with the PLO. Israel sought to solidify its power by encouraging the growth of Jewish settlements on the West Bank.

The *intifada* raged on. On October 8, 1990, Palestinians threw stones at Israeli police at a mosque in Jerusalem. Police opened fire, killing 19 Palestinians and wounding 100. It was the worst violence in Jerusalem since the 1967 war.

Lebanese Civil War

The Palestinian problem also became the fuel that ignited a long war in Lebanon. When Lebanon became independent in 1943, rival Christian and Muslim populations began vying for power. In the late 1960s tensions came to a head over the issue of Lebanon's 400,000 Palestinian refugees, most of whom lived in squalid camps in southern Lebanon. The government gave the PLO control of the camps. From there, the PLO shelled settlements in Israel. Israel retaliated, attacking deep inside Lebanon.

Unable to stop the PLO or prevent the Israeli attacks, the Lebanese government became

Civil war erupted in Lebanon in 1975. Today, much of the city lies in ruins and thousands of residents have fled.

Reflecting on the Times
What conditions led to the fighting in Lebanon?

Learning from Photographs *An Israeli armored vehicle patrols the Golan Heights.* ***What other land did Israel seize in the Six-Day War?***

Iran's Revolution

Throughout the 1960s and 1970s, Iran grew into a major military power in the Persian Gulf region. Shah Mohammed Reza Pahlavi built a capitalistic economy based on oil revenues. Muslim religious leaders resented his emphasis on Western materialism and values and sought a return to Muslim traditions. Through his hated police force, SAVAK, the shah silenced all protests and dissent.

During the late 1970s, opposition to the shah grew. Anti-shah forces rallied around 76-year-old Ayatollah Ruhollah Khomeini (koh MAY nee), a powerful Iranian Shiite Muslim leader living in exile in France. The ayatollah had long preached the overthrow of the shah and a return to Muslim traditions. By January 1979, widespread unrest forced the shah to flee the country. Khomeini triumphantly returned to form a new government run according to Islamic principles. He destroyed his enemies and kept power in his hands.

Iranian hatred for the shah then turned against the United States, where the shah had gone to receive medical help. Iran demanded that the United States return the shah to stand trial for his "crimes against the Iranian people." The United States refused, and the shah took refuge in Egypt, where he died in 1980. Anti-American sentiment in Iran exploded. On November 4, 1979, Iranians stormed the U.S. Embassy and took 52 U.S. diplomats hostage. The captives were not freed until January 1981.

Iran–Iraq War   Soon after Khomeini came to power, he condemned pro-Western and secular Arab leaders as enemies of Islam. Repeatedly he urged Arab masses in other nations to join a *jihad*, or holy war, against their leaders.

Determined to keep revolution from sweeping Iraq, President Saddam Hussein invaded Iran in September 1980. For eight years the two nations fought the bloodiest war in recent history. The war ended with a UN cease-fire in 1988. But the two nations lost about 1 million people and hundreds of billions of dollars in property.

Ayatollah Khomeini died in 1989. Iran's new president, Hashemi Rafsanjani, turned to rebuilding Iran's crippled economy.

paralyzed. Most Lebanese Muslims supported the PLO. The majority of Christians did not. Civil war broke out in 1975 among rival Christian and Muslim groups. Syria sent troops in response to requests from the Arab League and the Lebanese government. In 1982 Israel launched an offensive that further destabilized Lebanon. Israeli troops invaded southern Lebanon and drove out the PLO, damaging its morale and effectiveness.

Later that year, Western countries sent troops to try to keep the peace while free elections were held. Even so, terrorist strikes continued. Muslims despised the presence of Western troops, and in October 1983, Muslim suicide drivers bombed U.S. and French installations, killing 299 people. Early in 1984, Western forces withdrew from Lebanon, and immediately violence escalated.

In late 1990 some signs of hope appeared. Syrian forces ousted a Christian general who stood in the way of an Arab League peace plan for Lebanon. Meanwhile, a newly elected president was recognized by other nations as the new Lebanese leader. In late 1990 the various militias in Beirut agreed to pull out of the city so that a Lebanese government could be restored.

Iraq's Bid for Power

The war with Iran left Iraq's economy near collapse. Saddam Hussein needed a strategy for boosting oil revenues and for redirecting the blame for Iraq's worsening economy. His solution shocked the world. On August 2, 1990, Saddam Hussein invaded neighboring Kuwait. He claimed that Kuwait was a historic part of Iraq and that Kuwait had unfairly drilled Iraqi oil. Within days, Iraqi troops seized Kuwait and headed toward the border of Saudi Arabia.

The Saudis asked the United States for protection. President Bush, stating the need to protect a key Arab ally and to protect world oil supplies, sent troops to the Saudi desert. Western nations, the Soviet Union, and Japan imposed a trade embargo against Iraq. Eight Arab nations also sent troops to Saudi Arabia.

At U.S. urging, the UN set a deadline of January 15, 1991, for Iraq to withdraw from Kuwait and authorized the use of force if Iraq did not. Saddam Hussein vowed not to leave Kuwait until Israel pulled out of its occupied territories and Syria left Lebanon. He further threatened to attack Israel if Iraq were attacked.

War Breaks Out   Despite last-minute efforts by several nations to persuade Iraq to withdraw its forces, Saddam Hussein remained defiant. On January 16, one day after the UN deadline, the United States rained medium-range missiles on the Iraqi capital of Baghdad.

During the next month the allied forces—including troops from the United States, Great Britain, France, Syria, Saudi Arabia, Egypt, and Kuwait—conducted a massive air war aimed at destroying Iraq's warmaking ability. Communications facilities, supply lines, and the Iraqi air force were wiped out. Saddam Hussein responded by launching missiles at Israel, including its largest city, Tel Aviv. He hoped to draw Israel into the war and splinter Arab support for the coalition. Israel resisted retaliation, however, and the United States provided Israel with an antimissile defense system.

With most Iraqi military installations in ruins, the coalition began bombing Iraq's ground forces in and near Kuwait. In desperation, Iraq set hundreds of Kuwaiti oil fields afire to provide smokescreens.

Ground War   In mid-February the Soviet Union became involved in the war, trying to negotiate an Iraqi withdrawal. As talks stalled, there were new reports of Iraqi atrocities against Kuwaiti civilians. President Bush finally issued an ultimatum demanding that Iraq withdraw unconditionally from Kuwait by February 23 or face the consequences. Saddam Hussein refused, and the coalition staged a massive ground assault on Iraqi forces in Kuwait and southern Iraq.

In a campaign that took only 100 hours, allied troops swept into Kuwait, meeting only minor resistance from the Iraqis. With Kuwait freed, Bush ordered a cease-fire on February 27. Allied war deaths totaled just over 100, with tens of thousands of Iraqi soldiers believed killed.

Coalition nations immediately began focusing on the postwar role of Iraq and the restoration of Kuwait. They also planned to examine broader issues of Middle East security—such as the Palestinian question—which have remained unsolved for decades.

SECTION 4 REVIEW

Recall
1. **Define:** cartel, *intifada*
2. **Identify:** Camp David Accords, PLO, Saddam Hussein
3. **List:** What were the results of the Six-Day War?
4. **Explain:** What were the causes of the *intifada*?

Critical Thinking
5. **Apply:** How did Palestinian refugees in Lebanon contribute to the outbreak of civil war? What aspects of the war distinguished it from other modern-day conflicts?
6. **Analyze:** How do you think the Persian Gulf War will affect future Middle East politics?

Applying Concepts
7. **Conflict:** Explain how the growth of Israel into a military power both unified and split the Arab world.

Challenges Facing the Middle East

The tragic cycle of violence, wars between nations, and civil wars within nations have brought much suffering to the people of the Middle East since the end of World War II. Besides the lost lives, billions of dollars of precious resources are spent each year on weapons. If you speak to Middle Easterners about their hopes for the future, they undoubtedly include peace and stability. But peace and stability have been hard to achieve.

War and Peace   Although Egypt and Israel agreed to peace in 1979, Israel and the rest of the Arab world are still in a state of war. A leading issue between them is the future of the Palestinians who live in the Gaza Strip and on the West Bank of the Jordan River. If Israel keeps these areas, what will be the fate of the Palestinians who live there? They are either Muslims or Christians. If Israel extended citizenship to them, it would not remain a Jewish state. Israelis agree that their state should remain Jewish. Yet, if the Palestinians are free to determine their own future, they may decide to have an independent state of their own. Many Israelis fear that such a state may threaten their security.

The Golan Heights is another area of contention. Peace between Syria and Israel, depends in part, on the future of this territory, which has been in Israel's hands since 1967.

Lebanon's civil war has stopped for now, but Israeli troops in the south and Syrian troops in other regions still control large areas under their occupation. A truly free and prosperous Lebanon must be able to govern itself without foreign troops. Then, the massive effort to reconstruct the country and to restore its democracy may begin.

The Elusive Dream   Unity among Arab people has long been a powerful desire. For many centuries, millions of people throughout the Arab world have shared strong cultural ties, such as the Arabic language, tradition, religious beliefs, and a common history. British and French imperialism in the 1800s and 1900s increased division among the Arabs and created numerous states with artificial boundaries. Many Arabs thought that with independence from foreign powers they would be able to achieve unity. They began to take steps to strengthen the common links among them.

In 1944 political unity seemed within reach when Egypt, Transjordan, Syria, Lebanon, Iraq, Saudi Arabia, and Yemen formed the Arab League, a step toward unity. By 1991 membership in the Arab League had grown to 21 countries covering an area larger than the United States, with a population of about 200 million. But disagreements among governments and the unwillingness of some to give up their power frustrated any move toward further unity. In fact, bloody clashes have erupted between Arab states since the League was founded. The latest was Iraq's invasion of Kuwait in August 1990.

Some political leaders and government officials have advocated a cautious move toward unity. They formed cooperative councils among their countries to coordinate trade, economic development, and travel. Peoples' aspirations and political realities, in time, may lead to some type of loose union in which each state would retain independence and contribute to stability in the region.

Economic Developments

In the past 40 years the Middle East has seen greatly changed economic conditions. Light and heavy industry have been developed in most countries. Irrigation for agriculture spread as hydroelectric projects were constructed on major rivers, such as the Nile and the Euphrates. At the same time as production rose and jobs became available, the region's population grew rapidly. If the current rate of increase continues, the population will double in the next 25 years. The increase has been most apparent in major urban centers. By the early 1990s, more than 15 cities had populations exceeding 1 million each. The largest is Cairo with 12 million people. It is also the largest in the whole African continent. The needs and the challenges of rapidly growing populations are on the mind of every major leader in the Middle East.

Oil Wealth   Oil-producing countries of the Middle East have become well-developed and wealthy in recent years. But their wealth contrasts sharply with the poverty of other countries in the region. The per capita income of some Persian Gulf countries is about 15 times that of Egypt. Oil-producing countries have invested in and loaned large sums of money to the non-oil-producing countries. The poorer countries are asking for more assistance. They do not want the gap between the rich and the poor to be so wide.

Water Problem   Industrial development and rapidly increasing population have created a dangerous situation in several countries of the Middle East. Many of these problems are related to the uneven distribution of water. For ex-

ample, Turkey has a good deal of water in its western regions. Southeastern Turkey has large areas of fertile land but until recently did not have enough water. The Turkish government launched a massive project to build hydroelectric dams and other water facilities on the Euphrates River. The water from the dams would irrigate wide areas and solve Turkey's problem in that region. But Turkey's solution may deprive Syria and Iraq of water from the same river. Iraq would be worse off because it is the last country that is situated along the river. If the three countries do not come to an agreement on use of the river in the next few years, political disputes may lead to open warfare.

Another place with a water shortage is Israel. The country has been using its water resources and those of the West Bank and Gaza Strip close to their maximum capacity. But the anticipated settlement there of almost a million Soviet Jews will require quantities of water that Israel does not have. Israel's neighbors Syria and Jordan have themselves been experiencing shortages of water. If political differences among the three countries are settled, they will be able to coordinate their water resources, build desalination plants, and even import water from southwestern Turkey. Turkey has expressed a willingness to provide the three countries with water from its Ceyhan River, if they pay the cost of piping the water through Syria and Lebanon to Galilee. From there the water will be distributed to other parts of Israel and to Jordan.

Learning from Photographs *Mass demonstrations supported Khomeini on his return to Iran. His supporters denounced all foreign influences. Many women returned to wearing the traditional clothing pictured here, including the chador, a veil that covers the head.* **Why do you think women would want to return to a way of life that seems to place more restrictions on them?**

Social Change

Throughout the Middle East, modernization has turned traditional desert societies upside down. With the discovery of oil, desert cities boomed and new industrial areas were created. Arab cities sprouted high-rise offices, shopping centers, luxury apartments, and freeways. People in Arab countries have viewed these new influences in different ways.

Progress and Problems   Arabs welcomed some of the changes. Foreign investment created new jobs and raised standards of living. New wealth enabled countries to establish better education and health care systems, to build roads, and to provide utilities. Women were exposed to ideas of sexual equality and self-sufficiency, and many began to demand new freedoms. Families sent their children abroad to study, and many returned home with new skills in medicine, engineering, and other fields. Some countries adopted Western-style legal systems.

But other Arabs looked at these changes and saw a world that was morally and culturally disintegrating. In the cities they saw rising crime, alcoholism, and prostitution. In business life they observed greed, abuse of workers, and a growing gap between rich and poor. Traditional family structure and authority were shattered by changing values among women and young people. Religion, in particular, suffered. The secularization of society turned people away from the cherished beliefs and moral demands of Islam. Foreign influence was seen as the cause of many new social problems.

In addition, Arab people found themselves surrounded by more material goods such as cars, watches, videos, and Western television. The influence of these things became a source of resentment to Arabs who feared the spread of materialism. They blamed the West for this new emphasis in Arab society.

In Saudi Arabia, the birthplace of Islam, the Sunni majority has fiercely resisted Westernization, despite the influence of enormous oil wealth flowing into the country. Muslims are shielded from exposure to Western ideas through rigid censorship. By contrast more liberal lifestyles are permitted in Iraq, Lebanon, Syria, Jordan, and Egypt.

A Return to Religion   In recent years many Middle Easterners began to search for solutions to their problems by returning to **fundamentalism,** or the traditional values and practices of their religions. The reasons for their doing so may lead to several explanations. One could be that the people expected fast improvement in their lives after independence. But economic progress was not fast enough for them. Some found it difficult to accept the excessive materialism that closer ties to Western countries brought about. Others were dissatisfied with their governments and decided to use religion to oppose them.

Movements for reviving religious values have been active in the Muslim nations. In Iran, Shiite Muslim leaders are in control of the government. In Turkey and Egypt, the power of Muslim leaders is on the rise. In Jordan, 1990 elections brought many new Muslim fundamentalists into the parliament. Israel's Jewish religious parties are gaining strength. How these changes will affect the future of the Middle East remains to be seen.

SECTION 5 REVIEW

Recall

1. **Define:** fundamentalism
2. **Identify:** Name three challenges to Middle East stability.
3. **Explain:** What choices does Israel face in resolving the Palestinian question?

Critical Thinking

4. **Apply:** What impact has religious fundamentalism had on the Middle East?
5. **Evaluate:** Does Turkey have the right to build dams on the Euphrates? Why or why not?

Applying Concepts

6. **Nationalism:** Saddam Hussein justified Iraq's invasion of Kuwait in part on the grounds of Arab nationalism and unity. Analyze this reasoning. Do you think it is justified?

CONDUCTING INTERVIEWS

Reading about an event informs us but hearing about it from someone who was directly involved can provide a personal insight into current events. Often this insight is obtained through *interviews*, conversations between two people, one of whom is asking information from the other. You can also gain insight into events of historical interest through interviews. In your community there may be exchange students from Africa, families of business people who travel regularly to Europe or the Middle East, diplomatic personnel or immigrants. Through an effective interview, these people can tell you something not found in books.

Explanation

If during research on a topic you learn that someone knowledgeable about the topic is available to talk to you, follow these steps for a successful interview:

- Gather background information. Using library resources, find out all you can about the event your subject has experienced. If the person is a public figure—a political leader or writer—find biographical information about the person's life.
- Frame your questions. From what you know of the situation and your subject, what special insights could you hope to gain from the interview? An educator from Saudi Arabia, for example,

would know far more about schooling there than would a businessperson.

Make sure each question leads to more than a *yes* or *no* answer. Rather than ask, "Do girls in Saudi Arabia study different subjects than boys?" ask, "Please describe how the education of girls in Saudi Arabia differs from that of boys." Plan follow-up questions that will elicit further information about the event or topic.

- Assemble your equipment. If you plan to use a tape recorder during the interview, obtain your subject's permission.
- During the interview, begin asking the questions you prepared but stay flexible. Your subject's answers may lead to unexpected but valuable topics. You may need to have the person clarify or defend statements. It is essential to listen carefully and not to screen out things that don't fit into the pattern you anticipated.
- Take notes as quickly as you can without sacrificing accuracy. Even if you are using a tape recorder, keep some written record just in case the recorder malfunctions.
- After the interview, convert your notes or recording into a transcript, or written record. Do so as soon as possible, while details that you may not have written are still in your memory.
- If your interview is to be pub-

lished, as in a school newspaper, you should provide a preview copy to your subject for an accuracy check.

Example

A bookstore in your area advertises the upcoming visit of a novelist from Ghana. You contact the writer and arrange for an interview. Before her arrival, you read both of her novels, the biographical information on the book jackets, and several reviews. You plan to ask what influenced her to become a novelist and what she thinks Americans can learn from her work. However, the writer shows great enthusiasm for African folk tales. Your follow-up questions pursue the novelist's efforts to present African tribal folk tales to a world audience. Later you submit your interview to a local newspaper.

Application

Refer to the People to Meet on page 868. Choose one of the people, and using the outlined steps, write a mock interview with three questions and responses.

Practice

Turn to Practicing Skills on page 899 of the Chapter Review for further practice in planning and conducting interviews.

Modern Poems

by Nazim Hikmet, Jaime Torres Bodet,
and Gabriel Okara

*Modern poets have continued to explore both universal themes, such as
friendship and loneliness, as well as individual preferences for a particular
place or group of people. Nazim Hikmet, shown above, who lived from 1902 to 1963,
often criticized the government of his native Turkey for serving only the wealthy. In 1951
he left Turkey, never to return, and settled in Europe. His sympathy for the
peasants of his country, his love of nature, and his hope for
humanity are all suggested in the following poem.*

The World, My Friends, My Enemies, You, and the Earth

Translated from Turkish by Randy Blasing and Mutlu Konuk

I'm wonderfully happy I came into the world,
I love its earth, its light, its struggle, and its bread.
Even though I know its dimensions from pole to pole to the
    centimeter,
and while I'm not unaware that it's a mere toy next to the sun,
the world for me is unbelievably big.
I would have liked to go around the world
and see the fish, the fruits, and the stars that I haven't seen.
However,

I made my European trip only in books and pictures.
In all my life I never got one letter
                  with its blue stamp canceled in Asia.
Me and our corner grocer,
we're both mightily unknown in America.
Nevertheless,
from China to Spain, from the Cape of Good Hope to Alaska,
in every nautical mile, in every kilometer, I have friends and
     enemies.
Such friends that we haven't met even once—
we can die for the same bread, the same freedom, the same dream.
And such enemies that they're thirsty for my blood,
                   I am thirsty for their blood.
My strength
is that I'm not alone in this big world.
The world and its people are no secret in my heart,
             no mystery in my science.
Calmly and openly
         I took my place
               in the great struggle.
And without it,
       you and the earth
         are not enough for me.
And yet you are astonishingly beautiful,
        the earth is warm and beautiful.

*The following poem was written by one of Mexico's greatest writers,
Jaime Torres Bodet. Like Hikmet, Bodet was born in 1902 and
was active in politics. Bodet, however, served the government as an
administrator and diplomat rather than as a critic. In this poem,
Bodet urges people to take risks in their lives. Bodet died in 1974.*

The Window

Translated from Spanish by George Kearns

You closed the window. And it was the world,
the world that wanted to enter, all at once,
the world that gave that great shout,
that great, deep, rough cry
you did not want to hear—and now
will never call to you again as it called today,
asking your mercy!

The whole of life was in that cry:
the wind, the sea, the land
with its poles and its tropics,
the unreachable skies,
the ripened grain in the resounding wheat field,
the thick heat above the wine presses,
dawn on the mountains, shadowy woods,
parched lips stuck together longing for
cool water condensed in pools,
and all pleasures, all sufferings,
all loves, all hates,
were in this day, anxiously
asking your mercy . . .

But you were afraid of life.
And you remained alone,
behind the closed and silent window,
not understanding that the world calls to a man
only once that way, and with that kind of cry,
with that great, rough, hoarse cry!

*Gabriel Okara, born in 1921, is one of many
Nigerian writers to achieve international acclaim since
the 1960s. Others include Chinua Achebe, Christopher
Okigbo, and Wole Soyinka. Some of Okara's poems deal with the
problems of living in a country that is influenced by European
culture. Others deal with family, friends, and daily life.*

Once Upon a Time

Once upon a time, son,
they used to laugh with their hearts
and laugh with their eyes;
but now they only laugh with their teeth,
while their ice-block-cold eyes
search behind my shadow.

There was a time indeed
they used to shake hands with their hearts;
but that's gone, son.
Now they shake hands without hearts
while their left hands search
my empty pockets.

"Feel at home," "Come again,"
they say, and when I come
again and feel
at home, once, twice,
there will be no thrice—
for then I find doors shut on me.

So I have learned many things, son.
I have learned to wear many faces
like dresses—homeface,
officeface, streetface, hostface, cock-
tailface, with all their conforming smiles
like a fixed portrait smile.

And I have learned, too,
to laugh with only my teeth
and shake hands without my heart.
I have also learned to say, "Goodbye,"
when I mean, "Good-riddance";
to say "Glad to meet you,"
without being glad; and to say "It's been
nice talking to you," after being bored.

But believe me, son.
I want to be what I used to be
when I was like you. I want
to unlearn all these muting things.
Most of all, I want to relearn
how to laugh, for my laugh in the mirror
shows only my teeth like a snake's bare fangs!

So show me, son,
how to laugh; show me how
I used to laugh and smile
once upon a time when I was like you.

RESPONDING TO LITERATURE

1. **Comprehending:** In your own words, define "the great struggle" that Hikmet refers to near the end of his poem.
2. **Applying:** Explain whether you think the poem by Bodet is written just to the people of Mexico or whether it applies to people throughout the world.
3. **Synthesizing:** What is the main point of the poem by Okara?
4. **Thinking critically:** How does each poet view individuals who are willing to act boldly?

CHAPTER 33 REVIEW

HISTORICAL SIGNIFICANCE

The nations of Africa and the Middle East are very old—and very new. They have ancient cultures, but their political systems are still young. Most have been independent for only a generation or so. Their efforts to forge effective governments are complicated by monumental problems of debt, hunger, and ethnic strife.

In the early 1990s, political solutions for the Middle East seemed especially elusive. Progress was measured in gradual steps, such as the PLO's decision to abandon terrorism and the efforts to restore war-ravaged Lebanon.

Some factors weighed on the side of progress and peace. After decades of cold war competition that destabilized the regions, the superpowers began cooperating to find political solutions in nations such as Angola and Kuwait. And through trial and error, many countries were inevitably getting closer to finding their own answers for improving their future.

SUMMARY

For a summary of Chapter 33, see the Unit 8 Synopsis on pages 980–981.

USING KEY TERMS

Use the following key terms to complete the sentences below.

a. apartheid
b. cartel
c. fundamentalism
d. *intifada*
e. kibbutz
f. negritude

1. The _____ on the West Bank and the Gaza Strip brought the Palestinian cause to the world's attention.
2. _____ legalized the separation of races in South Africa.
3. Léopold Sédar Senghor helped found _____ , a literary movement that fostered African dignity.
4. In Palestine a _____ was a Jewish farming commune.
5. In 1973 OPEC, the oil _____ , raised its prices, crippling the world economy.
6. The strict following of the teachings of a religion, as practiced by many Shiite Muslims in Iran, is an example of _____ .

REVIEWING FACTS

1. **Define:** apartheid
2. **Identify:** Kwame Nkrumah
3. **Explain:** What caused the *intifada*?
4. **Locate:** Aswan High Dam
5. **Describe:** What was U.S. President Jimmy Carter's role in improving relations between Israel and Egypt?
6. **Explain:** What were the results of the Six-Day War?
7. **Locate:** Where is the Sahel?
8. **Define:** What is a *jihad*?

THINKING CRITICALLY

1. **Apply:** How would you solve the problem of food shortages in central Africa?
2. **Analyze:** How did the political boundaries drawn by Africa's colonial powers cause problems for many nations after they gained independence?
3. **Synthesize:** How would you respond if you lived under the system of apartheid?
4. **Evaluate:** Do you think that terrorism can be justified as a means of attaining political goals? Why or why not?

ANALYZING CONCEPTS

1. **Conflict:** Explain the issues that divide Israelis and Palestinians.

2. **Diversity:** Discuss the effects of ethnic diversity on Nigerian nationalism.
3. **Change:** How did the policies of the shah influence Iranian society?
4. **Nationalism:** What was the purpose of the Organization of African Unity (OAU)?

PRACTICING SKILLS

1. For a paper on apartheid, you want several statements from representatives of the U.S. government, either elected or with agencies, concerning the U.S. position toward South Africa. How would you identify and contact candidates for interviews? (Phone interviews are allowable.)
2. Two interviews are described below. Revise the question for each interview.
   a. Interview with Ahmed Sekou Touré after France's withdrawal from Guinea: "Mr. Sekou Touré, has your opinion of the French government changed in the past few weeks?"
   b. Interview with Anwar al-Sadat on his arrival in Israel to speak before the Knesset: "President Sadat, do you predict a speedy end to the Arab-Israeli conflict?"
3. Compare interviewing with reading as a source of information. Identify two characteristics of interviewing that make it preferable to reading. Identify two disadvantages you see in interviewing.

GEOGRAPHY IN HISTORY

1. **Location:** Refer to the map on page 882. In which direction does the Nile River flow from the Aswan High Dam?
2. **Movement:** Why is the Suez Canal important to European nations?
3. **Environment:** What effect resulted from the severe droughts that plagued Africa in the 1970s and 1980s?

TRACING CHRONOLOGY

Answer the questions using the time line below.
1. Nelson Mandela gained his freedom in 1990. For how long was he imprisoned?
2. How long after the Arab oil embargo did Khomeini come to power in Iran?
3. Algerians launched their war for independence in 1954. How long did the war last?

LINKING PAST AND PRESENT

1. In the 1970s, droughts brought widespread famine to Africa. What efforts to relieve food shortages continue there today?
2. In 1980, power passed relatively peacefully from the white minority government of Rhodesia to the black majority government of Zimbabwe. How might the Zimbabwe solution serve as a model for solving political problems in South Africa?

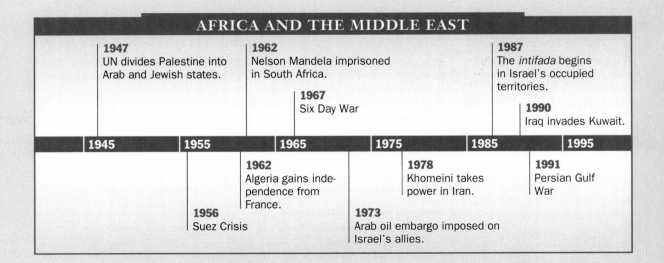

AFRICA AND THE MIDDLE EAST

1947 UN divides Palestine into Arab and Jewish states.	1962 Nelson Mandela imprisoned in South Africa. 1967 Six Day War	1987 The *intifada* begins in Israel's occupied territories. 1990 Iraq invades Kuwait.
1945 **1955**	**1965** **1975**	**1985** **1995**
1956 Suez Crisis 1962 Algeria gains independence from France.	1973 Arab oil embargo imposed on Israel's allies. 1978 Khomeini takes power in Iran.	1991 Persian Gulf War

Latin America

*O*n New Year's Day, 1959, the island of Cuba went mad with joy. Tall, bearded Fidel Castro, a lawyer turned soldier, and his band of guerrillas had driven dictator Fulgencio Batista out of Cuba. A people's revolution had been won, and years of repression were ending.

Along the road to the city of Santiago, crowds of people waved and cheered as Castro's ragtag troops passed by in battered jeeps and trucks. "Viva Fidel! Viva la revolución!" they cried. So delirious were the throngs, so swept away by the power of the moment, that a friend of Castro's later recalled, "It was like a messiah arriving. We were walking on a cloud."

Castro's revolution was not the first in Latin America, nor the last. Over the next few decades, tensions between rich and poor would erupt in violence repeatedly as nations of Latin America struggled toward modernity.

CHAPTER PREVIEW

Key Terms to Define: campesino, liberation theology, standard of living, death squad, hyperinflation

People to Meet: Anastasio Somoza, the Sandinistas, the contras, Monsignor Oscar Romero, Manuel Noriega, Juan Perón, Eva Perón, Salvador Allende, Augusto Pinochet

Places to Discover: the Bay of Pigs, Mariel Harbor, the Panama Canal, Medellin, the Falkland Islands, Buenos Aires

Objectives to Learn:
1. What problems did Latin American countries face after World War II?
2. How did Latin American leaders try to solve those problems?

The Santa Clara cloister and San Francisco church in Antigua, Guatemala

3. How did the cold war affect Latin America?

Concepts to Understand:
- Cooperation—New organizations promote economic ties in Latin America. Section 1
- Revolution—In Cuba and Nicaragua, the overthrow of U.S.-supported regimes opens the door to communism in the Western Hemisphere. Sections 2,3
- Conflict—Calls for land reform and political freedom lead to civil wars in Central America. Section 3
- Change—South American countries work to develop their struggling agricultural economies and to establish democracies. Section 4

Latin American Challenges

In the years after World War II, powerful changes began to reshape Latin America. Between 1940 and 1970, many Latin American nations industrialized as rapidly as did the United States in the late 1800s. Social changes followed this economic transformation. For example, schools and health-care facilities spread, and women won the right to vote.

Yet a dark cloud hung over these bright and hopeful achievements. Much of the region's newfound wealth flowed into the hands of the well-to-do, leaving millions of farmers and workers in the grip of desperate poverty. As the gap between rich and poor widened, the huge peasant class grew hungry and angry. Communism, with its appeal to the oppressed and its promise of social and economic equality, won many converts. As the peasants' demands increased, strong military dictators emerged to quell political upheaval through repression and terror.

These military leaders, in turn, were unable to solve mounting political and economic problems during the 1970s, and their tactics inspired calls for democratic reform. By the late 1980s, new civilian democratic governments began to overthrow the old, harsh regimes, and democracy had begun to return to the region.

Population Growth

Since World War II, Latin America's population has skyrocketed. In 1940 Latin America's population was 126 million. With a growth rate of 2.3 percent a year—about three times the rate of the United States and other industrialized countries—the region's population may expand to nearly 600 million by the year 2000.

Rapid growth has resulted from a combination of tradition and progress. Traditionally, families had many children. But because so many died in infancy, the population grew slowly. Latin American women still have many children. The average number of births per 1,000 Latin American women is twice the number in the United States, but improved health care has sharply lowered the infant mortality.

The rate of infant deaths, though five times that in the United States, is lower than in the past. Thus, more babies live to adulthood, and Latin America's population is increasing.

The population growth of Latin America has strained its economic and political systems. The expanding population requires increased supplies of food, clean drinking water, housing, schools, health care, jobs, and transportation.

Urbanization As the population of rural areas expanded, the poor farmers—known as **campesinos**—headed to cities in search of work in factories or stores and of better living conditions. With more schools, medical facilities, and other social services than rural areas have, larger cities continue to attract many rural people. In the 1950s about 10 percent of Latin Americans lived in a city of at least 1 million people. Today, over 25 percent do; another 45 percent live in smaller cities.

However, cities could not absorb easily the heavy flow of campesinos. The new residents clustered in sprawling, dilapidated shantytowns, many with no electricity, running water, or sanitary facilities. In his 1969 book *A Death in the Sanchez Family*, Oscar Lewis captured the bleakness of life in one such Mexico City slum:

The [place] where she [Guadalupe] lived consisted of a row of 14 one-room adobe huts about 10 feet by 15 feet, built along the left side and across the back of a 30-foot-wide bare lot. . . . Five of the dwellings had makeshift sheds, constructed by setting up two poles and extending the kitchen roofs of tarpaper, tin, and corrugated metal over the low front doorways. . . . Toward the rear of the yard, two large cement water troughs, each with a faucet, were the sole sources of water for the 84 inhabitants.

Such miserable surroundings offered little comfort or hope for the future. Even so, thousands of campesinos kept coming. The president of Venezuela observed, "The poor country peasant would rather come to the city and try to make a living selling lottery tickets than remain in the [countryside] where he has absolutely nothing."

Social Inequalities   Latin America's social structure—masses of poor people dominated by a small but wealthy elite—was established during the colonial period. Today the elite includes large landowners, successful industrialists, and military leaders. Many of the elite in Latin America today are the descendants of the Europeans who colonized the region centuries ago. The increase in wealth brought by industrialization simply made these families richer. Between 1964 and 1974, 75 percent of Brazil's newly generated wealth flowed into the hands of the wealthiest 10 percent of the people. The poorest 50 percent received less than 10 percent of the nation's income.

The majority of Latin America's population consists of poor people: peasants, landless farm workers, and factory workers. Many countries have a small but growing middle class consisting of professionals, managers, clerks, and government workers.

A more important change has been in the role of women in Latin America. Traditionally women had important but restricted roles in society. They were expected to work at home or else join a convent. In the late nineteenth century, women established their right to get an education and to enter a variety of careers. However, not until the mid-1960s did all Latin American women win the right to vote.

Economic Development

In recent decades many Latin American leaders pushed for increased industrialization. They hoped that their countries could manufacture their own products instead of importing them, thereby reducing their trade deficits. In just a few decades, Latin American steel production grew by 20 percent, while the production of metals, machines, and energy rose by 10 percent. Manufacturers flooded the markets with consumer products aimed at the upper and middle classes—fashions, sports cars, toys, appliances. Since industrialization did little to increase the buying power of the poor, the market

Learning from Photographs *Brasília, the capital of Brazil, is one of the world's leading examples of large-scale urban planning. It contains some of the most striking modern architecture in the world.* **In what ways are South American cities changing today?**

for consumer goods was limited to the small elite. Latin American firms quickly produced more than they could sell at home, so they turned to exporting goods to stay in business.

The efforts at industrialization brought results. Between 1950 and 1980, Latin American economic growth averaged over 5 percent a year. However, much of the money to finance industrial growth came from large multinational corporations and banks. For every dollar they invested in Latin America, they took out more than three dollars in profits and dividends.

Agricultural growth did not match industrial growth. More land was allocated for growing cash crops for export, such as coffee, bananas, and coca, which is used to make cocaine. For example, in the Central American country of Guatemala, acreage devoted to growing export crops increased 6.5 percent a year between 1950 and 1973. But as farmers converted more land to growing cash crops, they grew less food for the local population. Although the landowners prospered from selling their crops abroad, local people had to pay more to buy food from farther away. Most campesinos remained poor.

Hoping to stimulate economic growth, many Latin American leaders borrowed heavily from large banks in wealthy countries such as

CONNECTIONS: GEOGRAPHY IN HISTORY

Booming Buenos Aires

In no other part of the world has urbanization occurred as rapidly as in modern Latin America. For example, today more than 10 million people—well over one-third of all Argentinians—live in the port city and capital of Buenos Aires. One attractive feature of the city is the pleasant, temperate climate. Summers are long, and winters are mild. The people of Buenos Aires, called *portenos*, or port dwellers, are descendants of immigrants from all over the world—Spain, Germany, Italy, England, France, Poland, the Soviet Union, and the Middle East.

In the mid-1800s, British and Argentinian investors built a network of rail lines spreading outward from Buenos Aires. On these rail lines, wheat, corn, cattle, and sheep are now sent to Buenos Aires for export.

Building on its foundation of trade in agricultural products, Buenos Aires grew into a large industrial center. Among the major industries are food processing and textiles. Today the city enjoys a prosperous economy.

Buenos Aires' rapid growth typifies the recent expansion of cities throughout the region. In 1909 Buenos Aires topped the 1 million mark. During the 1920s and 1930s, a flood of immigrants pushed the population to well over 2 million. Just as the influx of immigrants began to slow, rural Argentinians began pouring into the city, seeking jobs. During the 1940s, Buenos Aires had 4.5 million people, and in forty years the population had doubled, reaching 10 million.

Making the Connection

1. What features of Buenos Aires have attracted immigrants?
2. Predict the consequences of growth on Buenos Aires' future.

the United States. Between 1975 and 1985, Latin American debt to other parts of the world increased 318 percent.

By the 1980s a worldwide recession made matters worse. It cut the demand for Latin American exports, forcing plants to slow production and lay off workers. At the same time, interest rates began to rise disastrously—from 9 percent in 1978 to 20 percent in 1981. As a result, Latin American debts also increased disastrously. Simply paying interest on huge debts lowered Latin America's export earnings. By 1984 the region's debt totaled $350 billion.

In early 1987 Brazil stated it would suspend payment on its massive debt and interest payments. This action had a chilling effect on U.S. banks, which held about 25 percent of the loans. Many observers believe that the Latin American debt remains one of the major problems for this hemisphere. If the debts are not paid, many banks may fail. The U.S. government has begun working with Latin American leaders to encourage an equitable rescheduling of loan payments to avoid a crisis.

Growth of Democracy

The economic problems of Latin America made the growth of democracy almost impossible. In most countries, the elite controlled the government as well as the economy. The elite did not trust the masses enough to allow any form of majority rule to take hold. And the majority of people, long dominated by a few powerful leaders, had little experience in making decisions or choosing leaders.

Political conflicts in most of Latin America were between liberals and conservatives. Liberals tried to help the masses through land and tax reforms. Conservatives wanted to maintain the traditional social structure and opposed any redistribution of wealth. Clashes between liberals and conservatives have often been bloody.

The failure of democracy and social reform prompted calls for more radical change. Armed guerrilla movements, that sought to change society by force, emerged in many countries. These groups often relied on the support and protection of campesinos. Many guerrilla organizations included at least some Communists. In Cuba, Nicaragua, and elsewhere, guerrilla movements successfully overthrew governments and took power themselves.

Fear of communism combined with outrage at the poverty of so many people caused changes in the Catholic Church. Since colonial times, the Church had generally supported rule by elites in most Latin American countries. Individual priests sometimes called for reforms to help the poor, but they were exceptions. After a meeting of Latin American bishops in Colombia in 1968, however, an increasing number of Catholic clergy began supporting land reform, democracy, and other changes that campesinos and workers had long demanded. They began emphasizing the role of Christianity in liberating people from oppression. Their beliefs became known as **liberation theology**. One Latin American religious worker explained the new movement this way:

For example, if, as the book of Genesis teaches, human beings have been created in God's image, they have a great dignity; hence, to torture another human being is to disfigure God's image. If the Lord gave the Earth to Adam and Eve, he meant it for all—not just a few plantation owners.

—Philip Berryman,
Inside Central America, 1985

The combined pressure of guerrillas, liberal Catholic clergy, and organized citizens began to bring changes in the 1980s. Argentina, Brazil, Chile, and other countries threw off their dictators and adopted democratic governments. However, these young democracies inherited foreign debts, widespread poverty, and social unrest. The most controversial issue in many countries has been land reform, which is still opposed by the military and wealthy landowners.

International Relations

Since the end of World War II, Latin America has become increasingly involved with the rest of the world, economically and politically.

Latin America has forged new trading relationships with Western Europe, Asia, Africa, and Japan. Today Japan provides consumer, chemical, and heavy industrial products to Latin America in exchange for food, copper, iron ore, and cotton.

In addition, many Latin American leaders have taken leadership positions in world diplomacy. For example, in the 1970s, Mexico's president, Luis Echeverría (ai cheh veh REE uh), was a leader in the nonaligned movement. And Peruvian diplomat, Javier Pérez de Cuellar, became the secretary general of the United Nations in 1982.

The most important relations of Latin American nations, however, have been with each other and with the United States. Discussions about hemispheric security during World War II led to a meeting in Rio de Janeiro, Brazil, in 1947. At that meeting the United States and most of the Latin American nations signed the Inter-American Treaty of Reciprocal Assistance. This defense pact, known as the Rio Treaty, provided that any attack on a member of the pact would be considered an attack on all of the members.

On April 30, 1948, the Organization of American States (OAS) charter was signed at Bogota, Colombia. The intent of the OAS was to nurture political and economic ties among the nations of the Western Hemisphere. The OAS grew out of efforts at hemispheric cooperation that started in 1889. One of its most important successes was in the late 1960s, when the OAS intervened to stop a war between Honduras and El Salvador shortly after fighting began. Today 31 countries belong to the OAS.

Relations between Latin America and the United States have been shaped by the cold war. The United States often provided financial aid and military support to unpopular military or authoritarian regimes. These governments agreed to protect U.S. investments and harshly suppressed reform movements that included Communists. Sometimes U.S. support meant overthrowing a popular government. In 1954 the U.S. CIA helped overthrow the government of Guatemala led by Jacobo Arbenz Guzman. Guzman's efforts to redistribute land to the peasants was viewed as a threat to American business interests.

Another way to fight communism was through financial assistance. In 1961 President John F. Kennedy launched the Alliance for Progress. This program provided $10 billion in aid for Latin American industry, housing, medical care, and military development. However, much of the money sent to Latin America was used to buy U.S.-made goods. The aid helped the United States as well as Latin America.

United States aid to Latin America continues today. However, much of it is military aid, which has little effect on economic development. Leaders in both the United States and Latin America, however, are realizing how intertwined the two regions are. Only a healthy Latin America can pay its debts, care for its people, and solve the international problems of drugs, environmental destruction, and mass emigration. "Far from becoming irrelevant," one U.S. observer wrote, "Latin America's problems and opportunities will increasingly be our own."

SECTION 1 REVIEW

Recall

1. **Define:** campesino, liberation theology
2. **Identify:** Jacobo Arbenz Guzman, Alliance for Progress
3. **Explain:** How did fast-growing populations and cities cause problems for Latin American nations?

4. **List:** What political and economic problems have confronted Latin American democracies in recent years?

Critical Thinking

5. **Analyze:** Examine the effects of U.S. involvement in Latin America after World War II.

6. **Analyze:** How has the role of the Catholic Church in Latin America changed since World War II?

Applying Concepts

7. **Cooperation:** How might increased U.S.–Latin American trade affect the campesinos?

Mexico and the Caribbean

Although Mexico and the Caribbean nations of Haiti and the Dominican Republic gained their independence in the early 1800s, they were independent in name only. The United States exerted great influence over the nations surrounding its southern borders. After World War II, these countries sought to assert more control over their industries and economies. But growing populations and political turmoil made these goals difficult to reach.

Mexico

Of all the countries in Latin America, Mexico was among the most stable after World War II. For decades, the Institutionalized Revolutionary Party (PRI) and a series of strong presidents had brought order to Mexico. The PRI welcomed the voices of business leaders and peasants, educators, and soldiers. Its drive to industrialize Mexico fostered a rapid increase in production and, in turn, a growing middle class.

From the end of the war until the 1960s, Mexico's **standard of living**—the overall wealth of its people—increased. In cities, more goods and services were available to a growing number of people. Rural areas did not prosper, however, and millions of people continued to live in poverty. To help the growing population pay for food, transportation, and basic needs, the government borrowed money, causing the nation's debt to soar. Because of the increased demand for goods, inflation jumped to 40 percent in 1975.

Economic Problems   In the 1970s, however, Mexico appeared to have a solution to its economic woes. New discoveries indicated that the country had at least three times as much oil as it had previously thought, and turmoil in the Middle East was driving the price of oil upward. As the oil industry prospered, so did the entire Mexican economy. The government borrowed money to finance economic development, assuming that oil revenues would make repaying it easy.

However, a worldwide recession in 1981 caused the oil boom to burst. A glut of oil on the world market sent oil prices plunging. Unemployment rose as the government cut jobs to save money. In an effort to stimulate exports, the government cut the value of the Mexican peso by 47 percent. With this, many wealthy families fled from Mexico, taking their fortunes with them.

Mexico's economic condition worsened throughout the 1980s. Mexico owed foreign investors nearly $65 billion in 1982. That amount soon rose to $100 billion, one of the highest debts among developing nations. Unemployment was high, and the gap between Mexico's rich and poor was widening. Rapid population growth meant increasing demands for goods and services and increasing competition for jobs. And in 1985 a devastating earthquake hit Mexico. The quake caused about $4 billion in damage and killed about 7,200 people.

Furthermore, relations with the United States had soured. The United States wanted the Mexican government to do more to stop Colombian drug producers from smuggling illegal drugs into the United States. In addition, many Mexicans, eager to obtain work, were coming to the United States in search of jobs. Some people in the United States resented the thousands of Mexicans who were entering the United States each year without visas.

A New Era   In 1988 Mexico's new president, Carlos Salinas de Gortari, advocated reforms to help solve Mexico's problems. For example, he began negotiating a free-trade agreement with the United States. This agreement would remove all quotas, tariffs, and other barriers to unrestricted trade between the two countries. Salinas hoped this plan would lure United States investors and their industries into Mexico, thereby increasing job opportunities.

To further enhance the economy, Salinas began to sell off government-owned industries to private investors. He was setting out to reverse the policy that had been followed between the 1930s and the 1980s, when the government of Mexico had purchased control of the oil industry, the system of railroads and other transportation systems, and most communications industries. Salinas hoped that private owners would run these industries with greater efficiency than had the government. One of the first industries sold to investors was the telephone company.

Cuba

Unlike Mexico, which has been politically stable since World War II, the Caribbean island nation of Cuba was the scene of a dramatic revolution. In 1953 Fidel Castro began a guerrilla movement against dictator Fulgencio Batista, who had ruled Cuba for most of the previous 20 years. Batista had allowed United States corporations to dominate the Cuban economy. By the early 1950s, United States companies, taking full advantage of this lenient policy, owned or controlled many of the island's mines and ranches as well as much of the oil and the sugar industries.

Castro attacked Batista's repressive and corrupt practices, calling for political and civil reforms. For six years he and his soldiers carried out guerrilla raids on Batista's forces. On January 1, 1959, Batista fled the country, and Cas-

IMAGES OF THE TIME

Mexico Today

With one of the world's biggest cities and a large rural population, Mexico is a land of great variety.

Traditional crafts are still highly valued today. These clay figurines are by a contemporary Mexican artist.

Mexico City, one of North America's oldest cities, is Mexico's cultural, governmental, and economic center.

tro assumed control. Many former political officials and army officers were tried and executed, and independent newspapers were closed. Many Cubans who opposed Castro left the country.

Castro's Domestic Policies Castro promised democratic reforms and a better standard of living for the Cuban people. Instead of establishing a democracy, however, Castro suspended elections. He did push through reforms to improve wages, health care, and basic education. He also began a program to redistribute ownership of land and businesses by nationalizing sugar plantations and major industries. He angered Americans by seizing American-owned property and by ignoring civil liberties of Cubans. As a result, relations between the two countries began to decline.

In retaliation for some of Castro's policies, the United States cut off all sugar imports from the tiny island in 1960. Castro turned to the Soviet Union for help. Soviet Premier Nikita Khrushchev agreed to buy Cuban sugar and sell arms to Castro. Two years after the revolution, Castro's dictatorship was openly Communist.

Cuba and the United States Castro's friendship with the Soviets made Cuba the key cold-war battleground in the Western Hemisphere. Castro supported bloody revolutions in Latin America and Africa by supplying military aid and troops and by calling on the people to support the revolts:

The revolution will triumph in America and throughout the world, but it is not for revolutionaries to sit in the doorways of their houses waiting for the corpse of imperialism to pass by.

—From a 1962 speech by Fidel Castro

Vibrant market days take place in many Mexican towns where people come to sell the foods they grow and the products they make.

Hand made textiles of wool and of cotton are an important industry in many rural areas.

Reflecting on the Times
What problems does the rising population in Mexico City pose?

Castro's defiance of the United States put him in danger. During this period there were at least 30 attempts to assassinate the Cuban leader, many of them ordered by the CIA.

In April 1961 the United States tried to overthrow Castro. About 1,500 anti-Castro exiles trained by the U.S. invaded Cuba at the Bay of Pigs, hoping to rally the Cuban people to revolt and topple Castro. The expected U.S. military support was canceled by President Kennedy, and they met stiff, armed resistance. In a matter of days, the Cuban army captured or killed most of the entire force. The failed invasion deeply embarrassed the United States.

A year later, the Soviets began installing nuclear missiles in Cuba. President Kennedy ordered nearly 200 U.S. warships to blockade Cuba and stop military shipments from the Soviet Union. American B-52 bombers with nuclear warheads took to the skies, and U.S. forces worldwide went on full alert. As Soviet ships steamed toward Cuba, a tense world waited in fear.

Four days later, after sleepless nights and tense negotiations, the crisis ended. Khrushchev agreed to dismantle the bases and pull the missiles out of Cuba if the United States promised never to attack Cuba again. The most dangerous encounter of the cold-war era had passed. Around the globe, people breathed a collective sigh of relief.

From 1963 to 1979, U.S.-Cuban relations were limited. Travel between the two countries was restricted. But in 1980 Castro allowed nearly 125,000 Cubans to sail to the United States from the small port of Mariel. Most of these people on the "Mariel boatlift" were political dissidents who opposed Castro's authoritarian rule. Some were criminals or mentally ill people whom Castro did not want in Cuba.

In the 1980s and 1990s Cuba faced major political and economic difficulties. Castro had promised to make Cuba independent, but it has become increasingly more dependent on Soviet assistance. Low sugar prices, a decline in Soviet aid, and inefficiencies in the state-run industries have stalled economic growth. As a result, Cuba and Castro are facing an uncertain future.

The Caribbean

To the east of Cuba is Hispaniola, a mountainous island divided between two countries. On the eastern end of the island is the Dominican Republic, a Spanish-speaking country. On

Learning from Maps
The Cuban missile crisis frightened the United States and the Soviet Union into improving relations with each other. In 1963 the "hot line," a special telephone connecting Washington and Moscow, was installed so the leaders of the superpowers could always contact each other instantly in a crisis. **From east to west, how large was the area covered by the U.S. blockade of Cuba?**

CUBAN MISSILE CRISIS 1962

Learning from Photographs *Fidel Castro has governed Cuba since his revolution more than 30 years ago.* **How does Castro's clothing relate to his background?**

the western end of the island is French-speaking Haiti. The two countries are among the poorest in the Western Hemisphere.

The Dominican Republic   Between 1930 and his assassination in 1961, General Rafael Trujillo Molina ruled the Dominican Republic as a military dictator. His family prospered during his reign, but few others did. In 1962 Juan Bosch was elected president, vowing to support land reform. Within a year, military leaders and large landowners threw him out of office. U.S. troops stopped an effort to restore him to power in 1965. In 1966 Joaquín Balaguer, a former leader under Trujillo, defeated Bosch in the race for president. However, the election was marred by charges of fraud. Balaguer served until 1978 and then returned to office again in 1986.

The main export of the Dominican Republic's agriculture-based economy is sugar. World sugar prices have been low in recent years, though, hurting the country's economy.

Haiti   Although independent since 1804, Haiti has always suffered poverty and political turmoil. Between 1844 and 1914, 32 rulers ran the country. Between 1957 and 1971, François Duvalier (doo vahl YAY) ran the country as a dictator. In 1971, when Duvalier died, his 19-year-old son, Jean-Claude, took power. In 1986 a popular revolution overthrew the Duvalier regime. For four years, the country suffered political strife. In 1990 a popular reform-minded priest, Jean Bertrand Aristide, was elected president. But his ability to take office and govern was threatened by Duvalier supporters.

SECTION 2 REVIEW

Recall

1. **Define:** standard of living
2. **Identify:** Carlos Salinas de Gortari, Fidel Castro, Fulgencio Batista, Rafael Trujillo, Joaquín Balaguer, the Duvaliers
3. **Locate:** Find Cuba on the map on page 910. Why might people in the United States have felt threatened by Castro?

Critical Thinking

4. **Evaluate:** Explain how Salinas's free-trade agreement with the United States could both help and hinder Mexico's economic growth.
5. **Apply:** Why did Mexico's huge oil reserves cause as many problems for Mexico as they solved?

6. **Analyze:** Compare the political development of Cuba and Mexico. Which seems better positioned to prosper in the coming century? Why?

Applying Concepts

7. **Revolution:** Explain why revolutions have been so common in Latin America since 1945.

Central America

Although the countries of Central America won their independence in the early 1800s, for almost two centuries those nations have suffered from wars, civil unrest, and interference by foreign powers. Since World War II, the problems confronting Nicaragua, El Salvador, and Panama have been representative of those nations throughout the region.

Revolution in Nicaragua

Nowhere was the hold of the wealthy elite tighter than it was in Nicaragua. There the Somoza family took power in 1957, and, with the exception of one four-year period, remained in control, backed by the U.S.-trained army known as the National Guard until 1979. By 1967, when Anastasio Somoza Debayle took over the presidency from his older brother, the Somoza family owned one-half of the land in Nicaragua and most of the country's industries, banks, and businesses.

The Somozas' domination of Nicaragua caused increasing resentment until 1978, when civil war broke out. A broad coalition of groups, including peasants, Catholic priests, middle-class merchants, socialists, and Communists, united to challenge Somoza. Leading the coalition was the Sandinista National Liberation Front (FSLN). The Sandinistas took their name from General Augustino Sandino, the popular hero who had waged guerrilla attacks on the U.S. occupation forces in Nicaragua in the 1920s. Sandino had been executed by the father of Anastasio Somoza in 1934.

After the Revolution The rebel coalition succeeded in overthrowing Somoza in 1979. Although the majority of Nicaraguans cheered the revolution, they differed on how the new government should operate. Some Nicaraguans believed in capitalism and wanted to maintain

Learning from Photographs *Civil war divided Nicaragua for many years, as the U.S.-backed contras attacked the left-wing Sandinista government.* **Why did the United States support the contras?**

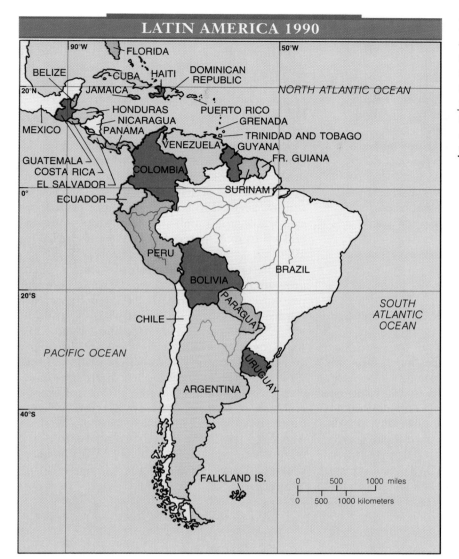

LATIN AMERICA 1990

FLORIDA
90°W
50°W
BELIZE
CUBA
HAITI
DOMINICAN
REPUBLIC
JAMAICA
20°N
NORTH ATLANTIC OCEAN
HONDURAS
PUERTO RICO
NICARAGUA
GRENADA
MEXICO
PANAMA
TRINIDAD AND TOBAGO
VENEZUELA
GUYANA
GUATEMALA
FR. GUIANA
COSTA RICA
COLOMBIA
EL SALVADOR
0°
SURINAM
ECUADOR
PERU
BRAZIL
20°S
BOLIVIA
PARAGUAY
CHILE
SOUTH
ATLANTIC
OCEAN
PACIFIC OCEAN
URUGUAY
ARGENTINA
40°S

FALKLAND IS.

0   500   1000 miles
0   500   1000 kilometers

Learning from Maps
Although Central America is a relatively small region of the Western Hemisphere, in recent years it has been the focus of more U.S. attention than the huge continent of South America. **Why do you think this is so?**

close ties with the United States. Others called for socialism and a lessening of dependence on the United States.

The Sandinistas, many of whom were Socialists or Communists, held control and began a series of popular reforms. They seized land that belonged to Somoza and turned it over to the peasants. With Castro's help, they taught people to read and write and improved rural health care. Within a year after taking power, however, the new Nicaraguan government faced growing opposition. Disgruntled former allies of the Sandinistas joined forces with former So-

moza supporters to try to overthrow the government. These opponents were called the contras, from the Spanish word meaning "against."

Civil War The Nicaraguan government received financial and military aid from Cuba, the Soviet Union, and many Western European countries. However, the United States, fearing the influence of the Soviets and the Cubans, decided to support the contras. In 1981 the United States government sent $19.5 million to the contras, the first official aid to the rebels. By 1985 contra forces numbered 15,000. From

FOOTNOTES TO HISTORY

NICARAGUA'S LITERACY CAMPAIGN

In 1980, soon after the revolution, the new Nicaraguan government attacked one of the key problems of the new country: illiteracy. Over one-half of the adults in the country were unable to read or write. The government decided that those who were literate must help those who were not literate. Over the next five months, almost 100,000 students helped teach 500,000 people, most of whom were peasants, how to read and write. At the end of the five months, the illiteracy rate was less than 15 percent.

bases in Honduras and Costa Rica, they attacked Nicaraguan military bases and businesses.

By 1985 the American public began to fear that the United States would be drawn into another conflict like that in Vietnam. The U.S. Congress banned military aid to the contras. Despite the ban, members of President Ronald Reagan's staff continued to send covert, or secret, funds to the contras. This illegal use of funds was part of the so-called Iran-Contra scandal that became public in 1987, embarrassing the Reagan administration and leading to indictments of some of the president's staff.

Through negotiations, which were led by Costa Rican president Oscar Arias, the contras and the Nicaraguan government agreed to a cease-fire and to hold presidential elections in 1990. Sandinista leader and Nicaraguan president Daniel Ortega ran for reelection against Violeta Chamorro, the widow of a popular newspaper editor killed by Somoza in 1978. Chamorro, with financial and political backing by the United States, led a wide-ranging coalition of parties. War-weary voters, many hoping that a change in government would bring about peace, elected Chamorro with 55 percent of the vote. With the Sandinistas out of power, the contras had little to fight against. Chamorro convinced them to disband. Though now at peace, Nicaragua continues to be divided by sharp political conflicts.

Conflict in El Salvador

During the 1960s and the early 1970s, El Salvador showed some signs of progress. The most industrialized nation in Central America, El Salvador boasted modern highways, railroads, hotels, and airports. However, the wealth of the country was held by a tiny elite group of people. One study in 1963 estimated that a group of 25 families, many of whom were related to one another by marriage, controlled about 90 percent of the wealth of El Salvador. And while the country seemed to be growing more prosperous as a whole, the number of landless peasants increased from 12 percent in 1961 to 40 percent in 1970.

The unequal distribution of wealth brought growing demands for change. Fearing a popular revolution like the one in Nicaragua, wealthy landowners hired **death squads**—bands of killers who murdered their political opponents. As many as 1,000 protesters, popular leaders, and their supporters were being killed a month. One of the leading critics of the murder of innocent civilians was El Salvador's Roman Catholic archbishop, Monsignor Oscar Romero. When a death squad killed him as he celebrated Mass on March 24, 1980, the country erupted into a civil war. In her poem "Because I Want Peace," Claribel Alegría described the feelings of many Salvadorans:

*B̲ecause there are clandestine
cemeteries
and Squadrons of Death
drug-crazed killers
who torture
who maim
who assassinate
I want to keep on fighting. . . .
Because there are liberated
territories
where people
learn how to read
and the sick are cured
and the fruits of the soil
belong to all
I have to keep on fighting.
Because I want peace
and not war.*

To stop the uprising, the military appointed José Napoleón Duarte as president in 1980. Duarte supported land reform, but he was powerless to stop the death squads. As the killing continued, the Farabundo Martí National Liberation Front (FMLN)–a coalition of guerrilla groups opposing the death squads and the military–won greater support. The United States, fearing Communist influence within the FMLN, gave military aid to the governments of Duarte and his successor, Alfredo Cristiani.

During the 1980s the war casualties totaled 70,000 people. The war also caused $3 billion in damage and forced more than 1.5 million Salvadorans into exile. However, in 1990 the FMLN and the military began to hint that they might agree to a negotiated settlement.

Power Struggles in Panama

Compared with Nicaragua and El Salvador, Panama has been relatively peaceful and prosperous since World War II. From 1968 to 1981, dictator Omar Torrijos (toh REE hohs) ruled Panama, bringing stability to the country. He gave government jobs to the country's poor, enabling them to move up the economic ladder. Under his rule, Panama became a center for banking and investment and the most prosperous country in Central America.

Much of Panama's prosperity came from the 50-mile-long canal that runs through the country. Despite the canal's location within Panama, it was controlled by the United States. Many Panamanians resented this foreign domination of their country's land. In 1977 U.S. leaders and representatives of 23 Latin American nations signed a new canal treaty. They agreed that Panama would take control of the canal by December 31, 1999, and that the canal would remain open to the ships of all nations.

After Torrijos died in a plane crash in 1981, Panama entered a period of political instability. In 1988 General Manuel Noriega, head of the National Guard, took power. A Panamanian CIA agent known for his brutality and his drug trafficking activities, Noriega put the National Guard on full alert, suppressing all protests.

Despite Noriega's ties with the CIA, tensions between Panama and the United States grew. Aware that Noriega was helping to smuggle drugs to the United States, a U.S. grand jury indicted him under international law. In response, Noriega arrested a group of U.S. citizens in Panama. In December 1989 President George Bush sent 9,000 U.S. troops into Panama, where they seized Noriega in January 1990 and brought him to Florida to stand trial. Between 300 and 2,000 Panamanian civilians died in the invasion, and 20,000 were left homeless. A year later, Noriega still awaited trial. The new U.S.-supported government of Panama, led by Guillermo Endara, struggled to rid itself of Noriega's legacy: rampant drug trafficking, political corruption, poverty, and economic decay.

SECTION 3 REVIEW

Recall

1. **Define:** death squad
2. **Identify:** Anastasio Somoza Debayle, Sandinistas, contras, Monsignor Oscar Romero, Manuel Noriega
3. **List:** Identify the causes of the civil wars in Nicaragua and El Salvador.
4. **List:** What were the terms of the 1977 Panama Canal Treaty?

Critical Thinking

5. **Apply:** President Kennedy once said of Central America: "Those who make peaceful change impossible make violent change inevitable." Show how events in El Salvador supported this observation.
6. **Analyze:** Compare the involvement of the United States in Nicaragua with the involvement of the United States in Panama. How were the actions of the United States different in the two countries?

Applying Concepts

7. **Conflict:** Propose a solution to the present conflicts in Central America. What role do you think the United States should play in solving these conflicts? What role do you think other countries should play?

South America

Since the end of World War II, South America has become a region of sharp contrasts. Rapidly growing cities include both prosperous tourist havens and vast neighborhoods of poor people. While new industries have developed in the coastal urban areas, traditional forms of agriculture still dominate much of the interior of the continent. The poverty of the continent's people, despite areas of modernization and prosperity, continues to shape its political and social structures.

Argentina

Before a world depression and the rise of fascism in Argentina in the 1930s, the country was one of the 10 wealthiest in the world. Since then, the country has often been under military rule, and its prosperity has declined.

The Perón Era   The dominant political figure in Argentina from the 1940s to the 1970s was Colonel Juan Perón (pay ROHN). When he was first elected president in 1946, Perón enjoyed great popularity, even though he was an authoritarian ruler. Perón and his glamorous wife, Eva, a former film and radio star, became the heroes of the downtrodden. By increasing the military budget and supporting pay raises for union members, Perón won the loyalty of soldiers and workers. By nationalizing foreign-owned industries, he appealed to Argentinian pride over controlling its own resources. Eva supported construction of hospitals, schools, clinics, and nursing homes and distributed millions of shoes, sewing machines, and other household goods to the poor.

However, Perón's popularity began to wane in the 1950s. The much-loved Eva died in 1952. His policy of taxing agriculture to fuel industrial growth led to a decline in food production. As the economy declined, anti-Perón protests increased. He responded by imprisoning more of his opponents. In 1955 the military forced him to leave office.

In 1972, after 20 years of military rule, Perón returned briefly to power. When he died in 1974, his new wife Isabel took over, becoming the first woman president in the Western Hemisphere. Poorly educated, conservative, and dull compared with Eva, Isabel failed to win the hearts of the people. Economic problems continued, and a coup ousted her in 1976.

Once again Argentina was under military rule. The three generals who jointly ruled Argentina managed to spark an economic turnaround. To slow inflation, they froze wages and cut government spending. To encourage farmers to increase food production, they boosted farm prices. However, the generals ruled brutally. Death squads roamed the country, torturing and killing those who dissented. As many as 20,000 people died or simply disappeared.

Falklands War   In 1981, governmental power shifted to General Leopoldo Galtieri. In an attempt to unite Argentina and to end one of the last outposts of colonialism, Galtieri sent Argentinian troops to seize the Falkland Islands, also known as the Malvinas. These islands off the coast of Argentina had been controlled by the British since 1833. Seventy-four days later, they returned home defeated by the British ships and troops sent by Margaret Thatcher. Public anger at the defeat, combined with continuing economic problems, forced Galtieri to resign. Nine generals and admirals involved in the war were tried and sentenced.

After the Falklands humiliation, free elections were held and democracy was restored. Through the rest of the 1980s, however, the economy of Argentina remained dangerously close to collapse. **Hyperinflation**—extremely sharp and rapid price increases—caused a severe depression, and much of the middle class fell into poverty. In 1989, for example, inflation reached 6,000 percent. The military staged several rebellions, but civilians remained in control of the government. In 1990 Argentinians elected Carlos Menem as president.

Chile

The long coastal country of Chile has one of the strongest traditions of democracy in Latin America. In 1970 the voters elected Socialist Salvador Allende to the presidency. He was the first Marxist in the Western Hemisphere to come to power through peaceful means.

To stimulate the faltering economy, Allende nationalized businesses, including U.S. copper-mining companies, and distributed land to the poor. He also boosted wages by 35 percent and put a ceiling on prices. In two years, the economy grew 13.5 percent and unemployment was cut in half.

Not all of Allende's policies were successful, however. For example, the breakup of big farms resulted in a decline in food production, which in turn caused food shortages. And the increased wages led to inflation.

More important, though, Allende's policies made him powerful enemies. Wealthy Chileans, frightened by Allende's concern for the poor, took their money out of Chile and invested it in other countries. In addition, the United States decided to undermine the Allende government by funding opposition candidates, promoting strikes and protests, and convincing the World Bank to halt loans to Chile. By 1972 Chile's economy was near collapse.

In 1973 Chilean military leaders who had worked closely with CIA led a coup against Allende. After the successful uprising, Allende was found dead in his office. The military leaders claimed Allende had killed himself with a machine gun that Castro had given him as a gift. It was reported that between 5,000 and 50,000 people died in the coup.

The new government was led by a ruthless dictator, General Augusto Pinochet. Immediately, Pinochet put an end to Chile's long-standing democracy. He dissolved the congress, censored the press, canceled civil liberties, and issued a new constitution. He killed or imprisoned as many as 1 in every 100 Chileans.

To improve the Chilean economy, Pinochet imposed higher taxes and encouraged foreign investment. Inflation, which had reached 600 percent in 1973, fell to 10 percent by 1981. Soon, store shelves were filled with consumer goods.

Learning from Photographs *Juan Perón salutes the crowds after taking the oath for a new presidential term in 1952. Within months, his wife Eva died of cancer. Without his strongest supporter and publicist, Perón's conflicts with his many opponents, particularly the Roman Catholic Church, intensified.* **What group finally ousted Perón from office?**

Bringing Back Brazilian Music

When European missionaries arrived in Brazil in the 1500s and 1600s, they taught people there to sing European tunes and play European musical instruments. As a result of this *deculturação*, or cultural reorientation, much of traditional Brazilian music was unknown to the world in following centuries. Traditional music was still played and passed on, but mostly at social gatherings in rural areas or on city street corners. Most professional Brazilian composers and musicians studied in Western Europe and produced works in the European style.

In the 1920s, however, a nationalist movement in the Brazilian arts began. Heitor Villa-Lobos (1887–1959) was one of the most important leaders of that movement. Throughout his life, Villa-Lobos studied and promoted the performance of Brazilian folk tunes on traditional instruments. He recognized the importance of Brazil's musical and cultural heritage and worked to educate the people of Brazil—and of the world—about that heritage.

As a child growing up in Rio de Janeiro, Villa-Lobos often heard popular songs, regional folk tunes, and street music. At age 18 he left home, in part because his mother objected to his decision to become a professional musician. For the next several years, he traveled throughout the regions of Brazil, playing cello, guitar and other musical instruments. More important, he listened to and wrote down hundreds of folk tunes and popular melodies.

In his own compositions, Villa-Lobos did not adhere to the traditional techniques of European folk and classical music. Instead, he took an intuitive approach to composition, much as improvisers of folk music might do. In much of his music, he incorporated traditional Brazilian melodies, often with variations, but still very recognizable.

In addition to his own musical achievements, Villa-Lobos helped transform the educational system of Brazil to include better music instruction. His methods of teaching and organizing large choral groups were adopted in the school systems of São Paulo and Rio de Janeiro and influenced music instruction all over the world.

Responding to the Arts

1. What was the effect of the nationalist movement in the Brazilian arts in the 1920s?
2. What contributions did Heitor Villa-Lobos make to Brazilian culture of the twentieth century?

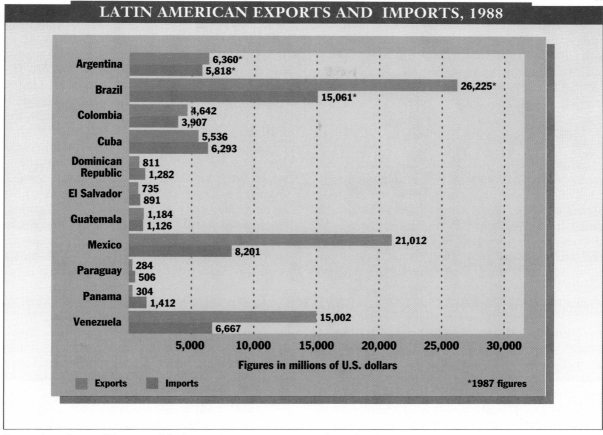

LATIN AMERICAN EXPORTS AND IMPORTS, 1988

Country	
Argentina	6,360* / 5,818*
Brazil	26,225* / 15,061*
Colombia	4,642 / 3,907
Cuba	5,536 / 6,293
Dominican Republic	811 / 1,282
El Salvador	735 / 891
Guatemala	1,184 / 1,126
Mexico	21,012 / 8,201
Paraguay	284 / 506
Panama	304 / 1,412
Venezuela	15,002 / 6,667

Figures in millions of U.S. dollars

■ Exports ■ Imports

*1987 figures

Learning from Charts *Nations strive to export more than they import, so they will not be in debt to foreign nations.* **Which nations export more than they import? Which import more than they export?**

Consumerism was the great work of Pinochet. He kept the country happy for almost ten years with color television sets from Hong Kong, dolls from Taiwan, automobiles from Japan, electronic games and computers from the United States. . . . Meanwhile torture and murder was the response to the heroism of the few Chileans who were not seduced.

—Jacobo Timerman,
Chile: Death in the South, 1987

Popular opposition to Pinochet remained strong. Many Catholic leaders continued to risk arrest, torture, and death by protesting against Pinochet's cruelty. In 1988, at long last Pinochet gave in to mounting pressure and allowed the people to have elections, which brought Patricio Aylwin to power. With the threat of another military coup still strong, Aylwin tried to revive Chile's democratic tradition.

Colombia

While Chile has had long periods of stability since World War II, Colombia has had long periods of instability. Between the late 1940s and the mid-1960s, battles between liberals and conservatives caused the deaths of about 200,000 people. Colombians refer to this period as *La Violencia*, or the violence.

In the past two decades, the ever-growing power of drug dealers has changed Colombian politics. Drugs, including marijuana and cocaine, became Colombia's largest export. Drug barons in the city of Medellin amassed tremendous fortunes. They murdered more than 350 judges and prosecutors who tried to stop the drug business. In 1990 César Gaviria, Colombia's new president, vowed to intensify the war against the drug lords.

Peru

Since the end of World War II, Peru has been run by military or by civilian dictators. One official who took bold steps to improve Peru's economy was General Juan Velasco, who ruled from 1968 to 1975. In ringing words he declared to the peasants of Peru, "the landlords will no longer eat from your poverty." He thereupon seized nearly 75 percent of the nation's wealthy estates and put the most fertile land into the hands of cooperatives.

Furthermore, General Velasco nationalized foreign-owned companies, thereby keeping profits in Peru, and he provided aid to the urban poor. By so doing, he hoped to unite Peruvians and to stimulate economic growth. However, inflation and unemployment continued to remain high. Military leaders removed Velasco from power in 1975.

Five years later, however, Peru fell into a deep economic depression as the world prices for sugar, copper, and other key Peruvian products plummeted. And as Peru's economy worsened, political unrest intensified. Today the country still remains divided, poor, and politically unstable.

Brazil

For two decades following World War II, Brazil was generally governed by freely elected leaders. Under their leadership, foreign investors opened auto factories and steel plants. However, when Joao Goulart became president in 1964 with the support of organized labor, the military feared he would begin reforms that would lead to communism. Military leaders therefore took control of the government.

In 1968 the military government launched a program to industrialize Brazil. Over the next seven years, they reduced social programs, sought investments by foreign companies, weakened the unions, and fixed wages at 50 cents an hour. With the economy growing 10 percent a year, businesses prospered. With wages kept low, however, workers remained poor.

In the 1980s the military allowed Brazil to return to democratic rule, but economic problems continued. In 1985 droughts destroyed much of the coffee crop, and devastating floods routed 1 million people from their homes.

In 1989 Fernando Collor de Mello became president of Brazil. He took strong steps to stabilize the country, encouraging increased mining of Brazil's rich stores of iron, bauxite, tin, gold, and other minerals. Most Brazilians supported the new president. He also won applause worldwide for his efforts to slow the destruction of the Amazon rain forest. Collor's concern about the rain forest reflects the growing importance of environmental issues throughout Latin America.

SECTION 4 REVIEW

Recall

1. **Define:** hyperinflation
2. **Identify:** Juan Perón, Eva Perón, Salvador Allende, Augusto Pinochet, Fernando Collor de Mello
3. **Describe:** What were political conditions like in Chile under the dictatorship of Augusto Pinochet?

Critical Thinking

4. **Analyze:** Why was Juan Perón's military government so popular in Argentina?
5. **Synthesize:** What conditions in Colombia would have to change in order to reduce the power of the drug barons?
6. **Analyze:** Compare the government of Argentina with that of Brazil during the 1970s.
7. **Apply:** How did international trade affect the economy of Peru?

Applying Concepts

8. **Change:** Explain how military governments both improved and damaged South American nations.

INTERPRETING STATISTICS

Your high school football coach has been at his job for ten years. A group of townspeople want him fired because they say he is on a losing streak. You know that last season's record was 0–10. Are they right?

Explanation

Often presented in tables and graphs, *statistics,* or numerical data, need to be carefully examined to determine their real significance. In the coach's case, for example, you would need to evaluate his entire record.

Use the following steps to interpret statistical information:

- Scan the table or graph, reading the title and labels to get an idea of what is being shown.
- Examine the statistics, looking for increases and decreases, similarities and differences. Determine if the data are relevant to a particular topic.
- Determine the conclusions you can draw from the statistics.

Example

Look at the graphs below, scanning titles and labeling. The bar graph focuses on imports and exports in Latin America in 1988 so you cannot make conclusions about trends over time. The line graph focuses on one country and shows changes over time. Since the graph shows that both imports

and exports dropped from 1980 to 1988, you could conclude that Guatemala did not have a healthy economy during the 1980s.

Application

Use the bar graph on page 919 to answer the following questions:
1. Which country imported the most in 1988?

2. Using this bar graph, can you make any conclusions about imports and exports in Latin America in the 1980s?

Practice

Turn to Practicing Skills on page 923 of the Chapter Review for further practice interpreting statistics.

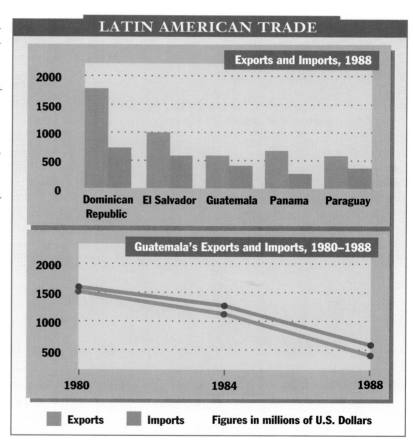

LATIN AMERICAN TRADE

Exports and Imports, 1988

Guatemala's Exports and Imports, 1980–1988

Exports   Imports   Figures in millions of U.S. Dollars

CHAPTER 34 REVIEW

HISTORICAL SIGNIFICANCE

The history of Latin America since World War II shows the difficulty of establishing democracy in societies that are dominated by a small elite. In most countries, the bitter conflict between the rich and the poor has prevented the growth of democracy. The history of Chile suggests that even in a relatively stable, democratic country, the danger of a military coup persists. And even in relatively stable countries, such as Argentina under Juan Perón and Mexico under the PRI, democracy has not always flourished.

A second significant limitation is the difficulty of economic development in such elite-dominated democracies. Efforts to boost agricultural exports or to develop industry in Latin America may bring some increases in total national wealth, but they do not necessarily help the majority of the population.

SUMMARY

For a summary of Chapter 34, see the Unit 8 Synopsis on pages 980-981.

USING KEY TERMS

Write one or two sentences that show how the key terms below are related to the concept of revolution.

1. campesino
2. death squad
3. hyperinflation
4. liberation theology
5. standard of living

REVIEWING FACTS

1. **Identify:** Who was Salvador Allende?
2. **Locate:** Where is the Bay of Pigs?
3. **Name:** What was the complete name of Nicaragua's FSLN?
4. **Describe:** Give an account of the impact of the assassination of Oscar Romero in El Salvador.
5. **Locate:** In which Caribbean nation did the 30-year rule by the Duvalier family end in 1986?
6. **Identify:** Who was Fulgencio Batista?
7. **Explain:** What is the purpose of the OAS?
8. **Identify:** Who overthrew the government of Jacobo Arbenz Guzman in Guatemala?

9. **Locate:** Where are the Falkland Islands?
10. **List:** What problems has rapid population growth caused in Latin America?
11. **Describe:** What was the role of Oscar Arias in Nicaragua's civil war?

THINKING CRITICALLY

1. **Analyze:** Why were foreign investors eager to invest money in Chile after General Pinochet overthrew the country's elected government?
2. **Evaluate:** Have the policies of the United States government had a positive or negative effect on the development of Latin America?
3. **Apply:** How would you solve the problem of the illegal drug trade between Colombia and the United States?
4. **Synthesize:** Imagine that you were a citizen of El Salvador in 1980. How would you feel about the United States providing support to your military government?
5. **Analyze:** How would you say that an overabundance of oil on the world market affected Mexico in 1981?
6. **Synthesize:** Why do you think so many Latin American governments have become dictatorships?
7. **Evaluate:** Do you think the U.S. policy toward Cuba since the end of World War II has been successful? Why or why not?

Analyzing Concepts

1. **Cooperation:** How has Latin American's interdependence with global and hemispheric markets affected its ability to develop economically?
2. **Revolution:** How did the United States' response to Cuba's revolution improve relations between Cuba and the Soviet Union?
3. **Conflict:** How has the cold war affected revolutionary developments in Latin America?.
4. **Change:** How have changes in the types of crops grown affected the standard of living of Latin American peasants?

Practicing Skills

Assume you see a newspaper article that shows four circle graphs, one each for 1960, 1970, 1980, and 1990. Each graph shows only the percentages of people living in rural and urban areas of Brazil. What types of conclusions could you draw from these graphs? Would you be able to tell if Brazil's population had grown between 1960 and 1990?

Geography in History

1. **Location:** Refer to the map on page 913. How many countries in Latin America are landlocked?

2. **Region:** Refer to the map on page 987. What physical feature dominates western South America?
3. **Movement:** Why have millions of campesinos moved to the many urban Latin American shantytowns?
4. **Place:** What is Cuba's most important crop?
5. **Environment:** How has Panama's location stimulated its economy?

Tracing Chronology

Refer to the time line below to answer these questions.
1. How long did the United States wait before first attempting to overthrow Castro's Cuban government?
2. For how many years did Chile remain under control of a dictatorship?

Linking Past and Present

1. How might the economic problems of Latin America cause problems for the United States in years to come? How might the United States have eased these problems?
2. In both the Monroe Doctrine and the regional defense pact of 1947, the United States pledged to protect Latin American nations from outside powers. But in the Falklands War, the United States quickly supported Great Britain. How do you think Latin Americans responded to this?

LATIN AMERICA

1946 Perón becomes Argentinian president.

1948 OAS founded.

1961 Bay of Pigs invasion

1962 Cuban missile crisis

1979 Sandinistas overthrow Somoza.

1982 Argentina loses Falkland Islands war.

| 1945 | 1955 | 1965 | 1975 | 1985 | 1995 |

1959 Castro overthrows Batista.

1954 Guatemalan government overthrown

1973 Allende overthrown in Chile

1989 United States invades Panama.

1988 Pinochet loses election.

Changes in North America and Europe

*G*orby! Gorby! Gorby!" chanted the freedom marchers in Dresden, East Germany, on October 8, 1989. Remarkably, the name of Soviet President Mikhail Gorbachev had become a rallying cry for democracy throughout communist Europe.

Marches like the one in Dresden took place throughout the Soviet satellite countries during 1989. To the amazement of people in the West, these new uprisings were being not only tolerated but encouraged by the Soviet leadership. The Communist Party's fortieth year in East Germany was its last, and most of Eastern Europe soon followed suit.

For a time, Gorbachev was hailed as the man who would dismantle the iron curtain, end communism, and stop the cold war. In later years, however, the course of Communist politics took some unexpected turns.

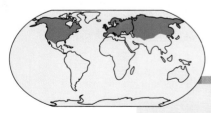

CHAPTER PREVIEW

Key Terms to Define: draft, imperial presidency, stagflation, budget deficit, separatism, détente, glasnost, perestroika

People to Meet: Presidents Gerald Ford, Jimmy Carter, Ronald Reagan, and George Bush; Mikhail Gorbachev; Lech Walesa; Pope John Paul II; Helmut Kohl; Margaret Thatcher; François Mitterrand

Places to Discover: the Watergate complex; Quebec; Afghanistan; the Baltic states; Gdansk, Poland

Objectives to Learn:
1. What conditions in the 1970s and 1980s caused the U.S.S.R. to retreat from communism?
2. How did the iron curtain fall?
3. In what ways is Europe becoming a more influential world power?

Eastern Europeans demonstrate against Communist regimes in 1989.

Concepts to Understand:
- Conflict—Concerns about U.S. involvement in Vietnam lead to widespread antiwar protests in the 1960s and 1970s. Section 1
- Nationalism—Ethnic movements arise in Eastern Europe and the Soviet republics. Section 2
- Change—The Soviet Union and its satellites undergo upheaval leading to greater economic and social freedoms. Sections 2,3
- Cooperation—The growth of the European Economic Community promises to unify the continent and make it a major economic power. Sections 3,4

925

The United States and Canada

During the 1970s and 1980s, the United States faced economic problems, internal political struggles, and continuing cold-war tensions with the Communist world. Despite blows to U.S. self-confidence, the United States remained committed to its role as a strong leader in world affairs. Meanwhile, Canada, its neighbor to the north, developed closer economic ties to the United States while dealing with internal threats to its national unity.

Ending the Vietnam War

President Dwight D. Eisenhower had involved the country in a cold-war conflict in Vietnam; President Kennedy had deepened that involvement; and President Johnson had expanded it into full-scale warfare. In 1968 the United States was choosing a new president, and the presidential race focused on Vietnam.

President Johnson, condemned for his handling of the lengthy, costly, and indecisive war, decided not to become a candidate for reelection. Instead, the Democratic National Convention of 1968 chose Senator George McGovern, a longtime opponent of the war. The Republican party chose former Vice President Richard Nixon, known for his strong anti-Communist stand. Nixon promised to restore America's self-esteem by ending the war in Vietnam. That promise won him a landslide victory.

Opposition to the War   President Nixon soon found that ending the war and "saving face" for America was difficult. As he struggled to find a politically acceptable solution, his administration was besieged by the antiwar forces that had overwhelmed Johnson's presidency.

Young men who were eligible for the **draft**—the mandatory enrollment in the U.S.

armed services—burned their draft cards, which was an illegal act. Many young men fled to Canada to avoid the draft, choosing to spend years in exile from their families and country rather than fight in the war. Demonstrators marched in front of the White House, carrying signs and shouting antiwar slogans. College professors canceled classes and held antiwar protests called "teach-ins." Most protests across the country were peaceful, but many incidents of violence occurred, including the bombing of military bases and other institutions that symbolized American government and power.

End of an Era   Nixon's plan for ending the war respectably was "Vietnamization"—a gradual withdrawal of U.S. troops while relinquishing control of war operations to South Vietnam. In a November 1969 speech, the president tried to counter the antiwar protests by appealing to what he called the silent majority of Americans who he said supported his policies.

Simultaneously with the U.S. withdrawal from Vietnam, Nixon ordered new attacks on Communist-held territory in neighboring Cambodia and Laos, including fierce bombing raids on Cambodia in 1970. The bombings prompted renewed protests, creating a superheated atmosphere of fear and distrust between supporters and opponents of the war. Those fears exploded in May 1970, when National Guard soldiers fired into a crowd of peaceful demonstrators at Kent State University in Ohio, killing four students.

In 1973, far later than Nixon had planned, the last U.S. forces withdrew from Vietnam, and the Paris Accords, discussed in Chapter 32, were signed. Of the 500,000 U.S. troops that had fought in Southeast Asia, about 58,000 died and 365,000 were wounded. The war cost the United States $150 billion. It made the nation more

Learning from Photographs *President Nixon's 1972 visit to the People's Republic of China opened a new relationship with the Communist regime.* **How did the imperial presidency affect U.S. foreign policy?**

cautious of foreign involvement during the 1970s and shook world confidence in U.S. military commitments.

The Changing Presidency

During the cold war, U.S. presidents gradually began to exercise powers beyond those spelled out in the Constitution. Claiming a need for a quick military response to counter communism, presidents began to assume the war-making powers of Congress, committing U.S. forces to combat without congressional approval. The two largest commitments to undeclared wars were in Korea and Vietnam.

The Imperial Presidency As the cold war continued into the 1960s and 1970s, many people felt that the increased presidential power was subject to abuses and a violation of the Constitution. The term **imperial presidency** came into use, reflecting this concern.

The term was most often applied to Presidents Lyndon Johnson and Richard Nixon, both of whom escalated the conflict in Vietnam without a congressional declaration of war, as called for in the Constitution, and often kept their actions secret from Congress. In 1973 Congress overrode Nixon's veto to pass the War Powers Limitation Act. The measure required the President to consult Congress before committing U.S. troops to combat.

The Watergate Scandal Early in Nixon's second term, when the imperial presidency was at its height, scandal engulfed his administration. Vice President Spiro Agnew was accused of taking bribes when he was governor of Maryland; he was forced to resign. Then the President himself came under fire in a scandal that brought to the nation's attention the possible abuses of power under the imperial presidency.

The Watergate scandal, as it was called, began on June 17, 1972, when five men were caught trying to plant electronic listening devices in the offices of the Democratic National Committee, located in the Watergate building in downtown Washington, D.C. The break-in was traced to Nixon's reelection committee.

A congressional probe revealed that the White House knew of the burglary and tried to cover it up. The President denied the charges at first, but tape recordings of Oval Office conversations proved that he had participated in the cover-up. Under the threat of impeachment, Nixon resigned on August 9, 1974. He was the first U.S. president ever to do so.

Gerald Ford, the Republican congressman from Michigan who had replaced Spiro Agnew as vice president, became president when Nixon stepped down in 1974. Ford was the first U.S.

President not to have been elected to either of the nation's top two offices. He assumed a presidency that had been weakened and tarnished. Watergate had shaken public confidence in the American political system. In addition, Ford had no personal mandate from the voters, since he had not been elected. As a former congressman, Ford maintained close ties with Congress. That, coupled with his acknowledged personal integrity, enabled him to function effectively. Both Ford and his Democratic successor, Jimmy Carter, a former governor of Georgia, worked to restore ethics to the presidency.

The U.S. Economy

The 1970s was a period of worldwide economic instability marked by high inflation. In the United States, inflation was aggravated by the costs of the Vietnam War. Inflation combined with high unemployment to produce an economic trend called **stagflation**. Low productivity in factories and competition from foreign companies also slowed the U.S. economy.

Another major economic problem in the 1970s was the growing trade deficit. As nations developed their industrial economies, their factories began to compete for sales to American consumers. In the automobile market, for example, rising gasoline prices caused buyers to choose more fuel-efficient cars from Japan instead of larger U.S. models. This trend contributed strongly to the U.S. trade deficit.

Soaring gas prices were part of an energy crisis that crippled economies around the world during the 1970s. In the United States, rapid economic growth had been dependent on cheap, abundant oil. The 1973 OPEC oil embargo, discussed in Chapter 33, was extremely damaging

---

The Sixties

The 1960s were a decade of change and, at times, turmoil for the United States. Students and minorities, in particular, challenged the nation's institutions and conventions.

Rebelling against the conservative ideals of society, many "hippies" adopted new fashions and hair styles.

Pop art like Andy Warhol's *Liz* explored the role of commercial images in modern culture, challenging traditional concepts of art.

to economic stability because it increased the cost of producing goods.

Meanwhile, the U.S. government found it difficult to live within its means. In 1980 Ronald Reagan was elected president in a campaign in which he promised to reduce the **budget deficit**—the condition in which the government spends more money than it earns in revenues, thus going into debt. Reagan cut government spending on social programs and lowered taxes to stimulate economic growth. During the course of his two terms, inflation began to slow and the economy began to improve. However, due to Reagan's emphasis on increased military spending, the budget deficit reached a new high.

George Bush came to office hoping to shift government spending from defense to social, educational, and environmental programs. But his plans were undercut by the need for increased military spending in the Middle East.

U.S. Foreign Policy

In the late 1970s and early 1980s, U.S.–Soviet relations gradually deteriorated. This period also saw growing problems for the United States in the Middle East.

Under Presidents Ford and Carter, nuclear arms reduction talks with the Soviets continued. But the Soviet invasion of Afghanistan later that year soured relations between the superpowers.

Events in the Middle East shattered the Carter presidency during this time. The taking of 52 American hostages by Iran and a failed U.S. attempt to rescue them turned public opinion against Jimmy Carter, who was seen as weak and ineffective. The episode demoralized the country and led to Carter's defeat in 1980.

Ronald Reagan promised to return the country to a position of respect and leadership abroad. He took a hard-line anti-Communist

Martin Luther King, Jr., led the civil rights movement (left). At Kent State University in Ohio, four students were killed during a protest over the bombing of Cambodia (below).

Reflecting on the Times
What were the key social and political issues of the 1960s in the United States?

Changes in North America and Europe **929**

A New Canvas

Just as handwriting can convey a mood—dramatic, hurried, or careful—a painter's brushstroke can communicate emotion. Artists of the abstract expressionism movement used lively brushwork to produce paintings that were highly emotional. Abstract expressionism was popular in the postwar years, but before long some artists tired of its powerful content.

One of the first postwar artists to explore cooler, more detached styles of painting was Helen Frankenthaler, a painter born in New York in 1928. Frankenthaler initiated a new technique of painting, one that rejected the highly expressive brushstroke of the abstract expressionists. The new method she developed was called the soak-stain technique. Traditionally, artists had covered the canvas cloth on which they painted with a very thin coat of gesso, or plaster, before beginning to paint. This coating smoothed out the surface of the cloth and provided a clean surface onto which the artist could apply paint with a brush.

Frankenthaler began painting on "raw," or untreated, canvas. Using thin paints, she poured colors onto the raw canvas instead of applying paint with a brush. The colors soaked deep into the cloth of the canvas. As a result, there was no "personal" brushstroke. The effect of this technique is that the colors Frankenthaler uses often appear to be transparent and intangible. Once soaked into the canvas, the paint seems to have no substance of its own.

Using this technique, Frankenthaler became one of the first artists of "color field" painting. In Color Field painting, emphasis was placed on the way areas of color were arranged on the canvas—meeting, blending, and overlapping. Frankenthaler's work is exceptional for its delicate quality. Veils of color give many of her paintings a beautiful lightness and transparency.

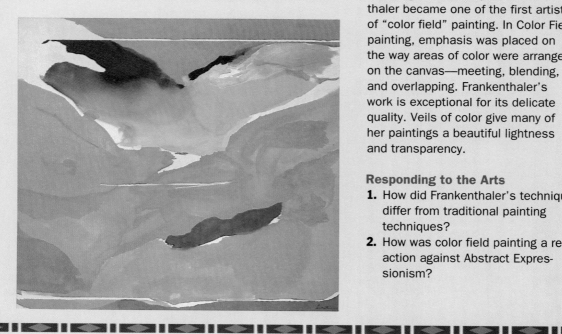

Responding to the Arts
1. How did Frankenthaler's technique differ from traditional painting techniques?
2. How was color field painting a reaction against Abstract Expressionism?

stand, calling the Soviet Union an "evil empire," and greatly increased military spending. One of his military initiatives was a major new weapons system called the Strategic Defense Initiative and nicknamed "Star Wars." With the support of NATO, Reagan also placed new nuclear missiles in Western Europe.

Later, however, as the Soviet Union under President Mikhail Gorbachev indicated a willingness to make massive weapons cuts and institute democratic reforms, Reagan developed a positive relationship with the Soviet leader.

Middle East problems proved to be as difficult for Reagan as they had been for Carter. Reagan sent troops to Lebanon during its civil war. But Arab resentment of the U.S. military presence was strong, and the force was withdrawn after terrorist attacks on U.S. targets.

With Reagan ineligible to run for a third term, his vice president, George Bush, won the election in 1988. He developed warm relations with Gorbachev that led to many new trade, technology, and immigration agreements. Bush relied heavily on Soviet support for his Middle East policies when the Allied coalition went to war with Iraq over its invasion of Kuwait.

Canada

Like the United States, Canada suffered many economic ills during the 1970s. This period was also marked by continual political controversy at home.

Canada's two major ethnic groups are people of British descent, who make up about 40 percent of the population, and those of French descent, who make up about 30 percent. French Canadians have sought recognition of their culture and special status in the province of Quebec, where 80 percent of the people are French-speaking.

In the late 1960s there was a growing debate over the issue of **separatism**, a movement favoring the establishment of Quebec as an independent country. The issue gave rise to the Parti Quebecois (kay beh KWAH), or Quebec party, sometimes known as the Separatist party.

In 1976 the separatists, led by René Levesque, won control of the Quebec assembly and declared French the official language of the province. In 1980 Levesque held a referendum to seek voter approval for Quebec to declare its independence. Under the plan, Quebec would have become self-governing and independent of the Canadian government. Amid widespread controversy and some violence, the plan was defeated at the polls.

Until 1982 Great Britain still had constitutional control over Canada. When Britain relinquished control, a new constitution was drafted, granting greater independence to all of the Canadian provinces and protecting the language and cultural rights of all Canadians.

However, Quebec refused to sign the new constitution without further guarantees. Prime Minister Brian Mulroney then met with the 10 provincial leaders at Meech Lake, Ontario.

The so-called Meech Lake Accords recognized Quebec as a "distinct society" within Canada. However, the measure failed to receive the ratification of all 10 provinces by the June 1990 deadline, placing strains on Canada's fragile national unity.

SECTION 1 REVIEW

Recall
1. **Define:** draft, imperial presidency, stagflation, budget deficit, separatism
2. **Identify:** Watergate scandal
3. **Explain:** What happened at Kent State University in May 1970?

Critical Thinking
4. **Apply:** Why do you think Reagan wanted to reduce the U.S. budget deficit? Why did he have difficulty reducing it?
5. **Analyze:** Do you think Quebec should secede from Canada? Why or why not?

Applying Concepts
6. **Conflict:** Describe President Nixon's "Vietnamization" policy. Develop a hypothesis for why the policy made it difficult to end United States involvement in the war quickly and easily.

The Soviet Union

The period from 1968 to the present time has been a difficult and tumultuous era in Soviet history. The centralized Soviet economy failed to provide basic goods, causing increasing disillusionment with the Communist system. This disillusionment spread to the Soviet satellite countries, creating upheaval and dissent and weakening the Soviet bloc. Political change in the Soviet Union forced repeated changes in relations with the United States as well—and that relationship is still changing today.

The Brezhnev Years

In contrast to Nikita Khrushchev—whose policies were increasingly seen by many Soviets as reckless and ineffective—his successor, Leonid Brezhnev, was a more cautious and traditional Communist leader. While Brezhnev took few risks that would provoke a nuclear war, he presided over a massive buildup of the Soviet military. With a strong army and secret police, he kept a tight grip on Soviet society and on the Soviet Union's satellite nations.

Military Might   Although by the late 1960s both the United States and the Soviet Union had enough nuclear missiles to annihilate each other several times over, Brezhnev was concerned about the missile gap: the greater number of U.S. missiles compared with the Soviet arsenal. Under Brezhnev the Soviet Union engaged in a massive buildup of nuclear weapons to close the gap. He also ordered vast increases in the stockpile of "conventional" weapons—that is, nonnuclear armaments such as guns, bombs, and tanks.

Dangers in all directions prompted Brezhnev to strengthen his forces. To the east, relations with China had grown increasingly hostile, and armed conflicts had erupted along the Chinese border. To the south, unstable regimes in Muslim countries such as Afghanistan were a constant worry. Looking westward, Brezhnev feared losing the Soviet hold on its satellites. He responded with the Brezhnev Doctrine, which prescribed the use of military force and the threat of force to crush dissent.

The Brezhnev Doctrine complemented the Soviet cold war strategy. In the East bloc the U.S.S.R. positioned new missiles aimed at targets in Western Europe. It also used its military resources to sustain Communist regimes in countries such as Cuba. Brezhnev took advantage of the U.S. preoccupation with Vietnam to extend Soviet influence in nonaligned countries in Africa and South America.

Trouble at Home   This military effort contributed to economic decay that would cripple the Soviet Union for years to come. The portion of the Soviet budget spent on the military was double that of the United States. As military spending grew, agricultural and industrial production suffered.

Policies from the Stalin era also caused the economy to suffer. The rigorously controlled system of production and distribution held few incentives for workers. During the Brezhnev years, Soviet steel production—the cornerstone of its economy—slackened. Production of other key industrial products, such as coal, cement, timber, and fertilizer also fell.

The collective farm system, which was poorly managed and running on outdated equipment, continually fell short of production goals. Grain was in particularly short supply, and the Soviet Union had to take the embarrassing step of buying wheat from the West. The grain shortage caused a reduction in the size of livestock herds, resulting in a shortage of meat for Soviet households.

As the economy deteriorated, waiting lines at the state-run stores lengthened. Even basic goods disappeared from the shelves. A thriving "black market" developed in which merchants bought and sold goods illegally. Items not available in state stores could often be bought on the black market—at a high price.

Communist party officials and other bureaucrats did not feel the economic pinch. Many enjoyed privileges—such as summer homes, new cars, and shopping at well-stocked stores—that were far beyond the dreams of most Soviet citizens. Soviet society had become anything but classless.

Zeal for Communist ideals was dimmed by resentment, hopelessness, and poverty. Worker apathy and a high rate of alcoholism were symptoms of the gloom that had descended on Lenin's revolution.

"Truce" in the Cold War   While facing problems and crushing opposition at home, Leonid Brezhnev sought closer ties to the West. For several reasons, an easing of superpower tensions was in the interest of the Soviet Union. First, a truce in the arms race would enable the Soviets to slow the rate of their military buildup without losing ground to the United States. A friendlier atmosphere between the two enemies might open the way for the Soviets to buy desperately needed consumer goods and technology from the West. Brezhnev was also concerned about a possible alliance between the United States and China, especially after President Nixon's visit to Beijing in 1972.

Brezhnev's foreign policy, as well as that of the United States at this time, was aimed at bringing about a thaw in the cold war. The policy was known as **détente**. Derived from the French word for "relaxation," détente means the improvement of U.S.–Soviet relations.

A 1972 summit meeting between Brezhnev and President Nixon in Moscow opened the seven-year period of superpower détente. The Nixon–Brezhnev summit led to the signing in 1972 of the Strategic Arms Limitation Agreement (SALT), under which both sides consented to limit the number of nuclear warheads and

THE ODD COUPLE

Learning from Political Cartoons *As cold war tensions eased in the early 1970s, friendlier relations developed between the United States and the Soviet Union.* **What does the "baby" in this cartoon represent?**

missiles each country could maintain. Although SALT was not a truce in the arms race, it did slow it significantly.

One result of the improved political atmosphere was the Helsinki Accords, signed in 1975 by the United States, Canada, and most of the countries of Europe. The signers recognized the postwar division of Europe into Eastern and Western spheres and pledged to work for peaceful cooperation in Europe, to support the United Nations, and to respect human rights.

The movement toward détente did not end the rivalry between the United States and the Soviet Union. The countries continued to compete for influence in various parts of the world. In 1979 the Soviets extended their influence, invading neighboring Afghanistan. Concerned by growing restlessness among the mainly Muslim

Afghans, Soviet troops moved in to bolster the Communist regime.

The move shocked the West and marked the end of détente. It also drew the Soviet Union into a 10-year guerrilla war against the tough Afghan nationalists. The occupation of Afghanistan became the Soviet Union's Vietnam—it drained the national treasury, killed thousands of young Soviet soldiers, and was extremely unpopular at home.

The Soviet military effort faced greater challenges in the early 1980s, when President Ronald Reagan launched a huge arms buildup. The Soviet Union could neither afford nor hope to match this escalation of the arms race.

Gorbachev

In 1982 Brezhnev died. During the next three years, the country's leadership changed three times, as one aging leader succeeded another. The leadership crisis opened the door for a power struggle between the "old guard" and a younger generation of Soviet leaders who saw that the Soviet Union could not maintain its superpower status while its economy collapsed.

Early Changes   In March 1985 the Communist party chose Mikhail Gorbachev, who at 54 was the youngest leader since Stalin. Gorbachev was willing to take risks and make drastic

PERSONAL PROFILES

The Two Faces of Mikhail Gorbachev

When Mikhail Gorbachev was nominated to head the Soviet Communist party, veteran diplomat Andrei Gromyko said, "Comrades, this man has a nice smile but he has iron teeth." His words were prophetic.

In the ensuing years, the man with the nice smile won the admiration of much of the world. Gorbachev's confidence, fresh speaking style, and cultural sophistication presented a contrast to the dour Soviet leaders who preceded him.

Gorbachev's personality was a key part of his foreign policy. He made overtures to Western Europe, where the peace movement was strong. Gorbachev impressed British Prime Minister Margaret Thatcher as someone she "could work with." Even Ronald Reagan eventually backed away from his "evil empire" rhetoric, strolling through Moscow's Red Square with his congenial host.

Recently, however, with his country's national unity crumbling and public opposition welling up around him, Gorbachev's iron teeth began to show. Now severe and often angry in his brief public appearances, he revived police powers in Russia and sent troops to the Baltic states. Did hard-liners force him to make the moves? Or was Gorbachev, who had grown up under Stalin and had served his party loyally, actually a traditional Communist at heart?

A comment by Winston Churchill in 1939 could easily be applied to Mikhail Gorbachev in the 1990s: "I cannot forecast to you the action of Russia. It is a riddle wrapped in a mystery inside an enigma."

Reflecting on the Person
1. Describe Gorbachev's personality.
2. What do you think is the explanation for the "two Gorbachevs"?

changes. Under his policy of *glasnost*, meaning "openness," he permitted new freedom of expression and eased harsh measures against dissidents, allowing some of them to leave the Soviet Union. In a move praised throughout the world, Gorbachev freed prominent dissident Andrei Sakharov from exile in Siberia.

Gorbachev realized that the only way to transform Soviet society was to lift the veil of secrecy, to expose the hidden problems of society, and to discuss them freely. "I do not pretend to know the absolute truth," he said. "We have to search for truth together."

There were other changes as well. Departing from rigid state controls, Gorbachev pushed for a rebuilding of the Soviet economy, a policy the Soviets called *perestroika* (pehr ehs TROY kah), or "restructuring." Gorbachev gradually began dismantling the national bureaucracy that controlled industrial production, allowing more decisions to be made at the local level. Plant managers were given more say on issues such as what products to make, how much to pay workers, and how to invest earnings. For the first time, workers could be laid off or fired. Quality, instead of quantity, was the goal.

For the first time since the 1920s, the government encouraged limited moves toward private enterprise. Gorbachev also negotiated new agreements with the West to buy badly needed farm technology such as milking machines and harvesting equipment.

Perestroika affected government structure as well. Gorbachev requested reforms to expand the authority of the president and limit the power of the Communist party. In his first six months he replaced 40 percent of the party's top leaders with his own loyal supporters. The military underwent a similar restructuring.

Foreign Policy Facing the enormous U.S. weapons buildup under President Reagan, Gorbachev needed to negotiate new arms-reduction agreements with the United States. Since Soviet economic progress depended on making military cutbacks, Gorbachev was willing to make large concessions in order to settle long-stalled treaty negotiations. His offers to cancel nuclear tests and to withdraw Soviet missiles from Eastern Europe were so sweeping that they took

---

FOOTNOTES TO HISTORY
BLACK MARKET MEAT

Amid widespread shortages of meat, Mikhail Gorbachev's rival, Boris Yeltsin, heard of a veal shipment that was to be delivered to a state store in Moscow. Yeltsin went to the store and joined the long line of customers waiting to buy meat. When he reached the counter, he asked for veal but was told there was none.

Knowing that the meat had been shipped there, Yeltsin insisted on buying some. Finally, the shopkeeper threatened to call the police. Instead, Yeltsin called the police himself. An investigation revealed that the meat had been sold to a black-market shop, where it would bring four times the price charged in the state-run store. The store managers illegally pocketed a big profit from selling to the black market.

Western leaders by surprise. To further ease global tensions, Gorbachev signed a new trade agreement with China and began to explore improved relations with Japan. He also withdrew Soviet troops from Afghanistan.

But the place where Gorbachev made his biggest mark on world politics was in the Soviet satellite countries of Eastern Europe. Gorbachev encouraged East-bloc leaders to try new methods to get their ailing economies moving and to lessen their dependence on Soviet aid. He was unexpectedly silent when some made attempts at liberalizing their repressive regimes.

Meanwhile, Gorbachev's rhetoric about glasnost and perestroika inspired discontented majorities in these repressed countries. Scattered demands for democratic reform grew into a wave of anti-Communist protest that eventually brought down the iron curtain.

New Challenges

Gorbachev's fresh outlook and genial personality made him a popular figure in the Western countries he visited. At one point his popularity rating among Americans was higher than

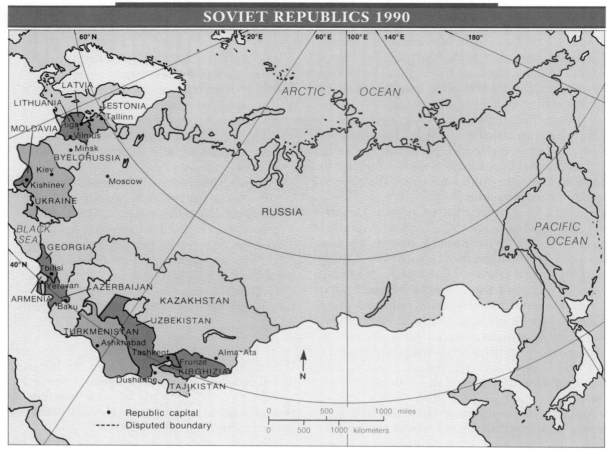

SOVIET REPUBLICS 1990

Learning from Maps *The Soviet Union is a federation of 15 republics, shown* above. ***What international political consequences could result if the re-publics became independent nations?***

that for President Reagan. Ironically, however, Gorbachev was increasingly criticized at home.

The promised perestroika came slowly. The enormous Soviet bureaucracy resisted change, fearing the loss of their jobs. Gorbachev had to move carefully to avoid backlash from hard-line Communists. He often zigzagged between reformist and hard-line positions, creating uncertainty throughout government and business. Economic problems continued, and worsened, while reforms were put in place. People became impatient. Gorbachev's popularity declined.

Political Rivals Another problem facing Gorbachev was one of his own making. Before glasnost he would have had no political rivals,

since dissent was not allowed. By 1990, however, the slow results of perestroika brought forward new challengers to Gorbachev's leadership.

Bureaucrats whose security was threatened by Gorbachev's demands for higher quality, production, and efficiency worked quietly to defeat his reforms. Military leaders opposed change as well. The ending of the cold war—with the reduction in weapons production and troop presence around the world—left the once-dominant military with reduced political influence.

By the end of 1986 Gorbachev had replaced all the top military leaders. His priorities were clear: "We are encircled not by invincible armies, but by superior economies." Ironically, Gorbachev's most visible rival was a former ally,

Boris Yeltsin. Yeltsin felt perestroika was moving too slowly. His vocal criticism of Gorbachev eventually earned him a severe reprimand and dismissal from his party positions.

Yeltsin took his case to the people, winning election to the presidency of the Russian Republic, the largest of the Soviet Union's republics. As an elected leader, Yeltsin had a stronger mandate than did Gorbachev, and he enjoyed greater popularity.

Eventually, Gorbachev's political balancing act alienated both liberals and conservatives. Facing strong criticism from his own people on one side and apparently losing control of the military on the other side, Gorbachev began a rollback of glasnost in the early 1990s and adopted new hard-line positions. Among them were the tightening of controls on the Soviet press to curb dissent and the restoration of powers to the KGB. Some of Gorbachev's liberal political aides began resigning in protest. Soviet citizens, led by Yeltsin, called for Gorbachev to step down.

Nationalities   The fuse that ignited the hard-line crackdown was a wave of uprisings in the Soviet republics. As its name reflects, the Soviet Union is a union of 15 separate republics, or states. The largest is Russia, which includes the Soviet capital, Moscow. In addition, the 15 republics—the result of Russian conquests from the 1600s through the 1800s—together comprise several leading nationalities and about 100 ethnic groups.

The republics have resented the dominance of the Russians over Soviet affairs. Many of the ethnic groups within the republics have had long-standing political and religious conflicts among themselves. A strong Soviet security force and army had long kept rival groups under control. But in the relaxed atmosphere of glasnost, old hatreds resurfaced. In the republics of Armenia and Azerbaijan, the reduced armed forces had difficulty quelling growing ethnic violence.

Throughout the republics there were strong demands for sovereignty, or self-rule, if not outright secession. In 1990 the Baltic republics—Latvia, Lithuania, and Estonia—declared their intention to become independent nations. Nationwide votes showed overwhelming support for self-rule. In Lithuania, the Soviets imposed an economic blockade to force compliance with Soviet rule. But anti-Soviet demonstrations grew and spread through the Baltics. The Soviet military attacked and killed demonstrators in Lithuania and Latvia in early 1991.

Western countries denounced the crackdown and threatened to withdraw trade agreements and financial aid recently granted to the Soviet Union. Gorbachev claimed that the military units had acted on their own, but he did not condemn the violence at first. Under mounting pressure, he eventually ordered the withdrawal of troops from the Baltic republics.

These events suggested two dangerous possibilities: that Gorbachev was losing power to the armed forces, or that he was returning to the repressive methods of his predecessors to hold the union together. Meanwhile, the freedom movements showed no signs of surrendering. Observers raised the specter of a military coup or a return to dictatorship. Others predicted the breakup of the Soviet Union.

SECTION 2 REVIEW

Recall

1. **Define:** détente, glasnost, perestroika
2. **Identify:** Mikhail Gorbachev, Boris Yeltsin
3. **Explain:** How did the policy of glasnost differ from previous Soviet policy?

Critical Thinking

4. **Apply:** How does Soviet military spending affect economic progress?
5. **Analyze:** Examine the seeming contradiction between Brezhnev's interest in détente and his huge military buildup.

Applying Concepts

6. **Nationalism:** Evaluate the ways in which Gorbachev's policy of glasnost contributed to ethnic violence in the Soviet republics and opened the way for independence movements there.

The Crumbling Wall

From 1968 to 1989 world leaders carried out cold-war politics in an atmosphere darkened by the threat of nuclear war. The cold-war view of the world was turned upside down in 1989, when the fortress of communism fell, as Ronald Reagan had predicted in 1981:

The West won't contain communism; it will transcend communism. It won't bother to denounce it; it will dismiss it as some bizarre chapter in human history whose last pages are even now being written.

The Rise of Dissent

By the time President Reagan took office in 1981, Communist economies were failing in the Soviet Union and Eastern Europe. Despite Moscow's efforts to tighten controls on its satellites, dissent swept the Soviet bloc, reaching a peak in 1989.

During the 1970s and 1980s reduced production, decreases in labor productivity, rampant inflation, and trade deficits virtually paralyzed the economies of Eastern Europe. This meant fewer goods at ever-increasing prices. The overly centralized economies caused widespread shortages of basic food commodities.

Economic problems led to upheaval in Poland during the 1970s, the first in a wave of uprisings that threatened Communist rule. The trouble began in 1970, when Poland tried to stabilize its economy by raising prices. Riots broke out, forcing the government to withdraw the increases. Instead, it resorted to food rationing, which was equally unpopular. Following the brutal suppression of the food riots in 1976, Polish workers raised funds to support families of workers who had been jailed, and secretly spread news about strikes and other labor activities.

Poland's antigovernment movement received a strong boost in the late 1970s, when the Roman Catholic Church selected a Polish

Learning from Photographs *Lech Walesa addresses a Solidarity meeting. His career has been remarkable—starting as an electrical worker at a shipyard; becoming president of the nation's first independent trade union, facing jailings and threats of violence; and triumphing to become Poland's first democratically elected president in the postwar era.* **Why do you think Walesa was awarded the Nobel Peace Prize?**

cardinal, Karol Wojtyla, as its pope. The elevation of Pope John Paul II, a staunch anti-Communist, inspired confidence among the Polish people and enabled them to take further steps toward liberation from Communist control.

In 1980 Polish workers in the Baltic part of Gdansk organized a trade union called Solidarity. Lech Walesa (vah WEN sah), an electrical worker at the Lenin Shipyard in Gdansk, was a founder and leader of Solidarity.

Solidarity backed up its demands for better living and working conditions with strikes, including one led by Walesa at the Gdansk shipyards. In a remarkable victory, the strikers forced the Polish government to officially recognize Solidarity in October 1980. Until this time, self-governing trade unions independent of Communist party control had not been allowed to exist in Communist countries.

Under Walesa's leadership, Solidarity expanded its activities, demanding free elections and a voice for workers in forming government policy. The Polish government responded by demanding that strikes and other "antistate" activities be ended. Under pressure from the Soviet Union, Polish authorities outlawed the union 16 months later and jailed many of its leaders. Despite this, Walesa and others continued their activities underground.

Although Solidarity's activities were not immediately successful, the courage of its members inspired people in other Eastern European countries. The revolt quickly spread across Eastern Europe. Walesa became a symbol of freedom and an international hero. The young electrician who boldly challenged communism was awarded the Nobel Peace Prize in 1983.

A Year of Miracles

As democratic movements gathered force across Eastern Europe during the late 1980s, the question on many people's minds was: Would Soviet President Mikhail Gorbachev exercise the terms of the Brezhnev Doctrine and assist Soviet satellite governments in putting down rebellions? In a speech on January 18, 1989, Gorbachev announced that he had ordered a cutback of 500,000 troops in the Soviet army—about

Learning from Photographs *John Paul II became the first non-Italian pope since 1523 and the first from a Communist country.* ***Why did his elevation have a big political impact on Poland?***

half of that number to come from troops stationed in Eastern Europe. The troops had been put there to enforce the Warsaw Pact and keep the Soviet satellites in line.

In March he pledged not to interfere with democratic reforms in Hungary. Referring to the 1956 and 1968 invasions of Hungary and Czechoslovakia, Gorbachev declared that "all possible safeguards should be provided so that no external force can interfere in the domestic affairs of socialist countries."

Gorbachev decided that most East-bloc governments—which lacked popular support—would continue to provoke opposition. The Soviet Union would be forced to intervene militarily at great cost. Soviet interests would be better served if he simply let these governments fall. Gorbachev would then establish friendly relations with the new governments.

The Wall Falls Throughout 1989, Communist regimes in Eastern Europe crumbled under the weight of staggering problems. Nearly all the satellite countries had ruined economies. Many had terrible environmental damage that had been ignored in the push to industrialize.

Other countries, such as Yugoslavia, were being shaken by internal ethnic conflicts.

In this atmosphere of political instability, Communist regimes either resigned or were overturned in East Germany, Czechoslovakia, Hungary, Poland, Romania, and Bulgaria. Throughout this remarkable year, Gorbachev astounded the world by not only refusing to intervene in democratic uprisings, but actually encouraging them along the way.

In mid-1989 Hungary, which had been quietly moving toward democratic reform for more than a decade, opened its sealed borders. Hundreds of refugees began pouring through this new "hole" in the iron curtain, seeking sanctuary in the West. Many of the refugees were from East Germany, and the exodus called attention to the failed regime of the country's aging leader, Erich Honecker.

Amid mass demonstrations and calls for democratic reform, Honecker's regime was toppled in October and replaced by a more moderate Communist government. The move did not satisfy the reform movement but made its supporters bolder and more demanding. The next month, in an attempt to defuse the situation, the government lifted all travel restrictions between East and West. It hoped the refugees would remain in East Germany under a reformed but still Communist government.

CONNECTIONS: GEOGRAPHY IN HISTORY

Culture

The political geography of Europe often does not reflect the cultural patterns of the population. Various national and ethnic groups are ruled by governments with whom they have no historical ties.

Sometimes this has occurred as the result of wars. Often the victors sliced up territory according to political considerations, ignoring cultural settlement patterns—as in the case of East and West Germany. Or they took control of territory embracing other ethnic groups, as the Russians did in creating their empire. Factors such as famine forced people to migrate, causing a mixing of peoples.

Yugoslavia, for example, is a federation of six republics: Bosnia, Croatia, Macedonia, Montenegro, Serbia, and Slovenia. The population includes Albanians, Bulgarians, Czechs, Hungarians, Italians, Romanians, Slovaks, and Turks.

These groups often resent living under the rule of others, and serious political tension results. Since World War II, Yugoslavia's various groups were kept together by the strong rule of the Communist party. But with the decline of communism in the late 1980s, old rivalries between the Serbians and the Albanians resurfaced. In the early 1990s, the Croatians made a bid to declare themselves an independent nation, threatening to split the country of Yugoslavia and change the map of Europe once again.

Making the Connection
1. Why do Europe's political boundaries conflict with the ethnic distribution of its people?
2. If you headed a government such as Yugoslavia's, how would you respond to ethnic clashes and the desire of republics to secede?

On the evening of November 9, 1989, the famous Brandenburg Gate at the Berlin Wall was opened. All through the night East Germans and West Germans, hearing the wall had been opened, rushed there to see for themselves, overwhelming the guards and passing through the gate in both directions. Others swarmed over the wall, dancing and singing atop it.

In the following days, people on both sides of the wall attacked it with picks and shovels, opening huge holes—even selling chunks as souvenirs. More gates were opened, and the flow of people increased. Families and friends who had not seen each other in decades were reunited. The government, helpless before this popular uprising, ordered the rest of the wall torn down.

Struggle in Romania The overthrow of Communist governments in Eastern Europe was, for the most part, nonviolent. The one grim chapter in the story took place in Romania, where dictator Nicolae Ceausescu (chow SHEHS koo) had ruled for 24 years. Ceausescu's methods had become increasingly brutal over the years, and his reaction to freedom protests in his country was violent. Thousands of people were killed before the Romanian army revolted and ousted the dictator in December 1989. Ceausescu and his wife, Elena, were tried and shot.

Throughout Europe and the West, euphoric crowds celebrated the fall of Ceausescu. They were also celebrating the end of Soviet domination in Eastern Europe and, in a larger sense, the possible ending of the cold war.

New Leaders in a New Age

Following the downfall of Communist governments, reformers looked for new leaders to bring democracy and stability to their countries. In East Germany, the fall of the Berlin Wall quickly led to calls for the reunification of Germany. On December 2, 1990, Helmut Kohl, riding a wave of pro-unification sentiment, was elected in a landslide victory as the first chancellor of a united Germany. Other countries looked to their national heroes to lead their new regimes. Czechoslovakia elected a dissident playwright, Václav Havel, who had been in jail only months before. And voters in Poland made a choice that surprised no one: Lech Walesa was elected president in 1990.

Even staunchly Communist Albania, the lone holdout against the reforms of 1989, was finally swept up in the wave of protests. It opened its sealed borders, allowed opposition parties to form, and scheduled elections for 1991.

Other nations, such as Romania, organized coalition governments that appeared fragile. After the euphoria of the rebellions cooled, the new regimes faced some daunting problems. Making the transformation from controlled economies to free ones would take years. Citizens indicated a willingness to wait for the reforms to work. But as Mikhail Gorbachev found out, the patience of impoverished people has its limits. Western governments, mindful of how the Marshall Plan buoyed Western Europe, began looking for ways to help the new democracies in Eastern Europe.

SECTION 3 REVIEW

Recall

1. **Identify:** Solidarity, Lech Walesa, Nicolae Ceausescu, Helmut Kohl
2. **Explain:** Why were some of the revolutions in Eastern Europe more violent than others?
3. **Retell:** Describe the fall of the Berlin Wall. What global development did its fall symbolize?

Critical Thinking

4. **Apply:** What kinds of changes may occur rapidly in Eastern Europe? Which do you think will occur more slowly?
5. **Analyze:** In the United States, a union strike would not threaten the collapse of the government. Explain why this happened in Poland.

Applying Concepts

6. **Change:** Evaluate Gorbachev's response to the uprisings in Eastern Europe. What might have happened if he had tried to stop the changes? How were changes in the Soviet Union and its satellites linked? How did Eastern European reforms differ from Soviet ones?

Changes in North America and Europe **941**

Western Europe

During the 1970s and 1980s, some European nations at first faced economic recession. Later they experienced significant recovery and growth. Others made political gains as dictatorships were replaced by democracies. By the early 1990s, Western Europe as a whole had made great strides toward complete economic and political unity and was ready to undertake a new role in world affairs.

Great Britain

The severe economic problems that plagued Great Britain in the postwar years have continued to the present, as the nation still struggles to regain some of its former power and prestige. British leaders have tried widely differing approaches to dealing with problems such as high inflation, aging industries, worker apathy, growing trade union demands, and frequent strikes. Prime ministers of both the Labour and Conservative parties during the 1970s had little success in stimulating the nation's economy. Voter dissatisfaction with high taxes helped bring the right-wing Conservative party leader Margaret Thatcher to power in 1979.

Thatcher, Britain's first woman prime minister, became a dominant figure in British politics. In an effort to lower inflation and stimulate the economy, Thatcher implemented free-market economic measures. She restricted the power of the unions, cut government spending and lowered taxes, dismantled welfare programs, and returned nationalized industries to private ownership. As a result of her huge cuts in social programs, many of Thatcher's opponents accused her of trying to end the welfare state created after World War II.

In addition to economic woes, Thatcher also faced the growing problem of terrorism.

Terrorist attacks had become one of the main tactics of Irish Roman Catholic radicals opposed to British rule over predominantly Protestant Northern Ireland. Clashes between Catholics and Protestants during the 1960s and early 1970s caused Britain to suspend the government of Northern Ireland and impose direct rule. Efforts to reestablish local control failed, and the outlawed Irish Republican Army (IRA) stepped up its attacks on British military targets in Northern Ireland. With support from groups in Europe and the United States, the heavily armed IRA extended its campaign of bombings and assassinations to Britain itself during the 1980s.

Thatcher took strong and controversial measures to stem terrorism. Britain suspended many civil liberties for suspected terrorists, such as the right to a trial by jury. Thatcher's methods were both cheered and widely criticized at home and abroad; the IRA responded by trying to assassinate her. Thatcher also took steps to ease tensions in Ireland, including a 1988 bill to curb job discrimination against Roman Catholics in Northern Ireland.

Thatcher's popularity slowly declined during the late 1980s, and a key issue once again was economics. Thatcher's policies had reduced inflation and aided business growth. However, high unemployment continued in hard-pressed industrial areas of the country, causing much hardship, dissatisfaction, and discontent. Meanwhile, tax increases and cutbacks in social programs also heightened opposition to her 11-year rule.

Finally, in 1990, Thatcher faced difficulties at home and abroad with her European policies. Although Great Britain had joined Europe's Common Market in 1973, Thatcher held steadfastly to the tradition of keeping England aloof from continental Europe. Her view of economic independence for Britain ran against the growing tide of support for a single European economy. When she lost the backing of many of her government colleagues, Thatcher resigned. Her successor, John Major, was committed to many Thatcher policies, but pledged to increase British participation in the movement toward European unity.

France

France experienced long-term economic growth despite the loss of its empire during the 1960s and 1970s. In the 1960s President Charles de Gaulle had sought to restore his nation's prestige by taking a strong role in world affairs. But his successors in the 1970s focused on domestic growth. President Georges Pompidou worked to improve industrial growth and efficiency. His death in 1974 brought Valéry Giscard d'Estaing into office. Giscard's pro-business policies were crippled by the worldwide economic downturn of the 1970s.

While British voters turned to a conservative to pull them out of this slump, the French elected a Socialist president, François Mitterrand, in 1981. Mitterrand introduced many socialist measures, nationalizing major industries and banks and raising taxes to pay for new social programs. But his measures heightened infla-

tion, and he eventually was forced to adopt many of the cost-cutting measures of his conservative predecessors.

Germany

For years before the fall of the Berlin Wall, East and West Germany had been seeking closer economic and political ties. In the early 1970s, West German Chancellor Willy Brandt worked to reduce tensions between his country and the Soviet bloc. This policy, known as *Ostpolitik* (German for "Eastern policy"), resulted in West German agreements with the Soviet Union and Poland in 1972. Brandt's initiative eventually led to the establishment of diplomatic ties between East and West Germany a year later.

Under Brandt and his successor, Helmut Schmidt, West Germany enjoyed economic prosperity but faced mounting difficulties with stagflation in the early 1980s. Promising a return to prosperity, a conservative chancellor, Helmut Kohl, came to power in 1982.

Despite economic problems, the overall strength of West Germany continued to attract the people of East Germany. With the overthrow of the Communist government in East Germany in 1989, the reunification of Germany, which many had hoped for but few dreamed possible, was suddenly a real possibility. In early

Learning from Photographs *Human rights injustices in Northern Ireland led to the rise of terrorist activities by the Irish Republican Army. The IRA attacked British and Protestant Irish targets to protest British rule.* **Do you think Margaret Thatcher's response to the terrorism was appropriate? Why or why not?**

Learning from Photographs *King Juan Carlos I and Queen Sofia restored the monarchy to Spain in 1975.* **Why was this a sign of progress?**

Mediterranean Europe

The push and pull of cold-war politics had a strong effect on southern Europe over the last two decades. The economic recession of the 1970s created hard times for many countries and increased political instability.

Weak leadership in Italy has brought repeated political shifts. During the 1970s, Italy came to have the largest Communist party in Western Europe. It was popular in part because it promoted a more democratic view of communism and sought to share power with the ruling conservative Christian Democrats. At the same time, the Catholic Church—for centuries a dominant political force in Italy—lost considerable influence among the increasingly secularized Italians. The Italian government defied church teaching by legalizing divorce in 1970 and abortion in 1978.

Adding to the political turmoil was a wave of terrorism by a leftist group called the Red Brigades. It carried out kidnappings and bombings, culminating in the murder of former prime minister Aldo Moro in 1978. Although economic and political problems remained, peace returned to Italy during the 1980s.

In Spain, after 36 years of the dictatorship of Francisco Franco, King Juan Carlos I inaugurated a new era of democratic rule. Assuming power after Franco's death in 1975, the king called for the nation's first free elections since the 1930s. The new legislature instituted a new constitution in 1978.

Terrorism has been a major problem in Spain in recent decades. For many years an ethnic group called the Basques has fought for independence from Spain. King Juan Carlos granted increasing measures of self-rule to the Basque provinces. Nevertheless, terrorist attacks by radical Basque separatists continue.

A turn toward democracy occurred not only in Spain, but in other Mediterranean countries as well. Decades of dictatorship in Portugal ended with a military coup in 1974, and in 1976 the nation held its first free elections in 50 years. During this time Portugal finally freed its African and Asian colonies, which had become so costly that the nation's economy nearly collapsed from the strain. The Social Democratic

1990, the reunification process moved forward rapidly. In February, Chancellor Kohl proposed a plan for monetary union with East Germany, establishing the West German deutsche mark as the common currency. That was followed by an agreement to merge the two economies.

In March 1990 East Germany held its first free elections in decades. With Kohl's support, Lothar de Maziere was elected to serve as the last East German leader. In July, Kohl called for an all-German parliamentary election, and East Germany agreed. Representatives of East and West Germany signed a reunification treaty in August. The treaty took effect on October 3, 1990, and that date became a national holiday.

After the euphoria wore off, Germans tackled some difficult problems. Issues ranged from the merging of banking systems and industries to whose athletes would represent Germany in the Olympic Games.

party, elected in 1983, has attempted to deal with persistent unemployment and inflation.

Greece, which had made great progress in the 1950s due to Marshall Plan aid, suffered a setback in the late 1960s and early 1970s under a repressive military regime. In 1974 democracy was restored as Greece held its first elections in 10 years. The elections brought to power the New Democratic party, led by Constantine Caramanlis. That was followed by the Socialist government of Andreas Papandreou (pah pan DRAI oo) in the 1980s. Amid charges of corruption, Papandreou was ousted in 1989.

European Unity

The trend toward democratic governments with free-market economies brought several new member nations into the European Economic Community, generally referred to as the EEC or the Common Market. Greece, Spain, and Portugal joined in the 1980s. During this time, the EEC undertook some significant changes in its policies and goals.

Despite the great success of the EEC, it became clear in the mid-1980s that there were still many barriers to trade in Europe. While EEC countries had made progress in lifting restrictive tariffs, other barriers—conflicting technical standards, quality standards, health laws, and environmental laws—made it difficult for manufacturers to sell products throughout the Continent. For example, if a car made in Germany did not meet France's antipollution standards, the car could not legally be sold in France. If an Italian car did not meet the seat-belt laws of Holland, the car could not be sold in Holland.

With more than 30 countries in Europe manufacturing thousands of products, there

Learning from Photographs *The leaders of West Germany, Canada, France, the United States, Japan, Great Britain, and Italy met in 1983 to discuss world economic issues.* **How might such a meeting be different after 1992?**

CHAPTER 35 REVIEW

HISTORICAL SIGNIFICANCE

Several challenges to the cold war arose between 1968 and the early 1990s. The Vietnam War caused a questioning of the containment theory in the United States. During the 1970s the superpowers engaged in détente to reduce the heavy military spending that was limiting domestic growth.

The idea of a world dominated by the two superpowers—the foundation of cold-war thinking—was challenged by nations such as France and Canada. Europe moved to put such a challenge into action with plans to create a unified economic bloc. Events in the Soviet bloc in the late 1980s led to what was hailed as the end of the cold war, although subsequent Soviet actions raised new concerns.

New directions are being considered around the world in light of changes in Eastern Europe. They include a shift in military emphases; policies to encourage positive change in Eastern Europe; and measures to ease the strains of the transition from communism to democracy.

SUMMARY

For a summary of Chapter 35, see the Unit 8 synopsis on pages 975–977.

USING KEY TERMS

Fill in the blank with the key term that best completes the sentence.

a. budget deficit
b. détente
c. draft
d. glasnost
e. imperial presidency
f. perestroika
g. separatism
h. stagflation

1. In 1991 the need for soldiers during the Persian Gulf war caused people to wonder if the United States would reinstitute the ___.
2. ___ means a relaxing of tensions between the United States and the Soviet Union.
3. A ___ occurs when a government spends more money than it collects in taxes.
4. ___ was a policy of information sharing and openness in Soviet government affairs.
5. French-Canadian ___ was led by René Levesque and centered in Quebec.
6. ___ occurs when there is simultaneous inflation and unemployment.
7. The Russian word ___ refers to a program of government restructuring.
8. The use of presidential powers not outlined in the Constitution was known as the ___.

REVIEWING FACTS

1. **List:** Name three Eastern European governments that collapsed during 1989 and 1990.
2. **Explain:** Why did Mikhail Gorbachev refuse to intervene when Eastern European countries broke with Communist rule?
3. **Identify:** Who is Boris Yeltsin?
4. **Explain:** What is the difference between Russia and the U.S.S.R.?
5. **Explain:** Name two factors that limited the effectiveness of Gerald Ford's presidency.

THINKING CRITICALLY

1. **Apply:** What was the major source of tension that led to the French Canadian separatist movement?
2. **Analyze:** How did the use of force in putting down the food riots in Poland actually assist the Polish people's drive for freedom?
3. **Synthesize:** What general trend or trends can you detect in the recent history of Europe?
4. **Evaluate:** Describe the effect of Watergate on the U.S. presidency.
5. **Analyze:** Briefly describe the contrast between the stated goals of Soviet communism and its actual performance.
6. **Apply:** Is the American presidency today an imperial presidency? Why or why not?

ANALYZING CONCEPTS

1. **Conflict:** Why did the United States stay involved in Vietnam for so many years, despite widespread protests at home?
2. **Nationalism:** What makes the union of Soviet republics fragile? How has this instability affected the political process in Moscow?
3. **Change:** Name three reasons for the rapid political change in Eastern Europe during the late 1980s.
4. **Cooperation:** Describe the benefits and drawbacks of European economic cooperation, both for Europe and for the world.

PRACTICING SKILLS

1. Refer to the first paragraph about Mikhail Gorbachev on page 934. Identify the style of writing used. Locate another passage of Chapter 35 written in the same style.
2. Most of this chapter is expository writing organized in chronological order. Choose one passage beginning with a boldface heading and containing at least four paragraphs. Identify all the words and phrases that indicate transitions and connections between ideas or events.
3. Choose one of the four styles of writing (expository, narrative, descriptive, and persuasive) and write about a current issue in world news using your chosen style.

GEOGRAPHY IN HISTORY

1. **Region:** Find the Baltic republics on the map on pages 990–991. Why were the Soviets willing to use military force to keep these small regions in the union?
2. **Movement:** What are some of the reasons that Europe's political boundaries do not match its ethnic distribution?
3. **Place:** Describe the ethnic makeup of Quebec, Canada.

TRACING CHRONOLOGY

Refer to the time line below to answer these questions.

1. In what years did events take place that contributed to the establishment of democracy in Eastern Europe?
2. What event in the 1980s led to the Soviet withdrawal from Afghanistan?
3. What events marked a lessening of cold-war tensions?

LINKING PAST AND PRESENT

1. Modern Europe is divided into many separate countries. Was it ever unified under one rule? When? What happened to cause its division?
2. How does the Europe 1992 plan differ from the alignment of Eastern Europe under the Warsaw Pact?

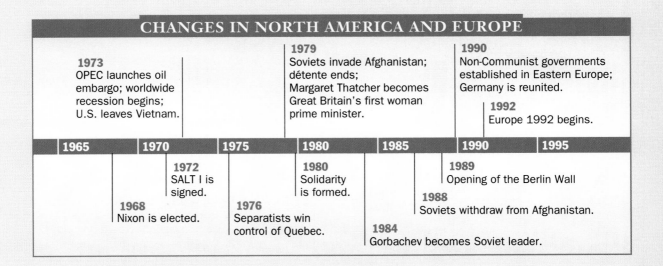

CHANGES IN NORTH AMERICA AND EUROPE

1973 OPEC launches oil embargo; worldwide recession begins; U.S. leaves Vietnam.

1979 Soviets invade Afghanistan; détente ends; Margaret Thatcher becomes Great Britain's first woman prime minister.

1990 Non-Communist governments established in Eastern Europe; Germany is reunited.

1992 Europe 1992 begins.

| 1965 | 1970 | 1975 | 1980 | 1985 | 1990 | 1995 |

1972 SALT I is signed.

1980 Solidarity is formed.

1989 Opening of the Berlin Wall

1968 Nixon is elected.

1976 Separatists win control of Quebec.

1988 Soviets withdraw from Afghanistan.

1984 Gorbachev becomes Soviet leader.

An Interdependent World

*F*ew people have had the privilege of gazing back at the shining orb of Earth from the black void of space. Those who have had the experience never forget it, as former astronaut Rusty Schweickart attests:

"As you pass from sunlight into darkness and back again every hour and a half, you become startlingly aware how artificial are the thousands of boundaries we've created to separate and define. And for the first time in your life you feel in your gut the precious unity of the earth and all the living things it supports."

More and more, the second half of the1900s is teaching the world to think like an astronaut—in global rather than national terms. In the decades since World War II, the world's technology, economy, environment, and culture have all become increasingly interconnected.

CHAPTER PREVIEW

Key Terms to Define: genetic engineering, multinational corporation, greenhouse effect, tropical rain forest, existentialism

People to Meet: Neil Armstrong, Jean-Paul Sartre, Betty Friedan, Alexander Solzhenitsyn, Rudolf Nureyev, Natalia Makarova, Pablo Neruda, Gabriel García Marquez, Octavio Paz, the Beatles

Places to Discover: Peru, Colombia, Chile, Zimbabwe, Kenya, Thailand

Objectives to Learn:
1. How have recent advances in technology affected the world?
2. Why have economic issues and environmental problems become a global concern?
3. What is the global culture that has emerged recently?

New technologies have brought the people of the world closer together in recent decades.

Concepts to Understand:
- Change—New developments in technology have increased communication and interaction between all parts of the world. Section 1
- Cooperation—Interdependent national economies have led to growing cooperation between the nations of the world. Section 2
- Relation to environment—Water and air pollution threaten the environment of the entire planet and require global as well as local solutions. Section 3
- Cultural diffusion—With increased interaction and cooperation between nations, cultural diversity has decreased and a global culture has appeared. Section 4

951

SECTION 1
The Technological Revolution

When the Berlin Wall was demolished in 1989, more than steel and mortar crumbled. "We feel as if we have walked into our television sets," said one East German man, stunned by the display of merchandise in West German shop windows.

Today, technology and politics are fused as never before. Where barriers of time and distance once stood, we now experience nearly instant connection. Events such as the fall of the Berlin Wall affect not only East and West Germans but also the world. Indeed, it is through technology that we glimpse the interdependent, or mutually dependent, nature of our world.

New Technologies

Since 1945 the world has undergone a technological revolution as significant as the Industrial Revolution of the early 1800s. People sepa-

rated by thousands of miles are now linked by supersonic air travel and the magic of fast, two-way electronic communication.

Advanced technology does not affect cultures and nations equally, however. For example, industrialized nations are more likely to have the resources to develop, improve, and benefit from technology. Developing nations often lag behind and do not necessarily derive the same benefits. As a result, the gap between affluent nations and developing nations is widening.

Consider computers, which are common tools for business and personal use in industrialized countries. Yet they remain relatively expensive, beyond the reach of businesses and individuals in many parts of the world. The affordability of advanced technology can affect the development and progress of a nation.

Computers process information, which may help analyze a nation's economy, forecast the weather, sift through political opinion polls, or

Learning from Photographs *Robots in Japan's Nissan factory replace human labor for many tasks.* **What other applications might industries have for robotic technology?**

calculate the flight path for a rocket. Nations that can afford the latest computer technology gain a distinct advantage—whether through increased productivity or ultimately a higher standard of living—over those still struggling with old-fashioned equipment.

International competition in computer technology has been fierce. In recent years the United States and Japan have engaged in a race to develop the world's first "supercomputer," capable of processing data much faster than current machines. Both countries have invested heavily in this research. The nation that succeeds is expected to gain the edge in space exploration, industrial design, and economic productivity.

The applications of computer technology are varied. The "brain" driving the computer is the microchip, a mesh of circuits etched on a silicon wafer. In medicine, doctors use these chips to power artificial limbs worn by accident victims. Industrial robots programmed to assemble machines and perform tasks like welding and painting represent another application.

Other technological changes have increased global linkages. A man walking on the coast of Maine can now whisk a cellular phone from his pocket, dial a friend in Mexico, and chat happily. An executive in Australia can receive a memo from Germany over a facsimile (fax) machine in minutes. Today, millions of such communications signals cross the world daily. They connect us as never before.

Learning from Photographs *Early rocket technology paved the way to put humans on the moon in 1969.* **How has the United States space program changed since then?**

Space Exploration

Since our Stone Age ancestors first marveled at the motion of the sun, moon, and stars, humans have dreamed of exploring the distant heavens. As the advanced technology for rocket propulsion became available in the 1950s and 1960s, the United States and the Soviet Union each launched ambitious space programs. The "space race," seen as a symbolic test of national will, became the focus of world attention.

In the late 1950s, the Soviet Union and the United States used rockets to place artificial satellites in orbit. The two superpowers boosted hundreds of satellites into space, making possible a worldwide communications and weather information network. They also launched unmanned scientific probes to gather information about the moon, the planets, and the sun.

Humans began strapping themselves into space capsules and rocketing aloft in the early 1960s. You have already read about the heroic contributions of Soviet cosmonauts Yuri Gagarin and Valentina Tereshkova and American astronaut John Glenn, Jr., in that period. The greatest challenge facing the United States and the Soviet Union at that time was placing a person on the moon.

As a feat of engineering, the mission to reach the moon stood alone. Nothing so complicated had ever been attempted in human history. United States President John F. Kennedy pronounced the challenge: an American would walk on lunar soil by the end of the 1960s.

Scientists at the National Aeronautics and Space Administration (NASA) struggled with and solved difficult problems in achieving Kennedy's goal. Finally, in July 1969, Neil Armstrong and Edwin Aldrin, Jr., became the first humans to explore the moon's surface. The pale disk in the heavens that had transfixed humans for centuries suddenly appeared close-up on television screens around the world.

The moon landing was the first step in our nation's plan to explore the universe. In the early 1970s, American scientists built the space shuttle, a reusable spacecraft that could take off like a rocket and land like an airplane. From the shuttle, astronauts could launch, retrieve, and repair satellites. NASA launched the first fully operational space shuttle, *Columbia*, in April 1981. It is hoped that in future years, astronauts will use space shuttles to build and maintain self-contained space stations that orbit the globe. NASA is also planning to send more space probes to distant planets.

Medical Advances

At the turn of the century, doctors had little more than aspirin and sympathy to offer sick patients. The medicines and machines that now monitor human health simply did not exist. Modern medicine has far surpassed the limitations that once were characteristic of the medical profession.

Around the world, people are living longer and enjoying better health than ever before. New medicines treat illness and suffering. Vaccines have virtually eliminated diseases such as smallpox during the past 50 years. In addition,

IMAGES OF THE TIME

Technology Today

Advances in technology influence almost every aspect of our lives today—from everyday life to global events.

Lasers are used to pick up sound on compact discs. Portable "CD" players produce top-quality sound.

Satellites transmit information that is picked up by satellite dishes all over the world. As a result, you can watch "live" coverage of world events.

the incidence of other illnesses, such as polio, has been dramatically reduced through the distribution of new drugs. Penicillin alone has saved millions from diseases and infections that were fatal in the past.

Revolutionary diagnostic devices are permitting doctors to identify and cure problems that would have been missed with older equipment. Laser technology allows doctors to perform delicate surgery with minimal discomfort and disruption. Current medicines can even correct chemical imbalances in the brain, thereby treating the severe depressions that can cripple some people's lives.

Organ transplants, too, have benefited from new technologies. Kidneys and livers are among the most commonly transplanted organs, but many people now live for years with transplanted hearts as well. Meanwhile, research continues on creating a safe and effective artificial heart.

Perhaps the most thrilling frontier in medicine today is the field of genetics. Modern genetics began in 1953, when American geneticist James Watson and British biophysicist Francis Crick discovered the spiral structure of the genetic molecule deoxyribonucleic acid (DNA). Once the structure of DNA was known, scientists had passed a milestone in understanding how cells reproduce themselves. Recent advances have deepened this understanding.

DNA appears to be central in providing answers to many mysteries. Further molecular research may yield insights into the origins and cure of cancer, or the causes of mutations and birth defects. Benefits of DNA technology are already in evidence, as the manufacture of insulin illustrates. Widely used in the treatment of diabetes, insulin has traditionally been made from the pancreas of animals. Using new techniques involving DNA, scientists have been able

Technology is always changing. At right, a monorail in Sydney, Australia, carries passengers through the city. Below, doctors use a computer to diagnose a patient's knee injury.

Reflecting on the Times
Think about what you have done since you woke up this morning. How have you used modern technology?

also poses unknown hazards. Some critics fear that tinkering with cell structure may create deadly new strains of disease that will defy treatment once outside the laboratory. At the same time, advances in DNA techniques could provide the cure for a disease such as cancer that affects millions of people worldwide.

Ethical Concerns

Many new technologies are raising serious ethical issues. Genetic engineering is one of the best examples. Some people believe that genetic engineering reflects the desire to play God. What are the limits—if any—they ask, of the applications of technology? Should we, as global citizens, be permitted to do anything we are capable of doing?

Ethical concerns are not merely abstract questions. While new technologies may lead us to uncharted regions, they also remind us that we as humans must assume responsibility for our actions and for the well-being of our world. Technology can be steered in any direction that humans desire. As astronaut Rusty Schweickart points out:

Our technology has progressed to where we can now manipulate energy and material to free ourselves from our earthly womb, or to destroy all life on it. Which will it be? I believe the right choice can only be made if we overcome our fears, our distrust of each other, our assumption of separateness. Our future— indeed, our survival—is closely tied to the idea of our common destiny. . . .

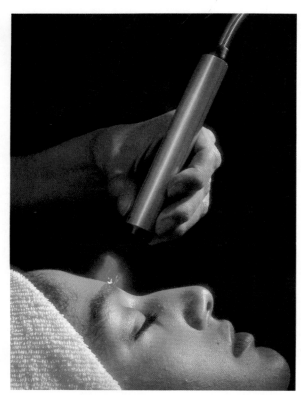

Learning from Photographs *The intense heat generated by lasers destroys diseased cells with little damage to surrounding tissue.* **How do medical patients benefit from laser technology?**

to duplicate human insulin cells. This approach yields a more effective form of the drug.

Recent DNA technology has led to the new field of **genetic engineering,** a process that involves the alteration of cells to produce new life forms. Research in this field, while promising,

---

SECTION 1 REVIEW

Recall
1. **Define:** genetic engineering
2. **Identify:** Rusty Schweickart, John F. Kennedy, Neil Armstrong, James Watson, Francis Crick
3. **Explain:** Why was the "space race" significant?

Critical Thinking
4. **Analyze:** How have recent developments in medical technology affected humans?
5. **Evaluate:** In what ways does history either disprove or confirm fears we may have regarding the effects of new technol-

ogy on our lives? Give some examples.

Applying Concepts
6. **Change:** Which technological change of the past 50 years has had the most far-reaching impact? Explain.

The Global Economy

For centuries, communities around the world were mainly self-sufficient. Nations produced what they needed, and trade was often limited by great distances and slow transportation. Cultural barriers—problems of language, local customs, and foreign business practices—were perplexing to many who might otherwise have engaged in international trade.

Since World War II, however, a revolution in technology and economics has transformed national and regional economies into a genuine global economy. Wide-ranging developments in transportation and communications have made international trade a booming business and an economic driving force in the modern world.

Economic Interdependence

Today no nation by itself can control its own economic health. The world is too complicated. This was proved again in October 1987 when the American stock market crashed and, within days, so did others around the world. Today, nations try to do the best they can with their resources, but they must cooperate with others.

The United States   Some nations have more advantages—and bargaining power—than others. At mid-century it was the United States that had the advantages: a high level of industrialization, a good supply of natural resources, and rich farm land. Its home market was so large that the United States did not think carefully about foreign markets. Not only could it support the economic recovery of Europe, but it could help other parts of the world as well. Above all it had a large trade surplus, meaning that it exported more goods than it imported.

By the late 1980s, the picture had changed. Americans were buying more products from other countries than the United States was selling abroad. Companies from other countries were buying American companies. American workers were upset because they were losing jobs to other nations and pressuring the government. Limit imports, they said. Raise tariffs.

Japan   Japan, on the other hand, had few natural resources and limited farm lands, so it had to buy oil, minerals, and food from other countries. The Japanese soon recognized how important it was to deal with an international market place. While Japan was recovering from its defeat in World War II, its leaders planned to make the most of what it had. Boosting overseas trade was part of the plan. By the late 1980s, Japan had the largest trade surplus in the world.

Europe   Japan was not the only one that thought about its economy after the war. The nations of Western Europe did, too. Would it be business as usual—competition among a number of small European countries? If this kept on, how could they compete against the efficiency of the large American market? One man—a French banker named Jean Monnet (zhahn moh NAY)—had a vision of a different Europe. He saw a European common market, one large market in which there were no trade barriers among European countries.

By small steps Monnet's vision has become a reality. From six original member nations in the 1950s, the European Economic Community (EEC) has now expanded to 12 member nations. Special provisions were worked out to protect groups, such as farmers, for a time. By 1992 there will be no economic barriers among the member nations. There will be one common currency and a central bank to regulate it. Western Europe has become a rival to the United States and Japan.

Learning from Photographs *Imported cars sit on a dock in Seattle, Washington.* **Why do industrial nations have the highest volume of trade?**

International Trade

World trade allows nations to specialize in producing certain goods if they have the resources to make specialization profitable. In this sense, international trade benefits people in two ways. First, consumers can purchase more goods at lower cost than if every country tried to be self-sufficient. Second, scarce resources can be used more efficiently if nations concentrate on making the items they can produce more easily than others.

The greatest volume of trade occurs between the industrial nations, which include the United States, Canada, Japan, Australia, and most Western European nations. This high volume of trade occurs in part because many people in these countries earn enough money to buy large quantities of goods. Moreover, these countries have the technical know-how to use and produce complex, high-demand items.

In any type of trade, goods are bought and sold based on price. Buyers want the cheapest goods available. The number of international transactions and their impact on national economies is best illustrated by the surge in growth of **multinational corporations**—companies that produce and market goods in more than one country. Today there are multinational banks, computer companies, airlines, and hotel and food chains.

While welcoming the benefits of multinational companies, countries frequently resent the loss of control that occurs when business ventures originate beyond their borders. Such economic linkage, however, can have its advantages. Interlocked economic fortunes ensure that the destiny of one country is increasingly tied to those of other countries. Such ties among nations might serve as a deterrent to war.

Developing Nations

Despite increasing interdependency among nations, many countries are still struggling to meet the basic needs of their citizens. The gap between rich and poor nations is a pressing global issue that continues to concern world leaders.

Developing nations in Asia, Africa, and Latin America are dependent on the economic systems of developed nations. Many of these developing nations supply raw materials to developed nations in exchange for manufactured goods. An example of this process can be seen in the South American nation of Peru, which trades its tin for such items as refrigerators and washing machines.

A developing nation will often try to raise its standard of living by diversifying, or increasing the variety of, the types of goods it supplies to the world. Diversification helps protect a nation's economy from depending on a single crop or commodity for its economic well-being. The transition to a diversified economy, however, can be long and difficult.

Lack of capital, or money, for such an economic transformation often leads developing nations to seek outside sources for funding. The World Bank and the International Monetary

Learning from Photographs *A business area of Guatemala City, Guatemala, has a jumble of signs. What familiar names do you see?* **What are the advantages and disadvantages of multinational corporations?**

Fund (IMF) are financial organizations that were established to provide a strong foundation for international trade. They, along with the United Nations and private banks, have loaned money to countries in need. Foreign corporations have also invested in developing nations.

Borrowing the money needed for economic growth has caused monumental debt. By the late 1980s, developing nations such as Mexico and Brazil were finding it very difficult to pay the interest charges on their loans. When loans cannot be repaid, banks often suffer huge losses. These losses can sometimes hurt businesses in, or even the total economy of, the country in which a bank is located.

Leaders of the industrialized world have struggled to solve the international debt crisis. Many strategies have been tried. In some cases, the banks involved have issued new loans to enable developing countries to pay off old debts. While such practices have helped to forestall immediate problems, the debt crisis remains a grave threat to the world's economic health.

The Arms Trade

The biggest share of international trade involves a product that most people are unlikely to own. Surprisingly, the product is armaments. Although it is difficult to fix a precise figure, some observers estimate the world sale of arms at $47 billion. In the United States, roughly one-quarter of the national budget goes to the military. The Soviet Union spends even more—about 40 percent of its budget—on the military.

The production and sale of arms have become a big business because of the large profits to be made selling weapons. The profits have enticed many developing countries into the business in recent years. Developing nations have been among the leading buyers of arms, and now they are sellers as well. By one recent count, at least 27 developing nations are competing in the world's arms market, supplying fighter planes, ships, missiles, and ammunition to other countries.

Nations have traditionally used the profits from the arms trade to offset the money they spend on imports. For example, France is one of the world's leading suppliers of arms. The weapons that it exports pay for one-quarter of the oil that the nation imports. For buying nations the real cost of arms is often hidden, especially in less developed nations. For every dollar that goes into the purchase of weapons, there is one less dollar to spend on education, public health, or the creation of jobs.

During the cold war, world attention was focused on the superpowers and the possibility of nuclear war. The world has changed in recent years. A reduction in tension has occurred between the superpowers, accompanied by meaningful efforts to achieve arms control and arms reductions. At the same time, dozens of small, deadly conflicts are in progress around the globe at any moment. It is possible that world attention may now swing to the growing menace of the arms buildup—including the proliferation of nuclear weapons—in developing countries.

Drug Traffic

The trade of illegal drugs throughout the world affects the global economy and threatens the social fabric of many nations. One of the nations most seriously affected by the drug trade is Colombia. In December 1989 a truck loaded with a half-ton of dynamite exploded outside the headquarters of the Colombian agency trying to end the nation's cocaine trade. The blast killed 52 people and injured a thousand more. It was later revealed that cocaine suppliers had planted the bomb to stop the agency's assault on its operations. Such events dramatize the challenge and dangers in attempting to curtail the trade and use of illegal drugs.

At the time of the blast, Colombia had been combating the powerful drug cartels, or coalitions of independent business organizations, for four months. By that time the drug dealers had carried out 265 bombings and killed 187 people, including a judge involved in the prosecution of drug dealers. The effort involved numerous attacks and counterattacks.

Many drug cartels survived by shifting their refineries to nearby countries, such as Bolivia and Peru, and altering shipping routes out of the country. Rather than follow their traditional smuggling route north through the Caribbean to the east coast of the United States, drug traffickers began going through Venezuela. Some shipments passed through Brazil, Uruguay, and Argentina on their way to Europe. Traffickers also moved drugs through Chile to points in Asia, where drug use was growing fast.

Illegal drug trafficking poses special enforcement problems. Aided by radar, ships, planes, and the latest communications technology, drug runners have forged a network that is difficult to eradicate. The tremendous sums of money involved complicate the matter further. A police officer earning a modest salary may be offered a million dollars to destroy a document, or merely to be absent when a drug shipment arrives. Not everyone will resist such offers.

It has not been any easier to reduce drug consumption than it has been to halt the trafficking and sale of drugs. The United States alone had 14.5 million users of Colombian marijuana, opium, and cocaine. That market was worth an estimated $100 billion annually. Despite aggressive government antidrug campaigns since 1980, the United States continues to suffer from the consequences of illegal drug use and from the crime associated with the drug trade.

Colombia's struggle with its powerful drug dealers illustrates that local or regional approaches do not solve a nation's internal drug problems. What is required, as with efforts to moderate the international arms trade, is increased cooperation among the nations of the world. Although a few instances of this cooperation have occurred, much more is needed to put a dent in the global drug trade.

SECTION 2 REVIEW

Recall
1. **Define:** multinational corporation
2. **Explain:** What are the benefits of international trade?
3. **Describe:** Why is the drug trade so difficult to stop?

Critical Thinking
4. **Apply:** In what ways does the growing trade in arms affect the world's political stability?
5. **Evaluate:** How does a global economy affect developing nations?

Applying Concepts
6. **Cooperation:** What needs to be done to increase the level of international cooperation in confronting the drug problem? What can the United States do to promote this?

The Environment

Presiding at a tree-planting ceremony in 1988, Prime Minister Robert Mugabe of Zimbabwe spoke the following words:

We take for granted that since we're born on a world with trees, on a world with animals, the animals and the trees shall always continue to be there—no matter how much devastation we do to them. No. Nature is not like that. When we devastate it, it will come back and devastate us.

Mugabe's point is much the same as that of astronaut Rusty Schweickart: "The future of our world is a shared destiny. Our problems are collective; so, too, are the solutions."

Current environmental issues illustrate this point. Toxins released from a smokestack in one part of the world can drift across national borders to cloud the skies and poison the forests of other countries. Garbage dumped into one corner of the ocean may sicken people thousands of miles away. Fluorocarbons sprayed into the air destroy the protective ozone layer in our atmosphere. Ultimately, there is no escaping the effects of environmental pollution. We all share the same air, land, and water.

World Population

Explosive population growth in recent decades makes it even more crucial that people live in harmony with their environment. Today the world's population stands at more than 5 billion. If the present growth rate continues, that figure is expected to top 10 billion by 2028. The most rapid rate of increase is occurring in Asia, Africa, and Latin America.

This rapid population growth has resulted in part from improvements in medical care during this century. Many of the world's deadliest diseases—including tuberculosis, smallpox, and polio—have been either completely eliminated or brought under control through vaccines. Fewer adults are dying from these diseases, and more babies are surviving to adulthood.

For developing nations, high growth rates cause considerable problems. In many countries the population is doubling every 20 or 30 years. To keep up, food supplies, housing, schools, and jobs need to double to maintain the standard of living. Yet this does not always happen.

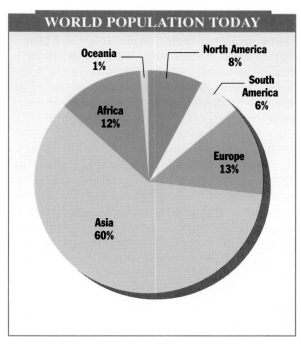

WORLD POPULATION TODAY

- Oceania 1%
- North America 8%
- South America 6%
- Africa 12%
- Europe 13%
- Asia 60%

Learning from Charts *In many countries the population is doubling every 20 to 30 years. **What is the estimated total world population for the year 2000, and how does that compare with the figures for 1950?***

Learning from Photographs *In 1973, central Africa suffered a devastating drought. Western foreign aid agencies distributed grain in an attempt to prevent famine.* **What programs have been set up to help developing countries increase their food supplies?**

The pressure created by rapid population increases has a particularly negative impact on urban areas. For example, a Kenyan farmer who is unable to make a living on his small farm may be tempted to move to the city. Yet the city is no more able to support him than the countryside was. He may be forced to live in a slum lacking toilets, sewers, or safe drinking water. These urban slums threaten not only public health but also the political stability of the regions where they are found.

Because of the problems that overpopulation creates, lowering the birthrate in developing nations is critical. Accomplishing this goal, however, is often difficult. In many rural areas, parents need help working the fields and consequently want large families. Religious and cultural prohibitions against birth control also hamper family planning programs.

Despite these obstacles, some countries have had notable success in slowing their population growth. In Thailand, an aggressive government program promoting birth control methods and changing public attitudes about family size have cut the nation's population growth rate in half in only 15 years. Today 70 percent of Thailand's couples practice family planning. Without the government program, Thailand would have been forced to support an additional 10 million people.

Other countries have taken more desperate measures. In 1979 China began a campaign to limit family size to one child per couple. Parents who fail to heed the official limit face penalties ranging from heavy fines and loss of jobs to forced abortion and even sterilization.

Resources

The struggle for resources has been a major theme in history. Water, gold, rich farmland, or concentrations of coal and oil—the resources in question may have changed, but the struggle has not. It has become clear, however, that the people of the world must share the earth's resources if those resources are to sustain the planet.

Food The world's food supply has been abundant for the past 50 years, but this supply has not been evenly distributed. Some developed nations such as the United States show food surpluses year after year, while many poorer nations routinely endure starvation.

Great advances have been made in food production and food storage in recent decades. Wheat production in India and Pakistan has tripled since 1967 because farmers have planted high-yield, disease-resistant strains. These strains are the result of long-term research and development programs carried out by scientists as part of the "Green Revolution." Other countries that have seen gains from Green Revolution techniques include Mexico, China, Brazil, Egypt, and Bangladesh.

Developing countries have also improved handling and storage methods. Until recently,

India lost more than three-quarters of its grain harvests to pests because the grain sat in the open air waiting to be taken to market. Now there are storage bins, insecticides, and better means of transportation. As a result, the waste in the grain harvest has fallen to 20 percent.

Despite these gains, world hunger remains a serious problem, largely because of difficulties in food distribution. If one region grows a surplus of food, yet that surplus never reaches the areas where there are shortages, what difference does the surplus make?

Famines in Africa have demonstrated how difficult food transportation can be. Because of severe droughts in recent years, starvation has killed tens of thousands of Africans. Relief agencies around the world have organized famine relief efforts to provide short-term help, but these efforts soon run into major obstacles.

Recent attempts to ship food from Kansas in the United States to the Sudan in Africa reflect the problems. Food must first be transported to the east coast of the United States, where it is loaded aboard ships or planes for Africa. Once in Africa, it must be unloaded in a major city and transported to the drought-stricken area. But roads in the Sudan are poor, distances vast, transportation limited, storage facilities scarce, and relief workers few. Much of the food may spoil before it reaches the starving people.

Population growth in some countries has far surpassed the food supply. At one time, Zaire exported food. Now it is importing hundreds of millions of dollars worth of food each year. Fourteen other African nations have also witnessed population growth that exceeds their ability to produce food.

It is estimated that nearly one-tenth of the world's people are starving at any time. Many more survive on inadequate diets. Failure to cope with global hunger may have serious consequences for the world—including economic and political chaos. "Developed nations should be deeply concerned about this problem," plant geneticist Norman Borlaug, the father of the Green Revolution, confirmed. "But not just for moral considerations," he added. "We should be concerned about the widespread hunger in the world because you can't build political stability on human misery. You can't build peace on empty stomachs."

Energy and Mineral Resources   Affluent countries consume a major share of the planet's resources. One recent study indicates that the United States, possessing 5 percent of the world's population, uses 26 percent of its oil. In doing so, our nation generates 26 percent of the world's nitrogen oxides and 22 percent of global carbon dioxide emissions. Michael Deland,

Learning from Photographs *Increasing demand for new sources of energy has led to important research in the field of energy. This solar furnace, operating in France, is the most powerful in the world.* **What other sources of energy are being explored and utilized?**

Learning from Photographs *Serious health hazards, caused by human carelessness in disposing of wastes in lakes, rivers, and oceans, threaten many people.* **What are nations doing about the problem of toxic waste disposal?**

chairman of the White House Council on Environmental Quality, acknowledged that "this country is the most wasteful on the face of this earth."

Environmental awareness has increased dramatically over the past 20 years. News stories about oil spills or acid rain have raised the public's consciousness and led to political action. In addition, many citizens in developed countries have now adopted conservation measures in their daily lives. They may carpool to work to save on fuel or recycle to reduce household waste.

Nations, too, have adjusted. In May 1989, 86 countries agreed to phase out their use of chlorofluorocarbons (CFCs), which are destroy-

ing the world's ozone layer, by the year 2000. To combat acid rain (rainwater containing poisonous industrial wastes), two dozen nations have pledged to cut their sulfur dioxide emissions from power plants by 30 percent.

Even with conservation and higher efficiency, large quantities of oil and other minerals need to be found to satisfy future needs. The search for new supplies of resources has prompted exploration of remote areas in Southeast Asia, Africa, and the polar regions. Scientists have even looked beneath the ocean floor, where cobalt, manganese, and nickel are embedded.

Nuclear power as an energy source has drawn both praise and criticism. The nuclear power plants currently in use depend on nuclear fission, or the splitting of nuclear particles, to generate energy. Unfortunately, this process yields radioactive wastes that remain dangerous for thousands of years. Critics also suspect that low-level radiation emitted from the plants may threaten the health of those nearby.

Severe systems failures in nuclear plants pose even greater risks. In 1986 a partial meltdown at the Chernobyl nuclear plant in the Soviet Union killed scores of people and released a radioactive cloud that drifted across Europe, contaminating crops and killing farm animals. Concerned over the safety of nuclear technology, many nations have moved away from nuclear energy. In the United States, construction of nuclear plants has virtually stopped. Sweden recently voted to declare a total ban on the use of nuclear power there.

Worldwide, the search has begun for clean, safe, renewable energy sources. Wind and solar power are being developed. Researchers are also studying ways to harness power from ocean tides and thermal springs. The world demands abundant energy for future needs. The concern now, for all inhabitants of this planet, is how that energy will be supplied without ruining the world's fragile environment.

Pollution

As the world population has grown and nations have become more industrialized, the volume of waste has grown. Affluent countries now produce mountains of garbage every day. On the average, each American discards 1,300 pounds (585 kilograms) of trash in a year. The challenge we now face is how to dispose of such a large volume of material cheaply and safely without endangering our planet.

Some garbage goes into local landfills, some is burned, and some is towed miles out to sea and dumped there. Each of these methods has problems. In some areas available landfill sites are now overflowing, and in others dangerous chemicals leaking from barrels and cans have seeped into the groundwater. On the other hand, burning huge volumes of garbage pollutes the air. Dumping waste into the oceans may poison plant life, kill fish and other sea creatures, and contaminate seafood.

Rivers and lakes have long served as dumping grounds in the United States and other countries. For a long time, industries discarded wastes in nearby bodies of water. After years of such abuse, pollution has either damaged or seriously threatened nearly half the rivers, lakes, and streams in the United States. Fishing and swimming are no longer possible in many of these bodies of water. Pollution has also contributed to freshwater shortages that have struck many regions of the country.

The cleanup of poisoned bodies of water and toxic dump sites is now a major goal of most

CONNECTIONS: HISTORY AND THE ENVIRONMENT

An Unnatural Disaster

Pressing economic and social problems have plagued the world's developing nations in the decades following World War II. The demand for natural resources, the creation of jobs, and the need for more open land to settle growing populations have led many nations to introduce deforestation programs.

Although a useful short-term solution to economic problems, deforestation has disastrous consequences. Deforestation can decrease soil quality and create erosion problems, reducing rich forests to wastelands. The destruction of the tropical rain forests in Brazil threatens to alter the world's climate and contribute to the greenhouse effect.

Deforestation recently led to a major disaster in Thailand. The Thai government's 30-year policy of encouraging logging resulted in the loss of fully half the nation's forests. A violent rainstorm that hit one of the deforested regions in November 1988 created flash floods on the bare, muddy hillsides. These floods killed 400 people and left thousands more injured and homeless.

If the forests had remained to absorb the downpour, floods would not have threatened the valley's residents. By ignoring the consequences of their actions, Thai officials and loggers not only destroyed a vital resource but also created a disaster. Experts say the destructive floods have set the region's economy back 20 years.

Making the Connection
1. How did extensive logging make the 1988 floods more deadly than they otherwise would have been?
2. Why do you think Thai officials encouraged logging during the past three decades?

FOOTNOTES TO HISTORY

HOLD THE PLASTIC!

In 1987 a fifth-grade civics class in Closter, New Jersey, decided to do battle with McDonald's, the hamburger giant. Their reason for attack? The company's excessive use of polystyrene (plastic foam) packaging.

Polystyrene takes decades to decompose, and emits toxic fumes when burned. Arguing that adding more than 1 billion pounds a year of the foam to global landfills was just too much, the students mounted a letter-writing campaign to change McDonald's policy. Their pressure tactics paid off. In November 1990 the world's biggest user of polystyrene announced it would begin phasing out the plastic foam in favor of paper wrapping materials.

industrialized countries. This task is essential if the earth and water we depend on for life are ever to be nursed back to health.

The Atmosphere

Travelers flying by jet to Paris, Los Angeles, or Tokyo see the same yellow-brown haze in the sky as they descend through the clouds to land. Smog has become a common feature of modern industrial life.

Unhealthful air can sicken those who regularly inhale it. Smog can promote lung disease and eye infections. Governments of the world now recognize air pollution as a serious health threat. Some countries have forced their industries to install pollution-control devices called scrubbers in their smokestacks. Governments have also passed laws requiring greater fuel efficiency for automobiles.

Certain trends in global air pollution are still more grave. Acid rain deadens the lakes and ponds that it touches and strips forests bare. The phenomenon was first observed in the Black Forest of Germany in the late 1970s when trees began to yellow and die. Acid rain has since affected parts of North America, South America, China, Japan, and Africa.

The billions of tons of carbon dioxide pumped into the air each year are causing average worldwide temperatures to rise alarmingly, some experts say. This warming trend, known as **the greenhouse effect,** could have drastic consequences if it continues unchecked. The wholesale clearing and burning of **tropical rain forests**—humid, densely overgrown areas such as in the Amazon region of Brazil—worsens world air quality in two ways. First, combustion adds more carbon dioxide to the air. Second, the loss of many thousands of acres of vegetation reduces the ability of the planet to purify its atmosphere by releasing oxygen.

Limited economic opportunities and the need for new farmland are two factors that lead people to burn tropical rain forests; however, the destruction of these forests threatens the entire planet. As a result, finding solutions to the greenhouse effect and other world environmental problems will depend on international cooperation. Just as the technological and economic progress of one country affects the well-being of its neighbors, so too do major environmental problems affect all the world's people.

SECTION 3 REVIEW

Recall
1. **Define:** greenhouse effect, tropical rain forest
2. **Identify:** Robert Mugabe, Norman Borlaug
3. **Explain:** How has Thailand responded to its population growth in recent years?

Critical Thinking
4. **Evaluate:** In what ways is food distribution a key problem in the fight to end world hunger?
5. **Analyze:** Why do you think the issue of industrial creation and control of acid rain creates conflicts between certain industries and many environmental groups?

Applying Concepts
6. **Relation to environment:** What should be the three highest priorities for global action to improve the environment?

SECTION 4

The Global Culture

Technological and economic changes following World War II have brought the people around the world into closer contact. Common environmental problems have provided another reason for people to meet and work together. With increased contact has come exposure to the customs, music, art, and literature of a wide variety of cultures.

As different cultures influence each other, a new global culture emerges. Distinct national and ethnic cultures still exist but boundaries between them are not as sharp as they were, and features they share are growing.

The Search for Meaning

Since 1945 changes throughout the world have affected our thoughts, actions, and expectations. The world has become more complex and fast-paced. Information from all over the globe bombards us daily, travel is faster than ever before, and communication is instantaneous. Keeping up in such a hectic and competitive world has become increasingly difficult.

Following World War II, the economic fortunes of peoples and nations differed sharply. Some countries recovered quickly from the conflict and rose to new heights of prosperity; other nations—particularly those that witnessed combat on their soil—faced many hardships.

Because America's cities and economy were not ravaged by war, many people were able to make a quick return to the "good life." A sustained economic boom lasting more than 20 years enabled Americans to buy consumer goods unavailable during the war. New technological advances also changed work patterns in the United States and other industrialized nations. Greater automation and shorter work hours led to more leisure time for many people.

Despite outward prosperity, there were signs of uncertainty in the West. The old political order, shattered by war, had given way to something new. But what that newness meant was unclear. Could the values that had guided the world in the first half of the twentieth century sustain it in the 1950s, 1960s, and beyond?

A shift toward personal expression was evident in many areas. This began, in a sense, with the French philosopher Jean-Paul Sartre, who originated a philosophy called **existentialism.** Each human being is essentially alone, Sartre said. Each person has the freedom to act, to chart an individual path through life, by saying yes or no to the world's choices.

Individual liberation was to become a key social concept in the postwar years. Many people sought a new degree of justice and freedom. Beginning in the mid-1950s, for example, those involved in the civil rights movement pressed for racial equality in the United States. They demanded an end to discriminatory practices that prevented African-Americans from going to good schools or voting. They protested, marched, and in some cases died to dramatize the unfairness that African-Americans were enduring every day. In more recent years, blacks in South Africa have been joined by sympathizers from all parts of the world in protesting the discriminatory policy of apartheid that keeps them in the position of second-class citizens.

American women also agitated to break free of traditional female roles. Betty Friedan's *The Feminine Mystique*, published in 1963, inspired a rebirth of the women's movement that had gone into eclipse after World War I. Women in the 1960s demanded more choices. They called for an end to sex discrimination and gender stereotyping. Women wanted the chance to be construction workers, executives, and politicians, as well as homemakers, wives, and mothers.

Learning from Photographs *Many people have supported a constitutional amendment guaranteeing equal rights for women.* **Judging from this photograph, what sections of the population seem to be backers of the ERA?**

Since Friedan's book was published, the women's movement has spread to countries around the world. Although the movement takes on its own character in each country, the push by women to expand their rights and opportunities has occurred worldwide.

Religion has not escaped global changes. As secular viewpoints have spread, many people have rejected traditional religious teachings. Numerous critics claim that mainstream religions have lost touch with modern human needs and problems. But, the decline of religion that some scholars had predicted has not occurred. Religious belief is still important to many people throughout the world. In addition, many religious groups have successfully applied their traditional teachings to the problems of the 1900s. Some of these religions have become involved in the issues of human rights, the environment,

and nuclear disarmament. Others promote understanding and cooperation among religions.

Religious fundamentalism has also been experiencing some growth around the world in recent decades. In the United States, for example, fundamentalist Christian denominations have grown rapidly since 1970, while older, more mainstream denominations have declined in membership. A response to technological advances and outside cultural influences in developing nations has sometimes been a return to more traditional beliefs. The Islamic world, for instance, has experienced a resurgence of fundamentalist religious faith since the 1970s. This resurgence has also been accompanied in some instances by a rejection of many Western ideas and developments.

The Arts

The spread of ideas and culture from one part of the globe to another has altered the art world in countless ways. The cultural isolation that existed before the advent of jet travel, television, and communications satellites no longer exists. Instead, changes move rapidly from one place to another, mixing and blending in a whirl of influences. Rock music that started in the United States now echoes in clubs in Eastern Europe and the Soviet Union. Indonesian folk dancers tour Scandinavia, and Brazilian poets entertain audiences in Tokyo.

Theater and Literature   Artists have always been influenced by other artists they encounter. What has changed in recent decades is the scope of this influence. Theater serves to illustrate this: Irish-born Samuel Beckett, Romanian-born Eugène Ionesco, and American Edward Albee were among the playwrights deeply influenced by philosopher Jean-Paul Sartre—a Frenchman. The plays of all three men have been labeled Theater of the Absurd for their vision of life as irrational and meaningless.

Beckett's play *Waiting for Godot* (1953) is a vivid example. The play consists of two tramps talking and waiting for somebody or something. By the end, it is still not clear who Godot is or what Godot stands for. This vision of modern

Cultural Exchange

Advances in technology have made the world much smaller. Transportation and communication systems enable people to travel and interact on an unprecedented scale. Yet as our technological ability has increased, other hindrances to collaboration among nations and cultures have emerged. After World War II, the cold war meant not only political and military confrontation between Western- and Eastern-bloc countries, but also cultural divisions.

One artist whose career bears testimony to this division is the dancer Mikhail Baryshnikov. Baryshnikov was born in 1948 in Riga in the Soviet Union. He began dancing at age 12 and four years later joined the famous Kirov Ballet. He soon became a star, with many fans and a comfortable apartment in Leningrad.

Although Baryshnikov was one of the premier dancers of the Kirov Ballet and received numerous awards, his work was restricted under the Soviet system. Production of new choreographic works was stifled by government censorship. Some artists were allowed to organize "creative evenings" at the Kirov, featuring the work of one dancer. The dancer was permitted to choose the pieces to be performed without state approval. Baryshnikov organized a "creative evening" in the early 1970s but found it discouraging. Although he was free to choose and direct the works, the atmosphere did not provide moral support or enthusiasm.

In 1974, at age 26, Baryshnikov defected from the Soviet Union. Although this meant banishing himself from his homeland, he was determined to seek artistic freedom. In the West, Baryshnikov was allowed to work with artists from many countries. The chance to collaborate gave him the challenge vital to artistic endeavor and a sense of fulfillment.

Baryshnikov was an immediate success in the United States. He has worked with the country's most prestigious ballet companies and continues to experiment with new works.

Responding to the Arts

1. Why did Baryshnikov defect from the Soviet Union?
2. How will recent developments in the Soviet Union affect its cultural exchanges with other nations?

Mikhail Baryshnikov

life as rootless, painful, and empty is clearly derived from the writings of Sartre.

A few decades ago, the Soviet Union and the countries of Eastern Europe were much more isolated from the West than they currently are. Censorship was a basic fact of artistic life in those nations during the years following World War II. But after the death of Stalin in 1953, writers began to push for greater freedom. The Soviet government responded by gradually easing restrictions. Poems by the once-disfavored poet Anna Akhmatova appeared, as well as new poetry by Andrey Voznesensky and Yevgeny Yevtushenko, members of the younger generation of Soviet writers. The government also permitted many formerly banned Western works to enter the Soviet Union. This relatively short-lived "thaw" ended in 1966 when another period of artistic repression returned. Since Soviet leader Mikhail Gorbachev introduced the policy of *glasnost* in the mid-1980s, however, Soviet writers have enjoyed far greater artistic freedom.

Writers from developing countries have gradually turned away from the literary trends they find in Paris, London, and New York. Instead, they have mined their own cultural heritage. They have created a literature that draws on rhythms, images, and experiences separate and distinct from the Western tradition, and the impact of their work has been felt worldwide.

Many African works in the postwar era explore the continent's conflicts with Western culture and its bitter history of colonialism. Chinua Achebe of Nigeria has received wide international acclaim for his novels dealing with these topics. In a similar vein, Ghanian playwright Ama Ata Aidoo describes the tensions that arise when a young Ghanian man marries an African-American woman in *The Dilemma of a Ghost* (1965). And Wole Soyinka of Nigeria, perhaps Africa's best-known playwright, wrote *A Dance of the Forests* (1963) to celebrate Nigerian independence from Great Britain.

Latin American writers are similarly determined to tap the riches of their own cultures. Their writing, in turn, has strongly influenced contemporary writers in the United States and Europe. Chilean poet Pablo Neruda and Colombian novelist Gabriel García Marquez are among the notable sources of this influence. Mexican poet and critic Octavio Paz is another. Paz, who won the Nobel Prize for Literature in 1990, combines modern language and ancient Aztec symbolism in his writings.

Music   Music has always had the ability to cross national borders. Since World War II, jazz and rock have become international favorites. People in all parts of the globe now listen to the work of such influential jazz musicians as Duke Ellington, Louis Armstrong, Charlie Parker, Thelonius Monk, and Miles Davis. Rock superstars such as the Beatles and the Rolling Stones in the 1960s, the Bee Gees and Elton John in the 1970s, and Michael Jackson and Bruce Springsteen in the 1980s have won worldwide followings.

In addition, regional music traditions have begun to spread beyond their original locales.

Learning from Photographs *The Beatles experimented with new musical forms and were widely imitated by other composers and performers.* **How do musicians and other artists contribute to the globalization of culture?**

Learning from Art *Op art became a global movement during the 1950s. This painting,* Arcturus II, *illustrates how artists can create the illusion of movement with color and geometric forms.* **Which quarter of the painting seems closest to you? Is this art?**

Popular Caribbean music—Jamaican reggae, for example—has gained a large following in North America and Europe. As musicians from one part of the world receive greater exposure to the regional music of other parts of the world, they often incorporate many features of that music into their own. Afro-pop is one example of this sort of musical blending.

Some Western musicians have traveled to countries in Asia, Africa, and Latin America to explore the rich diverse music. American songwriter Paul Simon has used both African and South American musicians on two of his best-selling albums, *Graceland* and *The Rhythm of the Saints.* Rock star Van Morrison has recorded an album with the Chieftains, a traditional Irish folk band.

Visual Arts   Since World War II, modern visual art has developed in many ways. Abstract expressionism flourished in the 1950s and took a revolutionary approach to painting. Experimenting with color, these artists believed that art did not have to represent objects; instead they used unusual, abstract forms to represent ideas.

Another movement called op art started in France in the 1950s and spread to the United States. Op art consisted of carefully arranged colors and patterns, which created the illusion of vibrating movement. Like abstract expressionism, it rejected realism in art.

After the 1960s many artists returned to realism. In photographic collages, David Hockney combined the realism of photography with the illusionary effect of Op Art. Today's artists are influenced by many cultures and aspects of modern life. New technology, environmental issues, and outer space may all be the topics of modern art.

Human Rights

Behind a locked door, in a dim, bare cell, a middle-aged woman sits sobbing. Her arms are bruised from the beatings that the jailhouse guards administer regularly. "I have been here, in the dark, for seven days," she tells a visitor. "They give me food only once a day."

Although a prisoner in Brazil, this woman might be found in countries where human-rights abuses occur. A recent report by Amnesty International, an organization that monitors human-rights violations, revealed the grim statistics. Of 135 countries where data was gathered in 1989, more than half still imprison people for speaking their minds. More than one-third torture political prisoners.

The nations that rely on imprisonment and torture for political control are familiar enough. Indonesia, Syria, Chile, Haiti, Ethiopia, South Africa, Cuba, Iran, Iraq, Bolivia, Guatemala, El Salvador—Amnesty International has cited these countries and more for human rights abuses.

The good news is that human-rights abuses are less prevalent today than they were. Standards of decency have been raised in recent decades. Human rights are becoming steadily more secure in the modern world. Today, an estimated 1,000 human-rights organizations document global abuses and apply public pressure to change the behavior of the offending governments. The increased visibility of each government's actions and the accompanying accountability that many nations feel is showing results.

Consider the Soviet Union. Until recently, this nation had always shrugged off world criticism of its treatment of political prisoners as inappropriate meddling. But in the late 1980s, in a startling change, the nation freed the majority of these prisoners. For a time, Soviet rulers tolerated widespread dissent. "Now, they've recognized that it *is* the world's business," says Aryeh Neier, executive director of the New York-based Human Rights Watch. "Almost every government around the world must now at least pretend that it respects human rights."

In 1948 the United Nations adopted what has become the most important human rights document of the postwar years—the Universal Declaration of Human Rights. The document talks about social and economic as well as political rights. It was a statement not of the way things were, but of the way things should be.

Great strides have been made in achieving some rights. With the backing of the United Nations, women's issues have won international attention, and nations have begun to discard barriers to women's equal participation in public and social life. Since the 1960s progress has occurred in educating citizens of developing nations and in raising the world's literacy rate.

Sigmund Freud wrote in his book *Civilization and Its Discontents:* "The mark of a civilization is how it cares for those in the dawn of life, those in the twilight of life, and those in the shadows." As the world's population grows, more will have to be done to provide the basic needs and a decent quality of life for the planet's inhabitants. But the United Nations Universal Declaration of Human Rights gives the world a common goal to aim for and the people of the earth an ideal to bring them closer together.

SECTION 4 REVIEW

Recall
1. **Define:** existentialism
2. **Identify:** Samuel Beckett, Jean-Paul Sartre, Gabriel García Marquez, Octavio Paz, Paul Simon
3. **Explain:** How have global life styles and social values changed in the decades following World War II?

Critical Thinking
4. **Analyze:** What is the status of human rights in today's world?
5. **Synthesize:** To what degree do foreign cultures influence contemporary American arts? To what degree does American culture influence others?

Applying Concepts
6. **Cultural diffusion:** What is the most powerful source of cultural diffusion today? Explain.

INTERPRETING CIRCLE GRAPHS

Have you ever sat at a dinner table and watched someone dish out pieces from an apple pie? As each person was served a slice, did you wonder if there would be a slice left for you?

Explanation

A sliced pie is like a *circle graph;* in fact, a circle graph is sometimes called a pie chart. Circle graphs present statistical data and show relationships among the parts of a whole. Thus, circle graphs are used to show proportion rather than absolute amounts. By looking at a circle graph, you can see how the sections compare with each other in size. The size of these sections is determined by converting percentages to degrees, based on a 360° circle.

Use the following steps to interpret a circle graph:
- Identify what whole unit the circle represents.
- Identify what the sections of the circle represent and what information is provided.
- Draw conclusions based on this information.

Example

In this circle graph, the whole—the uncut pie—represents the total amount of money given to Europe under the Marshall Plan. The sections represent the na-

tions that received the funds and how much they received.

A glance at the graph shows you which nations received the larger amounts. The sections for Great Britain and France are almost the same size. By looking at the numbers, you realize that Great Britain received 24% of the Marshall Plan funds, while France received 21% of the funds.

Application

Use the circle graph on page 961 to answer the questions:
1. What is the whole on which this graph is based?

2. Can you tell the total population of North America by looking at this graph?
3. Does any one region of the world have more than one half of the world's population? Is it easy to conclude the answer to this question without looking at the percentages?
4. Which continent, Africa or Europe, has more people?

Practice

Turn to Practicing Skills on page 975 of the Chapter Review for further practice interpreting circle graphs.

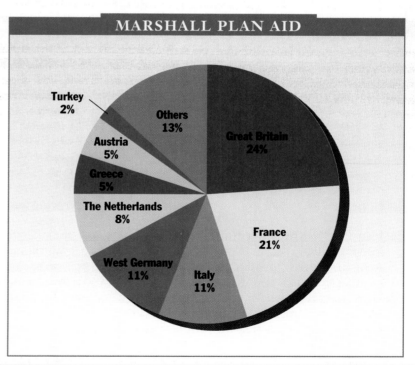

MARSHALL PLAN AID

Turkey 2%
Others 13%
Great Britain 24%
Austria 5%
Greece 5%
The Netherlands 8%
France 21%
West Germany 11%
Italy 11%

CHAPTER 36 REVIEW

HISTORICAL SIGNIFICANCE

Since World War II, the world has undergone many tremendous changes. The technological revolution has altered the way we live. Developments in communications technology and transportation have linked different parts of the world more closely than ever before and helped to create an interdependent global economy. Space exploration has led to far greater knowledge of our planet and universe. Advances in medicine have wiped out certain diseases and significantly prolonged the average life expectancy. Computers and robots are transforming the workplace.

While these advances occurred, the population of the world doubled between 1950 and 1986. By 2028 the world's population is expected to double again—from 5 to 10 billion people. This population explosion has strained developing countries' abilities to meet the needs of their people, widening the gap between rich and poor nations. Industrial growth and increased use of the earth's resources have contributed to the increase of air and water pollution and the emergence of global warming as a major new environmental problem.

Nations can no longer solve their economic and environmental problems alone, for the causes of the problems often lie beyond their borders. To solve the problems that threaten the entire world, nations must learn to cooperate.

SUMMARY

For a summary of Chapter 36, see Unit 8 Synopsis on pages 975–977.

USING KEY TERMS

Write the key term that best completes each sentence below.

a. existentialism
b. genetic engineering
c. greenhouse effect
d. multinational corporation
e. tropical rain forest

1. Jean-Paul Sartre is a central figure of a philosophy called___ .
2. A business that produces and markets a product in several countries is a ___.
3. Some scientists believe that emisions of carbon dioxide into the atmosphere will hasten the ____ causing average worldwide temperatures to rise.
4. Critics of ___ fear that altering cell structure might result in new diseases.
5. The destruction of the ___ reduces Earth's ability to purify its atmosphere through the release of oxygen.

REVIEWING FACTS

1. **Explain:** What is the Universal Declaration of Human Rights?
2. **Define:** What is the Green Revolution and who is its "father"?
3. **Identify:** Who is Mikhail Baryshnikov?
4. **Explain:** What is the international debt crisis? What are the costs of this crisis to the borrowing and lending nations?
5. **Locate:** Where in the Western Hemisphere can you find vast regions of endangered tropical rain forests?
6. **Explain:** What happened at Chernobyl in the Soviet Union in 1986?

CRITICAL THINKING

1. **Analyze:** What do you think brought about the changes in life styles throughout the world since World War II?

2. **Evaluate:** Name a current artist or performer who has global influence. What do you think accounts for this person's influence?

3. **Synthesize:** Why might developing nations argue that their rapid population growth should be of less concern than the high consumption rate of people in developed nations? What do you think is of greater concern and why?

ANALYZING CONCEPTS

1. **Change:** How has technology affected the level of global interaction?

2. **Cooperation:** How might an increasingly global economy foster peace and stability?

3. **Relation to environment:** Why do dangers to our planet require global solutions?

4. **Cultural diffusion:** What factors have led to the emergence of a global culture?

PRACTICING SKILLS

Imagine that you are trying to gather information about illegal drugs in the United States. You would like to know what kinds of drugs are sold here, the total amount of money spent on illegal drugs, and what foreign countries supply the most illegal drugs to this nation. Which of these pieces of information would be suitable for illustration in a circle graph?

GEOGRAPHY IN HISTORY

1. **Place:** Which economic activity created political instability in Colombia and posed a threat to world security?

2. **Environment:** How does the clearing of tropical rain forests affect the atmosphere?

3. **Movement:** How does overpopulation contribute to an increase in the percentage of people living in urban areas?

4. **Region:** Refer to the map on page 998. Which region in South America receives the greatest annual precipitation?

TRACING CHRONOLOGY

Use the time line below to answer these questions.

1. How many years after the start of the space race did astronauts first walk on the moon?

2. How long after the discovery of a hole in the ozone layer did countries agree to stop using chlorofluorocarbons?

3. How many years separated the launch of *Sputnik* and the launch of *Columbia*?

LINKING PAST AND PRESENT

1. How has the public's attitude toward natural resources changed over the past fifty years?

2. Placing a person on the moon was the primary goal of the space race. Has a new main goal for the space program emerged?

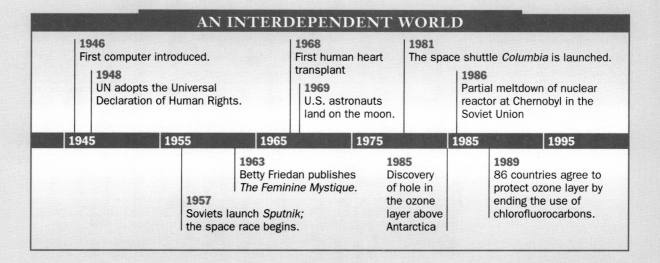

AN INTERDEPENDENT WORLD

1946
First computer introduced.

1948
UN adopts the Universal Declaration of Human Rights.

1968
First human heart transplant

1969
U.S. astronauts land on the moon.

1981
The space shuttle *Columbia* is launched.

1986
Partial meltdown of nuclear reactor at Chernobyl in the Soviet Union

| 1945 | 1955 | 1965 | 1975 | 1985 | 1995 |

1963
Betty Friedan publishes *The Feminine Mystique.*

1957
Soviets launch *Sputnik;* the space race begins.

1985
Discovery of hole in the ozone layer above Antarctica

1989
86 countries agree to protect ozone layer by ending the use of chlorofluorocarbons.

UNIT 8 SYNOPSIS

The period from the end of World War II to the present brought a major political realignment among the nations of the world. Weakened from war, the European colonial powers withdrew from Asia and Africa. The boundaries of many nations were redrawn, and new nations were created. These new nations struggled to establish their roles in the new world order.

The United States and the Soviet Union became superpowers, and much of the world divided itself into two blocs as smaller nations aligned themselves with one superpower or another. The superpowers became engaged in an ideological confrontation known as the cold war, which dominated world politics in the second half of the 1900s. The cold war was a race to establish spheres of influence in various parts of the world. As the Soviet Union sought to spread communism worldwide, the United States tried to resist its spread and to promote democracy.

For the most part, the cold war was not fought on bloody battlefields, although armed conflicts did occur. The main weapons in this confrontation were money, espionage, diplomacy, and the threat of nuclear war.

Each side sought to sway other nations to its point of view by offering economic aid and military protection. Each waged a global war of words, using propaganda and subversion to try to discredit the other and enhance its own stature. Occasionally the rival superpowers intervened with tanks and troops to establish control in weak or unstable countries. Nations found themselves having to choose sides in a world sharply divided between East and West.

With the introduction of the threat of nuclear annihilation, world leaders established many new organizations, such as the United Nations, to try to resolve world problems. However, the deep divisions of the cold war greatly hindered efforts toward lasting peace.

The cold war involved nations from Vietnam to Egypt to Cuba. It began, however, as a battle for control of the devastated countries of Europe.

Learning from Photographs *One weapon of the cold war was propaganda. The Berlin airlift, described in Chapter 31, was a propaganda victory for the United States, as it rescued millions of West Berliners from starvation by Stalin.* **Why did Stalin lift the blockade instead of using force to capture West Berlin?**

Learning from Photographs *A South Korean village prepares to welcome UN forces after MacArthur's strategic landing in Inchon in September 1950.* **Do you think the United States should have become involved in Korea?**

CHAPTER 31
The Cold War

The World War II alliance quickly dissolved when conflict arose over the postwar reorganization of Europe. As a result, Europe was divided into the Eastern bloc, dominated by the Soviet Union, and the Western bloc, tied to the United States and its allies. The division came to be known as the iron curtain, symbolized by the Berlin Wall.

Communist governments were established throughout Eastern Europe, either voluntarily or by force. The economies of these countries were reorganized to serve Soviet goals. The Soviet Union regarded the Eastern bloc as a buffer zone against Western aggression. Internal protests against Soviet domination were put down by force. In 1955 these nations allied for mutual defense under the Warsaw Pact.

In Western Europe, the price of victory had been almost as great as the price of defeat. Western nations turned to the task of rebuilding their shattered cities and economies with U.S. assistance under the Marshall Plan. They also formed the NATO alliance for mutual defense in 1949. At the same time they improved economic cooperation in order to eliminate competition for resources and thereby reduce the chance of future wars.

The United States and Canada survived the war with their economies intact and began a period of growth and prosperity. U.S. politics during the 1950s was dominated by the so-called red scare, in which Congress investigated the infiltration of government and industry by suspected Communists. During the 1960s women and minorities made new demands for equal rights.

CHAPTER 32
Asia and the Pacific

The post–World War II period brought profound changes to the nations of Asia and the Pacific Basin. Japan's political, economic, and social systems were immediately restructured, and the nation began its rapid rise to economic preeminence. During the 1950s, colonial nations from India to Indonesia achieved independence. They then faced new political and economic challenges.

In India the ancient Hindu–Muslim rivalry broke out when Great Britain relinquished control in 1947. The violence eventually resulted in the division of the Indian subcontinent into four new countries.

The withdrawal of colonial power from China led to civil war between the nationalists and the Communists. This resulted in the present Communist nation.

The cold war struggle for influence in Korea set off a war that left the country divided into two separate states. The war also caused a major shift in political and economic activity to the nations of the Pacific Rim. Their economic success has led some historians to refer to the 1900s as the Asian Century.

Learning from Photographs *The Palace of Fine Arts is one of Mexico City's impressive cultural sites.* ***How does Mexico City represent the nation's successes and challenges?***

CHAPTER 33
Africa and the Middle East

World War II gave new impetus to the African struggle for independence. Some European nations recognized this movement and began to give up their colonies voluntarily. Others fought bloody civil wars in Kenya, Algeria, the Belgian Congo, Angola, and Mozambique.

The newly independent nations faced serious problems: finding appropriate forms of government, resolving ethnic rivalries, and creating modern economies. Many had been left ill-prepared for those tasks by the former colonial powers. Some were dependent on a single crop or product to support their economies.

Many Africans sought to reestablish their cultural identity and began to throw off reminders of the colonial past. A Pan-African movement created new political and economic links among the nations on the continent.

A similar Pan-Arabic movement began in North Africa and the Middle East as the nations of this region gained their independence. Huge oil reserves brought tremendous growth to some nations, but these resources also made them a target for involvement by outside powers.

Arabs were unified in opposing the formation of the state of Israel in 1948. Egyptian president Gamel Abdel Nasser led the opposition. The Middle East has suffered continuing political violence and instability, in Egypt, Lebanon, Iran, and recently in Kuwait.

CHAPTER 34
Latin America

The nations of Latin America faced many challenges during the postwar period. Rapid industrialization brought new wealth to the region, but the population was sharply divided into groups of very rich and very poor. This disparity led to frequent social unrest.

In the late 1950s, Fidel Castro seized power in Cuba, confirming U.S. fears of Communist influence in the Western Hemisphere. In countries such as Nicaragua, Panama, and Argentina, repressive, often corrupt, dictatorships were the only powers able to keep order. The United States aided many of these regimes, seeing them as preferable to communism. Mexico has had the region's stablest democratic government.

During the 1980s democracy movements overturned dictatorships in several Latin American countries. Today the region faces rapid population growth and heavy foreign debt.

CHAPTER 35
Changes in North America and Europe

The Vietnam war was the United States' last major attempt at cold war containment. The war and the subsequent Watergate scandal led to congressional limits on the power of the president in order to curb the imperial presidency.

In the late 1960s tension between English-speaking Canadians and the French-speaking minority fueled a separatist movement in the province of Quebec. The conflict provoked a constitutional crisis that weakened the federal union and boosted provincial authority. The future of the Canadian union remains uncertain.

After 18 years of oppressive rule under Leonid Brezhnev, the Soviet Union opened a new era of political freedom under Mikhail Gorbachev in 1985. His policies of glasnost and perestroika brought economic and social reforms. But reactionary pressures and the threat of secession by the Soviet republics eventually forced Gorbachev to retreat somewhat from his liberal policies.

The reform movement spread to the countries of Eastern Europe, which threw off Soviet domination and launched new democracies. Protesters tore down the Berlin Wall in 1989 and brought down the East German government. The two Germanys were reunited in 1990.

The nations of Western Europe proceeded with postwar plans for economic integration, led by the European Economic Community. The EEC hoped to welcome the newly independent nations of Eastern Europe into the plan.

CHAPTER 36
An Interdependent World

As the world heads into the twenty-first century, the interdependence and common purpose of nations and peoples are gradually being recognized. Space exploration has permitted us to see the earth as a single unit with a shared environment. Advances in technology have enabled instantaneous communication across the globe, creating an electronic neighborhood of the world's people.

Such advances, however, are offset by rapid increases in world population and the accompanying industrial growth. These trends have created critical environmental problems that now affect the entire world. It is now apparent that global cooperation is essential to protecting the future of the planet.

SURVEYING THE UNIT

1. **Identifying Trends:** Has the postwar world seen a shift toward more or less political freedom? Explain, using examples from two continents.
2. **Relating Ideas:** How have global environmental problems such as deforestation changed people's thinking about the political relationships among nations?
3. **Making Comparisons:** Compare the results of nationalist movements in Africa and Asia. What forms of government did they lead to?

UNIT 8 REVIEW

REVIEWING THE MAIN IDEAS

1. **Explain:** The period from 1945 to 1990 was known as the cold war. What does this term mean?
2. **Identify:** What new concepts about relationships among nations emerged from World War II? What organizations embody these ideas?
3. **Explain:** Why did the European colonial powers lose their empires after World War II?
4. **List:** What are some of the major challenges facing developing nations?

THINKING CRITICALLY

1. **Apply:** Show how lessons that the United States learned in its relationship with the shah of Iran might be applied to U.S. foreign policy today.
2. **Analyze:** In the long run, what finally decided the cold-war conflict, ideology or economics? Explain your answer.
3. **Synthesize:** China, the world's most populous country, is still governed by an authoritarian communist government. In your opinion, will the collapse of Communist regimes in Europe be followed by similar events in China? Why or why not?
4. **Analyze:** Do you think the United States policy of containment was a good idea? What alternative strategies might Truman have adopted to counter the spread of communism?
5. **Evaluate:** Since World War II, many of the developing nations have adopted a program of rapid industrialization as the quickest route to economic success, following the example of the major Western industrialized countries. Discuss the advantages and disadvantages of this policy.
6. **Evaluate:** Imagine that the United States and the Soviet Union had remained allies in the postwar period, instead of competing for world dominance. How might that relationship have changed the course of events in the newly independent countries of Africa, Asia, and the Middle East?

A GLOBAL PERSPECTIVE

Refer to the time line on pages 808–809 to answer these questions.

1. What episode in history is marked by many of the events shown in the political sphere on the time line?
2. The Berlin Wall was built in 1961. How long did it remain standing?
3. What superpower competition peaked in 1969?
4. What is the relationship between the first and last events in the scientific sphere?
5. Choose two events on the time line that occurred in the United States and explain how they affected other countries.
6. What do you think are the three most important events on the time line? Explain your answer.

LINKING PAST AND PRESENT

1. Compare the Marshall Plan strategy of the 1950s to the economic embargoes imposed on South Africa in the 1980s and Iraq in 1990 and 1991.
2. In 1951, Rachel Carson published *The Sea Around Us*, and in 1961 she published *Silent Spring*. These two books helped launch a worldwide environmental movement. What kinds of progress have occurred since Carson's first warnings?
3. The cold war was marked by mutual suspicion and hostility between the United States and its allies. In 1989, the cold war seemed to end with the collapse of the Berlin Wall. Find examples of lingering cold-war attitudes in today's newspapers.

ANALYZING VISUALS

The poster shown here demonstrates how images and celebrations function in society. Just as revolutionary music can stir up public sentiment and support, images and parades can serve as unifying forces. This poster shows victorious Chinese Communist forces entering Beijing in 1949. Along with the tanks and trucks are crowds of people carrying Communist red banners and images of Mao. Political posters like this one are often mass-produced and inexpensive—making them available to a large, general audience. A poster such as this reminds people of an important event in Chinese history, providing a common experience or recollection for a wide, diverse public.

1. How can posters be effective tools in stirring up public support?
2. Compare this modern Chinese image with earlier Chinese paintings. Are the styles of picture-making similar or different? How?
3. This poster celebrates the Communist victory in Beijing. How would you compare it with national celebrations or images you know in the United States?

USING LITERATURE

Refer to literature selections on pages 894–897 to answer these questions.

1. How would you summarize the overriding theme or message of Hikmet's poem?
2. In Bodet's poem, what does the window symbolize?
3. Both poets adopt an informal, conversational tone, even though they are writing from far away and are conscious of a large audience. How does this tone relate to the message of the poem?
4. How do these poems reflect the theme of Unit 8?

WRITING ABOUT HISTORY

1. The war to liberate Kuwait has been praised as an effort to resist aggression and preserve democracy and criticized as a cynical effort to protect U.S. oil supplies. Choose one view and write a brief historical sketch outlining your views. Compare your sketch with those of your classmates. Can you find any middle ground among these views?
2. The unit describes many efforts at political and economic cooperation among nations, such as the European Economic Community. Do you believe such efforts will be successful? Why or why not? Examine both possibilities before giving your conclusion.
3. The withdrawal of Great Britain as a colonial power from India created a "power vacuum" that opened the way for renewed hostilities between Hindus and Moslems. Does the decline of Soviet power in Eastern Europe suggest a similar development there? Write a brief sketch on the history of Yugoslavia, describing the various groups in that country, their differences, and the prospects for the future.

APPENDIX

ATLAS KEY

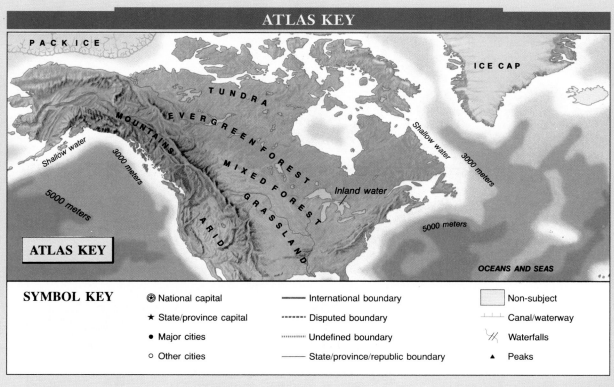

PACK ICE

ICE CAP

TUNDRA

EVERGREEN FOREST

MOUNTAINS

MIXED FOREST

ARID

GRASSLAND

Shallow water

Shallow water

3000 meters

3000 meters

5000 meters

5000 meters

Inland water

OCEANS AND SEAS

ATLAS KEY

SYMBOL KEY

⊛ National capital	—— International boundary	▭ Non-subject
★ State/province capital	------ Disputed boundary	⊢⊢⊢ Canal/waterway
● Major cities	·········· Undefined boundary	⫽ Waterfalls
○ Other cities	—— State/province/republic boundary	▲ Peaks

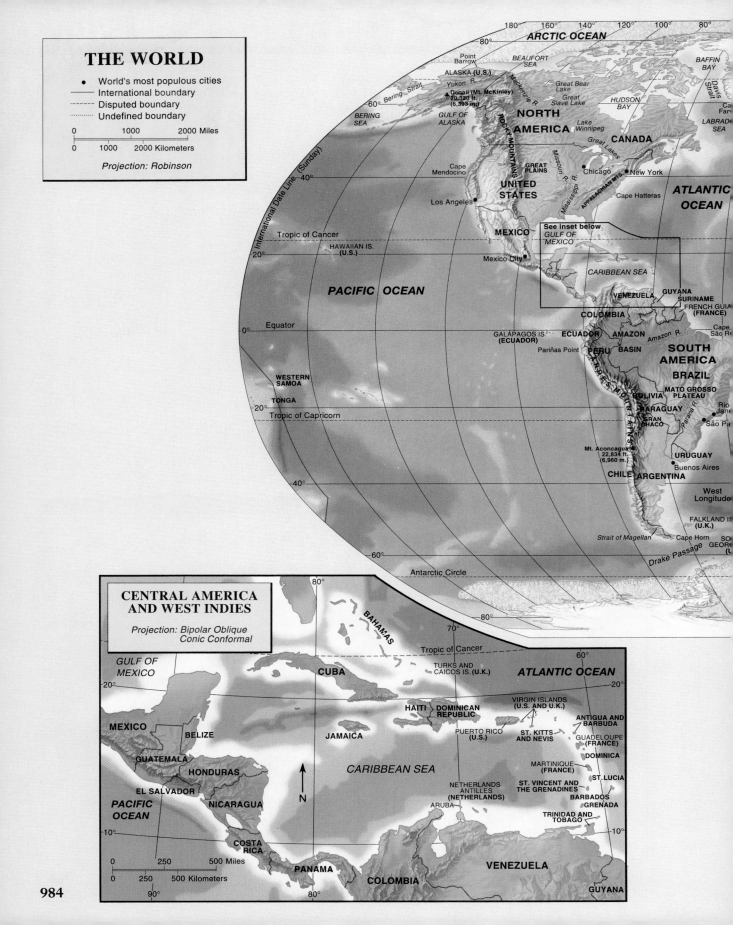

THE WORLD

- World's most populous cities
— International boundary
-- Disputed boundary
··· Undefined boundary

0 1000 2000 Miles
0 1000 2000 Kilometers

Projection: Robinson

ARCTIC OCEAN

180° 160° 140° 120° 100° 80°

Point Barrow
BEAUFORT SEA
BAFFIN BAY
Davis Strait
ALASKA (U.S.)
Yukon R.
Denali (Mt. McKinley) 20,320 ft. (6,393 m.)
Mackenzie R.
NORTH AMERICA
Great Bear Lake
Great Slave Lake
HUDSON BAY
CANADA
LABRADOR SEA
BERING SEA
Bering Strait
GULF OF ALASKA
ROCKY MOUNTAINS
Lake Winnipeg
Great Lakes
80°
60°
40°

Cape Mendocino
GREAT PLAINS
Missouri R.
Mississippi R.
Chicago
New York
Cape Hatteras
APPALACHIAN MTS.
UNITED STATES
ATLANTIC OCEAN

Los Angeles

International Date Line (Sunday)

Tropic of Cancer
20°
HAWAIIAN IS. (U.S.)
MEXICO
See inset below
GULF OF MEXICO
Mexico City
CARIBBEAN SEA
VENEZUELA
GUYANA
SURINAME
FRENCH GUIANA (FRANCE)
COLOMBIA

PACIFIC OCEAN

0°
Equator
GALÁPAGOS IS. (ECUADOR)
ECUADOR
AMAZON BASIN
Amazon R.
Cape São Roque
Pariñas Point
PERU
SOUTH AMERICA
BRAZIL

WESTERN SAMOA
TONGA
20°
Tropic of Capricorn
BOLIVIA
MATO GROSSO PLATEAU
ANDES MTS.
PARAGUAY
GRAN CHACO
Paraná R.
Rio de Janeiro
São Paulo

Mt. Aconcagua 22,834 ft. (6,960 m.)
URUGUAY
Buenos Aires
CHILE
ARGENTINA
40°
West Longitude

FALKLAND IS. (U.K.)

60°
Strait of Magellan
Cape Horn
SOUTH GEORGIA (U.K.)
Drake Passage

Antarctic Circle
80°

80°
BAHAMAS
70°
60°
Tropic of Cancer
ATLANTIC OCEAN
80°

GULF OF MEXICO
20°
CUBA
TURKS AND CAICOS IS. (U.K.)
20°

MEXICO
BELIZE
HAITI
DOMINICAN REPUBLIC
VIRGIN ISLANDS (U.S. AND U.K.)
ANTIGUA AND BARBUDA
JAMAICA
PUERTO RICO (U.S.)
ST. KITTS AND NEVIS
GUADELOUPE (FRANCE)
DOMINICA
GUATEMALA
HONDURAS
MARTINIQUE (FRANCE)
ST. LUCIA
CARIBBEAN SEA
N
EL SALVADOR
ST. VINCENT AND THE GRENADINES
BARBADOS
GRENADA
PACIFIC OCEAN
NICARAGUA
NETHERLANDS ANTILLES (NETHERLANDS)
ARUBA
TRINIDAD AND TOBAGO
10°
COSTA RICA
10°

0 250 500 Miles
0 250 500 Kilometers
PANAMA
VENEZUELA
COLOMBIA
GUYANA
90°
80°

984

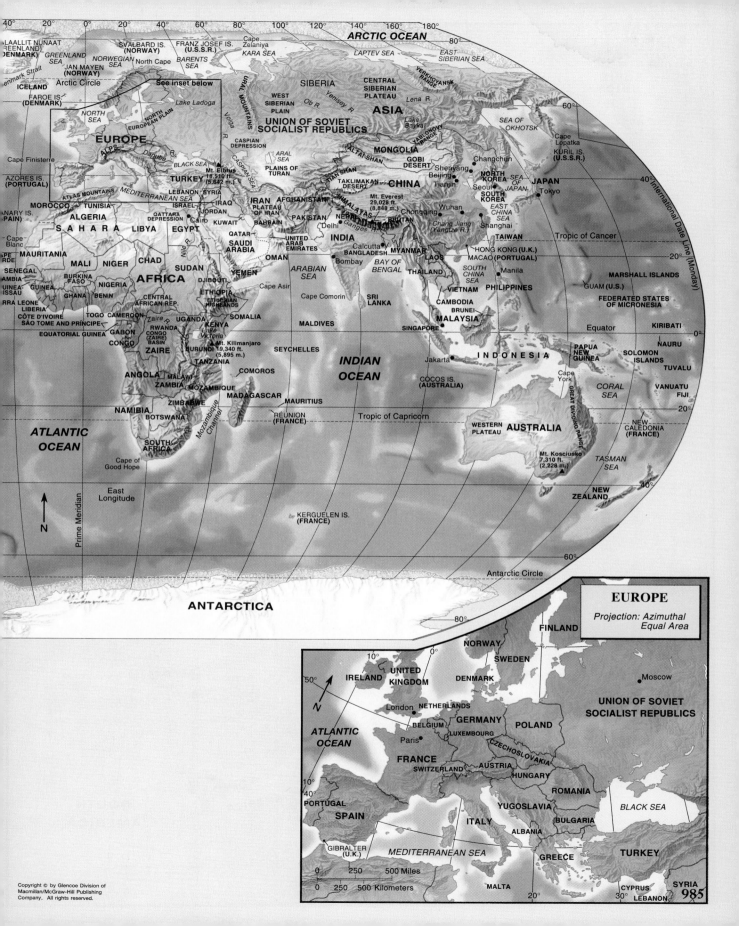

ARCTIC OCEAN

40° 20° 0° 20° 40° 60° 80° 100° 120° 140° 160° 180°

LAALLIT NUNAAT
(GREENLAND)
DENMARK)
GREENLAND
SEA
JAN MAYEN
(NORWAY)
Denmark Strait
ICELAND
FAROE IS.
(DENMARK)
Arctic Circle

SVALBARD IS.
(NORWAY)
NORWEGIAN
SEA
North Cape
Cape
Zelaniya
KARA SEA
FRANZ JOSEF IS.
(U.S.S.R.)
BARENTS
SEA
LAPTEV SEA
EAST
SIBERIAN SEA
80°

See inset below

NORTH
SEA
EUROPE
NORTH
EUROPEAN PLAIN
ALPS
Cape Finisterre
Danube R.
BLACK SEA
TURKEY
Mt. Elbrus
18,510 ft.
(5,642 m.)

URAL MOUNTAINS
Lake Ladoga
Volga R.
Ob R.
Yenisey R.
Lena R.

WEST
SIBERIAN
PLAIN
UNION OF SOVIET
SOCIALIST REPUBLICS

SIBERIA
CENTRAL
SIBERIAN
PLATEAU
ASIA
VERKHOYANSK
RANGE

60°

AZORES IS.
(PORTUGAL)
MOROCCO
TUNISIA
ALGERIA
SAHARA
LIBYA
EGYPT

CANARY IS.
(SPAIN)
Cape
Blanc

MAURITANIA
MALI
NIGER
CHAD
SUDAN
PE
VERDE
SENEGAL
GAMBIA
GUINEA-
BISSAU
GUINEA
SIERRA LEONE
LIBERIA
CÔTE D'IVOIRE
BURKINA
FASO
GHANA
TOGO
BENIN
NIGERIA
CAMEROON
CENTRAL
AFRICAN REP.
AFRICA

CASPIAN
DEPRESSION
ATLAS MOUNTAINS
MEDITERRANEAN SEA
LEBANON
SYRIA
ISRAEL
JORDAN
IRAQ
IRAN
QATTARA
DEPRESSION
Cairo
KUWAIT
Nile R.
QATAR
SAUDI
ARABIA
YEMEN
Cape Asir
DJIBOUTI
ETHIOPIA

CASPIAN
SEA
ARAL
SEA
PLAINS OF
TURAN
TIAN SHAN
ALTAI SHAN
TAKLIMAKAN
DESERT
PLATEAU
OF IRAN
AFGHANISTAN
BAHRAIN
PAKISTAN
HIMALAYAS
Mt. Everest
29,028 ft.
(8,848 m.)
NEPAL
Delhi
Ganges
UNITED
ARAB
EMIRATES
OMAN
ARABIAN
SEA
Cape Comorin
SEYCHELLES

MONGOLIA
GOBI
DESERT
Changchun
Shenyang
Beijing
Tianjin
CHINA
Chongqing
Wuhan
Chang Jiang
(Yangtze R.)
Shanghai
BHUTAN
INDIA
Calcutta
BANGLADESH
MYANMAR
Bombay
BAY OF
BENGAL
THAILAND
LAOS
VIETNAM
CAMBODIA
BRUNEI
MALAYSIA
SINGAPORE
SRI
LANKA
MALDIVES

YABLONOVY
RANGE
Lake Baykal
SEA OF
OKHOTSK
Cape
Lopatka
KURIL IS.
(U.S.S.R.)
NORTH
KOREA
SEA
OF
JAPAN
Seoul
SOUTH
KOREA
JAPAN
Tokyo
EAST
CHINA
SEA
Tropic of Cancer
TAIWAN
HONG KONG (U.K.)
MACAO (PORTUGAL)
SOUTH
CHINA
SEA
Manila
PHILIPPINES

40°

20°

International Date Line (Monday)

MARSHALL ISLANDS
GUAM (U.S.)
FEDERATED STATES
OF MICRONESIA

EQUATORIAL GUINEA
GABON
CONGO
ZAIRE
RWANDA
CONGO
(ZAIRE)
BASIN
UGANDA
BURUNDI
KENYA
Lake
Victoria
Mt. Kilimanjaro
19,340 ft.
(5,895 m.)
TANZANIA
SOMALIA
ETHIOPIAN
HIGHLANDS
Zaire

COMOROS
Jakarta
INDONESIA
PAPUA
NEW
GUINEA
Cape
York
SOLOMON
ISLANDS
Equator
KIRIBATI
NAURU
TUVALU

0°

INDIAN
OCEAN
COCOS IS.
(AUSTRALIA)
GREAT DIVIDING RANGE
CORAL
SEA
VANUATU
FIJI
NEW
CALEDONIA
(FRANCE)

ANGOLA
MALAWI
ZAMBIA
ZIMBABWE
MOZAMBIQUE
MADAGASCAR
MAURITIUS
Mozambique
Channel
NAMIBIA
BOTSWANA
RÉUNION
(FRANCE)
Tropic of Capricorn
WESTERN
PLATEAU
AUSTRALIA
Mt. Kosciusko
7,310 ft.
(2,228 m.)
TASMAN
SEA

20°

ATLANTIC
OCEAN
SOUTH
AFRICA
Cape of
Good Hope

East
Longitude
Prime Meridian

N

KERGUELEN IS.
(FRANCE)

NEW
ZEALAND

40°

60°

Antarctic Circle

80°

ANTARCTICA

Copyright © by Glencoe Division of
Macmillan/McGraw-Hill Publishing
Company. All rights reserved.

EUROPE
*Projection: Azimuthal
Equal Area*

FINLAND
NORWAY
SWEDEN
Moscow
UNION OF SOVIET
SOCIALIST REPUBLICS

10° 0°
50°
IRELAND
UNITED
KINGDOM
DENMARK
London
NETHERLANDS
N
BELGIUM
GERMANY
POLAND
ATLANTIC
OCEAN
Paris
LUXEMBOURG
CZECHOSLOVAKIA
FRANCE
SWITZERLAND
AUSTRIA
HUNGARY
ROMANIA
BLACK SEA
10°
40°
PORTUGAL
SPAIN
ITALY
YUGOSLAVIA
BULGARIA
ALBANIA
GIBRALTER
(U.K.)
MEDITERRANEAN SEA
GREECE
TURKEY

0 250 500 Miles
0 250 500 Kilometers

MALTA
CYPRUS
LEBANON
SYRIA
20°
30°

985

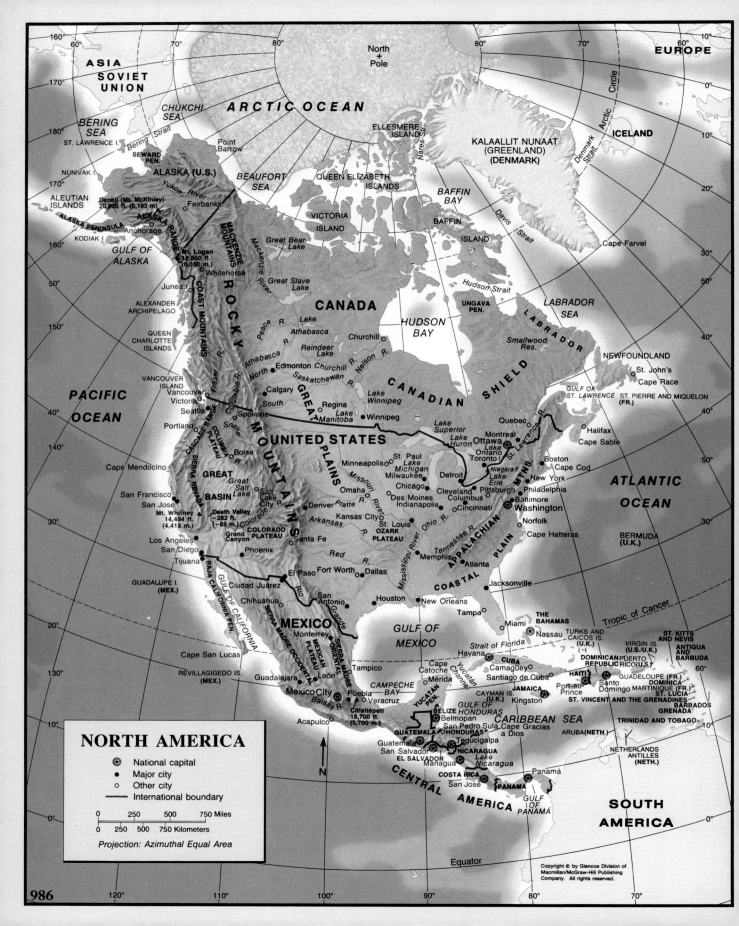

NORTH AMERICA

- ⊛ National capital
- • Major city
- ○ Other city
- —— International boundary

0 250 500 750 Miles

0 250 500 750 Kilometers

Projection: Azimuthal Equal Area

986

Copyright © by Glencoe Division of
Macmillan/McGraw-Hill Publishing
Company. All rights reserved.

SOUTH AMERICA

NORTH AMERICA
CENTRAL AMERICA

CARIBBEAN SEA

Pt. Gallinas
GUAJIRA PEN.
Barranquilla
Maracaibo
Maracay
MARGARITA I.
GRENADA
PARIA PEN.
TRINIDAD AND TOBAGO
Cartagena
Lake Maracaibo
Valencia
Caracas
Cumaná
Delta of the Orinoco

GULF OF DARIÉN
GULF OF PANAMÁ Medellín
Cúcuta
San Cristóbal
Bucaramanga
MERIDA RANGE
LLANOS
Orinoco River
Ciudad Bolívar
Ciudad Guayana
Guri Res.
Georgetown
Paramaribo
Van Blommestein Res.
Cayenne

VENEZUELA
Manizales
Tolima Peak 17,109 ft. (5,215 m.)
Bogotá
Cali
COLOMBIA
GUIANA HIGHLANDS
PACARAIMA MOUNTAINS
GUYANA
SURINAME
FRENCH GUIANA (FR.)
TUMUCUMAQUE MOUNTAINS

Cape San Francisco
Equator
Quito
Mt. Chimborazo 20,561 ft. (6,267 m.)
Ambato
Portoviejo
ECUADOR
Guayaquil
GULF OF GUAYAQUIL
Cuenca
Iquitos
Caquetá R.
Putumayo R.
Negro River
Branco R.
Essequibo R.
Delta of the Amazon
Cape Maguarinho
Belém
São Luis
Equator

Pariñas Point
Marañón River
PERU
Chiclayo
Trujillo
CORDILLERA ORIENTAL
Huascarán Peak 22,204 ft. (6,768 m.)
Chimbote
A M A Z O N
B A S I N
Manaus
Amazon River
Tocantins River
Teresina
Fortaleza
Cape São Roque
Natal

S E L V A S
Rio Branco
Purus R.
Madeira River
Tapajós R.
Xingu River
Araguaia River
Esperanca Reservoir
Sobradinho Reservoir
Recife
PLATEAU OF BORBOREMA
Maceió

Callao
Lima
Cuzco
Lake Titicaca
Ancohuma Peak 21,489 ft. (6,550 m.)
La Paz
BOLIVIA
Cochabamba
B R A Z I L
MATO GROSSO PLATEAU
Goiânia
Brasília
São Francisco R.
BRAZILIAN HIGHLANDS
Tres Marias Reservoir
Belo Horizonte
Bandeira Peak 9,481 ft. (2,890 m.)
Aracaju
Salvador
TODOS OS SANTOS BAY

PACIFIC OCEAN
Point Carreta
Arequipa
ANDES
BOLIVIAN PLATEAU
Oruro
Lake Poopó
Sucre
Potosí
A N D E S
Arica
Picomayo River
Simão Res.
Jupiá Res.
Campo Grande
Concepción
Campinas
Osasco
São Paulo
Ilha Solteira Res.
Furnas Reservoir
Volta Redonda
Santos
Santo André
Nova Iguaçu
Petrópolis
Niterói
Rio de Janeiro
Juiz de Fora

Tropic of Capricorn
Antofagasta
ATACAMA DESERT
Mt. Ojos del Salado 22,516 ft. (6,863 m.)
Salta
GRAN CHACO
PARAGUAY
Paraguay River
Asunción
Itaipú Res.
Iguazú Falls
Paraná River
Curitiba
Pôrto Alegre
Tropic of Capricorn

SAN FÉLIX I. (CHILE)
SAN AMBROSIO I. (CHILE)
Tucumán
Resistencia
Santiago del Estero
Corrientes
Salado R.
Uruguay R.
Rivera
Lake dos Patos
Lake Mirim

JUAN FERNÁNDEZ IS. (CHILE)
Mt. Aconcagua 23,834 ft. (6,960 m.)
Viña del Mar
Mendoza
Córdoba
CÓRDOBA RANGE
Rosario
Mar Chiquita Lake
Santa Fé
Paysandú
Negro Res.
URUGUAY
Montevideo

Talcahuano
Concepción
Temuco
Valparaíso
Santiago
CHILE
ARGENTINA
Buenos Aires
La Plata
PAMPAS
Punta del Este
RÍO DE LA PLATA
Cape San Antonio

Colorado River
Negro River
Mar del Plata
Bahía Blanca
Rasa Point
BLANCA BAY

ATLANTIC OCEAN

PATAGONIA
Chubut R.
VALDÉS DEPRESSION
VALDÉS PEN.
GULF OF SAN MATÍAS

CHILOÉ ISLAND
CHONOS ARCHIPELAGO
Comodoro Rivadavia
GULF OF SAN JORGE
Cape Tres Puntas

PEÑAS GULF
Lake Buenos Aires
Lake San Martin
Lake Argentino
GRANDE BAY

QUEEN ADELAIDE ARCH.
Strait of Magellan
Punta Arenas
TIERRA DEL FUEGO
ESTADOS ISLAND
Cape Horn
Stanley
FALKLAND ISLANDS (U.K.)
SOUTH GEORGIA I. (U.K.)

N

SOUTH AMERICA

- ⊛ National capital
- ● Major city
- ○ Other city
- ─── International boundary

0   250   500 Miles
0   250   500 Kilometers

Projection: Azimuthal Equal Area

Copyright © by Glencoe Division of Macmillan/McGraw-Hill Publishing Company. All rights reserved.

WESTERN EUROPE

- ⊛ National capital
- ● Major city
- ○ Other city
- —— International boundary
- ⊥⊤⊥ Canal

0   100   200   300 Miles

0 100 200 300
Kilometers

Projection: Azimuthal Equal Area

ICELAND
Akureyri
⊛ Reykjavík
Vatnajökull Glacier
Hvannadalshnúkur
6,952 ft.
(2,119 m.)

NORTH CAPE
Tromsø
Lake Inari
HIMNØY I.
Narvik
NORWEGIAN SEA
SCANDINAVIAN HIGHLANDS
Luleå
SWEDEN
FINLAND
Oulu
Lake Oulu
FAROE IS.
(DEN.)
Tórshavn
Trondheim
GULF OF BOTHNIA
Vaasa
L. Päijänne
Lake Saimaa
SHETLAND IS. (U.K.)
▲ Goldhöpiggen
8,097 ft.
(2,468 m.)
Bergen
Sundsvall
Tampere
ÅLAND I.
Turku
Helsinki ⊛
Espoo
Cape Wrath
ORKNEY IS.
MORAY FIRTH
NORWAY ⊛
Oslo
Stavanger
Orebro
Uppsala
GULF OF FINLAND
OUTER HEBRIDES IS.
SCOTLAND
Ben Nevis
4,406 ft.
(1,343 m.)
Skagerrak
Lake Vänern
Lake Mälaren
Stockholm ⊛
GOTLAND I.
Londonderry
Glasgow
Edinburgh
NORTH SEA
Ålborg
Lake Vättern
Norrköping
NORTHERN IRELAND (U.K.)
PENNINE RANGE
Belfast
ISLE OF MAN
UNITED KINGDOM
JUTLAND
DENMARK
Århus
Helsingborg
ÖLAND I.
BALTIC SEA
IRELAND
Dublin ⊛
IRISH SEA
Bradford
Leeds
Copenhagen ⊛
Malmö
BORNHOLM I.
Limerick
Liverpool
Sheffield
Odense
SJAELLAND
Cork
Manchester
Kiel
Rostock
Cape Clear
WALES
Birmingham
Coventry
NETHERLANDS
Hamburg
St. George's Channel
ENGLAND
Groningen
Bremen
Elbe R.
Berlin ⊛
Cardiff
Amsterdam
Weser R.
Hannover
Oder River
Bristol
Utrecht
Essen
Mittelland Canal
Magdeburg
EASTERN
Land's End
Southampton
London ⊛
The Hague
Rotterdam
Dortmund
Halle
Leipzig
EUROPE
English Channel
Strait of Dover
Gent
Cologne
GERMANY
Erfurt
Dresden
GUERNSEY I. (U.K.)
Le Havre
BELGIUM
Antwerp
Liège
Bonn
Frankfurt
Chemnitz
JERSEY I. (U.K.)
Seine R.
Brussels ⊛
LUXEMBOURG
Reims
Luxembourg ⊛
ATLANTIC
Raz Point
BRETON PEN.
Rennes
Paris ⊛
Marne R.
Rhine River
Stuttgart
Nürnberg
OCEAN
Nantes
Marne-Rhine Canal
Strasbourg
Danube
Munich
Linz
Loire
Salzburg
Vienna ⊛
FRANCE
CENTRAL MASSIF
Lausanne
Zürich
Bodensee
LIECHTENSTEIN
AUSTRIA
Graz
La Coruña
BAY OF BISCAY
Bordeaux
Lyon
Geneva
Bern ⊛
Vaduz ⊛
Innsbruck
Klagenfurt
Cape Finisterre
CANTABRIAN MTS.
Ebro R.
Bilbao
Garonne R.
Mt. Blanc
15,771 ft.
(4,807 m.)
SWITZERLAND
ALPS
Monte Rosa
(15,203 ft.)
(4,634 m.)
Venice
G. OF VENICE
Trieste
Porto
Duero R.
Valladolid
PYRENEES
Toulouse
Midi Canal
Rhône R.
Po
R. Padova
ADRIATIC SEA
PORTUGAL
Coimbra
SPAIN
Aneto Peak
11,168 ft.
(3,404 m.)
ANDORRA
Andorra
la Vella
Montpellier
Marseille
Nice
Turin
PO VALLEY
Milan
Genoa
Bologna
SAN MARINO
San Marino
Lisbon ⊛
Tagus River
IBERIAN PENINSULA
Madrid ⊛
Zaragoza
GULF OF LION
Toulon
MONACO
Monaco
LIGURIAN SEA
Florence
APENNINES
ITALY
Setúbal
Guadiana R.
Barcelona
ELBA I.
VATICAN CITY
Rome ⊛
SIERRA MORENA
Córdoba
Valencia
BALEARIC IS. (SP.)
MALLORCA I.
MENORCA I.
CORSICA (FR.)
Naples
Bari
G. OF TARANTO
Seville
Guadalquivir R.
Murcia
GULF OF VALENCIA
Cape Nao
Palma
IBIZA I.
SARDINIA (IT.)
TYRRHENIAN SEA
Taranto
Strait of Otranto
ASIA
Cape St. Vincent
Granada
Mulhacén
11,410 ft.
(3,478 m.)
Málaga
GIBRALTAR
(U.K.)
Strait of Gibraltar
Cagliari
Palermo
C. Spartivento
IONIAN SEA
Salonika
Larissa
AEGEAN SEA
GREECE
Patras
Piraeus
Athens ⊛
Strait of Sicily
Mt. Etna
10,858 ft.
(3,340 m.)
Catania
SICILY
PELOPONESE PEN.
RHODES
PANTELLERIA (IT.)
Valletta
IONIAN IS.
MALTA ⊛
Iráklion
AFRICA
MEDITERRANEAN SEA
CRETE (GR.)

Arctic Circle
Prime Meridian

N

Copyright © by Glencoe Division of
Macmillan/McGraw-Hill Publishing
Company. All rights reserved.

988

EASTERN EUROPE

⊛ National capital
● Major city
○ Other city
━━━ International boundary
⊥⊥⊥ Canal

0   250   500 Miles
0   250   500 Kilometers

Projection: Azimuthal Equal Area

Copyright © by Glencoe Division of
Macmillan/McGraw-Hill Publishing
Company. All rights reserved.

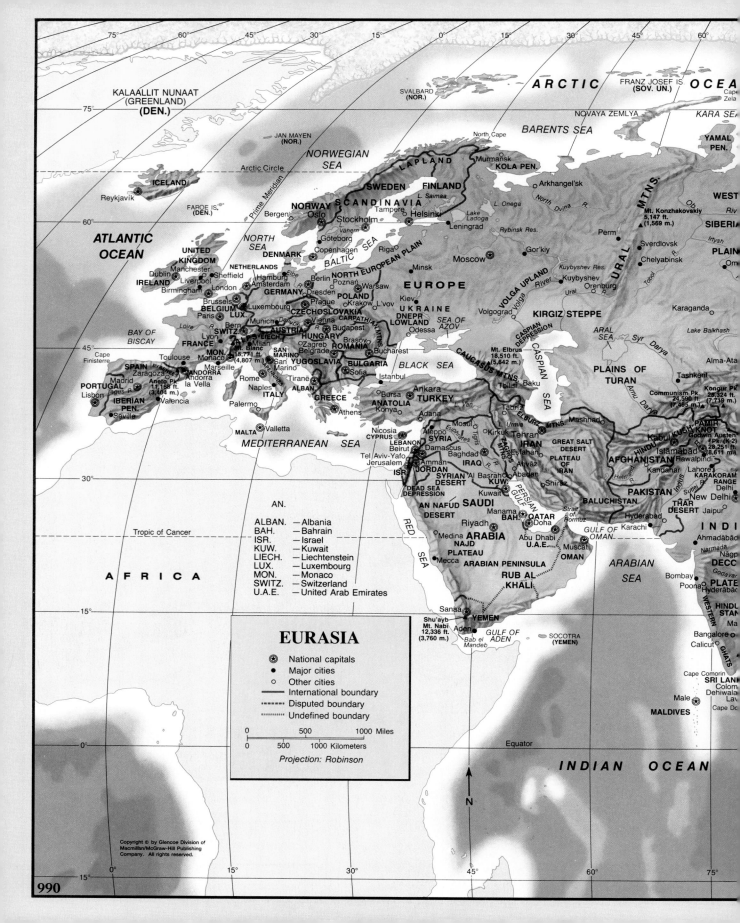

75°   60°   45°   30°   15°   0°   15°   30°   45°   60°

KALAALLIT NUNAAT
(GREENLAND)
(DEN.)

ARCTIC   FRANZ JOSEF IS   **OCEA**
                (SOV. UN.)
                            Cape
                            Zela
SVALBARD   NOVAYA ZEMLYA   **KARA SEA**
(NOR.)

75°   **BARENTS SEA**   **YAMAL
                                                                PEN.**

JAN MAYEN
(NOR.)
NORWEGIAN
SEA   North Cape
Arctic Circle   Murmansk   **KOLA PEN.**   **WEST**
ICELAND   LAPLAND   Arkhangel'sk   Riv
                                                                    Mt. Konzhakovskiy
Reykjavík   FAROE IS.   **SWEDEN FINLAND**   L. Saimaa   North Dvina R.   5,147 ft.   **SIBERIA**
             (DEN.)   **NORWAY SCANDINAVIA**   L. Onega   (1,569 m.)   Irtysh
60°   Bergen Oslo Tampere Helsinki   Leningrad   Perm   Sverdlovsk   **PLAIN**
ATLANTIC   Göteborg Stockholm   Rybinsk Res.   Kuybyshev Res. Chelyabinsk   Om
OCEAN   **NORTH   DENMARK** Copenhagen Riga   Gor'kiy   **URAL   MTS.**
             SEA   Hamburg Berlin **NORTH EUROPEAN PLAIN** Moscow   Kuybyshev   Orenburg   Tobol
UNITED Manchester Amsterdam Poznań Warsaw Minsk   **VOLGA UPLAND** Ural
KINGDOM Sheffield **NETHERLANDS GERMANY** Dresden **EUROPE**   Volgograd   **KIRGIZ STEPPE**   Karaganda
Dublin Liverpool London   **BELGIUM** Prague **POLAND** Kiev **UKRAINE**   **CASPIAN**   **ARAL** Syr Darya Lake Balkhash
IRELAND Birmingham   Brussels **LUX.** Kraków L'vov **DNEPR-**   **DEPRESSION**   **SEA**
             Paris Luxembourg **CZECHOSLOVAKIA** **LOWLAND** **SEA OF**   Volga   **PLAINS OF**
BAY OF   **BELGIUM** Munich Vienna **CARPATHIAN MTS.** Odessa **AZOV**   Mt. Elbrus   **TURAN** Tashkent   Alma-Ata
BISCAY   **FRANCE SWITZ. AUSTRIA HUNGARY** Budapest   18,510 ft.   Communism Pk. Kongur Pk
45°   Cape   Lyon Mt. Blanc **ZZagreb ROMANIA** Brasov **BLACK SEA** (5,642 m.) **CAUCASUS MTS.** 24,590 ft. 25,324 ft.
       Finisterre   15,771 ft. **SAN** Belgrade Bucharest   Tbilisi Baku   (7,495 m.) (7,719 m.)
             Toulouse (4,807 m.) **MARINO YUGOSLAVIA BULGARIA**   **ELBURZ**   **PAMIR**
       Milan **MON.** San **BULGARIA** Sofia Istanbul   Tabriz **MTS.** Mashhad   **KUSH KNOT**
SPAIN Monaco Marino   Tiranë   **CASPIAN**   Godwin Austen
Zaragoza **ANDORRA** Rome **ALBAN.** **GREECE** Ankara **TURKEY** L. Urmia **IRAN** **GREAT SALT** Kabul Pk (K-2)
Madrid Aneto Pk. la Vella **ITALY** Naples   **ANATOLIA** Konya Adana   Mosul Tigris Tehran **DESERT** **HINDU** Islamabad 28,251 ft.
PORTUGAL IBERIAN 11,168 ft.   Palermo   Athens   Nicosia   Aleppo Kirkuk Esfahan **PLATEAU** **AFGHANISTAN** Rawalpindi (8,611 m.)
Lisbon **PEN.** (3,404 m.) Valencia   **MALTA** Valletta   **CYPRUS SYRIA** Baghdad **OF** Ahvaz Kandahar Lahore **KARAKORAM**
       Seville   **MEDITERRANEAN SEA** **LEBANON** Damascus **IRAN** Shiraz   **PAKISTAN** **RANGE** Delhi
                                        Beirut **IRAQ SYRIAN** Al Basrah   **BALUCHISTAN** Hyderabad New Delhi
                                        Tel Aviv-Yafo **JORDAN DESERT** Abadan **KUW.** **PERSIAN** **THAR** Jaipur **INDI**
30°   Jerusalem **ISR.** Amman Kuwait **GULF** **DESERT** Karachi
                                        DEAD SEA **SYRIAN** Manama Strait Ahmadābād
                                        DEPRESSION **AN NAFUD** **SAUDI** **BAH.** of   Narmada Nagp
                    AN.   **DESERT** Riyadh Doha Hormuz **GULF OF** **DECC**
                    ALBAN. — Albania   **ARABIA QATAR** **OMAN** Bombay **PLATE**
Tropic of Cancer   BAH. — Bahrain   Medina **NAJD** Abu Dhabi Muscat   Poona Hyderābād
                    ISR. — Israel   **PLATEAU** **U.A.E. OMAN** **ARABIAN** **WESTERN**
                    KUW. — Kuwait   Mecca **ARABIAN PENINSULA**   **SEA** **HINDU**
AFRICA   LIECH. — Liechtenstein   **RUB AL**   **GHATS** **STAN**
                    LUX. — Luxembourg   **KHĀLI**   Bangalore Ma
                    MON. — Monaco   Sanaa   Calicut   **GHATS**
                    SWITZ. — Switzerland   Shu'ayb **YEMEN**
15°   U.A.E. — United Arab Emirates   Mt. Nabī Aden **GULF OF** **SOCOTRA** Cape Comorin
                            12,336 ft.   **ADEN**   (YEMEN)   **SRI LAN**
                            (3,760 m.)   Bab el   Colom
                    EURASIA   Mandeb   Dehiwala
                    ⊛ National capitals   Male ⊛   Cape Do
                    • Major cities   **MALDIVES**
                    ○ Other cities
                    ─── International boundary
                    ┈┈┈ Disputed boundary
                    ∙∙∙∙∙ Undefined boundary
                    Equator   **INDIAN OCEAN**
0°   0   500   1000 Miles
                    0 500 1000 Kilometers
                    Projection: Robinson
                            N

Copyright © by Glencoe Division of
Macmillan/McGraw-Hill Publishing
Company. All rights reserved.

15°   0°   15°   30°   45°   60°   75°

90°　　　　105°　　　　120°　　　　135°　　　　150°　　　　165°　　　　180°　　　　165°　　　　150°　　　　135°

SEVERNAYA ZEMLYA

TAYMYR PEN.　　　　LAPTEV SEA　　　NEW SIBERIAN ISLANDS　　　　EAST SIBERIAN SEA　　　　75°

WRANGEL ISLAND

Noril'sk

CENTRAL SIBERIAN

Yenisey

PLATEAU

KOLYMA
PLAIN

CHUKOTSK
PEN.

Bering Strait

VERKHOYANSK RANGE

Lower

Tunguska

R.

LENA PLATEAU

Anadyr'　R.

KOLYMA RANGE

Cape Navarin

SOVIET　UNION

SIBERIA

Lena

River

Yakutsk

Magadan

60°

Angara

R.

Kolyma

R.

BERING SEA

Krasnoyarsk

Bratsk Res.

SEA OF
OKHOTSK

KAMCHATKA
PEN.

Mt. Kluchevsk
15,584 ft.
▲(4,750 m.)

KOMANDORSKIY IS.

Novosibirsk
Novosibirsk Res.

SAYAN MTNS.

Lake Baykal

STANOVOY RANGE

Cape Lopatka

ALTAY SHAN

YABLONOVY RANGE

Amur

Komsomol'sk

La Pérouse Strait

KURIL
ISLANDS

45°

mipalatinsk

Lake
Zaysan

MONGOLIA

Ulaanbaatar

DA HINGGAN LING

R.

Khabarovsk

NGARIAN
BASIN

MONGOLIAN

NORTHEAST
(MANCHURIAN)

Songhua

Jiang

L. Khanka

Sapporo

Ürümqi

PLATEAU

Harbin

Vladivostok

AN SHAN

GOBI

Changchun

PLAIN

SEA OF
JAPAN

JAPAN

TURFAN
DEPRESSION

DESERT

Shenyang

Anshan

N.

JAPAN

ASIA

Huang

Beijing

KOREA

KLIMAKAN
DESERT

CHINA

Tianjin NORTH
P'yŏngyang

P'yŏngyang

Kawasaki

Tokyo

He

He

NORTH
CHINA

Seoul

Kyōto

Yokohama

NLUN SHAN

Wei

Xi'an

PLAIN

Inchon

S. Taegu

Osaka

BAYAN HAR
SHAN

YELLOW
SEA

KOREA

Kitakyūshū

HIMALAYAS

Annapurna Pk.
6,502 ft.
8,078 m.)

PLATEAU OF
TIBET

Chengdu

Chang

Jiang

Nanjing

L. Tai

Shanghai

EAST CHINA

PACIFIC

Mt. Everest
29,028 ft.
(8,848 m.)

Lhasa

Mt. Kang

29,29 CH

Hangzhou

L. Payang

Nanchang

SEA

OCEAN

hmandu

BHUTAN

Changsha

Fuzhou

RYUKYU IS.
(JAP.)

30°

rānas

Brahmaputra

YUNGUI

Guiyang

BANGLADESH

PLATEAU

Kunming

T'aipei

NGES

Khulna

Dhaka

Jiang

Guangzhou

TAIWAN

Tropic of Cancer

Calcutta

Chittagong

MYANMAR

Macao

Victoria

Kaohsiung

ANNAMITE MTNS.

Hanoi

MACAO
(PORT.)

HONG KONG
(U.K.)

Luzon Strait

Mandalay

Haiphong

BAY OF

Chiang

LAOS

Cape Engaño

BENGAL

Mai o

Vientiane

INDOCHINA

PHILIPPINE

Bassein

Rangoon

KHORAT

Savannakhet

SOUTH

LUZON

SEA

THAILAND

PLATEAU

Da Nang

Thonburi o

Ubon
Ratchathani

Quezon City

15°

ANDAMAN IS.
(IND.)

Krung Thep
(Bangkok)

VIETNAM

Manila

Tonle Sap

CAMBODIA

CHINA

MINDORO

PHILIPPINES

ANDAMAN

Phnom Penh

Cebu

SEA

Ho Chi Minh City

SEA

PALAWAN

MINDANAO

LON

Davao

NICOBAR IS.
(IND.)

MALAY

Bandar Seri
Begawan

George Town

PEN.

SULU ARCH. Point Tinaca
(PHIL.)

Ipoh

BRUNEI

Medan

MALAYSIA

Kuala Lumpur

BORNEO
HIGHLANDS

HALMAHERA

SUMATRA

Singapore

SINGAPORE

BORNEO

Equator

0°

BARISAN MTNS.

Pontianak

CELEBES

Cape d'Urville

Jayapura

Jambi

Banjarmasin

BANDA SEA

Jaya Pk.
16,499 ft.
(5,029 m.)

Palembang

JAVA SEA

Ujung Pandang

INDONESIA

NEW GUINEA

Sunda Str.

Jakarta

Semarang

Bandung

Surabaya

JAVA

90°　　　　105°　　　　120°　　　　135°　　　　150°　　　　165°

15°

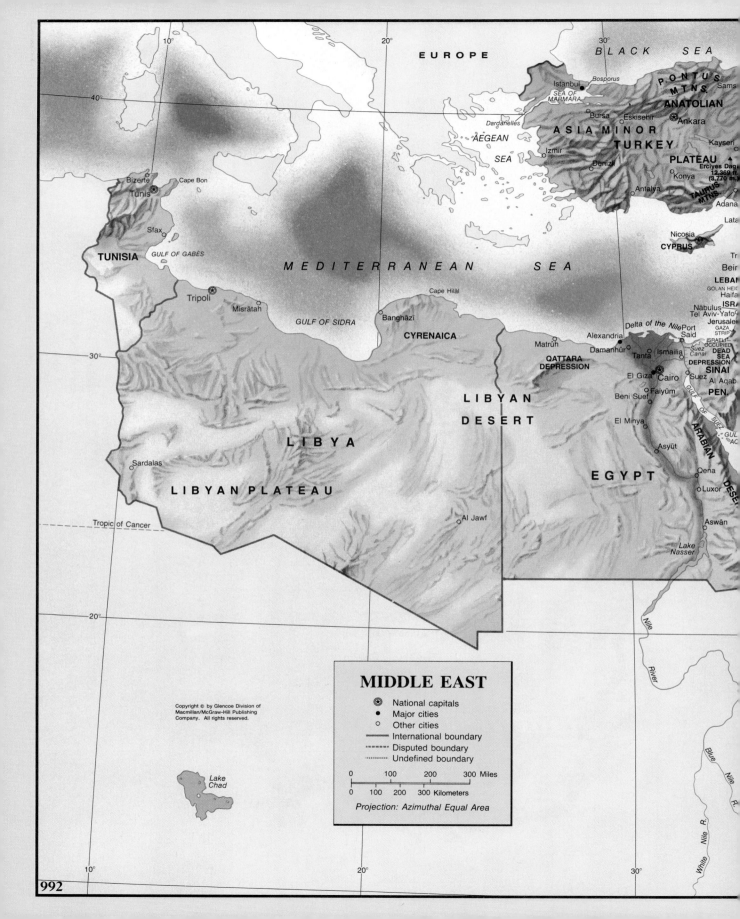

EUROPE

BLACK SEA

SEA OF MARMARA
Bosporus
Istanbul

PONTUS MTNS.
Sams

Dardanelles

ANATOLIAN

ASIA MINOR

Bursa
Eskisehir
Ankara ⊛

AEGEAN SEA

TURKEY

Izmír

Denizli

PLATEAU
Kayseri

Erciyes Dag
12,369 ft.
(3,770 m.)

Konya

Antalya

TAURUS MTNS.

Adana

Bizerte
Cape Bon

Nicosia ⊛

Lata

Tunis ⊛

CYPRUS

Tr

MEDITERRANEAN   SEA

Beir

Sfax

LEBA

GULF OF GABÈS

GOLAN HEIG
Haifa

TUNISIA

Cape Hilāl

Nábulus
Tel Aviv-Yafo

ISR

Tripoli ⊛

Banghāzi

Delta of the Nile
Port
Said

Jerusale

Misrātah

GAZA
STRIP

GULF OF SIDRA

CYRENAICA

Alexandria

Matrūh
Damanhūr

Tanta

ISRAELI
OCCUPIED
DEAD
SEA

Ismailia

*Suez
Canal*

Cairo ⊛

DEPRESSION

SINAI

QATTARA
DEPRESSION

Suez

Al Aqab

El Giza

LIBYAN

PEN.

Beni Suef
Faiyūm

ARABIAN

GUL
AC

DESERT

El Minya

LIBYA

Sardalas

EGYPT

Qena

LIBYAN PLATEAU

Luxor

DESE

Asyūt

Tropic of Cancer

Aswān

Al Jawf

*Lake
Nasser*

MIDDLE EAST

⊛ National capitals
● Major cities
○ Other cities
────── International boundary
┄┄┄┄ Disputed boundary
┈┈┈┈ Undefined boundary

0	100	200	300 Miles
0	100 200	300 Kilometers	

Projection: Azimuthal Equal Area

Copyright © by Glencoe Division of
Macmillan/McGraw-Hill Publishing
Company. All rights reserved.

*Lake
Chad*

Nile

River

Blue
Nile

R.

Nile R.

White

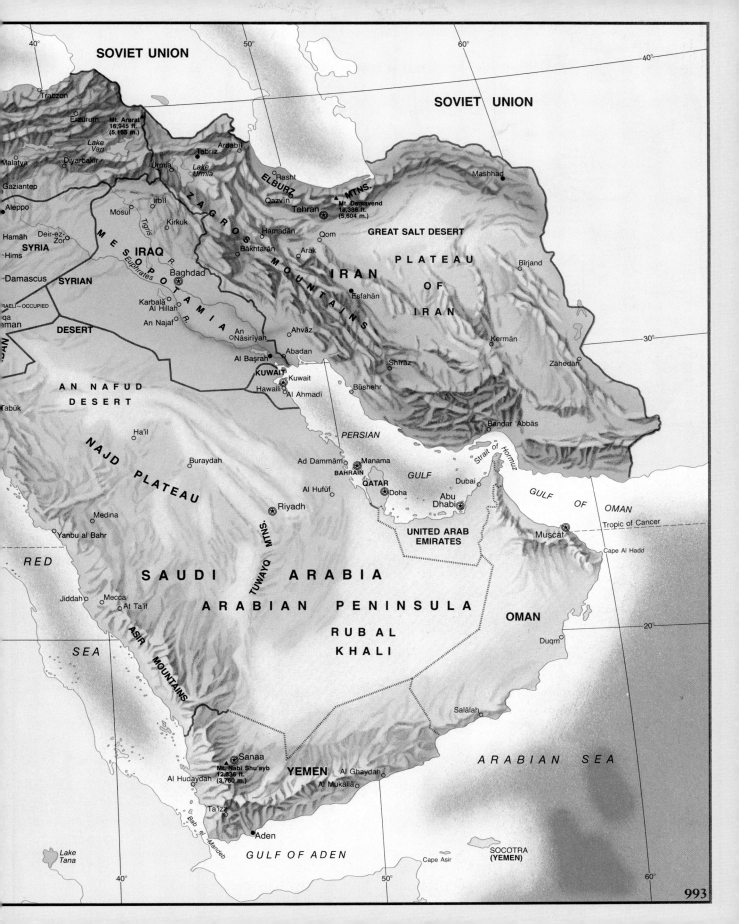

SOVIET UNION

SOVIET UNION

Trabzon

Erzurum Mt. Ararat
16,945 ft.
(5,165 m.)

Lake
Van

Tabrīz Ardabīl

Malatya Diyarbakır Urmia Lake
Urmia

Gaziantep Rasht Mashhad

Aleppo Irbīl Mosul Kirkuk Qazvīn ELBURZ MTNS.

Hamāh Deir-ez- Tehran Mt. Demavend
18,386 ft.
(5,604 m.)

Hims SYRIA Zor Tigris R. Hamadān GREAT SALT DESERT

Damascus SYRIAN MESOPOTAMIA IRAQ Baghdad Qom Arāk PLATEAU

ISRAELI—OCCUPIED Euphrates Bākhtarān OF Bīrjand

qa DESERT Karbalā An Najaf Esfahān IRAN

man Al Hillah Ahvāz ZAGROS MOUNTAINS

An
Nāsirīyah Abadan Kermān

Tabūk AN NAFUD Al Baṣrah Shīrāz Zāhedān

DESERT KUWAIT Kuwait

Hawalli Būshehr Bandar 'Abbās

Ha'il Al Ahmadī

NAJD PLATEAU PERSIAN Strait of Hormuz

Buraydah Ad Dammām Manama GULF GULF

Medina BAHRAIN QATAR Dubai OF OMAN

Al Hufūf Doha Abu Tropic of Cancer

Yanbu al Bahr Riyadh Dhabi Muscat

UNITED ARAB Cape Al Hadd

RED SAUDI ARABIA EMIRATES

Jiddah Mecca TUWAYQ MTNS. OMAN

At Ta'if ARABIAN PENINSULA

ASIR RUB AL Duqm

SEA KHALI

MOUNTAINS

Salālah

Sanaa ARABIAN SEA

Mt. Nabī Shu'ayb YEMEN Al Ghaydah

Al Hudaydah 12,336 ft. Al Mukallā

(3,760 m.)

Ta'izz

Lake Aden

Tana GULF OF ADEN Cape Asir SOCOTRA
(YEMEN)

993

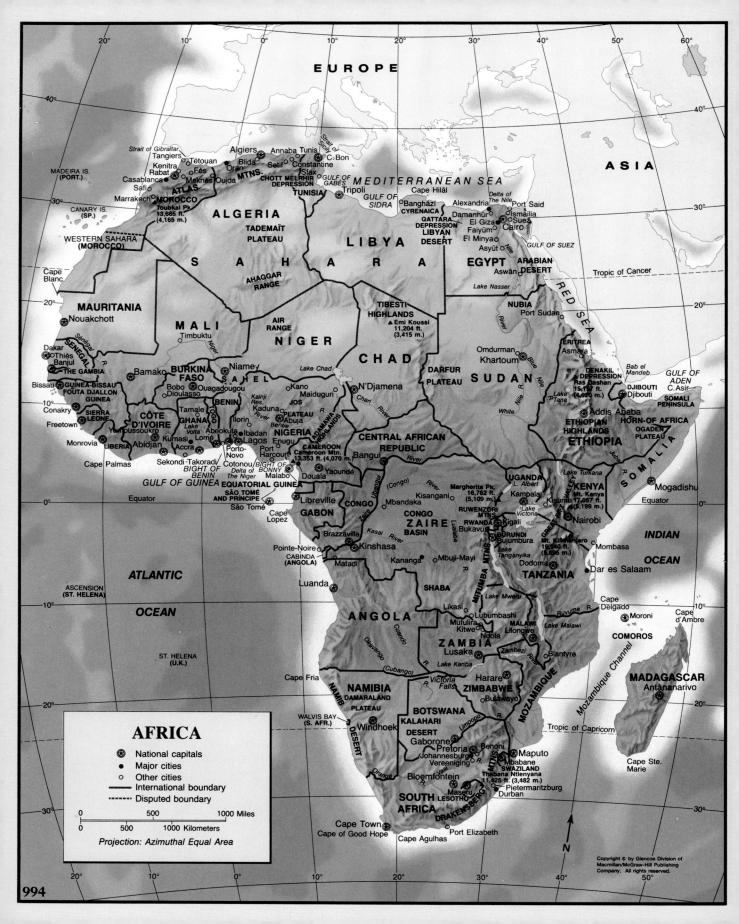

AFRICA

- ⊛ National capitals
- ● Major cities
- ○ Other cities
- —— International boundary
- - - - Disputed boundary

| 0   500   1000 Miles |
| 0   500   1000 Kilometers |

Projection: Azimuthal Equal Area

EUROPE

ASIA

MEDITERRANEAN SEA

Strait of Gibraltar
Tangiers
Tétouan
Algiers   Annaba Tunis
Kenitra   Fès   Oran Blida Sétif Constantine C. Bon
Rabat   Meknès Oujda   Stax
Casablanca
Safi   CHOTT MELRHIR   GULF OF   Tripoli
ATLAS   DEPRESSION   GABES
Marrakech   MOROCCO   TUNISIA
            Toubkal Pk.   Cape Hilâl
            13,665 ft.   Banghāzī
            (4,165 m.)   CYRENAICA
MADEIRA IS.
(PORT.)

CANARY IS.
(SP.)

WESTERN SAHARA
(MOROCCO)

Cape
Blanc

MAURITANIA
Nouakchott

ALGERIA

TADEMAÏT
PLATEAU

AHAGGAR
RANGE

MALI

S A H A R A

AIR
RANGE

NIGER

LIBYA

LIBYAN
DESERT

QATTARA
DEPRESSION

EGYPT

Delta of
The Nile
Alexandria   Port Said
Damanhûr   Ismâ'ilîa
El Gîza   Suez
Faiyûm   Cairo
El Minya
Asyûṭ

ARABIAN
DESERT

GULF OF SUEZ

Tropic of Cancer

TIBESTI
HIGHLANDS
▲ Emi Koussi
11,204 ft.
(3,415 m.)

NUBIA

Lake Nasser

Aswân

Port Sudan

RED SEA

Bab el
Mandeb

GULF OF
ADEN
C. Asir

ERITREA
Asmara

DENAKIL
DEPRESSION
Ras Dashan
15,157 ft.
(4,620 m.)

DJIBOUTI
Djibouti

SOMALI
PENINSULA

HORN OF AFRICA

SENEGAL
Dakar
Thiès
Banjul
THE GAMBIA
Bissau
GUINEA-BISSAU
FOUTA DJALLON
GUINEA
Conakry
SIERRA LEONE
Freetown

BURKINA
FASO
Bamako
Bobo
Dioulasso

Niamey

SAHEL

Ouagadougou

BENIN

Lake Chad

Kano
Maiduguri

N'Djamena

CHAD

Chari River

DARFUR
PLATEAU

SUDAN

Omdurman
Khartoum

Blue Nile

Lake
Tana

White Nile

ETHIOPIAN
HIGHLANDS

Addis Ababa

ETHIOPIA

OGADEN
PLATEAU

SOMALIA

Mogadishu

CÔTE
D'IVOIRE
Yamoussoukro
Monrovia
LIBERIA
Abidjan
Cape Palmas

Tamale
GHANA
Kumasi
Accra

Ilorin
Abeokuta
Lagos
Lomé
Porto-
Novo
Cotonou
Malabo

Kaduna
JOS
PLATEAU
Abuja
Benue River
NIGERIA
Enugu
Port
Harcourt

ADAMAWA
HIGHLANDS

CAMEROON
Cameroon Mtn.
13,353 ft. (4,070 m.)
Yaoundé
Douala

CENTRAL AFRICAN
REPUBLIC

Bangui

Ubangi River

Congo River

UGANDA
Lake Turkana

L. Albert
Kampala

Lake Turkana

KENYA
Mt. Kenya
17,057 ft.
(5,199 m.)
Nairobi
Mombasa

Equator

BIGHT OF
BENIN
Delta of
The Niger
BIGHT OF
BONNY
GULF OF GUINEA

SÃO TOMÉ
AND PRÍNCIPE
São Tomé
Cape
Lopez

EQUATORIAL GUINEA
Libreville

GABON

CONGO

Brazzaville

Mbandaka

Kisangani

CONGO
ZAIRE
BASIN

Margherita Pk.
16,762 ft.
(5,109 m.)
RUWENZORI
MTNS.
RWANDA
Bukavu
BURUNDI
Bujumbura

Kigali

Lake
Victoria
Kisumu

Mt. Kilimanjaro
19,340 ft.
(5,895 m.)

Dodoma

Dar es Salaam

INDIAN
OCEAN

ATLANTIC

ASCENSION
(ST. HELENA)

OCEAN

ST. HELENA
(U.K.)

Pointe-Noire
CABINDA
(ANGOLA)
Matadi
Kinshasa
Kananga
Mbuji-Mayi

Kasai River

Luanda

ANGOLA

SHABA

Likasi
Lubumbashi
Mufulira
Kitwe
Ndola

MITUMBA MTNS.

Lake Mweru

Lake
Tanganyika

Lake Malawi

MALAWI
Lilongwe

Blantyre

Ruvuma R.

Cape
Delgado

Moroni

Cape
d'Ambre

COMOROS

MADAGASCAR

Antananarivo

ZAMBIA
Lusaka

Zambezi River

Cape Fria

Okavango

NAMIBIA

DAMARALAND
PLATEAU

WALVIS BAY
(S. AFR.)
Windhoek

NAMIB
DESERT

KALAHARI
DESERT
Gaborone

Lake Kariba

Victoria
Falls

ZIMBABWE
Harare
Bulawayo

Limpopo R.

BOTSWANA

MOZAMBIQUE

Maputo

Mozambique Channel

Tropic of Capricorn

Cape Ste.
Marie

Orange R.

Pretoria
Johannesburg
Vereeniging
Bloemfontein

Benoni
Mbabane
SWAZILAND
Thabana Ntlenyana
11,425 ft. (3,482 m.)
Pietermaritzburg
Durban

DRAKENSBERG

SOUTH
AFRICA

LESOTHO
Maseru

Cape Town
Cape of Good Hope
Cape Agulhas

Port Elizabeth

N

Copyright © by Glencoe Division of
Macmillan/McGraw-Hill Publishing
Company. All rights reserved.

994

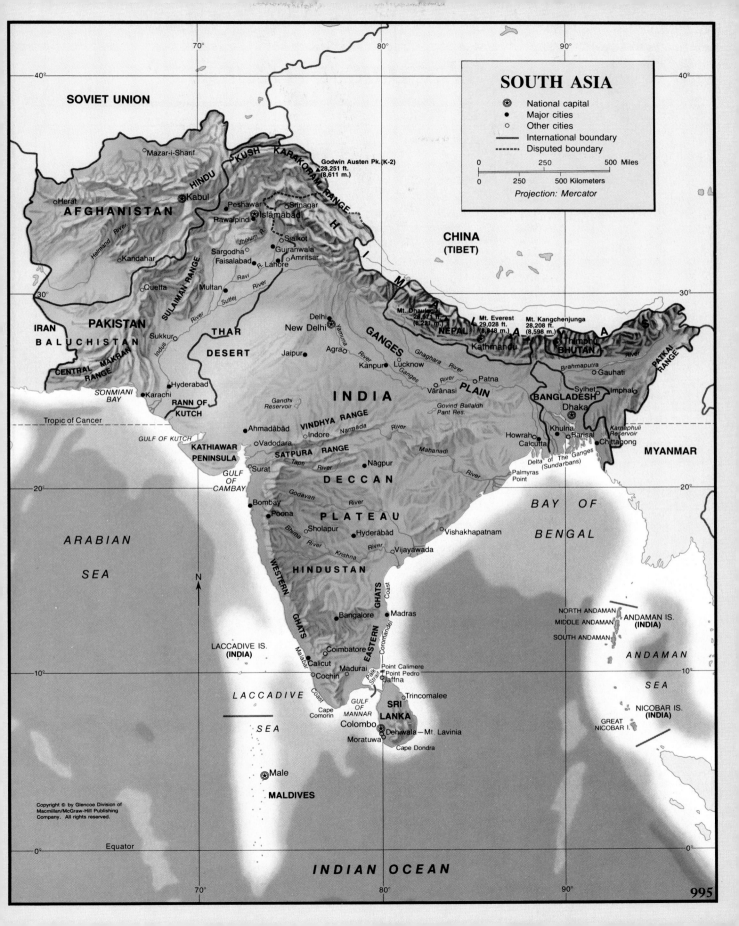

SOUTH ASIA

⊛ National capital
● Major cities
○ Other cities
— International boundary
---- Disputed boundary

Projection: Mercator

SOVIET UNION

Mazar-i-Sharif

HINDU KUSH KARAKORAM RANGE

Godwin Austen Pk. (K-2)
28,251 ft.
(8,611 m.)

Herat
○Kabul

AFGHANISTAN

Peshawar
Srinagar
Rawalpindi
⊛Islāmābād

Kandahar

Sialkot
Sargodha   Gujranwala
Faisalabad Amritsar
R. Lahore

Jhelum R.

Quetta   Multan

Ravi

IRAN   Sutlej   River

PAKISTAN   Sukkur   Delhi

BALUCHISTAN   **THAR**   New Delhi   Jaipur
Indus   **DESERT**
CENTRAL   Hyderabad
MAKRAN   Karachi   Agra
RANGE   **RANN OF**   Yamuna   River
SONMIANI   **KUTCH**
BAY   Kanpur

Tropic of Cancer

GULF OF KUTCH   Gandhi   Reservoir
KATHIAWAR   Ahmadābād   **VINDHYA RANGE**
PENINSULA   ○Vadodara   Indore   Narmada   River
GULF   Surat   **SATPURA RANGE**
OF   Tapti   River
CAMBAY   **INDIA**

**CHINA
(TIBET)**

Mt. Dhaulagiri
26,971 ft.
(8,221 m.)   Mt. Everest   Mt. Kangchenjunga
29,028 ft.   28,208 ft.
(8,848 m.)   (8,598 m.)

NEPAL   Kathmandu
Lucknow
Ghaghara   River
Vāranāsi   Patna   **BHUTAN**   Thimphu
GANGES   **PLAIN**   Brahmaputra   River   Gauhati
Govind Ballaldh
Pant Res.   Sylhet   Imphal
BANGLADESH
Dhaka   **PATKAI RANGE**
Howrah   Khulna   Barisal   Karnaphuli
Calcutta   Reservoir
Mahanadi   Chittagong
MYANMAR
River   Palmyras
Point   Delta of The Ganges
(Sundarbans)

DECCAN   Nāgpur

ARABIAN   Bombay
Poona
SEA   Sholapur   **PLATEAU**   Hyderābād
Bhima   River   Krishna   River
Godavari   Vijayawada   **BAY   OF**
River   **BENGAL**
Vishakhapatnam

HINDUSTAN

WESTERN   Bangalore   Madras

GHATS   **EASTERN**   **ANDAMAN IS.**
NORTH ANDAMAN   **(INDIA)**
Coimbatore   MIDDLE ANDAMAN
GHATS   SOUTH ANDAMAN

LACCADIVE IS.   Calicut   Madurai   **ANDAMAN**
(INDIA)   Cochin   Point Calimere
Palk   Point Pedro
Strait   Jaffna   **SEA**
Trincomalee   **NICOBAR IS.**
Malabar   **(INDIA)**
LACCADIVE   **SRI**   GREAT
Cape   GULF   **LANKA**   NICOBAR I.
Comorin   OF
SEA   MANNAR   Colombo⊛
Dehiwala—Mt. Lavinia
Moratuwa
Cape Dondra

⊛Male

MALDIVES

Equator

INDIAN OCEAN

0   250   500 Miles
0   250   500 Kilometers

Copyright © by Glencoe Division of
Macmillan/McGraw-Hill Publishing
Company. All rights reserved.

HISTORICAL ATLAS

THE WORLD ABOUT A.D. 200

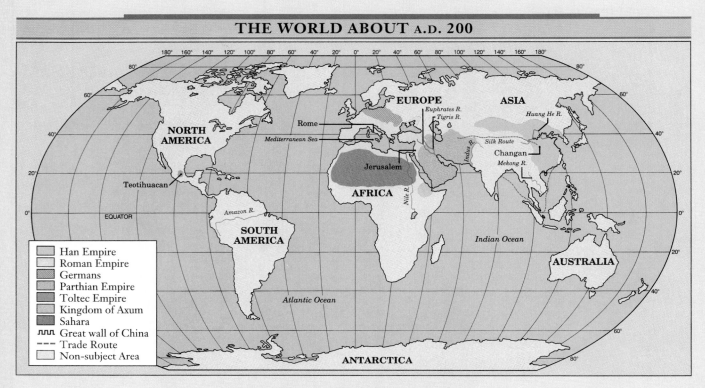

Legend:
- Han Empire
- Roman Empire
- Germans
- Parthian Empire
- Toltec Empire
- Kingdom of Axum
- Sahara
- Great wall of China
- Trade Route
- Non-subject Area

THE WORLD ABOUT A.D. 1300

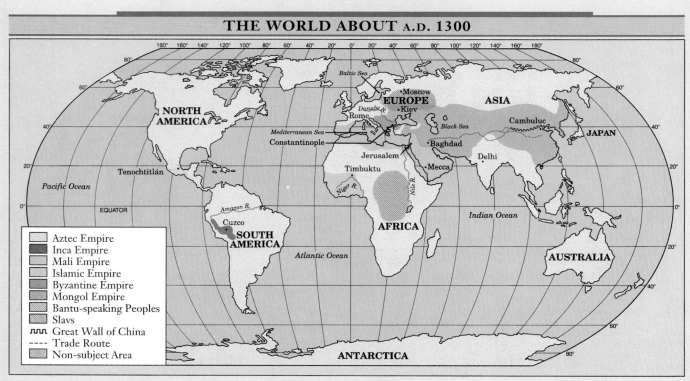

Legend:
- Aztec Empire
- Inca Empire
- Mali Empire
- Islamic Empire
- Byzantine Empire
- Mongol Empire
- Bantu-speaking Peoples
- Slavs
- Great Wall of China
- Trade Route
- Non-subject Area

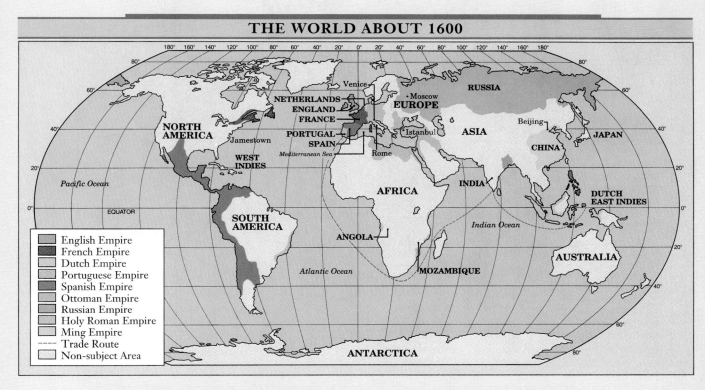

THE WORLD ABOUT 1600

180° 160° 140° 120° 100° 80° 60° 40° 20° 0° 20° 40° 60° 80° 100° 120° 140° 160° 180°

80°
60°

RUSSIA

Venice

NETHERLANDS
ENGLAND
FRANCE

EUROPE

• Moscow

NORTH AMERICA

Jamestown

PORTUGAL
SPAIN

Mediterranean Sea

Istanbul

Rome

ASIA

Beijing

CHINA

JAPAN

WEST INDIES

Pacific Ocean

EQUATOR

SOUTH AMERICA

AFRICA

INDIA

DUTCH EAST INDIES

Indian Ocean

ANGOLA

Atlantic Ocean

MOZAMBIQUE

AUSTRALIA

ANTARCTICA

Legend:
- English Empire
- French Empire
- Dutch Empire
- Portuguese Empire
- Spanish Empire
- Ottoman Empire
- Russian Empire
- Holy Roman Empire
- Ming Empire
- – – – Trade Route
- Non-subject Area

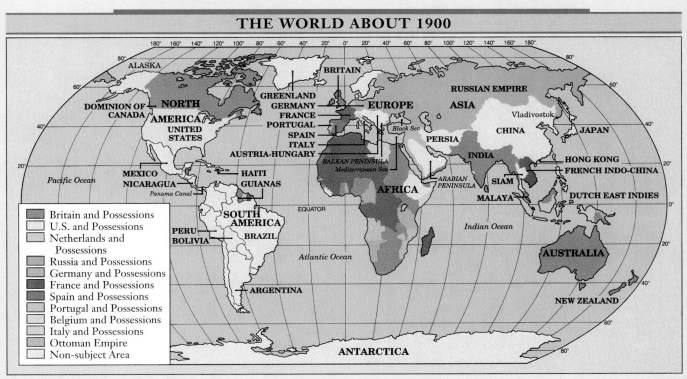

THE WORLD ABOUT 1900

180° 160° 140° 120° 100° 80° 60° 40° 20° 0° 20° 40° 60° 80° 100° 120° 140° 160° 180°

ALASKA

DOMINION OF CANADA

NORTH AMERICA

UNITED STATES

GREENLAND
GERMANY
FRANCE
PORTUGAL
SPAIN
ITALY
AUSTRIA-HUNGARY

BRITAIN

EUROPE

RUSSIAN EMPIRE

ASIA

Vladivostok

CHINA

JAPAN

Black Sea

PERSIA

INDIA

HONG KONG
FRENCH INDO-CHINA

MEXICO
NICARAGUA

Panama Canal

HAITI
GUIANAS

BALKAN PENINSULA
Mediterranean Sea

ARABIAN PENINSULA

SIAM

MALAYA

DUTCH EAST INDIES

Pacific Ocean

PERU
BOLIVIA

SOUTH AMERICA

BRAZIL

AFRICA

EQUATOR

Indian Ocean

AUSTRALIA

Atlantic Ocean

ARGENTINA

NEW ZEALAND

ANTARCTICA

Legend:
- Britain and Possessions
- U.S. and Possessions
- Netherlands and Possessions
- Russia and Possessions
- Germany and Possessions
- France and Possessions
- Spain and Possessions
- Portugal and Possessions
- Belgium and Possessions
- Italy and Possessions
- Ottoman Empire
- Non-subject Area

WORLD PROFILE

WORLD CLIMATES

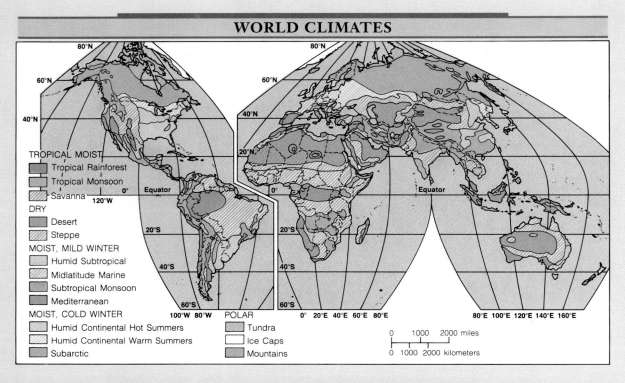

TROPICAL MOIST
- Tropical Rainforest
- Tropical Monsoon
- Savanna

DRY
- Desert
- Steppe

MOIST, MILD WINTER
- Humid Subtropical
- Midlatitude Marine
- Subtropical Monsoon
- Mediterranean

MOIST, COLD WINTER
- Humid Continental Hot Summers
- Humid Continental Warm Summers
- Subarctic

POLAR
- Tundra
- Ice Caps
- Mountains

0   1000   2000 miles
0   1000 2000 kilometers

NATURAL VEGETATION

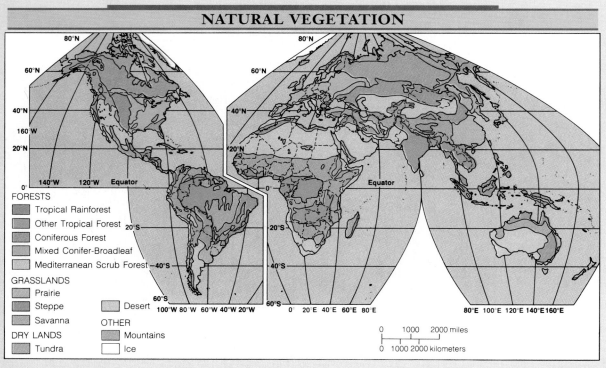

FORESTS
- Tropical Rainforest
- Other Tropical Forest
- Coniferous Forest
- Mixed Conifer-Broadleaf
- Mediterranean Scrub Forest

GRASSLANDS
- Prairie
- Steppe
- Savanna

DRY LANDS
- Tundra

- Desert

OTHER
- Mountains
- Ice

0   1000   2000 miles
0   1000 2000 kilometers

MAJOR RESOURCES

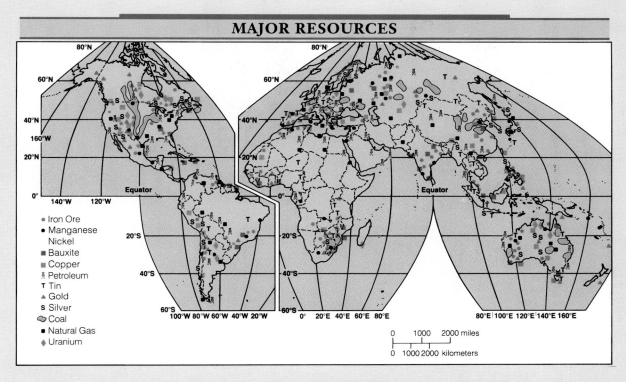

- • Iron Ore
- • Manganese Nickel
- ■ Bauxite
- ■ Copper
- ⚒ Petroleum
- T Tin
- ▲ Gold
- S Silver
- ◗ Coal
- ■ Natural Gas
- ♦ Uranium

0   1000   2000 miles

0   1000 2000 kilometers

WORLD POPULATION DENSITY

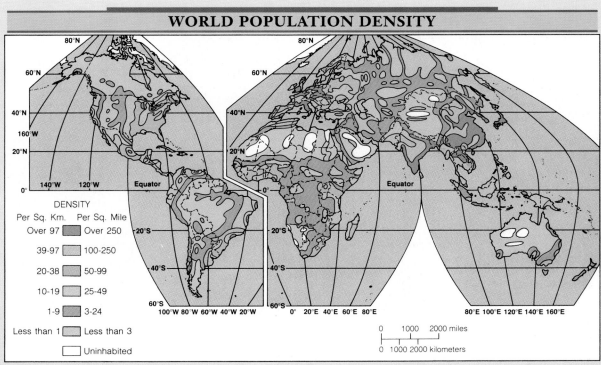

DENSITY

Per Sq. Km.	Per Sq. Mile
Over 97	Over 250
39-97	100-250
20-38	50-99
10-19	25-49
1-9	3-24
Less than 1	Less than 3
	Uninhabited

0   1000   2000 miles

0   1000 2000 kilometers

MAJOR RELIGIONS

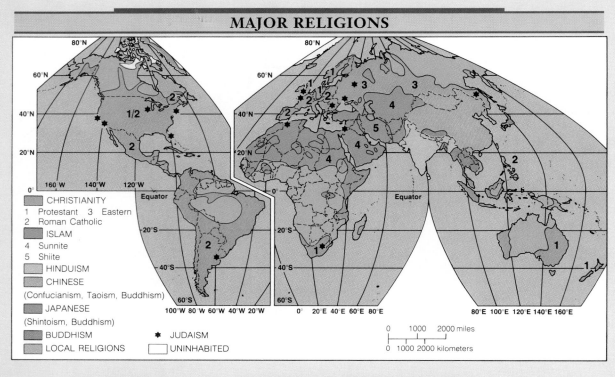

CHRISTIANITY
1 Protestant 3 Eastern
2 Roman Catholic

ISLAM
4 Sunnite
5 Shiite

HINDUISM

CHINESE
(Confucianism, Taoism, Buddhism)

JAPANESE
(Shintoism, Buddhism)

BUDDHISM ✦ JUDAISM

LOCAL RELIGIONS UNINHABITED

0   1000   2000 miles
0 1000 2000 kilometers

MAJOR LANGUAGES

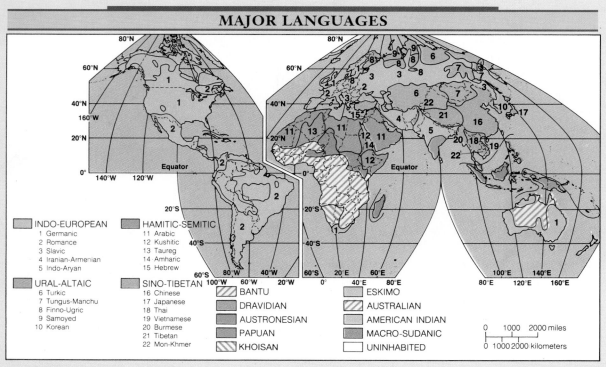

INDO-EUROPEAN
  1 Germanic
  2 Romance
  3 Slavic
  4 Iranian-Armenian
  5 Indo-Aryan

HAMITIC-SEMITIC
  11 Arabic
  12 Kushitic
  13 Taureg
  14 Amharic
  15 Hebrew

URAL-ALTAIC
  6 Turkic
  7 Tungus-Manchu
  8 Finno-Ugric
  9 Samoyed
  10 Korean

SINO-TIBETAN
  16 Chinese
  17 Japanese
  18 Thai
  19 Vietnamese
  20 Burmese
  21 Tibetan
  22 Mon-Khmer

BANTU
DRAVIDIAN
AUSTRONESIAN
PAPUAN
KHOISAN

ESKIMO
AUSTRALIAN
AMERICAN INDIAN
MACRO-SUDANIC
UNINHABITED

0   1000   2000 miles
0 1000 2000 kilometers

GLOSSARY

A

abbot the head of a monastery (p. 268)

absolutism political theory stating that monarchs hold supreme power and are responsible for their actions to God alone (p. 416)

acupuncture a traditional Chinese medical technique in which the body is pierced by fine needles at vital points (p. 200)

age set groups of males or females of similar age in sub-Saharan Africa who are assigned specific tasks (p. 335)

ahimsa (uh HIHM suh) Hindu doctrine of not harming any living animal or human (p. 175)

alliance system a formal defense agreement between two or more nations (p. 694)

alphabet system of symbols or characters that represent sounds or things (p. 68)

anarchy absence of any form of political authority or political institutions (p. 645)

animism the idea that both living and nonliving beings have spirits or souls (p. 311)

anthropologist (an thruh PAHL uh juhst) scientist who studies past human or prehuman civilizations (p. 16)

apartheid policy of strict racial separation and discrimination practiced in South Africa (p. 876)

appeasement the granting of concessions to another country to maintain peace (p. 777)

apprentice a person bound by legal agreement to work for another for a specific period of time in order to learn a trade, art, or business (p. 287)

aqueduct a pipe or channel to bring water from far away usually by gravity (p. 154)

arabesque (air uh BEHSK) geometric designs entwined with plant stems, leaves, flowers, and stars used by Islamic artists to decorate books, rugs, swords, and entire walls (p. 250)

arbitration the settling of a dispute by following the guidelines of an impartial person (p. 677)

archaeologist (ahr kee AHL uh just) scientist who studies the life and culture of ancient peoples by excavating ancient living sites (p. 16)

archipelago a group or chain of islands (p. 311)

aristocrat noble who owned land; in ancient Greece, a member of the upper class who pro-

vided cavalry to the king in time of war (p. 99)

armistice a mutual agreement to end a war or hostilities; truce (p. 711)

artifact an object made by humans, such as a tool, ornament, weapon, or pottery, that has historical or archaeological importance (p. 16)

artisan a skilled craftworker (p. 26)

assembly line a line of factory workers that stands in front of a conveyor belt assembling a product as it passes by (p. 561)

atomic theory the idea that all matter is made up of submolecular particles called atoms (p. 580)

autocracy rule by one person with unlimited power (p. 643)

B

balance of power a distribution of power such that no one nation is able to dominate or interfere with other nations (p. 422)

balance of trade the difference in value between what a nation imports and what it exports (p. 407)

baroque (buh ROHK) richly ornate, flamboyant art and architecture style developed in Europe in the 1550s (p. 384)

barter a system of trade in which one thing is exchanged for another (p. 68)

bishop a high-ranking clergyman having authority over other clergy and overseeing a church district or diocese (p. 160)

blitz an intensive air raid (p. 782)

blitzkrieg a swift, sudden Nazi offensive for the purpose of a speedy victory (p. 779)

boat people refugees from Southeast Asia who fled the area in crowded, often unseaworthy boats from 1975 to 1979 (p. 857)

bourgeoisie (boor zhwah ZEE) the middle class; social class between the very wealthy and the working class (p. 512)

boyar member of a council of landowners and wealthy merchants who assisted princes in early Russia (p. 225)

budget deficit a debt caused when a country spends more money than it earns (p. 929)

buffer state a neutral territory between two rival powers that lessens the danger of conflict (p. 533)

bullion gold or silver (p. 407)

bureaucracy in ancient Egypt, a group of government officials to whom the king delegated many administrative responsibilities (p. 38)

business cycle a cycle of business expansion and prosperity followed eventually by a period of decreased business activity (p. 561)

C

caliph (KAY lihf) Muslim supreme leader; successor of Muhammad (p. 241)

campesino a poor Latin American peasant or farm worker (p. 902)

capital money to invest in the labor, machines, and raw materials needed for industry (p. 555)

cardinal church official appointed by the pope and ranking directly below him (p. 270)

cartel an association of businesses formed to establish an international monopoly by price fixing and regulating production (p. 885)

cartographer a person who makes maps or charts (p. 394)

cash-and-carry policy a program in which Great Britain traded cash for needed supplies from the U.S. during World War II and transported them across the Atlantic in its own ships, thereby protecting American neutrality (p. 783)

cell theory a theory formulated by German scientists in 1858 that all living things are made up of cells (p. 578)

chancellor the chief minister of some European countries (p. 638)

charter formal document granting the right of self-rule (p. 289)

chivalry code of honor for an ideal knight including such characteristics as bravery, honor, courtesy, and generosity (p. 264)

choreographer a dance creator and arranger (p. 723)

chronicle an oral or written account in which events are arranged in the order they occur (p. 252)

circumnavigation sailing completely around the globe (first accomplished by Magellan) (p. 399)

citizen in ancient Greece, a male inhabitant of a city who took part in government (p. 98)

city-state an independent state consisting of a city together with surrounding land and villages (p. 45)

civil disobedience nonviolent opposition to an unjust law or practice by refusing to comply with it (p. 753)

civil service a system begun in China during the Han dynasty in which men who score high on examinations are permitted to become public officials (p. 192)

civilization highly organized society marked by knowledge of a written language, the arts, sciences, and government (p. 26)

classical relating to the culture of ancient Greece and Rome, characterized by simple, elegant, graceful balance (p. 116)

clergy people, such as priests and bishops, ordained for religious service (p. 216)

coalition an alliance or union of political factions to form one government (p. 729)

cold war political tension after World War II between the United States and the Soviet Union (p. 812)

collective bargaining negotiations between workers' representatives and employers to determine such things as wages, hours, rules, and working conditions (p. 568)

collective security negotiations between nations to take joint action against enemy attack (p. 774)

collectivization a farming system in which the land is managed and worked cooperatively by peasants under government supervision (p. 739)

colony a permanent settlement formed by a country in a distant land that remains under its control (p. 68)

comedy light, amusing story or play with a happy ending (p. 120)

common law the law of a country based on custom, usage, and the decisions of law courts rather than on codified written laws (p. 274)

commonwealth a nation or state governed by the people for the common good (p. 491)

communism a classless society with equal distribution of economic goods envisioned by Karl Marx and Friedrich Engels (p. 577)

concentration camp large prison camp in Nazi

Germany where war prisoners were held (p. 736)

conquistador Spanish conquerors who came to the Americas in the 1500s (p. 400)

conscription compulsory enrollment in the armed forces; draft (p. 523)

constitutional monarchy government in which a monarch's power is limited by a constitution (p. 492)

consul an executive official of ancient Rome, elected for one year (p. 143)

containment Truman administration policy designed to prevent the spread of communism (p. 816)

contraband goods forbidden from being transported that may be seized by an opposing nation during war (p. 704)

convoy ships traveling in a group surrounded by warships for protection (p. 710)

corporate state government in which each industry (rather than each political party or geographical area) is represented (p. 732)

corporation a company owned by many stockholders who buy shares in the company and share in the profits or losses (p. 561)

coup d'état a sudden overthrow of a government by people in authority in deliberate violation of the laws (p. 525)

covenant solemn agreement (p. 69)

creole a white aristocrat born in colonial Latin America (p. 620)

crusade military expedition by European Christians in the 11th–13th centuries to retake the Holy Land from the Muslims (p. 282)

cubism a style of art that reduces natural forms into abstract, often geometric forms (p. 722)

cultural differentiation the development of unique building styles, arts, and customs based on geography and natural resources (p. 341)

cultural diffusion the exchange of ideas, knowledge, skills, and customs among different civilizations (p. 27)

culture the ideas, customs, skills, and arts of a given people at a given time (p. 18)

culture system the use of forced labor to run a colony (p. 672)

cuneiform (kyoo NEE uh fawrm) Sumerian system of writing, believed to be the oldest in the world (p. 46)

D

daimyo (DY mee oh) most powerful samurai or nobleman in feudal Japan (p. 321)

death squad band of killers hired by a wealthy landowner to murder political opponents (p. 914)

democracy government by the people (p. 100)

depression a drastic decline in an economy, characterized by decreasing business activity, falling prices, and unemployment (p. 561)

developed country a nation with a high level of industrialization (p. 863)

developing country a poor, mostly agricultural nation with a very low gross national product (p. 863)

détente the lessening of tensions between the United States and the Soviet Union that began in 1972 (p. 933)

dharma Hindu set of rules that determines duties, virtues, and moral conduct of males (p. 173)

dictator an ancient Roman magistrate appointed temporarily to solve an emergency (p. 143)

dictatorship a government under the rule of someone having absolute authority (p. 526)

dictatorship of the proletariat control of the state by the working class in the U.S.S.R. (p. 737)

disarmament limitation, reduction, or elimination of armed forces or military weapons (p. 728)

disciple follower of a certain teacher or religious doctrine (p. 157)

disenfranchised deprived of the right to vote (p. 602)

dissident a person who criticizes, disagrees with, or opposes government policy (p. 823)

divine right of kings the doctrine that holds that monarchs derive their power directly from and are accountable only to God (p. 488)

division of labor a manufacturing system in which each person performs a specialized task on a product as it moves by on a conveyor belt (p. 561)

doge (dohj) the elected chief magistrate of the former republics of Venice and Genoa (p. 367)

domestic system a labor system in which entire families may work to produce goods in their homes (p. 554)

dominion one of the self-governing nations within the British Commonwealth (p. 607)

domino theory the belief that if one nation becomes Communist, nearby nations will also become Communist (p. 854)

draft to select from a group for compulsory military service (p. 926)

dual monarchy rule by one person over two kingdoms (p. 650)

duma an elected national legislature in the U.S.S.R. between 1905 and 1917 (p. 648)

dynasty a succession of rulers who are members of the same family (p. 37)

E

economy a system of producing, distributing, and consuming wealth to meet people's needs (p. 26)

emancipation freeing someone from oppression, slavery, or bondage (p. 644)

emigration permanently exiting a country or region to live elsewhere (p. 582)

émigré (ehm i GRAY) person who fled France in hopes of gaining support to restore Louis XVI to power (p. 519)

empire political unit made up of groups of territories ruled by one government (p. 41)

enclosure movement a move away from farming public lands to private ownership of larger farms occurring in England in the 1700s (p. 555)

enlightened despot a monarch with absolute power who uses it to improve society (p. 478)

entente a friendly agreement between two or more nations (p. 694)

entrepreneur (on truh pruh NYER) person who organizes and assumes the risk for a business venture hoping to make a profit (pp. 407, 556)

epic a long narrative poem celebrating the deeds of a legendary or historical hero (p. 171)

estate a class in France during the 1700s, such as the nobility, clergy, or commoners, possessing distinct political rights (p. 512)

ethics a system of moral principles; one system, begun by Kongzi in the 500s B.C., served as the basis for Chinese society and government for 2,000 years (p. 193)

evolution the development of a species from a simple state to a specialized state over great periods of time (p. 578)

excommunication a formal church censure that deprives a person of the right to belong to that church (p. 270)

existentialism philosophy that states that humans are unique and isolated in an indifferent world and that emphasizes freedom of choice and responsibility for one's actions (p. 967)

exodus departure of a large group of people (p. 69)

F

factory system an organized production method in which goods are manufactured by workers and machines in a factory outside of their homes under supervision of a manager (p. 557)

fascism (FASH ihz uhm) a system of government marked by strong social and economic control, usually headed by a dictator (p. 731)

federal system a form of government in which power is divided between a central authority and a union of states that retains some power (p. 506)

feudalism medieval social system in which serfs labored for landholders who protected them and were responsible to overlords (p. 262)

fief tracts of land with peasant laborers given by Frankish kings to warriors, counts, and local officials (p. 262)

friar a mendicant wandering preacher (p. 270)

fundamentalism religious movement characterized by rigid adherence to basic religious laws (p. 892)

G

geisha Japanese woman trained to entertain and provide company (p. 454)

general strike strike in which a large number of a nation's workers participate in order to pressure the government (p. 728)

genetic engineering the science of altering genes of living organisms to prevent hereditary defects or to manufacture useful new strains (p. 956)

glasnost term referring to the Soviet policy of openness and freedom of expression under Mikhail Gorbachev (p. 935)

grand jury a special jury that investigates accusations against a person suspected of a crime and if there is enough evidence brings the person before a petty jury (p. 274)

grand vizier a prime minister in Muslim countries during the Ottoman Empire (p. 440)

greenhouse effect a steady, gradual rise in the atmospheric temperature of the planet brought about by depletion of the ozone layer and the introduction of atmospheric pollutants (p. 966)

gross national product the total value of goods and services produced by a nation in a year (p. 841)

guerrilla warfare fighting by small, mobile groups that employ hit-and-run tactics (p. 632)

guild a medieval association of merchants, artists, or craftsmen (p. 287)

H

habeas corpus a law that prevents unlawful imprisonment by stating that a person cannot be jailed without a reason or a trial (p. 494)

haiku an unrhymed Japanese poem with a fixed three-line form (p. 454)

hajj Muslim pilgrimage to Mecca that every able-bodied Muslim is expected to make at least once in a lifetime involving three days of ceremony, prayer, and sacrifice (p. 240)

heresy disbelief in Roman Catholic doctrine by a Church member (p. 270)

hieroglyphics ancient Egyptian writing system employing picture symbols (p. 42)

Holocaust the mass extermination of more than 6 million people, especially Jews, in World War II (p. 786)

home rule allowing a dependent country to rule itself; self-government (p. 606)

humanism Renaissance movement influenced by ancient Greek and Roman literature that emphasized nonreligious concerns (p. 364)

hyperinflation extremely sharp and rapid price increases throughout an economy (p. 917)

hypothesis an explanation that accounts for facts and can be tested by investigation (p. 468)

I

icon a representation or picture of a sacred Christian person, itself regarded as sacred (p. 216)

iconoclast supporter of Emperor Leo III, who ordered all icons removed from churches because he believed they encouraged superstition and the worship of idols (p. 216)

illuminated manuscript the art of decorating a book page with elaborate designs, beautiful lettering, or miniature paintings as practiced by religious scholars of the Byzantine Empire and later adopted in western Europe (p. 220)

imam (ih MAM) a prayer leader in a mosque (p. 240)

immigration entering a new country or region to live permanently (p. 582)

imperial presidency term referring to a U.S. president who exercises powers beyond those spelled out in the U.S. Constitution (p. 927)

imperialism a policy of extending a nation's authority over other areas of the world (p. 658)

impressionism a school of painting whose aim is to capture a momentary glimpse of a subject and to reproduce the changing effects of light (p. 590)

indemnity payment for damages, losses, or injuries suffered (p. 146)

indulgence pardon sold by the Catholic Church until the Renaissance that released the buyer from time in purgatory (p. 376)

industrial capitalism system in which industrialists decide how best to make money by reinvesting profits and expanding factories (p. 560)

inflation an abnormal increase in currency resulting in sharp rises in prices (p. 161)

intendant public administrative officer who handles local government affairs (p. 424)

intercontinental ballistic missile a long-range explosive projectile capable of traveling from one continent to another (p. 822)

intifada an uprising by Palestinians against Israeli occupation (p. 887)

iron curtain a political barrier isolating Eastern-bloc countries from Western-bloc countries (p. 816)

J

janissary soldier in an elite guard of Turkish troops first established in the 1300s (p. 440)

jati the hundreds or thousands of groups, formed according to occupation, that made up each *varna* in India (p. 172)

jihad (jih HAHD) Muslim holy war against unbelievers or enemies of Islam (p. 241)

jingoism extreme nationalism usually characterized by a hostile or aggressive foreign policy (p. 652)

joint-stock company a means of financing trading voyages in which merchants investing money could share in any profits (p. 406)

journeyman a person who has finished an apprenticeship in a trade and is a qualified worker employable by someone else (p. 287)

justification by faith a Reformation idea promoted by Martin Luther that salvation can be achieved by faith in God alone (p. 376)

K

kaiser an emperor of Germany during the years 1871 to 1918 (p. 638)

kamikaze Japanese pilot and plane carrying explosives, dedicated to suicidal attack in World War II (p. 793)

karma a Hindu reincarnation principle that states that a person's actions in life influence what he or she is born as in the next life (p. 175)

kibbutz Israeli collective farm (p. 881)

kulak a landowning peasant in the U.S.S.R. who had become a well-to-do farmer (p. 739)

L

labor union a workers' organization formed to promote issues such as fair wages and decent working conditions (p. 568)

labor-intensive farming type of agriculture that relies more on human labor than on machines (p. 448)

laissez-faire (leh say FAYR) letting industry leaders fix the rules of competition, labor conditions, etc., without government regulation (p. 574)

laity lay members of a church who are not clergy (p. 216)

lay investiture when medieval secular rulers gave symbols of office, such as a ring and a staff, to bishops they appointed (p. 270)

lend-lease authorization to lend war equipment to a country whose defense is considered vital to national security (p. 784)

liberalism desire to change government to promote civil liberties, democratic reforms, and social progress (p. 533)

liberation theology a belief by Latin American Catholic priests that religion can be used to free people from oppression (p. 905)

line of demarcation an imaginary line drawn by the pope in 1493 that divided the world's unexplored lands between Spain and Portugal (p. 398)

logic science of correct reasoning and proof (p. 121)

M

madrasa Muslim theological school (p. 247)

maize corn (p. 341)

mandarin a class of well-educated civil servants who controlled the administration of the Chinese government until the twentieth century (pp. 192, 308)

mandate 1. authority from heaven to rule (in Chinese dynasties) according to the principle known as the Mandate of Heaven (p. 56) 2. authority from the League of Nations for one nation to rule a territory formerly ruled by a second nation (p. 712)

manorialism medieval social system in which lords owned both large estates and also the peasants who were bound to the land (p. 265)

martyr a person who chooses death rather than renounce religious principles (p. 158)

master a person who employs an apprentice (p. 287)

matrilineal tracing ancestral descent through the mother's ancestors (p. 335)

mayor of the palace Frankish government official in the A.D. 700s and later (p. 258)

mendicant a member of an order of friars that relies on gifts to live; a religious beggar (p. 271)

mercantilism policy of European nations in the 1600s of accumulating wealth, establishing colonies, and developing industry to achieve power (p. 407)

meritocracy a system (such as a bureaucracy) in which people are chosen and promoted for their talents and performance (p. 306)

messiah liberator of the Jews expected by them to arrive in the future (p. 157)

mestizo (meh STEE zoh) a Latin American of Indian and white ancestry at the bottom of the social order in colonial Latin America (p. 620)

middle class member of society occupying a position between the laboring class and the wealthy (p. 274)

middle passage the second of three legs of the triangular trade in which slaves were brought from Africa to the Americas in the 1600s (p. 405)

militarism national policy in which military preparedness is of ultimate importance (p. 694)

mobilization assembling and transporting military troops and equipment in preparation for war (p. 698)

monarchy rule by a king or a queen (p. 37)

money economy an economic system that uses money as the currency for buying and selling goods rather than relying on a barter system (p. 287)

monotheism belief in one god (p. 69)

monsoon seasonal wind of the Indian Ocean and southern Asia (p. 51)

mosaic a kind of picture that Byzantine artists excelled at creating, made by setting small pieces of glass or tile into mortar (p. 220)

mulatto a Latin American of African and white ancestry at the bottom of the social order in colonial Latin America (p. 620)

multinational corporation a company with operations or investments in more than one country (p. 958)

myth a traditional story that explains natural phenomena, such as the origin of people (p. 29)

N

nation-state a political organization composed of one nation inhabited by one group of people (p. 630)

nationalism yearning for national independence in a country under foreign domination (p. 528)

nationalization to convert an industry from private ownership to government ownership (p. 737)

natural law a universal moral law that can be understood by applying reason, first proposed in the 1600s (p. 473)

negritude a poetry movement that emphasizes and takes pride in African cultural heritage (p. 880)

nihilist a member of a Russian movement in the 1800s that rejected traditional values and advocated assassination and terrorism (p. 645)

nirvana state of complete oneness with the universe (p. 176)

nomad a person without a permanent home who moves about constantly in search of food (p. 19)

nonaligned not taking sides with any other nation or bloc in a conflict; neutral (p. 850)

O

oligarchy a government in which a small group holds political power (p. 100)

P

pacifist a person opposed to using violence to settle disputes (p. 753)

papal infallibility Roman Catholic doctrine stating that the pope is free from error when he speaks on matters of faith and morals (p. 640)

partition to divide a region into smaller parts (p. 662)

partnership two or more entrepreneurs who combine their money to create a business; each member shares responsibilities and debts (p. 561)

patriarch one of five leading archbishops in ancient Rome (p. 160)

patrician a member of one of the noble families of ancient Rome (p. 143)

peaceful coexistence Khrushchev policy in which the Soviet Union competed with the United States but avoided war or open confrontation (p. 821)

peninsular a man born in Spain or Portugal who held the most important positions in colonial Latin America (p. 620)

perestroika (pehr ehs TROY kah) term meaning "restructuring" that refers to the rebuilding of the Soviet economy under Mikhail Gorbachev (p. 935)

petty jury group of people that sit at trials to

determine the guilt or innocence of the accused (p. 274)

pharaoh ruler of ancient Egypt (p. 39)

philosophe (fee luh ZAWF) a philosophical, political, or social thinker of the Enlightenment who spread new ideas based on scientific reasoning (p. 476)

philosopher a thinker or lover of wisdom (p. 121)

plateau an elevated, relatively flat expanse of land (p. 332)

plebeian (plih BEE yuhn) a member of the lower class in ancient Rome (p. 143)

plebiscite a direct vote in which all people are allowed to participate (p. 526)

pogrom an organized slaughter of a minority group (p. 646)

polis city-state of ancient Greece (p. 98)

polytheism belief in or worship of many gods (p. 42)

pope the bishop of Rome and the head of the Roman Catholic Church (p. 160)

population explosion the great increase in the human population in modern times (p. 759)

post-impressionist school of art in the late 1800s that rejected the objective rendering of nature and emphasized and emphasized the artist's subjective viewpoint or the formal style of the painting (p. 592)

pragmatist a person in China who advocates modernization through increased westernization (p. 844)

predestination doctrine promoted by John Calvin that God preordains everything including who will be saved (p. 379)

prehistory history before recorded history, as learned from archaeology (p. 16)

prime minister the head of the cabinet and the chief executive of a parliamentary democracy (p. 496)

propaganda ideas, allegations, or rumors used to promote a cause or to damage an opposing cause (p. 701)

prophet religious leader who speaks or claims to speak the word of God (p. 72)

protectionism imposing tariffs or trade restrictions on foreign goods to protect domestic industries (p. 864)

protectorate a country that is protected and partially controlled, especially in foreign affairs, by another country (p. 661)

provisional government a temporary government set up pending permanent arrangements (p. 706)

purge to rid a nation of people considered undesirable (p. 740)

Q

queue long braid of hair worn hanging down the neck (p. 448)

R

radiocarbon dating measuring the age of once-living material by calculating the amount of radioactive carbon present in it (p. 17)

rajah an ancient Aryan tribal ruler or chief (p. 170)

ratify approve and so make valid, as of an amendment to the U.S. Constitution (p. 619)

reactionary one who opposes progress or liberalism (p. 533)

realism the picturing in art and literature of people and objects as they really are without idealizing them (p. 589)

reincarnation being reborn in another body (p. 175)

reparation compensation required from a defeated nation for war damage (p. 711)

republic government in which the power lies with the citizens who vote for people to represent them (p. 143)

revelation a vision of divine truth, which according to Islamic tradition was experienced by Muhammad in A.D. 610 (p. 236)

revolution overthrow of a government from within (p. 503)

rhetoric art of using words effectively when speaking (p. 105)

romanticism a movement in the 1700s and 1800s that emphasized freedom and originality, and the personality of the artist (p. 587)

royalist a Cavalier who supported the monarchy of Charles I (p. 490)

russification to make Russian in character (p. 646)

S

sacrament formal rituals of the Catholic Church including baptism, penance, receiving the eucharist, confirmation, matrimony, anointing of the sick, and holy orders (p. 267)

salon gathering of intellectuals during the Enlightenment to discuss philosophies and to engage in conversation (p. 476)

samurai feudal Japanese warrior responsible to the daimyo who practiced the bushido code of conduct (p. 321)

sanction coercive measures, frequently involving trade, taken by several nations against another nation that is breaking international law (p. 775)

sankin-kotai a system of control by a shogun to keep daimyos weak and unable to rebel by requiring them to travel and serve the shogun (p. 451)

satellite country a nation politically dominated by another (p. 814)

savanna a flat, treeless grassland in tropical or subtropical areas (p. 332)

schism a separation of the church in A.D. 1054 that created the Roman Catholic Church in the West and the Eastern Orthodox Church in the East (p. 218)

scholasticism medieval school of thought that reconciles classic philosophy with the teachings of the Roman Catholic Church (p. 290)

scientific method a way to test scientific truths through observation and through experimentation (p. 469)

scorched-earth policy a Stalin policy in which Soviet citizens destroyed anything that could be of use to Nazi invaders (p. 785)

secede to withdraw formally from an alliance or union (p. 616)

sect a religious group that has separated from a larger denomination (p. 157)

sectionalism excessive devotion to local political and economic interests without regard for interests in other regions (p. 616)

self-determination the right of a people to decide their own political status or government without outside influence (p. 746)

seminary theological school for the training of priests established by the Council of Trent (p. 384)

separatism a political movement favoring the secession of Quebec from the rest of Canada (p. 931)

serf feudal peasant laborer bound to the manor who could not leave it without permission (p. 265)

shamanism belief that living and nonliving beings have both good and evil spirits, with which shamans (medicine men) communicate (p. 315)

shari'ah (shuh REE uh) Islamic code of law that covers all the moral rules for private and public life (p. 239)

sheikh chief of a bedouin tribe (p. 234)

shogun "great general" or military governor of feudal Japan (p. 319)

shogunate military government in feudal Japan (p. 321)

socialism a society in which all members share in the work and the products (p. 576)

socialist realism art form that glorifies Communist ideology (p. 740)

sonnet a 14-line poem in a fixed verse and rhyme scheme that expresses a single theme or idea (p. 364)

soviet an elected workers' council in the U.S.S.R. (p. 648)

sphere of influence a territory in which a foreign power holds exclusive investment or trading rights (p. 661)

stagflation an economic condition in which high rises in prices are coupled with a decline in consumer demand and an increase in unemployment (p. 928)

stalemate situation in which further action by either of two opponents is impossible; deadlock (p. 847)

standard of living the level of wealth of a people in a region (p. 907)

steppe an immense semiarid grass-covered plain found in southeastern Europe and Siberia (p. 224)

stupa a dome-shaped Buddhist shrine built over the remains of holy people (p. 178)

suffragette a female advocate of voting rights for women; member of a 1903 British movement advocating women's voting rights (p. 604)

sultan ruler of a Muslim country, especially of the former Ottoman Empire (p. 440)

surrealism art movement that uses dreamlike images and unnatural combinations of objects to express the subconscious mind (p. 722)

symbolism art movement in which impressions are suggested indirectly through the use of symbols rather than directly statedly (p. 590)

syndicate a corporation of workers, employers, and government officials that helps set industry policies (p. 732)

T

technology the skills and knowledge available to a people (p. 18)

theocracy a government in which the ruler is both the religious and political leader (p. 38)

tithe a 10-percent tax on income paid to the clergy or church (p. 512)

trade deficit an economic imbalance occurring when a country imports more than it exports (p. 481)

tragedy a dramatic story or play that often represents a terrible struggle or calamity (p. 118)

trench a long, narrow ditch with soil piled in front from which soldiers fought during World War I (p. 701)

triangular trade the three legs of the journey (forming a triangle) traders made between Europe, Africa, and the Americas in the 1600s (p. 405)

tribune an ancient Roman official elected by the plebeians to protect their rights against the patricians (p. 144)

triumvirate three men with equal power in ancient Rome who shared public administration and authority (p. 148)

tropical rain forest a dense forest in a tropical region with an annual rainfall of 100 inches or more (p. 966)

troubadour a lyric poet of the Middle Ages in northern Italy attached to the courts who composed complex metrical songs (p. 290)

tsar an emperor of early Russia (p. 228)

tyrant a Greek leader who seizes power and who is harsh in exercise of authority (p. 100)

U

ultimatum a final offer in diplomatic circles that threatens severe penalties if not accepted (p. 696)

ultraroyalist an extremely conservative French aristocrat in the 1800s (p. 610)

unicameral legislature one-house legislature chosen by voters (p. 518)

urbanization to gradually transform an area from rural in character to citylike (p. 583)

utopia an ideal society with a perfect political and social system (p. 576)

V

varna one of the four main Indian social classes (p. 171)

vassal a feudal noble who served a lord of the next higher rank (p. 262)

vernacular writing in the native language of a region instead of in literary language (p. 290)

vocation a career in which people believe themselves to be called on by God to serve God and their neighbors (p. 378)

W

warlord a local military leader in China before World War II in a district where the government was weak (p. 755)

welfare state a social system in which the state assumes responsibility for the well-being of its citizens (p. 826)

westernization the spreading of European culture to other parts of the world (p. 672)

Z

zemstvo local council that governed in tsarist Russia (p. 645)

INDEX

An italic page reference indicates that there is an illustration on that page; A *c* or *m* following a page reference indicates a chart or map.

1023

ACKNOWLEDGMENTS

TEXT

Grateful acknowledgment is given authors and publishers for permission to reprint the following copyrighted material.
58 Herbert Mason, *Gilgamesh*, translated by Herbert Mason. Copyright © 1970 by Herbert Mason. Reprinted by permission of Houghton Mifflin Company; **132** Sophocles, "The Antigone of Sophocles," an English version translated by Dudley Fitts and Robert Fitzgerald. Copyright 1939 by Harcourt Brace Jovanovich, Inc.; renewed 1967 by Dudley Fitts and Robert Fitzgerald. CAUTION: All rights, including professional, amateur, motion picture, recitation, lecturing, performance, public reading, radio broadcasting, and television are strictly reserved. Inquiries on all rights should be addressed to Harcourt Brace Jovanovich, Inc., Copyrights and Permissions Department, Orlando, Florida 32887; **324** Li Po, "Letter to His Two Small Children Staying in Eastern Lu at Wen Yang Village Under Turtle Mountain" and "Hard Is the Journey" from *Li Po and Tu Fu*, translated by Arthur Cooper. Translation copyright © 1973 by Arthur Cooper. Reprinted by permission of Viking-Dutton, Inc.; **324** Li Po, "On a Quiet Night" from *The Works of Li Po the Chinese Poet*, translated by Shigeyoshi Obata. Published in 1965 by Paragon Book Reprint Corp.; **324** Li Po, "Taking Leave of a Friend" from *Personae* by Ezra Pound. Copyright 1926 by Ezra Pound. Reprinted by permission of New Directions Publishing Corporation; **386** Niccolò Machiavelli, *The Prince*, translated and edited by Thomas G. Bergin. Copyright © 1947 by F. S. Crofts & Co. Inc. Reprinted by permission of Viking-Dutton, Inc.; **536** Victor Hugo, *Les Misérables* translated by Lee Fahnestock and Norman MacAfee. Copyright © 1987 by Lee Fahnestock and Norman MacAfee. Copyright © 1985 by Cameron Mackintosh (Overseas) Ltd. Reprinted by permission of Viking-Dutton, Inc.; **594** Anton Chekhov, "The Beggar," translated by Marian Fell. Reprinted by permission of Random House, Inc.; **702** Wilfred Owen, "Dulce et Decorum Est" from *Collected Poems*, edited by C. Day Lewis. Copyright © 1963 by Chatto & Windus Ltd. Reprinted by permission of New Directions Publishing Corporation; **766** Santha Rama Rau, "By Any Other Name" from *Gifts of Passage*. Copyright © 1961 by Vasanthi Rama Rau Bowers; copyright © renewed 1989 by the author. Reprinted by permission of Harper & Row, Publishers, Inc.; **880** Michael Dei-Anang, "My Africa" from *Poems from Black Africa*, edited by Langston Hughes. Copyright © 1963 by Langston Hughes. Reprinted by permission of Indiana University Press; **894** Nazim Hikmet, "The World, My Friends, My Enemies, You, and the Earth" from *Things I Didn't Know I Loved*. Copyright © 1975 by Randy Blasing and Mutlu Konuk. Reprinted by permission of Persea Books, Inc.; **895** Jaime Torres Bodet, "The Window," translated by George Kearns. Translation copyright © 1974, 1963 by the McGraw-Hill Book Company, Inc.; **896** Gabriel Okara, "Once Upon a Time," from *African Voices*, edited by Howard Sergeant. Copyright © 1973 by Howard Sergeant. Used by permission of Evans Brothers Ltd, London; **914** Claribel Alegría, "Because I Want Peace" from *El Salvador: Testament of Terror*, edited by Joe Fish and Cristina Sganga. Copyright © 1988. Reprinted by permission of Olive Branch Press, an imprint of Interlink Publishing Group, Inc.

MAPS

Cartographic services provided by Intergraphics, Maryland CartoGraphics Incorporated, R.R. Donnelley and Sons Company.

PHOTOGRAPHS

Cover Lee Boltin; **Back Cover** Scala/Art Resource, NY; **i** Lee Boltin; **ii** © Erich Lessing/Magnum (bl); British Museum, London/The Bridgeman Art Library (tr); Robert Freck/Odyssey Productions (tl); Farrell Grehan/FPG (br); **ii–iii** Scala/Art Resource, NY; **iii** Scala/Art Resource, NY; **vi** © Erich Lessing/Magnum; **vii** Giraudon/Art Resource, NY (t); © Erich Lessing/Magnum (b); **viii** © Michael Holford; **ix** Victoria & Albert Museum/The Bridgeman Art Library (b); Kunsthistorisches Museum, Vienna/The Bridgeman Art Library (t); **x** © Erich Lessing/Magnum (b); Musée des Arts Decoratifs, Paris/Newsweek Books/Laurie Platt Winfrey, Inc. (t); **xi** The Bettman Archive; **xii** Smithsonian Institution Numismatics (l, r); **xiii** Kobal Collection/ SuperStock (t); Schlowsky Photography/Marianne Dunn (b); **xiv** Schlowsky Photography/Collection of Mary Schafer; **xv** © Erich Lessing/Magnum; **xvi** Laurie Platt Winfrey, Inc.; **xvii** Peabody Museum of Salem (b); **xviii** © Erich Lessing/Magnum (t); © Michael Holford (b); **7** By permission of The Folger Shakespeare Library (b); Maptec International Ltd., Science Photo Library/Photo Researchers, Inc. (t); **8** Robert Frerck/Odyssey Productions (tr); Wolfgang Kaehler (bl); Bernard P. Wolff/Photo Researchers, Inc. (cr); Wolfgang Kaehler (br); **9** COMSTOCK/George Gerster (b); Norman R. Lightfoot/Photo Researchers, Inc. (cr); SuperStock (t); **10** SuperStock (br); Robert Frerck/Odyssey Productions (tr); The Granger Collection (bl); **11** Wolfgang Kaehler (c); © Steve McCurry/Magnum (tr); Don W. Martin/FPG (b); **13** Borromeo/Art Resource, NY; **15** © Rene Burri/Magnum; **17** Des Bartlett/Photo Researchers, Inc.; **19** Wolfgang Kaehler; **21** French Government Tourist Office; **22** © Erich Lessing/Magnum (l); Tom McHugh/Photo Researchers, Inc. (r); **22–23** Wolfgang Kaehler; **23** Lee Boltin; **27** Dilip Mehta/Woodfin Camp & Assoc.; **28** Laurie Platt Winfrey, Inc.; **35** Farrell Grehan/FPG; **36** Farrell Grehan/Photo Researchers, Inc.; **37** © Erich Lessing/Magnum; **40** Lee Boltin; **42** The Granger Collection; **45** Lee Boltin; **46** Smithsonian Institution; **48** © Erich Lessing/Magnum (r); SuperStock (l); **49** British Museum, London/The Bridgeman Art Library (l); British Museum, London/The Bridgeman Art Library (r); **50** © Erich Lessing/Magnum; **53** Smithsonian Institution; **55** © Erich Lessing/Magnum; **58** Giraudon/Art Resource, NY; **60** © Erich Lessing/Magnum; **65** © Erich Lessing/Magnum; **66** Giraudon/Art Resource, NY (r); The Corning Museum of Glass, Corning, New York (l); **67** SuperStock (l); © Erich Lessing/Magnum (r); **71** Sonia Halliday Photographs; **75** Far Eastern Museum, Berlin; **76** SuperStock; **78** © Erich Lessing/Magnum; **83** French Government Tourist Office; **84** British Museum, London/The Bridgeman Art Library; **85** Far Eastern Museum, Berlin; **87** © Erich Lessing/Magnum; **89** © Erich Lessing/Magnum; **91** Art Resource, NY; **92** Don C. Nieman; **94** Scala/Art Resource, NY; **95** © Erich Lessing/Magnum; **99** The Granger Collection; **102** Ronald Sheridan/Ancient Art & Architecture (r); Newsweek Books/Laurie Platt Winfrey, Inc. (l); **103** William Hubbell/Woodfin Camp & Assoc. (l); Scala/Art Resource, NY (r); **105** © Erich Lessing/Magnum; **108** file photo; **115** Scala/Art Resource, NY; **116** COMSTOCK/Hartman-DeWitt; **117** British Museum, London/The Bridgeman Art Library; **119** Robert Frerck/Woodfin Camp & Assoc.; **120** Scala/Art Resource, NY; **122** The Granger Collection; **127** © Erich Lessing/Magnum; **128** © Erich Lessing/Magnum (l, r); **129** Art Resource, NY (l); Scala/Art Resource, NY (br); **132** Scala/Art Resource, NY; **134** Scala/Art Resource, NY; **139** SuperStock; **141** Scala/Art Resource, NY; **146** American Stock Photos/Tom Stack & Assoc.; **152** Alinari/Art Resource, NY (r); Scala/Art Resource, NY (l); **153** © Erich Lessing/Magnum (l); © Erich Lessing/Magnum (r); **154** Brian Brake/Photo Researchers, Inc.; **155** Travelpix/FPG; **156** SEF/Art Resource, NY; **158** National Gallery of Art; **160** © Erich Lessing/Magnum; **163** The Bettmann Archive; **169** SuperStock; **170** Ronald Sheridan/Ancient Art & Architecture; **172** SuperStock (r); © Michael Holford (l); **173** © Michael Holford (l); Robert Frerck/Odyssey Productions (r); **174** file photo; **177** Borromeo/Art Resource, NY; **181** Wolfgang Kaehler; **187** SuperStock; **191** Earl Dibble/FPG; **194** © Michael Holford; **198** © Erich Lessing/Magnum (l); Laurie Platt Winfrey, Inc. (r); **199** Laurie Platt Winfrey, Inc. (l, r); **205** British Museum, London/The Bridgeman Art Library; **206** National Gallery of Art; **207** Laurie Platt Winfrey, Inc.; **209** © Michael Holford; **211** Scala/Art Resource, NY; **213** © Erich Lessing/Magnum; **216** The Granger Collection; **217** © Erich Lessing/Magnum; **218** file photo; **220** Scala/Art Resource, NY (r); Robert Frerck/Odyssey Productions (l); **221** Byzantine Collection, Dumbarton Oaks (r); Sonia Halliday Photographs (l); **226** John Kohan; **227** The Granger Collection; **228** The Granger Collection; **233** American Stock Photos/Tom Stack & Assoc.; **235** Historical Pictures Service, Cgo.; **237** British Library, London/The Bridgeman Art Library; **238** SEF/Art Resource, NY; **239** Metropolitan Museum of Art; **240** Historical Pictures Service, Cgo.; **242** Freer Gallery of Art, Smithsonian Institution (l); Victoria & Albert Museum/The Bridgeman Art Library (r); **243** Victoria & Albert Museum/The Bridgeman Art Library (r); Robert Frerck/Odyssey Productions (l); **250** Robert Kohan; **251** SEF/Art Resource, NY; **252** Scala/Art Resource, NY; **257** Giraudon/Art Resource, NY; **263** Giraudon/Art Resource, NY; **265** Laurie Platt Winfrey, Inc.; **268** The Granger Collection (l, r); **269** Scala/Art Resource, NY (l); Robert Frerck/Odyssey Productions (r); **270** Photographie Giraudon, Paris; **273** Musée de la Reine, Bayeux/The Bridgeman Art Library; **275** Historical Pictures Service, Cgo.; **281** Art Resource, NY; **283** The Granger Collection; **288** SuperStock (l); © Erich Lessing/Magnum (r); **288–289** Scala/Art Resource, NY; **289** Canterbury Cathedral, Canterbury, Kent/The Bridgeman Art Library; **291** Giraudon/Art Resource, NY; **292** The Granger Collection; **295** Chartres Cathedral, France/The Bridgeman Art Library; **297** The Granger Collection; **300** Historical Pictures Service, Cgo.; **305** Bibliotheque Nationale, Paris; **307** The Granger Collection; **309** Ronald Sheridan/Ancient Art & Architecture; **312** SuperStock (l); © Michael Holford (r); **313** Leo Touchet/Woodfin Camp & Assoc. (l); SuperStock (r); **315** File Photo; **317** International Society for Educational Information, Tokyo; **319** SuperStock; **320** © Michael Holford; **324** Mary Evans Picture Library; **326** Freer Gallery of Art, Smithsonian Institution; **327** B. Norman/Ancient Art & Architecture; **331** The British Library; **334** B. Brander/Photo Researchers,

Inc.; **337** Victor Englebert; **338** The Granger Collection; **339** SuperStock; **342** British Museum, London/The Bridgeman Art Library (r); Robert Frerck/Odyssey Productions (l); **343** COMSTOCK/George Gerster (l); Courtesy of the School of American Research (r); **345** Historical Pictures Service, Cgo.; **348** Wayne Ettema; **349** Don W. Martin/FPG; **355** Laurie Platt Winfrey, Inc.; **357** The Granger Collection; **359** file photo; **361** © Erich Lessing/Magnum; **363** Scala/Art Resource, NY; **367** Oliver Radford; **368** Scala/Art Resource, NY; **369** Scala/Art Resource, NY; **370** Scala/Art Resource, NY; **371** Scala/Art Resource, NY; **372** Giraudon/Art Resource, NY (r); © Erich Lessing/Magnum (l); **373** Kunsthistorisches Museum, Vienna/The Bridgeman Art Library; **374** © Bruno Barbey/Magnum; **377** The Granger Collection; **378** German Information Center; **380** file photo; **382** The Bettmann Archive; **386** Art Resource, NY; **388** Scala/Art Resource, NY; **393** City Art Gallery, Bristol; **396** Belvoir Castle, Rutland/The Bridgeman Art Library (r); Giraudon/Art Resource, NY (l); © Erich Lessing/Magnum (c); **397** Rijksmuseum, Amsterdam/The Bridgeman Art Library; **398** Scala/Art Resource, NY; **399** The Granger Collection; **401** Index, Spain/The Bridgeman Art Library; **403** Historical Pictures Service, Cgo.; **404** New York Public Library; **407** The Granger Collection; **408** Coutesy of The Hispanic Society of America, New York; **409** Robert Frerck/Odyssey Productions; **415** Scala/Art Resource, NY; **417** MAS; **420** John P. Stevens/Ancient Art & Architecture (r); Christie's, London/The Bridgeman Art Library (l); **420–421** By permission of The Folger Shakespeare Library; **421** © Michael Holford; **422** © Erich Lessing/Magnum; **423** By kind permission of the Marquess of Tavistock, and the Trustees of the Bedford Estates, Woburn Abbey; **425** Scala/Art Resource, NY; **426** Bridgeman/Art Resource, NY (b); Private Collection/The Bridgeman Art Library (t); **430** Staatliche Museen zu Berlin; **431** The Granger Collection; **433** The Bettmann Archive; **434** The Granger Collection; **439** Giraudon/Art Resource, NY; **442** file photo; **444** Laurie Platt Winfrey, Inc. (r); Laurie Platt Winfrey, Inc. (l); **445** Wolfgang Kaehler (l); Giraudon/Art Resource, NY (r); **446** SuperStock; **448** The British Library; **451** The Granger Collection; **453** British Museum, London/The Bridgeman Art Library; **458** Oliver Radford; **460** The Granger Collection; **461** Wolfgang Kaehler; **463** file photo; **465** © Erich Lessing/Magnum; **467** National Gallery, London/The Bridgeman Art Library; **469** The Granger Collection; **470** The Granger Collection; **474** Kenwood House, London/The Bridgeman Art Library; **477** New York Public Library; **478** Musée des Arts Decoratifs, Paris/Newsweek Books/Laurie Platt Winfrey, Inc. (l); National Gallery of Scotland, Edinburgh/The Bridgeman Art Library (r); **479** Private Collection/The Bridgeman Art Library (l); The Granger Collection (r); **480** The Granger Collection; **481** The Granger Collection; **487** Forbes Magazine Collection, New York/The Bridgeman Art Library; **489** Scala/Art Resource, NY; **490** Giraudon/Art Resource, NY; **493** SuperStock; **494** The Bettmann Archive; **496** Historical Pictures Service, Cgo.; **498** Giraudon/Art Resource, NY (bl); Smithsonian Institution Numismatics (c, r); **499** Collection of the Maryland Historical Society (l); Newsweek Books/Laurie Platt Winfrey, Inc. (r); **500** The Granger Collection; **501** file photo; **503** The Granger Collection; **504** The Granger Collection; **511** Giraudon/Art Resource, NY; **513** Historical Pictures Service, Cgo.; **515** The Granger Collection; **516** Laurie Platt Winfrey, Inc. (l); **516–517** Giraudon/Art Resource, NY; © Erich Lessing/Magnum (r); **517** © Erich Lessing/Magnum; **518** Historical Pictures Service, Cgo.; **521** The Bettmann Archive; **522** Historical Pictures Service, Cgo.; **524** © Erich Lessing/Magnum; **525** Scala/Art Resource, NY; **529** The Granger Collection; **531** Historisches Museum der Stadt Wien; **533** Historical Pictures Service, Cgo.; **536** The Granger Collection; **537** Giraudon/Art Resource, NY; **538** © Erich Lessing/Magnum; **542** Private Collection/The Bridgeman Art Library; **544** Collection of the Maryland Historical Society; **545** Scala/Art Resource, NY; **547** National Gallery of Scotland, Edinburgh/The Bridgeman Art Library; **549** The National Motor Museum, Beaulieu; **551** Art Resource, NY; **553** The Granger Collection; **556** The Granger Collection; **557** Mary Evans Picture Library; **560** Smithsonian Institution; **562** Lauros-Giraudon/The Bridgeman Art Library; **565** Photograph by John Thomson from "Street Life In London" by John Thomson and Adolphe Smith, London, 1877; **566** The Granger Collection (r); Schlowsky Photography/Marianne Dunn (l); **567** Brown Brothers (c); New York Public Library (l); **573** New York Historical Society; **575** By Courtesy of the National Portrait Gallery; **577** The Bettmann Archive; **579** The Royal Institution; **580** © Erich Lessing/Magnum; **583** The Bettmann Archive; **584** The Bettmann Archive (r); Private Collection/The Bridgeman Art Library (l); **585** Culver Pictures (r); The Granger Collection (l); **587** From the collection at the Laing Art Gallery, Newcastle upon Tyne, England, reproduced permission of Tyne and Wear Museums Service; **589** Giraudon/Art Resource, NY; **591** Scala/Art Resource, NY; **592** Bridgeman/Art Resource, NY; **594** Culver Pictures; **596** Scala/Art Resource, NY; **601** By courtesy of Birmingham Museums and Art Gallery; **603** The Granger Collection (l, r); **605** The Granger Collection; **608** Texas Highway Dept., Austin; **611** Historical Pictures Service, Cgo.; **613** Science Museum/The Bridgeman Art Library; **616** Boston Athenaeum (r); © 1984, Time-Life Books Inc., from the Civil War series, *Decoying the Yanks*, photograph by Larry Sherer (l); **617** Boston Athenaeum (l); Library of Congress (r); **619** AP/Wide World Photos; **623** Museum of Modern Art of Latin America; **629** The Granger Collection; **631** The Bettmann Archive; **632** Scala/Art Resource, NY (l, r); **633** Scala/Art Resource, NY (l); The Bettmann Archive (r); **636** ADN/Zentralbild; **637** COMSTOCK/Michael Stuckey; **639** Archiv für Kunstund Geschichte; **642** Historical Pictures Service, Cgo.; **643** Tass from Sovphoto; **645** Brown Brothers; **647** © Stephane Korb/Magnum; **650** SEF/Art Resource, NY; **657** India Office/The British Library; **658** The Granger Collection; **658–659** Private Collection/The Bridgeman Art Library; **659** Peter Gottschalk (r); Mark Sexton/Peabody Museum of Salem (c); **660** Historical Pictures Service, Cgo.; **664** The Granger Collection; **665** Culver Pictures; **666** The Mansell Collection; **671** Sekai Bunka Photo; **673** Victoria & Albert Museum, London/The Bridgeman Art Library; **679** "Puck", August 15, 1900; **682** Brown Brothers; **685** The Granger Collection; **687** New York Public Library; **689** The Granger Collection; **691** Imperial War Museum; **692** Private Collection/The Bridgeman Art Library (l); UPI/Bettmann (r); **693** John Davies Fine Paintings, Stow-on-the-Wold, Glos/The Bridgeman Art Library (r); The Bettmann Archive (l); **695** The Granger Collection; **697** Art Resource, NY; **699** Library of Congress; **701** The Bettmann Archive; **703** Historical Pictures Service, Cgo.; **707** The Granger Collection; **708** The Granger Collection; **711** The Granger Collection; **714** John Frost Historical Newspaper Service; **719** File Photo; **721** Kansas State Historical Society; **723** Courtesy of Treasures of Westport Inc. Selectman's Office, Westport, CT; **724** Kobal Collection/SuperStock; **727** The Bettmann Archive; **729** Historical Pictures Service, Cgo.; **731** SEF/Art Resource, NY; **733** The Bettmann Archive; **734** UPI/Bettmann Newsphotos (r); FlexPhoto (l); **735** UPI/Bettmann (r); The Granger Collection (l); **736** Hugo Jaeger/*Life* Magazine © 1964, Time Warner, Inc.; **737** Tass from Sovfoto; **739** Sovfoto; **745** Carl Frank/Photo Researchers, Inc.; **746** The Granger Collection; **749** Art Resource, NY; **750** The Granger Collection; **751** Eliot Elisofon National Museum of African Art, Eliot Elisofon Archives, Smithsonian Institution; **753** The Granger Collection; **756** J.P. Laffont/SYGMA; **757** Library of Congress; **758** UPI/Bettmann (l); Historical Pictures Service, Cgo. (r); Imperial War Museum (c); **759** UPI/Bettmann (r); Schlowsky Photography (l); **762** The Granger Collection; **763** Historical Pictures Service, Cgo.; **766** UPI/Bettmann; **768** Robert Frerck/Odyssey Productions; **773** Naval Photographic Center/DAVA; **775** Wide World Photos; **777** Keystone Collection; **780** Mauritius/Black Star; **782** AP/Wide World Photos (l); The Granger Collection (r); **783** Bettmann/Hulton (r); Imperial War Museum (l); **785** Ullstein Bilderdienst; **787** Margaret Bourke-White/*Life* Magazine, © 1945 Time Warner Inc.; **788** UPI; **789** Library of Congress; **795** U.S. Coast Guard; **797** U.S. Air Force Photo; **803** Courtesy of Treasures of Westport Inc. Selectman's Office, Westport, CT; **804** Hugo Jaeger/*Life* Magazine © 1964, Time Warner, Inc.; **805** AP/Wide World Photos; **807** The Granger Collection; **809** Lee Boltin; **811** Jim Pickerell/FPG; 814 Frederic Lewis/R. Gates; **816** © Robert Capa/Magnum (l, r); **817** © Marilyn Silverstone/ Magnum (r); COMSTOCK/Adam Tanner (l); **818** German Information Center; **820** Sovfoto; **821** NASA; **824** Black Star; **827** AP/Wide World Photos; **828** Tate Gallery, London/Art Resource, NY; **830** © Elliot Erwitt/Magnum; **831** Owen Franken/Stock Boston; **837** Sovfoto/Eastfoto; **838** AP/Wide World Photos; **839** U.S. Army Signal Corps; **840** J.P. Laffont/SYGMA; **843** The Granger Collection; **844** © Henri Cartier-Bresson/Magnum; **846** UPI/Bettmann (r); Imperial War Museum (l); **847** UPI/Bettmann (l, r); **849** AP/Wide World Photos; **850** Wide World Photos; **852** Popperfoto; **856** file photo; **858** Wide World Photos; **859** Schlowsky Photography/Collection of Mary Schafer; **860** SuperStock; **869** J. Pickerell/Black Star; **873** Robert Frerck/Odyssey Productions; **875** © D. McCullin/Magnum; **877** Peter Magubane/AP/Wide World Photos; **879** SuperStock; **886** © Inge Morath/Magnum (r); © Rene Burri/Magnum (l); © Abbas/Magnum (c); **887** Pénélope Chauvelot/SYGMA; **888** D. Rubinger/Black Star; **891** C. Spengler/SYGMA; **894** AP/Wide World Photos; **901** Robert Frerck/Odyssey Productions; **903** Messerschmidt/FPG; **904** Christiana Dittman/Rainbow; **908** Nik Wheeler/Black Star (r); Schlowsky Photography/Collection of Mary Schafer (l); **908–909** Wayne Ettema (l, r); **911** AP/Wide World Photos; **912** © Susan Meiselas/Magnum; **917** UPI/Bettmann Archive; **918** Boston Symphony Orchestra Archives; **925** Orban/SYGMA; **927** White House Photo; **928** Schlowsky Photography/Collection of John Jenkins III (c); Schlowsky Photography/Courtesy of Mary Schafer (l); **928–929** UPI/Bettmann Newsphotos; **929** John Filo; **930** Private Collection, Courtesy André Emmerich Gallery, New York; **933** By permission of Bill Mauldin and Will-Jo Associates, Inc.; **934** P. Piel/Gamma-Liaison; **938** Chris Niedenthal/Black Star; **939** Wide World Photos; **940** Superstock; **943** M. Philippot/SYGMA; **944** © Jean Gaumy/Magnum; **945** © Alex Webb/Magnum; **951** NASA; **952** Eiji Miyuzawa/Black Star; **953** NASA; **954** Schlowsky Photography/Courtesy Amy Wrynn & Daniel Dineen (l); SuperStock (r); **955** SuperStock (r); Dan McCoy/Rainbow (l); **956** J.P. Laffont/SYGMA; **958** Doug Wilson/The Stock Solution; **959** Joe Viesti/Viesti Assoc.; **962** © Chris Steele-Perkins/Magnum; **963** Wide World Photos; **964** Jeffery Smith/Woodfin Camp & Assoc.; **965** James D. Nations/DDB Stock Photography; **968** Jean Louis Atlan/SYGMA; **969** Wide World Photos; **970** Zimmerman/FPG; **971** Scala/Art Resource, NY; **976** German Information Center; **977** UPI/Bettmann; **978** Nik Wheeler/Black Star; **981** The Granger Collection

WORLD UPDATE

Consultant: Alexey A. Pankin, Directorate of Foreign Relations
Academy of Pedagogical Sciences, Moscow, Russia

A Changing World

As 1992 DAWNED, the Soviet Union no longer existed; the cold war was at an end; and a new world order was emerging. Only a year earlier, the Soviet Union, although a troubled nation facing economic and ethnic problems, had been a superpower.

In an extremely short period of time during 1991, the 74-year-old Soviet experiment was swept away by an unforeseen series of events. First, an inept group of Communist party hardliners ousted Soviet President Mikhail Gorbachev and proclaimed a new government in the old Communist tradition.

They failed, however, to take into account Russian President Boris Yeltsin, who rallied the Russian people against the new leaders. When the coup collapsed and Gorbachev returned to Moscow, everything had changed: Yeltsin not Gorbachev—was the person in charge.

Gorbachev resigned as head of the Communist party three days later and urged that it be abolished, but nothing could stem the tide of change. First, the

Examining Photographs
Citizens of Moscow, riding a tank and carrying the white, blue, and red flag of pre-Communist Russia, celebrate the collapse of the coup staged by Communist hardliners in August 1991. One factor in the coup's failure was the refusal of the military to carry out the orders of coup leaders to suppress demonstrations.

Baltic republics won their freedom, and then the remaining 12 republics. By year's end, 11 of them had joined in a Commonwealth of Independent States. Russia and Yeltsin were dominant—Gorbachev was forced out of office.

While the Soviet Union entered history, profound changes heralded an uncertain future in eastern Europe. Yugoslavia, once held together by a loyalty to its own brand of communism, began to unravel as communist ideology throughout the region waned. As a result, the country plunged into Europe's first large-scale civil war since 1945.

Meanwhile, the opposite was occurring in western Europe, where the 12 members of the European Community took the first crucial steps toward complete economic and political union. With the forging of a large European market, the European Community hoped to emerge as a global trading power equal to the United States and Japan.

The Soviet Collapse

IN EARLY 1991, many of the Soviet republics were demanding independence from Moscow. To halt the breakup of the Soviet Union, Soviet President Mikhail Gorbachev proposed a new Union Treaty. The treaty was to establish a new constitutional basis for the relationship between the Soviet central government and the republics that made up the Soviet Union. Under the treaty, the republics would gain more control over their industrial and natural resources, while the Kremlin would have a say in economic and political reforms.

Hardliners Oust Gorbachev Fearing the loss of central government authority over the republics, Communist hardliners in August tried to force Gorbachev to declare a state of emergency. When Gorbachev refused, the hardliners ousted the Soviet President from power and formed a ruling committee.

The new leaders immediately clamped down on the press, banned demonstrations, and introduced curfews. After imposing a national state of emergency, the committee tried to use force to consolidate its power. Tanks, armored personnel carriers, and trucks loaded with soldiers swarmed through Moscow. The crackdown, however, was heaviest in the independence-minded Baltic republics. Soviet military officials took control of Lithuania, Latvia, and Estonia, and Soviet troops forced their way into TV and radio stations. Soviet warships blocked the main harbor in Estonia.

People Against the Coup As the coup leaders sought to consolidate their power, Soviet citizens began to respond. Small bands of Moscow residents built barricades of concrete blocks, iron bars, benches, and parked buses to prevent tanks from passing through the streets. In an afternoon of heated exchanges with civilians who climbed aboard their

Examining Photographs *Russian President Boris Yeltsin addresses a cheering crowd of pro-democracy supporters outside the Russian parliament building in Moscow, where he had led public resistance against the coup. As a result of the coup's collapse, Yeltsin emerged as the most powerful figure in the Soviet Union.*

Examining Photographs *During the days of the coup, supporters of Boris Yeltsin built barricades around the Russian parliament building to protect the Russian President and his staff inside. Many young citizens of Moscow were involved in the resistance to coup leaders.*

tanks, Russian soldiers stationed in Moscow said they did not want to shed Russian blood.

Russian President Boris Yeltsin rallied public support against the coup and for democracy. Appearing before a throng gathered in front of the Russian parliament building, he called for nonviolent resistance and urged military officials to refuse to carry out committee orders.

In response to Yeltsin's appeal, Moscow citizens set up barricades outside the parliament building and in neighboring streets. Tens of thousands of them defied the curfew to stand guard in the rain to protect Yeltsin and his aides, who remained holed up in the parliament building. Aside from a barricade of eight tanks that defected to the side of anti-coup forces, the protesters were unarmed.

Even though a column of tanks maneuvered nearby, no attack occurred. Inside the parliament building, Yeltsin supporters operated fax machines and photocopiers to print makeshift newspapers for distribution throughout the country. The resistance inspired by Yeltsin soon spread beyond Moscow, despite the ban on demonstrations. In Leningrad, 200,000 people jammed the city's main square and cheered for their liberal mayor, Anatoli Sobchak. About 400,000 demonstrators in Kishinev, the capital of Moldova, demanded the resignation of coup leaders and the return of Gorbachev. Coal miners in Siberia and the north carried out strikes, although in other parts of the country, industries were operating normally. In the Baltic republics, the parliaments of Estonia, Latvia, and Lithuania declared full independence from the Soviet Union.

In a startling development, many KGB (secret police) and military units throughout the nation refused to carry out orders from coup leaders.

Collapse of Coup In the face of public resistance, international condemnation, and growing splits within its ranks, the coup crumbled two days after it was announced. As troops and tanks withdrew from Moscow, the Soviet Parliament announced that it had formally reinstated Gorbachev as President. Meanwhile, Soviet police jailed many of the committee members and other conspirators.

Although Gorbachev was back in power, the coup and its failure had made him lose face. It was now

Examining Photographs After the coup's collapse, a wave of anti-Communist feeling swept the Soviet republics. In response to the public mood, Soviet President Mikhail Gorbachev resigned as Communist party leader and ended the party's 74-year rule of the Soviet Union. In Moscow and other Soviet cities, crowds cheered as statues of Lenin and other Communist leaders were removed from public squares and parks.

widely recognized that the coup stemmed from Gorbachev's inability to solve the Soviet Union's many problems and his unwillingness to break with the Communist old guard. The failed coup, on the other hand, had boosted the standing of Boris Yeltsin. Having rallied his people to resistance, Yeltsin was acclaimed as a world-respected leader.

End of Communist Rule Within a few days of the coup's collapse, Gorbachev and Yeltsin began forging a new relationship, one in which Yeltsin had the upper hand. Gorbachev removed from government posts the men who had tried to oust him and promised a renewed push for democratic reforms. He also announced the appointment of committed reformers to government positions. These people were chosen with the consent of Yeltsin and other leaders.

Meanwhile, anti-Communist demonstrations swept the Soviet Union. In Moscow, crowds cheered wildly as giant cranes toppled a large statue of the founder of the KGB. In other areas of the Soviet Union, statues of Communist leaders were removed from public squares. In the weeks that followed, many cities throughout the country began adopting their pre-1917 names. For example, Leningrad, the city that gave birth to the 1917 Bolshevik Revolution, reverted to its historic name: St. Petersburg.

Responding to the rising wave of anti-communism, Gorbachev on August 24 resigned as Communist party leader while remaining Soviet president. He urged the Central Committee—the Communist party's decision-making body—to disband, thus signaling the political collapse of the institution that had ruled the Soviet Union with an iron hand for nearly seven decades.

Gorbachev saw the further erosion of his authority as a number of Soviet republics declared their independence from the central government. Armenia, Georgia, Moldova, and the Baltic republics acted on earlier declarations and declared their full separation from the Soviet Union. The republics of Ukraine and Belarus took the first steps toward independence. The Baltic republics and eventually many of the other republics received recognition from the Soviet Union, the United States, and the European Community.

The Commonwealth

DURING LATE 1991, the Soviet republics faced a deepening economic and political crisis, and growing social tensions were erupting into ethnic conflicts. Declaring that the Soviet Union had ceased to exist, the leaders of the three Slavic republics of Russia, Ukraine, and Belarus announced the formation of a new Commonwealth of Independent States. They named themselves the first three members of the new union, and opened membership to all republics of the former Soviet Union.

The three cofounders of the Commonwealth—President Boris Yeltsin of Russia, President Leonid Kravchuk of Ukraine, and Stanislav Shushkevich, Chairman of the Belarus Parliament—stated that their authority to dissolve the Soviet Union rested on

Examining Photographs *Former Soviet President Mikhail Gorbachev gives a news conference following his resignation speech on December 25, 1991. Although Gorbachev's reforms had failed to halt Soviet economic decline, the Soviet leader won worldwide acclaim for his efforts to make the Soviet Union a freer society.*

the fact their countries were three of the four original cosigners of the 1922 treaty that had created the Union of Soviet Socialist Republics.

The new declaration—signed in Mensk, the capital of Belarus—nullified the Union Treaty proposed by Gorbachev. It stated that the Commonwealth assumed all international responsibilities of the former Soviet Union, including control over the Soviet nuclear arsenal.

In late December at Alma Ata in the republic of Kazakhstan, eight other former Soviet republics joined Russia, Ukraine, and Belarus in signing an accord that made them members of the Commonwealth of Independent States. Only the republic of Georgia did not join the new union.

New Beginning The loosely structured Commonwealth was intended to replace the highly centralized Soviet Union. Under the new arrangement, each member republic was sovereign and independent. A central administration, however, was established in Mensk to coordinate economic and monetary policies. In matters of defense, Commonwealth leaders agreed to a permanent unified command over the nuclear weapons held by Russia, Ukraine, and Kazakhstan, but each republic asserted the right to organize and maintain its own conventional military forces.

Resignation of Gorbachev On December 25, Mikhail Gorbachev resigned the Soviet presidency. "We are now living in a new world," he declared

COMMONWEALTH OF INDEPENDENT STATES

Examining Maps The Commonwealth of Independent States is a loose alliance of republics, shown above with their capitals. Formed in December 1991, the Commonwealth replaced the Soviet Union, which Mikhail Gorbachev had tried unsuccessfully to reform during the late 1980s and early 1990s.

THE EMERGING COMMONWEALTH

Republic (Date Independence Declared)	Capital	Population Estimates	Ethnic Groups	Major Products	Before Union Breakup
Armenia (9/23/91)	Erivan	3,305,000	90% Armenian 5% Azeri 5% Russian,	chemicals, machinery, textiles, grapes	0.2% land 1.2% pop. .9% GNP
Azerbaijan (8/30/91)	Baku	7,145,600	80% Azeri 8% Russian 8% Armenian 4% Daghestani	oil, copper, chemicals, cotton, rice, grapes, tobacco, silk	0.3% land 2.4% pop. 1.7% GNP
Kyrgyzstan (8/31/91)	Bishkek	4,372,000	52% Kirghiz 22% Russian 13% Uzbek 4% Ukrainian 2% Tatars	wool, livestock, machine and instrument production	0.9% land 1.5% pop. 0.8% GNP
Belarus (8/25/91)	Mensk	10,200,000	79% Byelorussian 12% Russian 4% Polish 2% Ukrainian 1% Jewish	chemicals, agri-cultural machinery, paper, building materials, potatoes, livestock	1.0% land 3.5% pop. 4.2% GNP
Georgia* (8/23/91)	Tbilisi	5,538,000	69% Georgian 9% Armenian 9% Russian	tea, citrus fruits, grapes, silk, tobacco, manganese, coal	0.3% land 1.9% pop. 1.6% GNP
Kazakhstan (10/26/90)	Alma Ata	16,538,000	36% Kazakh 41% Russian 6% Ukrainian	cotton, millet, coal, oil, lead, zinc, copper	12.1% land 5.7% pop. 4.3% GNP
Moldova (8/27/91)	Kishinev	4,321,000	64% Moldovan 14% Ukrainian 13% Russian	wines, tobacco, grain, vegetables	0.2% land 1.5% pop. 1.2% GNP
Russia (6/12/90)	Moscow	147,386,000	83% Russian more than 100 ethnic groups	chemicals, building materials, machine steel, cars, trucks, wheat, barley, rye, potatoes, sugar beets	76.6% land 51.4% pop. 61.1% GNP
Tajikistan (9/9/91)	Dushanbe	5,112,000	59% Tajik 23% Uzbek 10% Russian	cattle, sheep, fruit, hydroelectric power	0.7% land 1.8% pop. 0.8% GNP
Turkmenistan (8/22/90)	Ashkhabad	3,621,000	68% Turkmeni 13% Russian 9% Uzbek	oil, sulphur, cotton, dates, olives, figs	2.2% land 1.3% pop. 0.7% GNP
Ukraine (8/24/91)	Kiev	51,704,000	74% Ukrainian 21% Russian 1% Jewish	wheat, sugar beets, iron, oil, chemicals, machinery	2.7% land 18.0% pop. 16.2% GNP
Uzbekistan (8/31/91)	Tashkent	19,906,000	69% Uzbek 11% Russian 4% Tatar	cotton	2.0% land 6.9% pop. 3.3% GNP

*has not yet decided to join Commonwealth

Examining Photographs In late December 1991, leaders of the new Commonwealth of Independent States met in Mensk, the capital of Belarus, to discuss military policies. They agreed to have a permanent unified command over nuclear weapons, but allowed each republic the right to maintain its own conventional forces.

on state-run television. The former leader expressed concern for the new Commonwealth of Independent States: "I'm worried by the fact the people have lost the citizenship of a great country. The consequences can be unpredictable."

Following Gorbachev's speech, the red hammer and sickle Soviet flag that had flown over the Kremlin for 74 years was lowered and replaced with the white, blue, and red flag of Russia.

Yeltsin and Russia While signaling the end of Gorbachev's presidency, the formation of the Commonwealth confirmed Yeltsin's rise to power. Although the leaders of the 11 republics in the Commonwealth considered themselves equal, Yeltsin was the first among equals. His Russian Federation was the most powerful nation in the Commonwealth. By far the largest nation in land area and population, Russia produces about 90 percent of the oil and natural gas in the Commonwealth.

Just as his country far outstripped the other 10 in the Commonwealth, so did Boris Yeltsin's powers outstrip those of the other leaders—in fact, if not on paper. During the final months of the Soviet Union, Yeltsin assumed complete control over production and export of Russia's resources. He began monetary reforms designed to force the other republics to follow Russia's pace of change, and persuaded the Russian Parliament to vote him any powers necessary to implement reforms.

Yeltsin further expanded his leadership when he engineered the Commonwealth. As the new arrangement became more and more of a reality, Yeltsin took control of the Kremlin and all Soviet central government agencies. He assumed command of former Soviet President Mikhail Gorbachev's staff and office, and placed the Soviet Foreign Ministry and embassies under Russian control. With Gorbachev's resignation and Yeltsin's responsibility for the former Soviet Union's nuclear arsenal, Yeltsin, along with United States President Bush, became one of the world's most powerful leaders.

Although Yeltsin was the most influential Commonwealth leader, he had to assume responsibility for Russia's problems: a shattered economy, deteriorating public services, and ethnic strife. The Russian government had to carry the brunt of the Soviet Union's budget and debt load. As Russia's leader, Yeltsin also had to lead the Commonwealth into the international free market system, make good on his promise to revive a shattered economy, improve public services, and settle ethnic unrest. Finally, he had to demonstrate to the other republics and to the global community that Russia would not use its power to turn the Commonwealth into a new authoritarian Russian empire.

Economic Crisis Although the Commonwealth broke decisively with the Soviet past, its member republics faced a host of economic problems. These included rising prices, stagnant overseas trade, a decaying transportation system, and a declining standard of living. Continuing political instability also hindered the former Soviet republics from introducing workable economic reforms.

The economic crisis was particularly severe in the area of agriculture. Unresolved problems of food production and distribution, inherited from the previous centralized and subsidized system, had been heightened by months of political turmoil and governmental neglect.

Small farms and state-run complexes had long blamed the Soviet government for failing to deliver promised farm machinery and other equipment. In retaliation, farmers routinely "hid" thousands of tons of grain to use as barter on the black market. The results were seen in the fact that state stores had continual shortages of produce.

Examining Charts
In January 1992, Yeltsin and other Commonwealth leaders lifted long-standing price controls in an effort to bring more food to store shelves in their individual republics. As the figures here indicate, prices of goods in government-run stores immediately rose to high levels, while prices continued even higher in free-enterprise markets. Although ordinary citizens grumbled, Commonwealth leaders saw the ending of price controls as a necessary, though painful, step in the process of moving their economies toward capitalism.

Price Increases in Russia, January 1992					
	Old subsidized state price	Hours of work*	New price at state stores	Hours of work*	Price at private market stores	Hours of work*
Smoked sausage rubles per pound	35.5	17.8	49.1	24.5	68.2	34.1
Chicken rubles per pound	15.5	7.8	21.6	10.8	40.9	20.5
Butter rubles per pound	4.5	2.3	20.5	10.3	50	25
White bread rubles per loaf	.6	18 minutes	49.1	54 minutes	n/a	n/a
Milk rubles per quart	.69	21 minutes	2.1	1.1	37.1	18.6
Gasoline (93 octane) rubles per quart	.42	13 minutes	1.3	39 minutes	3.2	1.6

*Number of hours an average worker must work to earn that amount, based on about 175 hours of work per month.

Source: AP

Manufacturers of farm machinery also had complained of the same neglect and government disinterest as the farmers. During 1991, plants reported production drops of as much as 90 percent because of a lack of parts and supplies.

Another problem inherited from the past was the antiquated method of harvesting and getting crops to market. On many farms, harvesting was still done by hand; students and soldiers were drafted to pick, load, and unload crops. The poor transportation system also contributed its share to agricultural shortcomings. The system was not capable of delivering the goods.

Plagued by long-standing problems of machine shortages, outdated farming practices, and inadequate transportation, the agricultural sector was further afflicted by new problems arising from the political unrest of 1991. Many farmers, now free to sell crops to the highest bidder, refused to sell any to the crumbling state system at rock-bottom prices. As a result, government grain houses were empty during the months of the autumn harvest.

The collapse of Gorbachev's government meant that no central agency was in control of the flow of food and supplies between the republics. In the absence of central leadership, the republics began taking matters into their own hands. Early in October, Ukraine—the traditional "breadbasket" of the Soviet Union—banned grain exports to other republics. The other republics followed suit as winter approached. By December, a lack of food exports was causing serious food shortages in many of Russia's cities, most notably Moscow and St. Petersburg, and other nonagricultural areas. Some locations officially reserved all meat and milk supplies for schools and hospitals. Adding to food shortages was 1991's lowered grain production.

The economy's disintegration was seen in other areas. Inflation skyrocketed as government presses printed more currency to cover growing government expenditures. Fuel shortages led to cold living facilities, the shutdown of many airports, and the cancellation of most domestic flights. Consumers stood in long lines at stores, people foraged in fields, and older citizens and the poor combed garbage dumps for food and clothing.

In a rapid shift to free enterprise, the governments of Russia and the other republics lifted price controls

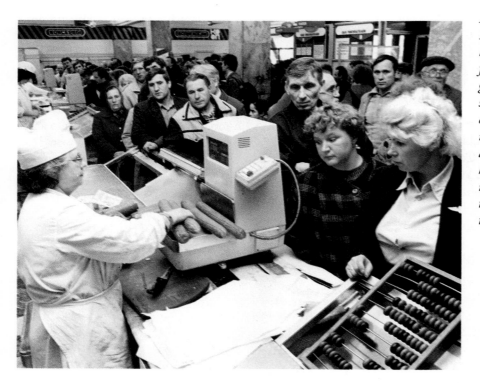

Examining Photographs
Russian shoppers form lines to purchase scarce food items in a government-run produce store. By early 1992, declining production, inadequate distribution, and widespread hoarding had led to food shortages in many towns and cities throughout Russia and the other republics.

Examining Photographs *A woman in the Georgian capital of Tbilisi stands in front of her house that was burned to the ground as a result of street violence between troops loyal to President Zviad Gamsakhurdia and opposition forces. Gamsakhurdia was later ousted from power, but he continued to resist the new military government that succeeded him.*

in early January 1992. Although prices rose significantly as a result, officials hoped that the move would in the long run spur production, stimulate competition, and lower prices. By late February, however, prices still had not declined, although more food had appeared in produce stores and emergency supplies were arriving from the United States and other foreign nations.

As the economic crisis continued, public opinion became divided. Many older Russians expressed a longing to return to the Communist system, while younger Russians preferred to support Yeltsin and to give his reforms more time to work. Meanwhile, critics of Yeltsin's reform plans emerged within the government. Vice-President Alexander Rutskoi led the attack, calling for an end to economic "shock therapy" and a return to government controls.

Future Prospects At the beginning of 1992, predictions about the future of the Commonwealth varied. Pessimists concluded that continuing economic distress could deepen into famine. Such a situation, they said, might lead to riots, civil war, and the return of dictatorship.

Optimists, while acknowledging the critical economic situation, did not expect widespread famine. They predicted continued shortages, long lines of dissatisfied shoppers, and perhaps "pockets of poverty" at the mercy of the decaying transportation system. They did not necessarily believe that the Commonwealth was headed for dictatorship.

Whether pessimists or optimists, experts agreed that the Commonwealth's job of converting to a free market economy would be long-term and would not bring prosperity for many years. During the transition, they stated, unemployment in the republics would rise as inefficient industries closed. Inflation would continue as the lifting of price controls took effect. Very few citizens anywhere in the Commonwealth would adjust easily to these changes.

Georgia Beset by internal conflict, Georgia was the only former Soviet republic that did not immediately join the Commonwealth of Independent States. In December 1991, heavy fighting flared between troops loyal to President Zviad Gamsakhur (zvee·AHD gahm·sah·KOOR·dee·ah) and rebel forces. Gamsakhurdia had become increasingly unpopular since his election in May. In recent months, the president had closed opposition newspapers, fired government officials who questioned his policies, and persecuted non-Georgian groups. Gamsakhurdia's opponents accused him of being a dictator and resorted to force to remove him from power.

Vowing not to resign, Gamsakhurdia sought refuge in the parliament building, while his troops battled rebels in the streets of Tbilisi, the capital. Finally, in early January 1992, Gamsakhurdia's forces were defeated by the rebels, and the president fled to neighboring Armenia. A military junta came to power, promising new elections in the spring for a civilian government that would establish a democratic system.

Support for the deposed president, however, re-mained strong, as daily pro-Gamsakhurdia rallies took place in Tbilisi. During the first week in January, gunmen loyal to the military junta fired on the demonstrators, killing at least two civilians and wounding as many as 30 others. The junta, which had declared a state of emergency, regretted the shootings but defended the need for law and order. Meanwhile, Georgia's political leaders continued to debate the country's future.

Changes in Europe

DURING THE PERIOD of the Soviet collapse, Europe underwent a number of significant changes. In eastern Europe, nations newly freed from Communist rule experienced difficulties adjusting to democracy and free enterprise economies. In western Europe, the nations of the European Community pushed for closer political and economic union.

Yugoslav Civil War In June 1991, the Yugoslav republics of Croatia and Slovenia declared their independence from Yugoslavia. Both had long-standing differences with the neighboring Yugoslav republic of Serbia. For months, both Croatia and Slovenia had demanded that they would leave the Yugoslav federation if Serbia did not meet their demands to transform the nation into a community of equal and sovereign republics. Serbia favored the present federal system, while Croatia and Slovenia wanted a looser

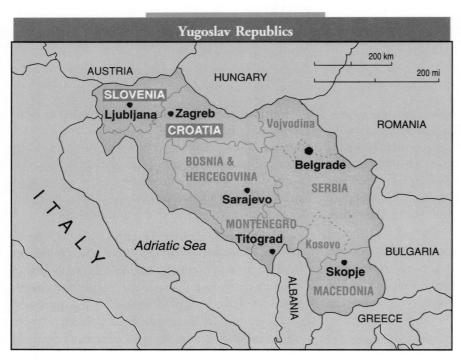

Examining Maps *Formed as a Communist republic in 1945, Yugoslavia until recently was a federation of six republics (Serbia, Croatia, Slovenia, Macedonia, Montenegro, and Bosnia and Hercegovina) and two provinces (Kosovo and Vojvodina). During the 1980s, Communist authority declined, the federal government weakened, and traditional ethnic rivalries surfaced once again. In 1991, civil war fragmented Yugoslavia following declarations of independence by Slovenia and Croatia. By early 1992, many foreign governments had recognized the independence of the individual Yugoslav republics.*

Examining Photographs
A young Croatian soldier fires on federal Yugoslav forces attacking a Croatian town. In early 1992, United Nations peacekeeping forces prepared to end the Yugoslav civil war, Europe's first full-scale conflict since 1945.

arrangement that would end what they regarded as Serb domination of their affairs.

The declarations of independence led to an outbreak of hostilities. Following Slovenia's announcement, Slovene citizens blocked many roads in their republic to prevent Yugoslav federal army units from reaching federal customs posts on the Italian, Austrian, and Hungarian borders. The federal troops, composed mainly of Serbs, battled Slovene militia units for control of the posts.

In early July, Slovenia freed captured federal troops, and the federal government stated that its army would not strike at Slovenia again. Federal and Slovene officials agreed to a cease-fire, accepting mediation from the European Community. Negotiators, who included the foreign ministers of Portugal, Luxembourg, and the Netherlands, agreed to start talks on aspects of Yugoslavia's future.

Meanwhile, Croatia's declaration of independence heightened already strained relations between the republic's Croatian majority and its Serb minority. The Serbs, who live in the northwestern part of Croatia, had declared their independence from Croatia in March, affirming their desire to unite with Serbia. Serb guerrillas then barricaded the roads, destroyed rail lines leading into their communities, and seized Croatian government buildings in the region.

In May, the Yugoslav federal government sent troops to Croatia in an effort to maintain order. The presence of the federal army, however, only fueled tensions between Serbs and Croatians. Because Yugoslavia's military was dominated by Serbs, Croatians accused the army of backing the guerrillas.

Fighting between the Croatians and ethnic Serbs continued into the early summer and intensified Croatian desires for independence. During July, the Serbs battled Croatian militia forces over a wide area of Croatia, thwarting the peace efforts of the European Community.

By late 1991, the conflict had become the first full-scale war in Europe since 1945. In November, Croatia appealed to the United Nations for help. By that time, Serb-dominated forces controlled more than a third of the republic. In January 1992, a cease-fire agreement finally was reached, and the United Nations prepared to send a peacekeeping force.

While peace efforts continued, various European nations became increasingly involved in the crisis. In January 1992, Germany announced that it was recognizing the independence of Slovenia and Croatia as well as any other Yugoslav republic that also requested such recognition. Other foreign ministers of the European Community followed Germany's lead, agreeing to diplomatic ties if the Yugoslav republics met a series of criteria, including respect for the rights of minorities within each republic's borders. Serbia warned that these moves would only deepen and expand the civil war.

European Unity While eastern Europe was torn by ethnic strife, western Europe took steps toward greater unity. During a December 1991 summit meeting at Maastricht in the Netherlands, leaders of the 12-nation European Community approved two treaties designed to move their countries closer to political and economic union. One treaty provided for the eventual creation of a common European currency and monetary system; the other paved the way for common defense, foreign, and economic policies. The heads of government also pledged Community economic assistance to the poorest members—Greece, Ireland, and Portugal.

Britain, which was very reluctant to cede any national sovereignty, succeeded in having removed from the second treaty a provision establishing common social welfare and labor policies. British Prime Minister John Major had insisted that each nation should set its own standards in each of these areas.

THE EUROPEAN COMMUNITY 1992

Examining Maps As it moves toward full economic and political unity, the 12-nation European Community is playing a larger role in European and world affairs. In late 1991, it intervened as a mediator in the Yugoslav civil war. In early 1992, the Community provided emergency aid to eastern Europe and the Commonwealth republics.

At Britain's request, members also removed from the treaties any references to the creation of a federal system for Europe, the expansion of the European Parliament's powers, and the requirement that all members must accept the change to a single currency.

"We have different traditions and different points of view," said Ruud Lubbers, Prime Minister of the Netherlands. "But if you take that into account, it is quite a miracle that we agreed." Although progress had been made on specific issues, European Community leaders still disagreed over how close a European union would be, what powers a central European government would have, and the steps to take toward union.

The European drive for economic and political union was powered by the desire to create a strong unit capable of competing with the United States and Japan in the global market. To many Europeans, a unified European economy was a necessity, particularly in light of

Examining Photographs *The European Community's flag, showing a circle of 12 stars on a dark blue background, flies outside Community headquarters in Brussels, Belgium. In February 1992, the European flag was flown for the first time at an Olympics ceremony when the 16th Olympic Winter Games opened in Albertville, France.*

recent American, Canadian, and Mexican moves toward a free trade area in North America, as well as Japanese efforts to strengthen trading links with the rest of the Pacific region.

WORLD UPDATE FOCUS

1. World History Why did the Soviet coup fail? How did it affect the Soviet Union?

2. Government & Civics How is the Commonwealth of Independent States politically organized?

3. Geography Which Commonwealth republic is the largest in land area?

4. Economics What problems did the economies of the Commonwealth republics face in early 1992? What steps did Commonwealth leaders take toward free market systems?

5. U.S. History How has the United States responded to the economic crisis in the Commonwealth republics? How do you think the breakup of the Soviet Union and the end of the cold war will affect the United States?

6. World History Why did Croatia and Slovenia declare their independence from Yugoslavia? What role have the United Nations and the European Community played in the Yugoslav civil war?

7. Geography Where are Croatia and Slovenia located?

8. Economics How are economies changing in the nations of eastern Europe?

9. Government & Civics What agreements were reached by European Community members at their recent summit conference? How did Britain's position differ from that of other members?

10. World History Based on current trends, what kind of world order do you think might emerge by the year 2000?

Photo Credits

P. 1 © 1991 Klaus Reisinger/Black Star.   P. 2 © Roberto Koch/Saba Press Photos.
P. 3 © Anthony Suau/Black Star.   P. 4 © Ricki Rosen/Saba Press Photos.   P. 5 © Shepard Sherbell/Saba Press Photos.
P. 8 © Georges de Keerle/Sygma.   P. 10 Reuters/Bettman Newsphotos.
P. 11 © Patrick Robert/Sygma.   P. 13 © Philip Horvat/Saba Press Photos.   P. 15 Pictor /Uniphoto.

G82267.01